GOOD

THE
GOOD
GARDENS
GUIDE 2000

EDITED BY PETER KING

BLOOMSBURY

Text copyright © Peter King 2000

This paperback edition published 2000

The moral right of the author has been asserted

Managing Editor: Katherine Lambert
Botanical Editor: Lizzie Boyd
Disk Editor: Emma Callery
Maps: Neil Hyslop
Design: Michelle Radford
Cover Illustration: Flowers & Foliage

Bloomsbury Publishing Plc,
38 Soho Square, London, W1V 5DF

A CIP catalogue record is available from the British Library

ISBN 0 7475 4541 3

10 9 8 7 6 5 4 3 2 1

Typeset by Hewer Text Ltd, Edinburgh
Printed in Great Britain by Clays Limited, St Ives plc

Contents

THE GARDENS

Illustrations: All the colour photographs in the *Guide* were chosen by Andrew Lawson from his portfolio.

Illustrations

The colour photographs, all by Andrew Lawson, have been chosen by him to illustrate gardens where a restoration programme has been completed, or where subtle changes have taken place over recent years.

Hestercombe, Somerset★ The restored eighteenth-century garden. The Jekyll garden here has also been restored and a 1880s shrubbery is being transformed in the style of Robinson.

RHS Garden Rosemoor, Devon★★ There is a new formal garden here and a foliage garden displaying the recent passion for grasses, proving that the RHS keeps up with the times.

Oxford University Botanic Garden★★ Although the oldest botanic garden in the country, it is far from the conventional image. Not only are there modern greenhouses, but also a restored bog garden and rockery, plus all kinds of extramural activities for visitors with a non-specialist interest in gardening.

Great Dixter, East Sussex★★ Although one of the most renowned gardens in the world, the plantings do not stand still. The owner, Christopher Lloyd, is an innovator whose life's work is to coax new and exciting effects from his plants.

Drummond Castle, Scotland★★ The garden is much older than the peacock, but it underwent dramatic changes in the nineteenth century, and subtle changes have been taking place ever since.

Hadspen Garden, Somerset★★ Distinguished gardeners have worked here, such as Margaret and Penelope Hobhouse, but the present owners have continued to embellish its classic 'country-house' look, particularly with new colourist plantings.

Herterton House, Northumberland★ The owners only took over here 25 years ago, but they have created 'a gem of a place' with interest throughout the season.

Hampton Court Palace, London★★ There have been many changes at the Palace since Cardinal Wolsey's time. For example, the kitchen garden now houses roses. The newest is the much-acclaimed Privy Garden, a Baroque formal garden from William III's time, now beautifully restored.

Iford Manor, Wiltshire★★ Although this is the creation of an early-twentieth-century architect and designer, it looks as if it is frozen in time. However, the fact is that some stonework has had to be replaced for technical reasons, but this is done so skilfully that externally it exactly matches Peto's original.

The Master's Garden, Lord Leycester Hospital, Warwick This is not a hospital garden in the modern sense, but a restored building with grounds going back over several centuries, splendidly converted for the modern visitor. The castle next door is ★.

Heligan, Cornwall★★ Existing here since 1603, the gardens were 'lost' until reclaimed by the energetic Tim Smit after 1991. One of the largest such projects in Europe, it will soon be joined by another Smit scheme, the Eden Project, also in Cornwall.

Waddesdon Manor, Buckinghamshire★★ The National Trust and the Rothschilds have done great things here, and the latter's newest project, for the Millennium, is to inject art and life into the extensive parterre, with participation by contemporary painters, aided by computers.

Introduction and Acknowledgements

This is the eleventh annual edition of the *Guide*, containing a considerable number of gardens which were not in the 1999 book, as well as some deletions of those that, for one reason or another, it was not appropriate to repeat. In all about 60 'new' gardens are listed this year. All the gardens described are open to the public and there is an emphasis on those that are open frequently or 'by appointment' over several months of the year. Some owners are only able or willing to open once or twice, and certain gardens of this kind are included on merit; we hope that such owners may be encouraged to open more frequently if they can.

Our thanks to everyone who has helped with the preparation of the *Guide* – to owners, custodians, professional gardening staff, and many others. In particular, we thank our inspectors and those who advised them. Some of those who have given advice do not wish to be listed and, although anonymous, they have been every bit as valuable. We are also obliged to staff of The National Trust, The National Trust for Scotland and English Heritage for their co-operation. The names which follow include inspectors and past inspectors (but not all of them) and advisors: Barbara Abbs, Jane Allsopp, Diana Atkins, Rosie Atkins, David Baldwin, Susan Barnes, Mr and Mrs Basten, Kerry Bate, Kenneth and Gillian Beckett, Lavender Borden, Kathryn Bradley-Hole, Hilary Bristow, Cecil Brown, Adam Caplin, Dr Joan Carmichael, Richard and Imogen Carter Jonas, Brian and Gillian Cassidy, Lady Cave, Liz Challen, Anne Chamberlain, Sir Jeremy and Lady Chance, Jeremy Cockayne, Sarah Coles, Anne Collins, E. Anne Colville, Beatrice Cowan, Simon Cramp, Jo, Penelope, Rosie and Trixie Currie, Wendy Dare, the late Michael Davis, Margreet Diepeveen-Bruins Slot, Marilyn Dodd, Rosemary Dodgson, Daphne Dormer, Lady Edmonstone, Matthew Fattorini, Daphne Fisher, Michael and Freda Fisher, Adrian and Audrey Gale, Lucy Gent, Alison Gregory, Elizabeth Hamilton, Camilla Harford, Anne Harrison, Sunniva Harte, Lance Hattatt, Jane Henson, Ronald Higgins, Steve Hipkin, Judith Hitchings, Hilary Hodgson, Mariana Hollis, Caroline Holmes, Jackie Hone, Sophie Hughes, Pam Hummer, Jill Husselby, David Jacques, Judith Jenkins, Valerie Jinks, Vanessa Johnston, Rosemarie Johnstone, Belinda Jupp, Mary Keen, Jo Kenaghan, Margaret Knight, the late John Last, Jean Laughton, Virginia Lawlor, Andrew Lawson, Anne E. Liverman, Malcolm Lyell, Charles Lyte, Janet Macnutt, Michael Mallett, Rhian de Mattos, Pat McCrostie, Anna McKane, Deirdre McSharry, Bettine Muir, Dr Charles Nelson, Hugh Palmer, Lucinda Parry, John and Carol Pease, Victoria Petrie-Hay, Lady Pigot, Stephen Player, Jocelyn Poole, Heather Prescott, Lorna Ramsay, Finola Reid, Anne Richards, Christopher Rogers, Dorothy Rose, Jane Russell, Alison Rutherford, Sarah Rutherford, Peter de Sausmarez, Kathy Sayer, George and Jane Scott, Barbara Segall, Marjorie Sime, Jill Skeet, Gillian Sladen, Dr Gordon Smith, Michael Smith, Lady Smith-Ryland, Elaine Snazell, Margaret Soole, Marlene Storah, Vera Taggart, Sally Tamplin, Bill Tobias, Caroline Todhunter, Michael Tooley, Annetta Troth, Marie-Françoise Valery, Mrs R.E. Vestey, Jackie Ward, Jennifer Wates, Sue Watts, Myra Wheeldon, Susan Whittington, Cynthia Wickham, John Wilks. The editor also expresses his appreciation of the dedicated assistance of Lizzie Boyd, Emma Callery, Angie Hipkin, Katherine Lambert and Wendy Turner.

The Garden Scene

The *Guide* has always had a heavy emphasis on parks as public gardens and perhaps some justification for our interest in them is overdue. Britain can with justice claim to have invented the urban park, those vital lungs of the smoke-laden industrial cities of the nineteenth century. Paxton's Birkenhead Park of 1843 has never been surpassed anywhere in the world for the brilliant way in which he created a *rus in urbe* which combined walks with drives, separated pedestrians from vehicles, opened up views, concealed movement and yet connected his park with the city.

Yet, a decade ago, Britain's public parks were in terminal decline. It took a report from the combined forces of the Garden History and Victorian Societies to present graphically the plight of the urban parks. They found an ardent ally in the Institute of Leisure and Amenity Management, from whose ranks many of the managers of city parks are recruited. Most importantly, they attracted the attention of Lord Rothschild in his last days as chairman of the Heritage Lottery Fund. He launched the Fund's £12m Urban Parks Programme of 1997, and that cash is starting to flow into rejuvenation schemes for existing parks up and down the country.

Just two years later Lord Rogers' Urban Renaissance initiative was announced. Alas, the only use of the word 'park' in his entire report was attached to that necessity of modern life, the car park. Yet, even if the Government's prophet of urban renewal chooses to ignore our cities' open spaces, all is not lost. Moves are afoot to rethink the way urban parks are conceived and managed. The most important idea to come out of this re-examination of their role in modern life is that they need an urban equivalent of the Countryside Commission – a government agency for urban parks which will have the money and the vision to place the park at the forefront of city thinking and life, to create as well as to restore urban parks, and the power to set standards for the next millennium.

The case has already been put to the Parliamentary Committee on Town and Country Parks. With strong support from the Lottery's New Opportunities Fund we may yet see the creation of a new agency for city parks, incorporating the royal parks too, which will accelerate this long-needed regeneration of the country's recreational spaces. And Britain's new urban parks of the twenty-first century might then match the achievements of Barcelona, Melbourne and Paris in the twentieth.

The vital element is of course upkeep. It is all very well voting large sums of money for a new park or a complete overhaul of an old one, but if the maintenance money is not there, the effort may be wasted. The fight against vandalism, in particular, needs ongoing financial support. Maintenance money is also necessary for that twenty-first-century invention, the wildlife park. The London Wildlife Trust has a scheme in hand for a *Survey of Garden Wildlife* aimed at improving the biodiversity of the capital – a trendy concept, but will the finance be there on a continuing basis?

How to Use the Guide

The *Guide* is **arranged by counties**. Within each of these the gardens are listed alphabetically by the normal name of the garden/house. The index at the end of the book can also be used to find a garden whose name only is known to the reader.

Maps at the beginning of each county section have numbers which refer to those given against each garden entry. Gardens in neighbouring counties may be close enough to the named county to be visited at the same time, so these are indicated by a flower symbol on the maps. Turn to the relevant county map to find the names of these nearby gardens. For detailed information about how to reach gardens use the data given in the garden entry itself.

Readers who do not have a specific garden in mind may like to take the following **procedure to discover gardens** in their particular area which are available for viewing:

1. Choose the county or neighbouring counties which will be your target area.
2. Search out (in these counties) the gardens which are open all year round, i.e. those marked with ○.
3. Having listed these gardens, pay particular attention to ★★ and then ★ gardens on the list.

Alternatively, readers can concentrate on the starred gardens, checking which of these are open on the days available to the visitor.

Symbols: Last year we expanded the use of these to convey some information at a glance.

For regular readers of the *Guide*, we have changed the symbol to denote entries new for 2000 to a NEW. Listed below are the other symbols, together with a brief explanation of their meanings:

○ open all year; ◕ open most of year; ◑ open for main season; ● open on a certain number of days and/or by appointment; 🍵 teas/light refreshments; ✗ meals; 🧺 picnics permitted; WC toilet facilities; <u>WC</u> toilet facilities, inc. disabled; ♿ garden partly wheelchair accessible; 🐕 dogs permitted on lead; 🌱 plants for sale; 🛍 shop; ♟ events held.

This list is repeated in various places throughout the book and further explanation of symbols is given under **Detailed Use of the Guide** (below).

Detailed Use of the *Guide*
(information listed in order used in entry)

Garden name The name of the garden, or the building with which it is associated.

Stars To help give the reader the opinion which inspectors and editors have formed about the status of certain gardens, over 100 properties have been marked with ★★ to indicate that in our opinion these are amongst the finest gardens in the world in terms of design and content. Many are of historic importance, but some of recent origin. Readers will appreciate that direct comparisons cannot be made between a vast estate like Chatsworth with its staff of professional gardeners and a tiny plantsman's garden behind a terraced house, although both may be excellent of their kind. Those gardens which are of very high quality, though not perhaps as outstanding as the ★★ ones, are given a single ★. The latter will be worth travelling a considerable distance to see, and sometimes the general ambience of the property as a whole will make the visit especially rewarding. The bulk of the gardens in the *Guide* are not given a mark of distinction, but all have considerable merit and will be well worth visiting when in the region. Some of them will have distinctive features of design or plant content, noted in the description, which will justify making a special journey. To give readers an idea of scale, we estimate that some 5000 properties in the UK are regularly open to the public, plus public parks and green spaces. We list well over 1000, of which over 100 have ★★ status, that is about ten per cent of the total listed. On the maps, those gardens given ★★ status are distinguished from the others by being boxed in bold.

Address This is the address supplied by the owner or some other reputable source. In the index, gardens with street numbers are listed at the beginning rather than under the initial letter of the street name.

Telephone/Fax Except where owners have specifically requested them to be excluded, telephone numbers to which enquiries may be directed are given for each property. To maintain the support and co-operation of private owners it is suggested that the telephone and fax be used with discretion. In all cases where visits by parties are proposed, owners should be advised in advance and arrangements preferably confirmed in writing. Where visits are by appointment, the telephone can of course be used except where written application is specifically requested. Code numbers are given in brackets. In 2000 codes change for London – (0171) is replaced by (020) followed by an 8-digit number, (0181) by (030) followed by an 8-digit number; Cardiff changes to (0290), Coventry to (02476), Portsmouth to (02392), Southampton to (02392). Visitors calling the Republic of Ireland from Britain should phone 00353 followed by the code (Dublin is 1) followed by the subscriber's 6-figure number. Northern Ireland and the Channel Islands follow the mainland system, but many Northern Ireland codes are changed. Details obtainable from Freephone Helpline 0808 22 4 2000. France has 9-figure numbers prefixed by 0033, Belgium prefixed by 0032 and Netherlands by 0031.

Owners Names given are those available at the time of going to press. In the case of The National Trust, some properties may be the homes of tenants of the Trust. Some other gardens are owned or managed by other trusts.

Location, travel and parking This information has been supplied by inspectors and is aimed to be the best available to those travelling by car. No specific details are given where to park because it is assumed that most owners make some convenient arrangement for visitors' cars. However, if special circumstances apply (i.e. if parking is a long walk away) this is usually mentioned under Other Information. The unreliability of train and bus services makes it unrewarding to include many details, particularly as most garden visits are made on Sundays. However, a number of properties can be reached by public transport.

Opening dates and times (see also symbols as opening indicators, below) Dates and times given of access to house (if open) and to garden are usually the best available at the moment of going to press, but some may have been changed subsequently. Some owners unavoidably cannot give their opening information before we go to press. The details given are the most helpful we can present. The dates and times given for all entries are inclusive – that is, an entry such as May to Sept means that the garden is open from 1st May to 30th Sept inclusive, and 2 – 5pm also means that visits will be effective during that period, although some gardens may close to visitors beforehand, and it is wise to arrive half an hour before closing time. Please note that many owners will open their gardens to visitors by appointment. They will often arrange to give a personally-conducted tour on these occasions.

Gardens in Great Britain which are open by courtesy of the owners for one of many charities are included where the gardens are of special interest even if, as on some occasions, they are open in this way on only one day in the year. However, many such gardens are also open at other specific times, such as for local charities or church restoration funds, and it is not generally possible to give dates for all these locally-publicised openings. Readers should note that other nearby gardens, not listed in this guide for one reason or another, may well be open at similar times to those of listed gardens. See also the *Salon des Refusés* on page XXII.

Entrance fees As far as is known, these are correct at time of going to press, but changes may be made without notice. Where there are variations, these will be upwards, but the amount of increase is usually small. Children are often charged at a lower rate, but are expected to be accompanied by an adult. Charges for parties are often at special rates. National Trust charges are explained in their literature with special concessions for members. The Trust is tightening its admissions policy: members who arrive without their membership card will have to pay the full entrance charges. Accompanied children are normally admitted by the Trust at half price and this is why no specific charge for children is usually listed for Trust properties. Figures for the Republic of Ireland are often given in punts (IR£). Some British gardens are open free to members of the Royal Horticultural Society.

Other information This section gives helpful information notified to us which we pass on to the reader. It includes: extra attractions in or near the garden (eg a museum or nursery); facilities outside the garden but nearby (eg toilet facilities); facilities which are limited either by availability (eg teas on charity open days only), or by location (eg picnics in park only); warnings (eg no coaches), and helpful hints (eg possible for wheelchairs but some gravel paths).

Disclaimer

The information given is believed to be correct at the time of going to press but changes do occur, properties sold or ownership varied. There may also be closures of over-visited properties, or limitations imposed on opening times. Prices of entry may be changed without notice.

Symbols

NEW New garden for 2000

○, ◔, ◑, ◕ **Opening times** These symbols indicate gardens are open as follows: ○ means open throughout the year; ◔ indicates open most of the year; ◑ shows open more or less throughout the season from Easter to October for several days (i.e. more than two or three) each week; and ◕ applies to those gardens open on a certain number of days and/or by appointment.

♨, ✕, 🧺 **Refreshments: a guide only** Where the symbol ♨ is given, this means that the owners have arranged to serve a simple tea or light refreshments on the property, or near at hand, at reasonable prices during opening hours. The symbol ✕ indicates that meals are served. 🧺 means that picnics are permitted.

WC, <u>WC</u> **Toilet facilities** The symbol WC indicates that access to a toilet or toilets is provided, while <u>WC</u> means that the toilet facilities are also suitable for disabled visitors. Where neither symbol is given, no specific toilets are available and enquiries will have to be directed to staff or owners.

♿ **Garden suitable for wheelchairs** Inspectors have told us where they believe a garden is partly or wholly negotiable by someone in a wheelchair and the symbol indicates this. This comment refers to the garden only and if a house or other building is also open, it may or may not be suitable for wheelchairs.

🐕 **Dogs** If dogs on lead are allowed in the property, a symbol is given.

🌱 **Plants for sale** The symbol means that plants are for sale. Often these are grown on the property, but some owners now buy in plants from a commercial source for re-sale.

🛍 **Shop** The symbol refers to shops on the premises, such as National Trust shops, those selling souvenirs, etc.

🎪 **Events** The symbol indicates that events may be held during, or additional to, normal garden opening times. Those wishing either to participate in, or to avoid, events should check before travelling.

No symbol means either that a certain facility is not available at a garden or that we have not been notified of it. However, it is worth checking under Other Information for details of partial availability.

Where to Stay

Our section to help those seeking accommodation while garden visiting has three main sources. First, there are those hotels which themselves have particularly fine gardens and therefore feature in the main text of the *Guide*. They are listed here by county with the appropriate reference. Second, there are hotels with gardens, some of which may also have particular distinction, but which, for one reason of another, have not been described in the main section of the *Guide*. Such hotels have probably not been visited by our garden inspectors, but they may be members of hotel groups such as *Pride of Britain* or listed in the Johansens Guide, *Recommended Hotels in Great Britain and Ireland*, published annually.

Next we have listed a number of pubs/inns which feature in *The Good Pub Guide* in their section detailing those houses with larger or more beautiful gardens, grounds or terraces than usual in their area *coupled with accommodation*. That guide points out that gardens in towns or cities may be more modest than the kind which would earn a listing in the countryside. Indeed, some of those listed may be horticulturally very modest indeed, since play areas for kids take precedence over plants nowadays.

Last, we list a range of B&Bs, taken from Mrs Sue Colquoun's publication called *Bed and Breakfast for Garden Lovers*. Those readers who wish to obtain her full list may do so by sending a 22cm x 11cm (A5) self-addressed envelope with four first-class stamps (loose or in a book) if within the UK, or three international reply-paid coupons with a self-addressed envelope if from abroad. These coupons are easily available from post offices around the world and can be used to purchase the appropriate stamps in this country. Queries, comments and suggestions are welcomed by *BBGL*, Handywater Farm, Sibford Gower, Banbury, Oxfordshire OX15 5AE. B&Bs in Ireland are listed in the booklet entitled *Friendly Homes of Ireland*, published by Tourism Resources Ltd of Dublin and available from the Tourist Board, P.O. Box 5451, Dublin 2 (IR£1).

This section is presented under counties for England, and countries for Scotland, Wales and Ireland. Accommodation is listed under these headings with the appropriate suffix: (H) for hotel, (P) for pub/inn, (BB) for Bed and Breakfast.

Bedfordshire
Knife and Cleaver (P), Houghton Conquest. Tel: (01234) 740387

Berkshire
Meadow House (BB) *(see entry)*
White Hart (P), Hampstead Marshall. Tel: (01488) 658201

Bristol Area
White Hart (P), Littleton upon Severn. Tel: (01454) 412275

Buckinghamshire
Cliveden (H) *(see entry)*
Five Arrows (H), Waddesdon. Tel: (01296) 651727.
Hartwell House Hotel (H),
Aylesbury. Tel: (01296) 747444.
Stag and Huntsman (P), Hambleden. Tel: (01491) 571227.
Walnut Tree (P), Fawley. Tel: (01491) 638360.

Cambridgeshire
Leeds Arms (P), Eltisley. Tel: (01480) 880283

Cheshire
Bears Head (P), Brereton Green. Tel: (01477) 535251.
Nunsmere Hall (H), Oakmere. Tel: (01606) 889100.
Sutton Hall (H), Macclesfield. Tel: (01260) 253211.

Cornwall

Long Cross (H) (see entry)
Meudon (H), Mawnan Smith. Tel:
(01326) 250541.
Trengilly Wartha (P), Constantine.
Tel: (01326) 340332.
The Well House (H), St Keyne. Tel:
(01579) 342001.

Cumbria

Leeming House Hotel (H),
Watermillock. Tel: (017684) 86622.
Linthwaite House Hotel (H),
Bowness-on-Windermere. Tel:
(015394) 88600.
The Mortal Man (H), Troutbeck.
Tel: (01229) 860291.
Sharrow Bay Country House (H),
Pooley Bridge. Tel: (018536) 301.
The Trout (P), Cockermouth. Tel:
(01900) 823591.

Derbyshire

The Clock Warehouse (P),
Shardlow. Tel: (01332) 792844.
Riber Hall (H), Matlock. Tel:
(01629) 582795.
Underleigh House (H), Hope.

Devon

Avenue Cottage (BB) (see entry)
Blue Ball (P), Sidford. Tel: (01395)
514062.
Buckland-Tout-Saints Hotel (H),
Kingsbridge. Tel: (01548) 853055.
Combe House (H), Gittisham. Tel:
(01404) 42756.
Docton Mill (BB) (see entry)
Endsleigh House (H) (see entry)
Gidleigh Park (H) (see entry)
The Knoll House, Studland Bay. Tel:
(0191) 450450.
Whitechapel Manor (H), South
Molton. Tel: (01769) 573377.

Dorset

Chedington Court (H), Chedington.
Tel: (01935) 891265.
Friars Way (BB), Upwey. Tel:
(01305) 813243.
The Knoll House (H) (see entry)
Langton Arms (P), Tarrant

Monkton. Tel: (01258) 830225.
The Manor (H), West Bexington.
Tel: (01308) 897616.
The Museum (P), Farnham. Tel:
(01725) 516261.
Plumber Manor (H), Sturminster
Newton. Tel: (01258) 472507.
Priory (H), Wareham. Tel: (01929)
551666.
Summer Lodge (H), Evershot.
Tel: (01935) 83424.
Thornhill Park (BB) (see entry)

Durham

Morritt Arms (P), Greta Bridge.
Tel: (01833) 627232.

Essex

The Queen's Head (P), Littlebury.
Tel: (01799) 522251.
The Rose (P), Peldon. Tel: (01206)
735248.

Gloucestershire

Burleigh Court Hotel (H), Burleigh.
Tel: (01453) 883804.
Calcot Manor (BB), Tetbury. Tel:
(01666) 890391.
Crown of Crucis (P), Ampney
Crucis. Tel: (01285) 851806.
Halewell Close (H), Withington.
Tel: (01242) 890238.
The Lygon Arms (H), Broadway.
Tel: (01386) 852255.
Upper Court (H), Kemerton. Tel:
(01386) 725351.
Village Pub (P), Barnsley. Tel:
(01285) 740421.
Wesley House (H), Winchcombe.
Tel: (01242) 602366.
The Wild Duck (P), Ewen. Tel:
(01285) 770310.

Hampshire

Esseborne Manor (H), Hurstbourne
Tarrant. Tel: (01264) 736444.
Lainston House Hotel (H),
Sparsholt. Tel: (01962) 863588.
Tylney Hall Hotel (H) (see entry)
The Vine (P), Stockbridge. Tel:
(01264) 810652.

Herefordshire
Broxwood Court (BB), Nr Pembridge. Tel: (01544) 340245.
Cottage of Content (P), Carey. Tel: (01432) 840242.
The Green Man (P), Fownhope. Tel: (01432) 860243.
Hope End Hotel (H), Ledbury. Tel: (01531) 633613.

Hertfordshire
Brocket Arms (P), Ayot St Lawrence. Tel: (01438) 850250.
Hanbury Manor (H) (see entry)
West Lodge Park Hotel (H) (see entry for The Beale Arboretum)

Kent
The Crown (P), Groombridge. Tel: (01892) 864742.
The Dering Arms (H), Pluckly. Tel: (01223) 840371.
Vine Farm (BB), Headcorn. Tel: (01622) 890203.

Lancashire
Parkers Arms (P), Newton. Tel: (01200) 446236.

Leicestershire
Neville Arms (P), Medbourne. Tel: (01858) 565288.

Lincolnshire
Black Horse (P), Donington on Bain. Tel: (01507) 343640.
The George (P), Stamford. Tel: (01780) 755171.

London Area
Grim's Dyke (H), Old Redding. Tel: (0181) 954 4227.

Norfolk
Beeches Hotel (H) (see entry for The Plantation Garden)
Beechwood Hotel (H), North Walsham.
Buckinghamshire Arms (H), Blickling. Tel: 01263) 732133.
Congham Hall (H) (see entry)
Manor Hotel (P), Titchwell. Tel: (01485) 210221.
Morston Hall (H), Morston. Tel: (01263) 741041.

Rose and Crown (P), Snettisham. Tel: (01485) 541382.
The Victoria (P), Holkham. Tel: (01328) 710469.

Northamptonshire
Olde Coach House (P), Ashby St Ledgers. Tel: (01788) 890349.
Red Lion (P), East Haddon. Tel: (01604) 770223.

Northumberland
Lord Crewe Arms (P), Blanchland. Tel: (01434) 675251.
Manor House (P), Carterway Heads. Tel: (01207) 255268
Warren House Hotel (H), Waren Mill. Tel: (01668) 214581

Nottinghamshire
Griff Inn (P), Drakeholes. Tel: (01777) 817206.

Oxfordshire
The Feathers (P), Woodstock. Tel: (01993) 812291.
The Lamb (P), Burford. Tel: (01993) 823155.
Le Manoir aux Quat' Saisons (H), Great Milton. Tel: (01844) 278881.
The Shaven Crown (P), Shipton-under-Wychwood. Tel: (01993) 830330.

Rutland
Fox and Hounds (P), Exton. Tel: (01572) 812403.

Shropshire
Hawkstone Park Hotel (H) (see entry for Hawkstone Historic Park and Follies)
The Hundred House (P), Norton. Tel: (01952) 730353

Somerset
Bull Terrier (P), Croscombe. Tel: (01749) 343658.
Brewers Cottage (BB). Tel: (01460) 281395
Charlton House Hotel (H), Shepton Mallet. Tel: (01749) 342008
Chinnock House (BB) (see entry)
Hunstrete House (H), Chelwood. Tel: (01761) 490490.

The Old Rectory (BB), Stanton
Prior. Tel: (01761) 471942.
Ralegh's Cross (P), Brendon Hills.
Tel: (01984) 40343
The Ship (P), Porlock. Tel: (01643)
862507.
Ston Easton (H) *(see entry)*

Staffordshire
The Greyhound (P), Warslow. Tel:
(01298) 84249.
Olde Dog and Partridge (P),
Tutbury. Tel: (01283) 813030.

Suffolk
The Angel (P), Lavenham. Tel:
(01787) 247388.
The Crown (P), Bidleston. Tel:
(01449) 740510.
Hintlesham Hall (H), Hintlesham.
Tel (01473) 652334.
Sun House (BB) *(see entry)*
The Swan (P), Lavenham. Tel:
(01787) 247477.

Surrey
Drummond Arms (P), Albury. Tel:
(01483) 202039.
Great Fosters (H) *(see entry)*
Langshott Manor (H) *(see entry)*
Nutfield Priory (H), Redhill. Tel:
(01737) 822066.
The Plough (P), Coldharbour. Tel:
(01306) 711793.

Sussex, East
Bates Green Farm (BB) *(see entry)*
The Griffin (P), Fletching. Tel:
(01825) 722890.
The Gun (P), Gun Hill. Tel: (01825)
872361.
King John's Lodge (BB),
Etchingham. Tel: (01580) 819232.
Lye Green House (BB), Lye Green,
Tel: (01892) 652018.
Netherfield Place (H), Battle. Tel:
(01424) 774455.
The Ram (P), Firle. Tel: (01273) 858222.

Sussex, West
Amberley Castle (H), Arundel. Tel:
(01798) 831992.
Gravetye Manor (H) *(see entry)*

The Half Moon (P), Kirdford. Tel:
(01403) 820223.
Little Thakeham (H) *(see entry)*
Ockenden Manor (H), Cuckfield.
Tel: (01444) 416111.
South Lodge Hotel (H), Lower
Beeding. Tel: (01403) 891711.
Three Horseshoes (P), Elsted. Tel:
(01730) 825746.

Warwickshire
Howard Arms (P), Ilmington. Tel:
(01608) 682226.
Red Lion (P), Little Compton. Tel:
(01608) 674397.
Welcombe Hall (H), Nr Stratford-
upon-Avon. Tel: (01892) 295252.

Wiltshire
Compasses (P), Chicksgrove. Tel:
(01722) 714318.
The Garden Lodge (BB), Chittoe.
Tel: (01380) 850314.
The Harrow (P), Little Bedwyn. Tel:
(01672) 870871.
The Horseshoe (P), Ebbesbourne
Wake. Tel: (01722) 780474.
Landford Wood (BB), Salisbury. Tel:
(01794) 390220.
The Rattlebone (P), Sherston. Tel:
(01666) 840871.
Red Lion (P), Axford. Tel: (01672)
520271.
Red Lion (P), Kilmington. Tel:
(01985) 844263.
Woolley Grange (H), Woolley
Green. Tel: (01225) 864705.

Worcestershire
The Elms, (H) Abberley.
Tel: (01299) 896666.
Grafton Manor, (H) Bromsgrove.
Tel: (01527) 579007

Yorkshire
Abbey Inn (P), Byland Abbey. Tel:
(01347) 868204.
Devonshire Arms (P), Cracoe. Tel:
(01756) 730237.
Middlethorpe Hall (H), York. Tel:
(01904) 641241.
Millgate House (BB) *(see entry)*

Ireland

Abbey Hotel (H), Roscommon. Tel: (903) 26505.

Assolas Country House (H), Kanturk, Co. Cork. Tel: (29) 50015.

Ballymaloe (H) (*see entry*)

Blessingbourne (H), Fivemiletown.

Caragh Lodge (H), Caragh Lake, Co. Kerry. Tel: (66) 69115.

Cashel Palace Hotel (H), Co. Tipperary. Tel: (62) 62707

Cuan Chalet (H), Newtownards.

Deer Park Hotel (H), Howth. Tel: (18) 332 624.

Dunloe Castle (H) (*see entry*)

Enniscoe House (H), Castlehill, Co. Mayo. Tel: (96) 31112.

Glin Castle (H) (*see entry*)

Gregans Castle (H), Ballyvaughan, Co. Clare. Tel: (65) 77005.

Hunter's Hotel (H), Rathnew, Co. Wicklow. Tel: (404) 40106.

Magheramorne House Hotel (H), Larne, Co. Antrim. Tel: (01574) 279444

Marlfield House (H), Gorey, Co Wexford. Tel: (55) 21124.

The Mustard Seed at Echo Lodge (H), Ballingarry, Co. Limerick. Tel: (69) 68508.

Newport House (H), Newport, Co Mayo. Tel: (98) 41222.

The Park Hotel (H), Kenmare, Co. Kerry. Tel: (64) 41200.

Rosleague Manor (H), Letterfrack, Co. Galway. Tel: (95) 41101.

The following private houses, buildings of architectural merit, offer the option of either full board or B&B accommodation. Further details are listed in *The Hidden Ireland* available from the Tourist Board at the address listed earlier.

Annesbrook, Duleck, Co. Meath. Tel: (41) 23293.

Ardnamona (*see entry*)

Ashbrook, Co. Londonderry. Tel: (01504) 349223

Avondale House, Scribblestown, Co. Dublin. Tel: (1) 838 6545.

Ballinkeele House, Ennisworthy, Co. Wexford. Tel: (53) 38105.

Ballyvolane House, Castlelyons, Co. Cork. Tel: (25) 36349.

Bantry House, Bantry, Co. Cork. Tel: (27) 50047.

Carnelly House, Clarecastle, Co. Clare. Tel: (65) 28442.

Castle Leslie, Co. Monaghan. Tel: (47) 88109

Clonalis House, Castlerea, Co. Roscommon. Tel: (907) 20014.

Cullintra House, Inistioge, Co. Kilkenny. Tel: (51) 423614 (10am – 2pm).

Delphi Lodge, Leenane, Co. Galway. Tel: (95) 42211.

Enniscoe Lodge, Ballina, Co. Mayo. Tel: (96) 31112.

Glendalough House, Caragh Lake, Co. Kerry. Tel: (66) 69156.

Glenlohane, Kanturk, Co. Cork. Tel: (29) 51100.

Hilton Park (*see entry*)

Kilrush House, Freshford, Co. Kilkenny. Tel: (56) 32236.

Lismacue House, Bansha, Co. Tiperary. Tel: (62) 54106.

Lorum Old Rectory, Bagenalstown, Co. Carlow. Tel: (0503) 75282.

The Manor, Manor Kilbride, Co. Wicklow. Tel: (1) 458 2105.

Martinstown House, The Curragh, Co. Kildare. Tel: (45) 441269.

Moycullen House, Moycullen, Co. Galway. Tel: (91) 555566.

Newbay House, Co. Wexford. Tel: (53) 42779.

Powerscourt (*see entry*)

Red House, Ardee, Co. Louth. Tel: (41) 53523.

Roundwood House, Mountrath. Tel: (502) 32120.

Streeve Hill, Limavady, Co. Londonderry. Tel: (015047) 66563.

Temple House, Ballymote, Co. Sligo. Tel: (71) 83329.

Tempo Manor, Tempo, Co. Fermanagh. Tel: (013655) 41450.

Tullanisk, Birr, Co. Offaly. Tel: (509) 20572.

Tyrella House, Downpatrick, Co. Down. Tel: (01396) 851422.

Scotland

Airds Hotel (H), Port Appin. Tel: (01631) 730236.

Ardanaiseig Hotel (H) (see entry)

Ardrannoch, Ledaig (BB), Tel: (01631) 720241.

Arisaig House (H), Beasdale. Tel: (01687) 450622.

Balbirnie Hotel Hotel (H), Markinch. Tel: (01592) 610066.

Balfour Castle (H), Shapinsay, Orkney. Tel: (01856) 711282.

Ceilidh Place (P), Ullapool. Tel: (01854) 612103.

Connoisseur Scotland (H), Edinburgh. Tel: (0131) 220 2729.

Creebridge House (P), Creebridge. Tel: (01671) 402121.

Creggans (P), Strachur. Tel: (01369) 86279.

Cringletie House Hotel (H), Peebles. Tel: (01721) 730233.

The Crown (P), Portpatrick. Tel: (01776) 810261.

Ferry Boat (P), Ullapool. Tel: (01854) 612366.

Fisherman's Tavern (P), Bloughty Ferry. Tel: (01382) 775941

Galley of Larne (P), Ardfern. Tel: (01852) 500284.

Glenborrodale Castle (H), Ardnamurchan. Tel: (01972) 500266.

Glenfeochan House (H), Kilmore. Tel: (01631) 770273.

Greywalls (H), Muirfield. Tel: (01620) 842144.

Kilberry Inn (P), Kilberry. Tel: (018801) 770223

Kildrummy Castle (H) (see entry)

Killiecrankie Hotel (P), Pitlochry. Tel: (01796) 473220.

Kilravock Castle (H), Croy. Tel: (01667) 493258.

Kinnaird, Dunkeld (H). Tel: (01796) 482440.

Knockinaam Lodge (H), Portpatrick. Tel: (01776) 810471.

Lion and Unicorn (P), Thornhill. Tel: (01786) 850204/850707.

Loch Melfont Hotel (P), Arduaine. Tel: (01852) 200233.

Murray Arms (P), Gatehouse of Fleet. Tel: (01557) 814207.

Plockton Hotel (P), Plockton. Tel: (01599) 544.

Prestonfield House (H), Edinburgh. Tel: (0131) 668 3346.

Riverside (P), Canonbie. Tel: (013873) 71512/71295.

Skaebost House Hotel (P), Skaebost, Skye. Tel: (01470) 532202.

Tibbie Shiels Inn (P), St Mary's Loch. Tel: (01750) 42231

Wheatsheaf (P), Swinton. Tel: (01890) 860257.

Wales

Abbey Hotel (P), Llanthony. Tel: (01873) 890487.

The Bear (P), Crickhowell. Tel: (01873) 810408.

Bodysgallen Hall (H) (see entry)

Halfway Inn (P), Aberystwyth. Tel: (01970) 880631.

The Harp (P), Old Radnor. Tel: (01544) 421655.

The Lion (P), Tudweiliog. Tel: (01758) 770244.

Llanerch (P), Llandrindod Wells. Tel: (01597) 822086.

Plas Penhelig (H) (see entry)

Portmeirion (H) (see entry)

Radnorshire Arms (P), Presteigne. Tel: (01544) 267406.

Trewern Arms (P), Nevern. Tel: (01239) 820395.

Tyddyn Llan (H), Llandrillo. Tel: (01490) 440264.

Ynyshir Hall (H) (see entry)

Two-Starred Gardens

BUCKINGHAMSHIRE
Ascott; Cliveden; The Manor House, Bledlow; Stowe; Waddesdon; West Wycombe

CAMBRIDGESHIRE
Anglesey Abbey; Christ's College; University Botanic Garden

CHESHIRE
Ness Botanic Gardens; Tatton Park

CORNWALL
Caerhays; Heligan; Pine Lodge; Trebah; Tresco; Trewithen

CUMBRIA
Holehird; Holker; Levens

DERBYSHIRE
Chatsworth

DEVON
Castle Drogo; Coleton Fishacre; Knightshayes; Marwood Hill; Rosemoor

DORSET
Cranborne Manor; Forde Abbey

ESSEX
The Beth Chatto Gardens

GLOUCESTERSHIRE
Barnsley House; Hidcote; Kiftsgate; Sezincote; Westbury Court; Westonbirt Arboretum

HAMPSHIRE
Exbury; Longstock Park Water Gardens; Mottisfont Abbey; Sir Harold Hillier Gardens and Arboretum; Ventnor Botanic Garden

HERTFORDSHIRE
Benington Lordship; Gardens of the Rose; Hatfield House

KENT
Goodnestone Park; Hever Castle; Sissinghurst

LANCASHIRE
Gresgarth Hall

LONDON AREA
Chiswick House; Hampton Court; Royal Botanic Gardens, Kew

NORFOLK
East Ruston Old Vicarage

NORTHAMPTONSHIRE
Cottesbrooke

NORTHUMBERLAND
Belsay Hall

OXFORDSHIRE
Blenheim Palace; Oxford Botanic Garden; Rousham; Westwell Manor

SHROPSHIRE
Hodnet Hall; Wollerton Old Hall

SOMERSET
Greencombe; Hadspen

STAFFORDSHIRE
Biddulph Grange

SUFFOLK
Helmingham Hall; Somerleyton Hall

SURREY
Painshill; RHS Wisley; The Savill Garden; Sutton Place; The Valley Gardens

SUSSEX (East)
Great Dixter; Sheffield Park

SUSSEX (West)
Leonardslee; Nymans; Wakehurst Place

WILTSHIRE
Iford Manor; Stourhead

YORKSHIRE
Castle Howard; Newby Hall; Studley Royal and Fountains Abbey

IRELAND
Butterstream; Castlewellan Arboretum; The Dillon Garden;

Earlscliffe; Glenveagh Castle; Ilnacullin; Mount Congreve; Mount Stewart; Mount Usher; Rowallane

SCOTLAND
Arduaine; Castle Kennedy; Castle of Mey; Crarae; Crathes Castle; Culzean; Drummond Castle; House of Pitmuies; Inverewe; Logan Botanic Garden; Manderston; Mount Stuart; Royal Botanic Garden Edinburgh; Younger Botanic Garden

WALES
Bodnant; Clyne Gardens; Powis Castle

FRANCE
Château de Brécy; Château de Canon; Parc Floral des Moutiers, Le Vasterival

BELGIUM
Annevoie

NETHERLANDS
Hof van Walenburg; Paleis Het Loo

New Gardens This Year

Putteridge Bury, Bedfordshire
Hazelby House, Berkshire
White Knights, Berkshire
Halfpenny Furze, Buckinghamshire
Island Hall, Cambridgeshire
Netherhall Manor, Cambridgeshire
Turf Maze, Cambridgeshire
The Old Hough, Cheshire
The Well House, Cheshire
Ince Castle, Cornwall
Ladock House, Cornwall
Charney Well, Cumbria
Fanshawe Gate Hall, Derbyshire
Castle Tor, Devon
Hartland Abbey, Devon
Rampisham Manor, Dorset
Brackenbury, Gloucestershire
Bryan's Ground, Herefordshire
Hampton Court, Herefordshire
Lower Hope, Herefordshire
Crittenden House, Kent
Clearbeck House, Lancashire
Gresgarth Hall, Lancashire
The Ridges, Lancashire
Woodside, Lancashire
Caythorpe Court, Lincolnshire
Grimsthorpe Castle, Lincolnshire
32 Main Street, Lincolnshire
5 Burbage Road, London
Down House, London
Elm Tree Cottage, London

26 Kenilworth Road, London
38 Killieser Avenue, London
4 Macaulay Road, London
48 Rommany Road, London
35 Rudloe Road, London
Lawn Farm, Norfolk
Lynford Arboretum, Norfolk
Magpies, Norfolk
Garsington Manor, Oxfordshire
Shellingford House, Oxfordshire
Old Hall, Rutland
10 Wing Road, Rutland
David Austin Roses, Shropshire
Manor Farm, Somerset
Manor House, Walton-in-Gordano, Somerset
Garden House, Suffolk
Ickworth, Suffolk
Gatton Park, Surrey
Wellingham Herb Garden, East Sussex
Stoneleigh Abbey, Warwickshire
Abbey House Gardens, Wiltshire
24 Alexander Avenue, Worcestershire
Shuttifield Cottage, Worcestershire
Cappoquin House, Republic of Ireland
Killineer, Republic of Ireland
Bolfracks, Scotland
University of Dundee Botanic Garden, Scotland
Wyndcliffe Court, Wales

Salon des Refusés

There are many reasons why certain splendid gardens are not listed in this *Guide*. Amongst them is the fact that a few owners prefer to control entry by arranging for groups to visit by appointment only. Sometimes such arrangements are described by the owners (or by commercial organisers) as 'private' visits, but this is a misleading term because the visiting group pays a fee, and the members are not generally personally known to the owner.

Quite understandably, some owners try to limit public visits to groups whose credentials can be established before entry, a major consideration being that this may narrow down the chances of their being burgled. We have recently heard from an owner who has opened her garden to the public for many years but is now restricting entry to groups. Not only were garden ornaments and valuable plants stolen, but a visitor who asked to use the loo pocketed several precious personal items before leaving.

Other owners who have not suffered such misfortunes nevertheless prefer visits by groups rather than individuals because, they admit frankly, they are more remunerative and more trouble-free to organise than 'open' days.

Having said all this, there are some owners to whom the term 'open to the public' is a red rag to a bull. The matter came to public attention when it was found that owners of works of art who had negotiated a tax-exemption concession had not entered into the proper spirit of commitment to allow public viewing of the tax-exempted works in question. Gardens sometimes fall into this category.

The desire to visit a 'forbidden' garden is a strong one, and perhaps it is therefore worth reprinting the hints given last year. Some regard Highgrove as their Mecca, if only they could reach it. Well, one can apply as a beagling club or some other recognised group, but the wait is likely to be a long one. Some exclusive gardens are open occasionally for charity. An example is Garsington. Alternatively, one may get in touch with one of the many commercial organisations that specialise in 'private' visits and can offer them a place on a favourable date. These companies include Border Lines (01590) 677994, Boxwood Tours (01341) 241717, the RHS's Gentle Journeys (0171) 720 4891, and Saga, which specialises in the over-50 age group, (0800) 300500.

To take just one area – middle England – the following gardens are, in the *Guide*'s opinion, worthy of such diligence, and all have been visited by our inspectors at so-called 'private' times:
DITCHLEY, Woodstock, Oxfordshire (now a conference centre, contains work by the Trees, Fowler, Jellicoe, etc.)
THE GARDEN HOUSE, Stow-on-the-Wold, Gloucestershire (owned by two ex-Sissinghurst gurus)
HASELEY COURT, near Oxford (former home of the late Mrs Nancy Lancaster, Mrs Ronald Tree, partner of John Fowler who also enticed Jellicoe, Roper and Page to work here)
THE LASKETT, near Hereford (home of Sir Roy and Lady Strong).

Glossary of Garden Terms

Arbour Any sheltered covered area open to one side which usually contains a seat. Arbours can be surrounded by masonry, hedging or by trellis work covered with climbing plants such as roses.

Allée or Alley A path either cut through a thick shrubbery or woodland or closely surrounded by a hedge or wall.

Bath house A rectangular sunken pool for cold water bathing, with seating approached by steps.

Belvedere A high point on a building, or a summer-house, which commands a beautiful view.

Bosket or bosquet A block of very closely planted trees.

Canal An ornamental water basin made in the form of an elongated rectangle. It can either be excavated into the ground or confined above ground within masonry walls.

Clair-voyée A gap in a wall or hedge which extends the view by allowing a glimpse of the surrounding countryside.

Exedra An area of turf within a semi-circular hedge which is usually used to display ornaments or locate a semi-circular seat; or the seat itself.

Eye-catcher A building such as a tower, temple, obelisk, etc. or sometimes merely a bench, large urn or an outstanding long-lived plant designed to beckon the eye towards a particularly rewarding view.

Finial An ornament such as an urn or a pointed sculptural form used to cap features like gateposts, the tops of spires, the top corners of buildings, etc.

Folly A decorative building with no serious function except perhaps to lure attention along a vista or to improve the composition of the garden 'picture'.

Gazebo Dog latin for 'I will gaze', used to describe a building usually sited on a high terrace from which the surrounding countryside can be enjoyed.

Grotto/Nymphaeum An artificial garden feature made to simulate an underground cavern and usually dimly lit from a single small natural light source such as the cave mouth or an oval occulus pierced through the roof or wall. When rather dank and simply lined with natural rock, a grotto can be a good example of art echoing nature. But when formally shaped and lined with statuary and a sophisticated encrusting of shellwork a grotto can become a nymphaeum and an example of art inspired by, and improving upon, nature. Such features are usually made by excavating into a natural hillside or are constructed on level ground then covered with earth to form a mound. Occasionally (as at Woburn Abbey) a grotto can be made as an extension to the house, so offering a cool area in hot weather. Other functions of grottos are to shock and surprise visitors, play upon their perception of the garden or provoke a fruitful melancholy.

Ha-ha A deep ditch separating the garden from the landscape beyond. It allows the unscreened view to be enjoyed from the house but is profiled in such a way that livestock cannot enter the garden.

Knot garden Geometric patterns of low-growing hedge plants such as box or shrubby germander which are made to appear as though they intertwine like knotted cord. The areas between the hedges are filled with plants or decorative gravels.

Mount An artificial hill usually surmounted by an arbour from which landscapes both inside and beyond the garden can be enjoyed from a different perspective.

Obelisk A tall, thin vertical column diminishing in width as it rises and frequently tapered to a pyramid. Large-scale examples have been built to commemorate great events or notable people and frequently to act as eye-catchers in great landscape schemes. Smaller *treillage* versions have been used to beckon for attention in smaller gardens or to act as vertical frames for climbing plants.

Pagoda A feature in a few great landscape gardens based on Buddhist multistorey towers of spiritual significance. In Britain they first were introduced during the eighteenth-century craze for things Chinese.

Palisade A tall hedge of deciduous trees or shrubs with interlaced branches.

Palladian bridge A bridge with a classical superstructure, usually open-sided with columns supporting a roof.

Parterre An intricately-patterned formal garden which usually includes other features such as statuary, water basins and fountains, much larger than a knot garden.

Patte d'oie Literally 'goose foot'; a series of usually three formal paths or grand avenues leading fanwise from a single point through densely-planted trees.

Pergola A framework of columns supporting beams which is usually clad with climbing plants such as roses, clematis or wisteria. If their parallel rows of columns are joined by cross beams and the cover of summer foliage, pergolas can become tunnels.

Pleaching Training the branches of a line of trees horizontally by pruning and attaching them to canes and wires, so that the remainder can be intertwined as they grow to form a screen of foliage.

Pylon A tower which is narrower at its squared-off top than at its base.

Ribbon bed A very narrow band of bedding plants which the Victorians were fond of using to border their lawns.

Rotunda Strictly a circle of classical columns on a raised circular plinth supporting a domed roof. Instead of a solid dome it may be topped with an open ironwork dome. Sometimes loosely called a kiosk.

Rustic work Garden features such as garden houses, fences or seats made from unbarked tree branches – frequently embellished with such decoration as patterns made from sectioned pine cones.

Souterrain An underground chamber usually in a grotto.

Stilt hedge Clipped trees, such as limes, which have all branches removed for several feet above the ground to reveal a line of bare trunks like stilts.

Tapis vert A long strip of lawns between paths or canals.

Théâtre de verdure Similar to but usually more spacious than an exedra, a turf 'stage' with a backcloth of trimmed hedge and sometimes other hedges disposed like the wings of a theatre.

Treillage Architectural features such as arbours, obelisks or ambitious screens made out of trellis.

Trompe-l'oeil A feature designed to deceive the eye, such as a path which narrows as it recedes from a viewpoint to exaggerate the perspective and make the garden seem larger.

Notes on Great Gardeners

SIR CHARLES BARRY (1795 – 1860) A highly successful architect (Houses of Parliament etc), he popularised the formal Italian style of gardening in the mid-nineteenth century, creating impressive designs incorporating terraces, flights of steps, balustrading, urns, fountains and loggias. His most notable gardens were at Trentham Park (Staffordshire), Dunrobin Castle (Highlands), Cliveden (Buckinghamshire), Shrubland Hall (Suffolk) and Harewood (West Yorkshire).

CHARLES BRIDGEMAN (d. 1738) Famous for the way in which he exploited the outstanding features of the sites for which he designed gardens, Bridgeman provides the link between the rigid formality of much of seventeenth-century garden design and the apparent freedom of the landscape movement pioneered by William Kent and 'Capability' Brown. While retaining features such as geometric parterres close to the house and straight alleys, he also incorporated wilderness and meadow areas linked by meandering paths. By his use of the ha-ha wall he made vistas of the surrounding landscape part of his designs. Apart from work for royal patrons in gardens such as Richmond and Kensington Gardens (where he was responsible for the Round Pond and the Serpentine), Bridgeman carried out important works at Blenheim (Oxfordshire), Claremont (Surrey), Rousham (Oxfordshire) and Cliveden and Stowe (both Buckinghamshire).

LANCELOT 'CAPABILITY' BROWN (1716 – 83) Having worked as head gardener and clerk of works at Stowe early in his career, Brown became familiar with the work of Bridgeman and Vanbrugh and helped to execute the designs of William Kent and James Gibbs. Their influence was particularly noticeable in the buildings he designed for his later schemes. However, he was much more radical than any of them, discarding formality when creating very natural-looking landscapes for his clients. Banishing all flowering plants and vegetables he confined them in walled gardens well away from the house and by using ha-ha walls to prevent the ingress of cattle he made the surrounding meadow land appear to run right up to the house walls. Making lakes by excavation and damming streams, he used the excavated soil to create slopes elsewhere which he clad with distinctive clumps of often quite large specimens of native trees to provide the type of park which seemed to flow naturally into the countryside and suited the hunting requirements of the sporting eighteenth-century squirearchy. To many people it seems that Brown strove to bring the rolling landscapes of his native north Northumberland to his client's parks in the flatter Midlands and South. Examples of his work in the *Guide* are: Audley End, Berrington, Blenheim, Bowood, Broadlands, Burghley, Burton Constable, Cadland, Charlecote, Chatsworth, Claremont, Corsham, Euston, Harewood, Highclere, Holkham, Leeds Castle, Longleat, Petworth, Ripley, Sheffield Park, Sledmere, St John's College (Cambridge), Sutton Place, Syon, Temple Newsam, Trentham, University Arboretum (Oxford), Warwick Castle, Weston, Wimpole Hall, Wrest Park.

PERCY CANE (1881 – 1976) He began as a writer in *My Garden Illustrated* which he owned from 1918 – 20; he also owned *Garden Design* from 1930 – 39. During this latter period he developed an influential international practice, and was a star performer at Chelsea Flower Shows in the thirties, where his curvy borders, now a common feature, were regarded as innovatory. Falkland Palace, Scotland and Dartington, Devon, show his imaginative horticultural skills at their best.

BRENDA COLVIN (1897 – 1981) Highly influential landscape architect who worked on large-scale projects such as land reclamation schemes and urban design. A founder member of the Landscape Institute, she became its president from 1951 to 1953, and her 1947 book *Land and Landscape* became a standard work for the professionals. Clipsham (Rutland) is an example of her work.

DAME SYLVIA CROWE (1901 – 98) Responsible for many large-scale projects such as the master planning for new towns like Warrington and Washington as well as being consultant on landscaping for the new towns of Harlow and Basildon. She became an acknowledged expert on the sympathetic integration of development schemes, such as the construction of power stations, with the surrounding landscape. She designed the roof garden for the Scottish Widows Fund in Edinburgh and a park in Canberra, Australia. She was President of the Landscape Institute 1957 -59. Examples of her work in the *Guide* are at Blenheim, Cottesbrooke and Lexham.

MARGERY FISH (1888 – 1969) An informed plantswoman and influential lecturer and author who was a great partisan of the nineteenth century designer William Robinson's naturalistic approach to gardening. This she developed in her own garden at East Lambrook Manor in Somerset which became a haven for endangered garden plants. Her style for the garden which mixed semi-formal features with traditional planting has been influential.

CHARLES HAMILTON (1704 – 86) Under the influence of William Kent between 1738 and 1773, when he was obliged to sell the estate at Painshill Park in Surrey to pay his debts, Hamilton created one of Britain's most picturesque landscape gardens which is now in the process of being restored. As well as being a talented designer, he was an exemplary plantsman, incorporating many exotics in his schemes, particularly those from North America. He also designed a cascade and grotto at Bowood in Wiltshire and advised on work at Holland Park in London and Stourhead in Wiltshire.

HENRY HOARE II (1705 – 85) He was the scholarly member of the banking family and greatly influenced the design of the great landscape garden at Stourhead in Wiltshire. A friend of Charles Hamilton, Lord Burlington and William Kent, he shared their naturalistic approach towards landscaping.

GERTRUDE JEKYLL (1843 – 1932) By both her writings and the examples of her work (much of it accomplished in partnership with the architect Sir Edwin Lutyens) during the last years of the last century and the first quarter of this, she has probably had as much influence on the appearance of British gardens as any other designer. As someone trained initially as a painter and an embroiderer, her great strength was in carefully considered and subtle use of plant colour. Finding inspiration in the happy informality of cottage gardens, she created large interwoven swathes of plants rather than confining them to precise 'spotty' patterns and in so doing she changed our attitude towards the way in which borders should be planted. One of the best examples of Gertude

Jekyll's work in partnership with Edwin Lutyens has recently been restored at Hestercombe Gardens (Somerset). Other examples, also in the *Guide*, are Barrington, Castle Drogo, Castle Tor, Folly Farm, Goddards, Hatchlands, Knebworth, Manor House (Upton Grey), Munstead Wood, Tylney, Vann and Yalding.

SIR GEOFFREY JELLICOE (1900 – 96) Shortly after becoming an architect, Jellicoe made an extensive study of Italian gardens with J.C. Shepheard, which led to their producing in 1925 what has become a classic book, *Italian Gardens of the Renaissance*. The publication of *Gardens and Design* in 1927 confirmed his understanding of basic principles and helped to bring him interesting commissions such as the design of a very large formal garden at Ditchley Park in Oxfordshire. After World War II he was given much public work, including the large water garden in Hemel Hempstead town centre, the Cathedral Close in Exeter, the Kennedy Memorial at Runnymede and a large theme park at Galveston in Texas. Among his work for private clients, the gardens at Sutton Place in Surrey and at Shute House in Dorset are notable. His witty designs have a strong architectural quality. In the past his late wife Susan suggested the planting for many of his schemes and she shared the authorship of the very authoritative *The Landscape of Man*, published in 1975, which discusses in great and informative detail the history and art of landscape design. His work may also be seen at Cliveden, Cottesbrooke, Mottisfont, Sandringham and Sutton Place.

LAWRENCE JOHNSTONE (1871 – 1948) One of the most outstandingly stylish twentieth-century gardeners, Johnston was an American who spent much of his youth in Paris and built two great gardens in Europe which influenced the design of a great many others, such as that of Harold Nicolson and Vita Sackville-West at Sissinghurst in Kent. He began to make the garden at Hidcote Manor in Gloucestershire in 1905 where he pioneered the creation of a series of sheltered and interconnected garden 'rooms', each of which surprised by its different content and treatment. Close to Menton in Southern France, at a property called La Serre de la Madone, Johnston could include in his planting schemes many southern-hemisphere plants which were not hardy enough to survive at Hidcote and allow his formal schemes to be softened by the terracotta, orange trees and bourgainvilleas of the Mediterranean.

INIGO JONES (1573 – 1652) Best known as a prolific architect, Jones brought formal Palladian ideas, acquired on two visits to Italy, to garden design at Arundel House in Sussex, Wilton House in Wiltshire and Lincoln's Inn in London. Apart from his own work, he strongly influenced William Kent (see below), who edited a book of his designs.

WILLIAM KENT (1685 – 1748) This former apprentice coach painter from Hull twice made the Grand Tour of Italy with his most influential patron, Lord Burlington. Heavily influenced by the paintings of Claude and Salvator Rosa, he later tried to introduce the type of romantic landscape encountered in their canvases into his gardens, freeing them from much of the formality which had dominated previous British gardening. His work at Rousham (Oxfordshire), Holkham Hall (Norfolk), Chiswick House (London), Claremont (Surrey) and Stowe (Buckinghamshire) had a great influence on Lancelot 'Capability'

Brown, Charles Hamilton of Painshill Park and Henry Hoare of Stourhead. Other examples of his work in the *Guide* are at Euston and Gunnersbury Park (London).

BATTY LANGLEY (1696 – 1751) A landscaper and architect who was an early partisan of the transitional garden in which a formal layout was allied to a slightly freer and more natural planting. While by no means advocating the totally natural approach to landscaping adopted by 'Capability' Brown later in the century, his book *New Principles of Gardening*, which was published in 1728, was probably responsible for changing attitudes. As an architect he remained attached to the idea that landscaped parks should contain temples, pavilions and folly ruins.

NORAH LINDSAY (1866 – 1948) A disciple of Gertrude Jekyll and a friend of Lawrence Johnston, she made the famous garden at the Manor House at Sutton Courtenay. Her style tended towards the theatrical and romantic, and gained favour with the then Prince of Wales (for whom she worked at Fort Belvedere) and Lord Lothian of Blickling Hall. An example of her work may be seen at Mottisfont.

GEORGE LONDON (d. 1714) and HENRY WISE (1653 – 1738) Towards the end of the seventeenth century, London took Wise as partner in his Brompton Park Nursery (now the South Kensington Museum area). London travelled, giving advice to great estates like Chatsworth, specialising in French-style layouts with plenty of clipped trees and shrubs. His design skills were pre-eminent for about 30 years. Wise, although involved in several projects for the Royals, stayed at home managing the 100-acre nursery. He was 'perfectly well skill'd in Fruit' such as oranges and lemons, and also saw that there was a plentiful supply of the fashionable bays and box. Wise moved to Blenheim in 1705. They planted Chelsea Hospital, Kensington Palace, Hampton Court, Longleat, Chatsworth, Melbourne Hall and Castle Howard, to name but a few.

JOHN CLAUDIUS LOUDON (1783 – 1843) A prolific author who founded the very successful *Gardener's Magazine* and published a popular and comprehensive *Encyclopedia of Gardening* (first published in 1822 and regularly updated), he had a considerable influence on the design of the middle- and small-sized villa gardens being made in their thousands by the burgeoning middle class. Initially a partisan of picturesque designs, he later favoured more formal arrangements and latterly advocated the adoption of the so-called gardenesque style in which each plant was isolated and displayed to its best advantage – an approach still favoured in the beds of many of our parks. Much of his design work has been lost, but there is a good surviving example in Derby Arboretum and also Gunnersbury Park, London.

SIR EDWIN LUTYENS (1869 – 1944) A fine architect who between 1893 and 1912 created approximately 70 gardens in partnership with Gertrude Jekyll. Her subtle planting always softened and complemented the strong architectural nature of his garden designs. And they in their turn splendidly integrated the house in the garden and its site. A fine example of the work of the partnership is at Hestercombe in Somerset, in process of being restored, where Lutyens' genius for using classical masonry forms in a highly imaginative and individual way is wonderfully displayed. Other examples of his work in the *Guide* are Abbotswood, Ammerdown, Castle Drogo, Folly Farm, Goddards, Heywood, Irish National War Memorial Park, Knebworth, Misarden, Munstead Wood and Parc Floral des Moutiers.

THOMAS H. MAWSON (1861 – 1933) A Lancastrian who trained in London and set up a landscape practice in Windermere in 1885, Mawson's reputation grew quickly and he was chosen by many of the rich northern industrialists to landscape the gardens of their Lakeland holiday homes. His distinctive designs there earned him many commissions elsewhere, and his garden and townplanning schemes were adopted as far afield as Greece and Canada. Examples of his work in the *Guide* may be seen at Brockhole, Dyffryn, Graythwaite, Hill Garden (London), Holker, Little Onn, Rivington, Thornton, Tirley Garth and Wightwick.

WILLIAM E. NESFIELD (1793 – 1881) In a long and adventurous life he was a soldier and talented watercolour painter specialising in the depiction of cascades in Europe and America before becoming a landscaper when he was over 40. He was persuaded by his brother-in-law, the famous architect Anthony Salvin, to use his talent for making pictures to help him design gardens. While his work was eclectic and the style he chose for his gardens usually reflected that of the houses which they surrounded, he was responsible for the reintroduction of the parterre as a garden feature in the nineteenth century. One of the best can still be seen at Holkam Hall in Norfolk. At the Royal Botanic Gardens at Kew, as well as a parterre, he made a pond and created the vistas from the Palm House. In total he is believed to have worked at 260 estates during his career. Those in the *Guide* include Alton, Blickling, Cliveden, Dorfold, Holkham, Rode, Shugborough, Somerleyton and Trentham.

SIR HAROLD NICOLSON (1886 – 1968) see Vita Sackville-West

RUSSELL PAGE (1906 – 85) Trained as a painter he quickly became absorbed by garden design and between 1935 and 1939 worked in asssociation with Sir Geoffrey Jellicoe. After the war he gained an international reputation and worked on many projects in Europe and America, including the garden at the Frick Gallery in New York and the Battersea Festival Gardens in London. He encapsulated many of his ideas about garden design in *The Education of a Gardener*, first published in 1962. Examples of his work in the *Guide* are at Longleat and Port Lympne.

JAMES PAINE (1716 – 89) Distinguished designer of garden buildings including the bridge at Chatsworth in Derbyshire, Gibside Chapel in Newcastle-upon-Tyne and the Temple of Diana at Weston Park in Shropshire.

SIR JOSEPH PAXTON (1803 – 65) Gardened at Chatsworth in Derbyshire for 32 years from 1826, where he made the great fountain and the great conservatory in which he pioneered ideas later used in the design of the Crystal Palace. One of the early designers of public parks including those at Birkenhead and Halifax, he was also influential as a writer and was one of the founders of *The Gardener's Chronicle*. Other examples of his work in the *Guide* are at Birkenhead, Capesthorne, Darley, Somerleyton and Tatton.

HAROLD PETO (1854 – 1933) A talented architect who worked for the partnership which later employed young Edwin Lutyens who undoubtedly influenced his style. A lover of Italianate formal gardens, one of Peto's best works was his own garden at Iford Manor in Wiltshire, but his canal garden at Buscot Park in Oxfordshire and at Ilnacullin, the garden on Garinish Island, Ireland, are also notable achievements. Other examples of his work in the *Guide* are at Easton Lodge, Greathed, Heale, Wayford and West Dean.

HUMPHRY REPTON (1752 – 1818) The most influential eighteenth-century landscaper after the death of Lancelot Brown, he was a great protagonist of Brown's ideas but he did tend to favour thicker planting than Brown, and the buildings he used to draw the eye into the landscape were rustic rather than classical. However, he restored formality to gardens in the form of terracing with flights of steps and balustrading near the house. His success in selling his ideas to clients was due to the production of excellent 'before and after' pictures of their parks, demonstrating the effects to be obtained if his schemes were adopted. These pictures with an explanatory text were bound into books which later became known as Repton's 'Red Books' because red was the colour of their binding. Repton was notable for his energy, producing over 400 Red Books and working on such fine estates as Holkham Hall in Norfolk, Sheffield Park in Sussex, Cobham Hall in Surrey, Woburn Abbey in Bedfordshire and Sheringham Park in Norfolk, which is his best-preserved work. Other examples of his work in the *Guide* are at Ashridge, Attingham, Bayfield, Catchfrench, Corsham, Endsleigh, Hatchlands, Holkham, Kenwood, Longleat, Rode, Sheffield Park and Ston Easton.

WILLIAM ROBINSON (1838 – 1935) An Irishman who settled in England and became one of the most prolific writers and influential designers of his epoch. By his teaching and his example he liberated gardeners from the prim rigidity which had begun to dominate garden design in the mid-nineteenth century. Instead of the tightly-patterned bedding displays which the Victorians had adopted in order to show off the host of annual bedding plants which the explorers were sending home, he advocated a very free and natural attitude towards the creation of herbaceous and mixed beds. It was Robinson's attitudes towards planting which early inspired Gertrude Jekyll. He founded a weekly journal, *The Garden* (later absorbed into *Homes and Gardens*), and wrote *The English Flower Garden* which ran to 15 editions during his life and more later. Examples of his work in the *Guide* are at Gravetye Manor, High Beeches, Killerton, Leckhampton College (Cambridge) and Shrubland Park.

LANNING ROPER (1912 – 83) A Harvard graduate from New Jersey who adopted Britain as his home and became one of the most popular landscapers in the 30 years after World War II. His best schemes, such as that at Glenveagh in Ireland, involved a subtle handling of plants combined with interesting formal features. One of his most controversial designs is the ornamental canal in the R.H.S. garden at Wisley. Other examples of his work in the *Guide* are at Anglesey Abbey, Broughton, Fairfield, Lower Hall, Old Rectory (Orford), Trinity College (Dublin) and Trinity Hospice (London).

VITA SACKVILLE-WEST (1892 – 1962) With her husband, Harold Nicolson, she made two notable gardens in Kent. The first, at Long Barn, Sevenoaks, was based on a Nicolson design which she planted during and after World War I. The second and most famous, at Sissinghurst Castle, was begun in 1932 and developed during the rest of her life. The Nicolsons were friendly with Lawrence Johnston, and their attitude to gardening was influenced by the ideas which he exploited at Hidcote. Another example of her work may be seen at Alderley, also in Gloucestershire. Although she was the propagandist of the pair, some think that her husband's conception of structure made a great contribution to twentieth-century garden design.

WILLIAM SHENSTONE (1714 – 63) An early partisan of picturesque gardening who bankrupted himself making a fine landscape garden of his own, Shenstone wrote an essay entitled 'Unconnected thoughts on gardening' which analysed picturesque gardening and contained advice from which hundreds of landscapers have subsequently benefitted.

SIR JOHN VANBRUGH (1644 – 1726) A considerable dramatist and spectacular architect of palaces like Blenheim in Oxfordshire and Castle Howard in Yorkshire. Although he did not design landscapes himself, he ensured that his houses were magnificently sited and often created buildings for their gardens, such as the bridge at Blenheim. He also adorned landscapes made by other designers of great gardens such as Stowe in Buckinghamshire, and Claremont in Surrey.

ELLEN WILLMOTT (1858 – 1934) She made a famous garden at Warley Place in Essex, part of which became a reserve for the Essex Naturalists' Trust in 1978, though little of her garden remains. She became renowned for her knowledge of plants, her patronage of plant hunters (notably Ernest Wilson), the book she published on roses, and her prickly temperament. One of her influential achievements was the development of the garden at Boccanegra on the Italian Riviera.

HENRY WISE see GEORGE LONDON and HENRY WISE

THOMAS WRIGHT (1711 – 86) Astronomer and adviser on about 30 gardens owned by great men of the time – including Badminton, Shugborough and Stoke Gifford. His variety of styles included primitive, Chinese, Gothic and classical, and he designed elaborate flower gardens when flower beds (other than parterres) were not common.

BEDFORDSHIRE

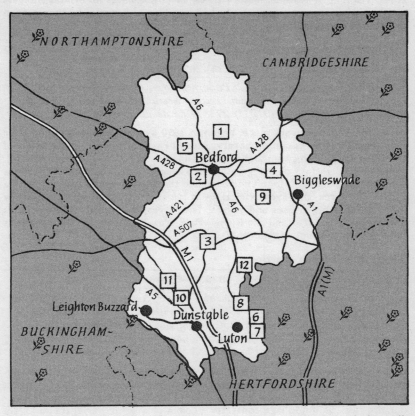

Some gardens have postal addresses in one county and are situated physically in another. If in doubt, a check in the index will direct the reader to the page on which the garden appears.

Broadfields

Keysoe Row East, Keysoe, Bedford MK44 2JD. Tel: (01234) 376326

Mr and Mrs Chris Izzard • Leave Bedford on B660 Kimbolton road. After 10m, turn right at Keysoe crossroads by White Horse pub, then ½ m on right • Open for charity Sun to Fri, 2 – 5pm, Sat 10am – 2pm (telephone for details) and by appt • Entrance: donation to charity • Other information: Cream teas served 1st June to 10th Sept ● ● WC & ◁▷

An immaculate two-acre garden. Mr Izzard has a full-time job and this is a hobby. Formal planting-out with wonderful standard fuchsias and clipped box trees. Vistas with heather, mature trees, shrubs, conifers for winter interest and beautifully grown begonias and bedding plants. A model kitchen garden and lots of spring bulbs.

Embankment Gardens 2

The Embankment, Bedford. Tel: (01234) 267422

Bedford Borough Council • Russell Park, near town centre • Open all year, daily • Entrance: free • Other information: Electric wheelchairs available for free hire during summer: telephone (01234) 271877 for details ○ 占 ◁◔

A charming Victorian set piece, begun in 1890 by the Corporation and later incorporated with its contemporary, Russell Park. It runs along the banks of the River Ouse with swans and a wonderful vista to Mill Meadows and John J. Webster's delightful iron bridge. A mature avenue of plane and lime trees lines the river embankment. John Lund designed the layout, which is formal, with a statue and urns and symmetrical beds of seasonal bedding balanced by miniature pampas grasses and yuccas. The 'Riverside Walks' leaflet includes Embankment Gardens and the Russell Park area. A children's boating lake is open during the summer months.

Kings Arms Path Gardens 3

Ampthill MK45 2QU. Tel: (01525) 402030/403945

Ampthill Town Council • Opposite Market Square, Ampthill, down Kings Arms Yard via public footpath • Open 13th Feb, 2 – 4pm; 23rd April, 28th May, 28th June, 27th Aug, 22nd Oct, 2.30 – 5pm and for parties by appt • Entrance: £1, children 25p • Other information: Teas served at adjacent Bowls Club on some open days, or at nearby hotel and tea shops in Ampthill ◐ 占 ℘

An unusual woodland walk created between 1968 and 1986 by the late William Nourish from an old hopground, later vegetable garden, which had become a rubbish dump. It is full of delightful surprises he planted for interest throughout the year. Skilful foliage contrasts – *Cornus controversa* 'Variegata', a lovely *Liriodendron tulipifera*, rodgersias and *Lysichiton americanus*. Good ground cover and underplanting including many varieties of snowdrops, narcissi, hellebores, primulas and epimediums. Collections of geraniums, hemerocallis, ilex, magnolias and many others. The *Acer tetramerum* is thought to be the finest of the species in the country. A peaceful place, maintained since 1987 by the 'Friends of the Garden'. On some open days there is music by the Ampthill Town Band.

The Lodge 4

Sandy SG19 2DL. Tel: (01767) 680551

Royal Society for the Protection of Birds • 7m E of Bedford, 1m E of A1 off B1042 Sandy – Potton road • Open all year, daily, dawn to dusk • Entrance: £2, OAPs £1, children 50p (1999 prices). RSPB members free ○ 🍽 **WC** 占 ℘ 🏬

One of over 100 reserves established by the RSPB throughout the country, where birds can be seen from woodland walks and nature trails. The RSPB

Memorial Garden is a tranquil spot where the names of those who have left bequests to the Society are honoured. The reserve, with a Victorian terrace and fine trees set in lawns, has seven acres of formal garden. It was developed in the 1930s by Sir Malcolm Stewart, who added a terraced fish pond on the south side. Its mature trees include a large weeping birch, Wellingtonias, acers, sweet chestnuts and large conifers. On the house is a huge wisteria and *Campsis radicans*. Azalea-lined walks lead to a woodland heath. Two small walled gardens have *Garrya elliptica*, old wisterias and many clematis. A major feature is a well-planted vista of old cedar trees. No peat is used and organic principles reign supreme. There is a new wildlife garden, a joint project between the RSPB and the Henry Doubleday Research Association.

The Manor House ★   5

Church Road, Stevington, Bedford MK43 7QB. Tel: (01234) 822064

Kathy Brown • 5m NW of Bedford off A428, through Bromham. In Stevington, right at crossroads, garden on left after ¼ m • Open 16th April, 9th July, 2 – 6pm and for parties by appt • Entrance: £2.50, children free ● ♨ ✕ 🏠 <u>WC</u> ♿ ⚘ 🧺

This is a garden of exuberant imagination, and reworked classic gardening themes: for example, a fine French-style, formal garden with clipped hedges and patterns in box punctuated by two fountains, one a splendid modern one. The Manor House itself is set off by a mound-strewn lawn and some old trees, but everything else is new, sometimes very new. Pots and containers of all sorts — some will make you blink and wonder if you really saw an iguana! Rectangular areas subdivided into patterns of succulents and grasses, and gravels of different colours provide foils for plants in the newest areas. The owner is known for her recipes for growing plants in containers, so there are confections of roses, violets, diascias, succulents, etc. In all, a splendid display of garden artistry.

Putteridge Bury   6

Putteridge, Luton LU2 8LE. Tel: (01582) 489069

University of Luton • 2m NE of Luton on A505 Hitchin – Luton road (south side of carriageway) • Open all year, daily • Entrance: £3, children £1 NEW ○

The Hertfordshire Garden Trust, backed up by the University of Luton, have restored these gardens to the original designs and planting plans of Lutyens and Jekyll, thus giving an exciting insight into their co-operation. Lutyens levelled the lawns and enclosed them in massive yew hedges, leading out to the rolling contours and views across the park. There are wide lawns with specimen trees, cut-leaved planes, mulberries and fine oaks. A magnificent rose garden, planted originally in 1911 with roses supplied by Harkness of Hitchin, has been restored with roses also from Harkness. There was originally an immense border backed by the fine old kitchen garden wall, but this is sadly no longer viable. The fine wilderness walk can, however, still be enjoyed. The original owners, the Sowerbys, employed 10 gardeners and many garden boys. The last Sowerby was killed by his pet stag, and there is a bronze statue to commemorate the event.

Seal Point ★   7

7 Wendover Way, Luton LU2 7LS. Tel: (01582) 611567

Mrs Danae Johnston • In NE of Luton. Turn N off Stockingstone Road into Felstead Way and take second turning on left • Open May to Sept, first Tues in month and some Suns, 2pm – dusk; at other times by appt. Small parties welcome • Entrance: £2.50 ◑ ▬ ▤ ℘

A most exciting small sloping town garden with many interesting plants and features. A sheltered paved patio contains *Jasminum mesnyi* and *Euphorbia rigida* (syn. *E. biglandulosa*) and original ornaments with a Japanese theme. A pool with a waterfall is surrounded by well-grouped contrasting foliage of giant rhubarb, cut-leaved elder, grasses, etc. There is a fern area and two beds, yin and yang: yin being blues and pale colours and yang berberis and brown sorrel. Trees include *Cercis canadensis* and a fine specimen of *Sophora japonica*, 20 years old and beginning to flower. *Clematis texensis*, a charming clipped box cat with tail, and much more. New wild garden.

Stockwood Park   8

Stockwood Craft Museum, Farley Hill, Luton LU1 4BH. Tel: (01582) 738714

Borough of Luton • From M1 take junction 10 to Luton. Take Farley Hill (Chapel Street) turn off A505 Dunstable road out of Luton. Signposted from A1081 • Open April to Oct, Tues – Sat, 10am – 5pm, Sun and Bank Holidays, 10am – 6pm; Nov to March, Sat and Sun, 10am – 4pm. Guided tours available by appt • Entrance: free • Other information: Stockwood Craft Museum in stable block ◔ ▬ ✕ ▤ <u>WC</u> ↺ ▦ ♀

A series of period gardens – medieval, seventeenth-century knot, cottage and Victorian – laid out within the walled gardens of the old house, designed by Robert Burgoyne, ably assisted by Peter Ansell, the head gardener. In the park is a landscape garden with sculpture by Ian Hamilton Finlay, whose work gives a convincing continuity to the landscape tradition by its location alongside the original ha-ha. Another of his sculptures is a curved inscribed wall, and his modern fragments of 'antique' buildings, partly buried, suggest the eighteenth-century ideal of a harmonious blend of planting, architecture and sculpture – arguably the greatest art form to have originated in Britain.

The Swiss Garden   9

Old Warden, Biggleswade SG18 9EA. Tel: (01767) 627666

Bedfordshire County Council • Take A1 to Biggleswade and follow signposts from A1 Biggleswade roundabout. Also signposted on A600 Shefford – Bedford road. Entrance in Old Warden • Open Jan to Oct: Jan, Feb and Oct, Sun only, 11am – 3pm; March to Sept, daily: Sun and Bank Holiday Mons, 10am – 6pm, other days 1 – 6pm (last admission 5.15pm). Guided tours available • Entrance: £3, concessions £2, family ticket £7.50, season ticket £12/£8. Special rates for parties • Other information: Restaurant in grounds of Shuttleworth Mansion. Disabled parking. Two wheelchairs available for loan ◔ ▬ <u>WC</u> ↺ ℘ ▦ ♀

This fascinating ten-acre romantic landscape garden is said to have been created in 1820 by the third Lord Ongley for his Swiss mistress. It was neglected for 40 years from 1939, then leased by Bedfordshire County Council and restored. It has wonderful trees: cedar of Lebanon, the largest Arolla pines in England, vast pieris 150 years old underplanted with *Helleborus orientalis*, and a most unusual variegated sweet chestnut. Innumerable rustic iron bridges cross over miniature ponds. Little Swiss cottage with sheets of bulbs in the spring underplanting azaleas, rhododendrons and spring-flowering shrubs. The gloom of the grotto and the dazzling light of the fernery provide a dramatic contrast.

Toddington Manor ★   10

Toddington LU5 6HJ. Tel: (01525) 872576

Sir Neville and Lady Bowman-Shaw • 1m W of M1 junction 12, 1m NW of Toddington. Signposted • Open by appt • Entrance: charge • Other information: Rare breeds of sheep, goats and pigs. Vintage tractor collection ◑

The Bowman-Shaws moved here in 1979 to find a wilderness, since reclaimed and planted with spring bulbs, flowering trees and other plants which lend colour well into the summer. They also inherited some wonderful old trees – beeches, ashes, yews and Wellingtonias – set in extensive lawns. The pleached lime walk, along a lovely old paved path, has a hosta/fern border on one side and a large herbaceous border on the other. Particularly beautiful are the varied shrub and climbing roses. A large walled garden is filled with many interesting and stylish plants, including delphiniums and peonies. There is a large, comprehensive herb garden beside the restored greenhouses which are home to vines and orchids. Water is important in both gardens and woods, with many streams, ponds and two lakes surrounded by paths providing excellent walks. Improvements continue: most recently a wildflower meadow has been sown in an old replanted orchard, and work on a new arboretum, featuring maples and cherries, has begun.

Woburn Abbey   11

Woburn MK43 0TP. Tel: (01525) 290666; Fax: (01525) 290271

The Marquess of Tavistock and Trustees of Bedford Estates • From M1 junction 13 follow signs • Open 2nd Jan to 19th March, Sat and Sun only, 10.30am – 3.45pm; 20th March to 26th Sept, daily, 10am – 4.30pm; Oct, Sat and Sun only, 10.30am – 3.45pm • Entrance: £5 per car, inc. all passengers' entry to park, can be exchanged for one entry to Abbey. Abbey and park £7.50, OAPs £6.50, children (12-16) £3, under 12 free(1999 prices) • Other information: Pottery and Antiques Centre ◑ 💬 ✕ 🖪 WC ◁ 🏠 ♌

Humphry Repton, who designed the park and garden, considered Woburn to be one of his finest achievements. Today, huge magnificent sweeping lawns are meticulously mown in diamonds and stripes lining up with the house. The private gardens, which are open to the public at stated times, contain a large hornbeam maze. They have good herbaceous borders, massed beds of 'Iceberg' roses edged with lavender, and a most successful new rose garden designed by Anita Pereire. Rare water lilies lie on the lovely ponds, and in the spring there are over 100 varieties of daffodils and narcissi, with fritillaries and orchids naturalised in the grass. The many fine trees include tulip trees. The owners are concentrating on viburnums and hope to hold a National Collection. An old camellia house (frost-free) contains large camellias, still with the odd flower in June. The deer park is landscaped down to the Shoulder-of-Mutton pond, with fine groups of trees, and with many species of deer. A wonderful, historic site.

Wrest Park 12

Silsoe, Bedford MK45 4HS. Tel: (01525) 860152

English Heritage • 10m S of Bedford, ¾ m E of Silsoe off A6 • Gardens open April to Sept, Sat, Sun and Bank Holidays only, 10am – 6pm; Oct, Sat and Sun only, 10am – 6pm (last admission 1 hour before closing) • Entrance: £3.20, OAPs £2.40, children (5-15) £1.60 ◑ 🚼 WC ♿ 🚭 🍴

An article in *Country Life* described this as 'little visited' and 'one of the most under-appreciated landscapes in England'. Wrest Park, 150 acres in total, is one of the few places in England where it is possible to see an early eighteenth-century formal garden in the manner of Bridgeman: the Great Garden, created for the 1st Duke of Kent. Bridgeman's layout dominates the main axis of the grounds, which feature an impressive, if slender, canal; many *allées* cut through thick blocks of natural and unrestrained woodland lead to statues and giant vases set in grassy glades. Later 'Capability' Brown worked here and made alterations without destroying the integrity of the earlier plan. He created a highly naturalistic artificial river to surround the grounds and loosened the planting at their perimeter. The woods on either side of the Long Water are intersected by avenues and dotted with unexpected temples, columns and other 'incidents of delight'. Amongst these are the Thomas Archer pavilion at the end of the Long Water, the Bath House, built as a romantic classical ruin, the Cascade Bridge and the exquisite Batty Langley Bowling Green House. Water catches the eye in every direction. In the nineteenth century, when the house was rebuilt in the French style, it was fronted by terraces with parterres. There are several fine buildings, including a large orangery designed by the French architect Cléphane. Two deep mixed borders, separated by a wide turf *allée*, have recently been refurbished and should look well for much of the summer if the rabbits can be kept at bay.

BERKSHIRE

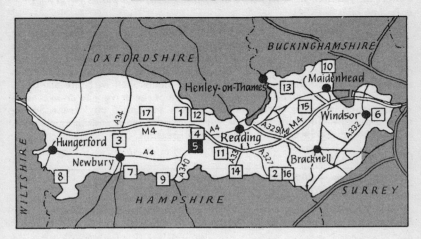

Some gardens have postal addresses in one county and are physically situated in another. If in doubt, a check in the index will direct the reader to the page on which the garden appears.

Two-starred gardens are marked on the map with a black square.

Ashdown House

(see Oxfordshire)

Basildon Park   1

Lower Basildon, Reading RG8 9NR. Tel: (0118) 984 3040

The National Trust • Between Pangbourne and Streatley, 7m NW of Reading on W side of A329; leave M4 at junction 12 and continue to Theale roundabout, then take Pangbourne road • House open April to Oct, Wed – Sun, 1pm – 5.30pm • Park open April to Oct, Wed – Sun, 12 noon – 5.30pm • Other information: Parking 400 metres from house ◑ ☕ ✕ 🗄 <u>WC</u> ♿ ⬗ 🏛 ♟

Within the park, with very old trees which frame a glimpse of the Thames, is a small formal garden with herbaceous borders. The early-nineteenth-century pleasure grounds, which are being restored, included a thatched 'Umbrello', probably based on an original design by J.B. Papworth.

Blencathra   2

Finchampstead, Wokingham RG40 3SS. Tel: (0118) 973 4563

Dr and Mrs F.W. Gifford • 3m S of Wokingham, 1m W of A321 near Crowthorne Station, at NW end of Finchampstead Ridges (B3348). Entrance 300 metres down joint private drive • Open 16th April, 21st May, 2 – 6pm and

by appt for individuals and parties • Entrance: £2.50, accompanied children free
• Other information: Park in joint private drive. Teas and plants for sale on
open days only ● ঙ ⬦

The owners started this 11-acre garden in 1964, when they purchased an unmanaged woodland site and built their house. Their enthusiasm for fresh ideas is inspiring. With minimal budget and help – none professional – the low-maintenance garden has evolved. Established shrubs, lawns, specimen trees and roses surround the house, whose design blends well with the plantings. Features include woodland areas on either side of the drive, and an extensive water garden including three pools, a stream and small 'bog' areas. Spring bulbs especially bluebells, together with rhododendrons and many conifers, ensure colour and interesting features in all seasons.

Chieveley Manor 3

Chieveley, Newbury RG20 8UT. Tel: (01635) 248208

Mr and Mrs C.J. Spence • 4m N of Newbury, ½ m from M4 junction 13 via
A34. In Chieveley, Manor Lane by church • Open 18th June, 2 – 6pm •
Entrance: £1, children free ● 🚌 WC ঙ ৶

Fine views over the paddock area from the stud with its imposing cedar tree. Two good herbaceous borders including newly planted purple sage beds interspersed with geraniums. Walled garden and swimming pool garden. Interesting shrubs and roses. Although open only one day, visitors have the benefit in the village of *Peasemore*, just down the road, of three grand houses which open their gardens for the NGS on the same afternoon, with teas at the Old Rectory, 2 – 6pm.

Englefield House 4

Englefield, Theale, Reading RG7 5EN. Tel: (0118) 930 2221

Sir William and Lady Benyon • 5m W of Reading. Entrance is on A340, near
Theale • Open all year, Mons; also April to July, Tues – Thurs; all 10am –
6pm • Entrance: £2, children free ◑ 📷 WC ঙ ৶ ✿

The car park is situated up a long drive past the church – and past several notices saying 'no parking'. The imposing house is set against a wooded hill, with grassy paths leading from a stream and water garden to a more formal area of roses and perennials. The terrace is particularly charming with a water feature set in an area of white and silver plants – the colours becoming stronger nearer the house – and a spectacular view overlooking the deer park. The seven acres of woodland have interesting trees and shrubs.

Folly Farm ★★ 5

Sulhamstead, Reading RG7 4DF.

7m SW of Reading, 2m W of M4 junction 12. Turn onto A4 and left at
road marked Sulhamstead at Mulligan's Fish Restaurant 1m after Theale

roundabout; entrance ¾ m on right • The house is being sold so do not visit without writing to the new owners to enquire about possible openings in 2000 ◐

A sublime example of the Lutyens and Jekyll partnership in its vintage years before World War I. The intimate relationship of house and garden personifies Lutyens' genius for design and craftsmanship. A complex arrangement of spaces and courts is linked by herringbone-patterned brick paths, enhancing the vernacular origins of an attractive Edwardian country house. The gardens retain much of their original character, although some planting has been chosen to suit the taste of the present owners. The mixed borders are mainly shrub roses, which look wonderful in the second half of June, with old-fashioned herbaceous plants in between giving colour as late as August. The formal sunken rose garden surrounded by a high yew hedge is particularly notable for its masterful design on several levels and this has been substantially replanted in subtle colours. Other features include formal entrance court, barn court, Dutch-inspired canal garden, flower parterre and tank cloister. This is one of the country's most important twentieth-century gardens, which it is hoped will remain open to the public.

Frogmore Gardens 6

Windsor SL4 2JG.

H.M. The Queen • At Windsor Castle. Entrance via signed car park on B3021 between Datchet and Old Windsor. Pedestrian access only from Long Walk • House open as garden in Aug • Garden open probably 29th to 31st Aug, 10am – 5.30pm and several dates in May, 10am – 7pm. Telephone for details (01753) 868286 ext. 2347 • Entrance: house, gardens and mausoleum £4.90, OAPs £3.90, children £2.90 (children under 8 not admitted) (1999 prices) ◐

Set amid the extensive Home Park of Windsor Castle, Frogmore House is surrounded by 30 acres of landscaped and picturesque gardens. Fine and unusual trees include a remarkable incense cedar planted in 1857. The house dates from the 1680s and was purchased in 1792 for Queen Charlotte, consort of George III. Frogmore then passed through a succession of royal owners, becoming a favoured retreat of Queen Victoria and later of King George V and Queen Mary. The peace of Frogmore drew Prince Albert and Queen Victoria to break with royal tradition and to choose a corner of the garden to build a mausoleum for themselves. Other architectural features include a charming wisteria-covered Gothick ruin by Wyatt, Queen Victoria's tea house and an Indian kiosk brought from Lucknow after the Mutiny. (Unfortunately, the limited opening means that the public will not see what must be one of the garden's chief glories, the 200,000 spring bulbs planted in Queen Mary's time.) The formal layout at the Castle, called the East Terrace, laid out by Sir Geoffrey Wyatville for George IV, is now open to the public. It has a somewhat municipal air, quite different from the private garden for the royal family behind its walls, or the gardens in the Great Park, begun after 1931, or, for that matter, Frogmore itself.

Hazelby House ★ 7

North End, Nr Newbury RG20 0AZ. Tel: (01635) 255011

Mr and Mrs P Swinstead • 5m S of Newbury from M4 junction 13. Take A34 to Newbury, then turn left to Ball Hill, and after 3m take left turning off Kintbury Rd • Open on some days for NGS, and by appt • Entrance: £3, children £1.50 NEW ●

Twenty-five years ago there was only a vegetable patch here – now there is a most impressive garden, planned on the Sissinghurst system of 'rooms'. The pergola is wreathed with the pale rose 'Paul's Himalayan Musk', jasmine and grape vines. Doorways in the hedges open onto two lily pools (one of pink lilies and one of white), a rose garden heavily underplanted with herbaceous perennials, and a long herbaceous border between beech hedges. A grass bank then leads down to the small lake with an islet showing a splash of colour from climbing roses, where a lakewood garden started some seven years ago is being steadily extended, the large hostas kept slug-free by the ducks. Meadows surrounding the intensively cultivated garden are a riot of indigenous wild flowers in midsummer. There are 20 acres of shaded woodland which include a magnificent oak over 430 years old.

Inkpen House 8

Inkpen, Hungerford RG17 9DS.

Mr and Mrs David Male • 3m S of A4, between Hungerford and Newbury. Go to Kintbury village centre crossroads, turn into Inkpen Road, after 1m turn right to Inkpen, then follow signs for thirteenth-century church. House is next to church • Open for NGS 19th July, 2 – 6pm • Entrance: £2, children free • Other information: Hungerford Town Brass Band may be performing ● ▣ WC ⚘

Here is an unusual opportunity to walk round a four-acre garden in the French style of Le Nôtre. The William and Mary house (not open) was built by the rector, later Master of Pembroke College, Oxford, about 1695. Miles Hadfield puts the pleached lime avenue and yew hedges at pre-1720 (the rector died of apoplexy in 1714) but Fleming and Gore date the planting as early as 1695 when the rector may have had the help of John Evelyn. Wonderful *allées* of yew, holly and beech, with pleached limes which may, therefore, be the oldest survivors in the UK – though a church at Westbourne in West Sussex claims to have a 1544 planting. Viewing mound. Statuary. Good herbaceous border. Walled kitchen garden. Restored and sensitively replanted by the previous owner, the late Sir Frederick Warner, the garden continues to be splendidly maintained.

Meadow House 9

Ashford Hill, Thatcham RG19 8BN. Tel: (0118) 981 6005

Antony and Harriet Jones • 8m SE of Newbury. From B3051 take turning at SW end of village to Wolverton Common. After 350 metres turn right down track to house • Garden open for NGS 18th May, 1st, 15th June, 6th, 20th July, 17th Aug, 11am – 4pm. Other times by appt. Parties of up to 40 welcome • Entrance:

£2, children free (1999 price) • Other information: Park cars in meadow and coaches at top of lane. Plants for sale in nursery ● ❺

Essentially a plantsman's creation. A small country house garden of just under two acres with lawn sweeping down to a small lake supporting ducks and waterside planting. The nursery and greenhouse are screened by a tall trellis smothered with clematis, rambler roses and honeysuckle. Woodland is under-planted with hostas, primulas, camellias and 'Annabelle' hydrangeas. Borders contain mixed shrubs, unusual herbaceous perennials and shrub roses.

Odney Club   10

Odney Lane, Cookham, Maidenhead SL6 9ST. Tel: (01628) 530011

John Lewis Partnership • Between Beaconsfield and Maidenhead, off A4094 near Cookham Bridge • Open one Sun in April, 2 – 6pm • Entrance: £2, children free 🍽 🏠 WC ❺ � ℘

Although only open one day a year, this huge 120-acre site along the Thames, well cared-for and continuously developing, makes a full afternoon visit. It was a favourite with Stanley Spencer, who often visited to paint the magnolia which featured in his work. There is a magnificent wisteria walk, and also specimen trees, herbaceous borders, small side gardens, and terraces with spring bedding plants.

The Old Rectory ★   11

Burghfield, Reading RG30 3TH. Tel: (0118) 983 3200

Mr A.R. Merton • 5m SW of Reading. Turn S off A4 to Burghfield village and right after Hatch Gate Inn • Open last Wed in each month Feb to Oct, 11am – 4pm and for parties by appt in writing • Entrance: £2, parties £2.50 per person ● 🍽 🏠 WC ❺ ℘

This garden has achieved wide renown, and its maturity and the amazing generosity of plants skilfully planted are remarkable in a site started from scratch in 1950. The late Mrs Merton described herself as 'a green-fingered lunatic' who collected plants from all over the world, notably some rare items from Japan and China. The terrace has a fine display most of the year, and the herbaceous border and beds are impressive, with collections of hellebores, pinks, violas, peonies, snowdrops, old roses and many others. In the spring there are drifts of daffodils and rather rare cowslips and so many other plants to see that it is well worth making a visit month by month if you live within reasonable range. Something here for every type of gardener.

Old Rectory Cottage ★   12

Tidmarsh, Pangbourne, Reading RG8 8ER. Tel: (0118) 984 3241

Mr and Mrs A.W.A. Baker • 5m NW of Reading, ½ m S of Pangbourne towards Tidmarsh (A340). Turn E down narrow lane • Open by appt for individual members of the RHS Lily Group, Alpine Garden Society, Hardy Plant Society and garden societies • Entrance: £2, children free (1999 prices) • Other information: Possible for wheelchairs but some grass and gravel paths ● WC ❺ ℘

This two-acre cottage garden is full of rare and exciting plants, many of them collected by the owners. It has an area with early spring bulbs and a wild garden round a small lake off the River Pang. Lilies, roses, wild geraniums, unusual shrubs and climbers. It is worth visiting on several occasions as there is always something new to stimulate the interest of a keen gardener. In addition there are ornamental pheasants, white doves and Arab horses. Quite rightly this garden has had much media coverage.

The Savill Garden

(see Surrey)

Scotlands ★   13

Cockpole Green, Wargrave, Reading RG10 8QP. Tel: (01628) 822648

Mr Michael and The Hon. Mrs Payne • 4m E of Henley-on-Thames. Off A4 at Knowl Hill, halfway between Warren Row and Cockpole Green • Open one Sun in May, 2 – 6pm for NGS and by appt • Entrance: £2, children free • Other information: Teas and plants for sale on NGS open day only. Picnics permitted on Cockpole Green ● 🅿 WC ♿ ⬦ 🐾

The attractive chalk-and-flint house, formerly a seventeenth-century barn, is surrounded by a series of courtyards, one with a lily pool. To the west is the oval swimming pool, guarded by yew hedges and the lead statue of a drummer boy. A herb garden with patterned paving and box, roses, lavender and choice vegetables such as artichokes is overlooked by a gazebo. To the east, a lawn sweeps down to the woodland and pond garden, the Repton-style summer-house signalling the merging of the landscaped water garden with natural woodland. Mown grass paths lead to a waterfall with rocks and a new gazebo. Fine specimen catalpa, cedars, Spanish chestnuts and copper beech mark the boundary of this four-acre site.

Swallowfield Park   14

Swallowfield, Reading RG7 1TG. Tel: (0118) 988 3815; Fax: (0118) 988 3930

Country Houses Association Ltd • 5m S of Reading in Swallowfield. Entrance in Church Road • Open May to Sept, Wed and Thurs, 2 – 5pm • Entrance: house and gardens £2.50, children £1, larger parties by appt ◑ 🅿 ♿ ⬦ 🍽

Twenty-five acres of garden, all maintained to the highest standard. There is a six-and-a-half-acre walled garden, much of it built by Thomas Pitt, grand-father of the Prime Minister, in which there are colourful herbaceous borders, scented roses, a small orchard and a laburnum-and-wisteria-cov-ered pergola. In other parts of the grounds are fine lawns and specimen trees, many of them brought to the park in the nineteenth century. There is a dogs' cemetery in which one of Charles Dickens' dogs is buried. Visitors are encouraged to walk past the croquet lawn (often in use) and a large decoy pond to the banks of the River Loddon, which forms the northern boundary of the park.

Virginia Water

(see VALLEY GARDENS, Surrey)

Waltham Place ★   15

White Waltham, Maidenhead SL6 3JH. Tel: (01628) 825517

Mr and Mrs N.F. Oppenheimer • 3½ m S of Maidenhead. From M4 take junction 8/9 to A423M and follow signs to White Waltham, watching for left turn to farm shop • Open June and July, Mon – Fri, 10am – 5pm, for NGS 28th May, 23rd July, 2 – 7pm, and for parties by appt all year (Tel: (01628) 824605) • Entrance: £2.50, children 50p • Other information: Refreshments served on NGS open days only ● WC ⬥ ℘ 🛍

Forty acres of organic gardens with woodlands and lake, integrated with the 100-acre farm. Look out particularly for the splendid weeping beech and Atlas cedar, and for a variety of herbaceous borders, including a long border framed by yew hedges, which is full of colourful perennials, and a 'hot' border. There is a butterfly garden, a knot garden, a traditional Japanese garden and a walled garden, complete with pergola, fountain and fish ponds. Bluebells, camellias and rhododendrons bring colour to the woods in season.

White Knights   16

The Ridges, Finchampstead, Wokingham RG40 3SY. Tel: (0118) 973 3274

Mrs Heather Bradly • 9m SE of Reading between A327 and A321, midway along Finchampstead Ridges on B3348. Turn in through white gate posts on right between Crowthorne station and war memorial • Open by appt only • Entrance £2.50 • Other information: Refreshments by arrangement for parties. Guide dogs only NEW ● WC ⬥ ℘

Over the last 16 years the owners have created a large garden designed to look interesting throughout the year with minimum upkeep. The beds around the house are mainly planted with dwarf conifers of all hues and many varieties of heathers. A noble wisteria covers the south-facing wall. A Japanese garden complete with flowing water and tea house in the Zen tradition, a Mediterranean area with cacti, both hardy and overwintered in the greenhouse, and a Chinese courtyard alongside the swimming pool graced by a fountain give the garden an international flavour. Indoors, a model of a Tudor village will appeal to all ages.

Wyld Court Rainforest   17

Streatley Road, Hampstead Norreys, Thatcham, Newbury RG18 0TN.
Tel: (01635) 200221; Fax: (01635) 202440

Wyld Court Rainforest • 7m NE of Newbury. Follow the signs from M4 junction 13 • Open daily except 25th, 26th Dec, 10am – 5.15pm (last admission ¾ hour before closing) • Entrance: £4, concessions £3, children (aged 5 – 14) £2.50 (1999 prices) ○ ▣ 🏠 WC ⬥ ℘ 🛍 🕯

A remarkable 1860-square-metre glasshouse with a fine collection of exotic plants, splendidly grown, which educates visitors in the beauty and diversity of the rainforest. A feature is the tasteful and imaginative way in which the plants are displayed in a carefully studied interior landscape with paths at various levels, allowing them to be enjoyed from above. There are two distinct environments – an area known as Lowland which mimics conditions in a coastal rainforest, and an area called Amazonica, which emphasises life in the forest canopy. In each is a representative collection of the animals found here, chosen to illustrate the symbiotic relationship between animals and plants in their natural environment.

GARDENING FOR THE DISABLED &

Demonstration gardens to assist the disabled are available at a number of properties open to the public. They include the following:

Battersea Park (see *Guide* under London) Horticultural Therapy Unit (Wandsworth Borough Council). For appt tel: (0171) 720 3419

Broadview Gardens, Hadlow (see Kent)

Capel Manor (see London) Tel: (01992) 763849

Disabled and Older Gardeners' Association, Herefordshire Growing Point, Herefordshire College of Agriculture, Holme Lacy, Hereford. Tel: (01432) 870316

Royal Horticultural Society's Garden, Wisley (see Surrey)

Ryton Organic Gardens, Ryton-on-Dunsmore (see Warwickshire)

Syon Park, Middlesex (see London).

Open days for the disabled are also held from time to time at the following gardens:

Dolly's Garden (see London)

Hillsborough Community Development Trust (see South & West Yorkshire)

Iden Croft Herbs (see Kent).

The Gardening for Disabled Trust is a registered charity which collects donations from the public and uses them to assist disabled people with improvements to their gardens, or to supply equipment which will enable them to continue to garden. Donations should be sent to Mrs Felicity Seton, Hayes Farmhouse, Hayes Lane, Peasmarsh, Rye, East Sussex.

WHEELCHAIR USERS &

Please note that the symbol denoting suitability for wheelchairs refers to the garden only. If there is a house open, it may or may not be suitable.

BIRMINGHAM AREA

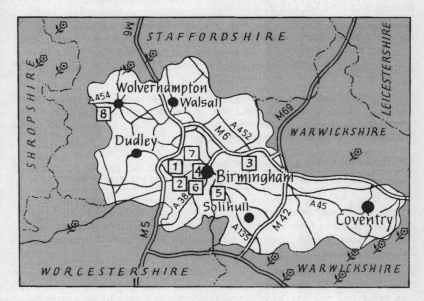

Botanical Gardens and Glasshouses ★   1

Westbourne Road, Edgbaston B15 3TR. Tel: (0121) 454 1860

2m from city centre. Approach from Hagley Road or Calthorpe Road, following tourist signs • Open all year, daily, 9am (10am on Sun) – 7pm (or dusk if earlier) • Entrance: £4.20 (£4.50 on summer Suns), OAPs, disabled, students and children £2.30. Parties £3.60 per person (£2.10 for concessions) (1999 prices) • Other information: Manual and electric wheelchairs available free of charge ○ ☕ ✕ 🖼 <u>WC</u> ♿ 🐾 🛍 🚻

This 15-acre ornamental garden will appeal to the keen plantsperson and also to the everyday gardener. In addition to the unusual plants in the Tropical House and the Orangery, there is a Cactus and Succulent House, cages with parrots and macaws, peacocks and a waterfowl enclosure with ducks, geese and other birds. Some beautiful old trees, a border for E.H. Wilson plants, a raised alpine bed and a sunken rose garden beside the lawn aviary. The rock garden contains a wide variety of alpine plants, primulas, astilbes and azaleas. There are also herbaceous borders, and a small display of carnivorous plants. The model domestic-theme gardens cover low-maintenance, children, colour and a plantsman's area. An attractive courtyard houses the National Collection of bonsai. The recently developed alpine yard has examples of the many ways to grow plants in a variety of raised beds and containers. A children's playground and adventure trail make this a pleasant place for a family outing. Bands play every Sunday in summer.

Cannon Hill Park 2

Moseley B13 8RD. Tel: (0121) 442 4226

Birmingham City Council • 2m from city centre opposite Edgbaston Cricket Ground • Park open all year, daily, 7.30am – dusk. Glasshouse open 10am – 4pm • Entrance: free • Other information: Midland Art Centre in park contains bookshop, gallery, theatre and restaurant and toilet facilities ○ 🍴 ♿ ⚓ 🎁 ♦

Eighty acres of park with formal beds, wide range of herbaceous plants, shrubs and trees. Glasshouse with collection of tropical and sub-tropical plants. Nature trails. Children's area. Also boating, miniature golf, bowls and tennis available. A model of the Elan Valley is set in the garden area.

Castle Bromwich Hall Gardens ★ 3

Chester Road, Castle Bromwich B36 9BT. Tel/Fax: (0121) 749 4100

Castle Bromwich Hall Gardens Trust • 4m E of city centre. 1m from junction 5 of M6 northbound. Southbound leave M6 at junction 6 and follow A38 and A452. Signposted • Open Easter to Sept, Tues – Thurs, 1.30 – 4.30pm, Sat, Sun and Bank Holiday Mons, 2 – 6pm. Guided tours daily • Entrance: £3, OAPs £2, children £1 ◐ 🍴 WC ♿ ⚓ 🌿 🎁 ♦

The hall, built at the end of the sixteenth century, was sold to Sir John Bridgeman in 1657, and his wife created the garden with expert help. It fell into decay, and now a series of formal connecting gardens is being restored to give them the appearance and content of a garden of 1680-1740. The perimeter wall, summerhouse and greenhouse have been rebuilt. There are fan- and espalier-trained fruit trees and an orchard, a kitchen garden, ponds, classical parterres, an archery lawn, a holly maze, a wilderness and historic borders. A formal vegetable garden is planted with historic and unusual vegetables, such as white carrots and blue 'Congo' potatoes. Ten acres in all.

City Centre Gardens 4

Cambridge Street B1 2NP.

Birmingham City Council • Off Cambridge Street, to rear of theatre and Symphony Hall on Broad Street • Open all year, daily during daylight hours • Entrance: free ◐ 🍴 ♿ ⚓

Approximately half an acre of rough ground remaining after building demolition and subsequently used as a car park has here been converted to a garden for all seasons. The flowering year begins with the earliest spring bulbs but there is something for gardeners to discover and enjoy throughout the year. The layout is formal, the planting skilful and exuberant, with a great variety of shrubs, perennials, roses and some annuals, many less usual but all blending harmoniously. Climbers cover the walls and fences, and the general effect on a summer's day is of colour and perfume.

16 Prospect Road 5

Moseley B13 9TB. Tel: (0121) 449 8457

Mr and Mrs Londesborough • Coming to Birmingham on A435 turn right in King's Heath just after Safeway supermarket and pedestrian lights, up Poplar Road to roundabout, second left into School Road, second right into Prospect Road • Open 16th April, 9th July, 2 – 6pm, and by appt all year • Entrance: £2 on open days, £1 by appt ● ● WC ♀

This is a plantsman's garden. The journey of discovery begins with a conservatory with collection of tender perennials; a collection of grasses, colour-filled pots and troughs of alpines on the terrace, and continues along winding paths between beds stocked with a remarkable display of usual and unusual plants showing colour at all seasons. At each turn of the path there are different plants to lead the eye on to a fresh discovery.

University Botanic Garden ★ 6

Winterbourne, 58 Edgbaston Park Road, Edgbaston B16 3TT.
Tel: (0121) 414 4944; E-mail: Unibotanic@bham.ac.uk

University of Birmingham School of Continuing Studies • Off A38 Bristol road leading out of city. On university campus • Open April to Sept, Mon – Fri, 11am – 4pm (closed Bank Holiday Mons) • Entrance: £2, children 50p ● ▦ WC ♿ ♀

About seven acres of garden originally belonging to a large house owing much to the landscape style developed by Edwin Lutyens and Gertrude Jekyll. Because of its wide range of plants and different features it should be of interest to the botanist as well as the ordinary gardener. There are geographical beds showing typical trees and shrubs from Europe, Australasia, the Americas, China and Japan. The pergola is covered with clematis and roses and there are herbaceous borders backed by brick walls covered with climbers. A miniature arboretum contains interesting specimens including giant oaks, acers, conifers and a *Ginkgo biloba* along with hedges of yew (*Taxus baccata*) and copper beech. In the Commemorative Garden is a black mulberry planted to mark the 100th anniversary of the City of Birmingham. The range of plants continues with the sandstone rock garden, troughs, rhododendrons, heathers and alpines. There is an unusual nut walk containing several varieties of *Corylus avellana* trained over an iron framework. A special feature is the walled garden laid out with beds of roses showing the history of the European rose, and elsewhere are more recent plantings of roses. Notable architectural features include a crinkle-crankle wall. Useful guide.

8 Vicarage Road 7

Edgbaston B15 3ES. Tel: (0121) 455 0902

Charles and Tessa King-Farlow • 1½ m W of city centre off A456 Hagley road. Going out of city, turn left into Vicarage Road • Open one afternoon and one evening for NGS (telephone for details) and by appt • Entrance: £1.50, children free ● ♿ ♀

A visit should give pleasure to most gardeners. There are several areas of interest and plenty of good planting ideas, with a clever use of colour and foliage combinations – a range of grey and variegated foliage. Roses and clematis scramble through old fruit trees and shrubs. There is a bank of shrub roses, and four mixed borders containing a wide range and some rare plants. Conservatory, pool and 1920s' rock garden providing year-round colour. The walled kitchen garden has fruit and vegetables mixed with colourful annuals and is laid out in a geometric pattern.

Wightwick Manor   8

Wightwick Bank, Wolverhampton WV6 8EE. Tel: (01902) 761400

The National Trust • 3m W of Wolverhampton off A454. Turn by Mermaid Inn up Wightwick Bank • House open Thurs – Sat, 2.30 – 5.30pm. Timed tickets • Garden open March to Dec, Wed, Thurs and Sat, Bank Holiday Suns and Mons, 2 – 6pm. Also open other weekdays by appt. Pre-booked parties accepted Wed and Thurs • Entrance: £2.40 (house and garden £5.40) • Other information: Possible for wheelchairs but sloping site. Braille guide available
🕐 💺 🏠 WC & ⬧ 🛍

This 17-acre garden, designed by Alfred Parsons and Thomas Mawson, surrounds an 1887 house strongly influenced in its design by William Morris and his Movement, which contains a collection of Pre-Raphaelite paintings. Large trees form a delightful framework to the garden, the main feature of which is the magnificent octagonal arbour in the centre of the rose garden, hung with climbing roses and clematis. This was based on garden designs in the 1906 Thomas Mawson catalogue. Through an old orchard is a less formal area with pools surrounded by shrubs and rhododendrons. There are herbaceous borders, two rows of barrel-shaped yews and beds containing plants from gardens of famous men. It is a surprise when, round a corner, one comes across a line of boulders from Scotland and the Lake District which were left when the great glaciers melted in the last Ice Age. The Peach House and the rose garden have been restored. The Mathematical Bridge, giving access to the Bridge Garden, with spring bulbs, is now reconstructed, all part of ongoing improvements.

HOW TO FIND THE GARDENS
Directions to each garden are included in the entry. This information has been supplied by the owners and garden inspectors. It is aimed to be the best available to those travelling by car, and has been compiled to be used in conjunction with a road atlas.

Some gardens can be approached by public transport, but alas these are few and far between. The unreliability of train and bus services makes it unrewarding to include details, particularly as many garden visits are made on Sundays. However, properties that can be reached by public transport feature in National Trust guides and the NGS Yellow Book, which sometimes give details.

BRISTOL AREA

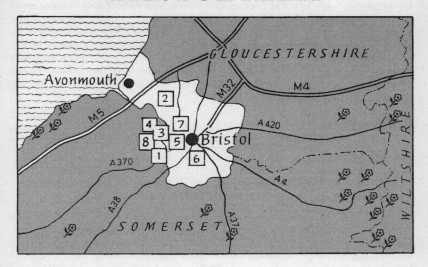

Ashton Court Estate 1

Long Ashton BS41 9JN. Tel: (0117) 963 9174

Bristol City Council • SW of city off A369 • Open daily, 8am – dusk • Entrance: free ○ 🍽 🧺 <u>WC</u> ♿ �️ 🛒🏪 ☕

Ashton Court Mansion dates from the early fifteenth century with the addition of a remarkable seventeenth-century wing, and some features of this period are incorporated in the predominantly Victorian gardens. The terraced lawn is bounded by an early eighteenth-century wall; steps lead down to the sunken garden with redwood trees and a pond. The pets' graves of the Smyth family overlook the ha-ha. A rose garden now graces an area that used to be greenhouses. The picturesque landscaped park, attributed to Humphry Repton, with its curving drive, tree belt and clumps, has a rare survival (one indebted to Bristol City Council for its maintenance) in the form of two deer parks. Nearby Clarkencombe Wood has ancient dramatic oaks.

Blaise Castle House ★ 2

Henbury BS10 7QS. Tel: (0117) 950 6789

Bristol City Museum • 4m N of city, W of Henbury, N of B4057 • House and first-floor museum open April to Oct, Sat – Wed, 10am – 5pm • Entrance: free access to Green ○ 🧺 ♿ 🚖 🛒🏪 ☕

A picturesque village owned by The National Trust in the form of a green surrounded by nine cottages with private gardens, designed by John Nash with George and John Repton in 1809 for the pensioners of John Harford's estate. The village pump and sundial of 1812 remain. Jasmines, ivies and honeysuckles were planted around the cottages to reflect their picturesque names ('Jessamine', 'Rose Briar'), with ornamental shrubs added to the woodland setting. A spectacular drive can be taken from Henbury Hill to the entrance lodge of Blaise Castle House – another charming *cottage orné* is half-way. The driveway into the gorge and up to the house passes a Robber's Cave and the Lovers' Leap. The view is exceptional. Near the house are the ornamental dairy (originally conceived by George Repton) and elegant orangery, both by Nash.

Bristol Zoo Gardens 3

Clifton BS8 3HA. Tel: (0117) 973 8951; Website: www.bristolzoo.org.uk

Bristol Zoo Gardens • Signposted from M5 junctions 17 and 18 and from city centre • Open daily except 25th Dec, 9am – 5.30pm (4.30pm in winter) • Entrance: £7.95, concessions £6.95, children (3-13) £4.50. Special rates for parties of 15 or more ○ 🍽 ✕ 🏬 WC ⬧ 👍 ⚲

Set up in 1835 as a garden as well as a zoo, the gardens will satisfy those with Victorian tastes for splashes of colour. Displays range from formal to informal, and botanically interesting plants are highlighted. The terrace bedding gives a 'rich tapestry of vibrant colours in an individual style using the choicest of plants'. The bedding is complemented by herbaceous borders, a lake, rose and rock gardens, indoor displays and numerous interesting trees and shrubs. Holder of two National Collections, actinidias and caryopteris. All well contrived, with evident love and care.

Emmaus House 4

**Retreat and Conference Centre, Clifton Hill, Clifton BS8 4PD.
Tel: (0117) 907 9950**

Sisters of La Retraite • From city centre take A4018 to Clifton, A4176 past Zoo and left into Clifton Down Road. Follow through to Regent Street. House is at bottom of drive on right • Open five times a year and on weekdays by prior appt • Entrance: £1.50, OAPs £1, children free (1999 prices) ◗ 🍽 ✕ WC ⚲

Covering one and a half acres, the gardens lie hidden from the road behind two imposing eighteenth-century merchants' houses. Walking down from the front entrance and around the side of the property the visitor enters a succession of separate gardens set on different levels, but all carefully linked and with extensive views towards the harbour and beyond. The gardens have been considerably altered in recent years but the Victorian kitchen garden is substantially intact, supplying fruit and vegetables to the house. The old greenhouses are still in use, containing apricots and a 150-year-old Black Hamburg vine. A formal herb garden framed by clipped box pyramids surrounds an ornamental fishpond. This leads down to a Zen Garden where large stones and running water are imaginatively used to represent the Zen concepts of life and rebirth. At a lower level, the visitor enters the Secret Garden containing many old apple trees and underplanted with spring bulbs. Then, continuing round the houses, the Courtyard Garden, reclaimed from the original stableyard, is enclosed by high walls with macleayas and vigorous euphorbias.

Goldney Hall 5

Lower Clifton Hill, Clifton BS8 1BH. Tel: (0117) 903 4873

University of Bristol • In city centre at top of Constitution Hill, Clifton • Garden open 7th May, 9am – 5pm • Entrance: £1, guided tours £2 ● ● WC ♿

The eighteenth-century garden (or what remains) is a thrilling discovery in the middle of this busy, once bombed city. Perched on a hillside, it is full of surprises, not least the small formal canal with an orangery at its head. From the largely nineteenth-century house the visitor is led through the shadows of an *allée* of yews to a dank grotto entrance whose façade is a striking example of early but sophisticated Gothick. The grotto itself, now justly famous, is astonishingly elaborate: water really gushes through it and the walls are liberally encrusted with shells and minerals. Passing through the grotto and out by narrow labyrinthine passages, suddenly there is a terrace, a broad airy grass walk with magnificent views over the old dock. At the far end of the terrace is a Gothic gazebo, and towering above the other end a castellated tower. Now owned by the University, Goldney has follies, a parterre and a herb garden packed into its nine acres.

The Red Lodge 6

Park Row BS1 5LJ. Tel: (0117) 921 1360

Bristol City Council • In city centre • House open • Garden open June and July, Sat – Wed, 10am – 4.30pm only. Opening hours are variable so telephone before travelling • Entrance: £1.05 ●

Good reconstruction of the early seventeenth-century town garden of a merchant's house. Trelliswork re-created from a seventeenth-century design and knot garden based on a plasterwork pattern in the house. Old varieties of roses, shrubs and other plants. A list of plant names is available for a small charge. Georgian *Queen Square* in the city is also subject of a major restoration with lottery funding. If you drive 6m south of Bristol on the A37 you reach *Blackmore and Langdon's Nursery*, open daily, a pleasure at any time, but particularly when the delphiniums are blooming.

9 Sion Hill 7

Clifton, Bristol BS8 4BA. Tel: (0117) 973 2761

Mr and Mrs R.C. Begg • In city, 100 metres from Clifton Suspension Bridge • Open by prior appt • Entrance: £1.50 ● ♫

This is not a typical town garden. On the contrary, 20 years of profuse planting have produced an overall impression of peace and plenty on a scale which belies the garden's true size. Entering through a working conservatory, a small grassed area dominated by a vigorous black mulberry tree (planted by the owners and for once not in King James' time) and surrounded by densely planted borders, leads to a central path whose axis is established by the 'temple', an ivy-clad terracotta architectural finial, from which paths radiate to various points. The timber pergola, unusual in spanning the entire width of the garden, is smothered in roses and clematis. The play of light and shade provides a constantly changing effect. Looking back from the house, the garden is terminated by a seven-metre-high wall which acts as a backdrop to a splendid Kanzan cherry tree. A town garden full of interesting ideas – the subtle placing of pots of various kinds is particularly successful.

University Botanic Garden 8

Bracken Hill, North Road, Leigh Woods BS8 3PF. Tel: (0117) 903 4873

University of Bristol • Cross Suspension Bridge from Clifton, turn first right (North Road) and go ¼ m up on left • Open all year, Mon – Fri except Bank Holiday Mons, 9am – 5pm. Parties welcome at other times by appt. Contact Superintendent for details • Entrance: free (guided tours for parties £3 per person) • Other information: Plants for sale on two NGS dates in June and Sept only. Friends of UBG (subscription £15) have out-of-hours access and members-only plant sales ○ WC ♿

The Botanic Garden relocated to this site in 1959 and is an interesting garden for the keen plantsman. Large collections of both New Zealand and South African flora as well as comprehensive collections of aeonium, cistus, hebe, paeonia, pelargonium, salvia and sempervivum are all cultivated in the attractive five-acre garden. Collections of native trees and shrubs and plants peculiar to the Avon Gorge, plus conservation collections of rare native south-west species. Glasshouses contain ferns, orchids, bromeliads, cacti and succulents, insectivorous plants and tender bulbs. Plants and borders are well labelled and arranged with various themes, such as poisonous, dye, economic, medicinal, sand dune and woodland. There are plans for a reference collection of Chinese medicinal plants, based on an existing collection in the city, the only such in Europe. Six miles south of Bristol off B3130 west of Chew Magna (follow sign to Bishopsworth) is probably one of the largest collections of aromatic, culinary and medicinal herbs, cottage plants and wild flowers in the west; this is the nursery of *Arne Herbs*, Limeburn Hill (Tel: (01275) 333399).

OPENING DATES AND TIMES

Times of access given are the best available at the moment of going to press, but some may have been changed subsequently. In the entries, the times given are inclusive – that is, an entry such as May to Sept means that the garden is open from 1st May to 30th Sept inclusive, and 2 – 5pm, means that entry will be effective during that period. Please note that many owners will open their gardens to visitors by appointment. They will often arrange to give a personally-conducted tour on these occasions. Unavoidably some owners cannot give their opening times before we go to press. In such cases we attempt to give the best guidance we can.

BUCKINGHAMSHIRE

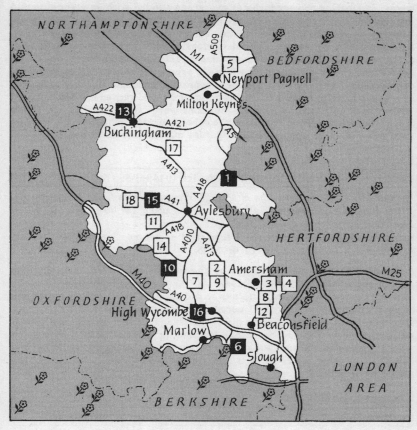

Two-starred gardens are marked on the map with a black square.

Ascott ★★ 1

Wing, Leighton Buzzard LU7 0PS. Tel: (01296) 688242; Fax: (01296) 681904

The National Trust • ½ m E of Wing, 2m SW of Leighton Buzzard on S of A418 • House and gardens open April and Sept, daily except Mon; 2 – 6pm (last admission 5pm). Gardens only open May to Aug, Wed and last Sun of month, 2 – 6pm (last admission 5pm). Parties must pre-book • Entrance: £4, children £2 (house and garden £5.50, children £2.50) (1999 prices) • Other information: Parking 220 metres from house ◐ **WC**

Thirty acres of Victorian gardening at its very best, laid out with the aid of Sir Harry Veitch and overlaid with designs and planting by Arabella Lennox-Boyd.

Formidable collection of mature trees of all shapes and colours set in rolling lawns. Fascinating topiary includes evergreen sundial with yew gnomon and inscription 'Light and shade by turn but love always' in golden yew. Wide lawns slope away to magnificent views across the Vale of Aylesbury glimpsed between towering cedars. Formal gardens include the Madeira Walk with sheltered flower borders, and the bedded-out Dutch garden. More topiary has been added to the garden, as shown in old prints, and there are new plantings of magnolias. The Long Walk has been reconstructed as a serpentine walk with new beech hedging leading to the lily pond, and a wild garden has been planted in Coronation Grove. Two stately fountains were created by Thomas Waldo Story – one a large group in bronze, the other a slender composition in marble. Interesting all year, spring gardens feature massed carpets of bulbs.

Blossoms 2

51 Cobblers Hill, Great Missenden HP16 9PW. Tel: (01494) 863140

Dr and Mrs Frank Hytten • 8m N of High Wycombe. From Great Missenden follow Rignall Road towards Butlers Cross. After about 1m turn right into Kings Lane and up to top of Cobblers Hill. At T-junction turn right at yellow stone marker in hedgerow. After 50 metres turn right at Blossoms sign • Open for NGS by appt only • Entrance: £1.50 ● 🍵 🖳 ዿ

A five-acre garden, mainly created by the owners since 1975, including one acre of beech woodland with bluebells. Spring-flowering bulbs flourish in the extensive woodland garden. There is an old apple orchard and new rock and cutting gardens. Collections of eucalyptus, acers and salix and many other specimen trees, including *Euodia hupehensis* (syn. *Tetradium daniellii*) and a magnificent ivy-leaved beech. Interesting features include a small lake with island where it is hoped mallards will make a home, and sculpture by the owner and friends; two other water gardens and a paved well garden with sundial are linked by woodland paths.

Campden Cottage ★ 3

51 Clifton Road, Chesham Bois, Amersham HP6 5PN. Tel: (01494) 726818

Mr and Mrs P. Liechti • On A416 between Amersham and Chesham. Turn into Clifton Road by Catholic Church (opposite primary school). Close to traffic lights at pedestrian crossing • Open 5th March, 9th April, 7th May, 11th June, 16th July, 8th Aug, 3rd Sept, 8th Oct, 2 – 6pm, and by appt for parties (no coaches) • Entrance: £1.50, accompanied children free • Other information: School car park available for parking on open days by arrangement ● 🎗

A generation ago the owner described herself as 'never having given gardening a thought', and started to 'tidy' the neglected garden while builders took over the house. Straight lines have given way to a design adapted to take advantage of a magnificent weeping ash, the original network of stone paths has become a sunny York stone terrace which has a large and ever-increasing collection of terracotta pots, planted for seasonal colour, and a new formal area with yew hedge, walled border and extended lawns has been created. The owner's speciality is rare and unusual plants, of which she has counted more than 500. She is also skilled in finding interesting associations of colour, shape and foliage. The busiest open day is in March for the well-known collection of hellebore species and hybrids, but the garden is worth visiting month by month to keep in touch with all developments.

Chenies Manor House ★ 4

Chenies, Rickmansworth, Hertfordshire WD3 6ER. Tel: (01494) 762888

Lt Col. and Mrs MacLeod Matthews • Off A404 between Amersham and Rickmansworth. If approaching via M25, take junction 18 • House open. Extra charge • Garden probably open April to Oct, Wed, Thurs and Bank Holidays, 2 – 5pm • Entrance: £2.20, children £1.10 ◑ 🍽 WC ⎣ ⚘ 🏛

The owners have created several extremely fine linked gardens in keeping with their fifteenth/sixteenth-century brick manor house. The gardens are highly decorative and maintained to the highest standards. Planted for a long season of colour and using many old-fashioned roses and cottage plants, there is always something to enjoy here. Formal topiary in the 'white' garden, collections of medicinal and poisonous plants in a 'physic' garden, a parterre, an historic turf maze and a highly productive kitchen garden. On her visits here, Queen Elizabeth I had a favourite tree and the 'Royal Oak' survives.

Chicheley Hall 5

Chicheley, Newport Pagnell MK16 9JJ. Tel: (01234) 391252

Trustees of The Hon. Nicholas Beatty and Mrs John Nutting • On A422 between Bedford and Newport Pagnell, 3m from M1 junction 14 • House only open • Telephone for details • Entrance: £6, children £1,50, parties of 20 or more £5 per person 🍽 WC

As we go to press, we learn that the garden and grounds here are no longer open to the public. However, visitors to the hall – one of the best and least altered Baroque houses in the country – will be able to glimpse the elegant park, with its fine avenues and views and mature trees, including recently planted formal avenues, and the C-shaped canal lake of 1709, attributed to London and Wise.

Cliveden ★★ 6

Taplow, Maidenhead, Berkshire SL6 0JA. Tel: (01628) 605069

*The National Trust • 6m NW of Slough, 2m N of Taplow off A4094 • * House (three rooms) open April to Oct, Thurs and Sun, 3 – 6pm (last admission 5.30pm) • Woodlands open all year; rest of estate open 15th March to 1st Nov, daily, 11am – 6pm; Nov and Dec, daily, 11am – 4pm. Closed Jan and Feb • Entrance: £5, family ticket £12.50 (house £1 extra, with entry by timed ticket) • Other information: Refreshments in Conservatory Restaurant, 15th March to Oct, Wed – Sun and Bank Holiday Mons. Dogs allowed in specified woodlands only* 🕒 🍽 ✕ 🏷 WC ⎣ 🏛 ♨

The original house was built in 1666 by the Duke of Buckingham in the grand manner overlooking the Thames, which flows at the foot of a steep slope (the cliff of 'Clif-den') below. The present house and terrace designed by Sir Charles Barry incorporates a famous balustrade brought by the 1st Viscount Astor from the Villa Borghese in Rome in the 1890s. The water garden, rose garden and herbaceous borders are attractive at the appropriate times of year; the formal gardens below the house and the Long Garden, fountains, temples and statuary are pleasing throughout the year. Amongst famous designers who have worked on the grounds are Bridgeman (walks and amphitheatre), Leoni (Octagon Temple), John Fleming (parterre), Nesfield (contribution uncertain) and Jellicoe (rose garden). The Trust has restored Jellicoe's rose garden of 1959, re-laying paths to the abstract design and incorporating the designer's secret garden in the shape of a cabbage rose. Other renovations include the Long Garden and the Borghese Screen lawn. An inner avenue of limes has been planted north of the house, and Yew Walk steps are in hand. There are stunning views of the mansion and parterre from woodland walks to the south of the estate. The house is now a luxury hotel, and there is an Open Air Theatre Festival in the summer. If you like to see where famous feet have trod, try to book an appointment to see part of nearby *Dorneywood Gardens*, a National Trust property used as an official residence for a Secretary of State, etc. Write to The Secretary, Dorneywood, Burnham SL1 8PY. Do not miss the colourful gardens in The Street, a row of sixteenth-century cottages discreetly renovated and occupied by the staff.

Gracefield 7

Main Road, Lacey Green, Princes Risborough HP27 0QU. Tel: (01844) 345560

Mr and Mrs B.C. Wicks • Take A4010 High Wycombe – Aylesbury road. In Bradenham turn right by Red Lion towards Walters Ash. Turn left at T-junction to Lacey Green. Brick and flint house is beyond church facing Kiln Lane • Open 1st May for NGS and for parties by written appt May to Aug • Entrance: £2, children free • Other information: Park at village hall. Lunches and teas on open day only ● ▆ ✕ ◁⊸ ℘

A steeply terraced water garden is a fine feature in this one-and-a-half-acre garden. Plants for the flower arranger; new designs for paved terraces and trough gardens; collections of clematis and shrub roses. Specimen trees include a special malus, M. 'Marshal Oyama', giving fantastic crab apple jelly. The owner is a self-confessed plantaholic and has thoughtfully labelled many specimens in her unusual collection.

Halfpenny Furze 8

Mill Lane, Chalfont St Giles HP8 4NR. Tel: (01494) 872509

Mr and Mrs R. Sadler • 5m NE of Beaconsfield off A413, ¼ m past mini-roundabout to Chalfont St Giles • Open with two other gardens one day in May and by appt • Entrance: £2 (£3 for all three gardens on open day) • Other information: Teas on open day only NEW ● ▆ WC ℘

Created from an old larch wood since 1956, this is a plantsman's garden containing a wide collection of shrubs and trees which provide colour nearly all year. Rhododendrons flourish in the soil made suitable by the needles from generations of larch trees. South of the house, the circular lawn is surrounded by beds, shrubs, perennials and roses. Grassy paths radiate to areas of particular interest, including a newly established Mediterranean garden.

Hughenden Manor 9

High Wycombe HP14 4LA. Tel: (01494) 755573; Fax: (01494) 463310

The National Trust • 1½ m N of High Wycombe on A4128 • House open as garden • Park and woodland open all year. Garden open March, Sat and Sun only; April to Oct, Wed – Sun and Bank Holiday Mons, 12 noon – 5pm, house 1- 5pm (last admission ½ hour before closing). No parties on Sat, Sun or Bank Holidays. Parties must pre-book at other times • Entrance: £1.50, children 75p (manor and garden £4.10, children £2.10, family ticket £10.20. Party rates on application) • Other information: Walled garden open for special events only

◑ ☕ ✕ 🖶 wc ♿ ⬦ 🎪 ♨

A high-Victorian garden created by Mrs Disraeli in the 1860s and recently restored. Particularly pleasing is the human scale of house and gardens. Five acres with lawns, terraced garden with new sub-tropical planting scheme, formal brightly coloured annual bedding (Mrs Disraeli's guests commented at the time on the blinding colour schemes she chose) and woodland walks. Orchard with old varieties of apples and pears. The unusual chimaera shrub *Laburnocytisus* 'Adamii' combines yellow and mauve flowers of *Laburnum anagyroides* and mauve sprays of *Cytisus purpureus* in late spring/early summer. The additional Victorian flower beds, usually at their best in July, have recently been restored.

The Manor House ★★ 10

Bledlow, Princes Risborough HP27 9PB.

Lord and Lady Carrington • 4m NW of High Wycombe, ½ m E of B4009 in middle of Bledlow • Manor House Garden open by written appt, 30th April to 18th June, 2 – 6pm. Lyde Garden open all year, daily • Entrance: Manor House Garden, £3, children free. Lyde Garden free • Manor House Garden: ● wc ♿ ♨ *Lyde Garden:* ○

With the help of landscape architect Robert Adams, Lord and Lady Carrington have created an elegant English garden of an exceptionally high standard. The highly productive and colourful walled vegetable garden has York stone paths and central gazebo. Formal gardens are enclosed by tall yew and beech hedges. Mixed flower and shrub borders feature many roses and herbaceous plants around immaculately manicured lawns. A garden approached through a yew and brick parterre, incorporating several modern sculptures (displayed with a wit typical of their owners), planned around existing mature trees on a contoured and upward-sloping site with open views, is now thoroughly established, with its trees and lawns fulfilling the original landscaping designs. *The Lyde Garden* is a water garden of great beauty and tranquillity supporting a variety of species plants. The formal gardens are children-friendly but in the magnificent water gardens they need watching on the difficult slopes.

Nether Winchendon House 11

Nether Winchendon, Aylesbury HP18 0DY. Tel: (01844) 290101

Mr and Mrs R. Spencer Bernard • 7m SW of Aylesbury, 5m NE of Thame. Near church in Nether Winchendon • Open 30th April, 25th June, 2 − 5.30pm for NGS and at other times by appt • Entrance: £2, children under 15 free (1999 prices) ● ▼ WC & ☝

The gardens surround a romantic brick and stone Tudor manor which is approached by an unusual line of dawn redwoods (*Metasequoia glyptostroboides*) planted in 1973, continuing a centuries-old tree planting tradition by the Spencer Bernard family. Small orchards on either side of the house combine with fine specimen trees, including mature acers, catalpas, cedars, paulownias, liquidambars and, dominating the lawns at the back of the house, an eighteenth-century variegated sycamore and a late-1950s' oriental plane of almost equal height. Well-kept lawns, shrub and flower borders, walled gardens including a productive kitchen garden.

Spindrift 12

Jordans, Beaconsfield HP9 2TE. Tel: (01494) 873172

Norma Desmond-Mawby • 1m NE of Beaconsfield, N of A40 in Jordans village. At far side of green turn right into cul-de-sac next to school • Open by appt • Entrance: £2, children under 12, 20p • Other information: Park in school playground on open days ● ▼ ✗ 🛍 WC & ⬥

A series of linked 'secret gardens' on different levels, with fine trees and hedges set off a wide range of unusual plants and shrubs. A miniature version of Monet's flower garden has been created recently and features iris, poppies, peonies and arches with climbing nasturtiums. A model fruit and vegetable garden is terraced on a hillside, and there are three greenhouses with vines. Large collection of hostas and hardy geraniums. Nearby is the small *Pleione* (orchid) nursery *Butterfields*, strongly recommended by Roy Lancaster. It is at Harvest Hill, Bourne End. Please telephone (01628) 525455 ahead of visit as there are no special facilities.

Stowe Landscape Gardens ★★ 13

Buckingham MK18 5EH. Tel: (01280) 822850

The National Trust • 3m NW of Buckingham via Stowe Avenue off A422 Buckingham − Brackley road • House (Stowe School) may be open in holidays. Check before visiting • Garden open 29th March to 29th Oct, Wed − Sun and Bank Holiday Mons (closed 27th May); 4th July to 5th Sept, Tues − Sun; all

10am – 5pm (last admission 4.30pm); 2nd to 23rd Dec, Wed – Sun, 10am to 4pm (last admission 3pm) • Entrance: £4.50, family ticket £11.50 (house, NT members must also pay, £2). All parties must pre-book • Other information: Refreshments for parties must be pre-booked through Property Manager. Picnics permitted in Grecian Valley only. Self-drive powered 2-seater batricars available, must be pre-booked ◐ 🍴 ✕ WC ⚓ 🛍 ⚲

Garden restoration on an heroic scale. The landscape at Stowe in the nineteenth century was diversified into distinct 'scenes', each having a character of its own. The aim now is to reinstate them. Initially the Trust had £13m to complete the project, including £2m from a mystery donor, and £5m to renovate the main house (now a school and not owned by the Trust). The public will have free access 365 days a year and greater access to the house. The concept is brilliantly planned, using the Trust's considerable management and computer resources to reinstate lost plantings or remove recent redundant additions. The work on the buildings alone deserves whatever medal the country gives to citizens who do fine work for posterity. Stowe has had enormous influence on garden design – starting from the mid-seventeenth century under a succession of distinguished designers including the owner, Viscount Cobham, Vanbrugh, Bridgeman, Kent, 'Capability' Brown, and then the new owner Lord Temple, who thinned out Brown's plantings after 1750. There are two ways of visiting Stowe – one is just to enjoy the wonderful views, the water, the trees and the buildings and sculpture. The other is to try to step back in time and understand what was meant by political/philosophical design which led to the landscape movement. This is exemplified at its finest by Stowe, influencing not only Britain but the gardening world at large. Whichever approach is adopted, the views are breathtaking and it is wise to allow a minimum of two hours to walk round, preferably with a map. Visitors must understand that the site has been a school since 1923, and that while the staff did their best to keep things going, what is now happening is a wondrous change of a quite different order. The Trust has also acquired the Home Farm and Deer Park with two large lakes, 320 acres in all, adjoining Stowe. The land was part of the original deer park and is an integral part of the designed landscape at Stowe; it includes the Wolfe Obelisk, the Gothick Umbrello and a superb set of farm buildings from the 1790s. This acquisition ensures that a substantial area of the Park will now be available for open access on foot without charge throughout the year. Finally to topical matters. The Trust has restored the Chinese House and returned it to Stowe in memory of the late Gervase Jackson-Stops, its advisor for 20 years who lived not far off at The Menagerie (see entry in Northamptonshire). When it was last seen at Stowe, the Chinese House stood on a little platform in the lake in the Elysian Fields. It is too fragile to be over water now and so it stands in a small grove in the Pheasantry. This area will gradually be developed to enhance the House in its new setting. A short walk away, the bases for the seven Saxon deities have been built and three copies installed on their respective 'months'. More statues will be replaced with the original or modern casts as funds permit. Planting continues – for example, 8000 trees and shrubs flanking one side of the Grecian Valley.

Turn End ★ 14

Townside, Haddenham, Aylesbury HP17 8BG. Tel: (01844) 291383/291817

Mr and Mrs P. Aldington • 7m SW of Aylesbury. From A418 turn to Haddenham. From Thame Road turn at Rising Sun into Townside. Turn End is 250 metres on left • Open 2nd April, 1st May, 2 – 6pm (for NGS); Weds in June, 10am – 4pm; 17th Sept (for NGS), 2 – 6pm. Parties by appt at other times • Entrance: £2, children under 14 50p. Party rates on application • Other information: No parking at garden. Teas on charity open days only ● WC &
⊲▷ ℘

Peter Aldington's RIBA-award-winning development of three linked houses (now listed) is surrounded by a series of garden rooms evolved over the last 30 years. A sequence of spaces, each of individual character, provides focal points at every turn. There is a fishpond courtyard, a shady court, a formal box court, an alpine garden, hot and dry raised beds and climbing roses. A wide range of plants is displayed to good effect against a framework of mature trees. This one-acre plantsman's garden, created within a village-centre site, is the subject of Jane Brown's book, *A Garden and Three Houses*.

Waddesdon Manor ★★ 15

Waddesdon, Aylesbury HP18 0JH. Tel: (01296) 651211; house bookings with charge, garden tours and events (01296) 653226

The National Trust • 6m NW of Aylesbury on A41, 11m SE of Bicester. Entrance in Waddesdon village • House (inc. wine cellars) open 29th March to 30th Oct, Thurs – Sun and Bank Holiday Mons (and Weds in July and Aug), 11am – 4pm (timed ticket system in operation from 10am; recommended last admission 2.30pm). No children under 6, except babies in front slings • Grounds (inc. gardens, aviary, restaurant and shops) open 1st March to 24th Dec, Wed – Sun and Bank Holiday Mons, 10am – 5pm • Entrance: £3, children £1.50 (house and grounds £10, children £7.50) (1999 prices) • Other information: Parking for disabled. Guide dogs only ◐ ☕ ✕ 🪑 WC & ℘ 👍 ♿

Baron Ferdinand de Rothschild's remarkable château (built 1874-1889), which houses a formidable art collection, is set in an appropriately grand park with fountains, vistas, terraces and walks. The gardens contain an extensive collection of Italian, French and Dutch statuary. An ornate, semi-circular aviary of sixteenth-century French style, erected in 1889, provides a distinguished home to many exotic birds. The area in front of it was designed by Lanning Roper. The park today benefits from its 100-year old plantings of native yews, limes and chestnuts with a liberal sprinkling of exotic pines, cedars, Wellingtonias and cypresses. The gardens continue to undergo changes, with old features being restored and new ones added: for example, Versailles boxes are obtained from the original Versailles manufacturers. The extensive parterre and fountains, intended to be viewed from the south side of the house, have undergone the most extensive restoration of all, requiring over 100,000 plants in the main summer display alone. The parterre is replanted twice a year, each changeover occupying 12 gardeners for two weeks. John Sales describes the south parterre as 'the central jewel of a rich Victorian scheme'. He recounts that one of the original head gardeners to the Rothschilds used to quote an aphorism describing how the rich showed their wealth by the size of their bedding-out plant list: 10,000 for a squire, 20,000 for a Bt., 30,000 for an earl and 50,000 for a duke. Waddesdon is truly regal. (If you want to show off to your chums, you can complain that the geraniums planted now are not the same colour as those originally planted.) Carpet bedding is indeed taken seriously at Waddesdon. The star of the show is a three-dimensional bird modelled on a 1910 diascope photograph of a bird originally sited on the private part of the estate at Eythrope. The 1999 bird is 3m tall and 4m from tail to beak, constructed on a galvanised steel skeleton with an inbuilt automatic irrigation system. The pheasant, named Ferdinand, requires 15,000 bedding plants with coloured foliage, clipped regularly for full effect. Elsewhere the exterior lighting scheme has won awards and can be enjoyed from the gardens on special evenings. Daffodil Valley is a major spring attraction with thousands of wild flowers, including cowslips, ox-eye daisies and a range of orchids, which are encouraged to seed. Close by over 20,000 camassias and colchicums have been naturalised into grassland and the woodland garden.

West Wycombe Park ★★ 16

West Wycombe HP14 3AJ. Tel: (01628) 488675

The National Trust • 2m W of High Wycombe, at W end of West Wycombe, S of A40 Oxford road • House open July to Aug, Sun – Thurs, 2 – 6pm (weekday entry by timed ticket, last admission 5.15pm) • Grounds open April to May, Sun and Wed; June to Aug, Sun – Thurs; also Bank Holiday Mons, all 2 – 6pm (last admission 5.15pm) • Entrance: £2.60 (house and grounds £4.50, family ticket £11.25) ◗ **WC**

The park was largely created by the second Sir Francis Dashwood and was influenced by his experiences on the Grand Tour, which included visits to Asia Minor and Russia. The first phase involved the creation of the lake with meandering walks, completed by 1739. Subsequently numerous classical temples and statues were added as well as delightful little flint and wooden bridges which span the streams. Later still, in the 1770s, the park was enlarged; Nicholas Revett was employed to design even more temples and follies, including a particularly fine music temple on an island. Thomas Cook, a pupil of 'Capability' Brown, was entrusted with the planting of trees and alterations to the landscape. There are splendid vistas, especially towards the lake which is in the shape of a swan. This is not the place to visit if you seek flower gardens and rose beds, but those who know a little about Dashwood's Hell Fire Club will enjoy seeing the other side of his nature.

Winslow Hall 17

Sheep Street, Winslow, Buckingham MK18 3HL. Tel: (01296) 712323

Sir Edward and Lady Tomkins • 9m N of Aylesbury, 6m S of Buckingham on A413 • House and garden open throughout the year by appt • Entrance: £2 (house and garden £4.50) • *Other information: Refreshments by arrangement. Teas served in village* ● &

The original gardens created around the house were completed in 1702. Apart from an English oak older than the house itself, the early London and Wise design has disappeared. Although set on a busy main road, the garden is exceptionally tranquil with a formal and high-walled terrace garden in front. Behind the house a sweep of lawn is bordered by shrubs and specimen trees, mainly planted over the last 30 years by the owners and providing an unusual example of dedicated and consistent pruning to show the trees to their best advantage; among them American scarlet oak, willow oak, a fascinating weeping 'creeping' cedar resembling a prehistoric animal, and an 'immature' sequoia only 100 years old. Where the 300-year-old oaks and elms have died, low stumps remain and provide a base for berberis, honeysuckle, roses, clematis and other climbers which are regularly clipped to make unusual flowering domes. Planted chiefly for foliage effect and autumn colour, but mixed shrub and flower borders and rose beds add summer interest.

Wotton House   18

Wotton Underwood, Aylesbury HP18 OSB.

David Gladstone • 8m W of Aylesbury off A41 • Open by application in writing
●

This remarkable landscape garden (250 acres) with over a dozen follies and the other attractions shares a history with Stowe (see entry). It was derelict after World War II but is slowly being restored. It is hoped to include a fuller description in next year's *Guide*.

HISTORIC GARDENS

A programme to update an authoritative record of the nation's historic landscapes has been started by English Heritage. The Garden History Society, created in 1965, began to compile a register of historic gardens in the '70s. Ten years later, when English Heritage was established, it took over the Garden History Society's register and today 1200 gardens are listed. There are three categories: an elite 10 per cent are classed as Grade I, 30 per cent as Grade II* gardens and the remainder as Grade II. Listing gardens does not oblige owners to apply for permission before altering anything; instead it encourages them to maintain and enhance the gardens. Owners of Grade I and Grade II* gardens can also apply for grants. Planning authorities are obliged to consult English Heritage or the Garden History Society on applications which could affect a garden on the register.

CAMBRIDGESHIRE

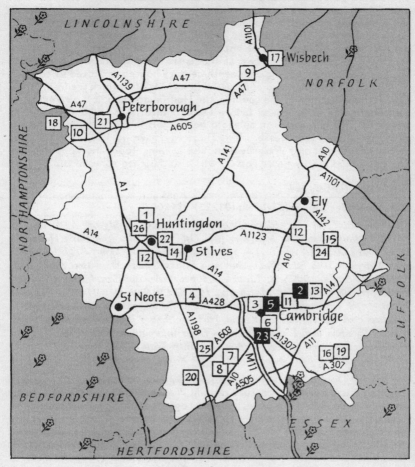

Two-starred gardens are marked on the map with a black square.

Abbots Ripton Hall ★   1

**Abbots Ripton, Huntingdon PE17 2PQ. Tel: (01487) 773555;
Fax: (01487) 773545**

*Lord and Lady De Ramsey • 2m N of Huntingdon, approached from B1090 •
Open 21st May, 25th June, 9th July, 23rd July, 6th Aug for charities, 2 – 5pm,
and for private visits by appt • Entrance: £3 on charity days; £6 (including
plant guide) for private visits* ● ☕ <u>WC</u> ⚙ 🌿 🛈

This superb garden was designed in the 1950s by Humphrey Waterfield. Fine lake, fishing hut like a Chinese pavilion, and a grey-leaved border with alpines and sun-loving perennials. Modern but rustic octagonal summerhouse, Doric loggia, and several timber bridges, including one of Chinese style. There is a circular rose garden: a ring of historic roses backed by grey foliage of sea buckthorn with a circular lawn at its centre. The spectacular herbaceous borders stretching from the eighteenth-century house are backed by columns of yew and philadelphus and punctuated by a circle of Gothick trellising. Look out for the tallest elm in the country, the Huntingdon elm; it is a reminder of the countryside as it looked before Dutch elm disease felled trees by the thousand. This elm seems in splendid health, but in fact survives on yearly injections to keep the disease at bay. Those who have worked in the park and garden include not only Waterfield but also Lanning Roper and Tony Venison. The two follies are by Peter Foster, who also designed some of the bridges.

Anglesey Abbey ★★   2

Lode, Cambridge CB5 9EJ. Tel/Fax: (01223) 811200

The National Trust • In village of Lode, 6m NE of Cambridge off A14, on B1102 • House open 25th March to 15th Oct, Wed – Sun and Bank Holiday Mons (but closed 21st April), 1 – 5pm (last admission 4.30pm) • Garden open 25th March to 10th July, Wed – Sun and Bank Holiday Mons (but closed 21st April); 3rd July to 10th Sept, 11am – 5.30pm (last admission 4.30pm). Winter Walk open 5th Jan to 25th March and 19th Oct to 24th Dec, Thurs – Sun, 11am – 4pm • Entrance: £3.50; winter £2.50 (house, garden and Lode Mill: weekdays and Sat £6, Sun and Bank Holiday Mons £7) (1999 prices). Charge is made for tours with Head Gardener • Other information: Two electric wheelchairs available. Gravel surfaces on Winter Walk paths. Lode Mill machinery working first Sat of month ○ 🍽 ✕ WC & ♨ 🏤 ♗

Magisterial! Do not rush around, because Anglesey Abbey's setting is one of England's finest twentieth-century gardens. You will need a whole day – many whole days – to absorb this place, its separate gardens, the parade of sculptures, trees and open spaces, and the changeful seasons. Avenues of mature trees lead the wanderer to intimate gardens enclosed by meticulous hedges; smooth lawns give way to meadows awash with cowslips, lady's bedstraw and ox-eye daisies; visitors will unexpectedly come upon dramatic vistas lined by superb trees, or glimpse the peaceful River Lode and Lode Mill. A semi-circular garden with a deep encircling herbaceous border is a highlight for the summer; the bold, imaginative planting of perennials is splendid, plumes of seakale and spires of delphinium mingling with mysterious sages. In another garden, 4500 hyacinths bloom in spring while dark-foliaged dwarf dahlias take their place in late summer. Narcissus gazes at his reflection surrounded by scented white- and yellow-blossomed shrubs. A curved border of randomly planted late-summer dahlias may not be to everyone's taste, but what garden is ever entirely perfect? This place is almost so, and is maintained with great panache. It is vast, too – 100 acres. The new one-mile-long Winter Walk is specifically designed for winter colour and fragrance. It features a serpentine walk, and other paths, including a recently rediscovered Victorian one.

Cambridge College Gardens 3

Most colleges are helpful about access to their gardens although the Masters' or Fellows' Gardens are often strictly private or rarely open. Specific viewing times are difficult to rely on because some colleges prefer not to have visitors in term time or on days when a function is taking place. The best course is to ask at the porters' lodge or to telephone ahead of visit. However, some college gardens will always be open to the visitor, by arrangement with porters, even if others are closed on that particular day. Several now charge for entry, but some will be open free this year in April for the City Gardens Open Day.

Amongst the College Gardens of particular interest are the following: *Christ's* (see entry). *Clare* (see entry). *Downing College*: Spacious neo-classical campus (founded 1800), covering 6 acres, with lawns and trees; a lot of recent tree planting. There are several fine old cedars of Lebanon and an interesting tulip tree with unusual leaves in the Master's Garden [Open most days and for charity at least one day a year]. *Emmanuel*: large gardens with herb garden designed by John Codrington. Also memorable for its fine trees, including a Caucasian wing nut (*Pterocarya fraxinifolia*), swamp cypress (*Taxodium distichum*), dawn redwood (*Metasequoia glyptostroboides*). The highlight must be the splendid plane tree, cloaked to the ground, one of the biggest in Britain, in the Fellows' Garden. Informal shrubberies and herbaceous borders skirt the lawns, and there is a pond with a restrained piece of modern sculpture nearby [Open daily, 9am – 5pm; College Gardens and Fellows' Garden open one day in summer]. *Jesus*: a must for those interested in sculpture to see the Flanagan Venetian horse. Sensitive planting elsewhere and do not miss the head in the cloisters. The new St Radegund's garden has planting derived from the 6th century saint's garden in Poitiers, France [Open daily, 9am – 4.30pm, but closed May to mid-June]. *King's*: one of the greatest British architectural experiences, set off by fine lawns. Spring bulbs [College and Chapel open daily until 6.30pm [£3, children (12-17) £2] but grounds closed mid-April to mid-June, 9.30am – 4.30pm and closed 23rd Dec to 3rd Jan &]. Fellows' Garden with magnificent old specimen trees [Open one day in summer for NGS, 2 – 6pm. £1]. *Leckhampton* (part of *Corpus Christi*) at 37 Grange Road: laid out by William Robinson, originally seven acres with two acres added [Open 5th June for charity ♥ WC]. *Magdalene*: Fellows' Garden [Open daily, 1 – 6pm. Closed May and June &]. *Pembroke*: extensive and varied garden, including orchard and winter bed, with notable range of unusual plants, most of which benefit from shelter provided by various walls. Lobster claw (*Clianthus puniceus*) cheek by jowl with tassel bush (*Garrya elliptica*), pomegranates and trumpet vine (*Campsis x tagliabuana*) form a mini-botanic garden. Good selection of herbaceous perennials. [Open daily during daylight hours. Closed May and June &]. *Peterhouse*: varied, smallish gardens and interesting octagonal court with hot and cool sides. Extensive naturalised daffodils in spring [Open Mon – Fri, 1 – 5pm. Closed 6th May – 16th June &]. *Robinson*: Warden and Fellows' Garden, Grange Road [Open daily, 10am – 6pm]. 10 acres surround this modern college, formerly grand Edwardian villas. Memorable trees, wild garden. *St John's*: huge park-like garden with eight acres of grass, fine trees and good display of bulbs in spring. Wilderness (two and three quarter acres) introduced by 'Capability' Brown, has spring bulbs including, from June to July, the spectacular Turk's cap lily (martagon lily). In the Master's Lodge Garden are quantities of *Arabus turnata*, probably the only specimens in the country. Rose garden [Open Mon – Fri, 10am – 5pm, Sat and Sun, 9.30am – 5pm. Entrance: £1.75, OAPs, students and children £1, family £3.50; Wilderness and Master's Lodge Garden restricted access]. *Trinity*: a garden and grounds of 45 acres with good trees. [Grounds open daily although restricted access, with charge for entry, March to Sept; opening times from Porter's Lodge. Fellows' Garden open 9th April, 2 – 6pm]. Nearby is *Little St Mary's Church*: wild and natural garden developed since 1925 [Open all year].

Childerley Hall   4

Dry Drayton, Cambridge CB3 8BB. Tel: (01954) 210271

Mr and Mrs John Jenkins • 6m W of Cambridge on A428 opposite Caldecote turn • Open mid-May to mid-July by appt • Entrance: £2 ●

The Hall lies between the sites of the two vanished villages of Great and Little Childerley, and the drive leading to the house, chapel and four-acre garden is nearly a mile and a half through flat open country, making it seem particularly still and remote. To one side is an ornamental Tudor moat and a yew hedge crowned by topiary birds. The south front of the house is on a raised terrace. From here the main garden, sunken and surrounded by raised grass walks, can be viewed. The corners of these walks were originally Tudor mounts. Here, flourishing in the boulder clay, are 350 shrub and species roses: planted beside straight paths, in the winding wilderness, and in the white rose garden, where they include 'Little White Pet', 'Boule de Neige' and 'Tynwald' as well as standard 'Iceberg'. Modern and historic roses grow together in harmony and with abandon. A further selection of roses, modern and old-fashioned, in the kitchen garden.

Christ's College ★★   5

St Andrew's Street, Cambridge CB2 3BU. Tel: (01223) 334900

In city centre • Open mid-June to Oct, Mon – Fri, 9.30am – 12.30pm; Oct to May, Mon – Fri, 2 – 4pm. Closed Bank Holidays, Easter Week and 23rd Dec to 2nd Jan ◐ &

First impressions are telling, and the court beyond the porter's lodge is a spectacle that proclaims excellence. The summer display of fuchsias and petunias in window boxes and tubs is tasteful, refined and peaceful. Tubs of hydrangeas welcome visitors into the gardens beyond. These are immaculate and maintain the impression of devoted, expert gardeners. The well-planned herbaceous borders are augmented with panache by bedded-out plants. The venerable mulberry, contemporary with Milton, on a mound in the far corner, sheds its fruit onto the exemplary lawn. There are many other lovely trees, including Indian bean trees (*Catalpa bignonioides*) in full bloom in mid-summer, and the cypress grown from seed from the tree on Shelley's grave in Rome. Charles Darwin's garden with canal intrigues the visitor with its false perspective.

Clare College Fellows' Garden 6

Trinity Lane, Cambridge CB2 1TL. Tel: (01223) 333200

In city centre. Entry from Queens Road and Trinity Lane • College open • Garden open April to Sept, daily inc. Bank Holidays (except on Graduation, May Ball and special events days), 10am – 4.30pm. Also one Sun in June, 5.30 – 7.30pm, with wine, and one afternoon in August for Red Cross with tea • Entrance: College and garden £1.75 ◑ &

Reached by crossing the oldest bridge over the Cam (from the College itself), or (from Queens Road) by walking along the avenue laid out in 1690. Between the college buildings and the bridge are two gardens – to the north the private Master's Garden and to the south the Scholars' Garden where the planting relies on silver, blue and purple and white. Professor E.N. Willmer designed the present, well-regarded planting scheme for the Fellows' Garden. Fine trees, including metasequoia, taxodium, davidia and *Aesculus pavia*, are mainly the legacy of his predecessors. At the garden's heart, concealed by hedges, is a formal pool. The double herbaceous borders have a yellow and blue theme, while along the northern boundary is a ribbon of silver with a mass of white flowers, including crambe, *Rubus* 'Benenden' and romneya that show up well against walls and hedges. Summer bedding is used to insert oranges and reds.

Crossing House Garden ★ 7

78 Meldreth Road, Shepreth, Royston, Hertfordshire SG8 6PS. Tel: (01763) 261071

Mr and Mrs Douglas Fuller • 8m SW of Cambridge, ½ m W of A10 • Open all year, daily, dawn – dusk • Entrance: by collecting box ○ **WC** & ⬥

Highly recommended, a delightful, eccentric place which proves that plantsmanship is alive and well in Cambridgeshire. A small garden, started by the present owners over 30 years ago, it is crammed full of plants and is an eye-opener about what can be achieved in a small space. There are little pools, excellent dwarf box edging, an arbour in clipped yew, rockeries and a lawn, and three tiny glasshouses full of orchids and alpines. In all there are estimated to be about 5000 different plants here, so a visit at any time of year will be rewarding. To walk to Docwra's Manor (see below), about 250 metres away, turn left and walk towards Shepreth village.

Docwra's Manor 8

2 Meldreth Road, Shepreth, Royston, Hertfordshire SG8 6PS. Tel: (01763) 261473/261557/260235

Mrs John Raven • 8m SW of Cambridge, ½ m W of A10. Opposite war memorial • Open all year, Wed, Fri, 10am – 4.30pm and 2nd April, 7th May, 4th June, 2nd July, 6th Aug, 3rd Sept, 1st Oct, 2 – 4.30pm. Also by appt. Parties welcome • Entrance: £2, accompanied children under 16 free. Extra charge for guided and out-of-hours parties • Other information: Park in village hall car park ◔ **WC** & ⚘

'Simply a garden as reasonably varied as could be' – that was John and Faith Raven's original intention, and this, more than 40 years later, is the result. The fascinating two-and-a-half-acre site is divided into unexpected compartments by buildings, walls and hedges, and contains many choice plants. Seedlings are left where they appear, so the effect is wild in parts; other areas are more formal with hosts of roses, spurges, clematis, eryngiums and philadelphus. John Raven (1914-1980), a lecturer in classics and an eminent field botanist, wrote about the plants he and his wife grew here in *A Botanist's Garden* (1971; re-issued), still a fascinating book and an invaluable guide to Docwra's Manor (and to Ardtornish – see entry in Scotland). Crossing House (see above) is within easy walking distance; turn right out of the Manor gate and walk towards the level crossing.

Elgood's Brewery 9

North Brink, Wisbech PE13 1LN. Tel: (01945) 583160; Fax: (01945) 587711

Elgood's Brewery • In Wisbech, at W end of North Brink • Brewery open for tours, Wed – Fri, 2.30pm. £4 inc. tasting (adults only) • Garden open May to Oct, Wed – Sun and Bank Holiday Mons, 1 – 5pm • Entrance: £2, OAPs and children £1.50 • Other information: Guide dogs only ◑ 🍽 🍴 **WC** ♿ 🌿 ⬛ 🌷

Wisbech is an elegant market town and among its delights are several splendid Georgian terraces. North Brink, along the River Nene, is arguably the most spectacular. Peckover House (see entry) is near the eastern end of the Brink, while Elgood's Brewery dominates the western end. Behind the brewery is a large enclosed garden with some superlative trees. The male maidenhair (*Ginkgo biloba*) near the public entrance first catches the eye. A few paces away stands a tulip tree (*Liriodendron tulipifera*) the like of which you will rarely see; in June every shoot bears a flower, a cup of orange and jade. Other dignitaries are a mulberry, a variegated sycamore, a weeping willow, a tree of heaven (*Ailanthus altissima*) and an oak. The recent restoration of the brewery garden has paid due respect to the garden's structure. The deep pool has been home for a colony of great crested newts. Paths have been reinstated, and colourful herbaceous borders, a rose garden, herb garden, a maze and a rockery planted. Above this new, sometimes incongruous floweriness, the trees retain their grace and dignity.

Elton Hall 10

Peterborough PE8 6SH. Tel: (01832) 280468 (during office hours)

Mr and Mrs William Proby • 8m W of Peterborough in Elton, just off A605 • Hall open • Garden open 28th, 29th May; June, Wed; July and Aug, Wed, Thurs, Sun and Bank Holiday Mons; all 2 – 5pm. Hall and garden open for tours by appt at other times • Entrance: £2.50 (hall and garden £5, accompanied children free) 🍽 🍴 ✕ 🍴 **WC** ♿ 🌿 ⬛ 🌷

Steps cloaked in aubretia and lavender, guarded by two sphinxes, rise to the low, pale gold castellated mansion, parts of which date from 1475. By the steps is a knot parterre in box, elegantly wrought, and in front a smooth lawn that rises to meet the surrounding pasture. A sunken pool, enveloped in a billow of whites and blues with some purple, is the first feature that visitors see as they enter this garden through an archway. Take the gravel path that encircles the lawn, which has an ornamental well-head offset in the middle, and wander past the low yew hedges and tumps of golden yew, and short ha-ha, to the restored rose garden, full of old-fashioned roses, summer scents and colours. The distant sound of water will eventually beckon you on, across a hornbeam-lined avenue punctuated with pyramids of box, into an informal silvery shrubbery, under a fine catalpa, to discover a new 'Gothick' orangery set in an ornamental garden. The hedges and lawns are immaculately clipped, creating a well-manicured spacious setting for a curious house, the exterior of which alone would keep any architectural historian happy for weeks.

Hardwicke House 11

High Ditch Road, Fen Ditton, Cambridge CB5 8TF. Tel: (01223) 292246

Mr J. Drake • 3½ m N of Cambridge off A14, ½ m from centre of Fen Ditton. From A1303 Newmarket road turn N by borough cemetery • Open 30th Aug for NGS, and by appt (if you are unable to keep appt please let owner know). Closed Aug • Entrance: £2, children 50p ● ⌾

Fenland gardens need shelter, and shelter is provided here by tall hedges, some of beech, some of conifers, with elderly pruned apple trees in between. The compartments formed by tall, clipped hedges are all different. Closely mown paths radiate through rougher grass providing vistas; the main vista is lined by birch trees alternating with yellow-blossomed roses. In late spring and early summer the garden is awash with columbines and cranesbills and filled with the fragrance of old roses; in autumn there are colchicums in abundance, while hellebores and daffodils provide late winter colour. Numerous unusual plants are scattered around because the owner collects old-fashioned and rare garden cultivars. In short, this is a plant-man's garden set within a sedate, formal design. Other gardens in Fen Ditton are open on the same days in May and June. If your passion is pelargoniums, watch out for two summer NGS openings at Netherhall Manor (see entry).

Island Hall 12

Post Street, Godmanchester PE18 8BA. Tel: (01480) 459676

Mr and the Hon. Mrs C. Vane Percy • In centre of Godmanchester • Open 28th May for NGS and Suns in July; parties by appt, May – July, Sept 1 – 5 pm • Entrance: £2 • Other information: refreshments on NGS day NEW ● ⌾

The garden is in two parts, separated by a mill-race yet linked by a Chinese-style wooden bridge erected in 1988; neglected for many years, it is now gradually being restored. The Island was the pleasure garden in Victorian times – today it has tall trees, mainly horse-chestnuts, underneath which cow-parsley and other wild flowers are being encouraged. There are lovely views across the River Ouse to Portholme Meadow. Returning via the bridge, another vista embraces two fine cedars of Lebanon, one of which stands in front of the eighteenth-century Hall. On the terrace is a formal parterre with clipped variegated box hedges, box spirals and yew pyramids; the Mill garden has a sundial ensconced in another parterre spilling over with white shrubby cinquefoil, white Scotch roses and columbines.

21 Lode Road ★   13

Lode, Cambridge CB5 9ER.

Richard Ayres • 6m NE of Cambridge. From A14 take B1102 to Lode • Open for charity 24th, 25th June, 8th, 9th July, 11am – 6pm • Entrance: £1.50 • Other information: Parking facilities at village hall. Possible for wheelchairs but narrow paths ● ☕ &

An open letter to Richard Ayres: "Thank you for the privilege, twice a year, of allowing us into your perfect garden. Your use of foliage in variety – glittering, golden, ferny, fulsome, silvery – and of the shapes and forms of shrubs and trees is masterful. The yellows and blues of the flowers, with occasional flashes of scarlet and crimson, and the subtle whites, create a brilliant tapestry through which the paths weave and wind, opening new views at every turn. Everything is compact; there is no sense of boundaries. Everything is immaculate – lawn, hedges – and you don't grow any weeds. You are a master-gardener of rare talent – no wonder Anglesey Abbey is magisterial under your head-gardenership."

The Manor   14

Hemingford Grey, Huntingdon PE18 9BN. Tel: (01480) 463134; Fax (01480) 465026

Diana and Peter Boston • 4m SE of Huntingdon off A14, in Hemingford Grey. Access off river tow path • House open by appt only • Garden open all year, daily • Entrance: £1, children 50p • Park in High Street ○ ⬤ ⅋ 🏛

A storybook garden – for children of any age – but there is much more than a garden here, for the wonderful moated Norman manor (c. 1130) is perhaps the oldest continuously inhabited house in England. It was the home of Lucy Boston from 1939 and the setting for her *Green Knowe* children's books. She designed the garden, intermixing old-fashioned roses with herbaceous perennials, creating parallel herbaceous borders, a formal rose garden and topiary in the form of chess pieces. Creditably, the roses and many of the irises are labelled. Trees in the lawns are underplanted with autumn crocuses. At the Norman front are ancient yews and a superb copper beech that has layered itself. Parts of the garden will be left wild deliberately for wildlife.

Netherhall Manor   15

Tanner's Lane, Soham. Tel: (01353) 720269

Timothy Clark • 6m SE of Ely on A142; pass church and war memorial and take second road on left. From Newmarket turn right in Soham at second road after cemetery • Open 23rd April, 7th May, 6th, 13th Aug for NGS 2 – 5 pm • Entrance: £1 NEW ☕

An elegant garden, touched with antiquity, and for those fond of old-fashioned plants a veritable joy. In high summer, the beds contain collections of nine-teenth-century variegated pelargoniums. In spring the garden blazes with Victorian hyacinths, crown imperials and old primroses, followed by the only display of florist's tulips and florist's ranunculus in the country. Entering through a courtyard with formal box-edged beds and a handsome fountain, visitors first glimpse the formal aconite garden later filled with old fuchsias; behind is the organic vegetable garden. To the right is a colonnade of lichen-encrusted columns linked by a balustrade on which pots of seasonal flowers are displayed; summer is for double lobelias, pelargoniums, yellow and golden-brown calceolarias and heliotropes. Old apples, trees, vast clumps of violets and hepatica and, most remarkably, the double-flowered ornamental black-berry (*Rubus ulmifolius* 'Bellidiflorus') trained against the gable wall, make this a most diverting garden.

Padlock Croft ★ 16

Padlock Road, West Wratting, Cambridge CB1 5LS. Tel: (01223) 290383

Mr and Mrs P.E. Lewis • 10m SE of Cambridge, N of A1307. On outskirts of village by West Wratting Park. House on Padlock Road on left • Open most days except Sun. Please telephone before travelling • Entrance: £1 ◓ 🖻 ⅋ ♉

Harebells, bellflowers, balloon flowers, sages, houseleeks cohabit happily at Padlock Croft with humans who are clearly enthusiastic gardeners. The Lewises have created tufa mountains, and added tubs of various sizes and small glasshouses, all for the sake of the National Collection of campanula species and cultivars, and the hundreds of other plants, which they collect avidly and cultivate superbly. It is a miraculous jumble, nicely chaotic, yet every plant is labelled. Keen gardeners will be content to spend hours here. Nearby property *Weaver's Cottage* (01223) 892399 open with Padlock Croft on charity open days.

Peckover House 17

North Brink, Wisbech PE13 1JR. Tel and Fax: (01945) 583463

The National Trust • In centre of Wisbech on N bank of River Nene • House open as garden • Garden open 27th March to Oct, Sat – Thurs and Bank Holiday Mons, 12.30 – 5.30pm • Entrance: £2 (house and garden £3.50) • Other information: Wheelchairs by prior application
◓ 🍴 ✕ wc ⅋ ♉ 🎁 ♉

Wisbech is a delightful town with handsome Georgian and Victorian build-ings lining the River Nene. Peckover House is a red-brick villa built in the 1720s, whereas the elongated, two-and-a-qaurter-acre garden has a distinctly late nineteenth-century Victorian ambience. Stepping from the house on to the croquet lawn, you are surrounded by greenery, tall trees and evergreen shrubs. The mature trees include ginkgo, tulip trees, *Sophora japonica*, yew, *Araucaria araucana* (monkey puzzle) and Chusan palms (*Trachycarpus fortunei*). Some bedding plants give summer colour. The scent of a host of roses in summer will draw you westwards, passing a new (reconstruction) formal pool, into compartments variously planted with flowering shrubs, perennials and those perfumed roses. Topiary peacocks overlook a second pool and summerhouse. Lilies, peonies, hydrangeas and 'Mrs Sinkins' pinks provide a succession of bloom in the elongated walled garden, at the end of which is the Orangery, full to bursting with flowering pot plants and three mature, fruiting orange trees. Further on, a new border, dominated by dark red, is maturing, backed by espalier pear trees. Everything is neat and tidy, bearing out the claim that this garden is 'the product of prudent tidiness, a period piece'. Elgood's Brewery Gardens (see entry), also on North Brink, is 10 minutes walk.

The Prebendal Manor House 18

Nassington, Peterborough PE8 6QG. Tel: (01780) 782575; E-mail: info@prebendal-manor.demon.co.uk; Web: www.prebendal-manor.demon.co.uk

Mrs Jane Baile • 8m W of Peterborough off A1, in Nassington opposite church • Open May and June, Sun and Wed; July and Aug, Sun, Wed and Thurs; Sept, Sun and Wed; all 2 – 5.30pm • Entrance: £3, children £1.20
◑ ⬛ 🍴 WC ᕕ ⚓

From a window sill of the early thirteenth-century tawny stone house a pair of carved heads gaze down, guardians of the secrets of this ancient place. Scattered around its six acres are reconstructions of various types of medieval gardens. The herber has grass seats, a fig tree and scented plants. The trellis garden's compartments overspill with poppies and mallows. Concealed by an ancient wall and protected by a fine withy fence is a vegetable patch with broad beans, herbs and wheat. A new nut walk leads to two fishponds. Patches of wild flowers sit in the lawn. Old willows, the other guardians of the manor's secrets, billow silvery in the breeze. The tithe barn contains an interpretative museum display with some look-alike farm tools. This is a new, commendable effort, diverting and informative. The latest addition is a small vineyard near the vegetable patch.

Scarlett's Farm 19

Padlock Road, West Wratting, Cambridge CB1 5LS. Tel: (01223) 290812

Mr and Mrs M. Hicks • 10m SE of Cambridge, N of A1307. On outskirts of village by West Wratting Park. House on Padlock Road at end • Open several dates for NGS, 2 – 6pm. Telephone for details • Entrance: £1, children 50p • Other information: Refreshments on charity open days only
● WC ⚓

A formal but irregular parterre, with a lovely mixture of summer plants, nestles cosily beside the red-brick farmhouse. Gigantic plume poppies and Miss Willmott's Ghost have the white and purple burning bush and Scotch thistles for company. The annuals add splashes of harmonious colour among the perennials, and interest is prolonged by beds of roses and irises, and tender shrubs in tubs. A small nursery is attached. Padlock Croft (see entry) is 100 metres away in the same road.

South Farm 20

Shingay, Royston, Hertfordshire SG8 0HR. Tel: (01223) 207581

Mr P. Paxman • 6m NW of Royston off A1198, via Wendy • Open 11th, 25th June, 9th July, 2 – 6pm and by appt • Entrance: £2.50 (joint entrance with Brook Cottage and other properties) ◑ 🍷 🖼 WC ♿ 🐾

A pair of black ducks crossed my path as I entered South Farm. The main flower garden is enclosed and protected by a tall cypress hedge, pierced frequently by gates that allow you to glimpse the long fields of wheat. The hedge even has a *trompe-l'oeil* cut into it – not a bad use for the loathsome 'Leylandii'. A lily pond in one corner is awash with sedges and monkey flowers and around it an informal garden with such beauties as *Rosa chinensis* 'Mutabilis'. Familiar flowers abound: Jacob's-ladders, day lilies, loosestrife, plume poppies. On the other side of the farmhouse is an exotic conservatory and a 1000-metre-square vegetable garden which contains three rotation plots, a nine-metre polytunnel, large hotbed, soft-fruit section and perennial vegetable plot. It is enclosed by espalier fruit trees, blackberries, loganberries, raspberries, etc. and totally netted. Each rotational plot is subdivided by gravel paths, parterre-style, into about 15 beds in which grow over 150 varieties of vegetables and fruit. Beyond is a small wildflower meadow, and more wheat. A happy, not-too-tidy garden – those lucky ducks and their companion 'rare breeds' have some well-trained humans to keep it for them. Plant list available. Nearby is a private nature reserve with a three-acre lake, which is open. *Brook Cottage* (Mr and Mrs Charvil), four minutes' walk away, is a much smaller garden with a crystal-clear stream embowered in poppies, harebells, toadflax, hollyhocks and larkspur. A real cottage garden with vegetables and poultry as well as honeysuckle and horsetails.

Thorpe Hall 21

Longthorpe, Peterborough PE3 6LW. Tel: (01733) 330060

The Sue Ryder Foundation • In Longthorpe, on W edge of Peterborough between A47 and A605 • Ground floor of house open for some events • Garden open all year, daily except 25th, 26th Dec and 1st Jan, 10am – 5pm • Entrance: by donation ○ 🍷 🖼 WC ♿ 🐾 🎁 ☕

A wooden door lets the visitor out of the courtyard into the L-shaped garden comprising a series of parterres and borders. Two elegant Georgian pavilions, far apart, are linked by a long vista which is interrupted as it pierces a third pavilion. A boldly planted herbaceous border and a restrained, lavender-hedged rose garden around an oval pond occupy parts of a longer axis. On the shorter axis, there is an architectural Victorian parterre planted with a strange mixture of perennials, including ornamental grasses, clipped bay laurel, box and yew, and bedded-out plants. A restoration programme of parts of this garden is continuing; what has so far been achieved is pleasing and worthwhile, providing a diverting small garden with echoes of former grandeur, especially in its Grade-II-listed pavilions, ancient yews and spreading cedar trees.

Turf Maze   22

The Green, Hilton, Huntingdon. Tel: (01480) 830137 (Clerk to Parish Council)

Parish of Hilton • On the green in centre of village • Open April to Nov • Entrance: free • Other information: Parking in parish hall nearby NEW ☾

Mazes are mysterious things, believed by some to be linked to fertility rites. This turf one, scheduled as an ancient monument, was created by one William Sparrow in 1660. It is circular, compact and intricate, and at its centre is an obelisk with Latin and English inscriptions about Mr Sparrow and his maze. When you've seen the maze, go on to Fenstanton (2m NE of Hilton) and inside the medieval parish church on the north wall of the chancel you will find a memorial to the famous landscape gardener Lancelot 'Capability' Brown, who owned the manor house and is buried in the churchyard.

University Botanic Garden ★★   23

Cambridge CB2 1JF. Tel: (01223) 336265

University of Cambridge • In S of city, on E side of A1309 (Trumpington Road). Entrance off Bateman Street • Open all year except 1st, 2nd, 3rd Jan, 25th, 26th Dec: summer 10am – 6pm, winter 10am – 4pm • Entrance: charge for March to Oct, Mon – Fri and weekends and Bank Holidays throughout the year; Nov to Feb, Mon – Fri, free ○ 🍴 🛍 WC ♿ 🏛

This garden covers 40 acres. It is so diverse that a brief description will not do it justice. It admirably fulfils its three purposes – research, education and amenity. A visit at any time is worthwhile, even in winter when the stem garden, especially on a sunny day, is dramatic. The various dogwoods with red, black, green and yellow-ochre stems contrast with *Rubus biflorus*, while the pale pink trunk of the birch *Betula albo-sinensis* var. *septentrionalis* is stunning. As this is primarily a research institute, there is a splendid collection of native trees, including willows, poplars and junipers, an illuminating display of rare and endangered British species, and ecological beds and rockeries. There are 'exotic' rockeries, too, both sandstone and limestone, so that plants with similar requirements can be seen growing together. Exotic trees include pawpaw (*Asimina triloba*), and good specimens of madroña (*Arbutus menziesii*), *Tetracentron sinense* and dawn redwood (*Metasequoia glyptostroboides*). The glasshouse range is always fascinating, and in winter, the tropical section can be a welcome retreat. It contains a green-flowered jade vine (*Strongylodon macrobotrys*), cycads, tropical economic plants and much more. In the alpine house, plants are changed regularly as they come into flower. The newest addition is the Dry Garden, which need never be watered even though it contains 80 species. Nearby is another novelty, a linear bed showing arable weed flora changes in UK agricultural history. A Genetic Garden is under development. The Botanic Garden should be visited more than once a year; it will certainly educate keen gardeners who may be astonished at the plants that will thrive outdoors in one of the coldest parts of Britain. A major benefactor was Reginald Cory (d. 1934) who was also responsible for Dyffryn in Wales (see entry). Seeds collected by Friends are on sale in the Gilmour Building refreshment room at only 50p a packet, and you can become a Friend and listen to lectures like 'Sex and the Wild Cabbage'.

Wicken Fen Cottage 24

Lode Lane, Wicken, Ely CB7 5XP. Tel: (01353) 720274; Fax: (01353) 720274

The National Trust • 9m SE of Ely, 3m SW of Soham, S of A1123, signed Wicken Fen National Nature Reserve • Fen Cottage open Mon • Entrance: Fen Cottage and Nature Reserve £3.50 • Other information: Light refreshments, toilet facilities and shop in Reserve visitor centre opposite open daily, 9am – 5pm (closed occasionally in winter) ● 🅑 🕸

A simple, effective garden with jumbles of foxgloves, hollyhocks, Shasta daisies, clary and golden yarrow in midsummer, a few roses, some butcher's broom, a patch of fruit and vegetables and lots of nettles – unpretentious, in keeping with the rural cottage. You can just peep over the garden hedge on your way to Wicken Fen National Nature Reserve, which is one of the wild treasures of Cambridgeshire.

Wimpole Hall 25

Arrington, Royston, Hertfordshire SG8 0BW.
Tel: (01223) 207257; Fax: (01223) 207838

The National Trust • 7m SW of Cambridge signed off A603 at New Wimpole • Hall open March to Nov as garden but open 1 – 5pm (Bank Holiday Suns and Mons 11am – 5pm) • Garden open 18th March to 5 Nov, Tues – Thurs, Sat, Sun and Bank Holiday Mons, 10.30am – 5pm (Tues – Sun in July and Aug); Nov to 17th March, Sat, Sun, 11am – 4pm. Pre-booked guided tours for parties with head gardener. Park walks open all year • Entrance: £2.50 (hall and garden £5.90, children £2.70) (1999 prices) • Other information: Disabled 'self-drive' vehicle available ◐ ☕ ✕ 🅑 WC & 🕸 ⚘ 🏤

The vast landscaped park of this house follows almost every fashion in land-scaping from the eighteenth to the nineteenth century; Charles Bridgeman (1720s), Lancelot 'Capability' Brown (1760s) and many others worked here. Today, their handiwork is in part immaculate, in part preserved, but else-where decrepit and in the process of restoration because, laudably, the Trust aims to restore the park to its 'former glory'. Restoration of the Walled Garden is progressing well too, and the glasshouses will be rebuilt. Apart from the parterre before the north front of the house, which is planted in Victorian style, this place is best seen using hiking boots, and with picnic in haversack. Vast avenues lead to the cardinal points of the compass, past lakes, bridges, a splendid 1770 folly, which can be seen in the distance from the parterre, trees in all stages from ancient to newly planted, and rare breeds of cattle and sheep everywhere. To reach the folly an hour is needed; other marked walks take longer. Be warned, the current Wimpole Park walks and rides leaflet (£1) is not entirely accurate.

Wytchwood 26

Owl End, Great Stukeley, Huntingdon PE17 5AQ.

Mr and Mrs David Cox • 2m N of Huntingdon off B1043. In Great Stukeley, turn at village hall into Owl End • Open for charity 23rd July, 1.30 – 5.30pm • Entrance: £1.50, children 50p • Other information: Parking at village hall
● ✕ ♨

The cascades of petunias and an 'ornamental' wheelbarrow filled with annuals are striking preludes. The brightly planted borders have manicured, matching golden cypress columns as backdrops. Even the magnolia has been clipped (Yes! Clipped!) A small pool, and a blue spruce in a heather bed frame the patio. A few steps further on and Wytchwood becomes altogether different. There is an acre of mown grass with large uncut islands full of wild grasses and native plants softly waving in the breeze – what a refreshing scheme, especially attractive to amphibians, butterflies and dragonflies. After the clichés of the front garden, which some will dislike but most will thoroughly enjoy, the restraint of the meadow islands full of lady's bedstraw and poppies, set with rowans and birches, is inspired. There cannot be many gardens like this, with such contrasting variety, all lovingly created and lovingly maintained, which is why it is included here – though sadly only open one day.

GARDENING FOR THE DISABLED ♿

Demonstration gardens to assist the disabled are available at a number of properties open to the public. They include the following:

Battersea Park (see *Guide* under London) Horticultural Therapy Unit (Wandsworth Borough Council). For appt tel: (0171) 720 3419

Broadview Gardens, Hadlow (see Kent)

Capel Manor (see London) Tel: (01992) 763849

Disabled and Older Gardeners' Association, Herefordshire Growing Point, Herefordshire College of Agriculture, Holme Lacy, Hereford. Tel: (01432) 870316

Royal Horticultural Society's Garden, Wisley (see Surrey)

Ryton Organic Gardens, Ryton-on-Dunsmore (see Warwickshire)

Syon Park, Middlesex (see London).

Open days for the disabled are also held from time to time at the following gardens:

Dolly's Garden (see London)

Hillsborough Community Development Trust (see South & West Yorkshire)

Iden Croft Herbs (see Kent).

The Gardening for Disabled Trust is a registered charity which collects donations from the public and uses them to assist disabled people with improvements to their gardens, or to supply equipment which will enable them to continue to garden. Donations should be sent to Mrs Felicity Seton, Hayes Farmhouse, Hayes Lane, Peasmarsh, Rye, East Sussex.

CHESHIRE

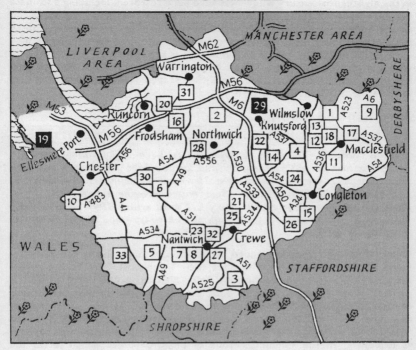

We have included some gardens with Cheshire postal addresses in the Manchester area for convenience. So before planning a day out in Cheshire it is worthwhile consulting pages 301–5.

Two-starred gardens are marked on the map with a black square.

Adlington Hall   1

Adlington, Macclesfield SK10 4LF. Tel: (01625) 820875

Mrs C.J.C. Legh • 5m N of Macclesfield off A523. Signed in Adlington • Hall and garden open to parties by appt • Entrance: hall and garden £4, children £1.50, parties of 25 or more £3.50 per person, children £1 (1999 prices) ● ☕ ✕ <u>WC</u>

To the porticoed Georgian south front of the house a gravelled carriage-sweep encircles an oval of lawn with a sundial at its centre. Beyond is a grass enclosure with a pair of iron gates leading to a short avenue of limes dating from 1688. At the end of the avenue a path leads eastwards to the shell house, a small brick building of 1794 which in the mid-nineteenth century was embellished with shells. To the west of the house is a wood through which there are walks open to the visitor; the walk along the small river bank is particularly pleasant. In the centre, close to the bridge, is a temple to Diana. Various follies in the eighteenth-century wilderness have been restored, including a Chinese bridge, a traditional Cheshire black-and-white timber-framed T'ing house and an old hermitage. In front of the black-and-white, early Elizabethan north front of the house more formal gardens have been created including a new maze and rose garden. East of the house across a cobbled area is a formal pool with a large statue of Father Tiber. Not much interest for the plantsperson, but an attractive woodland park, mostly landscaped in the eighteenth century in the style of 'Capability' Brown.

Arley Hall and Gardens ★ 2

Arley, Great Budworth, Northwich CW9 6NA. Tel: (01565) 777353/777284

Viscount Ashbrook • 5m W of Knutsford off A50, 7m SE of Warrington off A559. Signed from M6 junctions 19 and 20 and M56 junctions 9 and 10 • Hall open (times vary) • Garden open 21st April to 1st Oct, Tues – Sun, and Bank Holiday Mons, 11am – 5pm, but check before travelling • Entrance: £4, concessions £3.40, family £11 (hall extra) (1999 prices) • Other information: Arley Garden Festival 24th – 25th June, 10am – 5pm ◑ 🍵 ✕ 🖥 ⚒ ⬆ ✈ 🧺 🛕 ⚱*

One of the few remaining landed estates in Cheshire, this is the ancestral home of the Warburtons, who built their first house here in the seventeenth century, though the present Arley Hall dates only from 1840. The gardens cover 12 acres. It is thought that one of the earliest herbaceous borders in England was planted here in 1846, and the 'garden room' concept may have been adopted from Elvaston (see entry in Derbyshire). Bounded by old brick walls and yew hedges, there is a special predilection for topiary, as evidenced in the splendid avenue of pleached limes which forms the approach to the house, and the remarkable ilex avenue of 14 trees clipped to the shape of giant cylinders. The walled garden, once a kitchen garden, now contains a variety of cordoned fruit trees, shrubs and herbaceous plants. There is also a collection of hybrid and species shrub roses, a rock garden planted with azaleas and rhododendrons, and the recent addition of a woodland garden.

Bridgemere Garden World 3

Bridgemere, Nantwich CW5 7QB. Tel: (01270) 521100

Mr J. Ravenscroft • On A51 7m SE of Nantwich. Signed from M6 junctions 15 and 16 • Open all year, daily, 9am – dusk (summer 8pm, winter 5pm) • Entrance: free, but charge for television gardens ○ 🍵 ✕ 🖥 WC ⬆ ✈ 🛕 ⚱

Begun in 1961 with one field of roses, this 25-acre garden centre now claims to be one of Europe's largest. There are all types of plants for sale (including some rarely offered), pots and water features. The main area of interest is over 20 different gardens, including three Chelsea Flower Show Gold Medal winners and the *Gardeners' Diary* television garden where the weekly programme is filmed. There is the Hill containing dwarf or slow-growing plants, the cottage garden, rhododendron and azalea garden, winter garden, rock and water garden, silver-grey border, the French rose garden, folly garden, Victorian garden, Mediterranean garden, silver-grey, autumn, herbaceous and annual borders, a fruit and vegetable garden and a very early nursery. All this plus woodlands and lawns.

Capesthorne Hall and Gardens ★ 4

Macclesfield SK11 9JY. Tel: (01625) 861221; Fax: (01625) 861619

Mr W.A. Bromley Davenport • 7m S of Wilmslow, 1m S of Monks Heath on A34 • House open as gardens but 1.30 – 3.30pm only • Gardens open April to Oct, Wed, Sun and Bank Holidays, 12 noon – 6pm • Entrance: gardens and chapel £3.50, OAPs £3, children (5-18) £1.50 (hall extra charge) • Other information: Lunches, teas and suppers by arrangement. Dogs in park only
◑ ☕ WC ċ ☗

Capesthorne is one of East Cheshire's fine historic parks, showing the English style of eighteenth- and nineteenth-century landscape design, with belts of trees enclosing a broad sweep of park and with the house as the focal element. The gardens are best enjoyed by following the suggested woodland walks, because the outstanding features are the range of mature trees and the views and plants associated with the series of man-made lakes. There is much, too, to interest those with a taste for the history of gardens – for example, the site of a conservatory built by Sir Joseph Paxton. There is a pair of outstanding Rococo Milanese gates, and more conventionally a formal lakeside garden planned in the 1960s by garden designer Vernon Russell-Smith.

Cherry Hill 5

Malpas SY14 7EP.

Mr and Mrs Miles Clarke • 6m NW of Whitchurch, 2m W of Malpas off A41. From B5069 turn N at Cuddington Heath towards Chorlton and continue for 1m; garden is on left • Open one day second half June, 2 – 6pm and by appt • Entrance: £2.50, children under 16 £1 ● ☕ WC ċ ⬥

A pleasant mix of the formal and informal. The formal is to be found within an old walled garden divided into different areas all with a strong geometric design. A path through the centre leads under a rose-covered pergola, through a double border of peonies, another rose pergola and finally to a double herbaceous border, where the soft blues and pinks of lupins, geraniums, delphiniums and irises are picked out by a purple prunus hedge. On one side of the walk is a rectangle of lawn surrounded by lavender, shrub roses and cherry trees, and at one end a rose-covered arbour looks over a knot garden edged with low box hedging. On the other side of the walk is a neatly kept *potager*, a fine old greenhouse and a collection of shrub roses. A rill fed by a spring can be seen on the woodland walk. Outside the formal area a long sweep of lawn drops away from the house towards a trout pool surrounded by rhododendrons and woodland with the magnificent backdrop of the Welsh hills.

Cheshire Herbs 6

Fourfields, Forest Road, Tarporley CW6 9ES. Tel: (01829) 760578

*Libby and Ted Riddell • 9m E of Chester, on A49 close to crossroads with A54 •
Open daily except 24th Dec to 2nd Jan, 10am – 5pm • Entrance: free* ○ **WC** &
🌿 🧺 ♨

This is principally a nursery which stocks over 200 varieties of herbs, but there
is also a small garden in a lawned area enclosed by a yew hedge. It is a circular
knot garden small enough to be emulated by most gardeners; the raised bank
around it reminds us that such gardens are best seen from a higher level.
Beyond is a larger area of beds again circular in pattern containing many herbs
and planted in an informal manner. There is also a polytunnel full of large tubs
of plants. The aroma here and in other parts of the nursery makes a visit more
than worthwhile.

Cholmondeley Castle Gardens ★ 7

Cholmondeley Castle, Malpas SY14 8AH. Tel: (01829) 720383

*The Marquess of Cholmondeley • On A49 between Tarporley and Whitchurch •
Open 23rd April to Sept, Wed, Thurs, Sun and Bank Holiday Mons, 11.30am
– 5pm. Other days by prior arrangement for parties of 20 or more • Entrance:
£3, OAPs £2.50, children £1 (1999 prices)* ◑

Although the Cholmondeley family has lived here since the twelfth century,
the present castle was commenced only in 1801 and completed some 20 years
later. The splendid Baroque garden laid out by George London through the
1690s had already been swept away. The house is not open to the public, but
visitors may enjoy the park and gardens, which were laid out in the nineteenth
century and have been extensively replanted since the 1960s. As a site it is
magnificent, with the castle straddling a hill-top, a view across parkland to a
distant mere, and the classic ground in between. There are mature trees and
interesting (and acid-loving) plants in an attractive setting. In particular the
Temple Garden – bordered walkways around a water garden – is most
satisfying, with its rock garden and a fine view of the lake that leads to a
stream garden planted with moisture-lovers. The grass round the tea room is
filled with wild orchids and backing this is a good planting of rhododendrons –
indeed throughout the garden are many varieties of rhododendrons and
azaleas. The rose garden contains an interesting mixture of old and new.

Dorfold Hall 8

Chester Road, Acton, Nantwich CW5 8LD. Tel: (01270) 625245

*Mr R. Roundell • 1m W of Nantwich, S of A534 • Hall open • Garden open
April to Oct, Tues and Bank Holiday Mons, 2 – 5pm • Entrance: £4, children
£2* ◑ 🍴

The hall, impressive from the front, is approached along an avenue of limes
with open parkland to each side and a large pool just to the west. The approach
was laid out by William Nesfield, who was chosen to design various parts of

Kew. To the rear or south of the house is a large lawn, at the east side of which a statue of Shakespeare stands between two herbaceous borders, all the borders to the south having been replanted. Beyond a low wall is another large lawn from where there are views across a ha-ha to the flat countryside in the south. A broad grass walk leads eastwards to a dell, where the present owner has planted rhododendrons and other acid-loving shrubs amongst mature trees around a small stream. To the west is another grassed area with specimen trees and two fine gates.

Dunge Valley Gardens   9

Windgather Rocks, Kettleshulme, Whaley Bridge, High Peak SK23 7RF. Tel: (01663) 733787

David and Elizabeth Ketley • 12m SE of Stockport in Kettleshulme. Signed from B5470 Macclesfield – Whaley Bridge road • Open April to Aug, daily, 10.30am – 6pm, evening parties by appt • Entrance: May and June: Mon – Fri £2, Sat, Sun and Bank Holiday Mons £2.50, children 50p; other months: Mon – Fri, £1.50, Sat, Sun and Bank Holiday Mons £2.50 • Other information: Mini-buses up to 12 seats only ◑ 🍵 ✕ WC 🐾

Many gardens in Cheshire are magnificently situated but Dunge Valley Gardens perhaps comes out best of all. Nestling in a small valley high up in the Peak District, every view is provided with a marvellous backdrop by the surrounding hills. There is much of horticultural interest as well. Alpines grow around the terrace, and beds of diverse herbaceous plants and shrubs surround the old stone farmhouse from which a number of walks spread out. One leads into the rhododendron dell, where amongst a great variety of rhododendrons and azaleas there are also acers, magnolias and other shrubs. There are perennials, too: rodgersias, euphorbias, meconopsis, corydalis and others, mainly moisture-lovers as a small stream keeps this area damp. Another walk goes around the side of the valley and joins the stream further up. As well as more rhododendrons there are a number of seats positioned carefully at the best viewpoints back down the valley. Planting only began here in 1982 but the garden is already well worth a visit; shrub and species roses are plentiful, giving further interest after the rhododendrons have finished. Good bird life.

Dunham Massey

(see Manchester Area)

Eaton Hall ★   10

Eccleston, Chester CH4 9ET. Tel: (01244) 684400

The Duke of Westminster • 4m S of Chester off A483 Chester – Wrexham road • Gardens probably open three days in summer, 1.30 – 5.30pm • Entrance: £2.50, children £1 (1999 prices) • Other information: Chapel open ◕ 🍵 WC ♿

The gardens and parkland surrounding the modern hall are vast. There are several fine features: well-kept herbaceous beds, two laburnum tunnels and many stone statues and urns. A long, narrow greenhouse contains camellias, and a deep bed backing against the walled garden is planted for dramatic effect with 'hot-coloured' perennials and shrubs such as cotinus and dark-flowering buddleia. There is also a large lake covered with water lilies, and a small Gothic-style cottage set within its own small garden of herbs, with stone and brick paths. Close to the house is the imposing Italian garden surrounded by a high yew hedge; a large dragon fountain stands at the centre of a pool and there are beds of annuals and more statues. Arabella Lennox-Boyd has been working on the garden here for several years. Open days at Eaton Hall are few, but a visit is more than repaid. If you are in the area and the children are clamouring to visit *Chester Zoo*, it it has gardens with large beds of brightly coloured annuals, roses, etc.

Gawsworth Hall 11

Macclesfield SK11 9RN. Tel: (01260) 223456; Fax (01260) 223469

Mr and Mrs T. Richards • 3m S of Macclesfield off A536. Signposted • Hall open • Garden open probably early April to early Oct, daily, 2 – 5pm • Entrance: hall, park and garden £4.20, children under 16 £2.10, parties of 20 or more £3 per person (1999 prices) • Other information: Open-air theatre in garden mid-June to mid-Aug ◑ ☕ WC ₺ ♨ ♀

The hall is approached by a drive leading between two lakes to the north end, where there is a large yew tree and lawns sloping down to one of the lakes. A formal garden on the west side has beds of modern roses edged with bright annuals and many stone ornaments, including a sundial and circular pool with a fountain. Stone steps lead to a sunken lawn area with borders of shrubs and perennials. To the south is another lawned garden surrounded by a high yew hedge and herbaceous borders. A grassed area containing mature trees lies to the west of these formal areas, from where there is a view of the medieval tilting ground and site of the Elizabethan pleasure gardens. A path back to the house passes a small conservatory containing classical statues.

Hare Hill Gardens 12

Hare Hill, Over Alderley, Macclesfield SK10 4QB. Tel: (01625) 828981

The National Trust • 5m NW of Macclesfield, N of B5087 between Alderley Edge and Prestbury at Greyhound Road • Open April to Oct, Wed, Thurs, Sat, Sun and Bank Holiday Mons, 10am – 5.30pm. Special opening for rhododendrons and azaleas 10th to 30th May, daily, 10am – 5.30pm. Parties by written appt • Entrance: £2.50, children £1.25. £1.50 per car refundable on entry to garden (1999 prices) • Other information: Picnics at lakeside only ◑ WC ₺

There are two distinct areas here: a walled garden, once used for growing vegetables, and surrounding it a large woodland garden. The walled garden is rather sparsely planted. Climbing plants around the walls include vines, roses, ceanothus and wisteria, and in the centre are a few small rose beds. A seat set into the north wall is surrounded by a white trellis pergola, and nearby are two wire statues. The woodland garden is perhaps of greater interest. It contains over 50 varieties of holly, many fine rhododendrons and magnolias, spring-flowering bulbs and some climbing roses growing high into their host trees. In the centre is a pond spanned by two wooden bridges. Dredging work has been carried out to clear the woodland pools, and a new bridge links one of the garden paths to the island.

Henbury Hall ★ 13

Macclesfield SK11 9PJ.

Mr S.Z. de Ferranti • 2m W of Macclesfield on A537 • Open 28th May for charity, 2 – 5pm • Entrance: £2.50, children £1 ● ⚇ **WC**

The hall was built in 1986 based on Palladio's Villa Rotunda, and the French limestone goes well with its parkland setting. To the north the land slopes down to a lake with ornamental bridges at each end. The 12 acres are well-landscaped and planted with many mature trees, azaleas and rhododendrons. Further north the land rises again, and beyond more banks of trees and shrubs is a walled garden with a double herbaceous border and a laburnum arch. Close by is a unique design of tennis court and a large modern conservatory housing a swimming pool, a fernery and a grotto. At the other side of the walled garden is a cottage recently renovated in the Gothic style.

Jodrell Bank Arboretum 14

Jodrell Bank Science Centre and Arboretum, Macclesfield SK11 9DL. Tel: (01477) 571339

Manchester University • On A535 between Holmes Chapel and Chelford, 5m NE of M6 junction 18. Signposted • Open mid-March to Oct, daily, 10.30am – 5.30pm; Nov to mid-March, Tues to Sun, 11am – 4.30pm. Closed 20th – 26th Dec (1999 times) • Entrance: £4.60, OAPs £3.30, children £2.30 (under 5 free, but not admitted to Planetarium), family £13.50 (1999 prices) ⚇ ✕ 🛍 **WC** ♿ 👍 ☼

The arboretum was begun in 1972 largely at the instigation of Professor Sir Bernard Lovell and with financial support from the Granada Foundation. It is set in a flat landscape with all views to the south dominated by the massive radiotelescope. The large collection of trees covers 35 acres and includes a National Collection of malus with over 100 species and varieties and a National Collection of sorbus with over 70 species and varieties. There is a collection of hornbeams and fine specimens of *Ulmus minor* (syn. *U. elegantissima*) 'Jacqueline Hillier' and the cut-leaved form of the common walnut (*Juglans regia* 'Laciniata'). Broad grass walkways lead among the trees, and many small natural ponds are dotted around the garden. There are also beds of shrub roses, heathers and azaleas. A day out for the family and good value when all the attractions are considered.

Little Moreton Hall 15

Congleton CW12 4SD. Tel: (01260) 272018

The National Trust • 4m SW of Congleton on E side of A34 between Congleton and Newcastle-under-Lyme • Open 25th March to 5th Nov, Wed – Sun and

Bank Holiday Mons, 11.30am – 5pm (last admission 4.30pm). 11th Nov to 23rd Dec, Sat and Sun, 11.30am – 4pm • Entrance: £4.30, children £2.10, family £10.70 (hall and gardens); joint ticket with Biddulph Grange (see entry in Staffordshire) £6.50, children £3.20, family £16) • Other information: Wheelchair and scooter for loan. Guide dogs and hearing dogs permitted, but other dogs in areas outside moat only ◑ ☕ ✕ ⊞ WC ♿ ♨ ⛽ ⚚

The hall is one of the best-known timber-framed buildings in the country, and its gardens are pleasant in their own quiet way. Largely the creation of the Trust and a fitting complement to the house, they cover about an acre and are set within a moat. There is a cobbled courtyard in the centre of the hall and to the west a large lawn with fruit trees and an old grassed mound. To the north of the hall is a yew tunnel and the best feature of all, a knot garden, laid out under the guidance of Graham Stuart Thomas following a seventeenth-century model. It is a simple design of gravel and lawn separated by a low box hedge. Behind the knot garden, four new beds have been planted with medieval and culinary herbs and a selection of seventeenth-century vegetables. There are herbaceous borders around the hall and a gravel walk that follows the inside perimeter of the moat.

Lodge Lane Nursery and Gardens (Bluebell Cottage)   16

Lodge Lane, Dutton, Warrington WA4 4HP. Tel: (01928) 713718

Rod and Diane Casey • 4m SE of Runcorn, 6m NW of Northwich, S of A533. Signposted • Nursery open mid-March to early Oct, Wed – Sun and Bank Holiday Mons, 10am – 5pm. Gardens, meadow and woodland open May to Sept during nursery opening hours. Parties by appt • Entrance: Gardens, meadow and woodland £2, children free ◑ ⊞ WC ♿ ♨ ⚚

Set around an old cottage, these gardens have grown with their owners' interest in plants. They now include two acres of woodland, three acres of wildflower meadow and a large well-run nursery that stocks a good range of perennials. Clustered around the cottage are a number of small gardens divided by hedges and trellises covered in climbers. Each is devoted to a different theme: herb garden, yellow garden, raised vegetable garden, the mandatory area of grasses and a patio with a large collection of pelargoniums and other tender perennials grown in pots. In a larger open area to the side of the house a newly constructed scree bed runs down to a pool backed by a well-planted herbaceous border. Beds of penstemons and asters provide colour at the tail end of the year. A garden with interest for all.

Mellors Gardens   17

Hough Hole House, Sugar Lane, Rainow, Macclesfield SK10 5UW. Tel: (01625) 572345

Mr and Mrs A. Rigby • From Macclesfield take B5470 Whaley Bridge road. In Rainow turn off to N opposite church into Round Meadow. Then turn first left into Sugar Lane and follow down to garden • Open 29th May, 28th Aug, 2 – 5pm and by appt for parties of more than 10 • Entrance: £1.50, children free ◑ ☕ WC

Where can you pass through the Valley of the Shadow of Death, climb Jacob's Ladder, see the Mouth of Hell and visit the Celestial City, all within the space of 10 minutes? Here, in a small valley in a rugged but attractive part of the Peak District, in the second half of the nineteenth century, James Mellor, much influenced by Swedenborg, designed this allegorical garden which attempts to re-create the journey of Christian in Bunyan's *Pilgrim's Progress*. Most areas are grassed, with stone paths running throughout. There are many small stone houses and other ornaments to represent features of the journey. At one end a large pond is overlooked by a small octagonal summerhouse. Be sure to be shown round by the owner or buy one of the excellent guide books in order to get the best from this small garden.

The Mount   18

Andertons Lane, Whirley, Macclesfield SK11 9PB.

Mr and Mrs Nicholas Payne • 2m W of Macclesfield off A537. Turn into Pepper Street opposite Blacksmith's Arms, and left into Church Lane which becomes Andertons Lane. The Mount is 200 metres further on. Signposted • Open one day a year for NGS, and by appt at other times for parties of 10 or more. Parties by written appt • Entrance: £2.50, children 50p ● ☙ WC ☙ ℘

The garden, originally planted in the 1920s but enlarged, improved and replanted over the past 12 years by the present owners, is a fine setting for the Regency house. Each distinct area has its own individual style. The terraced garden has an Italian feel, with a swimming pool, many architectural features and brightly planted terracotta pots. The shade garden is more informal with rhododendrons, azaleas and camellias underplanted with hostas and other shade-lovers. A small lawned area has an herbaceous border containing some striking delphiniums. Opposite is another small border planted entirely with astilbes, and a small conservatory containing a climbing pelargonium. In one corner of the garden is an area where the grass has been cut to different heights, forming patterns and paths. It comes as a surprise to learn that the garden is only two acres.

Ness Botanic Gardens ★★   19

Neston Road, Ness L64 4AY. Tel: (0151) 353 0123

University of Liverpool • 10m NW of Chester, 2m off A540 between Ness and Burton • Open daily except 25th Dec: March to Oct, 9.30am – dusk; Nov to Feb, 9.30am – 4pm • Entrance: admission charge • Other information: Guide dogs only ○ ☙ ✕ ☙ WC ☙ ℘ ✍ ♔

Mr A. Bulley began gardening on this site in 1898, using seeds from plants collected for him by George Forrest, the noted plant hunter. His daughter, Lois Bulley, who gave the gardens to the University in 1948, was described in her *Times* obituary as 'an exceptional human being, born into wealth, which she rejected, a member of the Labour Party, Communist Party and Cheshire County Council, a Quaker, a fighter against racism and for social justice and equality, especially for women, a philanthropist with a shrewd business brain, a national benefactor of applied plant biotechnology and horticultural research'. Ness Gardens extend to over 60 acres. Those who have experience of the north-west winds blowing off the Irish Sea will marvel at the variety and exotic nature of the plant life. The secret is in the Lombardy poplars, holm oaks and Scots pines which have been planted as shelter belts shielding the specialist areas. The aim has been to provide all-year-round interest from the spring, through the herbaceous and rose gardens of the summer, to the heather and sorbus collections of the autumn. There are in addition areas of specialist interest such as the native plant garden, which houses plants raised from seed or cuttings from wild plants and used for propagation or the restocking of natural habitats. With the creation of an academic chair at the gardens in 1991 there has been a positive move to increase on-site research. Specialisms include sorbus, betulas, salix, rhododendrons and primulas. Maps, coloured guides and interest trails are available.

Norton Priory Museum and Gardens 20

Tudor Road, Manor Park, Runcorn WA7 1SX. Tel: (01928) 569895

The Norton Priory Museum Trust • From M56 junction 11 turn for Warrington and follow Norton Priory signs. From all other directions follow Runcorn then Norton Priory signs • Gardens open Nov to March, daily, 12 noon – 4pm; April to Oct, weekdays, 12 noon – 5pm, Sat, Sun and Bank Holiday Mons, 12 noon – 6pm. Walled garden open March to Oct • Entrance: £3.30, OAPs and children £2, family £8.80 • Other information: Museum open. Teas and snacks in Museum ○ 🍵 🖻 WC ♿ ⚲ 🛒 🔱

The priory was built as an Augustinian foundation in the twelfth century and transformed into a Tudor, then Georgian, mansion before being abandoned in 1921. The 38 acres of woodland gardens contain the ruins of the Priory, and also an authentic eighteenth-century walled garden. Originally built by Sir Richard Brooke in 1770, this eventually fell into disrepair, but since 1980 it has been restored to reflect both the Georgian and modern designs and tastes. Its range of specialities include a culinary and medicinal herb garden, plants for household uses, a fruit arch and cordon fruit, traditional vegetables, orchard and herbaceous borders. Holder of a National Collection of *Cydonia oblonga* (tree quince).

The Old Hough 21

Warmingham CW10 0HQ. Tel: (01270) 526232; Fax (01270) 526060

Mr and Mrs D.S. Varey • 2m S of Middlewich on A530 to Nantwich • Open 25th June for NGS, 2 – 6pm • Entrance: £2.50, children 50p NEW ◐ 💀 WC ♿

The two and a half acres of gardens are spacious in their conception. Broad stone paths surround the rambling old brick house enhanced by large stone troughs and small iron pergolas. A large sweep of lawn runs down the north side of the house. At one end is a set of borders containing plants chosen for their architectural effect and a wildlife pool surrounded by bullrushes. At the eastern end another large border contains an interesting collection of small trees and shrubs, including a ginkgo, a catalpa and a liriodendron. The area to the front of the house is more formal, with stone paths and yew hedges. An elegant black stone cat stands at the front door (there are some storks and dogs by the same artist elsewhere in the garden). One border has plants chosen for foliage colour, concentrating on reds, silvers and yellows. To the west of this area the land rises, and beyond a beech hedge an iris rill set in a lawn cascades through an arch into a pear-shaped lily pool in the lower garden. These gardens are still quite young but well worth a visit, especially for those with a taste for distinctive design.

Peover Hall 22

Over Peover, Knutsford WA16 6SW. Tel: Guide, I. Shepherd (01565) 632358; Estate Office (01565) 830395

Mr R. Brooks • 3m S of Knutsford on A50 • Hall open May to Sept, Mons only except Bank Holiday Mons, 2.30 – 4.30pm • Gardens open May to Sept, Mon and Thurs, 2.30 – 5pm • Entrance: £2, children £1 (hall, stables and garden £3, children £2) • Other information: Teas on Mons only. Possible for wheelchairs but many grass paths. Dogs in park only. Plants for sale on special occasions only ◑ WC

Peover Hall (pronounced Peever) and its gardens are surrounded by a large expanse of flat parkland laid out in the early eighteenth century, but the gardens are mainly Edwardian. On the northern side of the hall is a forecourt, from which a broad grass walk leads through an avenue of pleached limes to a summerhouse overlooking a small circular lawn; both are enclosed by a high yew hedge. On the west side of the gardens is a wooded area containing many rhododendrons and a particularly attractive grassy dell. Clustered around the south and west of the hall are several small formal gardens, separated by brick walls and yew hedges, some containing yew topiary. Rose garden, herb garden, white garden and pink garden. The lily-pool garden has a summerhouse with a tiled roof supported by Doric columns. Fine Georgian stables and a church to visit.

Queen's Park, Crewe 23

Victoria Avenue, Wistaston Road, Crewe CW2 7SE. Tel: (01270) 569176

Crewe and Nantwich Borough Council • 2m W of town centre, S of A530 • Open all year, 9am – sunset • Entrance: free • Other information: Parking off Queen's Park Drive ○ ▆ ▦ WC ᚕ ⬠ ꙮ

A well-landscaped Victorian park created in 1887-8 by the London & North Western Railway as a gift to the people of Crewe. It is oval in shape and covers 48 acres, with large grassed areas and a wide variety of mature trees. From an ornate entrance with two Gothick lodges and a clock tower, a drive leads through an avenue of birches to the centre of the park. Here a modern café with a terrace looks down upon the large boating lake surrounded by banks of trees and shrubs. From the west of the park a stream runs through a lightly wooded valley to join the four-and-a-half-acre puddled lake. A path linking the entrance to this valley passes some raised beds of heathers and goes through a tunnel of laburnum. There is a scented garden for the disabled. It merits a high grade for the quality of landscaping, the trees and the Victorian buildings, but in essence it is a large municipal park where the fight against vandalism and litter is fought hard.

The Quinta ★ 24

Swettenham, Congleton CW12 2LD.

Sir Bernard Lovell and Cheshire Wildlife Trust • 5m NW of Congleton, E of A535 Holmes Chapel – Alderley Edge road near Tremlow Green in Swettenham, next to church • Open daily, 2 – 6pm and for parties on weekdays by appt • Entrance: £2 • Other information: Teas on Sun openings only ☕

Sir Bernard Lovell began planting this garden in 1948 to satisfy his love of trees. It has expanded steadily and now contains a large variety of trees and shrubs. There are good collections of pines and birches, five of the six varieties of wingnut and an oriental plane directly descended from the Hippocratic tree on the island of Cos. Most areas are informally planted and interspersed with grassed glades; several avenues pass up and down the garden, including one of limes planted in 1958 to celebrate Sir Bernard's Reith lectures. Across the more recently planted areas to the west of the garden a walk (one mile from the car park and back) passes some marvellous views across the Dane Valley (SSSI). It leads to the 39 steps that descend into the wooded valley of a small brook. Take good walking shoes and a tree guide as some specimens have lost their labels and can be quite a challenge to identify.

Reaseheath College 25

Reaseheath, Nantwich CW5 6DF. Tel (01270) 625131; Fax (01270) 625665

Reaseheath College • 1½ m N of Nantwich on A51 • Open for College Open Days in May, and late May to July, Wed only, 1 – 5pm for NGS • Entrance: by donation. Guided tours available. Prices on application ☕ 🍵 🛍 WC ♿ 🛍 ⚲

The College is fortunate in being housed in the grounds of Reaseheath, for its attractive gardens must provide the students with constant inspiration. From the old brick hall a large lawn sweeps southwards to a lake, flanked on one side by a heather garden and on the other by a rockery. The lake is spanned by a wooden bridge and stocked with a good variety of water lilies and marginals. On the south side is a woodland garden, with many fine trees including a large cut-leaf beech. Underplanting is of primulas, hostas, azaleas and other shade-loving plants. To the west of the lake another lawned area has island beds with a variety of small trees, shrubs and perennials. There is also a formal rose garden enclosed by a berberis hedge. Other interests around the campus include a herb garden, a model fruit garden, a range of glasshouses and a nursery.

Rode Hall 26

Church Lane, Scholar Green, Stoke on Trent ST7 3QP. Tel: (01270) 882961

Sir Richard and Lady Baker Wilbraham • 5m SW of Congleton between A34 and A50 • House open as garden from 5th April, Wed and Bank Holidays only. Also for parties by appt at other times • Garden open 13th to 20th Feb (for snowdrops); 2nd March to Sept, Tues – Thurs and Bank Holidays, 2 – 5pm. Also for parties by appt at other times • Entrance: £2.50, OAPs £1.50 (house and garden £4, OAPs £2.50. Special parties at other times £6) ◑ 🍽 WC ♿ 🌱

A long drive leads through parkland to an attractive red brick house with fine stable buildings and a gravel forecourt. The gardens lie to the north and east of the house, with many areas remaining as planned by Repton in 1779. The rose garden and formal areas close to the house, however, were designed by Nesfield in 1860; these are mainly lawn, with gravel paths and clipped yews, and good views from here of the surrounding countryside and Repton's lake. In a dell to the west is a woodland garden with hellebores and flowering shrubs, rhododendrons, azaleas and some fine climbing roses. Old stone steps lead up the opposite side of the dell to a grotto and early nineteenth-century terraced rock garden. A small stream is dammed at the open end of the dell with the resulting pond surrounded by marginals. A path leads from here to the lake. The ice-house in the park is worth a visit and the two-acre Georgian walled kitchen garden, now open to the public, is at its best in June, July and August.

Stapeley Water Gardens 27

London Road, Stapeley, Nantwich CW5 7LH. Tel: (01270) 623868; Fax: (01270) 624919

Mr R.G.A. Davies • 1m SE of Nantwich on A51. Signed from M6 junction 16 • Open all year, daily except 25th Dec: summer, Mon – Fri, 9am – 6pm, Sat, Sun and Bank Holidays, 10am – 6pm; winter, Mon – Fri, 9am – 5pm, Sat, Sun, 10am – 5pm. The Palms open from 10am • Entrance: Display Gardens free. The Palms £3.50, OAPs £2.75, children £1.80, parties of 20 or more £2.85 per person, OAPs £2, children £1.50. Season tickets available (1999 prices) • Other information: Wheelchairs available ○ 🍽 ✕ 🏪 WC ♿ 🌱 🎁 ☕

Two acres of garden shopping under cover form the world's largest water garden centre. Within it a few areas are attractive gardens in their own right. At the back are many pools containing the largest display of aquatic plants (listed top by *Gardening Which?*) and the land around is landscaped with lawns and shrub borders. Another area has small demonstration gardens. Across the car park is The Palms Tropical Oasis. This huge greenhouse has none of the architectural merit of a Victorian palm house, but the main hall is impressive, with a long rectangular pool stocked with koi and flanked by huge palm trees. Display from the Manchester Museum of the World of Frogs, plus other exhibits. Those with an interest in water gardens might comment that this is a bleak description – think of the giant *Victoria amazonica* water lily from Brazil (they might say); the rare breeding sting-rays; the *Nymphaea gigantea* from Australia. Ooh-aah! And an angling centre for the non-horticultural.

Stonyford Cottage Garden 28

Stonyford Lane, Oakmere, Northwich CW8 2TF. Tel: (01606) 888128

Mr and Mrs Anthony Overland • Take A556 Northwich – Chester road, ³/₄ m W of crossroads with A49 turn N into minor road signed Norley and Kingsley. Garden is ½ m on left • Garden open April to Sept, Sun, Wed and Bank Holiday Mons, 12 noon – 5.30pm and by appt for individuals and parties at other times • Entrance: £2, children free • Other information: Refreshments on charity open days only. Plants for sale in nursery open Tues – Sun and Bank Holiday Mons ◑ 🍴 ♿ ✿

This nursery specialises in herbaceous perennials and grows most of its own stock. There is plenty of sound advice available and many of the plants are to be seen growing in the adjoining garden. This is divided into two parts by Stonyford brook and pool. The first part borders the pool, and moisture-lovers thrive here, hostas, mimulus, dicentras, primulas and ligularias among them. A wooden bridge leads to a small island covered with marsh marigolds growing wild, and a second bridge to the main part of the garden; this also has a damp area that borders the pool and a gunnera grows here, but higher up towards the cottage the land suddenly becomes quite dry. Here are plants such as salvias, diascias and penstemons. Gardening is not easy on this site as it is a frost pocket, but there are many interesting plants and the unusual situation makes for an attractive garden. The owners' plans for expansion promise greater things.

Tatton Park ★★ 29

Knutsford WA16 6QN. Tel: (01625) 534400

Cheshire County Council/The National Trust • 10m SE of Warrington. Signed from M6 and M56 • House open April to Oct, 12 noon – 4pm • Gardens open April to Oct, daily except Mon (but open Bank Holiday Mons), 10.30am – 6pm. Nov to March 2001, daily except Mon and 25th Dec, 11am – 4pm • Entrance: gardens £3, park £3 per car, Discovery Saver Ticket (to any two attractions excluding park entry) £4.50 (1999 prices). Note: NT members must pay some charges ○ 🍽 ✕ <u>WC</u> ♿ ✿ 🛍 🚻

The gardens here cover 50 acres and warrant an extensive exploration. However, as Tatton claims to be The Trust's busiest garden with over 100,000 visitors annually, choose your time carefully if you don't like crowds. On passing through the entrance visitors see to their left the Orangery. Built in 1820 by Lewis Wyatt, and recently restored to his original 1818 plan, it contains orange trees, lemon trees and plants of the period. Next door is Paxton's huge fernery of 1850, again recently restored. This has large New Zealand tree ferns in its distinctively Victorian interior. To the east, passing a large L-shaped herbaceous and shrub border, the Edwardian rose garden is formal in design with a pool at its centre and fine stone paths and ornaments around. To the south lie large informally planted areas, an arboretum with many conifers and rhododendrons and a lake containing water lilies with a good variety of marginal plants growing around its banks. On the west side of the lake is a unique Japanese garden built in 1910 by workers brought especially from Japan. Azaleas in season. The nearby Broadwalk leads to the Choragic Monument. To the south of the house is the Italian garden, possibly designed by Paxton and best viewed from the top floor of the house. Tatton Park has been awarded a grant by the Heritage Lottery Fund to restore its walled kitchen gardens. Work will take three years. The garden also contains a maze and is surrounded by attractive parkland.

Tirley Garth ★   30

Willington, Tarporley CW6 0LZ. Tel: (01829) 732301

Tirley Garth Trust • 9m E of Chester, 2½ m N of Tarporley, just N of Utkinton on Kelsall road. Signposted • Open 14th, 21st, 28th, 29th May, 4th June, 2 – 6pm. Parties welcome by appt at other times • Entrance: £3, children 50p ● 🍷 WC ⬥ 🐾

The magnificent Edwardian house has gardens that complement it perfectly. They are still in much the same layout as originally designed by T.H. Mawson and C.E. Mallows, and some of the stonework in the paths, ornaments and buildings is particularly notable. There is a circular courtyard at the western entrance and a small sunken garden to one side leading to the large terrace on the south front with lawns and rose beds. To the east is a lawned terrace with a view across the large semi-circular rose garden that spreads below it. In the centre of the house a courtyard has a circular pool and fountain. Outside these formal gardens are areas of parkland and woodland; to the east a stream runs through a small valley planted with fine azaleas, rhododendrons and other shrubs.

Walton Hall Gardens   31

Walton Lea Road, Higher Walton, Warrington WA4 6SN. Tel: (01925) 601617

Warrington Borough Council • 2m SW of Warrington on S side of A56 in Walton • Open daily, 8am – dusk • Entrance: free • Other information: Plants for sale on Suns only. Heritage centre, children's zoo and play area, pitch and putt, crazy golf ○ 🍷 🖼 WC ♿ ⬥ 🎪 ⛲

These gardens are dominated by the dark brick Victorian mansion with its distinctive clock tower. To one side of the building is a large pool containing carp and terrapins with, behind, an impressive rockery well planted with azaleas, rhododendrons, birch and other small shrubs and trees. Water cascades down the rocks to a pool planted with water lilies and marginals, including a clump of gunneras. Behind the hall is a series of formal gardens separated by yew hedges and low stone walls and containing beds of bright tulips and annuals. Beyond some large beech trees, modern roses are set out in formal beds. The walk back down the west side of the garden passes through light woodland with a collection of camellias and some fine acers and magnolias. The council keeps these gardens in good condition; a Ranger Service organises public events.

85 Warmingham Road   32

Coppenhall, Crewe CW1 4PS. Tel: (01270) 582030

Mr and Mrs A. Mann • 3m N of Crewe off A530 between Warmingham and Leighton Hospital near White Lion Inn • Open probably March to July by appt for parties of up to 40 • Entrance: £2, children free ● 🍵 WC 📷

Many and various alpines are to be found here, growing in just a third of an acre. In the first section of the garden, paths run among lushly planted beds that are lightly shaded by trees. There are perennials and small shrubs as well as a collection of lilies. A small pond in the centre has marginals such as golden sedge. Beyond this area is a brighter, more open section with gravel screes, a rock garden and a peat bed. Diascias, violas and geraniums are here in large numbers. There are also two greenhouses, one of which contains a good collection of cacti and succulents.

The Well House   33

Tilston, Malpas SY14 7DP. Tel: (01829) 250332

Mrs S H French-Greenslade • 12m S of Chester on A41. Turn right after Broxted roundabout, then on Malpas road through Tilston. Garden is at antique shop • Open two days for NGS, 2 – 5.30pm, and March to July by appt • Entrance: £2, children 25p (1999 prices) • Other information: Plants for sale sometimes NEW ● 🍵 WC

A one-acre garden set around a small natural stream. It is worth visiting both for the range of plants grown and the natural landscaping of the site. Close to the house is a geometric layout of beds containing perennials, campanulas and alstromerias amongst them, backed by a rose-covered pergola and with a sundial at the centre. There is also an area devoted to rock plants and a patio on which a large number of plants are grown in containers – a great inspiration for those with small gardens. Another area has plants chosen for foliage colour, including yellow robinia, purple berberis and silver pyrus. Moisture-lovers, including many ferns, line the stream that divides the garden, and a bridge leads across to a small hexagonal summerhouse. The land rises steeply from the stream, giving views back over the garden, and another fine view can be had from the balcony where tea may be taken.

GARDEN THEFTS
These now routinely include statuary, fencing, etc., and fish. There are two results of the increase in thievery – first that owners are reluctant to open their gardens except to pre-arranged groups who have provided references. Second, their entries in the *Guide* sometimes exclude mention of precious objects as owners do not wish to publicise their existence to the burgling fraternity or to other parties that cannot be identified in some way.

CORNWALL

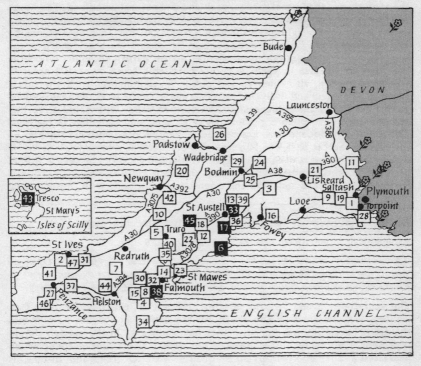

Two-starred gardens are marked on the map with a black square.

Antony

1

**Torpoint PL11 2QA. Tel: (01752) 812191 (NT office);
(01752) 812364 (Woodland Garden office)**

*The National Trust and Trustees of Carew Pole Garden Trust • From Plymouth
use Torpoint car ferry. Antony is 2m W of Torpoint on A374, 16m SE of
Liskeard • House open as formal garden • Formal garden open April to Oct,
Tues – Thurs and Bank Holiday Mons; also June to Aug, Sun, all 1.30 –
5.30pm (last admission 4.45pm). Woodland garden open March to Oct, Mon –
Sat, 11am – 5.30pm, Sun, 2 – 5.30pm • Entrance: £2.50; combined gardens
only £3 (house and formal garden £4, children £2, pre-booked parties £3.40 per
person) (1999 prices)* ◑ 🍽 WC ♿ 🛍

Antony is a little off the beaten track, but it is well worth the effort to visit one
of the country's finest eighteenth-century houses, in a truly magnificent
natural setting. The great garden designer, Humphry Repton, was consulted
by Reginald Pole Carew but they disagreed over the initial plans, and it has

been successive generations of the Carew Pole family who have presided over the evolution of the formal garden, parkland and natural woodland. The house and formal garden, with its terrace overlooking parkland which sweeps down to the River Lynher (glimpsed through a series of rides), are now owned by The National Trust. Be sure to see William Pye's cone water sculpture on the west lawn. Pye is one of our most talented water feature designers who stole the show at Chelsea in 1998. A family charitable trust owns 100 acres of woodland garden, also open to the public in conjunction with the house gardens. The woodland is divided into two areas: to the west of the woodland garden car park is the wilderness and Westdown Valley where, in late spring, one can ramble through a glorious array of specimen camellias (a National Collection), rhododendrons, azaleas and magnolias in a semi-wild setting. To the east of the car park are 50 acres of older natural woodland with lovely walks along the banks of the River Lynher. In these areas can be seen a 'fishful' pond, a fifteenth-century dovecot and the Bath House — built by Thomas Parlby between 1788 and 1790 and open by appointment with The National Trust.

Barbara Hepworth Museum and Sculpture Garden 2

Barnoon Hill, St Ives TR26 1AD. Tel: (01736) 796226

Administered by The Tate Gallery • In centre of St Ives. Signposted • Open all year, Tues – Sun, 10.30am – 5.30pm. Also open Mons in July and Aug • Entrance: museum/sculpture garden £3.50, concessions £1.80 ○ WC 👜 👤

The sculpture garden, within walking distance of the new St Ives Tate Gallery, was designed by the South African composer Priaulx Rainier and the artist herself. It was her wish that her sculptures in the garden should represent a permanent exhibition of her work. The whole garden, which possesses a distinct Mediterranean quality with its trees and bushes, is interconnected by intricate pathways. Native and semi-tropical flowers also enhance the setting.

Boconnoc 3

The Stewardry, Boconnoc, Lostwithiel PL22 0RG. Tel: (01208) 872546

*Mr and Mrs J.D.G. Fortescue • Between St Austell and Liskeard, S of A390. Well-signed on open days between Lostwithiel and Middle Taphouse • * Open for various charities 30th April, 7th, 14th, 21st, 28th May, 2 – 5pm • Entrance: £2, children free • Other information: special event on 28th May* ◑ 🖵 WC & ⬦ 🌳

The extensive grounds were first laid out by Thomas Pitt, Lord Camelford, in the eighteenth century. Great landscape effects. The magnificent woodland garden, covering some 20 acres, contains fine flowering shrubs and many large and unusual trees. It is best seen by taking a walk along the well-kept paths. Not far away in Lostwithiel is the *Duchy of Cornwall Nursery*, reputed to be the best garden centre in the county (Tel: (01208) 872668).

Bosahan ★ 4

Manaccan, Helston TR12 6JL. Tel: (01326) 231351

Mr and Mrs R.J. Graham-Vivian • 10m SE of Helston, 1m NE of Manaccan • Open 15th, 29th April, 2 – 5.30pm; also 16th, 30th April, 2 – 5.30pm. Parties of 6 or more by appt • Entrance: £3.50, OAPs £1, children under 14 free, parties £5 per person • Other information: Coach companies must confirm dates in advance ◕ ☕ WC

This valley garden of five acres, started 100 years ago, leads down to the Helford river and will give pleasure to the keen plantsman as it has both mature and more recently planted trees and shrubs, including some New Zealand and South American varieties. A giant magnolia stands near the house. Spring colour is provided by masses of camellias, rhododendrons, azaleas and magnolias along with bog plants in the water garden. There are a large number of palms (*Trachycarpus fortunei*) throughout the gardens. Walking down through the gardens is a valley leading to more mature specimens including pittosporums and dicksonias. Fine views from the top of the valley.

Bosvigo House 5

Bosvigo Lane, Truro TR1 3NH. Tel/Fax: (01872) 275774

Mr Michael and Mrs Wendy Perry • ¾ m W of Truro. From A390, turn into Dobbs Lane adjacent to Sainsbury foodstore roundabout. Entrance is 500 metres down lane on left, just after sharp left bend • Open March to Sept, Thurs – Sat, 11am – 6pm • Entrance: £2.50, children 50p • Other information: Rare and unusual plants for sale at nursery ◑ WC

A garden with subtle mixtures of colour and foliage where the plantsman will find many unusual and rare specimens. The three acres surrounding a Georgian house consist of several delightful enclosed and walled areas. The 'hot garden' displays red, yellow and orange plants. The Vean garden has white and yellow flowers, and the walled garden many rare plants. This is not a typical Cornish garden; it is at its best in summer when the mainly herbaceous plants start to flower.

Caerhays Castle Garden ★★ 6

Caerhays, Gorran, St Austell PL26 6LY. Tel: (01872) 501310; Fax: (01872) 501870; E-mail: caerhays@eclipse.co.uk; Website: www.eclipse.co.uk/caerhays

Mr F.J. Williams • 10m S of St Austell. On coast by Porthluney Cove between Dodman Point and Nare Head • Castle open for conducted tours 20th March to 28th April (excluding Bank Holidays), Mon – Fri, 2 – 4pm • Garden open 13th March to 19th May, Mon – Fri; also 2nd, 23rd April, 1st May, all 11am – 4pm • Entrance: £3.50 (castle only £3.50, castle and garden £6) ◕ ☕ WC

An internationally noted garden with unrivalled collections of magnolias and shrubs raised from seed and material brought back by such plant hunters as

George Forrest and E.H. Wilson, who were assisted financially in their expeditions by the Williams. The house, a vast romantic castle in the Gothic style, was built by John Nash between 1805 and 1807; the garden began to take on its present form from 1896. The woodland stretches down to the sea and the many rare specimens include tree ferns, acers, oaks, azaleas and nothofagus. J.C. Williams originally specialised in the cultivation and hybridising of daffodils, but turned his sheltered clearings over to a refuge for the nineteenth-century influx of new plants; many in British gardens today, including camellias which he bred, originated at Caerhays. A place to be visited by the family as well as the plantsman.

Carnowall 7

Black Rock, Praze, Camborne TR14 9NR. Tel: (01209) 831757

Mr and Mrs Smith • 5m N of Helston. Take B3297, then turning at Farms Common to T-junction, turn left 50 metres then left again into private lane • Open June to mid-Aug, Sun, Tues, Thurs, 2pm – evening • Entrance: £2 ◑ ☕ WC ⚘

This one-and-three-quarter-acre award-winning garden has been created by the present owners on open land at an altitude of 150 metres. Gravel paths connect the 'rooms', which contain a wide selection of shrubs and perennials and ornamental ponds and waterfalls. These are bordered by large stones and trees protecting the whole garden from the wind, a remarkable achievement in such an exposed spot. A large water feature has been created near the house.

Carwinion 8

Mawnan Smith, Falmouth TR11 5JA. Tel: (01326) 250258

Mr and Mrs H.A.E. Rogers • From Mawnan Smith, take left road by Red Lion. 500 metres up hill on right is white gate marked 'Carwinion' • Open all year, daily, 10am – 5.30pm • Entrance: £2, children free (1999 prices) ○ ☕ 🍴 WC ⚘ 🚗 ⚘

The Rogers family has been living at Carwinion since the eighteenth century. The garden, a conservation area, is some 12 acres with a wild sub-tropical woodland area leading to the River Helford. Here is the most comprehensive collection of bamboos in the UK (110 specimens), all labelled. Also a *Gunnera manicata* said to be one of the largest in the country, with a crown as big as a man's body, and some very fine examples of *Dicksonia antarctica*. An attractive and comprehensive fernery (45 specimens) has been added and a woodland walk cleared in which a profusion of snowdrops, daffodils and bluebells flower in spring.

Catchfrench Manor Gardens 9

St Germans, Saltash PL12 5BY. Tel: (01503) 240759

Mr and Mrs J.R. Wilks • 4m SW of Saltash. Take junction on A38 signed Catchfrench W of Trerulefoot roundabout • Open 6th March to 30th Sept, daily

except Sun, 10.30am – 4.30pm and at other times by appt. Closed 21st April •
Entrance: £2.50, children (5-14) £1 ◐ 🍵 🖻 🖺 WC ⚹

In his Red Book for Catchfrench, Humphry Repton remarked on the delightful scenery surrounding the mansion and he strove (successfully) to fit the new garden to the landscape. The scheme was carried out in 1792. The present house, built in the eighteenth century, was refurbished in 1913, and the garden is now being returned to its original glory. The secret quarry mentioned in the Red Book has been cleared in preparation for a fern garden and a pond. An Elizabethan herb garden has been created on the site of the Elizabethan house. A contemporary crypt has been revealed and has been dedicated as a chapel. The area above the Elizabethan terrace contains a magnificent collection of rhododendrons, magnolias, azaleas, camellias and conifers. A woodland area known as the Knoll, harmed by felling during the World War II has been replanted and the Elizabethan water channel has been restored.

Chyverton ★   10

Zelah, Truro TR4 9HD. Tel: (01872) 540324; Fax: (01872) 540648

Mr N. Holman • 12m NE of Redruth, 1m W of Zelah on A30. At end of bypass, turn N at Marazanvose; entrance is ½ m on right • Open by appt only March to Sept • Entrance: £5 (parties 10 – 20 £4; parties over 20 £3), bona fide horticultural students and children under 16 free. Visitors personally conducted around the garden ◐ 🖺 WC ⬥ ⚘

The outstanding feature of this garden, originally landscaped in the eighteenth century, is its collection of magnolias, including some bearing the name of the property and of the owner's father, 'Treve' Holman. Superb trees of copper beech, cedars of Lebanon, eucryphia and a collection of nothofagus make a beautiful backcloth to a large collection of camellias and rhododendrons. The garden, whose woodland area is divided into 29 different 'rooms', each containing rose trees, shrubs and flowers, is planned to give vistas and is always being further developed. A collection of acers is being planted and there are good colour combinations with azaleas and photinias. There is an unusual hedge of *Myrtus luma* and by the stream are gunneras and lysichitums. Note the new water garden and primulas. Trees and shrubs have room to develop freely here, but it is hard to realise that this extensive garden is maintained solely by the owner and yet has one of the best plant collections of woody plants from China still in private hands, including many introduced into cultivation by the owner in 1996. Plants are received and exchanged with such institutions as the Royal Botanic Gardens at Edinburgh and Kew. Visitors have also rated this one of the most beautiful of Cornish gardens because of its naturalness – no spraying, hence a profusion of wild flowers.

Cotehele ★   11

St Dominick, Saltash PL12 6TA. Tel: (01579) 351346

The National Trust • 8m SW of Tavistock, 4m SE of Gunnislake, 1m W of Calstock. Turn at St Anne's Chapel • House open April to Oct, daily except Fri but open 21st April, 11am – 5pm • Garden open daily, 11am – dusk • Mill open daily except Fri (but open 21st April and Fri in July and Aug), 1pm – 5.30pm (6pm in July and Aug; 4.30pm in Oct) • Entrance: garden and mill £3.20 (house, garden and mill £6, pre-booked parties £5 per person) • Other information: Presentation of estate history given in Film Room. Picnics and dogs in woodland only ○ 🍽 ✕ <u>WC</u> ⅋ ⚘ 🏚 ☕

This 15-acre garden with terraces falling to a sheltered valley has developed gradually from Victorian times. With its combination of formal courtyards, fine terraces, walled garden, pools, herbaceous borders and valley garden, it will give pleasure to most visitors. The grey granite walls of the house are a background to many climbers and from the rose terrace one walks down to the pool and dovecot. In the valley are giant conifers, hydrangeas, palms, acers and betulas. There is a small acer plantation and yew hedges. Nearby is a nineteenth-century river quay offering fine views.

Creed House   12

Creed, Grampound TR2 4SL. Tel: (01872) 530372

Mr and Mrs W.R. Croggon • Mid-way between St Austell and Truro. Take A390 to Grampound, then road in main street signed 'To Creed'. After 1m, opposite Creed church, turn left. Entrance to house and garden on left • Open all year, daily, 10am – 5.30pm, inc. two dates, probably in May and June, for charity, 2 – 5.30pm • Entrance: £2, children free • Other information: Teas and toilet facilities on charity open days only ○ ⅋ ⚐

A Georgian rectory garden of seven acres successfully restored over the past 20 years. The large lawn, originally the site of a bowling green and a tennis court, looks across to a magnificent view of the surrounding countryside. At the far end of the lawn is a delightful fish pond, and there are walled herbaceous gardens. From the stable yard a path leads down to a sunken cobbled area surrounded by flowers and small shrubs. The good collection of trees and rhododenrons has been supplemented by many new plantings; don't miss the woodland walk.

Eden Project   13

Watering Lane Nursery, Pentewan, St Austell PL26 6BE.
Tel: (01726) 222900

3m NE of St Austell off A390 🍽 ✕ <u>WC</u> ⅋ ⚘ 🏚 ☕

The plan, masterminded by Tim Smit of Heligan (see entry) is to build the 'largest greenhouse on earth' to house those plants which 'have changed the world'. Species will be housed in two 'biomes', one a tropical rainforest and the other Mediterranean. The site, a former china-clay pit, is 34 acres, and the domes will be up to 50 metres high. It is designed to handle 3500 visitors a day on a five-hour tour, all year round. The cost will be £74m, half of it financed by the Millennium Commission and £10m coming from Europe. Three million tons of earth have been removed so far, and work on the foundations and the building of the biomes will be completed by spring 2000;. the visitor centre will also then be open. Planting will start in September 2000 and is due to be completed by Easter 2001.

Fox Rosehill Gardens 14

Melville Road, Falmouth TR11 4DB. Tel: (01326) 319377

Carrick District Council • From A39 follow signs to beaches and hotels • Open all year, daily, 8am – dusk • Entrance: free • Other information: Plant sale in early June ○ &

A truly remarkable long-established small park of two acres, famous for its many exotic trees and shrubs, including an *Embothrium coccineum* (Chilean firebush) and a *Syragus romanzoffiana* (queen palm). Most shrubs and trees are labelled and set amongst paths and two lawns. A delight for the ordinary visitor and of great interest to the plantsman.

Glendurgan Garden ★ 15

Mawnan Smith, Falmouth TR11 5JZ. Tel: (01326) 250906

The National Trust • 4m SW of Falmouth, ½ m SW of Mawnan Smith on road to Helford Passage • Open 22nd Feb to 28th Oct (closed 21st April), Tues – Sat and Bank Holiday Mons, 10.30am – 5.30pm (last admission 4.30pm) • Entrance: £3.40, family £8.50 (1999 price) ◑ 🐾 WC 🌿 🛍

Glendurgan is one of the great sub-tropical gardens of the South-West. This 40-acre valley garden was originally planted by Alfred Fox in the 1820s alongside the Helford river, with the village of Durgan at its foot. The woodland valley contains many specimen trees and conifers, including two tulip trees and a swamp cypress; also sub-tropical plants, especially tree ferns. In spring camellias, rhododendrons and magnolias, including a fine *Magnolia campbellii alba*, flower as do wild flowers, including primroses, bluebells and daffodils. In summer there are drimys, eucryphias, embothriums and many hydrangeas, wild pink campions, aquilegias and foxgloves. There is also the fastest-growing tree recorded in Trust gardens, a *Populus* 'Androscoggin' which has reached 24 metres in 14 years. The 1833 laurel maze has been renovated and there is also a Giant Stride for children. Fine views of the Helford river.

Headland 16

3 Battery Lane, Polruan–by–Fowey PL23 1PW. Tel: (01726) 870243

John and Jean Hill • 8m E of St Austell off A3082. Passenger ferry from Fowey and 10 minute walk up hill. Or car ferry from Fowey to Bodinnick and follow signs for Polruan (3m). Ignore first car park, turn left for second car park, overlooking harbour. Turn left (on foot) down St Saviour's Hill • Open for charity May to Sept, Thurs only, 2 – 6pm • Entrance: £2, children £1 • Other information: Beach for swimming ◑ 🐾 WC

This cliff garden 30 metres above sea level, created from an old quarry on the headland, has been developed by the present owners since 1974. It is a credit to them that such an excellent range of plants flourishes on a site with sea on three sides where plants must withstand spray and gales. It is designed with narrow paths and archways leading round corners to secret areas with Australian and New Zealand plants (cordylines and olearias) and sub-tropical succulents (agaves, echeverias, crassulas and lampranthus). There is a path with various eucalyptus trees, and a flight of over 100 steps leads to a small sandy beach. In crevices are sempervivums, sedums, crinodendrons, erigerons and other colourful alpines. Monterey pines, Torquay palms, yuccas, tamarisks and fatsias all thrive, and there are good plant combinations.

Heligan ★★   17

Pentewan, St Austell PL26 6EN. Tel (01726) 845100; Fax: (01726) 845101

The Lost Gardens of Heligan • 4m S of St Austell. Take B3273 signed Mevagissey past Pentewan • Open all year, daily except 24th, 25th Dec, 10am – 6pm (last admission 4.30pm). Guided tours by arrangement • Entrance: £5.50, OAPs £5, children (5-15) £2.50, family (2 adults and 3 children) £15 ○ ☕ ✕ 🏠 WC ♿ 🐕 🌱 🛒 🌿

A garden has existed on this site since 1603; it was expanded gradually throughout the eighteenth century to its present size, a total of 80 acres. From 1914 the area was neglected and slowly covered over by arching brambles, thick ivy, laurels and fallen trees. Since reclamation began in 1991, Heligan has been recognised as the largest on-going garden restoration in Europe, and is becoming one of the most important gardens in the country. Undergrowth has been cleared, 1500 tons of timber removed, plants reinstated and 5000 trees placed in shelter belts, with work being done by a team of contractors and a constant supply of volunteers. Paths have been replaced in their original locations, and metal detectors used to find lead labels denoting the original position of plants. Among many outstanding specimens are a *Pinus thunbergii* (Japanese black pine), a *Cedrela sinensis*, a *Podocarpus totara* (Chilean yew) and a 'Cornish Red' rhododendron, all reputed to be the largest in Europe. Other features include a palm avenue, 450-foot rockery, fern ravine, crystal grotto, wishing well, melon garden with manure-heated pineapple pits, large productive vegetable gardens with glasshouses for citrus, peach and vines, tool and potting sheds, 300-foot herbaceous border, and Italian garden with pool and summerhouse. The beebole wall, with vaulted cells, is occupied by bees again. Meanwhile, an extensive new orchard has been planted. This is in keeping with one of the main aims of the project: to bring the area alive and to prevent it, after restoration, from stagnating into a mere showpiece. Beyond the Jungle, a further 30 acres called the Lost Valley have been discovered and cleared, revealing two large lakes and an old mill pond which existed there during the early eighteenth century. These have been restored in the Picturesque style and can be viewed from a long winding path interspersed with bridges. The Eden Project (see entry), also initiated by Tim Smit, is nearby.

The Hollies   18

Grampound, Truro TR2 4QS. Tel: (01726) 882474

Mr J.R. and Mrs N.B. Croggon • 6m SW of St Austell on A390 Truro road in Grampound next to post office • Open for charity 14th May, 11th June, 2 – 5pm and by appt. Private visits welcomed • Entrance: £1 ● ☕ 🏠 WC ♿ 🌱

This two-acre garden has a charming cottage-garden effect created by the unusual design. It consists of a number of sections, each different in character. Island beds contain a wide range of trees and shrubs with underplanting to provide interest throughout the year, although spring is the peak time. Many rare plants, including alpines, a white crinodendron and a black cow parsley (*Anthriscus sylvestris*).

Ince Castle 19

Saltash PL12 4QZ. Tel: (01752) 842249

Viscount and Viscountess Boyd of Merton • 3m SW of Saltash off A38 at Stoketon Cross. Turn at sign for Trematon and then Elmgate • Open 19th March, 16th April, 14th May, 11th June, 23rd July, 2 – 5pm and parties by appt • Entrance: £2.50, children under 14 free • Other information: Due to very narrow lanes, no large coaches NEW ● ☕ WC ♿ ✍

This five-acre garden is divided into small areas set around the castle. The paths are first-rate and there are friendly white peacocks. The bright colours vary throughout spring, summer and autumn, from daffodils and camellias to English and Mediterranean flowers. A large stretch of closely cut grass extends from the front of the castle towards the River Lynher – a magnificent view. The woodland area forms an integral part of the garden; inside, the grass is cut in the form of an ellipse. Another interesting feature is the shell house, whose internal walls are plastered with a great variety of seashells, collected in the 1960s.

The Japanese Garden and Bonsai Nursery 20

St Mawgan, Newquay TR8 4ET. Tel: (01637) 860116

Mr and Mrs Hore • 6m NE of Newquay, signed from A3059 and B3278 • Open all year, daily (closed 25th Dec to 1st Jan), 10am – 6pm, 10am – 5pm in winter (last admission 1 hour before closing time) • Entrance: £2.50, children £1 (bonsai nursery free) • Other information: Tea house does not serve refreshments. Toilet facilities nearby. Guide dogs permitted ○ ♿ ✍ 🧺

Within a single acre visitors can enjoy a water garden, a stroll garden, a Zen garden, a *Cha-Seki* (tea house) and a bamboo grove. The collections include *Acer palmatum* in variety, many unusual plants of Japanese origin and a wide range of bamboos and grasses.

Ken Caro 21

Bicton, Liskeard PL14 5RF. Tel: (01579) 362446

Mr and Mrs K.R. Willcock • 5m NE of Liskeard. Turn off A390 at Butcher's Arms, St Ive, take Pensilva road to next crossroads, then road signed 'Bicton' • Open 16th April to 28th June, Sun – Wed; July and Aug, Tues and Wed, all 2 – 6pm • Entrance: £2, children 50p ● WC ✍

These four acres are planted in two sections. One consists of a series of small enclosed areas interconnected by well kept paths, and contains shrubs, conifers, rhododendrons and flowers, all well labelled, and an aviary. Some rare shrub specimens include *Eucryphia* x *nymansensis* and *Lomatia ferruginea*. In contrast to the enclosed area, the second part is open to fine views of the surrounding landscape. Flower beds with a fine collection of roses are well kept, and there is a large fish pond. A good visit for plantsman and gardener alike.

Ladock House   22

Ladock, Nr Truro TR2 4PL. Tel: (01726) 882274

Mr G.J. and Lady Mary Holborow • 7m E of Truro on B3275. Entrance by church • Open 30th April, 2 – 5.30pm • Entrance: £2, children free NEW ☕ 🦽
WC & ⬦

The Georgian former rectory is set in six and a half acres of garden and woodland, all reclaimed and planted during the past 20 years. Spacious lawns are embellished with shrubs and flower beds, and a spring garden has clearings in wooded areas planted with rhododendrons, azaleas and camellias. The garden continues on the other side of a park-like field; here are bluebells and another shrub area.

Lamorran House ★   23

Upper Castle Road, St Mawes TR2 5BZ. Tel: (01326) 270800;
Fax (01326) 270801

Mr and Mrs R. Dudley-Cooke • Above St Mawes turn right at garage. Signposted at Castle. Continue for ½ m. Lamorran is on left set behind line of pine trees • Open probably April to Sept, Wed and Fri, and first Sat of each month, 10.30am – 5pm and at other times by appt • Entrance: £2.50, children free (1999 prices) • Other information: Coaches by prior appt ◑ WC &

This four-acre garden developed since 1980 contains a large and excellent collection of sub-tropical and warm temperate species which one would not expect to find on a hillside adjacent to the sea. In the main it has been designed in the Italian style with columns and other artefacts. Over 500 azaleas, many different palms and eucalyptus, yuccas, 250 rhododendrons, a wide range of conifers, a range of Australian and New Zealand plants, a large collection of tree ferns. There is a Japanese garden and many water features. Round every corner are unusual plants for the plantsman to enjoy, while all visitors will appreciate the various little gardens, good design features and interesting colour and foliage combinations. In St Mawes itself, the *Castle* (English Heritage) boasts a sub-tropical garden featuring plants from various parts of the world. Additional features added recently include cacti and succulent rockery and South African plantings. Views of St Anthony's Head and the lighthouse can be seen at many angles. This garden has been nicknamed 'An English Garden Abroad'.

Lancarffe ★   24

Bodmin PL30 4HU. Tel: (01208) 72756

Mr and Mrs R. Gilbert • 2m NE of Bodmin. Heading E, take second turning off A30 Bodmin bypass. Turn first left, first right then bear left • Open for charity for parties of 6 or more by appt only • Entrance: £1.50 per person ● WC ⬦

Walking through this four-and-a-half-acre garden one can enjoy one of the best collections of plants in the west of England, including *Davidia involucrata* (pocket-handkerchief tree) and beds of roses. Some beautiful trees form a backcloth to a fine collection of azaleas, camellias and rhododendrons. There is a delightful walled water garden with shrubs and climbers on the walls. Hydrangeas, eucryphias, acers, *Desfontainea spinosa* and *Campsis radicans*, one of the largest *Paulownia fargesii* (foxglove tree) in Britain, various cornus and embothriums are some of the many specimens.

Lanhydrock ★ 25

Bodmin PL30 5AD. Tel: (01208) 73320

The National Trust • 2½ m SE of Bodmin off A38 and A30, or off B3268 • House open April to Oct, Tues – Sun and Bank Holiday Mons, 11am – 5.30pm (Oct 5pm) • Garden open March to Oct, daily, 11am – 5.30pm (Oct 5pm); Nov to Feb, daily during daylight hours • Entrance: garden and grounds £3.20, children £1.60; free Nov to Feb (house, garden and grounds £6.40, children £3.20, family ticket (2 adults and up to 3 children) £16, pre-booked parties of 15 or more £5.50 per adult, £2.55 per child) (1999 prices) • Other information: Parking 600 metres but disabled park adjacent to garden ○ ● ✕ 🥄 WC & ℘ 🏠 🔦

This superb 30-acre garden, started in 1857, contains gardens within a garden and has some exceptional trees and shrubs in the park, the woodland and the more formal areas. The collection of trees was started before 1634. Banks of colour are provided by magnolias, camellias and rhododendrons and followed by roses in beds in the lawn adjacent to the house interspersed with cone-shaped Irish yews. In the terraces, beds of annuals are edged with box. A circular yew hedge surrounds the herbaceous borders, which contain a wide range of choice plants and provide summer colour. The woodland has walks amongst rare trees and hydrangeas and other flowering shrubs, and the stream is fringed with moisture-loving plants. The Victorian cob-and-thatch summer-house has been rebuilt.

Long Cross Victorian Gardens 26

Trelights, Port Isaac PL29 3TF. Tel: (01208) 880243

Mr and Mrs D.J. Crawford • 7m N of Wadebridge on B3314 near St Endellion church and Trelights. Signposted • Open all year, daily • Entrance: £1.50, accompanied children under 14 25p, season ticket £1.75 ○ ● 🥄 WC & ↩ ℘

In reconstructing the late-Victorian garden the former owners discovered paths which were not known to exist, also rockeries, steps, shrubs and plants. Hedges act as effective windbreaks against the strong west winds in this salt-laden coastal region. The layout produces a maze-like effect. Among the many sections is a central area with an ornamental pond, a pets' corner and a children's playground – in all, three acres. There is a good supply of attractive seats. Fine views of Port Quin to the west and Tintagel Head to the north. Long Cross is a hotel, open at all times.

Morrab Subtropical Garden 27

Penzance. Tel: (01736) 62341 ext. 3322 (Garden Manager)

*Penwith District Council • In centre of Penzance. Entrances in St Mary's
Terrace, Morrab Road and Coulson's Place • Open all year, daily, dawn – dusk
• Entrance: free* ○ WC & ⬠

The three-acre garden designed by Reginald Upcher, a well-known garden
architect in his day, remains exactly in accordance with his plan. The land was
bought by Penzance Corporation in 1888 and opened in 1889. The garden
contains two ponds, a large, highly ornamental fountain and a magnificent
bandstand. Many rare trees and plants, including a *Cordyline australis* (New
Zealand cabbage palm), a *Dicksonia antarctica* (tree fern) and a *Clethra arborea* (lily-
of-the-valley tree). The exceptional climate allows camellias to bloom as early
as mid-November. The garden is in two sections, the main one joined to a
smaller area beside the Morrab Library.

Mount Edgcumbe House and Country Park ★ 28

Cremyll, Torpoint PL10 1HZ. Tel: (01752) 822236; Fax: (01752) 822199

*Cornwall County Council and Plymouth City Council • Access from Plymouth by
Cremyll ferry (pedestrian) to Park entrance or Torpoint ferry (vehicle) via A374
and B3247. Access from Cornwall A38 to Trerulefoot roundabout then A374
and B3247 • House open as Earl's Garden • Park and formal gardens open
daily, 8am – dusk. Earl's Garden open April to Sept, Wed – Sun and Bank
Holiday Mons, 11am – 4.30pm • Entrance: Park and formal gardens free.
Earl's Garden and house £4.50, concessions £3.50, children under 15 £2.25,
family £10, season £7.50, party £3.50 per person • Other information: Coaches
must pre-book • Park and formal gardens:* ○ 🍴 WC & ⬠ 🌿 🏛 ♨ *Earl's
Garden* ◑ 🍵 ✕

The gardens and landscaped park were created by the Mount Edgcumbe family
in the eighteenth century. They were praised by William Kent and Humphry
Repton. The site covers 865 acres, and stretches from Plymouth Sound to
Rame Head. Surrounding the house, the Earl's Garden is an informal terrace
and shrub garden which contains a rare eighteenth-century shell grotto and on
the east front re-established late-Victorian flower beds. The formal gardens at
the lower end of the old tree-lined avenue encompass English, French and
Italian gardens (complete with ornamental orange trees) and two gardens to
commemorate the family's historical connection with America and New
Zealand. A useful leaflet describes all the allusions. In the amphitheatre is
the National Collection of camellias. Fine sea views to Drake's Island from the
park.

Pencarrow ★ 29

Washaway, Bodmin PL30 3AG. Tel: (01208) 841369

*The Molesworth-St Aubyn family • 4m NW of Bodmin. Signed from A389
Bodmin – Wadebridge road and B3266 at Washaway • House open as garden*

(except Fri and Sat), 1.30 – 5pm (June to 10th Sept and Bank Holiday Mon opens 11am) • Garden open 2nd April to 15th Oct, daily, 10am – 6pm • Entrance: £2, children free (house and garden £4.50, children £2, parties £4 per person) (1999 prices) • Other information: Dogs on lead near house only. Craft centre ◑ ☕ ✕ 🖻 WC ⅏ ⇗ 𝒴 ⬚ 🍵

The drive, one mile long, leads to the imposing Palladian mansion built in 1760. A formal garden with a circular lawn is laid out on two sides of the house. Nearby on a higher level, shrubs are placed in a rock garden made with boulders transported from Bodmin Moor when the gardens were designed by Sir William Molesworth from 1831 onwards. There are 50 acres of woodland and parkland with over 700 different varieties of rhododendrons and a large collection of camellias. Among the many trees stands a *Picea orientalis* (Caucasian spruce), the second earliest known to have been planted in Britain. There is a large number of *Araucaria araucana* (monkey puzzle trees). The English name is said to have originated when, in 1834, the parliamentary barrister Charles Austin, who was staying at Pencarrow, rashly touched the prickly leaves and quickly withdrew his hand, saying: 'It would puzzle a monkey'.

Penjerrick   30

Budock, Falmouth TR11 5ED. Tel: (01872) 870105

Mrs R. Morin • 3m SW of Falmouth between Budock and Mawnan Smith. Entrance opposite Penmorvah Manor Country Hotel • Open by appt March to Sept, Wed, Fri and Sun, 1.30 – 4.30pm • Entrance: £1.50, children 50p • Other information: Parking for one coach only, at gate. Plants for sale on charity days only ◑ ⇗

A 15-acre garden set in parkland created by the Fox family in the late eighteenth century. The home of the 'Barclayi' and 'Penjerrick' rhododendron hybrids. The upper garden with its large sloping lawns is planted with rhododendrons, camellias, tree ferns and bamboos and many rare trees (it also contains the second largest beech in Britain). The wilder lower garden has ponds enhanced by tree ferns, first planted c. 1824.

Penpol House   31

Penpol Avenue, Hayle TR27 4NQ. Tel: (01736) 753146

Major and Mrs T.F. Ellis • 4m SE of St Ives. Turn left at White Hart Hotel, Penpol Road, then second left into Penpol Avenue • Probably open by appt during June and July • Entrance: £2 ● ⅏ ⇗ 𝒴

Situated in the extreme south-west overlooking the Hayle estuary and surrounding the sixteenth-century house, the three-and-a-half-acre garden was formerly sheltered by a belt of elms which succumbed to Dutch elm disease. Old yew and fuchsia hedges and more recently planted trees and shrubs have reshaped a garden over a hundred years old. The garden leads from one colourful pocket to another, with old walls and low-growing box, fuchsia and yew dividing the various areas. The walled garden, with espaliered apple and pear trees surrounded by amaryllis lilies, contains a water garden, bordered by shrub and patio roses. Along one wall is a large bed of delphiniums grown from seed. The little grey garden planned years ago for quiet colours is now bright with shrubs and plants. An old lemon verbena fills one wall, japonica climbs another and beneath are crinum lilies. The main garden has roses over trellises, a garden of nineteenth-century roses and a formal rose garden. There are beds of flag iris, borders of herbaceous plants and peonies and more delphiniums, all set off by sweeping lawns and terraces. Plenty of ideas here for what can be done in alkaline soil.

Penwarne 32

Mawnan Smith, Falmouth TR11 5PH. Tel: (01326) 250585/250325

Mr and Mrs H. Beister • 3¼ m SW of Falmouth and 1¼ m N of Mawnan Smith off Falmouth – Mawnan Smith road • Open 9th April, 2 – 5pm • Entrance: £1.50, children 50p • Other information: Coaches by prior arrangement only ◐ WC

Many large trees, including *Cryptomeria japonica*, beeches and oaks, form a backcloth to this woodland garden planted about 1900 as the setting for a fine Georgian house. The old walled garden has roses, clematis and lilies and there are banks of azaleas, rhododendrons, camellias and magnolias, together with shrubs from New Zealand. The pool and stream running through the garden provide areas for primulas and tree ferns. Fruit trees and bushes, bamboos, many new plantings. Peacocks and dogs.

Pine Lodge ★★ 33

Cuddra, St Austell PL25 3RQ. Tel: (01726) 73500; Fax: (01726) 73500

Mr and Mrs R. Clemo • Just E of St Austell off A390 between Holmbush and turn to Tregrehan. Signposted • Open April to Sept, Wed – Sun and Bank Holiday Mons, 2 – 5pm. Guided tours for parties of 20 or more by appt all year • Entrance: £3.50, children £1.75 ◐ ◑ WC ♿

The 30-acre estate comprises gardens within a garden which hold a wide range of some 5500 plants, all of which are labelled. In addition to rhododendrons, magnolias and camellias so familiar in Cornish gardens there are Mediterranean and southern-hemisphere plants grown for all-year-round interest. Herbaceous borders, a fernery, a formal garden, a woodland walk and shrubberies. The water features include a large wildlife pond, an ornamental pond with cascades (stocked with koi carp), a lake with an island (home to black swans and many waterfowl) and marsh gardens. Trees are also a speciality with an acer glade, a collection of 80 conifers, all different, in a four-acre pinetum, and an arboretum. A Japanese garden is being prepared. Holder of National Collection of grevilleas. Plants for sale in the nursery raised from seed collected on plant hunting expeditions over the last 15 years.

Poldowrian 34

Coverack, Helston TR12 6SL. Tel: (01326) 280468

Mrs P.S. Hadley • Take B3293 Helston – St Keverne road. 2m after Goonhilly Earth Station, turn right at National garage at Zoar. Take second right signed

'Gwenter', then second left at Poldowrian sign • Open April to July by appt only • Entrance: by donation to charity ● 🖼

This is a four-acre woodland garden, well-pathed, leading to unspoilt coast. The area has remains which date from the Neolithic Age, such as an ancient roundhouse, and a museum of pre-history. The trees and shrubs include two Japanese umbrella pines, Norway maples, many camellias, hydrangeas and rhododendrons, and there are many woodland flowers. Other features are a pond with an island in the middle and a bog garden.

Polgwynne 35

Feock, Truro TR3 6SG. Tel: (01872) 862612

Mrs P. Davey • 5m S of Truro. Take A39, then B3289 to first crossroads. Continue on past garage on right following signposts to Feock. At T-junction turn left down steep hill and house is situated at bottom on right • Open 30th April, 28th May, 25th June, 2 – 5pm and by appt all year round • Entrance: £2.50 for charity, children free • Other information: Refreshments and plants for sale on open days only ● 🍵 WC ♿ 🐕 🅿

A three-and-a-half-acre garden in a beautiful setting with fine views and woodlands extending to the shore of Carrick Roads. Many unusual shrubs and fine trees including what is reputed to be the largest female *Ginkgo biloba* in Britain. Pleasing early-Victorian greenhouses stand in the large vegetable garden.

Porthpean House 36

Porthpean, St Austell PL26 6AX. Tel: (01726) 72888

Mr and Mrs C. Petherick • 1½ m S of St Austell. Take A390 and then road signed Porthpean, past Mount Edgcumbe Hospice, turn left down Porthpean Beach Road. Porthpean House is white building at bottom of hill just before car park • Open 12th, 19th March, 2nd, 9th April, 7th, 14th May for charity, 2 – 5pm. Also by appt • Entrance: £2, children free • Other information: Teas for parties only ● 🍵 🖼 WC ♿ 🐕 🅿

This three-acre garden was first developed by Maurice Petherick some 40 years ago. It contains a special collection of camellias, also many azaleas and rhododendrons. The grounds have access to the beach and from the main lawn there is a magnificent view of St Austell Bay; on spring days cherry blossoms stand out sharply against the blue of the sea. There is also a nursery garden with Victorian greenhouses.

St Michael's Mount ★ 37

Marazion, Penzance TR17 0EF. Tel: (01736) 710507; Fax: (01736) 711544

The National Trust • ½ m from shore at Marazion, ½ m S of A394. Access by ferry or across causeway • Castle open April to Oct, Mon – Fri, 10.30am – 5.30pm (last admission 4.45pm), and most weekends from June to Sept for charity when NT members are asked to pay for admission. Nov to March guided tours can be arranged if tide, weather and boating conditions permit. Check by telephone first • Gardens open April to May, daily and most weekends from June to Sept • Entrance: April and May gardens only £2 (otherwise castle and gardens £4.40, children £2.20, family ticket £11, pre-booked parties of 20 or more £3.50 per person) • Other information: Parking in Marazion ◑ ☕ ✕ WC ⚲ 👍

A unique and extraordinary 20-acre maritime garden which has been created in terraces just above the sea at the foot of a 90-metre perpendicular cliff. Here, in spite of apparent total exposure to gales and salt spray, sub-tropical species abound. The walled garden was planned in the eighteenth century by two young ladies, ancestors of the St Aubyn family, who still live in the Castle. A remarkable example of micro-climate effect is in itself a fascinating study for the keen gardener. Planting has been done amongst granite boulders, some weighing hundreds of tons. There are yuccas, geraniums, euryops, hebes, phormiums, fuchsias, puyas and in spring sheets of wild narcissi. Kniphofias grow wild in bracken – great splashes of colour. The climb to the castle is steep and rough and can be difficult for the elderly or handicapped. Sensible shoes are advised.

Trebah ★★ 38

Mawnan Smith, Falmouth TR11 5JZ. Tel: (01326) 250448

Major and Mrs J.A. Hibbert (Trebah Garden Trust) • 4m W of Falmouth. Signed from A39/A394 Junction at Hillhead roundabout, 500 metres W of Glendurgan Garden • Open all year, daily, 10.30am – 5pm • Entrance: £3.50, OAPs £3.20, disabled and children (5-15) £1.75, RHS members and children under 5 free (reduced rates Nov to Feb) • Possible for wheelchairs but paths steep in places ○ ☕ ✕ WC ⚲ 🏶 ⚲ 👍 ⚱

A 25-acre ravine garden started by Charles Fox in the 1840s which contains many beautiful and mature trees and shrubs providing an undulating carpet of colour. The deep ravine leads to a private beach on the Helford River. A stream runs through a water garden and a series of ponds with mature koi carp. Extensive plantings of sub-tropical Mediterranean plants at the top of the garden blend into the rainforest of the lower reaches with glades of giant tree ferns, bananas and bamboos. Three acres of blue and white hydrangeas carry the colour through to Christmas. A paradise for the artist, the plantsman and the family, and there is a fine playground for children.

Tregrehan ★ 39

Par PL24 2SJ. Tel/Fax: (01726) 814389

The Carlyon Estate/Mr T. Hudson • On A390 Lostwithiel – St Austell road. Entrance opposite Britannia Inn • Open mid-March to mid-June, Wed – Sun, also Bank Holiday Mons except 23rd April, 10.30am – 5pm • Entrance: £3, children free. Guided tours by prior arrangement ◑ ☕ WC ⚲ ⚲

The 20-acre garden contains many large and interesting trees and rhododendrons in addition to the large collection of camellias raised by the late owner.

There are woodland walks carpeted with bluebells in spring, and a walled garden. Other plants include clivias and nerines, but the camellias, rare trees and vast rhododendrons are of particular interest to the keen plantsman. A giant Monterey cypress. Much material grown from seed, and plants of known provenance. Magnificent Victorian greenhouses.

Trelissick ★ 40

Feock, Truro TR3 6QL. Tel: (01872) 862090

The National Trust • 4m S of Truro on B3289 above King Harry Ferry • Garden open 25th Feb to Oct, Mon – Sat, 10.30am – 5.30pm, Sun, 12.30 – 5.30pm (5pm in Feb, March and Oct) • Entrance: £4.30, children £2.20, family ticket £10.75, pre-booked parties £3.60 per person. Parking charge £1.50 (refundable) • Other information: Wheelchairs and Batricar available. Dogs in woodland and park only. Art and Craft Gallery. Open-air music and theatrical events during season ◑ 🍽 ✕ 🖪 WC ♿ 🐾 👍 ⚘

Trelissick is both a garden and an estate of rare tranquil beauty, set amidst more than 500 acres of sweeping park and farmland with glorious panoramic views down the Carrick Roads towards Falmouth and the open sea. The garden is famed particularly for its large collection of hydrangeas, camellias, rhododendrons and exotic and tender plants which thrive in the mild Cornish climate. National Collections of azaras and photinias are held here. The orchard will eventually contain the definitive collection of Cornish apple varieties and is particularly lovely in spring when the daffodils are in flower. The dell has tree ferns, hostas and hellebores, and there are some large trees, including *Quercus ilex*, *Fagus sylvatica* and a beautiful Japanese cedar (*Cryptomeria japonica*). Small walled garden with aromatic plants.

Trengwainton Garden ★ 41

Penzance TR20 8RZ. Tel: (01736) 363021

The National Trust • 2m NW of Penzance on B3312, or ½ m N of A3071 • Open March to Oct, Sun – Thurs and 21st April, 10.30am – 5.30pm (5pm in March and Oct) (last admission ½ hour before closing) • Entrance: £3.50, children £1.75, family £8.75 pre-arranged groups of 15 or more £2.80 per person • Other information: Teas at Trengwainton Farm, weather permitting ◑ WC ♿ ⬦

Trengwainton means 'House of the Spring' and was acquired by the Bolitho family in 1867. It will appeal to both the plantsman and the ordinary gardener for its magnificent collections of magnolias, rhododendrons and camellias and a series of walled gardens with many tender and exotic shrubs and plants that would not survive in less mild areas of England. The stream garden alongside the drive, backed by a beech wood, provides masses of colour from candelabra primulas, lilies, lysichitums and other bog plants. Many of the rhododendrons were raised from seed collected by Kingdon Ward's expedition to NE Assam and the Mishmi Hills of Burma. New Zealand tree ferns, pittosporums from China, Japanese maples, embothriums, olearias, acacias, eucryphias, and Chatham Island forget-me-nots are just a few of the beautiful plants to be seen during the spring and summer. The woodland walk also now features an ornamental pond. There are magnificent views of the hills leading down to the sea, and a space has been cut in the woodland to reveal St Michael's Mount.

Trerice 42

Kestle Mill, Newquay TR8 4PG. Tel: (01637) 875404

The National Trust • 3m SE of Newquay via A392 and A3058. Turn right at Kestle Mill • House open • Garden open 2nd April to 23rd July, daily except Tues and Sat; 24th July to 3rd Sept, daily; 4th Sept to 30th Oct, daily except Tues and Sat, all 11am – 5.30pm (5pm in Oct) (last admission $\frac{1}{2}$ hour before closing) • Entrance: garden only, free (house and garden £4, pre-booked parties £3.40 per person) • Other information: Guide dogs only

◐ ➤ ✕ 🖼 WC & 🌿 🏛 ♿

A small garden by Cornish standards, developed around an Elizabethan manor house, where the visitor can enjoy many unusual and rare plants. Shrubs, climbers and perennials provide good foliage and colour combinations. In the front walled courtyard are herbaceous borders. The back court has a range of cottage-garden plants – fuchsias, honeysuckles, roses and climbers on the house. An orchard has been planted with apples, pears, quinces, plums in the quincunx pattern used in the seventeenth century, and there are figs elsewhere in the garden. The design features of the garden are of particular interest. Lawn mowers of different sizes and from different periods are displayed in the former stable hay loft.

Tresco Abbey ★★ 43

Tresco, Isles of Scilly TR24 0QQ. Tel: (01720) 424105;
Fax: (01720) 422868 Mike Nelhams (Garden Curator)

Mr R.A. Dorrien-Smith • On Island of Tresco. Travel: by helicopter from Penzance Heliport to Tresco Heliport (reservations (01736) 363871 and (01720) 422646) or from St Mary's by launch • Open all year, daily, 10am – 4pm • Entrance: £5, children free, weekly tickets (7 days) £10 • Other information: Possible for wheelchairs but some paths very steep. Wheelchairs available at gate

○ ➤ 🖼 WC & 🌿 🏛 ♿

One of the most spectacular of all Britain's 'sub-tropical' gardens on an island which lies in the warming Gulf Stream. Usually protected from Atlantic gales, this was not the case in 1990, and as a result of the devastation several thousand trees have been replanted and massive clearance work done with financial assistance from English Heritage. Robin Lane Fox calls this 'a paradise...one of the most important recoveries in British garden history', and the amazing fact is that it is tended by a mere four full-timers. The garden is arranged on several terraces mounting a hillside linked by flights of steps. They serve as a home for myriad exotic plants like proteas from South Africa, the tender geranium G. maderense from Madeira and trees and shrubs from the North Island of New Zealand and Australia which could not thrive out-of-doors in many places on the British mainland. This 17-acre garden is both formal and informal. Many of the plants are self-seeded. The grounds also house the Valhalla collection of ship figureheads from the National Maritime Museum.

Trevarno Gardens ★ 44

Trevarno Manor, Helston TR13 0RU. Tel: (01326) 574274

Mr M Sagin and Mr N Helsby • 3m NW of Helston off A394 or B3302 • Open all year, daily except 25th Dec, 10.30am – 5pm • Entrance: £3, OAPs/disabled £2.50, children 5-14 £1.25, under 5 free ○ 💭 ✕ 📠 WC & 🗲 🌿 🛍 🍴

A vast restoration is taking place in a 60-acre woodland area, accessible throughout by well-kept paths. Here one can enjoy spectacular views, rare trees, shrubs and spring flowers. In other areas visitors will discover a lake, cascade, rockery, grotto and pinetum. (The large lake with a Victorian boat is now easy to approach since a further clearing of the earth around it.) The walled Georgian gardens are to be replanted and an Italian garden is now nearly returned to its original design. A large glasshouse containing vines planted in 1830 is another feature to be restored, while a large garden conservatory with a central fountain acts as a delightful tea room. A small museum has been built to exhibit what is believed to be the most comprehensive collection of gardening tools, implements, memorabilia and ephemera in the country.

Trewithen ★★ 45

Grampound Road, Truro TR2 4DD. Tel: (01726) 883647; Fax: (01726) 882301

Mr and Mrs A.M.J. Galsworthy • On A390 between Truro and St Austell • Walled garden open when house open • House open April to July, Mon, Tues, 2 – 4pm; rest of gardens open March to Sept, Mon – Sat, 10am – 4.30pm (also Sun in April and May) • Entrance: £3.50, children £2, parties of 20 or more £3.20 per person (house £3.50, children £2), joint ticket (house and garden) £6
◐ 💭 📠 WC & 🗲 🌿

This is an internationally famous garden, known for its great collection of magnolias, rhododendrons and camellias along with many other beautiful and rare trees and shrubs. It is fitting that its founder, George Johnstone, named a camellia after his daughter 'Elizabeth Johnstone', and there are rhododendrons 'Alison Johnstone' after his wife, 'Trewithen Orange', and 'Jack Skelton' after his head gardener. The lawn in front of the house is edged with banks of a wide range of shrubs including viburnums, azaleas, potentillas, euonymus, berberis. A sunken garden has tree ferns, azaleas and acers. Many nothofagus, embothriums, pieris, enkianthus, eucryphias, griselinias. The walled garden has a pool and some choice climbers including *Clianthus puniceus* and *Mutisia decurrens*, and there is a pergola hung with wisteria. Newly planted beds of young trees of sorbus and birch, mahonia, cornus, phygelius and roses, and island beds with heathers and dwarf conifers. Magnificent beech trees provide shelter. A half-hour video describes the creation of the garden over the years.

Trewoofe House   46

Lamorna, Penzance TR19 6PA. Tel: (01736) 810269

Mr and Mrs H.M. Pigott • 6m SW of Penzance. Take B3315 from Penzance via Newlyn towards Lamorna. At top of hill take sharp right turn signed Trewoofe • Open May to Sept by appt; May to July, Wed; June, Wed, Sun, 10th Sept for charity, 2 – 5pm • Entrance: £1.50, children under 16 free • Coaches by appt ● WC & ♪ ♫

This two-acre garden, situated at the head of the Lamorna valley, is planted informally with shrub and herbaceous beds that give colour all year round. An ancient mill leat runs through it, enabling a bog garden to be developed, planted with a wide variety of moisture-loving plants. The garden is on two levels, linked by two bridges over the leat and using local granite. There is a small fruit garden with cordon- and espalier-trained trees, and a conservatory with semi-tender climbers.

Trewyn Garden   47

St Ives TR26 1AQ. Tel: (01736) 362341 ext. 3322 (Garden Manager)

Penwith District Council • In St Ives, near Barbara Hepworth Museum (see entry) • Open all year, daily • Entrance: free • Other information: Special wheelchair slope in main section ○ & ◁◁

The garden is divided into three sections: a main garden with a superbly kept lawn, bright flowers and well-matured deciduous trees as well as numerous palms, a shrubbery, and a series of flower beds and a lawn leading to pensioners' flats – in all about one acre. About 150 metres away from Trewyn Garden is the Memorial Garden, under the same management (though not suitable for wheelchairs and locked at night). A rest haven, well furnished with benches, and with attractive flower beds. Another pleasant garden open all year is connected with the *Tregenna Castle Hotel* but is a public garden (Tel: (01736) 795254). It has several areas: a woodland, a well-stocked lavender garden and a rare plants section which includes Canary Island foxgloves and echium species. Pleasant seating. Though the trees hide the view from the garden, there are fine views towards St Ives Bay. In all, 72 acres.

NATIONAL COUNCIL FOR THE CONSERVATION OF PLANTS AND GARDENS
The NCCPG publishes a *National Plant Collections Directory*. Those interested in particular families of plants who want to see some of the rarer species and garden varieties will find this an invaluable publication. The latest edition, which offers information on about 550 collections comprising more than 50,000 plants and contains articles by holders of the collections, is available from NCCPG, The Pines, Wisley Garden, Woking GU3 6QB.

CUMBRIA &
THE ISLE OF MAN

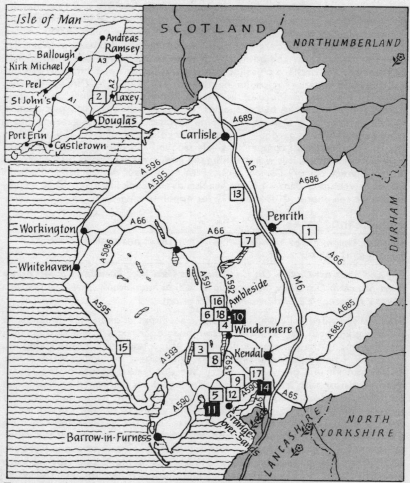

Two-starred gardens are marked on the map with a black square.

Acorn Bank Garden and Watermill

Temple Sowerby, Penrith CA10 1SP. Tel: (017683) 61893

The National Trust • 6m E of Penrith off A66 N of Temple Sowerby • Garden open April to Oct, 10am – 5pm (last admission 4.30pm) • Entrance: £2.30, children £1.20, family £5.80, pre-booked parties £1.70 per person • Other information: Guide dogs only in garden; other dogs in woodland only, on lead. Partially restored water mill open ◑ 🍴 🖼 WC ♿ ⟨⟩ 🐾 🛒 💧

The 'acorn bank' is the ancient oakwood sloping down to the Crowdundle Beck behind the house. In spring it is a carpet of daffodils and narcissi in many varieties planted profusely in the 1930s, and there are some 60,000 Lenten lilies. The walled gardens are then also a mass of blossom from the old varieties of apple, medlar, pear and quince, with their carpet of wild tulips, anemones and narcissi. The orchard trees include apple varieties which blossom late and are therefore suitable for cooler northern areas. Along the three sheltering walls are carefully modulated herbaceous and shrub borders, with good clematis and climbers. A bed of species roses flanks the steps to a picturesque sunken garden, with a pond and alpine terraces. Through a gateway lies a splendid walled herb garden – a well-tended collection of some 250 medicinal and culinary herbs, all comprehensively labelled and documented. For those interested in alpines, it is worth taking the A686 over the spectacular Hartside fell to *Hartside Nursery Garden* about 14m away near Alston [open daily in summer, weekdays, 9am – 4.30pm, weekends and Bank Holidays, 12.30 – 4pm, otherwise telephone (01434) 381372 for appointment].

Ballalheannagh ★   2

Glen Roy, Lonan, Isle of Man IM4 7QB. Tel: (01624) 861875; Fax: (01624) 86114

Clif and Maureen Dadd • On E of island in Glen Roy, 2m inland from Laxey • Open March to Oct, daily, 10am – 5pm, Nov to Feb variable (telephone first to check) • Entrance: £2, children free (1999 prices) ○ 🐾

Take a steep-sided valley, a ladder, some seedlings of exotic rhododendrons and forget all about digging pits to accommodate the roots. Just stick them into crevices among the mosses and ferns and wait a few years, never giving up. Outcome – paradise for plant-lovers. You expect to find a garden like Ballalheannagh in Cornwall or Kerry but this is the middle of the Isle of Man. No visitor with an interest in gardening who is marooned on that island need fear boredom. This is a botanical garden, not in name, but surely in content. Steep winding paths cling to the valley sides, and crystal water cascades below, carrying the bells of pieris to the Irish Sea. The lower portion is well stocked with lofty rhododendrons while the upper parts of the valley contain newer plantings that will certainly delight in years to come. Here are eucalyptus, drimys, epacris, epigaea, megacarpaea and betula (species with evocative names like *Betula tatewakiana*), and a host of others too, and the native mosses and ferns are a wonderful sight. The garden has been extended to more than 20 acres, with gravel walks exceeding four miles, and has new oriental features.

Brantwood   3

Coniston LA21 8AD. Tel: (015394) 41396

Brantwood Trust • E side of Coniston Water off B5285, signposted. Coniston Launch provides hourly service to Brantwood and other points around lake.

Steam yacht 'Gondola' sails regularly from Coniston Pier • House open • Garden open 13th March to 12th Nov, daily, 11am – 5.30pm; winter season Wed – Sun, 11am – 4.30pm, but closed 25th and 26th Dec • Entrance: garden £2, house and garden £4 (students £2.50), children under 18 £1 (1999 prices)
🕐 ☕ ✕ 🖼 WC ⬇ 🌂 🛍 🔦

This is a superb site with wonderful views, atmosphere and history. The rocky hillside behind the house is threaded with a wandering network of paths created by the social visionary, John Ruskin, to delight the eye and please the mind. A succession of small, individual gardens thread the landscape, exploring the many themes that fascinated Ruskin. Now in the capable hands of Sally Beamish, it is being returned to its former glory after many years of neglect. The structure of the allegorical Zig-Zaggy garden has been rebuilt and the Professor's Garden, fishpond and Harbour Walk have all been restored. A medieval-style herb garden will be opened soon. Among many other delights, there is a large collection of British native ferns, an ice-house, cascades and Ruskin's famous stone seat.

Brockhole ★ 4

Lake District Visitor Centre, Windermere LA23 1LJ. Tel: (015394) 46601

Lake District National Park Authority • 1½ m N of Windermere on A591 • Grounds and gardens open all year, daily, 10am – dusk • Entrance: parking fee only: private car £3 for 3 hours, £4 all day; minibuses and coaches free if pre-booked • Other information: Centre open April to Nov, with slide theatre and exhibition. Lake cruises from jetty ○ ☕ ✕ 🖼 WC ♿ ⬇ 🛍 🔦

A garden blessed with the Lakeland combination of western aspect and water to the hills beyond, in this case notably the Langdale Pikes. To frame this view Mawson worked closely (c.1900) with his architect colleague Gibson. The ornamental terraces drop through rose beds, herbaceous borders and shrubbery to a wildflower meadow flanked by mature woodland. The original kitchen and herb garden has been restored; other special features are herbaceous plants, Chilean and other tender shrubs and rarities and the constantly changing colour from spring rhododendrons and azaleas through to late Chilean hollies, maples and eucryphias.

Charney Well 5

Hampsfell Road, Grange-over-Sands LA11 6BE. Tel: (015395) 34526; Fax: (015395) 35765; E-mail: charneywel@aol.com

Richard Roberts and Christopher Holliday • Travelling W on A590, take B5277 to Grange-over-Sands. Continue up hill to mini-roundabout and turn right; at crossroads turn right, then left up Hampsfell Road. Gate in garden wall on left • Open for local charity 2nd June, 5pm onwards; for NGS 12th, 13th Aug, 10am – 5pm; and for parties by appt • Entrance: £2 [NEW] 🕐 ☕ 🌂

This remarkable half-acre garden has been developed by the owners over the past decade. It is on a steep limestone slope and surrounded on three sides by high limestone walls with magnificent views over Morecambe Bay. The sheltered situation and almost frost-free microclimate has made it possible to fill the site with tender exotica in a district normally given over to primulas, rhododendrons, meconopsis and other ericaceous plants. Amongst the profusion, ceanothus, pittosporum, corokia, *Melianthus major* and *Fatsia japonica* thrive; a National Collection of phormiums is held here. A useful list of unusual plants is available. This is a jewel in the crown of Lakeland gardens.

Copt Howe 6

Chapel Stile, Great Langdale, Ambleside LA22 9JR. Tel: (015394) 37685

Professor R.N. Haszeldine • 3m W of Ambleside on B5343 • Open 29th April to 1st May, 27th to 29th May, 12 noon – 5pm for NGS; also many other days mid-April to Sept (telephone for recorded weekly information). Private visits and parties by appt • Entrance: £2, OAPs £1.50, children free ● ◁▷ ℘

This plantsman's fellside woodland two-acre garden, with magnificent views of the Langdale Pikes and interesting geological features, has an exceptionally wide range of rare acid-loving plants from many mountainous countries, including expedition plants from Himalaya, China, Tibet, Japan, Bhutan, Tasmania, New Zealand and North and South America. The extensive collections includes acers, camellias, azaleas, quercus, fagus, large and dwarf conifers, pieris, kalmias, tilias, cercis and cercidiphyllums; among herbaceous plants are many bulbous species with orchids and species lilies, *Tropaeolum tuberosum* and *T. speciosum*. Alpine troughs; streams and woodland plantings with mountain primulas, cardiocrinum, *Myosotidium hortensia* and many types of meconopsis including *M. punicea*. Dramatic spring, early summer and autumn colours.

Dalemain Historic House and Gardens ★ 7

Dalemain Estate Office, Dacre, Penrith CA11 0HB. Tel: (017684) 86450; Fax: (017684) 86223

Mr and Mrs R.B. Hasell-McCosh • On A592 3m W of Penrith on Ullswater road • House open 11m – 4pm • Garden open 2nd April to 8th Oct, Sun – Thurs, 10.30am – 5pm • Entrance: £3 (house and garden £5, children (5-16) £3, family (2 adults plus own children) £13. Special prices for pre-booked parties) • Other information: Wheelchair and electric scooter available. Dogs outside garden only, on lead ◑ ● ✕ ⌷ WC & ℘ ⌸ ⍭

Dalemain has evolved in the most natural way from a twelfth-century pele tower with its kitchen garden and herbs. The Tudor-walled knot garden is there, as are the Stuart terrace (1680s) and the walled orchard where apple trees like 'Nonsuch' and 'Keswick Codling', planted in 1728, still bear fruit. The gardens were re-established by the late Mrs Sylvia McCosh during the 1960s and '70s with shrubs, species roses and other rarities, together with herbaceous replanting along the terraces and around the orchard, and since then developments are under the direction of her daughter-in-law. There is a wild garden on the lower ground featuring an outstanding display of Himalayan blue poppies in early summer and a walk past the Tudor gazebo into woods overlooking the Dacre Beck. Some thoughtful planting for future shapes and form in woodland. Further south off M6 junction 31 or 32 is the associated *Stydd Nursery*, Stoneygate Lane, Ribchester, Preston (Tel: (01254) 878797), which sells old-fashioned roses, including some unusual and rare varieties, as well as other plants, shrubs, etc [open Tues – Fri, 1.30 – 5pm].

Graythwaite Hall ★   8

Ulverston, Graythwaite LA12 8BA. Tel: (015395) 31248

Graythwaite Estate • 4m N of Newby Bridge on W side of Lake Windermere • Open April to June, daily, 10am – 6pm • Entrance: £2, children free ◗ ▣ WC ◁

Essentially a spring garden landscaped by the late Victorian Thomas Mawson in partnership with Dan Gibson in a beautiful parkland and woodland setting. Azaleas and rhododendrons lead to cultivars of late spring-flowering shrubs. Formal terraced rose garden. The finely wrought sundials and gate by Gibson, the Dutch garden and the stream and pond all add charm to this serene garden. For topiary admirers, Mawson employed interesting effects to contrast with his more billowy plantings. Notable are the battlemented yew hedge and some yew globes with golden yew in the top half and green in the bottom. While in Hawkshead, those interested in sculpture in nature should visit the *Grizedale Sculpture Trail*, organised by the Forestry Commission (Tel: (01229) 86029). The first piece was placed there over 20 years ago and there are now 80 sculptures.

Halecat   9

Witherslack, Grange–over–Sands LA11 6RU. Tel: (015395) 52229

Mrs M. Stanley • 14m SW of Kendal, off A590. Signposted • Garden open all year, Mon – Fri, 9am – 4.30pm, Sun, 2 – 4pm • Entrance: free • Other information: Plants, especially hydrangeas, for sale in adjoining nursery ○

These two acres are the front garden of the mid-nineteenth-century house which stands at the head of a small valley with distant views of Arnside Knott and the Forest of Bowland. Mrs Stanley has created this pleasing, personal garden over the past 45 years as a series of terraces and squares, and the limestone quarried from the borders has been used to build the retaining walls and the perimeter wall separating the garden from the surrounding woodland. An azalea bed has been made on the bottom terrace by removing rock and filling the beds with peat from a nearby bog. The mixed borders are well maintained and filled with many shrubs, clematis, herbaceous plants, and shrub and climbing roses. Look out for unusual wooden animals – particularly the bear. Beautiful gazebo with stained glass quarries, designed by Francis Johnson.

Holehird ★★   10

Patterdale Road, Windermere LA23 1NP. Tel: (015394) 46008

Lakeland Horticultural Society • 1m N of Windermere on A592 Paterdale road • Open all year, daily, sunrise – sunset. Garden guides available April to Oct,

11am – 5pm • Entrance: by donation (minimum £2 appreciated) • Other information: Annual plant sale first Sat in May in local school ○ 🖻 **WC**

Run by members of a Society dedicated to promoting 'knowledge on the cultivation of plants, shrubs and trees, especially those suited to Lakeland conditions', this garden is maintained to an exceptionally high standard. It lies on a splendid hillside site alongside Holehird mansion with a natural water course and rock banks looking over Windermere to the Langdale Pikes. The Society has five acres of attractive gardens and trial areas. Much of the earlier planting has been preserved, including many fine specimen trees. Highlights are the summer-autumn heathers, winter-flowering shrubs, alpines and National Collections of astilbes, hydrangeas and polysticum ferns. The walled garden has fine herbaceous borders, herbs and climbers.

Holker Hall ★★ 11

Cark-in-Cartmel, Grange–over–Sands LA11 7PL. Tel: (015395) 58328

Lord and Lady Cavendish • 4½ m W of Grange-over-Sands, 4m S of Haverthwaite on B5278 • Hall open. Extra charge • Garden open April to Oct, daily except Sat, 10am – 6pm (last admission 4.30pm) • Entrance: wide variety on offer (house, gardens, motor museum, potting sheds, exhibitions) so range of ticket prices depends on visitor requirements. Telephone for details • Other information: Motor Museum. Garden and Countryside Festival 2nd – 4th June. Dogs on leads in grounds but not gardens ◑ 🍽 ✕ 🖻 **WC** ♿ ℘ 🏛 ♉

Set in 125 acres of parkland, the award-winning 23 acres of woodland walks and formal gardens at Holker (pronounced Hooker) have been constantly developed by the family ever since Lord George Cavendish established his 'contrived natural landscape' over 200 years ago. The woods now contain many rare and beautiful specimens, all tagged and chronicled in the excellent guide to the walks. The National Collection of styracaceae is maintained here. Other features are the cascade, evocative of the Villa d'Este, and a beautifully contrived transformation of the croquet lawn into summer gardens. This combination of formal beds and inventive planting (e.g. spire lilies rising out of massed rue) makes a wonderful Italianate-cum-English garden that typifies the spirit of Holker. There is also Mawson's rose garden, which has been sensitively renewed (his pergola and balustrade still survive). Elliptical garden, rhododendron and azalea walk and wildflower meadow. New additions include a restored Victorian rockery.

Holme Cragg 12

Blea Cragg Bridge, Witherslack, Grange–over–Sands LA11 6RZ. Tel: (015395) 52366

Mr J. Watson • 14m SW of Kendal, off A590. From A590, follow signs to Witherslack. Past telephone kiosk in Witherslack, turn first left, first left again and follow signs Newton (past Halecat) for 1¼ m over small bridge to third gate on left • Open all year, daily • Entrance: by donation to Cumbria Wildlife Trust • Other information: Coaches must pre-book ○ **WC** ⬦ ℘

This is an amateur's and a plantsman's garden which has made magnificent use of natural features of the site. Every rocky outcrop is clothed in alpines, sedums, sempervivums and saxifrages. Azaleas and rhododendrons are an important feature as are the irises and candelabra primulas around the pond. The shaded areas are filled with the blue of the Himalayan meconopsis and a grass bank covered with double and single Welsh poppies in colours from deep orange to pale yellow. Interesting natural wildflower area. Rhododendrons are followed by shrub roses and later the foliage of acers provide colour interest. Well worth a visit after Halecat (see entry), with which it provides interesting contrasts and comparisons.

Hutton-in-the-Forest 13

Penrith CA11 9TH. Tel: (017684) 84449

Lord and Lady Inglewood • 6m NW of Penrith on B5305 (M6 junction 41) • House open: 20th April to 1st Oct, Thurs, Fri, Sun and Bank Holiday Mons, 12.30 – 4pm. Private parties by arrangement from April. Monthly tours with head gardener • Entrance: £2.50, children free (house and grounds £4, children (7-16) £2, family ticket £10) • Other information: Light lunches and teas when house open. Other meals on request ○ 🏠 WC 🚻 ⬇ 🍴 🌱

This garden is a mixture of seventeenth-, eighteenth-, nineteenth- and twentieth-century features. It has great visual appeal, with a magnificent view from the seventeenth-century terraces now embellished with Victorian topiary. The beautiful walled garden, dating from the 1730s, has excellent herbaceous borders, trained fruit trees and roses. Some of the mature woodland trees were planted by Henry Fletcher, an ancestor of the owners, in the early eighteenth century. A woodland walk has many fine specimen trees identified in a leaflet. Other features include a seventeenth-century dovecot and eighteenth-century lake, though the latter needs draining and some comments have been passed about maintenance.

Levens Hall ★★ 14

Kendal LA8 0PD. Tel: (015395) 60321

Mr C.H. Bagot • 5m S of Kendal on A6 (M6 junction 36) • House open as garden, 12 noon – 5pm • Garden and tearoom open, April to 14th Oct, Sun – Thurs, 10am – 5pm • Entrance: £3.90, children £2.10 (house and garden £5.30, children, £2.80). Party rates available (1999 prices) ◑ ☕ 🏠 WC 🚻 🌱

James II's gardener, Guillaume Beaumont, designed this famous topiary garden in 1694; it is one of very few to retain its original trees and design. The impeccably clipped yews and box hedges are set off by colourful spring and summer bedding and borders. The primroses in the seventeenth-century garden may be the start of a permanent collection. To celebrate the tercentenary of the gardens in 1994 a new area, the Fountain Garden, has been created with lime avenues meeting at the pool. Indeed there is much to see in addition to the topiary. Massive walls of beech hedge open to vistas over parkland. One avenue leads to the earliest English ha-ha. There is a picturesque herb garden behind the house. The record of only 10 head gardeners in 300 years, and the affectionate care by the Bagot family, account for the rare harmony of this exceptional garden, which clearly still has a stylish hand at the helm. A face-lift is in progress which includes two pairs of clematis gates, a green-oak ticket booth disguised as a garden pavilion, and a pair of gates with hearts as handles — celebrating the old legend that a gambler acquired the property in the seventeenth century by turning over the ace of hearts.

Muncaster Castle ★   15

Ravenglass CA18 1RQ. Tel: (01229) 717614

Mr and Mrs Gordon-Duff-Pennington • 15m S of Whitehaven on A595 • Castle open mid-March to 5th Nov, Mon – Fri, 12.30 – 4pm (last admission) • Gardens and owl centre open all year, daily, 11am – 5pm • Entrance: gardens and owl centre £3.80, children £2, family (2 adults and 2 children) £10, party of 12 or more £3.40, children £1 per person, (castle, gardens and owl centre £5.50, children £3.10, family £15, party of 12 or more £4.50, children £2.50 per person) (1999 prices) • Other information: Wheelchairs available for pre-booking ○ 🐾 ✕ 🏠 WC ⅙ ⬦ 🚲 👍 ☕

The castle is set against the splendid backdrop of Scafell and the hills, with a wide open view from the terrace. The acid soil and the Gulf Stream warmth provide ideal conditions for one of the finest collections of species rhododendrons in Europe, substantially from plant-hunting expeditions to Nepal in the 1920s (Kingdon Ward, Ludlow and Sheriff). There are excellent azaleas, camellias, magnolias, hydrangeas and maples, plus many unusual trees (e.g. nothofagus species). The gardens are at their best in May and June but intensive new planting is ensuring constant pleasure for visitors in all seasons. Extensive clearing and replanting continues and will take time to mature. A new Sino-Himalayan walk is being developed.

Rydal Mount   16

Ambleside LA22 9LU. Tel: (015394) 33002; Fax: (015394) 31738

Rydal Mount Trust • 1m N of Ambleside on A591 • House open • Gardens open March to Oct, daily, 9.30am – 5pm; Nov to Feb, daily except Tues, 10am – 4pm • Entrance: £1.50 (house and garden £3.50, OAPs and students £3, children (5-15) £1, parties of 10 or more pre-booked £2.50 per person, non-booked £3 per person. Reciprocal discounts with Dove Cottage and Wordsworth's House) • Other information: Limited parking with awkward entry/exit ○ 🏠 WC ⬦ 👍 ☕

The carefully maintained grounds of Wordsworth's house still follow the lines of his own plan, and it is easy to imagine the poet wandering along the upper terrace walk ('the sloping terrace') and down through winding, shaded paths to the lawns, or across a terrace to the ancient mound with its distant glimpse of Windermere. Apart from its poetic association the garden is also a visual delight, with good herbaceous borders, shrubs and unusual trees (e.g. the fern-leaf beech). A new terrace has recently been discovered and will be called Dora's Terrace, after the poet's daughter. An addition to the spring display is the bank of dancing daffodils in nearby Dora's Field. Wordsworth's other house at Cockermouth has a pleasant town garden, now restored, but it is only worth it if the house, too, is to be visited.

Sizergh Castle ★ 17

Kendal LA8 8AE. Tel: (015395) 60070

The National Trust • 3½ m S of Kendal on A590 (M6 junction 36) • Castle open 28th May to Oct, 1.30 – 5.30pm • Garden open 23rd April to Oct, Sun – Thurs, 12.30 – 5.30pm (last admission 5pm) • Entrance: £2.30, children £1.10 (castle and garden £4.60, children £2.20, family £11.20. Parties of 15 or more £3 per person. Other information: Manual wheelchair and powered buggy available. Enquire about guided walks with emphasis on different features ◑ ♨ 🖺 WC ﴾ ✍ 🏚 ⚱

An exceptionally varied garden with colour from early spring daffodils to summer borders and climbers, culminating in glorious autumn tints (the vine-clad tower all fiery red is a memorable spectacle). Other features encountered along shady paths are the herbaceous border, the terrace wall, with half-hardy shrubs and climbers not expected this far north, the south garden with many species roses, including Musk and Moss roses. The replanting of the rock garden is completed with excellent results. The maples and hardy ferns are of special interest with variety throughout the season. Also a restored 'Dutch' garden with its new avenue of 'Shirotae' flowering cherries, part of the 16-acre garden round the pele tower. There are wildflower banks with native lime-stone flora including six species of orchids, and a water garden and lake.

Stagshaw 18

Ambleside LA22 0HE. Tel/Fax: (015394) 46027

The National Trust • ½ m S of Ambleside on A591 • Open April to June, daily, 10am – 6.30pm, July to Oct, by appt (s.a.e. to NT Property Office, St Catherine's, Patterdale Road, Windermere LA23 1NH) • Entrance: £1.50 • Other information: Limited parking, access dangerous ◑

Created by the Trust's former Regional Agent, the late Cubby Acland, this is a carefully blended area of azaleas and rhododendrons among camellias, magnolias and other fine shrubs with unusual underplanting on a west-facing hillside of oaks looking over the head of Lake Windermere. A large area of pink erythroniums. Rather difficult of access, with the volume of traffic on A591 making the exit especially dangerous, but worth the effort.

WHEELCHAIR USERS ﴾
Please note that the symbol denoting suitability for wheelchairs refers to the garden only. If there is a house open, it may or may not be suitable.

DERBYSHIRE

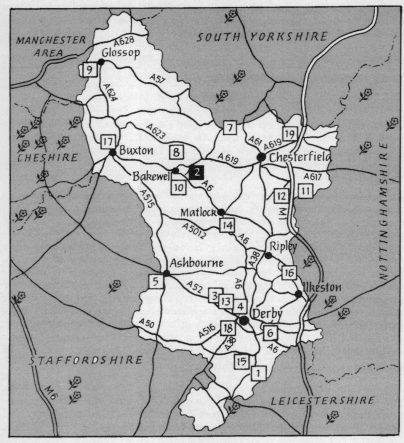

Two-starred gardens are marked on the map with a black square.

Calke Abbey
1

Ticknall DE73 1LE. Tel: (01332) 863822 (office); Fax: (01332) 865272

The National Trust • 10m S of Derby, off A514 at Ticknall • House open probably 1 – 5pm (ring for confirmation; tickets are timed and there may be some waiting) • Garden open 27th March to 1st Nov, Sat – Wed and Bank Holiday Mons, 11am – 5pm • Entrance: £2.30, children £1.10 (house and garden £5, children £2.50, family £12.50) (1999 prices). £2.50 vehicle charge entry to park, which is open during daylight hours all year, refundable on purchase of house and garden ticket • ◐ 🍺 ✕ <u>WC</u> ♿ 🏛 🕯

Previously owned by the Harpur Crewe family and taken on by the Trust in 1985, Calke Abbey gardens have a long history and with a sympathetic approach could be another Trust jewel. The Vinery in the Physic garden has been restored, as have the tomato house, frames, pits, and an auricula theatre. The gardeners are growing fruit, vegetables and flowers in the two walled compartments formerly kept for flowers and physic herbs. The third and biggest compartment is the old kitchen garden, now disused, overlooked by an orangery plus a head gardener's office of 1777. The exterior of the orangery is being restored, and the aim is to grow old varieties, including an apple and plum orchard, wherever possible, and the renewal of this garden will interest all those who yearn for traditional fruit and vegetables grown in the old manner. Garden produce on sale when available.

Chatsworth ★★ 2

Bakewell DE45 1PP. Tel: (01246) 582204; Fax: (01246) 583536

The Duke and Duchess of Devonshire • 4m E of Bakewell, 10m W of Chesterfield on B6012, off A619 and A6 • House open • Garden open 15th March to 29th Oct, daily, 11am – 6pm (last admission 5pm) • Entrance: £3.75, OAPs and students £3, children £1.75, family £9.50 (house and garden £6.50, OAPs and students £5.25, children £3, family £16.75) (1999 prices). Parking charge for cars only ◑ 🍽 ✕ 🏬 WC ♿ 🛍 🐾 🎁 🔦

The 100 acres of garden at Chatsworth have developed over 400 years and many areas still reflect the garden fashions of each century. The seventeenth-century gardens of London and Wise remain only as the cascade, fully restored now, the canal pond to the south and the copper 'willow tree' with water pouring from its branches. During the eighteenth century 'Capability' Brown destroyed much of the formal gardens to create a landscaped woodland park. Notable is the vista created by Brown from the Salisbury Lawn to the horizon, which remains unchanged, as does the lawn itself since no liming or fertiliser has been used, allowing many varieties of wild flowers, grasses, moss and sedges to thrive. The orange borders and blue and white borders are twentieth-century additions, as are the terrace, display greenhouse, rose garden and old conservatory garden which has lupin, dahlia and Michaelmas daisy beds, and a yew maze planted in 1963. The Duke and Duchess continue to work on the garden, improving the arboretum and pinetum by removing the suffocating rhododendrons, laurels and sycamores, and planting many new trees – labelling is excellent. The double rows of pleached red-twigged limes planted in 1952, and the serpentine hedge of beech planted in 1953, are both now rewarding features. Paxton's work still gives pleasure: there is the large rockery, some rare conifers, the magnificent 84-metre water jet from the Emperor Fountain. Alas, the Great Conservatory was a casualty of the 1914-18 war and metre-wide stone walls in the old conservatory garden are all that remain to give an idea of its size. The epitome of a cottage garden has been created near another recent addition, up the yew stairs to a 'bedroom' where the four poster is ivy and the dressing table privet, which future generations may regard as a folly. The kitchen garden has been resited and redesigned – it has been called 'indelibly British'. The first major piece of garden statuary to be placed in the garden for 150 years, 'War Horse' by Dame Elisabeth Frink, is sited at the south end of the canal.

Dam Farm House ★ 3

Yeldersley Lane, Ednaston, Ashbourne DE6 3BA. Tel: (01335) 360291

Mrs S.D. Player • 5m SE of Ashbourne on A52. Opposite Ednaston village turn, gate is 500 metres on right • Open April to Oct by appt only (also some Suns for NGS) • Entrance: £2, children free, parties £2.50 per person • Other information: Teas on charity open days only ● 🏠 WC ♿ 🌡

The scree garden has a large number of choice alpines. Climbers are used abundantly for clothing walls, trees, pergolas, even spilling down over high retaining walls – and all achieved since 1980. Collections of plants, shrubs and roses and an expanding arboretum. Plenty of informative labelling. This garden promises to be a most important one as it continues to develop.

Derby Arboretum 4

Arboretum Square, Derby DE23 8FN. Tel: (01332) 716644

Derby City Council • Between Reginald Street and Arboretum Square with entrances on either side of Royal Crown Derby Factory • Open all year, daily • Entrance: free ○ 🏠 WC ♿ 🔌

The first specifically designed urban arboretum in Britain, this was commissioned from John Claudius Loudon, whose original plans involved the planting of 1000 trees. A useful (and free) leaflet now lists 40 varieties, many from around the world, all individually numbered. The leaflet also describes other parks in Derby, including the well-known *Markeaton Park*. Those interested in that arcane floral pursuit of well-dressing will wish to visit Peak District villages such as Tissington and Youlgreave during May to Sept. Free leaflet with all places and dates from Chesterfield Tourist Office (Tel: (01246) 345777).

Dove Cottage Gardens 5

Clifton, Ashbourne DE6 2GL. Tel: (01335) 343545

Mr and Mrs S.G. Liverman • 1½ m SW of Ashbourne off A515. In Clifton turn right at crossroads then first left down lane (signed Mayfield Yarns). House is 200 metres on left by River Dove • Open by appt for party bookings of 10 or more and on certain Suns during May to Aug for charity, 1 – 5pm • Entrance: Parties £3 per person for guided tour and for charity £2, children free ● 🍴 WC 🌡

It is only to be expected that this richly stocked cottage garden is above the average for it has had the benefit of being developed and nurtured by an owner who is a qualified horticulturist. She began replanting it in 1979. There are several hardy plant collections including alliums, campanulas, euphorbias, geraniums and variegated plants. New experimental gravel bed.

Elvaston Castle Country Park ★ 6

Borrowash Road, Elvaston, Derby DE72 3EP. Tel: (01332) 571342; Fax: (01332) 758751

Derbyshire County Council • 6m SE of Derby on B5010 between Borrowash (A6005) and Thulston (A6). Signed from A6 and A52 • Park open all year, daily, dawn – dusk • Entrance: free. Estate Museum £1.20, children 60p. Parking charge • Other information: Estate Museum open 2nd April to 1st Nov ○ 🖪 WC ⬦ ⚲ ⚱

The estate's historic Grade-II gardens were designed by William Barron in the early nineteenth century and include the Italian, parterre and old English gardens, all of which were enclosed within 11 miles of hedges. It is probable that these were the first 'garden rooms', which influenced others when, 20 years after their establishment, they were opened to the public. Discover extensive topiary, tree-lined avenues and a large ornamental lake. Search out the golden gates, boat house and Moorish temple and wonder at the distinctive cedars of Lebanon. William Barron transplanted mature trees as high as 13 metres from as early as 1831, using his unique transplanting machines, one of which is housed at the Royal Botanic Gardens, Kew. For those who find a park out of scale with their own smaller gardens, a tiny 'romantic' garden nearby, *White Gate* at Arleston Meadows, is recommended. The owner, Mrs Judy Beba-Thompson, welcomes private visits and small parties by prior appointment (Tel: (01332) 763653).

Fanshawe Gate Hall 7

Holmesfield S18 7WA. Tel: (0114) 289 0391

Mr and Mrs John Ramsden • 6m NW of Chesterfield, 6m SW of Sheffield, 1m E of Holmesfield. Follow B6054 and turn first right after Robin Hood pub • Open for charity 2nd, 9th, 16th July, 11am – 5pm and for private visits by appt • Entrance: £1.50 NEW ● 🍽 WC ⬦ ⬦ ⚲

A very popular garden with visitors on charity days. The owners, who moved here over 40 years ago, have tried to choose plants appropriate to the age of the stone property (some 700 years). Topiary, mixed borders, a variegated border, an Elizabethan garden and a sixteenth-century dovecot are features of this two-acre garden. The upper walled garden displays herbaceous plants, shrubs, ferns, water features and roses while the lower courtyard has a knot garden and a herb border. A parterre to celebrate the millennium is being developed in the upper courtyard, and the orchard is to be replanted with old varieties of English fruit trees.

Fir Croft 8

Froggatt Road, Calver, Hope Valley S32 3ZD.

Dr S.B. Furness • 4m N of Bakewell. Between Power filling station and A625/B6001 junction • Open 7th, 21st May, 4th, 18th June, 2 – 5pm • Entrance: By donation • Other information: Plants for sale at adjoining nursery ● ⚲

The owner is a botanist and botanical photographer who has put his expertise into an extensive alpine garden – a 'must' to visit for those interested in alpine and scree gardens, particularly as the garden, started from scratch in 1985, now contains one of the largest collections of alpines in the UK.

Gamesley Fold Cottage 9

10 Gamesley Fold, Glossop SK13 6JJ. Tel: (014578) 67856

Mrs G. Carr • Off A626 Glossop – Marple road near Charlesworth. Turn down lane opposite St Margaret's School • Open 4th and 25th June for NGS and by appt for parties during June • Entrance: £1.50, children free ● ⬤ WC ♨

Although all gardeners will find much of interest here, those who like native or 'wild' flowers will be particularly impressed. The many loosely planted beds are crammed with primulas, violets, campions and poppies, a lot of which are self-seeded. Mixed in is a good variety of perennials, notably campanulas, euphorbias, geraniums, verbascums, meconopsis and others that go well with their wild neighbours. Much wildlife is to be found in this plantsman's garden, particularly butterflies lured here by the flowers, trees and shrubs. The extensive views of the surrounding countryside and hills are another bonus.

Haddon Hall ★ 10

Bakewell DE45 1LA. Tel: (01629) 812855

*Lord Edward Manners • 2m SE of Bakewell, 6½ m N of Matlock on A6 • * House open • Garden open April to Sept, daily, 10.30am – 5pm • Entrance: hall and gardens £5.50, OAPs £4.75, children £3, family (2 adults and 2 children) £14.75, parties £4.75 per person, school parties £2.50 per child (1999 prices). Parking charge for cars, coaches free* ◑ ⬤ ✕ WC ♿

The medieval castle and gardens of seventeenth-century origin – reconstructed this century – stand on a limestone bluff. The gardens are mainly on the south side and are laid out in a series of stone-walled terraces with the River Wye at their feet. The thick stone walls of the castle and terrace walls face south and west and look well as a background for the extensive collection of climbing and rambling roses. The plants, shrubs and roses all have legible labels. A garden for the active and fit, but worth the effort.

Hardwick Hall ★ 11

Doe Lea, Chesterfield S44 5QJ. Tel: (01246) 850430

The National Trust • 9½ m NW of Mansfield, 9½ m SE of Chesterfield. Approach from M1 junction 29 then A6175 • House open April to Oct, Wed, Thurs, Sat, Sun and Bank Holiday Mons, 12.30 – 5pm or sunset if earlier (last admission 4.30pm) • Garden open April to Oct, daily, 12 noon – 5.30pm. Country park open all year, daily, dawn – dusk • Entrance: £3, children £1.50 (house and garden £6, children £3). No reduction for parties • Other information: Refreshments in Great Kitchen on days hall is open. Dogs in park only, on lead. Limited access for wheelchairs ◑ ⬤ ✕ WC ♿ ♨ ♿

This famous Elizabethan mansion house was built by Bess of Hardwick and designed by Robert Smythson in the late sixteenth century. Mature yew hedges and stone walls provide necessary shelter to an otherwise exposed escarpment site. The borders of the South Court have spring-flowering shrubs to give colour for a longer period than herbaceous plants can provide. The West Court's herbaceous borders have strong, hot colours graduating to soft hues and are mainly late summer- and autumn-flowering. The herb garden is outstanding. The south-east quarter, originally part of the vegetable area, is now an orchard, and the north-east orchard has been progressively replanted with old varieties and crab apples. The grass is left long for the naturalised daffodils and other wild flowers.

The Herb Garden 12

Hall View Cottage, Hardstoft, Pilsley, Chesterfield S45 8AH.
Tel: (01246) 854268

Mrs Raynor • 3m SW of M1 junction 29, 6m SE of Chesterfield on B6039 Holmewood — Tibshelf road • Garden open 15th March to 28th Aug, daily except Tues, 10am — 5pm • Entrance: £1, children free ◑ 🍴 WC ♿ ⟳ ✿ 🛍

A rich herb garden in a rural setting with a now-established parterre. Three speciality gardens have been added: a physic garden, a scented pot-pourri garden and a lavender garden. A large range of herbs for sale, including some rare and unusual species. This garden is only a short distance from the other excellent herb garden at Hardwick Hall (see entry).

Kedleston Hall ★ 13

Kedleston, Derby DE22 5JH. Tel: (01332) 842191

The National Trust • 4½ m NW of Derby on Derby — Hulland road between A6 and A52. Signposted • Hall open 12 noon — 4.30pm • Garden open 11am — 6pm (opens 11am on Bank Holidays; last admission 4.30pm) • Park open April to Oct, daily, 11am — 6pm; Nov to 19th Dec, Sat and Sun only, 12 noon — 4pm. Garden open 3rd April to Oct, Sat — Wed, 11am — 6pm • Entrance: park (Thurs and Fri only) £2 per vehicle; park and garden £2.20, children £1; hall, park and garden £5, children £2.50, family ticket £12.50 (1999 prices) • Other information: Coaches must pre-book by writing to Property Manager. Electric stairclimber and Batricar available ◑ 🍴 ✕ WC ♿ 🛍 ☕

The ancient home of the Curzon family, their most famous member being George Nathaniel, Viceroy of India 1899-1905. The extensive gardens do not compete with this neo-classical Robert Adam palace, but are of mature parkland where the eye is always drawn to the house. The rhododendrons when in flower are worth seeing in their own right, otherwise visit the gardens as a pleasurable way not only to view Adam's magnificent south front but also the hexagonal-domed summerhouse, the orangery, the Venetian-windowed fishing house, the bridge across the lake, the aviary and slaughter-house — now a loggia — and the main gateway. The formal gardens have a sunken rose garden. The restored Sulphur Bath House, one of the earliest eighteenth-century landscape park features, is not accessible to the public.

Lea Gardens 14

Lea, Matlock DE4 5GH. Tel: (01629) 534380; Fax: (01629) 534260

Mr and Mrs Tye • 5m SE of Matlock E off A6 • Open 20th March to June, daily, 10am – 7pm; rest of year by appt • Entrance: £3, children 50p (season ticket £4) • Other information: Coaches by appt ◑ 🍵 WC 🔷 🅿️

This garden has a comprehensive collection of rhododendrons, azaleas, alpines and conifers all brought together here in a beautiful woodland setting. John Marsden Smedley started his rhododendron garden in 1935, inspired by his visits to Bodnant and Exbury. Under the Tye family the collection now comprises some 550 varieties of rhododendrons and azaleas in a much increased area. Excellent booklet with route for visitors.

Melbourne Hall Gardens ★ 15

Melbourne D73 1EN. Tel: (01332) 862502

Lord Ralph Kerr • 8m S of Derby between A514 and A453. off B587 in Melbourne • House open, Aug, daily except 4th, 7th, 14th, 21st, 2 – 5pm. £2.50, OAPs £2, children £1 • Garden open April to Sept, Wed, Sat, Sun and Bank Holiday Mons, 2 – 6pm • Entrance: £3, OAPs and children £2 ◑ 🍵 ✕ WC ♿ 🚻

There has been little alteration to the Rt Hon. Thomas Coke's formal plan so this is a visual record of a complete late seventeenth/early eighteenth-century design in the style of Le Nôtre laid out by London and Wise. It is in immaculate condition with avenues culminating in exquisite statuary and fountains, including a lead urn of The Four Seasons by van Nost, whose other lead statuary stands in niches of yew. A series of terraces runs down to a lake, the Great Basin. A grotto has an inscription thought to be that of Byron's troublesome mistress Caroline Lamb. Unique in English gardens is the Birdcage iron arbour of 1706 at the end of a long walk hedged with yews.

210 Nottingham Road 16

Woodlinkin, Langley Mill, Nottingham NG16 4HG. Tel: (01773) 714903

Mr and Mrs R. Brown • 12m NW of Nottingham, 4m N of Ilkeston on A610 • Open 11th June, 2 – 5pm • Entrance: £1.50 ◑

A plantsman's half-an-acre with an emphasis on shrub roses – the garden is packed with many good examples. Some rarer shrubs and trees. Geraniums, hellebores and hostas provide prolonged interest in the herbaceous section.

Pavilion Gardens 17

St John's Road, Buxton SK17 6XN. Tel: (01298) 23114

High Peak Borough Council • Near town centre • Open all year, daily • Entrance: free • Other information: Refreshments in complex ○ 🏪 WC ♿ 🔷 🚻

Twenty-three acres of landscaped municipal park, woodland and two ornamental lakes, this updated pleasure garden of 1871 has the distinction of having been laid out by Edward Milner of Sydenham (site of the Crystal Palace to whose designer, Paxton, Milner was chief assistant). The gardens are well maintained and the pleasing 1875 Octagon (now a conference centre) is a graceful backdrop. The conservatory is well stocked but, frankly, many find the colour schemes of the bedding plants harsh. However, there are band concerts to soothe shattered nerves. In the nearby Crescent, examples of the arcane art of well-dressing with flowers may be seen during July. A Heritage grant has aided a refurbishment programme costing £4 million over five years.

57 Portland Close   18

Mickleover DE3 5BR. Tel: (01332) 515450

Mr and Mrs A.L. Ritchie • From A5111 (Derby ring road) take A516. At first roundabout take B5020. In Mickleover turn right into Cavendish Way, then second left into Portland Close • Open by appt • Entrance: £1, children free ● ℘

A plantsman's small garden with something unusual in almost every inch. The knowledgeable owner propagates most of the huge variety of hostas, primulas, auriculas, violas and cyclamen. Alpines, sink gardens.

Renishaw Hall   19

Renishaw, Sheffield S21 3WB. Tel: (01246) 432042

Sir Reresby and Lady Sitwell • 6m SE of Sheffield, 5m NE of Chesterfield on A616. From M1 at junction 30, take A616 towards Sheffield for 3m through Renishaw • Open 21st to 24th April; then rest of April to 30th Sept, Fri – Sun and Bank Holiday Mons, all 10.30am – 4.30pm • Entrance: £3, OAPs/ children £2 • Other information: Sitwell museum, costume museum, gallery, craft workshops (combined ticket with garden, £5) ◑ ☕ ✕ WC ⅋ ⇪ ℘ 🛍 �️

For nearly 20 years Renishaw had 'the most northerly vineyard in western Europe'. Also astonishing to see at this northerly latitude and on top of a hill (albeit on a south-facing wall) are enormous specimens of *Acacia dealbata*, *Cytisus battandieri* and *Fremontodendron californicum*. There are other rare, slightly tender specimen shrubs, and presumably the fact that the soil is light, the aspect southerly and shelter provided by yew hedges and parkland trees, and the long, towering façade that acts as a windbreak against the north overcomes the disadvantages of latitude and height. Sir George Sitwell spent much of his life in Italy and hence this is the style he re-created at Renishaw nearly 100 years ago, all vividly described in Osbert Sitwell's memoirs. The sound of splashing water, always in the background, adds to the Italianate atmosphere, and the present owner has added a stupendous water jet to increase the effect. Good guide book by Sir Reresby Sitwell, who has enlarged the borders, introduced innovative planting (Sir George had rejected Miss Jekyll's designs as being too colourful) and linked the garden to the wood with new planting and paths. A nature trail leads into an avenue of camellias to classic temple, Gothick lodge, old sawmill, cave and lakes.

DEVON

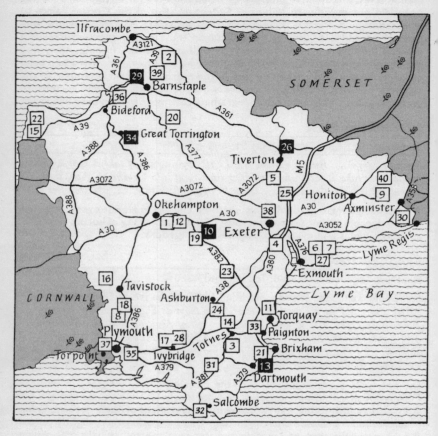

Two-starred gardens are marked on the map with a black square.

Andrew's Corner

1

Belstone, Okehampton EX20 1RD. Tel: (01837) 840332

Mr and Mrs R.J. Hill • 3m E of Okehampton off A30, signed to Belstone then Skaigh • Open 23rd, 30th April, 14th, 28th May, 4th, 11th June, 2.30 – 6pm, and by appt • Entrance: £1.50, children free • Other information: Teas on open days only ● ■ ᕼ ℘

Three hundred metres above sea level, on north Dartmoor, facing the Taw valley and across to the high moor, in only one and a half acres (amazing that it is not larger) grows a wide variety of plants of all sorts not normally seen at such an altitude. The sense of space is achieved by the division of the garden into different levels by rhododendrons and trees, each area being a small region with its own micro-climate, and all with glimpses through to other areas and to the wider landscape. Herbaceous plants and lilies, in spring flowering bulbs and meconopsis; in autumn colour from maples (many grown from seed) and gentians. There are dry-stone walls (a speciality of the area), a paved area and ponds with water plants; among the stone and paving are lewisias and other alpines. The owner does not like the description 'plantsman'; he says it is a hobby he loves.

Arlington Court   2

Arlington, Barnstaple EX31 4LP. Tel: (01271) 850296

The National Trust • 7m NE of Barnstaple on A39 • House open • Garden open April to Oct, daily except Sat (but open Sat of Bank Holiday weekends), 11am – 5.30pm (last admission $\frac{1}{2}$ hour before closing). Footpaths through woods and park open Nov to March during daylight hours • Entrance: garden and carriage museum £3.20, children £1.60 (house, museum and garden £5.20, children £2.60, family ticket £13 (2 adults and 2 children), parties of 15 or more £4.40 per person, children £2.20) (1999 prices) • Other information: Carriage Museum. Dogs in grounds only, on lead ◑ ☕ ✕ 🏠 <u>WC</u> ⅋ ⇪ ⏸ ♟

The Georgian house is set in a garden largely informal in design extending to 30 acres. The mild, damp climate, combined with acid soil, provides a perfect home for a wide range of plants, particularly rhododendrons, with many species of tree-like proportions. Hydrangeas also thrive here. In spring, drifts of bulbs carpet the grass, followed by wild flowers. The wilderness pond is surrounded by rhododendrons and offers views of the church. By contrast, the terraced Victorian garden is formal and symmetrical, with annual bedding. Double herbaceous border, rockery and conservatory. The one-acre walled kitchen garden is being restored, although at present the beds are cultivated.

Avenue Cottage Gardens   3

Ashprington, Totnes TQ9 7UT. Tel: (01803) 732769

Mr R.C.H. Soans and Mr R.J. Pitts • 3m S of Totnes. Take A381 from Totnes towards Kingsbridge, turn left to Ashprington. Facing Durant Arms in Ashprington turn left uphill past church; gardens are 300 metres on right • Open April to Sept, Tues – Sat, 11am – 5pm, and by appt • Entrance: £2, children 25p by collecting box ◑ 🏠 <u>WC</u> ⅋ ⇪

These were originally part of the eighteenth-century landscape gardens of Sharpham House, separated 50 years ago. They are approached along a splendid avenue of Turkey oaks planted in 1844. Many of the rhododendrons and azaleas planted in the last century are enormous and magnificent, but as parts of the garden had become very overgrown over the years a clearing programme was started. The new plantings are now developing and the garden is worth visiting at any time, although probably best in spring. The owners are always delighted to point out some of their more unusual treasures.

Bickham House 4

Kenn, Exeter EX6 7XL. Tel: (01392) 832671

Mr and Mrs John Tremlett • 6m S of Exeter on A38 before junction with A380. Leave dual carriageway at Kennford Services and follow signs to Kenn, then take first right and follow lane for ³/₄ m to end of no-through road • Open 19th, 21st, 22nd March, 16th, 18th, 19th April, 21st, 23rd, 24th May, 18th, 20th, 21st June, 16th, 18th, 19th July, 20th, 22nd, 23rd Aug, 10th, 12th, 13th Sept, 11am – 5pm and at other times by appt • Entrance: £2, children 50p ● ☕ 🍴 WC ♿ 🌿

Six acres of garden in a peaceful wooded valley, overlooking a small lake. The house has been in the family since it was built in 1682, but the garden has been extensively remodelled in the last few years, and new features are being added all the time. There are lawns and fine trees, spring-flowering shrubs and many naturalised bulbs. A box-hedged parterre around a lily pond is planted out with annuals twice each year. In the mixed borders great attention is paid to colour co-ordination. A colourful small water garden, and a walled garden of one acre with rose beds, a formal herb garden and a highly productive section, where vegetables and flowers are laid out in changing patterns every year, provide all-year-round interest.

Bickleigh Castle 5

Tiverton EX16 8RP. Tel: (01884) 855363

Mr O.N. Boxall • 4m S of Tiverton off A396. At Bickleigh Bridge take A3072 and follow signs • Castle and exhibitions open • Garden open 21st to 24th April; also 8th April to May, Wed, Sun and Bank Holiday Mons only; June to 3rd Oct, daily except Sat, all 2 – 5.30pm (last admissions 4.30pm) • Entrance: castle, garden £4, children (5-15) £2, family ticket £10, parties by appt ◑ ☕ ♿

Situated in the valley of the Exe around the ancient buildings, which are historically fascinating with much to see, the castle became the home of the Carew family, Sir George Carew being the Vice Admiral of the *Mary Rose*. Beyond the eighteenth-century Italian wrought-iron gates is a large mound planted in the 1930s with every known variety of rhododendron. There is a 300-year-old wisteria and many more mature trees including *Ginkgo biloba*, magnolias, a Judas tree and a tulip tree. Iris and water lilies in moat. The gardens are undergoing a five-year programme of restoration.

Bicton College of Agriculture 6

East Budleigh, Budleigh Salterton EX9 7BY.
Tel: (01395) 568353; Fax: (01395) 567502

2m N of Budleigh Salterton on A376 • Open all year, daily except 25th, 26th Dec, 11am – 4pm • Entrance: £2, children free (1999 prices) • Other information: Parking beyond student car park, short walk to garden ○ ☕ ⬦ 🌿

The gardens of this Georgian house form the horticultural department of Bicton College, and as such contain a large number of plants laid out for both study and general interest – truly a plantsman's paradise. As well as the fascinating herbaceous beds there is an arboretum with spring-flowering trees and an old walled garden with glasshouses, all approached by an avenue of araucarias (monkey puzzle trees). Amongst the plants which provide both information and effect are National Collections of agapanthus and pittosporums. Large area of parkland and a lake. Garden and arboretum guides available.

Bicton Park ★ 7

East Budleigh, Budleigh Salterton EX9 7BJ. Tel: (01395) 568465

Bicton Park • 2m N of Budleigh Salterton on B3178 • Open daily, 11am – 5pm. Closed for 2 weeks over Christmas and New Year • Entrance: £4.95, children (3-15) £2.95, family £13.75, concessions £3.95 ◗ 💷 ✕ 🖸 WC ♿ ♿ 🐾 🧺 ☕

There is much to see here in the 60 acres. The formal and informal gardens date from 1734; there is s Stream Garden with a 150-year-old mulberry, azaleas, camellias, flowering cherries and a peony border (bush and tree); an American Garden established in the 1830s with a snowdrop tree (*Halesia carolina*), calico bushes and a pocket-handkerchief tree (*Davidia involucrata*); a Hermitage Garden with lake and water garden; and a pinetum with some rare conifers, including a Mexican juniper, yuccas, Korean thuya and Tasmanian cedar. The pinetum was established in 1838 and extended in 1910 to take the collection of the famous botanist and explorer 'Chinese' Wilson. Perhaps Bicton's greatest glory is the Palm House, built between 1815 and 1820, one of the oldest in the country and recently refurbished; inside, Kentia palms up to seven metres, tree ferns and bromeliads, and outside an Assam tea plant. There are also geranium and fuchsia houses and a tropical and a temperate house for bananas, coffee trees and bougainvilleas. The new Museum of Garden History is due to open by Easter 2000, combining with the existing Museum of Country Life to make one of the largest museums in the West Country.

Buckland Abbey 8

Yelverton PL20 6EY. Tel: (01822) 853607

The National Trust and Plymouth City Council • 6m S of Tavistock, 11m N of Plymouth. Turn off A386 ¼ m S of Yelverton • Open April to Oct, daily except Thurs, 10.30am – 5.30pm, also Nov to Dec, Sat and Sun, 2 – 5pm (last admission ¼ hour before closing) • Entrance: £2.30, children £1 (abbey and grounds £4.40, children £2,20, family (2 adults, 2 children), £11). Increased charges (which also apply to NT members) when special events are in progress • Other information: Possible for wheelchairs but steep site. Motorised buggy may be available. Picnic in car park only ◑ 💷 ✕ WC ♿ 🧺 ☕

Buckland Abbey garden is largely a twentieth-century creation. There is a box hedge parterre between the 30-metre-long medieval barn and the abbey, its pockets filled with over 50 different herbs, reputedly inspired by Vita Sackville-West. *Magnolia delavayi* and *M. grandiflora* grow against the abbey. A line of ailing yews on the north border of the lawn is being replaced by an Elizabethan garden, and a thyme area has recently been created. Delightful estate walks. Close and distant views of Devon and Cornwall loom beyond the boundary.

Burrow Farm Gardens ★ 9

Dalwood, Axminster EX13 7ET. Tel: (01404) 831285

Mr and Mrs John Benger • 4m W of Axminster off A35 Honiton road. After 3½ m turn N near Shute garage onto Stockland road. Garden is ½ m on right • Open April to Sept, daily, 10am – 7pm • Entrance: £3, children 50p, parties (discount rate) by appt • Other information: Plants for sale in nursery ◑ 🐞 🗟 WC ♿ ⬥ ✑

These lovely gardens, created from pasture land, are the inspiration of Mary Benger and her family. The six-acre site is still being developed. Foliage effect was the prime consideration during the planning stages, and this has been admirably achieved with a colourful array of azaleas and rhododendrons. A former Roman clay pit is graded from top to bottom through mature trees and shrubs to an extensive bog garden with a marvellous show of candelabra primulas and native wild flowers during the early part of the season. In summer the pergola walk, with its old-fashioned roses and herbaceous borders, is a picture. A courtyard garden and a terraced garden have been added, with emphasis on late-flowering herbaceous plants. New for 2000 is the Rill Garden, a formal design with informal planting. The setting and sense of grandeur are more typical of gardens of greater repute. Magnificent views. Nearby, on the borders of Devon, Dorset and Somerset, is Homelea Farm, where *R&D Plants* has an inventive list of herbaceous and woodland plants. Open by appt in Feb for hellebores, then daily March to Oct 9am – 5pm (closed for lunch). Tel: (01460) 220206.

Castle Drogo ★★ 10

Drewsteignton EX6 6PB. Tel: (01647) 433306; Fax: (01647) 433186

The National Trust • 4m S of A30 or 4m NW of Moretonhampstead on A382, follow signs from Sandy Park • Shop • Castle open (but closed Fri) • Garden open April to Dec, daily, 10.30am – 5.30pm (last admission ½ hour before closing) • Entrance: £2.60 (castle extra). Reduced rate for parties by appt • Other information: Coaches by appt only. Disabled parking. Access for wheelchairs by arrangement at reception. Scented plants for visually handicapped. Croquet equipment for hire ◑ 🐞 ✕ 🗟 WC ✑ 🛍 ♨

The last castle to be built in England (begun 1910) was designed by Sir Edwin Lutyens. The plans for the planting of the garden were by George Dillistone of Tunbridge Wells. Apart from the evergreen oaks above the magnificent views over the Teign Gorge, and a valley planted with rhododendrons, magnolias, camellias, cornus and maples, there is a series of formal terraces and borders with walls of granite, sharp-edged yew hedges with rose beds and arbours of yew and *Parrotia persica* (the iron tree). In the main formal gardens, with galleries round a sunken centre, paths are serpentine (an Indian touch typical of Lutyens, who built New Delhi in the 1920s while he was supervising here), and herbaceous borders are full of old varieties of crocosmia (montbretia), lychnis, campanulas, iris and red-hot pokers. Under the granite walls are perennials – euphorbias, hellebores, alchemillas and veronicas – planted with spring bulbs. Steps lead to a second terrace with yuccas and wisterias and herb borders; more steps to shrub borders of lilacs, azaleas, magnolias and lilies; and finally comes a splendid circular lawn surrounded by a tall yew hedge at the top, a huge green circle and a perfect stage set for croquet.

Castle Tor   11

Oxlea Road, Wellswood, Torquay TQ1 2HF. Tel: (01803) 214858

Mr L. Stocks • In Torquay. From Higher Lincombe Road, turn E into Oxlea Road. Entrance is 200 metres on right with eagle-topped pillars • Open by appt • Entrance: £1, children 25p [NEW] ●

Half a century ago the then owner of Castle Tor approached Sir Edwin Lutyens and asked him to design a smaller version of Castle Drogo; being too busy himself, Sir Edwin nominated his pupil, Frederick Harrild, and the result is this fascinating architectural garden with magnificent views over Lyme Bay and Tor Bay. Gertrude Jekyll's ideas about garden colour – no violent juxtapositions or circular beds full of salvias – were incorporated, and the whole is framed in terraces of Somerset limestone (a pleasant change from granite) and cubic green walls of yew hedges; topiary is fashioned from both green and golden (Irish) yew. There are architectural-type follies: a pillared orangery with a domed roof, a tower with portcullis and gatehouse, and best of all a long ornamental water course or small canal. Over the years the owner has collected suitable statuary, and bright annual flowers are seen as acccents in urns and tubs against the stone background. About five years ago, Reg and Carole Burnside acquired the three lower terraces, flanking Lincombe Drive, and part of the round garden on the fourth terrace. They have constructed a magnificent residence in matching Somerset stone, called Lincombe Keep. It has received acclamation all round and won an architectural award. Visitors to Castle Tor are permitted to enter their part of the garden, which is maintained as a harmonious whole.

Cleave House   12

**Sticklepath, Okehampton EX20 2NN. Tel: (01837) 840481;
Fax: (01837) 840462**

Ann and Roger Bowden • 3½ m E of Okehampton on old A30 towards Exeter. House is in Sticklepath on left just past small right turn for Skaigh • Open for charity 29th, 30th April, 4th, 24th, 25th June, 10.30am – 5.30pm and at other times by appt • Entrance: £1.50 ● WC ⚥

For the Bowdens hostas are not just a business, they are an abiding passion. Their one-acre garden, tucked away at the heart of a small Devon village, boasts some delightful mixed planting – both trees and shrubs – but hostas are the dominant feature. Hostas are propagated by division from existing stock, while some are micro-propagated and grown on for two years. A few varieties, notably the brightly coloured, have been imported from the United States. This Mecca for the hosta enthusiast includes demonstration beds resplendent with over 500 different varieties, displaying fascinating variation of both colour and size. People from all over the world have made the pilgrimage to view the extensive range of plants on show and for sale, and to take advantage of the Bowden's specialist knowledge. The collection has been designated an NCCPG reference (of modern hybrids).

Coleton Fishacre Garden ★★   13

Brownstone Road, Kingswear, Dartmouth TQ6 0EQ. Tel/Fax: (01803) 752466

The National Trust • 3m E of Dartmouth, 4m S of Brixham off B3205. 2½ m from Kingswear, take Lower Ferry Road and turn off at toll house • House open as garden, 11am – 4pm. Possible timed tickets • Garden open March, Suns, 11am – 5pm; then April to Oct, Wed – Sun and Bank Holiday Mons, 10.30am – 5.30pm • Entrance: £3.60, children £1.80, pre-booked parties of 15 or more £2.90 per person (house and garden £4.60, children, £2.30, family ticket £11.50, pre-booked parties of 15 or more £3.80 per person) (1999 prices) ◑ ☕ WC ⅙ ⅌ 🛍 ♿

Oswald Milne, who was a pupil of Edwin Lutyens, designed the house and the architectural features of this garden for Rupert and Lady D'Oyly Carte; the house was completed and the garden begun in 1926. Exceptionally mild and sheltered, the setting is a Devon combe, sloping steeply to the cliff tops and the sea, and sheltered by belts of Monterey pines and holm oaks planted in 1923. The streams and ponds make a humid atmosphere for the moisture-loving plants like the magnificent bamboos (inch-thick canes) and mimosas, and many other sub-tropical plants rarely seen growing outside in this country. There is a collection of unusual trees like dawn redwood, swamp cypress and Chilean myrtle, and dominating all a tall tulip tree and tree of heaven (*Ailanthus altissima*) the same age as the house. The Paddock Woodland Walk runs from the Gazebo Walk near the house, through woodland to a main viewing area. Formal walls and terraces make a framework round the house for a large number of sun-loving tender plants. There are various water features, notably a stone-edged rill and a circular pool in the herbaceous-bordered walled garden. Scented herbs and plants. A brilliant garden.

Dartington Hall ★   14

Dartington, Totnes TQ9 6EL. Tel/Fax: (01803) 862367

Dartington Hall Trust • 2m NW of Totnes, E of A384 • Open all year, daily, dawn – dusk, parties by appt only • Entrance: by donation £2, guided tours by arrangement £4 • Other information: Coaches by appt ○ ☕ ✕ WC ⅙ ♿

In 1925, Leonard and Dorothy Elmhirst purchased the Dartington Hall estate to rescue it and the garden from decline. Over the years many notable garden designers have influenced the restoration, including the American Beatrix

Farrand, who was responsible for transforming the courtyard and opening up the woodland walkways. There are three walks, each using bay, yew and holly as background plantings for the collections of camellias, magnolias and rhododendrons. Percy Cane introduced such features as the glade, the azalea dell and the impressive magnolia steps. In more recent times Preben Jacobsen redesigned the herbaceous border and Philip Booth was commissioned to create the Japanese garden. The overall effect is strongly architectural, with the fourteenth-century tiltyard and its terraces at the heart.

Docton Mill ★   15

Lymebridge, Elmscott, Hartland EX39 6EA. Tel: (01237) 441369

Mr M.G. and Mrs E. Bourcier • 12m N of Bude, 14m W of Bideford off A39. From north Devon travel via Hartland to Stoke or from north Cornwall to West Country Inn, then turn left signed Elmscott towards Lymebridge in Spekes Valley • Open March to Oct, daily, 10am – 6pm • Entrance: £3, OAPS £2.75, children £1 ◖ ⬤ WC ⬤ ⬤

The garden was created from a derelict water mill of Saxon origin in 1980 by the previous owners, who embarked upon a large-scale clearance of the waterways; there are ponds, leats, footbridges over the river and many smaller streams as it is only 1500 metres from Spekes Mill Mouth coastal waterfall and the beach. A boggy area was drained to make a stream and a bog garden with ligularias, primulas and ferns; the whole purpose has been to make everything as natural as possible, integrating the garden into the wild. In spring there are displays of narcissi, camellias, primulas, azaleas and magnolias with bluebells; in summer the garden abounds in roses, mostly old shrub roses. There is a hedge of 'Felicia' and 'Pax' hybrid musk roses and a climbing 'Felicia' – a rarity. Roses are underplanted with many varieties of perennial geraniums, another favourite plant, and these are also used on the rockery (which is wet clay and north-facing and not suitable for alpines) together with hebes and dwarf conifers.

Endsleigh House and Gardens   16

Milton Abbot, Tavistock PL19 0PQ. Tel: (01822) 870248; Fax: (01822) 870502

Endsleigh Charitable Trust • 4m NW of Tavistock on B3362 • Gardens open April to Sept, Fri – Tues, 11am – 5pm, and by appt Wed and Thurs • Entrance: £3 (ticket machine) • Other information: Lunch and tea served at hotel by arrangement ◐ WC

Endsleigh was built, starting in 1811, for the 6th Duke of Bedford from designs by architect Jeffry Wyatville and landscape gardener Humphry Repton. The house is a good example of a *cottage orné* and was used as a fishing and hunting lodge by the Duke. It is now a quiet country house hotel popular with salmon fishermen. The house and the immediate garden have tight views overlooking the almost stream-like character of the upper Tamar, wooded on either bank. The garden is undergoing gradual restoration in an endeavour to re-establish the nineteenth-century vision. There is an uneasy truce between the rich wilderness that has invaded Repton's landscape and the slow process of ongoing authentication.

Rare tree species in the arboretum have largely survived the storms of the late 1980s. Buzzards and cormorants command the sky.

Fardel Manor   17

Ivybridge PL21 9HT. Tel: (01752) 892353; Fax: (01752) 894962

Dr A.G. Stevens • 1¼ m NW of Ivybridge off A38, 2m SE of Cornwood, 200 metres off railway bridge • Open 24th July, 11am – 4.30pm • Entrance: £1.50, children 50p ● 🖙 **WC** ♿ 🐾

A five-acre, all-organic garden, maintained with conservation and wildlife in mind. Small courtyards and a walled garden cluster around the fourteenth-century manor, with an orangery, herbaceous borders, a formal pond and a shrub garden. There are also enclosed fruit and vegetable gardens and an orchard with a wildflower meadow. A two-and-a-half-acre arboretum was planted during the 1980s, and a stream and lake with ornamental and native plantings create a habitat for waterfowl of all kinds.

The Garden House ★   18

Buckland Monachorum, Yelverton PL20 7LQ. Tel: (01822) 854769

The Fortescue Garden Trust • 10m N of Plymouth, 2m W of Yelverton off A386 • Open March to Oct, daily, 10.30am – 5pm • Entrance: £4, OAPs £3.50, children £1 ◑ **WC** 🐾

The Garden House occupies an unlikely spot, given its south Devon location, and provides a glorious summer show. It is largely north-facing and is nearly 150 metres above sea level; it also has to contend with up to 150 centimetres of rain per annum. The naturally acidic soil has become quite neutral due to the assiduous application of lime over the years – hence the great variety of plants. The evolution can be traced back to 1945 when Mr and Mrs Lionel Fortescue breathed life into a garden that had become derelict. Its walls, thatched barn and tower date from the sixteenth century, and, through years of painstaking restoration, this has now become one of the finest of its type in the country. In 1978, Keith and Ros Wiley came here and continued the work. The modification and planting programme since the 1980s has been quite remarkable. The walled garden now integrates with the remaining eight acres which, over the past two years, have been transformed by the planting of over 3000 trees and shrubs (most at least semi-mature), over 1000 herbaceous plants and thousands of spring bulbs. During the next two years the garden will undergo its final stage of evolution. There are plans for a stream and bog garden, a small lake, a peat garden, a wisteria wood and a water and courtyard garden. Lionel Fortescue, who died in 1981, would surely be impressed by the energy with which all this is being tackled.

Gidleigh Park ★   19

Chagford TQ13 8HH. Tel: (01647) 432367

Kay and Paul Henderson • Off A382 11m SE of Okehampton. In Chagford Square turn right into Mill Street by Lloyds Bank. In 150 metres fork right (virtually straight across junction). Go to end of the road – about 2m • Open all year except Bank Holidays, Mon – Fri • Entrance: £5 (inc. coffee or tea with biscuits) • Other information: Lunches and teas served in hotel ○ 🍵 ✕ WC ♿

Gidleigh Park, the acclaimed hotel and restaurant, is set in 45 acres of magnificent and secluded grounds on the north bank of the River Teign, within the Dartmoor National Park. The woodland garden and parkland were created between 1850 and 1930, but then fell into decay for the next 50 years. Since 1980, under the direction of head gardener Keith Mansfield, the owners have undertaken an extensive programme of restoration. Among the many interesting features is a delightful water garden rebuilt and planted in 1986, and extended significantly into the woodland in 1997. Visitors can take this in on their way round the Boundary Walk – a 45-minute stroll through natural mixed woodland, underplanted with azaleas and rhododendrons. The Teign is never far away, tumbling over granite boulders, past spring displays of rhododendrons. The mock-Tudor house gives way to a terrace resplendent with summer colour, while a parterre and herb garden add a touch of formality. There is an interesting avenue of young pleached limes (*Tilia platyphyllos*) adjacent to the front lawn and one must mention the croquet lawns, the very upmarket golf 'putting garden' opened in 1995 and extended in 1998, and the pavilion – the final decadent flourishes.

Glebe Cottage   20

Pixie Lane, Warkleigh, Umberleigh EX37 9DH.

Mrs Carol Klein • 10m SE of Barnstaple, 6m SW of South Molton, 1m N of Chittlehamholt on B3226 • Open early April to early Nov, Wed – Fri, 10am – 1pm, 2 – 5pm, but closed for two weeks in late May • Entrance: £1.50, children free ◑ ℘

Not far off the Tarka Trail, amid deepest Devon lanes and across a couple of fields it is a great delight to discover Carol Klein's romantic and exuberant cottage garden. The woodland glade with a trickling brook has ferns and shade-loving plants, while in front of the cottage are terraced beds and brick paths merging into each other, with traditional favourites and unusual plants rioting happily together in sympathetic colour schemes with many mauves and purples. There's a seat with roses and honeysuckle all around on which to sit, and hold hands should you feel so inclined. The nursery, which is small and intimate with a wide variety of irresistible and beautiful plants, has won five Chelsea gold medals.

Greenway House   21

Greenway Ferry, Churston Ferrers, Brixham TQ5 0ES.
Tel: (01803) 842382 (Greenway Gardens)

Mr and Mrs A.A. Hicks • 4m W of Brixham. From A3022 Paignton – Brixham road, take road to Galmpton, then towards Greenway Ferry • Garden opening times not agreed at time of going to press but will be different from 1999. Please check • Entrance: £2, children 50p (1999 prices) • Other information: Plants for sale in nursery. Parking limited ● ● WC ఈ ⊲ ♨

Another large (30-acre) and ancient Devon garden on a steep slope, here on the bank of the tree-lined Dart river which has woodland walks. There are many indigenous trees over 150 years old and a giant tulip tree. In the walled garden are many camellias, 30 varieties of magnolias, many ceanothus, wisterias and abutilons. The banks of primroses and bluebells make it magical in spring. On the Georgian façade are *Magnolia grandiflora, Akebia quinata* and *Mutisia oligodon*, in the natural glades foxgloves, white iris, herb Roberts, pennyworts, ivies and hart's tongue and male ferns. The house was Agatha Christie's home for many years.

Hartland Abbey   22

Nr Bideford, EX39 6DT. Tel: (01237) 441264/234 (administrator)

Sir Hugh and Lady Stucley • 15m SW of Bideford off A39 Bideford – Bude road. Follow signs to Hartland; drive through village, take road to Hartland Quay. Signposted • House and grounds open 23rd, 24th April, then May to Sept, Wed, Thurs, Sun (plus July and Aug, Tues), all 2 – 5.30pm. Other times by appt • Entrance: gardens and grounds £2.75, children £1.50 (house £4.50) [NEW] ◑ ● WC ♨ ⛪

Once an Augustinian monastery, the abbey is set across a narrow sheltered valley. Because of the gales, gardens were not created around the house – although a row of 100-year-old bay trees survives – but were planted either side of the valley with azaleas, rhododendrons, camellias, hydrangeas, gunnera and many other shrubs and trees. Some of the paths were designed by Gertrude Jekyll, and the Victorian fernery, also thought to be by Jekyll, who used to be a guest at the Abbey, was replanted in the spring of 1999. The series of walled gardens are set in a south-facing, gently sloping valley five minutes' walk away; vegetables, herbaceous plants, roses and clematis, plus self-seeded giant echiums, 12 feet tall. The walk to the Atlantic over a mile away gives stunning views of the rugged coastline.

Higher Knowle   23

Lustleigh, Newton Abbot TQ13 9SP. Tel: (01647) 277275

Mr and Mrs D.R.A. Quicke • 13m NW of Torquay, 8m NW of Newton Abbot, 3m NW of Bovey Tracey on A382 towards Moretonhampstead. After 2½ m, turn left at Kelly Cross for Lustleigh; after ¼ m left then right at Brookfield along Knowle Road; after ¼ m steep drive on left • Open Sun and Bank Holiday Mons from 26th March to 29th May, 2 – 6pm for NGS, and by appt between these dates • Entrance: £2.50, children free ● ● WC ⊲

A three-acre woodland garden surrounding a stone house built in 1914 with many Lutyens-style features by his pupil Fred Harrild as architect. Situated on a steep hillside with spectacular views over the Bovey valley to Dartmoor, the sheltered garden usually avoids late frosts and is home to tender plants. The old oak wood is carpeted with primroses and bluebells in the spring, with mature Asiatic magnolias providing a fine display in late March, followed by camellias, new hybrid magnolias, many rhododendrons and azaleas, and tall embothriums. Giant Dartmoor granite boulders add much natural sculpture to the woodland walks, which include a water garden. Plants are labelled. Not far away is *Pleasant View Nursery*, near Denbury, which also has a show garden for National Collections of abelias and salvias [Open May to Sept, Wed and Fri, 2 – 5pm].

Hill House Nursery and Garden ★ 24

Landscove, Ashburton, Newton Abbot TQ13 7LY. Tel: (01803) 762273

Mr and Mrs Raymond Hubbard • 17m SW of Exeter. From Plymouth-bound A38, take second exit signed Ashburton, then left signed 'Landscove' 2½ m, or from A384 Totnes – Buckfastleigh road follow signs to Landscove. Signposted • Open all year, daily, 11am – 5pm. Booking required for parties • Entrance: free • Other information: Tea room open March to Sept only ○ 🍴 🖼 WC ♿ ✿

The house and the adjoining church are Gothic-style buildings designed by the architect of Truro cathedral, John Loughborough Pearson. The garden is largely the brainchild of the late-lamented Edward Hyams, who featured Hill House in his book *An Englishman's Garden*. Since the early 1980s the present owners have been restoring Hyams's garden, endeavouring to continue his emphasis on the exotic and the unusual. In spring a giant cedar protects a mass of snowdrops and cyclamen, while daffodils stand like sentinels along peripheral woodland walks. Colour abounds right up to Christmas and it is quite amazing that so many tender varieties – salvias, unusual magnolias and vulnerable roses to name but a few – appear to flourish within sight of Dartmoor. The conservatory bordering the pond has been rebuilt to Hyams's original design and contains a grapevine, passion flowers and a lemon tree. The garden temple (thought to date from the eighteenth century) is to be restored. An integral feature of the garden is the commercial nursery. There are over 1670 square metres of glasshouses providing the ideal micro-climate for a colourful profusion of exotic plants. The display beds of fuchsias, rare passion flowers, salvias and many more are a joy to behold (note also the display beds in the car park).

Killerton ★ 25

Broadclyst, Exeter EX5 3LE. Tel: (01392) 881345

The National Trust • 7m NE of Exeter, on W side of B3181 • House and costume museum open 13th March to Oct, daily except Tues, 11am – 5.30pm (last admission ½ hour before closing) • Park and garden open all year, 10.30am – dusk • Entrance: £3.50, Nov to Feb reduced rate (house and garden £5) (1999 prices) • Other information: Licensed refreshments when house is open. Tea room limited opening in winter. Motorised buggies with drivers available for disabled. Dogs in park only, on lead ○ 🍴 ✕ 🖼 WC ♿ ✿ 🎁 🍺

This large hillside garden surrounded by woods, park and farmland extends to over 6000 acres. It was created by John Veitch in the 1770s and later involved the famous Victorian gardening writer William Robinson. The actual garden area of 18 acres will provide pleasure and interest to all but particularly to the tree and shrub enthusiast; it is a haven of delight. Beside the avenue of beeches, there are Wellingtonias (the first plantings in England), Lawson cypresses, oaks, maples and many fine broadleaved trees. Trees and shrubs introduced by Veitch are now reaching an imposing size. Terraced beds and extensive herbaceous borders provide summer colour. Killerton has a rhododendron collection with 95 different species, many brought back from China and Japan. The collection is currently undergoing restoration, propagating and renewing those that are under threat or already lost. There is also an early nineteenth-century summerhouse, the Bear's Hut, ice-house and rock garden. The fine chapel has its own grounds extending to three acres containing many other fine trees. Of note is the largest tulip tree in England. Nearby is *Little Upcot*, Marsh Green, a two-acre plantsman's garden, open by appointment (Tel: (01404) 822797).

Knightshayes ★★ 26

Bolham, Tiverton EX16 7RQ. Tel: (01884) 254665 (Property Manager); (01884) 253264 (Tel/Fax Garden Office)

The National Trust • 16m N of Exeter, 2m N of Tiverton. Turn off A396 at Bolham • House and gardens open 1 April to Oct, daily, 11am – 5.30pm. House closed Fri but open 21st April; Oct, 11am – 4.30pm (closed Thurs and Fri); Nov and Dec, Sun for pre-booked parties only, 2 – 4pm • Entrance: house and gardens, £5.20, children £2.60; gardens only £3.60, children £1.80 (1999 prices) • Other information: Dogs in park and Impey Walk only, on lead ◐ ☕ ✗ 🖻 <u>WC</u> & ⚘ 🎪 ⚑

This wonderful garden is the setting for a red sandstone house designed by the Victorian architect William Burges. His flamboyant style is seen in the stables with their fairytale Gothic tower clothed in yellow ivy. The garden was transformed from the 1950s by Sir John and Lady Amory. The terraces have shrub roses, tree peonies and herbaceous plants in soft colours and silvers. Yew encloses a paved garden planted in pink, purple and grey with two standard wisterias. Battlemented hedges frame the Pool Garden with a back-drop of *Acer pseudoplatanus* 'Brilliantissimum'. On the lower terrace, topiary hounds endlessly chase a fox. Good progress is being made with the Victorian walled garden. The Garden in the Wood is a magical place sheltering magnolias, rhododendrons, cornus, hydrangeas and many rare and tender plants, some grown in raised peat blocks. Drifts of pink erythroniums, white foxgloves and cyclamen appear in their seasons.

Lee Ford 27

Budleigh Salterton EX9 7AJ. Tel: (01395) 445894; Fax: (01395) 441100

Mr and Mrs N. Lindsay-Fynn • 3½ m E of Exmouth on B3178 Budleigh Salterton – Knowle road • Open 4th June, 1.30 – 5.30pm for charity, but by prior application only, and for parties by appt • Entrance: £2.50, OAPs £2, children £1.50. Pre-booked parties of 20 or more £2 per person • Other information: Teas on charity open day only. Coffee or teas for parties by arrangement ● WC ⬦

Inspired by the Savill Gardens at Windsor (see entry in Surrey), the present owner's father developed this woodland garden in the 1950s and 1960s; it is one of the longest-established open-to-the-public gardens in Devon. Although at its peak in spring, with acres of daffodils followed by rhododendrons, azaleas and magnolias, there is plenty to see later in the year. Following much recent landscaping, the formal garden round the house merges enchantingly into the woodland rising above it, with curving beds full of new planting that includes collections of hydrangeas and fuchsias, together with many grasses and a bog garden. In the woodland, with its fine tall trees and distant views of the sea, the mown glades are surrounded by masses of azaleas, species and ponticum rhododendrons, some rare, and there is a large collection of camellias, some from the Channel Islands, including white camellias which are often in flower on Christmas Day. The nineteenth-century walled garden is still run as a traditional vegetable garden, with flowers for cutting and greenhouses; there is also a conservatory, an Adam pavilion and a little herb garden, and further developments are promised.

Lukesland 28

Harford, Ivybridge PL21 0JF. Tel: (01752) 893390

Mr and Mrs B.N. Howell ● *1½ m N of Ivybridge off A38, on Harford road. On E side of Erme valley* ● *Open 16th April to 11th June, Wed, Sun and Bank Holiday Mons, 2 – 6pm* ● *Entrance: £2.90, children free. Other information: coaches by appt* ● ▉ WC ♿ ⬦

More a botanical park than a garden, on entering the grounds you could be forgiven for believing you were in the foothills of the Himalayas. Lying on the hem of Dartmoor, where an uneasy truce is preserved between the wilderness of the moor and the surrounding farmland, Lukesland is Victorian in both origin and taste. The house was built in 1862 in the Victorian Gothic style by W.E. Matthews. The delightfully secluded valley of the Addicombe Brook is the setting here for 15 acres of flowering shrubs, trees and carpets of wild flowers – a gem of its kind. This is primarily a spring garden, though recent planting has ensured a greater variety of all-year interest. But it is in spring that the profusion of rhododendrons, camellias and azaleas show the garden at its resplendent best. The magnificent *Magnolia campbellii*, over 21 metres tall, is one of the many fine specimen trees. The pocket-handkerchief tree, planted in 1936, is thought to be one of the tallest in the country. Addicombe Brook, which tumbles and gurgles its way over ponds and waterfalls, is criss-crossed by a series of delightful bridges which enable the visitor to wander at leisure amid scenes of great tranquillity. James McAndrew undertook the first major landscaping of the garden in the 1880s. In recent years Brian Howell (whose father continued McAndrew's work in the 1930s) and family have been involved in more planting, including a fine pinetum, and in the construction of more ponds and bridges, all in the spirit of the original. One of the finest gardens of its type in the South-West. Also near Ivybridge is the *Endsleigh Garden Centre*, worth a visit.

Marwood Hill ★★   29

Marwood, Barnstaple EX31 4EB. Tel: (01271) 342528

Dr J.A. Smart • 4m NW of Barnstaple off A361. Signposted • Open all year, daily except 25th Dec, dawn – dusk • Entrance: £3, accompanied children under 12 free • Other information: Teas on Sun and Bank Holidays or for parties by arrangement ○ 🍵 WC ⏤ 🔎

With its wonderful collection of plants this 20-acre garden is of special interest to the connoisseur but could not fail to give pleasure to any visitor. Five thousand different varieties of plants covering collections of willows, ferns, magnolias, eucryphias, rhododendrons and hebes, and a fine collection of camellias in a glasshouse. There is also a large planting of eucalyptus and betulas. Other features include a recently built pergola with 12 varieties of wisteria, raised alpine scree beds, and three small lakes with an extensive bog garden and National Collections of astilbes, clematis, *Iris ensata*, and tulbaghias. The garden has matured considerably in the last few years and the collections have been augmented continually. To quote the excellent guide book, 'there is an element of a botanic garden about Marwood Hill'. There is a wealth of interesting plants to discover and note, and the valley setting is a delight to the eye.

The Moorings   30

Rocombe, Lyme Regis, Dorset DT7 3RR. Tel: (01297) 443295

Mr and Mrs A. Marriage • 2m NW of Lyme Regis. Take A3070 out of Lyme Regis, turn right to Rocombe and Rhode Hill. After ½ m fork left (unsuitable for Heavy Goods Vehicles). Fourth house on right, drive is beyond house • Visitors welcome any time, but please telephone or call in advance • Entrance: £1, accompanied children free ● ⏤

Especially rewarding to visit in spring and autumn, this garden has been made by the owner since 1961 out of three small fields on a sheltered, steep, west-facing slope. Impressively, most of the newly planted arboretum trees have been grown from seed; there is a collection of eucalyptus, many unusual pines including umbrella and maritime pines (grown from seed gathered in the south of France) and nothofagus, including *N. obliqua* and *N. procera*, and the woodland is underplanted with snowdrops, daffodils and bluebells. *Hibiscus paramutabilis*, a hardy shrub with large flowers in August, is very rare in this country; there are camellias and a 10-metre-high magnolia, and a buddleia flowering rose-red in June. A great point of interest is the collection of many different species of fern, nearly all grown from spores.

The Old Rectory   31

Woodleigh, Loddiswell TQ7 4DG. Tel: (01548) 550387

Mr and Mrs H.E. Morton • 3½ m N of Kingsbridge off A381, E of Kingsbridge – Wrangaton road at Rake Cross (1m S of Loddiswell), 1½ m from Woodleigh itself • Open by appt only • Entrance: £1, children 20p ● ♿

A three-acre woodland garden, and walled garden, rescued from neglect nearly 40 years ago. In the woodland are several individual glades of mature trees, underplanted with magnolias, azaleas, camellias and rhododendrons. Evergreens and shrubs are planted for scent and winter effect, and the wild garden is most colourful in spring with crocus and daffodils, while the walled garden is designed with summer in mind. The garden is a haven for wildlife; no chemicals are used and it is managed without outside help.

Overbecks Museum and Garden ★ 32

Sharpitor, Salcombe TQ8 8LW. Tel: (01548) 842893

The National Trust • 1½ m S of Salcombe, SW to South Sands • Museum open April to Sept, daily except Sat (but open 22nd April and daily in Aug), 11am – 5.30pm; Oct, Sun – Thurs, 11am – 5pm • Garden open all year, daily • Entrance: £2.80 (museum and garden £4) • Other information: No coaches ○ 🐸 🖥 WC ♿ 🌿 🏢 ⚱

Palms stand in this exotic garden high above the Salcombe estuary, giving a strongly Mediterranean atmosphere. The mild maritime climate enables it to be filled with exotics such as myrtles, daturas, agaves and an example of the large camphor tree, *Cinnamomum camphora*, a great rarity. The Himalayan *Magnolia campbellii* is over 100 years old and 12 metres high and wide and a sight to see in Feb/March. The steep terraces were built in 1901 and lead down through fuchsia trees, huge fruiting banana palms and myrtle trees to a wonderful *Cornus kousa*. In formal beds near the house are Chatham Island forget-me-nots – *Myosotidium hortensia* (hydrangea-like) with flowers as clear as blue china – phormiums, and tender roses among the rocks. There is a new parterre of classical design, using the traditional coloured gravels surrounded by box, and enlivened with orange and lemon trees in season.

Paignton Zoo Environmental Park 33

**Totnes Road, Paignton TQ4 7EU. Tel: (01803) 697500;
Fax: (01803) 523457**

The Whitley Wildlife Conservation Trust • 1m W of centre of Paignton on Totnes Road • Open all year, daily except 25th Dec from 10am (closing times vary according to season) • Entrance: £7, OAPs £5.40, children £4.90 (1999 prices). Rates for parties available ○ 🐸 ✕ 🖥 WC ♿ 🏢 ⚱

Those with mixed views on zoos may be won over by Paignton; it is in the forefront of animal and plant conservation and one of the zoos worldwide involved in the breeding of endangered species. As well as the healthy and happy animals there are the plants. Over 100 acres in size, this was the first zoo in the country to combine animals and a botanic garden, laid out 60 years ago and added to over the years. There are six habitat areas: wetland, arid, savannah, forest, rainforest and Devon woodland. In addition an arboretum is being developed to a 25-year programme. The choice of plants has been dictated by their harmlessness to teeth and beaks and their ability to provide shade and perching, swinging and basking places. There are geographical collections of plants in the paddocks, and plants also make the fences safer. Hardy Chinese plants surround the baboon rocks. National Collections of sorbarias and buddleias. One of the large glasshouses contains a desert exhibit with plants from arid areas providing habitat for birds and reptiles. In the next few years, a new display will be added, a generic tropical forest, to give visitors the experience of this very different environment.

RHS Garden Rosemoor ★★   34

Great Torrington EX38 8PH. Tel: (01805) 624067

The Royal Horticultural Society • 7m SE of Bideford, 1m SE of Great Torrington on B3124 • Garden open all year, daily except 25th Dec • Entrance: £4, children £1 ○ 🍴 ✗ 🏠 WC ♿ ⚲ ♨ ♟

Given to the RHS by Lady Anne Berry, who created the original plantsman's garden here, Rosemoor was the Society's first regional garden and centre, second in importance only to Wisley, with which it has a certain stylistic affinity. Lectures, talks, garden walks and demonstrations are held throughout the year. The 40 acres include a new formal garden with 2000 roses in 200 varieties, colour-theme gardens, herb garden, *potager*, cottage garden, foliage garden, winter garden, alpine terrace and extensive herbaceous borders. The new foliage garden displays a wide range of plants grown mainly for their leaves, particularly grasses. Elsewhere are stream and bog gardens and a large walled fruit and vegetable garden. Lady Anne's original eight acres contain over 3500 plants from all over the world, many collected by her. National Collections of ilex (holly, over 100 kinds) and cornus (dogwood) are planted throughout. The *Rosemoor Explorer* and *Senior Explorer* are free guides to the garden for children aged 6 to 10 and 11 to 15. There are also many events, including a Roy Lancaster talk and an opera. A great 'Garden of Information' in the making, getting better every year.

Saltram House   35

Plympton, Plymouth PL7 1UH. Tel: (01752) 336546; Fax: (01752) 336474

The National Trust • 3m E of Plymouth. From A379 turn N to Billacombe. After 1m turn left to Saltram • House open as garden from 27th March at 12 noon • Garden open one weekend in March (please phone for details); 27th March to Oct, Sun – Thurs and 21st April, 10.30am – 5.30pm (last admission 5pm) • Entrance: £2.70 (house and garden £5.70). Parking £1.50 (1999 prices) ◑ 🍴 ✗ 🏠 WC ♿ ⚲ ♟ ♟

The original garden dates from the 1740s, with a Victorian and twentieth-century overlay; there are three eighteenth-century buildings – a castle or belvedere, an orangery (due to the mild climate the orange and lemon trees are moved outside in the summer) and a classical garden house named Fanny's Bower after Fanny Burney, who came here in 1789 in the entourage of George III. There is a long lime avenue underplanted with narcissi in spring and *Cyclamen hederifolium* in autumn, and a central glade with specimen trees like the stone pine and Himalayan spruce. There is a beech grove, a Melancholy Walk, and walks with magnolias, camellias, rhododendrons and Japanese maples which, with other trees, make for dramatic autumn colour. Tree walk guide available.

Tapeley Park ★   36

Instow EX39 4NT. Tel: (01271) 342558

Mr H.T.C. Christie • 2m N of Bideford S off A39 Barnstaple – Bideford road • House open for pre-booked parties. £2 per person • Gardens open 19th March to Oct, daily except Sat, 10am – 5pm • Entrance: £3.50, OAPs £3, children £2. Special rates for parties ◑ 🍵 🍴 WC ㅅ 🐦 🎪 🛍 ⚲

The house is basically William and Mary, set on a splendid site above the River Torridge and Bideford, with much to see and a family with a fascinating history – the Christies of Glyndebourne. There are three formal terraces, an Italian garden with ornamental water, yew hedges, an ilex tunnel, a shell house, ice-house, and a variety of roses, fuchsias, lavenders and dahlias, as well as more exotic plants like *Abelia floribunda*, sophora and feijoa from Brazil. On the south of the house are yuccas, *Magnolia grandiflora*, agapanthus and mimosas; on the east, wisteria and *Drimys winteri*, a fragrant evergreen. A woodland walk is lined with camellias, hydrangeas and rhododendrons, with primroses and primulas in spring under the giant beeches and oaks; this leads to a pond covered in late summer with water lilies, backed by tall firs and *Thuya plicata*. Walled kitchen garden. An exciting restoration of the gardens is underway with the help of Mary Keen.

Tudor Rose Tea Rooms and Garden   37

36 New Street, The Barbican, Plymouth PL1 2NA.

Plymouth Corporation • In old town centre • Open all year, daily, 10am – 6pm • Entrance: free ○ 🐦

An integral part of an area of Plymouth that is being refurbished, this is an interesting reconstruction of the type of Tudor garden that would have existed behind the house in this ancient street. As far as possible only plants which grew in Elizabethan England have been established. Elsewhere in Plymouth the Corporation commemorates great Victorian seaside gardening with colourful carpet bedding by traditional methods.

University of Exeter ★   38

Streatham Farm, Prince of Wales Road, Exeter EX4 4PX.
Tel: (01392) 263059; Fax: (01392) 264547

University of Exeter • On N outskirts of Exeter on A396, turn E on to B3183 • Gardens open all year, daily • Entrance: free • Other information: Coaches by appt only ○ 🐦

There is much to see on a one-mile tour of these extensive gardens based on those created in the 1860s by an East India Merchant millionaire who inherited a fortune made by blockade-running in the Napoleonic Wars. The landscaping and tree planting was carried out by Veitch, whose plant collectors (E.H. 'Chinese' Wilson among them) went all over the world, and at that time many of the trees were unique in Europe. There is a series of lakes with wildfowl, dogwoods, birches, hazels and alders, callistemon shrubs (bottle brushes), wingnut trees (*Pterocarya stenoptera*) brought from China in 1860, and a maidenhair tree (*Gingko biloba*) sacred in Buddhist China. Rockeries have collections of alpines; there is a banana tree (*Musa basjoo*), a large *Gunnera chilensis* and palm trees introduced by Robert Fortune in 1849. Formal gardens and bedding plants lead to a sunken, scented garden. Exeter will house the National Collection of azaras, evergreens from Chile, with scented yellow flowers. There are, of course, rhododendrons, magnolias, camellias in a woodland walk; roses, eucalyptus and *Opuntia humifusa*, the prickly pear cactus flowering in summer. A useful nursery is *St Bridgets*, of Old Rydon Lane and Clyst St Mary, Exeter. Palm enthusiasts should make an appointment to visit *Palm Garden*, Tel: (01392) 467015. The three small gardens cluster round the central palm house.

Woodside 39

Higher Raleigh Road, Barnstaple EX31 4JA. Tel: (01271) 343095

Mr and Mrs M. Feesey • Off A39 Barnstaple – Lynton road, turn right 300 metres above fire station • Open 9th July, 2 – 5.30pm for charity and at other times by appt • Entrance: £1.50, children 50p ☻

South-facing semi-woodland with intensive shrub planting and many ornamental grasses, bamboos and monocots (owner is author of RHS book on oriental grasses). Much is shaded and peaceful with good protection for tender shrubs. A collection of New Zealand flora and acid-loving shrubs; also raised beds and troughs, ornamental trees and conifers – all with emphasis on form and foliage colour.

Wylmington Hayes Gardens ★ 40

Wilmington, Honiton EX14 9JZ. Tel: (01404) 831751

Mr and Mrs P. Saunders • 5½ m N of Honiton. From A30 turn right, signed Stockland 3 and Axminster 10. After 3½ m entrance is on right, before Stockland TV mast • Open 14th, 28th May, 4th June, 2 – 5pm • Entrance: £3, wheelchair visitors and children £1 ☻ 🖾 WC ⚘ 🍴

Eighty-three acres of reclaimed gardens and woodland originally created in 1911. There is much to interest both the dedicated gardener and those who merely seek a quiet stroll amid lovely surroundings. For the gardener there are spectacular hybrid rhododendrons, azaleas, magnolias, camellias and acers; there are also some majestic trees, including numerous oaks, a pockethandkerchief tree, tree peonies, tulip trees and several sequoias. Two woodland walks – one short, one longer – extend to the extremities of the garden. Of particular interest is the Italian garden. The influence of water is apparent for all to see. There are several small ponds (some containing koi carp) and a fine lake which is home to an interesting collection of ornamental and domestic waterfowl, including black swans.

DORSET

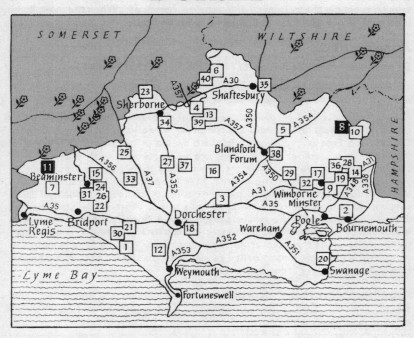

Two-starred gardens are marked on the map with a black square.

Abbotsbury Sub-Tropical Gardens ★   1

Abbotsbury, Weymouth DT3 4LA. Tel: (01305) 871387

Ilchester Estates • 9m NW of Weymouth, 9m SW of Dorchester off B3157 • Open March to Oct, daily, 10am – 6pm; Nov to Feb, daily except 25th, 26th Dec and 1st Jan, 10am – dusk • Entrance: £4.40, OAPs £4, children £2.50, family ticket £12 (1999 prices). Party bookings discount available ○ 🍽 ✕ 🖻 <u>WC</u> & ⬦ ⚘ 🛍 ⚘

Proximity to the sea helps to provide the micro-climate which makes Abbotsbury so special. Within its 20 acres there is much of interest to the plantsperson in the many rare species on display, while those less specialised can get pleasure from the banks of colour and the shaded walks – particularly in the spring, but also at other seasons. People travel a long way to visit these gardens – often called 'sub-tropical', but probably technically better described as 'wet Mediterranean'. The new visitor centre, shop and restaurant (called Old Colonial) are an excellent bonus for the many coach parties who come for both gardens and the nearby swannery (not to be missed when open); there is also a woodland trail and a children's play area. The redesigned plant sales area, while not extensive, has a range of healthy stock on display. There are several events in the evenings – Shakespeare, opera, etc. When the overall aim is so high it is a pity that the labelling is hit and miss.

Arnmore House 2

57 Lansdowne Road, Bournemouth BH1 1RN. Tel: (01202) 551440

Mr and Mrs David Hellewell • On B3064 just S of hospital • Open all year, by appt • Entrance: £1.50, children free ◐ ♿

This highly individual garden has been created over the past 25 years by its owner and reflects his interests as a composer who also has a strong feeling for Chinese art. Ease of maintenance has also been a priority as Mrs Hellewell is disabled. Shape, colour and texture are all-important, with many unusual specimen trees, topiary and box parterres. Trees and shrubs, many chosen for year-round colour and grown in pots, have been pruned and trained to give the desired effect. The formal parterre consists of neat diagonals of *Buxus sempervirens* complemented by clipped balls of *B.s.* 'Aureovariegata'. Visitors will be impressed with the garden's originality. A booklet, *Evolution of a garden*, is available. If you are an agapanthus fan, you can by appointment, all year, visit Dr and Mrs Slade's garden at *46 Roslin Road South*, also in Bournemouth; a plantsman's third-of-an-acre walled garden with many rare and unusual items as well as a kitchen garden and greenhouses.

Athelhampton House Gardens ★ 3

Athelhampton, Dorchester DT2 7LG. Tel: (01305) 848363;
Fax: (01305) 848135

Patrick Cooke • 5m E of Dorchester, 1m E of Puddletown on A35 • House and gardens open March to Nov, daily except Sat, 10.30am – 5pm; also Nov to Feb, Sun • Entrance: £3.50, children free (house and garden £4.95, OAPs £4.60, children £1.50, parties of 12 or more £3.95 per person) • Other information: Picnics in riverside area only ◐ ☕ ✕ 🖼 WC ♿ ♪ 🏬 ☇

The garden of this medieval manor house was rescued and redesigned by Alfred Cart de La Fontaine in 1891, a process continued by subsequent owners, latterly the late Robert Cooke. Courts and walls follow the original plan with beautiful stonework in walls and arches. Apart from some of the most impressive topiary in England there are also pools, fountains, a rectangular canal with water lilies and a pleached lime walk. Tulips, rambling roses, clematis and jasmine (in their seasons) make it memorable. The gardens are encircled by the River Piddle and on the west lawn stands a sixteenth-century dovecot.

Cartref 4

Station Road, Stalbridge, Sturminster Newton DT10 2RG.
Tel: (01963) 363705

Mrs Nesta Ann Smith • 10m SE of Shaftesbury. From A30 at Henstridge traffic lights turn S for 1m to Stalbridge. Turn left opposite PO; house is 80 metres on right • Open April to Sept by appt • Entrance: £2, children free ◐ 🖼 WC ♪

If one is to question what makes a good garden, a visit to this quarter acre behind an unassuming semi-detached village house has the answer for inveterate collectors. In this comparatively small area, winding paths, lawn and small woodland are crammed with clearly labelled rarities, each tree is a framework for interesting climbers, and the microclimate encourages plants such as *Cytisus battandieri*, *Poncirus trifoliata* and terrestrial orchids. The owner is happy to talk about plants from their provenance to maintenance; her vast knowledge is gleaned from experience gained by working in well-known nurseries under such masters as Jim Archibald and the hosta expert, Eric Smith. Many of the varieties are for sale.

Chettle House 5

Chettle, Blandford Forum DT11 8DB. Tel: (01258) 830209;
Fax: (01258) 830380

Mr and Mrs P. Bourke • 6m NE of Blandford on A354, turn left to Chettle • House open • Garden open 21st April to 2nd Oct, daily except Tues and Sat, 11am – 5pm. Closed 4th – 11th July • Entrance: £2.50, children free. Discount entry with Larmer Tree Gardens (see entry in Wiltshire) ◑ ☕ ✕ 🏠 WC ♿ 🐾 ⌖

Beyond the wide lawns framing this impressive Queen Anne house (designed by Thomas Archer of rounded style and inverted scrolls fame), vistas appropriate to that period are preserved, with a vineyard on the south slope. Lavish herbaceous borders contain many chalk-loving plants (some rare), including no fewer than 20 varieties of honeysuckle, a buddleia collection, and some fine clematis. The owners are always on the lookout for the unusual, and plants seen in the garden are sometimes available for sale in the plant centre. The tranquil site is approached through mature trees where a number of different horse chestnut species may be seen. There is an elegant church in the grounds.

Chiffchaffs 6

Chaffeymoor, Bourton, Gillingham SP8 5BY. Tel: (01747) 840841

Mr and Mrs K.R. Potts • 3m E of Wincanton. Leave A303 (Bourton bypass) at sign marked 'Bourton' and continue to end of village • Garden open April to Sept, Wed, Thurs; also 5th March, 2nd, 16th, 22nd, 24th April; 1st, 7th, 21st, 28th, 29th May, 4th, 18th June, 2nd July, 6th, 27th, 28th Aug, 3rd Sept, 1st Oct; all 2 – 5pm. Also by appt • Entrance: £2, children 50p • Other information: Refreshments and toilet facilities for groups only ◑ 🐾

An impressive avenue of flowering cherries leads to the house and garden, full of colour and interest, immaculately maintained, with an invitation to more pleasures at each turn of the path. The terraces and viewpoints afford glimpses of open country around, and the varied and colourful beds and borders are delightful. The underplanting in the woodland area is interesting and, in the garden, the collection of dwarf bulbs, dwarf rhododendrons, old-fashioned roses and a wide range of herbaceous plants is noteworthy. 12 acres in all. The nursery is well stocked with a wide variety of healthy-looking plants.

The Coach House ★   7

Bettiscombe, Bridport DJ6 5NT. Tel: (01308) 868560

*Mrs P. Hobhouse • 5m W of Beaminster off B3164 Broadwindsor –
Birdsmoorgate road. Take narrow lane S signed Shave Cross and Bettiscombe •
Open for garden tours for parties by appt only • Entrance: fee by arrangement* ☻

The owner has used her well-known professional skills to transform a simple
walled garden and small field into areas of elegance which reflect her particular
concern for structural plants with a painter's eye for colour associations.
Formal beds, laid on gravel, are packed with interest, and lavish climbers
adorn trellises and old brick walls. Grass avenues through wildflower planting
in the former field are punctuated with urns; secluded arbours have been
established to satisfy visitors wishing to observe this inspirational garden from
a quiet corner. Although open only rarely, this is a garden which plantspersons
should make every effort to see.

Cranborne Manor Garden ★★   8

Cranborne, Wimborne Minster BH21 5PP. Tel: (01725) 517248

*Viscount and Viscountess Cranborne • 10m N of Wimborne on B3078. Entrance
via garden centre • Garden open March to Sept, Wed only, 9am – 5pm and
some weekends for charity – telephone to check dates • Entrance: £3, OAPs £2.50
• Plants for sale in garden centre open all year* ☻ 🍴 WC ⚘ 🛒

Tradescant established the basic framework in the early seventeenth century,
but little is left of the original plan. Neglected for a long period, the garden has
been revived in the last three generations and now includes several smaller
areas surrounded by tall clipped yew hedges, a walled white garden at its best
in midsummer, wide lawns (again yew-lined) and extensive woodland and wild
areas. Best of all is the high-walled entrance courtyard to the south which is
approached through an arch between the two Jacobean gatehouses. Here the
plant selection along the lengthy borders is delightfully imaginative, providing
the perfect introduction to what has been called 'the most magical house in
Dorset' (not least for the garden which surrounds it). The excellent nursery
garden specialises in traditional rose varieties, but also carries a wide selection
of other plants, particularly clematis and herbaceous perennials.

Dean's Court   9

Wimborne Minster BH21 1EE.

*Sir Michael and Lady Hanham • In centre of Wimborne off B3073 • For open
dates and times contact Wimborne Tourist Information (Tel: (01202) 886116) •
Entrance: £2, OAPs £1.50, children 50p (1999 prices)* ☻ 🍴 WC ⚘ 🛒

A mellow brick house set in 13 acres of parkland containing a number of
interesting and very large trees. A swamp cypress towers near the house, also
a 28-metre tulip tree which flowers from June to July. The many fine specimens
include Wellingtonias, Caucasian wing nut, Japanese pagoda tree, blue cedars
and horse chestnuts. There are few formal beds, but a courtyard contains an

unusually comprehensive herb garden with over 250 different plants. The walled kitchen garden, in which many of the old varieties of vegetable are grown by chemical-free methods, is extensive and obviously successful. A monastic stewpond where the medieval monks bred their carp can still be seen in this peaceful haven just a few metres from a busy town centre.

Edmondsham House 10

Edmondsham, Cranborne, Wimborne Minster BH21 5RE. Tel: (01725) 517207

Mrs J. Smith • 1m S of Cranborne. From A354 turn at Sixpenny Handley crossroads to Ringwood and Cranborne • House open Easter Sun, Bank Hol Mons, also April and Oct, Wed, 2 – 5pm • Garden open probably April to Oct, Wed and Sun, 2 – 5pm. Also by appt • Entrance: £1, children 50p (house and garden £3, children £1, under 5 free) (1999 prices) • Other information: Refreshments April and Oct, Wed only ◑ 🍴 **WC** ⅋ ⅋

The visitor should allow time for a tour of the interesting family house and dairy before venturing out into the large walled kitchen garden. No chemical fertilisers or pesticides are used here. Beds of Russian comfrey, rhubarb, Jerusalem artichokes, asparagus, herb gardens and a fruit cage can all be studied before taking the path to the lean-to peach house. The 'Pit House' is the sunken greenhouse – restored in 1990. The arch of the walled garden leads to Cowleaze, the paddock and later the drive and the dell. The pond (dry in hot summers) has an island of *Sasa palmata* and a dawn redwood (*Metasequoia glyptostroboides*). (The 'dawn' is the common name and refers to the Dawn of Time). An unusual circular grass hollow is said to be a cockpit, one of only a very few 'naturalised' areas of the sort in the country. The massed spring bulbs together with the many spring-flowering shrubs make this the best season to visit, but the peaceful, mellow atmosphere pervades the garden at all seasons. Also allow time to visit the church to look for the clumps of mistletoe and two unusual trees, *Magnolia acuminata* (cucumber tree) and *Paulownia tomentosa* (foxglove tree).

Forde Abbey ★★ 11

Chard, Somerset TA20 4LU. Tel: (01460) 221290

Mr M. Roper • 7m W of Crewkerne, 4m SE of Chard off A30 • House open March to Oct, Wed, Sun, and Bank Holidays • Garden open all year, daily, 10am – 4.30pm • Entrance: £3.75, OAPs £3.50, children free. Parties £3.30 per person (house and garden £5, OAPs £4.70, children free. Parties of 20 or more £4 per person) (1999 prices) ○ 🍵 🍴 **WC** ⅋ ⅋ ⅋ ⅋ ⅋

This unique and fascinating former Cistercian abbey, inhabited as a private house since 1649, is set in a varied and pleasing garden. Old walls and colourful borders, wide sloping lawns, lush ponds and cascades, graceful statuary and huge mature trees combine to create an atmosphere of timeless elegance. There is something here for every gardener to appreciate: the bog garden displays a large collection of primulas and other Asiatic plants; the shrubbery contains a variety of magnolias, rhododendrons and other delightful specimens. The rock garden was revolutionised by the late Jack Drake, and a fine arboretum has been built up since 1947; at the back of the abbey is an extensive kitchen garden and a nursery selling rare and unusual plants which look in fine health. Allow plenty of time as the grounds extend to 30 acres in all.

Friars Way 12

Church Street, Upwey, Weymouth DT3 5QE. Tel: (01305) 813243

Les and Christina Scott • 4m N of Weymouth off A354. In Upwey opposite church • Open April to Sept, Thurs, 2 – 6pm, also some Thurs for NGS; parties and private visits by appt • Entrance: £1.50 ◗ ⌐

This half-acre garden on a steeply sloping, south-facing alkaline site is a treasure house of unusual plants. Work on the present garden was started in 1991, and every year since a new area has been developed. Visitors are greeted by a high rock wall planted to give colour from spring to late autumn. Walls, terracing and meandering gravel paths enhance the setting for the choicest of plants. An old apple tree provides dry shade for plants which thrive in such conditions. A scented garden contains perfumed roses such as R. 'Cécile Brünner', R. 'Ferdinand Pichard', R. 'Graham Thomas' and many others, together with daphnes, lavenders, thymes and nepetas. There is a small wildlife pond with appropriate planting, and a hot dry area planted with various cistus where the colours of larger shrubs are highlighted by underplanting with perennials such as *Knautia macedonica* and *Aster* x *frikartii* 'Mönch'. Over 100 varieties of geranium. A border with plants relating to the seventeenth century (when the cottage was built) has been developed. A wide range of plants seen in the garden is for sale in the garden nursery, many grown from seed.

Frith House 13

Stalbridge, Sturminster Newton DT10 2SD. Tel: (01963) 250232

Urban Stephenson • 12m W of Shaftesbury, between Milborne Port and Stalbridge, 1m S of A30 or turn west by Stalbridge PO, 2m along narrow lane, lodge on left • Open for parties in coaches or cars by appt only • Entrance: £1.50 children free • Other information: Plants occasionally for sale ◗ ⬤ 🏠 WC ♿ ⬦ ⌐

In an open valley surrounded by unspoilt pastoral views, this friendly Edwardian house lies beneath a shelter belt of woodland and looks south across sweeping lawns studded with orchard trees and fine old cedars. The four-acre grounds are very well maintained, in particular the immaculately trimmed yew hedges and the shrub borders within sunny walled areas. Below the terrace is a bed filled with a striking array of 20-year-old scarlet 'Frensham' roses; there is also an excellent kitchen garden, and shady avenues to enjoy on the woodland walk. Further down are two lakes, fed by a stone conduit, which have been developed as an ornamental area of shrubs and water plants. Pleasant grassy walks surround the lakes, where crayfish are bred.

Highbury 14

Woodside Road, West Moors, Ferndown BH22 0LY. Tel: (01202) 874372; Fax: (01202) 874370

Mr Stanley Cherry • 8m N of Bournemouth off B3072. In Woodside Road, last road at N end of West Moors • Open April to Sept by appt • Entrance: 75p (pre-booked parties for house and garden £1 per person inc. teas) ● WC ℗

A woodland garden of half-an-acre in a mature setting, surrounding an interesting Edwardian house, 1909, which is also shown. There are unusual plants and shrubs with ground cover. Good labelling.

Horn Park 15

Beaminster DT8 3HB. Tel: (01308) 862212

Mr and Mrs John Kirkpatrick • 1½ m N of Beaminster on A3066 on left before tunnel • Open probably April to Oct, Sun – Thurs, 2 – 6pm • Entrance: £3.50 • Other information: Teas for parties by arrangement ◖ 🕭 WC ᵭ ⬠ ℗

Although the impressive house by a pupil of Lutyens dates from 1910, the garden is a developing re-creation based partly on features discovered as the work progresses. A drive through parkland leads to the wide gravel sweep before the entrance porch, with terraced lawns to the front of the house and a panoramic view east and south towards Beaminster and the distant coast. Other features include rock areas, herbaceous and rose borders, unusual plants and shrubs, a water garden beneath a steep azalea bank, ponds, a woodland garden and walks with wild flowers, including orchids and bluebells in spring. The natural wildflower meadow is listed as a site of nature conservation interest, with over 160 different wild flowers and grasses.

Ivy Cottage ★ 16

Aller Lane, Ansty, Dorchester DT2 7PX. Tel/Fax: (01258) 880053

Anne and Alan Stevens • 12m NE of Dorchester, 10m W of Blandford, 6½ m N of Puddletown, 5m NW of Milborne St Andrew, 4m W of Milton Abbas. Take turning near Fox Inn, Ansty • Open April to Oct, Thurs, 10am – 5pm and some Suns for NGS. Parties by appt only • Entrance: on Thurs, £2, on Suns, £2.50 (combined with Aller Green – see overleaf) • Other information: Teas on Suns only ● 🕭 WC ⬠ ℗

Mrs Stevens trained and worked as a professional gardener before coming to her cottage over 30 years ago. Although chalk underlies the surrounding land, this one-and-three-quarter-acre garden is actually on greensand; it has springs and a stream that keep it well watered and is therefore an ideal home for plants such as primulas, irises, gunneras, and in particular trollius and moisture-loving lobelias. A thriving and ordered vegetable garden (which hardly ever needs a hose), large herbaceous borders giving colour all year round, drifts of bulbs and other spring plants surrounding specimen trees and shrubs, and three most interesting raised beds for alpines. This garden has justifiably been featured in print and on television, and merits a wide détour. Just up the road is *Aller Green*, a typical peaceful Dorset cottage garden of approximately one acre in an old orchard setting. The two share some charity opening days with a combined admission charge, and both cottages are particularly worth seeing in their autumn colours.

Kingston Lacy ★   17

Wimborne Minster BH21 4EA. Tel: (01202) 883402

The National Trust • 1½ m NW of Wimborne on B3082 • House open late March to Oct, Sat – Wed, 12 noon – 5.30pm (last admission 4.30pm) • Park and garden open late March to Oct, daily, 11am – 6pm; Nov to 17th Dec, Sat and Sun, 11am – 4pm; telephone for details of Jan to March opening • Entrance: £2.50, children £1.25 (house, garden and park: £6, children £3, family (2 adults and up to 3 children) £15, parties of 15 or more £5 per person, children £2.50) • Other information: Self-drive vehicle available for disabled. Dogs in park only, on lead ◐ 🍽 ✕ 🏠 WC ᕙ ⚲ 👍 ⚑

The garden has recovered well from tree loss in the 1990 storms, and there is a laurel walk and an ancient lime avenue. Spectacular roses near the restaurant. The Trust has planted extensive Victorian ground-cover, and overall the maintenance is to a high standard. In spring, there are many areas of bulbs in the 250-acre park to enjoy. The sunken garden has been restored to the 1906 plan. The terrace displays urns, vases and lions in bronze and marble. There are six interesting marble wellheads or tubs for bay trees, also an Egyptian obelisk and a sarcophagus. The small informal Dutch Garden was laid out in 1899 for the then Mrs Bankes in memory of her husband and is still planted in the seasonal schemes designed for her. The restored Victorian fernery leads to the once fine Cedar Walk, where one of the trees was planted by the Duke of Wellington in 1827, others by visiting royalty and family members. Good circular woodland walk.

Kingston Maurward Gardens ★   18

Dorchester DT2 8PY. Tel: (01305) 215003

Kingston Maurward Gardens • E of Dorchester off A35. Turn off at roundabout at end of bypass • Open 12th March to 29th Oct, daily, 10am – 5.30pm. Guided tours by appt • Entrance: £3.75, children £2, under 3 free. Family season tickets available (gardens and farm animal park) ◑ 🍽 ✕ 🏠 WC ᕙ ⚲ 👍 ⚑

The original parkland around Kingston Maurward encompasses 32 acres of specimen trees, water features and woodland, and overlooks the water meadows of the Frome Valley. The formal gardens to the west of the house were laid out between 1910 and 1915 by the Hanbury family, who also owned La Mortola in Italy. The splendid stone terraces, balustrading, steps and yew hedges have been used to create many intimate gardens and carefully planned vistas. Extensive refurbishment of the stone features has taken place, with the statuary on long loan from the Palace of Westminster and the Grecian temple recarved from the original design. The gardens contain a large collection of roses, herbaceous perennials and half-hardy plants, including National Collections of penstemons and salvias. Large drifts of spring bulbs, cyclamen and autumn crocus surround fine specimen trees. There is a tree trail with 65 different species represented and the original large lake has a nature trail around its margin, giving superb views of the gardens and water meadows. The garden is entered through the animal park, which has an interesting collection of unusual breeds, set in a beautiful wooded paddock overlooking Stinsford Church of Hardy fame. The author's birthplace, *Hardy's Cottage*, a National Trust property with a small garden and walk through the woods, is nearby (open 24th April to 1st Nov, daily except Fri and Sat (but open 21st April), 11am – 5pm or dusk if earlier).

Knoll Gardens and Nursery ★   19

Hampreston, Wimborne Minster BH21 7ND. Tel: (01202) 873931;
Fax: (01202) 870842; Web: www.knollgardens.co.uk

Mr Neil Lucas • Between Wimborne and Ferndown, off Ham Lane (B3073). Leave A31 at Canford Bottom roundabout. Signed 1½ m • Gardens open March, Wed – Sun, 10am – 4pm; April to Oct, daily, 10am – 5.30pm; Nov to 25th Dec, Wed – Fri, Sun, 10am – 4pm • Entrance: £3.50, OAPs £3, students £2.50, children (5-15) £1.75, family (2 adults and 2 children) £8.50 (1999 prices). Reductions for parties of 20 or more ⏲ ☕ ✕ <u>WC</u> ♿ ⚘ 🏪 ♀

Twenty-five years ago this was a private botanic garden, but is now laid out in an informal English setting with mature specimen trees and shrubs giving a relaxed and intimate atmosphere. Although only a little over four acres, the many different areas, winding pathways and constantly changing views give an impression of a much larger area. The owners continue to develop the garden and its plant collections, particularly with hardy perennials and grasses. The summer garden has a collection of exotic-looking tender perennials, the water garden has several waterfalls and large koi carp, and the penstemon walk is a summer-long delight. There are areas planted specifically for dry shade, for moisture, and most recently, a gravel garden for drought-tolerant plants. National Collections of deciduous ceanothus and phygelius. The attached specialist nursery, which predates the garden, was originally a market garden.

The Knoll House   20

Studland Bay BH19 3AH. Tel: (01929) 450450

Ferguson family • 2m NE of Swanage between Studland and Sandbanks ferry • Hotel open Easter to Oct • Garden open 20th, 21st May for NGS • Entrance: £2, children free ● ☕ WC ♿ ⬧ ♀

A family-run hotel with an interesting history and approximately 100 acres of grounds. The gardens, including eight acres at Studland Bay House across the road, have magnificent views over the bay to the Isle of Wight, and are surrounded by National Trust land, a nature reserve and Purbeck Heritage Coast. Following storm damage, the family replanted extensively and imaginatively, and the glades and clearings now impart a sense of intimacy, with carefully placed seating creating peaceful arbours for quiet reflection. There is a delightful azalea walk, magnificent rhododendrons and specimen trees.

Langebride House 21

Long Bredy, Dorchester DT2 9HU. Tel: (01308) 482257

Mrs Greener • Off A35 Dorchester – Bridport road, turn S to Long Bredy • Open two Suns for NGS and during March to July by appt • Entrance: £2 ● ➥ WC &

This garden has so many desirable features it is impossible to avoid making a list: 200-year-old copper beech rising from wide, lush lawns, underplanted with carpets of spring bulbs; a thriving enclosed vegetable garden of manageable size, backing onto a sloping grass area with colourful mixed borders along the tile-topped walls; a rising slope to the mixed wild woodland behind, where favourite trees have been planted in groups to allow for culling as they enlarge; a formal yew-lined lawn with pond, fountain and old stone features, from which steps descend through sloping shrubberies towards the front of the house; a miniature area of greensand allowing a patch of acid-loving plants to provide contrast; a long line of pleached limes running parallel with the bicolour beech hedge along the road. There is a sloping orchard, a tennis court with a tall rockery behind as a viewing point and sun-trap, beds and borders, trellises for climbing plants and low stone walls for those that prefer to hang. All around, thousands of bulbs hide in waiting for the spring explosion which, in the owner's opinion, is the best season to visit.

Loscombe House 22

Bridport DT6 3TL. Tel: (01308) 488361

Mr and Mrs Andrewes • 3m N of Bridport, 2m SE of Beaminster, 1m E of A3066. In Melplash take Loscombe turn opposite Half Moon Inn and after ½ m turn right at Loscombe sign. Continue 2m to bottom of lane • Open April to Sept, Sat – Tues, 11am – 6pm • Entrance: free (donations to RNIB welcome) ◐ 🖻

Once a 'lost combe', this is Dorset at its most rural. Set in a four-acre site, the garden has a background of hills which drop down close to the boundary. Hillside tree-planting undertaken in 1970 has now developed into woodland, improved from 1984 when the valley bog was drained. An attractive flowing stream is a focus, with winding grass paths among well-maintained and decorative shrubs and perennials, including roses, clematis and hostas, sustained by the micro-climate within this sheltered site. A delightful, peaceful scene, far indeed from the madding crowd.

The Manor House 23

Sandford Orcas, Sherborne DT9 4SB. Tel: (01963) 220206

Sir Mervyn Medlycott, Bt • 2½ m N of Sherborne, turning off B3148, next to village church • House open • Garden open 24th April, 10am – 6pm, then May to Sept, Sun, 2 – 6pm and Mon, 10am – 6pm. Also by appt for parties at other times • Entrance: £1 (house and garden £2.50, children £1). Reduced rates for pre-booked parties of 10 or more ◐ 🍴 WC ♨

Looked at purely as a garden, this is not exceptional. An old, flagged path slopes up between bordered lawns towards an open field. The stone walls at either side are attractive, and where they stop the eye travels on into the countryside beyond. There is a herb garden with small box-bordered beds and a pleasant view across a lower lawn along the south side of the house. At the end of this lawn another viewpoint back towards the south front allows the attractive planting below the herb garden to show at its best. Roses and other climbing plants clinging to the honey-grey walls harmonise well with this gracious setting. It is the house, ancient and redolent of its long history, which permeates the scene and transforms the garden.

Mapperton ★ 24

Beaminster DT8 3NR. Tel: (01308) 862645; Fax: (01308) 863348

The Earl and Countess of Sandwich • 5m NE of Bridport, 2m SE of Beaminster • House open to parties of 15 or more by appt • Plants for sale • Garden open March to Oct, daily, 2 – 6pm. Garden tours available by prior appt • Entrance: £3.50, children (5-18) £1.50, under 5 free. Tour with gardener can be arranged in advance ◐ 🍴 WC ♿ 🐾 🧺

A garden with a difference, running down a gradually steepening valley dominated by the delightful sixteenth/seventeenth-century manor house. Terraces in brick and stone descend through formal Italian-style borders towards a summerhouse, which itself stands high above two huge fish ponds. On all sides there is topiary in yew and box. Beyond the ponds, the valley becomes a shrubbery and arboretum, most of it planted since the 1950s. Some statuary depicting animals and birds, both natural and stylistic. Numerous ornaments (many supplied by a local firm founded in 1885) provide interest and surprise.

Melbury House 25

Melbury Sampford, Dorchester DT2 0LF. Tel: (01935) 83699 (Garden Office)

Mr James and The Hon. Mrs Townshend • 13m N of Dorchester on A37 Yeovil – Dorchester road. Signposted • Open 11th, 25th May, 8th, 22nd June, 6th, 27th July, 10th Aug, 2 – 5pm • Entrance: £3, OAPs and children £2 • Other information: Guided walks on normal open days at no charge, and by arrangement for parties of up to 15 at £3.50 per person ◑ 🍴 WC 🐾

This historic house (not open to the public) is approached by a long drive through open parkland. Visitors are directed to the west side and enter through the large walled garden, a good part still maintained as a productive kitchen garden. A walk through the western part of the arboretum leads to the bottom of the south lawn with fine views of the house and across the lake to the deer park. The main part of the arboretum with its massed spring bulbs lies to the east in the Valley Garden, overlooked by the ancient family church (open). Herbaceous borders along the south of the house lead to a colourful walled flower garden. Recent seasons have seen much replanting so this garden will be a source of continuous interest. *Frampton Roses* nursery (Tel: (01300) 320453) is 5m away off A356 Dorchester road.

Melplash Court 26

Melplash, Bridport DT6 3UH. Tel: (01308) 488418

Mr and Mrs T. Lewis • 5m N of Bridport on A3066 • Open probably May/ June, 23rd July, 2 – 6pm for charity and by appt • Entrance: £2.50 ● 💭 WC ☒ ⬚ ⚘

The elegant sixteenth-century house, set among the Dorset hills with the sea over the horizon, is approached through an avenue of mature trees. The owners have respected plans for the garden as laid out by the previous owner, Lady Diana Tiarks, but have extensively restored and extended the area so that new planting is a feature without disturbing the general concept. On the whole, muted colours are preferred and expressed in a wonderful variety of foliage, particularly on the banks above the stream garden. Each section, including the outstanding Japanese garden, is a surprise as the visitor progresses via walled areas into carefully planned bedding that dramatises the sloping contours. A walled kitchen garden features knots where again leaf shape, in the form of rhubarb, leek, cabbage, angelica, creates attractive patterns. Maintenance is first class and the overall effect impressive.

Minterne 27

Minterne Magna, Dorchester DT2 7AU. Tel: (01300) 341370

Lord Digby • 9m N of Dorchester, 2m N of Cerne Abbas on A352 • Open 28th March to 10th Nov, daily, 10am – 7pm • Entrance: £3, children (accompanied only) free ◗ WC ⬚

An interesting collection of Himalayan rhododendrons and azaleas, spring bulbs, cherries and maples. Many rare trees. One and a half miles of walks with palm trees, cedars, beeches, etc. Alas, no labelling to help the amateur. The first half of the walk can be disappointing in midsummer, although evidence remains of some spectacular spring colour and tree colour in autumn should be special. At the lower end of the valley the stream with its lakes and waterfalls is surrounded by splendid tall trees, among which the paths wind back towards the house. The lakes contain many water lilies and ducks have been introduced to deal with the duckweed. A restful and attractive atmosphere.

The Moorings

(see Devon)

Moulin Huet 28

15 Heatherdown Road, West Moors BH22 0BX. Tel: (01202) 875760

Mr H. Judd • 8m N of Bournemouth. Leave A31 at West Moors Garage into Pinehurst Road, take first right into Uplands Road, then third left into

*Heatherdown Road, then into cul-de-sac • Open May to Sept by appt only •
Entrance: 70p, children free ● WC ♛*

Mr Judd (over 90 years old) and his late wife built their garden from open heath
over 20 years. Although only a third of an acre and triangular in shape, it seems
to stretch and enlarge as the visitor is conducted from area to area through
archways and along winding paths. All the plants, some of them quite rare,
have been grown from seed or cuttings. There is also a fine collection of bonsai,
grown with great success by Mr Judd's own unique method which apparently
defies all the rules.

The Old Mill   29

Spetisbury, Blandford Forum DT11 9DF. Tel: (01258) 453939

*The Rev. and Mrs J. Hamilton-Brown • Take A350 Blandford – Poole road.
Opposite Spetisbury school, sign marked 'Footpath' • Open for charity 21st May,
9th July, 2 – 5pm, and on other days by appt. Parties welcome • Entrance: £2,
children free ● ● ● WC ⚘*

For best effect approach along the public footpath, a narrow concrete bridge
just over a metre above the undulating grass. From this vantage point the
visitor can immediately appreciate the quiet mill stream glowing with well-
chosen water-loving plants along its banks, the ponds and dips sheltering
lushly planted boggy areas, the graceful willows rising and weeping above
banks of balsam, rushes and tall grasses, the River Stour flowing clear and full
inches below the mown lawns. Water predominates (and sometimes overwhelms) in this appealing garden, developed over two decades.

The Old Rectory   30

Litton Cheney, Dorchester DT2 9AH. Tel: (01308) 482383

*Mr and Mrs Hugh Lindsay • 9m W of Dorchester, 1m S of A35, beside Litton
Cheney church • Probably open 23rd April and other days for charity in May
and June, 2 – 6pm. Also April to June by appt • Entrance: £2, children free
● ✕ WC ⚘ ⚘ ⚘*

The Rectory rests comfortably below the church and is approached by a gravel
drive which circles a small lawn. A thatched summerhouse stands to one side
like a massive beehive. A small walled garden has outhouses and a large barn on
two sides and borders around three, prolifically stocked with well-chosen and
favourite plants in specific colour bands. A steep path leads down into the four
acres of natural woodland, a surprisingly extensive area of mature trees with
many springs, streams and ponds – never a water shortage here, even in the
driest of summers. This area was reclaimed by the current owners, who are
adding new young trees and shrubs as well as successfully encouraging many
spring-flowering plant colonies, mostly native. Climbing back up to the house,
the visitor arrives at the belvedere giving views over trees to farmland on the
other side of the valley. Spring and autumn are the best times to see this
garden, from which Reynolds Stone, the wood-engraver, drew inspiration.

Parnham House ★ 31

Beaminster DT8 3NA. Tel: (01308) 862204

Mr and Mrs J. Makepeace • ½ m S of Beaminster on A3066 • House and workshop open • Open April to Oct, Tues – Thurs, Sun and Bank Holiday Mons, 10am – 5pm. Parties by appt only on Tues and Thurs • Entrance: £5, children (10-15) £2, under 10 free (house, workshop and garden) ◐ 💬 ✕ 🍴 WC ㋐ ⬧ 🏛 ♀

The imposing stone terracing to the south of the house frames the many large clipped yews through which descend spring-fed water channels. A wide lawn leads to a balustrade and a small lake. There are large woodland and wild areas to the north and east, and sheltered borders along the brick wall of the old kitchen garden – the earliest part. Here Mrs Makepeace has used her gift for colour and form to create some splendid displays, notable as much for their shape and texture as for the well-chosen colour schemes. There are also delightful small and large courtyards to the south with interesting plantings. John Makepeace is the noted furniture designer.

The Priest's House Museum 32

23–27 High Street, Wimborne Minster BH21 1HR. Tel: (01202) 882533

The Priest's House Museum • In centre of Wimborne • Museum open • Garden open April to Oct, Mon – Sat, 10.30am – 5pm; also June to Sept, Sun, 2 – 5pm • Entrance: £2.25, OAPs £1.75, children £1 (museum and garden) • Other information: Refreshments in summer only ◐ 💬 🍴 WC ㋐ 🏛 ♀

In the heart of this small town lies a 100-metre-long walled garden, hidden from the busy shopping thoroughfare by the frontage of the Museum. Both are well worth a visit. A long narrow level garden laid out with some formal beds but mostly lawn, herbaceous and herb borders. There are a few unusual plants (some unlabelled due to thieving visitors). In late spring the wisteria on the back of the house is particularly appealing. Sit on one of the seats dotted around and enjoy the peaceful atmosphere in this well-cared-for garden staffed by volunteers who are only too pleased to answer questions about the plants.

Rampisham Manor 33

Nr Dorchester DT2 0PT. Tel: (01935) 83612

Mr and Mrs Raymond Boileau • 12m NW of Dorchester off A37. After 7m turn right towards Evershot; in village turn left to Rampisham and follow signs into village. House is next to church • Open for NGS 26th April, 30th Aug, 2 – 5pm, 2nd July, 2 – 6pm • Entrance: £2.50, children 50p • Other information: coaches by arrangement [NEW] ◐ 💬

Set in a curve of hills in deep countryside, this three-acre garden complements the views beyond its boundaries. Laid out anew by its owners some eight years ago, it has now matured into a delightful meandering of formal and flowing planting. There is hardly a straight line anywhere, but hedges, distinctively shaped and immaculately pruned, provide both backdrop and windbreaks for excellent shrub planting. A parterre of 'Iceberg' roses on the level near the house leads towards a dominant feature – a giant stone arch that divides two areas. Beyond it, sloping lawns surround a large oval fish pond, with serpentine beds of roses and clever ground cover beyond. Good foliage contrast and harmonious colour schemes add to the pleasure. There is a little gravelled knot garden near the house, and a rockery.

Sherborne Castle 34

Sherborne DT9 5NR. Tel: (01935) 813182; Fax: (01935) 816727

The Wingfield Digby family • Signed from Sherborne • Castle open as garden Tues, Thurs, Sat, Sun and Bank Holiday Mons, 1.30 – 6pm (last admission 5pm) • Grounds open April to Oct, daily except Wed, 12.30 – 6pm • Entrance: £2.40, children £1.20 (castle and grounds £4.80, children £2.40, family (2 adults and 2 children) £12) (1999 prices) ◑ 🍵 🖻 WC ⅃ ⬦ 🎂 ♀

As they are seen today, the castle grounds are based on landscaping undertaken in the late eighteenth century by 'Capability' Brown for the sixth Lord Digby, when the lake was created out of the then-flowing River Yeo, and the famous hanging gardens enjoyed by Sir Walter Raleigh and his wife Bess a century earlier were lost forever. Nonetheless, many of the existing trees are descendants of those introduced by Raleigh from the Mediterranean and the New World, and the famous giant Virginia cedars he brought over still cling to life despite centuries of battering by westerly winds. Sweeping acres of deer park surround the castle, and masonry salvaged from the crumbling ruin of the old castle, destroyed during the Civil War in 1645, gave rise to fine stable blocks, courtyards and nearby Castleton Church. A charming walled flower garden has been designed within one of the courtyards near the Orangery, but the main attraction lies surely in the site's unique history, the colourful scene of water against graceful sloping lawns, and the ancient ruin visible across the lake. As Alexander Pope wrote with enthusiasm to a friend: 'This is so peculiar and its situation of so uncommon kind, that it merits a more particular description.' A visit to the delightful and comprehensive *Castle Gardens Plant Centre*, established in the original walled kitchen garden of the Castle and accessible from the main road, is worth a detour.

Shute House ★ 35

Donhead St Mary, Shaftesbury SP7 9DG . Tel: (01747) 828866

Mr and Mrs John Lewis • 5m NE of Shaftesbury, off A30. Near Donhead St Mary church • Open weekdays by appt for parties of 20 to 40 • Entrance: charge ◑ ⅃

The handsome historic house is surrounded by a garden of many springs and ponds – the source of a river. The marvellous site faces south, overlooking a slope to farmland. Behind, mysterious shrubberies have a magical hold on the visitor, who is led by paths through groves of camellias and rhododendrons into knot gardens and borders and by placid pools and canals. The late Sir Geoffrey Jellicoe designed the musical cascade that tumbles down the slope over projecting copper Vs set in concrete – an inspired statement of the Modern Movement of the 1930s. This famous feature is being revived and replanted, while other structural features are being created.

Stapehill Abbey, Crafts and Gardens 36

276 Wimborne Road West, Stapehill, Wimborne Minster BH21 2EB.
Tel: (01202) 861686

Mr and Mrs J. Pickard (Managers) • On old A31 Wimborne – Ferndown road,
½ m E of Canford Bottom roundabout • Abbey open • Garden open 21st April to
Sept, daily, 10am – 5pm; Oct to March, daily except Mon and Tues (but closed
21st Dec to 31st Jan) 10am – 4pm • Entrance: £5, OAPs and students £4.50,
children (4-16) £3.50, family ticket £13.50 (1999 prices) • Other information:
Guide dogs only. Craft workshops ○ 🍽 ✕ 🏠 WC ♿ ♨ 🏪 🎔

Formerly home for 200 years to Cistercian nuns, this lovely old abbey has now
been restored and the grounds transformed into gardens. Victorian cottage
garden, wisteria walk, tropical house, lake, woodland walk and picnic area,
large rock garden with waterfall and pools. There are a number of unique craft
shops in the old Abbey with demonstrations of traditional crafts on most days.
The restaurant is in the former refectory, off a lovely walled terrace so one can
eat out of doors in summer. The Country World museum has a good collection
of tractors etc, and looks on to the farmyard. Nearby is the long-established
Trehane Camellia Nursery, with a vast range of camellias, magnolias and other acid
lovers. (Open Mon – Fri, 9am – 4.30pm, spring weekends, 10am – 4pm).

Sticky Wicket ★ 37

Buckland Newton, Dorchester DT2 7BY. Tel: (01300) 345476

Peter and Pam Lewis • 11m from Dorchester and Sherborne, 2m E of A352, or
take B3143 from Sturminster Newton. At T-junction midway between church
and school • Open June to Sept, Thurs, 10.30am – 8pm and for parties by appt
(write for details) • Entrance: £2.50, children £1.50 ● 🍽 WC ♿ ♨

One of the four garden areas has a design of concentric circles and radiating
paths, which has enabled the creation of many separate beds showing different
planting styles. A fragrant and colourful display is bordered by species roses.
The garden is designed to attract birds, butterflies and bees and to provide
seed heads. There is a small pond and a wet area which is also attractive to
wildlife, an informal white garden with late-summer interest and a meadow.
This is very much the garden of conservationist-minded plant lovers and is not
suitable for most children; if the progress of recent years is maintained it is
destined to become outstanding.

Stour House 38

41 East Street, Blandford Forum DT11 7DU. Tel: (01258) 452914

Mr T.S.B. Card • In Blandford, 100 metres from Market Place on one-way
system • Open 19th March, 10th April, 2 – 5pm; 21st May, 18th June, 16th
July, 20th Aug, 2 –6pm;17th Sept, 15th Oct, 2 – 5pm • Entrance: £1, children
20p ● 🍽 WC ♿ ♨

A beautiful town garden, well worth a visit, appealing to both formal and
informal tastes. The formal part is walled with long wide-bordered lawns,

many unusual and some tender shrubs, long vistas towards modern sculptures and a wooden bridge of unusual design which leads to a delightful and romantic island in the River Stour. The island has many beautiful mature trees, both native and introduced species. The owner has planted many varieties of younger trees himself, and plans many new features.

Thornhill Park ★ 39

Stalbridge DT10 2SH. Tel: (01963) 362746

Mr and Mrs Richard Goode • 12m NW of Blandford, 1m S of Stalbridge opposite T-junction on A357 Blandford road • Open April to Sept, Thurs, Fri, 10am – 5pm, Sun, 2 – 5pm • Entrance: £3, children under 16 £1 • Other information: Teas on Suns only ◑ WC ℘

The eighteenth-century house is central to the garden and everywhere are spectacular views of the Blackmore Vale. Cary Goode trained at the English Gardening School and is a professional garden designer, holding courses on the premises from time to time. A few years ago she and her husband took on the estate, originally the home of Sir James Thornhill, and are now carefully restoring the 70-acre park. The six-acre garden has been planted with new trees and hedges. Gazebos and summerhouses have been constructed to catch the eye; there is a croquet lawn, rose garden and pond. Parterres (one of which, known as 'Bishops and Cardinals', is all purple and red), terraces and balustrading, along with shelterbelts of trellises, are already turning this into a remarkable site. There is also a willow garden with living willow sculptures, ornamental borders of distinct colours and all around a feeling of naturalism where self-seeding of flowers is encouraged.

Weston House 40

Buckhorn Weston, Gillingham SP8 5HG. Tel: (01963) 371005

Mr and Mrs E.A.W. Bullock • 4m W of Gillingham, 4m SE of Wincanton. From A30 turn N to Kington Magna, continue towards Buckhorn Weston and after railway bridge take left towards Wincanton. House is second on left • Open by appt May to Sept for NGS • Entrance: £1.50, children free ◐ WC ♿ ⊲⊳ ℘

It has taken 15 years of hard work and imaginative flair for the owners to transform a large area of grass to the rear of the Georgian farmhouse into an outstanding garden of vibrant colour, designed around an exceptional collection of old-fashioned and English roses. Central to the formal garden near the house is the York-stone path edged with a series of standard 'Polar Star' roses underplanted with blues and greys. The rose collection – currently there are 95 varieties on display, all clearly labelled – can be explored via a series of stepping stones thoughtfully arranged behind the border lines so that specimens may be closely examined and their scent appreciated. Clematis in variety intertwine at intervals, often in matching tones. Later in the season hot colours feature in herbaceous borders, and further from the house a small woodland, wildlife pond and wildflower meadow have been established, along with a new plantation of *Rosa rugosa*. The overall design is enhanced by a well-kept lawn and areas of rough-cut grass interspersed with some unusual trees.

DURHAM

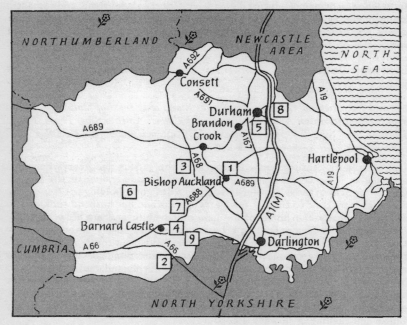

Some gardens have postal addresses in one county and are physically situated in another. If in doubt, a check in the index will direct the reader to the page on which the garden appears.

Auckland Park 1

Auckland Castle, Bishop Auckland DL14 7NR.
Tel: (01388) 765555 (Wear Valley District Council)

The Bishop of Durham; Managed by Wear Valley District Council • Leave A1(M) at Bishop Auckland sign and follow A689 W through Rushyford, past Windlestone Hall and Coundon into Bishop Auckland • Auckland Castle State Rooms and Chapel open. Admission charge • Gardens open all year daily: summer, 7.30am – 9pm; winter, 7.30am – dusk • Entrance: free ○ & ◁▷

A remarkable survival, poorly maintained, of an eighteenth-century and earlier deer park in the well-wooded valleys of the Coundon Burn and Gaunless River, tributary to the River Wear. Enter the park via a gatehouse designed by Sir Thomas Robinson with touches of Thomas Wright, and walk past Auckland Castle, glimpsed through a *clairvoyée*. Suddenly, through the gateway in James Wyatt's screen of 1796 for Bishop Barrington is a glimpse of the twelfth-century banqueting hall, converted to a chapel by Bishop Cosin in the late seventeenth century. The inner and outer park covers 80 acres, all that remains of a deer park that once extended to 500 acres. Within them the River Gaunless traces a meandering course with precipitate bluffs such as Kitty Heugh and craggy outcrops. The river has been canalised in places with a weir dating from the eighteenth century. There are avenues of Austrian pine and sweet chestnut and circular platoons of trees, groves of ancient alders and clumps of holly trees among which dog roses climb. The gnarled and ancient hawthorns are also a feature. Ornamental but functional buildings in the park include the deer shelter (now in the care of English Heritage) designed by Thomas Wright, the Wizard of Durham, in 1757.

Barningham Park   2

Barningham, Richmond, North Yorkshire DL11 7DW. Tel: (01833) 621202

Sir Anthony Milbank • 5m SE of Barnard Castle, 10m NW of Scotch Corner off A66 at A66 Motel crossroads • Open 21st May, 4th, 11th June, 9th July, 10th Sept and on several other dates, 2 – 6pm • Entrance: £2.50, children free • Other information: Coaches by appt ● ▆ WC ⬤ ℘

The house is set in an early eighteenth-century landscape on a steep, north-facing slope of the River Tees Valley, with remarkable views north and east to the North Sea. There are grass terraces to the south-east of the house, reminiscent of Claremont (see entry in Surrey), and a grass terrace walk to a mount, on the top of which was a bowling green, similar to the ascent to Wray Wood at Castle Howard (see entry in Yorkshire). Extensive woodland to the south and a deer park with circumvallating wall. Paths and mounts. A rock garden and stream with waterfalls were laid out by Sir Frederick and Lady Milbank in the late 1920s and 1930s.

Bedburn Hall Gardens   3

Hamsterley, Bishop Auckland DL13 3NN. Tel: (01388) 4888231

Mr I. Bonas • 9m NW of Bishop Auckland. W off A68 at Witton-le-Wear. 3m SE of Wolsingham off B6293 • Open by appt and as advertised on certain days in summer, 2 – 6pm • Entrance: £2, children 50p • Other information: Teas and plants for sale on NGS open day only ● ▆ ▤ WC ♿ ⬤ ℘

A medium-sized terraced garden, largely developed by the present owner, beautifully situated by Hamsterley Forest. It is dominated by a lake with associated rhododendrons and bamboos. A well-established conservatory contains figs, bougainvilleas, passion flowers and other exotics. Lilies and fuchsias a speciality.

The Bowes Museum Garden   4

Barnard Castle DL12 8NP. Tel: (01833) 690606

Durham County Council • In Barnard Castle about ¼ m E of market place • Garden open all year, daily, dawn – dusk except during occasional events when access to gardens may be restricted • Entrance: free (museum and gardens £3.90, OAPs and children £2.90) (1999 prices) • Other information: Refreshments, toilet facilities, inc. disabled, and shop in museum ○ ▤ ♿ ⬤ ♗

In front of the museum to the south side, beneath a stone balustrade, a traditional herbaceous border announces a formal parterre, laid out in 1981 to complement the style of the building designed in 1869 by Jules Pellechet for John Bowes. The raised beds of the parterre are edged with box, which if laid out would stretch for over one and a half miles. There are 20 acres of grounds, planted with 56 different species of tree. A double avenue starts behind the East Lodge and follows the park perimeter; the trees mark a carriageway which led from the main gate to the first site of the Bowes chapel. The low terrace wall and enclosed garden and tennis courts are on the site of this chapel, now a picnic area. The yew trees are a survival of this scheme. The trees continue as a windbreak round the whole of the northern edge of the grounds. In front of the native trees are planted exotic specimens, such as Wellingtonia. The mound behind the car park has been designed as a retreat, with arbours, shrubs and statues (removed from the Houses of Parliament during restoration work in the 1970s). A 15p leaflet, *A Walk through the Grounds*, lists all the trees.

East Durham and Houghall Community College   5

Houghall, Durham DH1 3SG. Tel: (0191) 386 1351

1m SE of Durham city S of A177 Durham — Stockton-on-Tees road. Or leave A1(M) at A177 signed Peterlee and continue towards Durham • Open all year, daily, 1 — 4pm • Entrance: free ○ 🍽 ✕ 🏠 WC 👤 🐾 ⚘

These campus grounds have been developed over the last 35 years as the county's main horticultural educational and training facility. They comprise some 24 acres of sports fields and ornamental features and contain one of the largest collections of hardy plants in north-east England. The gardens are in a frost pocket, where some of the lowest temperatures in the country are recorded annually. Ornamental features include a water garden, woodland garden, alpine house, display greenhouses, rock garden, raised beds, troughs, narcissi naturalised under trees, heather garden and arboretum. Since this is a working college the visitor may see empty beds and much work in progress. The College is holder of National Collections of sorbus and meconopsis.

Eggleston Hall Gardens   6

Eggleston, Barnard Castle DL12 0AG. Tel/answerphone: (01833) 650403; Fax: (01833) 650378

Mrs R. Gray • 18m NW of Darlington, 5m NW of Barnard Castle on B6278 • Garden open daily except 25th Dec, 10am — 5pm • Entrance: 50p (£1 for season) returnable if purchasing plants, guided tours for parties £1 per person • Other information: Catering and guides for parties by arrangement. Guide dogs only ○ 🍽 ✕ WC 👤 🐾 🛒

The house (not open but glimpsed) was designed by Ignatius Bonomi in the early nineteenth century for the antiquarian William Hutchinson. The lodge entrance, also by Bonomi, gives access to the gardens; Doric gate piers, a much later wrought-iron gate bought from The Great Exhibition by William Gray, and the lodge itself, with its pedimented, columned porch in warm stone greet the visitor. There are enjoyable walks along the stream with many unusual plants. The winding paths within the main garden continue to hold excitement as the visitor rounds corners to find colourful vistas which change with the seasons. The old churchyard, with gravestones dating from the seventeenth century, will soon be open to the public; curving stone steps have been built to lead into it from the main garden. Sadly the church was left to become a ruin, but there are plans for its future including a clematis walk. This area has a microclimate, so less hardy plants can be grown there. Three old greenhouses and several modern glasshouses and polytunnels hold plants of interest. In the sales area, celmisias are still a speciality, and soon the beautiful variegated lilac *Syringa emodi* will also be available. Organic vegetables and plants, trees, shrubs and perennials are for sale within the walled garden.

Raby Castle Gardens   7

Staindrop, Darlington DL2 3AY. Tel: (01833) 660202

The Rt Hon. The Lord Barnard • 1m N of Staindrop on A688 Barnard Castle – Bishop Auckland road • House open 1 – 5pm (extra charge) • Garden open May and June, Weds and Sun only; July to Sept, daily except Sat, 11am – 5.30pm. Bank Holiday openings Sat until following Wed • Entrance: £1.50, OAPs and children £1 • Other information: Dogs in park only, on lead ◑ ☕ 📷 WC & ♨ 🛍

One of the country's most impressive medieval castles, once the seat of the Nevills and home to Lord Barnard's family for over 350 years, is set in a 200-acre deer park and has an interesting walled garden. This formal garden, dating from the mid-eighteenth century, was designed by Thomas Wright (the Wizard of Durham) for the 2nd Earl of Darlington and has a wide array of trees, shrubs and herbaceous plants. Thomas White advised on the landscaping along with Joseph Spence. The garden walls from locally hand-made bricks have flues which used to enable sub-tropical fruits to be grown on the south terrace. The famous white Ischia fig tree, brought to Raby in 1786, still survives. Rose garden, shrub borders, original yew hedges, lakes and ornamental pond.

University Botanic Garden   8

Hollingside Lane, Durham DH1 3TN. Tel: (0191) 3742670

Durham University • 1m from city centre, E of A1050. Accessible from the A1(M). From S leave A177 and drive NW through Bowburn and Shincliffe to Durham. From N leave at A690 and drive SW to Durham. Garden off Hollingside Lane • Garden open all year. Glasshouses open daily, 9am – 4pm. Visitor centre open March to Oct, daily, 10am – 5pm; Nov to Feb, daily except Christmas week and bad weather, 11am – 4pm • Entrance: £1, concessions 50p • Other information: Wheelchair and map of wheelchair route available ○ ☕ WC & ♨ 🛍

Established in 1970 as a centre for botanical study, this is now one of the few botanical gardens in the north of England. Of special interest are woodland walks with exotic trees from the Americas and the Himalayas. There is little in the way of herbaceous borders because throughout the garden trees and herbaceous plants are grown together as they would be found in the wild. There are, however, individual features devoted to heathers and conifers and to woodland plants; there is a North American arboretum and a Himalayan valley and also a gazebo garden overshadowed by a huge monkey puzzle tree. Newly completed is an alpine/scree garden. The greenhouses contain tropical and Mediterranean plants and cacti, further details of which are available at the visitor centre. Near this centre is the Prince Bishop's Garden, comprising sculptures originally designed for the 1990 Gateshead Garden Festival; the six figures of some of County Durham's famous sons were carved by Colin Wilburn from elm trees, felled because of Dutch elm disease. While this has potential to be a very interesting botanical garden, some improvement in maintenance in specific areas will be required. Eighteen acres in all.

Westholme Hall 9

Winston, Darlington DL2 3QL. Tel: (01325) 730442

Mr and Mrs J.H. McBain • 10m W of Darlington on B6274 between Staindrop and Winston • Open 21st May, 2nd July, 27th Aug, 2 – 6pm. Parties by arrangement • Entrance: £2, children 50p ● ➴ ➴ WC ⅗ ➴ ⅋

The Jacobean house and the garden (which was laid out in 1890) are reached by a short drive of limes with mature hollies on the north side. To the south is parkland. Immediately inside the garden enclosure (about five acres), there are lawns: on the right an old tree supports a 'Félicité et Perpétue' rose and 'Comtesse de Bouchaud' clematis. From the front door in the south elevation, an axial line leads to a stone-flagged bridge over a stream, the Westholme Beck – a tributary of the Alwent Beck – and thence to the River Tees. A stone retaining wall parallel to and south of the house forms the backing for a grass walk running east-west; then a grass slope descends to a wide croquet lawn with bold plantings of rhododendrons. Beyond are grass walks with cherries and specimen trees. Cross the stream that bisects the garden and there is a paddock, and more walks through maturing woodland; one vista through what will one day become an avenue of beeches is closed by a massive stone plinth. Elsewhere in the garden, the long grass terrace walk is terminated by a wall and an urn. Stone parapets were salvaged from the Streatlam Park demolition sale of the 1930s, and now adorn this garden. There is a delightful shrub rose garden to the west of the house, partly sunken and overlooked by a summer-house, with a good collection of Albas, Bourbons, etc. At Headlam Hall about five miles east, excellent lunches and dinners are available.

A TOTALLY INDEPENDENT PUBLICATION
The *Guide* makes no charge for entries, which are written by our own inspectors. The factual details are supplied by owners. This is a totally-independent publication and its only revenue is from sales of copies in bookshops.

ESSEX

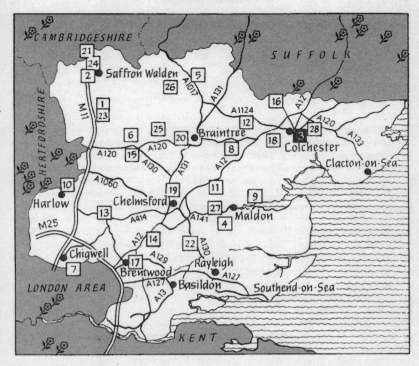

Two-starred gardens are marked on the map with a black square.

Amberden Hall ★   1

Widdington, Saffron Walden CB11 3ST. Tel: (01799) 540402

Mr and Mrs D. Lloyd • 6m S of Saffron Walden. E of B1383 near Newport. Follow signs to Mole Hall Wildlife Park. Hall is ½ m past park on right • Open 15th, 16th July, 2 – 6pm and for parties by appt • Entrance: £2.50, children free (1999 prices) ● WC ⓗ ☟

Some lovely old walls enclose this medium-sized garden set at one side of a fine house. The borders are well designed, so that not all of the garden is visible at once. All are planted in specific colours. The walls are covered in a variety of climbers, many rare. A *leylandii* hedge has been clipped and the sides corrugated. There is a good vegetable garden with raised beds to make it easier to cope with heavy clay soil. The garden has been extended beyond the walls with an ivy *allée* – this has two viburnum hedges with poles rising out of them each carrying different ivies. More recent additions are a secret garden inside a dismantled barn, a bog garden and a woodland walk.

Audley End   2

Saffron Walden CB11 4JF. Tel: (01799) 522399

English Heritage • 1m W of Saffron Walden on B1383 • House open. Guided tours only • Garden open April to Oct, Wed – Sun and Bank Holiday Mons, 11am – 6pm; Oct, Wed – Sun, 10am – 3pm • Entrance: £4, OAPs £3, children under 16 £2, family £10 (house and grounds £6, OAPs £4.50, children £3, family £15) (1999 prices) • Other information: Picnics in park only ◐ 💭 ✕ 🖥 WC 🚫 🔄 🍴 ♿

The Jacobean house has always been a gem but now visitors can enjoy an early version of the parterre garden restored to the plans developed by Lord Braybrooke and his wife c. 1830, advised by William Sawrey Gilpin. The design was inspired by the classic seventeenth-century French parterres, with sheltering shrubberies which relate to contemporary (1830) interiors, but the overall effect is rather Victorian. English Heritage has introduced the whole repertory of the flower garden of the period – irises, martagon lilies, roses, peonies and astrantias, violas, hypericums – all planted in some 170 beds. Restoration has taken 10 years and has been completed without interfering with the surrounding 'Capability' Brown landscape park, which features a circular temple, bridge and Lady Portsmouth's Column by Adam, also a cascade constructed in the same year on the site of an ancient mill dam. Fine plane, oak and tulip trees, and a pond garden, laid out in 1868, containing many scented old roses in a colour scheme of pinks and mauves. At one end there is a Pulhamite rock garden. The whole is immaculately maintained. The walled kitchen garden is now open to the public for the first time in 250 years. The area, known as Lady Portsmouth's Garden, includes a 170-foot-long vinehouse and is being developed into a working organic kitchen garden laid out in the Victorian style – a restoration by the Henry Doubleday Research Association, which has leased the garden from English Heritage. A wonderful start has been made with new fruit trees on the walls, a mile of box edging, and a splendid variety of Victorian vegetables, which are also for sale in season.

The Beth Chatto Gardens ★★   3

Elmstead Market, Colchester CO7 7DB. Tel: (01206) 822007

Mrs Beth Chatto • ¼ m E of Elmstead Market on A133 • Open March to Oct, Mon – Sat, 9am – 5pm; Nov to Feb, Mon – Fri, 9am – 4pm. Closed Sun and Bank Holidays • Entrance: £3, accompanied children free • Other information: Plants for sale in adjoining nursery. Parties by arrangement ○ 💭 🖥 WC ⌀ 🍴

Beth Chatto designed these gardens in the 1960s from a neglected hollow which was either boggy and soggy or exceedingly dry. She, more than anyone else, has influenced gardeners by her choice of plants for any situation – dry, wet or shady – and her ability to show them off to perfection. Her planting is a lesson to every gardener on how to use both leaf and flower to best advantage. The large new gravel garden which she planted to replace the old car park is maturing well as a home for beautiful plants which can thrive in very dry conditions. 'Tradescant' of *The Garden* says this should be compulsory viewing for everyone who lives in the rain-starved counties. It is completely English, he says, though the banks of plants recall the Mediterranean. A careful pruning programme has been undertaken 'to prevent that "ageing look" which creeps into mature gardens before you've noticed'. Changes have also been made to the herbaceous border. Handbook (£3), including fully descriptive catalogue with notes on the Chatto philosophy, a full page on the gravel garden and free price list. Adjoining is the excellent *Unusual Plants* nursery. All compulsory visiting.

Cameo Cottage 4

Chapel Lane, Purleigh, Chelmsford CM3 6PY. Tel: (01621) 828334

Mrs Joan Cook • 9m SE of Chelmsford, S of Maldon between B1010 and B1012. Locate hill that leads to church. Facing hill, turn right, take first left (Howe Green Road), then first right by black house (Chapel Lane). Cameo Cottage is first house on right • Open by appt for individuals and small parties • Entrance: £1.50 ●

Set around a cottage, the early part of which dates from the seventeenth century, this three-quarter-acre cottage garden is immediately captivating. It is entirely filled with plants that tumble and spill gloriously around a maze of narrow paths and small courtyards, yet the apparent informality is restrained within particular colour schemes, forming the cameos that give the cottage its name. Additional depth and texture are provided by a variation in levels and numerous raised troughs made by the owner's late husband. A diverted field ditch has allowed the creation of a bog garden. This is an enthralling place for the plantsman as it contains many rare treasures among more familiar herbaceous varieties. It is also known as a garden for all seasons, as it provides interest from February onwards. RHS Garden Hyde Hall (see entry) is nearby.

Cracknells ★ 5

Great Yeldham CO9 4PT. Tel: (01787) 237370

Mr and Mrs T. Chamberlain • 10m N of Braintree, on A1017 between Halstead and Haverhill • Open by appt • Entrance: by donation to collecting box ●

Mr Chamberlain started contouring this large garden even before he started building his house. The garden rolls away from the house down to the lake, also excavated at the start. This is not a garden in the accepted sense but 'a garden picture painted with trees', to use his own words. He has collected trees from all over the country and has an impressive collection. Here is the rare cut-leaf beech, *Fagus sylvatica heterophylla*, and its purple and pink-leaved forms, 'Rohanii' and 'Roseomarginata', as well as the variegated tulip tree *Liriodendron tulipifera* 'Aureomarginatum'. There are also collections of birches, acers, sorbus and oaks. If you are a lover of trees, make your pilgrimage.

Easton Lodge, The Forgotten Gardens 6

Easton Lodge, Little Easton, Great Dunmow CM6 2BB. Tel: (01371) 876979

Mr and Mrs B. Creasey • 1m N of Great Dunmow on B184. Signposted • Open Feb to Oct, Fri – Sun and Bank Holiday Mons, 12 noon – 6pm and at other

times by appt. • Entrance: £3.30, children under 12 £1, concessions £3.
Discount for parties • Other information: Teas at weekends only ◐ 💺 WC ♿
🐟 🐕 ♨

This is the old west wing of Warwick House, once home of 'Darling Daisy', Countess of Warwick. The main house was demolished and the gardens abandoned in 1950. The garden was designed originally by Harold Peto in 1903 and parts of it were described as some of his most outstanding work. Twelve acres have already been restored, including a nineteenth-century croquet lawn and formal lawns with flower beds. The cobbled herringbone courtyard is divided, with a fountain and raised brick beds, massed agapanthus, clematis, pots of orange and lemon trees, large azaleas, datura (brugmansia) and a good fernery. There are also pergolas supporting wisteria and clematis, a well-stocked conservatory and fine dovecot. In 1996, the pavilion was restored with financial assistance from Essex County Council, with a new formal pool and surrounding brickwork. A double terrace is located in front of the site of the original house, with two fine herbaceous borders with roses; good contrasting colours. In the Italian garden, the original flight of steps, paving stones and stone ornaments and balustrades were sold. This garden, together with the tree house, pergolas and large semi-circular seats will cost several hundred thousand pounds to replace, which can only be done with the help of grants. The Japanese garden has been cleared. As time goes on, improvements will be made but the tranquil, romantic atmosphere has returned. It is a most ambitious and important garden restoration project. The work is all being done on a tight budget with limited labour and will take several years to complete.

7A Ellesmere Gardens   7

Redbridge, Ilford IG4 5DA. Tel: (020) 8550 5464

Cecilia Gonzalez • Travelling E, off A12 Eastern Avenue between Redbridge
roundabout (M11 interchange) and Gants Hill roundabout • Open by appt only
(garden only takes two at a time) • Entrance: £2.50 ◐

A charming split-level courtyard garden, only six metres square, and a treasure trove of unusual plants. The owner knew little about gardening when she moved here at the beginning of the 1980s and the site was covered with paving stones, most now removed. The number of species here is remarkable, given the garden's size, but all growth is restricted and imaginative use is made of container planting. As a result, a real plant-lover can spend as much time here as in a far larger garden. Upper level filled with containers, dense tropical planting in lower level.

Feeringbury Manor   8

Coggeshall Road, Feering, Colchester CO5 9RB. Tel: (01376) 561946

Mr and Mrs Giles Coode-Adams • 6m E of Braintree between Coggeshall and
Feering • Open 4th May to 28th July, Thurs, Fri, 8am – 4pm and by appt •
Entrance: £2 ◑ 🍴 WC ♿ 🐟 ♨

A garden distinguished by detailed planting, all undertaken by the owners. There are bog-loving plants by two ponds and a stream as well as plants that prefer dry soil, and the season is prolonged with interesting bulbs and climbers such as sweet peas and clematis, the latter a speciality. Many plants have been grown from seed collected on expeditions with Kew Gardens. Notable, too, are the sculptured gates.

Folly Faunts House 9

Goldhanger, Maldon CM9 8AP. Tel: (01621) 788611; Fax: (01621) 788754 (office)

Mr and Mrs J.C. Jenkinson • On B1026 between Maldon and Colchester • Open for charity 30th April, 14th, 28th May, 11th, 25th June, 3rd Sept, 2 – 5pm. Parties of 12 or more at other times by appt • Entrance: £2 • Other information: Teas and plants for sale on open days only ● WC & ⬥

A large 20-acre garden and park created round an eighteenth-century manor house since 1963. The garden is divided into compartments, each with a different theme, and has a wide variety of unusual trees and shrubs. The plantings around the informal and formal ponds are a special feature. A further 20 acres of park and woodland divided by five double avenues provide attractive walks.

The Gibberd Garden ★ 10

Marsh Lane, Gilden Way, Harlow CM17 0NA. Tel: (01279) 442112

Gibberd Garden Trust • E of Harlow between A414 and B183. From M11 junction 7 take A414 to Harlow, follow signs to Old Harlow onto B183 (Gilden Way) and continue for 1m. Marsh Lane is on left • Open 23rd April to Sept, Sat and Sun only, 2 – 6pm • Entrance: £3, concessions £2, children free ● ▦ WC &

This is the extremely individual creation of the architect and art collector Sir Frederick Gibberd, who was appointed master planner of Harlow New Town in 1946. Considered an outstanding example of twentieth-century garden design, the nine-acre sloping site comprises a series of rooms designed to display his remarkable collection of modern sculpture and architectural artefacts. However, there is no rigidity of structure; tranquillity as well as drama is provided by glades, groves and *allées* as they open up vistas or focus on statuary. A waterfall and quiet pools have been incorporated into a small brook which borders the east of the property and towards which run lushly planted channels of water. At one end of the brook lies a moated castle. There are also natural ponds, a tree house, a labyrinth and a gazebo. Sir Frederick died in 1984, but the garden is now in the enthusiastic hands of the Gibberd Garden Trust, which is aiming to realise his wish that it be kept open to the public for recreation and study in perpetuity. Hugh Johnson claims that this 'must certainly be one of the most important [gardens] in the history of the twentieth century'.

Glen Chantry ★   11

Wickham Bishops, Witham CM8 3LG. Tel: (01621) 891342

*Mr and Mrs W.G. Staines • 9m NE of Chelmsford off A12, 2m SE of Witham.
Turn left off B1018 towards Wickham Bishops. Pass golf course, cross River
Blackwater bridge and turn left up track by Blue Mills • Open April to mid-Oct,
Fri and Sat, 10am – 4pm • Entrance: £2, children 50p • Other information:
D.I.Y. teas* ◑ ⚏ WC ⍤

A large undulating garden, started in 1977. The huge, informally shaped beds
are filled with an imaginative mixture of hostas, peonies, variegated grasses,
brunneras, white martagon lilies, crambes and variegated *Helleborus lividus* spp.
corsicus. The centres of some beds are raised, and this gives an excellent shape
to the planting. Large rock gardens, stream with waterfalls to a pond with
rodgersias and good foliage plants. An attractive white garden. Overall, the
plantings and colour schemes are really spectacular, due to Mrs Staines'
unerring eye for contrasting foliage and plant forms. A good nursery is
attached.

Hill House   12

Chappel, Colchester CO6 2DX. Tel: (01787) 222428

*Mr and Mrs R. Mason • 8m W of Colchester on A1124 between Colchester and
Earls Colne • Open by appt • Entrance: donation to charity* ◕

This large garden is now moving towards maturity. Designed by the owners on
formal lines using yew hedging and walls to create vistas, it has a lime avenue
sited to lead the eye out into the country. A mixed planting of tough native
trees, sorbus and hawthorn, etc., has been established as a windbreak. A small
courtyard, reminiscent of a London garden, with a raised pool has been
planted with green-leaved plants and white flowers only. Another feature
is a pond with two black swans. The bones of the garden are now in place
including urns, statues and seats, and all the colour and secondary planting is
being introduced gradually; some further land has been acquired and will be
planted out over the coming years.

Hobbans Farm   13

Bobbingworth, Ongar CM5 0LY. Tel: (01277) 890245

*Mrs Ann Webster • 6m SE of Harlow, N of A414 between Ongar Four Wautz
roundabout and N Weald Talbot roundabout, just past Blake Hall. First farm
entrance on right after church • Open for NGS 23rd April, 7th, 23rd May, 4th,
18th June, 2nd, 16th July, 20th Aug, 3rd, 17th Sept, 2 – 6pm. Private visits
and parties by appt • Entrance: £1.50* ◕ ⚏ WC ⍤

The Websters took over vacant farmland more than 30 years ago and have
transformed it into several romantic informal areas with great charm and
plenty of interest for the plantsperson. Good all-year-round shrubs and trees.
Clematis, old roses, herbs, aquilegias in abundance. The owner has a sensitive
feeling for design (obviously in the genes, as her son produces charming

outdoor furniture and ornaments which may be on display). This worthwhile garden is expanding further into adjacent farmland.

Hyde Hall

(see RHS GARDEN HYDE HALL)

Ingatestone Hall 14

Ingatestone CM4 9NR. Tel: (01277) 353010

Lord Petre • 7m SW of Chelmsford on A12. From Ingatestone main street, take Station Lane at SW end. Signposted • House open • Garden open 22nd April to 1st Oct, Sat, Sun and Bank Holiday Mons; also 12th July to 8th Sept, Wed – Fri, all 1 – 6pm • Entrance: £3.50, OAPs and students £3, children £2 ◐ ☕ WC &. ⛪ ☙

There have been buildings here since 950 AD, and the present house was built in the 1540s. A large stewpond, contemporary with the house, provided fish and fresh-water mussels; it is now bordered by huge gunnera and shady walks. The walled garden has magnificent standard roses and a lily pond. There are various walks: a nut walk and a grass walk, but the lime walk is haunted by Bishop Benjamin Petre's dog, which saved his life when he was set upon in 1740 and still patrols. The extensive, immaculate lawns have specimen trees: mulberries, *Magnolia grandiflora* and weeping beeches. The house, which is in a remarkable state of preservation, is well worth a visit.

Langthorns Plantery 15

High Cross Lane West, Little Canfield, Dunmow CM6 1TD. Tel: (01371) 872611

Mr and Mrs David Cannon • 5m E of M11 junction 8, on A120 • Plantery open daily, 10am – 5pm • Garden open by appt (telephone or ask at the plantery) • Entrance: free ● ⬳ ☙

The owners, avid collectors of unusual plants, propagate in the nursery, and Langthorns stocks one of the widest ranges of plants in the country: over 1200 varieties of herbaceous perennials, many unusual forms of tricyrtis, geraniums and salvias; 1300 varieties of shrubs and conservatory plants. Alpines, clematis and honeysuckles. The garden has now been re-vamped and is open to the public on a limited basis.

Lower Dairy House 16

Nayland, Colchester CO6 4JS. Tel: (01206) 262220

Mr and Mrs D.J. Burnett • 7m N of Colchester off A134. Left at bottom of hill before Nayland into Water Lane. Garden ½ m on left after farm buildings • Open 9th, 16th, 23rd, 24th, 30th April, 1st, 7th, 14th, 21st, 28th; 29th May, 4th, 11th, 18th, 25th June, 2nd, 9th July, 2 – 6pm and by appt • Entrance: £2, children 50p ● WC &. ☙

This plantsman's garden of one and a half acres is a riot of colour. Mrs Burnett fills any spaces in between the perennials with annuals – marigolds and

larkspur and geraniums – all old-fashioned plants. Many unusual plants inter-
mix with cottage-garden varieties, including a good selection of cistus, diascias
and other sun lovers. There is a pond where the thick planting consists of
primulas, hostas and mimulus. A natural stream runs along one side, feeding
bog gardens, a woodland dell, and bank of shrubs, roses and a variety of foliage
trees. Spring bulbs are also a feature.

The Magnolias 17

18 St John's Avenue, Brentwood CM14 5DF. Tel: (01277) 220019

*Mr and Mrs R.A. Hammond • From A1023 turn S to A128. After 300 metres
turn right at traffic lights, over railway bridge. St John's Avenue is third on
right • Open 19th, 26th March, 2nd, 16th, 23rd April, 7th, 14th, 21st May,
18th June, 16th July, 20th Aug, 17th Sept, 22nd Oct, 10am – 5pm. Parties by
appt • Entrance: £1.50, children 50p ● ⅋*

This fascinating half-acre plantsman's garden illustrates what can be achieved
in a small space. Lawns are minimal, and there are no fewer than seven ponds,
including raised pools. Paths wind through jungle-like borders filled with
acers, camellias and magnolias underplanted with smaller shrubs and ground-
cover plants. There is a large collection of hostas and unusual and rare
bamboos. Something of interest here at any time of the year.

Olivers 18

Olivers Lane, Colchester CO2 0HJ. Tel: (01206) 330575; Fax: (01206) 330366

*Mr and Mrs David Edwards • 3m SW of Colchester off B1022 Maldon road.
Follow signs to Colchester Zoo. From zoo continue ¾ m towards Colchester and at
roundabout turn right. After ¼ m turn right again into Olivers Lane. From
Colchester pass Shrub End church and Leather Bottle pub then turn left at
second roundabout • Open for up to three weekends and by appt for individuals
and parties • Entrance: £2, children free ● 🍽 WC & ⅋*

The moment visitors arrive at the attractive Georgian-fronted house and step
down onto the large York terrace, beautifully planted in soft sympathetic
colours, they are entranced. All around are 20 acres of garden and woodland.
From the terrace one can see down over the lawn, fine borders, pools and
woods to a natural meadow (cut only to encourage wild flowers and grasses)
and to trees bordering the river. A 'willow pattern' bridge crosses the first of a
succession of pools dropping down to an ancient fish pond. *Taxodium distichum*,
metasequoia and ginkgo flourish by the pools. There are yew hedges and a
delightful woodland walk, where mature native trees shelter rhododendrons,
azaleas and shrub roses in the rides.

Park Farm 19

Chatham Hall Lane, Great Waltham, Chelmsford CM3 1BZ. Tel: (01245) 360871

*Mr D. Bracey and Mrs J.E.M. Cowley • 5m N of Chelmsford. Take B1008 N
through Broomfield. On Little Waltham bypass turn left into Chatham Hall*

*Lane signed to Howe Street; Park Farm is ½ m on left • Open 9th, 10th, 23rd,
24th, 30th April, 1st, 14th, 15th, 28th, 29th May, 11th, 12th, 25th, 26th June,
9th, 10th July, 2 – 6pm for NGS. Parties by appt • Entrance: £1.50, children
50p* ◑ ▬ WC ⚲

Two acres of garden in separate 'rooms' formed by yew hedges with climbers
obscure the old farmhouse and dairy in the centre. There are many different
species of bulbs, shrubs, roses and herbaceous perennials – indeed, it is a
proliferation of plants, with amazing stands of colour, and the effect is unique.
The design is still evolving, with new projects underway, including a water
garden and a grotto.

Pound Farmhouse 20

Rayne, Braintree. Tel: (01376) 326738

*Mr and Mrs J.F. Swetenham • Off A120, 3m W of Braintree on Rayne –
Shalford road • Open by appt • Entrance: £1.50* ◑ ▬ WC ⚲

This medium-sized garden with its imaginatively planted and well-kept borders has been created over the last twenty years. The densely planted windbreak trees, producing shade and dry conditions, block a view of the
countryside from the house and consequently dictate the designs and choice
of plants. It is a garden which can be seen all year, either for the blossom and
bulbs in spring, the roses and pond a little later, the flame border in July or the
late-summer border in September.

Reed House 21

Manor Lane, Great Chesterford, Saffron Walden CB10 1PJ.
Tel: (01799) 530312

*Mrs Felicity Mason • 11m S of Cambridge, 4m N of Saffron Walden, 1m S
of Stump Cross M11 junction. On B184 turn into Chesterford High Street.
Turn left at Crown & Thistle into Manor Lane • Open by appt • Entrance:
£2.50* ◑

The owner moved to her present house a few years ago, leaving a large garden
crammed with treasures which used to be open to the public four times a year.
Her new garden is a revelation as to what can be achieved in a short time; she
designed and planted everything herself. Features include sink gardens, koi
carp in the pool, bulbs everywhere, clematis, a greenhouse bursting at its
panes, and a conservatory rapidly filling up with rare plants.

RHS Garden Hyde Hall ★ 22

Rettendon, Chelmsford CM3 8ET. Tel: (01245) 400256

*The Royal Horticultural Society • 7m SE of Chelmsford, signed from A130 •
Open 22nd March to 29th Oct, daily, 11am – 6pm (closes 5pm in Sept and
Oct) • Entrance: £3, children (6-16) 70p. Parties of 10 or more £2.50 per person
(1999 prices) • Other information: Guide dogs only* ◑ ▬ ✕ 🛍 WC ⚲ ⚲ 🎁 ⚱

This hilltop garden perched above the East Anglian wheatfields in a truly Tuscanesque manner has the potential to be magnificent. The eight acres are maintained to a very high standard and there are fine views to the Crouch Estuary to the south and rolling countryside to the north. Notable are the beds of species roses with white peonies and naturalised *Eremurus robustus* growing through them. There is much else to see: newly planted herbaceous border; an informal pond;: a spring garden of massed hellebores and many bulbs; an excellent rose garden with pillars behind and a superb *Clematis viticella* 'Mary Rose', gentian-blue and a very old variety; a broad planting of alliums and half-hardy salvias, behind which the greenhouse contains daturas, white *Cobaea scandens* and other tender plants. National Collections of viburnums and malus are here, so there is plenty for the plantsperson. Future plans could have exciting results: 3000 young trees have already been planted; paths are being adapted for wheelchairs, aiming for year-round access. The herbaceous border has been replanted most successfully, and there is a bed of contrasting foliage in yellow and green. The upper and lower ponds are being opened up and replanted, the terrace (entered through a massive new oak pagoda adorned with clematis and wisteria) is being enlarged, and the 12-acre field at the entrance is being replanted with new trees. In all quite a transformation.

R. and R. Saggers ★   23

Waterloo House, High Street, Newport, Saffron Walden CB11 3PG.
Tel: (01799) 540858

R. and R. Saggers • 8m N of Bishop's Stortford, on B1383 through Newport • Open all year, daily except Mon (but open Bank Holiday Mons), and Sun, Jan to March, and Aug, 10am – 5pm • Entrance: free • Other information: Possible for wheelchairs but gravel paths ○ 🍵 WC ♿ ⚲ 🏛

This small, immaculately kept nursery has a charming town garden running down to a stream between flint walls. The nursery stocks old-fashioned roses and rare and unusual plants, grown and propagated by Mr Saggers, a keen plantsman. Almost everything on sale is grown in the wide borders in front of the flint walls. Many exciting shrubs and herbaceous plants. A good range of statuary, lead urns, Whichford pots and Armillary sundials. On a small scale but excellent quality.

Saffron Walden: Bridge End Gardens   24

In Bridge Street, Saffron Walden • Open by pre-booked key from Tourist Information Office (01799) 510444 • Entrance: £10 key deposit (refundable) • Other information: Toilet facilities nearby ● 📷 ♿

The gardens were started in the mid-eighteenth century by Atkinson Francis Gibson. The yew hedge maze, planted in 1840 in the Italian Renaissance style, has 610 metres of pathways, originally embellished with statues and columns and entered by richly ornamented iron gates. It was opened to the public in 1905 (6d to the head gardener), but by 1949 it had fallen into neglect and by 1983 was an overgrown spinney. In 1984 the site was cleared again, the area surveyed and the original maze design marked out. It was replanted with 1000 yews, and officially opened in July 1991. On the common is the ancient turf maze, probably the largest of its kind in the world and one of eight in England. It was last restored in 1979. Tourist information from No 1 The Market Place, Saffron Walden CB10 1HR.

Saffron Walden: Turf Maze

On Saffron Walden Common • Open permanently ○ 🖶

This turf maze, one of eight such surviving turf mazes in England, is of great antiquity and importance, the largest example of its type in the world. The earliest known plan and drawings dated 1768 are in the Bodleian Library, Oxford. Circular, with 17 circuits, it has four bastions at equal distances round the circumference, giving it a diameter of 40 metres. Enclosed by a bank and ditch, the overall dimensions are 45 by 33½ metres. The pathway, one mile in length, follows grooves cut in the turf.

Saling Hall ★   25

Great Saling, Braintree CM7 5DT.

Mr and Mrs Hugh Johnson • 6m NW of Braintree, halfway between Braintree and Dunmow on A120 turn N at Saling Oak • Open for NGS May to July, Weds, 2 – 5pm. Parties by written appt • Entrance: £2, children free ● WC &

Hugh Johnson's wonderful garden is essentially for tree lovers. The huge elms died, and he turned the 12 acres of chalky boulder clay into an arboretum of genera that thrive on alkaline clay or gravel. A marvellous collection of pines, quercus, sorbus, aesculus, robinias, prunus, tilia, fraxinus, fagus, salix and betulas leads the eye to a classical Temple of Pisces. Many rarities like *Carpinus fangiana*, *Eriobotrya japonica*, *Staphylea pinnata*, an unknown weeping juniper, incense cedars from Oregon seed and unusual pines on the east slope. The walled garden faces south-west. Fruit trees are trimmed into mushroom shapes to contrast with a file of clipped cypress and a matching file of Irish junipers and pyramid box bushes. The borders are informal with grey and blue plants of rather typical Mediterranean associations – agapanthus, euphorbias, etc. The disciplined planting in the various sections creates a distinct atmosphere in each. There is a vegetable garden, a Japanese garden, a water garden (planted with rheums, primulas, iris, etc.), a valley garden and a strange menhir in its private glade. The old moat with its cascade boasts some substantial carp.

Shore Hall ★   26

Cornish Hall End, Braintree CM7 4HW. Tel: (01799) 586411

Mr and Mrs Peter Swete • 10m NW of Braintree off B1057, 2 ½ m W of Cornish Hall End on Great Sampford road • Open 14th, 17th, 18th May, 21st June, 2 – 6pm for NGS, and one other date for charity. Parties on weekdays only by appt • Entrance: £2.50 • Other information: Teas on Sun only ● WC 🐾 🏛

An immaculate, beautifully planted garden, with miles of wonderful mowing. There is a formal rose garden with flagged paths, another (newish) formal garden with timber edging and patterns of vegetables interplanted with variegated strawberries, leeks and red and green lettuces; adding an element of height are roses over arches and gooseberries and euonymus grown as standards. In the borders fine plants abound, and a feature of the planting are shrubs mixed with pink and grey. The hall itself sells excellent metal obelisks, rose arches, flower baskets and flower supports. A catalogue is available.

Stone Pine ★ 27

Hyde Lane, Danbury, Chelmsford CM3 4LJ. Tel: (01245) 223232

Mr and Mrs David Barker • 4m E of Chelmsford, 1m S of A414 leaving Danbury towards Maldon • Open by appt • Entrance: by donation to collecting box ● 🍽 ⬦

This small garden is owned by a former Chairman of the Hardy Plant Society. Mr Barker has filled it with choice and unusual varieties. The area of grass is minimal and paths wind around borders crammed with trees, acers being particularly popular, and shrubs. Surprising plants appear around each corner, like the rarely seen *Paris quadrifolia*. Mr Barker is also knowledgeable on lilies, hemerocallis, irises and grasses. National Collections of epimediums and Japanese anemones.

Tye Farm 28

Colchester Road, Elmstead Market, Colchester CO7 7AX. Tel: (01206) 822400

Mr and Mrs C. Gooch • 2m E of Colchester on A133, ½ m before Elmstead Market • Open 11th June, 2 – 6pm, and by appt • Entrance: £2 ● 🍽 WC ⬦ 🌂

This one-acre garden is cleverly planted with hedges to make compartments to break the prevailing wind. The shrubs and perennials are carefully chosen to complement one another and there are over 60 varieties of old and modern roses. Look for the gold area in the small walled kitchen garden. There is a formally planted, box-edged area for herbs. The conservatory contains many unusual plants.

2001 GUIDE
The 2001 *Guide* will be published before Christmas 2000. Reports on gardens for consideration are welcome at all times of the year, but particularly by early summer (June) 2000 so that they can be inspected that year.

All descriptions and other information are as accurate as possible at the time of going to press, but circumstances change and, if in doubt, it is wise to telephone before making a long journey.

GLOUCESTERSHIRE

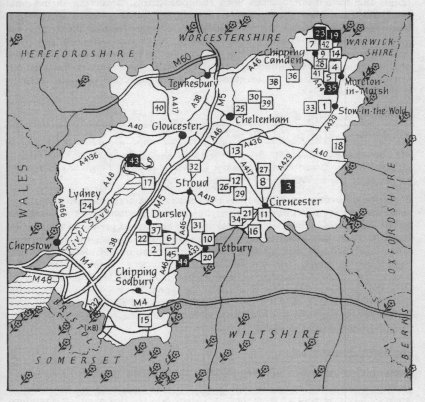

Some gardens have postal addresses in one county and are physically situated in another. If in doubt, a check in the index will direct the reader to the page on which the garden appears.

Two-starred gardens are marked on the map with a black square.

Abbotswood ★

Stow-on-the-Wold GL54 1EN. Tel: (01451) 830173

Dikler Farming Co • 1m W of Stow on B4077 • Open 24th April and some Suns in May and June, 1.30 – 6pm • Entrance: £2, children free • Other information: Coaches must drop passengers at top gate and park in Stow ● ☕ WC ♿

The house is in one of the most beautiful of Cotswold settings. From the car park it is approached via a descending stream and pools towards woodland carpeted in spring with flowers and bulbs, including one of the largest displays of fritillaries in season. The woods continue above and beyond the house and have been planted with rhododendrons, flowering shrubs and specimen trees. Near the house are terraces and formal gardens, including a box-edged rose garden and a water garden. Extensive heather plantings. The gardens round the house are by Lutyens. Note especially his lily pool running up to the house; there is a jet of water there which, if the angle of the sun is right, shimmers spectacularly. Alas, other vertical features by Lutyens were removed by an earlier owner, though the planting remains faithful to his design.

Alderley Grange ★ 2

Alderley GL12 7QT. Tel: (01453) 842161

Mr Guy and The Hon. Mrs Acloque • 2m S of Wotton-under-Edge. Turn NW off A46 Bath – Stroud road at Dunkirk • Open by appt during June • Entrance: £2, children free ● WC &

A garden of exceptional beauty and character in a tranquil walled setting, renowned for its collection of aromatic plants and scented flowers. Designed by the late Alvilde Lees-Milne and believed to be the last garden in which Vita Sackville-West had a hand, Alderley Grange was acquired by the present owners in 1974 and has been immaculately maintained and developed with discretion and style. The fine house and a mulberry tree date from the seventeenth century; a pleached and arched lime walk leads to a series of enclosed gardens. There is a notable hexagonal herb garden with many delightful perspectives of clipped, trained or potted shrubs and trees, and abundant plantings of old roses. Many tender and unusual plants flourish in this cherished and exquisite space.

Barnsley House ★★ 3

Barnsley, Cirencester GL7 5EE. Tel: (01285) 740561; Fax: (01285) 740628

Mr and Mrs Charles Verey • 4m NE of Cirencester on B4425 in Barnsley • Open 1st Feb to 16th Dec, Mon, Wed, Thurs and Sat, 10am – 5.30pm. Coaches and guided tours by appt • Entrance: £3.75, OAPs £3 children under 12 free. Season ticket £10. Guided tours extra ● WC & ⚘ 🏛

A splendid small garden of four acres, comprising many garden styles from the past, carefully blended by Rosemary and the late David Verey after they inherited the house from David's father, the Rev. Cecil Verey, in 1951. Management of the garden has now transferred to Rosemary Verey's elder son. The 1697 Cotswold stone house is set in the middle of the garden, surrounded on three sides by a 1770 stone wall. Borders create vistas and divide the garden into different areas with their own individual characters. The standard of horticulture and maintenance is very high. Great attention has been given to colour and texture. The kitchen garden, with its numerous small beds, ornate paths, box hedges, trained fruit trees, etc., is especially renowned. A very popular garden with visitors.

Batsford Arboretum ★ 4

Moreton–in–Marsh GL56 9QF. Tel: (01386) 701441

The Batsford Foundation • 1½ m NW of Moreton-in-Marsh on A44 to Evesham. Opposite entrance to Sezincote (see entry) • Arboretum open March to mid-Nov, daily, 10am – 5pm • Entrance: £3.50, OAPs £3, children under 16 free (1999 prices) • Other information: Aquatic Centre. Falconry Centre ○ ⬛ 📠 WC ☁ ⬧ ⅋ 🛍 ⓦ

Over 1500 different species and varieties of different trees, shrubs and bamboos in 50 acres of typical Cotswold countryside, plus an unusual collection of exotic shrubs and bronze statues from the Far East, originally collected for the garden by Lord Redesdale. It was expanded by the first Lord Dulverton in the 1960s. Fine collection of magnolias, Japanese cherries and spring bulbs in spring and early summer. Excellent autumn colour. Views of the house (not open).

Bourton House ★ 5

Bourton–on–the–Hill, Moreton–in–Marsh GL56 9AE. Tel: (01386) 700121

Mr and Mrs R. Paice • 2m W of Moreton-in-Marsh on A44 • Open 25th May to 20th Oct and Bank Holiday Mondays, 10am – 5pm • Entrance: £3.50, children free • Other information: Parking across road ○ ⬛ 📠 WC ⅋ 🛍 ⓦ

This exceptionally handsome eighteenth-century Baroque Cotswold village house with fine views is enhanced by a medium-sized garden largely created under the present ownership. The diminutive geometrical *potager* is a particular delight. Well-kept lawns, quiet fountains, a knot garden and Cotswold stone walls set off a number of herbaceous borders in which the choice and arrangement of plants and shrubs skilfully use current fashions in garden design. Each year there are new interests – the raised pond in the top garden, a topiary walk, and long terraces on the main lawn now planted with low-growing shrubs, perennials and roses. Entering the new shade-house is like entering a cocoon where novel shade-loving plants can flourish. Nearby Sezincote and Batsford, and Hidcote as well as Kiftsgate (see entries) are less than half an hour away and make Bourton House a sensible location to include while garden touring in this part of Gloucestershire.

Brackenbury 6

Coombe GL12 7NF. Tel: (01453) 842238

Mr and Mrs Peter Heaton • 1m NE of Wotton-under-Edge off B4058. From church go ½ m on Stroud road, turn right (signed 'Coombe'). From Stroud, go 300 yards past Wotton sign, turn left (signed 'Coombe') and garden is on right • Open for NGS 29th May, 25th June, 30th July, 28th Aug, 2 – 6pm • Entrance: £2, children free [NEW] ● ⬛ WC ⬧ ⅋

This small terraced garden with multi-layer planting is clearly designed by a plantsman with designer tastes. Foliage is a feature. There are good mixed borders, a cottage garden, a pool, 1000 different hardy perennials and 200 different shrubs. The vegetable garden is laid out on the deep-bed system. It is worth a visit in June and July just to see the National Collection of erigerons.

Burnt Norton 7

Near Chipping Campden GL55 6PR. Tel: (01386) 840162

The Earl of Harrowby • 1½ m N of Chipping Campden on road to Mickleton. As road goes downhill turn left into farm lane then through wood for ½ m • Open by appt (telephone caretaker) • Entrance: £2, children free; discounts for parties available ● ● & ♨

Burnt Norton is famous because T.S. Eliot, staying in 1934 at a nearby house (now a grand hotel), went over to see the estate in the belief that it belonged to a Birmingham businessman. In fact it was one of several residences of the Harrowby family, whose ancestor had purchased it in the mid-eighteenth century, and its extensive terraces, rose gardens, etc., appealed to the poet whose mind at the time was concentrating on the thought that 'Time present and time past/Are both perhaps present in time future/And time future contained in time past.' The result was the most famous poem in the *Four Quartets* series. Visitors with literary interests will find it useful to have a copy to hand. Others will enjoy the bluebell walk, the classical pavilion, the deserted pools and the brick terraces. Good views, reminiscent of Hidcote (see entry).

Cerney House Gardens 8

North Cerney, Cirencester GL7 7BX. Tel: (01285) 831300/831205; Fax: (01285) 831676

Sir Michael and Lady Angus • 3½ m N of Cirencester off A435 Cheltenham road. Turn left opposite Bathurst Arms, follow road up hill past church, and turn in through gates on right • Open April to Sept, Tues, Wed and Fri, 10am – 5pm and one Sun in May for charity. Open at other times and for parties by appt • Entrance: £3, children £1 • Other information: Lunches and high teas by arrangement ◐ ● WC & ♨ 🖐

Around the house, remodelled by Decimus Burton in 1791, goats and sheep graze and wild flowers flourish in their meadow. The pleasantly unmanicured garden is not for those who like everything tickety-boo – the plants are happy and unrestrained. There are lawns, shrubs and trees around the house, and behind it a three-and-a-half-acre sloping walled garden restored since the mid-1980s with riotous herbaceous borders, vegetables, many old-fashioned roses, clematis and a delightful children's story-book pig (a Gloucester Old Spot, of course) beneath the apple trees nearby. A woodland walk is carpeted with snowdrops in February and bluebells in May. There is a colourful rockery behind the house, with a waterfall. The herb garden, geranium and thyme bank, and pink border beside the swimming pool are now well established, and there is a genera-garden leading down to the pond, and a tree trail. Garden labels are packed with information, particularly those in the new beds to the side of the house which tell the stories of plant-hunters and famous nurserymen. The locality is rich in Roman history, with Chedworth Roman Villa a few miles away. The nearby twelfth-century church is well worth a visit.

Chipping Campden Gardens 9

Chipping Campden.

N of A44 between Evesham and Stow-on-the-Wold and S of Stratford-upon-Avon off A46 E of Broadway

Because of its position near Hidcote, Kiftsgate and Charlcote, the town is a popular holiday stopping-off point for garden visitors, so it is fortuitous that it has one garden permanently open. Watch out in local press for other gardens to visit, particularly those on N of main street. Open all year is the *Ernest Wilson Memorial Garden*, in the High Street. It was opened in 1984 in memory of 'Chinese' Wilson, who was born in Chipping Campden in 1876. The famous collector is estimated to have introduced 1200 species of trees and shrubs during his career, and the garden has several of his finds, including *Acer griseum* (the paperbark maple), *Davidia involucrata* (the pocket-handkerchief tree), and the plant for which he wished to be remembered, *Lilium regale*. It is a peaceful oasis, with seats and shade, backed by the beautiful church tower. Admission is free, with a box for contributions to its upkeep set in the stone wall beside the entrance arch. Other gardens in Chipping Campden and neighbouring Broad Campden are open for charity, and for the past few years a charity has arranged for 30 gardens to open over a June weekend. This will probably become an annual event. The choice of gardens appears to have been dictated by a desire for quantity rather than quality, and in general their appeal will be to those who like what is now called the traditional Cotswold style.

The Chipping Croft 10

The Chipping, Tetbury GL8 8EY. Tel: (01666) 503570

Dr and Mrs P. Taylor • In town centre proceed between The Snooty Fox and Barclays past parking in Chipping Square. Garden is at bottom on left behind wall with tall trees, entrance in driveway to courtyard • Open by appt • Entrance: £2.50 ● 🖼 ⅃ ⅃ 🖾 🌿

This is a most unusual town garden because of its size and character. Entering through a courtyard leading to a large and immaculately maintained lawn bordered by mature trees and a wooded walk, it extends to about two acres and is on three levels. At one time, the mostly Queen Anne house was used as a school, and since 1985 Dr Taylor has transformed a hard-surfaced playground area into a courtyard with a small rectangular raised pool and a conservatory. He has replanted extensively, constructed a summerhouse/potting shed and added new steps connecting the various levels. Three formal terrace-gardens contain a variety of cottage-garden flowers as well as unusual plants, vegetables and herbs, with the kitchen garden proper laid out as a *potager* on a higher level. Beneath the terraces is a wide walk with borders either side and arches covered with roses, honeysuckle and clematis leading back to the house.

Cirencester Park   11

Cirencester.

On W side of Cirencester, leading up to entrance to Cirencester Park • Open daily, 8am – 5pm ○ **WC**

The Park is open all the year round, courtesy of Lord Bathurst. Note the perimeter hedge, claimed to be the largest in the world, planted in 1720 by the first Earl Bathurst – it is over 12 metres. The Becks at 25 *Bowling Green Road*, just off A417, have what they call 'a floral jungle', with a wide range of perennials, including geraniums and more than 200 day lilies, roses and clematis, and will be open for NGS on certain Suns from June to Aug, all 2 – 5pm. Private visits also welcome from June to August but telephone (01285) 653778 first.

Conderton Manor

(see Worcestershire)

Cotswold Farm   12

Duntisbourne Abbots, Cirencester GL7 7JS. Tel: (01285) 653856

Major and Mrs P.D. Birchall • 5m N of Cirencester off A417. From Cirencester turn left signed Duntisbourne Abbots/Services, then immediately right and under underpass. Private drive straight ahead. From Gloucester turn left signed Duntisbourne Abbots/Services, past Centurion Garage. Private drive on left • Open by appt (adequate notice appreciated) • Entrance: £2.50 ● **WC**

A mature garden planted in grand style and sustained with sensitive artistry surrounding a fine old house in a superb Cotswold setting. The terrace was designed by Norman Jewson in 1938. The formal walled gardens have a pool and are planted with shrub, bush and climbing roses, alpines, lavender and a collection of scented flowers. There are also established plantings of shrubs, herbaceous perennials and many small treasures overlooking an unspoilt wooded valley. A charmed garden redolent of another age in a remote and lovely situation.

Cowley Manor   13

Cowley, Cheltenham GL53 9NL. Tel: (01242) 870540

The Cowley Manor Partnership • 5m S of Cheltenham. Approach from A435 Cheltenham – Cirencester road. Turn at sign for Cowley and, shortly after small bridge, turn left into drive for Manor • Open March to Oct, daily except Fri and Mon (but open Bank Holiday Mons), 10am – 6pm. Also at other times for individuals and parties by appt • Entrance: £3.50, OAPs £2, under 18s free, parties of 20 or more £3 per person, season ticket £20 • Other information: Dogs, Mon – Fri only, on lead ◑ 🐾 **WC** ⬧

Cowley Manor, gloriously situated on the edge of the Cotswolds, has 50 acres of Victorian landscaped grounds with woodland, four lakes and a dramatic

Italianate cascade (featured in Gertrude Jekyll's 1918 *Garden Ornament*). This is only the fourth year of the garden's return to life after a period of neglect: Noël Kingsbury intends gradually to restore the historic architectural features and to conserve the landscape as a whole. There are planting schemes inspired by contemporary Dutch and German design as well as perennials naturalised in grass alongside wild flowers, an idea first promoted by William Robinson at the end of the last century. It is also hoped to combine these schemes with new tree and shrub planting that concentrates on rare species and material collected from the wild; Cowley has been selected by Edinburgh Botanic Gardens as a site for a Conifer Conservation Programme Collection. This is an exciting project, and it is sheer delight to wander round the meadows, lawns and lakes with swans, Canada geese, tufted ducks, moorhens, coots and other wildlife. Lewis Carroll, when staying nearby, is thought to have found inspiration here for *Alice in Wonderland*. Perhaps there is a white rabbit in the undergrowth. At nearby *Colesbourne Park* are two weekends in February for snowdrop enthusiasts. For opening times, telephone (01242) 870264/870262.

Daylesford House ★ 14

Daylesford, Moreton–in–Marsh GL56 0YH. Tel: (01608) 659888

Sir Anthony and Lady Bamford • Off A436 between Stow-on-the-Wold and Chipping Norton • Open by appt on weekdays for parties only • Entrance: £5 per person ● WC ♿

Like nearby Sezincote, Daylesford House was designed by Samuel Pepys Cockerell. Warren Hastings, the first Governor-General of India, bought the Daylesford Estate in 1785; he was interested in gardening and built the large walled garden before the house was completed. This was stocked with exotic plants and fruits, and a yak which he brought back from India roamed around the extensive grounds. John Davenport was employed to design the layout of the garden, the lakes and the Gothick orangery. The garden is a delight, with its magnificent lawns and lakes complete with swans and Canada geese, woodland walks (carpeted with violets, primroses and many other wild flowers in spring, bluebells in May and wild orchids in the summer), orangery full of unusual shrubs, trellised rose garden and the decorative formal fruit and vegetable walled garden with orchid house, peach house and working glass-houses – a garden in the making. A great deal for the plantsman and others to see.

Dyrham Park 15

Chippenham SN14 8ER. Tel: (0117) 937 2501

The National Trust • 8m N of Bath, 12m E of Bristol on A46. Take M4 junction 18 in direction of Bath • House (including domestic areas) open as garden from 12 noon but closed 7th, 8th July • Garden open April to Oct, daily except Wed and Thurs, 11am – 5.30pm (last admission 5pm or dusk if earlier). Park open all year except 25th Dec, daily, 12 noon – 5.30pm or dusk if earlier (opens 11am on days when garden is open) • Entrance: park only £1.90, children 90p; park and garden £2.60, children £1.30; house, garden and park

£7.50, children £3.70, family ticket £18.50 • Other information: Possible for wheelchairs on terrace but park steep in places. All cars in car park at East Lodge, bus link to house and garden. Dogs in dog walking area only, on lead • Garden: ◐ ☕ ✕ WC ⚘ 🛍 ⛲ *Park:* ○ 🏛

Only a tiny fragment of the extensive London and Wise Baroque garden shown in the view by Kip in 1712 survives. The terraces were all smoothed out in the late eighteenth century to form an 'English' landscape with fine mature beech, Spanish chestnut, Lucombe oak, red oak and black walnut. Avenues of elms survived until the mid-1970s when they were wiped out by Dutch elm disease; they have since been replanted with limes. The cascade in the garden on the west side is still working and one can make out the form of the original garden and enjoy the terrace and Talman's orangery, all 30 metres now splendidly transformed and wonderfully scented. The views towards Bristol and the elegance of the 'natural' landscape, with the house and church tucked into the hillside make this an outstanding example of English landscape gardening. In all, 263 acres of ancient parkland. A transit link from car park to house enables visitors to enjoy the view of the house.

Ewen Manor   16

Ewen, Cirencester GL7 6BX. Tel: (01285) 770206

Lady Gibbs • 4m S of Cirencester off A429. Turn at signpost for Ewen, 1m • Open May to 10th July, Tues – Thurs, and probably for charity 30th April, 7th May • Entrance: £2 • Other information: Teas on charity days only ● 🏛 WC ⬦

In the late 1940s this was a run-down manor garden which had in part been used as a Dig-for-Victory patch. The Georgian house had been moved here from across the Thames 200 years earlier. Backed by magnificent trees, it now contains a series of gardens with architectural features, and everywhere the planting is profuse. There are views across the pattern-mown lawn to the circular summerhouse with its conical Cotswold stone-tiled roof, and to the 215-year-old cedars of Lebanon in the woodland area all around. The main herbaceous border is backed by a high yew hedge, behind which is a large rectangular lily pool surrounded by masses of helianthemums, overlooked by the garden room, once the stables, with its plant-filled terrace and pots. Daffodils and spring bulbs in May.

Frampton Court   17

Frampton–on–Severn GL2 7EU. Tel: (01452) 740267 (home); (01452) 740698 (office)

Mrs Peter Clifford • SW of Gloucester, 2m from M5 junction 13. Signposted. Left side of village green, entrance through imposing gates in long wall between two large chestnut trees • House open all year by appt with guided tours by owner. £4.50 per person • Garden open all year by appt • Entrance: £1 • Other information: Refreshments in village hall on selected days ● ☕ 🏛 WC ♿ ⬦

Home of Clifford lady ancestors, the botanic artists who painted The Frampton Flora 1830-1860, Frampton Court remains an elegant family establishment on land owned by the Clifford family since the twelfth century. The house, dating from the 1730s, is of the Vanbrugh school, with exquisite interior woodwork and furnishings which may be shown by appointment to visitors, preferably in parties, by the present owner. The five-acre grounds are maintained with a minimum of labour and contain a lake, fine trees and a formal water garden of Dutch design, believed to have been built by the architects of the larger Westbury Court Garden (see entry) on the other side of the Severn. A Strawberry Hill Gothic Orangery 1750 (not always open but available for holiday letting), where the ladies are believed to have executed their work, stands reflected in the still water, planted with lilies and flanked by a mixed border. This garden is open in association with that of *Frampton Manor*, also occupied by Cliffords, where a strongly planted walled garden with many old roses is set off splendidly by a fine fifteenth-century timbered house.

Great Rissington Farm   18

Great Rissington GL54 2LH. Tel: (01451) 820322

The Hon. John and Mrs Donovan • 4m SE of Stow-on-the-Wold, 6m NW of Burford off A424 onto Barrington road. From Stow, turn right after sign to 'Barn Business Centre' at lodge. From Burford pass sign left to Great Rissington and turn left at lodge • Open June and July, Tues, 2 – 5.30pm • Entrance: £2, children free ◐

On arriving at this sixteenth-century Cotswold house and its two acres, the visitor is assured of a warm welcome from the enthusiastic owner-gardeners. Three small walled gardens are filled with a large collection of roses and herbaceous plants and a long border runs behind here, which is partly shaded. A wide border on the edge of the lawn has bold planting of large shrubs and on the far side is a small spinney, partially cleared and being replanted with interesting new trees and shrubs. This is a most exciting young garden with lovely design and great potential complemented by marvellous views over surrounding countryside.

Hidcote Manor Garden ★★   19

Hidcote Bartrim, Chipping Campden GL55 6LR. Tel: (01386) 438333; Fax: (01386) 438817

The National Trust • 3m NE of Chipping Campden. Signposted • Garden open 1st April to 21st May, then Aug to 5th Nov, daily except Tues and Fri (but open Tues 22nd May to July), 11am – 6pm (5pm in Oct) (last admission 1 hour before closing). Parties by written appt only. Liable to overcrowding on Bank Holiday Mons and fine Suns • Entrance: £5.60, children £2.80, family (2 adults and up to 4 children) £14. No party concessions • Other information: Coaches by prior arrangement only ◐ ☕ ✕ WC ♿ ⚘ ▥

It is unnecessary to describe this garden in detail, as it is one of the most famous in Britain and an essential visit for garden lovers of every persuasion. It was created in the early years of the twentieth century by Lawrence Johnston with a strong sense of design and great skill in planting, using many new introductions, some of which he had collected himself. Many varieties now bear the name Hidcote. Given to the Trust in 1948, its splendid architectural effects and bold plantings have been retained, and those visitors who query the use of annuals may like to know that Johnston used many half-hardy varieties, even more of which are used today to prolong the flowering season in the Old Garden, Red Borders, etc. Johnston's achievement is all the more remarkable because of the isolation of the hill-top site, whose scale can be appreciated by the view from the entrance to Kiftsgate garden, which is within walking distance (see entry). See also Vale House, Chipping Camden and Sezincote. *Note:* For those lucky enough to be visiting the South of France, Lawrence Johnston's other garden, *La Serre de la Madone*, is being bought by a public conservation body. It is hoped they will restore the garden and open it to the public.

Hodges Barn ★   20

Shipton Moyne, Tetbury GL8 8PR. Tel: (01666) 880202

Mrs Charles Hornby • *3m S of Tetbury, 3m NW of Malmesbury just outside Shipton Moyne on Malmesbury side* • *Open 9th, 10th April, 21st, 22nd May, 4th, 5th June for NGS, 2 – 5pm. Also by appt* • *Entrance: £3, children free*
◐ 🏠 WC ♿ ⏏ ♨

In 1499 this was built as a dovecot or columbarium to a large house nearby, the latter burnt down in 1556. It was converted to a home in 1938 and bought by the Hon. Mrs Arthur Strutt, the late Mr Hornby's grandmother, in 1946. She set about creating the basic structure of the garden with good stone walls and topiary; she also planted most of the trees before her death in 1973. Another influence on the present garden was the once-famous Pusey House, near Faringdon, owned by Mr Hornby's parents, who supplied some of the fine plants at Hodges Barn. It is an extensive eight-acre garden, with plenty of interest for everyone – above all those who like roses (there are well over 100 different varieties). The spring garden, the water garden, the little wild wood-land, the large cleared wood, the topiary and the splendid lawns are all enjoyable. The plantings reflect a preoccupation with colour, scent and variety, uninhibited by a desire to prevent one flower or shrub from growing into another. Note the planting in gravel along some of the many beds, and the tapestry hedges. This is a garden which reeks of enthusiasm – long may it continue. On two weekends, in April and June, a rare opportunity to see a medieval castle with a marvellously romantic garden, only 2m W of Tetbury on the A4135, is offered by the owner of *Beverston Castle* (Mrs L. Rook). Rare because the castle is absorbed into the seventeenth-century house, looking down onto the paved terrace, moat and walled kitchen garden. Telephone (01666) 502219 for details of this year's opening. We hope to give a full description next year.

Hullasey House   21

Tarlton, Cirencester GL7 6PA. Tel: (01285) 770132

Mr and Mrs Jonathan Taylor • *5m SW of Cirencester off A433. In Tarlton, follow lane marked 'church'. Drive few 100 yds on right* • *Open 11th, 24th,*

25th, 26th June, 2 – 5pm for charity and Mon by appt • Entrance: £2, children free ● &

Mrs Taylor has achieved a well-established, medium-sized traditional Cotswold garden here in little more than five years, and overcome the problem of a windy situation. With spectacular views, the front of the house is a formal area with sweeping lawn and octagonal box-edged beds in purple, mauve, white and silver. The luxuriant herb garden is contained within a walled parterre, with fruit trees, yet more roses and a miniature camomile lawn. There is a splendid walled garden with an exuberant mixture of herbaceous plants and roses of every description, rambling around and beside the walls and over arches, intertwined with honeysuckle. Beyond is the spring garden, planted with wild daffodils and scillas, and the wild rose garden. A pond is in its infancy.

Hunts Court 22

North Nibley, Dursley GL11 6DZ. Tel: (01453) 547440

Mr and Mrs T.K. Marshall • 2m NW of Wotton-under-Edge near North Nibley. Turn E off B4060 in Nibley at Black Horse Inn and fork left after ¼ m • Garden open all year except Aug and 25th, 26th Dec, Tues – Sat, 9am – 5pm. Also Good Friday, Easter Monday, Spring Bank Holiday Mon and some Suns in June and July for NGS, 2 – 6pm. Telephone for details • Entrance: £2 • Other information: Teas on Suns only ○ **WC** & ♨

A must for those with a love of old roses. June sees in excess of 400 varieties – species, climbing and shrub – filling the borders, cascading the rails, pergolas and trees and spilling out over the informal grass paths which weave a passage through rare shrubs and herbaceous perennials. A more formal sundial garden, recently developed, the beds intersected with gravel paths, is colour co-ordinated and provides a home for hardy geraniums, penstemons and diascias. In another area mown paths draw the eye towards the Cotswold escarpment which commands the eastern landscape. Summer is inevitably dominated by roses but this is not to deny interest in other seasons, for this is a garden to provide something of note for the greater part of the year. In the adjoining nursery many of the plants growing in the garden are for sale, and the owner is on hand with helpful advice. A useful leaflet is available.

Kiftsgate Court ★★ 23

Chipping Campden GL55 6LW. Tel/Fax: (01386) 438777

Mr and Mrs J.G. Chambers • 3m NE of Chipping Campden and near Mickleton, very close to Hidcote, which is signposted • Open April, May, Aug and Sept, Wed, Thurs, Sun and Bank Holiday Mons, 2 – 6pm; June and July, Wed, Thurs, Sat, Sun, 12 noon – 6pm (Note: not identical opening times with Hidcote) • Entrance: £4, children £1 • Other information: Coaches by appt only ◑ ☕ WC ♨

The house was built in the late nineteenth century on this magnificent site surrounded by three steep banks. The garden was largely created by the present owner's grandmother, who with her husband moved there after

World War I. Her work was continued by her daughter, Diany Binny, who made a few alterations but continued the colour schemes of the borders. In spring, the white sunken garden is covered with bulbs and there is a fine show of daffodils along the drive. June and July are the peak months for colour and scent, but the magnificent old and species roses are the glory of this garden, home of *Rosa filipes* 'Kiftsgate'. Other features are perennial geraniums, a large wisteria and many species of hydrangea, some very large. In autumn, Japanese maples glow in the bluebell wood. This garden should not be missed, not only because of its proximity to Hidcote, but because of its profusion of colour and apparent informality. Unusual plants are sometimes amongst those available for sale. Vale House (see entry) is nearby.

Lydney Park Gardens 24

Lydney GL15 6BU. Tel: (01594) 842027

Viscount Bledisloe • 20m SW of Gloucester. N of A48 between Lydney and Aylburton • Gardens open 26th March to 4th June, Sun and Wed; also 23rd April to 1st May (but closed 29th April), 28th May to 2nd June, 4th June; all 11am – 6pm. Parties by appt • Entrance: £3 (except Wed when £2), accompanied children free • Other information: Picnics in deer park only. Roman site and museum ◑ ♨ ▤ WC ⬥ ⅋ ⊞

The park dates from the seventeenth century, and although it has been in the hands of one family since 1723, a new house was built in 1875 and the old one demolished. An area near the house has an interesting collection of magnolias, and a picturesque sight is the bank of daffodils and cherries, splendid in season. From 1955 a woodland garden was developed in the wooded valley, behind and below the house, with the aim of achieving bold colour at different times between March and June. Near the entrance to the main part of the gardens is a small pool surrounded by azaleas and a collection of acers. From here the route passes through carefully planted groups of rhododendrons and past a folly, brought from Venice. This overlooks a valley and bog garden. Crisscrossing the hillside are rare and fine rhododendrons and azaleas, including an area planted with un-named seedlings. Enormous effort has gone into the plant design, colour combination and general landscaping, and those who are enthusiastic about rhododendrons, azaleas and all varieties of shrubs and trees will find enough to enjoy for a whole day. Nearby is the Roman camp and museum containing the famous bronze Lydney dog, while the park contains a fine collection of trees and a herd of fallow deer. Guide book with map available.

13 Merestones Drive 25

Cheltenham GL50 2SU. Tel: (01242) 578678

Mr Dennis Moorcraft • In Cheltenham. From A46, follow signs to GLOSCAT (technical college). Turn off The Park to Merestones Drive • Open 4th, 18th June, 2 – 6pm for NGS and by appt • Entrance: £1.50, children 50p • Other information: Teas on charity days only ◑ ⅋

Merestones Drive, a suburban *cul-de-sac*, gives not the slightest hint of the pleasures and surprises to be found at the end of it, at Number Thirteen. Bordered by mature trees and with a small brook running through, the garden has an enormous variety of unusual plants, shrubs and trees, many propagated from seed brought back from the owner's travels abroad and now growing in profusion beside brick paths and terraces and/or in the dry shade under the trees. Species roses riot into and over the trees alongside the drive. There is a small scree garden. Hostas and ferns are a speciality (there are nearly 100 different varieties of hosta). In less than a decade, the owner has created a richly diverse plantsperson's garden.

Misarden Park Gardens ★ 26

Miserden, Stroud GL6 7JA. Tel: (01285) 821303

Major M.T.N.H. Wills • 3m NW of Cirencester, 3m off A417. Signposted • Open April to Sept, Tues, Wed and Thurs, 10am – 5pm. Parties by appt • Entrance: £3 (inc. printed guide), children free. Reduction for parties of 20 or more. Guided tour extra • Other information: Adjacent nursery open daily except Mon ◑ WC & ⬥ ⚲

This lovely, timeless English garden, which commands spectacular views over the Golden Valley, has most of the features one expects of a garden started in the seventeenth century. There are extensive yew hedges, a York-stone terrace, a Lutyens loggia overhung with wisteria, and a good specimen of *Magnolia x soulangeana*. The south lawn sports splendid grass steps. West of the house the ground ascends to the nursery in a series of grassed terraces. There are two good herbaceous borders leading to a traditional rose garden beyond. There are many fine specimen trees, and the spring show of blossom and bulbs is notable. A new rill and summerhouse have been added. The seventeenth-century manor house is not open.

Moor Wood 27

Woodmancote, Cirencester GL7 7EB. Tel: (01285) 831397;
Fax: (01285) 831859

Mr and Mrs Henry Robinson • 3½ m N of Cirencester off A435. In North Cerney through white gates on left beside lodge • Parking at end of drive • Open 25th June, 2nd July, 2 – 6pm and by appt • Entrance: £2, children free • Other information: Teas on open days only ●

With its attractive valley setting, this is the perfect home for a National Collection of rambler roses – 120 in all, crawling over every wall surrounding the gardens of this Cotswold family house and its cottages and stables. Since 1984 the owners have been gradually building up the collection and restoring the gardens, a continuing process. There are two acres of cottage gardens, formal lawn and borders, shrubs, orchard and terraced garden. What was the old walled vegetable garden is now a mass of wild flowers, all contributing to a delightfully natural atmosphere in keeping with the surrounding farmland.

Old Mill Dene 28

Blockley, Moreton-in-Marsh GL56 9HU. Tel: (01386) 700457; Fax: (01386) 700526; Website: http://www.SmoothHound.co.uk(hotels)/milldene.html

Mr and Mrs B.S. Dare • 3m W of Moreton-in-Marsh on A44 • Open April to Oct, Mon – Fri, (inc. most Bank Holiday Mons) 10am – 6pm. Also by appt. Parties welcome for tours • Entrance: £2.50, children £1. Special rates for parties ◑ ☕ 🖻 WC 🅿 🍴

The two-and-a-half-acre garden, built around the mill pond and stream, is crammed with innovations, such as a grotto and *trompe-l'oeil*. Climbing up the terraces which hug the steep hillside, the visitor finds that each has a different character and planting scheme, and there are splendid views from the top. New are a pergola by James Bolton, and a landscaped orchard. Up to a dozen gardens are open one or two days for charity in this picturesque hilly Cotswold village and they are well worth a visit, though some present steep climbs. Nearby is *Peartrees*, a small cottage garden, full of Mrs Beckwith's surprises, also open by appointment (01386) 700464.

The Old Rectory 29

Duntisbourne Rouse, Daglingworth, Cirencester GL7 7AP.

Charles and Mary Keen • 3m NW of Cirencester off A417. Via Daglingworth take narrow valley road for the Duntisbournes. After ½ m house is on right next to church • Open on several Mons for NGS and also by written appt for parties of 4 or more • Entrance: £2.50, children free. Parties negotiable. Light refreshments in winter ◑ WC

In an exceptional natural setting next to the Saxon church admired by John Betjeman, overlooking the little River Dunt, the Old Rectory was once the home of Katherine Mansfield's sister, Jean Renshaw. This is, however, by no means a typical Cotswold garden. Since 1993, Mary Keen, garden writer and designer, has created an unusual garden of many moods and different levels, full of year-round interest and surprising variety. Its one and a half acres combine informality within a formal framework of box and yew, as well as areas of lawn, orchard and meadow in miniature, a kitchen garden and a conservatory ablaze with unusual pelargoniums. An auricula cupboard and topiary. Unusual perennials, half-hardies and winter plants a speciality.

Orchard Cottage 30

Duglinch Lane, Gretton, Cheltenham GL54 5EX. Tel: (01242) 602491

Mr Rory Stuart • 6m NE of Cheltenham off B4078. In Gretton turn beside Bugatti Inn into Duglinch Lane. Cottage 300 metres on right opposite black railings • Open all year by appt only • Entrance: £1.50 for charity ◑

Well past the somewhat unpromising suburban beginnings of Duglinch Lane and tucked into the hillside near the famous Bugatti Club's Prescott Hill Climb is a romantic cottage garden created largely by the present owner's aunt, the late Mrs Nancy Saunders, in the 1950s. She was helped by John Codrington, whom she met on a botanical expedition. (She derived great pleasure from collecting plants during her travels abroad, bringing them home in her sponge-bag.) The approximately one and a half acres consist of an old orchard with a variety of unusual shrubs and trees, from which there is a splendid view towards Bredon Hill, and the garden around the cottage. The wide range of planting is for all-year interest, but if hellebores are your particular passion February to March would be the best time to see the extensive collection.

Owlpen Manor 31

Uley, Dursley GL11 5BZ. Tel: (01453) 860261

Mr and Mrs N. Mander • 6m SW of Stroud, 3m E of Dursley off B4066. 1m E of Uley. Signposted. Steep and winding drive • House open • Garden open April to Oct, Tues – Sun and Bank Holiday Mons, 2 – 5pm • Entrance: £2.75 (house and garden £4.50, children £2) ◑ ☕ ✕ 🍴 WC ♿

Situated in a remote Cotswold valley, the small hillside garden at Owlpen is an unusually complete survival of an early formal manorial garden, described by the late Sir Geoffrey Jellicoe as possibly the loveliest domestic garden in England, largely retaining its original form. Formal seventeenth-century gardens are laid out on seven hanging terraces with topiary yews, box parterres, old roses, and steep steps leading down to the mill pond. Making use of the old records, the gardens are being extended among open lawns, suggesting a plan of the early eighteenth century.

Painswick Rococo Garden ★ 32

Painswick GL6 6TH. Tel: (01452) 813204

Painswick Rococo Gardens Trust • ½ m from Painswick on B4073. Signposted • Open 12th Jan to Nov, Wed – Sun; also 24th April, 1st, 29th May, 28th Aug; and July and Aug, daily, all 11am – 5pm • Entrance: £3.30, OAPs £3, children £1.75 • Other information: Coaches by appt ◑ ☕ ✕ 🍴 WC ♿ 🐕 🛍 ♿

A great deal of time, money and effort is going into the restoration (almost complete redevelopment) of this rare Rococo survival. Much of the work is now completed with new plantings becoming established. At present, the best features are the eighteenth-century garden buildings, the views into beautiful surrounding countryside, and the marvellous snowdrop wood spanning a stream that flows from a pond at the lower end. This must be one of the best displays of naturalised snowdrops in England. There are some splendid beech woods and older specimen trees. Wild flowers are allowed complete freedom. Rococo gardening was an eighteenth-century combination of formal geometric features with winding woodland paths, revealing sudden incidents and vistas – in essence, a softening of the formal French style, apparent from about 1715 onwards in all forms of art. The basis for Painswick's present restoration is a painting by Thomas Robins (1716-1778) done in 1748 for Benjamin Hyett, who created the garden in the grounds of the house built by his father in 1735. To celebrate the 250 years of its existence, Painswick's owners have planted a yew hedge maze, designed by Angela Newing, in adjoining farmland; something to look forward to as it matures. In total it is a large estate and visitors (who should be fit for some steep inclines) must allow three-quarters of an hour or more even for a brisk walk round its many beauties.

The Priory

(see Worcestershire)

Rockcliffe   33

Lower Swell, Stow-on-the-Wold GL54 2JW

Mr and Mrs Simon Keswick • 3m W of Stow-on-the-Wold on B4068 • Open 7th, 8th, 14th, 15th, 21st June, 10am – 5pm • Entrance: £2.50, children under 15 free ● ▉ WC ✿

Tranquil Cotswold pastures with grazing sheep are the perfect setting for this immaculately cared-for five-acre garden which Mrs Keswick has created in the last 18 years. The walled and box-edged kitchen garden has pleached horn-beams, espaliered medlars and herbaceous borders, and to the side of it an intriguing bird topiary yew avenue flanking the path through the wildflower orchard which leads up to the site of the proposed dovecot. At the front of the house is a box parterre and well-kept lawns with a delightful pastoral view beyond the ha-ha. The sunken garden has a lily pond surrounded by variegated *Cornus controversa* to reflect in the water. The main herbaceous border leads on through a succession of yew-enclosed pink, blue, white and silver gardens, with vistas at every turn. The swimming-pool garden is exceptionally pretty, with rose-clad walls and hardy geraniums: the pump-house is covered with bright pink *Rosa* 'Zéphirine Drouhin', with blue *Nepeta* x *faassenii* all around – a simple but stunning effect.

Rodmarton Manor ★   34

Rodmarton, Cirencester GL7 6PF. Tel: (01285) 841253; Fax: (01285) 841298

Mr and Mrs Simon Biddulph • 6m SW of Cirencester, 4m NE of Tetbury off A433, halfway between Cirencester and Tetbury • House open to parties for tours by written appt • Garden open 10th May to 28th Aug, Weds, Sats and Bank Holiday Mondays, 2 – 5pm and at other times by appt. Conducted tours can be booked • Entrance: £2.50, accompanied children under 14 free (house and garden: parties of 15 or more £6 per person, children £3) • Other information: Coaches use Holly (west) drive. Large coaches need to reverse down drive. Tea and biscuits by prior arrangement and at extra charge ◖ WC ♿

Rodmarton Manor and its garden, designed by Ernest Barnsley for the Biddulphs from 1909, is an excellent example of the English Arts and Crafts Movement at its best and has been featured in numerous books and magazines over the years. The drive lies between impeccably clipped tapestry hedges, and the garden, which retains virtually all its original features, comprises a series of outdoor rooms, each with its own character, bordered by fine hedges of yew, beech, holly and box, for which it is famous. In front of the house is the terrace and topiary garden, the recently replanted trough garden, a sunken garden and white borders leading to the cherry orchard, which has a wide variety of snowdrops in early spring, as well as shrubs and roses. There is a good rockery, a wild garden with hornbeam avenue, and many attractive vistas. The large working kitchen garden features both culinary and ornamental plants, old apple arches, a new collection of old-fashioned and scented roses, and a row of sinks. Several areas have been replanted since 1991 when Mr and Mrs Simon Biddulph moved into the Manor, including parts of the leisure garden and the four large herbaceous borders, which are now quite magnificent. The shrubbery is currently undergoing renovation. Beautifully kept, this garden is full of romance and excitement. Helpful and interesting booklet available.

Sezincote ★★   35

Moreton–in–Marsh GL56 9AW.

Mr and Mrs D. Peake • 1½ m W of Moreton-in-Marsh on A44 just before Bourton-on-the-Hill • House open May to July and Sept, Thurs, Fri, 2.30 – 6pm (no children in house) • Garden open Jan to Nov, Thurs, Fri and Bank Holiday Mons, 2 – 6pm (or dusk if earlier). Also 10th July for charity • Entrance: £3.50, children £1, children under 5 free (house and garden £5) • Other information: Teas on charity open day only ☉ WC

The entrance to Sezincote is up a long dark avenue of holm oaks that opens into the most English of parks, with a distinct feel of Repton influence – fine trees and distant views of Cotswold hills. Turning the last corner is the surprise, for there is that fascinating rarity, an English country house built in the Moghul architectural style by Samuel Pepys Cockerell. The form of the garden has not changed since Repton's time, but the more recent planting was carried out by Lady Kleinwort with help from Graham Stuart Thomas, and on her return from India in 1968 she laid out the 'Paradise Garden' in the south garden, with canals and Irish yews. Behind this is the curved orangery, home to many tender climbing plants. The house is sheltered by great copper beeches, cedars, yews and limes, which provide a fine backdrop for the exotic shrubs. Streams and pools are lined with great clumps of bog-loving plants, and the stream is crossed by an Indian bridge, adorned with Brahmin bulls. The garden is planted for year-round interest. It is particularly strong on autumn colours, and the instructive guide to the garden, by Graham Stuart Thomas, is highly recommended. Nearby is *Compton Lane Nurseries*, open March to Sept, Wed, Thurs and Sat, 10am – 5pm. Tel: (01608) 674578.

Snowshill Manor ★   36

Broadway WR12 7JU. Tel: (01386) 852410

The National Trust • 3m S of Broadway off A44 • Manor open 1pm. Last admission 4.15pm. Timed ticket system • Garden open April to 1st Nov, daily except Tues, 1 – 5pm. Closed 21st April • Entrance: grounds £2.50 (manor and grounds £5.60, children £2.80, family ticket £14) (1999 prices) • Other information: Coaches by written appt only. No entry from Snowshill village. Car

*park 500 metres from Manor with entry via footpath. Braille guide available,
but otherwise unsuitable for disabled* ◑ ✕ 🏠

From a design by M.H. Baillie-Scott, the owner Charles Wade transformed a
'wilderness of chaos' on a Cotswold hillside into an interconnecting series of
outdoor 'rooms' in Hidcote style from the 1920s onwards. Wade was a believer
in the Arts and Crafts rustic ideal and the garden, like the house, expresses his
eccentricities. Seats and woodwork are painted 'Wade' blue, a powdery dark
blue with touches of turquoise which goes well with the Cotswold stone walls.
The simple cottage style conceals careful planting in blue, mauve and purple
motif. Organic gardening is employed here. The Visitors' Centre is not to
everybody's taste.

Stancombe Park ★   37

Stancombe, Dursley GL11 6AU. Tel: (01453) 542815

*Mrs Barlow • Between Wotton-under-Edge and Dursley on B4060 • Open by
appt for parties • Entrance: £3, children 50p • Other information: Plants
sometimes for sale* ● 🍽 🏠 WC

People still rush to view the most curious park and garden south of Biddulph
Grange (see entry in Staffordshire), built in the 1840s. Set on the Cotswold
escarpment, it boasts the ingredients of a Gothick best-seller. A narrow path
drops into a dark glen, roots from enormous oaks, copper beeches and
chestnuts trip your feet, ferns brush your face, walls drip water, and ammo-
nites and fossils loom in the gloom. Rocks erupt with moss. Egyptian tombs
trap the unwary. Tunnels turn into grottos. Even plants live in wire cages.
Folly freaks are in their element, though it has to be admitted that some
people do not find it gloomy since the droughts have stopped the springs;
indeed the secret garden can be light and friendly when it is not raining.
Everyone has a good time in this Victorian curiosity turned romantic vision
turned horror movie. But some think this description far too gloomy, and only
appropriate on drizzly days. There is another side to Stancombe – a pretty rose
garden, twentieth-century follies around the house, patterned borders and
extensive gardens with 'wonderful design and use of colour' created by the
owner and the designer Nada Jennett.

Stanway House   38

Winchcombe, Cheltenham GL54 5PQ. Tel: (01386) 584469

*Lord Neidpath • 1m E of B4632 Cheltenham – Broadway road, 4m NE of
Winchcombe • House open • Garden open Aug and Sept, Tues and Thurs, 2 –
5pm. Tours for parties at other times by appt • Entrance: £1.50 (house and
garden £3.50, OAPs £3, children £1)* ● WC ⇗

Stanway is a honey-coloured Cotswold village with a Jacobean 'great house'
which has changed hands once since 715AD. It was much frequented by
Arthur Balfour and 'The Souls' in the latter years of the last century. The
garden rises in a series of dramatic lawns and a (rare, picturesque) 'grass-
work' to the pyramid, which in the eighteenth century stood at the head of

a 190-metre-long cascade descending to a formal canal on a terrace above the house. This was probably designed by Charles Bridgeman or Stephen Switzer and exceeded in length and height (36 metres) its famous rival at Chatsworth (see entry, Derbyshire). The canal, the upper pond behind the pyramid, a short section of the cascade, and the upper fall below the pyramid have recently been restored, and it is hoped soon to restore the pyramid itself, a banqueting house from which guests on a summer evening could watch the sluices being opened and the water falling down towards the house. Other features include the fourteenth-century tithe barn, church and a dog cemetery whose inmates go back to 1898. Little for the plantsperson to study, but if you are suffering from a surfeit of National Trust manicuring, try this for sheer style.

Sudeley Castle ★ 39

Winchcombe, Cheltenham GL54 5JD. Tel: (01242) 602308;
Fax: (01242) 602959; E-mail: marketing@sudeley.ndirect.co.uk

Lord and Lady Ashcombe • 8m NE of Cheltenham off B4632 at Winchcombe • Castle open April to Oct, daily, 11am – 5pm • Gardens open March to Oct, daily, 10.30am – 5.30pm • Private guided tours in and out of season by arrangement • Entrance: castle and gardens £6, OAPs £5, children £3; party rates for 20 or more £5, £4, £3; season ticket £17, family season ticket £34. Other information: Picnics area ◑ ☕ ✕ 🖼 WC & ⚘ 🛍 ♀

There has been a house on this magnificent site, with views of the surrounding Cotswold hill at every turn, for over 1000 years, and today the emphasis is on tourism, with pleasant facilities and special exhibitions. The extensive grounds contain ten integrated but individual gardens, notably the Queen's Garden with its outstanding collection of old-fashioned roses, surrounded by immaculately clipped double yew hedges. These were laid out in the nineteenth century by an ancestor of the present owners on the site of the original Tudor parterre. In recent years Jane Fearnley-Whittingstall guided the restoration of this area, as well as designing the knot garden and newly planted buddleia walk, featuring 23 different varieties. The gardens surrounding the ruins of the banqueting hall and the tithe barn, with its carp pond, are exceptionally lovely, with old climbing roses and (should you be lucky enough to avoid the coachloads) a romantic atmosphere. There is a white garden, a secret garden designed by Rosemary Verey, a mulberry garden and a small Victorian kitchen garden, managed in collaboration with the Henry Doubleday Research Association to produce seed for propagation. Interesting colour booklet with descriptions of all the roses available.

Trevi Garden 40

Over Old Road, Hartpury, Gloucester GL19 3BJ. Tel: (01452) 700370

Gilbert and Sally Gough • 5m NW of Gloucester via A417. In Hartpury turn sharp back right into Over Old Road before war memorial • Open 2nd, 6th, 23rd, 24th, 27th, 30th April, 1st, 4th, 14th, 18th, 28th, 29th May, 1st, 11th, 15th, 29th June, 8th, 9th, 13th, 20th, 29th, 30th July, 3rd, 6th, 13th, 17th,

20th, 27th, 28th, 31st Aug, 3rd Sept, all 2 – 6pm. Coaches and parties at other times by appt • Entrance: £2, accompanied children free • Other information: Guide dogs only ◑ 🖵 WC ♿ 🐾

Completely designed by the owners, and maintained to a high standard, this one-acre garden reflects their enthusiasm and interest at every turning. Wandering grass paths beside a winding pond, across bridges, through arches and alongside thickly planted shrub and herbaceous borders that broaden out into enclosures of old and established trees. More formal elements include a clematis walk and an attractively set-out flower garden contained within a pole-and-rope garden featuring clematis, roses and other climbers, flanked with espaliered fruit trees. An alpine terrace and an expanding collection of epimediums. Careful arrangement of plants, many of which are of interest to the plantsperson, ensures colour and variety at every season. Not far away, although not open the same days, is *Cinderine Cottage*, where Daphne Chappell has over 100 varieties of snowdrops (3m NE of Newent off B4215, south of Dymock; look for sign Ryton/Ketford. After ¾ m cottage is on right.) Open frequently in February and March and at other times through to September, including every Tues. Telephone (01531) 890265 for details.

Upton Wold   41

Northwick Estate, Moreton–in–Marsh GL56 9TR. Tel: (01386) 700667

Mr and Mrs I.R.S. Bond • 5m NW of Moreton-in-Marsh on A44. Pass Batsford, Sezincote and Bourton House (see entries), continue up Bourton hill, pass Troopers Lodge Garage at A424 junction and drive is 1m further on right • Open for NGS 16th April, 25th June, 2 – 6pm; May to July, 10am – 6pm (telephone for details and appt) • Entrance: NGS openings £3, children free; May to July openings £4 ●

One would never know, travelling along the busy A44, that four fine gardens lie along this stretch of a few miles, the newest and best concealed of these being the garden set around a small seventeenth-century manor house hidden in a wold. The owners arrived here in the 1970s and have created, from scratch, what is now one of the most distinguished of typical Cotswold gardens. The view from the south-east façade of the house (not open) stretches out across a lawn and ha-ha to the valley. To the left is a long border, through which is the entrance to the pond and wild garden (fritillaries bursting through on our visit). The walk on the opposite side of the central lawn is bordered by a tunnel of yew. Beyond this the ground slopes up through the Hidden Garden and hedged croquet lawn to a long level area which hosts an ornamental fruit garden, fine vegetable garden and greenhouses. Imaginative planting everywhere (note the owners' passion for standards), with particular care taken to provide pleasing views from the house windows, such as the bank of old roses below the dovecot. Lots of interest for the plant enthusiast in this charming garden.

Vale House 42

Hidcote Boyce, Chipping Campden GL55 6LT. Tel: (01386) 438228

Miss Bettine Muir • On road from Chipping Campden to Hidcote and Kiftsgate (see entries) at edge of Hidcote Boyce • Open by appt only in May and June, any numbers welcome (telephone 12.45 – 2.15pm) • Entrance: £2.50, children free ● ᶑ ℘

Miss Bettine Muir is the second daughter of Heather Muir, the creator of Kiftsgate, and remembers the planting of the famous rose. She is a born gardener and her skill is reflected in the most unusual and exciting planting in her own garden. She moved to Vale House in the early 1970s, beginning work on the 'flat field' which surrounded it in 1972. Within dense windbreaks which do not impede the lovely view west across the Cotswolds to Bredon is a series of small gardens linked by paved paths. Around the house are climbers and borders of unusual plants; to the east a small enclosed garden with many interesting plants, shrubs and roses, edged with a border of nerines and shrub plantings.

Westbury Court Garden ★★ 43

Westbury-on-Severn GL14 1PD. Tel: (01452) 760461

The National Trust • 9m SW of Gloucester on A48, close to church • Open April to 29th Oct, Wed – Sun and Bank Holiday Mons, 11am – 6pm. Closed 10th April. Individuals at other times by appt and parties of 15 or more by written appt • Entrance: £2.80, children £1.40 (1999 prices) • Other information: Braille plan available ◐ 🍴 WC ᶑ ♀

A remarkable seventeenth-century Dutch water garden and, as such, one of the rarest types of garden to have survived more or less intact in this country. A contemporary Tall Pavilion dominates a long canal which is flanked by clipped yew hedges regularly spaced with pyramids and holly balls. Parallel to this is a T-canal where, in the centre of the arm, Neptune bestrides a dolphin, and where there is an elaborate seventeenth-century seat in the 'bowling green', a central area which appears, from the Kip engraving, to have been a vegetable garden. To the north-east is a charming gazebo, one side of which overlooks a small, walled garden where species of plants to be found growing in England prior to 1700 grow now in box-edged beds. Beyond is the parterre: beds of simple shape containing topiary, this time in box. This in turn is surrounded by the quincunx, a formal arrangement of small trees and clipped evergreens. A specimen of *Quercus ilex* is thought to be one of the oldest in the country, with a girth of eight metres at a point of one-and-a-half metres above ground. Westbury Court is a garden of *allée*, canal, *clairvoyée* and vista, all carefully restored and maintained to a high standard by the Trust. The historic houses on this site were destroyed, one as late as the 1950s, and there is now a home for elderly people here. If you then feel inclined for a completely different experience, take the *Forest of Dean Sculpture Trail*, on B4226 between Cinderford and Coleford.

Westonbirt Arboretum ★★ 44

Westonbirt, Tetbury GL8 8QS. Tel: (01666) 880220; Fax: (01666) 880559

The Forestry Commission • 3m SW of Tetbury on A433, 5m NE of A46 junction • Grounds open all year, 10am – 8pm or dusk • Entrance: £4, OAPs £3, children £1 (1999 prices) • Other information: Café and Visitor Centre closed Christmas week. Dogs in some areas only, on lead ○ 🍴 ✕ 🏠 WC ⚊ 🌡 🏛 🍴

This is perhaps the finest arboretum in Britain. Started in 1829 by Robert Stayner Holford, Westonbirt was expanded and improved by successive generations of the same family until it was taken over by the Forestry Commission in 1956. Numerous grass rides divide the trees into roughly rectangular blocks, within which are various open spaces and glades used for special plantings such as the famous Japanese maple collections. Westonbirt is noted for its vast range of stunning mature specimen trees. The Forestry Commission is continuing with planting, for example the Hillier Glade with ornamental cherries. Across the valley from the original arboretum is Silkwood, with collections of native, Asian and American species that in spring are carpeted with primroses, wood anemones and bluebells. There are in excess of 18,000 numbered trees and 17 miles of paths. Colour is best in May (rhododendrons, magnolias, etc.) and October (Japanese maples, fothergillas, etc.). From mid-Nov until Christmas the garden is illuminated with hundreds of twinkling lights, and many champion trees are floodlit.

Westonbirt School Gardens 45

Tetbury GL8 8QG. Tel: (01666) 880333; Fax: (01666) 880364;
E-mail: debbiesg@westonbirt.gloucs.sch.uk; Web: www.westonbirt.gloucs.sch.uk

Westonbirt School • 3m SW of Tetbury on A433 opposite Westonbirt Arboretum • Open 2nd April, 13th Aug for NGS, 2 – 4.30pm, and at other times by appt • Entrance: £2, children 25p (1999 prices) • Other information: Teas when open for events only 🍴 ⚊ 🔽 🍴

The house was built by the eminent Victorian plant collector Robert Stayner Holford, and modelled on Wollaton Hall, Nottinghamshire. A pioneer collector of trees, shrubs and flowers from around the world, he had already started to plant trees when he inherited the estate from his father in 1839, and the spectacular gardens which we see today had started to take shape before the house was completed in 1872. After his death in 1892, his son George, who had also inherited his father's love of horticulture, continued the development of both arboretum and garden, and became one of the most successful amateur gardeners of his time. He was particularly keen on orchids and exotics. The garden is designed to have leisurely walks and a few surprises. Sweeping lawns and terraces lead down to the fountain pool, with views across the ha-ha, which hides the road, to farmland beyond. The other axis leads from the church to the sunken garden, with its pond and statue of Mercury. An Italian garden with architectural features, knot garden and pergola walk complete the formal eastern side of the house, while the other side is more informal with irregular groups of trees and shrubs, many rare and exotic, a lake, grotto and rockery. Beautifully maintained. Fascinating illustrated booklet.

HAMPSHIRE &
THE ISLE OF WIGHT

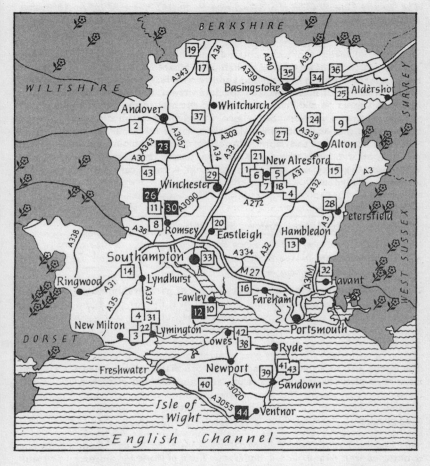

Gardens on the Isle of Wight will be found at the end of the Hampshire section.
Two-starred gardens are marked on the map with a black square.

Abbey Cottage   1

Rectory Lane, Itchen Abbas, Winchester SO21 1BN. Tel: (01962) 779575

*Col. Patrick Daniell • 3m E of Winchester on B3047, 1m E of Itchen Abbas •
Open 9th, 30th April, 1st May, 9th July, 27th, 28th Aug, 12 noon – 5pm and
by appt at other times. Parties welcome • Entrance: £2* ● 💭 📷 WC ♿ 🐾

A variety of levels above the cottage, each aligned with interlinking vistas,
results in a series of gardens within an old walled kitchen garden, leading into
each other by means of steps, slopes and corridors. It ends at the highest point
with a meadow of newly planted specimen trees, the whole comprising one
and a half acres on alkaline soil. In places the articulation of this immaculate
garden seems contrived, but there is much of inspiration and interest
throughout the year, including *Magnolia* x *loebneri* 'Merrill', stunning against
the yew hedge, bulbs and daphnes in spring, clematis, shrub and climbing roses
in summer and *Sorbus vilmorinii* in autumn. *Juniper chinensis* 'Aurea' and *Cornus
alternifolia* 'Argentea' are also very striking. A most carefully designed and
maintained garden.

Amport House   2

Chaplaincy Centre, Amport, Andover SP11 8BG.

*4m W of Andover, S of A303 • Open by written appt only to Rev. Barry
Hammett or Richard Jones • Entrance: £2.50 • Other information: Light
refreshments by arrangement* ● 💭 WC

This little-known garden of the Lutyens/Jekyll partnership has a great water
terrace on two levels, with rills, a central oval mirror pond and square lily
pools, and is said to be the prototype for the Lutyens water gardens at New
Delhi. Note the Lutyens/Jekyll hallmark of millstone and diaper paving.
Herbaceous borders, sunken rockery, pleached limes, splendid Victorian
parterre with the Winchester coat of arms, parkland and ha-ha. Since Lutyens
found the Victorian house, designed by Sir William Burn, unattractive, he
sought to distract the eye to his terraced gardens and waterways.

Apple Court   3

Hordle Lane, Hordle, Lymington SO41 0HU. Tel: (01590) 642130

*Mrs Diana Grenfell and Mr Roger Grounds • 200 metres N of A337 between
Lymington and New Milton along Hordle Lane opposite Royal Oak • Open Mar
to Oct, daily, except Wed, 10am – 1pm, 2 – 5pm • Entrance: £2, children 50p •
Other information: Plants for sale in adjoining nursery* 🕐 ♿ 🌱

The garden is a showcase for a National Collection of hostas and display
borders of day lilies. Pergola with hostas, fern path, herbaceous borders lined
with pleached limes and rose-covered rope swags. The day lily garden is at its
peak in July and August with beds of red, yellow, orange and pink day lilies,
most of them being American introductions, growing among agapanthus,
crocosmias, kniphofias and phormiums, backed by purple-leaved beech
hedges, and with a frothy rectangle of ornamental grasses at their centre.

The white garden is dramatic: a square holding an oval of white flowers and variegated-leaved shrubs, viewed through an inner oval of pleached hornbeam and dwarf box which frames them like a series of lit pictures. At the centre is an oval of mown grass. The effect is architectural, like entering a square with a circular colonnade or a theatre in the round.

Artsway 4

Station Road, Sway, Nr Lymington SO41 6BA. Tel: (01590) 682260; Fax: (01590) 681989

Mark Segal • 4m NW of Lymington. On Station Road, Sway behind Forest Heath Hotel • Gallery open all year • Garden open all year, Tues – Sun, 11am – 5pm • Entrance: free • Other information: Toilet facilities available at Gallery; refreshments at the Forest Heath Hotel ○ �& 👍

This Lottery-funded visual arts centre, originally a coach house, was landscaped by Sue Sutherland. Cleve West and Johnny Woodford have created a boules court which is not so much a garden as what they call 'an outdoor installation'. West, a designer of show gardens at Hampton Court, etc., attacks those who believe all show gardens are fantasies, so this one may well change many conceptions, as it is visited by over 200 people a week.

Bramdean House ★ 5

Bramdean, Alresford SO24 0JU. Tel: (01962) 771214; Fax: (01962) 771095

Mr and Mrs H. Wakefield • 9m E of Winchester on A272 in middle of Bramdean • Open 23rd, 24th April, 14th May, 11th June, 9th July, 13th Aug, 10 Sept, 2 – 5pm and by appt • Entrance: £2.50, children free ● ☕ WC ♚

The mellow brick eighteenth-century house is well protected from the main road by a huge undulating yew and box hedge. The six-and-a-half-acre garden on chalk slopes away from the house and is divided into three parts. One contains the famous mirror-image herbaceous borders, and surrounding beds have a large array of usual and unusual plants, shrubs and small trees. Fine wrought-iron gates lead through into the walled working kitchen garden, cultivated entirely by hand, and containing fruit and vegetables grown for the house, old-fashioned sweet peas, perpetual carnations, a peony walk and a trial area for plants. Ornamental flower beds along a central path lead through a second wrought-iron gate into the orchard area featuring fruit trees underplanted with massed daffodils. The orchard is terminated by a blue-doored apple house and belfry. To the east are interesting shrubs and trees, carpeted in spring with aconites, snowdrops and other bulbs.

Brandy Mount House 6

Brandy Mount, Alresford SO24 9EG. Tel: (01962) 732189; E–mail: MichaelBaron1@compuserve.com

Mr and Mrs M. Baron • In town centre. First right in East Street before Sun Lane • Open 5th, 6th, 9th Feb, 11am – 4pm; 5th March, 9th April, 7th May, 2 – 5pm (telephone to check) and by appt in snowdrop season • Entrance:

£1.50, children free • Other information: No vehicular access. Parking in station car park and Broad Street. Teas available except in Feb ● ও ⬦ ♨

This one-acre informal garden of trees, shrubs and lawns is essentially for the plantsman. Michael Baron is there to guide the visitors through his National Collections of snowdrops and daphnes, and there is also a wide variety of hellebores, pulmonarias and species peonies. You may wish to discuss the problems of growing shrubs on dry chalk soil and see a variety of alpine primulas, geraniums and lilacs. Amongst the well-labelled and rare plants in borders and spot beds are cardamine (dentaria), *Ornithogalum narbonnense*, *Fritillaria pyrenaica*.

48 Broad Street 7

New Alresford, Alresford SO24 9AN. Tel: (01962) 732441

Mr and Mrs David Ashdown • In town centre • Open by appt to individuals and parties • Entrance: £2.50 ●

This town garden, six to nine metres wide and 165 metres long, turns a typically narrow plot into a journey of light and dark through varied passages and rooms. Near the house are pots, paving, *Trachelospermum jasminoides* and clematis up the walls. Next comes the lawn, sculpture and box-edged beds of lilies, perennials and roses. Then you reach miniature woodland and an informal kitchen garden. The transition to Hampshire countryside is completed by a nut walk leading to a view of fields and a glimpse of Alresford pond.

Broadlands 8

Romsey SO51 9ZD. Tel: (01794) 505010

Lord Romsey • S of Romsey on A31. Signposted • Open June to Sept, daily, 12 noon – 5.30pm (last admission 4pm) • Entrance: £5.50, OAPs, disabled and students £4.70, children (12-16) £3.85, under 12 free ◑ 💷 🏠 WC ও 🍴 🍷

The eighteenth-century mansion, former home of Viscount Palmerston and, later, Lord Mountbatten, has a smooth lawn running from the steps of the porticoed west front to the River Test. Spreading parkland trees of beech and cedar come together in a composition that epitomises the eighteenth-century English Landscape School. The elegant Palladianism of Broadlands could only be the work of 'Capability' Brown.

Bury Court 9

Bentley, Farnham, Surrey GU10 5LZ. Tel: (01420) 23202; Fax: (01420) 22382

Marina Christopher and John Coke • 5m SW of Farnham, 1½ m N of Bentley on road signed Crondall • Open 23rd March to 28th Oct, Thurs – Sat, 10am – 6pm • Entrance: 50p • Other information: Plants for sale in adjacent nursery ◑ 💷 ✕ WC ও

The walled garden has been designed by Piet Oudolf, whose naturalistic style is well known in Holland. Although some planting is still to be done and much has yet to mature, the bones have originality and elegance. Surrounded by walls of brick and stone, curved oast houses and other buildings, with a glimpse of the countryside beyond, the asymmetrical geometric beds are dominated by robust perennials and various grasses. Stunning herbaceous borders in mid- and late summer. With cambered cobble paths, two water tanks, a gravel bed, several beds of small box bushes and some hedging, it is already a fine showcase for the owners' nursery, *Green Farm Plants*.

Cadland House ★ 10

Fawley, Southampton SO5 1AA.

Mr and Mrs Maldwin Drummond • 16m SE of Southampton off A326/B3053 • Open May, June, Sept and Oct by written appt for parties of 20 or more • Entrance: £3 • Other information: Teas by arrangement ● ▆ **WC** & ♨

This eight-acre 'cottage' garden designed by 'Capability' Brown for the banker Robert Drummond overlooks the Solent and since the 1987 storms has been restored using period plants such as cistus and rosemary, which thrive in dry gravel beside the sea. A path winds from the modern house (replacing the original *cottage orné* by Henry Holland) above the shore and back again, with glimpses of the sea. Kitchen garden with splendid glasshouses containing apricots, peaches, grapes, figs and other fruit. The modern walled garden with good shrubs (*Drimys winteri*, *Vestia foetida*, Chilean fire-bush and many more), bulbs (arum lily border) and perennials surrounding the hard tennis court makes a lively contrast to the eighteenth-century agenda. National Collection of leptospermums.

Croylands 11

Old Salisbury Lane, Romsey SO51 0GD. Tel: (01794) 513056

The Hon. Mrs Charles Kitchener • From Romsey take A3057 Stockbridge road, after 1m turn left at Duke's Head, fork left after bridge and garden is 1m further on right • Open May to early July by appt • Entrance: free ●

The lines of this informal plantsman's garden echo the curves of Florence Nightingale's wheelwright's cottage roof, and the vistas appear to be the result of happy chance but have been skilfully prepared. From the cottage there is a view across the lawn between shrubs to a stand of gold-leaved plants, and paths (brick from the local Michelmarsh works) wind through trees like *Arbutus unedo* and *Populus candicans* to reach glades furnished with arbours, pots of New Zealand cabbage or phormiums, shrubs wreathed in clematis, a large Australian mint bush, a white abutilon, and *Elaeagnus* 'Quicksilver'. There is a shade border and a white border with ornamental grasses, cerastium, etc. In June the former vegetable plot has 200 peonies in flower.

Exbury Gardens ★★ 12

Exbury, Southampton SO45 1AZ. Tel: (023) 8089 1203/8089 9422

Mr E.L. de Rothschild • 15 m S of Southampton. From M27 junction 2 take A326 then B3054. 2½ m SE of Beaulieu, after 1m turn right for Exbury. Signposted • Open 26th Feb to Oct, 10am – 5.30pm (or dusk if earlier) (last admission 5.30pm) • Entrance: main-season entrance: £5, OAPs £4.50 (£4 on Tues, Wed and Thurs), children (10-15) £4, parties of 15 or more £4.50 per person. Seasonal discounts available ◑ 💭 ✕ 🍴 WC ♿ ⟨⟩ 🌿 🏛 ♨

Established between the wars by Lionel de Rothschild, these gardens of rhododendrons and azaleas are the most outstanding of their kind in the south. Winding paths meander over 200 acres and proceed under a light canopy of trees, mostly oak and pine, over a bridge and beside ponds to the Beaulieu river. Many rhododendrons and azaleas like *R. yakushimanum* and Hawk 'Crest' were introduced here and are grown beside purple Japanese maples and candelabra primulas. At times the colour associations seem careless, harsh orange beside blush, metallic magenta beside pale blue, but a glade of towering white blooms, pink in bud, more than makes up for this. In March early rhododendrons, camellias and the daffodil meadow flower. In April the rock garden, miniature mountain scenery with screes and valleys, is at its peak with alpine rhododendrons among 'Skyrocket' junipers. May is Exbury's high season, and an early visit is recommended. In June and July the modern rose garden is a mass of bright colours, and the 'winter garden' (seen in autumn) has thick sinuous trunks of *Rhododendron sinogrande* and *Magnolia macrophylla*.

Fairfield House ★   13

East Street, Hambledon, Portsmouth PO7 4RY. Tel: (023) 9263 2431

Mrs Peter Wake • 10m SW of Petersfield in Hambledon • Open several days for charity and by appt. Suitable for parties • Entrance: £2.50, children 50p • Other information: Teas on open days and by arrangement only ◐ 💭 🍴 WC ⟨⟩ 🌿

This magnificent collection of species and old roses, climbers and ramblers, together with some modern roses, was established by Peter Wake 26 years ago with advice from Lanning Roper, and continues to flourish under the care of Marion Wake. The roses are planted informally on five acres, divided by yew hedges and brick walls, around the white Regency house. The lower stems of the species and larger shrub roses like 'Wolly Dodds' rose and *Rosa x alba* 'Maxima' are contained within stakes from which they rise and flower as if from giant urns. It is worth noting that none of these roses is sprayed. A map and list enables identification. On the spreading lawns are mature cedars, limes and copper beeches, as well as more recently planted sorbus, malus, robinia, *Ptelea trifoliata*, tulip tree and fern beech, indicating the range of trees which can grow on a thin chalk soil.

Furzey Gardens ★   14

Minstead, Lyndhurst SO43 7GL. Tel: (023) 8081 2464; Fax: (023) 8081 2297

Mrs M.M. Cole (Administrator) • 8m SW of Southampton, 1m S of A31, 2m W of Cadnam and end of M27, 3½ m NW of Lyndhurst • Gardens open daily except 25th and 26th Dec, 10am – 5pm (earlier in winter) • Entrance: summer: £3, OAPs £2.50, children £1.50, families £8; winter: £1.50, OAPs £1, children 50p, families £3. Reductions for parties by arrangement • Other information: Art and craft galleries. Sixteenth-century cottage open daily (weekends in winter) ○ 💭 🍴 WC ♿ 🌿 🏛 ♨

The eight acres of this well-maintained woodland garden were laid out by Hew Dalrymple in the early 1920s. In early March the acacia tree in full fragrant bloom, a group of *Corylopsis pauciflora* dripping with pale yellow flowers, species daffodils, *Magnolia stellata* and banks of heathers make a visit worthwhile. Among the plants which revel in the sandy acid soil of the New Forest are not only rhododendrons and azaleas, but the Chilean fire bush (*Embothrium coccineum*) flowering bright scarlet in May, and a host of shrubs and trees from Australasia. Pond and water garden with yellow skunk cabbage, ferns, etc. There is a fine church, where Sir Arthur Conan Doyle is buried.

Gilbert White's House and Garden 15

The Wakes, Selborne, Alton GU34 3JH. Tel: (01420) 511275; Fax: (01420) 511040

Oates Memorial Trust • 4½ m S of Alton, 8m N of Petersfield on B3006 • House open • Garden open daily Jan to 24th Dec, 11am – 5pm. Additional evening opening for parties • Entrance: £4, OAPs and students £3.50, children £1. Special rates for parties • Other information: Public car park behind Selborne Arms. Unusual plant fair 17th, 18th June and other non-horticultural events later ○ ☕ WC ⅙ ☞ ♨ ☕

Here the naturalist Gilbert White wrote his classic *The Natural History of Selborne* (published 1788). The garden is being restored and extended. The sundial and ha-ha beyond the lawn, with its splendid views of the beech-clad hangar, were there in White's day. The quincunx, a square pattern of five cypresses on a mound, was originally conceived by him. Borders and beds near the house contain many plants from his time including hollyhocks (which were called 'hollyoaks'), sweet Williams, pinks, species foxgloves, santolina, martagon lilies and old roses, Gallicas, Damasks, etc. Additions include a laburnum tunnel, a herb garden, a fine tulip tree planted in 1910 and some yew topiary. Historic varieties of fruit have been introduced, and there is a naturalist's garden for spring and summer wild flowers in the making.

Heathlands ★ 16

47 Locks Road, Locks Heath, Southampton SO31 6NS. Tel: (01489) 573598

Dr John Burwell • 5m W of Fareham. Leave M27 at junction 9. Locks Road runs due S from A27 at Park Gate • Open 19th March, 16th April, 14th May, 16th July, 27th Aug, 2 – 5.30pm • Entrance: £1.50, children free ● ☕ ⅙ ⇕ ☞

A row of paulownias, grown from seed by the owner, is a memorable sight in May, and raises the expectations of any visitor to this remarkable garden on the outskirts of Southampton. The lawn stretches through spring bulbs to a more wooded area. To the north a pond with small herbaceous border is separated from the kitchen garden by a yew hedge sporting topiary balls and a peacock, its tail in low relief, the head and crown rising above the hedge line. The kitchen garden has four bay cones and Worcesterberries grown espalier-fashion. A huge holly drum is one of over 1000 different plants, including the architectural *Yucca gloriosa* and *Phormium tenax*, ferns, pieris, *Rhododendron sinogrande*, corylopsis, and a National Collection of Japanese anemones. There is also a part-yew walk focusing on an obelisk, a secret garden with tiny pool, and a conservatory.

Highclere Castle and Gardens 17

Highclere, Newbury RG20 9RN. Tel: (01635) 253210

The Earl and Countess of Carnarvon • 4½ m S of Newbury, W of A34 • House open • Garden open probably early July to early Sept, Tues – Sun, 11am – 5pm (last admission 4pm) except Sat closes 3.30pm (last admission 2.30pm) • Entrance: £3, children £1.50 (castle and gardens £6, OAPs and students £4.75, children (5-14) £3, season ticket £25, parties of 20 or more £4.75 per person, children £3) (1999 prices) ◐ ☕ ✕ 🖺 **WC** ♨ 👜 ♿

At first glance it seems that the Houses of Parliament have flown and settled in a parkland setting of lawns and cedars. Not surprising, since Highclere Castle (1840) was designed by the same architect, Sir Charles Barry, who remodelled a Georgian mansion to create a fine Victorian home for the 3rd Earl of Carnarvon. Three follies, a rotunda beside the lake, a roofless temple called Jackdaw's Castle, and Heaven's Gate on Sidown Hill opposite the castle are remnants of the garden before 'Capability' Brown remodelled the grounds in 1774, giving a gloriously simple vista of valley and hills. Tucked out of sight is the walled garden and the flower garden, designed by the late James Russell.

Hillier Gardens

(see THE SIR HAROLD HILLIER GARDENS AND ARBORETUM)

Hinton Ampner ★ 18

Hinton Ampner, Bramdean, Alresford SO24 0LA. Tel: (01962) 771305; Fax: (01962) 793101

The National Trust • 8m E of Winchester, 1m W of Bramdean, on A272 • House open. Telephone for details • Garden open 19th, 26th March; then 1st April to Sept, Tues, Wed, Sat, Sun and Bank Holiday Mons, 1.30 – 5.30pm (last admission 5pm) • Entrance: £3.50, children (5-16) £1.75. Parties of 15 or more must pre-book • Other information: Coaches must use entrance through village. Plants usually for sale ◐ ☕ **WC** ♿

Approached through parkland, this quintessentially English garden has been well restored in recent years. It was created by Ralph Dutton, later Lord Sherborne, who inherited the estate in 1935. A dramatic series of terraces with downland views descends to the south, and from the cross axis of each terrace you see – as if by happy chance – urns, a temple, an obelisk or a silhouetted statue of Diana luring you to the garden's limits. The route leads through a series of secret gardens. Huge immaculately trimmed topiary mushrooms give a surreal *Alice in Wonderland* effect. Avenue of domed yews, good herbaceous plants, water-lily pond, garden of hexagons and dell with philadelphus, lilies, cotinus and others. In August, furnished with blue and white agapanthus, *viticella* clematis, species salvias and *Romneya coulteri*, the garden stays resplendent. The Trust claims the property as 'one of its undiscovered secrets'.

Hollington Herb Garden   19

Woolton Hill, Newbury, Berkshire RG20 9XT. Tel: (01635) 253759

Mr and Mrs S.G. Hopkinson • 4m S of Newbury E of A343. Next door to Hollington House Hotel • Open May, Wed; June, Wed, Sun, 12 noon – 5pm. Guided parties by appt • Entrance: £1.50, children 50p ○ ☕ WC & ⚘

The main border, first planted in the 1970s, leads to several small garden rooms. Designed as a maze, the various gardens are co-ordinated by paths ending with glimpses of topiary, fountain, bench or pot. A mixed double border with old roses and aromatic plants, a knot garden, a pergola covered with climbing roses, scented clematis, honeysuckles and golden hop, all lead to the culinary herbs and on through a small white garden to the Paradise Garden. This formal area is richly furnished with textural plants in shades of green and silver, purple and pink. Sixteen square beds surround four urns with bubble fountains; they are linked in pairs around a central knot by a rill of blue grass. Finally the visitor passes through waves of santolina and lavender to the thyme lawn, made up of several varieties and nearly 18 metres long.

53 Ladywood ★   20

Eastleigh SO50 4RW. Tel: (023) 806 15389

Mr and Mrs D. Ward • Leave A33/M3 at junction 12 signed A335 to Eastleigh, turn right at roundabout into Woodside Avenue, second right into Bosville, fifth right into Ladywood • Open for NGS on three Suns, 11am – 5.30pm and by appt April to Sept • Entrance: £1.50, children 75p • Other information: Parking in Bosville only ● ⚘

This suburban garden, four metres square, containing over 1200 different labelled plants, is subdivided into several more miniscule gardens. Water garden with water hawthorn (*Aponogeton distachyos*) and, later, water lilies, rock garden, shade garden with hostas and variegated plants, tiny oval lawn. Alpines, erodiums, hardy geraniums galore, the white *Clematis* 'Henryi', roses, grasses, the miniature *Philadelphus* 'Manteau d'Hermine', and many more. Good colour associations and contrasts, eg the black viola 'Molly Sanderson' and black grass *Ophiopogon planiscapus* emerging from pale shingle.

Lake House   21

Northington, Alresford SO24 9TG. Tel: (01962) 723820

Lord Ashburton • 3m NW of Alresford off B3046. Follow signs for Northington and the Grange, and turn sharp left before entrance to Grange • Open probably two Suns for NGS and also to parties of 10 or more by appt • Entrance: £3, children free ● ☕ ▤ WC & ⇔ ⚘

Lord Ashburton's modern single-storied house is situated in the old kitchen garden of the ruined Grange. A wall has been opened giving views of lake and parkland. An adjacent walled garden is filled with herbaceous borders and herringbone-pathed, box-edged plots growing old roses and perennials, as well as a rose-and-wisteria pergola and an avenue of Irish yews leading to a moon gate. This opens to a scenic walk round the lake, with views of the neo-classical shell of the Grange, a nineteenth-century cascade and ruined 'castle', and an arched bridge in oriental style. Near the house are conservatory, terrace, pots and small herb garden. The Grange, now English Heritage, former home to the Ashburton family, may be visited any time.

The Little Cottage 22

Southampton Road, Lymington SO41 9GZ. Tel: (01590) 679395

Wing Commander and Mrs Peter Prior • On outskirts of Lymington on A337 opposite Tollhouse Inn • Open June to Sept, Tues, 10am – 1pm, 2 – 6pm for NGS and at other times by appt • Entrance: £2 ●

This quarter-acre garden alongside a busy main road has been effectively divided into six rooms of formal design with informal planting. The first, in blue and yellow, has bay trees, *Euonymus japonicus* 'Aureus' and variegated holly all grown as standards, box edging and *Clematis* x *durandii* towers. Straight paths lead to focal points – urns, arbours and seats or a wall fountain. The other five rooms each have their own colour scheme, reflected in their artifacts as well as in their planting – white/green and lime; apricot and copper; red, purple and black; mauve, lilac, silver and turquoise; and pink and lime. The walkway from the front to the back is planted with blue and white and has a dramatic mixed pot collection on white gravel. *Rhinefield House Hotel*, near Lyndhurst, may be visited for tea and its Victorian garden.

Longstock Park Water Gardens ★★ 23

Longstock, Stockbridge SO20 6EH. Tel: (01264) 810894

John Lewis Partnership (Leckford Estate Ltd) • 2m N of Stockbridge. From A30 turn N on A3057. Signposted • Open April to Sept, first and third Sun of each month, 2 – 5pm and by appt for parties • Entrance: £3, children 50p (1999 prices) • Other information: Refreshments and plants for sale at nursery ● ☕
🏠 WC ♿ ✿ 👍

The seven acres of these superb water gardens, created by John Spedan Lewis in 1948, are fed from the River Test and surrounded by acid-loving trees and shrubs. They form an archipelago connected by narrow bridges and causeways. Gunnera, the swamp cypress (*Taxodium distichum*) surrounded by stilts, royal fern, giant white lily (*Cardiocrinum giganteum*) and Japanese angelica tree (*Aralia elata*) are just some of the plants reflected in the clear waters moving with gold carp, and a walk along the paths gives a succession of views followed by more intimate spaces. Aquatics include 48 different water lilies. Do not miss a visit to *Longstock Park Nursery* nearby (also open daily), set in a walled garden with climbing plants, and the fine herbaceous border reached through a gate in its wall. This runs parallel to a pergola planted with roses and an exquisite and extensive collection of *viticella* clematis. A National Collection of buddleias, with over 100 varieties, may be seen by request.

The Manor House ★ 24

Upton Grey, Basingstoke RG25 2RD. Fax: (01256) 861035

Mr and Mrs J. Wallinger • 6m SE of Basingstoke in Upton Grey, on hill immediately above church • Open April to Oct, Mon – Fri (but closed Bank Holidays) by appt only • Entrance: £3.50 (includes guide/leaflet) • Other information: Teas available if notice given ◐ WC ⅁

Over the past 13 years this garden has been meticulously restored by Mrs Ros Wallinger to the original 1908 Gertrude Jekyll planting plans, copies of which are on display, and the tender care invested makes it more than a unique museum piece. Here are formal beds with lilies, peonies and roses edged with lamb's ears, drystone walls clothed with plants, terraces, pergola and yew hedging, as well as Jekyll's only surviving restored wild garden with pond, daffodils and rambling roses. A living example of many Jekyll theories, it is worth noting her use of colour, with hot reds moving through yellows to distant greys and blues, the proportions of the steps, and the relation of the house (designed in grand vernacular style with hung tiles, etc by Ernest Newton for Charles Holme, founder and owner of *The Studio* magazine) to the garden. This is claimed to be the most authentic Jekyll garden reconstruction, supported by a useful booklet and plant list.

Marycourt 25

High Street, Odiham, Hook RG29 1LF. Tel: (01256) 702100

Mr and Mrs M.N. Conville • 7m E of Basingstoke, 7m W of Aldershot off A287 (M3 junction 5) • Open 25th June, 2nd July, 2 – 6pm; 5th July, 9am – 6pm for NGS and by appt • Entrance: £2, children free ◐ 🍽 WC ⅁

Large, long town garden, approached from the drive in the High Street. Splendid mixed borders (alpines, clematis, honeysuckles, roses, shrubs, bulbs, phormiums, perennials) along the walls open out to a riot of primary colours (ligularias, heleniums, bergamot, achilleas) beside the swimming pool. The detail and the variety of plants in the alkaline soil of this garden is remarkable. Near the grass tennis court, with its copper beech and climbing roses, are over 20 varieties of ivy, grown as ground cover, in pots, as shrubs and, best of all, 'Paddy's Pride' draping a shed. Blue and white beds with agapanthus, white roses and delphiniums, edged with lavender. Hostas grown with Solomon's seal and *Lilium regale* in a tunnel of overhanging apple trees are most effective.

Mottisfont Abbey Garden ★★ 26

Mottisfont, Romsey SO51 0LP. Tel: (01794) 340757

The National Trust • 10m NW of Southampton, 4¼ m NW of Romsey, ½ m W of A3057 • Garden open 25th March to Oct, Sat – Wed, 12 noon – 6pm or dusk if earlier; for rose season 11th to 25th June, daily, 11am – 8.30pm (last admission 1 hour before closing) (check recorded message, June only, for state of roses – (01794) 341220) • Entrance: £4.50, children £2.25, family ticket (2 adults and two children 5-18) £11. No reduction for parties • Other information: Coaches must pre-book. Picnics in grounds only. Four-seater golf buggy available. No smoking in walled garden during rose season ◑ ☕ ✕ ▨ WC ⅗ ℘ ♨ ♀

This famous collection of historic roses, based on the design and selection by Graham Stuart Thomas, was established in 1972. Stuart Thomas designed the garden, quartered with paths and box hedging and with a central pond and fountain, in the original kitchen garden. Fine herbaceous borders. Here are the Albas, Damasks and Gallicas of the Middle Ages, cabbage and moss roses, and the earliest Chinas, Bourbons, hybrid perpetuals, French nineteenth-century Gallicas and Albas as well as Rugosas, and ramblers up walls, arches and stands – in all, a National Collection of 300 old-fashioned roses (also a few species and New English roses) in the walled rose garden, now being renovated. The best time to visit is on midsummer evenings, when the coaches have gone. Sweeping lawns around the house, cedars, the largest London plane tree (*Platanus* x *hispanica*) in the country, and a spring running down to the River Test provide a tranquil contrast to the heady and scented delights of the roses. The pollarded lime walk was designed by the late Sir Geoffrey Jellicoe.

Moundsmere Manor 27

Preston Candover, Basingstoke RG25 2HE. Tel: (01256) 389207

Mr and Mrs Andreae • 6m S of Basingstoke on B3046. Manor gates on left just after Preston Candover sign • Open 2nd July, 2 – 6pm • Entrance: £2, children 50p • Coaches by appt ●

The 'Wrenaissance' house was inspired by Hampton Court and designed in 1908 by Sir Reginald Blomfield (1856-1942). To its south lies Blomfield's formal garden, with herbaceous borders backed by yew hedges and buttresses at either side, then yew avenues, and at the centre a sunken garden edged with roses and a central pool in which the house is pleasingly reflected from the far end. Ha-ha and views. Also pinetum, and good hothouses with streptocarpus, abutilons, figs, etc. This is Edwardian gardening on a grand scale, characteristically architectural, and exemplifies Blomfield's theories in *The Formal Garden in England*, in which he attacks the informal style supported by William Robinson. Other examples of Blomfield's work can also be found at Athelhampton House (Dorset) and Godinton Park (Kent) (see entries).

Petersfield Physic Garden 28

16 High Street, Petersfield. Contact: Helen Banham, 5 Church Road, Steep, Petersfield GU32 2DW. Tel: (01730) 233371

Hampshire Gardens Trust • Behind 16 High Street • Open daily except 25th Dec, during daylight hours • Entrance: free (donations welcome) • Other information: Teas or wine for pre-booked parties by arrangement ○ WC ⅗ ℘

This small secluded garden, planted since 1990 with plants known in the seventeenth century, is a welcome amenity in the centre of Petersfield. Knot garden, orchard, roses, box, topiary and herb garden with plants labelled according to their traditional uses.

12 Rozelle Close   29

Littleton, Winchester SO22 6QP. Tel: (01962) 880662

Mr and Mrs Tom Hyatt • 2m NW of Winchester. In Littleton, turn near Running Horse pub • Open 15th, 16th, 29th, 30th July, 9.30am – 5.30pm, and by appt during July only • Entrance: by donation ●

A celebration of seed catalogues and a place for *Amateur Gardening* to drool over. Here are over 10,000 bedding plants propagated by the owners: there are petunias, African marigolds, busy Lizzies, begonias, verbenas, in beds, borders, tubs, hanging baskets and around the two ponds in the third-of-an-acre garden. Particularly admirable is the vegetable patch beyond a screen of sweet peas, clematis and nasturtiums, where onions (from seed), cabbages and cauliflowers seem pumped with steroids. Glasshouses with magnificent melons, peppers, etc. The chalky soil is so enriched with compost each year that its rising level necessitates a periodic raising of paths. No weed stands a chance.

The Sir Harold Hillier Gardens and Arboretum ★★   30

Jermyns Lane, Ampfield, Romsey SO51 0QA. Tel: (01794) 368787; Fax: (01794) 368027

Hampshire County Council • 3m NE of Romsey, 9m SW of Winchester, ¾ m W of A3090 along Jermyns Lane. Signed from A3090 and A3057 • Open all year except 25th, 26th Dec, 10.30am – 6pm (Nov to March 5pm or dusk) • Entrance: £4, OAPs £3.50, children under 15 £1, parties of 10 or more £3 per person (Nov to March reduced rates) • Other information: Plants for sale and shop in adjacent nursery ○ 🍽 ✕ 🖼 WC ⅄ 🚻

Administered by Hampshire County Council since 1977, this enormous collection of trees and shrubs was begun in 1953 by the late Sir Harold Hillier, using his house and garden as a starting point. It extends to 180 acres and includes approximately 12,000 different species and cultivars, with many rarities. With a total of 40,000 plants it is impossible not to be impressed or to learn something about how, what and where to plant. Eleven National Collections are held here, including quercus and hamamelis. Seasonal-interest maps and labelling will lead the visitor to herbaceous, scree, heather and bog gardens. Amongst the trees and shrubs *Eucalyptus nitens* and *E. niphophila*, *Magnolia cylindrica* and the acers are worthy of note. The Winter Garden, on the site of the old rose garden, is claimed to be the largest such in the UK, specialising in plants at their best from November to March. Much more than an arboretum, this attractively laid-out garden can be enjoyed at many levels and can only increase in interest as the immense collection of young trees gains in maturity. Nearby at Broadlands (see entry) there is a 'Capability' Brown landscape. It is also worth the detour into Winchester to view *Queen Eleanor's Garden*, a small medieval plot designed and recreated by Dr Sylvia Landsberg, behind the Great Hall of Winchester Castle, and the *Dean Garnier Garden*, a secluded site with scented plants and fine views, reached by stairs from an oak door in the east wall of Winchester Cathedral.

Spinners ★ 31

School Lane, Boldre, Lymington SO41 5QE. Tel: (01590) 673347

*Mr and Mrs P.G.G. Chappell • 1½ m N of Lymington. From A337 Brockenhurst – Lymington road, turn E for Boldre. Signposted • * Open 14th April to 14th Sept, Tues – Sat, 10am – 5pm (Sun and Mon by appt); mid-Sept to March nursery and part of the garden open on same days. Telephone for details • Entrance: £1.50 • Other information: Plants for sale in nursery ◐ 🧺 WC 🚻*

This informal woodland garden on the acid soil of the New Forest, created by the Chappells, and praised by Roy Lancaster and other plantsmen, is remarkable for its plant associations and the owners' careful choice of scale. Nothing is over-large or dwarfs the smaller pleasures. In spring the sun shines through the canopy of trees, lighting camellias and dwarf rhododendrons, exochordas, magnolias, *Cornus kousa* and the brilliant coral leaves of *Acer palmatum* 'Shishio Improved'. At ground level, carpets of cyclamen, and *Erythronium revolutum* like pale pink stars, as well as white and strange maroon trilliums (a National Collection held here). Beside the spring near the house the yellow-greens of ferns and variegated iris synchronise with white and yellow skunk cabbage. Ferns, primulas, hostas in the bog garden. Good autumn colouring with *Nyssa sinensis* and other trees.

Staunton Country Park 32

Havant PO9 5HB. Tel: (023) 9245 3405

Hampshire County Council and eight other public bodies • 2m N of Havant on B2149. Signposted • Open daily: summer 10am – 5pm; winter 10am – 4pm • Entrance: £3.60, OAPs £3.20, children £2.60, family ticket £10.50 ○ 🍴 ✗ 🧺 WC ♿ 🌿 👍 🚻

Formerly the Leigh estate, belonging to the nineteenth-century horticulturist and orientalist Sir George Staunton. The walled garden has a crinkle-crankle wall to the south, and within it lies the largest restoration of Victorian green-houses in the country, costing over £1 million. Passion flowers, pepper vines and exotics grown by Staunton, including the giant *Victoria amazonica* lily in its original circular pool. The great house has gone and the park is split by a main road, but fine specimen trees remain, as well as the Gothick library and follies such as the shell house and the beacon, also the terrace and lakes, the Chinese bridge, and the remains of the lake fort where Staunton used to fire guns and fly the imperial yellow flag of China. There is also an ornamental Regency farm, stocked, as in the 1800s, with peacocks, deer, pigs, sheep, goats and horses.

The Tudor House Museum 33

Tudor House, Bugle Street, Southampton SO14 2AD. Tel: (023) 8033 2513

Southampton City Council • Near Docks. In Bugle Street, off Town Quay Road • Museum open • Garden open all year, Tues – Fri, 10am – 12 noon, 1 – 5pm, Sat, 10am – 12 noon, 1 – 4pm, Sun, 2 – 5pm • Entrance: free ○ WC ♿ 🌿 👍

This delightful museum, with its dark polished floors and gallery, includes a garden designed by Dr Sylvia Landsberg. It incorporates many features from Tudor gardens, such as heraldic beasts on poles, a camomile seat, a knot garden with twisting lines of santolina, germander and box, a skep for bees, a fountain surrounded by camomile and hyssop, an arbour hung with vines, and many herbs, labelled with details of their associations and uses.

Tylney Hall Hotel 34

Rotherwick, Hook RG27 9AZ. Tel: (01256) 764881

Access from M3 junction 5, take A287 via Newnham or from M4 junction 11, take B3349 via Rotherwick • Open for meals to non-residents and also open to public three Suns during summer for NGS • Entrance: £2, children free (1999 prices) • Other information: On garden open days main hotel closed except to guests with reservations, but refreshments available to garden visitors. Plants for sale on one open day only ☻ 🍵 WC ⚘

An Edwardian period piece. The house, with gardens stretching to 67 acres, was built by Seldon Wornum for Sir Lionel Phillips in 1900. In 1906 Wornum asked Gertrude Jekyll for designs and planting plans for the water garden. After the last war Tylney Hall became a Brent Council school. In 1984 the property was acquired by a hotel consortium, and since then the gardens have been restored, although not entirely. The original gates to the Dutch garden (which now has a modern swimming pool) have been recovered, the iris border has been replanted and the rose pergola in the kitchen garden rebuilt. Wornum's splendid Italian garden with terrace, herbaceous border and fountain overlooking parkland and lake has been restored. Jekyll's water garden to the south, with kiosk, two lakes, streams, stepping stones and bogside plants, has great charm. Avenue of Wellingtonias, specimen trees and fine vistas.

The Vyne 35

Sherborne St John, Basingstoke RG24 9HL. Tel: (01256) 881337

The National Trust • 4m N of Basingstoke between Sherborne St John and Bramley on A340, turn E at NT signs • House open as garden, 1 – 5pm • Garden open Feb and Mar, Sat, Sun; April to Oct, daily except Mon and Fri, 11 – 6pm • Entrance: £3 (house and garden £5, family ticket £12.50). Parties of 15 or more for house and garden £4 per person Tues – Thurs only • Other information: Picnics in car park only ◑ 🍵 ✕ WC ♿ 🛍 ♨

Classic English parkland of lawn, cedars, oaks and occasional clipped yews beside Wey Brook, widened here into a lake, complements the brick house with its handsome Corinthian portico added by John Webb, a harmonious *mélange* of sixteenth-, seventeenth- and eighteenth-century styles. The galleried Tudor chapel houses important stained glass windows depicting young Henry VIII and Catherine of Aragon, and rare encaustic floor tiles dating from around 1500. The garden house, also by John Webb, previously a dovecot, has the ground plan of a Greek cross. Small herbaceous beds to the west and a newly designed and planted summerhouse garden. Wild garden and woodland walk, from which the house is seen to advantage from across the water.

West Green House Garden ★   36

West Green, Hartley Wintney, Hook RG27 8JB. Tel/Fax: (01252) 844611

The National Trust, tenant Miss Marylyn Abbott • 10m NE of Basingstoke, 1m W of Hartley Wintney, 1m N of A30 • Open 21st to 24th April, May to Aug, Wed – Sun and Bank Holiday Mons, Sept, Sat, Sun; all 11am – 5pm • Entrance: £3 ◑ 🍽 WC ♿ ⚲ 🛍 ⛲

Nestling in a wooded corner of Hampshire is the attractive 1720s' manor, where busts of gods, emperors and dukes look down from the walls onto two major gardens. The inner gardens, enclosed by eighteenth-century walls, are all devoted to parterres. One is infilled with water lilies, another is in classical design of box topiaries and a third enacts the whimsy of *Alice in Wonderland* with the story's characters in ivy and box topiary surrounded by roses of red and white. The main walled garden is planted in subtle hues of mauve, plum and blues, contained in beds that have been faithfully restored to their original outlines. A decorative *potager* is centred around berry-filled fruit cages where herbs, flowers and unusual vegetables are designed into colourful patterns. All this is surrounded by a second garden, a neo-classical park studded with follies, birdcages and monuments hidden beside a tree-fringed lake, especially attractive in spring when carpeted with snowdrops, crocus and fritillaries. A grand water garden, the Nymphaeum, spills down rills and steps from a devil's mouth into serence ponds. A woodland planting leads to a new white serpentine garden. A green theatre, a picturesque orangery and long *allées* of green all add to this fine restoration that has been undertaken by the well-known Australian gardener Marylyn Abbott, who purchased a 99-year lease to remake this enchanted place after some years of neglect, and worse.

White Windows ★   37

Longparish, Andover SP11 6PB. Tel: (01264) 720222

Mrs J. Sterndale-Bennett • 5m E of Andover. Turn off A303 to Longparish on B3048 • Open two days for charity, 2 – 6pm and by appt April to Sept, Wed, 2 – 6pm • Entrance: £2 ◐ ♿ ⚲

Jane Sterndale-Bennett is Chairman of the Hardy Plant Society and crams a wealth of hardy perennials into the undulating beds of her immaculate garden. Three mini-gardens stretch in sequence from the house, each giving informal but theatrical views to adjacent areas. The fragrant white columbine grows among a mass of glaucous foliage, including *Artemisia ludoviciana* 'Valerie Finnis', and grasses like *Elymus (Leymus) hispidus* and *Festuca glauca*. Gold, variegated and purple-leaved shrubs, as well as unusual trees like *Malus transitoria* with its hawthorn-like leaves, make this a garden of interest throughout the year.

ISLE OF WIGHT

Barton Manor 38

Whippingham, East Cowes PO32 6LB. Tel: (01983) 292835

Robert Stigwood • From East Cowes take A3021, 500 metres beyond Osborne House on left • Garden open for themed charity days probably 4th June, 2th, 30th July, 3rd Sept, 10am – 5pm • Entrance: £2.50, OAPs £2, children £1, (1999 prices) • Other information: Coaches welcome. Guide dogs only ● ➍ 🐾 WC & 🏛

Prince Albert's original design included fine trees and the cork grove. The grand terraces were added by Edward VII and slope down towards Osborne Bay. There is also a secret garden planted with azaleas and roses and impressive herbaceous borders. In 1968 Hillier's laid out an intriguing water garden on the far side of the lake, home to carp and waterfowl, on what was originally Queen Victoria's skating rink. The present owner (a keen conservationist) has spared no effort in restoring and maintaining the estate. National Collections of red hot pokers (kniphofias) and watsonias are here. The most recent addition to the estate is a hedge maze which is the largest such attraction on the island – it is now large enough to get lost in. Another former royal residence, Osborne (see entry), is nearby.

Morton Manor 39

Brading, Sandown PO36 0EP. Tel: (01983) 406168

J.B., J. and J.A. Trzebski • 3m from Ryde on A3055, turn right at Brading traffic lights, signed 100 metres up hill • Manor open. Guided tours • Garden open April to Oct, daily except Sat, 10am – 5.30pm • Entrance: £4, OAPs £3.50, children (6-16) £1.75. Parties of 15 or more £3 per person (house and garden) (1999 prices) • Other information: Vineyard and winery ◑ ➍ ✕ 🐾 & ⬨ 🌿 🏛

The history of Morton dates from the thirteenth century. The Elizabethan sunken garden is surrounded by a 400-year-old box hedge and old-fashioned roses and shaded by a magnificent *Magnolia grandiflora*. The terraces are nineteenth-century with extensive herbaceous borders and a huge London plane. Masses of spring bulbs are followed by rhododendrons and traditional herbaceous displays. Among the wide range of fine trees is an Indian bean (*Catalpa bignonioides*) and a *Cornus kousa*. A particularly lovely tree in early June is *Robinia hispida*. Another feature is a pagoda covered with the vine variety 'Baco'. There are also 90 different varieties of Japanese maple. Little remains of the old walled garden, but in the corner behind the herbs are the restored bee boles; also a turf maze made for children, and a vineyard growing seven varieties of grape. Now selling several varieties of acer imported from New Zealand.

Northcourt ★ 40

Shorwell, Newport PO30 3JG. Tel: (01983) 740415; Fax: (01983) 740409

Mr and Mrs J. Harrison • 4m S of Newport on B3323. Entrance on right after rustic bridge, opposite thatched cottage • Open one day in May and June for

NGS, 2 – 5pm. Special opening for pre-booked parties of 10 or more • Entrance: approx. £2 (varies according to charity) ● ● ● WC ● ● ● ●

Twelve acres of wooded grounds surround a Jacobean manor house. There are varied gardens consisting of seventeenth-century landscaped terraces leading down to the stream and water gardens, herbaceous borders, woodland walks, walled rose garden and walled kitchen garden. In total there are 100 varieties of hardy geraniums and about 420 different shrubs and trees. Terraces with a south-easterly aspect have been made into a maritime garden with far-reaching views of the sea. The garden specialises in more tender plants. Abutilons, salvias, diascias and argyranthemums thrive, especially in the new Mediterranean garden. Shrub roses and later hydrangeas are a particular feature. The 'secret walled garden' at the top has been cleared and planted in sub-tropical style. A good leaflet describes all this. The garden of *Little Northcourt* is now open and has been planted in cottage garden style. This is a garden full of hidden delights. The owners welcome bed and breakfast guests and suggest May and June when the gardens are at their very best. Swinburne the poet stayed and wrote at the big house. The garden is being placed on the English Heritage register of parks and gardens of historic interest.

Nunwell House   41

Coach Lane, Brading PO36 0JQ. Tel: (01983) 407240

Col. and Mrs J.A. Aylmer • 3m S of Ryde, signed off A3055 in Brading into Coach Lane • House open, tours 1.30pm, 2.30pm, 3.30pm • Garden open 28th, 29th May, 4th June, then 3rd July to 6th Sept, Mon – Wed, 1 – 5pm • Entrance: £2.50 (house and garden £4, OAPs and students £3, accompanied children under 10 £1) ● ● WC ●

Nunwell House stands in six acres of gardens with wonderful views across the park to Spithead. The rose garden (a bowling green in the seventeenth century) is set at the top of a slope in front of the walled garden, which is now replanted with a double herbaceous border. The Long Walk leads down past the side of the house, where stand two very handsome paulownias, to the front. Among the varied shrubs and plants in the borders are several pretty *Lavatera* 'Barnsley', a notable acanthus, an enormous *Elaeagnus* x *ebbingei* and a *Cotoneaster* x *watereri* 'Cornubia'. There is also a 45-metre run of *Rosa* 'Frensham' and a *Cornus kousa*, and on the front of the house are three large myrtles. A steep flight of steps bordered by lavender leads up to the woods. To the rear of the house is an arboretum laid out by Vernon Russell-Smith in 1963. The gardens are gradually being restored to their former glory. The National Trust's *Mottistone Manor* is nearby and has good views of the Channel and a herb garden.

Osborne House   42

East Cowes PO32 6JY. Tel: (01983) 200022

English Heritage • 1m SE of East Cowes off A3021 • House open as grounds 10am – 5pm • Grounds open April to Oct, daily, 10am – 6pm (Oct closes 5pm)

• *Entrance: £3.50, OAPs £2.60, children £1.80 (house and grounds £6.90, OAPs 5.20, children £3.50. Discounts for parties of 11 or more) (1999 prices)*
◑ 🍽 ✕ 🗟 WC 🚻 ♨ ♀

Built by Queen Victoria 1845-51 as a family retreat, the royal apartments are open to the public and two wings are used as a convalescent home. The gardens, designed jointly by Victoria and Albert in the formal Italianate style, are now being restored and replanted to the original designs. Old cultivars are being used for the 'Victorian' bedding on the terraces, and the borders are being replanted with plants of the period. A wildflower meadow and orchard are being developed. A noteworthy feature of the park and gardens are the magnificent trees. The Swiss Cottage chalet, in what were the royal children's gardens, has nine plots, each with 14 beds, planted with old varieties of soft fruit, flowers and vegetables, with a carriage ride to and fro. The children's gardening tools and Queen Victoria's bathing machine can be seen. The walled garden, where fruit and flowers were grown during Queen Victoria's reign, will open to the public this summer. It has been remodelled by Rupert Golby, who has created a Contemporary Heritage Garden using historic plants within a modern design to celebrate the lives of Queen Victoria and Prince Albert.

Pitt House   43

Love Lane, Bembridge PO35 5NF.

L.J. Martin • Near village centre. Love Lane is near Maritime Museum • Open June to Aug, Sats, 2 – 5pm • Entrance: £1.50, OAPs and children 75p ● ♿

Four acres with lovely views of the Solent through the trees. On a lower level from the house is a delightfully shady dell with a waterfall, ponds and water plants. In the main part of the garden are pergolas hung with roses and honeysuckle, and a Victorian greenhouse with two magnificent yellow daturas. Interesting trees include a crinodendron and a paulownia.

Ventnor Botanic Garden ★★   44

The Undercliffe Drive, Ventnor PO38 1UL. Tel: (01983) 855397

Isle of Wight Council • SW of Ventnor. Signed from A3055 • Garden open all year, daily. Temperate House open: Jan to 20th March, Sun, 11am – 4pm; 21st March to 23rd Oct, daily, 10am – 5pm; 24th Oct to Dec, Sun, 11am – 4pm • Entrance: charge for car park but gardens free (Temperate House 50p, children 20p, parties of 15 or more 45p per person, school parties 15p per child subject to variation) ○ 🍽 ✕ 🗟 WC ♿ 🔊 ♨ ♀

Twenty-two acres, moderately sheltered from the south and north by *Quercus ilex* and escallonias. The shelter belt, which was decimated in the 1987 and 1990 gales, has been replanted. Many tender plants (including olives, *Berberis asiatica* and *Acer sikkimensis* from the Himalayas, *Cestrum elegans* from Mexico, *Pittosporum daphniphylloides* from China) all flourish in the mild climate. Banana plants from Japan and *Citrus ichangensis* are but a few of the rare plants displayed to maximum effect in surroundings which are now designed as a Victorian sub-tropical garden. There is also a magnificent temperate house with a worldwide collection of plants from the warm temperate zones, together with written and pictorial displays. There is an Australian section, a central bed of flowers from southern Africa, an island section concentrating on vulnerable and endangered species. New planting includes an extensive New Zealand garden, a Mediterranean terrace and, recently, a Japanese terrace. The medicinal garden, which contains plants used in folk medicine around the world, is outstanding. *Teucrium chamaedrys* (germander) makes an effective low hedge in the small formal area. The garden is particularly well supplied with seats throughout. The millennium project is under way, partly funded by the National Lottery. It is envisaged that there will be a Visitors' Centre (where exhibitions will be held), a gift shop and restaurant. The Plants for Sale area is well laid out with many unusual varieties. *Deacon's Nursery*, Godshill [open Oct – March, Sats only] has a large variety of fruit trees and bushes together with hops and nut trees. Their catalogue contains over 200 varieties of apples. A few miles inland is the ruined shell of the eighteenth-century *Appuldurcombe House*, which stands in grounds by 'Capability' Brown (English Heritage, open April to Oct, 10am – 6pm).

NATIONAL COUNCIL FOR THE CONSERVATION OF PLANTS AND GARDENS
The NCCPG publishes a *National Plant Collections Directory*. Those interested in particular families of plants who want to see some of the rarer species and garden varieties will find this an invaluable publication. The latest edition, which offers information on about 550 collections comprising more than 50,000 plants and contains articles by holders of the collections, is available from NCCPG, The Pines, Wisley Garden, Woking GU3 6QB.

POSTCODE PLANTS DATABASE
It is often difficult to find out which plants are local to an area. The Postcode Plants Database locates the names of flowers, trees, butterflies and birds for each of Britain's 26 million home addresses. Simply by typing in the first four characters of their Postcode, householders, schools, garden centres and councils can obtain tailor-made lists of local plants which are both hospitable and garden-worthy. Also included are the names of butterflies and birds most likely to visit gardens in each area. The lists come from innovative software, developed by Royal Mail and *FLORA-for-FAUNA* in conjunction with the Natural History Museum, which searches through hundreds of distribution maps of fauna and flora in the British Isles.

HEREFORDSHIRE

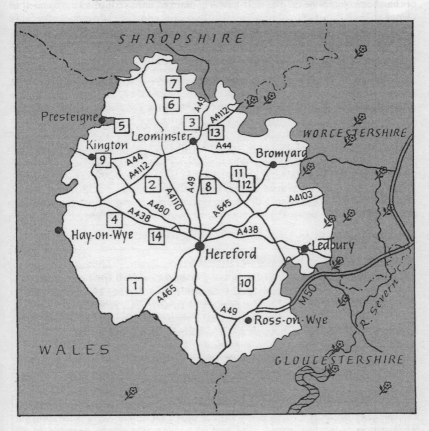

Abbey Dore Court 1

Abbey Dore, Hereford HR2 0AD. Tel: (01981) 240419

Mrs C.L. Ward • 11m SW of Hereford off A465 • Garden open 8th April to 1st Oct, daily except Mon and Wed, 11am – 6pm and by appt • Entrance: £2.50, children 50p ◐ ☕ WC ఉ ⚘

Mature trees, established lawns and a plethora of rare and familiar herbaceous plants all contribute to the established charm of Abbey Dore. The River Dore runs through the grounds and can be appreciated from the riverside walk and bridge. The original course of the river is now incorporated into an area being planted with a range of interesting trees. Planting throughout, whether formal or informal, is undertaken with flair and imagination. The gold and silver borders, which retain year-round interest, are particularly striking, but a

ond and rock garden, hellebores, herbs and a delightfully arranged
rd are also of note. There is a newly planted area of interest around the
cottage.

Arrow Cottage Garden ★ 2

Ledgemoor, Weobley HR4 8RN. Tel: (01544) 318468

*Mr and Mrs L. Hattatt • 10m NW of Hereford between A4110 and A480,
1½ m E of Weobley • Open April to Sept, Wed – Fri and Sun, 2 – 5pm and by
appt • Entrance: £2.50 • Other information: Unsuitable for children* ◐ 🍵 WC ✆

Formal design contrasts with careful plantings, mostly colour-themed, in this
two-acre plantsman's garden. The visitor is led through a series of distinct
enclosures, each with its own particular mood, to a summerhouse garden of
pastel hues and a kitchen garden where ordered vegetables are complemented
by a pair of hot, fiery borders, at their best in late summer. Water is never far
away, whether in the form of a natural stream and pond or a 52-metre, yew-
enclosed rill complete with a dramatic water spout. Long vistas, grass walks,
box parterres and unusual structures contribute to the delight.

Berrington Hall 3

Leominster HR6 0DW. Tel: (01568) 615721

*The National Trust • 4m N of Leominster, W of A49 • Hall open as garden,
1.30 – 5.30pm (last admission 5pm) • Grounds open April to Oct, Sat – Wed
and Bank Holiday Mons, 12.30 – 6pm (5pm in Oct) (last admission ½ hour
before closing). Park walk open July to Oct. Parties of 15 or more by written appt
• Entrance: £2 (hall and grounds £4.20, children £2.10, family ticket £10,
parties £3.50 per person) • Other information: Two wheelchairs and Batricar
available for pre-booking. Telephone for wheelchair access to restaurant. Picnics
in car park only and in play area in Walled Garden* ◐ 🍵 ✕ 🏠 WC ♿ 🍴 ☕

The late-eighteenth-century house designed by Henry Holland is set in mature
grounds landscaped by 'Capability' Brown. The gardens are well maintained
and formally organised, with many shrubs plus a woodland walk with unusual
trees, some recently planted. The walled garden is a young orchard of 50
varieties of pre-1900 apples. Park walk down to 'Capability' Brown's pool.
New attractions for children are an eye-spy trail, orienteering course and
outdoor quizzes, and a living willow tunnel in the children's play area. Croft
Castle (see entry) is nearby.

Brobury Gardens and Gallery 4

Brobury HR3 6BS. Tel: (01981) 500229

*Mrs L. Weaver • 11m NW of Hereford, off A438, at Bredwardine Bridge • Garden
open all year except 25th Dec and 1st Jan, Mon – Sat, 9am – 4.30pm (4pm in
winter) • Entrance: £2.50 • Other information: Gallery* ○ 🏠 WC ♿ ⟿ 🍴 ☕

The garden is what might be expected to be enjoyed by a well-to-do Victorian
gentleman. Conifers, some formal terracing, good trees, herbaceous borders

as well as modern planting, including a nice young stand of *Betula jacquemontii* and clever use of conifers to conceal electricity poles. More interesting plants can be found in antique prints in the Gallery, which has a wide selection, both horticultural and general. Brobury, facing, as it does, both Moccas and Bredwardine where the diarist Kilvert was vicar for the last few months of his life and where he is buried, is a convenient stop on the Kilvert Trail. The house offers bed and breakfast as well as self-catering cottages.

Bryan's Ground 5

Stapleton, Nr Presteigne LD8 2LP. Tel: (01544) 26001

Mr David Wheeler and Mr Simon Dorrell • 2m E of Presteigne between Stapleton and Kinsham • Open15th April to 18th Sept, Sat – Mon, 2 – 5pm, and Good Friday (21st April) • Entrance: £2.50, children £1 NEW ◑ ☕ WC ♿ ﹖

This ambitious new garden, created since 1994, is full of challenging ideas, variety and drama. The lines are already clearly drawn; no space is undefined by walls, hedges, fences or trim grass (sometimes with theatrically scalloped edges), no walk lacks its focal point, and the informality of the beautiful surrounding countryside is enhanced by the formal design of the garden. The comfortable and idiosyncratic Edwardian house is well integrated. Work continues in a newly developed woodland, where an extensive collection of hellebores already looks happy. Elements of the Edwardian garden remain – a brick terrace to the south of the house and a sunken garden with box dumplings and a circular pool. The walled kitchen garden has been subdivided into a smaller potager, an iris quarter, an orchard and a rose garden. From the Sulking House two suitably irascible dark red borders lead to a lovely view. The entrance is wonderfully bold – 30 varieties of apple, laid out formally in square beds with *Iris sibirica*. Bold to use apple in such a formal situation and bold to use only one other plant and in one colour. A garden well worth visiting on a regular basis.

Croft Castle 6

Leominster HR6 9PW. Tel: (01568) 780246

The National Trust • 5m NW of Leominster off B4362 • Castle open • Garden open 25th, 26th March; then April, Sat, Sun and Bank Holiday Mon, 1.30 – 5.30pm; May to Sept, Wed – Sun and Bank Holiday Mons, 1.30 – 5.30pm; Oct, weekends, 1.30 – 4.30pm (last admission ½ hour before closing). Parties of 15 or more by written appt. Parkland open all year • Entrance: grounds only: parking charge (castle and grounds £3.80, children £1.90, family £9.50) • Other information: Picnics in car park only. Braille guides available. Dogs in parkland only, on leads ◑ ☕ WC ♿ ﹖

The Welsh Marches castle dates from the fourteenth century and commands a spectacular landscape of open countryside. It is well kept and pleasant to walk through but lacks interest for the specialist, except for the walled garden which is in good condition. The park is notable for its fine avenue of Spanish chestnuts, possibly 350 years old, and for its venerable pollarded oaks. There charming walks in the Fishpool valley. Berrington Hall (see entry) is nearby.

Elton Hall   7

Elton, Ludlow, Shropshire SY8 2HQ. Tel: (01568) 770218; Fax: (01566) 770753

Mr and Mrs James Hepworth • 5m SW of Ludlow between B4361 and A4110 • Open to individuals and groups by appointment • Entrance: £2, children over 5 £1 • Other information: Plant fair 3rd September ● ▄ ℘

A 'must' for those who appreciate a slightly eccentric touch to their gardens. Also an opportunity to see a relatively young four-acre garden developing. Within the eccentricities (tortoise fort, Moorish sheep palace) lie a new kitchen garden and herbaceous borders filled, amongst others, with National Collections of echinaceas and rudbeckias, off-set with rich colourings of wine and purple-coloured foliage plants. There are brick-built gazebos, Doric columns and gracious urns, not to mention elephants and wigwams adding to the folly of it all.

Hampton Court   8

Hope under Dinmore, Leominster HR6 0PN. Tel: (01568) 797214. Fax: (01568) 797472

Hampton Court Estates (Herefordshire) Ltd • 5m S of Leominster, 200 yds S of junction with A417 • Open 24th June to Oct, Wed – Fri, Sun, 1 – 5pm • Entrance: £3.50 [NEW] ● ▄

The fifteenth-century castle was owned in the nineteenth century by the Arkwright family, but the Victorian gardens are not being restored. Instead we are promised an exciting variety of brand new gardens: a walled garden with fountains, a maze, a sunken garden with a cascade, and a Dutch garden. At the time of writing, much of the site is under construction, but it looks very promising. An ambitious project that deserves a visit.

Hergest Croft Gardens ★   9

Kington HR5 3EG. Tel: (01544) 230160

W.L. Banks • 14m W of Leominster, ½ m W of Kington off A44 • Open April to Oct, daily, 1.30 – 6pm • Entrance: £3.50, children under 16 free, season ticket £12, parties of 20 or more £2.75 per person ◑ ▄ 🥪 WC 占 ⬦ ℘ 👍 ♟

This has been the family home of the Banks family since 1896, and the garden design was much influenced by the writings of Robinson and Jekyll. Miles Hadfield rated the tree and shrub collection very highly, and the autumn colour from maples and birches is a great feature. Excellent kitchen garden. Half a mile through the park is a delightful 50-acre woodland containing vast sheets of rhododendrons nine metres high. By following the path at the top of the dingle you can look down on scenes not far removed from those of their native habitat. Wellington boots are usually necessary, not least in crossing the park in which many sheep safely graze. Fifty acres in all.

How Caple Court 10

How Caple, Ross-on-Wye, Hereford HR1 4SX. Tel: (01989) 740626

Mr and Mrs Roger Lee • 10m SE of Hereford on B4224, turn right at crossroads • Open all year, Mon – Sun, (closed Sun, Oct to Feb), 9am – 5pm. Parties by appt • Entrance: £2.50, children £1.25 • Other information: Shop open all year ○ 🍴 WC ♿ 🅿 🌿 ♨ ♀

A large house and medieval church set in 11 acres of grounds with fine trees lining a valley which flows down to a bend in the River Wye. Much of the Edwardian planting is being re-established, there are good formal terraces, and a big pool surrounded by a curious pergola. The Florentine garden and water supply have now been restored and the owners are working on the water steps below – a spectacular feature. Recent plantings in the valley are maturing well. In the stable yard is a small area selling some unusual shrubs, old roses and dried flowers.

Lower Hope 11

Ullingswick HR1 3JF. Tel: (01432) 820557

Mr and Mrs Clive Richards • 7m NE of Hereford. At roundabout on A465 near Burley Gate take A417 towards Leominster. After 2m turn right. Lower Hope is about ½ m on left. Signposted • Open for charity 2nd April, 28th May, 9th July, 13th Aug, 8th Oct • Entrance: £2, children £1 • Other information: Guide dogs only NEW ● ♨ WC ♿

Few gardens can rival this extensive south- and west-facing garden for summer colour and variety of design effects. Within the scope of five acres a number of artfully contrived water features are to be found, complete with oriental-style crossing points, a pergola, an exotic Mediterranean garden, a gazebo, a swimming pool with a patio surround, lushly planted conservatories and glasshouses. All of this is in addition to herbaceous borders, island beds, shrubs and trees (in part planted to form a woodland walk), vegetable and rose gardens. The whole is set off by immaculately maintained lawns which are, as is the rest of the garden, a tribute to the owners' gardeners. The surrounding fields are grazed by pedigree Hereford cattle and Suffolk sheep. A recent addition is a lime tree walk leading to a new lake landscaped with wild flowers and a bog garden surround.

Lower Hopton Farm 12

Stoke Lacy, Bromyard HR7 4HX. Tel: (01885) 490294

Mr and Mrs Giles Cross • 10m NE of Hereford off A465 Bromyard – Hereford road • Open for individuals and parties of 20 or more only, by personal introduction, to be confirmed in writing • Entrance: individuals £10 per person, parties £5 per person (minimum charge £100) ●

creation of a garden of this size and scale is an ambitious project, to say the y least. That so much has been achieved in so short a period of time is a testament to the owners' skill, determination and hard work. As the garden broadens out, formally designed areas in proximity to the house become much less so. Flair and good judgment are used in the placing of plant material everywhere, not least within the walls of a ruined barn where shelter is given to many tender perennials. A sunken garden, a white garden and an impressive grass walk, together with what will be a secret enclosure, are all well worth the (expensive) visit. So, too, are a red lacquer Chinese bridge, a moated island and a wealth of interesting and unusual plants. Three miles from Hereford is *Overcourt Nursery* at Sutton St Nicholas selling traditional and unusual cottage garden plants. Open March to Oct. Tel: (01432) 880845].

The Picton Garden

(see Worcestershire)

Stockton Bury Gardens   13

Kimbolton, Leominster HR6 0HB. Tel: (01568) 613432

Mr G. Fenn and Mr R. Treasure • 1m N of Leominster. From A49, turn right onto A4112 Kimbolton road. Garden is 300 metres on right. Signposted • Open April to Oct, Wed – Sun and Bank Holiday Mons, 12 noon – 5pm • Entrance: £3 ◐ 💭 🖻 WC ♿ 🐾

A series of interesting gardens, covering about four acres, set among the buildings of a working farm. The old walls and high hedges provide shelter for some of the more tender plants, such as *Abutilon megapotamicum*, tender buddleias and indigoferas. A superb specimen monkey-puzzle dominates the main lawn and a border of shrubs with interesting foliage. In the walled garden silver and golden box edge the beds of immaculate vegetables. A greenhouse contains such tender plants as hedychiums. The Dingle Garden, begun in 1995 and still under construction, has pools, flourishing marginal plants, including *Gunnera manicata*, and a grotto with shells and mirrors. Beautifully made stone paths lead to many hidden corners. The gardens are full of rare trees, shrubs and herbaceous plants, all immaculately cared for.

The Weir Garden   14

Swainshill, Hereford HR4 7QF. Tel: Infoline (01981) 590509.

The National Trust • 5m W of Hereford on A438 • Open 14th Feb to Oct, Wed – Sun and Bank Holiday Mons, 11am – 6pm • Entrance: £2, children £1 • Other information: No coaches ◐ 🖻

Mass upon mass of naturalised daffodils and other bulbs, and a spectacular setting along the banks of the River Wye, make this a memorable experience in the spring. Informal terracing, a small rock garden and, later in the year, colonies of wild flowers, are the principal charms of this understated garden. It is pleasant to walk and relax in, to enjoy the proximity of the river and to delight in the far-reaching views of the Black Mountains.

HERTFORDSHIRE

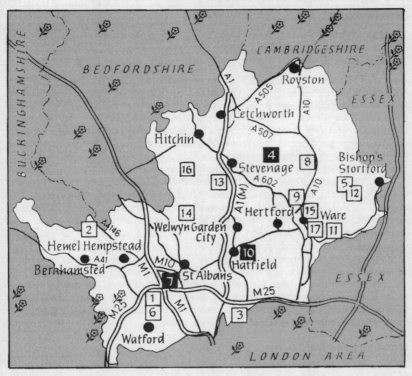

Two-starred gardens are marked on the map with a black square.

The Abbot's House 1

10 High Street, Abbots Langley WD5 0AR. Tel: (01923) 264946

Peter and Sue Tomson • 5m N of Watford, in Abbots Langley. Approach via M25 junction 19 (from W) and 21a (from E) or M1 junction 6 • Garden open 30th April, 9th July, 27th Aug, 2 – 5pm and by appt • Entrance: £2, children free • Other information: Plants for sale in nursery ● ➴ WC &

One and three quarter acres of plantsman's garden full of delights: *Mahonia gracilipes, Itea ilicifolia, Hoheria sexstylosa* 'Stardust' and *Halesia carolina*. Many outstanding shrub and tree specimens. The sunken garden has plants thriving between the brickwork. There is a new Mediterranean semi-formal garden, a shrub border with contrasting foliage, borders of differing colour schemes, a bog garden, an annual wildflower meadow and a conservatory.

Ashridge Management College 2

Berkhamsted HP4 1NS. Tel: (01442) 843491

Ashridge (Bonar Law Memorial) Trust • 3½ m N of Berkhamsted (A41), 1m S of Little Gaddesden off A4146 • Open 21st April to Sept, Sat, Sun and Bank Holiday Mons, 2 – 6pm • Entrance: £2, OAPs and children £1 ● WC & ⟁

A total of 150 acres comprising 90 acres of garden with the rest woodland. The nineteenth-century design was influenced by Humphry Repton, whose Red Book for the garden was presented to the 7th Earl of Bridgewater in 1813. Following the death of Repton the gardens were laid out by Sir Jeffry Wyatville, retaining many of Repton's suggested small gardens. An orangery with an Italian garden and fountain leads round to the south terrace dominated by clipped yew, appoximately 100 years old, and spring and summer bedding. The main lawn in front of the terrace links many small gardens and has within it a group of ancient yews and a large oak planted by Princess (later Queen) Victoria. The circular Rosarie is sited virtually where Repton intended. The Monk's Garden and Holy Well comprises box laid out to represent an armorial garden depicting the four families closely associated with Ashridge. The conservatory dates from 1864 and was used as a fernery. The grotto is constructed of Hertfordshire pudding-stone, and the *souterrain* leading from it of flints hung on an iron framework. This follows the original boundary between Hertfordshire and Buckinghamshire. Crossing the main lawn brings visitors to a sunken garden formerly used as a skating pond. Beyond a disused moat is an avenue of Wellingtonias planted in 1858 and underplanted with rhododendrons, leading to the arboretum with many specimen trees and a Bible garden featuring a circle of incense cedars.

The Beale Arboretum 3

West Lodge Park, Cockfosters Road, Hadley Wood EN4 0PY.
Tel: (0208) 216 3900

The Beale family • Leave M25 at junction 24 and take road S marked Cockfosters (A111). West Lodge Park 1m further on left • Open April to Oct, Wed, 2 – 5pm; also 21st May, 2 – 5pm and 29th Oct, 12 noon – 4pm, for NGS. Organised parties of 10 or more, including tour and luncheon or tea, by arrangement all year • Entrance: £2, children free • Other information: Possible for wheelchairs but undulating gravel paths ● ☕ ✕ WC & ⟁

The late Edward Beale bought the West Lodge Park Hotel in 1945 with the intention of enriching its fine eighteenth-century park with many more trees and creating the important arboretum which it has now become. To help him Mr Beale enlisted the professional advice of Frank Knight, a former director of the Royal Horticultural Society, consultant Derek Honour and Frank Hillier. Today, there are 10 acres of arboretum with some fine rare trees. The trees at West Lodge Park, the three acres of more formal garden, many azaleas, rhododendrons and a lake, coupled with the impressive four-star hotel, make a visit to this little-known gem, only 12 miles from central London, memorable. Certainly if he were to visit the property today, as he did in 1675, the diarist John Evelyn would still be able to say that it was 'a very pretty place – the garden handsome'. He would probably fail to recognise the strawberry tree which was believed to be there at the time of his visit and which has become one of the largest in England.

Benington Lordship ★★ 4

Benington, Stevenage SG2 7BS. Tel: (01438) 869668

Mr and Mrs C.H.A. Bott • 5m E of Stevenage • Open Feb/March for snowdrops (telephone end of Jan for recorded message on opening dates); April to Sept, Wed and Bank Holiday Mons, 12 noon – 5pm; also April to Aug, Sun, 2 – 5pm and 15th Oct, 2 – 5pm • Entrance: £2.80, children free ● ⬤ 🍴 WC ♨

Here is a garden that has almost everything: wonderful views, lakes to wander round, a Victorian folly and a Norman keep and moat, as well as a colourful rockery and big double herbaceous borders. Borders in the kitchen garden, one in shades of gold and silver, another full of penstemons. A great deal of the grass is not cut until July, by which time the wild flowers, notably the snowdrops, scillas, garlics and cowslips, have seeded. The newly planted rose garden has many shrub roses.

Bromley Hall 5

Standon, Ware SG11 1NY. Tel: (01279) 842422

Mr and Mrs A.J. Robarts • 6m W of Bishop's Stortford near A120 and A10 on Standon – Much Hadham road • Open 5th June and one other Sun in June (see local press for details), 2 – 5.30pm for charity • Entrance: £2, children free ● ⬤ WC & ♨

Mrs Robarts has created this four-acre garden entirely herself over the last 25 years, and improvements and alterations are going on all the time. It is both an architectural garden, making good use of walls and hedges, statuary and seats, and a plantsman's garden. Mr Robarts looks after the vegetable garden, and it is immaculate. The wide border on the edge of the drive, backed by a tall hedge, is a well-designed mixture of shrub and foliage planting with unusual and elegant perennials.

Capel Manor Horticultural and Environmental Centre

(see London Area)

Chenies Manor House

(see Buckinghamshire)

Cheslyn House 6

**54 Nascot Wood Road, Watford WD1 3SL.
Tel: (Watford Council) (01923) 235946**

Managed by Watford Council • In north Watford off A411 Hemel Hempstead road or Langley Road, near M25 junction 19 • Open daily except 25th, 26th

Dec, 1st Jan, dawn – dusk. Pre-booked tours with resident gardener available for parties • Entrance: free ○ WC ᵫ ⊲⅁

This three-and-a-half-acre garden has woodland, lawns, a bog garden and pond, herbaceous borders, a rock garden and an aviary, all bequeathed in 1965 by Mr and Mrs Colbeck, well-travelled collectors who chose and planted the trees. Among these are *Sequoiadendron giganteum*, *Catalpa bignonioides*, a particularly good *Diospyros kaki* and a large *Eucryphia* x *nymansensis* 'Nymansay', spectacular in late-summer bloom. The woodland, a haven for wildlife, is well planted with mature rhododendrons, azaleas, camellias and pieris, and there are drifts of spring and autumn bulbs amongst the trees. A renovation programme is presently underway to include structural features and plantings. The herbaceous borders have been redesigned and replanted and feature a collection of hemerocallis. Guide leaflets available free from the resident gardener or the town hall.

Gardens of the Rose ★★   7

Chiswell Green, St Albans AL2 3NR. Tel: (01727) 850461;
Fax: (01727) 850360

Royal National Rose Society • 2m S of St Albans on B4630. Signposted • Open 3rd June to 24th Sept: Mon, 9am – 5pm, Tues to Thurs, 9am – 8pm, Fri, Sat, 9am – 5pm, Sun and Bank Holiday Mon, 10am – 6pm • Entrance: £4, disabled £3.50, children (6-16) £1.50, parties £3.50 per person ◑ ▉ ✕ ▤
WC ᵫ ⊲⅁ ⅌ ⛨ ⚱

The Royal National Rose Gardens provide a splendid display of one of the best and most important collections of roses in the world. There are some 30,000 rose trees and at least 1700 varieties, including Hybrid Teas, Floribundas and climbing roses of every kind, miniature roses and ground-cover roses. Some are thought to differ little from those admired by writers in classical times. (Note: for those who wish to be up-to-date, Hybrid Teas and Floribundas are now known as large-flowered and cluster-flowered roses respectively.) Part of the gardens is the trial grounds for roses from all over the world. The Society has introduced many other plants which harmonise with roses and enhance the planting schemes to give a more natural effect, including clematis and hardy geraniums. H.M. The Queen Mother is particularly fond of old roses and the garden named for her contains a fascinating collection of Gallicas, Albas, Damasks, Centifolias, Portland and Moss roses. Here can be seen what is thought to be the original red rose of Lancaster and white rose of York. Among the Gallicas is the *Rosa mundi* said to have been named for Fair Rosamund, the mistress of Henry II. This is an historic wonderland which could be explored indefinitely by rose lovers and will have interest for all gardeners. The garden is being enlarged over the next 10 years from its current 12 acres to some 60 acres.

Great Munden House   8

Dane End, Ware SG11 1HV. Tel: (01920) 438244

Mr and Mrs D. Wentworth-Stanley • 7m N of Ware off A10. Turn off W of Puckeridge bypass • Open two days in late April, late May, 2.30 – 5.30pm, for

NGS and Red Cross. Small parties by appt • Entrance: £2, children 50p ● 🍵
WC ⚲

The charming small garden, beautifully planned and immaculately kept, is situated down the side of a valley with a backdrop of wheat fields and trees. Beech hedges act as necessary windbreaks, as the wind funnels down the valley. The mixed borders are imaginatively planted with shrubs, shrub roses and excellent foliage plants, and an island border is well established with various shrub roses and shrubs. A paved pond area is surrounded by silver plants, with a *Juniperus virginiana* 'Skyrocket' in each corner. Many climbing roses ramble through old apple trees, and there is an additional pond area with shade-loving plants and hostas. The kitchen garden is well planned with vegetables and flowers for picking.

Hanbury Manor Hotel 9

Ware SG12 0SD. Tel: (01920) 487722; Fax: (01920) 487692

Hanbury Manor Hotel • 2m N of Ware on A10 • Garden open all year • Entrance: free (charge on charity days) • Other information: Refreshments, toilet facilities and shop in hotel ○ ⅙ ⬦

Edmund Hanbury inherited the property (known then as Poles) in 1884. He pulled down the old house, replacing it with a Jacobean-style mansion designed by Sir Ernest George. The Hanbury family were gifted horticulturists and the original gardens, now part of the hotel complex, were widely acclaimed both for their species trees and orchid houses. Today, a colourful pre-Victorian walled garden with a listed moon gate shows off extensive herbaceous borders, herb garden and fruit houses. The original pinetum with its centuries-old sequoias still stands, and major restoration work has seen the revival of the period rose gardens and bulb-planted orchard. A more recent secret garden in a woodland setting is well worth a visit.

Hatfield House and Gardens ★★ 10

Hatfield AL9 5NQ. Tel: (01707) 262823

The Marquess of Salisbury • 2m from A1(M) junction 4 off A414 and A1000, opposite Hatfield railway station • House open as gardens, Tues – Thurs, 12 noon – 4pm, weekends, 1 – 4.30pm, Bank Holiday Mons 11am – 4.30pm • Gardens open 25th March to 24th Sept, daily except Mon (but open Bank Holiday Mons) and 21st April; West Gardens, daily except Mon, 11am – 6pm; all gardens and park open Fri, Connoisseurs' Day, 11am – 6pm; park, daily except Fri, 10.30am – 8pm • Entrance (1999 prices): park £1.50 and West Gardens supplement £2 (house, park and West Gardens £6, children (5-15) £3, under 5 free; Connoisseurs Day £5, no concessions) • Other information: Dogs in park only, on leads ◑ 🍵 ✕ 🗃 **WC** ⅙ ⚲ 🛒 🍴

Originally laid out in the early seventeenth century by Robert Cecil and planted by John Tradescant the Elder, the garden underwent various changes in the following centuries, particularly in the Victorian era, but in the past 28 years it has enjoyed a splendid transformation at the hands of the Marchioness of Salisbury. She began the work of restoration with an imaginative and bold stroke – a new garden as the setting for the Old Palace. From there she went from strength to strength. Not all her re-created gardens are actually open (the maze, for example, is a protected space) but all can be viewed on Fridays (Connoisseurs' Day). Lady Salisbury is well known for her creative work on other private gardens such as Castletown and Highgrove, but here at Hatfield are many splendours and new ones to come, such as the south-front inner courtyard shortly to be restored. The plantings are her particular skill – see the mop-headed *Quercus ilex* imported especially for the garden, and the wild garden around the New Pond (formed in 1607), landscaped and planted since the devastation by two hurricanes. Amongst the many features are the varied knot gardens and a charming herb garden in the scented garden, all planted by Lady Salisbury in the early 1980s following her own designs, and sited, like those in Tudor times, to be viewed from above, filled with plants used from the fifteenth to seventeenth centuries. There is an annual midsummer festival at Hatfield, part-country fair, part-garden party and part-flower show, which gives an opportunity to visit the gardens, including the splendid East Gardens mentioned above. Those interested in so-called wild gardens should spend time in the Wilderness and note that its splendours have not been achieved by throwing flower seeds about but by planting up to 20,000 bulbs a year. The whole 42 acres is gardened organically.

Hill House ★ 11

63 Cappell Lane, Stanstead Abbots, Ware SG12 8BX. Tel: (01920) 870013

Mr and Mrs R. Pilkington • Between Hertford and Harlow. From A10 turn E onto A414, and at roundabout take B181 for Stanstead Abbots. At end of High Street turn left and first right past church • Open 14th May, 4th, 11th June, 2 – 5.30pm, and by appt • Entrance: £2.50, children 50p • Other information: Picture gallery ● ● WC ◁ ◿

Nine acres of very varied garden including woodland, a bog garden, a fine herbaceous border and a highly recommended Victorian conservatory. Immaculate borders, extensive lawns and walls and a wide variety of plants. The position is an interesting one, on a south-facing slope with a magnificent view overlooking the Lea valley.

Hopleys ★ 12

Much Hadham SG10 6BU. Tel: (01279) 842509; Fax (01279) 843784

Mr A. Barker • 5m SW of Bishop's Stortford off B1004. 50 metres N of Bull pub in Much Hadham • Open March to Dec, Mon, Wed – Sat, 9am – 5pm, Sun, 2 – 5pm, and also on special days for charities • Entrance: £1.50, children under 16 free • Other information: Teas available May to Oct, Sun only, otherwise self-service refreshments ◐ ▦ WC ఈ ◿

The owner and his parents have been working on this four-acre plantsman's garden for many years and it has been expanding annually. The pool and bog area are well established. There are numerous borders filled with shrubs and hardy plants, most of which are for sale in the nursery. The long-established conifer bed illustrates the different sizes and shapes of mature conifers. The claim is that the fourth-largest ash tree in the country is here. Several new borders are being created. Not far away is the headquarters of Andrew Crace, who designs and sells a wide range of fine garden furniture and bronze and stone ornaments. Also nearby is *Dane Tree House*, Much Hadham, home of the *Henry Moore Foundation*. Moore lived here for 40 years and his collection, studios and workshops remain very much as they were in his lifetime, in a parkland with many native trees and particularly fine ancient hedgerows. Larger works are placed in the surrounding fields with sheep grazing round them — as he intended them to. [Open April to Sept, Tues — Thurs, mornings only by appointment or 2.30pm for tour. Tel: (01279) 843333]

Knebworth House ★   13

Knebworth, Stevenage SG3 6PY. Tel: (01438) 812661

Lord Cobbold • 2m S of Stevenage off B656. Access from A1(M) junction 7 • House open as garden • Garden open 15th April to 1st May, daily; 6th May to 21st May, Sat and Sun; 27th May to 4th June, daily; 10th June to 2nd July, Sat and Sun; 8th July to 3rd Sept, daily; 9th Sept to 1st Oct, Sat and Sun; all 11am — 5.30pm • Entrance: £5, family (4 persons) £17.50 (house and gardens £6, OAPs and children £5.50 • Other information: Guided tours available. Dogs in park only, on lead ◑ ☕ 🏠 WC 🅿 ♿ ⚲

As the historic home of the Lytton family, the garden evolved from a simple Tudor green and orchard to Sir Edward Bulwer Lytton's elaborate Victorian design of the mid-1800s. Edwin Lutyens redesigned the garden at the beginning of the twentieth century with twin avenues of pollarded lime trees leading to the rose garden, lily ponds and herbaceous borders with tall yew hedges behind. Beyond lies the Green Garden, Gold Garden, Brick Garden, with a blue and silver theme, and pergola. To one side is a pets' cemetery, to the other a malus (crab apple) walk. Other features are the maze (replanted in 1995), the ponds, and the Gertrude Jekyll herb garden, designed in 1907, but not laid out until 1982. The wilderness with its 'woodland walk' is a carpet of daffodils in spring followed by blue alkanet, foxgloves and other wild flowers. The walled garden is being redeveloped and should be open in the summer of 2000. In all there are 25 acres of gardens to explore. A few miles north at Hitchin are the rose gardens of R. Harkness & Co Ltd [open all year, Mon — Sat, 10am — 5.30pm, Sun and Bank Holiday Mons, 10am — 4.30pm].

Mackerye End House   14

Harpenden AL5 5DR.

Mr and Mrs David Laing • 3m E of Harpenden. From A1 junction 4 follow signs for Wheathampstead, or from M1 junction 10 follow B653 to Cherry Tree Inn and turn left to Wheathampstead. Follow signs for Luton and house is ½ m on right • Open 18th June, 11am — 5pm • Entrance: £3, concessions £2, children £1.25 ◑ ☕ WC ♿ ⚲

A Grade I manor house (1550) in 11 acres of park and garden. Its Victorian walled garden, filled with wonderful peonies of all shades, is now divided by magnificent yew hedges. There is a path maze, a cutting garden, a new garden enclosed by a pergola walk of old English roses and vines, a paved walk around the house with camellias and magnolias, and a patio with a large ginkgo. The rough grass in front of the house has a mass of wild daffodils and a vast tulip tree.

Scotts Grotto 15

Scotts Road, Ware SG12 9JQ. Tel: (01920) 464131

East Hertfordshire District Council • In Ware, off A119 Hertford road • Open April to Sept, Sat and Bank Holiday Mons only, 2 – 4.30pm. Party visits by prior arrangement • Entrance: £1 donation suggested ●

This eighteenth-century folly, restored by the Ware Society and described by English Heritage as 'one of the finest in the country', is decorated with exotic shells and lined with flints. It is truly 'grotto-esque'. Take a torch!

St Paul's Walden Bury ★ 16

Whitwell, Hitchin SG4 8BP. Tel: (01438) 871218

Mr and Mrs Simon Bowes Lyon • 5m S of Hitchin, ½ m N of Whitwell on B651 • Open probably four Suns in April, May or June, 2 – 7pm, and at other times by appt • Entrance: £2, children 50p ● ● & ●

The formal landscape garden has retained intact its original design of 1730, one of the few to survive. It covers an area of 40 acres. The long mown rides or *allées* are lined with clipped beech hedges. Originally they were planted with hornbeams, which shed all their leaves in winter, so the present owner's father, Sir David Bowes Lyon, President of the RHS and a famous gardener, replaced them himself with the help of his wife Rachel and an old-age pensioner. The three rides fan out from the eighteenth-century house – the heart of the layout – through *bosquets* to temples, statues, ponds and a medieval church. In one of the *bosquets* is an elegant green theatre. There are also woodland shrub gardens and masses of spring bulbs, and a lake with a temple and wonderful vistas. Although the borders and flower garden are no longer maintained, the layout and design remain truly wonderful.

Van Hage's Nursery ★ 17

Great Amwell, Ware SG12 9RP. Tel: (01920) 87081

Van Hage's Nursery • At M25 junction 25, take A10 towards Cambridge, A1170 towards Ware. On outskirts of Ware • Open daily except 23rd April: Mon – Sat, 9am – 6pm (opens 9.30am on Mon); Sun, 10.30am – 4.30pm • Entrance: free ○ ● ✕ WC & ● ● ●

A superbly run nursery with top-class plants, a vast selection of bedding plants, unusual perennials and exciting shrubs and trees. Exotica such as topiary elephants and bonsai trees. Imaginative tubs with catmint and lilies, and excellent indoor plants including wonderful orchids.

KENT

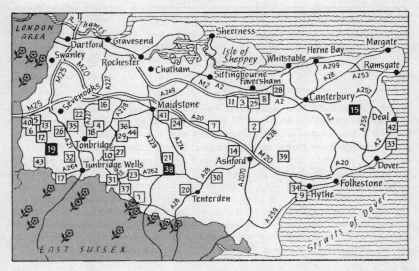

We have included some gardens with Kent postal addresses in the London section for convenience. So before planning a day out in Kent it is worthwhile consulting pages 259–300.

Two-starred gardens are marked on the map with a black square.

Bedgebury National Pinetum and Forest Gardens ★   1

Goudhurst, Cranbrook TN17 2SL. Tel: (01580) 211781 (Shop)

Forestry Commission • 10m SE of Tunbridge Wells off A21, on B2079 Goudhurst – Flimwell road • Arboretum open all year, daily, 10am – 7pm (4pm in winter) • Entrance: £2.50, OAPs £2, children £1.20, family (2 adults and 2 children) £7. Exact money required sometimes ○ 🍵 ✕ 🗏 WC ⟁ 🌿 🧺 💡

The modern pinetum was founded in 1921, but some of the larger specimen trees dating from 1850 are still flourishing. It has recently been listed as the best conifer collection in the world by the International Dendrological Research Institute based in America and Hungary. As well as conifers, it has many deciduous trees, including rare oaks and maples. The wide range of rhododendrons flowers from January to August. There is a newly planted Japanese garden containing trees from wild-collected seed, and an American garden is proposed with less common trees and shrubs from the southern states of North America. The pinetum has five National Collections: Lawson cypresses, Leyland cypresses, junipers, yews and red cedars. It is the top winter roost of hawfinches and crossbills.

Beech Court 2

Challock, Ashford TN25 4DJ. Tel: (01233) 740735; Fax: (01233) 740842

Mr and Mrs Vyvyan Harmsworth • 5m N of Ashford, W of A251/A252 crossroads, off The Lees • Open 28th March to 15th Nov, Tues – Fri, 10am – 5pm, Sat, Sun and Bank Holiday Mons, 12 noon – 6pm. At other times by appt. Closed 21st April • Entrance: £3, OAPs £2.50, children £1, parties of 12 or more £2.30 per person ◑ ◙ 🏠 WC & ♨ 🏺 ♀

One hundred and fifty metres above sea level in a pocket of acidic clay on the edge of the North Downs, this 10-acre woodland garden was designed with Inverewe (see entry in Scotland) in mind and has many acres of rhododendrons, azaleas, hydrangeas and viburnums. Spring colour from the rhododendrons, azaleas and acers is augmented by bulbs. Summer interest is provided by roses, philadelphus and hydrangeas, and the many specimen trees give good autumn colour. A *Prunus* 'Pink Perfection' is the largest tree of its kind in the country. Mature acers and various oaks, a rose walk, buddleia avenue and viburnum avenue encourage a natural feeling of tranquillity in this garden of meandering paths and surprising vistas. A small sunken pond has margins well planted with moisture-loving plants and is set in a lawn edged with a large variety of herbaceous plants. Most of the trees are labelled.

Belmont ★ 3

Belmont Park, Throwley, Faversham ME13 0HH. Tel: (01795) 890202

Harris (Belmont) Charity • 4m SW of Faversham, 1½ m W of A251 Faversham – Ashford road. From A2 or M2 junction 6, take A251 S towards Ashford. Signed at Badlesmere • House open • Garden open 23rd April to Sept, Sat, Sun and Bank Holiday Mons, 2 – 5pm • Entrance: £2.75, children £1 (house, clock museum and gardens £5.25, children £2.50) ● ◙ 🏠 WC & ♨ 🏺

The eighteenth-century house by Samuel Wyatt has been the seat of the Harris family since 1801 and, though somewhat off the beaten track down winding lanes, it is well worth a visit. It was built at a time when beautiful country-house architecture was required to blend in with equally beautiful and well-planned surroundings, exemplified here by 40 acres of formal and informal gardens blending with the 150 acres of parkland to give marvellous vistas of aged and noble trees. Yew walk and a pinetum. The walled garden includes borders, a pool, a rockery; note also the shell grotto and folly. There is a touching pets' cemetery for those who like that kind of thing.

Broadview Gardens 4

Hadlow, Tonbridge TN11 0AL Tel: (01732) 850551; Fax: (01732) 851957

Hadlow College • 8m SW of Maidstone, 3m NE of Tonbridge, on A26 • Open 20th March to 2nd Nov, Wed – Sun, 10am – 5pm • Entrance: £2 ◑ ◙ ✕ WC ♨ 🏺 ♀

This series of gardens in the grounds of Hadlow College was opened to the public in early 1997. Within an area of 40 acres are several new ideas in design and planting. The visitor enters an area of sub-tropical plants with four different varieties of musa and canna lilies, stooled paulownia and golden catalpa. An herbaceous border, 100 metres long, is bordered by an avenue of fastigiate oaks. There is an experimental garden with a modern steel wave sculpture and a low-maintenance gravel garden. The cottage garden has a wall of golden hop in contrast to the very dwarf trained fruit trees. In the sensory garden a water rill at waist height falls over cobbles and raised beds. The contrast between the Heaven and Hell gardens is achieved by planting the former with scented herbs and subtly varied foliage colour, while in Hell the hot colours of flowers and foliage convey an oppressive atmosphere, heightened by a black 'river' of *Ophiopogon planiscapus* 'Nigrescens' (lily turf). The seating alcoves in Hell are unusual, being lopsided and enclosed in intertwined willow stems. A half-acre Japanese garden has all the oriental elements and appropriate planting. There is a one-acre lake edged with bog plants and an area vibrant with colour in the autumn. The garden also contains National Collections of hellebores and Japanese anemones.

Charts Edge 5

Westerham TN16 1PL.

Mr and Mrs Bigwood • S of M25 and A25, ½ m S of Westerham on B2026 towards Chartwell • Open 7th, 21st May, 9th July, 2 – 5pm • Entrance: £2, children free ● 🍴 WC ⬦ ℘

The removal of some mature trees during storms over the last 10 years has opened up areas of this seven-acre garden to provide sweeping lawns, space for some interesting trees and the reclamation of some of the original Victorian features. Whilst a large part of the planting dates from the '60s – including many trees and rhododendrons – unusual examples of later plantings include *R. sinogrande*, *R.* 'May Day', and *R. Carita*. Recent additions include a *Paulownia tomentosa*, a cut-leaf beech and a weeping form of *Morus alba*. A 30-metre-long raised herbaceous border containing a wide selection of plants leads down to the atmospheric dell garden with acers, ferns, hostas and other bog plants. An interesting feature here, built into the hillside, is a Victorian grotto lined with flint. Adjoining is a brick-lined room with steps leading down to what was probably a bath with a lead pipe. Around the house are borders with roses, a large well-planted rockery, a terrace with views over the North Downs framed by two mature *Acer palmatum* var. *dissectum*, and an old mulberry. Squerryes Court and Chartwell (see entries) are both close by.

Chartwell 6

Westerham TN16 1PS. Tel: Infoline (01732) 866368; Fax: (01732) 868193

The National Trust • S of M25 between junctions 5 and 6, 2m S of Westerham off B2026 • House open • Garden open 1st April to Oct, Wed – Sun and Bank Holiday Mons; also Tues in July and Aug, all 11am – 5pm (last admission 4.15pm) • Entrance: house and garden £5.50, children £2.75, family £13.75 (1999 prices) ◑ 🍴 ✕ 🖼 WC ♿ ⬦ 🛍 ♀

Within this garden on a hill, with vast views over the Weald of Kent, the first feature at which the visitor arrives is a melodious waterfall. This enters the fish pool above the swimming pool (the latter constructed by Sir Winston Churchill and not in garish blue). Well-established trees along a path lead the way to a walled rose garden, the perimeter of which is planted with herbaceous plants such as hostas, peonies and penstemons. A cloud of shrub roses perfumes the terrace, and ceanothus, white potentillas and dark red double Rugosa roses invite the visitor on towards the house, one wing of which is covered by a huge *Hydrangea petiolaris*. The south wall has a large *Magnolia grandiflora*. A vine-covered pergola leads to a gazebo and viewpoint. A series of smaller terraces, one planted with silver-foliage plants, and a Golden Rose walk bordered by clipped beech hedges. Maintenance and labelling are excellent, but remember that Churchill bought Chartwell for 'that view'.

Church Hill Cottage Gardens ★ 7

Charing Heath, Ashford TN27 0BU. Tel/Fax: (01233) 712522

Mr and Mrs M. Metianu • From M20 junction 8 (from Maidstone) or junction 9 (from Folkestone) join A20. ½ m W of Charing, turn S from A20 dual-carriageway section to Charing Heath and Egerton. Fork right after 1m at Red Lion pub, take next right and gardens are 250 metres on right • Garden open 21st March to Sept, daily except Mon (but open Bank Holiday Mons), 10am – 5pm • Entrance: £2, children free ◑ 🏠 **WC** &. ℘

In these tranquil gardens there is a strong sense of design in the curves of borders and island beds, but they are so well matched by the fine and well-developed planting that the whole seems natural. Established birches form a central point. Beds are varied, some with colour themes, others with shrubs heavily underplanted with a wide range of unusual hardy plants and bulbs in season. Of interest to the plantsman are the large collections of dianthus and violas, which include between 30 and 40 types of old forms dating from the sixteenth to the eighteenth century. The woodland area has developed well and has been enlarged by the addition of two fine fern and hosta beds.

Copton Ash Gardens 8

105 Ashford Road, Faversham ME13 8XW. Tel: (01795) 535919

Drs Tim and Gillian Ingram • 1m S of Faversham. Just N of M2 junction 6 on A251 Faversham – Ashford road • Garden open March to Oct, Tues – Sun, 2 – 6pm, and by appt. There may be occasional closures so telephone before travelling • Entrance: £1.50, accompanied children free • Other information: Plants for sale in nursery ◑ &. ℘

Despite its position close to the M2 there is a pleasant atmosphere at Copton Ash. This a plantsman's garden created since 1978 on the site of an old cherry orchard. About one and a half acres in extent, it accommodates some 3000 species in herbaceous borders and island beds with specimen plantings. There is a collection of fruit varieties, alpines are grown in raised beds, and experiments are under way to examine the hardiness of species from Australia, New Zealand and South America. Helpfully, many plants and shrubs and the fruit varieties are labelled. From the garden, Tim Ingram has developed a specialist nursery with an emphasis on plants for dry situations, including cistus and umbellifers. Belmont and Longacre (see entries) are nearby. So is *Brogdale Horticultural Trust*, which has the National Collection of fruit — over 4000 varieties.

Country Flowers Wildflower Nursery 9

62 Lower Sands, Dymchurch, Romney Marsh TN29 0NF. Tel: (01303) 873052

Johanna Westgate • 4m SW of Hythe, 1m NE of Dymchurch signposted on A259 • Garden and nursery open March to Oct, daily, from 10.30am. Telephone answering machine for details • Entrance: free ◑ ℘

On the coast between Hythe and Dymchurch plants and wildlife flourish in harmony. Cottage-garden plants and wild flowers are grown to support wildlife and the ground is thickly planted with varieties, grown from seed collected on Romney Marsh and around Dungeness. There are 1500 species of wild flowers in Britain, and Johanna Westgate supplies about 150 of these as suitable for gardens. She also has a number of seed varieties available, including wild flowers for meadows, woodlands, ponds and coastal sites.

Crittenden House 10

Crittenden Road, Matfield, Tonbridge TN12 7EN. Tel: (01892) 832554

Mr B.P. Tompsett • 6m SE of Tonbridge on B2160. Turn left in Matfield along Chestnut Lane. House on right after 1m • Open 24th April, 2 – 5.30pm. Parties by appt • Entrance: £2, children under 12 25p [NEW] ◕ WC &

There is a wide variety of plants, all blending within the labour-saving concept of the owner's design; with its spring bulbs, rhododendrons, roses, lilies, waterside plantings and autumn colours, the garden teems with interest throughout the year. Curved lawns sweep to island beds and interestingly planted water fringes. The local native flora, such as *Primula vulgaris* and *Dactylorhiza fuchsii*, mingle strikingly with more rarified species like *Paeonia lutea* var. *ludlowii* ('Sherriff's Variety'), a gift from George Sherriff, and *Malus* 'Crittenden' (awarded a first-class certificate in 1971). Crataegus varieties – *C. monogyna* 'Pink May', *C x lavallei*, *C. laciniata*, *C. orientalis* – contrast with *Davidia involucrata* var. *vilmoriniana* (with its outstanding autumn colours) and *Rhododendron* 'Elizabeth', *R.* 'Unique', *R.* 'Exbury' and *R.* 'Lady Chamberlain'. Several trees have been raised from seed collected by the owner – *Pinus ayacahuite* from Popacatepetl, Mexico, and *Hippophae salicifolia* from Nepal, for example. The local stone in the garden has many fossil sand-ripples and even a fossil footprint of a dinosaur – possibly an iguanodon.

Doddington Place Gardens 11

Doddington, Sittingbourne ME9 0BB. Tel: (01795) 886101

Mr R. Oldfield • 6m S of Sittingbourne. From A20 turn N at Lenham. From A2 turn S at Teynham. Signposted • Open May to Sept, Wed and Bank Holidays, 11am – 6pm, Suns, 2 – 6pm. Other days for parties by appt • Entrance: £3, children over 5 50p, groups £2.50 per person • Other information: Picnics in park only ◑ ☕ ✕ WC & ⇦ ℘ ♨ ⚘

Ten acres of landscaped grounds in part designed by Markham Nesfield in the nineteenth century and further developed in the 1910s, 1960s and 1990s. The main attractions here are the views of open countryside and the spaciousness which offers pleasant walks at any time of year. Other features are a rather fine rock garden, excellent yew hedging (some cut to resemble undulating mountain scenery), a new *allée* and, in season, the woodland garden's collection of rhododendrons. A two-storey folly was built in 1997.

Edenbridge House 12

Main Road, Edenbridge TN8 6SJ. Tel: (01732) 862122

Mrs M.T. Lloyd • 1½ m N of Edenbridge on B2026 • Open April to Oct, Tues and Thurs, 2 – 5pm and for NGS some Sun and Wed and open by appt for parties • Entrance: £2 • Other information: Refreshments on charity open days only ◑ WC &. ⊕ ℘

This five-acre garden, originally made in the 1920s, is set on a south-facing slope. The part-sixteenth-century house is surrounded on three sides by a wide terrace on which a large variety of tender plants – datura, *Punica granatum*, *Streptosolen jamesonii* and *Cestrum elegans* – flourish in pots. A walled courtyard to one side of the house contains a parterre filled with scented herbs and violas. *Itea ilicifolia*, *Clerodendrum bungei*, wisteria, jasmine and a *Magnolia grandiflora*, together with roses, drape the walls. Garden 'rooms' are linked to the house by a lawn containing a fountain pool guarded by elegant drum-shaped golden yews. A small stream, crossed by two wisteria-clad bridges, meanders down to a small lower pool. The banks of the stream are edged with rocks and planted with moisture-loving plants. There is a large kitchen garden, a soft-fruit cage and an apple and cherry orchard. Part of the kitchen garden has been turned into an arboretum and planted with a selection of trees and shrubs to give a wide range of colour: *Amelanchier canadensis*, liquidambar, *Ginkgo biloba*, *Acer platanoides* 'Crimson King' and *Gleditsia triacanthos* 'Sunburst'. A 21-metre-long peach house now contains plumbago, passiflora and a large *Cobaea scandens alba*. This is a plantsman's garden with year-round interest provided by displays of bulbs from early spring to the colourful summer herbaceous borders and foliage colours of autumn.

Emmetts Garden ★ 13

Ide Hill, Sevenoaks TN14 6AY. Tel: (01732) 750367; Fax (01732) 868193

The National Trust • 1½ m S of A25, 1½ m N of Ide Hill off B2042 Edenbridge – Sundridge road • Open April to May, Wed – Sun and Bank Holiday Mons; June to Oct, Sat, Sun, Wed and Bank Holiday Mon; all 11am – 5.30pm (last admission 4.30pm) • Entrance: £3.20, children £1.60, family £8, pre-booked parties £2.50 • Other information: Buggy available from car park to entrance ◑ 🍽 🍴 WC &. ⊕ 🎋 ♿

Set on the top of Ide Hill, the garden gives a superb view over the Weald of Kent and provides an impressive setting for this plantsman's collection of trees and shrubs. It is a garden to visit at any time of the year, but is particularly fine in spring, with its bluebell woods and flowering shrubs. First planted by Frederick Lubbock, the owner from about 1890 until his death in 1926, it is noted especially for its rhododendrons and azaleas. It follows the late-nineteenth-century style of combining exotics with conifers to provide a 'wild' garden, all well listed in the Trust guide. Recent additions to extend the interest throughout the season include a rose garden, a rock garden and extensive planting of acers for autumn colour. The enforced clearance of some trees and shrubs after the gales of 1987 has enabled new planting to keep the traditions of the garden and also to expand it – the rock garden in particular has grown and is becoming established. It is still a wonderful site and a fascinating garden.

Godinton House and Gardens   14

Ashford TN23 3BP. Tel: (01233) 620773

The Godinton House Preservation Trust • 1½ m NW of Ashford off A20 at Potter's Corner (opposite Hare and Hounds) • Open 14th April to 15th Oct, Fri – Sun, 2 – 5pm • Entrance: £2, children £1 (house and garden £4, children £2) • Other information: Coaches by appt only ◑ WC ⑤

Godinton House reopened in April 1999 after major restoration. In the garden, the most visible element of the renovation is the cutting back of the great boundary hedge to encourage new growth. Godinton's hedge, planted to Blomfield's original design, is the garden's outstanding feature and one of the largest in the country. The treatment of cutting back to the yew trunks (doing one side at a time and leaving several years in between) has been tested in other historic gardens and it is estimated that Godinton's hedge will be re-established within five years. Other main features of the garden are the formal lawns, terraces, lily pond and topiary of Blomfield's first design. The wild garden with its huge tulip tree is famous for its show of daffodils and spring flowers. There is a walled Italian garden adjoining the main kitchen garden. Good views across the parkland. Restoration is continuing in parts of the garden.

Goodnestone Park ★★   15

Goodnestone, Canterbury CT3 1PL. Tel: (01304) 840107

Lady FitzWalter • 5m E of Canterbury on A257 turn S onto B2046, after 1m turn E • House open by appt for parties of 20 to 25. £1.80 per person • Garden open 27th March to 27th Oct, Mon, Wed – Fri, 11am – 5pm; also 2nd April to 20th Oct, Sun, 12 noon – 6pm. Closed Tues and Sat, except for pre-booked parties • Entrance: £3.50, disabled in wheelchairs £1, students £1.50, children under 12 50p, parties of 20 or more £2.50 per person (£3.50 per person for guided tour) • Other information: Teas available April to Sept only ◑ ☕ ✕ 🖥 WC ⑤ 🌿

Goodnestone (pronounced Gunston) Park is a 14-acre garden in a rural setting. Built in 1700 by Brook Bridges, the Palladian-style house was rebuilt and enlarged by his great-grandson, Sir Brook Bridges, 3rd Baronet, whose daughter Elizabeth married Jane Austen's brother, Edward. Jane Austen refers frequently to Goodnestone and her Bridges cousins in her letters. There are pleasant vistas within the garden and good views out to open countryside. The garden ranges in planting from the mid-eighteenth-century parkland with fine trees and cedars to the walled area behind the house, which dates from the sixteenth and seventeenth centuries. The garden tour leads along a broad terrace in front of the house, planted with a parterre for the millennium. Behind the house a small woodland garden, laid out in the 1920s, gives pleasant walks and welcome shade. Here are rhododendrons, camellias, magnolias and hydrangeas among many others. A cedar walk leads, between spring borders on the left and more roses on the right, to a walled garden overlooked by the church tower. Old roses mingle with mixed underplanting. Walls bear clematis, jasmine, climbing roses.

Great Comp ★   16

Platt, Borough Green, Sevenoaks TN15 8QS. Tel: (01732) 882669/886154

Great Comp Charitable Trust • From M20 junction 2, take A20 towards Maidstone. At Wrotham Heath take B2016. Signposted • Open April to Oct, daily, 11am – 6pm • Entrance: £3.50, children £1. Annual ticket £10, OAPs £7 • Other information: Teas on Suns and Bank Holidays or by arrangement for parties ◑ 🍴 WC ♿ ♨ ♟

A half-day is likely to be required to do justice to this imaginatively planned seven-acre garden, which offers all-year interest. Although the setting for an early-seventeenth-century house, it has only been created since 1957 by Mr Roderick Cameron and the late Mrs Joyce Cameron out of the neglected earlier garden, rough woodland and paddock. Long grass walks intersect the beds and borders, creating ever-changing views to tempt visitors to stray from their intended route. Focal points and interest are created by statuary, a temple and ruins built from the tons of ironstone dug up over the years. There are woodland areas, herbaceous borders, a heather garden, rose garden, formal lawns and a new Italianate garden, designed to set off a collection of Mediterranean plants. Hellebores are a feature, mainly *H. orientalis*. The *Taxus baccata* at the front of the house was planted in 1840. Other specimen trees include a young dawn redwood, *Metasequoia glytostroboides*, and a Californian redwood, *Sequoia sempervirens* 'Cantab'. A music festival is held here each year, with recitals in the former stables.

Groombridge Place ★   17

Groombridge, Tunbridge Wells TN3 9QG. Tel: (01892) 863999

Mr Andrew de Candole • 4m SW of Tunbridge Wells. Take A264 towards East Grinstead. After 2m take B2110 to Groombridge • Open April to Oct, daily, 9am – 6pm • Entrance: £6.50, OAPs, students and children £5.50, family ticket £20 (1999 prices) • Other information: Canal boat rides, birds of prey ◑ ☕ ✕ 🍴 WC ♿ ♨ ♨ ♟

This mid-seventeenth-century moated house (not open to the public) is set at the bottom of a valley with enclosed formal gardens sloping up to the north:

the Drunken Garden with topiary of drum yews and cypress leaning at angles; the Oriental Garden containing some very old gnarled cut-leaf acers; the Draughtsman's Garden (the eponymous film was filmed in the garden) and the White Rose Garden. These areas are subdivided by topiaried yews, a nut walk and a 'Bowling Alley'. There are many magnificent trees, such as the four nineteenth-century Wellingtonias to the east of the house and the two huge *Thuja plicata* 'Zebrina' flanking the steps leading to the first terrace. Beside the moat is a parterre knot from which a door in the wall leads into the Secret Garden — a small shady area planted with candelabra primulas alongside a stream flowing through mossy rocks. Dotted around are information boards giving details of the garden's historical and literary associations. Peacocks wander freely. A walk up through the vineyard gives access to 'The Enchanted Forest', through the Chime Walk and on up to the wooded hillside with magnificent views across the Weald. Several theme gardens designed by Ivan Hicks, plus an imaginative 'Spring of Life' by Myles Challis, are to be found along the walk which then brings the visitor back beside the canal to the formal gardens, and the newly-opened Golden Key Maze.

115 Hadlow Road   18

Tonbridge TN9 1QE. Tel: (01732) 353738

Mr and Mrs Richard Esdale • 1m N of Tonbridge. From High Street take A26 signed Maidstone. House is 1m on left in service road • Open by appt and 9th, 30th July, 27th Aug, 2 – 6pm • Entrance: £1.50 ◓ ☕

A third-of-an-acre terraced suburban garden with many interesting specimen trees such as *Catalpa bignonioides* 'Aurea', *Acer negundo* 'Flamingo', A. *japonicum* 'Aureum', golden elm and *Sorbus cashmiriana*. Herbaceous border, clematis, hardy fuchsias, ferns, grasses (*Stipa gigantea*), alpines, roses, shrubs and summer bedding provide additional colour, and a small pool with fountain contains a range of water-loving plants. There is a small, well-stocked fruit and vegetable garden.

Hever Castle and Gardens ★★   19

Hever, Edenbridge TN8 7NG. Tel: (01732) 865224

Broadlands Properties Ltd • 3m SE of Edenbridge, between Sevenoaks and East Grinstead off B2026 • Castle opens 12 noon • Gardens open March to Nov, daily, 11am – 6pm (last admission 5pm). Pre-booked guided tours for both castle and gardens available for parties • Entrance: £5.80, OAPs £4.90, children (5-16) £3.80, family (2 adults, 2 children) £15.40; castle and gardens £7.30, OAPs £6.20, children (5-16) £4, family £18.60. Rates for parties of 15 or more available (1999 prices) ◓ ☕ ✕ 🗟 <u>WC</u> & 🌺 ✿ 🛏 ☕

The gardens were laid out between 1904 and 1908 to William Waldorf Astor's designs. One thousand men were employed, 800 of whom dug out the 35-acre lake; steam engines moved rock and soil to create apparently natural new features and teams of horses moved mature trees from Ashdown Forest. Today the gardens have reached their maturity and are teeming with colour and interest throughout the year. Amongst the many superb features is an out-standing four-acre Italian garden, the setting for a large collection of classical statuary. Opposite is a magnificent pergola, supporting camellias, wisteria, crab apple, Virginia creeper and roses. It fuses into the hillside beyond, which has shaded grottos of cool damp-loving species such as hostas, astilbes and polygonums. Less formal areas include the rhododendron walks, Anne Boleyn's orchard and her walk, which extends along the full length of the grounds and is particularly attractive in autumn. In keeping with the Anne Boleyn connection a so-called Tudor herb garden has been added. Recently the 110-metre herbaceous border has been re-created and a water maze planted with a range of aquatic plants.

Hole Park   20

Rolvenden, Cranbrook TN17 4JA. Tel: (01580) 241251

Mr D.G.W. Barham • 4m W of Tenterden, on B2086 between Rolvenden and Benenden • Open April and June, Wed; and 2nd, 9th, 23rd, 30th April, 7th, 21st, 28th May, 8th, 15th Oct, all 2 – 6pm. Also private visits and parties by appt • Entrance: £3, children under 12 50p ● WC &

Situated midway between Sissinghurst and Great Dixter, Hole Park affords the visitor an opportunity to enjoy a peaceful garden of great beauty far away from the crowds and very different from its popular neighbours. The 14-acre gardens were designed and created by the owner's grandfather in the early 1920s, when extensive yew hedges were planted, and these, together with fine trees, broad lawns and old walls, provide the background for all varieties of plantings as well as pools, statuary and pleasant places in which to wander at will. There are splendid views over the beautiful parkland to Rolvenden's famous seventeenth-century postmill and out into the Weald of Kent beyond. In the wild garden to the north of the house, daffodils in great variety are followed by flowering shrubs, rhododendrons and azaleas, and the dell makes a cool feature throughout. In May bluebells fill the woodland walk and then, to close the season, autumn colours are a speciality, making the garden a sight for all seasons. Nearby is *Great Maytham Hall* (Country Houses Association), said to have inspired *The Secret Garden* and open Wed, Thurs, 2 – 5pm in August.

Iden Croft Herbs   21

Frittenden Road, Staplehurst TN12 0DH. Tel: (01580) 891432

Rosemary and David Titterington • 10m S of Maidstone. From Staplehurst at Elf Garage turn down Frittenden Road. Signed from A229 • Gardens open all year, Mon – Sat, 9am – 5pm. Also March to Sept, Sun and Bank Holiday Mons, 11am – 5pm • Entrance: £1.50, children (5-15) 50p (free to hospices and special parties by appt) ○ ♨ 🏠 WC & ⬦ ✿ 👜 ♟

Organic gardens situated in quiet backwater near Staplehurst. There are acres of herbs bordered by grass paths and a large walled garden. The 10-acre site contains a variety of plantings and includes several demonstration areas to help the planner. There is a special garden for the disabled so that texture, smell, shape and colour can be appreciated. A cottage garden near the refreshment patio demonstrates year-round colour and texture in a small area. A fifteenth-century walled garden built on the site of an ancient Wealden lake contains a variety of old-fashioned herbaceous plants. There are also beds of various scented-leaved pelargoniums. The garden has three National Collections: mint, marjoram and nepeta. One thousand varieties of herbs and aromatic plants are for sale; a new medicinal herb garden is planned for 2000. Plant names are provided in other languages for overseas visitors.

Ightham Mote 22

Ivy Hatch, Sevenoaks TN15 0NT. Tel: (01732) 810378; Fax: (01732) 811029

The National Trust • 6m E of Sevenoaks off A25, 1½ m S of Ightham off A227 • House open • Garden open 2nd April to 30th Oct, daily except Tues and Sat, 11am – 5.30pm (last admission 4.30pm) • Entrance: £5, children £2.50, family ticket £12.50, pre-booked parties of 15 or more £4.25 per person (1999 prices) • Other information: Disabled parking. Possible for wheelchairs but some slopes ◑ 🍽 WC ♿ ♨ ⚲

Situated in a wooded cleft of the Kentish Weald, this medieval and Tudor manor house lies in the valley of Dinas Dene, where a stream has been dammed to form small lakes and the moat which surrounds the house. The medieval design of the gardens has evolved over several centuries. The present lawn replaces the stew pond, which was used for breeding fish for the table. Further household needs were satisfied with vegetables and herbs for culinary and medicinal purposes, and flowers for decorating and scenting the house. During the nineteenth century the garden emerged as an excellent example of the ideal 'old English' garden, and the Trust is gradually restoring this with extensive replanting. Six acres of woodland walks with fine rhododendrons are re-established and the long border has returned to its former glory.

Ladham House ★ 23

Goudhurst TN17 1DB. Tel: (01580) 211203/212674; Fax: (01580) 212596

Mr and Mrs Alastair Jessel • 8m E of Tunbridge Wells, NE of Goudhurst off A262 • Open for NGS 30th April, 21st May, 2 – 5.30pm; also 6th July, 6 – 8pm, and by appt for individuals and parties at other times • Entrance: £3, children 50p, £3.50 for private visits • Other information: Teas must be pre-booked ● 🍽 🛗 WC ↩ ♨ ⚲

This Georgian house with additional French features has been in the family for over 100 years and the garden developed over that period. Interesting to see the bog garden, replacing a leaking pond, and the arboretum, replacing the old kitchen garden. The mixed shrub borders are attractive; notable are the magnolias – two M. x *watsonii* over 10 metres and a deep-red-flowering 'Betty Jessel', a seedling from Darjeeling. Amongst the other rarer trees and shrubs are *Cornus kousa*, embothriums, American oaks, *Aesculus parviflora*, *Carpenteria californica* and *Azara serrata*. The arboretum is maturing and has some unusual and interesting trees. Developments continue: the Fountain Garden has been completely reconstructed, the rock garden recently restored with a waterfall incorporated, a 200-metre-long Kentish ragstone ha-had built to the north of the house, and a woodland walk running down the side of the park opened up.

Leeds Castle Park and Gardens ★ 24

Maidstone ME17 1PL. Tel: (01622) 765400

Leeds Castle Foundation • 5m SE of Maidstone on B2163 near M20 junction 8 • Castle opens 11am (10.15am in winter) • Park and gardens open all year, daily, 10am – 5pm (Nov to Feb 3pm). Closed 26th June, 3rd July, 25th Dec, prior to occasional ticketed events and at times when hired out complete for c. £6000 a day • Entrance: £7.50, OAPs and students £6, children (5-15) £4.50, family ticket (2 adults and 2 children) £21 (castle, park and gardens £9.50, OAPs and students £7.50, children (5-15) £6, family ticket £26) • Other information: Transport available from car park to castle for wheelchairs

○ 🍽 ✕ 🏠 **WC** ♿ ♨ 🎁 🔔

Visit the castle and grounds for its romantic, wooded setting, covering some 500 acres. The woodland garden, with its old and new plantings of shrubs, is especially beautiful in daffodil time. The atmosphere is also much enhanced by wildfowl. The Culpeper Garden, in a secluded area beyond the castle, provides the main interest for the keen gardener. This is not a herb garden as often thought, though a small area does include some herbs, but is named after a seventeenth-century owner, distantly related to the herbalist. Started in 1980 by Russell Page on a slope overlooking the River Len, and surrounded by high brick walls of stabling and old cottages, the garden already has an established feeling of old-world charm. A simple pattern of paths lined with box contains areas of old roses, riotously underplanted with herbaceous perennials. Old greenhouses have been replanted with peach trees and there is an excellent fuchsia display. National Collections of nepetas and monardas. The spectacular grotto built in 1987 beneath the maze has been much publicised. The garden is complemented by some rare and attractive birds in the duckery and aviary which are well placed amid numerous shrubs and small trees. A new Italian-style terraced garden overlooking the Great Water has stunning sub-tropical plants like bananas and bamboos.

Longacre 25

Perry Wood, Selling, Faversham ME13 9SE. Tel: (01227) 752254

Dr and Mrs G. Thomas • 5m SE of Faversham. From A2 (M2) take A251 S signed Selling. Pass White Lion on left, second right, then left, continue for ¼ m. From A252 at Chilham, take road to Selling at Badgers Hill Fruit Farm, turn left at second crossroads, first right, next left, then right • Garden open April to Oct, daily, 2 – 5pm also for NGS 9th, 23rd, 24th, 30th April, 1st, 14th, 28th, 29th May, 11th, 25th June, 9th, 23rd July, 27th, 29th Aug, 10th Sept, and by appt • Entrance: £1.50, accompanied children free • Other information: Teas on NGS open days only ◑ 🏠 **WC** ♨

This is a jewel of a small garden in a tranquil country setting next to Perry Woods into which the borders of the garden melt. Created entirely by the present owners, it offers all-year interest of colour and form, replicating in miniature woodland, alpine and damp areas. There are new flower beds and a pond with running water. The enthusiast can spend an absorbing time in the nursery alone, which carries a wealth of unusual herbaceous plants.

Long Barn ★ 26

Long Barn Road, Weald, Sevenoaks TN14 6NH

Brandon and Sarah Gough • 3m S of Sevenoaks. From A21/B245 junction follow signs to Weald and continue through village • Open 18th June and 16th July, 2 – 5pm • Entrance: £2, OAPs £1, children 50p ◑ **WC**

An impressive three-acre garden set on different levels round the fourteenth-century Wealden hall that was the home of Harold Nicolson and Vita Sackville-West before Sissinghurst. Since 1986, keeping to the Nicolsons' basic design, the owners have renovated and replanted it extensively. Although formal areas give way effortlessly to the informal, romantic and classical, each is constrained within the linear control that reached its apogee at Sissinghurst. The garden has many fine features, including raised beds containing (in season) herbaceous plants that explode in vibrant but controlled bursts of colour, a cool and shady classical grove and a secret garden whose understated classical design gives it the air of an aesthete's study. A box parterre, terraces, banks, rose gardens, small courtyards, ponds and pergolas all add variety to this exciting garden, which continues to develop with new plantings of trees and shrubs. A nearby property with Sackville-West connections is *Knole*, where pedestrians can walk in the park. Lord Sackville's garden there is open on first Wed in each month, May to Sept only.

Marle Place 27

Brenchley, Tonbridge TN12 7HS. Tel: (01892) 722304; Fax: (01892) 724099

Mr and Mrs G. Williams • 5m E of Tunbridge Wells, 1m SW of Horsmonden, W of B2162. Signposted • Open April to Oct, daily, 10am – 5.30pm and also by appt • Entrance: £3.50, OAPs and children £3 (1999 prices) • Other information: Annual contemporary garden art exhibition (Tel: (01892) 724375) ◑ ➽ ▣ **WC** ᶘ ⚘ ☗

This 10-acre garden surrounding a seventeenth-century house hidden away in the byways contains a wide selection of garden features. Close to the house is a small shady fern garden and a border of several varieties of cistus (at their best in early June), set off by an old wall furnished with interesting climbers. A double herbaceous border leads into an area of alliums and ornamental grasses, also at its peak in June. Near the house is an old ornamental pool garden with a wildflower bank and aromatic plants, croquet lawn and several interesting specimen trees, such as an old *Acer brilliantissimum* and a weeping form of *Ginkgo biloba*. The use of different-coloured foliage hedges as a background to many of the borders illustrates the artistic flair of the owner (her studio is open to garden visitors). Other features include a Victorian gazebo, an ornamental pond, two lakes (one with sculpted head rising out of the water), and a red Chinese bridge over a boggy area planted with bamboos and a new mosaic terrace within the blue and yellow border. Areas of wild flowers both within the garden and in the 10-acre wood of native trees, as well as several large iron skeletal sculptures of horses and carved wooden furniture made by the owners' daughter, add to the eclectic charm.

Mount Ephraim   28

Hernhill, Faversham ME13 9JX. Tel: (01227) 751496

Mrs M.N. Dawes and Mr and Mrs E.S. Dawes • 6m W of Canterbury, 3m E of Faversham. NE from M2/A2 junction 7. Take A299, and at Duke of Kent pub turn to Hernhill. Garden through village on left. Signposted • Open 23rd April to Sept, Mon, Wed, Thurs, Sat, Sun, 1 – 6pm (Bank Holiday weekends 11am – 6pm) • Entrance: £3, children £1, parties £2.50 per person (1999 prices) • Other information: Craft centre shop on Suns only ◐ 🍽 ✕ 🏠 WC ⬥ ✿ ♨

Mount Ephraim is remarkable for the variety of its gardens on seven sloping acres with distant views of the Thames Estuary, surrounding fruit orchards and vineyard. With a backdrop of trees of outstanding shapes and contrasts, it includes rose gardens, a rock garden, water garden, arboretum, small Japanese garden and lake. Restored after years of neglect from 1950 onwards, it retains much of the original design of the 1800s. It was laid out again in 1912 by William Dawes, including topiary effects and the original rock garden. The house has been in the same family for 300 years. Spring bulbs, prunus in blossom and rhododendrons make spring to early June an ideal time to visit, but herbaceous borders and shrubs extend the interest through the seasons. At the end of June there are usually performances of Shakespeare. North-east of Mount Ephraim is *Busheyfields Nursery*, Herne, with National Collections of *Clematis montana, C. chrysocoma* and honeysuckles [open March to Oct, Tues – Sat and Bank Holiday Mons, 10am – 5pm].

Nettlestead Place ★   29

Nettlestead, Maidstone ME18 5HA. Tel: (01622) 812205

Mr and Mrs R.C. Tucker • 6m SW of Maidstone off B2015. Next to Nettlestead Church • Open for NGS 4th June, 17th Sept, 2 – 5.30pm, 21st June, 6.15 – 9.15pm, and by appt • Entrance: £3.50 ◕ 🏠 WC ♿

The thirteenth-century manor house is set in a seven-acre plantsman's garden. On entering through the early fourteenth-century gatehouse, an avenue of Irish yews leads into a lawned area edged with a large collection of sun-loving geraniums (155 different cultivars in the garden). The Kentish ragstone walls around two sides of this area are planted with many tender and rare plants from Tasmania, Malaysia and Asia, etc., such as *Buddleia auriculata* (South Africa), *Actinidia chinensis* (China) *Wattakaka sinensis* (China) and *Sophora tetraptera* (New Zealand). There is a small orchard with apples, pears and soft fruit, and a glen garden where the natural spring flowing down the hill is edged with hostas, primulas, dwarf pines, astilbes and shade-loving geraniums. A series of small canals separates the daffodil meadow from the new heather garden and salix collection – 28 in all. An 80-metre-long gravel garden planted with rock plants and dwarf bulbs lies along the eastern side of the house, which is clothed with akebia, sophora, fremontodendron and *Cytisus battandieri*. A large sunken pond bounded by a ragstone wall lies along the southern side and again provides a sheltered environment for tender plants. A large rose garden has an excellent collection of shrub roses. There is a comprehensive display of herbaceous plants in a series of island beds and also a diverse collection of shrubs mixed with other complementary plants in a further series of much larger island beds. Shade garden with hostas and ferns. A planting of trees overlooks a peaceful stretch of the river Medway.

Old Place Farm   30

High Halden, Ashford TN26 3JG. Tel: (01233) 850202

Mr and Mrs J. Eker • 10m SW of Ashford. From A28, opposite Chequers pub in High Halden, take Woodchurch Road and follow for ½ m • Open 11th June, 2 – 6pm and by appt • Entrance: £2.50 ● ● WC & ⚘

A three-acre garden surrounding a period house and farm buildings, created since 1968, mainly designed by Anthony du Gard Pasley. The lake of two-thirds of an acre provides a near focus from the house, and an elegant gazebo is an idyllic setting for contemplation. The borders behind have an apricot, gold and cream colour theme offset by blues, purples, silvers and greys. An avenue of *Crataegus* 'Prunifolia', underplanted with white-flowering bulbs from February to May, leads to a fine sheep statue. There is a nut plat, a philadelphus walk and, to provide summer shelter from the sun, two large *Catalpa bignonioides*. A parterre herb garden is linked to a circular brick feature with sundial by an avenue of *Malus* 'Golden Hornet'. A pergola draped with the rose 'New Dawn', white wisteria and purple vines divides the cutting garden from a small *potager*.

Owl House Gardens   31

Lamberhurst TN3 8LY. Tel: (01892) 890230

Estate of the late Maureen, Marchioness of Dufferin and Ava • 6m SE of Tunbridge Wells, S of Lamberhurst off A21. Signposted • Open all year, daily except 25th Dec and 1st Jan, 11am – 6pm • Entrance: £4, children £1 (1999 prices) • Other information: Coaches by appt ○ ▤ WC & ⬥ ⚘

In 1952 Lady Dufferin fell in love with a cottage which had the crookedest chimney in Kent and was the county's oldest building. In 1522 its tenants paid a yearly rental of one white cockerel to the monks at Bayham Abbey. During the sixteenth century it was a hiding place for wool smugglers who, at the approach of the law, hooted their warning, hence its name. It had no garden, just a cabbage patch and a plum tree, but within its 16½ acres a beautiful year-round garden was created over the years by the late Lady Dufferin, and is maintained as she left it. Swathes of bluebells and daffodils start the season, followed by camellias, azaleas and rhododendrons. The summer interest is maintained by large numbers of old roses, *R. longicuspis*, 'Bobbie James' and 'Rambling Rector', climbing into the many fine trees. Philadelphus and clematis also abound. Statues of owls are dotted about the garden, with seats placed strategically to overlook viewpoints. There is a wisteria temple, a grove of *Parrotia persica*, and four walks: of iris, apple blossom, laburnum and, for late summer, blue hydrangeas. Three lovely water gardens provide a peaceful setting for contemplation.

Penshurst Place ★ 32

Penshurst, Tonbridge TN11 8DG. Tel: (01892) 870307

Lord De L'Isle • 5m SW of Tonbridge on B2176, 7m N of Tunbridge Wells off A26 • House open 12 noon − 5pm (last admission 4.30pm) • Garden open weekends in March; April to Oct, daily, 10.30am − 6pm. Garden tours available for parties of 20 or more • Entrance: £4.50, OAPs and students £4, children £3.50, family ticket £13 (house and grounds £6, OAPs and students £5.50, children £4, family £16). Parties of 20 or more £5.30 per person • Other information: Guide dogs only ◑ 🍵 ✕ 🖳 WC & ⚘ ⛴ ♨

The 600-year-old gardens, contemporary with the house, reflect their development under their Tudor owner, Sir Henry Sidney, and the restoration by the present owner, his father and his grandfather. An example is the 640-metre double line of oaks, their planting completed in 1995 as part of a 15-year programme to re-create the historic parkland structure. The many separate enclosures, surrounded by trim tall yew hedges, offer a wide variety of interesting planting, with continuous displays from spring to early autumn. Just inside the entrance is a garden for the blind, with raised beds of aromatic plants, a small wooden gazebo and the constant music of water splashing on pebbles. The Italian garden with its oval fountain and century-old ginkgo dominates the south front of the magnificent house. Herbaceous borders are teeming with colour. Note also the borders designed by Lanning Roper in the late '60s and the blue and yellow border. Contrast is made by the nut trees and over a dozen different crab apples underplanted with daffodils, myosotis, tulips, bluebells, Lenten lilies, and a magnificent bed of peonies which borders the orchard. Even in late summer the rose garden is colourful with 'Aynsley Dickson' and 'Anna Olivier', and their perfumes mingle with that from mature lavender bushes. A new lake and nature trail have been developed so that the style of design so much enjoyed here by Gertrude Jekyll and Beatrix Farrand is fully recaptured. Numerous seats. Two medieval fish ponds have been reclaimed and stocked with fish. New and imaginative play area for children.

The Pines Garden 33

Beach Road, St Margaret's Bay CT15 6DZ. Tel: (01304) 852764; Fax: (01304) 853626

St Margaret's Bay Trust • 3m NE of Dover off A258, through St Margaret's at Cliffe, just before beach • Open all year, daily except 25th Dec, 10am − 5pm • Entrance: £1.50. children 35p • Other information: Teas and shop in St Margaret's Museum opposite open late May to early Sept only ○ 🍵 🖳 WC & ⬳ ⚘ 🍴 ♨

It is hard to believe that this well-stocked and perfectly maintained garden was a rubbish dump until 1970. Fred Cleary, founder of St Margaret's Bay Trust, and his wife transformed the original three acres, with a second three-acre site known as the Barrack Field, once home and training ground for soldiers during the Napoleonic Wars. Now the garden is established, with a good variety of trees, including conifers, flowering shrubs, bulbs and bog plants. An avenue of elms is an encouraging sight. The lake is well stocked with fish, and a rockery with waterfall provides further interest. An almost three-metre bronze statue of Sir Winston Churchill by Oscar Nemon looks across the garden to the 120-metre white cliffs at the end of the Bay. A Romany wedding caravan (as used by gypsies of Romney Marsh) stands under its shelter in the garden, and at the other end is a seventeenth-century façade from a London Cheapside property.

Port Lympne 34

Lympne, Hythe CT21 4PD. Tel: (01303) 264647

Mr J. Aspinall • 3m W of Hythe, 18m S of Canterbury on B2067 • House open • Garden open all year, daily, 10am – 5pm (summer) and to 1 hour before dusk (winter) • Entrance: £8.90, OAPs and children £6.90 (house, garden and wild animal park) (1999 prices) ○ 💭 ✕ 📠 WC 🌿 👜

This is one of those gardens which is hugely enjoyed by some people and leaves others cold. It stands in a 300-acre wild animal park with views across the Channel. Before World War I Sir Philip Sassoon began building a new Lutyens-style house and garden with the help of Sir Herbert Baker and Ernest Willmote and, after the war, with much assistance from the architect Philip Tilden. The interior is noted for the murals by Rex Whistler and Spencer Roberts. After a period of distinction in the 1920s and '30s it fell into decay until it was rescued in the 1970s by John Aspinall, who wanted the surrounding land for his private wild animal park. He has reconstructed the 15-acre garden to something like its original design with advice from experts, including the late Russell Page. Visitors enter down a great stone stairway of 125 steps, flanked by clipped, newly planted yews, to the paved West Court with lily pool. Beyond is the lime tree walk and a series of terraces planted with standard fig trees and vines. Everywhere there is fine stone paving and walls with appropriately placed urns, statues from Stowe, etc. There is extensive bedding and use of bedding-out. The late Arthur Hellyer admitted that 'for years it has been fashionable to denigrate Port Lympne' but he admired it; he also waxed lyrical about the beautiful wrought-ironwork by Bainbridge Reynolds.

Riverhill House Gardens 35

Sevenoaks TN15 0RR. Tel: (01732) 458802/452557

Rogers family (correspondence to Mrs John Rogers) • 2m S of Sevenoaks on A225 • House open to bona fide booked parties only. No children inside house • Garden open April to June, Wed, Suns and Bank Holiday Sats and Mons, 12 noon – 6pm • Entrance: £2.50, children 50p (house and garden for parties of 20 or more £3.50 per person) • Other information: Coaches by appt ● 💭 📠 WC 🌿 👜

This was originally one of the great smaller country-house gardens, housing a plantsman's collection of trees and species shrubs as introduced by John Rogers, a keen horticulturist, in the mid-1800s. Massive rhododendrons, many of them species, are topped by a cedar of Lebanon planted in 1815, and together with azaleas and outstanding underplanting of bulbs make a fine show in spring and early summer. Other features include a wood garden, a rose walk, an orchard with a Wellingtonia planted in 1860, magnolias, etc.

Rock Farm 36

Nettlestead, Maidstone ME18 5HT. Tel: (01622) 812244

Mrs P.A. Corfe • 6m SW of Maidstone. From A26 turn S onto B2015, then 1m S of Wateringbury turn right • Open April to 7th Aug, Wed and Sat, 10am – 5pm, Sun, 2 – 5pm. Private visits welcome by appt at other times • Entrance: £2 ◑ WC ⚲

This Kentish farmhouse, set on an east-facing slope, is surrounded by a two-acre plantsman's garden. Natural springs supply water for two ponds at different levels and for a small stream whose banks are planted with primulas and other bog plants. The soil is alkaline and there are excellent specimens of ceanothus, a huge *Solanum crispum*, a *Fremontodendron californicum*, a *Magnolia grandiflora* and climbing roses in an old pear tree. The best season is June to July when the large herbaceous border is at its height. An iris border provides a colourful entry to the garden. Of special interest is the *Chionanthus virginicus* or fringe tree. The two ponds are bordered with cupressus of various foliage colour. A *Catalpa bignonioides* 'Aurea' is cut annually to give huge golden leaves, and a *Sequoia sempervirens* is also pruned drastically, resulting in rarely seen new foliage of this coniferous forest tree. A small nursery sells a range of plants seen in the garden.

Scotney Castle Garden ★ 37

Lamberhurst, Tunbridge Wells TN3 8JN. Tel: (01892) 891081; Fax: (01892) 890110

The National Trust • 8m SE of Tunbridge Wells, 1m S of Lamberhurst on E side of A21 • Old Castle open May to 12th Sept same times as garden • Garden open 4th to 26th March, Sat, Sun, 12 noon – 4pm, April to 29th Oct (except 21st, 23rd, 24th April), Wed – Fri, 11am – 6pm, Sat, Sun, 2-6pm (last admission 5pm) • Entrance: £4.20, children £2.10, family ticket (2 adults and up to 3 children) £10.50. Pre-booked parties (weekdays only) £3.60 per person • Other information: Possible for wheelchairs but hilly approach ◑ 🍴 WC ♿ 🎁 ⚲

This is an unusual garden designed in the romantic manner by the Hussey family, following the tradition established by William Kent and using the services of William Gilpin, the artist and landscape gardener, who also advised on the site of the new house, completed in 1843. Of the fourteenth-century castle only one of the four towers remains, plus some of the sixteenth- and seventeenth-century additions. The landscape garden includes smaller garden layouts in the overall area. A formal garden overlooks a quarry garden and the grounds of the old castle enclose a rose garden. Herb garden. Lakeside planting adds an air of informality. Evergreens and deciduous trees provide the mature planting, linking shrubs and plants to give something in flower at every season. Daffodils, magnolias, rhododendrons and azaleas are the most spectacular; also notable are the kalmias and hydrangeas. In a good autumn, the colours are amazing. In some ways the planting seems occasional and haphazard, 'Picturesque' in the true sense, but visit this garden for its setting on a slope that gives fine views of open countryside, and for the romantic eighteenth- to nineteenth-century theme uniting it. The stream garden, developed by gardeners and volunteers, is new, planted with hostas, dactylorhizas, irises, lilies and large-flowered plants. This is fed by the River Sweetbourne, which also feeds the moat surrounding the romantic ruins of the castle. A great pity there are no refreshments as there is plenty of space.

Sissinghurst Castle Garden ★★   38

Sissinghurst, Cranbrook TN17 2AB. Tel: infoline (01580) 712850;
fax: (01580) 713911

The National Trust • 13m S of Maidstone, 2m NE of Cranbrook, 1m E of Sissinghurst on A262 • Garden open April to 15th Oct, Tues – Fri, 1 – 6.30pm (last admission 6pm), Sat, Sun and 2nd April, 10am – 5.30pm (last admission 5pm). Parties of 11 or more by appt. Timed ticket system in operation, and at peak times visitors may have short wait • Entrance: £6, children £3 (1999 prices) • Other information: Coaches by appt. Picnics beyond car park and in front of castle only. Wheelchairs restricted to two chairs at one time because of narrow, uneven paths; pushchairs not admitted ◑ 🍴 ✕ 🏬 WC ♿ ℘ ♿

'Profusion, even extravagance and exuberance within the confines of the utmost linear severity' was Vita Sackville-West's description of her design when creating Sissinghurst with her husband Harold Nicolson. It is a romantic garden with seasonal features throughout the year. Certain colour schemes have been followed, as in the purple border, the orange and yellow cottage garden, and the white garden, which is probably the most beautiful garden at Sissinghurst, itself one of the outstanding gardens in the world. The Nicolsons added little to, but saved much of, the Elizabethan mansion. The site was first occupied in the twelfth century, when a moated manor was built where the orchard now stands. The long library and Elizabethan tower are open and the latter is well worth climbing in order to see the perspective of the whole garden and surrounding area. The garden is in immaculate condition, well labelled, with changing vistas at every turn of the winding paths or more formal walks. The rose garden contains many old-fashioned roses as well as flowering shrubs such as *Ceanothus impressus* and *Hydrangea villosa,* which together with iris, clematis and pansies fill the area. There is a thyme lawn leading to the herb garden filled with fragrance and charm. It is a truly magnificent example of Englishness and has had immense influence on garden design because of its structure of separate 'outdoor rooms' within the garden. Long Barn (see entry) and *Knole* will also interest Vita's fans.

South Hill Farm 39

Hastingleigh, Ashford TN25 5HL. Tel: (01233) 750325

Sir Charles J. Jessel Bt • 6m E of Ashford, on Downs between Hastingleigh and Brabourne • Open 18th June, 2nd July, 2 – 6pm for NGS and for parties by appt • Entrance: £2, children 25p ● ☕ WC ♿ ☂

Originally a Jacobean farmhouse, to which a Georgian south front was added, the house (not open) stands nearly 200 metres above sea level. The two-acre garden, including a ha-ha, was replanned by the owner and his late wife in 1960 and everything has been planted since then, with one or two exceptions such as the lime tree in front of the house. There are around 60 different varieties of clematis, together with various unusual shrubs; also many roses, hydrangeas, hostas and hellebores. A series of raised beds, built of flint, was added in 1997 for plants needing well-drained soil. Walls have been added to the kitchen garden, which is entirely organic. Sculpture in steel and stone. Formal water garden. A garden of considerable charm and interest.

Squerryes Court 40

Westerham TN16 1SJ. Tel: (01959) 562345/563118; Fax: (01959) 565949

Mr and Mrs John Warde • ½ m W of Westerham on A25, near M25 junctions 5 and 6 • House open 1.30 – 5.30pm • Garden open April to Sept, Wed, Sat, Sun and Bank Holiday Mons, 12 noon – 5.30pm. Parties of 20 or more by appt any day • Entrance: £2.50, OAPs £2.20, children (under 14) £1.50 (house and garden £4.20, OAPs £3.80, children £2.50). Reduced rates for pre-booked parties ◑ ☕ 🛍 WC ♿ ♨ ♿

The 20 acres of gardens were originally laid out around 1700 in the formal Anglo-Dutch style and were landscaped again in the eighteenth century. The view over the large lake leads to a gazebo, built around 1740, from where a former member of the family used to watch his racehorses in training; nearby is a fine old dovecot. The main feature is the newly restored formal area to the rear of the house; a 1719 print has been used as an outline on which to base the changes. These reflect the mellow brickwork of this handsome house. Beds, edged with box, contain lavender, rue, purple sage and *Nicotiana affinis*, with contrasting magenta and pink of penstemon and verbena; all are framed by well-kept yew hedges. There are several rose gardens, a rockery and azalea and rhododendron shrubberies and fine examples of topiary, which, together with a broad variety of spring bulbs, make this a garden for all seasons. Many fine magnolias around the house and a cenotaph in memory of General Wolfe (a family friend) complete this most attractive garden. The house is worth a visit, too, for its collection of paintings. Those with a historical bent will wish to visit nearby Chartwell (see entry), although this, horticulturally speaking, has a much less interesting garden.

Stoneacre 41

Otham, Maidstone ME15 8RS. Tel: (01622) 862871; Fax: (01622) 862157

The National Trust • 3m SE of Maidstone, 1m S of A20 from Bearsted, at N end of Otham • House open • Garden open April to Oct, Wed and Sat, 2 – 6pm (last admission 5pm) and parties by appt • Entrance: house and garden £2.50, children £1.25 • Other information: Picnics in car park ◑ ﯼ

The Kentish hall house was restored and embellished from 1920 to 1926 by Aymer Vallance, Oxford aesthete, writer and friend of William Morris. Rosemary Alexander, as tenant of the Trust, has restored the garden after some years of neglect. The acre of cottage garden contains a ginkgo, mulberry, *Staphylea colchica*, roses and rare plants. There is a small *potager* with beds divided by low box hedging. A grass path leads to the summerhouse in the two-acre wild garden, which includes apple orchards and two ponds. She was helped in her work by old reports on the garden by Trust adviser Graham Stuart Thomas. The result is a charming cottage-type garden within the framework of yew hedges and ragstone walls, plus all the delights of the wild garden, a suitable setting for Mrs Alexander's English Gardening School, whose pupils spend some of their time here. A garden trail, suitable for children, has been devised in conjunction with the Kent Gardens Trust.

Walmer Castle and Gardens 42

Kingsdown Road, Walmer, Deal CT14 7LJ. Tel: (01304) 364288

English Heritage • On coast 2m S of Walmer on A258, off M20 at junction 13 or from M2 to Deal • Castle open • Garden open April to Sept, daily, 10am – 6pm; Oct, daily, 10am – 5pm; Nov, Dec and March, Wed – Sun, 10am – 4pm. Closed 24th to 26th Dec, and Jan and Feb. Also closed when Lord Warden in residence. Telephone in advance of visit to check if open, particularly in winter months and most especially Oct • Entrance: castle and garden £4.50, concessions £3.40, children (5-16) £2.30 (1999 prices). Discount for parties of 11 or more. English Heritage members free • Other information: Guided garden tours. Wheelchair available. Guide dogs only ◑ 🍵 🗋 WC ♿ ﯼ 🛒 🛈

English Heritage is restoring the gardens of this, the official residence of the Warden of the Cinque Ports, to their former status in the early twentieth century. The castle overlooks the sea and the 10-acre gardens are surrounded by shelter belts and meadows. There are walks with mature trees under-planted with shrubs. An enormous yew tree is several hundred years old and 18 metres in diameter. Good double herbaceous borders are backed by very old yew hedging. The old-fashioned kitchen garden has a cut-flower area, cold frames and a small orchard. A moat has been planted with shrubs against the castle walls and a wildflower area established in the mature arboretum. In the 1810 walled garden, Penelope Hobhouse has designed a new garden as a 95th birthday gift to H. M. The Queen Mother. It includes a 29-metre formal pond, pyramids of yew, a turf mound topped by a castle of clipped yew and sculpture, the whole screened by mature limes. There are also borders of shrubs, roses and herbaceous plants. Croquet for the initiated.

Waystrode Manor ★ 43

Spode Lane, Cowden, Tunbridge Wells TN8 7HW. Tel: (01342) 850695

Mr and Mrs Peter Wright • 8m W of Tunbridge Wells, 4½ m S of Edenbridge, off B2026 Edenbridge – Hartfield road • Open some Weds and Suns from May to July for NGS • Entrance: £3, children 50p ● 🍵 WC 🐾 ♿

This eight-acre garden on Wealden clay has been developed over the last 30 years and surrounds a beautiful half-timbered sixteenth-century house. An avenue of red-candled horse chestnut trees leads to the house, which is flanked on one side by an old barn supporting wisteria, clematis, actinidia and schizophragma. A stone-flagged area at the rear has herbs growing out of it and, as a central feature, an old mill grinding-wheel planted with low-growing plants. From the house the eye is led via the serpent fountain garden to a small yew-enclosed white garden. A large and decorative two-storey wooden building contains tender and tropical plants. Several pergolas of wisteria, laburnum and roses. Two small pools connected by a waterfall are crossed by a charming arched bridge. Borders of irises, old roses and geraniums are dotted around, and the whole is complemented by some excellent and unusual specimen trees, such as *Ulmus* x *hollandica* 'Dampieri Aurea', *Abies koreana*, *Betula utilis* var. *jacquemontii* and *Cedrus deodara* 'Pendula'.

Yalding Gardens 44

Benover Road, Yalding, Maidstone ME18 6EX. Tel/Fax: (01622) 814650

Henry Doubleday Research Association • 6m SW of Maidstone, ½ m S of Yalding on B2162 • Open weekdays in April and Oct, Wed, Sun and Bank Holiday Mons May to Sept, 10am – 5pm • Entrance: £3, accompanied children free, parties of 14 or more £2.50 (50p extra for garden tour) ◑ 🍵 ✕ 🏠 WC ♿ 🐾 ♿

The pergola of hop poles at the heart of the Yalding links it closely to the surrounding oasts and hop gardens of Kent. The gardens offer a tour of garden style through history, beginning with the natural woodland that once dotted our hills and valleys. Visitors pass through a thirteenth-century apothecary's garden, an Elizabethan Paradise Garden and Tudor knot, an early nineteenth-century cottager's plot, sweeping Edwardian borders and a utilitarian 1950s' allotment before being shown an organic vision of the future. A children's garden completes the tour. A fascinating experience for all the family; almost everyone will learn something new here.

LANCASHIRE

Two-starred gardens are marked on the map with a black square.

Ashton Memorial 1

Williamson Park, Quernmore Road, Lancaster LA1 1UX. Tel: (01524) 33318

E of Lancaster town centre. Signposted • Open daily except 25th, 26th Dec and 1st Jan: April to Sept, 10am – 5pm; Oct to March, 11am – 4pm • Entrance: park and ground floor of memorial with exhibition free; memorial viewing gallery 50p; butterfly house, mini-beast house, conservation garden and free-flying bird enclosure £2.95, OAPs £2.50, children £1.50 ○ ⊒ ✕ 🗄 <u>WC</u> ♿ ⬐ 🧺 ▯

Ashton Memorial, described by Pevsner as 'the grandest monument in England', stands at the highest point of Williamson Park looking down on the town of Lancaster. There are many views of the surrounding country from various points in the superbly landscaped park. Broad paths run through the grounds, much of which is woodland with an underplanting of rhododendrons and other shrubs. There is a small lake spanned by a stone bridge, and nearby a large stairway leads to the huge domed monument. Not far away is the butterfly house and pavilion. Both monument and butterfly house were designed in 1906 by John Belcher in Baroque Revival style.

Catforth Gardens ★ 2

Roots Lane, Catforth, Preston PR4 0JB. Tel: (01772) 690561/690269

Mr and Mrs T.A. Bradshaw and Mr and Mrs W. Moore • 5m NW of Preston. Turn S off B5269 to Catforth. Roots Lane is S of village. Signposted • Open 18th March to 10th Sept, daily, 10.30am – 5pm inc. some days for charity • Entrance: £2.50 (combined price), accompanied children 50p • Other information: Refreshments on charity open days only. Plants for sale in nursery
◑ 🍴 WC ♿ ℘

There are three gardens here, separated by a nursery which stocks an excellent range of perennials. *The Bungalow Garden* is informally laid out with grass paths running amongst well-planted beds. Some unusual small trees and shrubs provide height, and a good selection of ferns and grasses gives variety to the foliage, but it is perennials that will impress most. This is the home of a National Collection of geraniums, and the charm and usefulness of the genus is well demonstrated as they are grown in many different situations. Most other perennials are well represented too, flowering throughout the season. Euphorbias, pulmonarias and dicentras are particularly plentiful. There is also a pond surrounded by banks of alpines, and a small woodland area with hydrangeas and dwarf rhododendrons. *The Farmhouse Garden* was created as a cottage garden. It has a good collection of perennials, sidalceas, phloxes, lythrums and crocosmias, an alpine scree and newly made ponds. Constructed from 1994, the two-acre *Paddock Garden* has now developed into a summer flower garden with long, boldly planted herbaceous borders filled with unusual species and hybrids shading from hot colours to paler hues, three natural water-lily ponds and associated waterside planting, large raised banks planted with sun lovers, and a formal area with roses and complementary herbaceous plants.

Clearbeck House 3

Higher Tatham, Lancaster LA2 8PJ. Tel: (015242) 61029

Peter and Bronwen Osborne • From M6 junction 34 take A683 to Kirkby Lonsdale, turn right on B6480 and follow signposts from Wray village • Open 10th to 25th June (part of studio trail), also 25th June, 2nd July for NGS, 11.30am – 5.30pm. Private visits by appt • Entrance: £1.50, children free NEW
● 🖼 WC ♿ ⬥ ℘ 🍴

Art and water are the two key features of this garden, but there is plenty more in the way of plants and landscaping. The old stone house has a large balcony, from where tea can be taken overlooking much of the garden. Beneath the balcony is a terrace planted with shrubs and perennials – hebes, geraniums and heathers – and with an unusual glass sculpture. Below the terrace a large irregular lawn has grass paths radiating out. One path follows a series of pools planted with water lilies down to the two-acre wildlife lake with its lush margins (47 bird species were noted in a recent year); another leads to a pyramid, the entrance to a small secret garden with its own pool. Beyond a second, raised terrace are fine views over the garden and lake. There is a bog garden surrounding a small natural stream and throughout the garden many shrub roses, grasses and bamboos. But it is the sculpture that fits so well with the natural look of this distinctive garden.

Gawthorpe Hall 4

Padiham, Burnley BB12 8UA. Tel: (01282) 771004; Fax: (01282) 770178

*Lancashire County Council (on lease from National Trust) • 2½ m NW of Burnley, N of A671 just E of Padiham town centre • Hall open April to 7th Nov, daily except Mon and Fri but open 21st April and Bank Holiday Mons, 1 – 5pm (last admission 4.30pm) • Gardens open all year, 10am – 6pm • Entrance: free (hall £3, children £1.30, family £8; concessions £1.50) (1999 prices) • Other information: Refreshments when hall open only ○ 🍴 **WC** & ♿ 🔦*

This garden, though botanically not particularly special, does set off the Elizabethan hall. To the front is a formal layout of lawns and gravel paths, and to the rear a parterre by Barry in the form of a sunburst overlooks the River Calder. The woodlands that surround the formal garden are planted with rhododendrons and azaleas and traversed by many walks, with views back to the house and across the valley.

Gresgarth Hall ★★ 5

Caton LA2 9NB. Tel: (01524) 770313

Sir Mark and Lady Lennox-Boyd • From M6 junction 34 take A683 towards Kirkby Lonsdale, then turn right in Caton village, signed 'Quernmore' • Open 30th April, 28th May, 25th June, 30th July, 27th Aug, 24th Sept, 11am – 5pm • Entrance: £3 NEW ◐ WC 🐾 👍

You expect something special from the garden of such a renowned designer as Arabella Lennox-Boyd, and you will not be disappointed. Over this large area she has experimented with different styles of gardening and produced some superb results – all the more surprising since the weather in this part of northern Lancashire can be harsh. At the front of the house are formal areas herbaceous borders, protected by yew hedges, to the south a pool and bog garden with a large selection of moisture-lovers, including many ferns. An arboretum contains a large sequoiadendron, acers, lilacs and many other fine specimens, while the walled garden has a happy mix of vegetables, fruit and flowering plants. To the east an attractive terrace and belvedere overlook a rocky beck that rushes through this part of the garden. A Chinese bridge leads to a woodland garden where azaleas, cornus, magnolias and many unusual plants flourish in the light shade. Sculpture, classical and modern, is used creatively throughout. There are woodland walks, a huge variety of plants and so much else that this description can only serve as the briefest of introductions to a fine garden.

Hoghton Tower 6

Hoghton, Preston PR5 0SH. Tel: (01254) 852986; Fax: (01254) 852109

Sir Bernard de Hoghton, Bt • 5m SE of Preston, mid-way between Preston and Blackburn, on old A675 • House open for guided tours (£3, OAPs and students £2, children £1.25, family ticket £8) • Garden open Bank Holiday Suns and Mons (except Christmas and New Year); July to Sept, Mon – Thurs, 11am – 4pm, Sun, 1 – 5pm. Private tours by arrangement • Entrance: £1 (1999 price)
◑ ☕ 🖻 WC ⬠ 🏛 ⚲

Hoghton Tower, a sixteenth-century fortified manor house of local stone, occupies a hilltop position with good views to all sides and outwards to the surrounding countryside. The house and outbuildings are built around two courtyards which, although not qualifying as gardens, are fine spaces. Surrounding the house are three walled gardens. The first contains a large lawn and herbaceous borders. The second has a rectangular lawn flanked on two sides by clipped yews. At the centre is a raised square pond with an elaborate stone fountain; at one end is a statue and at the other a sundial on a stone pedestal. The third is mainly lawn with access to the tops of two crenellated towers. Around the walled gardens runs a long walk, which passes under large beech trees and is planted with shrubs, mainly rhododendrons and azaleas. There is a tradition that Shakespeare lived here during a formative period.

Leighton Hall 7

Carnforth LA5 9ST. Tel: (01524) 734474; Fax: (01524) 720357

Mr R.G. Reynolds • 1m W of Yealand Conyers, signed from M6 junction 35 • Hall open • Gardens open May to Sept, daily except Sat and Mon, 2 – 5pm (Aug, 11.30am – 5pm) • Entrance: £3.70, OAPs £3.20, children £2.50, parties of 25 or more £3 per person, schools £2 per child (hall and grounds) (1999 prices) • Other information: Dogs in park only, on lead ◑ ☕ 🖻 WC ♿ 🐾 🏛 ⚲

Very striking when first seen from the entrance gates, the white stone façade (c. 1822) shines out in its parkland setting with the hills of the Lake District visible beyond. The most interesting area of the gardens, which lie to the west of the house, is the walled garden with its unusual labyrinth in the form of a gravel path running under an old cherry orchard. Opposite is a vegetable garden made in a geometric design with grass paths. There are also herbaceous borders and an aromatic herb garden containing a wide variety of perennials with climbing roses on the wall behind.

Lindeth Dene 8

38 Lindeth Road, Silverdale LA5 0TX. Tel: (01524) 701314

Mrs B.M. Kershaw • 12m N of Lancaster. From M6 junction 35, turn right at Carnforth traffic lights and follow signs to Silverdale. ¼ m after level crossing turn left into Hollins Lane. At T-junction turn right into Lindeth Road and continue to fourth gateway on left • Open by appt • Entrance: £1.50, accompanied children free ●

A garden of one and a quarter acres set in an area of beautiful countryside with fine views over Morecambe Bay. Informal in layout, much of the garden consists of a large limestone rock garden planted with a wide range of perennials and alpines; there are many saxifrages and geraniums, and in the shadier parts (some large mature trees at this end of the garden) hostas, epimediums and varieties of ferns. Close to the house away from the trees are beds containing dwarf conifers and other small shrubs, also a heather garden, stone troughs and an organic kitchen garden. There is much of interest for the plantsman and for anyone looking for planting ideas for a small garden. Be sure to visit the excellent nursery next door, which stocks a large range of plant varieties, including ferns.

Mill Barn ★ 9

Goose Foot Close, Samlesbury Bottoms, Preston PR5 0SS. Tel: (01254) 853300

Dr C.J. Mortimer • 6m E of Preston on A677 Blackburn road, turn S into Nabs Head Lane, then Goose Foot Lane • Open 9th to 12th June, 1 – 5pm and for parties by appt • Entrance: £1.50, children free • Other information: Teas and plants for sale on open days ● ● WC

On the site of an old mill by the River Darwen, this garden has been designed to make the most of its superb setting. A path leads along a high stone embankment overlooking the fast-flowing river. It passes through a series of features: a unique temple created from an old sluice gate, a rose-clad pergola, a picturesque ruin constructed to hide a septic tank. Near here a fine 'Paul's Himalayan Musk' rose climbs high up into a tree. Finally there is a rectangular pool set into the wall containing a good variety of water plants and marginals, with a stretch of lawn and an heptagonal summerhouse beyond. A long herbaceous border runs back to the house, containing plants chosen for their contrasting foliage and architectural effects. Many schemes are still underway, including a spring garden in an old quarry area.

Pendle Heritage Centre 10

Park Hill, Barrowford, Nelson BB9 6JQ. Tel: (01282) 661701; Fax: (01282) 611718

The Heritage Trust for the North West • N of Nelson, near M65 junctions 13 and 14. In Barrowford at A682/B6247 junction • House and buildings open (£1.75, concessions 80p) • Garden open all year, daily except 25th Dec, 10am – 5pm. Parties welcome by appt • Entrance: museum and garden £2.75, concessions £1.50, family £6 • Other information: Plant sale in May with NCCPG stand ○ 🍵 ✕ <u>WC</u> ☕ 🌿 🏵 💧

In the centre of Barrowford among a group of fine old stone buildings (eight Grade-II-listed) is a walled garden dating from the 1780s. This has been restored and replanted under the guidance of the NCCPG, using only plants that were available in the eighteenth century. There are culinary and medicinal herbs and plants that were used in the production of dyes, as well as traditional varieties of fruit and vegetables. All plants are organically grown in beds divided by gravel paths and edged in clipped box. A woodland walk takes the visitor up a steep wooded bank planted with native wild flowers to a viewing point that looks back over the garden and surrounding countryside.

The Ridges 11

Limbrick, Chorley PR6 9EB. Tel: (01257) 279981

Mr and Mrs J. M. Barlow • From M61 junction 8 follow signs for Chorley on A6, then for Cowling and Rivington • Open Bank Holiday weekends, and at other times by appt • Entrance: £1.50, children 50p (1999 prices) NEW ● 🍵 <u>WC</u> ☕ ◁◻▷ 🌿

In the first area of this garden a herbaceous bed contains hemerocallis and geraniums, shaded by fruit trees. The seventeenth-century house has French windows leading onto a small lawn. This is part of the old walled garden; in one corner is a small pool set within a paved area. A path leads beneath a laburnum arch and between two large thujas into a separate part of the garden, where, in a large rectangular garden surrounded by woodland, are beds of perennials and shrubs, rather mean in proportion, that surround a large lawn. There is also a large greenhouse and a gravel area in the centre, currently being developed.

Rufford Old Hall 12

Rufford, Ormskirk L40 1SG. Tel: (01704) 821254

The National Trust • 7m NE of Ormskirk, N of Rufford, E of A59 • Hall open as garden (last admission 4.30pm) • Garden open April to 29th Oct, daily except Thurs and Fri, 12 noon – 5.30pm • Entrance: £2 (house and garden £3.80) (1999 prices) ◑ 🍵 ✕ 🏠 <u>WC</u> ☕ ◁◻▷ 🌿 🏵 💧

Rufford Old Hall is an exceptional sixteenth-century timber-framed house whose gardens complement it, having been laid out by the Trust in the style of the 1820 period. On the south are lawns and gravel paths designed in a formal manner. The many island beds are formal in layout, too, but the shrubs, small trees and herbaceous plants they contain are planted in a more relaxed way. In the centre a path leads from two large topiary squirrels to a beech avenue that goes beyond the garden towards Rufford. There are many mature trees and rhododendrons in this area. To the east of the house by the stables is an attractive cobbled space with climbing plants on the surrounding walls. When visiting, look for the cottage garden to the north side of the house, in which grow many old-fashioned plants enclosed by a rustic wooden fence.

Stonyhurst College 13

Hurst Green, Clitheroe BB7 9PZ. Tel: (01254) 826345

Stonyhurst College • 10m NE of M6 junction 31, just off B6243 Longridge – Clitheroe road on outskirts of Hurst Green • Parking • College open 17th July to 28th Aug, daily except Fri • Garden open July to 28th Aug, Sat – Thurs, 1 – 5pm • Entrance: house and garden £4.50, OAPs and children £3.50 ● 🍴 🏠 WC ♿

The rather severe stone buildings of Stonyhurst College are surrounded by long-established parkland. Two long rectangular pools flanking the drive date from the seventeenth century. An area of formal gardens to the south of the college is of less interest for the plants than for the stonework which, although in a state of poor repair, is still quite magnificent. Steps lead up to a circular pool, overlooked by an unusual cross-shaped stone building, and down to a gravel terrace with two gazebos placed symmetrically at each end and a fine view across the low connecting wall. Photographs in Gertrude Jekyll's book *Garden Ornament* show Stonyhurst in its former glory; it is hoped that the restoration will achieve something approximating to its previous bliss.

Swiss Cottage 14

8 Hammond Drive, Read, Burnley BB12 7RE. Tel: (01282) 774853

James and Doreen Bowker • 5m NW of Burnley on A671. In Read turn by Pollards Garage into George Lane, then at T-junction left into Hammond Drive • Open for parties by appt • Entrance: £2 per person ●

A modern garden of one and a half acres set on a steeply sloping south-facing site. The west side is backed by mature woodland and planted to enhance the woodland feel. Small trees such as sorbus, salix, acers and birch are here as well as a *Cornus nuttallii*, a particular favourite of the owners. Beneath the trees are rhododendrons, azaleas, camellias and skimmias, while hostas, tiarellas, helle-bores and other shade-lovers fill the remaining space. Close to the centre of the garden a small stream rises and is taken through a series of rock pools bordered by beds of astilbes, irises and calthas; there is also a bed of grasses. The east side of the garden close to the house has irregularly shaped beds meandering down the slope, which is much steeper here. They are mulched with gravel as the owners find that this breaks up the Lancashire clay better than bark or other mulches. Dwarf conifers, alpines and sun-loving perennials like the conditions. The planting is well considered; there is good variety and inspiration here.

Towneley Park 15

Todmorden Road, Burnley BB11 3RQ. Tel: (01282) 424213

Burnley Borough Council • 1½ m SE of Burnley on A671 • Hall open daily except Sat, weekdays, 10am – 5pm, Sun, 12 noon – 5pm. Closed Christmas week • Park open all year, daily during daylight hours • Entrance: free • Other information: Shop in hall ○ 🍴 🏠 WC ♿ 🚲 👶 ☕

The hall dates from 1500, but its exterior is largely the work of 1816 to 1820. The frontage looks out over a pond and beyond a ha-ha to open parkland laid out in the late eighteenth century. There are some formal beds to the east of the house planted with bright annuals. Herbaceous plants and shrubs have been chosen for the area around the hall, and the Small Lime Walk has been opened up by removing old rhododendrons, replacing them with a better selection of choice shrubs and ground cover. Further to the east, as well as to the south and west, are extensive woodlands containing many large rhododendrons, and long walks. There is also a museum of local crafts and industries, a nature centre and an aquarium.

Weeping Ash   16

Glazebury, Leigh. Tel (01942) 262066

John Bent • 14m W of Manchester. Turn S off A580 at Greyhound Hotel roundabout onto A574 to Culcheth. Garden is ¼ m further on left • Open 20th Feb, 26th March, 23rd April, 28th May, 25th June, 23rd July, 27th Aug, 24th Sept, 29th Oct, 26th Nov, 1 – 5.30pm • Entrance: £1.50, children 50p • Other information: Parking, teas, toilet facilities, plants for sale and shop at adjacent garden centre ● ➌ ✕ WC ✈ ◗ ♔

This garden has been created by a retired nurseryman, so it is only to be expected that a great variety of plants is found here. John Bent has a good collection of small trees, particularly sorbus, and many shrubs, especially roses. Ninety-metre-long herbaceous border. There is a large range of perennials, including over 50 hellebores and many bulbs; one large bed is devoted to lilies. But it is John Bent's ideas on design that bring so much to the garden. Broad grass paths snake around the mixed beds and small offshoot paths give interesting views back into the main areas. There are views over the whole garden from a ruined Doric temple on a mound – a feature inspired during a visit to Cyprus. Many structures have been created as hosts to climbing plants, the best being a rustic gazebo built entirely from scrapwood, which is now covered by a passion flower and a golden hop.

Woodside   17

Princes Park, Shevington, Wigan WN6 8HY. Tel/Fax: (01257) 255255

Barbara and Bill Seddon • 3m NW of Wigan. From M6 junction 26 or 27 follow signs for Shevington • Open 6th Aug for NGS, 11am – 5pm, and by appt • Entrance: £1.50, children free [NEW] ● ➌

This is a suburban garden of two thirds of an acre on an attractively undulating site, surrounded by mature trees. Broad grass paths designed to accentuate the landscaping lead round beds of mainly acid-loving plants. There are many azaleas, small rhododendrons, camellias, magnolias, acers and conifers. Of particular note is a large collection of peonies. An attractive water feature stands at the centre of the garden – a large stone trough with water bubbling up through stones guarded by a pair of stone geese. There is also a stone-banked dell excavated at one end of the garden. Everything is exeptionally well kept, and there is a surprising amount to see in what is not a vast garden.

Worden Park 18

Leyland PR5 2DJ. Tel: (01772) 421109

Borough of South Ribble • 4m S of Preston. Take B5253 S from Leyland. Signposted • Open daily, 8am – dusk • Entrance: free, except first Sat in June • Other information: Refreshments at craft centre ○ 🍵 ✕ 🏠 WC ♿ ☕

The gardens are set around part of an old house and a stable block that now contains craft and theatre workshops (the rest of the house was burnt down in the 1940s). The maze is unusual, being made of hornbeam hedges in a circular pattern. A little distance away is a large conservatory with a rockery to one side and a herbaceous border to the other. They face a formal sunken lawned area enclosed by a low balustrade and some fine ironwork gates. Large areas of open parkland surround the gardens, which contain a children's adventure play area, mini golf, a model railway, an ice-house and an arboretum. Areas in the parkland are being developed to attract wildlife. Full events programme (mostly without charge) – telephone for details.

COUNTY BOUNDARIES
Some gardens have postal addresses in one county and are physically situated in another. If in doubt, the index will direct the reader to the correct page.

DOGS, TOILETS & OTHER FACILITIES ♿ WC
If these are not mentioned in the entry, then facilities are probably not available at the property described. For example, if dogs are not mentioned, owners will probably not permit entry, even on a lead.

FEEDBACK
Readers are invited to advise the *Guide* of any gardens which in their opinion should be listed in future editions, and where possible arrangements will be made to review such suggestions. Readers who would like to add information about gardens listed are warmly invited to write to the *Guide* with their comments, which may be used in future editions without attribution. A report form is included at the back of the *Guide*, although letters will be welcome. Please send to the publishers, Bloomsbury Publishing plc, 38 Soho Square, London W1V 5DF. All letters are acknowledged by the editor.

LEICESTERSHIRE

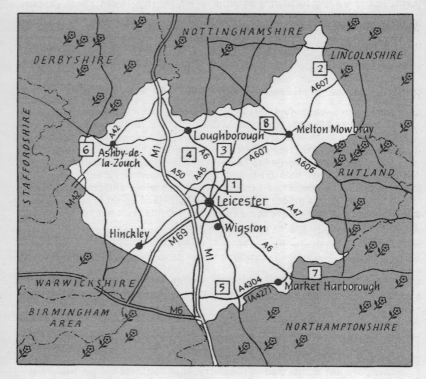

For gardens in Rutland, see pages 366–8.

Beeby Manor ★ 1

Beeby LE7 3BL. Tel: (01162) 595238

Mr and Mrs Philip Bland • 5m E of Leicester. Turn off A47 in Thurnby and follow signs through Scraptoft • Open by appt • Entrance: £1.80 ● **WC** ♿

Three acres of mature gardens in the form of a series of romantic rooms, enclosed with lofty yew hedges. Roses everywhere in soft colours, on frames and mellow walls, tumbling through arbours. A parterre, ancient-looking, though only 10 years old, leads to formal lily ponds and exuberant herbaceous borders which are overblown and carefully untidy. A charming old English garden in the grandest cottage style evoking a bygone age. Arboretum under development. *Kayes Garden Nursery* is nearby on A607 at 1700 Melton Road, Rearsby [open March to Oct, daily, 10am – 5pm, and Sun, 10am – 12 noon]. This one-acre garden is set in the lovely rural countryside of Leicestershire's Wreake Valley. It houses an extensive collection of interesting and unusual hardy plants. A long pergola, richly planted with clematis, roses and honey-suckles leads the visitor into the garden and forms a backdrop to the superb double herbaceous borders. Beyond are mixed beds, filled with a wide range of herbaceous plants, shrubs and shrub roses, combined in subtle, colour-co-ordinated groups. A stream with numerous small bridges dissects the garden and ends in a large wildlife pond. This is a garden for all seasons and a delight for the plantsman, gardener and naturalist.

Belvoir Castle 2

Belvoir, Grantham NG32 1PD. Tel: (01476) 870262

The Duke of Rutland • 10m NE of Melton Mowbray off A607 by Belvoir. Signposted • Castle open • Garden open April to Sept, Tues – Thurs, Sat and Sun; Oct, Sun only, 11am – 5pm (last admission to house 4pm). Open Bank Holiday Mons. Parties at other times by appt. Spring garden open all year for pre-booked parties • Entrance: castle and garden £5, OAPs £4, children £3. Spring garden £3.50 per person for pre-booked parties of 20 to 40 persons (1999 prices) ◑ 🍽 ✕ 🖼 WC ☕ 🏺 ⚘

From a distance this castle (pronounced Beaver) has all the appearance of a medieval fortress, although close to it is clearly a more substantial nineteenth-century edifice. The house is famous for its rooms by James Wyatt. The mid-nineteenth-century garden descends from the castle, with fine views of Belvoir Vale, in a series of terraces and slopes with some small gardens created by hedging. There are bulbs, early-flowering shrubs and roses, arbours and some seating, and friendly peacocks. Also available for viewing by pre-booked parties is the Duchess of Rutland's private woodland garden, known as the spring garden, a delightful informal spot situated in a natural ampitheatre in the middle of dense woodland. Don't miss the recently restored moss house. Overall, some people find the site rather 'municipal' in style.

Brinkfields ★ 3

Seagrave LE12 7NH.

Mr and Mrs John Gennard • Directions on application • Open by written appt only • Entrance: charge ●

Three acres, superbly maintained and visually satisfying, which after 30 years are just coming into the first flush of handsome maturity. Many acid-loving plants are amazingly robust, defying their clay surroundings. Large rock garden with alpines and water feature. Enchanting woodland glade with meconopsis and rare trilliums, carpets of spring bulbs and many rare specimens carefully placed together to give of their best. Nothing second-rate here.

Long Close ★ 4

60 Main Street, Woodhouse Eaves, Loughborough LE12 8RZ. Tel: (01509) 890616 (business hours)

Miss P. Johnson • S of Loughborough between A6 and M1 junctions 22 and 23 • Open on three Suns, 2 – 5.30pm for NGS. Also open March to July and in autumn, Mon – Sat, 9.30am – 1pm, 2 – 5.30pm. Tickets at Pene Crafts gift shop opposite. Private parties welcome by appt • Entrance: £2, children free • Other information: Park in adjacent public car park. Teas on NGS open days, and for parties by arrangement only ◑ 🍴 WC ⓑ 🧥 🌳 🏵

When Mr and Mrs George Johnson bought Long Close in 1949, they began a project of restoration on this five-acre garden, based on the framework and potential left by their predecessor, Colonel Gerald Heygate. Taking advantage of the lime-free loam they nurtured a large collection of rhododendrons, azaleas and magnolias, which are now in magnificent maturity. They added many camellias and other shrubs and trees to this collection. Formal terraces lead to more informal gardens, with winding paths between specimen trees and finally to a natural dappled pool. Many rare and interesting shrubs and plants. Formal and informal ponds. Drifts of snowdrops, daffodils and bluebells in spring. Prolifically planted herbaceous borders. A courtyard plays its sheltered part with magnificent wall-covering plants. Very old pasture wildflower meadow walk. This is sometimes described as a Cornish garden in Leicestershire due to the many quite tender trees and plants rarely to be found elsewhere so far north. Truly a plantsman's garden.

Orchards ★   5

Hall Lane, Walton, Lutterworth LE17 5RP. Tel: (01455) 556958

Mr and Mrs G. Cousins • 8m S of Leicester. Take A5199, turn right for Bruntingthorpe then follow signs for Walton • Open June to Aug, Suns, 2 – 5pm, and at other times by appt • Entrance: £1.80, children free ● 💭 WC 🌳 🍴

Tucked away behind a modern bungalow, this garden is a great success story: there are ideas here that relate to almost any medium-sized plot in town or country. Raised beds around a pool, old brick paths, island beds, a cottage garden with shrub roses, lavenders, verbascums and geraniums. Views through sculpted walks, vistas ending in unusual artistic interpretations; above all, a remarkably clever and original arrangement of enclosed spaces, carefully designed and planted.

Paddocks   6

Shelbrook, Ashby–de–la–Zouch LE65 2TU. Tel: (01530) 412606

Mrs Ailsa Jackson • 1½ m W of Ashby-de-la-Zouch on B5003 • Open five Sat and Sun, April to Aug, 2 – 5pm, and for parties of 10 or more by appt • Entrance: £1.50, children free ● 💭 ⓑ 🌳

A one-acre plantsman's garden and RHS award-winner, created as an exhibition to show the rarely seen to advantage.. A National Collection of primulas is closely planted with many new varieties and other unusual plants.

Stoke Albany House 7

Stoke Albany, Market Harborough LE16 8PT. Tel: (01858) 535227

Mr and Mrs Frederick Vinton • 4m E of Market Harborough. Turn S off A427 onto B669. Garden ½ m on left • Open 26th March (Daffodil Sunday), 17th, 24th, 31st May, 7th, 14th, 21st, 28th June, 5th, 9th, 12th July, 2 – 4.30pm (5.30pm on 9th July). Also for parties by appt • Entrance: £2.50, children free • Other information: Teas on Suns only ● WC & ⟨⟩ ⁹

A traditional country-house garden set in four acres with picturesque landscape sweeping beyond. There are fine trees and wide herbaceous borders, striped lawns, and good displays of bulbs in spring and roses in July. The walled grey garden shows splashes of white. The clever avenue of *Nepeta* 'Six Hills Giant' has 'Mme Alfred Carrière' roses skilfully trained over arches, the distances marked with carefully placed urns. A new box parterre filled with roses has been added to the side of the house. Beautifully maintained greenhouses. Everything one would expect to see in a perfect English setting.

Wartnaby Gardens ★ 8

Wartnaby, Melton Mowbray LE14 3HY. Tel: (01664) 822296

Lord and The Hon. Lady King of Wartnaby • 4m NW of Melton Mowbray. From A606 turn W in Ab Kettleby for Wartnaby • Open 30th April, 20th June, 11am – 4pm and for parties and individuals by appt (not Weds) • Entrance: £2.50, children free ● ⬛ 🔲 WC ⁹

The garden has delightful little gardens within it, including a white garden, a newly-laid-out rose garden and a purple border of shrubs and roses, and there are good herbaceous borders, climbers and old-fashioned roses. Two large pools have an adjacent bog garden with primulas, ferns, astilbes and several varieties of willow. There is an arboretum with a good collection of trees and shrub roses, and alongside the drive is a beech hedge in a Grecian pattern. Fruit garden with arches and cordon trees. Fine views.

POSTCODE PLANTS DATABASE
It is often difficult to find out which plants are local to an area. The Postcode Plants Database locates the names of flowers, trees, butterflies and birds for each of Britain's 26 million home addresses. Simply by typing in the first four characters of their Postcode, householders, schools, garden centres and councils can obtain tailor-made lists of local plants which are both hospitable and garden-worthy. Also included are the names of butterflies and birds most likely to visit gardens in each area. The lists come from innovative software, developed by Royal Mail and *FLORA-for-FAUNA* in conjunction with the Natural History Museum, which searches through hundreds of distribution maps of fauna and flora in the British Isles.

LINCOLNSHIRE

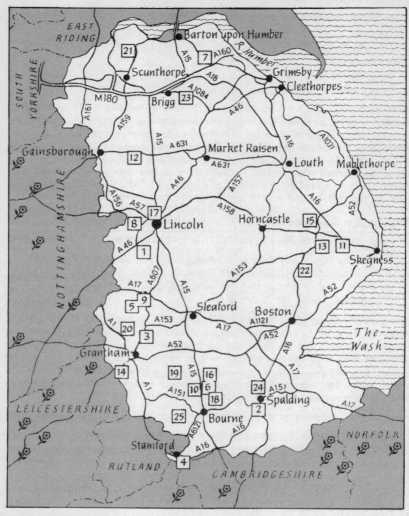

Aubourn Hall ★

1

Aubourn, Lincoln LN5 9DZ. Tel: (01522) 788270

Lady Nevile • 7m SW of Lincoln between A46 and A607 • House open •
Garden open for charity two or three times in early summer and July and Aug,
Wed only, 2 – 5.30pm • Entrance: £3, OAPs £2.50 • Other informaion: plants
for sale on some days ◑ WC ♿

First impressions of the gardens at this lovely red-brick hall (c. 1600) are of spacious simplicity. Glorious undulating lawns and borders sweep through rose arches or along grassy swathes to more lawns and gardens beyond. The enviably deep and diverse borders are carefully planted to give maximum effects of colour, shape and texture. There are, however, secluded areas in which to linger: the newly planted rose garden, the 'Golden Triangle' edged with yew and planted with ornamental crab apple trees and spring bulbs, the ponds and the woodland dell, and a swimming pool surrounded by a late-flowering rose-and-clematis-covered pergola. The nearby church, one of the smallest in Lincolnshire, is also open to visitors on garden open days.

Ayscoughfee Hall and Gardens 2

Churchgate, Spalding PE11 2RA. Tel: (01775) 725468; Fax: (01775) 762715

South Holland District Council • In centre of Spalding • Hall open daily, 9am – 5pm (opens 11am on Sun; closes 5pm on Fri). Closed Sat and Sun Nov to Feb and 25th Dec, 1st Jan • Gardens open all year, daily, 8am – dusk. Closed 25th Dec, 1st Jan • Entrance: free • Other information: Refreshments in main season only. Shop in Hall ○ 💭 ✗ WC ㋴ ⇪ 👜 ♀

The gardens of this medieval wool merchant's house are in a beautiful setting next to the River Welland. Entirely enclosed by lovely old walls, they are worth visiting for the bizarrely shaped clipped yew walks, the old rectangular fish pond with fountains, and the fascinating medieval red-brick hall, now housing the Museum of South Holland Life. In addition there are good bedding displays, lawns, pergola and wall shrubs, including a fruiting vine.

Belton House ★ 3

Belton, Grantham NG32 2LS. Tel: (01476) 566116

The National Trust • 3m N of Grantham off A607 • House open 1 – 5.30pm • Gardens open April to Oct, Wed – Sun and Bank Holiday Mons (but closed 21st April), 11am – 5.30pm (last admission 5pm). Free access to park on foot from Lion Lodge gates all year, but this does not give admittance to house, garden or adventure playground • Entrance: house and gardens £5.30, children £2.60, family ticket £13.20 ◑ 💭 ✗ 🖻 WC ㋴ 👜 ♀

The gardens and park at Belton are large and impressive. The extensive woodland area has two lakes, a small canal and good cedars; however, it is the formal area to the north of the house, completed with the superbly restored and replanted Jeffry Wyatville orangery, that makes a visit memorable. The 1870s' 'Dutch' garden has clipped yew hedging, formal beds with lavender edging, standard 'Iceberg' roses and well-planted urns. The earlier sunken Italian garden has a large central pond with fountain, a lion-headed exedra, lawns and clipped yews. A children's adventure playground makes it an enjoyable family visit.

Burghley House   4

Stamford PE9 3JY. Tel: (01780) 752451

Burghley House Preservation Trust. Custodian: Lady Victoria Leatham (née Cecil) • ½ m E of Stamford on Barnack road, close to A1. Signposted • House open • Garden and parkland open April to 8th Oct (except 9th Sept when closed), 11am – 4.30pm • Entrance: Free (house £6.10, OAPs £5.85, children (one child per adult) free • Other information: Limited access for wheelchairs. Dogs in park only, on lead ◑ 🍵 ✕ 📷 WC ♿

The main attraction at Burghley is the magnificent Elizabethan house with its immense collection of art treasures, built by William Cecil, created Lord Burghley by his Queen. The parkland, landscaped by 'Capability' Brown, is delightful and extensive, even though in the process he swept away the George London Baroque garden of 1700 which had 'canals, rising flights of terraces, ornamental fish-pools, a maze, vineyard and other conceits'.. In addition to creating a large serpentine lake, Brown built a new stable block, and an orangery. The finest surviving small building is Brown's recently restored lakeside temple. The planting, over the last few years, of nearly four acres of spring bulbs means that openings in April are quite spectacular. Otherwise Burghley is of limited interest to visitors with more botanical leanings, although a new area of garden to the east has been extensively planted with specimen trees, mature trees and shrubs. Here sculpture is displayed within the landscape, its most dramatic expression a group emerging Excalibur-like from the surface of the lake.

Caythorpe Court   5

**School of Agriculture, Caythorpe, Grantham NG32 3EP.
Tel: (01400) 272521/275686**

De Montfort University • 10m N of Grantham off A607 • Open for County Fair – ring for date • Entrance: £3 per car NEW ◑ 🍵 WC ♿ 🐾 🍴

This is one of three centres for the School of Agriculture in Lincolnshire. It is the original garden around the 1899 hunting lodge that makes a visit worthwhile. Three large terraces built on a west-facing slope are wonderfully romantic, with Ancaster stone walls, balustrades and stairways; for ease of maintenance all are quite simply planted. The upper terrace has a good shrub border and a lawn with a specimen monkey-puzzle tree. The middle terrace, a delight in spring, has walls covered in aubrieta, and a row of flowering cherries. The third has Virginia creeper and wisteria swathing the balustraded stairs, and a wide rose border underplanted with flag irises and backed by clematis-covered walls. From the upper terrace walks lead to woodland.

21 Chapel Street   6

Hacconby, Bourne PE10 0UL. Tel: (01778) 570314

Mr and Mrs C. Curtis • 3m N of Bourne off A15, turn E at crossroads to Hacconby • Open 19th, 20th Feb, 11am – 4pm, 6th April, 2 – 6pm, 23rd April, 11am – 5pm, 4th May, 1st June, 6th July, 3rd Aug, 7th Sept, 2 – 6pm, 8th Oct, 11am – 5pm; and by appt • Entrance: £1, children (under 16) free ● ☕ WC ✿

The gay and cottagey impression of this village garden has been achieved by minimising lawn area and replacing it with planting space. The circuitous path passes rockeries and scree beds, small trees and shrub roses, rustic arches, troughs and a pond, all exuberantly planted and underplanted to ensure year-round colour from snowdrops in February to red, yellow and gold herbaceous plants in late summer and asters to extend the season into October. There are hundreds of varieties of bulbs, alpines and herbaceous plants here to satisfy both the casual gardener and the seeker of the rare.

Croft House   7

Pitmoor Lane, Ulceby DN39 6SW. Tel: (01469) 588330

Mr and Mrs P. Sandberg • 9m NW of Grimsby, 7m SE of Barton-upon-Humber on A1077 • Open by appt for NGS, also for individuals and groups • Entrance: £1.50, children under 12 free • Other information: Refreshments and plants for sale on open days ● ☕ 🍴 ఈ ⬥ ✿

Although set within a formal design of high walls, clipped *Lonicera nitida* hedges, a pergola walk and gravel paths, this two-acre garden could not seem less formal. The eclectic planting of old favourites among sought-after varieties gives a refreshingly cottagey air, intensified by flowers allowed to seed freely in the gravel. The interesting variety of areas includes mixed, herbaceous and 'woodland' borders, a heather bed, rock garden, grassy meadow, gravel bed, kitchen garden and Victorian vinery.

Doddington Hall   8

Doddington, Lincoln LN6 4RU. Tel: (01522) 694308

Mr and Mrs A.G. Jarvis • 5m W of Lincoln on B1190 • House open as garden for May to Sept openings only • Garden open March and April, Sun only; May to Sept, Wed, Sun and Bank Holiday Mons, all 2 – 6pm. Parties at other times by arrangement • Entrance: £2.20, children £1.10 (house and garden £4.40, children £2.20, family £12.50), special rates for disabled in wheelchairs and parties of 20 or more ● ☕ 🍴 WC ఈ 🛍 ☕

The romantic gardens of the Elizabethan house successfully combine many different styles and moods. The simplicity of the gravel, box and lawned courtyard, the formal croquet lawn and the gravel walk along the kitchen garden wall contrasts with the walled west garden with its elaborate parterres of roses, iris and clipped box edging and its borders of herbaceous plants, flag iris and the sound of gently falling water from the fountains. The parterres were restored in Elizabethan style in 1900. Fine eighteenth-century Italian gates open onto a formal yew alley, more old roses and a good wild garden. Here the meandering walks take in a turf maze, a stream, ancient specimens of sweet chestnut, cedar, yew and holly, and the Temple of the Winds built by the present owner. The more recently planted herb garden, pleached hornbeams and dwarf box-edging continue to harmonise the different areas.

Fulbeck Hall 9

Fulbeck, Grantham NG32 3JW. Tel: (01400) 272205

Mr and Mrs Fry • 10m N of Grantham on A607 • Hall open • Garden open 4th to 7th, 11th to 14th April; 3rd to 5th, 31st May; 3rd July and each Sun — Wed in July; 30th Aug; all 2 — 5pm. Also 4th to 31st July, daily, 2 — 5pm. Parties by appt at any time • Entrance: £1.50, children £1 (hall and garden £3.50, OAPs £3, children £1.50) (1999 prices) • Other information: Refreshments for parties only ◗ 🖻 WC ♿ ♟

The 11-acre garden at Fulbeck is varied and interesting, with recent planting within the formal Victorian design laid out at the end of the last century. Many of the trees are as old as the house (1733). The top terrace with a gravel walk is backed by a superbly shaped clipped yew hedge. The bottom lawn has shrubs, roses, unusual clematis and ramblers climbing into the surrounding trees. Against a limestone wall at the south of the house is a herbaceous border with many choice plants. Beyond the immediate garden is a pleasant wild garden with a nature trail and pond.

Grimsthorpe Castle 10

Grimsthorpe, Nr Bourne PE10 0NB. Tel: (01778) 591205; Fax: (01778) 591259

Grimsthorpe and Drummond Castle Trust Ltd • 4m NW of Bourne on A151 Colsterworth — Bourne road • Castle open 1pm, last admission 4.30pm • Garden open Easter Sun; Sun, Thurs and Bank Holiday Mons to Sept; also daily in Aug, Sun — Thurs, 1 — 6pm • Entrance: Park and garden £3, OAPs £2, children £1.50 (additional £3 for castle, concessions £2.50) NEW ◗ ☕ ✕ 🖻 WC ♿ ♨ ♟

The impressive house, part-medieval, part-Tudor and part-eighteenth-century, of Vanbrugh design, is surrounded on three sides by good pleasure gardens in which 'Capability' Brown had a hand. The Victorian knot garden to the east of the house has beds of lavender, roses and catmint with edges of clipped box. To the south are two yew-hedged rose gardens with topiary, a yew 'broad walk' and a retreat. Leading to the west terrace is a double yew walk with classic herbaceous borders and beyond is a shrub rose border and row of 70-year-old cedars. The yew hedging throughout the garden is superbly maintained and differs in design from one area to another. Beyond the pleasure gardens are the arboretum, wild garden, an unusual geometrically designed kitchen garden with clipped box and bean pergola, and extensive parkland. Views of the old oak and chestnut avenues and of the parkland with its lake and Vanbrugh summerhouse are provided by cleverly positioned vistas and terraces.

Gunby Hall ★ 11

Gunby, Spilsby PE23 5SS. Tel: (01909) 486411

The National Trust • 7m NW of Skegness, 2½ m NW of Burgh-le-Marsh on S of A158 • Hall and garden open, Wed, 2 – 6pm (last admission 5.30pm) • Garden open 5th April to Sept, Wed and Thurs, 2 – 6pm. Also Tues and Fri by written appt to Mr and Mrs J.D. Wrisdale. Coaches and parties pre-book in writing • Entrance: £2.50, children £1.20 (hall and garden £3.50, children £1.70) (1999 prices) • Other information: Possible for wheelchairs but some gravel paths ● 🏠 WC ♿ 🐕 🌳 🍴

The early eighteenth-century hall, its walls smothered in fine plants, is set in parkland with avenues of lime and horse chestnut. The shrub borders, wild garden, lawns with old cedars and restrained formal front garden of catmint and lavender beds backed by clipped yew provide a startling contrast to the main attraction of Gunby – its walled gardens. The dazzling pergola garden with its apple-tree walkway has a maze of paths leading to beds of old roses, a herb garden and brimming herbaceous and annual borders. The second walled area houses an impressive kitchen garden reached after passing more borders of perfectly arranged herbaceous plants and hybrid musk roses. Backing onto its wall is another wonderfully classic herbaceous border and, beyond, an early nineteenth-century long fish pond and orchard complete an altogether enchanting garden. It is fitting that it was the subject of Tennyson's 'Haunt of Ancient Peace'.

Hall Farm and Nursery 12

Harpswell, Gainsborough DN21 5UU. Tel: (01427) 668412

Mr and Mrs M. Tatam • 7m E of Gainsborough on A631 • Open March to Oct, daily; Nov to Feb, Mon – Fri (and most Sat and Sun – telephone to check); all 10am – 6pm, and one day for NGS in Sept, 10am – 6pm (inc. free seed collection). Also by appt • Entrance: donation to charity • Other information: Coaches by appt. Teas on charity open day only ○ 🏠 WC ♿ 🐕 🌳

This garden combines the formal and the informal in a most imaginative way. The owners' sheer delight in plants, satisfied by their adjoining nursery, is evident everywhere. There are hundreds of varieties of unusual herbaceous plants, roses and shrubs. A santolina-edged rose pergola leads from a decorative paved area to the main garden at the rear of the farmhouse. Here the newly created walled top terrace has steps down to a classic double herbaceous border, a sunken garden with box edging and seasonal bedding, lawns, a rose garden and a large informal pond. A short walk away is an interesting medieval moat. A superb garden to visit in summer.

83 Halton Road 13

Spilsby PE23 5LD. Tel: (01790) 752361; Mobile: (0788) 791 3704

Mr and Mrs Gunson • 10m W of Skegness, in Spilsby on B1195 • Open mid-March to mid-Oct, Wed – Sun and Bank Holiday Mons, 10am – 5pm • Entrance: collection box for charity ◗ 🐕 🌳

A glorious place to visit in mid-summer. A gravel walk, flanked by deep borders, winds from a small scented cottage garden through plant-laden metal arches and trellises to a summerhouse and colour-themed garden beyond. Although the soft pastels of the borders are fairly restrained, the planting certainly is not. Bulbs, shrub roses and herbaceous plants (in particular scores of hardy geranium varieties supplied by the owners' specialist nursery) are densely planted, making a magnificent display. The few shrubs and conifers there seem lost amongst such a florid composition.

Harlaxton Manor Gardens 14

Grantham NG32 1AG. Tel: (01476) 592101; Fax: (01476) 592131

University of Evansville, USA • 2m SW of Grantham, 1m SW of A1 on A607 Melton Mowbray road • House occasionally open • Gardens open April to Oct, daily except Mon (but open Bank Holiday Mons), 11am – 5pm • Entrance: £3, OAPs £2, children under 12 £1.25, guided parties of 20 or more £3 per person

◑ 🍴 🍽 WC ⬦ 🅿 🏵 ✋ ♿

Salvin's fantastic Victorian mansion and garden was built to delight and impress – 'I have not read of such a place even in a fairy tale,' wrote Disraeli in 1846. The formal gardens were built on seven terraces and designed as a tour around Europe; these, and the cottage gardens of the estate, were held up as models of their time. Many of the original features remain: beautiful Ancaster stone steps, balustrades, colonnades, ponds and even a Tuscan-style tower. Sadly, most of the plantings and paths have been lost or overgrown over the last 50 years, but the landscape designer Alan Mason has begun the daunting task of renovating the gardens. Weeds, trees and undergrowth have been ruthlessly cut back, and the incredibly ornate six-and-a-quarter-acre walled garden has been partly replanted. Harlaxton will be of great interest to the garden historian or to anyone who likes a 'before and after' transformation.

Harrington Hall 15

Harrington, Spilsby PE23 4NH.

Mr and Mrs D.W.J. Price • 5m E of Horncastle, 2m N of A158 • Open 4th, 18th June, 9th, 23rd July, 2 – 5pm • Entrance: £2, children free ● 🍽 WC ⬦ 🏵

Red-brick Tudor and eighteenth-century walls provide the perfect backdrop for wall shrubs and a variety of borders. Referred to in Tennyson's 'Maud,' it is hard to imagine that these walled gardens and terrace have changed, although they were in fact replanted in the 1950s after wartime vegetable cultivation. The present owners have recently remade the formal one-acre vegetable garden with gravel paths, miniature box edging and espalier fruit trees. The tiny church is open to those visiting the garden.

25 High Street 16

Rippingale, Bourne PE10 0SR. Tel: (01778) 440693

Mr and Mrs Beddington • 6m N of Bourne off A15 • Open 19th, 20th Feb (hellebore and snowdrop Sat and Sun for NGS), 11am – 4pm; 10th June, 2 –

6pm, 11th June, 2 – 5pm (with other village gardens, for local charity). Also by appt • Entrance: Feb: £1, children free; June: £1.50, children free • Other information: Refreshments and plants for sale on open days only ◑ ☕ WC ♿ 🐾

What at first seems a small informal garden of lawn, borders and island beds in fact provides many delightful surprises. There are shady paths and secret corners, a bog garden, ponds, pergola and paved areas, and through a small gate there is an inspirational vegetable garden complete with fruit cage and rhubarb pots. The assiduous care of the knowledgeable owners ensures a display of unusual herbaceous plants, shrubs and bulbs throughout the year. The February opening is in conjunction with 21 Chapel Street, Hacconby and Manor Farm, Keisby (see entries), but in June usually about 12 gardens in the village are open together.

The Lawn 17

Union Road, Lincoln LN1 3BL. Tel: (01522) 560306

Lincoln City Council • Off Burton Road beside Lincoln Castle • Garden open: summer weekdays, 9am – 5pm; Sat and Sun, 10am – 5pm; winter Mon – Thurs, 9am – 5pm; Fri, 9am – 4pm; Sat and Sun, 10am – 4pm • Entrance: free, but charge for parking • Other information: Lincoln Archaeological Centre ○ ☕ ✕ 🗏 WC ♿

When Lincoln City Council bought this disused Georgian mental hospital in 1985 they aimed to establish a botanic collection to represent Lincoln's partnership with cities and countries around the world. Central to this is the Sir Joseph Banks conservatory. Here, excellent use of water, and arrangements of plants in areas corresponding with parts of the world visited by Banks on his three-year voyage with Captain Cook, have made this small area both exotic and interesting. The nearby walled *John Dawber Garden* continues this international theme, with mini-gardens representing England, Germany, China and Australia.

32 Main Street 18

Dyke, Bourne PE10 0AF. Tel: (01778) 422241

Mr and Mrs D. Sellars • 1m N of Bourne, off A15 • Open by appt. Parties especially welcome • Entrance: £1, children 25p NEW ◑ ⌐

This small area (30 x 15 metres) is subdivided into tiny compartments allowing an astonishing number of planting schemes. Every available space is crammed with a choice plant, ornament, trough or architectural feature, and careful planning and underplanting ensures continuous colour.

Manor Farm 19

Keisby, Lenton, Bourne PE10 0RZ. Tel: (01476) 585607

Mr and Mrs C.A. Richardson • 9m NW of Bourne, N of A151 between Lenton and Hawthorpe • Open 19th, 20th Feb, 11am – 4pm (snowdrops and hellebores) and 25th June, 2 – 5pm • Entrance: Feb £1, children free; June £1.50, children free ● 💬 WC ⚘

With its artistic planning and colour-harmonisation, this pretty, informal garden is a delight. The tiny paths to the herb garden, pergola and stream meander through the beds and so allow close inspection of the many choice plants, including herbaceous perennials, shrub roses, ramblers, clematis, and a large collection of snowdrops and hellebores. New formal herb garden and wildflower area in 'new naturalism mode' say owners.

Marston Hall 20

School Lane, Marston, Grantham NG32 2HQ.
Tel: (01400) 250225/250167 (Mrs Ballaam)

Reverend Henry Thorold • 6m NW of Grantham, 1½ m off A1 • House open • Garden open 18th, 25th June, 23rd July, 2 – 6pm. Other times by appt • Entrance: £2.50, children £1 (1999 prices) ● 💬 🗐 WC ﹠ ⟨⊕ ⚘

The gardens reflect the intimate nature of the beautiful and ancient Ancaster stone house. A series of small, walled and high-hedged gardens, courtyards and walks house formal rose beds, a cottage garden, a knot garden planted with herbs, and vegetables screened by herbaceous borders and trellising. To the south of the house are lawns, clipped yews and walks through the laburnum avenue and ancient trees, including an enormous laburnum and a 400-year-old wych elm. The avenue of Lombardy poplars stretches from the orchard to the river, perfectly uniting the garden with the parkland beyond.

Normanby Hall 21

Normanby Hall Country Park, Scunthorpe DN15 9HU. Tel: (01724) 720588;
Fax: (01724) 721248

Run by North Lincolnshire Council • 4m N of Scunthorpe on B1430 • Hall and Farm Museum open April to Oct, daily, 1 – 5pm • Park open all year, 9am – 5pm (up to 9pm in summer). Victorian walled garden open daily except 25th Dec, 1st Jan, 11am – 5pm (4pm in winter) • Entrance: £2.50, concessions £1.50, family £6.50, 50% discount for North Lincolnshire residents (1999 prices) ○ 💬 ✕ 🗐 WC ﹠ ⟨⊕ ⚘ 🛍 ♟

Although the parkland and woodland are extensive, with superb nature trails, rhododendron walks, lakes and an accessible deer park, the pleasure gardens are somewhat reduced. Next to the Regency house are formal rose beds and a lavender-edged sunken garden with a fish pond. Further away, however, are two lovely gardens partially enclosed by tall, mellow brick walls and old holly and conifer hedges. The first has double herbaceous borders, grass paths and good wall shrubs and climbers. The second, until recently a paddling pool, has been restored, with the help of the Heritage Lottery Fund and European Development Fund, as a Victorian kitchen garden. Faithfully re-created with peach cases, glasshouses, potting shed and bothy, and using Victorian varieties of fruit, vegetables and flowers, this garden promises to be both beautiful and educational. The garden is run totally organically using Victorian techniques.

Within the grounds is a farm museum which, like the house, has no entrance fee, thus allowing all the family to find something of interest at a minimal cost.

The Old Rectory 22

Church Lane, East Keal, Spilsby PE23 4AT. Tel: (01790) 752477

Mr and Mrs J. Ward • 12m W of Skegness, 2m SW of Spilsby on A16 • Open 16th March, 16th April, 11th May, 11th June, 2 – 5pm and Thurs by appt. For information on other open times please telephone • Entrance: £1.20, children free ● ● 🍽 ☜

Nestled on a hillside in the beautiful Wolds, this possibly boasts the best views of all the gardens listed in Lincolnshire. Over the last decade, the owners have kept the many old walls, paved areas and yew hedges, adding new plantings and creating a gorgeous three-quarter-acre garden. Taking advantage of the slope, the garden seems to flow naturally from one area to another. There are paths everywhere – grass, brick, stone and granite-sett – all meandering from one delight to another. Essentially the garden is cottagey, with lawn kept to a minimum and masses of flowers tumbling over rockeries, ponds, borders and retaining walls. There is still an old-fashioned, tranquil atmosphere appropriate to a former vicarage, probably due to the traditional front garden with lawn and borders, an extensive vegetable garden and orchard and a rhododendron walk.

Pinefields 23

Main Street, Bigby, Barnetby DN38 6ER. Tel: (01652) 628327

Mr and Mrs R. Hill • 10m SE of Scunthorpe, 4m E of Brigg off A1084 • Open by appt only • Entrance: £1.50 ● 🍽 WC ☜

From an extremely modest frontage, the rear of this three-quarter-acre village garden comes as a surprise. A paved terrace, complete with decorative tubs, has steps leading to a lawn and borders beyond. Each year a major feature is created, and the garden now boasts mixed and herbaceous borders, a gravelled alpine area, wildlife ponds and a wildflower area. Not having the advantage of old walls for the many climbing plants here (including at least 30 varieties of clematis), height has been achieved using wooden pillars with swagged ropes, pergolas and obelisks. With a passion for unusual and beautiful plants and great ingenuity, the owners have created a garden of interest and variety on a relatively long and narrow site.

Spalding Tropical Forest 24

Glenside North, Pinchbeck, Spalding PE11 3SD. Tel: (01775) 710882

Michael and Judy Mitchell • 2m N of Spalding off A16. Signposted • Tropical Forest open all year, daily except 25th, 26th Dec, 1st Jan, summer 10am – 5.30pm, winter 10am – 4pm • Entrance: £2.45, OAPs £1.99, children (5-16) £1.40, family (2 adults and 2 children) £6 (1999 prices) • Other information: Refreshments from March to Oct only (telephone for opening hours). Plants for sale in Rose Cottage water garden centre ○ 🍽 🛍 WC ☕ ☜ 🎁

Enclosed by half an acre of glass, the forest, designed by David Stevens, has been arranged into four zones – oriental, tropical, temperate and dry tropical – each with appropriate landscapes and plantings. The use of rock (over 500 tons of stone were used in its construction) and water is on a grand scale with streams, ponds and cascades. There is even a waterfall to walk through. The careful monitoring of temperature, light and humidity ensures a pleasant environment in which to linger, unlike the stifling atmosphere of most hothouses.

Walnut Cottage   25

Careby, Stamford PE9 4EA. Tel: (01780) 410660

Roy and Sue Grundy • 6m N of Stamford on B1176, 5m E of A1 at Stretton • Open May to Sept, Tues and Sat by appt only • Entrance: £1.50, children free

● ● WC ● ●

A narrow strip of tender plants and wall shrubs provides a cheerful frontage to these converted stone cottages and gives a taste of the wonderful half-acre garden to be found through the small gate. Here, on what was until recently a difficult south-west slope, the owners have used their construction expertise, imagination and love of plants to create several distinct areas. Using height to advantage for paths, viewing area and focal points, the gardens are at once both open yet full of delightful surprises. These include a gravel bed, a paved herb and flower garden, a small woodland area, a formal garden with yew and mixed borders and, a rare sight today, a well-made, well-planted and well-maintained rockery, with a cascade, pond and steps leading up to a summerhouse with a beautiful Tuscan pot. The garden, already a pleasure, can only improve as the herbaceous perennials, trellis plants, cordon fruit trees and hedges become more established and plans for a tropical lily house are realised.

2001 GUIDE
The 2001 *Guide* will be published before Christmas 2000. Reports on gardens for consideration are welcome at all times of the year, but particularly by early summer (June) 2000 so that they can be inspected that year.

All descriptions and other information are as accurate as possible at the time of going to press, but circumstances change and, if in doubt, it is wise to telephone before making a long journey.

SYMBOLS
[NEW] entries new for 1999; ○ open all year; ◐ open most of year; ◑ open during main season; ● open rarely and/or by appt; ● teas/light refreshments; ✗ meals ● picnics permitted; WC toilet facilities; **WC** toilet facilities, inc. disabled ● garden partly wheelchair-accessible; ● dogs permitted on lead; ● plants for sale; ● shop; ● events held

LIVERPOOL & WIRRAL

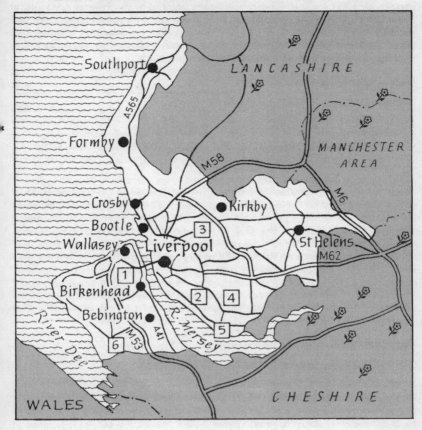

Birkenhead Park ★ 1

**Birkenhead, Wirral CH62 8BP. Tel: (0151) 647 2366 or
Ranger (0151) 652 5197**

*Metropolitan Borough of Wirral • 1m from centre of Birkenhead, S of A553 •
Open all year, daily, during daylight hours • Entrance: free* ○ **WC** 🚻

Birkenhead Park is rich in history. Opened in 1847, it was the world's first
urban park to be built at public expense. Designed by Joseph Paxton, it was
highly influential in the creation of New York's Central Park. Paxton's master-
stroke was to separate 'through' traffic from peripepheral traffic on roads
meandering around the perimeter of the park. He also banked up the edges of
the lakes to keep them hidden, and made them sinuous in shape to provide
walkers with a constantly changing view. No subsequent public park has

succeeded in fashioning a more subtle yet masterly landscape. The lake on the eastern side has its well-landscaped banks planted with trees and shrubs; a Swiss-style bridge links two islands, and to one end a fine stone boathouse has recently been restored. The lake in the west part has weeping willows and rhododendrons planted round its edge. Other restoration work includes entrances, railings and adjustments to tree plantings.

Calderstone Park ★ 2

Liverpool L24 0TR. Tel: (0151) 225 4835

Liverpool City Council, Environmental Services • 4m SE of city centre, S of A562 • Park open all year, daily. Old English garden and Japanese garden open all year, daily except 25th Dec: April to Sept, 8am – 7.30pm; Oct to March, 8am – 4pm • Entrance: free • Other information: Dogs in park only ○ ☕ WC &

This is a large landscaped park with mature trees, shrubs, a lake and rhododendron walk. In its centre, set around an old walled garden, are three gardens which are a credit to the city council gardener. The first, the flower garden, has semi-formal beds of perennials and grasses, formal beds of annuals and a long greenhouse. Next is the Old English garden, where amongst a formal layout of paths are beds containing a huge range of perennials, bulbs and shrubs. There is a circular pond at the centre, and pergolas carrying clematis, vines and other climbers cross the paths at various points. Finally the Japanese garden has a chain of rocky streams and pools around which are pines, acers and clumps of bamboos. A greenhouse contains the National Collection of aechmeas. Altogether this must be one of the best 'free' gardens in the country.

Croxteth Hall and Country Park 3

Croxteth Hall Lane, Liverpool L12 0HB. Tel: (0151) 228 5311

Liverpool City Council, Leisure Services • Turn N off A5058 Liverpool ring-road into Muirhead Avenue on NE side of city. Signposted • Hall and Victorian Farm also open • Garden open probably 21st April to Sept, daily, 11am – 5pm, winter times on request • Entrance: grounds free; walled garden £1, OAPs and children 50p; all facilities £3.20, OAPs and children £1.60, family ticket (2 adults and 2 children) £8 (1999 prices) • Other information: Dogs in outer park only. Shop in Hall ◑ ✕ WC &

The hall stands in 500 acres of its original parkland, in which there are large areas of woodland and many rhododendrons. The centre of interest to gardeners is the large walled garden to the north of the house. Interpreted as a working Victorian kitchen garden and divided up by gravel paths, this contains a great variety of fruit, vegetables and decorative plants, organically cultivated; espalier fruits are grown against the walls and trained on wire fences, and the south-facing wall has a broad herbaceous border containing a good variety of perennials and ornamental grasses. In the north-east corner several greenhouses and a mushroom house are all open to the visitor, while at the south end is a small herb garden.

Reynolds Park Walled Garden 4

Church Road, Woolton, Liverpool L24 0TR. Tel: (0151) 724 2371

Liverpool City Council (controlled by Environmental Services, Calderstone Park) • *4½ m SE of Liverpool city centre. Turn left off A562 up Beaconsfield Road to end and right into Church Road. Park is on left* • *Open all year, Mon – Fri, 9am – 4pm* • *Entrance: free* ○

A walled garden with herbaceous borders, large dahlia beds and excellent wall climbers. All in very good condition, litter-free and maintained with only two staff. Large grass area with mature trees. Unusual clipped yew garden. Small rose garden.

Speke Hall 5

The Walk, Liverpool L24 1XD. Tel: (0345) 585702 (Infoline) or (0151) 427 7231

The National Trust • *8m SE of city centre, S of A561. Signposted* • *Hall open as garden 27th March to Oct; then Nov to 13th Dec, Sat and Sun, 1 – 4.30pm* • *Garden open 28th March to March 2001, daily except Mon (but open Bank Holiday Mons), 12 noon – 5.30pm (closes 4.30pm 22nd to 31st Oct, 4pm Nov to Mar 2001). Closed 1st Jan, 21st April, 24th to 26th, 31st Dec, 1st Jan* • *Entrance: £1.60, children 80p, family £3.80 (hall and gardens £4.10, children £2.10, family £10.30)* • *Other information: Picnics in orchard only.* **Self-drive wheelchair available for grounds; accessible path around Stocktons Wood** ○ ☕ 🏪 WC ♿ 🏬 ♨

The gardens at Speke are neither as old nor as impressive as the Elizabethan hall. They are remarkable, however, for although they are situated amidst the industrial areas of south Liverpool and close to the airport, they seem to be set in the heart of the countryside. In front of the house is a large lawn with shrub borders to the sides containing mainly rhododendrons and hollies. On the side opposite the house a ha-ha allows views to the fields and woodland. A stone bridge leads over a drained moat to the ornate stone entrance of the hall. The moat continues to the west where there is a herbaceous border with a variety of perennials; a large holm oak stands opposite. To the south are new Victorian borders, and a formal rose garden contains fragrant varieties of old-fashioned roses. In the centre of the house is a large cobbled courtyard in which grow two enormous yews. The Trust is continuing to develop many areas of the gardens, and a mid-Victorian-style stream garden has been planted with rhododendrons, azaleas, camellias, ferns and other plants. New beds are being planted on the South Lawn (recapturing the image of J. Sukers' painting of 1865). A minibus service from Speke Hall will take visitors to the tiny garden at *20 Forthlin Road*, former home of Sir Paul McCartney, where the Beatles composed and rehearsed.

Thornton Manor ★ 6

Thornton Hough, Wirral L63 1JD. Tel: (0151) 336 4828 (Estate Office)

Leverhulme Estates • *3m S of Birkenhead, on minor road that links A5137 to the B5136 at Thornton Hough* • *Open two Suns in spring and two in summer,*

1 – 6pm (telephone for details) • *Entrance: £2, OAPs £1, children 50p* ◐ ☕ 🧺 WC ♿ 🐕 🌱

Thomas Mawson created two gardens for Lord Leverhulme. One, Rivington (see entry under Manchester Area) is perched high on a hillside; the other, Thornton Manor, lies in the very different flat, lush countryside of the Wirral. Here, instructed to create 'a garden for promenading and walking', Mawson came up with a wonderfully spacious design. In front of the house is a large lawn with a formal layout of broad stone paths; no planting, just good views of the surrounding countryside. To the east is a loggia and a lime walk. To the west, a long, straight path takes the visitor past some of the garden's main features. First the Forum, a rectangular lawn surrounded by a colonnade covered in climbers, then the tea house, an impressive stone building which was once the entrance to the walled garden; it, too, is covered in climbers. The path eventually reaches the most abundantly planted part of the garden, where gravel paths lead amongst mixed beds of shrubs, perennials and annuals. Starting here, a long walk leads to the lake and then to the east side of the house via a dell, an attractive planting of shrubs and trees surrounding a pool. A new arboretum has been planted.

OPENING DATES AND TIMES

Times of access given are the best available at the moment of going to press, but some may have been changed subsequently. In the entries, the times given are inclusive – that is, an entry such as May to Sept means that the garden is open from 1st May to 30th Sept inclusive, and 2 – 5pm, means that entry will be effective during that period. Please note that many owners will open their gardens to visitors by appointment. They will often arrange to give a personally-conducted tour on these occasions. Unavoidably some owners cannot give their opening times before we go to press. In such cases we attempt to give the best guidance we can.

SYMBOLS

NEW entries new for 2000; ○ open all year; ◔ open most of year; ◑ open during main season; ◐ open rarely and/or by appt; ☕ teas/light refreshments; ✕ meals 🧺 picnics permitted; **WC** toilet facilities; **WC** toilet facilities, inc. disabled ♿ garden partly wheelchair-accessible; 🐕 dogs permitted on lead; 🌱 plants for sale; 🧺 shop; 💡 events held

A TOTALLY INDEPENDENT PUBLICATION

The *Guide* makes no charge for entries, which are written by our own inspectors. The factual details are supplied by owners. This is a totally-independent publication and its only revenue is from sales of copies in bookshops.

LONDON AREA

29 Addison Avenue   1

London W11 4QS. Tel: (020) 7603 2450

Mr and Mrs D.B. Nicholson • Off Holland Park Avenue, W of tube station. Cars must enter via Norland Square and Queensdale Road • Open 30th July, 2 – 6pm • Entrance: £1.50 ◑

The meticulously kept and well-designed small walled garden of a charming stuccoed villa makes the best use of every inch of space, with a profusion of plants on every surface. A tiny lawn is dominated by two venerable pear trees. Beyond them are perennial borders, slightly raised, and formally laid out but informally planted with an emphasis on phlox and hardy geraniums. To one side of the studio workshop at the end of the garden is a small shade garden, complete with statue. In late summer *Solanum jasminoides* blooms profusely on one of the walls. The colour themes of the borders (pink, blue and white) and the variegated foliage help to unify the garden, which is an excellent balance between design and planting.

32 Atney Road   2

Putney, London SW15. Tel: (020) 8785 9355

Mrs Sally Tamplin • Off Putney Bridge Road • Visitors welcome by prior appt. Please telephone • Entrance: £1.50 ◑

A spacious London garden with an attractively planted terrace. Wide borders along the boundaries are packed with herbaceous plants, roses, hydrangeas and other shrubs to ensure a long season of interest. A central rose arch leading to the rear of the garden gives perspective.

Avery Hill Park   3

Eltham, London SE9. Tel: (020) 8850 3217

London Borough of Greenwich • Off Bexley Road (A210) and Avery Hill Road • Open all year, daily, 7.30am – dusk. Winter garden open Mon – Thurs, 1 – 4pm, Fri, 1 – 3pm, Sat and Sun, 10am – 4pm. Closed 24th, 25th Dec and 1st Jan • Entrance: free ○ 🍵 WC ♿

More remains of the gardens at Avery Hill than of the 50-room mansion, which was badly damaged in the Blitz. The house was built by Colonel John North, known as the Nitrate King because he made a fortune from Chilean nitrates, which were much in demand as fertiliser. Since 1906 it has been used as a teachers' training college, while the gardens are enjoyed by the local inhabitants. There are rose gardens and three giant conservatories, looking like icebergs which have come to a halt on the southern slope of Shooter's Hill. The domed temperate house is bursting with bougainvilleas and staghorn ferns. The tropical house attracts school parties to see bananas, coffee and ginger plants, camellias draw the crowds to the cold house in spring. Aviary.

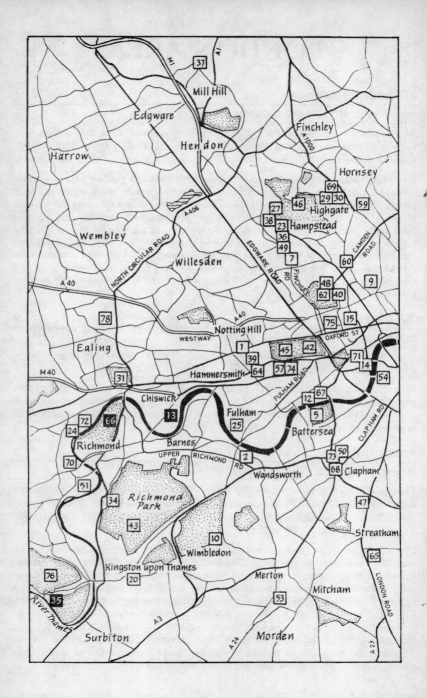

Barbican Conservatory 4

The Barbican, Silk Street, London EC2Y 8DS. Tel: (020) 7638 4141

City of London • In Barbican Centre, on 3rd floor via lift or stairs • Open Sat, Sun and Bank Holidays only, 12 noon – 5.30pm. Telephone to confirm opening times as conservatory is sometimes used for conferences • Entrance: 80p, OAPs and children 60p, family ticket (1 or 2 adults and up to 4 children) £2.25 (1999 prices). Pre-booked guided tours available – telephone for details ◐ WC ᕫ

The lift to the third floor of the Barbican propels you from the treeless streets of the City to a lush jungle of temperate and semi-tropical plants. Planted in the autumn of 1980-81 using 1600 cubic metres of soil, the conservatory was opened in 1984. Twin *Cupressus cashmeriana* grace the main entrance, while a vast banyan tree (*Ficus bengalensis*) in the eastern section threatens to burst through the roof. Many familiar houseplants like *Ficus benjamina* have reached gigantic proportions, and a colossal Swiss cheese plant (*Monstera deliciosa*) produces edible fruits after flowering. The Arid House on the second level, added in 1986, contains epiphyllum and cacti, including the largest *Carnegiea gigantea* in Europe. Fred, as it is affectionately known, was a gift from the Mayor of Salt Lake City. There are finches in the aviary and the ponds are alive with fish and terrapins. Natural predators and pathogens are used to keep down pests, and the hard Thames water is softened to stop nutrients becoming locked in the soil. Another interesting contemporary garden is at the *Broadgate Arena* at the far end of Liverpool Street Station concourse.

Battersea Park 5

Battersea, London SW11 4NJ. Tel: (020) 8871 7530/8800

Wandsworth Borough Council • S side of River Thames, from Chelsea Bridge to Albert Bridge • Open all year, daily, 7am – dusk • Entrance: free, but parking charge ○ ☕ ✕ 🏠 WC ᕫ ⬦ 🛍 🍷

With half a mile of Thames frontage, this 200-acre park still retains many of its original Victorian features, which will be restored over the next three years with a £6.9 million grant from the Heritage Lottery. Also to be restored are the remaining features from the Festival of Britain in 1951, including the Russell Page Garden, the Vista Lakes and a new jetty, which will connect the park to the Millennium Dome by river. The 15-acre boating lake has been revitalised, including replanting the banks in keeping with the original Victorian style. A borehole has been sunk to ensure fresh water at all times and a wildlife management programme put in place: Battersea Park is now one of only two sites in London where herons breed. Visitors can also enjoy the Old English Garden, the Cascade, the Children's Zoo, sculptures by Henry Moore and Barbara Hepworth and a modern Buddhist temple. Ancillary to all this are the 1930s' Lakeside Café, many sports facilities, and a long and refreshing river view.

Brockwell Park 6

Tulse Hill, London SE24 9BJ. Tel: (020) 7926 0105

London Borough of Lambeth • Take A204 then A215, entrances at Herne Hill Gate, Norwood Road, Brockwell Gardens Road, etc. • Open all year, daily, 9am – dusk • Entrance: free • Other information: Dogs outside walled garden only ○ ● WC &

A peaceful and attractive refuge from nearby Brixton shopping centre. (Radios, cassettes, and dogs are banned from the walled garden – and children under 14 have to be accompanied by an adult.) Within a surprisingly large park, Brockwell has a pretty and secluded Old English walled garden, with rose beds, and a delightful mixture of herbaceous bedding, providing almost year-round interest. On the hilltop surrounding the clock tower is a variety of shrubs and trees and formal bedding. There are three ponds. Both park and gardens are well maintained, and the parkland is well provided with benches. Good views to the north over a London of towers and spires.

15A Buckland Crescent ★ 7

London NW3 5DH.

Lady Barbirolli • Near Fitzjohn's Avenue at Swiss Cottage end. 5 minutes from Swiss Cottage tube station and various buses • Open 11th June, 2.30 – 6.30pm • Entrance: £2, children free ● & ♨

The strong sense of space and line that musicians often possess is expressed in this dignified third-of-an-acre town garden which has been described in several books. The ground plan combines flowing unfussy lines and ingenious geometry. Planting is everywhere discriminating, ranging from a functional but decorative vegetable patch to some unusual plants, citrus and other interesting shrubs, including a small bamboo 'grove'. A generous terrace is enhanced by boldly planted urns.

5 Burbage Road 8

Herne Hill, London SE24 9HJ. Tel: (020) 7274 5610

Crawford and Rosemary Lindsay • Close to Half Moon Lane. Nearest station: Herne Hill • Special open days for NGS (telephone for information); otherwise open by appt only • Entrance: £1.50 [NEW] ●

An attractive garden in a tranquil walled setting, with a well-kept lawn, quietly splashing fountain, vegetables and herb beds. There is year-round interest and a continual introduction of unusual plants; borders are filled with choice arrangements of herbaceous perennials and shrubs, and good use is made of a variety of pots housing climbers (clematis) and alpines (saxifrages).

Camley Street Natural Park 9

12 Camley Street, London NW1 0PW. Tel: (020) 7833 2311

London Borough of Camden; managed by London Wildlife Trust • Off Goods Way, near King's Cross railway station • Open all year, Mon – Thurs, 9am –

5pm, Sat and Sun: summer, 11am – 5pm, winter, 10am – 4pm • Entrance: free. Donations welcome ○ 🍴 **WC** ♿ 🎈

An innovative project created in the early 1980s and now a designated Local Nature Reserve (LNR), this is an example of an extremely successful urban wildlife park and garden created against all the odds. Plants, wildlife and people thrive in it. In two and a fifth acres set between the Regent's Canal and imposing black and red gasometers, it has been landscaped with a large pond and includes a visitors' centre with an environmental education classroom. This tranquil space has a fine sighting record of birds and other wildlife. Views of the canal and passing narrow boats are offset somewhat romantically by relics of Victorian industry.

Cannizaro Park 10

West Side Common, Wimbledon, London SW19 4UE. Tel: (020) 8946 7349

London Borough of Merton • West Side Common, Wimbledon • Open all year, daily, Mon – Fri, 8am – sunset, Sat, Sun and Bank Holidays, 9am – sunset • Entrance: free • Other information: Teas on summer Suns only. Top garden possible for wheelchairs ○ **WC** ♿ 🎈

Formerly the grounds of Cannizaro House and approached through imposing gates and a formal drive, lined with beautifully kept seasonal bedding. Cannizaro's trees are its principal attraction: cork oaks, mulberries and sassafras (until a few years ago it had the oldest sassafras in England). Some enormous and beautiful beeches, mature red Japanese maples, magnolias and rhododendrons (flowering May/June) are among the many attractions here. At the southern wooded end of the park, Lady Jane's Wood, the main feature is the magnificent azalea dell. Throughout the long spring-flowering season, the whole wood appears to be in flower; there is floral colour even in the coldest moments. In the midst of the trees a secluded picnic area, set with tables, contains – somewhat unexpectedly – a bust of the Emperor Haile Selassie of Ethiopia, who sought refuge in Wimbledon. There is a small aviary, a pretty walled rose garden, an azalea and rhododendron collection and a heather garden. The old garden, a formal garden and the pool are found down a steep slope directly in front of the house, with a wild garden in the same location. A sculpture exhibition is held in the park in June and an open-air theatre season in July and August. A group of local residents have formed the Friends of Cannizaro Park.

Capel Manor 11

Horticultural and Environmental Centre, Bullsmoor Lane, Enfield, Middlesex EN1 4RQ. Tel: (020) 8366 4442

Capel Manor Charitable Corporation • From M25 junction with A10, via Turkey Street/Bullsmoor Lane. Signposted. Or walk from railway station, which has ½-hourly services to Liverpool St except Sun • Open March to Oct daily, 10am – 5.30pm (last admission 4.30pm), Nov to Feb, Mon – Fri (times vary, so telephone before travelling) • Entrance: £4, OAPs £3.50, children £2. Special prices for Show weekends (1999 prices) • *Other information: Plants for sale at special events* ○ 🍴 🍵 WC ẑ 🛍️ 🏺

These busy gardens of the well-known horticultural college have several functions. They show the history of gardening from the sixteenth century to the present, and also serve as a design centre for the garden industry and as an instructional venue, with a wide variety of plants, combination planting and features such as water, paving and buildings. Although inevitably any sense of unity (such as at nearby Myddelton House – see entry) is lacking, great pleasure can be found in individual features. Allow time to find your favourites in this remarkable variety. Sponsors are found each year for the many small show gardens, such as the Japanese garden and flower arranger's garden. A large area has been established by *Gardening from Which?* which includes demonstration plots, an A-Z of shrubs, a theme garden, and even a selection of garden sheds with a 'best buy'. Also includes a low-allergen garden designed for the National Asthma Campaign by Lucy Huntingdon. Suitable for a family outing, enhanced by a maze and a few rare breeds of farm livestock including some strange pigs and Clydesdale horses.

Chelsea Physic Garden ★ 12

66 Royal Hospital Road, Chelsea, London SW3 4HS. Tel: (020) 7352 5646

Chelsea Physic Garden Company • *Entrance in Swan Walk, off Chelsea Embankment and, for wheelchair users only, in Royal Hospital Road* • *Open April to Oct, Wed, 12 noon – 5pm, Sun, 2 – 6pm; also during Chelsea Flower Show and Chelsea Festival Week, 12 noon – 5pm. There are some Sun openings and sales in winter (telephone for details)* • *Entrance: £4, students, children and unemployed £2* ● 🍵 WC ẑ 🛍️ 🏺

Founded in the seventeenth century to train London's apothecaries in herbal medicine, the Chelsea Physic Garden is still actively involved in research into herbal medicine, as well as playing an important botanical role. Its three and a half acres, tucked between Cheyne Walk and Swan Walk, are well worth visiting, not only for the fascinating range of medicinal plants, but also for the rare and interesting ones, including beautiful trees like the magnificent olive tree (*Olea europaea*). The garden also houses what is believed to be one of the earliest rock gardens in Europe, created with basaltic lava brought back by the botanist Sir Joseph Banks from Iceland in 1772. The main part of the garden is devoted to systematically ordered beds of plants, but there are also displays associated with the plant hunters and botanists who have played their part in the development of the garden, including Banks, Philip Miller, William Hudson and Robert Fortune, as well as an attractive woodland garden and a new Garden of World Medicine showing the use of medicinal plants by tribal peoples. A National Collection of cistus is housed here. You can become a Friend of the Chelsea Physic Garden for £20 *per annum*, entitling you and a guest to free entry on all public open days and to entry at other times during office hours.

Chiswick House ★★ 13

Burlington Lane, Chiswick, London W4 2RP. Tel: (020) 8995 0508

London Borough of Hounslow and English Heritage • 5m W of central London. Entrance on A4 • House open April to Sept, daily, 10am – 6pm (or dusk if earlier), Oct, 10am – 5pm, Nov to March, 10am – 4pm. Closed 24th, 25th Dec • Gardens open all year, daily, 8.30am – dusk • Entrance: garden free (house £3, concessions £2.30, children £1.50) (1999 prices) • Other information: Dogs outside Italian garden only ○ ☕ WC ₰ ♀

Handsome eighteenth-century gardens, stretching over many acres, with lake, statues, monuments and magnificent trees. Created from 1726 and extended by William Kent to complement the Palladian villa built by Lord Burlington in 1729, they are full of splendid vistas, avenues and changes of contour. Marcus Binney says that just as the house is a Veneto villa in miniature, so the grounds were planned as a microcosm of garden art. Drawings of the time show the degree of perfection the English lawn had reached even in the early eighteenth century. The Victorian garden with parterres is now filled with technicolour bedding plants in front of the handsome conservatory (both introduced after Kent's day) and has a large canal-shaped lake with a cascade at its southern end, recently restored, both by Kent who in 1738 designed the cascade to mimic an underground river flowing from a rocky hill. He failed to get the cascade to work but now English Heritage has succeeded, using information from archaeological excavation and from the archives at Chatsworth. English Heritage, in co-operation with the London Borough of Hounslow, plan the complete restoration of the gardens and have applied for Lottery funds. West of the lake, restoration of the Oriental Plane walk is in progress, the aim being to re-create the walk in the manner of the mid-nineteenth century, with holly hedges. There is an outstanding camellia collection, with some of the oldest specimens in England, dating from the early nineteenth century. A new outdoor camellia garden is planned to the south of the Italian garden. Other future plans include further work in Burlington's Orange Tree Garden and in the Northern and Western Wildernesses. Well worth visiting at any time of the year, but particularly in autumn and winter when many other gardens have lost their charm. From about Easter there are two return trips a day by boat from Westminster (for details telephone (020) 7930 4721).

College Garden and Little Cloister 14

Westminster Abbey, London SW1P 3PA. Tel: (020) 7222 5152; Website: http://www.westminster-abbey.org

Dean and Chapter of Westminster • Entrance via Broad Sanctuary (west end of Abbey) then Dean's Yard, Great Cloister and Fountain Court (signposted) • Garden open all year, Tues to Thurs, 10am – 6pm (Oct to March closes 4pm) • Entrance: suggested donation 20p • Other information: Band concerts (free) July and Aug, Thurs, 12.30 – 2pm as advertised ○ ☕ ₰ ♀

The eleventh-century College Garden (a little over one acre) has been under cultivation for more than 900 years, and therefore qualifies as one of the oldest in England. Originally the source for herbs used in the monastic infirmary of the Benedictine Abbey, it is now a private garden for the Abbey staff and members of Westminster School. Landscaping by John Brookes encourages visitors to move towards the south and east, from where some of the best architecture of the Abbey may be viewed. In the south-west corner is a shaded area with a crucifixion group in bronze. Some interesting small gardens with topiary and intensive planting adjoin the buildings to the north of the area. The Little Cloister Garden is a miniature study in green and white, with a fountain and fish pond in the centre. Fine trees throughout and good labelling.

Colville Place   15

London W1.

London Borough of Camden • Between Charlotte Street and Whitfield Street, near Tottenham Court Road • Open all year, daily, 7.30am – dusk • Entrance: free
○ &

Fortunate houses in Colville Place look across a paved path onto what is a cross between a *hortus conclusus* and a small piazza. This imaginative tiny public garden was created on a bomb site. There is a lawn, a pleasing pergola, fruit trees and, slightly tucked away, a children's play area. Planting is bold, simple and pleasing, with lots of lavender. This seems to be London's nearest equivalent to modern garden design in the public arena, and has great charm, even if somewhat neglected in winter. If you are there when it is looking past its best, go round the corner to one of the many galleries for inspiration. A haven from Oxford Street.

Crystal Palace Park   16

Crystal Palace Road, London SE22. Tel: (020) 8313 4407 (Bromley Leisure Services)

London Borough of Bromley • Entrance at junction of Thicket Road and Crystal Palace Road • Open all year, daily, 7.30am – dusk • Entrance: free (charge for farmyard) ○ ☕ WC &

After the success of his Crystal Palace at the Great Exhibition of 1851 Sir Joseph Paxton was asked to re-erect it in Sydenham in what has become known as Crystal Palace Park. He was also responsible for creating the fine gardens which surrounded his 'glass cathedral'. Sadly the Crystal Palace was burnt down in 1936, but the terraces remain and give a true impression of the massive scale of the former building. There are plenty of features remaining from the 200-acre park's glory days, particularly the 29 life-sized statues of pre-historic monsters, the world's first dinosaur theme park. See also the large maze, the farmyard with live animals, the symphony concerts and fireworks. A day out for all the family.

133 Crystal Palace Road   17

London SE22 9ES. Tel: (020) 8693 3710

Sue Hillwood • On Crystal Palace Road near North Cross Road. On bus routes 12, 40, 176 and 185 • Open for NGS 21st May, 6th Aug and by appt • Entrance: £1.50 ◐ ☕

A small secluded garden, only 11 x 5 metres, with confident, exuberant planting. A pergola with its main arches painted in blue and gold adds height for the wisteria, roses and clematis that climb its posts. This is a shade garden, with only the central Victorian brick terrace, stone water feature and pots with blue grass and sedums receiving any sun. Stylish ideas here.

Dolly's Garden 18

43 Layhams Road, West Wickham, Kent BR4 9HD. Tel: (020) 8462 4196

Mrs Dolly Robertson • Layhams Road is off A232 and A2022. Semi-detached house with small sunken garden in front opposite Wickham Court Farm • Open all year by appt only • Entrance: by donation to collecting box ● <u>WC</u> �& ⬥

This is a raised vegetable garden purpose-built for the disabled owner with easy access to wide, terraced walkways. The owner, who maintains the entire 8 by 23 metres herself, is pleased to pass on her experiences as a disabled gardener so that others, even if they are wheelchair gardeners, may share her joy and interest.

Down House 19

Luxted Road, Downe, Kent BR6 7JT. Tel: (01689) 859119

English Heritage* 2m NE of Biggin Hill off A21 • Open April to Sept, Wed – Sun, 10am – 6pm (closing time 5pm Oct, 4pm Nov to March). Open Bank Hols, closed 24th – 26th Dec, New Year's Day and Feb • Entrance: £5.50, OAPs £4.10, children £2.80 (1999 prices). Entry by timed ticket only; pre-book at least one day in advance (Tel: (0870) 603 0145) [NEW] ○ ☕ <u>WC</u> �& 🛍

Charles Darwin and his family lived at Down House for 40 years from 1842, and his daughter claimed, 'Many gardens are more beautiful and varied but few could have greater charm or repose.' Darwin used the garden, woodland and meadows as his 'open-air laboratory' as he formulated the theories which culminated in his ground-breaking work, *On The Origin of Species*. For visitors one of the most famous features of the garden is the 'Sand-walk' or 'thinking path' where Darwin walked every day pondering his ideas. The greenhouse where he studied plant growth and pollination has been restored and now houses orchids and carnivorous plants. The flower garden outside the drawing room, replanted with fritillaries, forget-me-nots and begonias, was used by the family as an extra room. Outside, on the lawn, is a 'wormstone' laid out here by Darwin's son Horace in an experiment to measure soil displacement. The estate is home to 170 species of fungi, including rare grassland species such as wax-caps (hygrocybe).

The Elms 20

13 Wolverton Avenue, Kingston upon Thames, Surrey KT2 7QF. Tel: (020) 8546 7624

Professor and Mrs R. Rawlings • 1m E of Kingston on A308, 100 metres from Norbiton station. Entrance opposite flats in Manorgate Road • Open several dates in March, April and May, 2 – 5pm and for parties of 10 or more by appt • Entrance: £1.50 ◐ ⚘

This is a true collector's garden with some rare and unusual plants, featuring rhododendrons, magnolias, camellias, dwarf conifers and a wide range of evergreen and deciduous shrubs. Small trees, herbaceous ground cover, a two-level pool with geyser and well-planted margins. This very small garden (only 16½ x 7½ metres) even has plums, pears and soft fruit. A roof garden has recently been created (open to private visitors only) which is an object lesson in the possibilities of such gardens.

Elm Tree Cottage   21

85 Croham Road, Croydon CR5 7HJ. Tel: (020) 8681 8622

Michael Wilkinson and Wendy Witherick • Take B275 from Croydon, then turn off A2022 at Selsdon Road. Nearest station: South Croydon • Open several days for NGS, and for private groups (10 people min) and individuals by appt • Entrance: £2 • Other information: Unsuitable for people unsteady on their feet NEW ◐

A cottage garden with an abundance of old roses and unusual plants. Each year brings new interests – look out for tree ferns, badgers' runs and unusually painted pots. Plants and shrubs are cleverly and imaginatively arranged, and there is a pond and a bog garden in pots.

Eltham Palace Gardens   22

Court Road, Eltham, London SE9 9QE. Tel: (020) 8294 2548

English Heritage • Near Eltham High Street. Palace is ½ m from Eltham railway station (Bus 161) or ¾ m from Mottingham railway station (then Bus 126 or 131) • Palace open as garden • Garden open 16th June to 30th Sept, Wed – Fri, Sun, 10am – 5pm; Oct, Wed – Fri, Sun, 10am – 5pm; Nov to March, Wed – Fri, Sun, 10am – 4pm. Telephone (020) 8294 2548 for further information ☕ 🍴 WC ♿

Despite its proximity to Eltham High Street, the approach to Eltham Palace, over the medieval bridge spanning a moat of water lilies and small islands, is a far cry from the bustle. The palace is one of the oustanding Art Deco properties in London, though little is now left of the medieval palace except the hall. The gardens were laid out in 1936 for Stephen and Virginia Courtauld, and a major programme of garden repair and restoration has started in the areas where most of the structures and features of the Courtauld design still remain. The rose garden has been replanted using early hybrid tea and hybrid musk varieties, a permanent planting scheme created in the Triangle Garden, and the cascade in the rock garden revealed. Widely mown paths have been created in the wild meadows and framed views of the palace opened up on the route from the new car park. A Contemporary Heritage Garden in the 100-yard-long South Moat Border and the banks at either end is being re-designed in the spirit of the 1930s' garden by designer Isabelle Van Groeningen.

Fenton House   23

**Hampstead Grove, London NW3 6RT. Tel: (020) 7435 3471;
Fax: (020) 7435 3471**

*The National Trust • In centre of Hampstead in Holly Hill behind Heath Street
• House open (closes ½ hour earlier than garden) • Garden open March, Sat
and Sun, 2 – 5pm; April to 1st Nov, Sat, Sun and Bank Holiday Mons, 11am
– 5pm and Wed – Fri, 2 – 5pm (last admission ½ hour before closing). Parties
at other times by appt • Entrance: house and garden £4.10, family ticket £10.25
• Other information: Toilet facilities if house is also visited* ◑ &*

Handsome seventeenth-century house and walled garden (about one acre).
The formal south garden is seen through an impressive iron gate. The entrance
to the house is via the side door. Directly behind, the walled garden is formal,
with gravel walks and herbaceous borders edged with neatly-clipped box.
Standard hollies are an unusual feature, and here the walls are particularly well
planted; note the interesting collection of *Clematis viticella* varieties. There are
terraces on several levels with yew hedges dividing the areas, which become
less formal further from the house. Herb border. The sunken rose garden has
secluded seating, good vistas and many scented plants, and the far wall hosts a
beautifully trained *Magnolia grandiflora*. Adjacent to the main garden, below
another wall, is an old orchard, carefully cut at three mower heights, and a
small kitchen/cottage garden. The re-instated vine house occupies part of the
herb border at the end of the orchard path. Particularly good views are to be
had from the attic floor of the house. It is remarkable what the Trust has
achieved in the first decade of Fenton House's development, and improvements continue.

The Ferry House   24

**Old Isleworth, Middlesex TW7 6BD. Tel: (020) 8560 6769;
Fax: (020) 8560 0709**

*Lady Caroline Gilmour • 2m W of Kew Bridge, bus 267 from Hammersmith
and Bus 37 from Richmond. Signed from A315/310 at Bush Corner.
Adjacent to Syon Park gates • Open 10th, 11th June, 2 – 6pm for NGS and
for parties by appt • Entrance: £2.50, OAPs £1.50, children 50p, parties £4
per person for charity • Other information: plants for sale sometimes* ◑ ▨
WC & ◁

A three-acre garden of exceptional charm on the bend of the Thames opposite
Richmond Old Deer Park, with Kew to the south-east. A terrace commands a
view of a completely unspoilt stretch of the river, framed in spring by white
cherry. The terrace itself, flanked by pleached lime trees, is planted mainly in
white, with a profusion of plants in urns and tubs and splendid mature climbers
on the old brick walls around the house. The borders are full of old-fashioned
roses and other scented flowers, aromatic herbs and variegated and golden
shrubs. On one side of the house is a large walled area, to which the fine old
trees of nearby Syon Park provide a backdrop. Here there are avenues of
whitebeam, groups of well-chosen trees and shrubs, winding paths with

shaded seats, wildflower areas and, in spring, carpets of bulbs. Fine gazebo, attractive vegetable and fruit cage.

Fulham Palace 25

Bishops Avenue, London SW6 6EA. Tel: (020) 7736 3233

London Borough of Hammersmith and Fulham • Off Fulham Palace Road down Bishop's Avenue • Museum open Wed – Sun and Bank Holiday Mons, 2 – 5pm (Nov to Feb, Thurs – Sun, 1 – 4pm) • Garden open all year, daily except 25th Dec, 1st Jan, 8am – dusk. Tours of Palace and garden every second Sun of the month, 2pm. Other tours by appt • Entrance: free (museum 50p, concessions 25p, children free; tours £2) (1999 prices) • Other information: Plants for sale in nearby nursery. Annual plant sale 7th May, 11am – 4pm. Garden walks run once a season ○ 🖰 ⚒ ⬇ 🍴

The palace, surrounded in its prime by a moat, was the former home of the Bishops of London; in the seventeenth century Bishop Compton used his missionaries to help him establish here a collection of shrubs and trees sent back from America. It is a charming place for a peaceful walk, far superior to many other open spaces in London. The Museum tells the story of the site including its garden history. The east front of the house looks over lawns with enormous cedars and other trees, including an ancient evergreen oak. The ancient holm oak has been nominated as a Great Tree of London, estimated at over 500 years old. Tree maps available. The romantic old walled garden contains a very long (if ruined) vinery built along a curved wall, and an elliptical box-edged herb garden enclosed by a magnificent old wisteria pergola. Another part has order beds as well as an orchard which has recently been replanted using historic varieties of apple, pear and other fruit trees. The small courtyard at the front of the house (part Henry VII, part Victorian) has euphorbias, some climbers and other plants and a fountain. Do not mistake Fulham Palace for Bishop's Park, next to it with a fine riverside walk.

Geffrye Museum Herb Garden 26

Kingsland Road, London E2 8EA. Tel: (020) 7739 9893

Geffrye Museum Trust • 200 metres N of Shoreditch Church • Front garden open all year, daily except 1st Jan, 21st April, 24th to 26th Dec; herb garden open April to Oct, daily except Mon (but open Bank Holiday Mons), 10am – 5pm, Sun, 12 noon – 5pm • Entrance: free • Other information: Guide dogs only ○ ☕ ✕ 🖰 <u>WC</u> ⬇ ⬇ 🍴

For nearly three centuries citizens of Hackney in east London have enjoyed the fine green space around what were the almshouses of the Ironmongers' Company and now is the Geffrye Museum. After a period of fluctuating fortunes the management of the museum (which has a magnificent display of English furniture in period settings) and its grounds were taken over by a charitable trust in 1990. Shortly afterwards garden and art historian Christine Lalumia was appointed as deputy director and set about reviving the garden. Nowadays the planting round the fine front lawn studded with magnificent

London planes is an exercise in flawless taste and conviction. Long beds in front of the Georgian building are planted with Virginia creeper, which is kept clipped at the first-floor level, and a solid stand of hydrangeas. Lateral beds are dominated by formally arranged hostas and red and white pelargoniums. Lalumia's best trick so far has been the creation of an attractive walled herb garden – with fountain – designed by her. The rear gardens have been developed into a series of period 'rooms', based on research into the design and planting of urban middle-class gardens from the seventeenth to the twentieth centuries. These will be complementary to the museum's displays of period rooms.

Golders Hill Park 27

North End Way, Hampstead, London NW3 7HD. Tel: (020) 8455 5183

Corporation of London • From Hampstead, past Jack Straw's Castle on road to Golders Green, opposite Bull and Bush pub. Flower garden is on right of park, past café • Greenhouse open weekends, 2 – 4pm • Park open all year, daily, 7.30am – dusk • Entrance: free • Other information: Refreshments, at North End Way entrance, from March to Oct only. Brass band/jazz concerts in June and July, Suns, pm. Children's shows in Aug, Tue, Wed, Thurs, 3 – 4pm ○ 🏠 **WC** ♿ ⬇ 🐾 ☕

The manicured 36-acre park was created in 1899 in the grounds of a manor house (bombed in World War II). The two-acre flower garden on the north side is claimed to be as good as you will see anywhere in London, with a mixture of perennial and bedding plants. With its neat, brilliantly coloured displays of flowers, it has an almost Victorian feel. The colour schemes and designs are different and exciting, though some feel they err on the vulgar side. On a less strident note is the canal feature, planted with water-loving and woodland plants, leading down to the ornamental pool with its ducks. A water garden is being developed with a spring theme, featuring rhododendrons, azaleas and primulas. Plenty of seats at strategic points ensure that the garden is much used by elderly local residents. The park itself has a large menagerie with deer, goats, wallabies, blackbuck and many birds.

Greenwich Park 28

Greenwich, London SE10. Tel: (020) 8858 2608

Royal Parks • Entrances in Greenwich (Romney Road) and in Blackheath (Charlton Way). Good service to Greenwich by river; telephone (020) 7376 3676 or (020) 8305 0300 for winter timetables • Park open all year, daily, dawn – dusk • Entrance: free • Other information: Parking easier at Blackheath entrance. Possible for wheelchairs but steep in places. Observatory and Maritime Museum, Greenwich Theatre and Ranger's House. Ships at Greenwich pier. Thames Barrier Visitors' Centre ○ 🍽 ✕ 🏠 **WC** ♿ ☕

Situated on a hilltop overlooking London, Greenwich is the oldest enclosed royal park. Covering 183 acres, it is associated with a pageant of kings and queens and provides a setting for several historic buildings, including the Old

Royal Observatory, recently restored. The park was particularly popular with Henry VIII and his daughter Elizabeth I, who, legend has it, took refreshment within the hollow oak that bears her name. Probably open to the public from George IV's reign, it continues to be popular with the local community and tourists, as does the flower garden, with its brilliant displays of summer colour. Sunday afternoon band performances and entertainments for children. Boating pool (summer only) and large playground.

4 The Grove ★ 29

Highgate Village, London N6 6JU.

Mr Cob Stenham • In Highgate Village, off Hampstead Lane • Open one Sun in June, 2 – 5pm • Entrance: £1. Other information: Teas may be available at 5 The Grove on open day ● ♨

The seventeenth-century house sits behind a dignified front courtyard, beautifully paved with brick and surrounded by lush plantings of evergreens such as skimmias and ivy grown along the railings, with spring-flowering magnolias in the borders. A side passage brings the visitor through to an outstanding vista: the terrace, with a formal pool surrounded by dramatic planting, is the foreground to an immaculate lawn with well-planted mixed borders. Beyond this is an extensive backdrop to the wooded slopes of Hampstead Heath. An arbour of silver pears overlooks this stunning view, and a ceanothus arch leads one down, through a tunnel of *Vitis coignetiae*, to the lower garden. This comprises an orchard with an old mulberry tree and some good statuary. One yew hedge conceals the well-ordered compost/bonfire area, and another balances this to enclose a secret garden dominated by a *Cladrastis lutea*. *Rosa laevigata* 'Cooperi' flourishes on the south wall of the house, and the whole garden, which is beautifully designed and maintained, has exceptional charm. Two other gardens, *No 5* and *No 7* (see below) The Grove, are usually also open on the same charity day in June.

7 The Grove ★ 30

Highgate Village, London N6 6JU. Tel: (020) 8340 7205

Thomas G. Lyttelton • In Highgate Village, off Hampstead Lane • Open 2nd April, 11th June, 24th Sept, 2 – 6pm • Entrance: £1.50, OAPs and children £1 (£3, OAPs and children £2 for all three gardens) • Other information: Teas available at 5 The Grove ● 🖼 &

A half-acre London walled town garden behind a handsome Victorian house c.1830, splendidly designed by the owner for low maintenance, but with lots of interest. Tunnels, arbours, screens abound, providing inspiration for busy garden-owners who would still like to have an interest outside the house. A series of nineteenth-century brick-built arches across the width of the garden separates it into two compartments. The area near the house is formal with a lawn, the area beyond the screen much less so, with fine compartments and features. Secret paths and unexpected views make this a magical place for children. Much use is made of evergreens and there are some exquisite shrubs, including a row of camellias down one wall and a massive *Hydrangea petiolaris* with a trunk as thick as a boxer's biceps. There are many species and varieties of a particular genus – five varieties of box and even more of ivies, for example. The owner describes it as a gold, green, yellow and red garden. The canal feature was restructured and enhanced into a water garden in autumn 1996. Two other gardens, No 4 (see above) and *No 5 The Grove*, are usually also open on the charity day in June.

Gunnersbury Park   31

London W3. Tel: (020) 8993 2055

London Borough of Ealing and Hounslow • ½ m N of Chiswick roundabout turn left off A406. Entrance in Popes Lane • Open all year, daily, 7.30am – dusk • Entrance: free • Other information: Gunnersbury Park Museum open afternoons. Tel: (020) 8992 1612. No coaches ○ 🍽 ✕ 🏛 **WC** 🚽 ⟁ 🍴

Little remains of the grandiose gardens of the Rothschild days except the rose gardens in the traditional clock pattern, with a background of parkland. Alas, the formal beds have been grassed over and planted with shrubs. Beyond the trees the sports grounds, golf course and tennis courts are hidden from view from the terrace, where it is difficult to realise one is only a few miles from Marble Arch. Thanks to the Lottery, considerable restoration is afoot. Following surveys, a programme of urgent remedial repairs, including tree work, was agreed for the park. Amongst the gardeners who have toiled here were William Kent and J.C. Loudon. For children, there is a boating pool and two play areas.

Hall Grange   32

Shirley Church Road, Croydon, Surrey CR9 5AL. Tel: (020) 8777 3389

Methodist Homes • In Shirley Church Road, near junction with Upper Shirley Road • Open 21st May, 2 – 5pm (last admission 4.30pm) • Entrance: £1.50, children free ● 🍽 **WC**

The garden at Hall Grange, originally called the Wilderness, was created by the Reverend William Wilkes, breeder of the Shirley poppy and secretary of the Royal Horticultural Society from 1888 to 1920. He acquired seven acres of Shirley Common in 1910 to build his retirement home, and planted the garden with informal groups of trees, shrubs, rhododendrons and tree heathers in the existing turf, adding British wild plants. To botanists the most interesting area is the sphagnum bog which the London Ecology Unit has designated a Site of Metropolitan Importance. There are 126 species of wild flowers and native shrubs and trees in the garden and 22 mosses, including four types of sphagnum.

Hall Place   33

Bourne Road, Bexley, Kent DA5 1PQ. Tel: (01322) 526574

Bexley Council • Just N of A2 near A2/A223 junction • House open summer: Mon – Sat, 10am – 5pm, Sun, 2 – 6pm; winter: Mon – Sat, 10am – 4.15pm • Garden open all year, daily, Mon – Fri, 7.30am – dusk, weekends and Bank

Holidays, 9am – dusk. Model allotment, parts of nursery and glasshouses open all year, daily except 25th Dec, Mon – Fri, 9am – 6pm (4pm in winter) • *Entrance: free* ○ 💭 ✕ 🖥 <u>WC</u> ⑃ ♨ 🎋 ♀

Surrounding a splendid Jacobean mansion, this is arguably the most interesting and best-kept public garden in south-east London. Although there is a strong emphasis on municipal annual bedding plants like ageratum, *Senecio* x *hybrida* and African marigolds to provide summer colour, they are used with great restraint and good taste, as are the roses in the large classical rose garden. So, too, are the herbaceous plants in two splendid borders separated by a turf *allée* and backed by a characterful old brick wall on one side and a tightly clipped yew hedge on the other. Features include a raised walk overlooking one of Britain's finest topiary gardens, several rich shrubberies, a large and beautifully designed patterned herb garden, a rock garden, meandering stretches of the River Cray, a heather garden and acres of lawn studded with an interesting mixture of evergreen and deciduous trees to provide vistas.

Ham House ★   34

Ham Street, Richmond, Surrey TW10 7RS. Tel: (020) 8940 1950

The National Trust • *On S bank of Thames, W of A307 at Petersham* • *House open probably 25th March to Oct, Sat – Wed, 1 – 5pm* • *Garden open all year, Sat – Wed, 10.30am – 6pm (or dusk if earlier)* • *Entrance: £1.50 (house £5, children £2.50, family £12.50)* • *Other information: Parking 400 metres by river, disabled on terrace. Refreshments March to Oct, and weekends only in Nov, Dec and March* ○ 💭 ✕ 🖥 <u>WC</u> ⑃ ♨ 🎋 ♀

Seventeenth-century formality predominates in the gardens at Ham House. The Trust is now launching a fundraising appeal and embarking on a comprehensive restoration of part of the garden. In the south garden, below a wide gravel terrace, are eight square lawns divided by paths. The strong architectural nature of the wilderness, gravel terraces and parterres of box, lavender and cotton lavender, as well as replicas of seventeenth-century garden furniture, add to the charm of the restoration. The border has now been replanted in formal seventeenth-century style with clipped yew cones, standard hibiscus and pomegranate trees. Pots and tubs copied from seventeenth-century originals decorate the terrace and the grass plats. A cut-flower border of period plants has been established. The orangery is late seventeenth-century, the earliest surviving example of its type in the country, and in front of it is a wide lawn with rose beds and a peony border. During the summer months, orange trees in period-style boxes are displayed on the orangery terrace. The garden is well maintained – for example the Cherry Garden has been replanted with 1000 lavender and santolinas and now displays one of the garden's original seventeenth-century marble statues. A useful guidebook, although mostly about the house, gives details of the garden's history. Marble Hill (see entry) is across the river and can be reached by ferry.

Hampton Court Palace ★★   35

East Molesey, Surrey KT8 9AU. Tel: (020) 8781 9500

Historic Royal Palaces Trust • On A308 at junction of A309 on N side of Hampton Court bridge over Thames • Palace open (admission charge) • Gardens open all year, daily, dawn – dusk • Entrance: Rose Gardens, Wilderness and East Front Gardens: free; Maze £2.30, children £1.50; King William III Privy Garden, Sunken Garden and Great Vine £2.10, children £1.30 (free to Palace ticket-holders). Afternoon garden tours, including entrance to King William III Privy Garden, daily from April to Oct, £5 (£3 to Palace ticket-holders); special pre-booked morning tours can also be arranged. ○ 🍴 ✕ 🛍 **WC** ♿ ⬇ 🛒 ♻

Hampton Court Palace is worth a visit to study the activities of British monarchs from Henry VIII onwards, and the gardens, which provide the setting for the palace, are an exciting and eclectic mixture of styles and tastes, with many different character areas of interest. Most famous for its Great Vine, planted in 1768 (probably the oldest in the world), which still produces hundreds of 'Black Hamburg' grapes each year (for sale to the public when harvested in September), and its maze, the oldest hedge-planted maze in Britain, originally planted in 1691. The Pond Gardens offer a magnificent display of bedding plants, and there is a 1924 knot garden with interlocking bands of dwarf box, thyme, lavender and cotton lavender infilled with bedding plants. On a truly grand scale, the great Fountain Garden, an immense semi-circle of grass and flower beds with a central fountain, is probably the most impressive element, but the Wilderness Garden in spring, with its mass of daffodils and spring-flowering trees – principally cherry and crab apple – has the most charm. The laburnum walk – a tunnel of trained trees with butter-coloured rivulets of flowers in May – off the Wilderness Garden is another great attraction. The former kitchen garden now houses a rose garden. The newly restored Privy Garden of William III is a spectacular example of the Baroque, with parterres, cutwork, clipped yews and spring and summer displays of seventeenth-century plants. It now forms a magnificent setting for Sir Christopher Wren's south front of the palace and the elaborate gilded ironwork railings by Jean Tijou. Though this restoration has been much praised, it probably does not compare favourably with the design and main-tenance of its model, Paleis Het Loo, in the Netherlands. An area of the gardens sometimes missed by visitors is the secluded twentieth-century garden, an area developed originally for the training of apprentices, but now also open to all. It is located just over the canal next to the Fountain Garden (signposted) and is open daily, 7am to dusk or 9pm whichever is earlier. Too much to see in one day – plan at least two trips; one in spring and one in summer to walk in only part of the 66 acres of gardens and the informal deer park 10 times that size. By-the-by, try taking the boat from Westminster pier down to Hampton Court – the most charming approach to the garden. The Park is also the venue for the annual Hampton Court Palace International Flower Show in July, which has established itself alongside Chelsea as a major horticultural event.

37 Heath Drive 36

London NW3 7SD. Tel: (020) 7435 2419

*Mr C. Caplin • Off Finchley Road • Open 14th May, 16th July, 2.30 – 6pm •
Entrance: £2, children 50p* ● ☕ ♿ ♻

Large square garden (about one-fifth of an acre) with a vast number of plants
packed into it. There is an attractive pergola walk and unusual and interesting
plants. Lots of abutilons, tree peonies, rhododendrons, palms (trachycarpus),
broom trees, large and black bamboos, a tamarisk tree, figs and a mulberry tree.
Other features of the garden include pools and rockeries, a fruit tree pergola
(apples, pears and plums), raised beds and a greenhouse and conservatory for
exotics. The garden has an effective compost heap hidden behind a hedge of
delightful cut-leaved alder. In the front garden there is a highly scented
stauntonia flowering in spring, and a very large *Pieris formosa forrestii*. The Caplins
have won the Frankland Moore Trophy (for gardens with help) eight times.

Highwood Ash 37

Highwood Hill, Mill Hill, London NW7 4EX. Tel (020) 8959 1183

*Mr and Mrs Roy Gluckstein • From central London via A41 (Watford Way) to
Mill Hill Circus, turn right up Lawrence Street, bear left at top up Highwood
Hill. House is at top on right • Open 13th, 14th, May, 2 – 6pm, and by appt
May to Sept for charity • Entrance: £1.50, children 50p • Other information:
Refreshments on 13th, 14th May only* ● ◁▷

This is a surprising country-sized garden in north London – some three and a
half acres in all. The house (not open) dates from the sixteenth to eighteenth
centuries, during which time it was home to, amongst others, the noted
traveller Celia Fiennes (d. 1741). The garden, however, is the result of the
careful attention of the owners over the past four decades. A spacious lawn
takes the eye to boundaries of mature trees with a brick wall on one side
fronted by a broad mixed border. On the opposite side are headlands of
juniper planned by the late Percy Cane, who assisted Mrs Gluckstein with the
design in its early phases. His main feature was a formal rose garden. Another
noted designer, John Brookes, assisted with the late 1980s' water features in
the lower garden. Two large pools have imaginative planting at their edges,
with an old mulberry over one bank and ornamental trees elsewhere. Behind a
copper beech are white-barked birches, *Betula jacquemontii*, partially shielding
the 'secret garden' with its spring bulbs. Other surprises include a new terrace
with a raised herb bed and a covered arbour leading to the swimming pool.
Rhododendrons and azaleas in spring.

The Hill Garden 38

Inverforth Close, North End Way, London NW3 7EX. Tel: (020) 8455 5183

*Corporation of London • From Hampstead past Jack Straw's Castle on road to
Golders Green, on left hand side. Inverforth Close is off North End Way (A502)
• Open all year, daily, 9am – dusk • Entrance: free* ○ ♿

Overgrown in parts, the chief charm here lies in the secluded setting. A major restoration project is underway at the pergola, built between 1906 and 1925 to a design by Thomas H. Mawson to screen Lord Leverhulme's house, The Hill (now known as Inverforth House), from its kitchen gardens and to shield it from people walking on the Heath. It is one of the best examples of a pergola fully restored with all its columns and timber features intact. Planting of the pergola walk is complete and is open to the public at the same times as The Hill Garden. The former kitchen garden, now laid out and planted, is also open. Wonderful views across the Heath from many points in the garden. Large formal lily pond, herbaceous borders, undulating lawns, many shrubs and trees.

Holland Park   39

Kensington, London W8/W11. Tel: (020) 7471 9813

Royal Borough of Kensington and Chelsea • Between Kensington High Street and Holland Park Avenue, with several entrances • Parking (pay and display) from Abbotsbury Road entrance • Open all year, daily, 7.30am – dusk • Entrance: free • Other information: Dogs in some areas only, on lead ○ 🍵 ✕ 🏠 WC ♿ ♻

Most of the famous Holland House was destroyed by bombs in World War II, but the formal gardens, created in 1812 by Lord Holland, have been maintained. The 53-acre park contains some rare trees such as Pyrenean oak, Chinese sweet gum, Himalayan birch, violet willow and the snowdrop tree, which flowers in May. The rose walk has now been replanted with a variety of azaleas. There is a small iris garden round a fountain. Peacocks strut the lawns and drape the walls with their tail feathers, and in the woodland section birds and squirrels find sanctuary from London's noise and traffic. Excellent children's play areas. In 1991 the charming and beautifully maintained one-acre Kyoto Garden was opened as a permanent souvenir of the Japanese Festival. One of the most pleasant small London parks, although paths and grass can look worn and tired after the busy summer period.

The Holme   40

Inner Circle, Regent's Park, London NW1 4NT.

Crown Estate Commissioners • In Regent's Park, just W of Inner Circle • Open several days for NGS • Entrance: £2.50, children £1 • Other information: Metered parking in Outer Circle. Refreshments and toilet facilities in café opposite ◑ ♿

A garden designed to enhance the setting of one of the best-positioned houses (by Decimus Burton) in central London, overlooking Heron Island in Regent's Park Lake. Wisely, the waterfowl are excluded. A gravel path leads down through a well-maintained shrubbery towards sweeping lawns and herbaceous beds at the back of the house. Mature trees. A spectacular rock garden with grotto, bridge and waterfall are not to be missed. Find time to sit at some of the many vantage points to admire the good planting schemes and outstanding views.

Horniman Gardens 41

Hornimans Drive, London SE23 3BT. Tel: (020) 8699 8924

Horniman Museum • On South Circular at Lordship Lane/London Road junction • Open all year, daily except 25th Dec, Mon – Sat, 7.15am – dusk, Sun, 8am – dusk • Entrance: free • Other information: Horticultural demonstrations March to Sept, first Wed in the month at 2.30pm ○ 🍵 📷 WC 🔦

This charming, rather old-fashioned park has a fine setting, with extensive views over the North Downs, St Paul's and west London, and its attractions include formal bedding, a rose pergola, a bandstand – with a band on summer Sunday afternoons and children's entertainment in August – and a steep hill garden with rocks, stream, conifers, etc. The large and impressive Victorian conservatory was rebuilt recently behind the Horniman Museum, which does not contain any plants in winter but is used for functions from time to time and for the concert series held in spring and autumn. At the end of June, the annual international Horniman Music Festival runs for a week. There are two nature trails, one in the gardens and one along a stretch of disused railway line with a pond and wildflower meadow, also an animal enclosure and a new natural history building, the Centre for Understanding the Environment (CUE). Not far away is Dulwich Art Gallery (not to be missed).

Hyde Park 42

London SW1 1NR. Tel: (020) 7298 2000

Royal Parks • Hyde Park Rose Garden • Open all year, daily, dawn – midnight • Entrance: free • Other information: Dogs in general parkland areas only ○ 🍵 ✕ 📷 WC ♿ 🔦

The final phase of construction of the new rose garden involved the completion of a footpath layout threading through beds which have been planted with many varieties of roses and herbaceous plants. A pergola has been constructed on the southern border of the site and will be covered with climbing roses and clematis. As with all rose gardens, its season is short – arguably too short to be occupying such a prominent position in such an important park. The whole area is enclosed to keep out dogs and cyclists. New shrub beds have been planted to provide shelter along the northern edge and to screen the toilet block. The Diana Fountain has been refurbished and is relocated in a more accessible site within the garden. North-west of the rose garden, in the centre of Hyde Park, is a large enclosure called The Ring. This was the focus of fashionable London life in the seventeenth century, the first ornamental feature of the park, indicating a move from a military and hunting role to that of a public pleasure ground. The re-creation of the original line of The Ring was undertaken in 1986 with the planting of limes. The Royal Parks in general have for some years been subject of concern. *The Royal Parks Review – Final Conclusions* states: 'In terms of overall public expenditure the needs of the Royal Parks are infinitesimal. But if savings continue to be made the task of covering up cash shortages will soon prove impossible. Recent improvements will be overtaken by decay. The Department for Culture, Media and Sport must stand fast.' At the time of going to press, plans are afoot to create a new National Parks Agency to include the Royal Parks. Proper funding will be the test of true governmental resolve.

Isabella Plantation ★ 43

Richmond Park, Richmond, Surrey. Tel: (020) 8948 3209

Royal Parks • Richmond Park, Broomfield Hill • Open all year, daily, dawn – dusk • Entrance: free • Other information: Parking in Broomfield Hill car park, Pembroke Lodge, Roehampton Gate, disabled at north entrance by way of Ham Gate. Refreshments at Pembroke Lodge. Toilet facilities in summer only. Motorised wheelchair available weekdays. Telephone to book by 12 noon previous day ○ ♿ ⬦

The remarkably rich wooded plantation features many fine indigenous forest trees – oaks, beeches and birches – as well as more exotic specimens like magnolias, camellias, witch hazels and styrax trees. The principal glory is the collection of rhododendrons and azaleas, the earliest rhododendron 'Christmas Cheer' blossoming in the New Year, but the garden is at its best from April until June, when the dwarf azaleas and the waterside primulas around the pond are also in flower. The garden is a notable bird sanctuary – nuthatches, tree-creepers, kingfishers, woodpeckers and owls have all been spotted, and herons fish regularly in the ponds. The Waterhouse Plantation (see entry) in neighbouring Bushy Park is also very fine.

26 Kenilworth Road 44

Penge SE20 7QG. Tel: (020) 8402 9035

Mr and Mrs S. Clutson • Off A234 Beckham Road; 10-min walk from Kent House station • Open by appt only • Entrance: £1 [NEW] ●

This garden (10 x 6 metres) is a must for anyone with young children and little space. Created by a designer and especially for children, it has a Mediterranean theme, with paved patio, pots and interesting borders. A well-pruned *Buddleia alternifolia* is the central focus; cardoons and alliums stand tall above woodruff.

Kensington Gardens 45

London W2 4RU. Tel: (020) 7298 2000

Royal Parks • Entrances off Bayswater Road, Kensington Gore and West Carriage Drive, Hyde Park • Palace State Apartments open May to Sept, daily, 9am – 5pm. £9.50, OAPs/students £7.70, children £7.10, family £29.10. Outdoor sculpture sometimes on display at Serpentine Art Gallery open weekdays, 10am – 6pm (dusk in winter). Orangery open daily. For information telephone (020) 7937 9561 • Gardens open all year, daily, 6am – closing times displayed at gate • Entrance: free ○ 🍴 🏪 WC ♿ ⬦ ♟

These 274 acres of finest park, adjoining Hyde Park, have their own pleasures, including sculpture by Henry Moore and G.F. Watts and, for children and older enthusiasts, the Peter Pan statue. The Albert Memorial, now officially reopened, is a treat. The elegant Baroque orangery by Hawksmoor and Vanbrugh, with decoration by Grinling Gibbons, is well worth a visit. So, too, is the sunken water garden surrounded by beds of bright seasonal flowers, which can be viewed from 'windows' in a beech walk. From the Broad Walk south to the Albert Memorial, semi-circular flower beds are kept planted against a background of flowering shrubs. Recently installed at the Serpentine Gallery are some fine works by one of the nation's greatest gardeners, Ian Hamilton Finlay, in his classic style.

Kenwood 46

Hampstead Lane, London NW3 7JR. Tel: (020) 8348 1286

English Heritage • N side of Hampstead Heath, on Highgate – Hampstead road • House open April to Oct, 10am – 6pm (5pm in Oct); Nov to March, 10am – 4pm. Closed 1st Jan, 24th, 25th Dec • Park open all year, daily, summer: 8am – 8.30pm, winter: 8am – 4.30pm • Entrance: free • Other information: Parking at West Lodge car park, Hampstead Lane ○ ☕ WC ᴖ ⟁ ▯

A picturesque landscape laid out by Humphry Repton at the end of the eighteenth century. Vistas, sweeping lawns from the terrace of Kenwood House and views over Hampstead Heath (and London) predominate. Magnificent mature trees, mainly oak and beech. There is also some worthwhile modern sculpture, including a Henry Moore and a 1953 Barbara Hepworth. The pasture ground slopes down towards two large lakes known as the Wood Pond (the largest) and the Thousand Pound Pond (where open-air concerts are held in summer). Woods to the south of the lakes fringe the heath side of the pasture ground, with several gates onto the heath itself. A good place to walk at any season, but particularly when the trees are turning in autumn, to recall that the lime walk was a favourite of that great gardener of the eighteenth century, Alexander Pope. Look out also for the ivy arch which opens out on to the lakes, one of Repton's famous 'surprises'; walks which follow Repton's originals; haymeadows on the western side which change colour from May to July; kitchen garden with walls once heated. The sham bridge on the Thousand Pound Pond, site of the concert stage, has been faithfully rebuilt with its single upside-down baluster, and natural regeneration of the ancient woodlands is being encouraged.

38 Killieser Avenue 47

Streatham, London SW2 4NT. Tel: (020) 8671 4196

Mrs Winkle Haworth • Off Streatham High Street, turn into Telford Avenue, then take second turning. Streatham station is nearby • Open to groups of 5 or more by appt • Entrance: £1.50 NEW ● ᴖ ৶

This much visited South London garden is immaculately kept and full of carefully chosen plants and shrubs. The skilful planting of a variety of roses, perennials and annuals all blend harmoniously – creamy nasturtiums beneath phormiums, old-fashioned roses, clematis and *Viola cornuta*. An obelisk, a Gothic arbour and a water feature give architectural interest, and pots of agapanthus by a delightful arbour introduce visitors to a second level with a parterre and wall fountain.

London Zoo   48

Regent's Park, London NW1 4RY. Tel: (020) 7722 3333

London Zoo • In Regent's Park to N of Outer Circle. Take Bus 274 from Camden/Baker Street to Prince Albert Road and walk across bridge to main gate; tube to Camden Town/Baker Street; waterbus from Camden Lock or Little Venice • Open all year, daily except 25th Dec, 10am – 5.30pm (4pm in winter) • Entrance: £9, OAPs and students £8, children (4-14) £6, under 4 free. Saver tickets available • Other information: Car park at zoo or metered parking in Outer Circle. Wheelchairs and buggies available from information kiosk at main gate ○ ☕ ✕ 🍽 WC ♿ 🛍 ♨

Hear the dramatic cries of the macaws in the distance as you enter the main gate and notice the mixed carex planted in front of their enclosure. All the enclosures are designed to provide the conditions which the animals need. The keepers choose the most appropriate materials (willows, bamboos, etc., all grown on site) for each species: sand or earth for burrowing animals, hard surfaces for hoofed animals, branches and perches for arboreal species. Note the tree of heaven (1870) with the listed Penguin Pool built around it, and the old black mulberry (wrongly labelled 'white' a century ago), whose leaves are fed to silk worms. Find time to walk over the timber bridge below the 'stream' of blue slate in the Thames Water Water-wise Garden. Bright seasonal bedding and hanging baskets are planned to complement the zoological role. As part of the '*Web of Life*' exhibition, housed within the Millennium conservation centre, a new native wildlife garden has been created. This includes enclosures for field crickets and great crested newts as well as habitats such as meadows, woodland and hedgerow along with ideas for a domestic garden including a rockery and a herb garden, showing ways that birds, butterflies and animals can be attracted to a city garden.

8 Lower Merton Rise   49

London NW3 3SP. Tel: (020) 7722 5107

Mr and Mrs Peter Gravett • Close to Swiss Cottage tube station • Open by appt • Entrance: charge ☕

Inspired by oriental gardens and Chinese pottery, this meticulously kept small area reflects calm and space. It is on two levels with a pond and a bamboo water-drip. A stylish bamboo fence and red corner pergola catch the eye when entering the garden and a *Tai-chi* area of wooden decking, large mirror and green planting complete this thoughtful part of the L-shaped space. The colour theme of turquoise and blue continues in the collection of well-placed pots and urns to give balance between design and planting, cleverly uniting the garden with the house.

4 Macaulay Road   50

Clapham, London SW4 0QX. Tel: (020) 7627 1137

Mrs Diana Ross • Off Clapham Common Northside • Open by appt. Parties of 8 or more welcome • Entrance: £2.50 per person [NEW] ● ℘

A walled garden (24 x 15 metres) set out in strong, clear lines with formality heightened by box hedges, topiary and lots of pots. Two circular lawns are surrounded by dense mixed planting, arches and a pergola. There is a grotto with a fernery around it and many exotic shrubs and herbaceous plants chosen for their strong foliage. The garden has been designed to look as good in winter as in summer; with a large range of plants, many grey or variegated, the overall effect is of profusion and soft colours.

Marble Hill   51

Richmond Road, Twickenham, Middlesex TW1 2NL. Tel: (020) 8892 5115

English Heritage • S of Richmond Bridge off Richmond Road. Additional access by river launch • House open April to Sept, daily, 10am – 6pm; Oct, daily, 10am – 5pm; Nov to March, Wed – Sun, 10am – 4pm. Closed 1st to 18th Jan, 24th to 26th Dec • Park open all year, daily, 7.30am – dusk • Entrance: £3, concessions £2.30, children £1.50 (1999 prices) ○

English Heritage is still in the process of reviving these gardens, originally laid out for the Countess of Suffolk in the 1740s. Alexander Pope, a neighbour of the Countess, took an interest in the layout and recent excavations have revealed one of the two grottos known to have been constructed. Traces of pebble and flint patterns exist, though hard to see; the main objective of the grotto would have been the view of Richmond Hill, now obscured by an over-mature landscape There is an ice-house and a young 'Sweet Walk'. The gardens (if they can be called that, as now they are largely sports pitches and a venue for summer music concerts) lay claim to the largest and probably the oldest black walnut in the country and also the tallest bay willow and Italian alder trees. Take the ferry to Ham House (see entry) over the river. You can also visit Strawberry Hill (station of the name nearby) where Horace Walpole's 'little Gothick castle' can be seen on a tour from Easter to Oct on Sunday afternoons (parties by appointment, Tel: (020) 8892 0051).

Mile End Park   52

Mile End Road, London E3.

Beside Regent's Canal on either side of Mile End Road/Bow Road, W of Grove Road • Open all year, daily • Entrance: free ○ 🍵 ♿

This 90-acre 'lung' created in 1947 to give breathing space to half a million residents of the East End is marred through being divided by the five-lane busy Mile End Road. However, Tower Hamlets Council has commissioned architect Piers Gough to build a steel green bridge (to unite the north and south parts) surrounded by earth and trees with shops and cafés below. A man-made mountain will offer views of Limehouse. Cost £24 million, target for completion the millennium.

Morden Hall Park 53

Morden Hall Road, Morden, Surrey SM4 5JD. Tel: (020) 8648 1845; Fax: (020) 8687 0094

The National Trust • S of Wimbledon, N of Sutton, off A24 and A297. ½ m from Morden Road station and Morden tube station and on tramlink Phipps Bridge and various bus routes • Open all year, daily, except 25th, 26th Dec, 1st Jan, 9am – 5pm. Guided tours by arrangement • Entrance: free • Other information: Wheelchairs available ○ 🍵 ✕ 🏠 WC ᕿ ⬗ 🌿 ♿ ⌖

In the heart of London suburbia, the former deer park of Morden Hall Park is a green oasis with a newly restored rose garden coming along. The ancient hay meadows, waterways and an impressive collection of stables, mills and cottages make this a welcoming place to visit. An independently managed garden centre, a city farm [open daily except Mon, but open Bank Holiday Mons, 9am – 5.30pm] and craft workshops [closed Tues] are all in the vicinity.

Museum of Garden History 54

Lambeth Palace Road, London SE1 7LB. Tel: (020) 7261 1891; Fax: (020) 7401 8869

The Tradescant Trust • Lambeth Palace Road, parallel to River Thames on S bank, hard by Lambeth Bridge • Open 5th March to 10th Dec, daily except Sat, 10.30am – 4pm (Sun 5pm) • Entrance: free, donations requested • Other information: Antique collection of garden tools and artefacts which include Gertrude Jekyll's desks and other memorabilia. Courses, exhibitions, lectures, plant fairs and concerts ◑ 🍵 ✕ WC ᕿ ⬗ 🌿 ⌖

The garden in the churchyard was created in 1981. It commemorates the two John Tradescants (father and son), gardeners to Charles I and II, who are buried in a fine tomb in the replica seventeenth-century garden. The garden contains examples of plants brought back by the Tradescants from their plant-hunting travels in Europe and America in the seventeenth century. Lady Salisbury's knot garden design incorporates some of the Tradescants' imported plants which are now thought of as indigenous to this country. Well-labelled herbs abound amongst pretty perennials, making a delightful backcloth for the table tombs, whilst the walls are clothed in Virginia creeper, ivy, roses and clematis. Although small, the garden has a few well-placed benches. A planting plan of the knot is available in the shop, and some of the plants featured are on sale. Nearby the large garden of *Lambeth Palace* is open one or two days in summer for NGS. Because it is so very big it needs big vision and extensive maintenance. Is it a park or a garden? Does it need Royal Parks' support, or a simpler plan? Beth Chatto planted the herbaceous bed 15 years ago; her area is good but the outer regions beyond are a muddle of obscurity. She should be persuaded to return and complete her vision.

Museum of London Nursery Garden   55

**The Museum of London, London Wall, London EC2Y 5HN.
Tel: (020) 7600 3699; Fax: (020) 7600 1058**

*Museum of London • Underground: St Paul's or Barbican, then follow signs •
Garden open 30th March to Oct, Mon – Sat, 10am – 5.50pm, Sun, 12 noon –
5.50pm (last admission 5.30pm) • Entrance: £5 (annual ticket), concessions £2
(museum) • Other information: Possible for wheelchairs but shallow steps make
assistance necessary* ◗ 🍽 ✕ 🖺 WC 🦽 🐾

Garden designers Colson and Stone totally revamped the internal courtyard in
1990 to coincide with the exhibition of London's gardens. The team transformed an almost lifeless area into a living history of plantsmanship in the City
from medieval times to the present day. Legendary names like Henry Russell,
who sold striped roses in Westminster, and James Veitch, who sold exotica like
the monkey puzzle tree from his nursery in Chelsea, are represented. This tiny
roof garden is flanked on four sides by high buildings yet the designers have
still managed to incorporate a tumbling rill and a rock garden.

Myddelton House Gardens ★   56

Bulls Cross, Enfield, Middlesex EN2 9HG. Tel: (01992) 717711

*Lea Valley Regional Park Authority • S of M25 on A10 (junction 25), first right
on to Bulls Moor Lane, left into Bulls Cross and Myddelton House is on right at
junction with Turkey Street • Open all year, Mon – Fri, 10am – 4.30pm; also
23rd April to Oct, Sun, Bank Holiday Mons and NGS open days, 2 – 5pm •
Entrance: £1.90, concessions £1.30 •* ○ 🍽 WC 🦽 🐾

A magnificent, diverse plant collection set in four acres was built up by the
famous E.A. Bowles and is now restored. Splendid spring bulbs, followed by
iris, followed by autumn crocus and impressive varieties of autumn-remontant
iris make this garden a joy all year round. Zephyranthes and nerines are but a
few of the autumn bulbs and there is a fine *Crinum moorei* near the conservatory.
This is by no means a municipal garden, and the impressive plant collection is
displayed attractively in a well-designed garden surrounding the Regency
house of mellow golden brick. The garden is still unified by Bowles's plants and
vision and it is worth reading details of his plan, which included a Lunatic
Asylum planted with botanical misfits. Other attractions include the carp lake,
rock garden and part of the old London Bridge.

The Natural History Museum Wildlife Garden   57

Cromwell Road, London SW7 5BD. Tel: (020) 7938 9111

*Natural History Museum • On corner of Cromwell Road and Queen's Gate.
Access via information desk in Museum • Open April to Oct for tours and
special interest parties; book by calling (020) 7938 9461. Weekday schools
activities pre-book by calling (020) 7938 9090 • Entrance: £6.50, concessions
£3.50, children free, (museum and garden)* ◗

Set in the Museum's grounds, unfortunately bordered by busy roads to the south and west, the wildlife garden covers one acre and visitors will nonetheless be able to enjoy the sights, sounds and smells of the country-side in the heart of London. One thousand trees and 20,000 wild flowers have been planted and tonnes of limestone, chalk and topsoil landscaped to re-create British nature sites, including an ancient hedged lane, grass meadows, ponds, a reed bed and a marsh. It was designed by Museum scientific staff working in collaboration with landscape architects and ecology advisors.

17A Navarino Road   58

Hackney, London E8 1AD. Tel: (020) 7254 5622

John Tordoff • Off London Fields, near Hackney Central station. Buses 30, 38 • Open by appt • Entrance: £2 for parties of 10 or more ●

An imaginative explosion of designs in a space 25 x 8 metres, yet this garden visit must not be hurried, starting with the Italianate courtyard with its fountain guarded by white pottery doves — the doves, archways, Mount Fuji, tea house and mirrored alcove are recycled or made by the owner. Clipped yews lead to a new perspective — a Japanese garden. Do not miss the seating area on the right which shares the pool with neighbours. Miniature conifers and well-placed rocks bring the eye down to the small scale of the design, and the whole is kept together by the rich green carpet of *Soleirolia soleirolii* (baby's tears). The clear stream is a haven for many birds. Memorable.

Noel–Baker Peace Garden   59

Elthorne Park, Hazelville Road, London N19.

London Borough of Islington • Entrances to Elthorne Park in Beaumont Road and Sunnyside Road • Open all year, daily, Mon – Fri, 8am – dusk, Sat, 9am – dusk, Sun, 10am – dusk • Entrance: free • Other information: Toilet facilities in adjacent playground ○ &

This is a small, well-designed formal garden within a London park, created in 1984 in memory of Philip Noel-Baker, winner of the Nobel Peace Prize in 1959. It is an interesting example of late twentieth-century garden design and planting, centering on a water feature and a striking bronze figure (with horizontal bronze reflection). Much use is made of brick and York stone paving, and raised beds together with lawns; the overall effect is softened and enlivened by the excellent planting, with many unusual species (e.g. *Feijoa sellowiana, Clerodendrum bungei, C. trichotomum*). The emphasis is on green, grey and white, lifted here and there by splashes of colour and linked by the strong lines of the asymmetrical design. There are several secluded sitting areas. The garden receives extensive use and support from the local community, and although the results of limited maintenance are sometimes apparent, the overall impression is of well-loved amenity. In adjacent *Elthorne Park* is a good children's playground and a fitness trail.

1F Oval Road 60

Flat 1, 1F Oval Road, London NW1 7EA. Tel (020) 7267 0655

Sheila Jackson • On Oval Road. Nearest tube Camden Town. Buses to Camden Town or Camden High Street, stops C2 and 274 very near • Open by appt only • Entrance: £1, children 50p • Other information: Parking difficult, especially on Suns ◐

A tiny space squeezed between a tall Victorian house and the Euston railway line has been transformed into a miniature garden of great charm and horticultural interest by the owner. Despite its small size one needs to walk through and around the garden to explore all the hidden places and vistas, and to appreciate the huge variety of unusual plants. Most of these grow in containers and have thrived this way for years. The garden is the subject of the book *Blooming Small, a City Dweller's Garden*.

Priory Gardens 61

Orpington, Kent. Tel: (020) 8464 3333 ext. 4471

London Borough of Bromley • Off Orpington High Street • Open all year, daily, 7.30am – dusk (weekends and Bank Holidays 9.30am – dusk) • Entrance: free • Other information: Separate area for dogs ○ 🏠 WC & 🍴

Adjacent to an attractive medieval priory building (now Bromley Museum), this is one of the most tastefully gardened public spaces in outer London, whose documentation dates from 1634. Pre-1939 the gardens were extended in the formal Arts and Crafts style. It has an excellent example of patterned annual bedding, a recently replanted herbaceous garden, a rich rose garden, fine mature trees and shrubs and a refurbished lake. Considering the recent cutbacks in public spending, the level of husbandry and maintenance in these gardens is exemplary.

Regent's Park (inc. Queen Mary's Rose Garden) ★ 62

Inner Circle, Regent's Park, London NW1. Tel: (020) 7298 2000

Royal Parks • Off Marylebone Road. Many other entrances to park • Open all year, daily, dawn – dusk • Entrance: free • Other information: Dogs in parkland only ○ 🍽 ✗ 🏠 WC & 🍴

These sedate, well-laid-out and beautifully manicured gardens are justly famous. Playing host to more than 60,000 roses – dominated by hybrid teas and floribundas, although also including old-fashioned, shrub and species roses – the sight and scent of the gardens in high summer is a magnet for thousands of visitors. It must be said, however, that this style of rose garden is not to everyone's taste. The roses are grown with almost military precision and are in perfect condition. Swagged and garlanded climbers surround the circular rose garden, but the herbaceous borders are also worth visiting, particularly in late July and August, as is the large ornamental lake with its central island. It attracts many varieties of waterfowl, including herons which nest on the island. The Broad Walk (five minutes from the Rose Gardens) between the Inner and Outer Circle towards Cambridge Gate is another exquisitely maintained Victorian-style area of planting. Its side walks are lined with urns and fountains following Nesfield's originals. Cypress lookalikes line the paths. There are 32 ornamental vases and tazzas (shallow bowls) and eight fountains. Nesfield's planting precision has been described as performing the same function as a military band – it provides entertainment for park visitors. Do not miss the charming little St John's Lodge garden. Nearby, at 66 Portland Place, W1 (a short walk from Oxford Circus) is the *Royal Institute of British Architects* (RIBA). The delightful new roof garden on the first floor adjoining the café is open to the public during office hours. Designed by Helen McCabe and Elsie Josland, it features gleaming steel containers with clipped box and other architectural foliage plants; the sophisticated sculpture fountain is by William Pye.

48 Rommany Road   63

Gipsy Hill, London SE27 9PX. Tel: (020) 9766 7587

Dr Belinda Barnes and Ronald Stuart-Moonlight • Off Salters Hill and Gipsy Hill, 1/2 m from Gipsy Hill mainline station. Buses 3, 322 • Open for NGS, inc. some evenings, and by appt (max. 15 persons) • Entrance: £2.50 NEW ●

This small gem of a garden (10 x 7 metres) was started from scratch in 1995. The owners designed and built every feature – garden walls, paving, pergola and arbour. The careful planting includes climbers such as muehlenbeckia intertwined with *Clematis armandii*. Hostas and ferns flourish in large pots; white-flowered wisteria, a small mulberry tree, *Acacia dealbata* and much more prove an object lesson in imaginative planting in a small space.

The Roof Garden   64

99 Kensington High Street, Kensington, London W8 5ED. Tel: (020) 7937 7994

Virgin Group • In Derry Street off Kensington High Street by lift • Telephone to check gardens open before attempting to visit • Entrance: free ● ♀

Fantasy one-and-a-half-acre garden 30 metres above the ground on the sixth floor of what was Derry and Toms 1938 department store. A Grade II on the *English Heritage Register of Parks & Gardens of Special Historic Interest in England* and a private members' club with restaurant facilities, the gardens which surround the bar and dining room are also used for functions and conferences. Ralph Hancock designed them to give three distinct illusions – a formal Spanish garden with canal, an English woodland garden and a Tudor garden. The soil is nowhere thicker than a metre so it is remarkable that more than 500 varieties of trees and shrubs, including palms, figs and vines, survive up here. Ducks swim about in their high-rise ponds, watched over by flamingos, and there is a delightful maze of small paths, bridges and walkways, with peepholes in the outer walls giving glimpses across the city skyline.

The Rookery   65

Streatham Common South, London SW16. Tel: (020) 8671 0994

Lambeth Council • Streatham High Road, then Streatham Common South • Open all year, daily except 25th Dec, 9am – dusk • Entrance: free • Other information: Parking top of Streatham Common. Dogs on lead on top terrace only ○ 🍵 WC &

A secluded and beautifully kept mixed garden. Formerly the walled garden of a private house and the surrounding hillside, with sloping lawns and terraces, it now runs down to the busy High Road a quarter of a mile below, and has views of Croydon – alas no Elysium. There is a walled garden, the attractive white garden best seen in July, an extensive rock garden with a small stream and goldfish pond, and a delightful Old English garden, beautifully scented, with a large variety of annual and perennial plants. Adult visitors will appreciate the tables in the orchard picnic area, the abundance of benches donated by grateful Streatham residents, and the plethora of litter bins; children will also enjoy the orchard (but no ball games), the dense shrubbery and hidden, winding paths leading up through the rock garden area and stream. Not far away in SE27 is *10A The Pavement* (Tel: (020) 8761 565), which its owner claims is 'the smallest garden in London, a hidden oasis behind the All Seasons Fish Bar'. Mostly containers but 'country type'. Featured in *The Observer* and *The Times*; the latter warns visitors may have to queue.

Royal Botanic Gardens ★★   66

Kew, Richmond, Surrey TW9 3AB. Tel: (020) 8940 1171 (24–hour message)

Trustees • Kew Green, S of Kew Bridge • Kew Palace closed for refurbishment but Queen Charlotte's Cottage open summer weekends and public holidays (April to Sept) • Gardens open all year, daily, except 25th Dec and 1st Jan, 9.30am – 4/ 7.30pm depending on season, glasshouses, 9.30am – 5.30pm. Guided tours daily from the Victoria Gate visitor centre, 11am and 2pm • Entrance: £5 (last hour of admission £3.50), OAPs, students £3.50, children (5-16) £2.50, under 5 free, blind, partially sighted and wheelchair occupants free (attendant at appropriate rate), family day ticket (2 adults and up to 2 children) £13, season ticket (for Kew and Wakehurst Place) £19, family season ticket £38 (1999 prices). Other season tickets and Friends of Kew Membership available. Guided tours £1 per person (1999 prices) • Other information: Parking Kew Green/ Brentford Gate car park in Ferry Lane. Coach parking Kew Road. Wheelchairs may be reserved in advance free of charge. Guide dogs permitted ○ 🍵 ✕ 🖼 WC & 🚻 🏮

Internationally renowned, and primarily a botanic research institution collecting, conserving and exchanging plants from all over the world, Kew's delightful and varied gardens and grounds of more than 300 acres have something for everyone. In spring, the flowering cherries, crocuses, daffodils, and the lovely rock garden; in May and June, the bluebell wood, the lilacs (made famous by the song) and the water-lily house; in summer the Duke's garden, the rose garden; in autumn bulbs and trees; in winter, the winter-flowering cherries and (indoors) the alpine house. Year-round pleasures are Decimus Burton's Palm House, the Temperate House, and the Diana, Princess of Wales Conservatory with its computer-controlled microclimates. Kew's grounds also contain four temples — the famous Pagoda, a Campanile, the Marianne North Gallery (filled with over 800 oil paintings of plants) and the Kew Gardens Gallery — besides Kew Palace (still closed for internal renovation, although the exterior is now completely refurbished), and the charming Queen Charlotte's Cottage. The grass garden has over 500 taxa of grasses, besides those of the bamboo garden. A large percentage of the herbaceous stock is of known wild origin. There is a somewhat formal rose garden, a delightful rock garden, originally of limestone, but completely replaced by sandstone. The Filmy Fern House should not be missed. The Queen's Garden (in the style of a seventeenth-century garden) has been renovated and re-opened. The Japanese Gateway has been completely re-stored and the area around newly landscaped. The huge glasshouses, some of which are kept at tropical temperatures, are well worth visiting in winter, with their unique collections of exotic and unusual plants, ranging from banana trees to giant water lilies. Evolution House. Museum No. I (opposite Palm House) exhibits the Economic Botany Collection. The trees range from ash and birch collections, through conifers, eucalyptus and mulberry to walnut. The lake, once a disused gravel pit, has an abundance of wildfowl. The Orangery does not contain oranges — which are to be found in the Citrus Walk in the Temperate House. The Orangery now has a shop and a restaurant. It is well worth buying the souvenir guide and planning a route for the elderly or unenergetic. The disabled will find all parts of Kew except the Marianne North Gallery easily accessible; indeed there is a Secluded Garden, designed by Anthea Gibson, created with the partially sighted and disabled in mind, with easy access and many displays at waist height. Call (020) 8332 5622 for details. Children will particularly enjoy the Princess of Wales Conservatory, with its imaginative mangrove swamps, Mohave desert and carnivorous plants, as well as the Palm House with its bananas and the Marine Display showing seaweeds and fish from around the world. Alas, tree-climbing, ball games and other sports are not allowed; neither are radios, cassettes, etc.

Royal Hospital, Chelsea (Ranelagh) Gardens   67

Royal Hospital Road, London SW3 4SR. Tel: (020) 7730 0161

Royal Hospital Chelsea • Through Chelsea Hospital London Gate in Royal Hospital Road, and through next gate into South grounds, then through small gate on left • Open all year, daily (except 1st Jan, 25th Dec and May and June due to Chelsea Flower Show), Mon − Sat, 10am − 1pm, 2pm − sunset, Sun, 2pm − sunset • Entrance: free ○ WC &

Elegant and attractive gardens to one side of the Royal Hospital, with over a mile of wide walkways through undulating park-like grass and handsome tree and shrub planting, with a few perennial and shrub borders. Formerly the pleasure grounds of Ranelagh, complete with a large rotunda (now demolished) and laid out in formal style, they were redesigned by Gibson in the nineteenth century, turned into allotments for pensioners between the World Wars, and later reconstructed according to Gibson's plan. A summerhouse by Sir John Soane, near the entrance to the garden, houses several seats plus glass cases with a history and a map of the gardens with the major trees marked on it. These include many species of poplar, birch, beech, holly, cherry, chestnut, lime, oak and so on, with a couple of more exotic ones – the tree of heaven and the maidenhair tree. The serenity of the gardens is marred by traffic in Chelsea Bridge Road. To one side of the park is the area used to house the Chelsea Flower Show. A long avenue of plane trees marks the western edge of the gardens.

35 Rudloe Road   68

Clapham, SW12 0DR. Tel: (020) 8673 2437

Judith Sharpe • Off A24 Clapham Common South, directly off Ponders Road (A205 South Circular). Clapham South station is 10 mins' walk • Open by appt only • Entrance: £2 NEW ●

This 10 x 6 metre garden is an excellent example of good design and imaginative planting. Chelsea winner Judith Sharpe nips and tucks a wide variety of plants with complementary shapes into this small space. Clematis, climbing roses, metallic-leaved phormiums and myrtle share abundant good health. A variety of pots, an antique garden seat and Scottish pebbles complete an unusual garden.

Southwood Lodge   69

33 Kingsley Place, Highgate, London N6 5EA. Tel: (020) 8348 2785

Mr and Mrs Christopher Whittington • Off Southwood Lane, Highgate • Open by appt April to July and for NGS one Sun pm in May and one evening in June • Entrance: £1.50, children 50p • Other information: Plants for sale on NGS Suns only ●

An imaginatively designed garden created in 1963 from a much larger, older one, set at the highest part of London with a magnificent view to the east 'as far as the Urals'. In approximately a third of an acre on a fairly steep site, there is much variety of mood and planting. By the house, which is clad in clematis and a rather sick rose, a densely planted paved area is enclosed on two sides by a high beech hedge, through which steps lead down to a grassy walk planted with shrubs, more clematis and herbaceous plants. A wooded area in the lowest part of the garden, with many shade-loving plants, leads up past two pools with the soothing sound of trickling water and suitable bog plants. There are alpines growing in troughs on a low wall.

7 St George's Road ★   70

St Margaret's, Twickenham, Middlesex TW1 1QS. Tel: (020) 8892 3713

Mr and Mrs R. Raworth • Off A316 between Twickenham Bridge and St Margaret's roundabout • Open 28th May, 11th June, 2 – 6pm, 1st June, 6 –

8pm, and by appt • Entrance: £2, children 50p, evening opening £3.50 including wine • Other information: Teas on open days only ● ● ♨

A most successful result of garden design, inspired by Hidcote (Gloucestershire) and Tintinhull (Somerset) on a miniature scale. This is one of the most interesting and impressively maintained private gardens in the West London area and well worth going out of one's way to see – though close to one of London's main routes to the west, it is a haven of grace and peace. Among its many striking features are impressive hedges of privet, yew, box and hornbeam which enclose various rooms and a knot garden. Entering through a sunken Mediterranean garden and a sink garden full of interesting small plants, you pass under a rose-covered pergola to an emerald grass carpet, flanked by flower borders backed by old trees in a private park. In one corner is a newly added water feature, a pool with waterside planting surrounded by wooden decking and crossed by a charming bridge. There are many old roses, rare shrubs and containerised plants to interest the plantsperson, who will also be drawn to the large, elegant conservatory on the north-facing wall, where old-fashioned Victorian plants, such as schizanthus, and interesting pelargoniums are cultivated.

St James's Park ★   71

London SW1A 2BJ. Tel: (020) 7298 2000

Royal Parks • Extends from Buckingham Palace on W to Horse Guards Parade on E, The Mall on N and Birdcage Walk on S • Open all year, daily, 5am – midnight • Entrance: free ○ ● 🖼 WC ♿ 🛶 ♨

One of the smaller royal parks but one of the prettiest, though the Garden History Society and the Victorian Society criticise those who have replaced its original path system with 'a crude and quite unplanned overlay' of tarmacked straight lines. It was Henry VIII who turned this swampy field into a pleasure ground and nursery for deer. After the Restoration in 1660, Charles II employed the French garden designer Le Nôtre, who planned the gardens at Versailles, to refashion the park into a garden. Le Nôtre gave advice, via his nephew, Claude Desgots, on a formal canal and included a pitch for King Charles to play the old French game of *paille maille* (a crude form of croquet). The game gave its name to Pall Mall. Nash remodelled the lake and gardens in 1827-29. The islands are still home to a wide variety of birds from ducks to pelicans. The park is also a sanctuary for politicians and civil servants as well as weary sightseers who can doze on deckchairs. Free band performances in summer and café open from 10am.

Syon Park ★   72

Brentford, Middlesex TW8 8JF. Tel: (020) 8560 0881

The Duke of Northumberland • 2m W of Kew Bridge, road marked from A315/ 310 at Bush Corner • Telephone for house opening dates, times and entrance charges • Garden open all year, daily except 25th, 26th Dec, 10am – 5.30pm or dusk. Entrance: charge ○ ● ✗ 🖼 WC ♿ ♨ 🛍 ♨

The Tudor house, with interiors redesigned by Robert Adam c.1760, is the London seat of the Percy family. Syon Park shows British gardening on a grand scale and is one of the oldest landscapes in the country. A few statistics: 3200 trees here – one in four of these are over 100 years old and about one in seven over 200 years old. There are wonderfully mature oaks and swamp cypresses among the 211 different species in this park landscaped by 'Capability' Brown, but the most glorious asset here is a great curving conservatory designed by Charles Fowler, which is said to have inspired Paxton when he was working at Chatsworth. One wing is full of scented flowers, the other is planted with vines leading to a fern-covered waterfall. The central part is not planted as it is used for receptions. The formal garden in front of it has recently been simplified and now has an austere Italianate feel. The brashly commercial architecture of the garden centre and the crude, unshielded parking area in front of the house have done great damage to the setting, yet the house remains serene and the direct view to the river from it is remarkably untouched. The surrounding park and lakeside walk are of great interest and a new path was opened in 1999 to allow visitors to walk the complete circuit of the lake. In spite of economic restraints much work has been done in eliminating unsuitable 1960s' planting and in trying to bring the garden closer to Brown's original vision. Wildflower areas are being developed, and the rose garden has been redesigned and replanted with old varieties. One of the glories of Syon has always been the view from the ha-ha across water meadows towards the Thames; here new vistas and the famous axis to the Palm House at Kew are being opened up, and soon it will be possible to see across to the Observatory and the Pagoda. Much work still needs to be done, but there is a continuing programme for improvement and conservation. The future is bright indeed. Nearby *Osterley Park* is improving [open March onwards or by arrangement. Tel: (020) 8560 3918].

Trinity Hospice ★   73

30 Clapham Common North Side, London SW4 0RN. Tel: (020) 7787 1000

Trustees of the Hospice • Off N side of Common • Open for charity 15th, 16th April, 17th, 18th June, 29th, 30th July, 2nd, 3rd Sept, 2 – 5pm and by appt at other times • Entrance: £1, children free ● 🐝 WC & 🌿

The gardens at Trinity Hospice were designed primarily for the benefit of patients, their families and the staff. Stretching over nearly two acres, they are set out on slightly rolling park-like terrain and designed by John Medhurst and David Foreman of London Landscape Consortium on the principles laid down by Lanning Roper. The latter had originally been asked by the Sainsbury Family Charity Trust to design these gardens on a dilapidated site but his illness caught up with him before he could do much. The gardens were finished thanks to donations made by his friends and called the Lanning Roper Memorial Garden. Perennials and shrubs predominate but there is also a wild garden at one end, a large pool with a mobile sculpture by George Rickey and a smaller pool with a water feature by William Pye.

Victoria and Albert Museum (The Pirelli Garden) 74

Cromwell Road, London SW7 2RL.

Cromwell Road, close to South Kensington tube station • Open all year, daily except 24th to 26th Dec, 10am – 5.45pm • Entrance: £5, concessions £3, Friends of the V&A, students and children under 18 free (entrance free after 4.30pm) • Other information: Refreshments during summer only

○ WC ♿ ♨ ☕

This large area within the splendid Victorian pile originally had a large number of cherry trees which had reached the end of their natural life and a big ash tree. At the time, the early 1980s, the then-director of the museum, Sir Roy Strong, had just staged an epoch-making *The Garden* exhibition. Thanks to the sponsorship of Pirelli it was possible to employ two architects, Douglas Childs and Maggie Davies, who produced a design of classic geometry sympathetic to the Italianate style of the museum buildings. It is elegant and maintained to a high standard. The central fountain is floodlit in the evening. Music, wine and food lectures, etc. available on Wed evening openings (seasonal) (Tel: (020) 7942 2209).

Wallace Collection 75

Hertford House, Manchester Square, London W1M 6BN. Tel: (020) 7935 0687

Trustees of the Wallace Collection • N of Wigmore Street, behind Selfridges • Garden open all year, daily, 10am – 5pm, Sun, 2 – 5pm. Closed 1st to 3rd Jan, 21st April, 1st May and 24th to 26th Dec • Entrance: free • Other information: Gallery open ○ WC ♨

A secluded paved courtyard in the centre of Hertford House, a mansion built in 1776-88 for the then Duke of Manchester. When this storehouse of paintings, furniture and other treasures, collected by the Marquess of Hertford, was bequeathed to the nation in 1897, the government bought the family mansion to display them. This stylish courtyard is like a stage set, dramatised by eight magnificent bronze urns, all of which once stood in the Château de Bagatelle, the French home of the Marquess. Sponsorship of flowers and plants for the urns would be warmly welcomed, according to the Museum. The centrepiece is an elegant fountain with a golden snake recoiling from the fish in the pool. The planting is kept simple with beds edged with clipped box. Some Sunday mornings there is music, and wine and croissants are available to embellish the garden visit. Other garden developments are planned, and the central courtyard is undergoing major works due to be completed June 2000. From that date, the courtyard will be glazed over at second floor level and will become a sculpture garden with café facilities.

The Water Gardens

(see COOMBE WOOD, Surrey)

Waterhouse Plantation
(also known as Woodland Garden) ★ 76

Bushy Park, Hampton, Surrey. Tel: (020) 8979 1586

*Royal Parks • On A308 Hampton Court road, ½ m W of Hampton Court
roundabout. Short walk from car park, gate on main road alongside • Open all
year, daily, 9am – dusk • Entrance: free (park and plantation)* ○ &

There are two Plantations, both in Bushy Park, adjoining Hampton Court.
Planting similar to the Isabella Plantation in Richmond Park (see entry)
concentrating on masses of shrubs – rhododendrons, azaleas and camellias.
The paths wind round shrubs and open onto small lakes and the Longford
River with many small bridges. The gardens are sensitively cared for and
worth seeing at all times of year. Investment has been made in seating. There is
an extensive programme of events in both parks – leaflet available from Royal
Parks Agency.

West Ham Park 77

Upton Lane, Forest Gate, London E7 9PU. Tel: (020) 7472 3584

*Corporation of London • 6m E of the City. Nearest underground Plaistow (15
minutes) • Open all year, daily, 7.30am – dusk • Entrance: free • Other
information: Refreshment van on Sat, Sun, Bank Holidays and daily during
school holidays from 23rd April to Sept* ○ 🍽 🏢 WC & ⬦

Since 1566 the ground covered by what is now the park has been well
cultivated, but the main development of interest to gardeners took place
in the second half of the eighteenth century, when Upton House and its 30-
acre garden were owned by a Doctor Fothergill. He built a 67-metre-long
glasshouse and filled it with exotic species which he encouraged sea captains
sailing out of the nearby London docks to bring back from abroad. His
collection grew to more than 3400 species and was considered to be the most
wide-ranging outside that of Kew Gardens. In 1775/6 Fothergill and a friend,
Doctor Pitcairn, sent two Scottish gardeners to the Alps to collect alpines so
that they could make one of Britain's earliest true rock gardens, and this has
recently been re-created. But what is probably one of the original and oldest
ginkgo trees in Britain remains the pride of a fine tree collection which
features some good, rarish hollies. Elsewhere in this well-maintained park
there has been a revival of imaginative Victorian bedding schemes with some
charming and amusing carpet bedding.

42 Woodville Gardens 78

Ealing, London W5 2LQ. Tel: (020) 8998 4134

*J. Welfare • Off Hanger Lane (off A40) • Open by appt only • Entrance: By
donation to charity* ● ⬦

Larger than the average town garden, this is laid out predominantly to
accommodate the owner's love of plants: the beds surrounding the lawn have

increased in size to keep pace with the need for more plant space. There are a number of interesting and unusual ones, including a *Cestrum parqui* on the house wall, a small bed under an apple tree with four different pulmonarias and a large number of silver-leaved and variegated perennials and shrubs. The small raised terrace by the house is interplanted with low-growing silver-foliage plants and geraniums. Below it is a densely planted bed of dwarf alpines, with a small bog garden at the bottom.

London's Open Spaces

CITY OF LONDON PARKS AND GARDENS

Although there is inevitably a certain similarity in the design and planning of any group of gardens administered by a public body, those within the City of London (numbering around 150), being principally located on bomb sites, churchyards and former churchyards, perhaps have more variety than might be expected. An excellent free English Tourist Board leaflet, produced in conjunction with the Corporation of London, entitled *Open Spaces in the City of London*, gives details. For tourists and workers these gardens provide a welcome respite from the dirt and noise of the City and almost all are provided with lots of benches. *They are open 8am – 7pm or dusk, 7 days a week unless otherwise stated.* 🚍 &

EC1: *Christchurch – Greyfriars Rose Garden*, Newgate Street. A collection of hybrid teas and climbing roses trained up wooden pillars with rope linking them. *Postman's Park*, Aldersgate Street. Close to St Paul's Cathedral. Formal bedding in the centre with mature trees and shrubs, a small pool with fountain and goldfish, together with tombs and headstones as the area is still a churchyard. An arcade protects the Watts Memorial, a tiled wall commemorating the deeds of those who died in their efforts to save others.

EC2: *Finsbury Circus*. [Closed Oct to March at weekends] The largest public open green space in the City and London's first public park (1606). Apart from the ubiquitous London plane trees, it also boasts the only bowling green in the City, surrounded by low box hedges, bedding plants, shrubs, a drinking fountain and a small bandstand. *St Anne and St Agnes Churchyard*, Gresham Street. [Permanently open] Here the church still stands, alongside the remains of part of London Wall and those of a Roman fort, surrounded by trees and shrubs. *St Botolph-without-Bishopsgate Churchyard*, Bishopsgate. [Permanently open] Apart from the usual planting, there is also a tennis court (summer) and netball courts (winter) and a former school house, restored in 1952 by the Worshipful Company of Fan Makers to serve as a church hall. *St Mary Aldermanbury*, Love Lane. [Permanently open] Made within the low ruined walls of a Wren church destroyed in the Blitz, the stumps of remaining pillars mark different levels of the garden. A shrubbery encloses a monument to Shakespeare's pals, John Heminge and Henry Condell. There is also a small knot garden. *St Mary Staining*, Oat Lane. [Permanently open] Another patch of grass surrounded by shrubs, roses and benches. A rare opportunity to see a design by the late David Hicks is available at *Salter's Garden*, Fore Street, re-opened with funding from the Salters and the Corporation of London. Now maturing, it is worth peeping in to register the progress of the planting. Paved areas alternate with grass alleys dividing rectangular box-edged beds. Formally placed obelisks in the beds have been planted with climbing roses and some of the alleys run below honey-suckle-clad tunnels. Three fountains introduce the sparkle and murmur of running water. *St Alphage Highwalk Garden*, London Wall is nearby [Permanently open]. This roof garden beside London Wall can be reached via the escalator at Moorgate station and consists of a series of raised beds and extensive trellis work. The planting is a mixture of shrubs, climbers and herbaceous plants with an interesting collection of grasses as a centrepiece.

EC3: *Pepys Garden*, Seething Lane. [Open weekdays only, 9am – 5.30pm] A splinter of garden on the site of the Navy Office, where Samuel Pepys lived and worked. A surprising number of trees in a tiny area. *St Dunstan-in-the-East Church Garden*, St Dunstans Hill. The most romantic garden in the City, it has been created within the walls of a Victorian Gothick church which was bombed during World War II. Only the Wren tower survived and was restored. The remaining walls, containing arched windows and doorways, are covered with creepers and climbing plants and the spaces between planted with small trees and shrubs. There is a small fountain surrounded by benches and large tubs with standard fuchsias and bedding plants.

EC4: *Bow Churchyard*, just off Cheapside [Closed weekends], will interest US visitors as in its small garden is the statue of Captain John Smith, 'citizen and cord-wainer', who was leader of the first settlers in Virginia. *St Laurence Pountney*, Laurence Pountney Hill. Two pocket-handkerchief patches of green-ery with benches on the site of St Laurence Pountney Church and Corpus Christi College, destroyed in the Great Fire, 1666. *St Paul's Churchyard*. [Open 6am – 7.30pm] Winding paths surround the back of the Cathedral with welcome shade and a resting place for the weary tourist. Apart from the usual municipal planting, there is a rose garden in the SE corner with hybrid teas and climbing roses on the fine early wrought-iron railings.

E1: *Portsoken Street Garden*, between Portsoken Street and Goodman's Yard. A tiny oasis with a bubbling fountain, brick walls, small trees and shrubs in raised beds behind low brick walls.

LONDON SQUARES

Other cities have squares but probably none has more than London's 400. They were mostly built in the eighteenth and nineteenth centuries to provide an outlook for the fashionable houses which surrounded them and in not-so-fashionable areas like Pimlico so that the lesser classes could imitate the behaviour of their betters. A few squares still remain the joint property of the owners of houses (and today, flats) round them, the grandest being Belgrave Square built by Basevi in 1825, Cadogan Square and Eaton Square. Other private squares, hardly less grand, include Brompton, Carlyle, Edwardes, Lowndes, Montpelier, Onslow, Pembroke and others to the west of Hyde Park Corner. One enthusiast, Roger Phillips of Eccleston Square, says that in order to keep the squares going for the benefit of the residents and the visual pleasure of others passing by, it is necessary to wage a horrendous battle against potential developers. By contrast, the ageing Tory whiz-kid Michael Heseltine says that 'someone, somewhere, should get a grip' on London squares. There should be tree-planting schemes, seats for the elderly, statues or water features – possibly provided by sponsors. For the first time, in 1998, a number of London's private square gardens were persuaded to open to the public on a single day in June. It was such a success that the scheme is now likely to be an annual event. More gardens have joined the scheme, including Eaton Square, the Inner and Middle Temple gardens, Little Venice along the canal in Paddington and Portman Square in the heart of the West End. Tickets for 2000 are available giving access to all the gardens in the scheme, for £3 (adults) and £1 (children) by post from: London Squares Day, c/o London Historic Parks and Gardens Trust, Duck Island Cottage, St James's Park, London SW1. A list of participating squares and further information is available from English Heritage (Tel: (020) 7973 3434). Some squares (and 'gardens' as other areas are called) have over the years become places where the public may be admitted and these include the following:

Northern area: Despite its name probably the least romantic is the home of the Bloomsberries, *Bloomsbury Square*, now more litter-full than literary; *Russell Square*, recently restored after a period of neglect; *Queen Square*, with its statue of Queen Charlotte, after whom it is named; *Brunswick Square* beyond which is the walled garden, usually a haven of peace; *Tavistock Square* (quietest in the area); *Gordon Square*, closed weekends; and *Fitzroy Square*, the work of Sir Geoffrey Jellicoe, not open but viewable. Further north is *Gibson Square* in Islington, with plenty of seats, much grass, fine trees and too many municipal roses.

Central area: *Berkeley Square*; *Cavendish Square*; *Grosvenor Square*. *Phoenix Gardens*, a community-run site with a 20-year lease which shows what can be done by London residents, and, unlike many others, is open 24 hours a day, and *St James's Square* (this is the earliest, begun 1665, and the quietest). *Mount Street Gardens* is a well-hidden leafy retreat much loved by locals while the throng of the city seems to pass it by. Tasteful planting and lofty trees make it the perfect spot to take your ease after shopping. Versailles tubs planted with palms, beds of sugar-pink and white geraniums or other interesting and varied schemes can be enjoyed from dozens of wooden benches donated by those who have enjoyed this garden's charm [Open spring and summer, weekdays, 8am – up to 9.30pm; autumn and winter, 8am – 4.30pm. Suns and Bank Holidays, open from 9am. Free]. Also within walking distance are *St Paul's Churchyard*, *Covent Garden* and *Soho Square*.

Eastern area: *Embankment Gardens*, if rather municipal, are leafy and tranquil. At *Gray's Inn* Field Court is open to the public during weekday lunchtimes in the summer. *Inner and Middle Temple Gardens* stretch up from the Embankment (no entrance here) to Fleet Street. Their fourteenth-century origins are recalled by names of some of the individual squares. The Inner Temple's Great Gardens were extended in the early eighteenth century, with majestic trees, and again in the nineteenth century. The smaller Middle Temple has fine borders and a small rose garden. Alas, the future of these beautiful, historic and unique gardens is in jeopardy because of a plan to build a bridge, with twin towers as high as the dome of St Paul's, on their very doorstep. At *Lincoln's Inn* one of the 'squares', New Hall, is open to the public Mon – Fri, 12 noon – 1.30pm only. The newest square in London is surrounded by offices, not houses. This is *Arundel Great Court*, which may be viewed from The Strand, south of Aldwych and entered from Arundel and Norfolk Streets. To the south is the luxurious courtyard garden of the *Norfolk Hotel*.

Southern area: *Eccleston Square* in Pimlico [Open two or three times for NGS. Tel: (020) 7834 7354 for details]. This three-acre square, run by a committee of residents, and normally reserved for the use of the residents, has something for everyone – a tennis court, areas for children to play in and a paved patio. It is also of considerable horticultural interest and contributes to the National Collection of ceanothus. More than 400 different roses and 110 different camellias.

OTHER LONDON 'PUBLIC' SPACES

EC1 (London Borough of Islington): *Angel/Upper Street*. Three charming court-yard gardens have been built below the new office block, Regent's House, in Upper Street, just a few metres from the Angel tube exit. Nowhere to sit, but pleasant strolling space. *Bunhill Fields Burial Ground*, between Bunhill Row and City Road. [Open Mon – Fri, 7.30am – 7pm (4pm Oct to March), weekends 9.30am – 4pm] A burial ground, unused since 1853, containing many fine tombs and memorials, including those of William Blake and John Bunyan. Most of the tombs are behind railings, but part of the grounds which were bomb-damaged has been planted with grass, trees and shrubs. Fine planes and a mulberry. *Fortune Street Garden*, NW of the Barbican between Beech Street and Old Street. *Myddleton Square*, St John Street, which houses St Mark's Church.

EC3 (London Borough of Tower Hamlets): *Trinity Square*, Tower Hill, home to Wyatt's Trinity House.

E10: *Lee Valley Regional Park* total 10,000 acres. Telephone information Centre at Waltham Abbey Gardens (01992) 702210.

E16: *Thames Barrier Park*. Exciting new park on Thames at N end of the Barrier, designed by Alain Provost, raised above the river on a plateau. 'Green dock' incorporates hedges cut into waves echoing an impressive water feature. Altogether *nouvelle vague* and fun.

N1: *New River*, a narrow man-made stream and park off Canonbury Road. *St Mary Churchyard Gardens*, Upper Street, opposite the King's Head Theatre.

SE1: The new *Globe* theatre is to have an Elizabethan knot-garden on its one-acre site. For further details contact Shakespeare Globe Trust, Bear Gardens, London SE1 (Tel: 020 7928 7710).

SE15: *London Wildlife Garden Centre*, 28 Marsden Road, near East Dulwich railway station, gives information and sells plants for gardeners who want to attract wildlife. Open Tues – Thurs and Sun, 11am – 4pm, but telephone first (020) 7252 9186.

SE23: *Sydenham Hill Woods*, near Forest Hill railway station. Over 180 species of trees and plants.

SW1: *Whitehall Court*. Parallel to N bank of River Thames, between Horse-guards Avenue, Whitehall Place and Victoria Embankment. A Grade-II-listed garden, owned by Westminster City Council, re-created in 1994 after a decade of neglect. The excellent planting plan takes into account the proximity of heavy traffic along Victoria Embankment and gives occasional views of the River Thames. Cross over Northumberland Place and visit the rest of *Victoria Embankment Gardens*, especially Bryant's small lily pond and Sullivan's Victorian memorial, which are well supported by planting. Maintenance is to a high standard.

W9: *Clifton Nurseries* is a commercial establishment for the sale of plants and garden paraphernalia, but for all that it has the charm of a small enclosed London green space, well worth visiting at all times of year (nearest tube station: Warwick Avenue). Nearby is *Rembrandt Gardens*, a small municipal triangle by the side of the canal where, if the weather is suitable, the newspaper can be read in pleasing surroundings.

W10: Some London cemeteries have a gardenesque style, or have acquired one over the centuries. Highgate is one of the best known. The longest-surviving cemetery still in private ownership is the 77-acre *Kensal Green* (Harrow Road. Tube to Kensal Green on Bakerloo line or bus No 18. Parking access via West Gate WC ♿ ⬦ 🚻), and it also has more free-standing mausoleums than any other in England – the majority were constructed to the owners' approved designs before being put to use. Several are Grade II listed. There are fine trees here as well as grand graves. The company which established Kensal in 1832 aimed to create a spacious park that would complement the fine monuments. They succeeded, and their work is now assisted by subscription-paying 'Friends'. [Open April to Sept, 9am – 5.30pm, Sun, 10am – 5.30pm; Oct to March, 9am – 4pm, Sun, 10am – 4pm; Bank Holidays, 10am – 4pm/5.30pm. Guided tours on Sundays at 2pm throughout the year.]

TELEPHONE AND FAX NUMBERS

Except where owners have specifically requested that they be excluded, telephone and (where applicable) fax numbers are given for each property. To maintain the support and co-operation of private owners, it is suggested that the telephone and fax be used with discretion. In all cases where visits by parties are proposed, owners should be advised in advance and arrangements preferably confirmed in writing. Where visits are by appointment, the telephone may of course be used except where written application, particularly for parties, is specifically requested. Code numbers are given in brackets. Note that several UK and Northern Ireland codes change in 2000.

HOW TO FIND THE GARDENS

Directions to each garden are included in the entry. This information has been supplied by the owners and garden inspectors. It is aimed to be the best available to those travelling by car, and has been compiled to be used in conjunction with a road atlas.

Some gardens can be approached by public transport, but alas these are few and far between. The unreliability of train and bus services makes it unrewarding to include details, particularly as many garden visits are made on Sundays. However, properties that can be reached by public transport feature in National Trust guides and the NGS Yellow Book, which sometimes give details.

MANCHESTER AREA

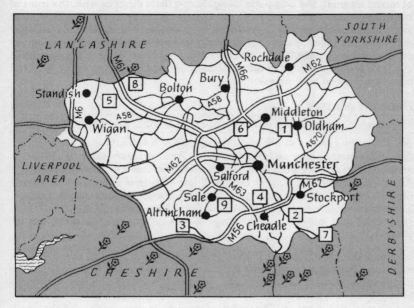

A few gardens with Cheshire addresses are included in the Manchester section for convenience, but check pages 47–62 as another beautiful garden may be nearby. For the same reason, check other neighbouring counties.

Alexandra Park   1

Oldham.

More than 85 per cent of the users of this park have no garden of their own. Some of the terrace houses they live in can be seen nearby, remnants of the day when they housed cotton workers. Today, with the help of Millennium funds, their municipal gardens are being put back into shape. Watch for progress and a report here next year.

Bramall Hall   2

Bramall Park, Bramhall, Stockport, Cheshire SK7 3NX
Tel: (0161) 485 3708; Fax: (0161) 486 6959

Stockport Metropolitan Borough Council • 3m S of Stockport on A5102 between Bramhall and Stockport. Signposted • Hall open April to Sept, daily, 1 – 5pm; Oct to Dec, daily except Mon and 25th, 26th Dec, 1 – 4pm; Jan to March, weekends only • Grounds open all year, daily • Entrance: free (hall £2.95, OAPs and children £2) (1999 prices) • Other information: Dogs in some areas only, on lead. Shop in Hall ○ 🍽 WC &*

The gardens round this magnificent black-and-white timber-framed house are of mixed interest, the best parts being those a little distance from the front of the house where, in a narrow strip of land, formal beds contain bright annuals and a herbaceous border is enclosed by a hedge. The parkland is another matter. In the valley of a small river broad areas of grassland encircle a number of small lakes. Woods, which contain some very large beech trees, surround the park and hide all sign of the suburbs of Stockport. The riverside walk has banks covered in wild flowers.

Dunham Massey ★   3

Altrincham, Cheshire WA14 4SJ. Tel: (0161) 941 1025; Fax: (0161) 929 7508

The National Trust • 3m SW of Altrincham off A56 • House open April to 1st Nov, daily except Thurs and Fri, 12 noon – 5pm (last entry 4.30pm). 30th Sept to 1st Nov, access by guided tour only. Garden open April to 1st Nov, daily, 11am – 5.30pm (closes 4.30 in Oct). Mill open 1st April to 1st Nov, Wed and Sun, 2 – 4pm. Park open daily; guided walks • Entrance: car park £3, garden £3, house and garden £5 (1999 prices) • Other information: Manual wheelchairs and Batricar available. Dogs in park only, on lead ◐ 🍽 ✕ WC ♿ ✍ 🎫 ♨

Between the conurbations of Liverpool and Manchester sits the 3000-acre estate of Dunham Massey, where fallow deer still roam free in extensive parkland. A miraculous survival, the avenues predate the English Landscape School of the eighteenth century. It belies the long history of the estate. The park is medieval in origin. The broad stretch of water curling round the north and west sides of the house is an Elizabethan moat, and the semi-circular promotory jutting out into the moat the site of the Elizabethan mount. The house, described as of 'beautifully proportioned austerity', is an eighteenth-century replacement of the Elizabethan mansion. Enough of the formal seventeenth-century Baroque lay-out of the park to the west and the south remained for The National Trust to repair and replant the six long avenues which radiate out from a *patte d'oie* in front of a triple row of lime trees each side of the southern forecourt. Other historical layers remain, including an Edwardian parterre planted in purple and gold by the north front of the house an eighteenth-century orangery and an old well-house on a large lawn bordered by shrubs and trees. The east park has been restored to re-create its later existence as a Victorian pleasure ground, complete with individual hosta, moss and bog gardens of special interest, and a woodland area for late-flowering azaleas. Visitors to the house will find an attractive courtyard in the centre with four beds of shrubs and herbaceous plants. Inside the house, be sure not to miss John Harris Jr's spectacular birds-eye views of one of the finest English Baroque gardens.

Fletcher Moss Botanical and Parsonage Gardens ★   4

Mill Gate Lane, Didsbury M20. Tel: (0161) 445 4241

Manchester City Council Education Leisure Department • 5m S of Manchester city centre on Mill Gate Lane, S of A5145, close to centre of Didsbury • Open all

*year, daily, 9am – dusk • Entrance: free • Other information: Refreshments in
small café (the building where the first meeting of the RSPB took place) but
opening times uncertain. Dogs in certain areas only* ○ 🍵 🏠 **WC** ♿

Much of this well-maintained garden is set on a steep south-facing bank planted
with a variety of shrubs, heathers, bulbs, alpines, azaleas and small trees.
Rocky streams run down to a water garden and lawned area where there are
moisture-loving plants including gunneras. Across some grass tennis courts a
large grass area contains specimen trees. Within a short walking distance the
Parsonage Gardens, laid out in Victorian times and more formal, contain
lawns, good herbaceous borders, camellias and rhododendrons. Also some fine
trees, notably a swamp cypress and a mulberry.

Haigh Hall Gardens 5

Haigh Country Park, Haigh, Wigan WN2 1PE. Tel: (01942) 832895

*Metropolitan Borough of Wigan (Department of Leisure) • 2m NE of Wigan, N
of B5238. Signposted • Parkland open all year, daily during daylight hours •
Entrance: free, but parking charge during summer • Other information:
Wheelchairs available from information centre. Craft gallery. Children's rides,
model village and railway* ○ 🍵 **WC** ♿ 🖐 🏛

The hall is set in the midst of mature parkland, and a short distance to the east
are formal gardens, probably of Victorian and Edwardian origin. In an open
area of lawn rose beds and specimen shrubs surround an oval pool. Three
walled gardens adjoin. The middle one contains a good herbaceous border and
a well-stocked shrub border. The second, to the south, has shrubs around the
walls and young specimen trees planted in a lawn in the centre; the low wall to
the south gives a view across a wild garden with a pond. The third, at the
northern end, can only be entered at peak times, and here against the south-
facing wall is a cactus house. On the west side a landscaped area has heathers
and conifers. The rest of the layout is formal, with roses, yew hedges and lawns
and, against the east wall, a border of shrub roses. The arboretum featuring
acers set in woodlands is developing well.

Heaton Hall 6

**Heaton Park, Prestwich, Manchester M25 2SW.
Tel: (0161) 236 5244 (Hall enquiries); (0161) 773 1085 (Park enquiries)**

*Manchester City Council • 4m N of city centre on A576 just S of junction with
M66 • House open summer months only • Garden open all year during daylight
hours • Entrance: free, but parking charge on Sun and Bank Holiday Mons •
Other information: Some areas possible for wheelchairs but telephone first* ○ 🍵
WC 🖐 🏛

The hall, designed in 1772 by James Wyatt, was described by Pevsner as 'the
finest house of its period in Lancashire'; the restored interiors include fine
contemporary plasterwork, paintings and furnishings. The 650-acre park,
landscaped between 1770 and 1830, contains a number of other neo-classical
buildings. To the front of the hall are formal, brightly planted Edwardian

gardens. The stables to the west have a small heather garden in front and a large formal rose garden behind. A path leads through a tunnel to an attractive dell of mature trees and many rhododendrons, then follows a stream through a series of pools and waterfalls to a large boating lake. On the Prestwich side of the park small demonstration gardens are enclosed within old walls.

Lyme Park ★ 7

Disley, Stockport, Cheshire SK12 2NX. Tel: (01663) 762023/766492

The National Trust • 6m SE of Stockport just W of Disley on A6 • Open 24th March to Oct, Fri – Tues, 11am – 5pm, Wed and Thurs, 1 – 5pm; Nov to 20th Dec, Sat and Sun, 12 noon – 3pm. Guided tours by arrangement • Entrance: garden £2 (park: pedestrians free, car and occupants £3.50) ◑ ☕ ✕ 🍴 WC ♿ 🎁 🔱

Lyme Hall, a Palladian-style mansion, is set in spectacular parkland in the foothills of the Pennines with panoramic views of the Cheshire Plains. The 17-acre gardens are of great historic importance, retaining many original features from Tudor and Jacobean times. Lyme Park is regarded as the foremost National Trust garden for high-Victorian-style bedding in magnificent formal beds, using many rare and old-fashioned plants including *Penstemon* 'Rubicunda' (bred at Lyme in 1906). Important features include a well-planted orangery (Lewis Wyatt, 1814) containing two venerable 150-year-old camellias; a spectacular Dutch garden with a rare example of a *parterre de broderie* using Irish ivy and golden box hedging; a fine Gertrude Jekyll-style herbaceous border designed by Graham Stuart Thomas; a wooded ravine garden with a stream and fine collections of rhododendrons, azaleas, ferns and other shade-loving plants; a collection of rare trees and plants associated with the eminent plantsman, the Hon. Vicary Gibbs; a large reflection lake; a 300-year-old lime avenue; extensive lawns and a recently restored rose garden.

Rivington Terraced Gardens 8

Bolton Road, Horwich, Bolton BL6 7SB.
Tel: (01204) 691549 (Rivington Information Centre)

North West Water • 1m NW of Horwich. Follow signs to Rivington from A673 in Horwich or Grimeford. Gardens are 10-min walk from Rivington Hall and Hall Barn • Open all year, daily • Entrance: free • Other information: Parking, refreshments, toilet facilities at Hall Barn and refreshments, toilet facilities and information at Great House Barn ○ ☕ 🍴 WC ⬷

These are not gardens as such but the remains of gardens built by Lord Leverhulme and designed by Thomas Mawson in the early part of this century. Set mainly in woodland on a steep west-facing hillside, they have fine views across Rivington reservoirs. Particularly impressive is a rocky ravine, the remains of a Japanese garden and the restored pigeon tower. The number and variety of mature trees and rhododendrons indicate that this must once have been a very grand estate. When visiting be prepared for a stiff walk and take care on the paths which can be slippery when wet or icy. It is worth buying the guide which leads the visitor round and explains the various features.

Wythenshawe Horticultural Centre   9

Wythenshawe Park, Wythenshawe Road M23 0AB. Tel: (0161) 998 2117

Manchester City Council • 7m S of Manchester city centre, ¼ m S of M63 junction 9, ½ m SE of M56 junction 3, S of B5167 • Open all year, daily, except 25th Dec, 10am – 4pm • Entrance: free ○ 🍵 🖶 WC ♿ ☙ 🏬 ☕

Once this nursery grew bedding stock for the city's parks; now it is a demonstration garden where a large number of different plants can be seen growing. To the right of the entrance a large lawned area runs along a chain of pools planted with many moisture-lovers, including irises and astilbes, in large effective clumps. The developing area, backed by mature woodland, already looks attractive. The Safari Walk through a long array of greenhouses leads past a series of plant collections – cacti, tropical plants, carnivorous plants, a fernery and some unusual displays, including one on rice growing. Behind the greenhouses is an area of demonstration gardens – a heather garden, a pool and rockery, a collection of shrubs and small trees, a well-labelled herbaceous border and a section of dwarf conifers. Another area is devoted to fruit, with many of the bushes and trees grown as cordons. Be sure to visit the Hall, an attractive timber-framed building surrounded by formal areas.

A TOTALLY INDEPENDENT PUBLICATION
The *Guide* makes no charge for entries, which are written by our own inspectors. The factual details are supplied by owners. This is a totally-independent publication and its only revenue is from sales of copies in bookshops.

WHEELCHAIR USERS ♿
Please note that the symbol denoting suitability for wheelchairs refers to the garden only. If there is a house open, it may or may not be suitable.

GARDEN THEFTS
These now routinely include statuary, fencing, etc., and fish. There are two results of the increase in thievery – first that owners are reluctant to open their gardens except to pre-arranged groups who have provided references. Second, their entries in the *Guide* sometimes exclude mention of precious objects as owners do not wish to publicise their existence to the burgling fraternity or to other parties that cannot be identified in some way.

NEWCASTLE-UPON-TYNE
AREA

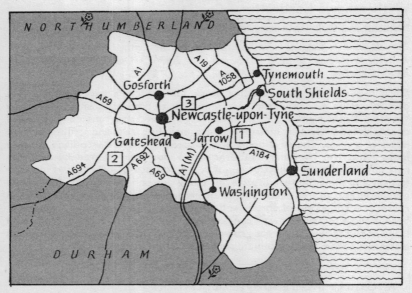

Some gardens have postal addresses in one county and are physically situated in another. If in doubt, a check in the index will direct the reader to the page on which the garden appears.

Bede's World Herb Garden

Church Bank, Jarrow, South Tyneside NE32 3DY. Tel: (0191) 489 2106

Bede's World • 8m NE of Gateshead off A185, or S entrance to Tyne Tunnel off A19 • Museum open all year • Garden open daily except Mon (but open Bank Holiday Mons): April to Oct, 10am – 5.30pm; Nov to Mar, 11am – 4.30pm (Suns all year, 2.30 – 5.30pm) • Entrance: garden free (museum, Anglo-Saxon farm and garden £2.50, concessions £1.25, family ticket £6) (1999 prices)
○ ☕ WC ♿ 🐕 🌿

A small garden, of great interest to the herbalist, with a wide range of herbs in four sections: culinary, Anglo-Saxon medicinal, aromatic and medicinal. There are also narrow beds in a second part of the garden based on the plans of a medicinal herb garden found at St Gall (c. AD 816), and a bricked area at the top of the garden with seating, planted around with rosemary, lavender and with two banks of herbs below it leading down to the 'St Gall' area. An 'Anglo-Saxon' farm has been developed on adjacent land – an 11-acre site with fields, crops and animals and Anglo-Saxon timber buildings. Some herbs and early vegetable strains will be grown here together with pond and stream plants and trees of species available at the time of the Venerable Bede (AD 673-735). The adjacent museum building has a courtyard with four raised beds planted in the style of a late-medieval formal garden. Some construction work is in progress.

Gibside 2

Burnopfield, Gateshead NE16 6BG. Tel: (01207) 542255

The National Trust • 6m SW of Gateshead, 20m NW of Durham from B6314, off A694 at Rowlands Gill. Signed from A1(M) • Open April to Dec, daily except Mon (but open Bank Holiday Mons), 11am – 5pm • Entrance: summer £3, children £1.50; winter £2 • Other information: Picnics in car park only. Chapel open, service first Sun each month. Concerts, guided walks and events ◐ 🍵 WC ◁ 🛍 ♀

One of the finest eighteenth-century designed landscapes in the North. There is no real flower garden but the fine avenue of mostly Turkey oaks is memorable. The Palladian chapel is surrounded by woods leased to the Forestry Commission. There is a walled kitchen garden dating from the 1730s which is an open space waiting to be filled. Walks have been opened up with views to the ruined hall, orangery and other estate buildings in the grounds. In all, the Trust, assisted by the National Heritage Memorial Fund, has acquired 354 acres to secure the future of this great eighteenth-century landscape garden and protect the setting for the chapel. Restoration is taking place to re-open the eighteenth-century vistas.

Jesmond Dene 3

Jesmond NE2 2EY. Tel: (0191) 2810973

Newcastle City Community and Leisure Services Department • 1m E of city centre along Jesmond Road • Open all year, daily • Entrance: free • Other information: Parking in Benton Bank. Visitor Centre open at weekends ○ 🍵 WC ♿ ◁

Presented to the city in 1883 by Lord Armstrong, the famous engineer, and only a mile from the city centre, this steep-sided, thickly-wooded dene provides extensive walks in an entirely natural setting, complete with a waterfall, a ruined mill and some fine old buildings. There is a well-run pets' corner, and from Freeman Road the upper park has a children's play area and pond. Quite exceptional condition for a city park. Those who want to drive out to the country may like to visit the National Trust's *Cherryburn*, some 11 miles west at Station Road, Mickley, the birthplace of Thomas Bewick, where they can see his splendid engravings and picnic in the garden. See Cragside (Northumberland), also created by Lord Armstrong.

SYMBOLS
[NEW] entries new for 2000; ○ open all year; ◑ open most of year; ◐ open during main season; ● open rarely and/or by appt; 🍵 teas/light refreshments; ✕ meals 🛋 picnics permitted; WC toilet facilities; WC toilet facilities, inc. disabled ♿ garden partly wheelchair-accessible; ◁ dogs permitted on lead; 🌿 plants for sale; 🛍 shop; ♀ events held

NORFOLK

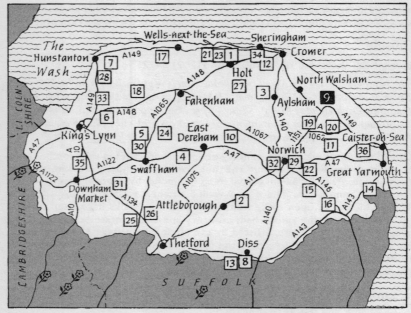

Two-starred gardens are marked on the map with a black square.

Bayfield Hall   1

Bayfield, Holt N25 7JN. Tel: (01263) 712219

*Mr and Mrs R. Combe • 1m N of Holt off A148 • Open 18th June, 2 – 5pm for charity
and by appt • Entrance: £2, children (under 10) free • Other information: Teas on
charity open day only. Plants for sale at adjacent Wildlife Garden* ● 🖼 🌳 ♿

The house commands one of the most beautiful views in Norfolk. The grounds
are thought to have been landscaped by Repton and the wooded valley of the
Glaven has been dammed to form a lake; a ruined Saxon church forms part of
this arrangement. The gardens immediately around the house are well planned
and contain many unusual plants, including a mature *Schizophragma hydrangeoides*. Above the church is a Victorian dogs' graveyard with woods beyond. A
tranquil and peaceful place.

Besthorpe Hall ★   2

Besthorpe, Attleborough N17 2LJ. Tel: (01953) 452138

*Mr J.A. Alston • 14m SW of Norwich, 1m E of Attleborough on Bunwell Road.
Entrance on right, past church • Open 10th June for NGS, 2 – 5pm, and by
appt • Entrance: £2* ● WC ♿

A pool and fountain occupy the centre of the entrance forecourt. Beyond the house, more pools and fountains are set among lawns skirted by high clematis-hung walls of Tudor brick which form a backdrop to long herbaceous borders. The largest lawn, believed to have been a tilt yard once, has developing topiary, while on another is an enormous and shapely Wellingtonia. There are many other fine trees, among which are paulownias and a variety of birches, acers and magnolias, including the sumptuous M. *delavayi*. Walled kitchen gardens, a nuttery, a herb garden, and a small lake with wildfowl. On another pool lives a pair of black swans. Bearded irises are the June feature. *Peter Beales Roses*, London Road, Attleborough is not far away and open Mon – Sat, 9am – 5pm, daily and Sun, 10am – 4pm.

Blickling Hall ★   3

Aylsham, Norwich NR11 6NF. Tel: (01263) 738030; Fax (01263) 731660

The National Trust • 15m N of Norwich, 1½ m NW of Aylsham on N side of B1354 • House open 8th April to Oct, Wed – Sun, 1 – 4.30pm • Garden open 8th April to July, Wed – Sun and Bank Holiday Mons; Aug, daily except Mon; Sept and Oct, Wed – Sun; all 10.30am – 5.30pm; Nov to March, Sat and Sun, 11am – 4pm • Entrance: £3.70 (house and gardens £6.50) • Other information: Picnics in walled garden only. Dogs in park only, on lead
◐ ☕ ✕ WC க ⚘ 🎂 ☕

Although the gardens seem so suited to the style and beauty of the Jacobean house, they consist of a blend of features from the seventeenth to the twentieth centuries. From the earliest period come the massive yew hedges flanking the south approach. To the east is the parterre planned by Nesfield and Wyatt in 1870 with its topiary pillars and blocks of yew shaped like grand pianos. Complicated flower beds were replaced in 1938 with Norah Lindsay's four large square beds of herbaceous plants in selected colours with surrounding borders of roses edged with catmint. The central pool has a seventeenth-century fountain bought from nearby Oxnead Hall. A high retaining wall bounds the southern side, while in the centre of the eastern side flights of steps mount to the highest terrace with a central vista through blocks of woodland to the Doric temple of 1730 raised above parkland beyond. The two blocks are intersected by *allées* in seventeenth-century style planted in 1861-64. Gales did much damage but replanting has been completed using Turkey oak, lime and beech. On the southern side the orangery of 1782 by Samuel Wyatt houses half-hardy plants and a statue of Hercules by Nicholas Stone made for Oxnead in the 1640s. In the corner of the northern block is the secret garden, a remnant of a larger eighteenth-century garden for which Repton made recommendations. It now consists of a lawn with a central sundial surrounded by high beech hedges. The shrub border through which it is approached is by Norah Lindsay, who was also responsible for the planting of the dry moat around the house. North of the parterre is a raised grassy area, possibly a remnant of the Jacobean mount; here grows an enormous, sprawling Oriental plane. To the north-west is landscaped parkland where woods descend to the curving lake formed before 1729 and later extended. West of the house cedars of Lebanon and a collection of magnolias around a nineteenth-century fountain. Elsewhere in the park are the Gothick

Tower of 1773 and the Mausoleum of 1796, a pyramid nearly 14 metres square by Joseph Bonomi. The Trust has recently restored the park to its 1840 limits and replanted 30 acres of the Great Wood.

Bradenham Hall ★ 4

West Bradenham, Thetford IP25 7QP. Tel: (01362) 687279

Mrs Allhusen • 8m E of Swaffham, 5m W of East Dereham S off A47 • Open April to Sept, 2nd, 4th and 5th Suns in month, 2 – 5.30pm. Coach parties on Sun or other times by written appt with meals if requested • Entrance: £3, children under 12 free • Other information: Plant sale on 1st Sun in Oct (entrance £1) ● ➤ WC ও ♨

The gardens sit near the top of Norfolk's arguably highest hill and give a fine view to the south over rolling farmland. The garden and arboretum comprise about 27 acres and surround a fine early-Georgian brick house (not open). Since the site is windy, the gardens are divided by many yew hedges screening 90 yards of herbaceous borders, backing onto shrubs and the Philosophers' Walk. There is a paved garden and a large old-fashioned rose garden. The other borders have a plantsman's collection of shrubs, flowers and trees, all labelled. The house and garden walls are covered with a wide range of shrubs, climbers and fruit (some slightly tender). In the walled kitchen garden are vegetables, cut flowers and a mixed border backed by laburnums. Two glasshouses and an attractive old barn. The arboretum, of about 1000 varieties, all named, includes many rare and interesting specimens. In spring there are large plantings of naturalised daffodils (some 90 selective cultivars, all labelled) in groups that drift through part of the arboretum; there is also an area of fritillaries. Noted gardeners have described Bradenham as 'exceptional' and 'a must' for visitors.

Castle Acre Priory 5

Castle Acre, King's Lynn PE32 2AF. Tel: (01670) 755394

English Heritage • 5m N of Swaffham, ¼ m W of Castle Acre, off A1065 • Open summer, daily, 10am – 6pm; winter, Wed – Sun, 10am – 1pm, 2 – 4pm • Entrance: £3.10, concessions £2.30, children £1.60 (1999 prices) ○ ➤ ▣ WC ও ⇗ ⌂ ♨

This is a walled herb garden divided into four sections containing medicinal, decorative, culinary and strewing herbs. Lavenders line the walls, where there are also three apple trees dating from the sixteenth century. A central circular bed contains a bay tree. The Old Rectory, South Acre (see entry) is nearby, and *West Acre Gardens*, a commercial nursery for rare plants set in a two-acre walled kitchen garden, is about four miles away.

Congham Hall Hotel 6

Lynn Road, Grimston, King's Lynn PE32 1AH. Tel: (01485) 600250; Fax: (01485) 601191

Mr and Mrs T. Forecast • 7m NE of King's Lynn. From A149/A148 interchange, follow A148 signed Sandringham/Fakenham/Cromer for 100 metres. Turn right for Grimston. Hotel is 2½ m on left • Open April to Sept, daily except Sat, 2 – 4pm. Small parties by arrangement at other times • Entrance: free • Other information: No coaches ◑ **WC** ♿ ☙

The hotel, set in 40 acres of parkland with a neat parterre full of bright bedding at the entrance, is listed in the *Good Food Guide*. It merits an entry in this *Guide* for its formal herb garden with about 650 varieties of both culinary and medicinal herbs, each labelled in an eccentric manner, although it also has some herbaceous plantings and pergolas with roses. The herb garden was started about 12 years ago to supply the hotel kitchen, and is thus a working garden. A 'Woodery' has been added to accommodate the increasing collection of herbs, utilizing timber salvaged from fallen trees instead of rocks.

Courtyard Farm ★ 7

Ringstead PE36 5LQ.

Lord Melchett • 16m NE of King's Lynn, 3½ m E of Hunstanton, 2m E of Ringstead, on road crossing Ringstead Common to Chosely and Burnham Market • Open all year, daily • Entrance: free ○ ▤ ⟁

The primeval gardener was a stone-age farmer who enjoyed the poppies and cornflowers that spattered his little fields of ripening grain. Farming in the computer age is altogether different, but Courtyard Farm harks back to those prehistoric days of marigolds and corncockles. The best time to visit is in July. Take a circular walk through fields of ripening grains and ramble back in time, through acres of cornfield wild flowers. Ninety-three plant species have been identified in the grassland areas, and 29 in the cornfields. This is not gardening on a small scale, but it is a most praiseworthy effort to retain our natural heritage of wild and cultivated plants. On many farms the cornflowers have been exterminated as weeds – there are no weeds here! Most heartening.

The Dell, Bressingham
(Bressingham Steam Museum and Garden) ★ 8

Bressingham, Diss IP22 2AB. Tel: (01379) 687386/382 (24 hours)

Mr Alan Bloom • 3m W of Diss on A1066 • Open early April to late Sept, daily, 10am – 5.30pm • Entrance: £4.50 (museum and garden) • Other information: B&B at Bressingham Hall from April to Oct ◑ ☕ ✕ ▤ **WC** ♿ ☙ 🛍 ☕

Alan Bloom's two passions are on display side by side here – steam engines, including trains, and fine plants – a superb collection of nearly 5000 species and cultivars. The famous island beds, often with cleverly placed snaking flint walls to provide extra height, are planted with a collection of herbaceous perennials for continual colour from spring to autumn. Differences in heights and textures, as well as in the colour of the blossoms, provide rich variety. In the middle of summer the colours are striking: blue agapanthus and lemon yellow daisies, fiery crocosmias and rich magenta loosestrifes. Willow, birch and oak trees provide cool shaded patches, and a pool lies at the garden's heart. Many of Bressingham's famous plants are in these five acres, and as everything is labelled keen gardeners will find this garden an inspiration and an education. Entry is through the steam museum where engines and trains chug away and whistle in the background, but Mr Bloom claims that these nostalgic sounds do not detract from the peace of the garden. For complete quiet also visit Adrian Bloom's Foggy Bottom (see entry), a 5-minute walk away.

East Ruston Old Vicarage ★★ 9

East Ruston, Norwich NR12 9HN. Tel: (01603) 632350 (daytime)

Graham Robeson and Alan Gray • 15m NE of Norwich, 4m E of North Walsham. Turn off A149 signposted Bacton, Happisburgh, then left at T-junction. Ignore 3 signs to East Ruston; vicarage is next to church • Open 23rd April to 29th Oct, Sun, Wed, Fri and Bank Holiday Mons, 2 – 5.30pm, and by appt for coach parties • Entrance: £3.50, children £1 ◑ 🍽 **WC** & ⚘ 🌢

This garden has as much to offer in style as in substance, for its twin strengths are the architectural framwork of walls and hedges and an astonishing profusion of plants. Two Norfolk churches are visible from the garden, and play a fundamental role as focal points at the end of skilfully crafted vistas. Within the garden the value of theatre is not forgotten: tall dark hedges with openings beckon the visitor on to yet further discoveries from box parterre to sunken garden, superb herbaceous borders, Mediterranean garden and, one of the most striking elements, the tropical border. How rare to find bananas growing one and a half miles from the North Sea, their leaves intact, surrounded by equally luxurious foliage of cannas and many other exotics. Rare plants are everywhere, set in gravel or in borders; because of the garden's coastal setting, many are semi-hardy, and shrubs from the southern hemisphere are well represented. On the perimeter, a cornfield achieves an astonishing density and brilliance of summer colour, and the garden continues to be developed with apparently limitless energy on the part of the owners, the most recent alteration being the creation of a Desert Wash.

Elsing Hall ★ 10

Elsing, East Dereham NR20 3DX. Tel: (01362) 637224

Mr and Mrs D.H. Cargill • 14m NE of Norwich, 5m NE of East Dereham. Signed off A47 • Open June to Sept, Sun only, 2 – 6pm and by appt • Entrance: £3, children free ● 🍽 🏠 **WC** & ⟵⟶ 🌢

The romantic appearance of the garden is in complete harmony with the moated half-timbered and flint house which it surrounds. It is rich, lush and unrestrained and in mid-summer is filled with the scent of the old garden roses which cover the walls and fill the borders. The lawn between the house and the moat has been abandoned to wild orchids; wildfowl nest among the reeds. Both the moat and a nearby stewpond are encircled by moist borders supporting luxuriant growth. On the walls of the kitchen garden grow old roses, many of which seem unique to this place, and more are continually being added. A large variety of trees has been planted, a formal garden developed, and an avenue of ginkgos established.

Fairhaven Garden Trust ★   11

School Road, South Walsham, Norwich NR13 6DZ. Tel: (01603) 270449

*Fairhaven Garden Trust • 9m NE of Norwich off B1140 at South Walsham •
Open daily except 25th Dec, 10am – 5pm, May to Aug, Wed, Thur, 10am –
9pm. Guided walks for parties • Entrance: £3, OAPs £2.70, children £1, under
5 free. Season tickets £10, family season ticket £25, wildlife sanctuary £1.
Discounts for parties • Other information: Boat trips available* ◑ 🍲 ✕ 🏚 WC
& ⟁ ⳾ 👍 ⚲

A garden created in natural woods of oak and alder extending to about 230
acres surrounding the unspoiled (private) South Walsham Inner Broad. Paths
wind among banks of azaleas and large-leaved rhododendrons and lead to the
edge of the broad itself. Much of the area is wet and supports a rich variety of
primulas, especially candelabras, with lysichitums, hostas, astilbes, ligularias
and gunneras of exceptional size merging into the natural vegetation, among
which are many royal ferns and some majestic oaks. Although particularly
colourful during the flowering of the azaleas and rhododendrons in the spring,
this garden gives pleasure at all times of the year when natural beauty is
preferred to man-made sophistication.

Felbrigg Hall ★   12

Felbrigg, Norwich NR11 8PR. Tel: (01263) 837444; Fax: (01263) 837032

*The National Trust • 2m SW of Cromer off A148. Main entrance on B1436 • Hall
open as garden, 1 – 5pm (Bank Holiday Mons, 11am – 5pm) • Garden open
March to Oct, Sat – Wed, 11am – 5pm. Park and woodland walks all year daily,
dawn – dusk • Entrance: £2.20, children £1 (house and gardens £5.50, children
£2.75, parties £4.50 per person, children £2.25) (1999 prices) • Other information:
Self-drive scooter available • Garden:* ◑ 🍲 ✕ 🏚 WC & ⳾ 👍 ⚲ *Park:* ○ ⟁

The Jacobean house faces south across the park, which is notable for its fine
woods and lakeside walk. William Windham III, the great-grandson of the
builder of the hall, was Humphry Repton's landlord and patron. Felbrigg may
have been Repton's first large-scale essay in landscape design. A ha-ha separates the park from the lawns of the house where there is an orangery planted
with camellias. To the north the ground rises and there are specimen trees and
shrubs. At some distance to the east a large walled kitchen garden is now richly
planted with a combination of fruit, vegetables and flowers in a formal design
behind clipped hedges. Vine house and great brick dovecot. In early autumn
there is a display of many varieties of colchicums: a National Collection is kept
here. The gardens are in immaculate order, and restoration, renewal and
replacement continue at a brisk pace. Sheringham Park (see entry) is nearby.

Foggy Bottom ★   13

Bressingham, Diss IP22 2AA. Tel: (01379) 688402; Fax: (01379) 687788

*Mr Adrian Bloom • 3m W of Diss on A1066 adjoining The Dell, Bressingham
and close to Bressingham Plant Centre • Open 2nd April to Oct, daily except Sat*

*and Mon, 12.30 – 4.30pm, and 4th, 5th March, 2nd, 3rd Sept, 10.30am –
4.30pm. Parties by appt • Entrance: £3, OAPs £2.50, children (under 16) free •
Other information: food and toilet facilities available at Bressingham Plant
Centre* ◑

Foggy Bottom is a wicked name for a splendid garden – don't think of dull,
dank days, think of sunshine and blue skies. It sparkles with colour, principally
from the excellent collection of gold and blue conifers. Does that sound awful?
Go to be converted into a fan of colourful conifers! (Take a notebook; most
plants are labelled.) The trees, now mature but still youthful, have been
combined with excellent herbaceous perennials and shrubs planted in bold
clumps. Heathers in many colours and shades form cushions of colour at all
seasons. Numerous grasses have been planted to great effect. Spacious, with
marvellous vistas through the islands of trees and a soft lawn for ambling, this
is a quiet place, full of brightness, a place to linger before, or after, the Steam
Museum and Garden just 300 metres away.

Fritton Lake Countryworld   14

Fritton, Great Yarmouth NR31 9HA. Tel: (01493) 488208

*Lord and Lady Somerleyton • 5m SW of Great Yarmouth off A143 • Garden
open April to Sept, daily, 10am – 5.30pm • Entrance: £5, OAPs £4.50, children
£3.80 (includes all attractions except miniature railway 80p, children 60p).
Discounts for parties • Other information: Falconry, heavy horses, golf, putting,
boats, children's farm, pony rides, miniature tractors and craft workshops* ◑ 🍽
✕ 🏪 <u>WC</u> ♿ 🏧 ▤

The large lake remains almost unspoilt and separate from the tea rooms and
other commercial attractions of this country park. An unusual feature is a
Victorian garden of about half an acre in the gardenesque style with irregular
beds surrounded by clipped box hedges and filled with shrubs and herbaceous
perennials that give a colourful display in the summer. In addition to the
formal lakeside gardens there are woodland walks and gardens, including the
Lost Gardens of Fritton Hall. The Victorian hall was burnt down in 1957, not
rebuilt, and the gardens left to go wild. They contain a large collection of
rhododendrons and azaleas intersected by paths.

The Garden in an Orchard   15

Mill Road, Bergh Apton, Norwich NR15 1BQ. Tel: (01508) 480322

*Mr and Mrs R.W. Boardman • 6m SE of Norwich off A146 at Hellington
Corner • Open 29th, 30th April, 1st May, 27th – 29th May, 26th – 28th Aug;
11am – 6pm; also other weekends May to Sept (check before visiting) • Entrance:
£1.50 • Other information: Refreshments on Suns only* ● WC 🏪 ♿ 🐕 ▤ ▤

The garden started as a three-and-a-half-acre commercial orchard and over the
years has been planted up bit by bit with rare and unusual plants and trees.
Narrow paths meander through dense plantings of species roses, giving eye-
to-eye contact with their flowers, then open up to similar plantings of
herbaceous walks, imbuing the garden with an atmosphere of mystery. Mr

Boardman is a professional plantsman and among his rare trees are *Phellodendron amurense*, *Prunus padus* 'Colorata', *Paulownia tomentosa* and nine species of eucalyptus. *Lonicera ledebourii* catches the eye, along with *Malva sylvestris mauritiana* and many special clematis scrambling through trees. A half-acre wildflower meadow, with a wide range of British flora, is now maturing.

Hales Hall 16

Hales, Loddon NR14 6QW. Tel: (01508) 548395

Mr and Mrs Terence Read • 12m SE of Norwich, off A146. Signposted • Open all year, Tues – Sat, 10am – 5pm, Sun and Bank Holiday Mons, 11am – 4pm. Closed 21st April. Parties by arrangement • Entrance: £1.50 (Great Barn and gardens) • Other information: Fifteenth-century thatched Great Barn ○ 🍴
WC & 🐾 💡

A moat surrounds the remaining wing of a vast house of the late fifteenth century and a central lawn with well-planted borders and topiary of box and yew (grown from cuttings) backed by high brick walls. Work is continuing on the restoration of the garden after centuries of neglect, and a new fruit garden has been planted. The owners specialise in growing rare and unusual perennial plants, and look after National Collections of citrus, figs and greenhouse grapes. The associated century-old nurseries offer an extensive range of conservatory plants, vines, figs, mulberries, and many peach, apricot, nectarine and greengage varieties.

Holkham Hall ★ 17

Wells–next–the–Sea NR23 1AB. Tel: (01328) 710227 or (01328) 711707; (01328) 711636 (Holkham Nursery Gardens)

The Earl of Leicester • 23m W of Cromer, 2m W of Wells on A149 • Hall open as terrace gardens plus 4th June to 24th Sept, Sun, 1 – 5pm. Also 23rd, 24th, 30th April, 1st, 28th, 29th May, 27th, 28th Aug, 11.30am – 5pm • Terrace gardens open 30th May to 28th Sept, Mon – Thurs, 1 – 5pm. Nursery gardens open daily except 25th, 26th Dec, 10am – 5pm • Entrance: Terrace and nursery gardens free (hall and bygones museum £6, children £3; either hall or bygones museum separately £4, children £2) • Other information: History of farming exhibition • Terrace gardens: ◐ 🍽 ✕ 🍴
WC & 🐾 💡 👜 *Nursery gardens:* ○ 🐾

The vast park, famous for its holm oaks, was laid out originally by William Kent but altered by 'Coke of Norfolk' and the 2nd Earl. On the west side of the house, lawns sweep down to the great lake. The terrace which fronts the south façade was added in 1854, but the scale of the house and park is so large that, from a distance at least, this does not seriously disrupt the vision of the two. The formal beds designed by W.A. Nesfield flank a great fountain representing St George and the Dragon said to be designed by R. Smith. The nursery gardens, in the original eighteenth-century walled kitchen garden in the grounds, extend to over six acres, subdivided into six areas with perennial borders and the original greenhouses. Alpines, shrubs, perennials, herbs, roses, bedding and house plants are for sale. About five miles away is another nursery worth visiting, the *Creake Plant Centre* at South Creake.

Houghton Hall ★ 18

King's Lynn PE31 6UE. Tel: (01485) 528569

The Marquess of Cholmondeley • 13m NE of King's Lynn off A148 • Hall open, as garden, 2 – 5.30pm • Park and gardens open 23rd April to 24th Sept, Sun, Thurs and Bank Holiday Mons, 12 noon – 5.30pm • Entrance: £3.50, children £2 (hall, park and gardens £6, children £3) (1999 prices) ◐ ☕ 🏠 WC ⅙ ☼ ▥

One of the most magnificent houses in Britain, built between 1721 and 1735 by Colen Campbell and James Gibbs. The five-acre walled kitchen garden has, over the last few years, been transformed by the Marquess of Cholmondeley and his enthusiastic head gardener, Paul Underwood, into an exciting and ambitious new garden. A 120-metre-long double herbaceous border, edged with catmint and backed by yew hedges, spans it and there will be a garden room at one end, with a Kent seat closing the view. The rose garden is based on the design of the ceiling in the White Drawing Room. New English and old-fashioned roses, underplanted with lavender, fill the beds and climb over metal arches painted in verdigris, as in Monet's garden. The centrepiece is a sunken pool, flanked by antique statues. There are roses everywhere, and it is said that the scent can be detected as far away as the park. The vegetable and fruit garden is as perfect as the flower garden. Orderly rows of produce supply the house (fifteen varieties of vegetables are available each day during the summer season) with a useful herb border nearby. Wide grass paths are edged with 100 different varieties of cordon apples, 30 varieties of pears, red and white currants in double cordons and fan-trained cherries. These will eventually form tunnels. Blocks of raspberries, gooseberries and hybrid berries and strawberries fill the beds. An ambitious area of pleached hornbeam walks and a water garden with fountain surrounded by topiary are both coming along well. It is seldom one can see a garden being developed on this scale.

Hoveton Hall Gardens 19

Wroxham, Norwich NR12 8RJ. Tel: (01603) 782798

Mr and Mrs Andrew Buxton • 9m NE of Norwich, 1m N of Wroxham on A1151 • Open 23rd April to 13th Sept, Wed, Fri, Sun and Bank Holiday Mons, 11am – 5.30pm. Coach parties and tours by arrangement • Entrance: £3, children (5-14) £1, season tickets £8, family £18 ◐ 🏠 WC ⅙ ☼

Set in the Norfolk Broads area, the gardens are amply supplied with water and streams. For mid-May and early June the rhododendrons and azaleas, many rare varieties, are spectacular, dominating and scenting the woodland walks. The formal walled garden, planted and enclosed in 1936, with herbaceous borders of that period, is now in the process of additional planting. A delightful gardener's cottage is set picturesquely in one corner, covered in roses. The adjoining walled kitchen garden is a good example of traditional vegetable planting, with herbaceous plants from the garden for sale. The entrance to the two walled gardens has an intriguing iron gate in the shape of a spider, hence the formal garden is called the Spider Garden. A water garden, leading to the lake, has good water plants, vast examples of *Gunnera manicata*, peltiphyllums, hostas and good stands of bamboos. The whole area is laced with streams and interesting bridges, adding calm and reflection at every corner. Birds, both migratory and native, abound.

How Hill Farm ★ 20

Ludham, Norwich NR29 5PG. Tel: (01692) 678558

Mr P.D.S. Boardman • 15m NE of Norwich, 1m W of Ludham off A1062. Follow signs to How Hill. Farm Garden S of How Hill • Open 21st May, 2 – 5pm. Party visits at other times by arrangement • Entrance: £2, children free ● � ▣ WC ₺ ⬦ ❧

The garden around the farm is comparatively conventional, with a new garden and pond in the old bullock yard and a large Chusan palm planted in a dog cage from which it threatens to escape. Here, too, is a collection of over 100 varieties of *Ilex aquifolium* as well as many rare species of the holly genus. Over the road in the river valley is a rich combination of exotics mingled with native vegetation. Around a series of pools, banks of azaleas merge into reed beds, rhododendron species rise over thickets of fern, wild grasses skirt groves of the giant *Arundo donax*, with birches, conifers and a collection of 50 different bamboos against a background of a recently created three-acre broad, thick with water lilies. The soil acidity in some places is as exceptionally low as pH 2.8, other parts varying up to pH 7.5, supporting a wide variety of trees and shrubs.

Kettle Hill ★ 21

Blakeney NR25 7PN. Tel: (01263) 741147

Richard and Frances Winch • 11m W of Cromer, just outside Blakeney on B1156 Langham road • Parking • Open for charity 6th Aug, 2 – 6pm, and by appt • Entrance: £3, children free ● ▣ WC ₺ ❧

One could be forgiven for thinking that gardening on the north Norfolk coast was a daunting task, but Kettle Hill dispels all that. With the help of Mark Rumary, the owners have transformed this garden into a luxurious and elegant delight. A box-edged rectangular parterre with heart-shaped beds, heightened with topiary spirals and mop heads, reflects their interest in the *Romantic Garden Nursery* at Swannington. A cleverly sited brick wall shelters a long mixed border packed with colour and unusual plants and leads to a circular secret garden. A large lawn, featuring a delightful Gothick summerhouse by George Carter, extends from the house to mature woodland, to which many ornamental trees have been added and which is carpeted in spring with bluebells and naturalised lilies. The walks cut through the wood hold many surprises, but the triumph is the short downward slope to a semi-formal fenced garden full of fragrant shrub roses.

Lake House Water Gardens 22

Brundall, Norwich NR13 5LU. Tel: (01603) 712933

Mr and Mrs Garry Muter • 5m E of Norwich. From A47 roundabout take Brundall turn and turn right at T-junction into Postwick Lane • Open 23rd, 24th April, 11am – 5pm. Private parties by appt • Entrance: £2, accompanied children free • Other information: Sale of unusual plants on open days ◕ ☕ 🗄 ⊲🏠

Two acres of water gardens set in a steep cleft in the river escarpment. From the top of the hill the gardens fall away to a lily-covered lake at the bottom. They were once part of a 76-acre private estate and arboretum planted about 1880. The fascinating history has been researched and written by the owners and can be purchased by visitors. Plant associations are a feature throughout the garden, reflecting Mrs Muter's talent as a flower arranger. Surrounding the formal areas are drifts of primroses, bluebells and daffodils in season; wild flowers abound. The formal planting has many rare and interesting species: *Zantedeschia* 'Green Goddess' and *Z. aethiopica* 'Crowborough' in a large clump cool down a flamboyant *Hemerocallis* 'Frans Hals'. A wide variety of hardy geraniums blooms in succession and a good collection of hybrid helianthemums awaits those who visit by appointment in June.

Lawn Farm 23

Cley Road, Holt NR25 7DY. Tel: (01263) 713484

Mr and Mrs G.W. Deterding • Take Cley road out of Holt opposite King's Head in High St. After 1m house is turning on right, after Holt Hall School gates • Open April to July by appt • Entrance: £3, children free NEW ◕ WC

The six-and-a-half acre garden was laid out by the owners in 1987. There are four natural ponds with two planted water gardens, while a damp wooded area is home to hydrangeas and azaleas. A completely different garden is contained in two medieval flint-walled courtyards with roses, plus many interesting and unusual shrubs and climbers which flourish in the warm and sheltered conditions. The owners have a magpie's eye for the rare and difficult to find, and the collection of trees is of the same high and eclectic standard.

Lexham Hall 24

East Lexham, King's Lynn PE32 2QJ. Tel: (01328) 701288/701341; Fax (01328) 700053

Mr and Mrs Neil Foster • 6m N of Swaffham, 2m W of Litcham off B1145 • Open 21st May, 18th June, and May to July mid-week by appt for parties of 25 or more • Entrance: £3 ◕ ☕ 🗄 WC ♿ 🐕

The seventeenth- and eighteenth-century hall sits well amid beautiful parkland with sheep and interesting trees. The ground falls away to the river forming a lake and canals crossed by elegant bridges, largely the creation of the Wodehouse and Keppel families. The garden was the inspiration of the present owner's mother who, with the help of the late Dame Sylvia Crowe, laid out its bones. Massive yew hedges reveal intimate views of the park, taking the eye to the distance beyond. Wide terracing to the south of the house is well planted and colourful, and a long grass walk edged with herbaceous plants and shrubs progresses to woodland full of rhododendrons, azaleas and spring bulbs. (In early spring, the parkland and adjoining churchyard are awash with snowdrops.) Colourful rose garden. The kitchen garden, maintained in the old style, has an early eighteenth-century crinkle-crankle wall covered with fruit, a cutting border, greenhouses with plants for the house and tender vegetables, the whole a picture of health. A wood to the south, known as the American Gardens, is reputedly planted from seeds collected in America.

Lynford Arboretum   25

Lynford Road, Mundford, Nr Thetford IP27 0TJ. Tel: (01842) 810271

Forestry Commission • 8m N of Brandon on Swaffham road (A1065); signposted • Open daily during daylight hours • Entrance: free NEW ○ 🍴 ⅙

This small arboretum, with recently renewed paths and well-labelled trees (vandals have removed some labels), is a diverting place for a gentle stroll; you could spend an hour or more here. The trees are little more than 50 years old, so none is of special note. Combine your visit with one to another part of Thetford Forest, perhaps the King's Forest (between Brandon and Bury St Edmunds) where the beech trees are especially splendid in late spring and in autumn. Less than a mile from the arboretum, on the outskirts of Mundford, is Magpies garden and nursery (see entry).

Magpies   26

Green Lane, Mundford IP26 5HS. Tel: (01842) 878496

Patricia Cooper • ½ m N of A134 Downham Market – Thetford road at Mundford roundabout, or off A1065 Swaffham road • Open May to July, daily, 12 noon – 5pm; nursery open March to Sept, daily except Wed, 12 noon – 5pm (closed 27th, 28th Aug) • Entrance: £1 (for charity) • Other information: Groups welcome, but please check in advance for picnic facilities NEW ◑ ⅙ ⊕ ⍭

The garden in midsummer is a living display of vegetable fireworks, but for all that it is a tranquil, subtle garden. Shimmering fountains of golden oats (*Stipa gigantea*) are its hallmark. Larches and birches provide a light canopy over irregular island beds boldly planted with perennials. Tall mulleins and evening primroses are mixed with chicories and plume poppies, while the fragrance of jasmine and honeysuckle hangs in the air. It is a real cottage garden composed of informal rooms, each filled to the brim with interesting plants. There is a pond and shady nooks and crannies where you may even chance to see a wandering hedgehog snuffling about under the billowing cranesbills. Many of the excellent, modestly priced plants are for sale. Nearby is Lynford Arboretum (see entry), and the vast expanse of Thetford Forest.

Mannington Hall ★ 27

Saxthorpe, Norwich NR11 7BB. Tel: (01263) 584175

Lord and Lady Walpole • 18m NW of Norwich off B1149. Signposted • Open May to Sept, Sun, 12 noon – 5pm; also June to Aug, Wed – Fri, 11am – 5pm • Entrance: £3, OAPs and students £2.50, children free ◐ 🍵 🍴 WC ♿ 🌿 🏛 ♨

The romantic appearance of this garden of 20 acres is only matched in Norfolk by Elsing Hall (see entry), where the house is also of the fifteenth century. Lawns run down to the moat, crossed by a drawbridge, to herbaceous borders backed by high walls of brick and flint. The moat also encloses a secret, scented garden in a design derived from one of the ceilings of the house. Outside the moat are borders of flowering shrubs flanking a Doric temple, and beyond are woodlands containing the ruins of a Saxon church and nineteenth-century follies to deceive the visitor, if only temporarily. Within the walls of the former kitchen garden, a series of rose gardens has been planted following the design of gardens from medieval to modern times and featuring roses popular at each period. A twentieth-century rose garden incorporates planthouse, vegetable plot and children's garden as well as numerous roses. There are now more than 1500 varieties of roses in the gardens. A lake, woods and meadowland with extensive walks are other features.

Norfolk Lavender 28

Caley Mill, Heacham, King's Lynn PE31 7JE. Tel: (01485) 570384; Fax: (01485) 571176; E-mail: admin@norfolk-lavender.co.uk

Norfolk Lavender Ltd • 13m N of King's Lynn on A149 • Open all year except 25th, 26th Dec, 1st Jan, daily, 9.30am – 5pm • Entrance: free ○ 🍵 WC ♿ 🌿 🏛 ♨

Fields of lavender, stretching into the distance like giant stripes of corduroy, are a splendid sight in July and August. There is a more intimate display of named lavender (designated as a National Collection) near the Victorian watermill that serves as the visitor centre for this major commercial enterprise. A small herb garden is well tended and labelled, and the beds in the rose garden are lavender-edged. The four-acre fragrant garden has helped to reduce the pressure caused by coach loads of visitors, particularly in July and August.

Oak Tree House 29

6 Cotman Road, Thorpe, Norwich NR1 4AF. Tel: (01603) 623167; Fax (01603) 617661

Mr W.R.S. Giles • In E Norwich off A47 Thorpe road, ¼ m from Norwich Thorpe station. From Yarmouth follow one-way system towards city centre, turn right at traffic lights opposite MAFF building and after 300 metres turn left opposite Barclays Bank • Open for parties by arrangement only • Entrance: £3, children free (1999 prices) • Other information: Wheelchairs by arrangement ● 🍵 🌿

An exotic garden of half an acre on a hillside. The owner (who is also an illustrator) is creating a garden full of hidden corners. The air is filled with the mysterious scents of daturas, jasmines, lilies, hedychiums, cordylines and the like. Hemerocallis glow in the evening light, whilst a host of different cannas with large leaves and iris-like flowers in shades from pale yellow to intense red, gently nod in the breeze. Tall banana plants with two-metre leaves tower above tithonias and purple-leaved *Ricinus communis* 'Carmencita'. Everywhere there are terracotta pots filled with aeoniums, agaves, aroids, citrus. Giant scabious and fetid dracunculus are to be found near a recently rebuilt thatched Victorian root house, crowned with a hat of golden hop. Towards the back of the house, on a steeper incline, a grotto-cum-vertical-rockery covered in ferns and mosses is one of the projects under construction. Above and beyond this is the woodland garden with raised flint wall beds containing chain ferns (woodwardia), tree ferns and variegated ground elder.

Old Rectory   30

South Acre, King's Lynn PE32 2AD. Tel: (01760) 755469

Mr and Mrs Clive Hardcastle • 3m N of Swaffham off A1065, opposite South Acre church • Open for NGS one Sun in June, 2 – 5pm, and from May to July by appt • Entrance: £2.50, private visits £3 ◑ 🏠 WC ♿ ⬧ ✿

A three-acre garden where a long lawn with mixed herbaceous borders on each side leads the eye past a huge willow tree to a fine view of the eleventh-century Castle Acre Priory (see entry). To one side clipped peacocks guard the entrance to the herb garden, and beyond lies a small vineyard with lavender bushes at each end of the rows. Clipped box and climbing roses edge the well-tended vegetable garden, with fruit trees trained against the wall. To the other side of the lawn, behind a yew hedge, there is a pool garden which leads into a wild area, with specimen shrubs, ancient box trees and many bulbs in spring. Behind the house is a newly planted rose garden. The house was the childhood home of Margaret Fountains of *Love among the Butterflies* fame.

Old Vicarage, East Ruston

(See EAST RUSTON OLD VICARAGE)

Oxburgh Hall   31

Oxborough, King's Lynn PE33 9PS. Tel: (01366) 328258; Fax: (01366) 328066

The National Trust • 7m SW of Swaffham off A134 • House open 1st to 26th April, 1st to 29th Oct, Sat, Sun, Tues, Wed and Bank Holiday Monday; 29th April to July, Sept, Sat – Wed; Aug, daily; all 1 – 5pm except Bank Holiday Mondays, 11am – 5pm • Garden open 4th to 26th March, Sat, Sun, 11am – 4pm; April to July, Sept to 29th Oct, Sat – Wed, Aug, daily, 11am – 5.30pm • Entrance: £2.60 (hall and garden £5.20, pre-booked parties £4.20 per person) ◑ ☕ ✕ 🏠 WC ♿ ⛪ ✿

This romantic mellow red-brick manor house seems to float in its rectangular moat above a haze of fringed water lilies. Both house and garden are concealed from view until you have walked past the orchard of quince, plum and greengage trees. Then you look down over the formal parterre, a Victorian copy of a Le Nôtre design consisting of a moderately restrained pattern of beds edged with clipped box hedges, punctuated by clipped tumps of yew. Yellow, red, violet and silver are the colours of the annual bedding – a colourful carpet. Behind a long yew hedge is a narrow border edged with wispy catmint, with carefully repeated clumps of perennials: loosestrife, golden-rod, daisies and mallows. There are some fine trees, and circular walks lead into the park and woodland, full of snowdrops and winter aconites in spring.

The Plantation Garden   32

4 Earlham Road, Norwich NR2 3DB. Tel: (01603) 611669
(Trust chairman: Mrs E. Bickerton)

Plantation Garden Preservation Trust • Entrance off Earlham Road, between Beeches Hotel and Crofters Hotel • Open mid-April to Oct, Suns, 2 – 5pm and several days for charity. Guided parties by arrangement • Entrance: £1, accompanied children free (£1.50 special openings). Parties £20 minimum ◐ ▣ WC ♿ ◁ ℘ ⛯

An unusual surviving example of a high-Victorian suburban garden, framed by mature trees. It was created by Henry Trevor in a disused chalk quarry just outside the medieval walls of Norwich. The first feature in his garden, an idiosyncratic Gothick fountain over nine metres high, was built in 1857. There followed terraces with walls in the medieval style (random rubble), built using an extraordinary conglomeration of materials: industrial waste, locally made fancy bricks, flint and stone. Flights of steps with Italianate pedestals and balustrades, a replica rustic bridge (1998), flower beds and woodland paths combine to make a garden simultaneously typical of its period and the personal vision of one individual. Conservation and restoration is an on-going process. It is also an area of ecological interest with birds and lime-loving wild flowers. Grade II English Heritage registered.

Sandringham House ★   33

Sandringham, King's Lynn PE35 6EN. Tel: (01553) 772675

H.M. The Queen • 9m NE of King's Lynn on B1440 near Sandringham Church • House open as garden • Garden and park open 15th April to 8th Oct, daily except 21st April and closed dates, probably 22nd July to 3rd Aug; then weekends only in Oct, all 11am – 4.45pm • Entrance: museum and grounds £4.50, OAPs £4, children £3, family £12 (house, museum and grounds £5.50, OAPs £4.50, children £3.50, family £14.50) ◑ ▉ ✕ WC ♿ ℘ ⛯

The house stands among broad lawns with an outer belt of woodland through which a path runs past plantings of camellias, hydrangeas, cornus, magnolias and rhododendrons, with some fine specimen trees including *Davidia involucrata* and *Cercidiphyllum japonicum*. The path passes the magnificent cast- and wrought-iron Norwich Gates of 1862. In the open lawn are specimen oaks planted by Queen Victoria and other members of the Royal Family. To the south-west of the house is the upper lake whose eastern side is built up into a massive rock garden using blocks of the local carrstone, and now largely planted with dwarf conifers. Below the rock garden, opening onto the lake, a cavernous grotto was intended as a boathouse, while above is a small summerhouse built for Queen Alexandra. There are thick plantings of hostas, agapanthus and various moisture-loving plants around the margin of the lake. The path passes between the upper and large lower lake set in wooded surroundings. To the north of the house is a garden designed by the late Sir Geoffrey Jellicoe for King George VI: a long series of beds surrounded by box hedges, divided by gravel and grass paths and flanked by avenues of pleached lime, one of which is centred on a gold-plated statue of a Buddhist divinity.

Sheringham Park ★ 34

Upper Sheringham NR26 8TB. Tel: (01263) 823778

The National Trust • 4m NE of Holt off A148 • Park open all year, daily, dawn – dusk • Entrance: Probably £2.60 per car inc. parking and all occupants. Coaches £7.80 • Other information: Coaches must pre-book with Warden during rhododendron season. Refreshments available April to Sept only
○ 🍽 🛍 WC ♿ ⌖

Located in a secluded valley at the edge of the Cromer/Holt ridge, close to the sea but protected from its winds by steep wooded hills, house and park, both designed by Humphry Repton, are now the property of the Trust, although the house remains in private occupation. The park is remarkable not only for its great beauty and spectacular views but also for an extensive collection of rhododendrons which thrive in the acid soil. Crowning an eminence is a modern classical temple based on a Repton design and erected to mark the 70th birthday of Mr Thomas Upcher, the last descendant of the original owner to live at Sheringham. This is the most-admired and best-preserved work of Repton.

Stow Hall ★ 35

Stow Bardolph, King's Lynn PE34 3HU. Tel: (01366) 383194

Lady Rose Hare • 2m N of Downham Market, E of A10 • Open 14th May, 18th June for NGS, 1 – 5pm and parties by appt • Entrance: £2.50, children free • Other information: Possible for wheelchairs but some gravel paths 🍽 🛍
WC ♿ ⌖ ✿

Majestic plane trees, beeches and cedars of Lebanon, certainly two centuries old, provide a changing backdrop for a garden that is in effect a long series of imaginative and interesting gardens linked by a straight path of red bricks and gravel. The high, warm walls of the old stableyard and the house are swathed in roses and wisteria – this is a paradise for anyone enthralled by old roses. Shrubs more usually seen in milder gardens also have congenial homes in the shelter of these walls – vanilla-scented *Azara microphylla*, white and blue abutilon, sun roses, Californian lilac, and many others. Amble along the path from the house to the nineteenth-century walled kitchen garden and you pass small elegant formal gardens, an iris garden, a Dutch garden, cloisters with more roses, and a croquet lawn. Inside the kitchen garden, as well as fine vegetables in season, you will find gnarled apple trees and pear trees, a venerable mulberry, and more roses. A new collection of antique apple trees has recently been planted. Everything is carefully maintained. Even if none of this existed, the astounding, self-layering fern-leaved beech would make any visit to Stow Hall worthwhile.

Thrigby Hall Wildlife Gardens   36

Filby, Great Yarmouth NR29 3DR. Tel: (01493) 369477

Mr K.J. Sims • 6m NW of Great Yarmouth on A1064. Signposted • Open all year, daily, 10am – 6pm or dusk • Entrance: £5.50, OAPs £4.90, children (4 – 14) £3.90 ○ 💷 🍴 WC ♿ 🛍

The chief attraction here is a collection of Chinese plants arranged to form the landscape of the willow-pattern plate, complete with pagodas and bridges across a small lake. Complementing the collection of Asiatic animals, the plants are those particularly associated with temple gardens and include *Ginkgo biloba*, *Pinus parviflora*, *Paeonia suffruticosa*, *Nandina domestica* and *Chimonobambusa quadrangularis*, set against a background of willows of many species. Otherwise Thrigby is a wildlife park with many facilities for children.

2001 GUIDE
The 2001 *Guide* will be published before Christmas 2000. Reports on gardens for consideration are welcome at all times of the year, but particularly by early summer (June) 2000 so that they can be inspected that year.
   All descriptions and other information are as accurate as possible at the time of going to press, but circumstances change and, if in doubt, it is wise to telephone before making a long journey.

COUNTY BOUNDARIES
Some gardens have postal addresses in one county and are physically situated in another. If in doubt, the index will direct the reader to the correct page.

DOGS, TOILETS & OTHER FACILITIES 🐕 WC
If these are not mentioned in the entry, then facilities are probably not available at the property described. For example, if dogs are not mentioned, owners will probably not permit entry, even on a lead.

NORTHAMPTONSHIRE

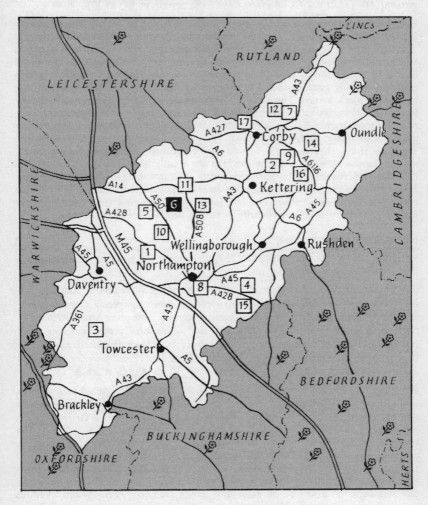

Two-starred gardens are marked on the map with a black square.

Althorp House

1

Althorp, Northampton NN7 4HQ. Tel: (01604) 770107;
Fax: (01604) 770042 (house and park office)

*Earl Spencer • 6m NW of Northampton on A428 Northampton – Rugby road •
House open • Gardens open some days in the year, and July to August. Please*

telephone for opening times and events details • Entrance: £3 (house and gardens £6, OAPs £4.50, children £3) (1999 prices) ● 🍲 📷 WC & 🏠

Because this was the home of Diana, Princess of Wales, its future will inevitably be dedicated to her memory and to those who visit out of respect or curiosity. The Earl, her brother, recognising this, has engaged Dan Pearson to produce an unusual memorial – a two-mile walk in the grounds through the park and house to the island where the Princess is buried, leading through a green meadow of long grasses and wild flowers by the lake with 1000 white water lilies, and black swans. The original Elizabethan building was surrounded by formal gardens probably swept away during the fashionable eighteenth-century improvements by the architect Henry Holland, helped by Samuel Lapidge, 'Capability' Brown's assistant. The present gardens were laid out in the 1860s by the architect W.M. Teulon and enclosed by stone walls and balustrades. To the side and rear the gardens are mainly laid to lawn, although Dan Pearson has recently planted beds with a subtle blend of bronze fennel, aconitum, potentillas and *Verbena bonariensis* outside the stable block, which now houses a tasteful shop, and the same restricted palette is used in other borders, harmonising wonderfully with the honey – coloured stone.

Boughton House Park   2

Kettering NN14 1BJ. Tel: (01536) 515731; E-mail: llt@boughtonhouse.org.uk; Web: www.boughtonhouse.org.uk

The Duke and Duchess of Buccleuch and Queensberry • 2m NW of Kettering off A43, entry via Geddington. Signposted • House open as garden • Garden open Aug to 1st Sept, 2 – 5pm (last admission 4.30pm). Park open May to 15th Sept, daily except Fri, 1 – 5pm. Specialist and educational parties welcome at other times by prior arrangement • Entrance: £1.50, OAPs and children £1 (house, gardens and park £6, OAPs and children £5) (1999 prices) • Other information: Dogs in park only, on lead ◐ 🍲 ✕ 📷 WC & 🐾 🏠 🍷

Although with only limited formal gardens remaining, Boughton will be attractive to garden enthusiasts and the whole family. The large sixteenth- and seventeenth- century house, with monastic origins and a strong French influence, contains an extensive collection of paintings and furniture. The magnificent surrounding park, with its lakes and canalised river, and avenues of trees, was laid out by the first Duke of Montagu before 1700 with the help of a Dutch gardener, Van der Meulen, who had experience of reclamation work in the Fens. The second Duke, known as 'John the Planter', added a lake and the network of avenues of elms and limes in the 1720s. These avenues originally extended to 70 miles before Dutch elm disease took its toll. Many elms are being replanted with limes. Planting close to the house includes herbaceous borders and some fine planted vases. To the south of the house a small circular rose garden leads on to the outstanding rectangular lily pond, beyond which the walled garden houses a long herbaceous border and well-stocked plant centre. In the 350-acre park are walks and trails, including one for the disabled, and a woodland adventure play area for children.

Canons Ashby House 3

Canons Ashby, Daventry NN11 3SD. Tel: (01327) 860044

*The National Trust • 6m S of Daventry off A361 Daventry – Banbury road •
House open • Garden open April to Oct, Sat – Wed, except 21st April, 12 noon
– 5.30pm or dusk if earlier (last admission 5pm) • Entrance: garden free (house
and garden £4, children £2, family ticket £10. Reductions for pre-booked parties)
• Other information: Parking 200 metres from house. Disabled telephone in
advance and park near house. Wheelchairs available. Taped guide for visually-
handicapped. Picnics in car park. Dogs in home paddock only, on lead* ◑ ☕
WC ♿ ▯

The romantic house where Spenser wrote part of *The Faerie Queene* was rescued
by the National Heritage Memorial Fund. Now its well-maintained garden is
being extensively restored by the Trust. Formal, with axial arrangements of
paths and terraces, high stone walls, lawns and gateways, it dates almost
entirely from the beginning of the eighteenth century. It is maturing well, with
trees and shrubs beginning to give the required height and scale. Hexagonal
beds, part of the later Inigo Trigg's plan of 1901, have been reinstated and
feature seasonal bedding. Borders have majestic plants such as acanthus,
cardoons and globe artichokes. The yew court contains fine topiary. Old
varieties of soft fruit bushes and pear, apple and plum trees include espaliers
grown from original stock planted in 1710 by Edward Dryden, whose family
owned the house. Cedar planted in 1781.

Castle Ashby Gardens 4

Castle Ashby, Northampton NN7 1LQ. Tel: (01604) 696232

*The Marquess of Northampton • 5m E of Northampton, between A45
Northampton – Wellingborough road and A428 Northampton – Bedford road •
Gardens open daily, 10am – dusk, with occasional closures when the whole
10,000 acres and house can be hired as a 'corporate venue' for £10,000 a day.
Tours for parties by appt • Entrance: (tickets from machine when entrance
unattended) £2.50, OAPs £2, children £1.50 • Other information: Refreshments
at tea rooms in village, 400 metres. Possible for wheelchairs but uneven paths.
Farm shop and rural craft centre in village. Country fair first week July*
○ ◁▷ ▯ ▯

Originally Elizabethan, then a park landscaped by 'Capability' Brown, and later
a Matthew Digby Wyatt terrace, Italian garden and arboretum. The house is
never open to the public, but there is access to most of the gardens (except the
east terrace, although there are good views from near the church) which
present a glorious combination of views. A nature walk past mature trees leads
over a terracotta bridge and to the 'knucklebone arbour', a summerhouse
with what are probably sheep or deer knuckles set in the floor. Among the
wild and naturalised plants are carpets of aconites and snowdrops, winter
heliotropes, butterburs, daffodils, bluebells, wood anemones, celandines, bush
vetches, wood buttercups and a wide selection of lake and pondside plants.
Features include an orangery and archway greenhouses, topiary and well-

planted large vases. Restoration of the garden and architectural features is continuing.

Coton Manor Gardens ★   5

Guilsborough, Northampton NN6 8RQ. Tel: (01604) 740219; Fax: (01604) 740838

Mr and Mrs Ian Pasley-Tyler • 10m NW of Northampton, 11m SE of Rugby near Ravensthorpe Reservoir, signed from A428 and A5199 • Open April to Sept, Wed – Sun, 12 noon – 5.30pm • Entrance: £3.50, OAPs £3, children £2
◑ ☕ ✕ <u>WC</u> ♿ ☈ 🧺 ⛪

Dating from the 1920s, when the original seventeenth-century farmhouse was bought and added to by Mr Pasley-Tyler's grandparents, this is a beautifully maintained garden of exceptional charm, with unexpected vistas at every turn. There is something for everyone here: a most attractive assortment of pelargoniums in pots on the terrace by the house leading to the rose garden, a contrastingly shady woodland garden, a water garden, lush lawns sloping down to a large pond complete with black swans and moorhens, and magnificent mixed borders, particularly striking in July with campanulas and philadelphus. There is a surprise around every corner (do not rub your eyes should you think you see a real crane or flamingo beside the neatly-clipped yew hedge – no verdigris imitations here) and strategically placed seats from which to enjoy the views and effects of Mrs Pasley-Tyler's marvellous eye for colour. The garden has continued to develop since the present generation moved into the house in 1991: a Mediterranean bank planted three years ago is well established, as is a most attractive herb garden. The bluebell wood is magical in May and the path through the wildflower meadow, as yet in its early stages, makes a pleasant walk. This garden could not fail to inspire and manages to retain its atmosphere of family involvement. A helpful and interesting booklet and plant list is available; don't miss a visit to the extensive nursery.

Cottesbrooke Hall ★★   6

Cottesbrooke, Northampton NN6 8PF. Tel: (01604) 505808; Fax: (01604) 505619

Captain and Mrs J. Macdonald-Buchanan • 10m N of Northampton between A5199 and A508 (A14 – A1/M1 link road) • House open as garden, but Thurs and Bank Holiday Mons only; also 7th May, 4th June, 2nd July, 6th Aug, 3rd Sept • Gardens open 24th April to Sept, Tues – Fri and Bank Holiday Mons; also Sats and Suns in Sept, 2 – 5.30pm (last admission 5pm). Parties by appt • Entrance: £2.50, children £1.25 (house and gardens £4, children £2)
◑ ☕ 🖼 <u>WC</u> ♿ ☈

An excellently maintained formal garden surrounding a fine Queen Anne house, set in a large park (also open) with lakes and a stream, vistas and avenues. Designs by Edward Schultz, Geoffrey Jellicoe, Dame Sylvia Crowe and the late Hon. Lady Macdonald-Buchanan are being continued by the present owners – particularly the planting. The result is a series of delightful enclosed courtyards and gardens around the house with superb borders, urns and statues. Be sure to visit the intriguingly named Dilemma garden and to examine the Statue Walk. The spinney garden is at its best in spring with bulbs and azaleas. New trees, borders, yew hedges, gates and vistas have recently been added. Beyond the thatched Wendy house the wild garden surrounds a running stream and cascades, with azaleas, rhododendrons, acers, cherries, spring bulbs and wild flowers. The magnolia, cherry and acer collections and the ancient cedars are notable. The house contains fine paintings, including distinguished Stubbses, and was possibly the model for Jane Austen's Mansfield Park.

Deene Park 7

Corby NN17 3EW. Tel: (01780) 450278/450223

Mr Edmund Brudenell • 6m N of Corby off A43 Kettering – Stamford road • House open • Gardens open 21st, 24th, 30th April, 1st, 28th, 29th May; then June to Aug, Sun and 28th Aug, all 2 – 5pm. Parties by appt • Entrance: £2.50, children (10-14) £1.25, accompanied children under 10 free (house and gardens £4.50, children (10-14) £2, accompanied children under 10 free) (1999 prices) • Other information: picnics permitted in car park ● ☕ WC ♿ ☕

The glory of Deene, which was created by generations of the Brudenell family, is its trees. Fine mature specimens and groups fringe the formal areas and frame tranquil and enchanting views of the parkland and countryside. The main features of the garden are the long borders, old-fashioned roses, parterre and the lake. The gardens, parkland, church and house together provide a delightful, interesting and relaxing afternoon for visitors in what was the home of the Earl of Cardigan who led the Charge of the Light Brigade in 1854.

Delapre Abbey 8

London Road, Northampton NN4 8AW. Tel: (01604) 761074

Northampton Borough Council Leisure Department • 1m S of Northampton on A508 • Open March to Sept, daily, 10am – dusk. Park open all year • Entrance: free ◑ WC ♿ ⬦

Largely rebuilt in the seventeenth century, the house, on the site of the former nunnery of St Mary of the Meadow, together with 500 acres of land, passed into public ownership in 1946. With improving standards of maintenance (although some associated buildings are in need of repair), it is still possible to glimpse the hey-day of a lovely garden. Beyond the walled former kitchen garden, well-tended lawns, perennial, annual and rose beds and an eighteenth-century thatched game larder are walks through the wilderness garden with fine trees, shrubberies and lily ponds. There are lakes and a golf course in the park, and at the roadside close to the entrance, one of the Queen Eleanor Crosses commemorates the funeral procession in 1290 of Edward I's queen.

Hill Farm Herbs 9

Park Walk, Brigstock, Kettering NN14 3HH. Tel: (01536) 373694

Eileen and Mike Simpson • 8m NE of Kettering via A43, 5m SE of Corby, 6m NW of Thrapston. In Brigstock, just off A6116. Signposted • Open April to Sept, daily, 10.30am – 5.30pm (telephone for details of winter opening) • Entrance: free ◑ 🍽 WC 👵 🐾 🧺

Set at the back of an old stone farmhouse, many herbs and cottage-garden plants are grown in a number of areas, some in informal cottage mixtures, others laid out with specific themes, such as the cook's garden, full of culinary herbs, and the lavender and thyme garden. Those planning a new or remodelled cottage or herb garden will find these areas a great inspiration.

Holdenby House Gardens and Falconry Centre 10

Holdenby, Northampton NN6 8DJ. Tel: (01604) 770074

Mr and Mrs James Lowther • 7m NW of Northampton, signed from A5199 and A428 • House open 24th April, 24th May, 28th Aug and by appt. Garden and falconry centre open April to Sept, Sun, 2 – 6pm, July and Aug, daily except Sat, 2 – 6pm • Entrance: £3, OAPs £2.50, children £1.75 (house and gardens £4, children £2) • Other information: Meals by appt. Special events Easter, May Day, Whitsun and Aug Bank Hols, 1 – 6pm ◑ 🍽 🖼 WC 👵 ◁ 🧺 ♿

Two grassed terraces, a fish pond and the palace forecourt with its original arches remain of the extensive Elizabethan garden which surrounded the vast mansion built by Elizabeth I's chancellor, Sir Christopher Hatton, in the late sixteenth century. The gardens still link the surviving remnant of the house (one-eighth of its former size) to its past, especially the delightful Elizabethan garden, planted in 1980 by Rosemary Verey as a miniature replica of Hatton's original centrepiece, using only plants available in the 1580s. Other garden features include the fragrant border (now replanted by Rupert Golby), part of the nineteenth-century garden, the silver border and kitchen garden, the Falconry Centre, an authentically re-constructed seventeenth-century farmstead and children's amusements.

Kelmarsh Hall ★ 11

Kelmarsh, Northampton NN6 9LU Tel: (01604) 686543

Kelmarsh Hall Estate Preservation Trust • 5m S of Market Harborough, 11m N of Northampton, on A508 near A14 junction • House and garden open 23rd April to 27th Aug, Sun and Bank Holiday Mons, 2.30 – 5pm. Garden open 4th April to 28th Sept, Tues, Thurs, 2.30 – 4.30pm • Entrance: £2 (house and garden £3, OAPs and children over 12 £1, children under 12 free) ◑ WC ◁

The Palladian house, designed by James Gibbs and built in 1730, is set in an eighteenth-century landscape and has twentieth-century gardens made by Nancy Lancaster, who was advised by Norah Lindsay in planting the lavish herbaceous borders. The deep terrace on the garden front of the house, designed by Geoffrey Jellicoe, looks out across the lake and has rows of pleached limes on either side. A sunken garden, surrounded by billowing box hedges, is filled with sweetly scented plants in pale pastel colours. The fan-shaped rose garden, filled with old-fashioned roses, looks across a meadow towards the church; a herd of British White Cattle grazes. Early in the year, the garden is rich with spring flowers, from fritillaries naturalised down the drive to large drifts of daffodils in the woodland walk. A great sense of peace pervades this very private garden, and its well-articulated design and sure sense of style are re-emerging as the restoration programme unfolds.

Kirby Hall   12

Deene, Corby NN17 5EN. Tel: (01536) 203230

English Heritage • 4m NE of Corby off A43 on road W of Deene • Open all year: April to Oct, daily, 10am – 6pm (5pm in Oct); Nov to March, Sat and Sun, 10am – 4pm. Closed 1st Jan, 24th to 26th Dec • Entrance: £2.50, concessions £1.90, children £1.30 (1999 prices) ○ ☕ 🏠 WC ↻ 🐕 🧺 🍷

The gardens date from at least the period when Sir Christopher Hatton owned the hall in Elizabethan times. However, it was in the late seventeenth century that they achieved considerable fame through the work of the fourth Sir Christopher Hatton, who devoted his energies to the gardens until his death in 1705. In the 1930s the Great Garden was laid out following the pre-war idea of how a Baroque formal garden would have appeared. Since then, following extensive research of the period, the 1930s' garden is being buried and the parterre re-created using a design based on Longleat (see entry in Wiltshire) which will provide a more accurate view of how this garden would have looked in 1686. Over 80 two-metre-high clipped yew cones, holly mopheads and box balls, many placed in oak barrels similar to those used in the Hampton Court restoration, surround the dramatic geometric design of the 'gazon coupé' parterre of wide gravel paths and cut-through patterns of lawn. The north border was replanted in 1995 with species following as closely as possible those mentioned by Hatton in his notebooks. These include old varieties of fruit trees – apples, pears and cherries – trained against the walls.

Lamport Hall Garden   13

Lamport, Northampton NN6 9HD. Tel: (01604) 686272

Lamport Hall Trust • 8m N of Northampton on A508 • Hall open • Garden open 23rd April to 1st Oct, and 21st and 22nd Oct, Sun and Bank Holiday Mons, 2.15 – 5.15pm (last admission 4pm). Details of other days available on request. Coach parties at any time by arrangement • Entrance: £3.80, OAPs £3.30, children £2 (house and gardens) (1999 prices) • Other information: Dogs in picnic area only, on lead. Gift, craft, antique and doll fairs every month except Nov. School study centre and agricultural museum ● ☕ WC ↻ 🐕 🧺 🍷

The principal façade of the hall is by John Webb and the Smiths of Warwick. The grounds, initially laid out by Gilbert Clarke in 1655, have been the subject of comprehensive restoration. There are now extensive herbaceous and mixed borders and lawns, and the lily pond and rose garden are mature. Sir Charles Isham's local ironstone rockery, the home of the first garden gnome, has been painstakingly restored and his box bowers are growing back to their original style. The unusual shell and coral fountain at the centre of the Italian garden is in working order again after many years. There is also public access to the park.

Lyveden New Bield   14

Oundle, Peterborough PE8 5AT. Tel/Fax: (01832) 205358

The National Trust • 4m SW of Oundle off A427, 3m E of Brigstock • Lodge open all year, Tues – Sun during daylight hours • Water garden open for parties by prior arrangement with custodian • Entrance: £2, children £1, family £4.20 • Other information: Access on foot only, ½ m along farm track. Teas by prior arrangement ● 🖺 ⟁

The Bield is a strangely compelling, roofless architectural shell, with mullioned and transomed windows which stare sightlessly over a rolling landscape of woods and cornfields. This unique structure was built by Sir Thomas Tresham between 1595 and 1605 as a garden lodge for his main residence, the Old Bield. Although staunchly loyal to Queen Elizabeth I, who knighted him in 1575, Sir Thomas converted to the Catholic faith in 1580 and spent 15 of his last 25 years either in prison or under house arrest for his religious beliefs. Destined never to be completed, the New Bield remains unaltered since Sir Thomas's death in 1605. The three-storey structure was devised in the shape of an equal-armed cross as a celebration of the Passion of Christ. It is constructed from local oolitic limestone with superb ashlar masonry, an outstanding example of Elizabethan craftsmanship. The Trust is undertaking a project to reveal the extensive remains of an elaborate water garden, containing a series of truncated pyramids and circular mounds, surrounded by moats and terraces.

The Menagerie   15

**Horton, Northampton NN7 2BX. Tel: (01604) 870957
(Leave message for Administrator)**

Mr A. Myers • 6m SE of Northampton, on B526 turn left 1m S of Horton into field. Watch out for tiny notice on gate • Open April to Sept, Mon and Thurs, 2 – 5pm, also last Sun of these months, 2 – 6pm • Entrance: £3.50, children £1.50 ● 🍽 WC �& 🌣

The informal approach through a farm gateway and across uncultivated fields gives no hint of the delights of the fascinating journey beyond. This is a garden still in the making, with formal water gardens and wetlands surrounding the house, an eighteenth-century folly, where Lord Halifax had his private zoo. The house is one of the most important surviving works of Thomas Wright of Durham. The garden created by the late Gervase Jackson-Stops and Ian Kirby is a recent development, attractively sited with views across to where Horton Hall once stood. The central lime avenue, planted in the 1980s, provides a vista to a mount with a spiral path to the obelisk on top. Two hornbeam *allées* end in eighteenth-century ponds with fountains. Two thatched arbours have been built – one circular and classical, the other triangular and Gothick – with newly planted shrubberies designed to hide them from the house. The charming rose garden enclosed by yew hedges was designed by Vernon Russell-Smith in 1989. A most unusual garden, in which most of the plantings are now well established.

The Old Rectory ★ 16

Sudborough, Kettering NN14 3BX. Tel: (01832) 733247; Fax: (01832) 733832

Mr and Mrs Anthony Huntington • 7m SE of Corby off A6116 Corby – Thrapston road, A14 junction 12 • Open April to Sept, Tues, 10am – 4pm and by appt. Parties welcome • Entrance: £3 (£4 with tea and biscuits), children under 16 free ● ● WC & ✿

A delightful three-acre rectory garden in beautiful stone and thatch village. Much has been accomplished in recent years to develop plantings throughout the year, with a fine collection of hellebores in spring and many containers, especially in summer. Copious planting in the mixed borders, around the pond and many climbers. The *potager*, begun by Rosemary Verey and completed by Rupert Golby, is fascinating, with small beds and brick paths leading to a central wrought-iron arbour; standard roses, gooseberries and tents of runner beans and marrows provide vertical features. A small wild garden with interesting trees and a woodland walk along the stream completes the picture, with excellent labelling throughout.

Rockingham Castle Gardens 17

Corby LE16 8TH. Tel: (01536) 770240

Commander James Saunders Watson and family • 2m N of Corby on A6003. Signposted • House open • Garden open 24th April to 15th Oct, Sun and Thurs, Bank Holiday Mons and the Tues following, also Tues in Aug, 1 – 5pm (grounds open 11.30am on Sun and Bank Holiday Mons). Parties by appt on other days • Entrance: £2.80 (castle and gardens £4.40, OAPs £3.90, children £2.80, family ticket (2 adults and 2 children) £12, parties of 20 or more £3.90 per person) • Other information: Disabled may park near entrance ◑ ● ✕ ▣ WC & ⬱ ⬛ ☗

Rockingham sits on a hilltop fortress site with stunning views of three counties. It has remains from all periods of its 900-year history, with major features ranging from formal seventeenth-century terraces and yew hedges to the romantic wild garden of the nineteenth century. There is a circular rose garden surrounded by a yew hedge and also good herbaceous borders. The wild garden was replanted with advice from Kew Gardens in the late 1960s and includes over 200 species of trees and shrubs. The result is a delightful blend of form, colour, light and shade. Recommended for party/family outings and for those who combine interest in horticulture with history.

NORTHUMBERLAND

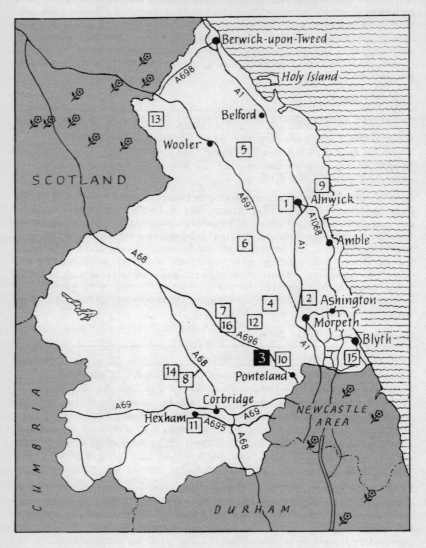

Two-starred gardens are marked on the map with a black square.

Alnwick Castle   1

Alnwick NE66 1NQ. Tel: Mon – Fri (01665) 510777; Sat/Sun (01655) 603942

Duke and Duchess of Northumberland • 30m N of Newcastle upon Tyne. Take A1 and turn W at Alnwick. Signposted • Castle open 12 noon • Grounds open Easter to Sept, daily except Fri, 11am – 5pm (last admission 4.15pm) • Entrance : £4.50, children £2.50, family £11 (1999 prices) • Other information: Fuseliers Museum in castle ◑ 🍵 🛍

Most of the existing landscape is by 'Capability' Brown, plus a 12-acre Italianate walled garden (now derelict) by Nesfield. But the Duchess has plans for an exciting new development, for which details are awaited.

Ashfield   2

Hebron, Morpeth NE61 3LA. Tel: (01670) 515616

Mr B. and Mrs R. McWilliam • 3m N of Morpeth, 1m E of A1 on C130 S of Hebron • Open all year by impromptu appt • Entrance: £1.50 ◑ 🍵 🛍 WC ♿

The house looks out onto a terrace dense with bulbs and a carpet of alpines, many, including *Androsace lanuginosa*, tumbling over the supporting wall. The lawn slopes gently down beyond, sheltered by beech and prunus hedges and punctuated by small island beds planted with bulbs, shrubs and small trees, including many varieties of sorbus. The owner is a keen plantsman and the garden reflects his enthusiasm. On the east side is a mixed border, including an area for bog plants. Beyond this is a 'three-acre garden', an expanse of lawn with colourful herbaceous borders, a small pinetum, and beds of shrubs and bulbs. On the west side, a one-and-a-half acre woodland deeply planted under mature trees. The woodland walks wind past beds planted with spring bulbs, hellebores, hostas and other shade-loving plants and small trees (sorbus, betulas, acers, etc.). Many plants come from abroad and have been grown from seed, as in the scree-bed planted with Sino-Himalayan alpines beside the entrance. Total area five acres.

Belsay Hall ★★   3

Belsay, Newcastle upon Tyne NE20 0DX. Tel: (01661) 881636;
Fax: (01661) 881043

English Heritage • 14m NW of Newcastle on A696 • Hall and Castle open • Gardens open April to Sept, daily, 10am – 6pm; Oct, daily, 10am – 5pm; Nov to March, daily, 10am – 4pm. Closed 1st Jan, 24th to 26th Dec. Pre-booked evening tours in summer include joint natural history and gardening tours • Entrance: £3.80, OAPs £2.90, children £1.90. Reductions for parties of 11 or more (1999 prices) • Other information: Advance notice preferred for coaches. Refreshments Easter to Oct only. Wheelchairs available for loan. Annual NCCPG plant sale in June ◑ 🍵 ✕ 🛍 WC ♿ 🐕 ✿ 🛍 ♨

The 30-acre gardens are the creation of two men who between them owned the Hall in succession from 1795 to 1933. Sir Charles Monck built the severe neo-classical mansion with formal terraces leading through woods to a 'garden' inside the quarry from which the house was built. Sir Arthur, his grandson, took over in 1867, adding Victorian features. Both were discerning plantsmen. The result is a well-cared-for collection of rare, mature and exotic specimens in a fascinating sequence. The terrace looks across to massed June rhododendrons. Other areas (flower garden, magnolia terrace, winter-flowering heathers) lead to woods, a wild meadow and the quarry garden itself. Reminiscent of the ancient Greek quarries in Syracuse, this was carefully contrived and stocked to achieve a wild romantic effect and give shelter to some remarkable specimens, dramatically beautiful in the light and shade of the sandstone gorge. The winter garden, with its heathers, also has a 28-metre Douglas fir, and some rhododendrons can bloom as early as December. An unexpected pleasure is the grand croquet lawn on which white-clad figures pleasure themselves with their strange sport. The one-and-a-half-mile Crag Wood walk is a stepped, serpentine path which passes by the lake and through the hanging woodlands opposite the Hall.

Bide-a-Wee Cottage ★ 4

Stanton, Netherwitton, Morpeth NE65 8PR. Tel: (01670) 772262

Mark Robson • 5m NW of Morpeth, 3m SW of Longhorsley, off A697 Morpeth − Coldstream road towards Stanton • Open 29th April to 2nd Sept, Sat and Wed, 1.30 − 5pm. Parties by arrangement, except Sun • Entrance: £2 ● ℀

One of the most enchanting and richly planted gardens in the North-East. Combining formal, informal and wild features, it occupies a long-abandoned stone quarry and some of the higher surrounding land. The beauty of the natural rock faces has been exploited to the maximum and they have been enriched by truly sympathetic planting. Unusual for this type of garden, there are three pools which with their margins provide a fine habitat for marsh-loving and aquatic plants. As well as being a highly refined plantsman, the owner is also a splendid mason whose stonework has done much to embellish the garden. About 3m N of Morpeth is a well-known garden centre, *Heighley Gate*, open seven days a week, with coffee shop.

Chillingham Castle 5

Chillingham NE66 5NJ. Tel: (01668) 215359/215390; Fax: (01668) 215463

Sir Humphry Wakefield, Bt. • 12m NW of Alnwick between A1 (signposted), A697, B6346 and B6348 • House open • Gardens open 21st to 24th April and May to Sept, daily except Tues (daily in July and Aug), 12 noon − 5pm or by appt • Entrance: £4.30, OAPs £3.50, accompanied children free, parties of 20 or more £3.50 per person. Guided tours £25 ◐ ☕ 🏛

Since the 1200s this has been and continues to be the family home of the Earls Grey and their relations. Sir Humphry is vigorously restoring the castle and garden along with the grounds, landscaped in 1828 by Wyatville (of Windsor Castle and Royal Lodge fame). The Elizabethan-style walled garden has been virtually excavated to rediscover its intricate pattern of clipped box and yew (enlivened by scarlet tropaeolum), with rose beds, fountains, a central avenue and a spectacular herbaceous border running the whole length of the garden. Outside are lawns and a rock garden, delightful woodland and lakeside walks through drifts of snowdrops and spring displays of daffodils, bluebells and, later, rhododendrons. The medieval castle and wide mountain views provide a spectacular backdrop.

Cragside House, Garden and Grounds 6

Rothbury, Morpeth NE65 7PX. Tel: (01669) 620333

The National Trust • 13m SW of Alnwick off A697 between B6341 and B6344 • Estate open 1st April to 29th Oct, daily except Mon (but open Bank Holiday Mondays), 10.30am – 7pm (last admission 5pm) • House open as estate, 1 – 5.30pm (last admission 4.30pm) • Nov to 17th Dec: estate and garden only Wed – Sun, 11am – 4pm • Entrance: garden, grounds and exhibition £4, family (2 adults and 3 children) £10; house, garden, estate and exhibition £6.50, family £16 • Other information: Main car parks either near to house (with ½ m walk to formal garden) or near formal garden, with further car parks along the estate drive. Visitor centre and Armstrong Exhibition (some distance from garden) with toilet facilities and shop. Dogs in grounds only, on lead ○ 🍽 ✕ 🏠 WC ♿ 🌢 🎖 ♨

Lord Armstrong, one of the greatest of Victorian engineers, clothed this hillside above the Coquet Valley with millions of trees and shrubs as the setting for a house designed by R. Norman Shaw (the first ever lit by hydro-electricity) that was then the wonder of the world. From the car park nearest to the house the path (signposted 'Garden') affords views of the rock gardens below the house. These have been cleared after years of neglect and are now planted with an impressive display of heathers, shrubs and alpines. The path descends sharply into the Debdon gorge, crosses the river by a rustic bridge (magnificent views of the elegant iron bridge soaring above) and climbs through majestic conifers to the clock tower (1864) which overlooks the formal garden. This walled area, laid out in high-Victorian style, is set in three terraces and restoration is continuing. On the upper terrace are rock fer-neries, grottos and a small canal. The middle terrace contains the imposing orchard house, with its rotating fruit pots of peaches, cherries and tomatoes, to one side of which is a carpet bed (2 x 18 metres) planted with small foliage plants in a formal star-and-diamond pattern typical of the 1870s. Carpet bedding is taken literally at Cragside: two of the beds mirror the design of floor-coverings in the house. In the formal beds some 6000 tulips are planted in autumn for spring colour. On the lower terrace is a cast-iron rose loggia built at Lord Armstrong's works and now planted colourfully. The walk back through the gorge impresses on the visitor the contrasting forces of wild romanticism and industrial technology which influenced this estate in equal measure. Two hundred rare North American coniferous species, given to the Trust by the Royal Botanic Gardens in Edinburgh, have been planted here. The climatic conditions and historic landscape of the property make it an ideal site for a collection of specimen conifers, which include *Abies magnifica* and *Pinus ponderosa*. It has to be said that the replanting and rerouting and all the infrastructure here subtract somewhat from the romance which must have characterised the original. Helpful leaflets.

Herterton House ★ 7

Hartington, Cambo, Morpeth NE61 4BN. Tel: (01670) 774278

Frank and Marjorie Lawley • 11m E of Morpeth, 2m N of Cambo off B6342, signed Hartington • Open April to Sept, daily except Tues and Thurs, 1.30 – 5.30pm • Entrance: £2.20 (1999 price) ◑ **WC** ℘

The Lawleys took over this land and near-derelict Elizabethan building, with commanding views over picturesque upland Northumberland, in 1976. With vision and skill they have created four distinct areas. In front, a winter garden with tranquil vistas; alongside, a cloistered 'monastic' knot garden of mainly medicinal, occult and dye-producing herbs; and to the rear, their most impressive achievement, a flower garden with perceptively mingled hardy flowers chosen with an artist's eye. Many are unusual traditional plants (including many species from the wild) that flourish within the newly built sheltering walls. A fourth area is nearly ready, with the two-storey gazebo already open in the Fancy Garden. A gem of a place, of great interest to the plantsperson.

Hexham Herbs 8

**The Chesters Walled Garden, Chollerford, Hexham NE46 4BQ.
Tel: (01434) 681483**

Kevin and Susie White • 5m N of Hexham, ½ m W of Chollerford on B6318 • Open March to Oct, daily, 10am – 5pm, reduced hours in winter. Also by appt • Entrance: £1.50, children (under 10) free (1999 prices) • Other information: Ices, cold drinks available. Possible for accompanied wheelchairs, but gravel paths ◑ ও ℘ 📠

The tall brick walls of the old kitchen garden slope gently south from the very line of Hadrian's Wall, echoing the Roman forts that lie to east and west. Within these ramparts, still with vestiges of the Victorian glasshouses and heating system, the Whites have fashioned a large herb collection (over 900 varieties), including most fittingly a unique Roman garden with plants (myrtle, etc.) identified by archaeologists through pollen analysis. A major feature is the National Collections of thymes and marjorams. A rose garden (over 60 species), extensive herbaceous borders (with some 1500 varieties) and terraced lawns against the architectural backdrop of Norman Shaw's Chesters mansion fill out this splendid intriguing 'fort'. A new feature is a formal round pool with fountain set in a gravelled area with benches and a knot garden laid out in box and yew to William Lawson's design of 1617. A woodland walk with wild flowers and a secluded pond are also open.

Howick Hall ★ 9

Howick, Alnwick NE66 3LB. Tel/Fax: (01665) 577285

Lord Howick of Glendale (Howick Trustees Ltd) • 6m NE of Alnwick, 2m N of Longhoughton, off B1339 • Open early April to Oct, daily, 1 – 6pm • Entrance: £2, children and concessions £1 (1999 prices) ◑ **WC** ও

Acquired by the Grey family in 1319, the accident of woodland which sheltered this site from the blasts of the North Sea enabled Lord and Lady Grey to start building a fine collection of tender plants, which would do credit to a Scottish west-coast garden. Although the main house is unoccupied, Stephen Anderton describes the ambience as 'a genial lived-in garden of the best kind'. The lower terrace has a pond and excellent borders and the lawns run down through shrubs to a stream. Winding paths lead through shrubbery or parkland to Silverwood, under whose magnificent trees the visitor passes among numerous fine shrubs and woodland flowers planted by Lord and Lady Grey from 1931, the year of their silver wedding. There are good varieties of rhododendron and azalea, and outstanding species hydrangea (H. villosa) apart from other unusual varieties. A large pond-side garden is maturing well, with a great variety of moisture-loving plants making an impressive display. A catalogue of plants would be helpful. This is a plantsperson's garden, but there are many delights for the aesthete, such as the agapanthus of varying blues on the terrace. In early April visitors will be impressed by the spectacular view of drifts of daffodils in the meadow and parkland. One of the signed walks is the 'Long Walk', a one-and-a-half-mile path to the sea.

Kirkley Hall College   10

Ponteland NE20 0AQ. Tel: (01661) 860808; Fax: (01661) 860047

11m NW of Newcastle off A696, right at Ponteland on C151 for 2½ m. Signposted • Open April to Sept, daily, 10am – 3pm • Entrance: free ◗ **WC** ⚘

The 10-acre grounds with their three-acre Victorian walled garden form a showcase for all the gardening arts from propagation onwards. Inside the walls are climbers, borders and bedding plants in profusion, all pleasingly grouped. The grounds contain a succession of beds, skilfully shaped to follow the rolling contours of the land, each carefully composed for variety of profile and continuity of colour. Then to the Hall with its outstanding array of beautifully planted containers on terraces down to a most attractive sunken garden and a wildlife pond. National Collections include beeches. The whole is thoroughly professional.

Loughbrow House   11

Hexham NE46 1RS. Tel: (01434) 603351

Mrs Kenneth Clark • 20m E of Newcastle, 1m S of Hexham. Take B6306 off Whitley Chapel road and at fork is brick lodge and long drive to house • Open 17th May, 21st June, 19th July, 12 noon – 3pm, one Sun in late June, 2 – 5pm for charity, and by appt at other times • Entrance: £2, children free ● 🍵 **WC** ♿ ⚘

There is a large terrace and lawn with inspirational ideas both for plantspersons and those who enjoy original design concepts. On the terrace is an interesting canal. Roses and shrubs. The two large herbaceous borders show Mrs Clark's colour concepts to great advantage, and beyond is a newish woodland garden. Kitchen garden. A new pond has been constructed and planted and the bog garden extended.

Meldon Park 12

Morpeth NE61 3SW. Tel: (01670) 772661

*Mr and Mrs M.J.B. Cookson • 7m W of Morpeth on B6343 • House open •
Garden open 20th May to 18th June, 26th to 28th Aug, 2 – 5pm • Entrance:
£3, OAPs £2, children 50p • Other information: Light refreshments on Sun and
Bank Holidays only* ● 🅱 WC ♿

When, in 1832, Newcastle glassmaster Isaac Cookson purchased a 700-acre
estate enclosing a stretch of the steep Hartburn dene, he simply asked John
Dobson to pick his spot and design the house. His trust was rewarded.
Dobson created a broad plateau on which he placed a fine neo-classical
house facing squarely south over terrace and ha-ha to the dene below. This
was flanked by shrubberies and mature imported trees, of which at least
one fine cedar still survives – as does the serene charm of the original
vision, a tribute to the continuing care of the Cookson family. Attractions
include rose beds, a small orangery, woodland and wild meadow walks, and
in particular the walled garden, quartered by pathways, in part apple-
hedged, where kitchen beds and venerable plums are accompanied by much
innovative planting. Rose beds bordered by trim box hedges give colour
later, and there is a well-planted herbaceous border on the east side of the
house with an attractive variety of plants, including notable peonies and
iris.

Mindrum 13

Cornhill-on-Tweed TD12 4QN. Tel: (01890) 850246

*The Hon. P.J. Fairfax • 14m SW of Berwick-upon-Tweed. From A697 turn onto
B6351 at Akeld, join B6352 towards Kirk Yetholm and continue 3m to
Mindrum • Open for charity probably 25th June, 9th July, 2 – 6pm, and by
appt • Entrance: £2 • Other information: Teas and plants for sale on open days
only* ● 🍽 🅱 WC ⟁ 🌿

From the nineteenth-century house built on flat ground there are fine views to
the valley of the Bowmont Water (you can actually see the Scottish Borders to
the south), and the creators of the three-acre garden have taken good
advantage of the different levels of the site. From the lawn at the side of
the house – over 90 metres above sea level – a path leads down a gentle slope to
a walled garden with many flowering shrubs, roses and a fine white abutilon.
Opposite this, and separated from it by a sage hedge, is a rose garden with yew
hedges on the far sides. The path then descends steeply, winding down beside a
small stream which tumbles over dramatic rocks into a still pool at the foot of
the bank and joins a tributary of the Bowmont Water. The rocky bank above is
densely planted with colourful perennials, shrub roses, many varieties of acer
and golden yew, irises and candelabra primulas by the water – the whole a feast
for the eyes. The tributary is crossed by wooden bridges which lead to the
riverside walk. The far bank has rhododendrons, azaleas, acers, and planting
still continues.

Nunwick ★ 14

Simonburn, Hexham NE48 3AF.

Mrs L.G. Allgood • On B6320 8m NW of Hexham • Open 18th June and for parties by appt • Entrance: £2 • Other information: Teas and toilet facilities on open days only ☕

This is one of the most interesting gardens in a county full of remarkable ones. The house (not open) is described by Pevsner as perfect for its date (1760). It looks out over lawns and parkland, with fine trees which the owners have been meticulous in caring for and replacing when necessary. Walking down to the gardens (when the house was built it was fashionable to place these well away from the park) it is clear that the owners combine a clever sense of colour and shape with an interest in unusual plants. The herbaceous borders are cut back from their sheltering wall to ease maintenance, and there are fine beech hedges and shrub roses to provide shelter on the orchard side. The large Victorian walled kitchen garden is excellently maintained. Mrs Allgood experiments with varieties of vegetables – there were about 12 named potato varieties when our inspector visited. Good flowers, too, along the walks. Behind one wall is a small and elegant orangery containing a camellia over 100 years old. The other fascinating feature is the woodland path to the recently planted bog garden (*en route* note the stone wellhead newly moved here), where the visitor first becomes aware of the owner's passion for hostas. The latter become evident again after crossing one of the rustic bridges over the burn and reaching the eighteenth-century Gothick kennels. Its four rooms, now open to the sky, house a spectacular collection of hostas, and the walls are planted with purple erinus, ivies of many kinds, toadflax and ferns. Trees and plants are well labelled. Back beside the house is a large collection of stone farm troughs with alpines, and a newly installed fountain. It is difficult to do justice in words to the charm of this garden, but it is a 'must' for anyone within miles of Hexham who can arrange an appointment – there will be interest all year round.

Seaton Delaval Hall 15

Seaton Sluice, Whitley Bay NE26 4QR. Tel: (0191) 2371493

Lord Hastings • 10m NE of Newcastle, ½ m inland from Seaton Sluice on A190 • Parts of house open together with coach house, stables and ice-house • Garden open 1st, 28th, 29th May; June, Wed and Sun; July and Aug, Wed, Sun and 28th Aug; Sept, Wed, Sun; all 2 – 6pm • Entrance: £3, OAPs £2.50, children £1 ◑ 🍴 WC ♿ ⬇ 🏛

The original grounds of this architectural masterpiece by Vanbrugh no doubt matched its magnificence, but little is known save for an early painting showing a swan lake. A notable weeping ash survives from that time, and there is a venerable and impressive rose garden, its beds outlined by box hedges 60 cm high and 30 cm wide. Since 1948 an excellent parterre has been laid out, now embellished by a large Italianate pond and fountain. An attractive shrubbery (rhododendrons, azaleas, etc.), herbaceous borders and a laburnum walk have been established on the south side towards the fine Norman chapel. Replanting continues and the garden is obviously in good hands.

Wallington ★ 16

Cambo, Morpeth NE61 4AR. Tel: (01670) 774283

The National Trust • 20m NW of Newcastle off A696 (signed on B6342) • House open April to Oct, daily, except Tues, 1 – 5.30pm (4.30pm in Oct; last admission ½ hour before closing) • Walled garden open April to Oct, daily, 10am – 7pm (Oct 6pm; or dusk if earlier); Nov to March, daily, 10am – 4pm. Grounds open all year, daily, during daylight hours • Entrance: £3.80, children £1.90 (house and grounds £5.20 children £2.60, family £13) • Other information: Self-drive scooters available ○ 🍽 ✕ 🗄 WC ⬤ ⬤ ⬤ ⬤ ⬤

The superb house in a 100-acre landscape of lawns, terraces and flower beds has an excellent walled garden, with a great variety of plants. There is a garden house designed in Tuscan style by Daniel Garrett. Lancelot 'Capability' Brown, growing up locally, would have been aware of the first 'landscaping' works at Wallington and he later made partly extended plans for a separate park on the estate at Rothley. The Victorian peach house in the walled garden is now restored, and the Edwardian conservatory is home to many treasures. Outside, the walks step down from a classical fountain past beds re-designed by Lady Trevelyan in the 1930s, including notable heathers and many herbaceous perennials. Trees planted by the Duke of Atholl in 1738 include a great larch, the survivor of six, by the China Pond.

DOGS, TOILETS & OTHER FACILITIES ⬤ WC

If these are not mentioned in the entry, then facilities are probably not available at the property described. For example, if dogs are not mentioned, owners will probably not permit entry, even on a lead.

FEEDBACK

Readers are invited to advise the *Guide* of any gardens which in their opinion should be listed in future editions, and where possible arrangements will be made to review such suggestions. Readers who would like to add information about gardens listed are warmly invited to write to the *Guide* with their comments, which may be used in future editions without attribution. A report form is included at the back of the *Guide*, although letters will be welcome. Please send to the publishers, Bloomsbury Publishing plc, 38 Soho Square, London W1V 5DF. All letters are acknowledged by the editor.

NOTTINGHAMSHIRE

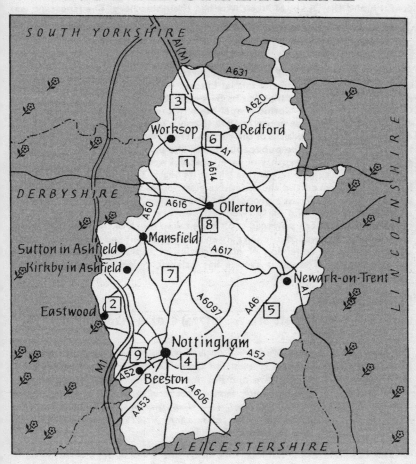

Clumber Park

Clumber Estate Office, Clumber Park, Worksop S80 3AZ. Tel: (01909) 476592

The National Trust • 4½ m SE of Worksop off A1 and A57, 11m from M1 junction 30 • Park open all year, daily during daylight hours, except 15th July, 19th Aug, 25th Dec • Walled kitchen garden open April to Sept, Wed, Thurs, 10.30am – 5.30pm, Sat, Sun and Bank Holiday Mondays, 10.30am – 6pm • Entrance: 70p. Vehicle charge for park: cars £3, caravans and mini-coaches £4.30 (1999 prices) • Other information: Wheelchairs, inc. those for children, available. Bicycles for hire. Chapel open (telephone for details). ○ ♥ ✕ 🖻 WC 🚶 ⟨♿⟩ 🐾 ⛲ 🔦*

The park of 3800 acres was enclosed from Sherwood Forest in the eighteenth century, and the Dukes of Newcastle had their seat here. The landscape was variously shaped by three famous pairs of hands – those of 'Capability' Brown, Humphry Repton and Richard Payne Knight, who completed the eighteenth-century lay-out as late as 1794. Stephen Wright designed two temples and a bridge for the lake, which remain today. In the 1830s William Sawrey Gilpin planted the two-mile-long lime avenue, extended the formal gardens in front of the house and created the formal Lincoln walk (now restored). From the nineteenth century also are Charles Barry's stable block and clock tower, and G. F. Bodley's ornate Gothic chapel built in the pleasure garden. Since the demolition of the great house in 1938 (Barry's being the last in the line), the chapel has become the focus of the garden. The Trust, with contributions from local authorities and the public, purchased the park in 1946 and have kept in good order the wide expanse of park, peaceful woods, open heath and rolling farmland with a superb serpentine lake at its heart. The vinery and palm house have been restocked and the extensive glasshouses (138 metres) are the best and longest in the Trust's properties. The kitchen garden exhibition of late nineteenth-century and early twentieth-century tools is fascinating and re-minds us that modern powered tools have taken much of the heavy work out of gardening. The walled kitchen garden contains a fruit and vegetable border, a herb border, a collection of old varieties of apple trees and a working Victorian apiary. The cedar avenue has Atlantic cedars and sweet chestnut trees of breath-taking size.

Felley Priory ★   2

Underwood, Jacksdale NG16 5FL. Tel: (01773) 810230/812056; Fax: (01773) 580440

The Hon. Mrs Chaworth Musters • 10m NW of Nottingham, ½ m SW of M1 junction 27. Take A608 for Heanor and Derby. Garden on left • Garden and nursery open all year Tues, Wed and Fri, 9am – 12.30pm; also March to Oct: second and fourth Weds in month, 9am – 4pm, and third Sun in month, 11am – 4pm. Also open for NGS 9th April, 11 – 4pm, and by appt for parties • Entrance: £1.50, children free. Other information: NCCPG Plant Fairs 4th June, 1st Oct, 12 noon – 4pm ⏰ ☕ <u>WC</u> ♿ 🐾 🌱

Despite the M1 being only half a mile away, above the house but out of sight, the first impression is of a garden with quiet English countryside as a backdrop. The owners have, with the use of hedging, created several gardens within the one, the original ancient walls unifying the parts as well as providing shelter and support for many unusual and slightly tender shrubs and climbers. The new rose garden with its domed pergola is now mature and a glorious sight in full bloom.

Hodsock Priory ★   3

Blyth, Worksop S81 0TY. Tel: (01909) 591204; Fax: (01909) 591578

Sir Andrew and Lady Buchanan • 6m NE of Worksop, 2m W of A1 at Blyth off B6045 Blyth – Worksop road • Open Feb/March for 4 weeks, daily (weather permitting – telephone before travelling), 10am – 4pm • Entrance: £3, children free • Other information: Coaches must book. Hot refreshments. Dogs in park only ◐ 🍵 ✕ WC ও ⚘

An historic five-acre private garden with Grade-I-listed gatehouse c. 1500 and a dry moat but open only in the winter for the Snowdrop Spectacular. Choose your time to visit carefully as there were over 20,000 there in the 1999 winter. The part-acid, part-neutral soil allows a wide range of plants and there is an unusual mix of garden styles. Fine trees include a huge variegated cornus, a very old catalpa (Indian bean), a tulip tree and a swamp cypress, and there is an interesting holm oak hedge. The Snowdrop Spectacular covers one and a half miles, though the dates when this is at its best vary from year to year. The walks beyond the small lake and bog garden and into the old moat are also accessible to the disabled. Some of the turn-of-the-century gravel paths have been restored, and three new arbours built.

Holme Pierrepont Hall

4

Radcliffe–on–Trent NG12 2LF. Tel: (0115) 933 2371

Mr and Mrs R. Brackenbury • 5m SE of Nottingham off A52/A6011. Continue past National Water Sports Centre for 1½ m • Hall open • Garden open some days for NGS in April and May; also 23rd, 24th April, 28th, 29th May; then June, Thurs; July, Weds and Thurs; Aug, Tues, Weds, Thurs; also Summer Bank Holiday Suns, Mons; all 2 – 5.30pm. Parties by appt all year, inc. evening visits • Entrance: £1.50 (house and garden £3.50, children £1) ◐ 🍵 WC ও ⚘ 🧺

The hall is a medieval brick manor house, but the listed garden and parterre of 1875 have been restored by the present owners. The box parterre is the outstanding feature of the gardens, and the herbaceous borders next to the York stone path (replacing old rose beds) enhance the courtyard garden further. (The Jacob sheep are friendly lawnmowers.) The owners work hard with improvements to this peaceful house and garden and willingly provide ample information. Their innovations include a winter garden, outer east garden, yews, shrubs and roses. Recent years have seen great improvements as the collection of plants matures and increases.

Mill Hill House

5

Elston Lane, East Stoke, Newark NG23 5QJ. Tel: (01636) 525460

Mr and Mrs R.J. Gregory • 5m SW of Newark. Take A46, turn left into Elston Lane (signed Elston) and house is first on right • Open April to Sept, Wed – Sun and Bank Holiday Mons; Oct, Fri – Sun, 10am – 6pm, some for NGS. Parties and individuals welcome by appt • Entrance: £1.50 (by donation to collecting box), accompanied children free • Other information: Parking 100 metres past house in nursery ◐ 🌿 WC ⬅ ⚘

A half-acre cottage garden generously filled with a wide variety of plants provides year-round interest and tranquillity. The garden is well screened from the road and visitors have often commented 'What a beautiful surprise' or 'One of the best kept secrets in Nottinghamshire'. This garden uplifts the spirit as it demonstrates how to overcome the problems of an exposed northward-sloping site. The plants provide a wealth of propagating material for the adjacent nursery.

Morton Hall 6

Ranby, Retford DN22 8HW. Tel: (01777) 702530

Lady Mason • 4m E of Worksop, 4m W of Retford. Entrance on A620/ southbound A1 link road • Open for charity 26th March, 21st May, 15th Oct, 2 – 6pm • Entrance: £2.50 per car or £1.50 per person, whichever is least • Other information: Nurseries adjacent ◐ ☕ 🏠 WC ⅙ 🐾 ♟

'The gardens are celebrated,' wrote Henry Thorold in his *Shell Guide to Nottinghamshire*. It is not surprising, for there is a large number of mature and rare specimen trees and shrubs in a relatively small park. They were planted over 100 years ago by the Mason family, all amateur botanists. The well-stocked nursery next to the gardens was started 30 years ago by Sir Paul and Lady Mason and is run by Mrs McMaster. The soil is sandy and poor but obviously suits the slightly more tender shrubs – romneyas thrive next to the house. Enjoy the rare and unusual and the colours in spring and autumn in this peaceful garden but do not expect immaculate lawns and flower beds. The forestry walks feature some modern planting by William Mason, the present landowner.

Newstead Abbey ★ 7

Newstead Abbey Park, Nottingham NG15 8GE. Tel: (01623) 455900

Nottingham City Council • 11m N of Nottingham on A60 • House open April to Sept, 12 noon – 5pm (last admission 4pm). Contains Byron memorabilia and 30 period rooms • Gardens open all year, daily, 10am – dusk • Entrance: £4, children £2 ○ ☕ ✕ 🏠 WC ⅙ ◁ 👍 ♟

Water predominates in this estate which the poet Byron inherited but in which he could rarely afford to live. In most of the extensive and immaculate gardens there is much of interest. The Japanese gardens are justly famous and the rock and fern gardens worth visiting. Indeed the waterfalls, wildfowl, passageways, grottos and bridges provide plenty of fun for children, but in addition there is an excellent, imaginatively equipped play area with bark mulch for safety. The tropical garden and the monks' stewpond are visually uninteresting but they are of laudable age. It is a pity that the large walled kitchen garden is now a rose garden – rose gardens, however pretty, are commonplace, but large kitchen gardens to the great houses are now rare. The old rose garden, now the iris garden, is in the process of development. Alas, the gardens are currently under threat from underground mining.

Rufford Country Park 8

Ollerton, Newark NG22 9DG. Tel: (01623) 823148

Nottinghamshire County Council • 9m NE of Mansfield, 2m S of Ollerton on A614 • Rufford Abbey Cistercian area open • Park open all year, daily, dawn –

dusk • Entrance: free. Parking charge from April to Oct at weekends and Bank Holidays, and through school holidays in summer • Other information: Four wheelchairs available for pre-booking. Conducted walks (telephone for dates and times) ○ ♨ ✕ 🖿 ♿ ⬨ ⬛

This contains almost everything that might be expected of an important country park, e.g. lakes, lime avenues, mature cedars, etc. A visit to the eight themed gardens within the formal gardens is well worthwhile, and there is a new rose garden in front of the abbey ruins. Large areas are managed with wildlife in mind, but ball games are allowed on the lawns beneath cut-leaved beeches and cedars. The Reg Hookway arboretum, established in 1983, shows promise with a good collection of oaks and birches – all well labelled.

Wollaton Park   9

Nottingham NG8 2AE. Tel: (0115) 915 3900

Nottingham City Council • W of city centre on A609. From M1 junction 25 take A52, turn left onto A614 and left onto A609 • Natural history museum in Hall open Mar to Nov, daily except Fri, 11am – 5pm. Closed 25th Dec to 1st Jan. Free except small charge on Sun and Bank Holidays • Garden open all year, daily, 11am – 5pm • Entrance: free but small charge for parking ○ ♨ 🖿 **WC** ♿ ⬨ 🌱 ⬛ ⚲

This large park and garden – the setting for Smythson's masterpiece – is surrounded by the city but because of its size the visitor feels deep in the country, although near the park periphery the roar of traffic dispels that illusion. The polyanthus in spring are spectacular, as is the summer bedding, where castor-oil plants and ornamental cabbages have their place in the schemes. The formal gardens at the top of the hill afford views of huge cedars and holm oaks, lime avenues and the deer in the park.

FEEDBACK
Readers are invited to advise the *Guide* of any gardens which in their opinion should be listed in future editions, and where possible arrangements will be made to review such suggestions. Readers who would like to add information about gardens listed are warmly invited to write to the *Guide* with their comments, which may be used in future editions without attribution. A report form is included at the back of the *Guide*, although letters will be welcome. Please send to the publishers, Bloomsbury Publishing plc, 38 Soho Square, London W1V 5DF. All letters are acknowledged by the editor.

OXFORDSHIRE

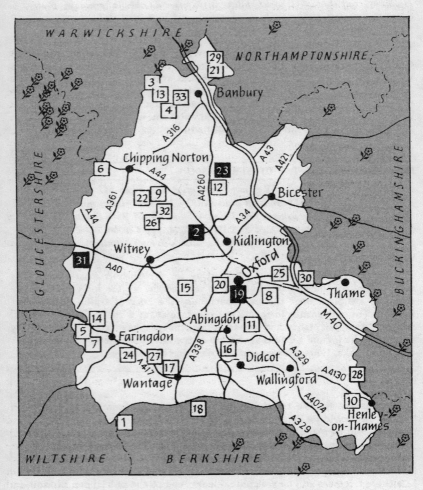

Two-starred gardens are marked on the map with a black square.

Ashdown House

Lambourn, Newbury, Berkshire RG16 7RE. Tel: (01488) 72584 (Estate Office)

The National Trust • 9m E of Swindon, 3½ m NW of Lambourn on W side of B4000 • House (hall, stairway and roof) open as garden, by guided tour only, starting at 2.15, 3.15 and 4.15pm • Garden open April to Oct, Wed and Sat only, 2 – 5pm. Woodlands open all year, Sat – Thurs, dawn – dusk. Parties must pre-book in writing • Woodlands free (house £2.10). No reduction for parties • Other information: Parking 250 metres from house. Dogs in woodland only, on lead ◐

Seen from the main road, the house appears to have a tall central section complete with cupola flanked by two lower wings. It is only when the visitor approaches the front entrance that it becomes obvious that the wings are quite separate from the central block – one was the kitchen and the other the servants' quarters of this exquisite hunting lodge built by the first Lord Craven for Elizabeth of Bohemia. The remains of a large formal park are present in a western lime avenue. A complementary lime avenue planted in 1970, to the north of the house, is now maturing well. Sadly the avenue west of the parterre was practically destroyed in the 1990 storm; it has now been replaced new new planting. An appropriately intricate parterre, designed by A.H. Brookholding-Jones, was planted by the Trust in the 1950s. The garden is best enjoyed in spring when thousands of snowdrops, naturalised in the avenue and woodland, are at their showiest.

Blenheim Palace ★★   2

Woodstock, Oxford OX20 1PX. Tel: (01993) 811091

The Duke of Marlborough • 8m NW of Oxford. At Woodstock on A44 • House open as garden • Park open all year, daily except 25th Dec, from 9am. Garden open mid-March to Oct, 10.30am – 5.30pm (last admission 4.45pm) • Entrance: park only (inc. herb garden, butterfly house, train and nature trail) pedestrians £2, children £1. Cars inc. occupants: £6; gardens only £3.50; house and gardens £8.50, OAPs £6.50, children £4.50 (1999 prices) • Other information: Rowing boats for hire • Park: ○ 🍴 & 🐕 🛍 ♿ *Garden:* ◑ 🍵 ✗ WC &

The visitor who walks through Hawksmoor's Triumphal Arch into Blenheim Park sees one of the greatest contrived landscapes in Britain. The architect Vanbrugh employed Bridgeman and Henry Wise, Queen Anne's master gardener and the last of the British formalists. Wise constructed a bastion-walled 'military' garden, kitchen gardens, planted immense elm avenues and linked Vanbrugh's bridge to the sides of the valley. The gardens were ready when the first Duke of Marlborough moved into the palace in 1719. Major alterations were made by the 4th, 5th and 9th Dukes, one of the earliest of which was the grassing-over of Wise's formal gardens by 'Capability' Brown after 1764. Brown also landscaped the park, installing the lake and cascade, and removed Wise's military garden. The gardens include formal areas designed by Achille Duchêne early this century to replace those grassed by Brown. He made formal gardens to the east and west, the latter as two water terraces in the Versailles style. To the east of the palace is the elaborate Italian garden of patterned box and golden yew, interspersed with various seasonal plantings. To the south-west from the terraces are the rose garden and arboretum. From the vast south lawn 'one passes through a magnificent grove of cedars... part shrubberies of laurel and an exedra of box and yew, the whole exemplifying the Victorian pleasure grounds', in the words of the *Oxford Companion*. It is possible to spend several hours walking through the grounds. In 1991, as a contribution to the celebration of the 300th anniversary of the replanting of the maze at Hampton Court, the Duke of Marlborough planted a maze which is maturing well in part of the kitchen garden; in a few years it should provide visitors with a puzzling and pleasurable experience. The former garden centre has been redeveloped as a lavender and herb garden. Not far off is *Kiddington Hall*, only open for a few hours one Sunday, but interesting because it was 'Capability' Brown's first garden project when he came south from his northern home. Very rarely, *Heythrop House* gardens are open.

Brook Cottage ★ 3

Well Lane, Alkerton, Banbury OX15 6NL. Tel: (01295) 670303/670590

Mrs D. Hodges • 6m NW of Banbury. From A422 Banbury – Stratford-upon-Avon road, turn W signed Alkerton. With small war memorial on right, turn left into Well Lane and right at fork • Unusual plants for sale • Open 24th April to Oct, Mon – Fri, 9am – 6pm. Other days, including Bank Holiday Mondays, 9am – 6pm, all parties by appt only • Entrance: £2.50, OAPs £2, children free, partly for NGS • Other information: Refreshments for parties must be pre-booked. DIY tea or coffee on weekdays ◐ 🍽 🍴 WC ♿ ୬

A four-acre garden of genuine originality, created since 1964 as a series of interconnecting informal enclosures, all of them heavily planted. It is the work of a plantswoman and an architect who together have embraced Alexander Pope's credo 'Consult the Genius of the Place in all', for the garden is moulded to the topography of the steeply sloping, west-facing site. Once past the terrace below the house, slivers of paths force visitors into single file, making their emergence onto open lawn above the stream and lower pond all the more exciting. Here, the planting is bold and confident, grouped tellingly in individual clumps or in beds with skilful combinations of colour. In the bog garden a splendidly-broad band of foliage plants contrasts with feathery or piercing flower spikes. The hanging garden of shrub roses is the garden's most famous feature in its season, but for those who wish to see a profusion of plants, many of them rare, disposed in a masterly way, Brook Cottage is a living workshop of ideas at all times of year.

Broughton Castle ★ 4

Broughton, Banbury OX15 5EB. Tel: (01295) 262624

Lord Saye and Sele • 2½ m SW of Banbury on B4035 • Castle open • Garden open 23rd, 24th April, 1st May; then 17th May to 13th Sept, Weds, Suns and Bank Holiday Mons; also Thurs in July and Aug, all 2 – 5pm. Also by appt for parties all year • Entrance: £4, OAPs and students £3.50, children £2 • Other information: Teas on open days only. Refreshments for parties by arrangement ◐ 🍴 WC ♿ ୬ ⛪

More of a house than a castle, with gardens that are unexpectedly domestic within the confines of the moat. In 1900 there were 14 gardeners, now there is one maintaining the overall splendour. The most important changes were made after 1969 following a visit from Lanning Roper, who suggested opening up the views across the park. There are now two magnificent borders, where great planting skill is evident in the serpentine flows of colour. The west-facing border, backed by the battlement wall, has a colour scheme of blues and yellows, greys and whites. The other long border is based on reds, mauves and blues. On the south side is the walled 'ladies garden' with box-edged, fleur-de-lys-shaped beds holding floribunda roses; a scene from *Shakespeare in Love* was filmed there. Another wonderful border rises up to the house wall. Everywhere is a profusion of old-fashioned roses and original planting.

Buscot Park ★ 5

Faringdon SN7 8BU. Tel: (01367) 240786; Fax: (01367) 241794

Administered by Lord Faringdon on behalf of The National Trust • On A417 between Lechlade and Faringdon • House closed Mons and Tues • Open April to Sept, Mon – Fri and every second and fourth Sat and following Sun in the month, 2 – 6pm (last admission 5.30pm). Closed Bank Holiday Mons • Entrance: £3.30, children £1.65 (house and grounds £4.40, children £2.20)
◑ 🍽 WC 🌿

Although the house was built in 1780, the garden has been developed during the twentieth century. The water-garden-within-a-wood was created by Harold Peto in 1912; later, avenues linking lake to house were cut through, branching out from a goose-foot near the house, with fastigiate and weeping varieties of oak, beech and lime. The Egyptian avenue created by Lord Faringdon in 1969 is guarded by sphinxes and embellished with Coade-stone statues copied from an original from Hadrian's Villa. Two new gardens at *allée* intersections – the Swinging Garden and the Citrus Bowl – provide enclosed areas of great charm. The large walled kitchen garden was rearranged in the mid-1980s, and is now intersected by a pleached avenue of ostrya (hop hornbeam) and a Judas tree tunnel. Deep borders under the outside walls have unusual and skilled planting by Tim Rees, mixing old roses and climbing vegetables (gourds, marrows, beans, cucumbers) which lay themselves out over the rose bushes after their flowering is over. Walkways both outside and inside the kitchen garden are between wide borders which use the exterior and interior walls and trellises as screens. In the latter the planting by the late Peter Coats and, over the years, imaginative development by Lord Faringdon, is exceptionally effective. The planting of the kitchen garden and the double borders is so skilful that even in drought conditions none of the effect is lost. The small garden at *Buscot Old Parsonage*, also a Trust property, has different opening times.

Chastleton House 6

Chastleton GL56 0SU. Tel: (01608) 674355; Fax: (01608) 674355

The National Trust • 6m NE of Stow-on-the-Wold off A436 • The Trust is trying to limit attendances, so admission, inc. NT members, is strictly by prior appt. Pre-booked timed ticket system for all visitors: telephone (01608) 674284. Pre-booked guided tours available • Entrance: £5, children £2.50, family ticket

£12.50, parties of 11 to 25 (max) by prior written appt only £7 per person (inc. NT members) (1999 prices) • Other information: Parking 270 metres from house. No coaches. Picnics permitted in car park. Braille guide available ● WC ⑤

This charming house was, it must be admitted, somewhat in disarray when it was in private hands, but all the more magic for that. The Trust is trying to retain some of the charm by restricting public entrance by such cunning means as having no teas or shop. The garden was at its peak at the turn of the century and survived intact until the 1940s, but the topiary, probably a Victorian re-creation of a seventeenth-century design, is well worth a view. There will be some detailed planting in specific areas. The rules of croquet were originally codified at Chastleton and the Trust is restoring at least one of the original croquet lawns. The house and garden still retain some of their original magic, and a pre-booked visit is well worthwhile if you are nearby.

Clock House 7

Coleshill, Swindon, Wiltshire SN6 7PT. Tel: (01793) 762476

Denny Wickham and Peter Fox • 3½ m SW of Faringdon on B4019 • Open 21st May, 18th June, 10th Sept, 8th Oct; also April to Oct, Thurs, all 2 – 5pm, except June, Thurs, 2 – 8pm; also by appt • Entrance: £1.50, children free • Other information: Teas in courtyard in fine weather ● WC ⑤ ✣

Situated on a hillside with inspiring views over the Vale of the White Horse, this exuberant, delightful garden was created by the present owners in the last 30 years in the grounds of Coleshill House (burned, then demolished in the 1950s). The ground-plan of the original house is planted out in box and lavender, to show the layout of walls and windows. The gravel 'rooms' are full of self-sown poppies in June and *Verbena bonariensis* in late July. There is a courtyard with a collection of plants in pots, and a sunny walled garden in the old laundry-yard with roses and mixed planting and a fine greenhouse. The lime avenue at the front of the house sweeps down to the views, and a pond and terrace are sheltered by tall shrubs. The mixed herbaceous borders are filled with interesting and unusual plants. This is an original garden, designed by an artist, with a large collection of plants in imaginative settings, the atmosphere being prolific rather than tidy.

Garsington Manor 8

South End, Garsington OX9 9DH. Tel: (01865) 361234

Mr and Mrs Ingrams • 5m SE of Oxford between A40 and B480 • Open 7th May and 30th Sept, 2 – 5pm for NGS and local charities • Entrance: £2, children free NEW ●

Created by Lady Ottoline Morrell early this century, the magnificent gardens at Garsingon Manor have been lovingly restored by the present owners over the last 15 years. The sixteenth-century house of mellow Cotswold stone (not open), is sited at the top of a steep hill, with glorious views over the Berkshire Downs and the gardens, each with their distinct style, radiating below. To the east of the house is the flower garden, its honeyed walls creating a calm, intimate atmosphere for the 24 square beds filled with bright annuals and herbaceous perennials; and below is a large lawn, formerly a tennis court, on which the annual village play is performed. Borders of lavender, pinks, shrub roses are to be found, together with a dovecot and a juniper walk leading to an Italianate garden, complete with formal pool, fountain and statuary. Beyond is a wooded dell with a natural spring, wild flowers and bogside plantings; an imposing *allée* of majestic lime trees, carpeted in spring with bulbs, leads back to the house. During the summer, opera productions are staged on the stone terrace by the house.

Gothic House   9

Charlbury, Chipping Norton OX7 3PP. Tel: (01608) 810654

Mr and Mrs Andrew Lawson • In centre of Charlbury on B4022 Witney – Enstone road • Open 28th, 29th May, 2 – 6pm for NGS and for parties by appt • Entrance: £2, children 50p (combined admission with The Priory) • Other information: Teas at church on open days ● ⚘

A third-of-an-acre walled town garden, designed by one of the country's leading garden photographers and his sculptress wife. Artistic flair is evident everywhere, from the entrance through a fine Gothick glass structure to the tour round the many gems picked out in miniature. The planting is highly imaginative and so is the clever use of green wood structures in *treillage* style, including a romantic seat, and the railway sleepers which define the pond. Andrew Lawson usually has a new floral theme such as masses of alliums – so there is a different inspiration each year. Note the *trompe-l'oeil* painting on wood. Briony Lawson's sculptures are everywhere, numbered and for sale. *Objets trouvés* amid the foliage and the whole effect delightful. The Priory (see entry) often open on the same days, is nearby.

Greys Court ★   10

Rotherfield Greys, Henley-on-Thames RG9 4PG. Tel: (01491) 628529

The National Trust • W of Henley-on-Thames, E of B481. From town centre take A4130 towards Oxford. At Nettlebed mini-roundabout take B481. Signposted to left shortly after Highmoor • House open April to Sept, Mon, Wed, Fri, 2 – 6pm. Closed 21st April • Garden open 24th April to Sept, Mon – Wed, Fri and Sat, 2 – 6pm (last admission 5.30pm). Closed 21st April • Entrance: £3.20, children £1.60, family ticket £8 (house and garden £4.50, children £2.20, family ticket £11.20) • Other information: Plants for sale on certain days only ◑ 🐶 WC ♿

The statue symbolising St Fiacre, the protector of gardeners and commemorating Charles Taylor, a former head gardener, stands modestly in this beautiful garden, or several gardens, set against the ruins of a fourteenth-century fortified house. The largest area, an orchard, is divided by lines of morello cherries and parallel hedges of *Rosa mundi*. An ancient wisteria forms a canopy over a walled area, approached on one side through a tunnel of younger wisterias in pinks and blues. The impeccably kept peony bed and rose garden glow against the ancient walls. Beyond the kitchen garden – now a new ornamental garden of unusual vegetables – across the nut avenue, is the flat Archbishop's Maze, interesting for its symbolism. Donkey wheel and restored ice-house open; work continues to restore the ha-ha.

The Harcourt Arboretum 11

Nuneham Courtenay, Oxford OX44 9PX. Tel: (01865) 343501; Fax: (01865) 341828

Oxford University Botanic Garden • 6m S of Oxford off A4074 • Open all year except 21st to 24th April and 22nd Dec to 3rd Jan: May to Oct, daily, 10am – 5pm; Nov to April, Mon – Fri, 10am – 4.30pm • Entrance: free • Other information: No coaches ○ 🏠 ら

The village and church of Nuneham were demolished in the 1670s to make way for a classical landscape to be seen from the house; Oliver Goldsmith's poem *The Deserted Village*, written in 1770, may be based on that upheaval. Horace Walpole, in 1780, described the gardens, designed by 'Capability' Brown and William Mason (the poet-gardener), as the most beautiful in the world. The garden was then full of flowers, not only along the walks, but in carefully planted beds. This 85-acre site, now owned by Oxford University Botanic Garden, dates from 1835 when the Harcourt family, who owned the Nuneham estate at the time, planted a pinetum. Many of those plantings are now magnificent mature specimens underplanted with camellias, rhododendrons, bamboos, magnolias and a collection of acers. There is also a 10-acre bluebell wood and a 22-acre meadow.

Hill Court 12

Tackley. (Enquiries to Court Farm, Tackley, Kidlington OX5 3AQ. Tel: (01869) 331221)

Mr and Mrs Andrew C. Peake • 9m N of Oxford, off A4260. From Oxford turn opposite Sturdy's Castle; from S turn off at Tackley sign • Open 10th, 11th June, 2 – 6pm • Entrance: £2, children free ● 🍴 WC ら ぷ

A two-acre, sixteenth-century walled garden, formerly attached to the house, which was demolished c. 1960. Remains of the manor house, also demolished, can be seen across the park, which dates from 1787. The garden, the design of which was influenced by Russell Page, is unusual because it is terraced uphill from the entrance. The rose beds had to be removed about a decade ago and the sensitive and original planting which replaced them is the work of Rupert Golby. Designers will find it of great interest.

Home Farm 13

Balscote, Banbury OX15 6JP. Tel: (01295) 738194

Mr and Mrs G.C. Royle • 5m W of Banbury, ½ m off A422 • Open March to Oct by appt and on NGS open days with other village gardens • Entrance: £2 • Other information: Teas on open days only, otherwise light refreshments if pre-booked ● 🍴 🏠 WC ら ぷ ぷ

This sophisticated hilltop garden of half an acre has been created by the Royles since 1984 from a farmyard on a gently sloping site, with soft pastoral views of grazing sheep. There is nothing mimsy here. Mrs Royle has a firm way of using colour, and the garden is abundantly planted with unusual flowering shrubs, bulbs, herbaceous plants, alpines and roses – designed to give all-year interest, with a special love of coloured or contrasting foliage. Combine with a trip to nearby Brook Cottage (see entry).

Kelmscott Manor 14

Kelmscott, Lechlade, Gloucestershire GL7 3HJ. Tel (01367) 252486

The Society of Antiquaries • 2m E of Lechlade in Kelmscott • House open as garden • Garden open April to Sept, Wed, 11am – 1pm, 2 – 5pm, first Sat of July and Aug, and third Sat of each month, 2 – 5pm. Tours for parties by appt on Thurs and Fri • Entrance: £6 ● ☕ ✕ 🏠 WC ♿ 🏛 ☕

Described by *Country Life* as a magical house in a remarkably unchanged village, its strange atmosphere will be relished by those who are attracted by William Morris in particular, or the Pre-Raphaelite Brotherhood in general. The magazine says the impression one forms of all Morris's gardens is that they had an unruly beauty where weeds might well have been encouraged if they were decorative. Above all his choice of flowers was essentially artistic and romantic because, for him, gardens were places of magic and mystery, fairy tale worlds where lovers met under rose-covered arbours. The present owners have tried to re-create some of that romanticism – what Morris himself described as 'a heaven on earth... and such a garden! Close down on the river, a boat house and all things handy.' Details of Morris's gardens and the inspiration for his flower designs will be found in Derek Baker's book *The Flowers of William Morris* (Barn Elms, 1996).

Manor House ★ 15

Stanton Harcourt, Witney OX8 1RJ. Tel: (01865) 881928

Mr and The Hon. Mrs Gascoigne • 9m W of Oxford, 5m SE of Witney off B4449 • House open • Garden open 23rd, 24th, 30th April, 1st, 11th, 14th, 25th, 28th, 29th May, 8th, 11th, 22nd, 25th June, 6th, 9th, 20th, 23rd July, 3rd, 6th, 17th, 20th, 24th, 27th, 28th Aug, 7th, 10th, 21st, 24th Sept, all 2 – 6pm • Entrance: £3, OAPs and children under 12 £2 (house and garden £5, OAPs and children £3) ◐ ☕ WC ♿ ☕ 🏛

Twelve acres of gardens incorporated in and around the ruins of a fourteenth- and fifteenth-century manor house. An avenue of clipped yew leads from the house to the chapel, and there are herbaceous and rose borders, with clematis, hydrangeas and roses clambering up the magnificent old walls. The kitchen garden is still in the process of redesign as a formal rose garden, using David Austin's New English roses, espaliered apple trees, and a fountain in the middle. The stewponds are sadly low in water, but covered with water lilies in high summer and fringed with water-loving plants, and are crossed by some enchanting old bridges. It would take an army of gardeners to keep this garden immaculate, so enjoy it for its nostalgic atmosphere and history, magnificent walls and urns, and romantic paths winding through nut-walks underplanted with bulbs and primulas in the spring. Don't miss the teas in the medieval kitchens. For contrast, see a completely different kind of garden, more of a museum really, a walled garden laid out as it was in Victorian times, at *Cogges Manor Farm Museum* between Witney and the A40 to the south. All produce is organic. Various events and plenty for the kids to see, too.

The Mill House 16

Sutton Courtenay, Abingdon OX14 4NH. Tel: (01235) 848219; Fax: (10235) 848959

Mrs Jane Stevens • 1½ m S of Abingdon off B4016. Leave town over river bridge, entrance gates in main street opposite Fish pub • Open 9th April, 11th June, 24th Sept, 2 – 6pm and at other times by appt for parties of 10 or more • Entrance: £2, children £1, under 4 free, parties £4 per person ● ▆ × wc & ◁▷ ⌾ 👍 ♀

Although the stone house behind high walls suggests promise, the romantic experience of the garden cannot be guessed at as the visitor approaches it through the winding main street of the village. Of course, few gardeners have the gift of the Thames in their territory, but the use which Mrs Stevens has made of it since she acquired the garden in 1981 is quite remarkable. She had the benefit of a structure laid out by Colonel Peter Laycock, a colleague of Eric Savill, who planted some splendid trees around the ruined paper mill, and she has added highly imaginative touches of her own like the circles of comfrey. This is a garden to be walked in, sat in and savoured, so do not attempt to rush around the eight and a half acres. There are formal areas on either side of the early Georgian house, but once past these, the wanderer will be lost in a sylvan idyll amongst the water, trees and groves. Fine bulbs in spring, old-fashioned roses in summer, and charming colours in autumn. High standard of maintenance. For those who like to conjure up dreams of previous owners, Herbert and Margot Asquith lived here before 1916 while he was Prime Minister and entertained all the great figures of the day for Fridays-to-Mondays. The nearby *Manor House*, with garden by Norah Lindsay, is open once a year, usually mid-May, for the NGS.

Old Church House 17

2 Priory Road, Wantage, Berkshire OX12 9DD. Tel: (01235) 762785

Dr and Mrs Dick Squires • Near Wantage Market Square next to parish church and opposite Vale and Downland Museum • Open April to Oct, Tues – Sat, 10.30am – 4.30pm, Sun, 2 – 5pm. Private visits by appt • Entrance: £1 or donation to church (tickets available at Museum). Children welcome • Other information: Park in nearby public car park. Refreshments and toilet facilities at Museum ◐ 🍴 wc & ◁▷ ♀

An unusual and exciting town garden running down to Letcombe Brook. Dr and Mrs Squires have transformed his childhood garden into a series of rooms leading away from the existing lawns and mature trees. There is a sunken water garden, a Mediterranean garden, a pergola garden and a wild garden, all filled with unusual plants and shrubs, follies and highly imaginative building. It is an inspiration to see what can be achieved in less than three years. Some fascinating documentation shows the development of the planning and the work itself in before-and-after style.

The Old Rectory ★ 18

Farnborough, Wantage, Oxfordshire OX12 8NX. Tel: (01488) 638298

Mr and Mrs Michael Todhunter • 4m SE of Wantage off B4494 • Open 16th April, 14th May, 25th June, 2 – 6pm and by written appt • Entrance: £2, children free on open days, and £4 by appt • Other information: Teas nearby on charity open days and for parties ● WC & ☙

At nearly 250 metres, and despite being prey to winds from the Downs, this four-acre site has been created over 30 years on a good original structure of large trees and hedges, with magnificent views. Deep, parallel herbaceous borders are backed by yew hedges. The planting by the front of house is subtle and effective, and smaller areas have been laid out for sun- or shade-loving plants. Woodland contrasts with shrubs and lawns, and the fast-growing arboretum now contains over 100 trees.. The swimming pool is surrounded by a large *Hydrangea sargentiana* and potted lilies, with mixed roses and clematis around the outside walls. There is a collection of old roses and small-flowered clematis, and wild flowers line the front lawn by the ha-ha. The tennis court has been turned into a *boule à drôme* - a place in the middle to play boule – with four large beds, pretty wrought-iron gates and a gazebo. Those who like John Betjeman's poetry will be interested to know that he lived here from 1945 to 1950 and can look for the ghost of Miss Joan Hunter Dunn in the shrubberies. A John Piper window in the church is in his memory.

Oxford Botanic Garden ★★ 19

Rose Lane, Oxford OX1 4AX. Tel: (01865) 276920

University of Oxford • In city centre opposite Magdalen College near bridge • Open all year, daily: April to Sept, 9am – 5pm (glasshouses 10am – 4.30pm); Oct to March, 9am – 4.30pm (glasshouses 10am – 4pm). Closed 21st April and 25th Dec • Entrance: April to Aug £2, children under 12 free; Sept to March by donation to collecting box • Other information: Professional photography and music prohibited ○ 🏠 WC &

This is the oldest botanic garden in Britain and one of the most attractive to the general visitor as nowhere else on earth, it is claimed, are there so many different plants in four and a half acres, 8000 species in all, and representatives of over 90 per cent of families of flowering plants. Founded in 1621 for physicians' herbal requirements, it is surrounded by a high wall and entered through a splendid gateway by Nicholas Stone. One yew survives from the early plantings, and there is a series of beds containing herbaceous and annual plants in systematic and labelled groups. The old walls back beds with tender plants, including roses and clematis. To the left are the greenhouses, modern ones replacing those built in 1670. A rock garden is currently being renovated, as is the bog garden. A National Collection of euphorbias. The site, currently looked after by 10 gardeners, amply justifies its original purpose 'to promote learning and glorify the works of God'. Outside the front entrance is a large rose garden donated by Americans in memory of those university staff who developed penicillin. Several miles away at Nuneham Courtenay (south of the A423) is the Harcourt Arboretum (see entry) opened in 1968.

Oxford College Gardens 20

Most colleges are helpful about access to their gardens, although the more private ones, such as the Master's or Fellows', are rarely open. Specific viewing times are difficult to rely on because some colleges prefer not to have visitors in term time or on days when a function is taking place. The best course is to ask at the porter's lodge or to telephone ahead of visit. However, it is fair to say that some Oxford college gardens will always be open to the visitor, by arrangement with porters, even if others are closed on that particular day. Some colleges have a policy of allowing public entrance on official guided tours only and others now make a charge for entry.

Amongst the College gardens of particular interest are the following: *Christ Church*: although famous for Lewis Carroll's reference to the Cheshire Cat's chestnut tree in the Deanery garden and the Oriental plane planted 1636, neither of these horticultural heritages can be visited by the public. However, they can visit the Memorial Garden on St Aldates [Memorial Garden open daily except 25th Dec, Mon – Sat, 9am – 5.30pm, Sun, 1 – 5.30pm. Master's, Cathedral and Dean's Gardens only open once a year for NGS, usually mid-Aug. Meadow open daily]. *Corpus Christi*: the smallest college, with an attractive small garden overlooking Christ Church Meadow [Closed 21st to 24th April, 21st Dec to 3rd Jan 2001 but otherwise normally open 1.30 – 4pm]. *Exeter*: Fellows' Garden [open most days, 2 – 5pm] is walled on all sides with part of boundary formed by the old Bodleian Library and Divinity Schools. The mound at the end gives excellent views across Radcliffe Square with Camera, Church of St Mary the Virgin and All Souls College all clearly visible. Visitors are requested to keep to the paths. Herbaceous borders, shrubs and mature trees. Also the Rector's private garden [open for NGS in conjunction with New College Warden's Garden one Sun in late June/early July, 2 – 5pm]. *Green College*: alas this institution with its environmental name is only open to the public once a year. *Holywell Manor*, part of Balliol: a restful, well-maintained garden of one acre [Open 10.30am – 6.30pm]. *Kellogg College*: an unusual and pleasant inner courtyard with three separate walled gardens at the back situated in Rewley House, Wellington Square [Open all year – telephone (01865) 270360 WC &]. *Lady Margaret Hall*: eight formal and informal acres, mainly designed by the Victorian architect Blomfield, who was also responsible for some of the buildings. Fine specimen trees and good borders [Open 2 – 6pm or dusk if earlier. All visitors are requested to call at the Porter's Lodge &]. *Magdalen College*: 100 acres of meadows including a deer park adjacent to the College buildings and Fellows Garden (open to the public). The water meadows bounded by the River Cherwell and circled by Addison's Walk, named after the eighteenth-century essayist and garden enthusiast, are famous for the display of fritillaries in April/May [College and gardens open all year, 2 – 6pm (12 noon – 6pm, July to Sept). Entrance: April to Sept £2.50, OAPs, students and children £1.25; Oct to March free. Refreshments sometimes available WC &]. *New College*: admirers of the writings of Robin Lane Fox will be able to see examples of his plantings, outstanding mixed borders against Oxford city wall, rose borders, cloister garden. The mound was completed in 1649. [Open Easter to Oct at New College Lane Gate, 11am – 5pm (admission charge of £2 including chapel, hall, quadrangles, cloisters and gardens); winter at Holywell Gate, 2 – 4pm, no charge]. *Nuffield*: formal gardens in two quadrangles with water features [Open Mon – Fri, 9am – 5pm, but closed Christmas, Easter and August Bank Holiday. No large parties]. *Queen's*: a garden with a fourteenth-century history, today pleasantly modernised. Good herbaceous borders in the Fellows' Garden [Open once a year for charity but not to casual visitors during year except those on guided tours through the Information Centre]. *Rhodes House*: not a college and not a pretty building but an unexpectedly pleasant garden behind [9am – 5pm weekdays only]. *St Catherine's*: in the midst of so much ancient charm in garden design it is pleasing to be able to recommend a modern garden (1960-4) created by the distinguished Danish architect Arne Jacobsen (1902-71). Noted for his concern for integrating building and landscape, this is a remarkable example. It has a fine water feature, and John Brookes says that, later in the season, when the water planting is at its best, the canal comes into its own – there is a marvellous transition throughout the building to a little floating platform which gives onto a beautiful three-dimensional concept. [Open except Easter, August and Christmas]. *St Hilda's*: five acres of lawns and beds; flood plain meadow with interesting wild flowers [Open one Sun in March, 2 – 5pm for NGS]. *St Hugh's*: an interesting 10-acre garden largely created by Annie Rogers, a Fellow. [All visitors are requested to call at the porters' lodge &]. *St John's*: landscaped in the eighteenth century and still immaculately kept. Striking in spring when bulbs in flower. See also the new Garden Quad, opened in 1993, designed by MacCormac Jamieson & Pritchard and described as 'one of the most important buildings of the 'nineties anywhere in Britain' [Open daily, 1 – 5pm or dusk if earlier. Better to go during the week, rather than at weekends, to avoid crowds &]. *Trinity*: broad sweeping lawns, magnificent herbaceous borders and informal woodland carpeted with bulbs in spring; interesting trees including 1737 catalpa and a splendid fraxinus. [Open daily, 10.30am – 12 noon, 2 – 5pm. £2, OAPs £1, concessions for parties, includes Chapel and Hall &]. Trinity Fellows' and President's Gardens, recently developed with choice plants, statuary and fountain [Open for NGS, one Sun in late March or early April and 6th Aug, 2 – 5pm 💷 WC ♨]. *Wadham*: herbaceous borders, new 'fragrant' garden, rare and fine old trees [Open 1 – 4.30pm WC &]. *Wolfson*: nine acres designed around modern college buildings by Powell and Moya. Mature beds of perennials and shrubs, formal lawns and mature trees in a peaceful riverside setting. [Open daily, daylight hours & ⬦]. *Worcester*: the only true landscaped garden in Oxford, including a lake, made from a swampy area in 1817. Brightly coloured beds in front quad [Open term time 2 – 6pm, vacation 9am – 12 noon and 2 – 6pm. Organised parties not admitted except by prior written arrangement]. The Provost's Garden, open on special occasions, has a charming rose garden stretching to wooded lakeside walks and orchards. *The University Parks* (a short walk from Rhodes House past the amazing museum): these were laid out in 1864 and are the perfect place for walking in all weathers and across the bridges to Mesopotamia or the Spalding nature reserve. The herbaceous border near South Lodge Gate is laid out in colour themes. The borders along the West and North Walks contain a broad collection of shrubs and groundcovering plants chosen especially for their drought tolerance, grouped in strong associations to create a focus in the middle distance. The newly extended pond provides a habitat for moisture-loving plants while Cox's Corner has an emphasis on winter colour. The Parks have a fine collection of mature trees mixed with newer plantings [Open daily, except St Giles Fair on 6th Sept, 8am – dusk 🍴 **WC** ⅊ ⬥].

Pettifers 21

Wardington, Banbury OX17 1RU. Tel: (01295) 750232

Mr J. and The Hon. Mrs Price • 5m NE of Banbury on A361 from M40 junction 11. Opposite Lower Wardington church • Open for NGS probably three Suns, 2 – 6pm, and by appt • Entrance: £2 ◕

Created over 15 years and still evolving, this garden is pervaded by an air of maturity and peace which stems partly from the stunning view dominating the landscape. Interesting foliage plants ensure plenty of colour all year round. Bold planting of some more unusual plants, and attention to detail – for instance in the elegant patterns made in the paths – make this a garden to linger in now, and to watch mature with pleasure. There is a box-edged herb and kitchen garden, and large mixed borders with an emphasis on plant association: herbaceous, green and white foliage shrubs, old roses, and an autumn border. Good plan and plant list supplied.

The Priory 22

Charlbury OX7 3PX. Tel: (01608) 810417

Dr D. El Kabir and others • On B4022 Witney – Enstone road. In Charlbury adjacent to church • Open 28th, 29th May, 2 – 6pm • Entrance: £2, children 50p (combined admission with Gothic House) ◕ 🍴 ⬥

The basic structure is a formal terraced topiary garden with Italianate features. The owners have aimed to create a poetic and contemplative atmosphere through terraces, parterres, foliage colour schemes, statuary and water features. Over one acre is planted with many unusual specimen trees and shrubs mainly in various 'rooms'. There is a newly planted three-acre arboretum which has about 200 different trees. Gothic House (see entry), often open at the same time, is nearby.

Rousham House ★★ 23

Steeple Aston OX6 3QX. Tel: (01869) 347110 or (mobile) (0860) 360407

Charles Cottrell-Dormer • 11m N of Oxford, 2m S of Steeple Aston off A4260 and B4030 • House open April to Sept, Wed, Sun and Bank Holiday Mons, 2

– 4.30pm • Garden open all year, daily, 10am – 4.30pm • Entrance: £3, no children under 15 ○ 🏠 WC ♿

This is much admired because William Kent's design of 1738 is effectively frozen in time. Historical enlightenment can be combined with the enchantment of the setting and the use he made of it. In fact, before Kent it was already a famous garden, described by Alexander Pope as 'the prettiest place for water-falls, jetts, ponds, inclosed with beautiful scenes of green and hanging wood, that ever I saw'. Kent's design, influenced perhaps by stage scenery, created a series of effects. There are splendid small buildings and follies, fine sculpture, water and many seats and vantage points. The best way to view the garden is to follow these one by one, in the order Kent intended, and for this a guidebook is necessary. By taking the effects *seriatim*, a feeling for the whole will then gradually emerge. This was also one of the first places where the garden took in the whole estate, 'calling-in' the surrounding countryside, to use Pope's words. Walled gardens next to the house, which pre-date Kent, have been made into a major attraction with herbaceous borders, parterre, rose garden and vegetable garden. Even those who are not particularly interested in the historic splendours of Rousham will find this walled area rewarding.

Shellingford House   24

Shellingford, Faringdon SN7 7QA. Tel: (01367) 710612

Mr and Mrs Nicholas Johnston • 2m SE of Faringdon off A417 Faringdon-Wantage road • Open: one Sun in April for charity and other days by prior appt
[NEW] ● 🍴 🏠 WC ♿ ⟐ ⚲ ⚱

This two-acre garden has some eccentric features inspired by the late Robert Heber Percy's Faringdon House, alas no longer open. There is a stream, and orchard, and spring features include fritillaries and bulb carpets. Also a wooden crocodile, gnome garden and other sculpture fantasies for children, which will soon include a bamboo house. One of the garden 'rooms' is, logically, furnished, weather permitting, with rugs and pictures; it will be interesting to see how far this is taken by other gardeners who have gone mad about 'rooms'.

Shotover House   25

Shotover Estate, Wheatley, Oxford OX33 1QS.

Lt Col Sir John Miller • 6m E of Oxford on A40 (S carriageway) • Open probably April and July for NGS, but check Oxford Times for dates • Entrance: £1, children free • Other information: Possible for wheelchairs but some unsurfaced paths ● 🍴 🏠 WC ⟐ ⚲

Rare cattle and sheep, including black varieties, greet visitors as they walk from the car park at the end of the drive round to the colonnaded back of the eighteenth-century house (not open). Pevsner calls the exterior dull, but the owner is doing much to enliven the planting in the formal garden surrounding it and to revive the statuary. From the rear arcade the view is of a long canal ending in a Gothick folly, which can be reached by walking via the pet cemetery and interestingly decorated wooden chalet. From the west front of the house, visitors will enjoy strolling down the long avenues carved out of what was once part of the royal forest of Wychwood. The garden was begun c. 1718 and William Kent was involved in the design in the 1730s, constructing a domed octagonal temple, said to be the first example of a Gothic Revival building, now ringed by cherry trees, and, on another axis, an obelisk (Kent was working at nearby Rousham (see entry) from 1738). Allow an hour to explore this pleasant park.

The Skippet ★   26

Mount Skippet, Ramsden, Chipping Norton OX7 3AP. Tel: (01993) 868253

Dr and Mrs M.A.T. Rogers • 4m N of Witney off B4022 Charlbury road. At crossroads signed Finstock turn E and almost immediately turn right. After 500 metres turn left up No Through Way lane • Open April to Sept by appt • Entrance: £1 for charity • Other information: Refreshments for parties by appt
● & ♨

Tucked away between the village pond, with its multi-racial ducks, and ancient ridge-and-furrow farmland not far from Akeman Street, Dr Rogers, a retired research chemist now in his eighties, has developed a two-acre garden of exceptional interest over the last 25 years. It is literally crammed with rare and fascinating plants of every description, in luxuriant herbaceous borders reminiscent of Monet, in rockeries, in greenhouses and in an enormous number of pots and containers of all shapes and sizes. There are exotic and unusual climbers both in the conservatory and all around the largely seventeenth-century house. A courtyard with a profusion of annuals, mostly self-sown, and bulbs in spring, leads to the prolific vegetable garden. Across the lawn, surrounded by a large variety of shrubs, are attractive vistas, and the alpine house contains a collection of treasures. In another greenhouse Dr Rogers demonstrates a revolutionary method of growing tomatoes in straw bales, and there is an interesting tufa collection. There are unusual shrubs and trees in the wild garden, a mass of bulbs in the orchard in spring, and snowdrops beside the pond. Almost everything in the graden is labelled, some rare plants are for sale, and, if you are lucky, Dr Rogers will delight in giving you an enthusiastic and highly informative tour.

Stansfield ★   27

49 High Street, Stanford–in–the–Vale, Faringdon SN7 8NQ.
Tel: (01367) 710340

Mr and Mrs D. Keeble • 16m SW of Oxford, 3½ m SE of Faringdon. Turn off A417 opposite Vale Garage • Open by appt, parties and evening visits welcome • Entrance: £1.50 ● ▆ 🗃 ♨

A one-acre-plus plantsman's garden, not yet finished, with many island beds and borders, and a large collection of plants for both damp and dry conditions. All-year round interest is provided by a wide use of foliage and seasonal flowers, starting with species spring bulbs – indeed, attention is focused on number and variety of plants rather than layout and design. New areas under development include woodland, a grass border and a scree garden, and alpines in sinks and troughs give interest on a smaller scale.

Stonor Park

28

Stonor, Henley–on–Thames RG9 6HF. Tel/Fax: (01491) 638587

Lord Camoys • 5m N of Henley-on-Thames on B480 • House open • Garden open: 23rd April to June, Sun, Bank Holiday Mons and 30 April, 27th May; July to Aug, Wed, Sun and 26th, 28th Aug; Sept, Sun, all 2 – 5.30pm. Parties by arrangement, Tues, Wed or Thurs (am and pm) and Sun pm (dates may vary) • Entrance: £2.50 (house and gardens £4.50, children under 14 in family parties free) (1999 prices). Party rates on application • Other information: Lunches for parties by arrangement. Wheelchairs by arrangement ◑ 🍺 🍽 WC ♿ 🍴 ♀

The house, a red-brick, E-shaped Tudor building with twelfth-century origins, is set in a bowl on the side of a hill with open parkland and large trees in front. Behind and to the side of the house on higher land, sheltered against the hill, are flower and vegetable gardens. Lawns lead up to a terrace with pools, stone urns and planting along the steps. The orchard, with its cypresses and espaliered fruit trees, and the lavender hedges are attractive features.

University Arboretum

(see HARCOURT ARBORETUM)

Wardington Manor

29

Wardington, Banbury OX17 1SW. Tel: (01295) 750202/758481; Fax: (01295) 750805

Lord and Lady Wardington • 5m NE of Banbury off A361 from M40 junction 11 • Open for groups by appt only • Entrance: £2 (£3 with Pettifers) ◑ 🍺 WC ♿ ⬇

Great lawns spread themselves in front of the Carolean manor house with its wisteria-covered walls. The topiary is impeccable too, and there are attractive borders. Away from the house, the owners have created a flowering shrub walk with interesting ground cover, which leads to a walled area planted with hostas. To the left is a rockery and a large pond with a peripheral walk.

Waterperry Gardens ★

30

Wheatley, Oxford OX33 1JZ. Tel: (01844) 339226; Fax: (01844) 339883

9m E of Oxford, 2½ m N of Wheatley off M40 junction 8. Signposted • Garden open daily, March to Oct, 9am – 5.30pm; Nov to Feb, 9am – 4.30pm. Closed Christmas and New Year holidays. For 20th to 23rd July open only to visitors to Art in Action (enquiries (020) 7381 3192) • Entrance: Nov to March, £1; April to Oct, £3.25, OAPs £2.75, children £1.75, coach parties (of 20 or more) by appt only £2.75 per person (1999 prices) • *Other information: Art and Craft Gallery. Saxon Church* ○ 🍵 ✕ <u>WC</u> ♿ 🐕 🌿 🏛 🕯

Waterperry has to be included in this *Guide* although its 20 acres are difficult to categorise. There is a strong educational atmosphere going back to the 1930s when a Miss Havergal opened up a small horticultural school. There is also a commercial garden centre which occupies large areas of the walled garden. The herbaceous nursery stock beds are in the ornamental gardens and form a living catalogue, the plants grown in rows and labelled. Intermixed with this are major features of the old garden, lawns and a substantial herbaceous border – also new beds containing collections of alpines, dwarf conifers, other shrubs and a new rose garden. The south field is a growing area for soft fruit. The clay bank is planted with shade-lovers. Almost all the plants are labelled and the owners describe the place as one where 'the ornamental and the utilitarian live side by side'. The greenhouses in the nursery are interesting too, containing a good stock of houseplants for sale, usually including orchids and tall ficus; another, in the old walled garden, has an enormous citrus tree (it's worth the détour just to catch the scent of blossom) and other Mediterranean specimens, which are not for sale. Several hours need to be spent here to do it justice, especially if the visitor wishes to stroll down the shady path by the little River Thame. A guide is sold at the shop. Several Wheatley gardens are also open in spring for charity, including Shotover House (see entry). A few miles east down the M40 is *Le Manoir aux Quat' Saisons*, in Church Road, Great Milton (off A329 Thame – Stadhampton road). The 12-acre garden surrounding Raymond Blanc's renowned hotel includes an impressive potager providing herbs and vegetables for the restaurant, a water garden, Japanese garden, orchard etc. It is open one day for NGS and can be viewed by patrons, who are offered a lower-price set lunch Mon – Fri.

Westwell Manor ★★   31

Burford OX18 4JT.

Mr and Mrs T.H. Gibson • *10m W of Witney, 2m SW of Burford off A40* • *Open 11th June, 2 – 6.30pm* • *Entrance: £3, children 50p* ● WC 🌿

Although this garden is open only once a year, it is worth a special effort to see it, both for the originality of its design and the high standard of its maintenance. At first sight it may appear merely one of the gems of the Cotswold manor genus, but Mrs Gibson has achieved a feeling of modernity by clever touches throughout a series of seemingly conventional rooms – over 20 at the last count. A useful plan (£1) leads the visitor round the six complex acres; more is being taken in to the garden each year. There are too many fine features to list in their entirety – they include good borders, lavender terrace, sundial garden, vegetable garden, rose garden, fine topiary, water garden, knot garden, lily pond and so on. Clever design ideas will be found in the alder basket area, moonlight garden, secret garden, two rills lined by a pleached lime *allée* and in a new *pièce d'eau* complete with rowing boat in place of the grass tennis court. Interesting wild garden or field beyond, and plenty for the plantsperson everywhere.

Wilcote House ★ 32

Wilcote, Finstock, Chipping Norton OX7 3DY. Tel: (01993) 868606

The Hon. and Mrs Charles Cecil • 6m N of Witney, 3m S of Charlbury E off B4022 • Open by written appt • Entrance: £2, children free, parties negotiable. • Other information: conducted tours for private parties on weekdays by arrangement ● WC ♿

Surrounding and complementing a fine sixteenth- to nineteenth-century Cotswold stone house, the large garden is itself a period piece, with extensive beds of old-fashioned roses and mixed borders and a nearly 40-metre laburnum walk at its best at the end of May. An unusual feature is the large wild garden intersected by grass paths, planted within the last two decades with an increasing selection of trees now beginning to feature, particularly with autumn colour. Mount Skippet (see entry) is nearby.

Wroxton Abbey 33

Wroxton, Banbury OX15 6PX. Tel: (01295) 730551

Wroxton College of Fairleigh Dickinson University of New Jersey USA • 3m W of Banbury off A422 • House (now used for academic purposes) open only by appt • Grounds open all year, daily, dawn − dusk • Entrance: free • Other information: Parking in village. Vehicles not permitted in grounds ○

The historical interest of this garden and park is that in 1727 Tilleman Bobart (a pupil of Wise) was commissioned to construct a Renaissance-style garden with canals by the owner of the large Jacobean manor house, the 2nd Baron Guilford. But by the late 1730s his son had this grassed over to convert it to the then-fashionable landscape style, and Sanderson Miller designed some of the garden buildings c. 1740. The present American owners have restored much of this early landscape garden since 1978. On entering the long drive up to the house, it appears to be a conventional park, but beyond are interesting features including a serpentine river, lake, cascade which can be seen from a viewing mount, Chinese bridge, Doric temple, Gothick dovecot and ice-house, all restored from their derelict state. There is a rose garden and a knot garden. The steps have all been renovated. Alas, an unsightly wire fence is erected to deter vandals. In all, the grounds cover 56 acres and offer many hours of pleasant walks. A garden guide is available.

RUTLAND

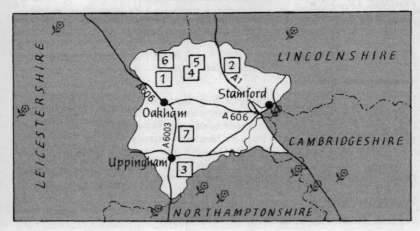

Ashwell House

1

Ashwell, Oakham LE15 7LW. Tel: (01572) 722833

Mr and Mrs S.D. Pettifer • 3m N of Oakham via B668 towards Cottesmore, turn left to Ashwell • Open by appt and one Sun in June for NGS • Entrance: £1 per person ● ● WC & ℘

An old walled garden, well planned with combinations to provide all-year colour, together with a well-stocked vegetable garden. There is a wide range of shrubs and perennials in the borders, with new plantings. The pleasure garden has a pavilion in classical style and architectural features by George Carter.

Clipsham House ★

2

Clipsham, Oakham LE15 7SE. Tel: (01780) 410238

Mr and Mrs R. Wheatley • 10m NE of Oakham, E of A1 Stamford – Grantham road on B668 • Open for charity in June for parties by appt only • Entrance: £2, children 25p ● ● WC &

This romantic three-acre garden is at one with the pretty Regency rectory (1820) set in parkland with fine trees and rolling pasture. The exceptional walled garden, laid out in 1939 and designed by Dame Brenda Colvin, features old-fashioned roses, shrubs with contrasting foliage and hardy perennials in muted colours. An elevated summerhouse with pool gives added dimension, and a pleached hornbeam walk takes the eye to the perfect folly. A mile away is *Clipsham Yew Tree Avenue*, 150 yew trees clipped into topiary which are nearly 200 years old. Formerly the carriage drive to Clipsham Hall, but now owned by the Forestry Commission, it commemorates many important events since 1870. Beautifully maintained. Enjoy a stroll and discover the anchor, the three bears, the deer, the elephant and other surprises. Nearby is *Barnsdale Plants*,

The Avenue, Exton, formerly owned by the late Geoff Hamilton. The nursery has a series of show gardens, such as town paradise, rose, woodland, stream, bog and modern estate gardens, which are excellent aids to planning or redesigning green spaces.

Lyddington Bede House 3

Blue Coat Lane, Lyddington LE15 9LZ. Tel: (01572) 822438

English Heritage • In Lyddington, 7m S of Oakham, 1m E of A6003 • Open April to Oct, daily, 10am – 1pm, 2 – 6pm • Entrance: £2.50, concessions £1.90, children £1.30, under 5s free (1999 prices) • Other information: Parking off road, 20 metres from entrance via cobbled alley ◑ 🖼 ⅋ ⇗ 🛒 ⚕

Originally a medieval palace of the Bishops of Lincoln, the Bede House, now over 900 years old, still has many of its original features. It was later converted into an almshouse. This delightful palace is set in small gardens among picturesque golden stone cottages and beside the handsome parish church of St Andrew. Situated in a sunny corner at the entrance to the palace and backed by walls, the herb garden forms an L-shape, with culinary herbs on the longer side of the L, medicinal herbs on the shorter side. The herbs have been carefully chosen from those which would have been here originally. Beds are edged with low box hedging. There are around 42 culinary and 20 medicinal herbs.

The Old Hall 4

Market Overton, Oakham LE15 7PL. Tel: (01572) 767276

Mr and Mrs T. Hart • 6m NE of Oakham, 2m N of Cottesmore off B668 • Open one day for NGS, 2 – 6pm, and by appt only • Entrance: £2, children 50p (combined admission with The Old Manor House – see entry) on open day **NEW** ◑

Five acres of softly agreeable grounds. Carefully coloured borders lead from a sunken lawn which falls away gently to distant vistas and trickling stream, and the formal enclosed swimming pool in the walled kitchen garden has views through ornamental gates and avenues of mature trees. There are many interesting focal points, including a raised pond with enchanting tiny frog sculptures that spout from lily leaves into the jaws of a lion mask. The pleached lime screen now coming into its own is elegant and well-placed. The whole is at one with its beautiful surroundings of Rutland stone and rolling landscape.

The Old Manor House 5

Market Overton, Oakham LE15 7PW. Tel: (01572) 767270

Dr and Mrs Evans • 6m NE of Oakham, 2m N of Cottesmore off B668 • Open one day for NGS, 2 – 6pm • Entrance: £2, children 50p ◑ 🖼 WC

An inspiring artist's garden, planned by a respected teacher of botanical painting, gives a glorious display of thickly planted flowers and shrubs within a disciplined but generous one-acre structure. Roses, roses everywhere, scrambling, tumbling and sitting politely. 300 different shrub varieties. In their season there are tulips, prolific as a Dutch Old Master. The creamy stone of an eighteenth-century house (not open) is the backdrop. Another corner has mirrors used with *trompe-l'oeil* effect; pleached limes mark a boundary. A pond and knot gardens are of an accomplished design, with vistas that delight the eye at every turn. Simply enchanting.

The Old Rectory 6

Teigh, Oakham LE15 7RT. Tel: (01572) 787681

Mr and Mrs D.B. Owen • 5m N of Oakham between Wymondham and Ashwell • Open 30th April, 2 – 6pm and by appt in April, June and July. Parties welcome • Entrance: £1 🌑 🍽 ⬥ ⬥ 🐾

An enchanting, partially walled garden of three-quarters of an acre, the perfect setting for the BBC production of *Pride and Prejudice*. First laid out in the 1950s, the existing garden has evolved from its original design over the last 25 years under the present owners, with much successful thought given to colour and juxta-position of plants. There is a good show of spring bulbs and blossom, but perhaps the best month is July. Roses used cleverly, connecting shapes and contrasts of foliage. Fine trees and climbing plants everywhere to complement the mellow walls of the eighteenth-century stone rectory. Special Strawberry-Hill-Gothick church next door, a testament to the grandeur of an earlier incumbent.

10 Wing Road 7

Manton LE15 8SZ. Tel: (01572) 737538

Betty Hunt • 5m SW of Oakham off A6003 • Open by appt only • Entrance: charge [NEW] 🌑

This colourful, densely planted garden, where wild areas successfully combine and contrast with more formal plantings, is the creation of an artist and plant collector who was runner-up in a recent Daily Mail/RHS national competition. It is a narrow, south-facing plot, roughly 55 x 20 metres, sheltered behind a tall hedge of conifers. The exuberant planting of trees, shrubs, perennials and wild flowers reflects her enthusiasm for conservation and wildlife, attracted espe-cially to the pond and woodland, and reflects also the rolling landscape that surrounds the garden.

FEEDBACK
Readers are invited to advise the *Guide* of any gardens which in their opinion should be listed in future editions, and where possible arrange-ments will be made to review such suggestions. Readers who would like to add information about gardens listed are warmly invited to write to the *Guide* with their comments, which may be used in future editions without attribution. A report form is included at the back of the *Guide*, although letters will be welcome. Please send to the publishers, Blooms-bury Publishing plc, 38 Soho Square, London W1V 5DF. All letters are acknowledged by the editor.

SHROPSHIRE

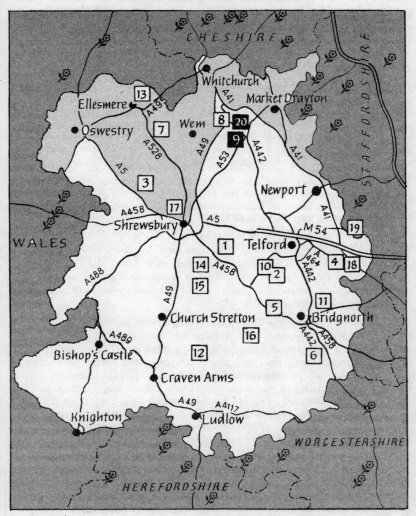

Two-starred gardens are marked on the map with a black square.

Attingham Park

1

Attingham, Shrewsbury SY4 4TP. Tel: (01743) 709203; Fax: (01743) 709352

The National Trust • 4m SE of Shrewsbury. Turn off B4380 at Atcham • House open 31st March to 30th Oct, Fri – Tues, 1.30 – 5pm; Bank Holiday Mons,

11am – 5pm (last admission 4.30pm). Parties by arrangement • Deer park and grounds open all year except 25th Dec, 9am – 9m (closes Feb 5pm) • Entrance: £2, children 90p (house and grounds £4.20, children £2.20, family £10.20). Party and out-of-hours rates available • Other information: Picnics on Mile Walk only. Self-drive electric scooter available by pre-booking. Dogs in grounds only (not deer park) on lead ○ 🍽 WC & 🏛

The grand neo-classical house is really the main attraction, but after the tour visitors can enjoy a mile-long walk by the River Tern, with daffodils in spring followed by azaleas and rhododendrons; autumn colour is provided by dog-woods and American thorns. There are a few perennials near the house, but this is a landscape mainly of large trees and shrubs, including a magnificent grove of Lebanon cedars. A longer walk through the deer park affords fine views of the house and the Repton landscape. The eighteenth-century oran-gery has been restored.

Benthall Hall   2

Broseley TF12 5RX. Tel: (01952) 882159

The National Trust • 1m SW of Broseley off B4375, 4m NE of Much Wenlock, 4½ m S of Telford • Part of house open same times as garden • Garden open 2nd April to 24th Sept, Wed, Sun and Bank Holiday Mons, 1.30 – 5.30pm (last admission 5pm). Coaches and parties by arrangement only, Tues and Wed am • Entrance: £2 (house and gardens £3) (1999 prices) • Other information: Parking 150 metres down road ◑ WC &

A small garden containing some interesting plants and features and some topiary. George Maw and Robert Bateman both lived in the house and contributed to the garden design and plant collection. The rose garden has fine plants and a small pool and there is a delightful raised scree bed. A good collection of geraniums and ground-cover plants, together with a peony bed, clematis and roses through trees and shrubs create a pleasant garden to stroll through. The old kitchen garden now contains a collection of crab apples, roses, wall plants, etc. In spring the crocus introduced by George Maw and daffodils provide interest, and the large specimens of Scots pine, beech and chestnut are stunning features. A monument to botanical history.

Brownhill House   3

**Ruyton XI Towns, Shrewsbury SY4 1LR. Tel: (01939) 261121;
Fax: (01939) 260626; E-mail: brownhill@eleventowns.demon.co.uk;
Web: www.eleventowns.demon.co.uk**

Roger and Yoland Brown • 10m NW of Shrewsbury on B4397 • Open for NGS several times in summer, 1.30 – 5.30pm and by appt May to Aug • Entrance: £2, children free • Other information: Parking at Bridge Inn 100 metres away. Bed and breakfast accommodation ● 🍽 WC ⚘

Out of an impossible north-facing cliff a most unusual and distinctive garden of great variety has been created since 1972. The slope has been transformed from a scrap-covered wilderness to a series of terraces and small gardens connected by over 550 steps that wander up and down the hill through plantings of trees and shrubs, patches of wild flowers and open flower-filled spaces. At the bottom a riverside garden runs from an open lawn to a bog garden. A series of formal terraces includes a laburnum walk, and at the top there are paved areas with a pool, gazebo, parterre, a long walk with herbaceous border, flower beds and a large kitchen garden with glasshouses. Also a folly, Thai spirit house and sculptures. Work on the grotto and terracing is progressing, but meanwhile a new summerhouse, a large Arabic arch and a unique design of Menorah have been built and steps completely resurfaced. A few miles away just W of the A5 at Kinnerley is *Hall Farm Nursery*, which has an award-winning selection of herbaceous perennials.

David Austin Roses 4

Bowling Green Lane, Albrighton, Wolverhampton WV7 3HB.
Tel: (01902) 323931; Fax: (01902) 372142

Mr and Mrs David Austin • 8m NW of Wolverhampton, 6m SE of Shifnal, between A41 and A454. Take Junction 3 off M54 towards Albrighton, turn right at sign 'Roses and Shrubs', then second right • Open all year, Mon – Fri, 9am – 5pm, Sat, Sun and Bank Holiday Mons, 10am – 6pm (closes dusk from mid-Oct to mid-March). Closed 24th Dec to 1st Jan. Entrance: free NEW ○ ☕
WC ♿ ⌖ ⌖

David Austin is one of the country's leading rose breeders, so this is an ideal place for inspecting roses. There are about 900 varieties, including shrub, climbing, species and old roses. At flowering time there is a riot of colour. For the past 15 years Mrs Austin has presided over the hardy plants department, which stocks more than 1000 species and varieties of hardy perennials and grasses. The nursery also has one of the most comprehensive selections of irises and peonies, including tree peonies.

The Dower House 5

Morville Hall, Morville, Bridgnorth WV16 5NB. Tel/Fax: (01746) 714407

Dr Katherine Swift • 3m NW of Bridgnorth at A458/B4368 junction, within Morville Hall grounds • Open April to Sept, Wed, Sun and Bank Holiday Mons, 2 – 6pm; 16th April, 18th June, 2 – 5pm with other local gardens for NGS; and at other times, inc. evenings, by appt. Guided tours for parties • Entrance: £2, children under 16 50p, guided tours £2.50 per person • Other information: Parking in churchyard. Special Rose Days in late June/early July. Period Garden Design workshops ◑ ☕ ♿ ⌖ ⌖ ☕

Starting in 1989, the present owner has transformed a one-and-a-half-acre site within the grounds of Morville Hall, with the aim of relating the history of English gardens in a sequence of separate features: a turf maze, a medieval cloister garden, a knot garden, a seventeenth-century plat and flower beds, a William and Mary canal garden with formal water feature and a box-edged *plates-bandes*, an eighteenth-century flower garden, a Victorian rose border, a nineteenth-century wilderness and, finally, an ornamental fruit and vegetable garden. Particular attention is given to the use of authentic plants and construction techniques; old roses are a speciality. The gardens of *Morville Hall* (National Trust) are said to be an attractive four acres but are open by written appointment only with the tenants, Dr and Mrs J.C. Douglas.

Dudmaston 6

Quatt, Bridgnorth WV15 6QN. Tel: (01746) 780866; Fax: (01746) 780744

The National Trust • 4m SE of Bridgnorth on A442 • House open • Garden open 2nd April to 1st Oct, Wed, Sun and Bank Holiday Mons, 12 noon – 6pm (last admission 5pm); also 31st May, 2 – 6pm for NGS. Special opening for pre-booked parties only, Thurs, 2 – 5.30pm. Estate open free of charge for pedestrian access throughout the year • Entrance: £2.50 (house and garden £4, children £2, family £8) • Other information: Batricar available. Dogs in Dingle only, on lead ◑ 🍴 ✕ 🏛 WC ♿ ⬦ 🏪 🍽

An eight-acre garden of appeal and interest with its large pool and bog garden and the associated plants, along with island beds with shrubs, azaleas, rhododendrons, viburnums and good old roses. Some large specimen trees bring an air of peace to the garden, and old fruit trees, including mulberries and medlars, add to the interest of old shrubs. Alas, no plant labels to help identify the specimens. The rock garden has been restored and the Big Pool has attractive plantings. There are two estate walks of between four to five and a half miles starting from Hampton Loade off A442. This is one of half-a-dozen gardens near Bridgnorth, and, if there is time to spare, it is worth going into town to see Telford church and the town gardens beside it.

Gate Cottage 7

English Frankton, Ellesmere SY12 0JU. Tel: (01939) 270606

G.W. Nicholson and Kevin Gunnell • 10m N of Shrewsbury on A528. At Cockshutt take road to English Frankton, garden 1m on right • Open 14th May, 4th June, 1 – 5pm for NGS, and for parties by appt • Entrance: £1.50, children 50p • Other information: Teas on charity open days only ◑ 🍴 ⬦ 🌿

This garden is changing and developing all the time to accommodate a vast range of plants. Roses and clematis scramble through old fruit trees, and there are many other fine roses along the exterior fence and in the herbaceous borders, which contain hellebores, hostas, aquilegias, digitalis, delphiniums, poppies, iris and euphorbias. Pools and a bog garden with primulas. In the extended area shrubs have been planted for colour effect. Large pebbles have been used to create attractive features and, because one of the owners is a flower arranger, there are unusual brown and black foliage plants and some interesting grasses. New rock and gravel plantings are being extended.

Hawkstone Historic Park and Follies 8

Weston–under–Redcastle, Shrewsbury SY4 5UY. Tel: (01939) 200611; Fax (01939) 200311

13m NE of Shrewsbury via A49, 6m SW of Market Drayton on A442 Telford – Whitchurch road. Entrance on road from Hodnet to Weston-under-Redcastle. Signed from Hodnet • Park open April to 27th Oct, daily; Jan – Mar, Sat and Sun; all 10am – 6pm • Entrance: park £4.50, OAPs £3.50, children £2.50, family (2 adults and 3 children) £12 (1999 prices). Reduced rates for pre-booked parties ◗ 🍴 📠 <u>WC</u> ⑃ ⬳ 🏠 ⚲

What Marcus Binney describes as 'a heroic new chapter' in the rescue of this historic park has taken place. In its day it was as famous as Stowe and Stourhead, and through the generosity of the proprietors of the Hawkstone Park Hotel the grounds have been returned to their eighteenth-century grandeur and sublimity (the latter was supposed to induce awe if not fear). A series of monuments, now reconstructed, is linked by winding paths and tunnels. Ascending towards the White Tower, the visitor passes the thatched buildings, in one of which was a mechanical hermit famous for his artificial cough (now replaced by a hologram), then a grotto (used to house Santa at Xmas) and a so-called Swiss bridge, a fallen tree across a gorge. Much remains to be done to the Red Castle, which is genuinely medieval. The whole thing is a triumph for all involved, including English Heritage, who rate this Grade I. A walk through the park is approximately three and a half miles, but visitors should be warned that it involves climbing and descending many steps. Nearby are the restored Victorian gardens of *Hawkstone Hall* open to the public in August.

Hodnet Hall ★★ 9

Hodnet, Market Drayton TF9 3NN. Tel: (01630) 685202; Fax: (01630) 685853

Mr A.E.H. and The Hon. Mrs Heber-Percy • 12m NE of Shrewsbury, 5½ m SW of Market Drayton, at A53/A442 junction • Open April to Sept, Tues – Sun and Bank Holiday Mons, 12 noon – 5pm • Entrance: £3, OAPs £2.50, children £1.20, (1999 prices) ◗ 🍴 ✕ 📠 <u>WC</u> ⑃ ⬳ 🌿 🏠

From its spring opening, the 60-acre parkland offers a constant succession of interest, although the greatest overall effect is in autumn when the acers, sorbus and birches present their display. The grounds are grouped around a series of lakes and water gardens, home to black swans. This is essentially splendid large-scale parkland planting: magnolias, azaleas, rhododendrons in late spring are followed in summer by fuchsias, astilbes and gunneras, matched with water lilies on the lakes. For the herbaceous gardener there are shrub roses, tree peonies and the more traditional border plants.

Limeburners   10

Lincoln Hill, Ironbridge, Telford TF8 7NX. Tel: (01952) 433715

Mr and Mrs J.E. Derry • 4m SW of Telford. Turn off B4380 W of Ironbridge up Lincoln Hill and garden on left at top • Open April to Sept by appt • Entrance: £2, children free ● **WC** &

Walking round this delightful garden there are always surprises in store and a wealth of interesting plants to see. The wildlife garden has a wide range of trees and shrubs, and the use of ground-cover plants must help to reduce maintenance. Note the roses climbing through shrubs. The planting combinations are excellent, and there is colour even on a limestone bank. A new water feature incorporates a waterfall and stream splashing into the large pool.

Lower Hall ★   11

Worfield, Bridgnorth WV15 5LH. Tel: (01746) 716607; Fax: (01746) 716325

Mr and Mrs C.F. Dumbell • 4m NE of Bridgnorth. Take A454 Wolverhampton/ Bridgnorth road, turn right to Worfield and after village stores and pub turn right • Open 29th June, 1st, 2nd July, 2 – 6pm. Also by appt from April to July and for a limited number of horticultural parties • Entrance: £3, children under 12 free • Other information: Access for coaches difficult. Garden room available for parties of up to 40 for lunches or evening meals ● ● × ▤ **WC** & ⬦ ₰

This modern plantsman's garden has been created by the present owners since 1964, helped originally by the designer Lanning Roper. The walled garden has a magnificent display of iris in season. Old-fashioned and modern shrub roses as well as climbers on walls and through trees are a feature in late June. Beyond the walls the village cottages and the Tudor house provide a fine backcloth to the garden. Everywhere the use of colour combinations and plant associations is good – a red border, another of white and green giving a cool effect. The water garden is separated from the woodland garden by the River Worfe with two bridges and two weirs. The view across the candelabra primula island and pond with the sixteenth-century house as its backdrop is much used for calendars. The woodland garden includes rare magnolias, a collection of birches with bark interest, acers, amelanchiers – all-year variety and colour.

Millichope Park   12

Munslow, Craven Arms SY7 9HA. Tel: (01584) 841234

Mr and Mrs L. Bury • 10m SW of Telford, 8m NE of Craven Arms, 11m N of Ludlow on B4368 • Open 1st May, 25th June, 2 – 6pm for NGS, and for parties by appt • Entrance: £2 per person • Other information: Teas on open days only. Picnics in woodland only ● **WC** ⬦ ₰

The glory of Millichope Park is its magnificent landscaping, commissioned in the 1760s by a father seeking a fitting memorial to his four sons, all of whom had predeceased him. The main memorial was an elegant Ionic temple now dramatically sited away from the house across a lake. The present owners have commissioned a fine Chinese-style bridge across one of the gorges and Mrs Bury has added a set of herbaceous borders disposed in elegant 'rooms' framed by yew hedges. Away from Georgian classicism, romantic wilderness plantings of roses and philadelphus combine to make this a most beautiful park and garden.

Oteley 13

Ellesmere SY12 0PB. Tel: (01691) 622514

Mr and Mrs R.K. Mainwaring • 8m NE of Oswestry, 1m E of Ellesmere near A528/495 junction. From N past The Mere turn left opposite convent • Open 16th April, 29th May, 2 – 6pm, and by appt • Entrance: £2, children 50p • Other information: Possible for wheelchairs if dry ● 🍵 WC ⌁ ℘

The magnificent 10-acre garden, set in park and farmland with glimpses of The Mere beyond surrounding trees, has extensive lawns with architectural features, interesting and old handsome trees set about the lawns, a grey/ silver border, decorative island beds, rhododendrons, azaleas, roses and shrubs in a gracious setting, with a collection of peonies flowering simulta- neously. Herbaceous borders are backed by high walls covered with roses, clematis and other climbing plants, and a folly and a walled kitchen garden provide the finishing touches. All this plus what an inspector describes as 'one of the best plant stalls we have come across in 20 years of garden visiting, both for unusual plants and modest prices'.

The Patch 14

Acton Pigott, Acton Burnell, Shrewsbury SY5 7PH. Tel: (01743) 362139

Mrs Margaret Owen • 8m SE of Shrewsbury between A49 and A458. From Acton Burnell take Cressage Road. After ½ m turn left signed Acton Pigott • Open 27th Feb for charity, 11am – 3pm and for parties by appt • Entrance: £1.50, children free ● 🍵 WC ♿ ℘

Do not be deceived by this half-acre garden – allow time. It is filled with beauties, starting in spring with snowdrops, hellebores, erythroniums, dicen- tras, trilliums and violas. On into summer go *Paeonia mlokosewitschii* and *P. daurica*, followed by dictamnus, veratrums (National Collections applied for), roses, and to set all these in context Mrs Owen holds National Collections of camassias and epimediums. Other specialities include nerines, schizostylis and veratrums. The garden is bordered by a broad grassy path, and at its centre lies a white garden. It is graced with tree rarities such as *Eucalyptus pauciflora* spp. *debeuzevillei*, *Styrax obassia* and *Toona sinensis*.

Preen Manor ★ 15

Church Preen, Church Stretton SY6 7LQ. Tel: (01694) 771207

Mr and Mrs P. Trevor-Jones • 5m SW of Much Wenlock on B4371. After 3m turn right for Church Preen and Hughley; after 1½ m turn left for Church Preen, over crossroads. Drive is ½ m on right • Open several dates in summer and autumn for NGS and by arrangement for parties of 15 or more in June and July only • Entrance: £2.50, children 50p ● 🍵 WC ℘

The grounds of Preen Manor are blessed with a beautiful south-east aspect facing Wenlock Edge. Despite the attractions of the more formal part of the gardens, it is the wooded landscaped walks beside the pools and natural stream which are the most outstanding feature. Rodgersias, *Primula japonica*, *Rhododendron ponticum* hybrids and magnificent yews and cedars create a noble setting on the banks which fall away from the former manor house. The more formal part of gardens is akin to a pretty cottage garden, with roses, deutzias and violas. Other gardens, including a chess garden, pebble garden and gazebo complete with parrot and cat demonstrate an esoteric style of gardening which may appeal to some. Slightly east of Preen is *Wenlock Priory* (English Heritage), a large ruin featuring imaginative topiary [open all year].

Ruthall Manor   16

Ruthall Road, Ditton Priors, Bridgnorth WV16 6TN. Tel: (01746) 712608

Mr and Mrs G.T. Clarke • 7m SW of Bridgnorth. Ruthall Road signed near garage. Manor garden ³/₄ m further on • Open by appt and for parties • Entrance: £2 (1999 price) ● 🅱 WC & 🕭

The severe winter of 1982 resulted in a complete reorganisation of this garden. Set below the heights of Abdon Burf, its renewal is now coming to maturity. It offers a mixture of settings, from a prettily planted romantic pool to more formal plantings near the house, a woodland area and a vegetable garden. Well-sited trees and shrubs are mixed with climbers and perennials.

The Shrewsbury Quest   17

193 Abbey Foregate, Shrewsbury SY2 6AH. Tel: (01743) 243324

The Shrewsbury Quest Ltd • In central Shrewsbury in Abbey Foregate, opposite Shrewsbury Abbey • Garden open daily except 25th Dec and 1st Jan, 10am – 5pm (Nov to March last admission 4pm) • Entrance: Quest and garden £4.50, OAPs and students £3.80, children £2.95, family ticket (2 adults and 2 children) £13.40 (1999 prices) ○ 🍽 ✕ 🅱 WC & ℘ 🏛

The Brother Cadfael novels have become so popular that a commercial presentation has been installed for his fans opposite the Abbey. It contains a herb garden, laid out by Dr Sylvia Landsberg in the same spirit as the one at the Abbey of Fontevraud in France. Gallica roses and honeysuckles are framed within what is developing into an attractive trellised walk. There is an interesting (and not at all gimmicky) herbarium with dried herbs.

Swallow Hayes ★   18

Rectory Road, Albrighton, Wolverhampton WV7 3EP. Tel: (01902) 372624

Mrs Michael Edwards • 9m SE of Telford, 7m NW of Wolverhampton. Use M54 junction 3. Turn off A41 into Rectory Road after Garden Centre • Open one day in mid-Jan (for National Collection of witch hazels), 11am – 4pm. Also for parties by appt; telephone for details • Entrance: £2 (on open day), parties £2.50 per person (incl. tea and biscuits), children 10p • Other information: Teas on open days only ● 🅱 WC & 🕭 ℘

A delightful two-acre modern garden with many design features, colour and foliage contrasts, and a beautiful display of plants, shrubs and trees. Although planted for easy maintenance, it contains nearly 3000 different types of plants and gives year-round interest. The alpine border is divided into various soil conditions, and the Mediterranean wall has tender plants. Small pools, ferns and a woodland area provide contrast. National Collections of witch hazels and lupins are here, plus an interesting area of small gardens to copy at home, vegetables and fruit trees, nursery stock beds and a hardy geranium trial.

Weston Park ★ 19

Weston–under–Lizard, Shifnal TF11 8LE. Tel: (01952) 852100

Weston Park Enterprises • 6m E of Telford on A5, 7m W of M6 junction 12 and 3m N of M54 junction 3 • House open at 1pm. Extra charge • Garden open April to Sept (please enquire for days, times and events list) • Entrance: park and gardens £3.80, OAPs £2.80, children £2.20 (house, park and gardens £5.50, OAPs £4.30, children £3.40) ◑ 🍷 ✕ 🖼 WC ⇔ 🏪 🦮

A distinctive 'Capability' Brown creation covering almost 1000 acres of delightful woodland planted with rhododendrons and azaleas, together with beautiful pools. Magnificent trees form a handsome backcloth to many shrubs. A rose walk leads to the deer park. The rose garden by the house and the Italian parterre garden have been restored. The many architectural features – Temple of Diana, Roman bridge and Orangery – were all designed by James Paine. For those who wish to spend more time at Weston there are gourmet dinners and open-air cultural events in the park and gardens. Adventure playground, railway, pets' corner.

Wollerton Old Hall ★★ 20

Wollerton, Hodnet, Market Drayton TF9 3NA. Tel: (01630) 685760 (daytime)

John and Lesley Jenkins • 12m NE of Shrewsbury off A53. Signed from A53/ A41 junction • Open May to Aug, Fri, Sun and Bank Holiday Mons, 12 noon – 5pm • Entrance: £2.50, children 50p ◑ 🍷 ✕ WC & 🦮

Artistry, vision and discipline combine here to make a garden of exceptional quality. Within a little over three acres is a series of beautifully planted rooms, each distinct in character yet very much part of the whole. This effect is achieved through the careful positioning of a number of principal and secondary axes upon which the overall plan of the garden depends. Contrasts are much in evidence. Fiery borders in the hot garden, stunning in August, are tempered with cool whites in a scented garden. Openness, in the form of a broad expanse of lawn, contrasts with the intimacy of a pergola dripping with roses and clematis. But this garden is not just about plantsmanship and design. It is charged with atmosphere, enhanced by a number of most appealing structures; in recalling the Arts and Crafts Movement of the early years of the last century, this garden is redolent of many fashionable ones of the present.

SOMERSET

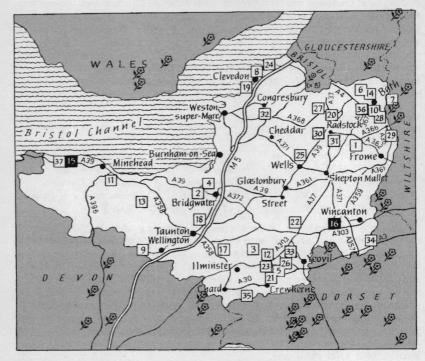

Two-starred gardens are marked on the map with a black square.

Ammerdown House ★   1

Radstock, Bath BA3 5SH.

Lord Hylton • 10m S of Bath, on B3139, ½ m off A362 Radstock – Frome road • Open for charity 24th, 29th May, 11am – 5pm • Entrance: £3, children free • Other information: Pre-booked catering for parties at Ammerdown Study Centre. Tel: (01761) 433709 ● ● 🖿 **WC** ⬤ ◁▷

The Bath-stone house was designed by James Wyatt, with panoramic views on one side and a garden on the other; the garden was a brilliant conception by Lutyens, who wanted to link the house with the orangery. Walking through the Italianate 'rooms' of yew and sculpture and parterre, one is unaware of the tricks of space that are being played. Massive yew planting, now mature and nearly four metres high, creates enclosed formal areas which lead irresistibly one from another – the spaces between being almost entirely filled with hedging. The originality and grandeur remain, as do some particularly clever details such as the clipped Portugal laurels, honeysuckles trained over wire umbrellas, ancient lemon verbenas in pots in the orangery, and on terraces.

Daffodils, narcissi and cowslips are spring features, together with fountains and statues at all seasons. For those who enjoy music in the garden, there is the Great Elm Music Festival, Great Elm, Frome BA11 3NY. Write for details of the three July weekend concerts.

Barford Park ★ 2

Spaxton, Bridgwater TA5 1AG. Tel: (01278) 671269

Mr and Mrs M. Stancomb • 5m W of Bridgwater. From Bridgwater – Spaxton road, turn to Enmore • House open by appt • Garden open for individuals and parties by arrangement from May to Sept • Entrance: £3, children free (house and garden) ● WC �& ⬠

This is a garden in the eighteenth-century style developed over the last 32 years, set in parkland and protected by a ha-ha on three sides. After watching the golden orfe darting around the lily pond, stroll down a sweep of lawn to a stand of tall trees. There, in the woodland glade, is a carpet of many shades of primulas. The eighteenth-century walled garden is unusually sited in view of the house – a lawn with deep herbaceous borders on each side makes a colourful vista.

Barrington Court Garden ★ 3

Barrington, Ilminster TA19 0NQ.

The National Trust • 5m N of Ilminster, on B3168 in Barrington • Parking • House open as garden • Garden open March and Oct, Fri, Sat, Sun, 11am – 4.30pm; 1st April to 30th June and Sept, daily except Fri, 11am – 5.30pm; July and Aug, daily, 11am – 5.30pm (last admission 5pm) • Entrance: £4.20, children £2.10, family ticket £10.50, parties of 15 or more, by arrangement with Visitor Reception Manager (Tel: (01460) 241938) • Other information: Self-drive buggy and wheelchairs available ◑ 🍽 ✕ 🖻 WC �& ✿ 👜 ♀

In 1917, at the end of her career, Gertrude Jekyll planned the planting for the Lyle family, the Trust's first tenants at Barrington. It ranks among her best work and is one of the best-preserved of her gardens. It is currently being restored to the Jekyll plantings and design – as is best illustrated by the rose and iris garden completed in 1996. Set in a park with avenues of mature chestnut trees, the gardens are in the Hidcote style of separate 'rooms'. The lily garden has a central pool with surrounding beds of annuals and perennials planted with a 'hot' theme of oranges, reds and yellows. The white-flowering and silver-leaved plants are seen in the White Garden *à la* Sissinghurst, though this is a Lyle, not a Jekyll, scheme. It is fascinating that this was part of the farm before the Lyle lease, and the cattle troughs can still be seen in the beds. Beyond, a pergola, also not Jekyll, supports clematis, wisteria and honey-suckles in profusion. Note the cattle sheds c. 1800 of considerable visual appeal. The vast walled kitchen garden produces a wide variety of fruit and vegetables. Further afield a cider orchard provides raw material for the liquid refreshments.

Cannington College Gardens ★   4

Cannington, Bridgwater TA5 2LS. Tel: (01278) 655000

Cannington College • 3m NE of Bridgwater on A39 • Open April to Oct, daily, 9am – 5pm. Parties by appt • Entrance: £2, OAPs and children (5-16) £1 • Other information: Teas for parties by arrangement. Guide dogs only ◐ ☕ 🗌 WC ♿

The gardens, enclosed within a medieval priory wall surrounding the fifteenth-century Cannington Court, contain one of the largest collections of rare and unusual plants in the South-West, including the National Collections of abutilons, argyranthemums, osteospermums and wisterias. The gardens are planted individually on various botanical themes, including an Australasian Garden and the Bishop's Garden, featuring plants from the Eastern Mediterranean. In total, the college gardens cover an area of approximately two-and-a-half acres, including various glasshouses. Plant centre nearby sells some National Collection species and a range of others.

Chinnock House   5

Middle Chinnock, Yeovil TA18 7PN. Tel: (01935) 881229

Guy and Charmian Smith • Between Crewkerne and Yeovil off A30 • Open 28th, 29th May, 2 – 6pm and by appt for parties of 2 or more • Entrance: £2, children free ● ☕ ⚘

The rose-covered double-fronted Regency house (c. 1820) was once a linen manufacturer's dwelling. Its intimate two-acre garden, recommended by American landscape architect Hope Rehlaender as 'one of the most perfect private gardens we have seen', invites the visitor to wander from one walled section to another, taking in the close planting and effective colour schemes. The Hockneyesque blue swimming pool is framed in white, silver and green; the main border dominates a pear-tree-spangled lawn with blues, pinks and yellows like Edwardian hats. A small vegetable plot is managed organically. The best views of the Somerset landscape and lawn and borders are from the gravel and Westmoreland slate terrace. The present owners, benefiting from the sheltering walls, have created a scented garden worth making a detour for, and there are intriguing views of the garden of Manor Farm (see entry) just below the east wall.

City of Bath Botanical Gardens   6

Royal Victoria Park, Upper Bristol Road, Bath BA1 2NQ.

City of Bath • In Royal Victoria Park • Open all year, daily, 9am – dusk • Entrance: free • Other information: Toilet facilities nearby in park ○ ♿ ⚐

Located in the city's Royal Victoria Park, the botanical gardens were formed in 1887 to house a collection of plants assembled over a lifetime by Mr C.E. Broome of Batheaston, an enthusiastic amateur botanist and plant collector. It has become one of the finest collections, certainly in the West Country, of plants on limestone. To mark the centenary in 1987, the gardens were extended to take in the adjacent Great Dell in the Park itself. The herbaceous border was replanted in 1990. A 10-year improvement scheme was begun in 1992 to develop and create new collections and improve labelling. A nine-and-a-half-acre refuge from busy city life.

Claverton Manor 7

Claverton, Bath BA2 7BD. Tel: (01225) 460503

The American Museum • 2m SE of Bath off A36, signed American Museum • Garden open 25th March to 29th Oct, daily except Mon, 1 – 5pm; Bank Holiday Suns and Mons, 11am – 5pm. Pre-booked private garden tours by arrangement • Entrance: grounds and galleries: £3, children £2. House, grounds and galleries: £5.50, OAPs £5, children £3. Garden tours £3 per person • Other information: Museum and New Gallery ◑ ☕ 🖪 WC ⟳ ⚘ 🎪 ♿

The house, designed by Jeffry Wyatville, and garden are set on the side of the valley of the Avon in a stunning position with splendid views from the terrace. The rather stark high walls of the house and the terrace support honeysuckle, clematis and old rose climbers, and fastigiate yews make strong buttress shapes up the south-facing wall. The Colonial Herb Garden is modest in size but the little herbarium is popular for seeds, herbs, tussie-mussies and so on. The Mount Vernon Garden, a colonial interpretation of George Washington's famous garden, with rampant old-fashioned roses, trained pear trees and box and beech hedges, is surrounded by white palings. There is a replica of the octagonal garden house used as a school room for Washington's step-grand-children. The seven-acre arboretum, which contains a fine collection of exclusively native American trees and shrubs, is believed to be the only one of its kind outside the US. Labelling is extensive and a map listing trees and shrubs is available. An orchard contains American apple varieties, and there is also a fernery, a cascade and a waterfall.

Clevedon Court 8

Tickenham Road, Clevedon, Bristol BS21 6QU. Tel: (01275) 872257

The National Trust • 1½ m E of Clevedon on B3130. M5 junction 20 • House open • Garden open April to 28th Sept, Wed, Thurs, Sun and Bank Holiday Mons, 2 – 5pm (last admission 4.30pm) • Entrance: £4, children £2 (house and garden) (1999 prices) • Other information: Coaches by appt ◑ ☕ WC

The fourteenth-century house is magnificently sited with steeply terraced gardens. The upper terrace is backed by ornamental woodland of ilexes and holm oaks, London planes and a mulberry tree said to be 'ancient' in 1822. The bowling green on one of the terraces is flanked by a Gothick gazebo which counterbalances an eighteenth-century octagonal summerhouse on the other. The Trust suggests these south-facing terraces may have housed apricots and figs, but they have been replanted with species such as the strawberry tree (*Arbutus unedo*), *Canna iridiflora*, palms, myrtles, fuchsias, a Judas tree and fine magnolias (best in spring) which flourish in the sheltered microclimate. Nearby is *Passiflora*, Lampley Road, Kingston Seymour (Tel: (01934) 877255) [open Mon – Sat, 9am – 1pm, 2 – 5pm], with over 200 species of seeds and plants available.

Cothay Manor ★   9

Greenham, Wellington TA21 0JR. Tel: (01823) 672283

Mr and Mrs Alastair Robb • 5m W of Wellington. From A38 at Beambridge Hotel turn right signed Thorne St Margaret. Continue straight for ¾ m and at next crossroads turn right signed Thorne St Margaret. Take first left, follow lane for m and at junction bear right for ¼ m. Entrance on left • House open for parties by appt • Garden open May to Sept, Wed, Thurs, Sun and Bank Holiday Mons, and for NGS 25th June, 30th July, all 2 – 6pm • Entrance: £3 • Other information: Coaches by appt ● 🍵 🖻 WC ﾟ 🌶 💡

The house is reputed to be one of the finest small medieval manors in the country, and its outstanding garden appears integral to the house, each a natural extension of the other. In fact the gardens seen today were laid out only in the 1920s. Now they have been redesigned and replanted over the last few years, within the original yew hedges which constitute a serene seventeenth-century promenade complete with 'conversation' arbours. Surrounding meadows, planted with specimen trees, shrubs and spring bulbs, lead on to herbaceous borders, a cottage garden and a magical white garden. There is also a bog garden. Masterly planting is everywhere, exuberance balanced by restraint, as the owners are never afraid to repeat a theme within an enclosed space. Particularly unusual is the effective way that complementary greys and mauves flow into the house walls. Plants propagated from the garden are for sale. If you are heading back to Taunton, 3m south-west is *Broadleigh Gardens Nursery* [open Mon – Fri only], where bulbs and herbaceous plants may be ordered after viewing them in flower in the garden.

Crowe Hall ★   10

Widcombe Hill, Bath BA2 6AR. Tel: (01225) 310322

Mr John Barratt • Behind Bath Spa station off A36 within walking distance of station • Open 19th March, 16th April, 7th, 21st May, 11th June, 16th July, 2 – 6pm and for parties by appt • Entrance: £2, children £1 ● 🍵 WC ⟨⟩

These gardens, which extend to 11 acres on the hillside above Widcombe, are some of the most mysterious and beautiful in Bath. Through the gates there is an intriguing view of a drive, portico and terrace, and once inside the grounds few gardens in the area offer so many surprises and delights. As the owner says, 'The garden is an island of classical simplicity surrounded by romantic wilderness.' Around the Regency-style house are Italianate terraces, a pond, grottos, tunnels, woods, glades, kitchen gardens and a long walkway with a stone statue facing a stunning view of Prior Park, a Palladian mansion (see entry). Vistas and views are a feature of this steeply banked garden, where down one walk you suddenly come upon the roof of the fifteenth-century church of St Thomas à Becket. The loss of 20 trees in storms is regarded as an improvement by the owner because new vistas have opened up. Beyond the recently restored grotto is a new meadow garden and an amusing garden dedicated to Hercules, with a theatrically ferocious hero. This garden has been redesigned and Hercules now appears in a mosaic pool, as well as on dry land. Magnificent trees include mulberries, beeches and limes. The charming little enclosed Sauce Garden, with its trelliswork and canal-like pool, was created in 1995. The 1852 greenhouse has been restored to its former glory. For its stunning setting in the meadows above and facing away from Bath and for the romantic ambience Crowe Hall is an experience not to be missed.

Dunster Castle ★ 11

Dunster, Minehead TA24 6SL. Tel: (01643) 821314

*The National Trust • 3m SE of Minehead on A39 • Castle open Sat – Wed • Garden and park open daily: April to Sept, 10am – 5pm; Oct to March, 11am – 4pm (last admission ½ hour before closing). For Christmas period telephone (01643) 823004 • Entrance: £3, children under 16 £1.30, family ticket (2 adults and 3 children) £7.30 (castle, garden and park £5.50, children under 16 £3, family ticket £14, pre-booked parties £4.80 per person) • Other information: Picnics in park only. Electrically operated self-drive Batricar, and volunteer-driven multi-seater available for disabled and infirm. Dogs in park only ○ *
WC & 👍 ⚲

The Luttrell family, who had lived here since the fourteenth century, gave the castle and gardens to the Trust in 1976. A fine border of rare shrubs surrounds a lawn by the keep and is well worth the steep climb to view. On the formal terraces below and along the river thrives a variety of sub-tropical plants, camellias and azaleas. Thousands of bulbs have been planted, and after the daffodils and snowdrops come fine displays of forsythias, camellias and early rhododendrons. There is a National Collection of arbutus and a huge 18-metre *Magnolia campbellii*. Views across to Exmoor, the Quantocks and the Bristol Channel. The park totals 28 acres in all.

East Lambrook Manor Gardens ★ 12

South Petherton TA13 5HL. Tel: (01460) 240328; Fax: (01460) 242344;
E-mail: ELambrook@aol.com

Robin and Marianne Williams • 3m SW of Martock off A303, 2m NE of South Petherton • Open March to Sept, Mon – Sat, 10am – 5pm • Entrance: £2.50, OAPs and students £2, children 50p • Other information: Art gallery throughout summer ● 💻 WC ⚲ 👍 ⚲

Margery Fish established the garden for endangered species, and it still houses a remarkable collection of plants, many of which she saved from extinction. Thanks to the previous owner, Andrew Norton, the National Collection of geraniums (cranesbill) species and cultivars also remains here. An extensive restoration programme was started by the present owners and their head gardener, Mark Stainer, in 1999, with the aim of improving historically important areas of the Grade-I-listed garden, famous not only for its plants but also for its controlled luxuriance of growth, colour and scent. This will include restoring the green garden, replacing the pudding trees and clearing the top terraces and the colosseum. The second stage for the coming year is to follow Margery Fish's interest in medicinal herbs and create an enclosed herb garden, which will also incorporate a return to her vegetable garden. The attached nursery has been moved and upgraded; plants in season in the garden will also be on sale.

Forde Abbey

(see Dorset)

Gaulden Manor ★ 13

Tolland, Lydeard St Lawrence, Taunton TA4 3PN. Tel: (01984) 667213

Mr J.H.N. Starkie • 9m NW of Taunton off A358 • House open July to Aug • Garden open 8th June to 28th Aug, Sun, Thurs and Bank Holiday Mons, 2 – 5pm. Also parties at other times by prior arrangement • Entrance: £3 (house and gardens £4.25) • Other information: Teas on Sun and Bank Holiday Mons only, and for parties by arrangement ● ▨ ☕ 🅿 WC ♿ 🌿 🏛

Garden seats at vantage points give the visitor a chance to appreciate the many different vistas provided in this country garden, which includes a bog garden, herb garden, butterfly garden and herbaceous borders of selected colour. A short walk through a woodland glade leads to a secret garden of white-flowering plants. Visitors should not miss the small duck garden near the tea house with carvings on the fence posts.

The Georgian Garden 14

Gravel Walk, Bath BA1 2EW. Tel: (01225) 477752

Heritage Services, Bath and North East Somerset • Entrance on Gravel Walk • Open May to Oct, Mon – Fri except Bank Holiday Mons, 9am – 4.30pm • Entrance: free • Other information: Parking in Charlotte Street, a few minutes' walk across Royal Victoria Park. Toilet facilities in park ◗

Anyone interested in seeing how a Georgian town garden looked should not miss the fully restored garden behind The Circus. Designed to be seen from the house, the garden plan is based on excavations conducted by the Bath Archaeological Trust of the original garden, laid out in the 1760s. Surprisingly simple, there is no grass but a bed of yellow gravel edged with stone paving. Three flower beds are on a central axis. The planting sets out to show how a Georgian garden might have evolved between 1760 and 1836. Box-rimmed borders are planted starkly with scented varieties of phlox, stocks, asters and a good deal of love-lies-bleeding. Honeysuckle clings to a central white pole. An eye-catcher is a curious bench copied from an eighteenth-century original. Another pleasant garden in Bath is at the *Holburne Museum*, Great Pulteney Street. Meanwhile, if you are looking for garden tools, pots or, indeed, anything 'from a trowel to a 50 ft fountain', it may be worth seeking out David Bridgwater at *Heather Cottage*, Lansdown, Bath (Tel: (01225) 463435), who will also search for specific items if he does not stock them.

Greencombe ★★ 15

Porlock TA24 8NU. Tel: (01643) 862363

Greencombe Garden Trust (Miss Joan Loraine) • 7½ m W of Minehead, ½ m W
of Porlock off B3225 • Open April to July, and Oct to Nov, Sat – Wed, 2 – 6pm
• *Entrance: £3, children 50p* • *Other information: Coaches by arrangement*
◑ ☕ WC ♿ ⚘

Created in 1946 by Horace Stroud, this garden has been extended by the
present owner over the last 30 years. Overlooking the Bristol Channel, set on
a hillside where the sun cannot penetrate for nearly two months in the winter,
it glows with colour. The formal lawns and beds round the house are
immaculate. Roses, lilies, hydrangeas, maples and camellias thrive. By contrast
the woodland area, terraced on the hillside, provides a nature walk of great
interest. A wide variety of rhododendrons and azaleas flower in the shelter of
mature trees, where ferns and woodland plants also flourish. No sprays or
chemicals are used in the cultivation of this completely organic garden, which
contains National Collections of erythroniums, gaultherias, polystichums and
vacciniums.

Hadspen Garden and Nursery ★★ 16

Castle Cary BA7 7NG. Tel/Fax: (01749) 813707

Mr N.A. Hobhouse and N. and S. Pope • 3½ m NW of Wincanton, 2m SE of
Castle Cary on A371 • Open March to 1st Oct, Thurs – Sun and Bank
Holiday Mons, 10am – 5pm • Entrance: £3, children 50p • Other information:
Coaches by arrangement ◑ ☕ ✕ 🏠 WC ♿ ⚘

The basic plan in this garden was devised by Margaret Hobhouse in the
Victorian gardening 'boom' days, to provide a setting for the eighteenth-
century hamstone Hobhouse home. Over the years the garden became overgrown and formless, with an interval in the 1960s when Penelope Hobhouse
endeavoured to restore some order. In the last few years the present owners
have reclaimed the garden, retaining the best of the original plan and
embellishing it with a variety of planting to provide colour, shape and interest.
It is now a classic country-house garden, with carefully colour-schemed
herbaceous borders, a lily pond in a formal setting, shrub walks, a curved
walled garden contrasted with wild flowers in the meadow, all framed in
parkland. Visitors have noted an amazing display of colour and interest in
July. Hostas are a speciality.

Hatch Court 17

**Hatch Beauchamp, Taunton TA3 6AA. Tel: (01823) 480120;
Fax: (01823) 480058**

Dr and Mrs Robin Odgers • 5m SE of Taunton off A358 Ilminster road. In
Hatch Beauchamp, turn left at Hatch Inn • Open April to Sept, daily, 10am –
5.30pm. Parties for house and garden at any time by appt • Entrance: £2.50,
children under 16 £1, under 12 free ◑ 🏠 WC ♿ ⚘

Anyone interested in the process of reviving old gardens and in intriguing decisions being made about planting and vista-making should not miss Hatch Court and its five-acre garden and 30-acre deer park. Ancient cedars, a looming copper beech and sentinel Irish yews frame a Palladian mansion of 1750, and the Menil fallow deer and sweeping views of Taunton Vale complete the eighteenth-century picture. For 50 years it was a scene of neglect, until in 1984 the present owners began to revitalise the garden and park. No plans or drawings existed, so the re-creation is a contemporary interpretation of the classic eighteenth-century park. Already giving pleasure and promise are the lime *allée*, horse chestnut avenue, new yew hedges and walk to the church bordered by clematis-hung wall and towers of rambling roses. In the vast walled kitchen and cutting garden the previous bramble-infested jungle echoes to bees zooming along perfectly clipped box hedges, foams of lavender and huge vegetable and fruit beds. Not far away, at Curry Mallet, is *Mallet Court Nursery*, the well-known tree nursery of James Harris, known as 'Acer' Harris for his speciality. [Open all year, Mon – Fri (closed lunch 1 – 2pm) Tel: (01823) 480748].

Hestercombe Gardens ★   18

Cheddon Fitzpaine, Taunton TA2 8LG. Tel: (01823) 413923; Fax: (01823) 413747

HGP Ltd/Somerset County Council • 4m NE of Taunton off A361, just N of Cheddon Fitzpaine. Signposted • Garden open all year, daily, 10am – 6pm (last admission 5pm). Parties by written appt only • Entrance: £3.50, children (5-15) £1, under 5 free (1999 prices) • Other information: Coaches by arrangement

○ 🍽 ✕ 🖼 WC ⅃ ⬳ 🌿 🏛 🔦

This is a superb product of the collaboration between Edwin Lutyens and Gertrude Jekyll, blending the formal art of architecture with the art of plants. *The Oxford Companion* describes it as Lutyens at his best in the detailed design of steps, pools, walls, paving and seating. The rills, pergola and orangery are fine examples of his work. On a limited budget the Somerset County Council has endeavoured to maintain the gardens, respecting the colour groupings of the original designs and keeping the water courses flowing as they would have in Edwardian days. The Council's programme to restore the gardens to Gertrude Jekyll's original plant design is proceeding well, and the guide which details this and Lutyen's stonework is most useful. To the north of the house is the Combe, laid out two centuries earlier than the main gardens and a unique example of eighteenth-century pleasure grounds unchanged until the timber was felled in the 1960s. Visitors are now able to see the eighteenth-century parkland designed between 1750 and 1786 by Coplestone Warre Bampfylde, who was noted for his use of water features in a 'picturesque' setting. Note the newly restored 'Great Cascade' and recall that Bampfylde also designed the cascade from the lake at Stourhead (see entry in Wiltshire). He described this as one 'that will rivet you to the spot with admiration'. This ambitious restoration of a Grade-l-listed landscape will continue until after the millennium, and will form a 35-acre landscape garden in its own right. The Chinese seat is being restored and the Victorian Terrace completed, including the fountain. A programme is underway to restore the Victorian shrubbery in the style of William Robinson, c 1880. Be sure to see the Doric temple, the mausoleum and the rebuilt witch's hut. Tim Richardson writes of the remarkable way in which the gentleness of Bampfylde's vision has endured. There is still a sense of nature enhanced rather than transformed, with the set pieces so well sited and spaced that they seem to relax into the natural setting.

Jasmine Cottage   19

26 Channel Road, Clevedon BS21 7BY. Tel: (01275) 871850

Mr and Mrs Michael Redgrave • 12m W of Bristol. From M5 junction 20, take road to seafront, continue N on B3124 and turn right at St Mary's church • Open by appt May to Aug, daily • Entrance: £1.50, children free • Other information: Plants for sale in nursery ● WC & 🌱

Here is something for everyone: old-fashioned roses, climbers, mixed shrubs, herbaceous borders, island beds, a pergola walk and a vegetable garden – all crammed into one-third of an acre. An inspiration for suburban enthusiasts, especially as it is only about 100 metres from the sea. The rectangular shape is cleverly disguised, with island beds in one area, and a pond enclosed by a hedge over three and a half metres high and cut annually. Through the hedge is the so-called cottage garden with unusual climbers, including *Rhodochiton atrosanguineum* and *Dregea sinensis*.

Lady Farm ★   20

Chelwood, Bristol BS18 4NN. Tel: (01761) 490770

Malcolm and Judy Pearce • 9m S of Bristol on A368, ½ m E of Chelwood roundabout (A37/A368) • Open for parties by appt • Entrance: £3, children free but under 14s not encouraged ● 🐶 WC

Set on the side of a valley and covering approximately six acres, the area beyond the farmhouse has been planted only recently, yet it is amazing what has been achieved in a short time. A spring-fed water course with marginal planting and waterfalls flows into a lake with adjacent rock features. The water flows on down to join a further lake, made by damming a stream in the valley bottom. Here, a lakeside and woodland walks are being developed. A large area of new-style perennial planting (prairie), including many ornamental grasses and North American plants, was started in 1997 and already looks fascinating. There are wildflower meadow areas, a meandering walk of birch species underplanted with hostas, hellebores, grasses and bulbs. New is a formal garden with a thatched summerhouse and herbaceous perennials in a four-square design with a circle in the centre. This is a garden with a future, and one for all seasons.

Lower Severalls   21

Crewkerne TA18 7NX. Tel: (01460) 73234; Fax (01460) 76105

Mary Cooper • 1½ m NE of Crewkerne off A30 • Open March to 15th Oct, Mon – Wed, Fri – Sat, 10am – 5pm and in May to June, Sun, 2 – 5pm • Entrance:

£1.50 • Other information: Coaches by appt. Teas for pre-arranged parties only. Plants for sale in nursery ◑ 🏬 **WC** ♿

A typical cottage garden of some two and a half acres with an herbaceous border against the stone-walled house. The garden extends through stone pillars which make a frame for the view of the valley over lawn and varied shrubs and a bog garden. Additional features include arches made from recycled farm machinery, and a 'willow basket' (woven willow growing in a circle with a large structure forming the handle). A water garden has now been created, fed from a spring in adjacent farmland, together with a wadi or dry garden built up to form a windbreak for a sheltered valley.

Lytes Cary Manor   22

Charlton Mackrell, Somerton TA11 7HU. Tel: (01458) 223297

The National Trust • 2½ m NE of Ilchester, signed from A303 • Open April to Oct, Mon, Wed and Sat, 2 – 6pm or dusk if earlier (last admission 5.30pm) • Entrance: £4.10, children £2.10 ◑ **WC** ♿ ♿

Once the house of the medieval herbalist Henry Lyte, the main feature is a long, wide border which has been replanted in line with Graham Stuart Thomas's original design, with a mixture of roses, shrubs and herbaceous plants. There are also pleasing lawns with hedges in Elizabethan style and some topiary, as well as a large orchard with naturalised bulbs and mown walks with a central sundial. At Kingsdon, 2m SE of Somerton, is *Mrs Marrow*'s renowned old-fashioned nursery, open daily but check (Tel: (01935) 840232).

Manor Farm   23

Middle Chinnock, Crewkerne TA18 7PN. Tel: (01935) 861895

Simon and Antonia Johnson • 5m W of Yeovil off A30 • Open 28th May, 2 – 6pm, and by appt • Entrance: £2. Children free • Other information: Teas at Chinnock House on open day NEW ●

Despite being the recent creation of the owner, designer Simon Johnson, the garden succeeds in making the visitor feel that it could always have been here, and that its scale and proportion are right for both the site and the family life that goes on in and around it. The hamstone farmhouse has architectural distinction without being grand, and this is reflected in the garden spaces. There is a traditional framework of stone walls and hedges – yew and hornbeam – allowing areas for plants and colours, for fruit- and vegetable-growing and for architectural austerity and lush wildness. Contrasts appear throughout, and everywhere there are seats from which to take in the views of the landscape beyond the garden. Despite its air of timelessness and maturity, the garden is still evolving, with structures and new plantings appearing as time and funds allow.

The Manor House ★ 24

Walton-in-Gordano, Clevedon BS21 7AN. Tel: (01275) 872067

Mr and Mrs C. Wills and Mr and Mrs S Wills • 2m NE of Clevedon on N side of B3124 Clevedon – Portishead road • Open by appt all year • Entrance: £2, children under 14 free NEW ● WC

A truly remarkable garden, created behind a largely early eighteenth-century farmhouse by the present owners over the past 20 years. Expanding on the plantings, mostly of trees, which remain from the eighteenth century onwards, it definitely *vaut le détour*. Ornamental trees, shrubs, herbaceous plants and bulbs are used to give form and colour throughout the year, particularly in autumn. The informal design disguises the thought and knowledge that lie behind the sensitive planting of a seemingly endless variety of specimen trees, some of them grown from seeds brought back by the Wills from their travels to Chile, Nepal and elsewhere. South of the house, the white and silver beds retain something of their original layout. A formal pool garden, hedged with yew, contains rectangular pools and fountains framed by an explosion of delicate pinks, blues, white and silver. The owners have given a new and different meaning to the term 'a plantsman's garden', combining scholarship with an eye for light and shade, texture, form and understated colour to make a visit a deeply satisfying experience.

Milton Lodge ★ 25

Wells BA5 3AQ. Tel: (01749) 672168

Mr D.C. Tudway Quilter • ½ m N of Wells. From A39 Wells – Bristol road turn N up Old Bristol Road • Open 23rd April to Oct, Tues – Thurs and Bank Holiday Mons, 2 – 5pm • Entrance: £2.50, children under 14 free • Other information: Parties and coaches by special arrangement. Teas on Sun and Bank Holidays only ◐ WC ⌨ 👍

The Grade-II-listed terraced garden, replanted by the present owner in the 1960s, is cultivated down the side of a hill overlooking the Vale of Avalon, affording a magnificent view of Wells Cathedral. A wide variety of plants, all suitable for the alkaline soil, provides a succession of colours and interest from March to October. Many fine trees can be seen in the garden and in the seven-acre arboretum opposite the entrance to the car park. In the centre of Wells is the *Bishops Palace*, whose pleasant garden is open Easter to Oct, Tues – Thurs and Bank Holiday Mons, 11am – 6pm, Sun, 2 – 6pm, and Aug, daily, 10am – 6pm (last admission 5pm).

Montacute House ★ 26

Montacute TA15 6XP. Tel/Fax: (01935) 823289

The National Trust • 4m W of Yeovil. Signposted from A3088 and A303 near Ilchester • House open April to Nov, daily except Tues, 12 noon – 5.30pm (last admission 5pm) • Park and garden open all year: April to 1st Nov, daily except Tues, 11pm – 5.30pm (or dusk if earlier); Nov to March 2001, Wed – Sun,

11.30am – 4pm or dusk if earlier. Other times by arrangement with the property manager • Entrance: garden and park £3, children £1.30; Nov to March 2001, £1.50 (house, garden and park £5.40, children £2.70, family £13.40) (1999 prices) • Other information: Picnics in designated areas only. Dogs in park only, on lead. Plants for sale April to Sept ○ 🍵 ✕ WC ⑤ ⌂ 🧺 ♿

This Elizabethan garden of grass lawns surrounded by clipped yews set in terraces is a triumph of formality. The surrealism of the topiary, which some claim was inspired by a dramatic snowfall, adds immensely to the effect. A large water feature has replaced the original Elizabethan high circular mount. Colours are provided by herbaceous borders from mid-summer. There is a charming raised walk, two original pavilions and an arcaded garden house probably devised by George Curzon during his tenancy, when he lived here, first with Elinor Glyn, then with his second American wife. The gardens are surrounded by graceful parklands giving vistas and an impression of space. A new avenue of 72 limes is now established.

2 Old Tarnwell   27

Upper Stanton Drew BS39 4EA. Tel: (01275) 333146

Mr and Mrs K. Payne • 6m S of Bristol, W of Pensford between A368 and B3130 • Open June and July for parties by appt • Entrance: £2 ◐

An astonishingly interesting and praiseworthy garden, tiny in scale but highly imaginative in the use of colour and texture. Three beds in the front garden use yellow as the dominant colour. The rear garden manages to include a tiny trickling pool enclosed by rampant clematis and climbing plants.

Prior Park ★   28

Ralph Allen Drive, Bath BA2 5AH. Tel: (01225) 833422 (general enquiries)

The National Trust • No parking at garden or nearby, so use public transport from city centre or walk up A3062 from Widcombe • Open 22nd April to Sept, daily except Tues, 11am – 5.30pm, Dec, Fri – Sun, 12 noon – 5.30pm. Closed 25th, 26th Dec and 1st Jan • Entrance: £3.80, children £1.90 (£1 discount, on production of ticket, for those arriving by public transport or pre-booked coach) • Other information: Small area for disabled parking (must be pre-booked), with limited access for disabled ○ 🏬 WC ⑤

This remarkable restoration by the Trust, when completed, will have transformed Prior Park. The Palladian mansion, designed by the architect John Wood from 1735 for Bath's leading entrepreneur and philanthropist Ralph Allen, dominates the steeply sloping landscape and provides stunning views of the city. While the mansion is used by Prior Park College and is not open to the public, the grounds below are well worth the circular walk (allow 1½ hours) from the entrance gate off Ralph Allen Drive. Allen landscaped and planted continuously over a period of 30 years from 1734 to 1764, helped by several gardeners, notably 'Capability' Brown, who eliminated areas of formality. Earlier, it is highly probable that Alexander Pope inspired the area known as the Wilderness, which includes a Rococo sham bridge and the ruins of Mrs

Allen's grotto (but full restoration of the Wilderness is a future project). The walk continues from the mansion viewpoint down the east side of the valley to the lakes and the Palladian bridge of 1755, returning by the west side of the valley via the rock gate. Undoubtedly two-star are the views — sensitively created by the Trust — of the Palladian bridge.

Rode Tropical Bird Gardens 29

Rode, Bath BA3 6QW. Tel: (01373) 830326

Mrs E.S. Risdon • 5m NE of Frome, signed off A361 • Gardens open all year, daily except 25th Dec, summer 10am – 6pm, winter 10am – dusk (last admission 1 hour before closing) • Entrance: £5.50, OAPs £5, children (3-16) £2.90, family (2 adults and 2 children) £16 ○ � × é WC é ê ê

The gardens have been developed to provide the background and natural habitat, as far as possible, for the birds. The clematis collection was started in 1985 and is now established — the owner is a member of the British Clematis Society. Underplanting in the tree trail is going on continuously. The Rode woodland railway runs from Easter to October.

Sherborne Garden 30

Pear Tree House, Litton BA3 4PP. Tel: (01761) 241220

Mr and Mrs J. Southwell • 15m S of Bristol, 7½ m N of Wells on B3114 ¼ m beyond Litton and The Kings Arms • Open 5th June to 25th Sept, Mon and occasional Sun, 11am – 6pm. Other days by appt • Entrance: £2, children free ● é é WC é ê é

A largeish, rather surreal garden that displays a very personal choice of specimen trees, grasses and water garden features in a four-and-a-half-acre site reclaimed from farmland. The owners are compulsive tree people who since 1963 have planted hundreds of native and exotic trees, expanding the original cottage garden and paddock into a mini-arboretum. The garden now boasts a pinetum, nut hedges, a collection of species roses and the latest manifestation, new gravel beds with collections of giant and miniature grasses and about 100 varieties of hemerocallis, a Prickly Wood that offers 150 varieties of holly, and a collection of over 250 ferns. Most trees and plants are clearly labelled. This garden is an interesting example of how natural pasture land may be tamed and surface water channelled into ponds.

Ston Easton Park ★ 31

Ston Easton, Bath BA3 4DF. Tel: (01761) 241631

Peter and Christine Smedley • 11m SW of Bath, 6m NE of Wells on A39 • Open by appt only • Entrance: free • Other information: Teas and toilet facilities in hotel. Property for sale at time of going to press, so check before travelling ● × é WC é ê é

The Grade-I-listed Palladian house is set in a park replanned and replanted by Humphry Repton in 1792-93. A suitably impressive drive winds past old stables to the plain Palladian magnificence of the house. The glory is the view from inside the great Saloon, or from Repton's terrace immediately outside, over the River Norr with a bridge and cascades. Repton made a Red Book with his proposals for improvement, and Penelope Hobhouse worked with the Smedleys on the restoration of the park to Repton's plans. Beyond the terrace are wide lawns, woods, cedars, beeches, oaks, willows and some newly planted yew hedges. The vast kitchen garden, with its glasshouses, cutting garden and metres of beautifully presented fruit and vegetables, now has a rose garden, recently completed with the help of Mrs Hobhouse. It took seven years to repair the kitchen garden walls, three and a half years for each side. It is worth making an appointment to study the restoration in progress – the owners now run the house as a hotel.

Stonewell House 32

Duck Street, Churchill Green, Churchill BS25 5QJ. Tel: (01934) 852919

Mrs Ursula Dornton • 14m SW of Bristol off A368 towards Weston-super-Mare. Go through Churchill past school and take first turning on right • Open all year by appt. • Entrance: £1.50 ● WC & 🔾

A well-designed garden of one and a half acres with good planting, constantly added to and improved. Good spring display of tulips, bulbs, bearded iris and rhododendrons. Many species roses, honeysuckles and intertwining clematis appear in profusion in summer, followed by autumn colour provided by a good selection of trees and shrubs.

Tintinhull House Garden ★ 33

Farm Street, Tintinhull, Yeovil BA22 9PZ.

The National Trust • 5m NW of Yeovil, ½ m S of A303. Signposted • Open April to Sept, Wed – Sun and Bank Holiday Mons, 12 noon – 6pm • Entrance: £3.70, children £1.80 (1999 prices) • Other information: Disabled parking by arrangement ◑ 🥄 WC

A relatively small modern garden, barely one and a half acres, which achieves an impression of greater size with a series of vistas created under the influence of Hidcote. Developed from the 1930s by Phyllis Reiss, it was later in the hands of Penelope Hobhouse; there has been some recent replanting which has yet to achieve an established appearance. The Eagle Court near the house has fine borders and leads through to a small white garden. From here, an opening leads to the stylish kitchen garden with orchard beyond. The pool garden is particularly splendid, with its iris-bordered canal and 'hot' and 'cool' borders. The Cedar Court has some old trees, including a yew said to be 400 years old. The wide variety of plants is not labelled in order to retain the charm of a private garden but an inventory is available for interested visitors.

Ven House 34

Milborne Port DT9 4PR.

Thomas Kyle and Jerome Murray • 8m E of Yeovil on A30, E of Milborne Port • Open once or twice on Suns for charity • Entrance: £1.50 (1999 price) ●

Some 100 acres of grounds, mainly farmland, have been extensively redesigned to conform to eighteenth-century style, and the river has been diverted to create waterfalls and stone channels through decorative woodland. Recently built balustrading extends the existing lines of the terrace and surrounds a sunken garden with herbaceous plants around a central water feature. There are courtyards and a knot garden, and conical topiaried yews adorn the lawn before the main entrance. Extensive views southwards beyond the terrace and sunken garden with imaginative tree-planting in avenues carry the eye to fields and woodland and sweep uphill northwards to the line of woodland on a hilltop originally designed by 'Capability' Brown. The extensive orangery has been renovated and enhanced by rows of standard fuchsias and pots of nearly two-metre-high pelargoniums in full flower in season, copious screens of osmanthus and daturas, all perfect specimens. Sheltered courtyards will feature *Cytisus battandieri* in profusion, with white irises and yellow roses, while the knots are a mix of vegetables and herbaceous plants. All this is cared for by four gardeners.

Wayford Manor ★ 35

Crewkerne TA18 8QG. Tel: (01460) 73253

Mr and Mrs R.L. Goffe • 3m SW of Crewkerne off B3165 at Clapton • Open 9th, 30th April, 14th, 28th May, 2 – 6pm. Parties by appt • Entrance: £2, children 50p ● 🅿 WC ⟨⟩ 🌿

A well-maintained garden of flowering shrubs and trees (including some rare and colourful maples), rhododendrons and spring bulbs, against the stonework of an Elizabethan house. This is a fine example of the work of Harold Peto, who redesigned the garden in 1902 and whose original plans are being restored by the present owners. The loss of mature trees and larger shrubs in the 1990 gale opened up an area which led to the discovery of a previously buried waterway. This has been cleared and now runs from the lower of a series of small pools down to a much larger pool whose original shape had been lost by the force of peltiphyllum rhizomes pushing out the retaining stonework. Order has now been restored. Restoration of the winter garden is another project.

William Herschel Museum 36

19 New King Street, Bath BA1 2BL. Tel: (01225) 311342/446865; Web: www.bath.preservation–trust.org.uk

Trustees of the Museum • On New King Street close to Queen's Square and Green Park Station • Museum open • Garden open March to Oct, daily, 2 – 5pm; Nov to Feb, Sat and Sun, 2 – 5pm. Closed 21st April • Entrance: £2.50, children under 18 £1, family (2 adults and up to 4 children) £5 ◐ WC ⟨⟩ 🏛 🖋

This is one of the smaller and more fascinating museums, from whose garden William Herschel discovered the planet Uranus in 1781. Over the years the garden has suffered from neglect, but recent replanting has now re-created a charming small town garden such as might well have existed in Herschel's time. Before leaving the Bath area, visit *The Hannays of Bath*, Sydney Wharf

Nursery, Bathwick, described as 'renowned for being first with unusual plants', entered via Sydney Mews on A4 ring road [open daily except Tues or by appointment until 1st Nov, 10am – 5pm].

Woodborough 37

Porlock Weir TA24 8PE. Tel: (01643) 862406

Mr and Mrs R.D. Milne • 6m W of Minehead. From A39 take B3225 towards Porlock Weir. At Porlock Vale House on right, take left tarmac lane uphill. Garden first on right • Open by appt only • Entrance: £2, children under 10 free • Other information: No coaches ● ◁D

This fascinating garden created on a steep (1 in 4) hillside has magnificent views over Porlock Bay. The wide variety of shrubs includes some of the lesser-known hybrid rhododendrons and a number of Ghent azaleas. A bog garden and two pools add interest over a longer season. The owners will happily share with visitors their hard-won experience in garden restoration and their battle with the dreaded honey fungus.

GARDENING FOR THE DISABLED ♿

Demonstration gardens to assist the disabled are available at a number of properties open to the public. They include the following:

Battersea Park (see *Guide* under London) Horticultural Therapy Unit (Wandsworth Borough Council). For appt tel: (0171) 720 3419

Broadview Gardens, Hadlow (see Kent)

Capel Manor (see London) Tel: (01992) 763849

Disabled and Older Gardeners' Association, Herefordshire Growing Point, Herefordshire College of Agriculture, Holme Lacy, Hereford. Tel: (01432) 870316

Royal Horticultural Society's Garden, Wisley (see Surrey)

Ryton Organic Gardens, Ryton-on-Dunsmore (see Warwickshire)

Syon Park, Middlesex (see London).

Open days for the disabled are also held from time to time at the following gardens:

Dolly's Garden (see London)

Hillsborough Community Development Trust (see South & West Yorkshire)

Iden Croft Herbs (see Kent).

The Gardening for Disabled Trust is a registered charity which collects donations from the public and uses them to assist disabled people with improvements to their gardens, or to supply equipment which will enable them to continue to garden. Donations should be sent to Mrs Felicity Seton, Hayes Farmhouse, Hayes Lane, Peasmarsh, Rye, East Sussex.

STAFFORDSHIRE

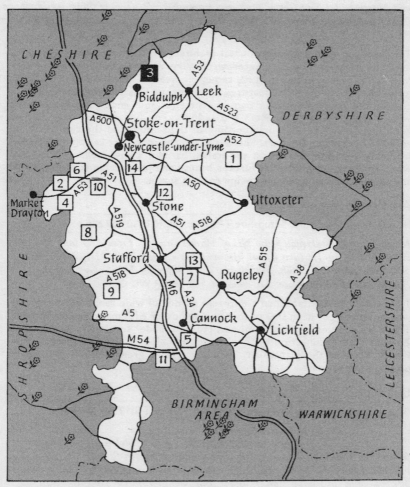

Two-starred gardens are marked on the map with a black square.

Alton Towers ★

Alton ST10 4DB. Tel: (0990) 204060

Alton Towers • From N take M6 junction 16 or M1 junction 28, from S take M6 junction 15 or M1 junction 23A. Signposted • Theme park, ruins and grounds open all year, daily, 9.30am – 5pm, 6pm or 7pm according to time of year (1 hour before rides open until 1 hour after they close). Telephone for opening times Nov to mid-March (when probably grounds only open) • Entrance: mid-March to 1st Nov (theme park and grounds) £19.50, OAPs £10, children (4-13) £15, family season ticket £59. Towers Two ticket allows second day at Park for £8. Party rates available (1999 prices) ○ ⬤ ✕ 🗟 WC ♿ 🛒

This fantastic garden of ornamental architecture was one of the last great follies, created in the early nineteenth century. W.A. Nesfield was active here (one of his parterres is still *in situ* though in need of restoration). It contains many beautiful and unusual features, including the Chinese pagoda fountain, a copy of the To Ho pagoda in Canton. The enormous rock garden is planted with a range of conifers, acers and sedums. The fine conservatory houses geraniums and other colour according to the season, and the terraces have rose and herbaceous borders. There is a Dutch garden, Her Ladyship's Garden featuring yew and rose beds, the Italian garden, a yew-arch walkway and woodland walks. Water adds further beauty and interest. In addition, there are all the attractions of the theme park in season.

Arbour Cottage   2

Napley, Market Drayton, Shropshire TF9 4AJ. Tel: (01630) 672852

Mr and Mrs D.K. Hewitt • 4m NE of Market Drayton. From A53 take B5415 signed Woore. In 1m turn left at telephone box • Open 14th, 21st, 28th April, 5th, 19th May, 2nd, 16th, 30th June, 2 – 5.30pm for NGS; also by appt. Parties welcome • Entrance: £2, children 50p ⬤ ⬤ WC ♿ 🌿

The owners have established a two-acre garden of wide-ranging interest and year-round colour in an area of countryside beauty with many species of trees. There are peonies, grasses, bamboos, etc. and tender specimens such as New Zealand flax. A collection of shrub roses and alpines, screes and rockeries. Plenty here for the plantsman, including a large greenhouse with tropical plants, some for sale.

Biddulph Grange Garden ★★   3

Grange Road, Biddulph, Stoke–on–Trent ST8 7SD. Tel: (01782) 517999 (Garden Office)

The National Trust • 3½ m SE of Congleton, 7m N of Stoke-on-Trent. Access from A527 Biddulph/Congleton road • Open 25th March to 29th Oct, Wed – Fri (but closed 21st April), 12 noon – 6pm, Sat, Sun and Bank Holiday Mons, 11am – 6pm (last admission 5.30pm); 6th Nov to 19th Dec, Sat and Sun, 12 noon – 4pm or dusk if earlier. Guided tours by appt only • Entrance: £4.30, children £2.20, family £10.70, parties of 15 or more £3.50 per person; Nov and Dec: £2, children £1, family £5 • Other information: Limited wheelchair access ◐ ⬤ ✕ 🗟 WC 🌿 🛒 🔦

This is one of the most remarkable and innovative gardens of the nineteenth century. There is an Egyptian garden with a pyramid and obelisks of clipped yew. The Chinese garden has a joss house, a golden water buffalo overlooking a dragon parterre, a watch tower and a temple reflected in a calm pool. In front of the house terraces descend to a lily pond. The Stumpery demonstrates an innovative Victorian way to display suitable plants. The verbena, araucaria and rose parterres and the Shelter House and Dahlia Walk (with over 600 dahlias) have now been restored just as they were in the middle of the nineteenth century. A courageous effort was the felling and replanting of the fine, long Wellingtonia avenue. In all, one of the country's most unusual gardening rediscoveries and restorations — it should not be missed.

The Covert 4

Pheasant Walk, Burntwood, Loggerheads, Market Drayton, Shropshire TF9 2QZ. Tel: (01630) 672677

Mr and Mrs Leslie Standeven • 5m NE of Market Drayton. Turn off A53 Newcastle-under-Lyme — Market Drayton road onto Burntwood, S of Loggerheads crossroads. Follow Burntwood until Pheasant Walk opens off • Open 6th April to 28th Sept, Thurs, 2 – 5pm, 28th May, 2 – 5pm, 24th, 25th June, 1 – 5pm, 30th July, 27th Aug, 1st Oct, 2 -5pm • Entrance: £2, children 50p ◓

Everyone will enjoy the patterns, colours and vistas here, but for the plantaholic it is a box of delights. The owner is a designer and has brought her training to the display of plants. In three-quarters of an acre there is an extraordinary variety, starting with a scree garden of Mediterranean plants at the front of the house and continuing through a bog garden, a pool garden, alpines in scree and tufa beds and in alpine house, architectural and herbaceous plants (many of uncommon species), shrubs and trees. A slate area. Labelling is excellent.

12 Darges Lane 5

Great Wyrley, Walsall WS6 6LE. Tel: (01922) 415064

Mrs A. Hackett • 2m SE of Cannock. From A5 (Churchbridge junction) take A34 towards Walsall. First turning on right over brow of hill. House on right on corner of Cherrington Drive • Open 30th April, 2 – 6pm, 21st June, 6.30 – 9.30pm, 10th Sept, 2 – 6pm and by appt • Entrance: £1.50 • Other information: Plants for sale on open days and third Mon in months March to Sept only ◓ � ⚘

A quarter-acre garden on two levels, well stocked and of great interest to plantsmen. Attractive trees and large variety of shrubs and foliage plants are the background to a comprehensive collection of flowering plants and small shrubs, some unusual, even rare. Holder of a National Collection of lamiums. There are borders and island beds, and a small water garden. Every inch is used to grow or set off the plants, and there is year-round appeal for flower arrangers. The overall effect is attractive as well as enticing to the plant lover. Plants for sale include some more unusual ones.

The Dorothy Clive Garden ★ 6

Willoughbridge, Market Drayton, Shropshire TF9 4EU. Tel: (01630) 647237

Willoughbridge Garden Trust • 7m NE of Market Drayton, 1m E of Woore on A51 between Nantwich and Stone • Open April to Oct, daily, 10am – 5.30pm •

Entrance: £3, OAPs £2.50, children (11-16) £1, under 11 free • Other information: Disabled parking ◑ 🍺 🪑 WC ♿ 🔱

Created by the late Colonel Clive in memory of his wife, with the help of distinguished gardeners including the late John Codrington, this garden has wide appeal both because of its design and because of its inspired planting. The coloured guide identifies the highlights season by season. These include the rhododendrons and azaleas in the quarry garden and the pool with the scree garden rising on the hillside above it. In spring there are unusual bulbs and primulas, in summer colourful shrubs, unusual perennials and many conifers; other trees provide autumn colour. The scree garden must give gardeners many good ideas. The garden has been extended and new features include a laburnum arch with roses and other climbers, and a small pool with a bog garden.

The Garth   7

2 Broc Hill Way, Milford, Stafford ST17 0UB. Tel: (01785) 661182

Mr and Mrs David Wright • 4½ m SE of Stafford. On A513 Stafford – Rugeley road, at Barley Mow turn right, then left after ½ m • Open 4th, 25th June, 2 – 6pm and by appt for parties • Entrance: £1.50, children 50p ◑ 🍺 WC 🔱 ☯ 🍷

This half-acre garden surrounded by countryside contains specialist areas which should give inspiration and ideas to any gardener. The visitor moves down the different levels to discover old caves at the bottom of the slope. The range of plants includes six unusual beeches, 20 different ferns, 30 different clematis, magnolias, rhododendrons, pulmonarias, hostas, azaleas, penstemons and astilbes, berberis, fothergillas, garryas, amelanchiers and *Holodiscus discolor*, all planted to provide foliage interest and colour combinations. Archways are covered with roses and loniceras, and in the herbaceous borders are heathers, campanulas and osteospermums. There is also a pool and a bog garden.

Heath House   8

Offley Brook, Eccleshall ST21 6HA. Tel: (01785) 280318

Dr and Mrs D.W. Eyre-Walker • 10m NW of Stafford, 3m W of Eccleshall. Take B5026 towards Woore. At Sugnall turn left and after 1½ m turn right immediately by stone wall. After 1m go straight across crossroads and garden is on right in few metres • Open probably 14th May, 16th July, 2 – 5.30pm, 7th June, 2 – 9pm for NGS and for individuals and parties by appt • Entrance: £2, children free ◑ 🍺 WC ☯

A one-and-a-half-acre garden round a country house with varied features, including a delightful bog garden, wide well-planted herbaceous borders providing a succession of colour, a fruit and vegetable garden, a raised alpine bed, an old mulberry tree, and a rose border. The woodland area with various ground-cover plants makes a good contrast to the formal front garden. There are large shrubs and a wide selection of unusual plants.

Little Onn Hall 9

Church Eaton, Stafford ST20 0AU. Tel: (01785) 840154

Mrs I.H. Kidson • 6m SW of Stafford, 2m S of Church Eaton, midway between A5 and A518 • Open by appt only • Entrance: £3, children 50p ● 💻 🏠 WC 🚾 ⬤

The driveway to this six-acre garden is flanked by long herbaceous borders backed by yew hedges. The large rose garden contains standards, shrub and hybrid teas. An unusual-shaped pool known as the Dog Bone is planted with water lilies; bog plants reside elsewhere in the medieval moat, a delightful feature. Since 1971 the present owner has been planting new trees and is trying to maintain the original design by Thomas H. Mawson. Many rhododendrons, spring bulbs and large beeches and conifers ensure colour for a long season..

Manor Cottage 10

Chapel Chorlton, Newcastle-under-Lyme ST5 5JN. Tel: (01782) 680206

Mrs Joyce Heywood • 6m SW of Newcastle-under-Lyme. From A51 Nantwich – Stone road turn behind Cock Inn at Stableford. House on village green • Open 24th April to 28th Aug, Mon only, 2 – 5pm, and at other times by appt • Entrance: £1.50, children 50p ● ✕ WC 🚾 ⬤ ⚘

This two-thirds-of-an-acre garden has been created by the present owner over several years and is beautifully designed with excellent colour combinations and varieties of foliage, including many variegated forms. It is a flower arranger's paradise, with a wide range including collections of ferns, geraniums, hellebores, grasses and hostas. Small paths lead to surprises round each corner, and there are roses climbing through old fruit trees, a broad range of conifers and a good alpine area. All-year-round colour and interest and continual introduction of unusual plants.

Moseley Old Hall 11

**Moseley Old Hall Lane, Fordhouses, Wolverhampton WV10 7HY.
Tel: (01902) 782808; Fax: (01902) 782808**

The National Trust • 4m N of Wolverhampton. From S on M6 and M54 take junction 1 to Wolverhampton. From N on M6 take junction 11 then A460. Coaches must use A460 • House open • Garden open 25th March to May, Sat and Sun; June to Oct, Wed, Sat and Sun (and Tues in July and Aug), 1.30 – 5.30pm. Also Bank Holiday Mons, 11am – 5pm and Tues following (except 2nd May), 1.30 – 5.30pm; Nov and Dec, Sun only, 1.30 – 4.30pm • Entrance: £4, children £2, family ticket (2 adults and 3 children) £10 (house and garden) • Other information: Light lunches available July and Aug, Sun ◑ 💻 ✕ 🏠 WC 🚾 ⬤ ⚘ 🛍 ☕

Around the Elizabethan house where Charles II hid after the Battle of Worcester is a garden mainly for the specialist interested in old species, as all are seventeenth-century except for a few fruit trees. The knot garden is from a design of 1640 by the Reverend Walter Stonehouse. A wooden arbour is covered with clematis and *Vitis vinifera* 'Purpurea'. Fruit trees include a mulberry, medlars and a morello cherry. The walled garden has topiary and herbaceous borders, and fritillaries grow in the nut walk. There is a small herb garden and boles for bees. It is interesting to see plants grown in times past to provide dyes and for cleansing and medicinal purposes.

Oulton House   12

Oulton, Stone ST15 8UR. Tel: (01785) 813556

Mrs M. Bridger • 8m N of Strafford, ½ m NE of Stone. From Stone take Oulton road and after Oulton village sign turn left. After houses turn right up long drive • Open April to July by appt • Entrance: £2, children 75p ◐ 🍽 WC ℘

This three-acre garden with fine views, surrounded by parkland, has been developed by the present owner over more than 20 years. A range of large trees provides shelter. The conservatory contains vines, camellias and roses. There is a rhododendron walk, large rockery, herbaceous borders containing interesting colour combinations and a wide range of plants including geraniums, delphiniums, euphorbias and astrantias. Old shrub roses abound, and a grey-and-silver border has been planted by the house, which has clematis and roses climbing its walls. A new border has yellow, blue and white perennials including superb delphiniums, and the bank behind is covered with ivies, loniceras and roses. Patio area, golden corner, white area, large vegetable and fruit garden. Although not a weed-free garden, there is plenty to delight the eye and it is hoped it may be open more often as the borders contain a mass of snowdrops and tulips which must be a delight to see in spring, extending to June.

Rode Hall

(see Cheshire)

Shugborough ★   13

Milford, Stafford ST17 0XB. Tel: (01889) 881388; Fax: (01889) 881323

Staffordshire County Council/The National Trust • 6m E of Stafford on A513 • House, museum and Park Farm open • Garden open 25th March to 24th Sept, daily except Mon, 11am – 5pm; Oct, Sun only. Open for pre-booked parties all year from 10.30am • Entrance: £2 per vehicle to parkland, gardens, picnic area, walks and trails. House, County Museum (includes servants' quarters) and Park Farm £8, concessions £6, children under 5 free; or £4, concessions £3 for single-site ticket. NT members free to house, reduced rate to museum and farm • Other information: Batricars available. Dogs in park only, on lead ◐ 🍽 ✕ 🧺 WC ♿ ⬛ ℘

Shugborough is of interest to garden historians because Thomas Wright of Durham worked here. Many of the buildings and monuments are ascribed to James 'Athenian' Stuart and were built for Thomas Anson from the 1740s onwards. These are some of the earliest examples of English neo-classicism, and there is also an early example of Chinoiserie based on a sketch made by one of the officers on Admiral Anson's voyage round the world. The *Oxford Companion* suggests that the buildings were 'randomly scattered', but another view is that they were put in place as 'hidden architectural treasures' to surprise. As for the garden, the Victorian layout with terraces by Nesfield was revitalised for the Trust in the mid-1960s by Graham Stuart Thomas, who also worked on the Edwardian rose garden. Seasonal attractions include azaleas, rhododendrons and a fine herbaceous border. The first stage of a major tree-planting scheme has begun with over 1000 young oaks, the aim being to restore Shugborough to its original eighteenth-century layout with more hedgerows and wooded areas. There is also a woodland walk and guided tours of the garden.

Trentham Gardens 14

Stone Road, Trentham, Stoke–on–Trent ST4 8JG. Tel: (01782) 657341

Trentham Leisure Ltd • On A34 S of Stoke-on-Trent. 2m from M6 junction 15 • Open early April to early Oct, daily, 10am – 6pm • Entrance: £1, concessions and children 50p (1999 prices) • Other information: Conference centre adjacent ◑ 🍽 🛍 WC ♿ ⬦ 👁

The 750 acres of parkland were designed by 'Capability' Brown. Nesfield added a large Italian garden and Sir Charles Barry laid out formal gardens for the Duke of Sutherland. The gardens have been greatly simplified but still retain many features, such as Brown's large lake, on which one can now enjoy water sports (including waterskiing). There is a rose garden, a good selection of shrubs including hebes, potentillas and buddleias, magnificent trees alongside the River Trent, which flows through the gardens, and in the woodland area by the lake. A good place for a family day out, as there are picnic areas, a play area and a funfair. However, the buildings and hundreds of acres of parkland have been neglected and are currently subject to a planning application for a major refurbishment by the new owners.

POSTCODE PLANTS DATABASE

It is often difficult to find out which plants are local to an area. The Postcode Plants Database locates the names of flowers, trees, butterflies and birds for each of Britain's 26 million home addresses. Simply by typing in the first four characters of their Postcode, householders, schools, garden centres and councils can obtain tailor-made lists of local plants which are both hospitable and garden-worthy. Also included are the names of butterflies and birds most likely to visit gardens in each area. The lists come from innovative software, developed by Royal Mail and *FLORA-for-FAUNA* in conjunction with the Natural History Museum, which searches through hundreds of distribution maps of fauna and flora in the British Isles.

SUFFOLK

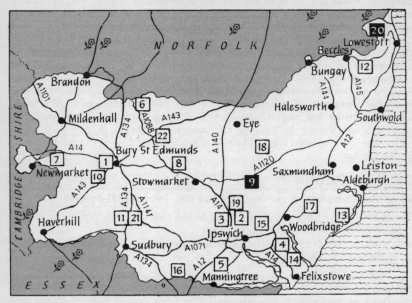

Some gardens have postal addresses in one county and are physically situated in another. If in doubt, a check in the index will direct the reader to the page on which the garden appears.

Two-starred gardens are marked on the map with a black square.

Abbey Gardens   1

Bury St Edmunds.

Borough of St Edmondsbury • In town centre • Open: daily • Entrance: free
○ ☕ WC ♿ 🏛

This is a very surprising garden. In 945 the Benedictines founded the Abbey, and undoubtedly this had gardens for herbs and vegetables. The Abbey ruins (it was dissolved in 1539) form the extraordinary 'bones' of the present-day landscape; if for no other reason, visit this place to see the great abbey walls, like some extraordinary geological feature, now dissolving into flinty stumps. Then think forward 900 years and bring to mind that one Nathaniel Hodson actually formed a botanic garden on this site in 1821. The present arrangement of formal beds on the site of the Great Court of the Abbey mirrors Hodson's botanic garden, of which perhaps only a few trees remain. The planting in the formal garden may be brash – lots of begonias and busy lizzies in summer – but in its way it is the modern equivalent of Hodson's garden. You will learn more about the hstory of the gardens by asking for the excellent free leaflet at the Bowling Green office; there is also a leaflet (25p) about the small 'medieval' herb garden. So this is a special place, of historical interest, much used by the townspeople, and certainly worth a visit when you are in the town perhaps to see 'The Hidden [private] Gardens of Bury'.

Barham Hall ★ 2

Church Lane, Barham, Ipswich IP6 0QF. Tel: (01473) 830055

Mr and Mrs Richard Burrows • 5m NW of Ipswich off A14 (A45). Take third turning to Claydon, ½ m up Church Lane • Open 26th March, 25th June, 2 – 5pm for charity • Entrance: £2 ● ☕ ✿

The garden, which is seven acres in all, includes a water garden and lake surrounded by bog plants, a woodland shrub garden, many herbaceous borders and a collection of Victorian roses, all kept to the highest standard. The whole impression is of immaculate care and attention to detail, achieved during the past 10 years, with extensive remodelling over the past five. If the perfection of maintenance will not make you green with envy you must see this garden – if it does, go anyway to see the Henry Moore sculpture in the church.

Blakenham Woodland Garden 3

Little Blakenham, Ipswich. Tel: (01473) 833249

4m NW of Ipswich, 1m off B1113. Signed from The Beeches in Little Blakenham, 1m off old A1100 (now B1113) • Open March to June, daily except Sat, 1 – 5pm and for a couple of days in May for charity. Parties welcome by appt – telephone number above • Entrance: £1 ◑

Set in five acres of bluebell wood, planted with a huge variety of ornamental trees and flowering shrubs, it is at its best in spring, full of cornus, azaleas, magnolias and rhododendrons, followed later by roses, hydrangeas and abutilons. Camellias. As summer advances it gets more overgrown, which only adds to its charm. Grass paths wind through and one can sit on one of the many seats, listening to the birds in perfect peace. It is a pity that the opening times cannot be extended through high summer.

Bucklesham Hall ★ 4

Bucklesham, Ipswich IP10 0AY. Tel: (01473) 659263

Mr and Mrs D.R. Brightwell • 6m SE of Ipswich, ½ m E of Bucklesham. Entrance opposite and N of primary school • Open by appt • Entrance: £2.50 • Other information: Coaches by appt. Refreshments by arrangement ● ☕ 🍴 ♿ 🔦

The great interest of Bucklesham is how these seven acres of interlocking gardens, terraces and lakes have been created from scratch since 1973 by the previous owners and added to and further improved by the present owners since 1994. Round the house are secret gardens so packed with flowers that no weed could survive; beds of old-fashioned roses overflow their borders, and a courtyard garden has been created with the use of every kind of container.

Descending terraces of lawns, ponds and streams lead to the woodland and beyond; round each corner is a new vista. Skill, wide horticultural knowledge and imagination have resulted in a remarkable display of plants, shrubs and trees.

East Bergholt Place 5

East Bergholt, Suffolk CO7 6UP. Tel: (01206) 299224

Mr and Mrs Rupert Eley • 8m SW of Ipswich, 2m E of A12 on B1070 • Open March to June and Oct to Nov, daily, 10am – 5pm. Closed 23rd April • Entrance: £2, children free ◑ 🍴 **WC** ♿ 🐾

The garden was originally laid out between 1900 and 1914 by Charles Eley, the present owner's great-grandfather, and many of the existing plants originate from the great plant collector George Forrest. The 15 acres are an interesting blend of the formal and informal, and are particularly lovely in the spring. The yew topiary and terrace area are linked to undulating informal walks by water features, including a pool and stream. The large collection of rare specimen trees and shrubs includes many camellias, magnolias and rhododendrons. There is an extensive plant centre in the attractive walled garden.

Euston Hall ★ 6

Thetford, Norfolk IP24 2QP. Tel: (01842) 766366

The Duke and Duchess of Grafton • 3m S of Thetford on A1088 • House open as garden • Garden open June to 28th Sept, Thurs, 2.30 – 5pm, and 27th June and 5th Sept, 2.30 – 5pm • Entrance: £3, OAPs £2.50, children 50p, parties of 12 or more £2.50 per person ● 🍴 🍴 **WC** ♿

Fronted by terraces, the Hall stands among extensive lawns and parkland along a winding river, the work of William Kent in the 1740s (followed by 'Capability' Brown), as is the splendid domed temple isolated on an eminence to the east, and also the pretty garden house in the formal garden by the house, developed by the present Duke. The pleasure grounds, laid out in the seventeenth century by John Evelyn, have grown into a forest of yew, but straight rides trace out the original formal layout. Also from this period are the stone gate piers which, together with the remnants of a great avenue, mark the original approach to the house. A small lake reflects the house across the park, and there are many fine specimen trees and a wealth of shrub roses.

Garden House 7

Brookside, Moulton, Newmarket CB8 8SG. Tel: 01638 750283

Mr and Mrs J. Maskelyne • 3m E of Newmarket on B1085 in Moulton village • Open for charity, for parties by appt • Entrance: £2 [NEW] ● 🍴 **WC** ♿ 🐾

A midsummer afternoon; an English village quaint with time; the gentle rustle of the leaves in a soft breeze; exotic perfumes wafting over the green; a quiet murmuring of voices wondering what that rose might be, or where might we get such-and-such a clematis. Bliss. And this is the kind of relaxing, near-perfect garden we all want to live in. A veritable, vibrant pot-pourri. There are too many plants to mention, arrayed in beds and borders, but the principals are old roses and clematis. There is a stunning *Carpenteria californica*, and overhead a variegated maple (not everyone's favourite, but here just right). Sages and geraniums, delphiniums and day-lilies, all fitting into place and all looking healthy and happy. In spring the hellebores and epimedium in the shaded nooks will be a joy. The summer colour combinations are subtle and immaculate: creams and dark crimsons, lilacs and blues. Not to be missed, especially in midsummer, when you can linger for afternoon tea on the patio.

Haughley Park ★　　　　　　　　　　　　　　　　　　8

Stowmarket IP14 3JY. Tel: (01359) 240205

Mr R.J. Williams • 4m NW of Stowmarket, signed 'Haughley Park' (not 'Haughley') on A14 • House open by appt • Garden open 30th April, 7th May (Bluebell Suns), and May to Sept, Tues, 2 – 5.30pm • Entrance: £2, children £1 • Other information: Coaches by appt. Teas provided on Bluebell Suns ● 🅑 WC ♿ ⬦

A hundred acres of rolling parkland at the heart of 100 more acres of woodland surround the seventeenth-century Jacobean mansion. Unexpected secret gardens with clipped hedges or flint and brick walls hide immaculate flower beds, climbers and flowering shrubs; each garden has its own character. The main lawn is surrounded by herbaceous borders, with, at the end, a splendid lime avenue drawing the eye across many miles of open countryside. Rhododendrons, azaleas and camellias grow on soil which is, unexpectedly for Suffolk, lime-free. The trees include a splendid *Davidia involucrata*, a 12-metre-wide magnolia and a flourishing oak over nine metres in girth, reputed to be 1000 years old. Beyond are the walled kitchen garden (much improved), the greenhouses and the shrubbery. In spring the broad rides and walks through the ancient woodland reveal not only the newly planted trees, specimen rhododendrons and other ornamental shrubs, but 10 acres of bluebells and, more remarkably, two acres of lilies-of-the-valley, and half a mile of mauve *ponticum* rhododendrons.

Helmingham Hall Gardens ★★　　　　　　　　　　　　9

Stowmarket IP14 6EF. Tel: (01473) 890363 (Contact Jane Tresidder)

Lord Tollemache • 9m N of Ipswich on B1077 • Open 30th April to 10th Sept, Sun, 2 – 6pm. Also Wed, 2 – 5pm for parties and individuals by prior appt • Entrance: £4, OAPs £3.50, children £2.50, parties of 30 or more £3.50 per person (Wed parties £4 per person) • Other information: Safari rides to see deer, Highland cattle and Soay sheep ● 🍽 WC ♿ 🐾 ♨

Nineteen generations of Tollemaches have lived here, and though there have been many changes over the past five centuries the property retains a strong Elizabethan atmosphere. The double-moated Tudor mansion house of great splendour and charm, built of warm red brick, stands in a 400-acre deer park. A nineteenth-century parterre, edged with a magnificent spring border, leads to the Elizabethan kitchen garden which is surrounded by the Saxon moat with banks covered in daffodils. Within the walls the kitchen garden has been transformed into an enchanting *potager* most subtly planted; the meticulously maintained herbaceous borders and old-fashioned roses surround beds of vegetables separated by arched tunnels of sweet peas and runner beans. Beyond is a meadow garden with, leading from it, a yew walk with philadelphus and shade-loving plants. On the other side of the Hall is a newly created garden dating from 1982. It is an historical knot and herb garden, with a magnificent collection of shrub roses underplanted with campanulas and geraniums, framed by a yew hedge. All the plants are chosen to be contemporary with the house.

Ickworth Park and Gardens 10

Horringer, Nr Bury St Edmunds IP29 5QE. Tel: (01284) 735157

The National Trust • 3m SW of Bury St Edmunds; signposted • Park open daily • Garden open all year, daily, except 25th Dec, 10am – 5pm • Entrance: £2.20, children 80p NEW ☾ ▆ ✕ ▣ WC ᚛ ⬯ ⟡ ⬚ ⬛ ⬦

The vast park, safely grazed by sheep, is in part the work of Lancelot 'Capability' Brown, and it provides a formidable setting for the late eighteenth-century Ickworth House. At first the building is not obvious, but the great rotunda soon looms large, a monster of a building, grandiose and gaunt, with vast curving wings. A formal garden, in the Italian style, fronts the south façade. A cavernous orangery, adorned with pots of agapanthus in summer, peers across the lawn. There is box everywhere (including the National Collection of buxus). Swags of Jerusalem sage and catmint, and bedded-out scarlet pelargoniums provide occasional colour. Hidden behind the clipped hedges you can discover Spring and Silver and Gold gardens, and the extraordinary Stumpery complete with bits of the Giant's Causeway (signalling Ickworth's builder, the Earl-Bishop of Bristol's other stupendous creation, Mussenden Temple at Downhill, on the north coast of Northern Ireland). Ickworth park has follies that pre-date the house (an ornamental canal and Summer House (1703)), a vineyard, miles of paths, and an enclosure with fallow deer. Even if the formal garden does not excite you, there is plenty of scope for walking in a peaceful tree-filled landscape.

Melford Hall 11

Long Melford, Sudbury CO10 9AA. Tel: (01787) 880286

The National Trust/Sir Richard Hyde Parker, Bt • 14m S of Bury St Edmunds, 3m N of Sudbury, on E side of A134 • Hall open with special Beatrix Potter exhibition • Garden open April, Sat, Sun and Bank Holiday Mon; May to Sept, Wed – Sun and Bank Holiday Mons; Oct, Sat and Sun; all 2 – 5.30pm • Entrance: principal rooms and garden £4.30 • Other information: Disabled driven to hall. One wheelchair provided. Picnics in car park only. Dogs in park only, on lead ◑ ▣ WC ᚛

The magnificent sixteenth-century house of mellow red brick is set in a park and formal gardens. A plan by Samuel Pierse of 1613 shows that the park was separated from the Hall by a walled enclosure, outside which was the moat; part of this is now the sunken garden. The avenue at the side of the house is currently being replanted with oaks grown from acorns taken from the existing trees. The octagonal brick pavilion on the north side of the path, a rare and beautiful example of Tudor architecture, overlooks the village green and the herbaceous borders inside the garden, which are being restored to their original Victorian and Edwardian design and planting. Outside the pavilion clipped box hedges and a bowling-green terrace lead past dense shrubbery. The garden has many good specimen trees, including the rare *Xanthoceras sorbifolium*. Great domes of box punctuate the lawns, and an interesting detail is the arrangement of yew hedges to the north of the house. Outside the walls are topiary figures. Round the pond and fountain are beds originally planted with herbs in 1937 and now being gradually improved. Some recent visitors have complained about the general standard of maintenance.

North Cove Hall ★ 12

North Cove, Beccles NR34 7PH. Tel: (01502) 476631

Mr and Mrs B. Blower • 3½ m E of Beccles, 50 metres off A146 Lowestoft road • Open for charity 25th June, 2 – 6pm and by appt • Entrance: £2, children free
● ● ● WC & ● ●

Climbing roses adorn this sunny Georgian house set in lawns surrounded by mature park trees. The walled garden partly encloses the half-acre pond studded with water lilies and bordered by majestic *Gunnera manicata*, *Taxodium ascendens nutans*, a group of *Betula jacquemontii* and *Alnus glutinosa* 'Imperialis'. A small stream with waterfalls has recently been constructed and planted. Inside the walls are herbaceous and shrub borders, pergolas and the kitchen garden. Small scree garden. Outside are woodland walks among mature trees and various younger conifers. About 10 miles south of Beccles is *Woottons* of Wenhaston, a small garden of one acre attached to a nursery run by Mr Loftus. Well laid out and labelled, full of rare and unusual plants.

The Old Rectory 13

Orford, Woodbridge IP12 2NN. Tel: (01394) 450063

Mr and Mrs Tim Fargher • 10m E of Woodbridge. Take B1084 Woodbridge – Orford road. Old Rectory on left behind church • Open 12th June to 14th July, Mon – Fri, 10am – 4pm, Sat, 10am – 12 noon, by appt only • Entrance: £5, OAPs and children £2.50 • Other information: Parking for disabled only. Visitors asked to make themselves known to the gardener, Mr Denny ●

This extensive five-acre garden, tucked behind Orford church, is immaculate, secluded and unexpected. It was designed for the owners' parents by Lanning Roper, with additions by Mark Rumary, and its beautifully planned borders and vistas surround the house, which has a large conservatory.

Peter's Garden 14

**The Mill, 194 Kirton Road, Trimley St Martin, Felixstowe IP11 0QL.
Tel: (01394) 448241**

*Diana Hewett • 8m SE of Ipswich. From A14 (A45) Ipswich – Felixstowe road
turn left at roundabout signed 'Kirton'. Pass Trimley St Martin school, and Mill
on right • Open by appt only • Entrance: donations towards upkeep appreciated*
◑ WC ℗

The half-acre plantsman's garden was developed over 45 years around a
converted post-mill by literature teacher and poet, Peter Hewett. It is now
funded largely by an anonymous donor and maintained by local volunteers. It
features an orchard, vegetable plot, pond, bog garden and lavender border.
Dominating the garden are deep beds of shrubs and old roses underplanted
with cottage-garden flowers.

Playford Hall 15

Playford, Ipswich IP6 9DX. Tel: (01473) 622509

*Mr and Mrs Richard Innes • 3m NE of Ipswich, 1m N of A1214 between
Ipswich and Woodbridge, on edge of Playford • Parking • Open by appt only •
Entrance: £3* ◑ 🖻 ♿ ⟨⟩

A beautiful moated Elizabethan house set in 10 acres of outstanding gardens.
Trees, lawns and a lake surround the house, with yew hedges dividing
herbaceous and shrub borders full of unusual plants. Roses cascade over
the house and moat walls, and there is also a pergola rose garden underplanted
with lavender and other old favourites. Small vegetable and herb garden in
orchard.

The Priory ★ 16

Stoke by Nayland CO6 4RL. Tel: (01206) 262216

*Mr and Mrs Henry Engleheart • 8m SE of Sudbury on B1068 • Open 21st
May, 25th June, 2 – 6pm • Entrance: £2.50, children free* ◑ 🍵 🖻 WC ♿ ⟨⟩
℗

An exceptional nine-acre garden, with fine views over Constable countryside.
Around the house is a splendid selection of plants and roses in terraces and
mixed borders. Lawns slope down to a series of six small lakes, planted with a
mass of water plants and water lilies. A Chinese bridge links to a tea pavilion by
one of the lakes. In the spring rhododendrons and azaleas ring the lakes under
large trees. A garden of mixed planting in the walled garden leads into the
greenhouse/conservatory, with its colourful collection of tender plants.

The Rookery ★ 17

Eyke, Woodbridge IP12 2RR. Tel: (01394) 460226

*Captain and Mrs Robin Sheepshanks • 5m E of Woodbridge. Turn N off B1084
Woodbridge – Orford road signed 'Rendlesham 2' before double bend sign • Open*

9th, 30th April, 14th May, 4th, 18th and 25th June, 16th July, 17th Sept, 2 –
5.30pm • Entrance: £2.50, children 50p • Other information: Vineyard ● ●
● WC & ● ●

The informal garden of about eight acres designed on differing levels has a wide
variety of trees and shrubs. The owners have increased the already large stock
of roses, and have made new vistas. The visitor's curiosity is constantly aroused
as to what is round the next corner. A fish pond, waterfall and Japanese water
garden all add interest to the peaceful grass walks, with rhododendrons, bulbs
and flower beds.

Rumah Kita   18

Church Lane, Bedfield, Woodbridge IP13 7JJ. Tel: (01728) 628401

Mr and Mrs Ivan Dickings • 18m N of Ipswich, 2½ m NW of A1120 between
Earl Soham and Saxtead • Open by appt for NGS • Entrance: £2 ● WC & ●

The main garden has long formal borders and a formal lawn. There is a parterre
and a water feature, curved borders, including a late-summer border with
grasses and late-flowering herbaceous plants. But the main point is that Rumah
Kita is a paradise of rare and unusual plants, such as *Paeonia suffruticosa* 'Joseph
Rock' grafted by Ivan Dickings, *Emmenopterys henryi* and *Sequoiadendron giganteum*
'Pendulum'. Different areas of the garden are enclosed with a variety of
hedging plants, including the purple-leaved *Prunus cerasifera* 'Nigra', which
makes a good backdrop on one side of a sunny late-flowering hot border. On
the other side is a cool silvery garden of plants whose foliage and flowers are
predominantly grey, blue and white. Informal curved beds, once packed with
half-hardy perennials, are now used for a more mixed, less labour-intensive
planting. New features include a rose-covered pergola lining a new bark-
mulched walkway into the garden. This one-and-a-half-acre garden reflects the
enthusiasm of the owners for plants which are rare and/or difficult to
propagate – Mr Dickings is a propagator by profession. If your interest is
hostas, there are over 300 varieties at *Park Green Nurseries*, Wetheringsett, six
miles NE of Stowmarket [open March to Sept, daily].

Shrubland Park ★   19

Coddenham, Ipswich IP6 9QQ. Tel: (01473) 830221 (Estate Office)

Lord de Saumarez • 4m N of Ipswich. Turn off A140/A14 interchange slip road
towards Ipswich and turn to Barham • Open 9th April to 24th Sept, Sun and
Bank Holiday Mons, 2 – 5pm. Guided tours for parties of 10 or more at other
times by arrangement • Entrance: £2.50, OAPs and children £1.50 ● ● WC

The magnificence of Shrubland Hall is reflected in the Victorian gardens, laid out
by Sir Charles Barry and later modified by William Robinson. They are amongst
the most important of their type remaining in England. From the upper terrace
outside the house one descends by a stunning cascade of a hundred steps and
terraces to a garden of formal beds, fountain and eye-catcher loggia. Beyond is
the wild garden which merges into the woods and is bordered by the park with
its many fine trees, some reputed to be 800 years old. The gardens are

punctuated by a series of enchanting follies ranging from a Swiss chalet to an alpine rockery and magnificent conservatory. The extensive ongoing programme of restoration includes the box maze and the old dell garden.

Somerleyton Hall and Gardens ★★ 20

Somerleyton, Lowestoft NR32 5QQ. Tel: (01502) 730224 (732950 during opening hours); Web: www.somerleyton.co.uk

Lord and Lady Somerleyton • 8m SW of Great Yarmouth, 5m NW of Lowestoft on B1074. Signposted • House open 1.30 – 5pm. Telephone for details of running times of miniature railway • Gardens open 23rd April to 25th Sept, Thurs, Sun and Bank Holiday Mons; July and Aug, Tues, Wed, Thurs, Sun and Bank Holiday Mon, 12.30 – 5.30pm. Private tours of hall and gardens for parties by arrangement with the Administrator • Entrance: £4.80, OAPs £4.60, children £2.40, family (2 adults and 2 children 5-16) £13.50, parties of 20 or more rates on application (1999 prices) ◑ 💬 ✕ 🍴 WC ᕫ ✍ 🎫 ♿

The former Jacobean house was extensively rebuilt in the mid-nineteenth century by Sir Morton Peto as a grand Italianate palace, and the gardens splendidly reflect this magnificence with 12 acres of formal gardens, a beautiful walled garden, an aviary, a loggia and a winter garden surrounding a sunken garden displaying statues from the original nineteenth-century winter garden. Special features include the 1846 William Nesfield yew hedge maze and the 90-metre-long iron pergola covered in wisteria, vines and roses. Not to be missed are the extraordinary peach cases and ridge-and-furrow greenhouse designed by Sir Joseph Paxton, now containing peaches, grapes and a rich variety of tender plants. The Victorian kitchen garden and a museum of 'bygone' gardening equipment are being developed.

Sun House ★ 21

Hall Street, Long Melford, Sudbury CO10 9HZ. Tel: (01787) 378252

Mr and Mrs J. Thompson • 3m N of Sudbury. In centre of Long Melford opposite Cock and Bell and next to Swags and Bows shop • Open 23rd April, 1st May, 4th, 11th, 17th, 25th June, 2nd, 9th July, 2 – 6pm, and by appt • Entrance: £2.50 ◑ ✍

The gardens consist of a large central section created over the past decade. They have a notable false acacia tree, a stone courtyard with formal pond near the house and a small, less formal pond at the far end. Weathered statues and busts make strong focal points, as do weeping pear and birch in mixed shrub and herbaceous borders. Over 100 clematis wind through old apple trees or grow against the mellow brick walls of the 'secret' garden. Old roses, lilies, peonies and irises are contained in neat box-edged beds within this new garden, with its colonnaded summerhouse and lion wall fountain. Compost heap and tool area are cunningly disguised by a flint wall, complete with shell mosaic; ferns and ivy add romantic enchantment to this recently created 'ruin'. The garden cottage is available as part of the 'Bed & Breakfast for Garden Lovers Scheme' (see Hotels list).

Wyken Hall ★ 22

Stanton, Bury St Edmunds IP31 2DW. Tel: (01359) 250287/250240

Sir Kenneth and Lady Carlisle • 9m NE of Bury St Edmunds on A143. Leave A143 between Ixworth and Stanton. Signed Wyken Vineyards • Garden open April to 1st Oct, Thurs, Fri, Sun and Bank Holiday Mons, 10am – 6pm • Entrance: £2.50, OAPs £1.50, children under 12 free • Other information: Vineyard 🕐 ☕ ✕ <u>WC</u> ♿ 🐕 ✿ 🛒

This outstanding garden covers four acres, most of which have been planted in the last dozen years. It is divided into a series of rooms, starting with the wild garden and winter garden, which leads into the south and woodland garden, and so into the dell. Mown paths meander between shrubs and into the newly planted copper beech maze next to the nuttery and gazebo. Then to the rose garden, enclosed on three sides by a hornbeam hedge and on the fourth by a rose-laden pergola. Beyond the wall are the knot and herb gardens, separated by yew hedges and designed by Arabella Lennox-Boyd. An 'edible garden' and a kitchen garden have been planted to the north of the house, and there is a new pond just beyond the garden. Remarkable for its colours and scents, particularly in high summer. Amongst the latest additions are an eccentric dog kennel, a chapel (with armchair), a contemplation garden and a curious veranda with rocking chairs. One might well describe these as the 'personal touches' of Lady Carlisle.

HOW TO FIND THE GARDENS

Directions to each garden are included in the entry. This information has been supplied by the owners and garden inspectors. It is aimed to be the best available to those travelling by car, and has been compiled to be used in conjunction with a road atlas.

Some gardens can be approached by public transport, but alas these are few and far between. The unreliability of train and bus services makes it unrewarding to include details, particularly as many garden visits are made on Sundays. However, properties that can be reached by public transport feature in National Trust guides and the NGS Yellow Book, which sometimes give details.

OPENING DATES AND TIMES

Times of access given are the best available at the moment of going to press, but some may have been changed subsequently. In the entries, the times given are inclusive – that is, an entry such as May to Sept means that the garden is open from 1st May to 30th Sept inclusive, and 2 – 5pm, means that entry will be effective during that period. Please note that many owners will open their gardens to visitors by appointment. They will often arrange to give a personally-conducted tour on these occasions. Unavoidably some owners cannot give their opening times before we go to press. In such cases we attempt to give the best guidance we can.

SURREY

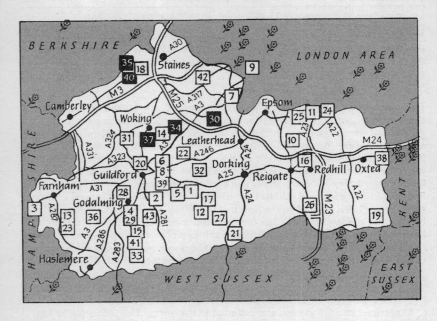

We have included some gardens with Surrey postal addresses in the London section for convenience. So before planning a day out in Surrey it is worth consulting pages 259–300.

Two-starred gardens are marked on the map with a black square.

Albury Park Gardens ★   1

Albury, Guildford GU5 9BB. Tel: (01483) 202964; Fax: (01483) 205013

Trustees of the Albury Estate and Country Houses Association Ltd • 5m SE of Guildford. Turn off A25 onto A248 (signed Albury). After ¼ m, turn left and entrance immediately left • Mansion open as grounds • Grounds open May to Sept, Wed and Thurs, 2 – 5pm • Entrance: £2.50 ● � ✧

John Evelyn designed the 14 acres of pleasure grounds in the mid-seventeenth century. Today the gardens to the south of the River Tillingbourne belong to the Country Houses Association, while the grounds to the north belong to the Trustees of the Albury Estate. Two dramatic terraces, a quarter of a mile long, extend across the grounds; at the centre of the upper terrace is the entrance to the tunnel through the hillside and a semi-circular pond which was originally fed by water from the Silent Pool. On the lower level is a bathhouse dated 1676. In the grounds are about 70 different species of trees, a lake and a small canal, both restored in 1990/91. The gardens around the house have impressive trees, a bank of azaleas and a formal rose garden. In 1882 William

Cobbett on one of his rural rides described the gardens as 'without exception the prettiest in England; that is to say, that I ever saw in England'.

Barnett Hill 2

Wonersh, Guildford GU5 0RF. Tel: (01483) 893361

Barnett Hill Conference Centre Ltd • Leave Guildford on A281 S towards Horsham. After 1½ m cross railway bridge and turn left at Shalford village green for Wonersh. Continue for 1½ m and turn left signed 'Conference Centre'. Entrance at top of hill on right • Open 14th May, 2 – 5.30pm • Entrance: £2.50, children under 14 free ● 🍽 🏠 WC ⚙ 🌳

The attractive house was built in 1906 by the grandson of Thomas Cook, founder of the travel agents. On a 26-acre site with 10 acres of formal and planted gardens he employed 14 gardeners. Now there are three. After World War II, Mrs Cook gave the property to the British Red Cross for eventual use as a training and conference centre. The garden stands on a levelled hill top, the ground falling away on all sides, giving panoramic views. There is an azalea walk and banks of mature rhododendrons; a formal sunken garden with a fish pool; a charming period Wendy house; a new area with grasses; specimen trees and a woodland walk. On open days a band plays on the wide lawn, and other entertainment is laid on for visitors. Extensive plant sale with many unusual plants.

Birdworld 3

Holt Pound, Farnham GU10 4LD. Tel: (01420) 22838

Forest Lodge Garden Centre • 3m S of Farnham on A325 • Open 1st to 5th Jan, daily; 6th Jan to 12th Feb, weekends; 13th Feb to early Nov, daily: summer 9.30am – 6pm, winter 9.30am – 4.30pm (last admission 1 hour before closing) • Entrance (includes admission to aquarium 'Underwater World' and Jenny Wren Farm): £7.50, OAPs £5.95, children £3.95, family ticket (2 adults and 2 children) £19.95. Reduced rates for parties (1999 prices) • Other information: Wheelchairs for hire. Guide dogs only 🕐 🍽 ✕ 🏠 WC ♿ 🛍 🌱

First-time visitors to 26 acres of Birdworld will be surprised by the extensive gardens which provide a backdrop to the bird sanctuary. House and gardens are well cared for and in good condition. With its wide flat paths and ample seating there is plenty of space to enjoy the planting on show. The gardens around the aviaries have been replanned and replanted. Wide level paths wind past bright summer bedding, a cottage garden, borders of shrubs and perennials, a herb garden and amusing topiary. Other features include hanging baskets, wall baskets, a rose garden, a heather bed, an ornamental grass border, a pergola and climbing roses, a pond and a white garden.

Busbridge Lakes 4

Hambledon Road, Godalming GU8 4AY. Tel: (01483) 421955

Mr and Mrs Douetil • 1½ m S of Godalming off B2130 Hambledon road • Open 16th to 24th, 30th April, 1st, 28th, 29th May, 19th to 28th Aug,

10.30am – 5.30pm • Entrance: £3.60, OAPs and children £2.60 • Other information: Refreshments at weekends and on Bank Holidays only. Guide dogs only ● ● ● WC & ●

Parkland was created here in the 1650s and the grounds were landscaped in 1750 by Philip Webb M.P. It is now a Grade-IIA-Heritage garden. Beside the largest of the three lakes stands an early nineteenth-century Gothick boat-house, recently restored, with delicate blind windows, a room with a fireplace and two verandahs. At the end of the lake, what appears to be a bridge, multi-arched and built of rocks, proves to be an illusion. Huge plane trees dominate the lakeside; the Restoration chestnuts, probably planted in 1660, may be the tallest in England at over 30 metres. Tulip trees (*Liriodendron tulipifera*) and a fine cedar of Lebanon stand near the orchard; a sequoia towers above the house. Across the canal lake from the house is a hermit's cave, excavated in 1756 as a tomb for the then owner's wife and two of their children. Further up, a late eighteenth-century Doric temple with two porticos has recently been re-stored; below it a grotto contains the spring which feeds the lakes. There are peacocks on the lawns, and the site abounds with attractive, rare and endangered species of ducks, geese, swans and pheasants, all flourishing – as are the gardens.

Chilworth Manor   5

Chilworth, Guildford GU4 8NL. Tel: (01483) 561414

Lady Heald • 3m SE of Guildford on A248. Turn off in Chilworth up Blacksmiths Lane • House open on garden open days only • Garden open 8th, 9th April, 13th, 14th May, 10th, 11th June, 8th, 9th July, 12th, 13th Aug, 2 – 6pm and by appt • Entrance: £2 (house £1), children free • Other information: Teas on open days only ●

A lovely old garden, particularly in spring and summer, but something to see all the year round. Laid out in the eighteenth century, a walled garden was carved in three tiers out of the side of the hill by Sarah, Duchess of Marlborough. The high walls, backed by wisteria, shelter many fine plants, a herbaceous border, lavender walk and shrubs. There is also a woodland area with magnolias, rhododendrons, azaleas, an oak tree reputed to be 400 years old and a Judas tree. Our inspector, who visited in spring, was impressed by the candelabra primulas along the stream and golden carp in the monastic stew-ponds. The house is decorated by various Surrey flower clubs in turn. The ideal time to visit is on a day warm enough to sit on one of the strategically placed seats so as to absorb the atmosphere created by time past and time present.

Clandon Park   6

West Clandon, Guildford GU4 7RQ. Tel: (01483) 222482; Fax: (01483) 223479

The National Trust • 3m E of Guildford on A247 at West Clandon; or take A3 to Ripley then join A247 via B2215 • House open 2nd April to Oct, Tues – Thurs, Sun, Bank Holiday Mons and 21st, 22nd April, 11.30am – 4.30pm (last admission 4pm). Parties, Tues – Thurs only, must book • Garden open all year, daily during daylight hours • Entrance: free (house £4.40, children £2.25, family £11, parties of 15 or more £3.80 per person, combined ticket with Hatchlands (see entry) £6.40) • Other information: Disabled parking near front of house. Dogs in picnic area only, on lead ○ 🍵 ✕ 🏠 WC ♿ 🚻 ⏷

Clandon was built by the Venetian architect Giacomo Leoni in the early 1730s for the 2nd Lord Onslow, whose family still owns the park, although the house and garden are owned by the National Trust. The seven-acre garden is on a hillside and gives a fine view of the lake in the park. An interesting feature is the Maori meeting house, known as 'Hinemihi', brought from New Zealand over 100 years ago by the then Lord Onslow. Note also the grotto, parterre and new herbaceous border plus the new bedding and colours in the Dutch Garden.

Claremont Landscape Garden ★ 7

Portsmouth Road, Esher KT10 9JG. Tel: (01372) 467806

The National Trust • E of A307, just S of Esher • House (not NT) and Belvedere open for the first weekend in each month Feb to Nov • Garden open all year: Jan to March, daily except Mon, 10am – 5pm; April to Oct, Mon – Fri, 10am – 6pm, Sat, Sun and Bank Holiday Mons, 10am – 7pm; Nov to March 2001, daily except Mons, 10am – 5pm or sunset if earlier (last admission ½ hour before closing) but closed 15th July, 25th Dec, 1st Jan. Coach parties must book • Entrance: £3, children £1.50, family (2 adults and 2 children) £8, pre-booked parties of 15 or more £2.50 per person (1999 prices) • Other information: Dogs, Nov to March only, on lead ○ 🍵 ✕ 🏠 WC ♿ 🚻 ⏷

The Oxford Companion describes this as one of the most significant historic landscapes in the country. The great landscape designers of the eighteenth century each adapted it in turn for the owner, the immensely wealthy man who eventually became Duke of Newcastle. He bought the house from Sir John Vanbrugh, who also designed the belvedere for him (the views from the top are amazing). The Duke employed Bridgeman in 1716, then Kent in the 1730s. The latter adapted the garden to create picturesque settings, evoking various moods, and also enlarged the pond to make the lake, with pavilion (recently restored). When the Duke died, Clive of India purchased the estate. He brought in 'Capability' Brown, who also designed the house and, in typical form, diverted the London-Portsmouth road to improve the viewpoints, the most striking of which is the grass amphitheatre. In the nineteenth century it was a favourite retreat of Queen Victoria and her younger son. The 50 acres restored by the Trust are only part of the original estate, which was broken up in 1922 when part of the house became a school. A useful leaflet describes the various contributions to the park, which will appeal to everyone with its sensitive reconstruction of the eighteenth-century English style, even if it has nothing specific to offer the plantsperson, except perhaps the camellia terrace. The garden is popular with local families, sunbathers and picnickers.

The Conservatory   8

Gomshall Gallery, Gomshall GU5 9LB. Tel: (01483) 203019

*Marceline and Chris Siddons • 6m E of Guildford, 5m W of Dorking on A25,
in Gomshall • Open all year, Mon – Sat, 10am – 5.30pm; also April to Sept,
Sun and some Bank Holiday Mons, 2 – 5pm, but closed 21st, 23rd April, 25th,
26th Dec, 1st Jan • Entrance: free • Other information: Gallery adjacent ○ ⚲ ▥*

Opened in 1995, this large conservatory has an attractive display of both
unusual and easy-to-grow plants, all suitable for indoor rooms and conservatories, all bursting with health and vigour, and all for sale. There are large
well-established specimens as well as young plants in a wide range of varieties:
nine abutilons, four bananas, 16 bougainvilleas, 14 citrus and five passion
flowers, for example. Clear information is given about the height a plant may
reach, conditions required and pests and problems it may be prone to. Further
advice is available, and there is an informative free plant list.

Coombe Wood ★   9

Warren Road, Kingston Hill, Kingston upon Thames KT2 7LF.

*The Water Garden's Residents Association • From Kingston take A308 (Kingston
Hill) towards London. About 1½ m on right, turn right into Warren Road •
Open probably 30th April, 15th Oct, 2 – 5pm for NGS. Write for details •
Entrance: £2, OAPs £1, children 50p (1999 prices) ◗ ⚲*

An unusual and historic Japanese water garden. It was the original site of
Veitch's famous nursery, to which the owner's eldest son, resident in Japan,
sent hundreds of plants for commercial development. This was in the 1860s and
at the turn of the century more oriental plants arrived from Ernest Wilson's
expeditions to China. When the nursery was sold in 1914, General Sir Arthur
Paget and his wife, who lived next door, bought the two acres containing the
stream and a pond, which they incorporated within their own Japanese-style
garden, saving many Veitch plantings. The Paget estate changed hands again
and today part is a residential development of 10 acres, of which the water
gardens form a most beautiful area. The Japanese features have been retained
and improved. First-rate and well-restored bridges, tea house, etc. in the
Japanese style induce a sense of excitement for visitors exploring the winding
paths, as the maturity of the planting creates a full woodland effect. The
rhododendrons are a particular attraction and include many Wilson species.
Note also the fine magnolias, camellias and Japanese maples, which show to
advantage at the spring and autumn openings. The blue hydrangeas are a
remarkable sight and there are many unusual trees. The upkeep is above
average. (Note: the NGS calls these The Water Gardens, London.)

Copt Hill Shaw   10

Alcock's Lane, Kingswood KT20 6BB. Tel: (01737) 355979

*Mr and Mrs M. Barlow • 3m N of Reigate, 6m S of Sutton. From A217 after
Burgh Heath traffic lights, take first left (signed Coulsdon) to Waterhouse Lane,*

then first left into Alcock's Lane • Open 20th May, 2 – 5.30pm • Entrance: £2, children free • Other information: Parking in Furze Hill nearby ● ● WC ⅙ ♨

Immaculate yew hedges and topiary divide the different levels of this one-and-a-half-acre garden laid out in 1906. The lawn is bordered by a bank of azaleas with an exedra at one end and a yew arch at the other. Flights of brick steps lead up to a curved terrace with a pergola covered with clematis and old-fashioned roses. Through the yew arch is a small, hidden fruit and vegetable garden. All is meticulously maintained.

2 Court Avenue   11

Old Coulsdon CR5 1HF. Tel: (01737) 554721

Dr K. Heber • S of Croydon in Old Coulsdon, opposite Tudor Rose pub • Open by appt • Entrance: £1, children 50p ● WC ⅙ ⍟

From the corner of a busy road, visitors step into a colourful oasis. Dr Heber began this garden nearly 30 years ago and now grows around 3000 different plants in a level third of an acre. Against a background of shrubs, roses and clematis are many unusual varieties of herbaceous and foliage plants. The design is open and informal, with every inch of earth covered by plants, leaving no room for weeds. Knightsmead (see entry) is nearby.

Coverwood Lakes, Garden and Farm   12

Peaslake Road, Ewhurst, Cranleigh GU6 7NT. Tel: (01306) 731 1031

Mrs C.G. Metson and Mr and Mrs N. Metson • 7m SW of Dorking, 6m SE of Guildford, ½ m S of Peaslake off A25 • Gardens and farm open 23rd, 30th April, 7th, 14th, 21st May, 4th June, 2 – 6pm; 22nd Oct, 11am – 4.30pm • Entrance: £2.50, children £1 (share to NGS). Large or private parties by prior arrangement • Other information: Hot soup and sandwiches available on Oct open day ● ● WC ⅙ ♨ ♀

The original gardens were designed in 1910 by a rich Edwardian businessman. Now it is a woodland estate surrounding four lakes, the water for which comes from the natural springs in the bog garden. Each lake has a different character, from the towering rhododendrons reflected in the calm water of the highest to the largest alongside the arboretum. This was planted early in 1990 and contains 100 different kinds of trees, which are prospering in this natural setting. Bordering the paths are a great many varieties of hostas, trilliums and candelabra primulas. Lilies-of-the-valley form a carpet below a dazzling display of rhododendrons and azaleas. There is a marked trail to see pedigree Poll Hereford cattle, sheep, horses and wonderful views.

Crosswater Farm   13

Millais Nurseries, Crosswater Lane, Churt, Farnham GU10 2JN.
Tel: (01252) 792698

Mr and Mrs E.G. Millais • 6m SE of Farnham, 6m NW of Haslemere, ½ m N of Churt off A287. Signed 'Millais Nurseries' • Open May to 9th June, daily,

10am – 5pm 1st, 28th, 29th May for charity) • *Entrance: £2, children free* •
Other information: Teas on charity open days only ◐ 🍴 <u>WC</u> & ♫ ⚱

These six acres of woodland gardens were begun in 1946 by the present
owners, who specialise in azaleas and rhododendrons and have assembled an
exceptional collection from all over the world. Among the mature and some
more recent plantings are rare species collected in the Himalayas and hybrids
raised by them, including *Rhododendron* 'High Summer'. The plants are labelled
and most are available from the adjoining nursery, which grows more than 750
different varieties. There is also an excellent collection of sorbus trees. The
surrounding garden features a stream, ponds and companion plantings including young rare species, some being the first to be grown outside China and
Bhutan.

Dunsborough Park 14

Ripley, Woking GU23 6AL.

Baron and Baroness Sweerts de Landas Wyborgh • *3m NE of Guildford. Take
A247 or A3 to Ripley. Entrance across Ripley Green* • *Open by appt* • *Entrance:
£2.50, children £1.25 (1999 prices)* ◐ WC

The garden of the Georgian house has recently been restored. Herbaceous
borders lead to the extensive walled gardens, now redesigned as pleasure
gardens; a row of ginkgo trees, grown originally for sale, became too big to
move and now forms an unusual feature. A hidden garden encloses an ancient
mulberry. At the end of the water garden the bridge, with its belvedere, is
now accessible, and the fine Victorian glasshouses are being restored. The
Antique Garden Ornament Centre is open by appointment (Tel: (01483)
225366).

Feathercombe Gardens 15

Feathercombe, Hambledon, Godalming GU8 4DP. Tel: (01483) 860264/860257

The Campbell and Murray families • *4m S of Godalming, E of Hydestile –
Hambledon road* • *Open probably several days in May, 2 – 6pm and by appt* •
Entrance: £2, children 50p (1999 prices) ◐ 🍴 WC & ➬ ♫

The garden is notable for its good display of rhododendrons and azaleas, yew
topiary and tree heaths, and for the fine views across three counties. The
original design of 1910 was by Eric Parker, whose wife Ruth was one of Ludwig
Messel's daughters; there were strong links between Feathercombe and the
Messel garden at Nymans in West Sussex (see entry).

Gatton Park 16

Reigate RH2 0TW. Tel: (01737) 645826/644968

The Royal Alexandra and Albert School • *3m NE of Reigate. From A23, ⅓ m
NE of junction with A242, turn left into Rocky Lane. Entrance is almost 1 m
on left* • *Open: Feb – Oct, 1st Sun each month, 1 – 5pm* • *Entrance: £1.50* •
Other information: plants for sale on some Suns NEW ◐ ☕ WC ➬

The Domesday Book records a manor and deer park at Gatton. In the fifteenth century it became a rotten borough: a diminutive town hall still stands opposite the impressive portico. This is all that remains of the Italianate mansion, burnt down in 1934 and rebuilt in plainer style in 1937. There are magnificent cedars and sequoias around the house, and ancient oaks below in the parkland. In the eighteenth century, 'Capability' Brown swept away earlier formal gardens and created the 28-acre lake as well as a chain of smaller ones, the parkland, woods and vistas, enhancing the spectacular setting on the North Downs. This was one of his larger commissions for which he was paid £3000. In the late Victorian and Edwardian eras Jeremiah Colman, the mustard magnate, developed the gardens. He built a dramatic rock and water garden on a slope, with Pulhamite pools, massive rocks and curving steps. This is now being restored and is shaded by yews and appropriately planted. Coleman also created a Japanese garden restored in 1999, with interlacing pools and paths with waterside plants. It is overlooked by a thatched tea house. Future plans include the restoration of the lakes, extensive stone-walled kitchen gardens and dry arch. The owners also intend to remove the tennis courts from below the house and re-create the original parterre. Much of the work has been done by volunteers; others would be welcome.

Goddards   17

Abinger Common, Dorking RH5 6JH. Tel: ticket bookings during office hours (01306) 730871

The Landmark Trust • From Guildford take A25 Dorking Road E. At Wotton take right turn for Abinger Common. House on green opposite Victorian well • Open 26th April to 25th Oct, Wed only, 2 – 6pm, strictly by appt • Entrance: £3 • Other information: Limited parking ◑

Sir Edwin Lutyens designed the house originally in 1898 as a home of rest for ladies of small means. He planned it around a courtyard garden, facing slightly west of south and overlooked by all the principal rooms – in effect an outdoor room. Gertrude Jekyll collaborated on the structure of the garden, which remains intact; a three-year restoration programme is underway. A dipping well in the centre provides water for the plants and around it are paved paths, low walls, curved beds and a raised sundial. There are flower borders under the windows and vines and wisteria grow against the house walls. Architectural yew hedges enclose the formal gardens around the house, and yew arches give vistas over lawns, a ha-ha and across a meadow to a curving backdrop of woods.

Great Fosters ★   18

Stroude Road, Egham TW20 9UR. Tel: (01784) 433822; Fax: (01784) 472455

Great Fosters (1931) Ltd • Off M25 junction 13, 1m S of Egham. From railway station follow Manorcroft Road into Stroude Road and continue 1m. Hotel on left • Open all year, daily during daylight hours • Entrance: free • Other information: Refreshments and toilet facilities in hotel ○ ⑤

Built in the late sixteenth century, possibly as a Windsor Forest hunting lodge, this has been a hotel since 1929. The Grade-II garden, developed in 1918, has recently been restored. Behind the hotel, a long, paved terrace gives views of a wide semi-circular lawn and a lime avenue truncated at the far end by the M25. Steps lead down to four knot gardens with box edging, topiary and statues surrounding a sixteenth-century sundial, the whole outlined by a U-shaped Saxon moat. Wisteria drapes the Japanese bridge, which arches over the moat and leads to a pergola underplanted with lavender. A circular, sunken rose garden with an octet of steps down to a lily pool and fountain is bordered by rose arches and a paved path and surrounded by yew. Two square iris and peony gardens, also enclosed by yew hedges, are on a more intimate scale. At the side of the hotel a new vista garden with serpentine yew hedges is developing. An orangery has been built at the southern end, and orange trees in containers stand on the terrace in summer.

Greathed Manor 19

Ford Manor Road, Dormansland, Lingfield RH7 6PA. Tel: (01342) 832577; Fax: (01342) 836207

Country Houses Association • 8m SW of Edenbridge, $2\frac{1}{2}$ m SE of Lingfield. Take B2028 to Plough Inn, Dormansland. Follow Ford Manor Road opposite for about 1m • Open May to Sept, Wed and Thurs, 2.30 – 4.30pm • Entrance: £2.50, children £1 (1999 prices) ◐ **WC**

The main feature of these four acres of gardens, set in parkland, is the sunken garden on a grand scale, attributed to Harold Peto and created early this century. Curving terraces and wide steps lead down to an oval pool surrounded by decorative paving. Beds of azaleas and roses give spring and summer colour, with borders on the higher level. The enclosing sandstone wall is balustraded, as is the terrace running the length of the house. Elsewhere are rhododendrons, azaleas, spring flowers and specimen trees, all carefully maintained.

Guildford Castle Gardens 20

Castle Street, Guildford GU1 3TU. Tel: (01483) 505050

Guildford Corporation • From High Street walk through arches into Tunsgate. Castle opposite at far end • Castle keep open 10am – 5pm. Admission charge • Gardens open all year, daily, dawn – dusk • Entrance: free ○ க ⬠

This ruined keep built by William the Conqueror (close to the present city centre) once formed part of the garden of a private house bought by Guildford Corporation in 1885. Clever use has been made of the original moat. A path runs around the bottom, and shaped beds, retaining their interesting Victorian designs, are cut into the sloping, turfed sides. They are bedded-out for spectacular spring and summer display with much the same plants as the Victorians would have used. There are plenty of seats here in a wider level area for the weary or contemplative. A tunnel, its damp, shady approach brightly planted, leads up to a bandstand and a bowling green with attractive borders and clipped hedges, well maintained like the whole of the garden.

Hampton Court Palace

(see London Area)

Hannah Peschar Sculpture Garden 21

Black and White Cottage, Standon Lane, Ockley RH5 5QR.
Tel: (01306) 627269; Fax: (01306) 627662

Hannah Peschar • 6m S of Dorking, 1m SW of Ockley off A24. Follow signs 'Golf and Country Club'. Entrance on right in Standon Lane 400 metres past low bridge over stream • Open May to Oct, Fri and Sat, 11am – 6pm, Sun and Bank Holiday Mons, 2 – 5pm. Other days, except Mon, by appt only • Entrance: £7, OAPs £5, children under 16 £4 • Other information: Refreshments and meals for parties by arrangement only. Possible for wheelchairs in outdoor gallery only. Details of lecture tours, party and school visits on request ◑ 🏠 WC

The heart of this garden was part of the Leith Vale Estate, planted with rhododendrons and camellias, and later belonged to Dick Trotter, a former treasurer of the R.H.S. But it had been neglected for many years when the present owners arrived. The garden was opened in 1984 and has been extended and redesigned on informal lines with woodland, streams, lakes and grassed areas. Planting is architectural and large scale to provide a background for the display, for sale, of contemporary sculpture.

Hatchlands 22

East Clandon, Guildford GU4 7RT. Tel: (01483) 222482

The National Trust • 5m NE of Guildford, E of East Clandon, N of A246 • House open • Garden open April to Oct, Tues – Thurs, Sun and Bank Holiday Mons, also Fri in Aug, 2 – 5.30pm (last admission 5pm); park walks and grounds open April to Oct, daily, 11am – 6pm. Parties Tues – Thurs • Entrance: park walks and grounds £1.80 (house and garden £4.40, family £11, parties of 15 or more £3.80 per person, combined ticket with Clandon (see entry) £6.40) ◑ 🍴 WC &

The restoration of these gardens has now been successfully completed and the Gertrude Jekyll garden returned to its original size and planted to her 1914 plans. Plants were specially propagated, some having come from abroad, and the result is very effective. Beside the garden is a magnificent mature London plane tree. A wildflower meadow is left uncut until July. The garden at the front has been restored from the Italianate to a Reptonian original design of lawns and vistas. There are three woodland walks and the park has also been restored to Reptonian principles.

High Meadow 23

Tilford Road, Churt, Farnham GU10 2LN. Tel: (01428) 606129

Mr and Mrs John Humphries • 3m N of Hindhead. Take A287 from Hindhead then fork right to Tilford. House nearly 2m on right • Open 23rd, 24th April,

28th, 29th May, 27th, 28th Aug, 2 – 5pm. Parties by appt • Entrance: £2, children free • Other information: Parking and toilet facilities at Avalon PYO farm on left past turning to house. Disabled parking in drive to house. ◑ ☕ ⚘

As the name suggests, this garden is situated high on a meadowside protected by a series of hedges of beech, holly and cupressus. A small terrace is overlooked by a pergola with a variety of climbers. Unusually shaped beds surround grass of putting-green quality and contain a wealth of colour-co-ordinated shrubs, roses and herbaceous plants cleverly graded by height. There is a small pool set in a rock garden, a bog plant section, a rockery and a small peat garden. A plantsman's garden.

The Homestead 24

Old Lodge Lane, Kenley CR8 5EU. Tel: (020) 8660 9816

Mr and Mrs P. Wallace • Between Croydon and Caterham. From A23 SE from Reedham railway station, or from A22 SW from Kenley station. Take Hayes Lane for 1½ m and into Old Lodge Lane in right. Homestead is third house past Wattendon Arms on left • Open July by appt • Entrance: £1 ☕ ☕ ⚘

Colour throughout the season is the aim and achievement of the owners of this half-acre prize-winning garden, which they designed, created and maintain themselves. A patio shelters a profusion of hanging baskets filled with named varieties of begonias. The walls are covered with more than 30 different kinds of tender plants in containers – mainly fuchsias. High, dense hedges enclose the garden, creating a background for climbing roses, clematis and shrubs. Tightly packed borders of hardy and tender plants, including exotic cannas, provide continuous colour. In the centre of the lawn a stream and waterfall flow from a group of rocks and trees. Beds of colourful plants, raised in the greenhouses, surround small clipped trees. An occasional glimpse of a glider from Kenley aerodrome close by gives an added surreal element.

Knightsmead 25

Rickman Hill Road, Chipstead CR5 3LB. Tel: (01737) 551694

Mrs C. Jones and Miss C. Collins • 1m SW of Coulsdon, 3m SE of Banstead, off B2032 • Open 12th April, 10am – 4pm, 10th, 11th June, 2 – 5.30pm, and by appt • Entrance: £2, accompanied children 50p ☕ ☕ WC ⚘

When the present owners came here over a decade ago, the half-acre garden was overshadowed by vast Lawson cypresses. Now there are shrub roses and clematis, with arcs of smaller trees underplanted with spring bulbs and woodland plants such as erythroniums, trilliums and pure-colour-bred hellebores. A graceful 18-metre Deodar cedar dominates this well-designed plantsman's garden, and a lily pond, rose arch and beds of shrubs and perennials give year-round interest. On heavy clay soil, a bog garden, peat bed and limestone scree provide ideal conditions for choice plants. Walls support climbers and a conservatory extends the range. 2 Court Avenue (see entry) is nearby.

Langshott Manor 26

Langshott, Horley RH6 9LN. Tel: (01293) 786680; Fax: (01293) 783905

Mr and Mrs Peter Hinchcliffe • 4m N of Crawley. From Horley on A23 turn right at Chequers Hotel roundabout into Ladbroke Road and continue about 1m. Manor is on right • Open all year • Entrance: free ○ ☕ ✗ WC ⅙ ⟨⟩ ⚲

This beautifully restored Grade II Elizabethan manor house, draped in roses, clematis and a huge *Magnolia grandiflora*, is tucked away down a country lane; it is now a hotel. The peaceful setting is enhanced by a garden whose design complements the house. A sunken rose garden with borders edged in box contains an interesting star-shaped brick-and-tile feature with roses growing up a central pillar. The terrace of mellow stone and brick is edged with lavender. A pleached lime avenue curves around one side of the croquet lawn, and a hornbeam pergola leads from the entrance drive down towards it. A small orchard of old varieties of fruit on dwarf rooting stock contains a turf seat and a colourful mixed bed of herbs and salad plants. There is also a small lake with swans, cygnets and ducks and a rustic stone bridge separating the birds' domain from the ornamental part, planted with water lilies and moisture-loving plants.

Leith Hill Rhododendron Wood 27

Tanhurst Lane, Coldharbour. Tel/Fax: (01306) 712711/712153

The National Trust • 5m S of Dorking. Take Coldharbour Road and continue to Leith Hill. At next junction keep right, then fork left. Wood immediately on left • Leith Hill Tower open April to Sept, Wed, 12 noon – 5pm, Sat, Sun and Bank Holidays, 11am – 5pm (last admission 4.30pm). Also weekends Oct to March, 11am – 3.30pm (last admission 3pm) • Rhododendron Wood open all year, daily, during daylight hours • Entrance: £1.50 per car for the wood and 80p, children 40p, for the tower (1999 prices) • Other information: Light refreshments when tower open ○ WC ⅙ ⟨⟩

The wood was originally part of the estate of Leith Hill Place, once the home of the composer Ralph Vaughan Williams. Beside the car park is an extensive picnic area, and below this the rhododendrons and azaleas are a blaze of colour in April and May. There has been some replanting and the paths have been improved. An immense tulip tree, *Liriodendron tulipifera*, can be seen in the field beyond, and there are spectacular views. Further on, the mature trees create a shady area for rhododendrons in soft colours.

Loseley Park ★ 28

Compton, Guildford GU3 1HS. Tel: (01483) 304440
(enquiries to the Leisure Department); Fax: (01483) 302036

Mr and Mrs M.G. More-Molyneux • 3m SW of Guildford, W of A3, off B3000 • House open June to Aug, Wed – Sat, 2 – 5pm • Garden open 1st May to 30th Sept, Wed – Sat and 28th Aug, 11am – 5pm • Entrance: £2.50, OAPs/disabled £2, children £1.50 (house and garden £5, OAPs/disabled £4, children £3) (1999 prices) ◑ ☕ 🖪 WC ⅙ ⚲ 🏪 ⚲

The Elizabethan house is set in a sweep of lawn surrounded by parkland. Hidden away at the side of the house, the vast walled garden has been transformed: the old yew hedges have been cut back drastically and extensive new gardens created. The old mulberry is still there and a medlar with a group of palms. An enchanting rose garden with low box hedges is filled with old-fashioned roses, carefully labelled; box balls and circles emphasise the design, while pillars of roses and hollies give height. Along one side is an arcade of vine and clematis. A herb garden displays culinary, medicinal and ornamental herbs in triangular beds and others used in cosmetics, lotions and dyes, all well labelled. Quartets of domed acacias stand at the intersections of the main paths, and golden malus (crab apple) form a square avenue in the flower garden. Beyond is a large, productive vegetable area. The fountain garden is a new addition, planted with white and silver flowers and foliage to create a romantic atmosphere. Future plans include a wild flower meadow. The moat walk shelters a long border of sun-loving plants, including yuccas (don't step back while admiring them). Near the entrance to the garden are an ancient wisteria and a good herbaceous border. Trailer rides to the farm are available (June to August, Sats and Bank Holiday Mondays only).

Munstead Wood ★   29

Heath Lane, Busbridge, Godalming GU7 1UN. Tel: (01483) 417867

Sir Robert and Lady Clark • From Godalming take B2130 to Busbridge. Heath Lane is on left opposite church • Open 16th April, 21st May, 16th July, 2 – 6pm • Entrance: £3, OAPs £1.50 ● ☕ WC & ⬦ ℘

The house was designed by Edwin Lutyens for Gertrude Jekyll in 1896, but she had begun the garden 13 years earlier with no definite plan. She lived here until her death in 1932; Sir Robert and Lady Clark have been here 30 years. *Hydrangea petiolaris* clothes the wall around the unusual entrance. There are narrow borders and wall plants against the house and a cool courtyard at the back with paving and a pool. Well-kept lawns lead to a rock garden, a pergola and a wall; sun-loving plants grow on the south side and shade-lovers on the north. The southern part of the garden has been restored to Jekyll's original design with spring and summer gardens, a nut walk and a primula garden. In the lawn at the front of the house, the original Jekyll beds have been replanted and grass paths lead through massed mature rhododendrons and azaleas to shady woods. In Gertrude Jekyll's day, eight gardeners tended 15 acres; now 10 acres are worked by two gardeners.

Painshill Landscape Garden ★★   30

Portsmouth Road, Cobham KT11 1JE. Tel: (01932) 868113 (for information) or (01932) 864674 (for opening times); Fax: (01932) 868001

Painshill Park Trust • From M25 junction 10, take A3 and A245. W of Cobham on A245. Entrance 200 metres from A245/A307 roundabout • Garden open all year: April to Oct, daily except Mon (but open Bank Holiday Mons), 10.30am – 6pm; Nov to March, daily except Mon and Fri, 11am – 4pm (or dusk if earlier). Closed 25th, 26th Dec. Parties of 10 or more by appt • Entrance:

£3.80, concessions £3.30, children (5-16) £1.50. Children under 16 must be accompanied. School parties welcome • Other information: Wheelchairs available by prior booking ⏲ 🍽 🖼 WC ♿ 🐾 🛍 ⚗

The Hon. Charles Hamilton created Painshill – contemporary with Stowe and Stourhead – between 1738 and 1773, when it was sold after he ran out of funds. Until World War II, the Park was well maintained, then in 1948 it was sold off in lots and all but lost. Between 1974 and 1980 Elmbridge Council bought up most of the land; the following year the Painshill Park Trust was formed and began the task of restoration. The landscaped park, which now covers 160 acres, was designed around a winding 14-acre lake fed from the River Mole by a spectacular water wheel. The restored Chinese bridge, opened in 1988, leads to an island and a magical grotto, still being restored, the main chamber of which is 12 metres across, hung with stalactites and lined with shards of glistening feldspar. The mausoleum, near the river, was depicted on one of the plates of Catherine the Great's Wedgwood 'Frog Service'; a further reach of the lake reflects an abbey ruin. The focal point of the garden is the elegant Gothick temple on higher ground. It is approached across a grassed 'amphitheatre' encircled by formal eighteenth-century-style shrubberies. A dramatic blue-and-white Turkish tent with a gold coronet stands on a plateau among informal plantings. In the distance is the Gothick Tower. The great cedar of Lebanon, 36½ metres high and with a girth of 10 metres, is reputedly the largest in Europe. A vineyard has been replanted on a southern slope as it was in Charles Hamilton's day. The future depends on a satisfactory solution to the location of a visitors' centre and car park – to be viable Painshill needs 80,000 visitors annually. Finance, probably from the Heritage Lottery Fund, may be the key.

Pinewood House   31

Heath House Road, Woking GU22 0QU. Tel: (01483) 473241

Mrs Van Zwanenberg • 5m NW of Guildford. Turn off A322 opposite Brookwood Cemetery wall • House open with hand-embroidery exhibits • Garden open April to Oct by appt for parties of 2 to 25 persons • Entrance: £3 (house and garden) ⏲ 🍽 🖼 WC ♿ ⚗

In 1986, Mr and Mrs Van Zwanenberg built a new house in four acres of their original garden, retaining the water garden and rhododendrons massed against a backdrop of Scots pines, cedars and other fine trees. There is a young arboretum and a charming new walled garden with a fountain. An automated conservatory displays exotic plants.

Polesden Lacey ★   32

**Great Bookham, Dorking RH5 6BD. Tel: (01372) 452048
or Information line (01372) 458203; Fax: (01372) 452023**

The National Trust • 5m NW of Dorking, 2m S of Great Bookham off A246 Leatherhead – Guildford road • House open 31st March to Oct, Wed – Sun, 1.30 – 5.30pm and Bank Holiday Mons, 11am – 5.30pm (last admission ½ hour before closing) • Grounds open all year, daily, 11am – 6pm, or dusk if earlier (last admission 5pm) • Entrance: £3, family ticket £7.50 (house and grounds £6, family ticket £15, pre-booked parties of 15 or more £5 per person) • Other information: Parking 150 metres away. Disabled parking area. Batricar available on pre-booked basis. Braille guide available. Picnics and dogs permitted outside formal garden only. Open-air theatre and concerts mid-June to early July

○ ☕ ✕ WC ⭑ ⚘ 📷 ♿

This 30-acre garden has grown up over several centuries. Richard Brinsley Sheridan, the dramatist who owned the house for over 20 years, lengthened the Long Walk before he died here in 1816. The present house was built a few years later by Cubitt in the Greek classical manner for an owner who made extensive alterations and planted over 20,000 trees. In the Edwardian era the society hostess Mrs Greville laid out the formal walled gardens. Her tomb stands near the house in the centre of a lawn surrounded by yew hedges. The garden was further developed early in the twentieth century and given to the Trust in 1944. The walled rose garden is in four square areas divided by paths and covered by wooden pergolas, and the area is dominated by a water tower covered by an ancient Chinese wisteria. Small gardens of peonies, bearded irises and beds of different kinds of lavender lead to a winter garden over-shadowed by three ironwood trees (*Parrotia persica*), a long herbaceous border and a sunken garden. The fragrant evergreen *Clematis armandii*, flowering in April, grows on the wall of the house. A detailed garden guide is available. Stunning walks through the landscape of the North Downs have been constructed on the estate, one built with a hard surface for wheelchair-users with strong pushers to enjoy.

Ramster 33

Chiddingfold, Godalming GU8 4SN. Tel: (01428) 654167

Mr and Mrs P. Gunn • NE of Haslemere, 1½ m S of Chiddingfold on A283 • Open 22nd April to 5th July, daily, 11am – 5pm, and for parties by appt • Entrance: £3, children free • Other information: Teas daily in May. Possible for wheelchairs in dry weather only ◑ ☕ 🍴 WC ⭑ 🐟 ⚘

Owned by the same family for over 70 years, these are 20 acres of peaceful woodland with views of lakes and hillsides filled with colour and interest. Planting includes Californian redwoods, cedars, firs, camellias, rhododendrons and azaleas, plus the rarer *Styrax obassia*, *Tetracentron sinense* and *Kalopanax pictus*. A camellia garden, magnolia bed and widespread bluebells and daffodils ensure flowers are on view throughout the spring. Especially notable is an avenue of *Acer palmatum* 'Dissectum'.

RHS Garden Wisley ★★ 34

Wisley, Woking GU23 6QB. Tel: (01483) 224234

Royal Horticultural Society • 20m SW of London, 7m NE of Guildford, on A3. Signed from M25 junction 10 south. Trains to Esher, West Byfleet or Woking; taxi service usually available at stations • Garden open to non-members of the RHS, Mon – Fri, 10am – sunset (6pm during British

Summer Time); Sat, Sun, 9am – sunset (6pm during British Summer Time); (Sun for RHS members and a guest only). Glasshouses close 4.45pm (4.15pm Nov to Feb) • *Entrance: by membership or £5, children (6-16) £2, under 6 free; companion for wheelchair-bound or blind visitor free (1999 prices)* • *Other information: Disabled and shaded parking* ○ ☕ ✕ 🖶 WC ♿ 🐾 🛍 🌵

Wisley Garden was presented to the R.H.S. in 1903 by Sir Thomas Hanbury, who created the famous La Mortola in Italy. The Society's first major development was the rock garden, which was fashionable at the time and sections of which were reconstructed in the 1980s. The laboratory, built in 1916 in Tudor style, is the hub of the Society's advisory service to members: identifying plants, answering queries on pests and diseases and gardening problems. Talks and demonstrations of gardening techniques are given, informative walks conducted, and a training programme run for students. The combination of learning with pleasure is the essence of Wisley, as 750,000 visitors discover each year as they explore the 240 acres. The Broadwalk, between double mixed borders, each over 120 metres x 5½ metres, leads to a new Country Garden designed by Penelope Hobhouse, to the Rose Gardens and onwards to Battleston Hill and East Battleston, with azaleas, rhododendrons, hydrangeas and lilies. Over the crest of the hill, on the southern slope, is the Mediterranean Garden, planted since the Great Storm of 1987 and, beyond it, the Portsmouth Field. Here the Society, as the leading international trials institution, holds trials of plants, flowers and vegetables, including, every year, delphiniums, sweet peas and dahlias. To the east is the Winter Garden. To the west, the 32-acre Jubilee Arboretum encircles the Fruit Field, where growing trees can be compared. In 1980 displays of hedging and ground cover were planted between the Arboretum and the Glasshouses to compare rates of growth. The Temperate House, the central section of the main glasshouse, has been completely redesigned: at one end is a curved area for subjects preferring arid conditions; at the other end a water feature with plants enjoying moisture, and in the centre a circular seasonal display area. The Orchid House is naturalistic, with a stream and bridge. Nearby the popular model gardens offer ideas for different types of garden; others display herbs, fruit and vegetables – 1000 varieties of top, bush and soft fruit are grown. The peaceful pinetum, the riverside walk and new heather garden in Howard's Field lie beyond the restaurant. The Canal and Loggia in front of the Laboratory were designed by the late Sir Geoffrey Jellicoe. The area beside it has recently been redeveloped as part of a continuing programme of improvements. The latest is a new Garden of the Senses with a major collection of bonsai, on the site of the former Garden for the Disabled so it is easily accessible for wheelchairs. A Reading Room, for RHS Members and visitors, is now open and is situated near the restaurant with direct access from the garden. The Royal Horticultural Society Garden Wisley is acclaimed by gardeners throughout the world, but you do not have to be a keen gardener to appreciate its virtues. Whatever the season, the garden is a place that people return to time and time again.

The Savill Garden ★★ 35

Wick Lane, Englefield Green TW20 0UU. Tel: (01753) 847518

Administered by the Crown Estate Commissioners • 5m S of Windsor. From A30, turn into Wick Road and follow signs, or follow signs from Englefield Green • Open daily: March to Oct, 10am – 6pm; Nov to Feb, 10am – 4pm. Closed 25th, 26th Dec • Entrance: £3–£5 (seasonal), OAPs £2.50–£4.50, accompanied children under 16 free. Parties of 20 or more £3.30 per person. Guided tours available – apply to Keeper of the Gardens ○ ☕ ✕ WC ⅃ ℘ 📇 ♀

A particularly fine woodland garden. Covering some 35 acres, it contains a wide range of rhododendrons, camellias, magnolias, hydrangeas and a great variety of other trees and shrubs producing a wealth of colour throughout the seasons, especially in spring and summer with splendid meconopsis and primulas in June. A wonderful collection of hostas and ferns flourishes in the shadier areas. Daffodils in impressive drifts dominate in the spring while lilies are the highlight of high summer, and the tweedy autumn colours are almost as satisfying in their mellowness as the jauntier spring hues. A more formal area is devoted to modern roses, herbaceous borders, a range of alpines and an interesting and attractive dry garden. An imposing temperate house was opened in 1995; on fine days the whole of one of its walls can be raised so that the garden continues into the house. Tender subjects – the weeping Kashmir cypress, tree ferns, mimosas, eucryphias and delicate shrubs – are arranged in tiered beds and underplanted with exotics. Metal obelisks support non-hardy climbers; *Lapageria rosea* is on the main wall. The minimum temperature maintained in this $36\frac{1}{2}$ x 18-metre glasshouse is only 2°C (38°F), easily achieved in a conservatory. Windsor Castle and Frogmore (see entries in Berkshire) are nearby.

Street House 36

The Street, Thursley, Godalming GU8 6QE. Tel: (01252) 703216

Mr and Mrs B.M. Francis • 6m SW of Godalming, just W of A3 between Milford and Hindhead, near road junction in Thursley • Open several times April to July for charity (telephone for details). Private parties welcome by appt • Entrance: £2, children 50p • Other information: Parking on recreation ground, behind house from A3 ● ☕ WC ⅃ ⏷ ℘ ♀

Sir Edwin Lutyens spent his early years at this listed Regency house, and it was said that he first met Gertrude Jekyll here. There are three separate gardens around the house. A walled garden is full of interesting plants, trees and shrubs, including an immense false acacia (*Robinia pseudoacacia*), a Japanese snowball tree (*Viburnum plicatum* 'Sterile') and *Rubus* 'Benenden'. The main lawn is surrounded by shrubs with a curving backdrop of fine limes, while the lower lawn is framed by dazzling rhododendrons and azaleas and has splendid views. There is an unusual astrological feature constructed with Bargate stone unearthed from the garden and local ironstone.

Sutton Place ★★ 37

Guildford GU4 7QV. Tel: (01483) 504455

Sutton Place Foundation • 3m N of Guildford off A3 (directions will be given when appt is made) • Open by appt for pre-booked parties ◐ 🍽 WC ♿

Henry VIII gave Sutton Place to Sir Richard Weston in the early sixteenth century and it remained in the family until this century. Paul Getty lived here in the 1960s and '70s; in 1980 Stanley Seeger, the oil magnate, arrived and commissioned the late Sir Geoffrey Jellicoe to design a new garden on a grand scale; in 1986 Sutton Place was sold again and the gardens closed. Now the new owner, Sutton Place Foundation, has reopened the mansion and the gardens. The restoration and development of Jellicoe's series of gardens have been successfully achieved and some areas replanned. There is a new rose garden in soft colours with a central arbour, the beds divided like a cake and edged with box. The walls are clothed in climbers and the borders punctuated by conical yews. A long rose arch separates it from a *potager*. Beyond the wall a Jellicoe path with false perspective passes huge decorative urns bought from Mentmore. Thoughtfully surrounded by yew hedges is Ben Nicolson's *White Wall* sculpture. A new Ellipse garden is approached by curving paths through a shrubbery planned to give scent throughout the year; in the centre is a pool with a funereal fountain bordered by an ellipse of pleached hornbeams. As well as a camellia garden and an 18-acre woodland garden going down to the River Wey, there is an orchard of different varieties of apples, pears and plums, underplanted with daffodils. Across the south front of the house is a vast lawn with mature trees, including a magnificent Atlas cedar, its branches sweeping the ground; a dramatic Victorian fountain has been placed as the focal point of a yew bauble avenue leading from the mansion. Citrus trees grow in boxes in front of the house, with herbaceous borders on either side, one in hot and one in cool colours. High-arching pleached limes lead to Jellicoe's two-storey summerhouse, designed to balance a sixteenth-century one in the old walled garden. His Paradise Garden, now prosaically renamed the East Walled Garden, is a delight of rose arbours around little fountain pools, curving brick paths, tall laburnum arches and mixed planting. A moat with water lilies divides it from the house. Jellicoe's secret moss garden has gone, and now the enormous, central plane tree, with its welcome circular seat, stands on a square lawn with borders planted in purples and blues. The pool garden has a silver and old gold scheme and a Gertrude Jekyll shelter. At the front of the house, beyond a double avenue of American oaks, is a vast lake designed by Jellicoe in the shape of a foetus, part of his allegorical theme.

Titsey Place 38

Titsey Hill, Oxted, Surrey RH8 0SD. Tel: (01273) 407077/407056 (Information line); Fax: (01273) 478995

Trustees of the Titsey Foundation • 9m W of Sevenoaks. Leave M25 at junction 6. From A25 E of Oxted, turn left into Limpsfield (signed Warlingham). At end of High Street fork left into Blue House Lane and first right into Water Lane • House open • Garden open mid-May to Sept, Wed, Sun and Bank Holiday

Mons, 1 – 5pm (last admission 4pm) • Entrance: £2, children £1 (house and garden £4.50, no concession for children) • Other information: Parking through park near walled garden, or by gate for woodland walks with long walk to garden ◐ WC

The recently restored 18-acre gardens and grounds have been in the same family for 400 years. The walls of the one-acre Victorian kitchen garden were damaged by a World War II bomb and now, rebuilt, support espaliered fruit behind deep borders of old-fashioned roses. The garden is divided classically at crossing points, two ironwork gazebos giving height in the centre. Box-edged beds are filled with organically grown vegetables, salad crops and herbs, raised from unusual varieties of seed collected from all over the world. There are strawberries too, and flowers for cutting. Against the south wall greenhouses shelter collections of alstroemerias, pelargoniums and unusual varieties of tomatoes and peaches. The central glasshouse displays exotic and more familiar plants in pots, and from here the central path leads out into the gardens. An unusual knot border stretches across the front of the house, and below it herbaceous borders curve round a fountain. An ancient yew guards old gravestones. Two modern rose gardens are attractively planned, but the colour schemes are unappealing. Magnificent mature trees dominate the lawns, which lead down to two lakes divided by a bridge and a cascade. The larger lake has an island, the smaller a fountain. Two woodland walks are open, free, all the year.

Vale End   39

Albury, Guildford GU5 9BE. Tel: (01483) 202594

Mr and Mrs J. Foulsham • 4½ m SE of Guildford. From Albury take A248 W for ¼ m • Open 18th June, 10am – 5pm, 21st June, 6-9pm, 30th July, 10am – 5pm • Entrance: £2, children free ◐ ◑ WC ⬧ ⬦

In an idyllic setting with views of a mill pond backed by woodland, this one-acre walled garden is arranged on different levels. The sloping lawn is bordered by old roses and old favourites as well as less familiar perennials. The terrace in front of the house is a sun trap, the border filled with subjects that thrive in hot, dry conditions. Beyond a yew hedge, a cool area is shaded by a spreading magnolia, and above, edging a walk, stand clipped yew boxes and a catenary of posts and rope swags, festooned with roses, wisteria and vines. An attractive courtyard is hidden behind the house. Up a flight of steps, level with the roof, is a fruit, vegetable and herb garden.

The Valley Gardens (Windsor Great Park) ★★   40

Wick Road, Englefield Green. Tel: (01753) 860222

Administered by the Crown Estate Commissioners • 5m S of Windsor. From A30 turn into Wick Road and follow signs for Savill Garden (1m to W) and drive to car park adjoining Valley Gardens, avoiding a 2m round walk • Open all year, daily, 8am – 7pm or dusk if earlier. Possible closure if weather inclement • Entrance: car and occupants £3 (10p, 20p, 50p and £1 coins only) (1999 price) • *Other information: Refreshments and plants for sale at Savill Garden (see entry)* ○ WC ⬦

One of Britain's most discriminating and experienced garden visitors, the late Arthur Hellyer, suggested that The Valley Gardens are among the best examples of the 'natural' gardening style in England. With hardly any artefacts or attempts to introduce architectural features, they are merely a tract of undulating grassland (on the north side of Virginia Water), divided by several shallow valleys, that has been enriched by the introduction of a fine collection of trees and shrubs. It was started by the royal gardener Sir Eric Savill, when he ran out of room in the Savill Garden, to continue making 'natural' landscapes. One of the valleys is filled with deciduous azaleas. In another, the Punchbowl, evergreen azaleas rise in tiers below a canopy of maples. Notable too are collections of flowering cherries, a heather garden which amply demonstrates their ability to provide colour during all seasons, and one of the world's most extensive collections of hollies. Lovers of formal gardening might be forgiven for suggesting that the Valley Gardens have something of that rather too open, amorphous, scrupulously kept feel found in America. *Virginia Water Lake*, off the A30, adjacent to the junction with the A329, was a grand eighteenth-century ornamental addition to Windsor Great Park by the Duke of Cumberland, who became its ranger in 1746. It had dams, rockwork, a cascade and grotto. There was a fake 'Mandarin yacht', a Chinese pavilion and a Gothick belvedere with a mighty single-arch bridge. Alas, almost all have disappeared, but the woodland and the lovely one-and-a-half-mile lake, full of fish and wildfowl, survive, and there is still a colonnade of pillars and a nine-metre waterfall.

Vann

41

Hambledon, Godalming GU8 4EF. Tel: (01428) 683413

Mr and Mrs M.B. Caroe • *11m S of Guildford, 6m S of Godalming. Take A283 to Wormley, turn left at Hambledon crossroads into Vann Lane and continue for 2m* • *Open for three to four weeks between 23rd April and June (telephone for details) and by prior appt. Parties by arrangement* • *Entrance: £2.75, children 50p* • *Other information: Refreshments for parties by prior arrangement and on some open days only. Toilet facilities at weekends only. Limited access for wheelchairs. Plants for sale at weekends* ◑ 🍽 WC 🐾

The Grade-II-listed house dates from the sixteenth century and the name derives from the word 'fen'. The oldest part of the garden is at the front, divided by paths and planted in cottage-garden style. Clipped yew hedges enclose it and lawns spread around the house. A stone pergola, underplanted with shade lovers, strides out towards an old field pond. The woodland water garden was designed with Gertrude Jekyll who supplied the plants in 1911. It has a winding stream, crossed and recrossed by stone paths and swathed in lush planting. Above the pond a narrow, stone-walled stream is enclosed by a yew walk. A serpentine crinkle-crankle wall supports fruit trees and there are new double borders in the vegetable garden and island beds in orchard.

The Walled Garden   42

**Sunbury Park, Thames Street, Sunbury–on–Thames. Tel: 01784) 451499
(Community Services)**

*Spelthorne Borough Council • In Sunbury-on-Thames via B375 Thames Street.
Entrance through car park • Open all year, daily except 25th Dec, 8am – dusk •
Entrance: free • Other information: Wheelchair available on request* ○ WC &

The original house was built for a courtier of Elizabeth I, and the hearth return
for 1664 shows it, with its 27 hearths, to have been the largest domestic
building in Sunbury. A later house was pulled down in 1946 and the site bought
by Surrey County Council; the local borough council began to develop the
walled garden in 1985. A pergola leads to beds of roses of the Victorian era.
Adding interest are knot gardens of lavender and box, parterres, modern
roses and island beds of plants from all over the world. There are climbers
against the walls and gates which lead through to Sunbury Park. During the
summer, exhibitions of sculpture, paintings, etc. are on view and a band plays
at published times.

The Water Gardens, Kingston upon Thames

(see COOMBE WOOD)

Winkworth Arboretum   43

**Hascombe Road, Godalming GU8 4AD. Tel: (01483) 208477;
Website: www.cornuswweb.co.uk**

*The National Trust • 2m SE of Godalming, E of B2130 • Open all year, daily,
dawn – dusk (but may be closed in bad weather, especially high winds) •
Entrance: £2.50, children (5-16) £1.25, family (2 adults, 2 children and one
other family member) £6.25. Pre-booked guided tours available • Other
information: Coaches must pre-book. Disabled parking. Possible for wheelchairs
but some steps and steep paths* ○ ☕ 🛍 WC ◁▷ 👜 ☗

Winkworth is open 365 days of the year, so is a great place to take the family
for a walk on Christmas Day or any other. The 60 plant families and 150 genera
grown here provide variety and interest throughout the year. In the spring
there are slopes carpeted in bluebells, then azaleas, rhododendrons, cherries,
and in the autumn sorbus, liquidambars, acers and nyssas. The arboretum
contains a National Collection of whitebeams. Hillside setting and two lakes
give pleasing views from almost all of the site. A newly renovated boathouse is
a tranquil resting place with balcony views over the water. Nearby, in
Hambledon, *Oakhurst Cottage*, a small timber-framed cottage restored and
furnished as a simple dwelling in the 1800s, has a delightful cottage garden
with a variety of contemporary plants [open strictly by appointment with
Witley Common Information Centre, Tel: (01428) 683207].

Wisley

(see ROYAL HORTICULTURAL SOCIETY GARDEN)

SUSSEX, EAST

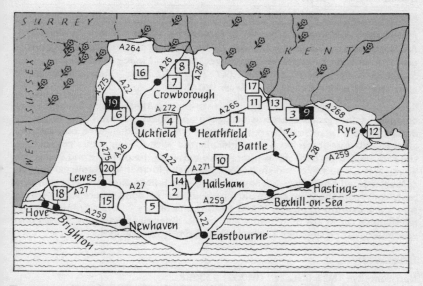

Two-starred gardens are marked on the map with a black square.

Bateman's 1

Burwash, Etchingham TN19 7DS. Tel: (01435) 882302; Fax: (01435) 882811

The National Trust • 10m SE of Tunbridge Wells, 6m SW of A21/A265 junction, ½ m S of Burwash off A265 • House and mill (which grinds flour every Sat in open season) open, 11am – 5pm (last admission 4.30pm) • Garden open April to 1st Nov, Sat – Wed, 11am – 5.30pm • Entrance: £5.10, children £2.55, family £12.75, pre-booked parties of 15 or more £4.30 per person (house, mill and garden) • Other information: Picnics in area provided. Dog creche available ◖ 🍵 ✕ <u>WC</u> ♿ 🛍 ♨

Kipling may be more screened than read these days, but his home from 1902 to 1936 is much visited. The house was built in 1634 and the rooms and study remain as they were during the period when Kipling wrote many of his best-known works. Much of the garden was his doing and contains formal lawns with yew hedges, a rose garden and pond, a wild garden, and, on the right as you descend from the car park, an exceptional herb garden. Not far away in Rottingdean is the *Grange Museum* [open weekdays, 10am – 4pm and Sun, 2 – 4pm], opposite which are two acres of garden, formerly part of the house the Kiplings rented on their return from India, and where he wrote the *Just So Stories*, *Kim* and *Stalky & Co.* These *Kipling Gardens* are open all week.

Bates Green Farm 2

Arlington, Polegate BN26 6SH. Tel: (01323) 482039

Mrs Carolyn McCutchan • 7m NW of Eastbourne, 2½ m SW of A22, 2m S of Michelham Priory (see entry) at Upper Dicker. Approach Arlington passing Old Oak Inn on right, continue for 350 metres, turn right along small lane. Signposted • Open 6th April to 12th Oct, Thurs, 10.30am – 6pm. Parties on other days by appt • Entrance: £2 ● 🏠 WC & ♫

Successful and original groupings of plants express the owner's flair for using colour and foliage to create atmosphere and effect. Overall this might be described as a 'plantsman's artistic garden'. A splendid mature oak isolated after the '87 hurricane has been underplanted with foliage plants rejoicing in the dappled shade. Bark paths interweave between the planting and under the young trees. The warm and sheltered area of the former vegetable garden has colour-themed borders of sun-loving plants and foliage contrast. A serpentine path leads from the front of the old farmhouse to the pond where water-loving plants are skilfully grouped. Views from the pond are of the adjoining woodland where there are delightful walks in the bluebell season (but allow up to one hour); other specified walks extend from ½ m upwards.

Brickwall 3

Northiam, Rye TN31 6NL. Tel: (01797) 253388

The Frewen Educational Trust • 9m N of Hastings, on B2088 Rye road • House open • Garden open April to Oct, Sat, 2 – 5pm by appt only • Entrance: £3, children under 10 free • Other information: Coaches by arrangement during school holidays ● & ♫

This is an interesting example of a Stuart garden, and care has been taken to use the plants chosen by Jane Frewen when she was making and planting it between 1680 and 1720, such as day lilies, bergamots, *Lychnis chalcedonica*, Cheddar pinks and columbines. There are two old mulberries, groups of clipped yew, and a superb pleached beech walk. A striking modern addition is the Chess Garden with green and golden yew chessmen in iron frames, set in squares of white and black limestone chips. This garden is not far from Great Dixter (see entry).

Cabbages and Kings ★ 4

Wilderness Farm, Hadlow Down, Uckfield TN22 4HU. Tel: (01825) 830552; Fax: (01825) 830736

Ryl and Andrew Nowell • 4m E of Uckfield, ½ m S of Hadlow Down off A272 at Wilderness Lane • Open 20th April to Oct, Thurs – Mon and Bank Holiday Mons, 10.30am – 5.30pm, and at other times by appt • Entrance: £3, OAPs £2.50 • Other information: Guided talks and tea for parties by arrangement ① 🍵 WC & ♫ ♀

This imaginative contemporary garden has been developed by designer Ryl Nowell to demonstrate the art of garden design and to help people realise the full potential of their own gardens. Construction started in 1989. The strength and originality of the design were such that within two years the garden began to feature in the media. A stunning transformation has been achieved, from a windswept east-facing slope to a series of small terraced gardens, which embrace and enhance subtle water features, urns, statuary, a swimming pool and trelliswork. The garden opens out to the beautiful landscape of the High Weald beyond. The difficult transition from garden to countryside has been skilfully achieved with soft colours and balanced planting. Nearer to the buildings richer colours in the plants and more exotic foliage effects set off the fine detail of the paving and the warmth of the brickwork. The 13-acre flower meadow has recently been opened up with mown walks, and there is a new permanent undercover exhibition on garden design.

Charleston 5

Firle, Lewes BN8 6LL. Tel: (01323) 811265/811626

The Charleston Trust • 6m E of Lewes on A27 • House open (guided tours Wed – Sat) • Garden open April to Oct, Wed – Sat, 2 – 6pm (July and Aug, 11.30am – 6pm); Sun and Bank Holiday Mons, 2 – 6pm (last admission 5pm) • Entrance: £2, children £1 (farmhouse and garden £5.50, children £3.50)

◗ ☕ WC �& ⚲ ⏍ ⚑

The garden is of special interest because it was created by artists of the Bloomsbury Group. The walled garden has been meticulously restored through painstaking research and from memories of people who visited when Vanessa Bell and Duncan Grant lived at the farmhouse and of those like Angelica Garnett and Quentin Bell who spent their childhood there. It is a delightful example of an artist's garden created during the 1920s by an idiosyncratic group of highly creative people. Useful notes available.

Clinton Lodge ★ 6

Fletching, Uckfield TN22 3ST. Tel: (01825) 722952

Mr and Mrs Hugh Collum • 4m W of Uckfield from A272. Turn N at Piltdown and continue 1½ m to Fletching. Lodge in main street surrounded by yew hedge • Open 11th, 12th, 21st June, 5th July, 2 – 5pm, and for private parties by appt • Entrance: £3. Minimum agreed entrance fee for private parties

◑ ☕ WC ⚲

This Caroline house was enlarged by the Earl of Sheffield for his daughter, who married Henry Clinton, one of the three generals of Waterloo. The eighteenth-century façade is set in a tree-lined lawn, overlooking parkland. The 1987 storm removed the old oaks but these have been replanted in a Repton-style landscape which in future will lead to a temple. The garden itself is of about six acres of clay soil divided into areas by period. The Elizabethan herb garden has well-tended camomile paths and turf seats, and four knot gardens. The Victorian era is represented by a tall white, yellow and blue herbaceous border; the Pre-Raphaelites by an *allée* of white roses, clematis, purple vines and lilies; the twentieth century by the area surrounding the swimming pool encircled by an arcade of apples. There are also various walks of quince, pleached limes and a rose garden of old and English roses complete with dovecot. A *potager* along medieval lines has been developed and recently a yew *allée* has been planted with early statuary and a 'secret' way out. Pillars of ceanothus and roses cover the walls in early summer, and less formal areas of orchard and wild flowers complete a garden of outstanding imagination and charm.

Cobblers 7

Mount Pleasant, Tollwood Road, Jarvis Brook, Crowborough TN6 2ND. Tel: (01892) 655969

Martin and Barbara Furniss • On A26 at Crowborough Cross take B2100 towards Crowborough and Jarvis Brook station. At second crossroads take Tollwood Road • Open 14th, 29th May, 11th, 25th June, 9th, 23rd July, 6th, 20th Aug, 3rd, 10th Sept, 2.30 – 5.30pm • Entrance: £4 (inc. home-made tea), children £1 ◐ ☕ ✕ WC ♿

Martin Furniss, an architect, created the garden from old meadows nearly 25 years ago. He is fascinated by the architectural forms of plants and this is reflected in the inspired planting and the creation of vistas in all directions. Over 2000 varieties and species, ranging from rock plants and alpines on the terrace to magnificent mixed borders and beds and, at the lowest part of the garden, a rhododendron walk. An outstanding feature is the water garden, which is full of surprises and delights, and this, together with the 14 other mixed and herbaceous borders, is bound together visually by ingenious brick paths and stone steps.

Crown House 8

Eridge Green, Tunbridge Wells TN3 9JU. Tel: (01892) 864389

Major L. Cave • 5m NE of Crowborough, 3m SW of Tunbridge Wells off A26. In Eridge take Rotherfield turn S, and house first on right, 300 metres from bus stop • Open for NGS 8th, 9th July and by appt May to Oct; small parties welcome • Entrance: £2, children under 14 free ◐ ☕ WC ♿

This gently sloping one-and-a-half-acre garden contains several different areas. At the front of the house are lily ponds surrounded by rare shrubs; on the east side the principal lawn is dominated by a raised, round bed which has as its centrepiece an umbrella of old-fashioned musk roses, surrounded by *Spiraea japonica* 'Goldflame' and nepetas. On the south side are two more lily ponds, an alpine garden leading to a grass walk, which is flanked on one side by a herbaceous border and on the other by a heather garden. The walk ends in a paved seating area enclosed by a trellis of roses and sweet peas surrounding an ornamental pond with fountain. On the east side is a developing arboretum and a croquet lawn, on the south-west and west sides a formal rose garden, a herb garden and a rose walk leading to a further lawn and shrubbery. Panoramic views of the surrounding countryside.

Great Dixter ★★ 9

**Dixter Road, Northiam, Rye TN31 6PH. Tel: (01797) 252878;
Fax: (01797) 252879**

*Christopher Lloyd and Olivia Lind • 10m N of Hastings, ½ m N of Northiam.
Turn off A28 at Northiam post office • House open • Garden open April to mid-
Oct, daily except Mon (but open Bank Holiday Mons), 2 – 5pm • Entrance: £4,
children £1 (house and garden £5, children £1.50) (1999 prices) • Other
information: Plants for sale at nursery* ◑ 🍵 🈂 WC ⅃ ⚲ ⛪

One of the best-known gardens in Britain belongs to the fifteenth-century
house bought by Nathaniel Lloyd in 1910, and restored by Lutyens. The
Sunken Garden was designed and constructed by Mr Lloyd, and his son
Christopher has continued his family's great gardening tradition, backed up
by a strong team under head gardener Fergus Garrett. Composed of a series of
gardens, including fine topiary, a magnificent mixed Long Border, and an
Exotic Garden (spectacular in autumn) replacing the roses. The latest development is a pebble mosaic of two reclining dachshunds. Throughout the
complex of gardens are pockets of wild flowers. Spring at Great Dixter is
famous for the huge drifts of naturalised bulbs. Truly a plantsman's garden, but
a joy for anyone who enjoys gardening in the finest tradition. Over the past
decade, when many might have thought of him as an established pioneer of the
British garden, Lloyd has made it clear that he regards his life's work as being
to coax new and exciting effects out of plants of all kinds, and the best place to
see what this means is Dixter.

Groombridge Place

(see Kent)

Herstmonceux Castle 10

Hailsham BN27 1RN. Tel: (01323) 833816

*Queen's University (Canada) • 14m N of Eastbourne, off A271 Hailsham –
Bexhill road • Open 15th April to 29th Oct, daily, 10am – 6pm (last admission
5pm) but check before travelling • Entrance: £3, children (6-15) £2, (under 5)
free, concessions £2, family ticket £8.50 (1999 prices)* ◑ 🍵 🈂 WC ⟳ ⚲ ⛪ 🍽

The approach to the impressive fifteenth-century castle is past the science
centre housed in the erstwhile observatory buildings. The path continues
alongside the moat and under gnarled but stately 300-year-old sweet chestnuts. The garden proper is contained within yew hedges (some castellated) and
ancient walls comprising a knot garden, a chequer-board herb garden, rose
gardens and herbaceous borders. A new orchard has been planted with old
varieties of fruit trees with detailed labelling. A woodland area with azalea
walk and lake includes a newly planted folly garden. In all 550 acres of
woodland and gardens, including a nature trail. A visit could be combined
with one to Michelham Priory (see entry).

King John's Lodge   11

Sheepstreet Lane, Etchingham TN19 7AZ. Tel: (01580) 819232

Mr and Mrs R.A. Cunningham • 10m NW of Hastings, 2m SW of A21/A265 junction. In Etchingham, turn into Church Lane leading to Sheepstreet Lane • Open April to Sept, daily, 11am – 6pm, and by appt • Entrance: £2, children free • Other information: Shop selling statuary ◐ ☕ 🍴 WC ♿ ✈ 🧺

This romantic three-acre garden has been developed since the present owners came here more than a decade ago. The 80s' hurricane removed sixty per cent of the mature trees, leaving some rhododendrons, a small number of formal and informal water features and a wild garden incorporating bulbs in spring and roses in summer. Main borders include softly coloured old roses and herbaceous plantings. The secret garden, a favourite area, leads to the attractive garden house, which in turn leads through a meadow to a fine barn covered in roses and honeysuckle. The historic Jacobean house forms a delightful backdrop. More recently the garden has been increased to feature a large pond near the wild garden with a bridge leading to a shaded garden and then through gates to the parkland with its many fine trees.

Lamb House   12

West Street, Rye TN31 7ES. Tel: (01892) 890651; Fax (01892) 890110

The National Trust • In centre of Rye, in West Street, near church • House open • Garden open April to 28th Oct, Wed and Sat, 2 – 6pm (last admission 5.30pm) • Entrance: house and garden £2.50, children £1.25. No reduction for parties • Other information: No parking near house ◑

Although the author Henry James professed to have no horticultural knowledge, with help from Alfred Parsons he left a town garden of charm and interest. An oasis of calm in this crowded town, there are unusual trees and shrubs, vegetable and herb gardens and herbaceous plantings enclosed within a one-acre walled garden.

Merriment Gardens ★   13

Hawkhurst Road, Hurst Green TN19 7RA. Tel: (01580) 860666

Mr and Mrs Mark Buchele and Mr David Weeks • 7m N of Battle, on A229 (formerly A265) between Hawkhurst and Hurst Green • Garden open 1st April to 10th Oct, daily, 10am – 5pm • Entrance: £2.50, children £1 • Other information: Plants for sale in adjoining nursery ◐ ☕ ✕ WC ♿ ✈ ✈ 🧺

The extravagant planting of the swirling beds and waterside areas of this sloping garden reveals the growth potential and indicates the appropriate placing of plants, which can be acquired from the excellent adjoining nursery. Tall, rustling ornamental grasses, dramatic shrubs grown for foliage effect, skilled combinations of form and colour, extensive exotic and indigenous tree planting, make this a garden of ideas and inspiration. A few years ago it was a field. Innovative ideas have included a yellow/orange border at the far end of the garden. In late summer, the golden colours of over-two-metre-tall *Rud-*

beckia laciniata and the equally tall *Helianthus salicifolius* complement the glowing tones of autumnal leaves. In mid- to late-summer also, the new, brightly-painted Monet pergola rises amidst the jewelled colours of clematis, nasturtiums, dahlias and rudbeckias, with the ruby foliage of *Ricinus communis* 'Carmencita' against the uprights. The most recent development is a gravel garden using blue flowers. Colour and form are the keynotes of this exciting new garden.

Michelham Priory ★ 14

Upper Dicker, Hailsham BN27 3QS. Tel: (01323) 844224

Sussex Past • 10m N of Eastbourne off A22 and A27. Signposted • House, museum and gardens open 15th March to July, Wed – Sun and Bank Holiday Mons, 10.30am – 5pm (11am – 4pm in March); Aug, daily, 10.30am – 5.30pm; Sept to 29th Oct, Wed – Sun, 10.30am – 5pm (11am – 4pm in Oct) • Entrance: £4.20, OAPs and students £3.50, children (5-15) £2.20, disabled £2.10, family (2 adults and 2 children) £10.80. Rates available for pre-booked parties of 20 or more (1999 prices) • Other information: Guide dogs and hearing dogs for the deaf only. Watermill, blacksmiths and rope museum ◗ ☕ ✕ 🗏 WC ♿ ℘ 🏪 ♨

Initially, the main horticultural interest of this historic monastic site – more a Tudor manor than a monastery – was the Physic Garden. This contains medicinal plants well labelled as to their original uses. Every visit reveals new areas of interest within the moated site of the old priory. The stewponds have been re-excavated and planted with exotic waterside plants, particularly those with dramatic foliage. The widely sweeping herbaceous border is planted in swathes of bold colour and form and leads into new areas of mixed planting alongside the moat and adjoining the buildings. A fine ornamental *potager* of vegetables, flowers and central pergola lies behind the walls of a yew hedge. Young liquidambars and catalpas are gaining strength and enliven the foreground to the more natural moatside planting. A recent addition has been a cloister garden in the well courtyard, inspired by illustrations of medieval 'Mary' gardens. It includes an arbour, turf seat and raised beds for medicinal plants. Herstmonceux Castle (see entry) is nearby.

Monk's House ★ 15

Rodmell, Lewes BN7 3HF. Tel: (01892) 890651; Fax: (01892) 890110

The National Trust • 4m S of Lewes off old A275, now C7. In Rodmell follow signs to church and continue 400 metres to house • House open • Garden open 1st April to 28th Oct, Wed and Sat, 2 – 5.30pm (last admission 5pm) and pre-booked parties, Thurs • Entrance: £2.50, children £1.25, family £6.25 ◑ WC

The cottage home of Virginia and Leonard Woolf from 1919 until his death in 1969. Leonard Woolf had kept the village self-sufficient in vegetables, as well as showing them, and the original vegetable area is still thriving. There are three ponds, one in dewpond style. An orchard, underplanted with spring and autumn bulbs, contains a comprehensive collection of daffodils. Flint stone walls and yew hedges frame the more formal herbaceous areas, leading to a typical Sussex flint church at the bottom of the garden. The one-and-three-quarter-acre garden is a mixture of chalk and clay, nurturing a wide variety of species. Among the interesting specimen trees are *Salix hastata* 'Wehrhahnii', Chinese lanterns over six metres tall, *Magnolia liliiflora*, walnut, mulberry, and *Catalpa bignonioides* (Indian bean).

Moorlands   16

Friar's Gate, Crowborough TN6 1XF. Tel: (01892) 652474

Dr and Mrs Steven Smith • *2m N of Crowborough on St John's Road to Friar's Gate or turn left off B2188 at Friar's Gate onto road signed 'Narrow road to Crowborough and Horder Centre for Arthritis'* • *Open April to Oct, Weds, 11am – 5pm and 21st May, 16th July, 2 – 6pm* • *Entrance: £2, children free* ● �wc ⬥ ⚲

It is fifty years since work commenced on this fine wetland garden in the Ashdown Forest. When it belonged to the present owner's parents it was surrounded by boggy meadows and there was no garden as such at all. Over the years a fine terrace has been made by the house, its flatness contrasting sharply with the precipitous slope behind and the undulating slopes down to the river and ponds below. In spring, the ponds and waterside are fringed with primulas, irises, lysichitons, rheums and rodgersias, backed by azaleas and rhododendrons and set among more unusual shrubs and trees. Autumn colour is provided by the rich red tones of liquidambar and scarlet oak, set against the russet foliage of a group of larches. A new riverside walk has been constructed to enable visitors to look back at the garden across its own lush valley.

Pashley Manor ★   17

Ticehurst TN5 7HE. Tel: (01580) 200692

Mr and Mrs James A. Sellick • *10m SE of Tunbridge Wells on B2099 between Ticehurst and A21. Signposted* • *Open 8th April to Sept, Tues – Thurs, Sat and Bank Holiday Mons, 11am – 5pm. Coach parties by appt only* • *Entrance: £5, OAPs £4.50* ◑ ▾ ✕ wc ♿ ⚲ ⛟ ♞

Pashley Manor is a Grade-I-listed Tudor timber-framed ironmaster's house of 1550 with a George I rear elevation dated 1720, standing in some eight acres of formal garden. Since 1981 Mr Sellick has undertaken, with advice from Antony du Gard Pasley, a complete renovation of what was largely a Victorian garden. The planting is subtle with emphasis on colour and form, pale colours blending with the carefully chosen foliage. From the terrace and over the magnificent fountain there is a view of the Mad Jack Fuller obelisk at Brightling Beacon several miles away. A series of enclosed gardens is surrounded by some beautiful eighteenth-century walls. Grass paths, some concealing the original Victorian gravel beneath, lead through camellia and rhododendron shrubberies. Natural springs feed a series of ponds falling away from the house and medieval moat. These springs, together with the large fountain, ensure that the sound of falling water is heard over most of the garden. Access to a small island with classical temple is by a decorative iron bridge. A golden garden has been created, and other projects include an extensive planting of tulips to complement the Tulip Festival held in April; an avenue of pleached pear trees underplanted with box so arranged as to give a view through to the existing magnificent hydrangeas; and a garden of old-fashioned roses which will complement the Summer Flower Festival to be held in June. New herbaceous borders, designed by Antony du Gard Pasley, totalling 110 metres long and over four metres wide, divided into four beds, have been planted with strong colours and sculptural plants for late-summer flowering. The new garden, approximately one and a half acres, lies to the south-east of the old walled garden and has wonderful views across to the Weald and the new ha-ha.

Royal Pavilion Gardens 18

Brighton BN1 1EE. Tel: (01273) 290900; Fax: (01273) 292871

Brighton & Hove Council • In central Brighton • Royal Pavilion open June to Sept, daily, 10am – 6pm; Oct to May, daily except 25th, 26th Dec, 10am – 5pm • Garden open all year, daily • Entrance: gardens free (Royal Pavilion £4.50, concessions £3.25, children under 16 £2.75) (1999 prices) ○ ☕ WC ♿

The gardens surrounding the Royal Pavilion have been restored to their original Regency splendour, closely following John Nash's plans of the 1820s; this involved removing the tarmac road which had crept across the gardens. Nash conceived the building and grounds as a unity, and his vision will be fully realised as the plants and shrubs continue to flourish and mature. The beds are of mixed shrubs and herbaceous plants, a combination first applied in the Regency period. Species and varieties have been selected to conform as closely as possible to the original lists of plants supplied to the Prince Regent, later King George IV. The gardens and grounds reflect the great revolution in landscape gardening that began in the 1730s, when straight lines and symmetrical shapes were banished, and in their place appeared curving paths and 'natural' groups of trees and shrubs undulating gracefully over the lawn. As visitors pass through the grounds, the magical Royal Pavilion is disclosed by a succession of varying views through the shrubs and thickets.

Sheffield Park Garden ★★ 19

Uckfield TN22 3QX. Tel: (01825) 790231; Fax: (01825) 791264

The National Trust • 5m NW of Uckfield, midway between East Grinstead and Lewes E of A275. Bus connects with Bluebell Railway which links with Connex South Central services • Garden open Jan to Feb, weekends; 10.30am – 4pm, March to Oct, Tues – Sun and Bank Holiday Mons; 10.30am – 6pm, Nov to Dec, Tues – Sun, 10.30am – 4pm (last admission 1 hr before closing) • Entrance: £4.50, children £2.25, family (2 adults and up to 3 children) £11.25, pre-booked parties £3.80 per person, children £1.9o. No reductions for parties on Sat, Sun or Bank Holiday Mons • Other information: Teas at Oak Hall (not National Trust). Picnics adjacent to car park only. Wheelchairs and four self-drive powered vehicles available ◔ WC ♿

One-hundred-and-twenty-acre landscape garden and arboretum with two lakes installed by 'Capability' Brown for the Earl of Sheffield in 1776. Repton also worked here in 1789 and was responsible for the string of lakes up to the mansion. Later still, the lakes were extended to four and a waterfall and cascades made. Between 1909 and 1934 a collection of trees and shrubs notable for their autumn colour was added, including many specimens of *Nyssa sylvatica*. These and other fine specimen trees, particularly North American varieties, provide good all-year-round interest. Features include good water lilies in the lakes, the Queen's Walk and, in autumn, two borders of the Chinese *Gentiana sino-ornata* of amazing colour. The Trust is continuing to develop new areas, including the stream garden and a National Collection of Ghent azaleas. Stewards are on duty to answer questions.

Wellingham Herb Garden   20

Wellingham Lane, Nr Lewes BN7 5SW. Tel: (01435) 883187

Grant Brickell • 2m N of Lewes off A26 • Open 23rd April to Sept, Sat and Sun, 10.30am – 5.30pm • Entrance: free NEW ◑ & ☞

Enclosed within a walled garden is a delightful and aromatic example of a herb garden created since 1992. Herbs are displayed in four main box-edged beds. The walls are clothed with fruit, including medlars and accompanied by old roses and perfumed shrubs.

2001 GUIDE
The 2001 *Guide* will be published before Christmas 2000. Reports on gardens for consideration are welcome at all times of the year, but particularly by early summer (June) 2000 so that they can be inspected that year.

All descriptions and other information are as accurate as possible at the time of going to press, but circumstances change and, if in doubt, it is wise to telephone before making a long journey.

COUNTY BOUNDARIES
Some gardens have postal addresses in one county and are physically situated in another. If in doubt, the index will direct the reader to the correct page.

DOGS, TOILETS & OTHER FACILITIES ☜ WC
If these are not mentioned in the entry, then facilities are probably not available at the property described. For example, if dogs are not mentioned, owners will probably not permit entry, even on a lead.

SUSSEX, WEST

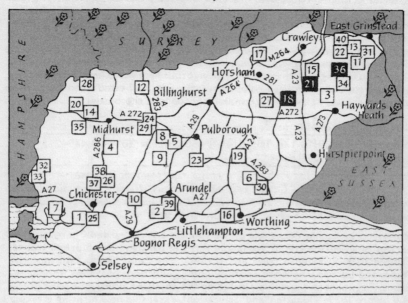

Two-starred gardens are marked on the map with a black square.

Apuldram Roses 1

Dell Quay Road, Chichester PO20 7EF. Tel: (01243) 785769

Di Sawday • 1m SW of Chichester. Turn off A259 (old A27) at sign to Dell Quay, Apuldram • Open all year, daily except 24th Dec to 9th Jan, Mon – Sat, 9am – 5pm, Sun and Bank Holidays, 10.30am – 4.30pm • Entrance: charity collection box • Other information: Plants for sale in nursery ◐ 🍵 ⅏ ⌖ 🛍 ♬

Here are the brightest and latest Hybrid Teas, Floribundas, miniature and patio roses, as well as climbers, several old varieties, modern shrub roses and standards. Every rose sold in the nursery is shown in a delightful enclosed garden with grass paths. Visitors can also wander through the rose field, a sheet of fragrance and colour in July. If visiting in April, it would be worth checking when Rymans open (see entry).

Berri Court 2

Yapton, Arundel BN18 0ED. Tel: (01243) 551663

Mr and Mrs J.C. Turner • 8m E of Chichester, 5m SW of Arundel on B2233, in Yapton between PO and Black Dog pub • Open some days during summer – check local press for details • Entrance: £1.50, children free ◐

A series of sheltered gardens within a one-and-a-half-acre garden of great interest to plant enthusiasts. A mass of daffodils flowers in spring, with the azaleas and rhododendrons. The borders have an impressive display of herbaceous plants, many varieties of shrubs and climbing roses. Around the house are magnificent *Magnolia grandiflora*, *Drimys winteri* and *Clematis rehderiana*. Elsewhere, *Clematis x jackmanii* clambers through trees, and different varieties of eucalyptus are grown throughout the garden. The vigorous *Rosa glauca* (syn. *Rosa rubrifolia*) provides spectacular foliage colour contrast, and well-established *Tropaeolum speciosum* creates splashes of vermilion throughout the borders.

Borde Hill Garden ★   3

Haywards Heath RH16 1XP. Tel: (01444) 450326; Fax: (01444) 440427; E-mail: info@bordehill.co.uk

Borde Hill Gardens Ltd • 1½ m N of Haywards Heath on Balcombe – Haywards Heath road • Garden open all year, daily, 10am – 6pm; guided tours by arrangement • Entrance: £4.50, children £1.75, family ticket £11, family season ticket £27.50 ○ ▆ ✕ 🖻 <u>WC</u> ⅃ ⏦ ⌕ 🖤 ⚱

Described by *Country Life* as one of the country's great gardens, here is a rich variety of all-season colour set in 200 acres of parkland and bluebell woods. Planted from 1893 with trees and shrubs from China, Asia, Tasmania, the Andes and Europe, there are award-winning collections of azaleas, rhododendrons, magnolias and camellias, including the popular cultivars raised at Borde Hill before 1939, 'Donation' and 'Salutation'. Extensive new planting is taking place, with rose, herbaceous and water gardens designed by Robin Williams, plus an ongoing 'Garden Renaissance' using a grant from the Heritage Lottery Fund. Attractions include coarse fishing, children's fishing, Pirates adventure playground, extensive woodland walks and lakes with a picnic area.

Casters Brook   4

Cocking, Midhurst GU29 0HJ. Tel: (01730) 813537

Mr and Mrs John Whitehorn • 3m S of Midhurst on A286 to Chichester. Turn sharp E at Cocking PO and garden is 100 metres on right, next to church • Open 25th June, 2nd July, 2 – 6pm. Also by appt • Entrance: £2, children free ◑ ▆ WC ⅃

Extensive ponds with islands, trout, sculptures and a small bridge are memorable features of this imaginative garden under the South Downs. The site slopes from the house down to the millpond and is on a series of levels, separated by beds and banks of lavender, musk and Rugosa roses (both of which do well on chalk), santolina and fragrant philadelphus. There is a riot of roses, including old-fashioned and climbing varieties, and dramatic plantings of iris, ferns and wild flowers round the ponds. Near the house are small secluded areas, including a fig court, a fruit and herb garden and a *potager*. A shady walk between the garden and the churchyard, beside a fence decorated with shells, ends in a secret garden. Dramatic pieces of sculpture – which may change from year to year – and a *trompe-l'oeil* mirror in the front drive add elements of surprise.

Champs Hill 5

Coldwaltham, Pulborough RH20 1LY. Tel: (01798) 831868

Mr and Mrs D. Bowerman • 2m S of Pulborough. From A29 at Coldwaltham turn W towards Fittleworth. Champs Hill is 300 metres on right • Open 12th, 15th, 19th, 22nd, 26th, 29th March, 2nd April, 3rd, 7th, 10th, 17th, 24th May, 6th, 9th, 13th, 16th, 20th Aug, 11am – 4pm (Sun 2 – 6pm). Private parties welcome – please telephone • Entrance: £2.50, children free ◑ ☕ WC &

This fascinating heathland garden, with over 300 varieties of heather grown alongside dwarf conifers and other interesting plants, is complemented by spectacular views of the Arun Valley and South Downs. The heathers are best viewed in March and August, but a walk in May through the 27 acres of natural woodland interplanted with a wealth of rhododendron and azalea species is a real bonus. A new stream has been constructed to flow down the ravine, kept very shallow to make sure that the owners' grandchildren come to no harm.

Chantry Green House 6

Church Street, Steyning BN44 3YB. Tel: (01903) 814824

Mr R.S. Forrow and Mrs J.B. McNeil • 8m N of Worthing, 10m NW of Brighton off A283. From Steyning High Street, opposite White Horse Inn, turn into Church Street. House is 150 metres on left • Open 10th, 11th June, 2 – 5pm • Entrance: £2, children 50p • Other information: Parking in Fletchers Croft car park opposite church ● ☕ ⚲

A sheltered and well-maintained town garden with some interesting features and many uncommon trees within its one acre. In a corner, an old wall fountain is the focus of a shady area planted with ferns and hostas. There is a water garden, a kitchen garden, an American garden and an arboretum with unusual trees, including *Liriodendron tulipifera* 'Aureomarginatum', *Lagerstroemia indica*, the crape myrtle, and *Eriobotrya japonica*, the Japanese loquat. Also of note are the many varieties of cistus.

Chidmere House 7

Chidham Lane, Chidham, Chichester PO18 8TD. Tel: (01243) 572287/573096

Mr T. Baxendale • E of Emsworth, W of Chichester, S off A259. Turn right at southern end of Chidham • Open certain days for charity in spring and summer and by appt, 2 – 6pm • Entrance: £2, children free (1999 prices) ● WC & ⬥

The house is excitingly situated next to Chidmere Pond, so much so that the well-filled greenhouse which borders the mere almost feels like a houseboat. The garden was laid out in 1930-36 by the present owner's father, and is divided into separate compartments by tall hedges of hornbeam and yew. Flowering cherries, sheets of daffodils and bluebells ensure that it is spectacular in the spring. There are other flowering trees – magnolias, *Cornus kousa* var. *chinensis*, *Davidia involucrata* and *Ginkgo biloba* – while the house supports a

Banksia rose and two wisterias. Later, roses, a tulip tree, herbaceous border and *Taxodium distichum* are features. The house (not open) is Tudor in origin.

Coates Manor 8

Fittleworth, Pulborough RH20 1ES. Tel: (01798) 865356

Mrs G.H. Thorp • 3m W of Pulborough, ½ m S of Fittleworth off B2138 • Open 15th Oct, 11am – 5pm, and by appt • Entrance: £1.50, children 20p ● 🍵
WC 🌀

This one-acre garden has trees and shrubs which give long-term pleasure in the form of interesting foliage, berries and autumn colour. There are ferns such as *Polystichum setiferum* 'Divisilobum', grasses such as *Stipa gigantea* like frozen waterfalls, *Phlomis italica* and *P. chrysophylla*, blue and white agapanthus, a golden *Catalpa bignonioides* 'Aurea', a white-trunked *Betula jacquemontii* var. *utilis*, and a *Liquidambar styraciflua* 'Worplesdon' giving autumn colour. A small paved walled garden has *Clerodendrum trichotomum*, clematis, pinks and other scented flowers. The owner, who has lived here for over 35 years, is particularly interested in colour contrasts, light and shade, and goes to considerable lengths to find the best possible species available. Look out for a variegated ivy contrasting well with *Cotinus coggygria* 'Notcutt's Variety' on a wall by the house; a mature copper beech tree stands nearby. The delightful Elizabethan house is partly covered in variegated ivy and euonymus, linking it with the surrounding countryside.

Cooke's House ★ 9

West Burton, Pulborough RH20 1HD. Tel: (01798) 831353

Miss J.B. Courtauld • 5m SW of Pulborough. Turn W off A29 at foot of Bury Hill and continue for ¾ m • Open 26th to 28th March, 2nd to 4th April, 1 – 5pm, and by appt • Entrance: £1.50, children under 14 free ● 🍵 WC

This delightful garden, surrounding an Elizabethan house (not open) with views of wooded downs, has the components of a great garden in miniature, each section perfectly articulated to vistas leading the eye beyond. There is a tiny paved rose garden and herb garden, a meadow filled in spring with cowslips, and an orchard. The yew topiary of cubes, cones and birds about to take flight is overlooked by a stone heraldic lion. Steps lead up to a path between borders of tulips, yielding later to herbaceous plants. Shrubs are underplanted with snake's-head fritillaries, Solomon's seal and bluebells. Notable are the Judas tree, tulip tree and magnolias.

Denmans ★ 10

Fontwell, Arundel BN18 0SU. Tel: (01243) 542808

John Brookes • 5m E of Chichester. Turn S off A27, W of Fontwell racecourse • Open March to Oct, daily, 9am – 5pm • Entrance: £2.80, OAPs £2.50, children over 4 £1.50, parties of 15 or more £2.20 per person if pre-booked (1999 prices) ◑ 🍵 ✕ WC ♿ 🌀 🏛

Described by Penelope Hobhouse as 'a really important garden'. John Brookes moved here in 1980, taking over the areas converted from 1946 by the late Mrs Robinson and her husband, who originally grew commercial crops under cover in the space where unusual frost-tender plants are now grown. Brookes now owns the garden and runs his School of Garden Design from the clock house. The whole site relies for its drama on foliage plants – even in spring, in spite of the early flowering bulbs, one comes away with one's mind full of euphorbias, yuccas, phormiums and mounds of clipped box. The centre of the garden is a 'river' of pebbles and gravel against which the leaves of thistles and bamboo show up dramatically. There are some choice tulips and other spring bulbs, interesting primulas and spring-flowering shrubs, including a *Stachyurus praecox*. The walled garden contains many old roses as well as a herb garden and perennials and is at its finest in late June and July. Outside the house is the South Garden. Very tender species are planted in another gravel area near a circular pond. In late summer a large border of *Romneya coulteri*, the Californian tree poppy, is at its best, while autumn and winter interest are given by the stems of willow and cornus, and by the leaves of *Parrotia persica* and staphylea, the bladder nut.

Duckyls 11

Sharpthorne, East Grinstead RH19 4LP. Tel/Fax: (01342) 811038

Lady Taylor • 4m SW of East Grinstead, 6m E of Crawley. Take B2028 S at Turners Hill and fork left after 1m to W Hoathly. Left at sign to Gravetye Manor (see entry) on right • Open 29th, 30th April, 1st May, 2 – 6pm, and for small parties by appt • Entrance: £3, children £1 ● ● ● WC ◁ ℘

These 14 acres of terraced and hilly garden, with breathtaking views of woods and Weir Wood Reservoir, are established with rhododendrons and azaleas among carpets of bluebells, daffodils, fritillaries. Later come dogwoods, *Kalmia latifolia* and rambling roses. The rose garden, vegetables and the white Rugosa 'Blanche Double de Coubert', is being made into a parterre garden; some beds are underplanted with irises. There are ponds and a bog garden with gunnera and philadelphus. Only a portion of the garden is maintained to the same standard as that around the house, yet the place stays immensely attractive.

Frith Hill 12

Northchapel, Petworth GU28 9JE. Tel: (01428) 707531

Mr and Mrs P. Warne • 8m NE of Midhurst, 7m N of Petworth on A283. In Northchapel turn E into Pipers Lane by Deep Well Inn; after ¾ m turn left into bridleway past Peacocks Farm • Open six times a year for charity (send s.a.e. for further details) and for parties of 10 or more by appt • Entrance: £2.50, children free ● ● WC & ℘

A one-acre garden of variety and charm surrounding a brick-and-tile-hung house and relating effortlessly to the countryside beyond, with surprises in every corner. The first walled garden has a huge herbaceous border to the north and leads to another walled area with an arbour and old-fashioned roses enclosed by clipped box, then proceeds in shade past a quince through a gate to splendid views of the rolling weald. Overlooking the view is a third garden with a paved area and beside the gazebo a shady white garden with massed Rugosa roses ('Blanche Double de Coubert'), water bubbling over a millstone, and a herb garden with alliums, mallows and almost black opium poppies as well as culinary herbs. There are also massive white ramblers, lilies, good hydrangeas and interesting pots everywhere. The millennium project is a pond facing views of the rolling Weald.

Goodwood House and Sculpture Park

(see SCULPTURE AT GOODWOOD)

Gravetye Manor   13

Vowels Lane, East Grinstead RH19 4LJ. Tel: (01342) 810567

Mr P. Herbert • 4m S of East Grinstead between M23 and A22. By M23, take exit 10 onto A264 towards East Grinstead. After 2m, at roundabout, take 3rd exit on B2028. 1m after Turners Hill turn left and follow signs • Open all year to hotel and restaurant guests; perimeter footpath only for public on Tues and Fri • Entrance: free • Other information: Parking in drive in lay-by before gates. Hotel restaurant open to non-residents for lunch and dinner, but reservations essential. Toilet facilities for hotel and restaurant guests only ☻

This historically important garden has been carefully restored in the style pioneered here by William Robinson. The area around the hotel (which can only be visited by guests or visitors having lunch or dinner) can be viewed from a public footpath which passes through wildflower meadows to the north and south. There are several large shrubs and trees – parrotias, rhododendrons and pines – which may be part of the original planting. The path to the west edged with hydrangeas and large camellias leads down through a wooded area to a large lake, continues along the lake and completes the circumnavigation back to the entrance. For those interested in the Robinsonian doctrine, it is well worth giving yourself a treat, either by spending a night at Gravetye or simply going for a meal, though do not plan a visit without asking about prices and availability beforehand. For a complete contrast, not far away is *Birch Farm Nursery*, open all year for the sale of Ingwersen's renowned alpines – 1800 different varieties (formerly part of the original Robinson estate).

Hammerwood House Garden   14

Iping, Midhurst GU29 0PF. Tel: (01730) 813635

The Hon Mrs Lakin • 3m W of Midhurst, 1m N of A272 • Open 7th, 14th May, 2 – 5.30pm • Entrance: £2, children free ☻ ☻ WC ᕫ ᐊᑞ ᛦ

This is a peaceful country garden, formerly part of a Regency vicarage, planted with care and a fine eye for good plants. Although the rhododendrons and azaleas give it its most spectacular flowering season, there are some good camellias, magnolias, cornus and other specimen trees. Across a meadow from the main garden is the woodland walk by a stream. Bluebells and other wild flowers abound.

High Beeches Gardens ★ 15

Handcross RH17 6HQ. Tel: (01444) 400589; (01444) 401543

High Beeches Gardens Conservation Trust • 5m S of Crawley, 1m E of Handcross, S of B2110 • Open 24th March to June, Sept and Oct, daily except Wed, all 1 – 5pm. Event days 24th April, 1st, 29th May, 10.30am – 5pm • Entrance: £4, accompanied children under 14 free. Guided parties of 10 or more by appt any day or time, £5 per person with lunches, etc. by arrangement • Other information: Refreshments and plants for sale on event days ◑ 🍵 🖻 WC 🌿

This is an important woodland and water garden of over 20 acres where the visitor will find a continually renewed collection of rare trees and shrubs. Originally designed by Colonel Loder in 1906, the garden was influenced by the son of the painter John Millais, by Arthur Soames of Sheffield Park and by William Robinson. The collection is well labelled. The woodland, carpeted with bluebells and other wild flowers, extends over a series of valleys, often with ponds and streams. Plenty of benches for enjoying the different woodland pictures. Rhododendrons, amelanchiers and magnolias are splendid in spring, and autumn colour is particularly fine. Plants to look for, amongst a wide collection, include *Cyclamen hederifolium* flowing over the roots of a tall oak tree near Centre Pond, adding to an explosion of autumn colour. *Disanthus cercidifolius*, a late-flowering shrub, its bluish-green round leaves attractive from spring until they colour brilliantly in autumn. *Elaeagnus angustifolia* 'Quicksilver' is another small tree to look out for. National Collection of stewartias.

Highdown 16

Littlehampton Road, Goring–by–Sea BN12 6PE. Tel: (01903) 501054

Worthing Borough Council • 3m W of Worthing, N of A259 • Open April to Sept, Mon – Fri, 10am – 6pm, Sat, Sun and Bank Holidays, 10am – 6pm; Oct to March, Mon – Fri only, 10am – 4.30pm (4pm Dec to Jan) • Entrance: free – donation box • Other information: Refreshments at peak times only. Toilet facilities available to wheelchair users only with key ○ 🍵 ✕ 🖻 WC ♿

Gardeners everywhere, but particularly those who garden on chalk, must be grateful to Worthing Council for their continuing high standard of care for Sir Frederick Stearn's chosen site in 1910 in and around a bare chalk pit donated to Worthing in 1968. The season starts with a mass of hellebores; narcissi and cowslips follow, and then peonies and iris. Brilliant scarlet anemones are naturalised in the grass; later there will be agapanthus, eremurus and autumn crocus. And these are just the flowers. There are also fine specimen trees – davidia, arbutus and cornus – and many shrubs, including roses, ceanothus, kolkwitzia and laburnum, with buddleia and paulownia to follow. Dramatic banks of pittosporum are a striking feature. Highdown is a plantsman's garden – it doesn't have a lot of shape – and unfortunately there are few labels. There is, however, an explanatory display at the entrance.

6 Holbrook Park   17

Old Holbrook, Horsham RH12 5PW. Tel: (01403) 252491

*Mr J. Pollard • 3m N of Horsham, ½ m N of A264 Horsham northern bypass.
From Horsham take A24 towards Dorking. At roundabout where dual
carriageway ends, turn right onto A264 signed Gatwick. Follow dual
carriageway, take second left marked Old Holbrook (formerly Northlands Road) •
Open April to Sept, Thurs, 2 – 5pm • Entrance: £2, children free* ● ☕ ⏧

The house and garden form part of a large country mansion, now divided. The
two and a half acres at No. 6 are a delightful reminder of how the garden must
have been, with informal walks through beds of trees and shrubs, including fine
groups of rhododendrons. The planting near the house is more formal, with
mixed borders and a circular lawn edged with a drystone wall and planted in part
with azaleas. From here, a path leads to a pond and a stone-built pergola,
generously planted with roses and clematis, mostly *viticella*, and thence to a small
bridge. Beyond this is a new herbaceous border. A recently planted collection of
bamboos will eventually make a grove through which a path will be mown. A
shrub border with golden foliage looks particularly effective during the early
months of the year. New steps (to match existing flights) lead up the bank into
what was the formal rose garden. The centre bed has been retained and planted
up for spring and summer. A large herbaceous bed runs along the south side
planted with shrub roses, peonies, campanulas and phlox edged with *Nepeta* x
faassenii. The south wall of the house shelters a fine *Magnolia grandiflora*, a wisteria,
Rosa 'New Dawn' and clematis. The garden is still evolving.

Leonardslee Gardens ★★   18

**Lower Beeding, Horsham RH13 6PP. Tel: (01403) 891212;
Fax: (01403) 891305**

*The Loder family • 4m SW of Handcross and M23 on B2110 (A279)/A281 •
Open April to Oct, daily, 9.30am – 6pm (May, 9.30am – 8pm) • Entrance:
April: £4, May: £6, June to Oct: £4, children £2.50. Season tickets £12 • Other
information: Victorian motor car collection* ◑ ☕ ✗ 🏠 WC ⏧ 🎁 ⚱

The garden was enlarged by Sir Edmund Loder, who raised the famous
Rhododendron 'Loderi' hybrids, with their huge scented flowers. This 240-acre
valley with its seven lakes, its collection of rhododendrons (some are 190 years
old), azaleas, camellias, acers, magnolias, snowdrop tree and other shrubs, and
sweeps of bluebells, combines to form a beautiful landscape in a peaceful
setting. Wallabies (used as mowing machines) have lived semi-wild in parts of
the valley for over 100 years. The immense scale and the mature trees give the
garden a special quality. In the late afternoon and early evening light the
colours of the rhododendrons and azaleas glow and their heady scent fills the
air. The rock garden has ferns and Kurume azaleas in perfect small scale. Nor
should visitors miss the excellent bonsai exhibition, the alpine house with 400
species of alpines including lewisias and other miniatures, the temperate
greenhouse with banana, *Ceanothus thyrsiflorus repens* like a blue umbrella,
and the miniature landscape of the 'Behind the Doll's House' exhibition.

Little Thakeham ★ 19

Merrywood Lane, Storrington RH20 3HE. Tel: (01903) 744416

*Mr and Mrs T. Ratcliffe • 10m SW of Horsham. Take A24 towards Worthing.
2m S of Ashington, at roundabout, return N up A24 for 200 metres. Turn left
into Rock Road for 1m. At staggered crossroads turn right into Merrywood Lane.
House is 300 metres on right. From Storrington, take B2139 to Thakeham. After
1m turn right into Merrywood Lane • Open probably two days in April and two
in June for NGS. Telephone for details • Entrance: £2 (1999 prices)* ● ▆

The superb Edwin Lutyens house is surrounded by an almost equally fine garden,
recently restored. The original owner, Tom Blackburn, was a lover of words who
chose flowers for the beauty of their names, especially tulips, and planned orchards
with trees full of exotic-sounding fruits – it was he, not Lutyens, who planted the
garden. He sold the house, completed in 1904, in 1919. It is now a hotel. Clematis,
roses, romneyas and grey-leaved plants grow against the house walls. The
entrance court is very simple: squares of lawn, low pots overflowing with ivy,
ferns and hostas against the walls. At the side of the building, a double herbaceous
border in soft colours owes a lot to Gertrude Jekyll: peonies, thalictrums,
columbines, geraniums, dicentras and catmints combine to form an archetypal
English border. In front of the house, a paved parterre has a large Arts and Crafts
urn as a centrepiece. A long pergola walk, planted with roses and almost blocked
by two handsome acers at the beginning, leads to the apple orchards which
surround the garden. In spring you look over a sea of blossom. There is a small
water garden: a square pond with a fountain is linked by a rill planted with ferns to
another square, filled in and planted with primulas, ferns and astilbes as a bog
garden. There are also lawns, specimen trees and banks of wild flowers.

Malt House 20

Chithurst, Rogate, Petersfield GU31 5EZ. Tel: (01730) 821433

*Mr and Mrs Graham Ferguson • From A272, 3½ m W of Midhurst, turn N
signed Chithurst. Or leave A3(M) at Liphook and follow old A3 W for 2m, turn
SE to Milland then follow signs to Chithurst for 1½ m • Open probably 7th,
14th, 21st May, 2 – 6pm • Entrance: £2, children 50p • Other information:
Teas probably available* ● ▩ WC ◁▷ ☞

Five-acre garden of flowering shrubs and trees, including fine prunus, rhododendrons and azaleas on steep slopes leading down to the Malt House and its
outbuildings. The pretty cottage is thickly hung with wisteria, one roof
intriguingly smothered with cotoneaster. Interesting underplanting includes
hostas, ferns, and the pink purslane, *Claytonia sibirica*.

Nymans ★★ 21

Handcross, Haywards Heath RH17 6EB. Tel: (01444) 400321/400161/400157;
Fax: (01444) 400253

*The National Trust • 4m S of Crawley. At southern end of Handcross, off A23/
M23 and A279. Signposted • House open as garden March to Oct, 12 noon – 4pm*

• *Garden open March to Oct, Wed – Sun (but open Bank Holiday Mons), 11am – 6pm or dusk if earlier (last admission 5.30pm); Nov to Feb 2000 weekends only, weather permitting (telephone for details)* • *Entrance: house and garden £5, family £12.50, parties of 15 or more £4 per person, joint ticket available for Nymans and Standen (see entry) Wed – Fri only, £7, children £3.50* • *Other information: Coaches must pre-book. Batricar, wheelchairs and braille/audio guide available to borrow, free. Map of wheelchair route available* ◑ 💬 🏚 WC ♿ ♨ 🛍 ♨

An historic collection of trees, shrubs and plants in a beautifully structured setting, full of outstanding and almost theatrical effects: sheets of white narcissi under sorbus trees, a circle of camellias around a lawn with an urn in the centre, a vista down a lime avenue with a 'prospect' at the end and several borders of great splendour. Originally started by Ludwig Messel in 1890, it was continued by his son Leonard, and daughter-in-law Maud, and then by his granddaughter, Anne, Countess of Rosse. Although the garden was given to the Trust in 1954, Lady Rosse continued to live there until her death in 1992. The library, drawing room and walled garden have been preserved and opened to the public. These rooms lead out to the forecourt and a knot garden. The picturesque ruins of the original building (built c. 1928 to resemble a medieval manor house and largely destroyed by fire in 1947) are planted with clipped yew and other topiary. The Messel creations include a pinetum, sunken garden with stone loggia, laurel walk, croquet lawn, heather garden, roses in beds and over arbours, and magnificent herbaceous borders. Some of these areas can be viewed from on high, from the Mound. Bedding is always beautifully done and the whole is exceptionally well maintained. *Magnolia* x *loebneri* 'Leonard Messel' and *Eucryphia* x *nymansensis* were both raised at Nymans. On the opposite side of the road is The Rough, a wild garden. Overall, there are many fine, rare, well-labelled trees and only the very sharp-eyed could spot signs today of the hurricane which cut such a swathe through the South Weald in 1987. The Trust also have in hand some 600 acres of park. This is one of the most outstanding gardens in an area of interesting gardens. A final thought. One of our leading designers calls Nymans 'very crisp and gardenesque', and it may therefore be asked if in the process of making it meet the needs of the Trust it has not lost the romance it once had? If a garden is manicured to such a degree, what happens to the mystery it must have had in Messel's day?

Orchards   22

Off Wallage Lane, Rowfant, Crawley RH10 4NJ. Tel: (01342) 718280

Penelope S. Hellyer • *4m E of Crawley. From Turners Hill crossroads, turn N on B2028 for 1½ m, left into Wallage Lane and in ¼ m right immediately after railway bridge, up farm track* • *Open 1st March to 25th Oct, Wed – Sat, 12 noon – 4pm; Mon and Tues by prior appt only* • *Entrance: £2, accompanied children free* ◑ 💬 WC ♨

The late Arthur Hellyer acquired this plot of south-facing land in 1934. Working on the site at weekends only, he and his wife camped out in a small wooden hut while building their house and, initially, developing a market garden. Full use has been made of the sloping terrain. Viewed from the house, an open area with magnificent conifers on either side leads down to a small pond with lush marginal plantings of *Gunnera manicata*. Mainly a woodland garden, *Juniperus recurva* var. *coxii*, liquidambar, *Picea omorika* (Serbian spruce) and *Liriodendron tulipifera*, the tulip tree, are just a few of the striking mature specimen trees to be found here. Penelope, the Hellyer's daughter, now runs the small nursery and is restoring and maintaining the garden with the help of her husband. They have added interesting herbaceous borders, a herb and vegetable garden and an avenue of stunning variegated willows, *Salix integra* 'Hakuro-nishiki'. Beneath an old apple tree is a meadow planted with wild flowers including orchids. Numerous camellias, a bluebell wood, apple orchards, rhododendrons, conifers and a heather border make this a year-round garden.

Parham House and Gardens ★   23

Pulborough RH20 4HS. Tel: (01903) 742021/744888;
Fax: (01903) 746557/744888 (Information line);
E-mail: Parham@dial.pipers.com; Web: htlp.//www.parhaminsussex.co.uk

4m SE of Pulborough on A283, equidistant from A24 and A29 • House open as garden but 2 – 6pm (last admission 5pm) • Garden open April to Oct, Wed, Thurs, Sun and Bank Holiday Mons, 12 noon – 6pm (last admission 5pm); also 15th, 16th July for Garden Weekend. Private parties and guided tours on other days • Entrance: £3, children 50p, season ticket £17.50 (house and garden £5, OAPs £4, children £1, family £10, season ticket £27.50). Pre-booked parties per person: unguided of 20 or more £4; guided of 30 or more £5.50 (1999 prices) • Other information: Advance notice required for wheelchairs ◑ ☕ ▣ WC ♿ ⚲ ♿ ⚕

Set in the heart of a medieval deer park on the slopes of the South Downs, the gardens of this Elizabethan house are approached through Fountain Court. A broad gravelled path leads down a gentle slope through a wrought-iron gate guarded by a pair of Istrian stone lions to a walled garden of about four acres, which retains the original quadrant layout divided by broad walks and includes an orchard and teak walk-through greenhouse. In 1982 the walled garden was redesigned, retaining its character and atmosphere; the borders were replanted to give interest for many months, with shrubs as well as herbaceous plants. Recent additions are a potager, a rose garden and a green border, planted along the outer west wall. In one corner is an enchanting miniature house, a delight for both children and adults. The pleasure grounds of about seven acres provide lawns and walks under stately trees to the lake, with views over the cricket ground to the South Downs. Veronica's brick and turf maze is a feature here. This is a garden for all seasons, and in spring it is dominated by the splendid 'sacred' grove of 'Mount Fuji' white-flowering cherry, over 50 years old.

Petworth House ★   24

Petworth GU28 0AE. Tel: (01798) 342207

The National Trust • 6½ m E of Midhurst on A272 in Petworth • House open as Pleasure Ground from April, 1 – 5.30pm (last admission 4.30pm) • Pleasure

*Ground open 18th, 19th, 25th, 26th March, 12 noon – 4pm, April to 1 Nov,
daily except Thurs and Fri (but open 21st April), 12 noon – 6pm. July, Aug
and Bank Holiday Mondays Pleasure Ground opens 11am. Deer park open all
year, daily (except 25th to 27th June), 8am – dusk • Entrance: £6, children £3,
family £15. Pre-booked parties of 15 or more £5.50 per person (house and
grounds). Deer park free, pleasure ground £1.50 • Other information: Parking ½
m N of Petworth on A283. Disabled visitors by arrangement with Administration
Office, special parking available. Refreshments on days house open only •
Pleasure Ground:* ◑ ⬛ ✕ 🍽 WC ♿ 🎂 ⬤ *Deer park:* ○ ⬥

Petworth is a stately palace, with one of the finest late-seventeenth-century
interiors in England. It sits in a magnificent park. The deer park grew from a small
enclosure for fruit and vegetables in the sixteenth century to its present size of
705 acres over centuries, and is enclosed by an impressive five-mile-long stone
wall. George London worked here, as did 'Capability' Brown. The latter toiled
from 1751-63 for the 2nd Lord Egremont, modifying the contours of the ground,
planting cedars and many other trees and constructing the serpentine lake in
front of the house. It was one of Brown's earliest designs, planned while he was
still at Stowe. Turner painted fine views of the park (as well as the interior of the
house) and it is interesting to see these and have them in one's mind when
strolling around the park, as he must have done many times while staying at
Petworth. This is not a garden for the botanist, but it is a splendid experience, all
year round, for any lover of man's improvements over nature, and individual
trees and shrubs, including Japanese maples and rhododendrons, deserve close
study. It is interesting to contemplate that at the turn of the century Petworth
had over two dozen gardeners (they were always counted in dozens). Far fewer
men have now planted 10,000 trees in a 10-acre area, thanks to the development
of the diesel engine and the American tree spade. Opposite Petworth, in North
Street, is Somerset Lodge (see entry).

Rymans 25

Apuldram, Dell Quay, Chichester PO20 7EE. Tel: (01243) 783147

*Mrs Suzanna Gayford • 1m SW of Chichester. Turn off A259 (old A27) at sign
to Dell Quay, Apuldram, garden on left • Open two days in April, May, Sept 12
noon – 3pm for NGS, and by appt • Entrance: £2, children 50p* ⬤ 🍽 WC ♿
⬥

Previously owned by Lady Anne Phillimore, a member of the Dorrien-Smith
family of the famous Tresco Abbey Gardens, Isles of Scilly (see entry in
Cornwall), the garden holds a number of plants with Tresco connections.
Surrounding a fifteenth-century house with mellow Ventnor stone exterior,
the garden is being developed by its new owner. A walled garden filled with
flowering shrubs and roses, including *Rosa chinensis* 'Mutabilis', leads to a
modern architectural water feature. Seen from within the walled garden
an avenue of black poplars, *Populus nigra*, stretches beyond a magnificent
wrought-iron gate to nearby twelfth-century Apuldram church. Planted with
massed daffodils, the avenue is a picture in springtime. Apuldram Roses (see
entry) is nearby.

Sculpture at Goodwood ★ 26

Goodwood, Chichester PO18 0QP. Tel: (01243) 538449;
Fax: (01243) 581853; Web: www.sculpture-org.uk

*Mr and Mrs Wilfred Cass • 7m N of Chichester, 3m S of East Dean, between A286
and A285 (telephone (01243) 77114 for directions) • Open March to Nov, Thurs –
Sat, 10.30am – 4.30pm • Entrance: £10, students and children £6* ◑ **WC** ◕

Twenty acres of woodland on the Goodwood Estate have been shaped to
provide a finer setting for British contemporary sculpture than any indoor
gallery. The quality of sculpture is superb, and the trees act as screens, giving
each piece its own stage. Some are framed by copses, some are the focus of
walks, and at the end of one walk the spire of Chichester cathedral is included
as sculpture. Pieces, mostly for sale, vary, as works are commissioned to
provide about fifteen new works a year. It is well worth following the
directions of the printed guide on a tour of the wood – at present the visitor
begins walking down to a gallery designed by architect Craig Downie through
Glynn Williams' *Gateway of Hands*. Sculptures include Cathy de Monchaux's
boudoirlike *Confessional*, William Furlong's audible *Wall of Sound*, David Mach's
huge swaying *Garden Urn* made from coathangers and William Pye's *Miss Prism*, a
triangular steel pillar veiled with running water which both reflects and
contrasts with the rustic setting. (Pye's garden work won awards at Chelsea
1998.) *Goodwood House* is open on Sundays and Mondays from Easter, and has a
private landscape garden opening from the new wing.

Selehurst 27

Lower Beeding, Horsham RH13 6PR. Tel: (01403) 891501

*Mr and Mrs M. Prideaux • 4½ m SE of Horsham on A281, opposite
Leonardslee (see entry) • Open 14th May, 1 – 5pm • Entrance: £2* ● ▆ ▤
WC ♿ ⚲

The 20-acre woodland garden is now emerging as a romantic landscape garden in
the skilful hands of garden designer and novelist Sue Prideaux. Near the house a
30 metre rose and laburnum tunnel is underplanted with ferns, phormiums,
artichokes and hostas in a striking tapestry of foliage. The Italian border has
purple old-fashioned roses and darkest delphiniums. A box-patterned herb knot
is scented with lilies and moss roses. The walled garden has a huge white wisteria
and herbaceous borders. The woodland shelters a collection of tender scented
rhododendrons and specimen trees including the tallest eucalyptus in the
Kingdom, according to Alan Mitchell. A series of ponds linked by waterfalls
leads ultimately to Pope's Vale, a green theatre with urns and a spring-fed tear-
drop pond. A Gothick folly tower is being decorated with shells.

Shulbrede Priory 28

Linchmere, Haslemere, Surrey GU27 3NQ. Tel: (01428) 653049

*Laura Ponsonby and Ian and Kate Russell • 2m SW of Haslemere off B2131 •
Open 28th, 29th May, 27th, 28th Aug, 2 – 6pm and by appt • Entrance: house*

and garden £2, children £1, parties (maximum 30) £3 per person (guided tour included) ● ☕ 🗄 WC ♿ 🧺

Originally an Augustinian priory, twelfth-century Shulbrede became the home of Lord Ponsonby, a writer and former pacifist MP early this century. He and his wife Dorothea created the garden here which delighted Dorothea's father, Sir Hubert Parry, the composer and Director of the Royal College of Music, who often visited Shulbrede and composed the *Shulbrede Tunes* for piano. Their grand-daughter, Laura Ponsonby, recently retired as Education Officer at Royal Botanic Gardens, Kew, continues to improve the garden. Cottage-style borders are seen and smelt from the house, a sunken garden gives an Italianate air, a waterside walk in the wild garden inspires a sense of mystery, and vast yew hedges enclose a series of individual gardens planted to great effect. A gem on the Sussex/Surrey borders.

Somerset Lodge   29

North Street, Petworth GU28 0DF. Tel: (01798) 343842

Mr and Mrs R. Harris • 6½ m E of Midhurst on A272 in Petworth, 100 metres N of church • Open some days in early June, 12 noon – 6pm and for parties by appt • Entrance: £1.50, children 25p ● ☕ WC ◁

This seventeenth-century house near Petworth House (see entry), has a steeply sloping garden with splendid views towards the North Downs. In just over a decade the present owners, retired architects, have transformed an ancient orchard by creating different elements on several levels. An abundance of clearly marked roses include *Rosa mundi* (*Rosa gallica* 'Versicolor') and *R. moyesii* planted with *Clematis* 'Mrs Cholmondeley'. Add herbaceous borders, a wild garden leading to an impeccable vegetable garden, ponds and a gazebo, to find a peaceful yet exuberant atmosphere. The superb woodwork in the gazebo, trellises and fences, all with fine finials, has been designed and built by Mr Harris.

St Mary's House   30

Bramber BN44 3WE. Tel: (01903) 816205

Peter Thorogood • 8m NE of Worthing off A283 in Bramber, 1m E of Steyning • Open April to Sept, Thurs, Sun and Bank Holiday Mons, 2 – 6pm (last tour 5pm). Parties by appt daily, 9am – 6pm except during public open times • Entrance: formal gardens £2, children 50p; Lost Gardens £1, children 50p (house and formal gardens £4) ◑ ☕ WC ♿ 🧺 ♟

Around the fifteenth-century timber-framed house, the established formal gardens contain topiary in the shapes of animals and birds. There is also a mysterious ivy-clad 'Monks' Walk' and an exceptional example of the living fossil tree, *Ginkgo biloba*. The adjacent 'Lost Gardens', until recently an overgrown and impenetrable jungle of brambles, nettles and saplings, are currently being restored. Originally laid out in the 1890s, the pleasure and kitchen gardens have been 'asleep' for the last 50 years. Clearance has revealed that one of the three Victorian glasshouses has survived intact, as well as a magnificent 40-metre fruit wall, a rare circular orchard, heated pits with their stove-house, and a

Boulton and Paul potting shed with its apple store. Plans for restoration include the re-creation of herbaceous borders, fruit-wall planting, the re-establishment of woodland area as a nature reserve, the creation of a wildflower meadow and small lake for wildfowl, and the conversion of the potting shed into a rural museum. Two magnificent herbaceous borders, designed by students on the Intermediate Diploma Garden Design course at Brinsbury College, Pulborough, should come into their full glory in the millennium. Brinsbury students have also been responsible for re-planting in the Lost Gardens.

Standen 31

East Grinstead RH19 4NE. Tel: (01342) 323029; Fax: (01342) 316424

The National Trust • 2m S of East Grinstead signed from A22 at Felbridge, and also B2110 • House open days as garden March to Nov, 12.30 – 4pm • Garden open 29th March to 5th Nov, Wed – Sun and Bank Holiday Mons, 11.30am – 6pm; 10th Nov to 17th Dec, Fri – Sun, 1 – 4pm • Entrance: £3 (£2 Nov and Dec), children £1.50 (£1 Nov and Dec) (house and garden £5, children £2.50, family £12.50); joint ticket available for Standen and Nymans (see entry) Wed – Fri only, £7, children £3.50 • Other information: Picnics in picnic area only. Dogs in woodland walks only 🕐 ☕ ✕ 🖼 WC ♿ 🔫

The house and estate have close connections with William Morris, and the late-Victorian garden reflects much of the Arts and Crafts period of the latter part of the nineteenth century. It is made up of a succession of small, very English gardens, and the helpful leaflet lists 12 different areas or features including bamboo and rose gardens. Perhaps the most outstanding is the little quarry (with its newly restored bridge), which has survived as a Victorian fernery. There are good views from this hillside garden across the Medway Valley. Two walks are described in the leaflet, but these can be muddy. The house, designed by Philip Webb, will be of interest to architectural pundits.

Stansted Park 32

Rowlands Castle, Hampshire PO9 6DX. Tel: (023) 9241 3090

Penhill Nurseries • 7m W of Chichester, 2m N of Westbourne, off B2149 • Garden centre and walled gardens open May to Oct, daily, 12 noon – 5pm, Sun 10.30am – 4.30 • Entrance: free 🕐 ☕ WC ⚥ ♿

Now a garden centre, the Victorian glasshouses, conservatories and complex of walled gardens, and the circular well head garden in the arboretum have recently been restored. The Garden in Mind in the Lower Walled Garden is unaffected (see entry below).

Stansted Park Victorian Walled Garden (The Garden in Mind) 33

Rowlands Castle, Hampshire PO9 6DX. Tel: (023) 9241 3350

7m W of Chichester, 2m N of Westbourne, off B2149. Signposted. In Lower Walled Garden of Stanstead House • Open July to Sept, Sun only, 2 – 5pm or by appt • Entrance: Walled Garden £2. Surreal Garden £2.01 or a suitably surreal object ◑ ⚘

Ivan Hicks is now widely known for his imaginative work at Groombridge (see entry in Kent) and elsewhere, but his intriguing design in what was a walled kitchen garden, incorporating old iron, wood and stone objects, remains as a shrine for the Sunday afternoon *cognoscenti*. Lilies grow in a room with a telephone, bed, wardrobe and fireplace, a chair is perched in the air, a pair of legs is all that is left of someone who has dived into a dell of ferns. Underworlds and overworlds, a source of inspiration to many and a thought-provoking place.

Stonehurst 34

Ardingly, Haywards Heath RH17 6TN. Tel: (01444) 892488 (Nursery)

Mr and Mrs D.R. Strauss • 7m SE of Crawley, 4m N of Haywards Heath on B2028, 800 metres N of South of England Showground, Ardingly • Open some days in spring. Telephone for details. The Druid's Rocks may be seen by appt • Entrance: £2.50, children £1 • Other information: Plants for sale in nursery on charity open days ● ● **WC** ⬠ ⚘

The Edwardian house is set above a valley, with contemporary brick balustrading, a terrace, gazebos, an observatory and summerhouses. Nearby are herbaceous border and lawns, with views of South Downs, valley and lakes, while the slopes below are informally landscaped with steps, paths, a grotto and a rock garden, and are planted with shrubs, camellias, azaleas and specimen trees. Five lakes constructed before World War I fall into each other by a series of waterfalls, and are enjoyed by the black swans. A woodland walk leads to a weird rock formations nearby, mentioned in the Domesday Book and Cobbett's *Rural Rides;* the woodland itself is a designated Site of Special Scientific Interest because of its lichens, liverworts and ferns. Thirty acres in all.

Trotton Old Rectory 35

Trotton, Petersfield GU31 5EN.

Captain and Mrs John Pilley • 3m W of Midhurst on A272 • Open for parties by appt • Entrance: £2 ●

Set in the pretty Rother valley, the one-and-a-half-acre garden consists of several different areas of varying shapes and sizes, each with its own character. Many are lavishly planted, and they are separated from each other by hedges of yew, holly and beech as well as a trellis screen and walls. To the north of the house are newly planted pleached limes and box, to the south a terrace leads out into a formal rose garden. This is planted with attractive pink and white roses, contrasting with the old roses in the circular rosarium in the garden beyond, which is surrounded by mixed borders where lavender, delphiniums, campanulas and many other plants provide a riot of colour. A restful enclosure dominated by a venerable oak has gunneras, clipped yew and a lawn speckled with bulbs in spring to give variations of texture and shades of green; against the hedge are the graves of family pets. Another garden surrounds the croquet lawn. To the east of the house at a lower level is a large pond surrounded by clumps of handsome *Iris ensata*. Linking the different areas are walks lined with shrubs and hostas, hemerocallis and lilies.

Wakehurst Place Garden ★★ 36

Ardingly, Haywards Heath RH17 6TN. Tel: (01444) 894000; enquiry line (01444) 894066

The National Trust/The Royal Botanic Gardens, Kew • 5m N of Haywards Heath. From London take A(M)23, A272, B2028 or A22, B2110 • Part of house open • Garden open all year, daily, except 25th Dec and 1st Jan: Nov to Jan, 10am – 4pm; Feb and Oct, 10am – 5pm; March, 10am – 6pm; April to Sept, 10am – 7pm (last admission ½ hour before closing). Guided walks available 11.30am and 2.30pm most weekends • Entrance: £5, OAPs, students and UB40 £3.50, children (5-16) £2.50, under 5 free, family ticket (2 adults and up to 4 children) £13 (1999 prices). Season tickets and Friends of Kew membership available • Other information: Plants for sale, in summer only ○ ✕ 🏪 WC ⟨ 🖐 ⚲

Dating from Norman times, the estate was bought by Gerald W.E. Loder (Lord Wakehurst) in 1903. He spent 33 years developing the gardens, a work carried on by Sir Henry Price. The gardens have been managed by the Royal Botanic Gardens, Kew, since 1965. They have a fine collection of hardy plants arranged geographically and display four comprehensive National Collections – betulas, hypericums, nothofagus and skimmias. Unique is the glade planted with species growing at over 3000 metres in the Himalayas. Wakehurst is a place for the botanist, plantsman and garden lover, offering features of year-round interest, particularly the winter garden which bursts into colour about late November after autumn's has gone. Indeed it has been said that this garden, designed primarily 'for winter effect', will 'bewitch the senses' at the turn of the year.

Weald and Downland Open Air Museum 37

Singleton, Chichester PO18 0EU. Tel: (01243) 811363

Weald & Downland Open Air Museum • 5m N of Chichester on A286 • Open March to Oct, daily, 10.30am – 6pm (last admission 5pm); Nov to Feb, Wed, Sat and Sun, 10.30am – 4pm • Entrance: £5.20, children £2.50, under 5 free, family (2 adults and 2 children) £14 (1999 prices) ○ 🍽 ✕ WC ⟨ ⟨⟩ 🖐 ⚲

Set in 50 acres of countryside, the museum (founded 1967) not only has over 40 buildings restored to their original form but also an orchard and garden laid out around the Bayleaf Farmhouse and Hangleton. The replica fifteenth-century garden is required to produce vegetables, herbs and fruit, just as its predecessor would have been. Then there may have been a turf seat and a small vine arbour, served by a well of Wealdstone sandstone, and the area would have fulfilled the gastronomic and medical needs of six adults, their children and servants from beds over four metres long and a metre wide. An educational experience for those keen to experience medieval husbandry. Toll Cottage and the house from Walderton also have gardens and there is a Victorian replica cottage garden beside Whittaker's. Useful books and magazines.

West Dean Gardens ★   38

West Dean, Chichester PO18 0QZ. Tel: (01243) 818210

Edward James Foundation • 5m N of Chichester on A286 • Open March to Oct, daily, 11am – 5pm (last admission 4.30pm) • Entrance: £4, OAPs £3.50, children £2. Pre-booked parties of 20 or more £3.50 per person ◑ ☕ ✕ 🖶 WC ♿ 🐾 👜 ☕

There have been gardens here since 1622; in 1836 a number of rare trees were mentioned by J.L. Loudon, and in 1891 William James bought the property and Harold Peto designed the magnificent 100-metre-long pergola. The advent of Jim Buckland as head gardener has resulted in another burst of activity with the laying out of new paths and much new planting. The restored pergola has roses, clematis and honeysuckle and is underplanted with pulmonarias, ferns, the attractive double primula 'Marie Crousse' and dicentras in quantity, followed by hostas and alchemillas. The south side of the pergola is planted with sun-loving Mediterranean plants. At one end is a stone pavilion, at the other a sunken garden with beds of glowing tulips and wallflowers in spring, a pool and a fountain. There is a new woodland walk, with flowering trees and shrubs. Particularly noteworthy, however, is the recently restored walled garden with a large collection of trained fruit trees, three large herbaceous borders, and a large vegetable and cut-flower garden – the *Victorian Kitchen Garden* come to life. An extensive range of Victorian glasshouses, with displays of flowers, ferns, peaches, figs and melons, together with a circular thatched apple store, makes this whole area especially memorable. It is all immaculately maintained. The house, which is now an Arts and Crafts college, and its gardens are surrounded by parkland and it is possible to follow a marked path of two and a quarter miles to *St Roche's Arboretum*, which has a good collection of rare trees and shrubs. The garden borders the Weald and Downland Museum of traditional rural life (see entry). If you are returning through Chichester, you may like to look in on the *Bishop's Palace* garden, near the cathedral, palace gatehouse and city walls or, if you are interested in garden history, to visit *Fishbourne Roman Palace*, Salthill Road, Fishbourne, where the garden has been replanted to a simple plan as revealed by archaeological research (Tel: (012473) 785859).

The White House   39

Burpham, Arundel BN18 9RH. Tel: (01903) 884833

Elizabeth Woodhouse • ½ m S of Arundel, turn off A27 Arundel – Worthing road and continue for 2m through Wepham to Burpham • Open by appt • Entrance: free ●

The owner, RHS medallist in botanical illustration, has turned her attention to garden design consultancy, and her artist's eye shows to full effect in her own garden of just under an acre. The form and colour of each plant are minutely thought through. Steeply sloping to the foot of the South Downs (a ramblers' paradise), the garden is arranged in three tranches. Two circular layers with wide, colourful beds lead to a third, wild area. This runs down to a pond and folly through masses of self-seeding verbascum, including *Verbascum chaixii* 'Album'. Such transformation of a basically untended garden shows what can be done in ten years or so.

Yew Tree Cottage ★   40

Turner's Hill Road, Crawley Down RH10 4EY. Tel: (01342) 714633

Mrs Hudson • Between Crawley and East Grinstead 1m S of A264 on Down Lane opposite Grange Farm entrance on B2028, turn right and cottage is second of semi-detached on left • House open for small parties 50p extra per person • Garden open by appt for small parties • Entrance: £1.50, children free ◐ ⚘

A plantsman's delight and an encouragement to all with small gardens; it is not surprising that this third-of-an-acre plot has been a prizewinner. Changes to reduce maintenance include the use of gravel and the introduction of drought-resistant plants. A number of grasses has been added, such as the low-growing, feathery *Stipa tenacissima*, which has proved most successful. Developments continue: the front garden is now given over to clipped shrubs, and the vegetable garden, inspired by the Dutch designer Piet Oudolf, to ornamental grasses and natural planting. To the rear of the house a mature quince, underplanted with hellebores, stands over a well, while the borders are bursting with colour and unusual plants. *Geranium cinereum* 'Felicia', *Mertensia asiatica*, pink phlomis, *Baptisia australis*, toad lilies, and *Cheiranthus mutabilis* (*semperflorens*), sweet rocket and *Rhododendron impeditum* are but a few of the interesting plants in this exceptional garden.

HOW TO FIND THE GARDENS

Directions to each garden are included in the entry. This information has been supplied by the owners and garden inspectors. It is aimed to be the best available to those travelling by car, and has been compiled to be used in conjunction with a road atlas.

Some gardens can be approached by public transport, but alas these are few and far between. The unreliability of train and bus services makes it unrewarding to include details, particularly as many garden visits are made on Sundays. However, properties that can be reached by public transport feature in National Trust guides and the NGS Yellow Book, which sometimes give details.

SYMBOLS

[NEW] entries new for 2000; ○ open all year; ◑ open most of year; ◐ open during main season; ● open rarely and/or by appt; ☕ teas/light refreshments; ✕ meals 🧺 picnics permitted; **WC** toilet facilities; <u>WC</u> toilet facilities, inc. disabled ♿ garden partly wheelchair-accessible; ⚐ dogs permitted on lead; ⚘ plants for sale; 🛍 shop; ⚑ events held

WARWICKSHIRE

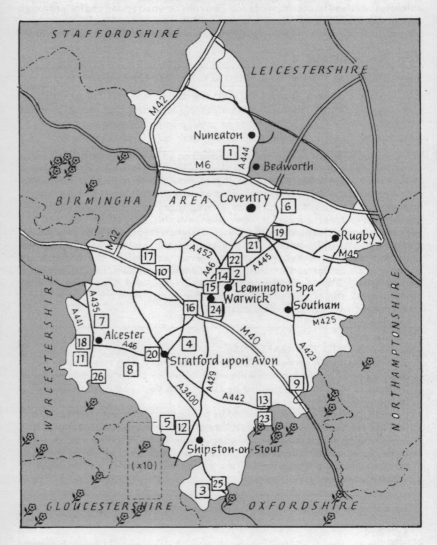

Arbury Hall ★

Arbury, Nuneaton CV10 7PT. Tel: (024) 7638 2804

Viscount and Viscountess Daventry • 10m N of Coventry, 3½ m SW of Nuneaton off B4102 Fillongley/Nuneaton road • House and garden open 23rd,

24th, 30th April, 1st, 28th, 29th May, 27th, 28th Aug, 2 – 6pm (last admission 5pm) • *Entrance: £3, children £2 (hall and gardens £4.50, children £2.50), family £10* ● ▣ ✕ WC ♿ ⟡ 🖐 ⬤

A formal rose garden and climbing roses are features of this delightful, peaceful garden, distinguished also by the lakes with their wildfowl, the parkland, the drive and the bluebell woods. Especially memorable are the pollarded limes, the old walled garden and the beautiful old trees. Bulbs at the start of the season are followed by rhododendrons and azaleas, then roses in June and autumn colour from trees and shrubs. A canal system was installed years ago as a method of transport.

Avon Cottage   2

Ashow, Kenilworth CV8 2LE. Tel: (01926) 512850

Neil Collett • *5m NE of Warwick, 1½ m E of Kenilworth. From A452 Kenilworth – Leamington road turn onto B4115 (signed Ashow and Stoneleigh), after ¼ m turn right into Ashow and right again. Continue to end of Ashow. Cottage is beside church with drive opposite Village Club* • *Open 18th, 19th March, 13th, 14th May, 24th, 25th June, 19th, 20th Aug, 21st, 22nd Oct, 10am – 6pm* • *Entrance: £1.50, children 50p* • *Other information: Refreshments and toilet facilities available in Village Club on Suns* ◑ ✿

A delightful one-and-a-half-acre garden surrounding a picturesque eighteenth-century listed cottage in a lovely riverside setting. The owner, a landscape architect, has worked organically to protect valuable wildlife habitats. Although only in its seventh year, it is extraordinarily well established, with sensitive use of reclaimed materials and varied plantings providing interest all year round. There are riotous mixed herbaceous borders, with vegetables and herbs growing among the flowers, an orchard area with domestic and water fowl, a rhododendron walkway, a collection of old-fashioned shrub roses and masses of daffodils in spring. Don't leave without crossing the footbridge to the twelfth-century church, or you will miss a sensational view of the garden.

Barton House   3

Barton–on–the–Heath, Moreton–in–Marsh, Gloucestershire GL56 0PJ. Tel: (01608) 674303

Mr and Mrs I.H.B. Cathie • *6m S of Shipston-on-Stour off A3400, 4m E of Moreton-in-Marsh off A44* • *Open for NGS 28th May, 2 – 6pm and for parties by appt* • *Entrance: £2.50, children £1* • *Other information: Refreshments in village on open day. Catering for parties, by arrangement, can range from tea on terrace to champagne in Great Hall or a banquet* ● ▣ WC ♿ ✿

This five-acre garden around a manor house by Inigo Jones (not open) has many varied features and surprises. Borders of rhododendrons greet the visitor, and throughout the garden an excellent collection of American, species and hybrid types provides a long flowering period. A secret garden planted for colour and form has magnolias, maples with camellias, geraniums for ground cover. Viewing points have been made to enjoy the surrounding countryside, and there are some fine mature Scots pines, Wellingtonias and Douglas firs. Other features are a catalpa walk, a collection of mountain tree-peonies, a rose garden with beds of individual colours surrounding an oblong lily pool, a Himalayan garden, a Japanese garden, herbaceous and shrub beds, statues, archways and a copy of the portico of St Paul's, Covent Garden. There are many rare specimens plus National Collections of nothofagus and stewartias, and masses of spring bulbs. A paved roundel has been built, surrounded by new planting in the centre of the walled kitchen garden. The ornate cast-iron atrium from the Royal Exchange in Threadneedle Street has been purchased and forms the roof of a new orangery. Also worth seeing is *Whichford Pottery* off the other side of the A3400 [open all year, daily except Sun]. This is not a garden, although the owner, Jim Keeling, has his own charming one adjoining.

Charlecote Park 4

Charlecote, Wellesbourne, Warwick CV35 9ER. Tel: (01789) 470277

The National Trust • 5m E of Stratford-upon-Avon, 1m W of Wellesbourne • House open as garden, 12 noon – 5pm (last admission 4.30pm) • Garden open 21st April to 5th Nov, Fri – Tues, 11am – 6pm. Parties by prior arrangement only. • Entrance: house and garden £5.40, children £2.80, family ticket (2 adults and up to 3 children) £13.50. Party rates for parties of 15 or more and introductory talk available weekdays only by prior arrangement • Other information: Picnics in deer park only. Plants for sale in nursery opposite entrance ◑ ☕ ✕ 🖻 WC ♿ 👜 ☂

Home of Lucy family since the thirteenth century. Shakespeare reputedly poached the deer, descendants of which still populate the park alongside Jacob sheep. The pink brick gatehouse is the only remnant of the early Tudor house left untouched. The park was laid out by 'Capability' Brown, who was directed not to destroy the avenues of elms, but they were later eliminated by Dutch elm disease. The Orangery is now a restaurant, a parterre has been re-instated, the wild garden is interesting and the cascade will attract those who like water features – these include a pond in the small wilderness garden, full of wildlife. The Shakespeare border has plants which feature in the plays, ranging from herbs to quince and medlar, old roses and carnations. A new courtyard garden has been designed in front of the house. Useful leaflet with map.

Compton Scorpion Farm 5

Ilmington, Shipston-on-Stour CV36 4PJ. Tel: (01608) 682552

Mrs T.M. Karlsen • 8m S of Stratford-upon-Avon, 4m NW of Shipston-on-Stour off A3400. Take left fork uphill at Ilmington village hall. After 1½ m turn left down steep narrow lane and house is on left • Open Mon and by appt • Entrance: £2, children free ◒ WC

One of the most stunning views in the county unfolds as you drive along the ridge from Ilmington towards this farmhouse, which in 1989 was surrounded by a mere meadow, sloping steeply towards the house. The owner has worked wonders, from the small walled garden behind the house aiming at Jekyll-inspired single colour schemes, to the rose-encrusted slope up beyond and the rabbit-proof vegetable garden around the old sheep shed. A spring-fed pond has been established in the orchard. In countryside as beautiful as this you could say that she started with an advantage, but her stylish planting must be seen. Combine with a visit to Ilmington Manor (see entry).

Coombe Country Park   6

Brinklow Road, Binley, Coventry CV3 2TL.
Tel: (024) 7645 3720 (Ranger Service)

Just E of Coventry on B4027 • Open all year, daily, 7.30am – dusk • Entrance: free but pay-and-display parking charge all year
○ 🍽 ✕ 🏠 WC Ꮬ ⬦ 🏮 ☕

Nearly 400 acres of beautiful parkland including woodland and lakeside walks, all-weather pathways, wildflower meadows and historic gardens by William Andrews Nesfield and William Miller. There are also the remains of a duck decoy and an arboretum. Facilities include information centre, history video, wildlife discovery centre, bird hide and play areas.

Coughton Court ★   7

Alcester B49 5JA. Tel: (01789) 400777; Fax: (01789) 765544

Mrs C. Throckmorton • 10m NW of Stratford-upon-Avon, 2m N of Alcester on A435 • House open • Garden open 18th, 19th, 25th, 26th March; April to Sept, Wed – Sun and Bank Holiday Mons; 1st to 29th Oct, Sat and Sun only, all 11am – 5.30pm (Oct 5pm). Parties of 15 or more by arrangement • Entrance: £4.60, children £2.30; walled garden £2 (charge for NT members) (house and garden £6.40, family ticket £19.50) • Other information: Dogs in car park, on lead ◑ 🏠 WC Ꮬ ⚘ 🏮 ☕

The garden complements the mid-sixteenth-century house and includes a variety of gardens both formal and informal. The main garden, courtyard and walled garden were designed by Christina Williams. The replanted orchard contains many old local varieties of apples, plums and cherries. The large lawn is bordered by cloistered lime walks, and there is a herb garden. A peaceful stroll beside the River Arrow reveals willows, wild garlic and native trees and shrubs, and the lake has various types of wild duck; in spring there is a bluebell wood and many bulbs to enjoy. A second lake has been drained to form a bog garden, with a collection of ferns, hostas, gunnera and *Dicksonia antarctica*; this area is being planted further. One of the finest features is the large walled garden with hot and cold herbaceous borders dedicated to Professor d'Abreu – Mrs Throckmorton's father – containing a superb display of plants to give colour and interest through the seasons. There is a red and white garden; hornbeam hedges surrounding them are being trained to provide windows. There are masses of beautiful roses and clematis growing over arches and pedestals. Pale colours change to deeper shades of blue and red. Good architectural features. A pond and fountain is surrounded by benches and green and white planting gives a peaceful place for contemplation. Wisteria growing over raised hoops with peonies beneath. The garden is continually being developed. Gunpowder Plot, children's clothes and garden exhibition have been arranged in the stable buildings.

Elm Close 8

Binton Road, Welford–on–Avon CV37 8PT. Tel: (01789) 750793

Mr and Mrs E.W. Dyer • 5m SW of Stratford-upon-Avon on B439. Turn left after 4½ m to Welford • Open for NGS and by appt • Entrance: £1.50, children free ● ● WC & ☺

It is fascinating to see the wide range of plants in a relatively small garden. Clematis are trained over pergolas and climb through trees and shrubs, and there are dwarf conifers, a rock garden, hellebores, a pool, alpine troughs, raised beds and an excellent variety of bulbs. Herbaceous plants and shrubs provide interest and colour throughout the year. All visitors are likely to be stimulated by new ideas.

Farnborough Hall 9

Farnborough, Banbury OX17 1DU. Tel: (01295) 690002

The National Trust/Mr and Mrs Holbech • 5m N of Banbury, ½ m W off A423 or 1½ m E off B4100 • House open • Grounds open April to Sept, Wed and Sat and 30th April, 1st May; terrace walk only open Thurs and Fri, 2 – 6pm (last admission 5.30pm) • Entrance: garden and terrace walk £1.50, children 75p; terrace walk only (Thurs and Fri) £1, children 50p (house and grounds £3, children £1.50) • Other information: Terrace walk steep. Possible for wheelchairs in grounds only. Dogs in grounds only, on lead ◐ WC & ⬦

The grounds were improved in the eighteenth century with the aid of Sanderson Miller, the architect, landscape gardener and dilettante who lived at nearby Radway. The fine S-shaped terrace walk climbs gently along the ridge looking towards Edgehill. The owner, William Holbech, built the walk in order to greet his brother on the adjoining property. *The Oxford Companion* describes it as a majestic concept marking the movement towards the great landscaped parks at the end of the eighteenth century. There are two temples along the walk and an obelisk at the end. The trees are beeches, sycamores and limes. Beyond the cedar tree is part of the site of the former orangery, a rose garden, and a yew walk with steps at the end leading into a field, where there is a seat with a fine view over the river and towards Edgehill. The cascade fountain suppresses the otherwise-invasive hum of the M40. A uniquely interesting site.

Hickecroft 10

Mill Lane, Rowington CV35 7DQ. Tel: (01564) 782384

Mr and Mrs Pitts • 6m NW of Warwick, 15m SE of Birmingham on B4439 between Hockley Heath and Hatton. Turn into Finwood Road (signed

Lowsonford) at Rowington crossroads and first left into Mill Lane • Open 18th June, 2 – 5.30pm • Entrance: £2, children 50p ● ☕ 💭 WC ♿

This well-designed garden uses hedges to divide the different sections, and there are surprises round most of the corners. A National Collection of digitalis is matched by a good range of euphorbias, grasses, geraniums and potentillas. The owners' flair shows itself in their use of colour contrasts, topiary, well-sited pools, and trees planted at strategic points with roses growing up through them. Different materials are used for paths. There is also an orchard with daffodils and a fruit and vegetable garden to enjoy.

The Hiller Garden 11

Dunnington Heath Farm, Alcester B49 5PD. Tel: (01789) 490991

Mr and Mrs R. Beach • 9m W of Stratford-upon-Avon, 3m S of Alcester at former A441/A435 junction, now B4088 • Open all year, daily, 10am – 5pm • Entrance: free • Other information: Plants for sale at adjacent garden centre
○ 💭 ✕ WC ♿ 🐕 🌳 🏛

An established two-acre garden with year-round interest. Large beds of herbaceous perennials with frequent new introductions enable visitors to the garden centre to see mature, well-labelled plants in good colour combinations and so judge their suitability for personal use. The garden also embraces an extensive rose garden which includes more than 200 varieties and has a Victorian rose garden as its centrepiece. The owners' adjacent private garden is also open for pre-booked visits by horticultural societies. Ragley Hall (see entry) is nearby.

Ilmington Manor 12

Ilmington, Shipston-on-Stour CV36 4LA. Tel: (01608) 682230

Mr D. Flower and Lady Flower • 4m NW of Shipston-on-Stour, 8m S of Stratford-upon-Avon • Open by appt and for NGS 9th April, 14th May, 18th June, 9th July, 2 – 6pm. Other gardens in village may be open on one or more of these dates. Parties welcome • Entrance: £2, children free ● 💭 WC ♿ 🐕 🌳

Created from an orchard in 1919, this is now a mature garden full of surprises with a strong formal design; there is also much to interest the plantsperson. To the right of the drive is a paved pond, with thyme of many varieties ornamenting the stones; scented and aromatic climbers surround this area. Next, a walk by the pillar border presents an unusual combination of shrubs and herbaceous plants in colour groups. Then, up stone steps, is the formal rose garden and the long double border planted with old and modern shrub roses and herbaceous plants. The so-called Dutch garden is really an informal cottage garden with a profuse mixture of colour. There is much more – a trough garden, iris and foliage beds, a rock garden and, in the spring, plenty of daffodils and crocus. A charming gazebo was built to celebrate Mr Flower's 80th birthday, and new plants and trees are still being added.

Ivy Lodge ★ 13

Radway CV35 0UE. Tel: (01295) 670371/670580

Mrs M.A. Willis • 14m SE of Stratford-upon-Avon, 7m NW of Banbury via B4100 and B4086 • Open for parties by appt • Entrance: £1.50, OAPs £1, children free ◐ ☕ WC ♿

Radway nestles below Edgehill, and the garden of Ivy Lodge runs back across the former battlefield. Above on the skyline can be seen the mock castle by Sanderson Miller, who lived in the village. Mrs Willis has developed a splendid 'natural' garden with bulbs and blossom in spring, in summer an outstanding number of old roses, many rambling through the trees, and in autumn, wonderful October colours. Nearer the mock-Gothic house are interesting plants and two attractive beds. The village contains many cottages with well-maintained gardens, and in 2000 about a dozen will be open to the public.

Jephson Gardens 14

Leamington Spa CV32 4AD.
Tel: (01926) 450000 (Amenities Department, Warwick District Council)

Warwick District Council • In Leamington Spa, main entrance off Parade • Open all year, daily, 8am (9am Sun and Bank Holidays) to ½ hour after dusk • Entrance: free • Other information: Parking in adjacent Newbold Terrace ○ ☕ WC ♿

This spa town has always made a great effort to provide floral displays in its streets, and this vibrancy can also be enjoyed at its peak in the intensive bedding-out of the principal formal public garden. It is fine enough to be listed by English Heritage and, besides flowers, contains a remarkable collection of trees. Leamington has a string of parks and gardens running along the River Leam right across the town – an almost unique piece of town planning of a century ago. It is possible to walk their length: Mill Gardens, Jephson Gardens, Pump Room Gardens, York Promenade and Victoria Park. There are some fine listed examples of Victorian iron bridges, as well as earlier stone ones. On the outskirts of nearby *Kenilworth* is the ruined castle whose reconstructed Tudor garden is worth a visit in memory of what it once was.

The Master's Garden 15

Lord Leycester Hospital, Warwick CV34 4BH. Tel: (01926) 491422

Board of Governors of Lord Leycester Hospital • In High Street • Open 22nd April to Sept, daily except Mon (but open Bank Holiday Mons), 10am – 4.30pm • Entrance: £1 ◑ ☕ ✕

The restoration work of this garden is remarkable. Old cobbles from the summerhouse have been relaid in the new circular house with its thatched roof of Norfolk reeds. Archways dating from the 1850s have been copied to support roses, clematis and other climbers. A brick pathway through the centre of the garden repeats the feathered pattern. The 150-year old pleached lime avenue remains, and on the walls is a fig tree, along with gooseberries and red currants. An eighteenth-century dovecot has been converted into a gazebo, and a pineapple frame is to be restored. A circular herb garden has a sundial at its centre, and there is a vegetable and fruit area. Through the seasons the borders are filled with 4000 tulips and various perennials. A twelfth-century Norman arch leads into the other half of the garden, which includes a Victorian rock garden, shrubs, roses and perennials. The large 2000-year old vase was intended by the Earl of Warwick for use in the grounds of nearby Warwick Castle (see entry). A peaceful place to walk, and the Hospital is well worth a visit.

The Mill Garden 16

55 Mill Street, Warwick CV34 4HB. Tel: (01296) 492877

Mr A.B. Measures • Mill Street is off A425 to W just before reaching Castle • Open 8th April to 18th Oct, daily (except in emergency), 9am – dusk. Parties by appt • Entrance: £1, children free ◑

A garden of great variety and charm, nestling below the great towers of Warwick Castle (see entry) and beside the River Avon. The toll-stocks in the garden recall the history of days gone by, and one can see the old bridge across which Shakespeare is said to have ridden to London. Good use has been made of roses and clematis climbing through trees and large shrubs. There is something of interest all year, including herbs, alpines and unusual plants.

Packwood House ★ 17

Lapworth, Solihull B94 6AT. Tel: (01564) 782024

The National Trust • 11m SE of central Birmingham, 2m E of Hockley Heath on A3400 • House open, 2 – 6pm • Garden open 1st to 29th Oct, Wed – Sun and Bank Holiday Mons: March, April, Oct, 10am – 4.30pm (closed 21st April), May to Sept, 10am – 5.30pm (last admission ½ hour before closing). Parties of 15 or more by written arrangement • Entrance: £2.20 (house and garden £4.40, children £2.20, family £11) • Other information: Picnic site opposite main gates ◑ 🍽 📷 WC ♿ 🛍 🔦

Hidden away in a rather suburban part of Warwickshire, this garden is notable for its intact layout, dating from the sixteenth and seventeenth centuries when the house was built. Courtyards, terraces, brick gazebos and mount. Even more remarkable is the almost surreal yew garden, unique in design. Tradition claims that it represents the Sermon on the Mount, but in fact the 'Apostles' were planted in the 1850s as a four-square pattern round an orchard. Never mind, the result is now homogeneous. A spiral 'mount' of yew and box is a delightful illusion. Note also the clever use made of brick. G. Baron Ash, who gave the property to the Trust, made a sunken garden in the 1930s and restored earlier design features. He also introduced colourful border planting, and now the gardens are worth seeing at all seasons of the year. In spring drifts of daffodils follow the snowdrops and bluebells carpet the copse, while shrubs flower on red-brick walls. The herbaceous border, the sunken garden, the terrace beds and climbing roses and honeysuckle are a riot of colour in summer, and autumn brings changes in foliage. *Baddesley Clinton* is nearby, visited particularly by those who enjoy the restaurant. It is a medieval moated manor house with walled garden containing herbaceous borders and climbers. In the corners are collections of herbs and the greenhouses contain a vine and collection of pelargoniums. Pleasant walks round the lake, a new Wilderness Walk and Discovery Trail quiz for the young.

Ragley Hall 18

Alcester B49 5NJ. Tel: (01789) 762090

Marquess and Marchioness of Hertford • 8m W of Stratford-upon-Avon, 1m S of Alcester off A435 • House open 13th April to 1st Oct, Thurs, Fri, Sun, 12.30 – 5pm (last entry 4.30pm), Sat 11am – 3.30pm (last entry 3pm) • Park and Garden open July, Aug, daily, 10am – 6pm • Entrance: £5, OAPs £4.50, children £3, family (2 adults, 4 children) £17 (1999 prices) • Other information: Dogs in park only, on lead ◐ 🍵 🏠 WC ♿ 🛍 ⛾

Visitors come to Ragley to enjoy the handsome house and the oasis its park provides in this outpost of Birmingham. The garden is not well cultivated, but the climbers on the pillar by the house, the rose garden and some old trees are worthy of a visit. There is also a beautiful lake surrounded by lawns with picnic tables, an adventure area with good facilities, and woodland walks and country trails. A popular outing.

Ryton Organic Gardens 19

(National Centre for Organic Gardening) Ryton-on-Dunsmore, Coventry CV8 3LG. Tel: (024) 7630 3517

The Henry Doubleday Research Association • 7m NE of Leamington Spa, 5m SE of Coventry. Turn off A45 onto Wolston road • Open all year, daily except Christmas period, 9am – 5.30pm (or dusk if earlier) • Entrance: £3, accompanied children free, parties of 14 or more £2 per person (50p extra for guided tour) • Other information: Guide dogs only ○ 🍵 ✕ 🏠 WC ♿ 🖉 🛍 ⛾

Ryton was set up in 1985 to be a centre of excellence for organic horticulture. Since then the 10 acres have been steadily developed, in a beautifully land-scaped setting, to provide a wide range of inspirational and educational displays of herbs, roses, unusual vegetables, fruit, wildlife gardening and plants for bees. The individual gardens include demonstrations of organic methods of looking after soil, and pest and disease control. There are also gardens for the visually impaired and those with other special needs, and a children's play area with a growing willow structure that invites exploration. At the centre of the garden is a vibrant display of herbaceous perennials in an informal drift of form and colour. The most recent additions are a garden for the enthusiastic cook and a highly acclaimed Paradise Garden created in memory of the late Geoff Hamilton.

The Shakespeare Houses and their Gardens 20

Stratford–upon–Avon. Tel: (01789) 204016; Fax: (01789) 296083

Shakespeare Birthplace Trust • Located in Stratford-upon-Avon and surrounding area • All properties open all year except 23rd to 26th Dec. Opening and closing times vary – times and prices on application • Other information: Parking on site at Anne Hathaway's Cottage and Mary Arden's House, otherwise in town car parks. Restaurant/tea shop at Hall's Croft and café and picnic area at Mary Arden's House ○ WC & ⚘ 📖

Some claim that little is known about Shakespeare and less still about his gardens. The Trust has made them interesting adjuncts to the houses. They include: *The Birthplace Garden*, a small informal collection of over 100 trees, herbs, plants and flowers mentioned by the Bard. *Mary Arden's House*, the front a *mélange* of box, roses and flowers, the rear a stretch of lawn with a wild garden beyond. Country Museum with tools, etc. *Anne Hathaway's Cottage*: a typical English cottage garden dating from the end of the nineteenth century, including a small garden with varieties of Victorian vegetables, and a nearby tree garden with examples of those mentioned in the *Works*. Garden Centre with plants and herbs for sale grown by the Trust's gardeners, and a small display of Victorian and Edwardian garden tools. *Nash's House and New Place*: the house Shakespeare bought for his retirement, demolished in the eighteenth century; the foundations are planted with a garden beyond which, it is suggested, his orchard and kitchen garden lay. Reconstructed Elizabethan knot garden with oak palisade and 'tunnel' or 'pleached bower' of that time. *Hall's Croft*: walled garden with little resemblance to its probable form in the period when it was owned by the Bard's son-in-law. All the above are Trust properties and fee-charged. Beyond the knot garden is a the *Great Garden* with free access. Also free are *Bancroft Gardens* in front of the Theatre and the long stretch owned by the Royal Shakespeare Theatre, along the River Avon between the Swan Theatre and the church where Shakespeare is buried. Charlecote (see entry) is nearby.

Stoneleigh Abbey 21

Kenilworth CV8 2LF. Tel: (01926) 858585; Fax: (01926) 859724;
E-mail: enquiries@stoneleighabbey.org; Web: www.stoneleighabbey.org

Stoneleigh Abbey Ltd (Charitable Trust) • 4m N of Leamington Spa, 5m NE of Warwick, 7m S of Coventry, off M40 junction. Turn off A46 onto B4113, then follow signs to Ashow; entrance on right between two lodges • Opening Easter 2000. Please telephone for details • Other information: Dogs allowed in park only, on lead NEW ◐ ☕ WC & 📖 ☂

Stoneleigh Abbey is to reopen to the public at Easter 2000. The Baroque west wing and its grand state rooms have been magnificently restored. The renaissance of the fourteenth-century gatehouse, the conservatory overlooking the River Avon, and the early nineteenth-century stables and riding school is set for the millennium following extensive restoration since 1997 by the charitable trust in which ownership is vested. Its park and gardens will also be made accessible as one of Humphry Repton's most imaginative and picturesque landscape plans is gradually reinstated. Stoneleigh was the focus in 1809 of one of Repton's finest and largest 'Red Books'. Not all his proposals were executed but the Avon was widened, his stone bridge was built, his inspirational reflective pool was created to mirror in its stillness the south façade, and next to it, as counterpoint, his weir was built to churn noisily the waters of the river. Later hands responsible for shaping the landscape included a pupil of Wyatville — C. S. Smith — who in the 1810s and 1820s provided many of the buildings in the park, and Percy Cane in the twentieth century who restored and replanted the western terrace. Their efforts may not be rewarded with restoration until the twenty-first century is well under way. W.S. Nesfield's strident Italianate garden, created overnight for a visit by Queen Victoria in 1858, may be left as a footnote in gardening history. Instead, Repton's flower beds may make a reappearance as a western parterre. Be sure to visit this great landscape.

University of Warwick   22

Gibbet Hill Road, Coventry CV4 7AL. Tel: (024) 7652 3523

Warwick University • Nearer to Coventry than Warwick, most direct access is off A46 signed 'University of Warwick/Stoneleigh' just S of Coventry • Open all year. Term dates: 10th Jan to 19th March, 26th April to 1st July, 4th Oct to 11th Dec • Entrance: free • Other information: Parking difficult in term-time although there are short-term pay-and-display spaces ○ ☕ ✕ WC ♿

The Oxbridge college gardens are much publicised, so it is interesting to see what a new university makes of its campus in botanical terms. The buildings here have been the subject of early controversy, but the landscaping of the surrounding area has done something to mellow their impact. The continuing work includes the creation of new landscaped sportsfields south of Gibbet Hill Road and the use of trees in landscaping larger areas; interesting in a smaller space is a wisteria-covered pergola in the Social Sciences quadrangle. Formal gardens are being created in connection with the latest student residential development, known as Claycroft residences. Located around the Arts Centre and at sites across the University is a sculpture trail which features work by Richard Deacon, Liliane Ljin, Keir Smith, Bettina Furnée and William Pye, amongst others. Staff are available to give pre-booked tours (Tel: (024) 7652 4732). The university now has five lakes with a wetlands environment and nature reserve. There are several walks through and around the extensive grounds and all are illustrated in an attractive leaflet 'Campus walks'. This and the sculpture trail leaflet are available from reception in the Rootes Social Building and Senate House.

Upton House ★   23

Banbury, Oxfordshire OX15 6HT. Tel: (01295) 670266

The National Trust • 12m SE of Stratford-upon-Avon, 7m NW of Banbury on A422 • House open (timed tickets at peak times) • Garden open early April to Oct, Sat – Wed, 2 – 6pm (last admission 5.30pm). Parties of 15 or more and evening guided tours by arrangement • Entrance: £2.70 (house £5.40, children

£2.70). No reductions for parties • Other information: Coaches by arrangement with property manager. Possible for wheelchairs in parts but very steep in places. Motorised buggy with driver available for access to and from lower garden ◑ ☕ WC ⚲ ♿ ⚑

The house itself, which dates from 1695, contains a fine collection of paintings including three superb Stubbs. More interesting to the garden visitor is that it stands on limestone, over 210 metres above sea level, on Edgehill, near the site of the famous battle. Below a great lawn, the garden descends in a series of long terraces, along one end of which is an impressive flight of stone steps leading down to the large lake. In the centre of the terraced area is a huge sloping vegetable garden, well labelled to indicate varieties. The grand scale of the plan is the main interest, but there are many unusual plants, particularly perennials and bog plants. This is a fine example of terraced gardening, beautifully maintained by the Trust. *The National Herb Centre*, with small display gardens, good herb nursery, research glasshouses, exhibition and herb bistro, is nearby on B4100 at Warmington [open March to Dec, daily from 9.30am. Tel: (01295) 690999].

Warwick Castle ★ 24

Warwick CV34 4QU. Tel: (01926) 406600

The Tussauds Group • In Warwick • Castle open • Grounds open all year, daily except 25th Dec: April to Oct, 10am – 6pm; Nov to March, 10am – 5pm • Entrance: £9.50, OAPs £7.25, children (4-16) £5.80, family ticket (2 adults and 2 children) £27.00 ○ ☕ ✕ 🖼 WC ♿ ⚑ ⚑

The castle stands on the banks of the River Avon, surrounded by 60 acres of beautiful grounds landscaped by 'Capability' Brown. He had previously been in employment as gardener to Lord Cobham at Stowe, but after the latter's death in 1749 he decided to take on commissions of his own. His work at Warwick Castle for the first Earl (Francis Greville) is thought to have been his first independent commission, for which he received much praise, encouragement and publicity. He removed the old formal garden outside the wall and shaped the grounds to frame a view using an array of magnificent trees, notably cedars of Lebanon. In 1753 he began to landscape the courtyard. He removed steps, filled in parts of the yard and made a coachway surrounding the large level lawn. Brown then worked on the creation of the park on the other side of the eleventh-century mound. In 1779, when Brown's remodelling was barely 20 years old, the 2nd Earl embarked on a grandiose scheme of expansion which involved demolishing several streets in the town. In 1786 he constructed the conservatory at the top of Pageant Field, which today houses a replica of the famous Warwick Vase. From here visitors can view the panorama before them – the Peacock Garden and the tree-lined lawn of Pageant Field which meanders down to the gently sloping banks of the River Avon. On the other side of the castle entrance is the Victorian rose garden re-created in 1986 from Robert Marnock's designs of 1868. One interesting way to see the castle walls is to go first to The Mill Garden (see entry), in Mill Street, Warwick, south of the town, then, from the castle grounds, view this same area from the riverside by crossing the bridge near the boathouse. Also in the town is The Master's Garden at Lord Leycester Hospital (see entry). The castle itself is ★★. A splendid family day out.

Wheelwright House 25

Long Compton CV36 5LF. Tel: (01608) 684478

Richard and Suzanne Shacklock • 6m S of Shipston-on-Stour on A3400. At S end of Long Compton take road signed Little Compton and continue 300 metres. House on left • Open 9th July, 2 – 5.30pm for NGS and by appt • Entrance: £2, children free • Other information: Teas on open day only and for parties by arrangement ● WC ᐸ ⬦ ℘

The central feature of this attractive one-acre garden surrounding the early eighteenth-century Cotswold stone house is a natural stream, with little waterfalls, distinctive bridges and banks covered in moisture-loving plants. In seven years the owners have created a garden with a variety of moods, aspects and colour themes, containing many interesting and unusual plants. There is a formal lily pond with surrounding rose pergola, woodland garden, shady areas with ferns, hostas and pulmonarias, a Mediterranean garden in a sheltered sunny spot, a collection of pots, and several mixed borders designed for year-round colour. Seats are strategically placed to enjoy the various vistas. The garden continues to develop: the latest project just completed is a box wheel in the front garden accompanied by a topiary wheelwright, and there are plans for a snowdrop collection. Barton House (see entry) is nearby.

Woodpeckers ★ 26

The Bank, Marlcliff, Bidford–on–Avon B50 4NT. Tel: (01789) 773416

Dr and Mrs A.J. Cox • 7m SW of Stratford-upon-Avon off B4085 between Bidford and Cleeve Prior • Open by appt • Entrance: £2.50, children free • Other information: Wheelchair users must be accompanied ● 🍴 ᐸ ℘

This two-and-a-half-acre garden contains a wide range of design and planting ideas and blends well with the surrounding countryside. It was planned for year-round interest. A small arboretum with betulas, eucalyptus and ilex provides contrast in form and colour. Moving around the garden, there are many surprises – a collection of old roses, with clematis climbing through; a small *potager* with archways covered with apple trees at the corners; colourful and unusual herbs, soft fruits and vegetables. A knot garden has been created from three varieties of box. Other features are an ivy arbour with statue, a fern border, a white and apricot bed, several island beds with splendid ranges of colour and plants, a Mediterranean garden, a cactus and succulent green-house and a round greenhouse for tender plants including mimosas, abutilons, salvias and clematis. The terrace has a range of troughs and alpine plants, and there is a delightful pool and bog garden. A belvedere of framed English oak affords fine views of the garden, including a wildflower area in spring. New features, including topiary, are always being added.

WILTSHIRE

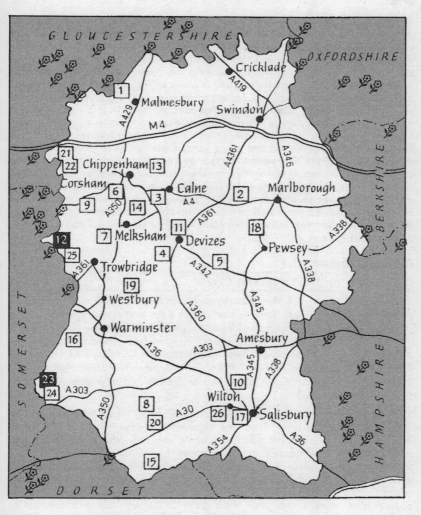

Two-starred gardens are marked on the map with a black square.

The Abbey House Gardens ★   1

Malmesbury SN16 9AS. Tel: (01666) 822212; Fax: (01666) 822782

Barbara and Ian Pollard • In town centre next to Abbey • Open March to Oct, daily, 11am – 6pm, and to parties by appt • Entrance: £4.50, children £2 •

Other information: long-stay free car park close to garden [NEW] ◑ ☕ 🍴 WC ⚲ 🐾 ☺

A remarkable five-acre garden, now acquiring a national and international reputation, has been created in only five years. The owners' passion and enthusiasm are reflected in its immaculate design and exuberant planting schemes. The setting around a late Tudor house beside the Abbey is unique, the effect overwhelming, with thousands of roses, an enormous arcade-encircled herb garden with ingenious oak plank edging and hundreds of herbs, a generously proportioned laburnum tunnel and many other triumphs. Also included are a Celtic cross knot garden echoing the historic surroundings, huge herbaceous borders in riotous colours with many unusual plants, water features, a river and woodland walk (with kingfishers and water voles if you are lucky), rhododendrons, and a bog garden with an exceptional display of meconopsis in spring. The season starts with a dazzling display of thousands of tulips and continues right through to the autumn. As well as clematis and climbing roses, there is a large and interesting variety of fruit trees around the arcade, with sweet peas for added colour, a foliage walk, a maple walk and seats pleasantly situated from which to enjoy it all. No detail has been overlooked, from the excellent yet unobtrusive plant labelling to the tucked-away children's play corner.

Avebury Manor 2

Marlborough SN8 1RF. Tel (01672) 539250

The National Trust • 6m W of Marlborough, 1m N of A4 Bath road on A4361. Manor on N side of High Street, behind church • Parts of manor open as garden, Tues, Wed, Sun and Bank Holiday Mons, 2 – 5.30pm • Garden open April to Oct, daily except Mon and Thurs (but open Bank Holiday Mons), 11am – 5.30pm (last admission 5pm) • Entrance £2.25, children £1 (manor and garden £3, children £1.50) (1999 prices) • Other information: Parking in outer village. Alexander Keiller Museum, refreshments and shop adjacent. Toilet facilities in village ◑ ⚲

The house and gardens were purchased by the Trust in 1991 after a chequered recent history. The fine eighteenth-century walls are in need of repair, and the statuary which originally enhanced the garden has been sold. But the rose garden in the shadow of the church tower is well maintained, herbaceous borders are set neatly behind low box hedging, and there is a splendid lavender walk at the main entrance to the house, which on the south and west is framed by lawns and topiary. There is much conservation work under way, with trees to be replaced and substantial replanting of the herbaceous beds. This will be undertaken by the Trust over the next few years, a project well worth watching. An orchard has been replanted with old apple varieties from Wiltshire. The topiary garden pond is being restored and its box topiary hedges are being cut back to re-define the design of overlapping diamonds, which was inspired by a plaster ceiling in the Manor.

Bowood House and Gardens ★   3

Bowood House, Derry Hill, Calne SN11 0LZ. Tel: (01249) 812102

The Earl and Countess of Shelburne • 8m S of M4 junction 17, 4½ m W of Calne, 5m SE of Chippenham. Off A4 in Derry Hill. Separate rhododendron walks off A342 Chippenham – Devizes road midway between Derry Hill and Sandy Lane • House open. Adventure playground for children 12 and under • Garden open April to Oct, daily, 11am – 6pm or dusk if earlier. Rhododendron walks open daily for 6 weeks in May and June depending on flowering season • Entrance: house and gardens £5.50, OAPs £4.50, children £3.20 (parties £4.60 per person, OAPs £3.90, children £2.60); rhododendron walks £3 (£2 if combined with visit to house and gardens), children free (1999 prices) ◗ ⬤ ✕ ▩ WC ♿ ⌖ 🧺

The house and its pleasure grounds cover over 100 acres and lie in the centre of 'Capability' Brown's enormous park. Other splendours include a tranquil lake, arboretum and pinetum, Doric temple, cascade waterfall and hermit's cave. Thousands of bulbs bloom in spring. The Robert Adam orangery (converted into a gallery) is particularly fine, and in front of it are formal Bath stone terraces with rose beds, standard roses and fastigiate yews. *Fremontodendron californicum* flourishes on the Italianate terrace. The upper terrace was laid out in 1817 and the present fountains were added in 1839. In the twentieth century, when elaborate bedding schemes became too time-consuming, the parterre was planted with hybrid tea roses, thus blurring the edges. Mary Keen advised replacing the grass paths with gravel and compensating for the loss of green by putting box hedges around the beds. New planting has ensured that the flowering season starts almost three months earlier than it used to do. In the nineteenth century it was the aim of every garden to be 'as clean as a drawing room', and Bowood is now in this class once again. The rhododendron walks are situated in a separate 50-acre area, which is only open when the rhododendrons are flowering. Robert Adam's mausoleum (a little gem well worth a visit) is in this area.

Broadleas Garden   4

Broadleas, Devizes SN10 5JQ. Tel: (01380) 722035

Lady Anne Cowdray/Broadleas Garden Charitable Trust • Signed from Devizes town centre or 1m S of Devizes on A360 • Open April to Oct, Sun, Wed, Thurs, 2 – 6pm • Entrance: £3, children under 12 £1. Parties of 10 or more £2.50 • Other information: Coaches must use Devizes town centre approach. Teas on Sun until end of Aug only ◗ ⬤ WC ◁▷ ⌖

This garden was bought just after World War II and started from nothing by Lady Anne Cowdray in a combe below Devizes. Mature and semi-mature magnolias grow on each side of a steep dell. As good as any Cornish garden, it is stuffed with fine things that one would think too tender for these parts. Large specimens of everything (much of it now over 40 years old) – *Paulownia fargesii*, *Parrotia persica*, all manner of magnolias, azaleas, hydrangeas, hostas, lilies and trilliums of rare and notable species – all carefully labelled. There has also been much planting in recent years, including many rhododendrons and camellias. It is a garden of tireless perfectionism, at its most stunning in spring when sheets of bulbs stretch out beneath the flowering trees. Rarely seen in such quantities for instance are the erythroniums or dog-tooth violets. Many of the more unusual plants, both shrubs and perennials, are grown for sale at Broadleas. There is also a woodland walk, a sunken rose garden and a silver border. This is serious plantsmanship and dendrology.

Chiffchaffs

(see Dorset)

Clock House

(see Oxfordshire)

Conock Manor

5

Conock, Devizes SN10 3QQ.

Mr and Mrs Bonar Sykes • 5m SE of Devizes off A342 • Open 21st May, 2 – 6pm • Entrance: £2, children under 12 free • Other information: cream teas available ● & WC ℅

Set between distant views of Marlborough Downs and Salisbury Plain, the Georgian house looks on to the lawns with specimen trees, ha-has and a recently planted arboretum. From a Reptonesque thatched dairy near the house, a long brick wall and mixed shrub border lead to the stable block, in early Gothic-Revival style, with a copper-domed cupola. Beyond, yew and beech hedges and brick walls frame the meticulously kept kitchen garden and 1930s' shrub walk. Beech forms attractive bays and box makes clipped balls. Pleached limes, a magnolia garden including malus, sorbus, prunus and many eucalyptus. Woodland walk. Small new arboretum of unusual trees in kitchen garden.

Corsham Court

6

Corsham SN13 0BZ. Tel: (01249) 701610/701611

James Methuen-Campbell • 4m W of Chippenham on A4 • House open • Garden open Jan to 20th March, Sat and Sun, 2 – 4.30pm; 20th March to Sept, daily except Mon (but open Bank Holiday Mons), 11am – 5.30pm; Oct and Nov, Sat and Sun, 2 – 4.30pm (last admission ½ hour before closing). Closed Dec. Also open by appt for parties of 15 or more • Entrance: £2, OAPs £1.50, children £1, garden season tickets £10 (house and garden, inc. 1 hour guided tour: £4.50, OAPs £3.50, children £2.50, parties £3.50 per person) ● ₤ WC & ◁▷

Approaching from Chippenham, look out for a glimpse of this house on your left, once framed by an avenue of elms now replaced by some lime trees. Inside the house is a fine collection of pictures and furniture. Surrounded by a landscape of 'Capability' Brown's devising finished off by Humphry Repton (the lake and boat-house particularly), it is an example of this kind of gardening at its best. Rare and exotic trees look entirely at home: black walnuts, Californian redwoods, cedars, Wellingtonias, and the most astonishing layered Oriental plane tree, shading beeches, oaks, sycamores and Spanish chestnuts. There are 340 species of trees and 75,000 daffodils in the 20-acre arboretum. The bath-house designed by Brown is a treat and one can get through it into a world of entirely different mood – the Bradford porch leads out into a small enclosed flower garden with catalpa trees. Repton's roses trained over metal arches encircling a round pond are a rare surviving example of the elegance of early nineteenth-century flower gardens. Here the flower borders contain the unusual *Clerodendrum trichotomum* and enormous iron supports for roses and *Clematis* x *jackmanii*. There is a box-edged garden, hornbeam *allée*, urns, arbours and seats.

The Courts 7

Holt, Trowbridge BA14 6RR. Tel: (01225) 782340

The National Trust • 3m SW of Melksham, 3m N of Trowbridge, 2½ m E of Bradford-on-Avon on B3107 • Open April to 2nd Nov, daily except Sat, 1.30 – 5.30pm, and out of season by appt • Entrance: £3.10, children £1.60 • Other information: Parking at village hall ◑ &

Created by Sir George Hastings in 1900-1911, this has been an impressive garden and is still well worth visiting for both ideas and plants, including a wide range of bog and water plants. The eighteenth-century house is set in formal areas of garden which give place to wild, bog and orchard gardens beyond. There are many lawns, much topiary, beguiling nooks and lots of good Edwardian features such as stone walls and paths, hedges, lily ponds and terraces. A garden in the Hidcote mould, it is being substantially restored under the care of the present head gardener. The large terrace has been rebuilt and recently replanted; the lower pond has been restored and will be replanted. There are some superb specimen trees. A large part of the garden is given over to wild flowers, with close-cut pathways winding through. Three miles away is Europe's biggest provider of chalk-tolerant plants, specialising in foxgloves, *The Botanic Nursery*, on A36 towards Bath, just past Atworth.

Fonthill House 8

Tisbury, Salisbury SP3 5SA. Tel: (Estate Office) (01747) 820246

Lord and Lady Margadale • 12m W of Salisbury, E of Hindon on B3089. Entrance is S of Fonthill Bishops, on farm road over bridge and through deer park • Parking • Open one day April, May, June, July for charity, 2 – 6pm – see local press • Entrance: £2, children free ◑ ⚌ WC & ⬦ ℘

The 1970s neo-Georgian house, built on the site of a demolished Detmar Blow masterpiece on the estate, stands at the head of a combe with fine views and is backed by mature beech and oak trees. Throughout this woodland grow camellias and rhododendrons and, in spring, a carpet of bluebells. The front of the house is framed by stone walling and new planting. The charm and isolation of the place add to its magic, particularly in spring when the woodland is a mass of colour. Five acres in all.

Hazelbury Manor 9

Box, Corsham SN13 8LB. Tel: (01225) 812952

5m SW of Chippenham. From Box take A365 towards Melksham, turn left onto B3109, next left, and right immediately into private drive • Open one weekend for NGS and by appt • Entrance: £2.80, OAPs £2, children £1, under 6 free

◐ WC ⅙ ♀

The extensive formal gardens, surrounding a sprawling Elizabethan house, are undergoing restoration based on evidence from old photographs. The rock garden at the front of the house is impressive, although it couldn't be called in keeping with the house and makes as big a twentieth-century statement as the earlier Edwardian garden. The formal garden has a large lawn, with a chess set and other topiary sculpture, banked up on either side by high walks between clipped beeches. In spring the *allées* are all carpeted with bright polyanthus, cowslips and wallflowers. Mammoth herbaceous borders blaze in summer. There is a beautiful arched laburnum walk, and other notable features include a lime walk and, nearer the house, a terraced alpine garden.

Heale Gardens ★ 10

Middle Woodford, Salisbury SP4 6NT. Tel: (01722) 782504

Mr and Mrs Guy Rasch • 4m N of Salisbury between A360 and A345 • Gardens open all year, daily, 10am – 5pm • Entrance: £3, children under 14 free ○ 🍴 🍵 WC ⅙ ♨ 🛒 ♀

This is an idyllic garden with mature yew hedges, much of it designed by Harold Peto. A tributary of the Avon meanders through it, providing the perfect boundary and obvious site for the sealing-wax red Japanese bridge and the thatched tea-house which straddles the water. This was made in 1910 with the help of four Japanese gardeners and extends under the shade of *Magnolia* x *soulangeana* along the boggy banks planted with bog arums, *Rodgersia aesculifolia*, candelabra primulas and irises. There are two terraces immediately beside the house. One is rampant with alchemilla, spurges and irises; the other has two stone lily ponds and two small borders given height by nearly three-metre-high wooden pyramids bearing roses, clematis and honeysuckles. The Long Border contains roses backed by a simple but effective rustic trellis, and also many interesting herbaceous plants. Behind it is a border of musk roses. The walled kitchen garden is possibly the most successful part, achieving a satisfying marriage between practicality and pleasure. It is not a regimented vegetable garden: the formal nature of rows of potatoes etc. are made into a feature, and plots are divided by espaliered fruit trees forming an apple and pear tunnel, and by pergolas and hedges. The wonderful flint-and-brick wall provides protection for many plants including *Cytisus battandieri* and an ancient fig. This is a walled garden where one is encouraged to linger on the seats and in the shaded arbours and enjoy and admire the extraordinary tranquillity of the place. The plant centre is comprehensive and the shop appeals to the discerning. Unique wrought-iron plant supports can be bought here. Look out for the ancient mulberry, the very old *Cercidiphyllum japonicum* (the second tallest known in Europe), and the *Magnolia grandiflora*.

Home Covert ★   11

Roundway, Devizes SN10 2JA. Tel: (01380) 723407

Mr and Mrs John Phillips • 1m N of Devizes. Turn off A361 on edge of built-up area NE of town, signed 'Roundway'. In Roundway turn left towards Rowde. House is ¼ m on left. Signposted • Open 1st May, 6th Aug, 2 – 6pm for charity, and by appt. Guided parties (12-40 persons) welcome • Entrance: £2, children free • Other information: Teas and plants for sale on charity open days only ● ● ● ● ● ●

This garden, developed in the 1960s, has been created by the present owners out of amenity woodlands of the now-demolished Roundway House. In front of the house is a large lawn on a plateau edged with grasses, herbaceous plants and alpines producing much colour throughout the year. Beyond this, grass pathways meander through an informal collection of trees and rare shrubs. A steep path drops from the plateau to a water garden, lake, waterfall and bog garden, rich with colour from bog primulas and other moisture-loving plants. This area is shaded by fine specimen trees. Excellent collections of hostas and hydrangeas are scattered informally throughout, and roses and clematis scramble over walks and through trees. Described as 'a botanical madhouse', this garden offers wonderful contrasts.

Iford Manor ★★   12

Bradford-on-Avon BA15 2BA. Tel: (01225) 863146

Mrs Cartwright-Hignett • 2m S of Bradford-on-Avon off B3109, 7m SE of Bath via A36. Signposted • Open April, Sun; May to Sept, Tues – Thurs, Sat, Sun and Bank Holiday Mons; Oct, Sun; all 2 – 5pm. Other times and parties by appt • Entrance: £3, OAPs, students and children over 10 £2. Children under 10 admitted Tues – Thurs only • Other information: Teas May to Sept, Sat, Sun and Bank Holiday Mons only ● ● WC ● ●

It is always illuminating to see a famous architect and landscape gardener's own garden. Harold Peto found himself a near-ideal house in the steep valley through which the River Frome slides langorously towards Bath. The topography lends itself to the strong architectural framework favoured by Peto and the creation of areas of entirely differing moods. The overriding intention is Italianate with a preponderance of cypresses, junipers, box and yew, punctuated at every turn by sarcophagi, urns, terracotta, marble seats and statues, columns, fountains and loggias. In a different vein is a meadow of naturalised bulbs, most spectacularly martagon lilies. A path leads from here to the cloisters – an Italian-Romanesque building of Harold Peto's confection made with fragments collected from Italy. From here one can admire the whole, and the breathtaking valley and the walled kitchen garden on the other side. Westwood Manor (see entry) is nearby.

Kellaways   13

Chippenham SN15 4LR. Tel: (01249) 740203

*Miss J.A. Hoskins • 3m NE of Chippenham off B4069 on East Tytherton road •
Open by appt • Entrance: £2, children 20p* ●

June is a rewarding time to visit because of the old roses which, cleverly
underplanted, predominate throughout. Winter is another outstanding time,
because of the profusion of winter-flowering shrubs. The Cotswold-stone
seventeenth-century house has a stone terrace on the walled garden side
bursting with thyme and wild strawberries. The clemency of the walls means
that the owner can grow joyous things like sun roses, *Carpenteria californica* and
other frailties. A serious cottage garden.

Lacock Abbey   14

Lacock, Chippenham SN15 2LG. Tel: (01249) 730227

*The National Trust • 3m S of Chippenham off A350 • Grounds, cloisters and
Museum of Photography open 26th Feb to 29th Oct, daily, 11am – 5.30pm.
Closed 21st April • Entrance: grounds, cloisters and Museum £3.70, children
£2.20, family £10.60 (abbey, grounds, cloisters and Museum £5.80, children
£3.20, family £15.90, parties £5.30 per person, children £2.70) • Other
information: Refreshments and shop in village. Batricar available. NT Shop in
village. Abbey open April to 29th Oct, daily except Tues, 1 – 5pm. Closed 21st
April. Cloisters and Museum of Photography • Other information: Teas and
meals avilable in village* ◑ WC & ♀

The thirteenth-century abbey, set in meadows beside the River Avon, was
turned into a private house by Sir William Sharington after the Dissolution,
and was later gothicised by John Ivory Talbot in the eighteenth century. The
romantic Victorian woodland garden is best viewed in spring when sheets of
crocuses, daffodils, and later, fritillaries, replace the large drifts of snowdrops
and aconites. Lady Elisabeth's Rose Garden, originally created for the mother
of William Henry Fox-Talbot, inventor of photography, has been re-created
from the original photograph of 1840, which is probably the earliest known
photograph of a garden. Fox-Talbot was also an eminent botanist, and planted
many unusual trees which can still be seen today, including specimens of the
American black walnut, the Judas tree and the swamp cypress. His walled
'Botanic Garden', once fallen into use as allotments, has reopened after
restoration. An eighteenth-century grotto will also be restored.

Larmer Tree Gardens   15

Rushmore Estate, Tollard Royal, Salisbury SP5 5PT. Tel: (01725) 516228

*Mr Michael Pitt-Rivers • 16m SW of Salisbury, 7m SE of Shaftesbury off B3081
• Open April to Oct, Sun – Thurs, 11am – 6pm • Entrance: £3, OAPs £2.50,
children £1. Discount entry available with Chettle House (see entry in Dorset)*
◑ 🍴 & ♨

Larmer's 12 acres were first laid out in 1880 by the owner's grandfather, General Pitt-Rivers, for the enjoyment of the local populace (there was no house to match). His descendant's aim has been to provide similar facilities with extensive areas of lawn and a playground for the young, plus large tea room and hall which can accommodate conferences and parties. The Roman temple and an Indian room with Nepalese carving were introduced by the General as points of interest for his less fortunate contemporaries with small knowledge of the outside world. Now, after restoration, they form a striking backdrop for newly planted flower borders, dells, arbours and a water garden. Free-flying macaws and peacocks add flashes of brilliant colour. Musical events are held throughout the summer in the outdoor theatre, some of them in co-operation with nearby Bryanston School. A visitor centre has been set up, displaying the work of the General, who was devoted to anthropology, archaeology and the excavation of antiquities. A maze is proposed for future enjoyment.

Longleat   16

Warminster BA12 7NW. Tel: (01985) 844400

The Marquess of Bath • 3m SW of Warminster, 4½ m SE of Frome on A362 • House open • Garden open all year, daily except 25th Dec, 8am – 6pm (Nov to March closes 4pm) • Entrance: £2, OAPs and children £1, coaches free (house extra) (1999 prices) • Other information: Helicopter landing pad available by prior request ○ 🍽 ✕ 🏪 WC ⅚ 🛒 ⚲

This garden has been rearranged and developed by most of the great names in English landscape history. There is nothing left to show today of the two earliest gardens here, the Elizabethan and that created by London and Wise in the 1680s-1690s, which must have been one of the most elaborate ever made in England. Sadly it was barely half a century before 'Capability' Brown ironed out the formality and created a chain of lakes set amongst clumps of trees and hanging woods, best admired today from 'Heaven's Gate'. The park was slightly altered by Repton in 1804 and added to in the 1870s when it became fashionable to collect exotic trees such as Wellingtonias and monkey puzzles and to make groves of rhododendrons and azaleas. It remains both beautiful and rewarding for all who delight in trees. In this century the fortunes of the garden came under the guiding hand of Russell Page. The nineteenth-century formal garden in front of the orangery to the north of the house was simplified and improved upon by Page to great effect, although, alas, most of his work has since been swept away. The orangery itself is a dream of wisteria and lemon-scented verbenas. A quarter of a mile to the south there is a pleasure walk in a developing arboretum, with many spring bulbs and wild flowers. To the immediate west of the house the small private garden is not open to the public. Lord Bath says this was designed by Lawrence Fleming in 1965 around the two commas within the Yin and Yang symbols: bulbs and fruit trees in the first and a lily pond in the second. There is a large dovecot in one corner – inspired by the turrets on the roof at Longleat. Elsewhere, the Safari Park and other attractions are available to visitors. The amazing Lord Bath planted the world's largest maze at Longleat in 1975, and new mazes are currently at various stages of growth, from the Sun Maze and Lunar Labyrinth to the east of the house to the Maze of Love in front of the orangery. Future mazes will encompass a variety of styles and materials.

Mompesson House 17

The Close, Salisbury SP1 2EL. Tel: (01722) 335659

The National Trust • In city centre, N of Choristers' Green in Cathedral Close • House open • Garden open April to Oct, daily except Thurs and Fri, 12 noon – 5.30pm (last admission 5pm) • Entrance: 80p (house and garden £3.40, children £1.70, parties £2.90 per person) • Other information: Charge for parking in the Close. Teas when house open. National Trust shop nearby
◑ WC ⅋

If visiting Salisbury, the Cathedral and the Close are a must, and if you have been fortunate enough to find a parking space, take time also to visit this small walled garden, which is in the Old English style. Its reposeful atmosphere is very refreshing. Summer is best, with the old-fashioned roses in bloom, but it is attractive throughout the open season.

Oare House ★ 18

Oare, Marlborough SN8 4JQ. Tel: (01672) 562613

Mr H. Keswick • 2m N of Pewsey on A345 • Open 16th April, 23rd July, 2 – 6pm • Entrance: £2, children 20p ◑ 🦽 WC ⅋ ⬥

The 1740 house was extended by Clough Williams-Ellis in the 1920s and the garden created from 1920 to 1960 by two successive owners, Sir Geoffrey Fry and Henry Keswick. The house is seen as the backdrop to a cathedral-like nave of limes, a worthy overture to many good things. The main garden is approached through a wisteria-covered pergola enlivened by a lily pond and tinkling fountain. Great yew hedges enclose a 'library' garden, from which an elegant loggia (where splendid teas are served on open days) can be spied along a formal axis of pleached limes. Below is a long, corridor-like secret garden, known as 'the slip', where good brick walls have been used for interesting planting. The lawns to the west of the house are very much in the grand manner. The eye rises over an immaculate lawn to the sweep of the Marlborough Downs seen at the end of a woodland ride. Substantial borders on either side of this lawn lead down to a swimming pool of equally grand proportions flanked by great herbaceous borders, one all gold achilleas and heleniums and the other filled with dahlias. In the impressive kitchen garden fruit and vegetables are arranged around the edge in purposeful manner behind their lavender hedges, espalier fruit trees and shrub roses. The two axial paths are magnificent: one is dominated entirely by white roses, while in the other a mossy gravel path threads its way through a stunning tunnel of herbaceous plants with yellow and white violas spilling out beneath clumps of richly coloured phlox and heleniums of many varieties. This is a garden worth every mile of a long detour.

The Old Vicarage ★ 19

Edington, Westbury BA13 4QF. Tel/Fax: (01380) 830512

*J.N. d'Arcy • 4m NE of Westbury on B3098 to West Lavington. Signposted •
Open once for charity in mid-June and by appt • Entrance: £3.50, children free
(includes other neighbouring gardens) • Other information: Parking in church
car park* ● ● WC & ⬦ ⁊

Every year new discoveries mark the travels of this peripatetic gardener,
who has created a varied, scented garden on a two-and-a-half-acre escarpment set high on the north side of Salisbury Plain. To be shown round by Mr
d'Arcy is a treat as he mixes wit with erudition. Swags of clematis, cistus
and mahonias enliven the plain façade of the former vicarage, where a wide
lawn — croquet of course — leads to a meadow artful with wild flowers
beneath rare varieties of chestnut, sorbus and maple. National Collection of
evening primroses gives pleasure after dark. Stunning views towards Edington Church lift the visitor's eyes through well-planted vistas. Dividing the
garden is a dense yew hedge, only 14 years old, which is clipped so that the
base gets the light. "For a mature hedge it is agreeably slim," he says. An
allée of fastigate hornbeams points the view towards Devizes. Newly built
brick walls create rooms and shelter exotic plants and trees, and a base of
natural greensand over clay and mulch from elaborate bays of compost
ensure vigorous plants. Waves of *Phlomis bovei* mark the hot garden, while a
sunken garden to the rear of the house is cool and romantically planted
round a 15-metre well. Nepetas, a particular passion, run riot. Towards the
end of the tour a gravel bed is a sea of agapanthus and eryngium, including *E.
bourgatii* (from the Atlas mountains), and everywhere seedlings push through
the gravel — phlomis, dierama, *Acanthus discoridis* and *Oenothera caespitosa*
'Marginata', an unusual evening primrose with white flowers. And the
strong salvia, *S. darcyi*, a souvenir of his Mexican tour — 400 species there.
It is worth noting that the Old Vicarage opens together with a dozen other
gardens in Edington in July every other year.

Old Wardour Castle 20

Tisbury, Salisbury SP3 6RR. Tel: (01747) 870487

*English Heritage • 2m SW of Tisbury, off A30 • Open all year except 1st Jan,
24th to 26th Dec: April to Oct, daily, 10am – 6pm (5pm in Oct); Nov to
March, Wed – Sun, 10am – 1pm, 2 – 4pm • Entrance: £1.90, concessions
£1.40, children £1 (1999 prices)* ○ ● ● WC & ⬦ ● ⁊

In a picture-book setting, the ruins of this fourteenth-century castle stand
overlooking a lake and surrounded by woodland. The gardens and park were
laid out in the eighteenth century when the nearby New Wardour castle was
built, and remnants of this landscape can still be seen in some fine trees and
shrubs. There is a pavilion in Gothic style and a picturesque grotto built of
stone, brick and plaster by Josiah Lane, a noted creator of rockwork grottos in
Wiltshire in the eighteenth century. Paths and tunnels twist between ancient-
looking weathered rocks containing nooks and alcoves. Notable among the

trees are a stand of yews around 400 years old, Atlas Mountain cedars of between 150 and 200 years old, and a cedar of Lebanon.

Pound Hill House 21

West Kington, Chippenham SN14 7JG. Tel: (01249) 782781

Mr and Mrs Philip Stockitt • 8m W of Chippenham, 2m NE of Marshfield between A420 and M4 • Open Feb to Dec, daily, 2 – 5pm. Parties by arrangement • Entrance: £2 • Other information: Plants for sale in adjacent nursery ◑ 💺 WC ♿ ⬨ 🌿 🛍

An interesting update on the theme of the Cotswold garden, in two acres around a sixteenth-century stone house. Mrs Stockitt believes 'it's not contrived – gardening should be a refining process. And every year we have a new development.' The viewer takes in the effect from the yard through to an 'old-fashioned rose garden' (planted and labelled David Austin roses) leading to a Victorian vegetable garden with espaliered fruit trees, then through a wisteria, rose and clematis tunnel, culminating in a statue. Beyond there is an orchard, a Cotswold garden with topiary, yew-screened tennis court, herbaceous border and drystone walls showing off 'Ballerina' roses, topiary and two trelliswork obelisks. A water garden, with many shade-loving as well as moisture-loving plants, is surrounded by yew hedging to create another small garden. Another walk area, using *Betula utilis* var. *jacquemontii*, underplanted with *Pulmonaria officinalis* 'Sissinghurst White' and tulips, leads on to a rose walk lined with clipped sweet chestnuts and planted with old-fashioned roses. The courtyard has many interesting planters. The nursery sells progenies from 2000 varieties of rarer plants as well as roses, topiary and specimen plants.

Ridleys Cheer 22

Mountain Bower, Chippenham SN14 7AJ. Tel: (01225) 891204

Mr and Mrs Antony Young • 8m W of Chippenham S on A420. Turn N at Shoe pub, take second left, then first right • Open 26th March, 30th April, 21st May, 18th June, 2 – 6pm. Parties welcome by appt • Entrance: £2, children under 14 free. £3 per person for group visits • Other information: Picnics in arboretum only, from 1pm ● 💺 🖻 WC ♿ 🌿

The garden, created over the past 20 years, covers some three acres, two of which hold a young and interesting arboretum, and there is also a three-acre wildflower meadow. The garden is on two levels, connected by a broad flight of steps and a grass walk, and contains many fine examples of rarer shrubs and trees. The shrub roses, including many species and hybrids seldom encountered, are a major summer feature. There is a small *potager*, and a recent addition is a small gravel garden in box and yew outside the conservatory. Autumn colour is given by a growing number of maples, beeches, tulip trees, oaks and zelkovas. In the main, this in an informal garden, full of appeal for plantsmen, who can derive much information from the knowledgeable owners. A small nursery sells trees, shrubs and perennials, many of them unusual. Pound Hill House (see entry) is nearby.

Stourhead ★★ 23

Stourton, Warminster BA12 6QF. Tel/Fax: (01747) 841152

The National Trust • 3m NW of Mere (A303) at Stourton off B3092 • House open April to 29th Oct, daily except Thurs and Fri, 12 noon – 5.30pm or dusk if earlier (last admission 5pm) • Gardens open all year, daily, 9am – 7pm (or dusk if earlier), except 20th to 23rd July when gardens close at 5pm with last admission 4pm • Entrance: House or garden, April to Oct: £4.60, children (5-16) £2.60, family ticket £10; garden only, Nov to Feb, £3.60, children £1.50, family ticket £8; house and garden £8, children £3.80, family ticket £20 • Other information: Refreshments in village hall restaurant or at Spread Eagle Inn at garden entrance. Wheelchairs available. Buggy service from car park to house and garden entrances in peak season. Dogs Nov to Feb only ○ 🏠 WC ⅋ ⅋ 🎁 🌡

An outstanding example of an English landscape garden, designed by Henry Hoare II between 1741 and 1780, a paragon in its day and almost the greatest surviving garden of its kind. The sequence of arcadian images is revealed gradually if one follows a route anti-clockwise around the lake, having come from the house along the top route, so seeing the lake from above. Each experience is doubly inspiring: visitors glimpse classical temples across the lake, almost unattainable and mirage-like, and when they reach their goal some other vision always attracts the eye – the boat-house, Temple of Flora, turf bridge, Temple of Apollo, rock bridge, cascade (these two are tucked away and very surprising), Pantheon (now restored), rustic cottage and grotto. The view from the Temple of Apollo (1765) was described by Horace Walpole as 'one of the most picturesque scenes in the world', by which he meant that it was as fine as a painting. To gain a better idea of how these buildings would have looked had the surrounding planting remained as it was originally, take a walk by Turner's Paddock Lake below the cascade. Between 1791 and 1838 Hoare's grandson Richard Colt Hoare planted many new species, particularly from America, including tulip trees, swamp cypresses and Indian bean trees. He also introduced *Rhododendron ponticum*. From 1894 the sixth Baronet added to these with the latest kinds of hybrid rhododendrons and scented azaleas, and a large number of copper beeches and conifers, such as the Japanese white pine, Sitka spruce and Californian nutmeg, of which many are record-sized specimens. In the early nineteenth century Stourhead boasted one of the best collections of pelargoniums in the world, over 600 varieties. The latest effort to emulate Richard Colt Hoare's interests consists of over 60 varieties of pelargoniums in a 1910 lean-to greenhouse. A new footbridge leads into the lower terrace of the walled garden, recently opened, and begins the route through to the house and garden. Especially wonderful in winter when quiet.

Stourton House Flower Garden ★ 24

Stourton House, Stourton, Warminster BA12 6QF. Tel: (01747) 840417

Elizabeth Bullivant • 3m NW of Mere (off B3092). Follow signs to Stourhead, then immediately before Stourhead car park, signed Stourton House • Open April to Nov, Wed, Thurs, Sun and Bank Holiday Mons, 11am – 6pm or dusk if

earlier. Also for parties of 12 or more on other days by arrangement • Entrance:
£2.50, children 50p, parties £2 per person • Other information: Parking in
Stourhead (NT) car park ◗ 🍵 WC ♿ ⏛ 🧺

This colourful five-acre garden contains treasures in friendly, small spaces: a
wild garden, woodland garden, secret garden, delphinium walk. Seats abound.
Rare plants and imaginative designs are everywhere; 270 different varieties of
hydrangea, many species of magnolia, unusual daffodils and camellias; euphorbias, chocolate plants and a profusion of flowers for drying. A switchback
hedge of Leyland cypress encloses a herbaceous garden of island beds, lavishly
planted, and a lily pond with many carnivorous plants and a great urn full of
flowers. All-year-round interest.

Westwood Manor   25

Bradford–on–Avon BA15 2AF. Tel: (01225) 863374

The National Trust • 5m SE of Bath, 1½ m SW of Bradford-on-Avon off
B3109. In Westwood beside church • Open April to Sept, Sun, Tues and Wed, 2
– 5pm and at other times for parties of up to 20 by written appt with s.a.e. •
Entrance: £3.60. No reduction for children or OAPs ◗

Turning from the Italianate glories of Iford Manor (see entry) one mile away,
topiarists and others might like to contemplate the dense green geometry of
the topiary garden here. Mrs Azis says 'There are no flowers'. And, other than
the lilies in the pond set into the lawn and the swathes of wisteria on the wall
leading to the entrance, there are none. A small garden links the ancient barns
to the medieval manor house which the yew hedges enfold and enclose. This
simple design looks centuries-old but dates from the early part of this century,
when Mr Edgar Lister purchased and restored the house and created and
designed the garden, both of which he later left to the Trust. The late James
Lees-Milne wrote that the exquisite manor in its present form 'was his
[Lister's] creation and should be his memorial'. It must be emphasised that
this garden should be visited as an adjunct and a complement to the house,
which is lived in and administered by the tenant.

Wilton House ★   26

Wilton, Salisbury SP2 0BJ. Tel: (01722) 746720

The Earl of Pembroke • 3m W of Salisbury on A30 • House open • Grounds
open 10th April to 29th Oct, daily, 10.30am – 5.30pm (last admission 4.30pm)
• Entrance: £3.75, children £2.50 (house, grounds and exhibition areas £6.75,
OAPs £5.75, children (5-15) £4.50, parties £5.25 per person) (1999 prices) •
Other information: Plants for sale in nearby garden centre ◗ 🍵 ✕ 🏠 WC ♿
🧺 ♨

The first garden the visitor sees, in the north courtyard, was designed by David
Vickery in 1971. It incorporates formal pleached limes in rectangular layout, the
geometry being further emphasised by a box parterre infilled with lavender and
a central, torrential fountain which provides a cool haven in summer. It has
created a green space with immense style which manages to answer the

architecture of the house. A wrought-iron gate adjoining the courtyard leads to the east front with wall-trained shrubs and extensive herbaceous borders. Looking to the south, the Palladian bridge built in 1737 spanning the River Nadder is a focal point. Beside this stands a fine golden oak, *Quercus robur* 'Concordia', raised and grafted in 1843 at a nursery in Ghent. Going east along the broad gravel walk among many specimen trees set in eighteenth-century landscaped parkland, the visitor reaches the walled rose garden containing a large collection of old-fashioned English roses. This adjoins a pergola clothed with climbing plants and a water garden containing roses, aquatic species and ornamental fish. Beyond is the Whispering Seat with its unusual acoustic properties and a loggia facing the statue from the Arundel collection, all enclosed by a short avenue of *Quercus ilex*, with the River Nadder a glistening vista in the distance. Within the central courtyard of the house, the current, 17th, Earl has completed the fourth new garden. Echoing designs from the central, ninth-century Venetian wellhead, a border of cotton lavender encloses quadrants of clipped box hedge. For children there is fun and excitement in a large adventure playground; for historians, there is interest in searching out those parts of the garden which show the work of Isaac de Caus (*c.* 1632), the 8th Earl, the 9th 'Architect Earl', Sir William Chambers and James Wyatt (1801). Tree-trail leaflet available. Nearby is *Philipps House*, Dinton (Tel: (01985) 843600), a National Trust house by Wyatville *c.* 1816, open all year with 100-acre *Dinton Park*. The house (ground floor only) is open 23rd April to Oct, Mon, 1 – 5pm and Sat, 9am – 1pm. Walks in the park and woodland start from the car park.

COUNTY BOUNDARIES
Some gardens have postal addresses in one county and are physically situated in another. If in doubt, the index will direct the reader to the correct page.

DOGS, TOILETS & OTHER FACILITIES ⬥ **WC**
If these are not mentioned in the entry, then facilities are probably not available at the property described. For example, if dogs are not mentioned, owners will probably not permit entry, even on a lead.

FEEDBACK
Readers are invited to advise the *Guide* of any gardens which in their opinion should be listed in future editions, and where possible arrangements will be made to review such suggestions. Readers who would like to add information about gardens listed are warmly invited to write to the *Guide* with their comments, which may be used in future editions without attribution. A report form is included at the back of the *Guide*, although letters will be welcome. Please send to the publishers, Bloomsbury Publishing plc, 38 Soho Square, London W1V 5DF. All letters are acknowledged by the editor.

WORCESTERSHIRE

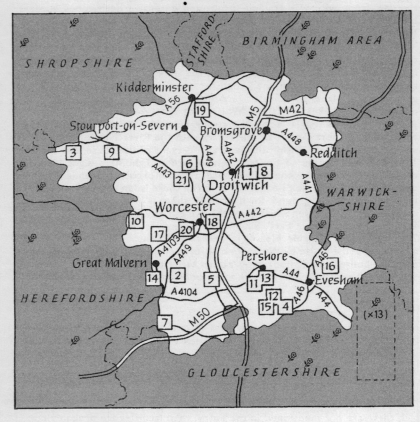

24 Alexander Avenue

1

Droitwich WR9 8NH. Tel: (01905) 774907

Owners: David and Malley Terry • Take M5 exit 5 or 6, then A38 • Open for NGS and by appointment • Entrance: £1.50 for charity NEW ●

This 40 x 10m garden is a lesson in what can be done in a small space and a short time. The present owners moved here in the winter of 1995 and have turned a barren patch of grass into a paradise. High hedges obscure the views of neighbouring houses, and through them climb some of the 100 clematis the garden boasts. The borders are stuffed with a dazzling array of interesting plants, many of them rare; most shrubs have climbers growing through them. There is a fine collection of ferns, and alpines grow in troughs or the gravel bed in front of the house. A garden of immaculate artistry.

Barnard's Green House 2

10 Poolbrook Road, Barnard's Green, Great Malvern WR14 3NQ.
Tel: (01684) 574446

Mr and Mrs Philip Nicholls • Just E of Great Malvern at B4211/B4208 junction • Open April to Sept, Thurs, 2 – 6pm and one spring, one autumn opening for NGS. Other times by appt • Entrance: £2, children free ● ☕ WC ⚿ ✍

Wide, well-kept lawns surround a Grade-II-listed house dating from 1635, and among many fine trees are two mature cedars. Elsewhere established yew and box hedges contribute both structure and style to what is, in terms of design and atmosphere, a period piece. Of particular interest is the immaculate vegetable garden, laid out with a series of fine herring-bone brick paths and containing a splendid glasshouse and a series of cold frames. Here Mrs Nicholls grows an imaginative array of plants which are used to support a flourishing dried-flower enterprise. Formal herbaceous borders, winding paths, a rose garden, a small pond and woodland area, particularly good in spring, complete this quintessentially English garden.

Burford House Gardens 3

Tenbury Wells WR15 8HQ. Tel: (01584) 810777; Fax: (01584) 810673

Mr C. Chesshire • 19m SW of Kidderminster, 1m W of Tenbury Wells on A456 • Open daily, 10am – 5pm • Entrance: £3.50, children £1. Parties of 10 or more by prior arrangement £3 per person • Other information: Plants for sale, especially clematis, at Treasures Plant Centre opposite ○ ☕ ✕ 🏪 WC ⚿ ✍ 🛖 ⛲

This was the four-acre plantsman's garden created by the late John Treasure. The present owner inherited the island beds with generous plantings of clematis, and his careful redesigns and new planting schemes are coming into their own. A superb vista from the front of the Georgian house and plantings of echinaceas, heleniums and hemerocallis are a part of imaginative design schemes. The restoration of a bridge over the River Teme (to commemorate the Treasure brothers) has given scope for new riverside plantings.

Conderton Manor 4

Conderton, Tewkesbury GL20 7PR. Tel: (01386) 725389

Mr and Mrs William Carr • 8m SW of Evesham, 5½ m NE of Tewkesbury between A46 and B4079. Opposite Yew Tree Inn in Conderton • Open for NGS by appt for individuals and parties • Entrance: £3 • Other information: Refreshments at Yew Tree Inn and silk shop in Conderton. Toilet facilities by arrangement ● WC ⚿

The seven-acre garden of this fine seventeenth-century manor house has spectacular views over the Cotswolds, the Vale of Gloucester and the Malverns. Completely restructured over the last ten years, it has an attractive parterre containing foliage plants on the terrace, an old vegetable garden transformed with rose arches and mixed borders, and an enormous 135-metre long border with unusual shrubs. There is a new quarry garden and bog bank, with cornus and salix for winter stem colour. The vistas through the box avenue and apple orchard (producing organic cider) and through the fountain garden are quite magnificent, and the whole garden is planted with many unusual trees, the owner's special interest. Although at its best between April and June and September and November, this remains a garden for all seasons.

Croome Park   5

High Green, Severn Stoke WR8 9JS. Tel: (01905) 371006

The National Trust • 8m S of Worcester, E of A38 and M5 • Pleasure Grounds open May to Oct, Sat – Sun and Bank Holiday Mons, 11am – 5pm (last admission 4.30pm). Also Thurs and Fri in July and Aug, 11am – 5pm. Guided tours by prior application in writing • Entrance: Park (pay-and-display car parking charge, excl. NT members) £2. Pleasure Grounds £3 (car park refund on entry). Pre-booked guided tours £4 (inc. NT members) • Other information: For disabled access, telephone in advance ◑ 🏠 WC ⬤

The Trust describes Croome as the first complete landscape designed by 'Capability' Brown, which made his reputation. The elegant park buildings and other structures are mostly by Robert Adam and James Wyatt. The Trust acquired 670 acres of the park with substantial grant aid from the Heritage Lottery Fund and a substantial donation from Royal & Sun Alliance and has embarked on a 10-year restoration plan, which includes dredging the water features and clearing and replanting the pleasure grounds, and there is now limited opening of the Western Pleasure Grounds, including the lake garden.

Eastgrove Cottage Garden Nursery ★   6

Sankyns Green, Shrawley, Little Witley WR6 6LQ. Tel: (01299) 896389

Malcolm and Carol Skinner • 8m NW of Worcester on road between Shrawley (B4196) and Great Witley (A443) • Open April to July, Thurs – Mon; 1st Sept to 14th Oct, Thurs – Sat, all 2 – 5pm. Closed Aug • Entrance: £2, children free ◑ WC ර ⚘

This delightful cottage garden with a profusion of colour has been carefully planted to give each plant maximum impact, the interaction of variegated foliage and strongly coloured shrubs creating backdrops for a variety of perennials. A collection of flowers and foliage by the front door, looking stunningly casual, turns out to be all in pots. The brick paths lead through areas of clever colour combinations. The romantic Secret Garden, concentrating on pinks, mauves, silver and strong burgundy, leads into the Great Wall of China, a raised bed stuffed with sun lovers and backed by old apple trees – a different atmosphere altogether. The arboretum, now extended, is artistically planted to give maximum effect to the variously coloured foliage. Most plants are labelled, and the owners are always on hand with helpful advice. A wide range of well-grown, less usual plants is for sale, all propagated at the nursery. Witley Court (see entry) is nearby.

Eastnor Castle 7

Eastnor, Ledbury HR8 1RL. Tel: (01531) 633160; Fax: (01531) 631776

Eastnor Estate • 8m SW of Great Malvern, 2m E of Ledbury on A438 • Castle open selected days for collections of armour, tapestries and fine art. Parties of 20 or more by appt any day • Garden open 23rd April to 1st Oct, Sun; also July and Aug, daily except Sat; open Bank Holiday Mons, all 11am – 5pm (last admission 4.30pm) • Entrance: £2.75, children £1.50 (house and garden £4.75, children £2.50) • Other information: Refreshments on castle open days
◑ 🏠 WC ⬦ ⚲ 👜 ♨

Essentially an arboretum, Eastnor has one of the best nineteenth-century plantings in the country with many mature specimens. It is worth visiting early in the year for the display of spring bulbs. The house is an early nineteenth-century castle in medieval style by Sir Robert Smirke surrounded by grounds now brought under control as an extensive restoration and replanting plan gathers momentum (maintenance until recently was largely confined to the vicinity of the castle). A path around the lake gives striking views of the castle, although an area of the water is covered in summer with 'Pattypans', *Nuphar lutea*, the common yellow water lily, and around the edges are clumps of khaki shelters which, by day, partially conceal the common cold fisherman. There is a great variety of both conifers and broad-leaved trees, most with discreet aluminium labels, relating to the tree guide. Paths have been kept clear, and the keen tree enthusiast will enjoy the long walks in the woodland. From time to time the park is the venue for a variety of large events, craft fairs, Land Rover and mountain bike rallies. Just outside Ledbury is *Rushfields*, sellers of 'choice garden plants' [open Wed – Sat or by appt].

Hanbury Hall 8

Droitwich WR9 7EA. Tel: (01527) 821214

The National Trust • 4½ m E of Droitwich, 1m N of B4090, 6m S of Bromsgrove, 1½ m W of B4091 • House open • Garden open 2nd April to 29th Oct, Sun – Wed, 2 – 6pm (last admission 5.30pm or dusk if earlier) • Entrance: £2.90 (house and garden £4.60, children £2, family ticket £11.60) • Other information: Batricar available. Dogs in parkland only, on paths, on lead
◑ ☕ 🏠 WC ♿ ⚲ 👜 ♨

The Trust has restored much of the early eighteenth-century garden design by George London. The formal garden, typical of the period, comprises a sunken box-edged parterre, fruit orchard and a wilderness. Structural additions include two summerhouses and two planned bowling pavilions. Lawns spread round to the Orangery housing citrus trees. Further on a cedar walk leads to a fine ice-house. The final stages of the project includes rebuilding two bowling green pavilions (in timber instead of brick) and an obelisk two-and-a-half metres high. An almost three-metre pond has its fountains operated by solar panel.

Kyre Park 9

Kyre, Tenbury Wells WR15 8RP. Tel: (01885) 410282

Mr and Mrs J. Sellers • 22m SW of Kidderminster, 4m S of Tenbury Wells, 7m N of Bromyard off B4214 • Open probably Easter to Dec, daily, 11am – 6pm • Entrance: £2.50, children 50p ① 💺 🏠 WC 🔥 ⟨⊅ ♟

To describe this as a garden is somewhat misleading. More accurately it should be seen as a mid-eighteenth-century landscaped pleasure ground and shrubbery. It extends to some 29 acres and includes a number of Georgian features, not least of which are winding lakes, waterfalls, rapids and romantically placed ruins. Restoration work is taking place, although the scale of the task is daunting. Of particular interest are National Collections of hardy ferns – cystopteris, dryopteris, polypodiums and thelypteris – which form a major part of the plantings, and some of which are for sale in the nursery. A former tithe barn now houses 'Toy City' and a Norman dovecot also remain on the site.

Lakeside 10

Gaines Road, Whitbourne, Worcester WR6 5RD. Tel: (01886) 821119

Mr D. Gueroult • 9m W of Worcester off A44. Turn left at county boundary sign, signed 'Linley Green' (ignore sign to Whitbourne) • Open by appt for parties of 10 or more • Entrance: £2, children free ● 💺 WC

The first glimpse of this six-acre garden is a moment of sheer delight: a dramatic vista of the lake at the bottom of a steep grassy slope. The main part of the garden lies within the walls of what was the fruit garden of Gaines House nearby and consists of mixed beds and borders with many unusual plants, including bulbs and climbers. It has been created by the present owner and the late Mr C. Philip since 1984 and is now well established, with continuing expansion, particularly the bog garden. The main lake – complete with fountain – is the largest of three medieval stewponds which are thought to have provided fish for the Bishop of Hereford's palace nearby at Whitbourne Court. A small pinetum is now maturing well. A short woodland walk, bordered with ferns and different varieties of holly, leads to the attractive lakeside walk, where there are various kinds of daffodil in spring. A garden on an exceptional site, with great variety and interest. Don't miss the view from the top of the heather garden.

The Manor House 11

Birlingham, Pershore WR10 3AF. Tel: (01386) 750005

Mr and Mrs D. Williams-Thomas • 8m W of Evesham, 2m SW of Pershore, off A4104 in Birlingham • Open 30th April, 1st, 4th, 11th, 18th, 25th May, 1st, 8th, 15th, 22nd, 29th June, 6th, 13th July, 7th, 14th Sept; all 11am – 5pm • Entrance: £2, children free • Other information: Rare plant sale 25th June
① 💺 🏠 WC 🔥 ♟

The charm here lies in the successful blend of spacious, informal areas, made up of sweeping lawns, wide, well-stocked borders and splendid views over open countryside, with more enclosed, formal gardens where a sense of secrecy and intimacy is maintained. Most notable of these is a partly walled white garden where old brick paths weave a pattern amongst massed plantings of roses, hardy geraniums and campanulas complemented by grey foliage plants. On the south side of the house an expanse of lawn carries the eye over a ha-ha and meadow to the river beyond, a view echoed from the windows of a pretty little summerhouse retreat. Throughout, mature trees and hedges, climbing roses and free-flowering clematis give an air of tranquillity.

Overbury Court ★   12

Overbury, Tewkesbury, Gloucestershire GL20 7NP.
24hr Answerphone/Fax: (01386) 725528

Mr and Mrs Bruce Bossom • 9m SW of Evesham, 5m NE of Tewkesbury, 2½ m N of Teddington (A46/A435) roundabout • Open by appt only • Entrance: £2, children free • Other information: Parking in field off lane by church ● &

The south side of this magnificent Georgian house boasts a fine stone terrace overlooking a great sweep of formal lawns with hundreds of metres of clipped hedges, specimen clipped yews and a formal pool. To the east, the lawn is framed by a silver and gold border designed by Peter Coats with a crinkle-crankle edging of golden gravel, leading to a gazebo overlooking the road and the country to the south. On the west the frame is completed by more hedging and a sunken garden of attractively underplanted species roses leading to the west side of the house. There, under enormous plane trees, a stream winds its way from a grotto over vast lawns, falling gently into pools before disappearing underground. Elsewhere, shrub and flower borders and aged cherries merge and blend into the adjacent churchyard; the Norman church is usually open for visitors. Everything speaks of a continuity rare today, from the family totem-pole near the grotto (now being restored) to the polished plate on the estate office door.

Pershore College   13

'Avonbank', Pershore WR10 3JP. Tel: (01386) 552443

7m SE of M5 junction 7, 1m S of Pershore on A44 • Gardens open 3rd June for College Open Day, 10am – 5pm, and weekdays by appt for large parties • Entrance: £1, coaches £50 on Open Day (1999 prices) ● ● ● WC & ◁▷ ♨ ⬗

The grounds are working areas designed with an educational bias, and include an area designated as 'model gardens' created by students. The plant collections are well labelled. There are also specialist gardens such as an alpine garden, the Hardy Plant Society garden, the Bradstone garden and a wedding garden. Additionally, the grounds include an arboretum, orchards, automated glasshouses and a hardy plant production nursery. The RHS Pershore Centre is on the college campus and the Alpine Garden Society has its national HQ here; the college also holds the National Collections of penstemons and philadelphus.

The Picton Garden   14

Old Court Nurseries, Colwall, Great Malvern WR13 6QE. Tel: (01684) 540416

Mr and Mrs P. Picton • 3m SW of Great Malvern on B4218 • Garden open Aug, Wed – Sun; Sept, daily; 1st – 15th Oct, daily; 16th – 31st Oct, Wed – Sun, all 11am – 5.30pm • Old Court Nurseries open as garden and April to July, Wed, Sun • Entrance: £2, children under 15 free ◑ ꝯ

A one-and-a-half-acre plantsman's garden on the site of Ernest Ballard's Old Court Nurseries. Alpine and rose gardens, together with the existing large collection of herbaceous perennials, ensure plenty of summer interest, while shrubs and shade beds create year-round diversity. The National Collection of Michaelmas daisies is here, a genus on which the owner, Paul Picton, the son of the late Percy Picton, is an acknowledged expert. At the end of September and in early October it is possible to see a vast array of these useful autumn-flowering plants in every imaginable variety.

The Priory ★   15

Kemerton, Tewkesbury, Gloucestershire GL20 7JN. Tel: (01386) 725258

The Hon. Mrs Healing • 8m NW of Evesham, 5m NE of Tewkesbury off B4080 • Open 27th May to Sept, Thurs and Sun, and 18th June, 8th July, 6th, 27th Aug, 10th, 24th Sept, 2 – 6pm • Entrance: May and June: £1.50; July to Sept: £2, children free • Other information: Refreshments on Suns only. Plants for sale at nursery ◑ 🍴 WC & ⟳ ꝯ

The fine eighteenth-century house (not open) provides a handsome backdrop for this splendid garden of wide lawns, abundant borders and fine trees, where artistic planning and high maintenance are the keynotes. Of interest throughout the year, the packed herbaceous borders come into their own in July and August in a carefully co-ordinated arrangement of colour, form and texture. Quieter, but no less exciting, areas include a delightful, formal fountain garden and a yew-buttressed sixteenth-century ruin. The swimming pool has been converted into a lily pond, the walled garden has been redesigned, and a traditional knot garden planted in 1997 adjoins the herb garden.

Red Gables   16

The Parks, Offenham Road, Evesham WR11 5JP. Tel: (01386) 446775

Derrick and Rowlatt Cook • 2m NE of Evesham. Off Evesham bypass signed 'Offenham B4035'. Turn onto Offenham Road (B4510), then into The Parks (private road) • Open 8th, 9th April, 28th, 29th May, 29th, 30th July, 27th, 28th Aug, 10am – 5.30pm. Parties and individuals by appt at other times • Entrance: £1.50 ◐ 🍽 🍴 WC & ⟳ ꝯ

Situated on what, over 30 years ago, was a two-acre plum orchard, this garden is now a Mecca for plants. Paths meander through densely planted areas. Old fruit trees play host to roses, honeysuckle and clematis. Pools and raised beds are filled with interesting species, many of which have been collected on the owners' extensive travels abroad. Good plant combinations and textural contrasts.

Shuttifield Cottage 17

Birchwood, Storridge, Malvern WR13 5HA. Tel: (01886) 884243

Angela and David Judge • 8m SW of Worcester off A4103. Pass Storridge church and follow signs to Brickwood; after 1m stop at top of steep tarmac drive on left. Park in road and walk down slope • Open: 25th June, 2 – 6pm • Entrance: £2 NEW ●

Lawns lead down a two-acre sloping site, from borders and beds planted with shrubs and flowering plants, many of them unusual, in a succession of pleasure and interest, to the rose garden and a wood beyond. The rose garden has space for a large collection of old varieties to spread, sprawl, climb and bloom abundantly in what is almost a secret garden. In other parts are colour-themed beds, splendid trees, herbaceous plants, a woodland walk, a vegetable garden, a deer park and a pond. The planning and planting are so skilful that the overall effect is a natural, unstudied garden where everything grows happily.

Spetchley Park 18

Spetchley, Worcester WR5 1RS. Tel: (01905) 345224/213

Trustees of Spetchley Gardens Charitable Trust • 3m E of Worcester on A422 • Open April to Sept, Tues – Fri, 11am – 5pm, Suns, 2 – 5pm, Bank Holidays, 11am – 5pm. Closed other Mons and all Sats • Entrance: £3.20, children £1.60 ◑ 🍽 WC ও

For gardens which are, after all, of considerable size, there is an alluring intimacy about the grounds of Spetchley Park. Linked romantically with Ellen Willmott whose sister Rose Berkeley was responsible for the gardens in her day, they retain a wonderful sense of the past. Mellow brick walls, clipped yew hedges hiding secret enclosures, unfolding walks and vistas, antique statues and an ornate fountain are but a few of the delights to be discovered. Fine trees abound, as does interesting planting, including drift after drift of the handsome *Lilium martagon* along the walk to the horse pool in summer. Within the old kitchen garden, a new development, part sunken, shows great promise.

Stone House Cottage Gardens ★ 19

Stone, Kidderminster DY10 4BG. Tel: (01562) 69902

Mr and Mrs James Arbuthnott • 2m SE of Kidderminster via A448 • Open March to Sept, Wed – Sat, 10am – 5.30pm; Oct to March by appt • Entrance: £2, children free ◑ WC ও 🌒

The garden has been created since 1974, and looking round it now, it is difficult to believe that the whole area was once flat and bare. The owners have skilfully built towers and follies to create small intimate areas and at the same time provide homes for many unusual climbers and shrubs. Yew hedges break up the area to give a vista with a tower at the end, covered with wisteria, roses and clematis. Hardly anywhere does a climber grow in isolation – something will be scrambling up it, usually a small late-flowering clematis. Raised beds are full to overflowing, shrubs and unusual herbaceous plants mingle happily. In a grassed area shrubs are making good specimens. All plants are labelled so the visitor knows what to look for in the adjacent nursery. In June during two evenings of music the towers have a secondary purpose as platforms for the wind ensembles. You are invited to picnic in the garden for a modest fee – the effect is akin to non-pretentious Glyndebourne transplanted to San Gimignano. At other times you may ascend the towers to view the garden as a whole for the price of a donation to the Mother Theresa charity.

21 Swinton Lane   20

Worcester WR2 4JP. Tel: (01905) 422265

Mr A. Poulton • 1½ m W of city centre off B4485 from St Johns to Rushwick. Swinton Lane is between Portobello pub and Worcester golf course • Open 25th May, 18th June, 13th, 16th July, 13th Aug, 7th Sept, 11am – 6pm • Entrance: £1.50 ● ⚘

Behind this 1930s' house, in a space no greater than one third of an acre, the owners have created a most imaginatively planned, splendidly planted, atmospheric garden. Clever use of divisions, hedges, trees, shrubs and trelliswork has resulted in distinct areas or enclosures, notably a beautifully conceived and executed silver and white garden, designed for all-year interest, a hot late-summer border and an area devoted to shade-loving plants. Throughout, herbaceous borders are supplemented with pot-grown, tender perennials, which are moved in and out of key positions according to flowering season.

Witley Court   21

Worcester Road, Great Witley, Worcester WR6 6JT. Tel: (01299) 896636

English Heritage • 10m NW of Worcester on A433 • Open April to Oct, daily, 10am – 6pm (5pm in Oct); 3rd Nov to March 2001, Wed – Sun, 10am – 4pm. Closed 1st Jan, 25th, 26th Dec. Entrance: £3.50, OAPs £2.60, children £1.80 • Other information: Disabled parking ● 🍽 🏪 WC ♿ 🐕 👶 ♨

English Heritage describes Witley Court as an early Jacobean manor house, turned in the nineteenth century into a vast Italianate mansion with porticos by John Nash. It is now a spectacular ruin. The elaborate gardens, William Nesfield's 'Monster Work', still contain immense stone fountains. From the new visitor centre there are newly restored woodland walks around the lake and through the Wilderness to the magnificent ruined house. The Jerwood Foundation Sculpture Park is being installed at Witley Court. Elizabeth Frink's 'The Walking Man' is the first permanent installation.

COUNTY BOUNDARIES
Some gardens have postal addresses in one county and are physically situated in another. If in doubt, the index will direct the reader to the correct page.

YORKSHIRE (N. & E. RIDING)

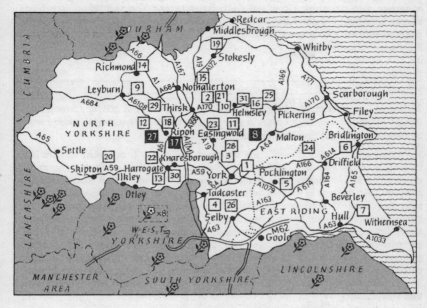

Two-starred gardens are marked on the map with a black square.

Aldby Park ★

Buttercrambe, York YO41 1XU. Tel (01759) 371398

Mr and Mrs G.M.V. Winn • 7m NW of York off A166 Bridlington road. Turn left at sign to Buttercrambe and continue ½ m past Gate Helmsley • Open 4th, 18th June, 2 – 5.30pm for charity or by appt • Entrance: £2, children £1 • Other information: Teas and other refreshments on open days only. Plants for sale in adjacent nursery ● 🍵 📷 <u>WC</u> ❤ ⬦ 🐾

A fine house dating from 1726 on a wooded hillside site which includes the mound and dry moat of King Edwin's seventh-century castle. The original terraced garden was created by Thomas Knowlton in 1746. In 1964 Mr Winn, who had known and loved the pre-war garden as a child, took over the house, and with a single gardener began the huge task of restoring what was by then a jungle to the garden we see today. The result is a triumph – a truly romantic garden which lifts the heart as it reveals itself to you. A glimpse through ornamental trees leads to a grassy terrace around a mound, decked on the sunny side with day lilies, yuccas and agapanthus. Pale colours contrast with the dark yews and box and range from white and yellow to silver and pink. In shady areas electric-blue geraniums take over, and a band of hostas flourishes free of slugs, thanks to hungry hedgehogs. Golden elders, *Hypericum* 'Hidcote' and corkscrew hazels add interest. Now a steep drop to the river is revealed, and the path leads down to a grassy walk along the water's edge, where kingcups and primulas glow and dark ferns thrive. On the water are black swans, greylag geese and ducks. Back up towards the house, a 'Kiftsgate' rose has smothered a large yew tree, and fine shrub roses, selected for looks and fragrance, abound.

Arden Hall   2

Hawnby, York YO6 5LS. Tel: (01439) 798348

Earl and Countess of Mexborough • 11m NE of Thirsk, 9m NW of Helmsley off B1257 • Open two or three times a year for charities and possibly by prior appt to suitably interested parties • Entrance: charge ●

Formerly the site of a Benedictine convent, the house (not open) was built in the eighteenth century, and the gardens are a series of formal terraces, dominated by a massive yew hedge at least 250 years old. A natural spring supplies four gallons of water a minute, a bonus imaginatively developed under the direction of gardener Stephen Mead. A formal Italianate pond is fed through a series of rills in stone troughs which pass through the terraces. Splendid new borders have been made by the old croquet lawn. A 1920s' swimming pool (too cold for use) has been converted into a wildlife-oriented pond which flows into a stream and then a series of pools disappearing down the valley. There are wildflower grazing meadows on the steep slopes beyond the garden walls. The valley has abundant wild plants, especially wood garlic, and the philosophy of Stephen Mead is to progress from the naturally informal environment – an 'Arden' indeed.

Beningbrough Hall and Gardens   3

Shipton–by–Beningbrough, York YO30 1DD. Tel: (01904) 470666; Fax (01904) 470002

The National Trust • 8m NW of York off A19 York – Thirsk road at Shipton • House open (last admission 4.30pm), with National Portrait Gallery loan exhibition • Gardens open April to 29th Oct, Sat – Wed; also Fri in July and Aug; all 11am – 5.30pm (last admission 5pm) • Entrance: gardens and exhibitions £3.50, children £1.70, family £8.70 (house, gardens and exhibitions £5, children £2.50, family £12.50). Party rates available and discount ticket for cyclists • Other information: Picnics in walled garden only. Annual regional NCCPG plant sale 10th Sept ◑ ☕ ✕ WC & ⚘ 🏛 ☕

The main formal garden, comprising geometrically patterned parterres, was laid out at the time the house was built in 1716, but was replaced during the late eighteenth century by sweeping lawns and specimen trees, part of an estate of 365 acres. This is essentially a pleasure garden with an historic framework, amongst which considerable recent planting has been integrated. The wilderness and two privy gardens have been restored to the original standards, and there is a nineteenth-century American garden and a Victorian conservatory. The main border has been planted as part of a three-stage redevelopment project. New planting has brought the walled garden back to life, including more than 5000 lavender plants, flowers for cutting, blocks of vegetables, and soft fruit, with vegetables surplus to the restaurant requirements sold in the shop. In total, the restoration has cost about £75,000.

Betula and Bolton Percy Churchyard   4

Bolton Percy, York YO23 7BA. Tel: (01904) 744383

Roger Brook • 7½ m SW of York, 5m E of Tadcaster. Bolton Percy signed from Tadcaster and from A64 (travelling York-Leeds direction only) • Betula open probably one Sunday in April, June and Sept, 1 – 5pm but telephone to check before travelling. Parties by appt • Entrance: combined admission with Windy Ridge and The White House £3, children free (1999 prices) • Betula: ● ● × WC ☺ *Bolton Percy Churchyard:* ○

The enthusiasm of Roger Brook has brought a wilderness under control in the splendid one-acre village churchyard at Bolton Percy, and it is now in all respects a paradise of garden plants growing in the new perennial style of gardening, with limited maintenance required – a lesson for churchwardens the country over. In Roger Brook's own garden, Betula, the National Collection of dicentras is also on view on open days.

Burnby Hall Gardens and Museum ★   5

The Balk, Pocklington, East Riding. Tel: (01759) 302068

Stewart's Burnby Hall Gardens and Museum Trust • 13m E of York off A1079 in Pocklington • Open April to 1st Oct, daily, 10am – 6pm • Entrance: £2.40, OAPs £1.90, children (5-15) £1, under 5 free. Parties of 20 or more £1.50 per person (1999 prices) ◐ ● × 🖻 WC ☺ ☺ 🎪 ☕

When the gardens were established on eight acres of open farmland in 1904 by Major Stewart, the original ponds, which covered two acres, were constructed for fishing, but in 1935 they were converted to water-lily cultivation. The large collection of hardy water lilies here forms part of the National Collection. They may be seen from June to mid-September in a normal year, and in July and August the two lakes are covered in colourful blooms from 80 different varieties.

Burton Agnes Hall   6

Burton Agnes, Driffield, East Riding YO25 4NB. Tel: (01262) 490324

Mrs Susan Cunliffe-Lister/Burton Agnes Preservation Trust Ltd • 5m S of Bridlington, 5m NE of Great Driffield on A166 • House open • Garden open April to Oct, daily, 11am – 5pm • Entrance: £2.25 (hall and garden £4.50, OAPs £4) ◐ ● × 🖻 WC ☺ ⬥ ☺ 🎪 ☕

The beautiful Elizabethan hall – designed by Robert Smythson, master mason to Elizabeth I and builder of Longleat and Hardwick – is approached through the gatehouse archway, up a wide gravel drive flanked by rows of fig-shaped yew hedges, with lawns beyond. Little evidence remains of the garden's history, any former flower planting in sight of the Hall having succumbed to lawn on all sides. However, the walls of the former enormous kitchen garden conceal a riot of colour (including campanulas, thymes, clematis, hardy geraniums and old roses). The *potager* of vegetables and herbs supplies the needs of the household. There are two herbaceous borders, a scented garden, a jungle of bamboos and giant exotic species, and also a maze. A series of large-scale games (including chess, draughts and snakes and ladders) is laid out on paving at the far end of the walled garden. Behind the hall is a woodland garden, and also an arboretum walk of approximately one mile. Adjoining is the English Heritage *Burton Agnes Manor House*, a rare example of a Norman house open 'any reasonable time'.

Burton Constable Hall   7

Burton Constable, Hull, East Riding HU11 4LN. Tel: (01964) 562400

Burton Constable Foundation • 7½ m NE of Hull off A165 • Hall open as garden, 1 – 5pm • Garden open 23rd April to Oct, daily except Fri, 12 noon – 5pm. Parties at any time by arrangement • Entrance: hall and grounds £4, OAPs £3.70, parties £3.50 per person ◑ 💻 WC ♿

The fine Elizabethan house is surrounded by parkland laid out in the 1770s by 'Capability' Brown, whose plans can still be seen. His 20 acres of lakes are spanned by a good stone bridge, and while not all his trees have survived they are being replaced by new plantings, still in their infancy. Around the house is a four-acre garden with a handsome eighteenth-century orangery, statuary and borders. This is one of the grandest establishments in the North-East and with the help of a £3.5m endowment from the National Heritage Memorial Fund should soon regain its former glory.

Castle Howard ★★   8

York YO60 7DA. Tel: (01653) 648444 ext. 220; Fax: (01653) 648501

Castle Howard Estates Ltd • 17m NE of York, 5m SW of Malton off A64 • House open • Garden open 17th March to Oct, daily, 10am – 4.30pm. Special tours of woodland garden and rose gardens available for pre-booked parties • Entrance: £4.50, children (4-16) £2.50, (house, gardens and grounds £7, OAPs £6.50, children (4-16) £4.50) (1999 prices). Special rates for garden tours on request • Other information: Dogs permitted, on lead, but no dogs in Ray Wood ◑ 💻 ✕ 🏠 WC ♿ ⟁ ♨ 🎁 ❦

Described as one of the finest examples of the heroic age of English landscape architecture, the house and grounds were first designed by Sir John Vanbrugh, assisted by Nicholas Hawksmoor. This architectural framework still basically exists, although in recent times features have been added, for example the impressive fountains designed by Nesfield. Although known principally as a fine landscape with remarkable park buildings, there is also much for the enthusiastic garden lover. There is one of the largest collections of old-fashioned and species roses in Europe, with the soil of the two gardens having been completely replaced in recent years and 2000 new roses planted. Ray Wood and the adjacent area accommodate fine collections of magnolias, rhododendrons, sorbus and vaccinium, an adjunct to the newly extended arboretum, which will soon be one of the largest and most important in the United Kingdom. A new association has been formed between the Royal Botanic Gardens, Kew and Castle Howard to manage the wood. Most of the plants are well labelled. Some distance from the house is an area devoted to shops with a wide range of goodies, including some produce. The arboretum is open on selected dates; telephone for information.

Constable Burton Hall 9

Leyburn, North Yorkshire DL8 5LJ. Tel: (01677) 450428

Mr Charles Wyvill • 16m NW of Ripon, 3m E of Leyburn on A684 • Open 19th March to 18th Oct, daily, 9am – 6pm • Entrance: £2.50, OAPs £2, children 50p ◑ WC ⚹ 🐾 ♿

In a walled and wooded parkland setting is a perfect Palladian mansion designed by John Carr of York in 1768. Built in beautiful honey-coloured sandstone, it rises from the lawns shaded by fine mature cedars. The owners have made a great effort to replant and develop. A delightful terraced woodland garden of lilies, ferns, hardy shrubs, roses and wild flowers drops down to a lake enhanced by an eighteenth-century bridge (no access). Near to the entrance drive are a stream and rock garden, and a new lily pond has been added. This substantial garden is a pleasure to visit because, after placing their entry coins in the honesty box, visitors can follow the numbered directional arrows using the concise notes to pass from one area of the garden to another (it is a technique that many other gardens could use with advantage). Surprises abound, such as *Lilium monadelphum* (yellow Turk's cap) in profusion and many mad climbers and shade-loving ground-cover plants. Several grand borders and a herbaceous garden have replaced the old formal rose garden. A fine morning or afternoon outing at all times of year.

Duncombe Park 10

Helmsley, North Yorkshire YO62 5EB. Tel: (01439) 770213/771115 (during open hours); Fax: (01439) 771114; E-mail: sally@duncombepark.com; Website: www.duncombepark.com

Lord Feversham • 12m E of Thirsk, 1m SW of Helmsley off A170 • House and garden open 2nd April to 29th Oct, April and Oct, Sun – Thurs, May to Sept, Sun – Fri, all 10.30am – 6pm or dusk if earlier (last admission 4.30pm). Parkland Centre and National Nature Reserve open as above, 10.30am – 5pm. Please telephone to check • Entrance: parkland and country walks £2; grounds £4; house and grounds £6. Discounts for pre-booked parties visiting house and grounds • Other information: Parking at Parkland Centre. Alternative entrance for wheelchair users ◑ 🍽 ✕ 🏪 WC ⚹ 🚻 ♿

Home of the Duncombes for 300 years, the mansion has recently been restored as a family home by Lord Feversham. Its 35-acre garden, set in 300 acres of dramatic parkland, dates from c. 1715 and was described as 'the supreme masterpiece of the art of the landscape gardener' by Sacheverell Sitwell. Impressive are the tree-lined terraces, classical temples, statues, vast expanses of lawn and magnificent trees mostly dating from the original eighteenth-century planting, including the tallest ash and lime trees, according to the *Guinness Book of Records*. The ha-has is one of the earliest ever built, pre-dating Bridgeman's at Stowe. Yew walk, orangery. Views from terrace of the North York Moors.

Gilling Castle   11

Gilling East, North Yorkshire YO62 4HP. Tel: (01439) 788238

The Right Reverend The Abbot of Ampleforth • 20m N of York on B1363 York – Helmsley road • Great chamber and entrance hall of castle (boarding school) open during term only • Garden open daily, 10am – 4pm • Entrance: £1.50, children free ○

A lovely garden in outstanding scenery. The terraces have been constructed on the south-facing side, four of them tumbling down the slope from an expansive lawn at the top. Many old-fashioned flowers grow in the borders, with a backdrop of majestic trees.

Hackfall Wood   12

Grewelthorpe, North Yorkshire.

Woodland Trust • 6m NW of Ripon off A6108, between Grewelthorpe and Masham • Open all year, daily • Entrance: free ○ ⬦

The site is a spectacular gorge, over 100 metres deep, cut out by the River Ure. Now battered by neglect, this romantic woodland garden, once painted by Turner and praised by Wordsworth, was laid out by William Aislabie between 1750 and 1765 as a counterpoint to the splendour of Studley Royal (see entry) created by his father. In the 112 acres of entirely overgrown semi-natural scenery, paths lead to a pool, a grotto and a number of small Arcadian ruins. The crumbling banqueting hall, which may in time be restored, commands magnificent views over the gorge. Restoration of the paths, sometimes soggy, is underway. Spring sees masses of flowering wild garlic and bluebells, and tall ferns flourish in late summer amid beech, Turkey oak, elder and elm. English Heritage Grade-I status.

Harlow Carr Botanical Gardens ★   13

Crag Lane, Harrogate, North Yorkshire HG3 1QB. Tel: (01423) 565418; Fax: (01423) 530663

Northern Horticultural Society • 1½ m W of Harrogate on B6162 Otley road • Open all year, daily, 9.30am – 6pm or dusk if earlier • Entrance: £3.60, OAPs £2.70, accompanied children free. Parties of 20 or more £2.70, children under 16 free (1999 prices) • Other information: Manual and electric wheelchairs for loan. Guide dogs only ○ ☕ ✕ 🍴 WC ♿ ⚘ ♨ ♨

The 68-acre site, established in 1949 by the Northern Horticultural Society as a centre for garden plant trials, now also provides a wide range of horticultural courses for amateurs. It is said that if a plant prospers here it will grow anywhere in the north. The garden hosts National Collections of heather and rhubarb cultivars as well as those of dryopteris and polypodium ferns, and there are large collections of rhododendrons and alpines. The streamside planting boasts one of the best collections of moisture-loving plants in the north of England. There is also a fine alpine house and two extensive rock gardens.

Millgate House ★ 14

Richmond, North Yorkshire DL10 4JN. Tel: (01748) 823571;
Fax: (01748) 850701

Austin Lynch and Tim Culkin • In Richmond, in corner of Market Square opposite Barclays Bank • Open mid-March to mid-Oct, daily, 10am – late evening, and at other times by appt • Entrance: £1.50 ◐ ⟁ ⚲

This small but outstanding award-winning town garden is walled on two sides, with the continuous sound of waterfalls on the River Swale in the background. Clematis, roses and jasmine jostle for place against the walls. Hostas and ferns are at the roots of the rose 'Boule de Neige', while 'Maigold' hangs in fragrant swags from the Regency balcony that runs across the first floor of the house. The lower garden houses over 28 varieties of roses, the clematis list is equally spectacular, and there is a specialist collection of hostas. A jewel offering plenty of ideas for the small garden.

Mount Grace Priory 15

Saddle Bridge, Northallerton, North Yorkshire DL6 3JG. Tel: (01609) 883494

English Heritage • 12m N of Thirsk, 7m NE of Northallerton on A19 • Open April to Oct, daily, 10am – 6pm (5pm in Oct); Nov to March, Wed – Sun, 10am – 1pm, 2 – 4pm (last admission 3.30pm) • Entrance: £2.80, concessions £2.10, children £1.40 (1999 prices) ◑ ▦ WC ⚲ 🏛 ⚲

The ruins of the priory guest house, incorporated into a seventeenth-century manor, were combined with a larger house in 1900-1901, which is an important example of the Arts and Crafts Movement. The monks' cells in the monastery were occupied from 1398 to the dissolution in 1539, and each monk's cell had its own garden. Recently some have been replanted, with the latest crop of herbs illustrating varieties used for medicinal purposes. The scheme is so popular that English Heritage now sell more herbs than guidebooks. The design of the cell-garden is in the form of paths and raised beds. A low box hedge surrounds the central bed, which is filled with blocks of herbs; each year these follow a different theme. The one-acre turn-of-the-century garden of stepped terraces falling away from the house has been re-created, with rock plants spilling over the edges. There are shrubberies and narrow borders and a Japanese garden with small pond, colourful maples, rhododendrons and azaleas.

Nawton Tower ★ 16

Highfield Lane, Nawton, York YO62 7TU. Tel: (01439) 771218

Mrs Sylvia Ward • 14½ m E of Thirsk, 2½ m NE of Helmsley, off A170 Scarborough road. In Nawton and Beadlam, turn left up Highfield Lane. After 2m entrance through white gates • Open May and June, weekends only, 2 – 6pm and at other times by appt • Entrance: £1.50, children 75p ● ⬦ ⚲

This remarkable atmospheric 12-acre garden on the edge of the North York Moors was created during the 1930s by the Earl of Feversham. It consists of a series of formal grassy walks between living tapestries woven from a masterly selection of trees, rhododendrons, azaleas and old shrub roses. Every junction from the central walk leads to a fresh surprise: a statue on a pedimented gazebo as the focal point of another pathway; a yew-hedged topiary garden; a quiet contemplative clearing with a silent stone fountain at its centre. A magical experience.

Newby Hall and Gardens ★★ 17

Ripon, North Yorkshire HG4 5AE. Tel: (01423) 322583; Fax: (01423) 324452

R. Compton • 4m SE of Ripon on B6265, 3m W of A1 • Open April to Sept, daily except Mon (but open Bank Holiday Mons), 11am – 5.30pm • Entrance: £4.50, OAPs £3.90, children £3 (house and gardens £6.30, OAPs £5.20, children £3.80) (1999 prices) • Other information: Wheelchairs provided. Dogs in area adjacent to picnic area only ◑ ☕ ✕ 🛍 WC ♿ ⚲ 🛒 ⚱

The much-loved home of the Compton family, who have restored this famous Adam house to its original beauty and have renovated and developed 25 acres of award-winning gardens. Some features remain from the eighteenth century, such as the east-to-west walk marked by Venetian statuary and backed by yew and purple plum. The south face has long wide green slopes down to the River Ure, with herbaceous borders on either side backed by clipped hedges and flowering shrubs. Cross-walks lead to smaller gardens full of interest. These include species roses and tropical, autumn, rock and stepped water gardens, as well as a fine woodland area attributed to Ellen Willmott. A National Collection of cornus is here. There is also a garden restaurant, children's adventure garden and a miniature railway. Events are held in the summer, such as craft fairs, with special admission prices. The Newby plant stall is operated in conjunction with *Oland Plants*, a nursery and garden five miles west of Ripon on B6265.

Norton Conyers 18

Ripon, North Yorkshire HG4 5EQ. Tel: (01765) 640333

Sir James and Lady Graham • 4m N of Ripon, near Wath. From A1 turn off at Baldersby flyover, take A61 to Ripon and turn right to Melmerby • House open, 2 – 5pm. Admission charge • Garden open 23rd April to 3rd September, Sun and Bank Holiday Mons; also 3rd to 8th July, daily; all 11.30am – 5pm. Parties at other times by appt • Entrance: free, though donations welcome (house and garden £3, OAPs and children £2.50) • *Other information: Teas on charity open days only. Pick Your Own fruit during summer; intending pickers should check beforehand* ❶ 🍴 WC ♿ ⤴ 🐕 ♌

The lure of both house and garden lies with the past, especially the association of the house with Charlotte Brontë, who made it one of the models for Thornfield Hall in *Jane Eyre*. The eighteenth-century walled garden, with its orangery and herbaceous borders, covers two and a half acres. The plantings are modest but pleasant and give an historic feel.

Ormesby Hall   19

Ormesby, Middlesbrough TS7 9AS. Tel: (01642) 324188

The National Trust • 3m SE of Middlesbrough, W of A171 • Open 2nd April to 29th Nov, Tues – Thurs, Sun and Bank Holiday Mons, 2 – 5.30pm • Entrance: £2.20, children £1 (house, garden, railway and exhibitions £3.50, children £1.70). Party rates available • Other information: Disabled parking near house. Braille guide available. Dogs on leads, in park only ❶ 🍽 🍴 WC ♿ 🐕 🚽 ♌

There have been recent developments in the gardens, including the replanting of the main rose beds, incorporating standards, bush and shrub roses, and much new ground cover and planting in the Holly Walk. A new glasshouse will help with the propagation of plants for the garden and the sales shop. Spring and summer mini garden guides available. The head gardener officiates at garden tours on the last Thursday of the month. The Hall itself is licensed for wedding ceremonies, and the impressive stable block is used by the local Mounted Police.

Parcevall Hall Gardens ★   20

Skyreholme, Skipton, North Yorkshire BD23 6DE. Tel: (01756) 720311

Walsingham College (Yorkshire Properties) Ltd • 10m NE of Skipton, 1m NE of Appletreewick off B6265 Pateley Bridge – Skipton road • Open 21st April to Oct, daily, 10am – 6pm; in winter by appt. Also open for charity • Entrance: £2, children (5-12) 50p (1999 prices) • Other information: Picnics in orchard only ❶ 🍽 🍴 WC ⤴ 🐕

A garden of great interest to the plantsperson all year round, many of Sir William Milner's treasures having survived years of neglect. Much of the garden has been renovated – and each year another area is restored, currently the old rose garden. There are red borders, an extended woodland walk, fish ponds and a rock garden. It is well worth a visit to enjoy the spectacular views of Simon's Seat and Wharfedale from the terrace. A fine range of rhododendrons, many originally collected in China, still grows happily in the walk here.

Rievaulx Terrace and Temples ★ 21

Rievaulx, Helmsley, North Yorkshire YO6 5LJ. Tel: (01439) 798340

The National Trust • 10m E of Thirsk, 2½ m NW of Helmsley on B1257 • Open probably April to Oct, daily, 10.30am – 5pm (April and Oct 4pm). Ionic temple closed 1 – 2pm • Entrance: £3, children £1.40, family ticket (2 adults and up to 3 children) £7 • Other information: Coach park. Possible for wheelchairs but steps to temples. Electric 'runaround' available for pre-booking; one manual wheelchair also available. Exhibition of landscape design in basement of Ionic temple ◗ 🏠 WC ♿ ⬦ 🎟 ☕

This is a unique example of the eighteenth-century passion for the romantic and the picturesque – that is, making landscape look like a picture. The work was done at the behest of the third Thomas Duncombe around 1754 and consists of a half-mile-long serpentine grass terrace high above Ryedale with fine views of the great ruins of one of the finest of all of Britain's Cistercian abbeys. At one end is a Palladian Ionic temple-cum-banqueting-house with furniture by William Kent and elaborate ceilings. At the other is a Tuscan temple with a raised platform, from which are views to the Rye Valley. The concept is wonderfully achieved. Those who want to see flowers will have to concentrate their attention on the grass bank below the terrace which is managed for wildflower content – fine displays of cowslips, primroses, orchids, violets, bird's foot trefoils, ladies' bedstraws, etc. There is also blossom throughout the spring season, such as cherry (bird and wild), blackthorn, rowan, whitebeam, elder and lilac.

Ripley Castle 22

Ripley, Harrogate, North Yorkshire HG3 3AY. Tel: (01423) 770152; Fax (01423) 771745

Sir Thomas Ingilby, Bt • 3½ m N of Harrogate off A61 Harrogate – Ripon road • Castle open all year (telephone for dates). Extra charge • Garden open all year, daily , 10am – 5pm • Entrance: £2.50, OAPs £2, children £1. Parties of 25 or more £2 per person. Season ticket £15 • Other information: Guide dogs only ◷ ☕ ✕ 🏠 WC ♿ 🐾 🎟

The mid-eighteenth-century 'Capability' Brown landscape with formal gardens has been developed by Peter Aram for a family that has been here since the fourteenth century. Magnificent specimen trees. The formal areas have recently been almost completely restored and the huge herbaceous borders – a total of 110 metres long – are amongst the most spectacular in the north of England. Other features include a lake with an attractive Victorian iron bridge, an eighteenth-century orangery and summerhouses. There are magnificent specimen trees. A woodland walk leads to a temple with fine views, and a lakeside walk takes the visitor through the deer park. Extensive new plantings of a rich variety of spring-flowering bulbs have been made to complement a National Collection of hyacinths here, and the tropical plant collection formerly owned by Hull University at Cottingham Botanical Gardens is now at Ripley and is open to the public in the newly restored listed greenhouses. The vegetable garden has rare species adopted from the Henry Doubleday Research Association. Nearby, at the new arts centre in Knaresborough, is 'a garden of the senses' built for Henshaw's College for children with disabilities. Telephone (01423) 886451 for details.

Shandy Hall 23

Coxwold, York YO61 4AD. Tel: (01347) 868465

The Laurence Sterne Trust • 18m N of York, 7m SE of Thirsk. From York, take A19 towards Thirsk, turn off to Easingwold and follow signs to Coxwold. From crossroads go 150 metres past church • House open June to Sept, Wed, 2 – 4.30pm and Sun, 2.30 – 4.30pm • Garden open May to Sept, daily except Sat, 11am – 4.30pm • Entrance: £2.50 (house and garden £3.50, children £1.50) • Other information: Refreshments in village nearby. Art and pottery gallery ◐ **WC** ♿ ⚲ ⛟ ⚱

A delightful small-scale, three-part garden, full of year-round interest, surrounds the pretty fifteenth-century cottage in which Laurence Sterne wrote *Tristram Shandy* during the 1760s. In the Stackyard Garden, borders of herbaceous plants and shrub roses enfold on three sides, with a view out to Byland Abbey and the North York Moors beyond. The Old Garden is approached through a small orchard in which gnarled trees are covered with climbing roses including 'Kiftsgate', 'Sanders' White Rambler' and 'Louise Odier'. A wide selection of old-fashioned roses in raised beds against drystone walls is interspersed with herbaceous planting in which careful thought is given to plant associations for colour and form. The foliage of a silver poplar provides a perfect backdrop for shrub roses such as 'Kassel', 'Fantin-Latour' and 'La Reine Victoria'. The third section is a sunken garden, created in a long-since-abandoned adjacent quarry. Four magnificent ash trees form a centrepiece for plantings of shrubs, bulbs and other perennials, a wildflower meadow, bluebells, and species roses and clematis climbing through trees.

Sledmere House 24

Sledmere, Great Driffield, East Riding YO25 3XG. Tel: (01377) 236637

Sir Tatton Sykes, Bt • 9m NW of Great Driffield off A166. Signposted • House open • Garden open 21st to 24th April; then May to Sept, Tues – Fri and Bank Holiday Mons, 11am – 5pm • Entrance: £1.50, children £1 (house, park and garden £4.50, OAPs £4, children £2) (1999 prices) ◐ ☕ **WC** ♿ ⚱

A listed garden, Sledmere is among the best-preserved of 'Capability' Brown's landscape schemes. Dating from the 1770s, it clearly reveals his characteristic belting and clumping of trees and carefully controlled diagonal vistas to distant 'eye-catchers'. His use of a ha-ha allows the park to flow up to the windows of the house (whence it is best seen) across extensive tree-planted lawns. To the rear of the house is a well-stocked herbaceous border, a newly planted knot garden and an interesting Italian paved sculpture court (1911) which is undergoing restoration. The eighteenth-century walled gardens, now grassed over and planted mainly with roses and herbaceous plants, are entered through a small but attractive rose garden set off by garden urns.

Sleightholme Dale Lodge 25

Fadmoor, Kirbymoorside, North Yorkshire YO62 7JG. Tel: (01751) 431942

Dr and Mrs O. James • 20m NE of Thirsk, 3m N of Kirbymoorside, 1m from Fadmoor off A170 Thirsk – Scarborough road • Open by written appt and a few days for NGS and NHS • Entrance: £2, children 50p ● WC ⟁

This garden occupies a unique position on the side of a wooded valley opening on to the moors. In the spring there is a blaze of blossom, wild daffodils and azaleas, and through the summer the walled garden, which runs steeply up the hill to the north, is breathtaking in the colour and exuberance of the parallel borders. This is described as 'a gardeners' garden' and there are many rare plants to be seen, notably meconopsis. Descending terraces, built at the beginning of the century to the south of the house, have deep shrubberies. The lowest of them is a grass platform separated from the meadow beyond by a ha-ha. A fine series of steps runs down through the terraces.

Stillingfleet Lodge ★ 26

Stillingfleet, York YO19 6HP. Tel/Fax: (01904) 728506

Mr and Mrs J. Cook • 6m S of York. From A19 York – Selby road take B1222 signed Sherburn in Elmet. In Stillingfleet turn opposite church. Garden at end of lane • Open for Pulmonaria Day on 16th April, 1.30 – 5.30pm; May, June, Aug, Sept, Wed and Fri, 1 – 4pm; and 14th May, 25th June, 1.30 – 5.30pm for NGS • Entrance: £2, children free • Other information: Parking and plants for sale at nursery ● 🖼 WC ໒ ৶

A plantsman's garden of about one and a half acres constructed by the owners since 1977 and subdivided into small gardens, each with a colour theme. Many climbing roses and clematis, and a good use of foliage plants in soft colours give the garden a romantic feel. There is also a 45-metre double herbaceous border, a wildflower meadow and a pond. A National Collection of pulmonarias is here.

Studley Royal and Fountains Abbey ★★ 27

Ripon, North Yorkshire HG4 3DY. Tel: (01765) 608888

The National Trust • 2m SW of Ripon, 9m N of Harrogate. Follow Fountains Abbey sign off B6265 Ripon – Pateley Bridge road • Deer park open all year during daylight hours. Abbey and garden open all year, daily except 24th, 25th Dec and Fri in Nov to Jan, as follows: April to Sept, 10am – 7pm; Oct to March, 10am – 5pm or dusk if earlier. Free guided tours April to Oct, daily • Entrance: Deer park free. Abbey and garden £4.50, children £2.10, family ticket £10.50. Special rates for pre-booked coach parties • Other information: Parking free at main visitor centre car park but £2 at Studley park (pay-and-display, NT members free). Self-drive powered 'runarounds' available by prior booking ○ 🍵 ✕ 🖼 WC ໒ ⟁ 🍺

The gardens of Studley Royal were created by John Aislabie, who had been Chancellor of the Exchequer but whose finances were 'ruined' by the South

Sea Bubble in 1720; he retired here to his estate in 1722 and worked until his death in 1742 to make the finest water garden in the country. The lakes, grotto springs, formal canal and water features, plus buildings such as the Temple of Piety, turn what is essentially a landscape with large trees and sweeping lawns into one of the most stunning of green gardens. The views from Colen Campbell's Banqueting House must also be savoured. Furthermore, there is its intimate and dramatic landscape relationship with Fountains Abbey, the largest and most complete Cistercian foundation in Europe, described by the *Oxford Companion* as probably the noblest monastic ruin in Christendom. This can be seen in the distance from the 'surprise view', through a door in a small building, although it is a pity that the necessity for a new car park means that visitors to Fountains no longer have as their indelible first impression the Abbey floating on a green sward, but instead look down on the roofless shell from above. Restoration of Anne Boleyn's seat, a timber gazebo with a fine view, is now complete. A further £3 million is being collected for the next phase of conservation, which includes the repair of river banks, fords and bridges, the restoration of Fountains Hall and Abbey Mill, and an on-going programme of woodland management and tree planting. Tent Hill, a once-lost area of the garden, is now open.

Sutton Park ★ 28

Sutton-in-the-Forest, York YO6 1DP. Tel: (01347) 810249/811239; Fax: (01347) 811251

Sir Reginald and Lady Sheffield • 8m N of York on B1363 • House open 21st to 24th April; then April to Sept, Wed, Sun and Bank Holiday Mons; all 1.30 – 5pm. Private parties Thurs, Fri and Sat by appt. Also ice-house • Gardens open 21st April to Sept, daily, 11am – 5pm • Entrance: £2, children 50p (house and gardens £4, parties £5 per person (£4.50 for parties of 25 or more)) • Other information: Coaches by appt. Teas available for booked parties when house open ◑ WC &

The distinguished English garden designer, Percy Cane, came in 1962 to this Georgian house and its terraced site with views over parkland said to have been moulded by 'Capability' Brown. Cane started the elegant planting which has been most carefully expanded by the present owners. There are several fine features on the terraces – a tall beech hedge curved to take a marble seat, ironwork gazebos and everywhere soft stone. The woodland walk leads to a temple. A new water feature has been created in the old walled garden. New herb garden and fernery.

Thorp Perrow Arboretum ★ 29

Bedale, North Yorkshire DL8 2PR. Tel: (01677) 425323

Sir John Ropner, Bt • 10m N of Ripon, 2m S of Bedale, signed off B6268 Masham road • Arboretum open all year, daily, dawn – dusk • Entrance: £3.50, OAPs and concessions £2.50, children (5-16) £2, family tickets £10 and £14 • Other information: Electric wheelchair available ○ ☕ 🍴 WC & ⟨⟩ ♦ ⏻

The arboretum was established many years ago and is one of the finest collections of trees in the north of England, containing over 2000 species. In the 85 acres is a Victorian pinetum, sixteenth-century woodland and National Collections of ash, limes and walnuts. You can follow the tree trail, the nature trail or simply amble at your own leisure. Thousands of naturalised daffodils and bluebells in spring, glorious wild flowers in summer and stunning autumn colour. There are new plantings and continual improvements in the arboretum.

Valley Gardens ★ 30

Valley Drive, Harrogate, North Yorkshire. Tel: (01423) 500600

Harrogate Borough Council • In centre of Harrogate; main entrance near Pump Room Museum and Mercer Art Gallery • Open all year, daily during daylight hours • Entrance: free ○ 🍵 🧺 WC ♿ 🐕 🎪

One of the best-known public gardens in the north of England, laid out earlier this century at the time Harrogate was fashionable as a spa. The refurbishment of the Sun Pavilion is now complete, while a programme for the renovation of the main rockery and gardens is being planned. The standard of formal bedding remains high, and a fine dahlia border display is an annual feature.

Wytherstone House 31

Pockley, York YO62 7TE. Tel: (01439) 770012

Lady Clarissa Collin • 15m E of Thirsk, 2½ m NE of Helmsley off A170. In Pockley, past church • Open for individuals and parties by appt • Entrance: £2.50 🌙 🧺 WC 🌿

A large and expanding plantsman's garden with a wide range of rare shrubs, perennials and roses, consisting of a series of interlinked compartments, each with its own character. The garden has been created from a green-field site over the course of 30 years. The spring garden has a tapestry of azaleas and rhododendrons and newly installed peat terracing. Next to the spring garden is a rock garden with some rare alpines. A sunken garden of mixed shrubs and herbaceous plants is enclosed by tall beech hedges and leads through to other delights beyond, past a newly planted arboretum and pond to a woodland walk. Back in the conservatory garden, climbing roses smother trees, and fine herbaceous plants and old roses create borders full of interest and colour, along with plants not normally thought to be hardy in the North of England, such as *Melianthus major*, thriving and flowering year after year.

SYMBOLS

[NEW] entries new for 2000; ○ open all year; 🌓 open most of year; 🌗 open during main season; 🌙 open rarely and/or by appt; 🍵 teas/light refreshments; ✕ meals 🧺 picnics permitted; WC toilet facilities; **WC** toilet facilities, inc. disabled ♿ garden partly wheelchair-accessible; 🐕 dogs permitted on lead; 🌿 plants for sale; 🏠 shop; 🎪 events held

---

YORKSHIRE (S. & W. AREA)

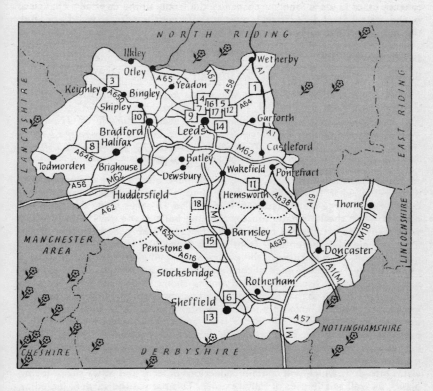

Bramham Park ★   1

Wetherby LS23 6ND. Tel: (01937) 844265

Mr G. Lane Fox • 10m NE of Leeds, 15m SW of York, 5m S of Wetherby just off northbound A1 • House open by written appt only • Garden open Feb to Sept, daily, 10am – 5.30pm (closed 5th to 11th June) • Entrance: £2.50, OAPs £2, children £1 (house and gardens £4, OAPs £3, children £2). Reduced rates for parties of 20 or more ◑ 🍽 **WC** ♿ ⟁ ☕

Created by Robert Benson after the style of Le Nôtre nearly 300 years ago, this is one of the few formal landscape gardens in the French style to survive in this country. Although a great storm early in 1962 destroyed many mature beeches and extensively damaged the avenues, the original concept has been maintained and the layout restored. Apart from their unique design, the gardens also have a substantial rose garden which provides summer-long colour, and an interesting herbaceous border. However, it is the splendid architectural features, with trees and water, which would have been familiar to the garden's creator, that are outstanding. In 1991 the remains of a massive eighteenth-century cascade were found. Apparently the family of the day had a change of mind, so they carefully grassed it over without ever starting to build a pond at the bottom of the valley.

Brodsworth Hall 2

Brodsworth, Doncaster DN5 7XJ. Tel: (01302) 722598; Fax (01302) 337165

English Heritage • 5m NW of Doncaster. Access from A1(M) junction 37 off A635 • House open April to Oct, 1 – 5pm • Garden open April to Oct, Tues – Sun and Bank Holiday Mons, 12 noon – 6pm, Nov to 26th March, 11am – 4pm • Entrance: summer £2.60, concessions £2, children £1.30; winter £1.60, concessions £1.20, children 80p (hall and gardens £4.70, concessions £3.50, children £2.40) (1999 prices) ◐ ☕ ✕ 🖾 WC ⧫ ♨ ☕

As the restoration continues, the grounds here offer a rare opportunity of discovering what it was like to stroll among the shrubberies and formal bedding of a large-scale Victorian layout. The 15 acres were designed and planted when the Italianate house was being built in the mid-1860s, on land with many fine established trees. It also featured a long, deep quarry dating from the eighteenth century, from which stone had been taken to build a previous hall. Main features in the garden are tamed evergreen shrubberies, a mixed border with trimmed shrubs and Japanese anemones, day lilies, aconites, ferns and fuchsias, all planted among them. Wide gaps have been left between the plants so that each type has sufficient space in which to display its full beauty. Beyond, around a marble fountain, an intricate bedding scheme uses the original shapes cut in the lawn and is now planted with modern pelargonium varieties, with cordyline palms and the standard roses 'White Pet' as additional tall spot-plants. Trees overhanging the old quarry shade a maze of walkways and bridges in fine rockwork; these offer a baffling series of vistas into dells which will contain collections of ferns and other shade-loving plants, as well as glimpses of folly temples. This part of the garden, including the rose garden and flower dell, is undergoing further restoration. There is a thyme garden with nearly 100 varieties, commemorating a unique variety found in the lawns, which are rich in natural flora. The only complete collection of the Portland group of roses has been planted here, along with other historic roses, all underplanted with herbaceous plants, while a large herbaceous border provides a fine backdrop to this mixture of colour and scents. Special events include music in the summer and at Christmas.

East Riddlesden Hall 3

Bradford Road, Keighley, Bradford BD20 5EL. Tel: (01535) 607075

The National Trust • 1m NE of Keighley on N side of A650 and 3m NW of Bingley • House open • Garden open April to Oct, Sat – Wed; also July and Aug, Thurs, 12 noon – 5pm and Sat, 1 – 5pm (last admission 4.30pm). Pre-booking required for parties • Entrance: £3.40, accompanied children £1.90 • Other information: Dogs in grounds only, on lead ◐ ☕ ✕ WC ⧫ ♨ ♨ ☕

A traditional seventeenth-century Yorkshire manor house with oak furniture and fine embroideries. The small garden has herbaceous borders, an abundance of lavender and herbs. There is a magnificent oak-framed Great Barn considered one of the finest in the north of England. Various events most of the year.

Golden Acre Park ★   4

Otley Road, Leeds. Tel: (0113) 246 3504

Leeds City Council • NW of Leeds off A660 Leeds — Otley road at approach to Bramhope • Open all year, daily, during daylight hours • Entrance: free ○ ☕ WC ♿ ⬧ 🏠

Until 1945, when it was purchased by Leeds Corporation for £18,500, this was a privately owned pleasure park. Since then it has been developed as an important public park and minor botanic garden. It stands on a pleasant undulating site leading down to a lake, and the extensive tree collection has most specimens labelled. Rhododendrons are a feature in the spring, along with alpine plants both in the rock garden and in the alpine house. The park is noted for its fine collection of houseleeks (sempervivums) as well as its heather collection. Demonstration plots are maintained where instruction is provided for home gardeners; the quality of planting and vegetables improves annually.

Harewood House ★   5

Harewood, Leeds LS17 9LQ. Tel: (0113) 288 6331; Fax: (0113) 288 6467

The Earl and Countess of Harewood • 7m N of Leeds on A61 • House open, 11am – 4.30pm • Grounds open April to Oct, daily; Nov to mid-Dec, Sat and Sun, all 10am – 6pm (or dusk if earlier) • Entrance: Terrace Gallery, Bird Garden and grounds £5.75, OAPs £4.75, children £3.25, freedom ticket £6.95, OAPs £6.25, children £4.50; family Harewood Card £40) (1999 prices) • Other information: Art gallery, bird garden and adventure playgrounds. Regular garden tours and talks programme ◐ ☕ ✕ 🏠 WC ⬧ 🅿 🏠 ♨

Originally laid out in the 1770s by 'Capability' Brown, the gardens and park still retain many of his characteristic features, most notably a majestic lake and a well-wooded horizon. Sir Charles Barry's terrace of the 1840s contains formal parterres and fountains, herbaceous borders and bedding. The terrace has been restored and the intricate patterns of the parterre have been re-created to Barry's original designs after decades under grass. The west garden on the upper terrace has been reconstructed to an elegant new design typical of the work of the late David Hicks. Nineteenth-century rhododendrons enrich the edge of the lake and make a fine sight reflected on its surface when flowering in early June; splendid views can be seen from the boat which is launched in good weather. Other features in this woodland setting are a vaguely Japanese bog garden housing a good collection of hostas below the lake's cascade. Parkland, excellently maintained with trees and shrubs, is being further replanted.

Hillsborough Walled Garden 6

Middlewood Road, Sheffield S6 4HD. Tel: (0114) 281 2167

Hillsborough Community Development Trust • Adjacent to Hillsborough Library • Garden open Mon – Fri, 9am – 4pm, weekends by appt • Entrance: free but donations welcome • Other information: Parking for disabled only. Guide dogs only ○ 🥤 🍴 WC ♿ ⚘

The site embraces four different gardens: a wildlife area, a lawn with herbaceous borders, a woodland glade and a formal garden with raised beds for easy use by disabled gardeners. The many features include a pergola, pool, wallspout, arbour, herb garden, vegetable and nursery garden, greenhouse, and a garden for the visually handicapped. There is a Victorian heated garden wall, thought to be the most extensive in the Sheffield area. Planned as a project for children's nature studies, it now has strong links with arts bodies and provides employment training and community entertainments; it was awarded a Community Enterprise Scheme award in 1993. The garden was planned, created and is run by the community. As such it is not just an area to look at and enjoy, but everyone is encouraged to help with its upkeep. Tools are available on site and plants are always welcomed.

The Hollies Park ★ 7

**Weetwood Lane, Leeds LS16 5NZ. Tel: (0113) 247 8361
(Parks and Countryside)**

Leeds City Council • In NW Leeds off Weetwood Lane, off A660 Leeds – Otley road • Open all year, daily, during daylight hours • Entrance: free ○ 🍴 WC ♿

The original layout is Victorian, and the gardens were given to Leeds Corporation in 1921 by the Brown family in memory of a son killed during World War I. The fine informal, largely woodland garden features woody plants, especially rhododendrons, many rarely seen growing in this part of the North. Ferns flourish throughout the gardens and a varied collection of hydrangeas provides late summer colour. Many slightly tender subjects, such as eucryphia, embothrium and drimys, thrive in the pleasant microclimate. A number of National Collections maintained by Leeds City Council is grown, including those of hemerocallis, hostas and deutzias, and probably the most comprehensive philadelphus collection in Europe.

Land Farm 8

Colden, Hebden Bridge, Calderdale HA7 7PJ. Tel: (01422) 842260

Mr and Mrs J. Williams • 3½ m NE of Todmorden, off A646 between Sowerby Bridge and Todmorden. Call at Visitors' Centre in Hebden Bridge for map • Open May to Aug, Sat, Sun and Bank Holiday Mons, 10am – 5pm. Parties welcome • Entrance: £2.50 ◑ ✕ WC ♿ ⚘ 🛍 🌡

A four-acre garden created by the owners on a north-facing site 300 metres up in the Pennines. Designed as a low-maintenance garden, it nevertheless contains a wide diversity of shrubs, herbaceous plants and alpines. There is a newly created woodland garden with rhododendron and cornus underplanted with herbaceous plants. *Tropaeolum speciosum* runs in glorious riot through parts of the garden. There is also an art gallery in the former barn.

30 Latchmere Road 9

Leeds LS16 5DF. Tel: (0113) 275 1261

Mr and Mrs Joe Brown • NW of Leeds off A6120 (ring road to Bradford), turn up Fillingfir Drive, right at postbox, then left into Latchmere Road • Open for horticultural societies, garden clubs and tourist parties by appt only • Entrance: £2, children 50p • Other information: No parking in Latchmere Road ● WC ⚲

A garden of exceptional merit created from scratch over the last 30 years, a good example of inspired design on a small scale. Herbaceous plants, ferns, climbers and shrubs all contribute to a series of mini-features through which the visitor passes in a controlled circuit of the garden. These include a clematis collection, sink gardens, pools, a patio and an alpine garden.

Lister Park 10

Keighley Road, Bradford. Tel: (01274) 751535

City of Bradford Metropolitan Council • 1½ m N of Bradford centre (Forster Square) on A650 Bradford – Keighley road • Open all year, daily, during daylight hours • Entrance: free • Other information: Cartwright Hall, City Art Gallery and Museum open all year, daily except Mon ○ 🍽 ✕ WC ♿ ⟡ 🌳

A pleasant city park with an old botanical garden, currently being restored through a Heritage Lottery funded grant. There is an attractive formal bedding display in front of the Cartwright Hall and an interesting floral clock: a rare example of Victorian ingenuity which is worth seeing. The latest phase of restoration includes a new garden reflecting the simplicity of Mughal design, a symmetrical synthesis of Islamic and Hindu styles, due for completion summer 2000. Why go to India when you can experience Bradford?

Nostell Priory 11

Doncaster Road, Nostell, Wakefield WF4 1QE. Tel: (01924) 863892

The National Trust • 6m SE of Wakefield on A638 • House usually open from 12 noon • Garden open probably April to June, Sat and Sun; July and Aug, daily except Fri; Sept and Oct, Sat and Sun, all 12 noon – 5pm (last admission 4.30pm) • Entrance: £2.50, children £1.50, family £6.50 (house and garden £4, children £2, family £9.50) [Note: House and garden closed in 2000] ◑ 🍽 🍱 WC ♿ ⟡ 🌳

The dark, brooding eighteenth-century mansion by Robert Adam sits in open parkland with an attractive lake and a variety of well-established trees. A fine, well-tended and well-labelled rose garden is the main gardening feature, together with extensive lakeside gardens including magnolias (March to

April), rhododendrons (May), summerhouse, Gothick archway and cock-fighting pit. One of the most attractive Gothick buildings, with later additions by Robert Adam, once occupied by a couple who looked after the animals, has been restored. There is a children's playground and a picnic area. At the time of going to press, we learn that both house and garden will be closed during 2000, due to extensive building works, and will reopen in 2001.

Roundhay Park (Tropical World Canal Gardens) ★   12

Roundhay Road, Leeds LS8 2ER. Tel: (0113) 266 1850

Leeds City Council • S of A6120 northern ring, off A58 Roundhay Road from city centre • Open all year, daily, except 25th Dec, 10am – dusk • Entrance: £1, children (8-16) 50p, under 8 free • Other information: Dogs in park only, on lead ○ 🍴 🍽 WC & ♿ ☕

A wonderful day out for all the family. The intensively cultivated canal gardens area was formerly the kitchen and ornamental gardens of the Nicholson family who sold the site to the Leeds Corporation in 1871. The extensive parkland with its fine trees is an extravagant setting for the pure horticultural extravaganza of the canal gardens with their formal bedding and generous collections. The exotic houses have the largest collection outside Kew, with exotic butterflies and birds. Waterfalls and pools are surrounded by tropical plants, and a new arid house holds a large collection of cacti and succulents. There is an underwater world of plants and fish, an insect house and a nocturnal house where bush babies, monkeys and other animals can be seen.

Sheffield Botanical Gardens   13

Sheffield S10 2LN. Tel: (0114) 267 1115

Sheffield Council • ½ m from A625, 1½ m SW of city centre • Open all year, daily except 25th, 26th Dec and 1st Jan, 10am – dusk • Entrance: free ○ 🍽 WC & ♿ ☕

These historic gardens (opened in 1836) are owned by the Sheffield Town Trust and managed by Sheffield City Council, with considerable input from local garden societies, notably The Friends of the Botanical Gardens (FOBS). It is popular with visitors for the peace and seclusion of 19 sheltered acres so close to the city centre. Enjoyment will be vastly improved by the conversion of the erstwhile Curator's House into a café/restaurant. This is just one of many proposals to be supported by a Heritage Lottery Fund award (£5.06m). Others include the complete restoration of the irreplaceable 'Paxton' pavilions and re-instatement of the greenhouses which once joined them together. The resulting 90-metre conservatory will house plants from the southern hemisphere. Clearing and replanting is already taking place and there are improvements all the time; the lottery-funded work over the next five years will see the gardens completely revitalised.

Temple Newsam 14

Leeds LS15 0AE. Tel: (0113) 264 5535

*Leeds City Council • 3m E of Leeds, signed off A63/A6120 ring road junction •
House open daily except Mon, 10.30am – 6.15pm. Extra charge • Park open all
year, daily, 9am – dusk; National Collections open Mon – Fri, 11am – 3pm,
Sat and Sun, 11am – 2pm • Entrance: free* ○ ☕ WC & ⊞

A pleasant oasis surrounded by urban Leeds. Set in the remnants of a
'Capability' Brown landscape of the 1760s (much reduced by a golf course
and open-cast mining) is a wide diversity of gardens. Around the house are an
Italian paved garden and a Jacobean-style parterre surrounded by pleached
lime walks. A rhododendron and azalea walk leads to small ponds with a bog
garden and arboretum, beyond which is a large walled rose garden and
greenhouses containing collections of ivies, cacti and some rather dashing
climbing pelargoniums. National Collections of delphiniums, phlox and asters.
Also within the large walled garden are traditional herbaceous borders
considered to be amongst the best in England.

Wentworth Castle Gardens ★ 15

Lowe Lane, Stainborough, Barnsley S75 3ET. Tel: (01226) 731269

*Barnsley Metropolitan Borough Council • 3m SW of Barnsley off M1 junction
37, 2m along minor roads signed 'Oxspring, Gilroyd and Northern College' •
Gardens open mainly for guided tours, probably from mid-April to June.
Telephone for times and prices • Other information: House and main buildings
occupied by Northern College* ● WC & ⬯

One of the most exciting gardens in Yorkshire, laid out mainly under
the direction of William Wentworth between 1739 and 1791, which is
currently undergoing a complete review of its activities. It contains one
of the finest collections of rhododendrons in the north, which has been
established during the past 15 years to form an invaluable educational
resource. Barnsley Council are putting together an important development package in conjunction with the Northern College (who own the
house), for which a grant has been requested from the National
Heritage Lottery Fund; this will restore the fabric of the garden and
also enable its collections to be expanded. It has the National Collection
for large-leaved rhododendrons. There are also extensive new plantings
of camellias, especially the *C. x williamsii* hybrids which have National
Collection status. The eighteenth-century landscape has been designated
Grade 1 by English Heritage. Among the many features are a three-
quarter-mile-long serpentine lake, monuments to Queen Anne and Lady
Mary Wortley Montagu, and the stunning Gothick folly of Stainborough
Castle, constructed on the highest point of the estate, which forms a
fitting dramatic climax to the garden layout. Noise from the M1 in the
valley is the only intrusion.

5 Wharfe Close 16

Adel, Leeds LS16 8JE. Tel: (0113) 261 1363

Mr and Mrs C.V. Lightman • E of A660 Leeds – Skipton road and N of north Leeds ring road (A6120). Turn off ring road into Adel along Long Causeway/ Sir George Martin's Drive to Derwent Drive • Open some Suns from June to Aug, 2 – 5pm and by appt • Entrance: £1.50 • Other information: Parking between bus terminus and shop ◑ ▣ WC ℗

An interesting garden of about three-quarters of an acre which includes three ponds and a woodland glade. There are large collections of both ivies and conifers and an amazing array of planted sinks and troughs, a passion of the gardener responsible for laying out the site.

York Gate ★ 17

Back Church Lane, Adel, Leeds LS16 8DW. Tel: (0113) 267 8240

The Gardeners' Royal Benevolent Society • Off A660 Leeds – Otley road, behind Adel Church • Open 13th Feb, 12th March, 9th April, 14th May, 4th, 25th June, 16th July, 6th, 28th Aug, Thurs June to Aug, 2 – 5pm, 13th June, 5th, 27th July, 6 – 9pm • Entrance: £2.50, children free • Other information: Coaches by appt only ◑ ▣ WC ℗

A garden created by the Spencer family and bequeathed by the late Sybil Spencer to the Gardeners' Royal Benevolent Society. Bought by the Spencers in 1951, this was a bleak farmhouse and unpromising area of land. When her husband died, her son took over the design and in a tragically short life he achieved a garden of impeccable taste and style, using local stone, cobble stones and gravel to create a structure of style and great interest. As to the design, the late Arthur Hellyer remarked on its debt to Hidcote, but noted that many of the ideas used there in 10 acres are here confined to barely one. He also commented on the clever use of eye-catching ornaments and topiary. 'This is a garden made for discovery,' he said, as 'from no vantage point is it possible to see the whole... Nor is any route of exploration specially indicated.' It is also a plantsperson's garden, maintaining a quality collection arranged in clearly defined model features. These include an extraordinary miniature pinetum as well as fern, peony and iris borders, and an exquisite silver and white border, now showing a hint of pink in it. A garden of rare delight. Also in Adel is the Wainwright's garden at *8 Dunstarn Lane*, open three times a year for charity. Strong on delphiniums and other summer flowers, Tel: (0113) 267 3938.

Yorkshire Sculpture Park 18

Bretton Hall, West Bretton, Wakefield WF4 4LG. Tel: (01924) 830302

Yorkshire Sculpture Park, Independent Charitable Trust • 6m NW of Barnsley, 6m SW of Wakefield at West Bretton. Leave M1 at junction 38 • Open all year, daily, except 24th, 25th, 31st Dec: summer, 10am – 6pm, winter, 10am – 4pm • Entrance: free but donation welcomed. Parking charge • Other information:

Coaches by prior arrangement. Access Sculpture Trail suitable for wheelchairs.
Information Centre gallery ○ 🍽 ✕ 📷 <u>WC</u> ♿ ⟨⟩ 🏧 ♨

Britain's first permanent sculpture park was established in 1977, and is now considered to be one of Europe's leading open-air galleries. The Palladian-style house and its 260 acres of formal gardens, woods, lakes and parkland provide a fine setting for temporary and permanent exhibitions. Work is not bought or given, but available on extended loan from artists, collectors, the Arts Council and the Tate Gallery. The layout makes it possible to view sculpture in 'garden' as well as 'public' settings that demand a more monumental approach by the sculptor. Note the imaginative use of colour on the wooden fencing which leads to the Access Sculpture Trail designed by Don Rankin with emphasis on access for disabled visitors. The sculptures here are being worked upon *in situ*, evolving with the gardens – an example of the subtle relationship between art and nature. Maintenance is patchy, and a difficult balance has to be kept between jolly areas for school parties and a certain amount of dignity round pieces by the likes of Henry Moore.

HOW TO FIND THE GARDENS
Directions to each garden are included in the entry. This information has been supplied by the owners and garden inspectors. It is aimed to be the best available to those travelling by car, and has been compiled to be used in conjunction with a road atlas.

Some gardens can be approached by public transport, but alas these are few and far between. The unreliability of train and bus services makes it unrewarding to include details, particularly as many garden visits are made on Sundays. However, properties that can be reached by public transport feature in National Trust guides and the NGS Yellow Book, which sometimes give details.

OPENING DATES AND TIMES
Times of access given are the best available at the moment of going to press, but some may have been changed subsequently. In the entries, the times given are inclusive – that is, an entry such as May to Sept means that the garden is open from 1st May to 30th Sept inclusive, and 2 – 5pm, means that entry will be effective during that period. Please note that many owners will open their gardens to visitors by appointment. They will often arrange to give a personally-conducted tour on these occasions. Unavoidably some owners cannot give their opening times before we go to press. In such cases we attempt to give the best guidance we can.

NORTHERN IRELAND &
THE REPUBLIC OF IRELAND

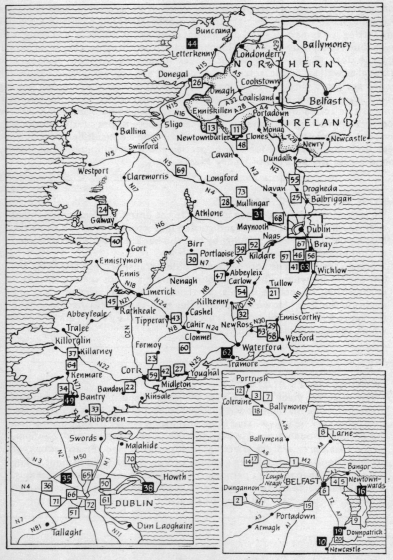

Two-starred gardens are marked on the map with a black square.

NORTHERN IRELAND

Antrim Castle Gardens ★ 1

Randalstown Road, Antrim, BT41 4LH. Tel: (028) 9442 8000; Fax (028) 9446 0360

Antrim Borough Council Arts and Heritage Service • Access from A6 Randalstown Road, Antrim • Grounds open all year, daily, 9.30am – dusk. Guided tours for parties at any time by arrangement • Entrance: £2, concessions £1. Parties of up to 40, £1 per person, school parties 50p per child, accompanying adults free (1999 prices) • Other information: Refreshments by arrangement for parties. Interpretive display in Clotworthy Arts Centre ○ 🍵 🗟 WC ௯ ⬦ ⓧ

A rare example of an estate where the main elements survive as they were when laid out for a late-seventeenth-century castle (now demolished). The canals, connected by a cascade, are lined with clipped lime and hornbeam hedges. Paths crisscross through the wooded wilderness, the main avenue of which leads to an airy clearing with a round pond reflecting sky and trees. Following a restoration project, a large parterre has been planted with varieties known in the seventeenth century and is set off by a quincunx grove of standard hornbeam (new) and an immense yew hedge (old). The adjacent Anglo-Norman motte retains its spiral path; although difficult to access it is worth a climb to the top to see the lower course of the Sixmilewater river, the centre of the town of Antrim, and the 37-acre ornamental site below – a fraction of a once-vast desmesne stretching as far as the eye can see.

The Argory 2

Moy, Dungannon BT71 6NA. Tel: (028) 8778 4753; Fax: (028) 8778 9598

The National Trust • 4m NE of Moy, 3m from M1 junction 14 • House open • Grounds and garden open April, May, and Sept, Sat, Sun and Bank Holiday Mons; June to Aug, daily except Tues, all 2 – 6pm • Entrance: £2.60, children £1.30 (includes guided tour of house). Parking charge £1.50 (1999 prices) • Other information: Coaches must use M1 junction 13 because of weight restrictions. Parking 100 metres from house ◑ 🍵 🗟 WC ௯ ⬦ 🏪 ⓧ

The lawns of the pleasure ground slope down past yew arbours to two pavilions, one a pump house, the other a garden house. Beyond, the visitor can walk under pollarded limes along the banks of the Blackwater river, and there are other woodland walks in this tranquil landscape. A splash of summer colour near the house attracts the eye to a pretty, enclosed early nineteenth-century sundial garden of box-edged rose beds. There is a new riverside walk of 1½ miles.

Ballylough House 3

Bushmills, Antrim BT57 8TP. Tel: (028) 7073 1219; Fax: (028) 7073 0156

Mr and Mrs Traill • S of Giant's Causeway. From Bushmills take B66 Dervock road past old distillery for 1½ m and turn right • Open June to Sept by appt • Entrance: £3 • Other information: PYO raspberries ⬤ 🗟 ௯ ⌖

Traills have lived in this eighteenth-century house and gardened here for 200 years. A meadow containing dozens of different wild flowers surrounds the picturesque ruins of a fifteenth-century castle. Many interesting plants for the enthusiast are informally planted within the shelter of the two-and-a-half-acre walled garden, which still retains traditional box-edged beds in the lower fruit and vegetable section.

Ballyrogan Nurseries 4

The Grange, Ballyrogan, Newtownards, Down BT23 4SD.
Tel: (028) 9181 0451 (6 to 6.30pm)

Gary Dunlop • Write or telephone for directions from Newtownards or Belfast • Open by appt evenings and weekends • Entrance: donation to charity • Other information: Plants for sale by order ◐ ♿ ◁▷ ℘

This unusual garden covers three acres of rocky outcrop surrounded by farmland and wonderful views. Merging compartments crammed with a superb plant collection undulate from watery depths full of beardless iris, via beds of herbaceous and woody material, to rugged heights faced with alpines. Each section is decorated with statues and seats. Paths strike out to newly planned areas of this ever-evolving garden. Three National Collections (celmisias, crocosmias and euphorbias) join with many other well-represented genera such as agapanthus, astelia, dierama, erythronium, eucalyptus, iris, kniphofia, libertia, meconopsis, phormium, rhododendron, rodgersia, roscoea, schizostylis, watsonia, etc., and variegated plants. The nursery can supply enthusiasts with a large range of plants in limited quantities from most of these genera and others.

Ballywalter Park 5

Ballywalter, Newtownards, Down BT22 2PA. Tel: (028) 4275 8264

Dunleath Estates • 20m E of Belfast, 10m SE of Newtownards off B5 between Greyabbey and Ballywalter. Turn right at T-junction facing gates and follow wall to entrance on left opposite farm • Open by appt only. Please ring Mon — Fri between 9am and 1pm • Entrance: house or garden £3.50 each (house and garden £6) • Other information: PYO in season ◐

The fine mid-nineteenth-century Italianate house by the architect Lanyon, with an elegant conservatory wing, was praised by Sir John Betjeman. The surrounding grounds are an amalgam of two earlier 'landscaped' desmesnes, embellished for the present house with a rock garden around a stream with bridges, also by Lanyon. The notable rhododendron collection is provided with shelter from mature trees throughout the park. A rose pergola and newly restored glasshouse decorate the walled garden.

Belfast Botanic Garden 6

Stranmillis Road, Belfast City BT9 5BJ. Tel/Fax: (028) 9032 4902

Belfast City Council Parks Department • Between Queen's University and Ulster Museum, Stranmillis. Buses 69, 84 and 85 • Open all year, daily, 7.30am —

dusk. Palm House and Tropical Ravine, summer, weekdays, 10am – 5pm, weekends and public holidays, 2 – 5pm (closes 4pm in winter). Guided tours and parties at any time by arrangement • Entrance: free. Guided tours £10 • Other information: Refreshments in Ulster Museum ○ 🍴 WC ♿ ☕

Established in 1828, this became a public park in 1895. As well as two magnificent double herbaceous borders and a rose garden with 8000 roses, there are two other reasons to visit this otherwise unexceptional park – the curvilinear iron and glass conservatory (1839-52), and one of the finest Victorian glasshouses (Richard Turner built only the wings; the dome is by Young of Edinburgh). It was restored in the 1970s and contains a collection of tropical plants with massed displays of 'pot mums' and the like in season (again well grown and finely displayed, but not everyone's favourite). The Tropical Ravine House is the greater delight, and also recently restored. This is 'High Victoriana', with ferns, bananas, lush tropical vines and tree ferns, goldfish in the Amazon lily pond, and a waterfall worked with a chain-pull. Marvellous, evocative of bygone crinoline days.

Benvarden 7

Dervock, Ballymoney, Co. Antrim BT53 6NN. Tel: (028) 2074 1331; Fax (028) 2074 1955

Mr and Mrs Hugh Montgomery • 4m E of Coleraine off B67. Signposted • Open June to Aug, daily, 2 – 6pm and at other times by appt • Entrance: £2 (1999 prices) ◑ 🍴 WC ♿ ☕

The walled garden has a curved and brick-faced three-metre wall, lined with old espalier-trained apple and pear trees and focused on a round goldfish pond and fountain. Vertical interest is achieved by climbers scrambling over former glasshouse frames, beneath which seats are provided. The adjoining one-acre traditional kitchen garden is in full production and contains melon and tomato houses, potting sheds and gardener's bothy, fruit trees and box hedges. The eighteenth-century house is set in lawns where the visitor can wander along the banks of the Bush River, which is spanned at this point by an elegant Victorian iron bridge, 36 metres long, to a pond surrounded by yews, rhododendrons and azaleas.

Carnfunnock Country Park 8

Coast Road, Drains Bay, Larne. Tel: (028) 2827 0541

Larne Borough Council • 4m N of Larne on A2 Antrim coast road • County park and walled garden open all year, daily: April to Sept, 8am – 9pm; Oct to March, 8am – 5pm. Maze (deciduous) open June to Sept, daily • Entrance: country park £2 per car • Other information: Guide dogs only in walled garden ○ 🍴 ✕ 🍴 WC ♿ ☕ 🏪 ☕

The main attraction is the Time Garden, a display of the history of time, with more than a dozen different sundials catching the sun in the shelter of the old walled garden. This steep site was planted and landscaped, complete with post-modernist pergolas and many hardworks, in 1990. Nearby, 9000 hornbeams were used to make a maze in the shape of Northern Ireland. Both features are in the centre of parkland with walks among mature trees high up to an ice-house and fine views of the sea. Activity centre with free children's play area.

Castle Ward 9

Strangford, Downpatrick, Down BT30 7LS. Tel: (01396) 881204; Fax: (028) 4488 1729

The National Trust • 7m NE of Downpatrick, 1½ m W of Strangford on A25, on S shore of Strangford Lough. Entrance by Ballyculter Lodge • House open April to Oct, weekends (June to Aug, daily except Thurs) • Estate, gardens and grounds open all year, daily, dawn – dusk • Entrance: parking charge £3.50 (£1 when house and other facilities closed) ○ 🍵 ✕ 🗁 WC ৬ ⟨⊞ 🎐 ✿

A beautifully situated landscape park on a peninsula near the mouth of Strangford Lough enhances the 1760s' house with its classical west front and Gothick east front. Both house and decorative Lady Anne's Temple command the heights. Below lie an impressive canal and yew walks, features retained from the gardens of a previous early eighteenth-century house. The sunken Windsor Garden has lost much of its intricate bedding but there are colourful borders containing an interesting range of plants, some quite rare, leading to the rockery and a sentinel row of cordylines and Florence Court yews.

Castlewellan National Arboretum ★★ 10

Castlewellan, Down BT31 9BU. Tel: (028) 4477 8664; Fax (028) 4477 1762

Forest Service, Dept of Agriculture (Northern Ireland) • 25m S of Belfast, 4m NW of Newcastle, in Castlewellan • Open all year, daily • Entrance: cars £3.50, minibuses £7, coaches £20 (1999 prices) • Other information: Disabled parking. Refreshments in summer only ○ 🗁 WC ৬ ⟨⊞ ✿

The walled garden, now called the Annesley Garden, contains an outstanding collection of mature trees and shrubs, many planted before the turn of the century by the Earl Annesley. Original specimens of some of Castlewellan's cultivars thrive here, in fine condition. In the spring and summer there are many rhododendrons in bloom, and scarlet Chilean fire bushes (*Embothrium coccineum*). In mid-summer, the snow-carpet is the fallen petals of an unequalled collection of eucryphia. In all, there are 38 champion specimen trees in one area of just nine acres: *Cupressus macrocarpa* 'Lutea', *Dacrycarpus dacrydioides* (syn. *Podocarpus dacrydioides*), *Dacrydium colensoi*, *Juniperus recurva* and *Picea breweriana*. Castlewellan has 17 southern-hemisphere broad-leaved champions, including *Pittosporum tenuifolium*, *Crinodendron hookerianum*, *Eucryphia cordifolia* and *Pseudopanax crassifolius*. Half of these specimens are also thought to be the oldest examples in cultivation. Apart from the trees there are rhododendrons, bulbs, herbaceous borders, a new fragrant garden, a small glasshouse display range with canaries, as well as topiary of Irish yew and, in summer, probably one of the largest displays of tropaeolum. The 12-acre walled garden has a formal axis, with an herbaceous border and two recently restored fountain pools with water lilies. Beyond the walls the arboretum extends for a further 85 acres in the Forest Park, planted with heathers, dwarf conifers and birch, and flowering trees (malus, prunus, etc.). Signposted walks lead into the forest and round the magnificent lake. A caravan and camping ground within the park provides a wonderful base for exploring this part of Ireland and for visiting the other famous County Down gardens. Castlewellan is well known to everyone for the golden Leyland cypress that came from here — don't be dismayed, the arboretum contains many more wonderful plants, some unique, all in their prime. You will not see decrepit trees here — the maintenance and labelling are exceptionally good. Red squirrels all year. A programme of restorative regeneration is taking place in the garden — for example, the 'lost vista' of the Mourne Mountains from the viewing terrace has been reinstated.

Crom Estate   11

Newtownbutler, Fermanagh. Tel: (028) 6673 8174; Visitor Centre (028) 6673 8118

The National Trust • 3m W of Newtownbutler on Crom road • Estate open April to Sept, Mon — Sat, 10am — 6pm, Sun, 12 noon — 6pm. Guided walks by arrangement • Entrance: £3 parking charge for cars and boats • Other information: Batricar available. Visitor Centre with jetty to allow cruiser access. Boat hire available. Castle not owned by the National Trust — please respect areas marked 'Private' ◑ ☕ 🖻 WC ⬦ ♨ ⚱

Many lovely walks can be enjoyed at this heavily wooded lough shore and island desmesne, though no formal gardens remain. Beautiful rhododendron woodland walk in April/May and spectacular autumn colours. The Trust's aim is to keep up this estate as a nature conservation site. The notable features to visit are a pair of ancient and venerable yew trees. Cross the White Bridge to Inisherk Island and survey the naturally picturesque landscape enhanced by W.S. Gilpin in the 1830s for the present house. The many interesting estate buildings, such as the boat house, tea house and the island folly, Crichton Tower, are used as eye-catchers and surprises, and the local church and ruins of the seventeenth-century Old Castle are incorporated into the vistas.

Downhill   12

Castlerock, Coleraine, Limavady BT51 4RP.

The National Trust • 6m W of Coleraine, 1m W of Castlerock on A2 coast road • Mussenden Temple open April, May, June and Sept, Sat, Sun and Bank Holiday Mons; July and Aug, daily, all 12 noon — 6pm • Grounds open all year, daily • Entrance: free ○ ⬧ ⬦

The gaunt ruins of Downhill, one of the houses of the Earl-Bishop, Frederick Hervey, sit amidst rough grass, his gardens having long since gone, but at one of the gate lodges, The Bishop's Gate, is a gem of a garden created by the former custodian, Miss Jan Eccles. Startling clumps of *Iris kaempferi*, embothriums, crinodendrons and many other unusual trees and shrubs are planted up a glen. Dressed stones from tumbledown buildings and armless statues are enveloped with happy plantings of lithospermum, bergenia and fuchsia, with roses spilling from a rickety pergola. The late eighteenth-century Mussenden Temple, designed by Sir William Chambers and sited on the clifftop with spectacular views along the coast, must be one of the most extraordinary libraries in the world and certainly one of the most outstanding garden buildings. There are walks to a mausoleum, a fish pond, a walled garden, a belvedere and woodland.

Florence Court   13

Florencecourt, Enniskillen, Fermanagh BT92 1DB. Tel: (028) 6634 8249; Fax (028) 6634 8873

The National Trust • 8m SW of Enniskillen, via A4 Sligo road and A32 Swanlinbar road, 4m from Marble Arch Caves • House open April and Sept, Sat, Sun and Bank Holiday Mons; May to Aug, daily except Tues, all 1 – 6pm • Estate open all year, daily, 10am – 7pm (Oct to March 4pm). Closed 25th Dec. Parties by arrangement • Entrance: Forest Park and Pleasure Gardens £2 per car (house £3, children £1.50, parties £2.75 per person) • Other information: Batricar available ○ 🍽 ✕ 🖺 WC ᕼ 🔄 🖐 🚻

The original, the mother of all Irish yews (*Taxus baccata* 'Fastigiata'), still grows in the original garden site – accessible by well-marked woodland paths and about a quarter of a mile from the splendid mansion at Florence Court, although strong shoes are essential (especially in rainy season) if you wish to pay respects to the venerable 250-year-old tree. Well worth the walk, the gravel path allows glimpses of the mountains and the handsome 'Brownian' park in front of the house. Some fine weeping beeches, Japanese maples and old rhododendrons grow in the pleasure grounds. There are ponds and a rose garden in the walled garden. Ice-house, water-driven saw mill and recently restored summerhouse, eel bridge and hydraulic ram. The three-acre walled garden at Florence Court, including the listed Rose Cottage and Gate Lodges, has recently been acquired by the Trust. The nearby caves (open to public) are worth visiting too, making a rewarding day out.

28 Killyfaddy Road   14

Magherafelt, Londonderry BT45 6EX. Tel: (028) 7963 2180

Ann Buchanan • 10m NE of Cookstown off A31. From Magherafelt, take Moneymore road. After ¼ m Killyfaddy Road is second on left opposite filling station. Gardens 1m further along, both sides of road • Open all year, Tues – Sat, 1 – 5pm and by appt • Entrance: donation to charity ◐ 🖺 WC ᕼ 🔄 🚻

An acre of informal country garden created over nearly three decades, densely planted with an extensive range of herbaceous perennials plus trees, shrubs, alpines, fruit, vegetables and a small orchard. A 'wild' garden in a separate site across the road has woodland and shade areas, and a wildlife pond with associated bog plants.

Kilwarlin Battle Garden 15

Kilwarlin, Hillsborough, Lisburn.

Moravian Church • 4m SW of Lisburn between Moira and Hillsborough. Difficult to find but follow signs to Moravian Church (OS ref J209588) • Open all year, daily ○

One of Ireland's strangest 'gardens', comprising a series of grassy mounds representing the site of the Battle of Thermopylae. Tucked away in the countryside near Moira, and reached by narrow country roads, the battle garden, created in the nineteenth century by the Rev. Zula (1834-44), is sited in the grounds of a small church. A place for those intrigued by the eccentricities of mankind.

Mount Stewart ★★ 16

Greyabbey, Newtownards BT22 2AD. Tel: (01247) 788387/788487; Fax: (01247) 788569

The National Trust • 15m E of Belfast, 5m SE of Newtownards on A20 Portaferry road • House open different times • Garden open 17th March, April to Sept, daily, 11am – 6pm; Oct, Sat and Sun only, 11am – 6pm • Entrance: house and garden £3.50, children £1.75, family £8.75, parties £3 per person (1999 prices) • Other information: Parking 300 metres. Two battery wheelchairs available ◑ ⬤ ✕ 🏠 WC ⬤ ⬤ ⬤ ⬤

Of all Ireland's gardens this is the one not to miss. Any adjective that evokes beauty can be applied to it, and it's fun too. In the gardens in front of the house is a collection of statuary, depicting British political and public figures – dodos, monkeys and boars. The planting here is formal, with rectangular beds of 'hot' and 'cool' colours. Beyond in the informal gardens are mature trees and shrubs, a botanical collection with few equals, planted with great panache and maintained with outstanding attention to detail. Spires of giant lilies (cardiocrinum), aspiring eucalyptus, banks of rhododendrons, ferns and blue poppies, rivers of candelabra primulas – and much more. Walk along the lakeside path to the hill that affords a view over the lake to the house. Rare tender shrubs such as *Metrosideros umbellatus* flourish here outside the walled family cemetery. Leading from it is the Jubilee Avenue and its statue of a white stag. Mount Stewart is a whole day for those keen on plants; it should be seen several times during the year truly to savour its rich tapestry of plants and water, buildings and trees. The Temple of the Winds, James 'Athenian' Stuart's banqueting hall of 1785, is also memorable.

Moyola Park 17

Castledawson, Magherafelt BT45 8ED. Tel: (028) 7946 8606

Lord Moyola • 3m NE of Magherafelt, 3m W from NW shore of Loch Neagh, in Castledawson. Main entrance in Bridge Street • Open by appt for parties • Entrance: £2 per person • Other information: Plants for sale from nursery by appt ◑ ⚘

The imposing mid-eighteenth-century house surrounded by lawns sits above the Moyola River. Behind is a succession of beautifully planted woodland compartments merging above and beside its banks, enhanced by tall old trees. Planting is interesting throughout the seasons, beginning with swathes of daffodils, followed by camellias and rhododendrons, later giving way to the paler shades of old roses, meconopsis and primulas. Numerous specimen trees and shrubs planted since the 1960s serve as a backdrop within the glades.

O'Harabrook 18

Ballymoney BT53 7PN. Tel: (028) 8066 6273

Mr and Mrs Sandy Cramsie • 1m SW of Ballymoney on B66 Garvagh road, on right at black and white gate • Open 28th May, 30th July, 2 – 6pm and for parties by appt • Entrance: £2.50, children £1, parties of 10 or more £2 per person • Other information: Teas for parties by appt. PYO in season ● ☕ 📖 WC ♿ ⚲

Set amongst rhododendron-edged woodland and parkland, the eighteenth-century house, once a coaching inn, surprisingly has a garden fenced in with corrugated iron, heavily disguised by plant growth. This former formal garden is now attractively informal, with plants cascading over paths and around seats, the whole enclosed by tall trees. A pond is has been planted up in a separate area.

Rowallane Garden ★★ 19

Saintfield, Ballynahinch, Down BT24 7LH. Tel: (01238) 510131; Fax (028) 7951 1242

The National Trust • ½ m S of Saintfield on A7 Belfast – Downpatrick road • Open April to Oct, Mon – Fri, 10.30am – 6pm, Sat and Sun, 2 – 6pm; Nov to March 2001, Mon – Fri, 10.30am – 5pm. Closed 25th, 26th Dec and 1st Jan. Parties of 15 or more at other times by appt • Entrance: April to Oct, £2.50, children £1.25; Nov to March, £1.25, children 80p, parties during opening hours £1.75 per person; out of hours £3 per person (1999 prices) ○ ☕ 📖 WC ♿ ⬳ ⚲

While famous as a 52-acre rhododendron garden and certainly excellent in this regard, Rowallane has much more to interest keen gardeners. In summer, the walled garden blossoms in lemon and blue while hoherias scatter their white petals in the wind, and in secluded places a pocket-handkerchief tree blows. There is restored Victorian bandstand (music-filled on some summer weekends) and a rock garden with primulas, meconopsis, heathers, etc. Any season will be interesting, and for the real enthusiast there are rhododendron species and cultivars in bloom from October to August. A National Collection of large-flowered penstemons is here. A feature is made of *Hypericum* 'Rowallane' at the entrance to the walled garden; within are the original plant of *Viburnum plicatum* 'Rowallane' and the original *Chaenomeles x superba* 'Rowallane'; Recent additions are wildflower meadows that are becoming famed for such comparative rarities as wild orchids. The garden is almost organic in cultivation, so wildlife abounds.

Seaforde 20

Downpatrick, Down BT30 8PG. Tel: (028) 4481 1225; Fax: (028) 4481 1370

Mr Patrick and Lady Anthea Forde • 22m S of Belfast on A24 Belfast –
Newcastle road • Garden open all year except 25th Dec to 1st Jan, Mon – Sat,
10am – 5pm, Sun, 1 – 6pm (Nov to Feb, Mon – Fri only) • Entrance: £2.20,
children £1.30 • Other information: Plants for sale in nursery. Shop at butterfly
house ○ 🍴 ✕ 🖻 WC ♿ 🐾 🛒

The fine landscaped park can be glimpsed on the way to the vast walled garden,
half of which is a commercial nursery with the attraction of a butterfly house
displaying a collection of tropical plants. The other half is an ornamental
garden bedecked in late summer with blooms of eucryphia that make up a
National Collection. The hornbeam maze has a rose-clad arbour at the centre,
the vantage point for which is a 1992 Moghul tower. Beyond the walled garden
is the Pheasantry, a verdant valley enclosed by mature trees, full of noteworthy plants collected over many years and still expanding.

REPUBLIC OF IRELAND

Altamont 21

Tullow, Co. Carlow. Tel: (0503) 59444

Duchas, the Heritage Service • 12m SE of Carlow, 5m S of Tullow, 1m off
Tullow-Bunclody road (N80/81) near Ballon • Open all year, Wed – Sun,
11am – 7pm • Entrance: IR£2, OAPs IR£1.50, students IR£1, children IR£1,
family IR£5, groups IR£1.50 per person • Other information: Garden centre.
Coaches welcome ◑ 🖻 WC 🐾

The lily-filled lake, surrounded by fine, mature trees, forms a backdrop for a
gently sloping lawn. A central walkway formally planted with Irish yews and
roses leads from the house to the lake. There is a beautiful fern-leaved beech,
and other ancient beeches form the Nun's Walk. A long walk through the
desmesne leads to the River Slaney with diversions to a bog garden, through an
Ice-Age glen of ancient oaks undercarpeted with bluebells in spring. The late
owner Mrs North's passion for trees, old-fashioned roses and unusual plants is
evident.

Amergen 22

Walshestown, Ovens, Co. Cork. Tel: (21) 331326

Mrs Christine Fehily • 10m W of Cork. Take N22 Cork – Killarney road, turn
right at Tatler Jack's Pub, follow road to crossroads, turn right into cul-de-sac for
about 1m. Garden on right • Open for parties by appt • Entrance: IR£3 ● 🖻
WC ♿ ⟁

A magnificent setting overlooking the valley of the River Lee. Behind the
house is a modest arboretum that merges into mixed borders interspersed

with informal lawns and a small orchard. The driveway divides the main garden from a slope thickly planted with shrubs and trees. Paths meander through this area where lush *Geranium maderense* and handsome dogwoods vividly demonstrate the mildness of the Cork climate. Many tender plants can be grown outdoors, including *Melianthus major*, *Acacia melanoxylon* and correa, so interesting and unusual shrubs and perennials – *Viburnum harryanum*, *Mimulus aurantiacus* – abound. The garden, started only in the early '80s, is an object lesson in informality and variety.

Annes Grove ★   23

Castletownroche, Near Mallow, Co. Cork. Tel: (22) 26145

Mr and Mrs F.P. Grove Annesley • 1m N of Castletownroche, between Fermoy and Mallow • Open mid-March to Sept, Mon – Sat, 10am – 5pm, Sun, 1 – 6pm • Entrance: IR£3, OAPs and students IR£2, children IR£1 (1999 prices). Reductions for pre-booked parties ◑ 🏠 WC ⅊ ⬦ ℘

This is an archetypal 'Robinsonian' (alias wild) garden, but such tags are not helpful. Rhododendron species and cultivars arch over and spill towards the pathways, carpeting them with fallen blossoms. Steep, sometimes slippery paths descend at various places into the valley of the Awbeg river (which inspired Edmund Spenser). The statuesque conifers planted in the valley make a colourful tapestry behind the river garden, with mimulus, day lilies and candelabra primroses in profusion. The walled garden has a weird contorted birch, emulating a willow-pattern tree, over the pool, a short herbaceous border and some formal features. The glory of Annes Grove is, however, the collection of rhododendron species, among which visitors may see hidden surprises – a superb *Juniperus recurva* 'Castlewellan', a mature pocket-handkerchief tree (*Davidia involucrata*) and other exotic, flowering trees. Here are bird-song and the crystal-clear Awbeg, water-buttercups and giant rhubarb – peaceful groves.

Ardcarraig ★   24

Oranswell, Bushypark, Co. Galway. Tel: (91) 524336

Mrs Lorna McMahon • From Galway – Oughterard road, take second left past Glenlo Abbey Hotel, continue ¼ m and garden is on left • Open 24th May, 10am – 9pm, and by appt • Entrance: IR£3, parties of 15 or more IR£2.50 per person • Other information: Refreshments and plants for sale on open day only ◑ WC

A garden full of surprises, created and maintained by a veritable enthusiast. In front of the house is a collage of heathers and conifers, with spring and autumn-flowering bulbs; ordinary but attractive. Beside it is a formal, sunken garden, with pergola covered by clematis and a terracotta *pithoi* as the focal point; handsome, but not unusual. The path then enters a wild hazel wood carpeted with bluebells, ramsons and ferns; nature's garden, and you begin to wonder 'What's next?' A clearing ablaze with scented azaleas in spring and roses and geraniums in summer is the first surprise. The path winds on to a pool surrounded by blue Himalayan poppies, hostas and candelabra primulas. And on... to a bubbling peat-stained stream that chatters over granite rocks to a bog garden with heathers and skunk cabbage, to a stunning tranquil Japanese hill and pool garden in which a snow-viewing granite lantern sits by a pool, while the boulder beyond suggests Mount Fuji. And on... to Harry's Garden, the newest part, started in 1997, full of plants given to Lorna in memory of her late husband, and planted (with a pick!) among the natural granite boulders. And on... back to the house and a formal herb garden. A magical lesson on how to improve Nature's wilderness.

Ardgillan Desmesne Gardens 25

Ardgillan Castle, Balbriggan, Co. Dublin. Tel: (1) 849 2212; Fax: (1) 849 2786

Fingal County Council • 15m N of Dublin. Signed off N1 • Castle open all year, daily except Mon (but open Bank Holiday Mons and Mons in July and Aug). Closed 23rd Dec to 2nd Jan • Park and gardens open all year, daily except 25th Dec, opens 10am, closes: Jan, 5pm, Feb, March, 6pm, April, 7pm, May, 8pm, June to Aug, 9pm, Sept, 8pm, Oct to Dec, 7pm. Conducted tours in June to Aug, Thurs, 3.30pm • Entrance: £1.50 (castle tours £2.75, OAPs and parties per person £1.50) ○ 🍽 🏦 WC ♿ ⬅ 🏮 ⚘

The approach to the castle is one of the most spectacular in Ireland, with views northwards along the coast to the Carlingford and Mourne mountains and the castle itself nestled in a hollow. When the north wind blows it can cut to the bone, so retreat quickly to the handsomely restored wooden Victorian conservatory, planted with a variety of traditional fruits and the spectacular magenta *Passiflora antioquiensis* (banana passion-flower). In front of the conservatory is a rose garden, colourful in summer. In the walled garden, remarkable for its unique alcove wall, are four compartments, each containing a different type of garden. These 'reconstructions' include a herb garden, *potager*, cottage garden and new four-seasons garden, all well maintained. A Robinsonian garden has recently been added, and there is an extensive herbaceous border along an early nineteenth-century yew walk. Little-known and out-of-the-ordinary, a great credit to its most enthusiastic head gardener.

Ardnamona ★ 26

Lough Eske, Co. Donegal. Tel: (73) 22650; Fax: (073) 22819

Kieran and Amabel Clarke • On NW shore of Lough Eske, approached from Donegal, following signs for Harvey's Point • Open all year, 10am – 8pm by appt • Entrance: IR£2 ○ 🍽 🏦 WC ⬅ ⚘

William Robinson would have been proud of this garden created by the Wallaces between 1880 and 1932. Ardnamona is wild gardening at its most exuberant and refined. Imagine a Himalayan mountain slope cloaked with primeval rhododendron forest, 18 metres tall, with a carpet of fallen leaves underfoot embroidered in discarded flowers – you are close to imagining Ardnamona. The rhododendrons are mainly over 100 years old, and they proclaim their age with proud clean trunks, coloured from cinnamon to purple, and canopies well beyond reach. Opened in 1992, this garden (once neglected, now again cared for) will welcome visitors – bed and breakfast is offered in the house. Rhododendron enthusiasts will need little more encouragement than the prospect of being in paradise.

Ballymaloe Cookery School Gardens ★ 27

Shanagarry, Co. Cork. Tel: (21) 646785; Fax: (21) 646909

Tim and Darina Allen • 23m E of Cork, between Cloyne and Ballycotton • Open April to Sept, daily, 9am – 6pm (café 9am – 9pm). Guided tours for parties by arrangement • Entrance: IR£3 • Other information: booking essential for café

◑ ◪ ✕ WC ⬠ ⬛

Take the bones of an old Quaker garden and begin afresh – that is what Darina Allen has done at Kinoith (and she hasn't finished yet). The antique beech hedges are being clipped again, and within their shelter are compartments, each different and refreshing. The first is the flower garden with short herbaceous borders, and beside a small pool is a summerhouse, the floor of which is patterned with shards of delft. Beyond is the almost-new herb garden, where dwarf box hedges delineate a formal pattern of beds planted mainly with culinary herbs. These compartments can be enjoyed from ground level and from a viewing platform – a splendid idea. The pool garden lies outside the old hedges, and has an incomplete folly. A double herbaceous border, planted in 1996, leads to a plain garden house with Gothic windows. 'Please do not touch my insides' is a friendly piece of advice, for this unassuming building's interior is decorated with myriad shells, a fantastic work of art that deserves to last for centuries. The organic vegetable garden appeals directly to the eye with its tapestry of vegetables and edible flowers. These are working gardens used by the students and Ballymaloe is itself also a hotel.

Belvedere 28

Mullingar, Co. Westmeath. Tel: (44) 40861/42820

Westmeath County Council • 4m S of Mullingar on N52 Tullamore road • Garden open May to Sept, daily, 12 noon – 6pm • Entrance: IR£1, children IR50p, season ticket IR£15 ◑

The Jealous Wall is one of those typically Gothic-Irish follies, built in 1760 to separate two squabbling brothers. It looks antique and is impressive. Otherwise this garden does not abound in interest, but there are some fine trees and a large walled garden, containing some bedding displays, and it is pleasant to be on the terraces, which drop in steps to the shores of Lough Ennel with views of its waters and islands. A pets' corner is included for children.

Berkeley Forest House 29

New Ross, Co. Wexford. Tel: (51) 421361

Count Gunnar Bernstorff • 16m SW of Enniscorthy, 4m NE of New Ross on N79 • Open for parties by appt • Entrance: IR£3 ◕

The walled garden, built in 1780 and named in honour of an uncle-by-marriage, the philosopher Bishop Berkeley, has been through several manifestations. Part is now an Italianate garden, part a small fernery and part a bonsai collection. The focal point is a fairy-tale thatched summerhouse overlooking a small knot garden.

Birr Castle Desmesne 30

Birr, Co. Offaly. Tel: (509) 20336

The Earl and Countess of Rosse • 82m SW of Dublin, 24m S of Athlone, on N52 in Birr • Desmesne open all year, daily. Guided tours by arrangement • Entrance: IR£5, OAPs and students £3.50, children IR£2.50, family IR£12, parties of 25 or more IR£3.50 per person • Other information: Parking outside castle gates. Exhibition daily. Picnics in walled garden only. Castle not open. Historic Science Centre ○ 🍺 🏠 **WC** ♿ 🐕 ᎓ 👍 🍴

The Victorian Gothic castle dominates vistas which strike through the park and at whose centre is the restored 'Leviathan' (the Great Telescope which made Birr famous in the last century and which operates regularly throughout the day). Around, in profusion, are rare trees and shrubs, many raised from seed received from central China in the 1930s. Over one of the rivers is a beautiful suspension bridge, and hidden amongst laurels is a Victorian fernery with recently restored water-works. Evergreen conifers, golden willows, carpets of daffodils, and world-record box hedges, magnolias in the river garden, a newly replanted cherry avenue and the original plant of *Paeonia* 'Anne Rosse' are mere selections of the many attractions. It is invigorating to walk around the lake, glimpsing the castle, examining the shrubs and trees (many of which are specially labelled) and revelling in the peace and quiet of central Ireland – two counties can be visited in one brief walk. The beauties of this garden owe so much to the late Anne, Countess of Rosse and gave her international fame as a gardener.

Butterstream ★★ 31

Trim, Co. Meath.

Jim Reynolds • Write for directions • Open April to Sept, daily, 11am – 6pm • Entrance: IR£3 ◑ 🍺 **WC** ᎓

Like all the best gardens, this is a single-handed work of art. A series of compartments contains different arrangements of plants, ranging from a formal box-hedged garden of old roses and lilies to an informal gold garden carpeted with ferns and hostas. In the main garden a selection of choice herbaceous perennials in an island bed encircled by wide borders processes through the summer from whites and blues to yellows and reds – phlox, kniphofia, lobelia, macleaya and allium are just a few of the genera represented. A formal pool, replete with water lilies and carp, is flagged in Liscannor stone, and large terracotta pots of box topiary stand sentinel. A view across the rich pastures of adjoining farmland adds to the sense of a Tuscan villa garden. The large tennis lawn has a restrained gallery of clematis, deep purple hedges and a rustic summerhouse. New features include a

Gothick pavilion, a small laburnum archway skirted by box and a maturing yew obelisk still caged in its wooden trellis. Still being developed with great enthusiasm and style.

Cappoquin House and Gardens 32

Dungarvan, Co. Waterford. Tel: (058) 54004

Lady Keane • On N72, immediately N of Cappoquin • Open April to July, Mon – Fri, 9am – 1pm. Entrance: charge NEW ◑

In the Blackwater River Valley as it turns towards Cork, you will find the house and garden prettily situated on a wooded hillside. We have not visited it, but will do so next year, despite the fact that the *Rough Guide* says the village seems strangely neglected. It recommends a friendly, central B&B, Mrs Flynn's Riverview guesthouse (Tel: (058) 54073).

Creagh Gardens 33

Skibbereen, Co. Cork. Tel/Fax: (28) 22121

Gwendoline Harold-Barry Trust • 4m SW of Skibbereen on R595 Baltimore road. Entrance on right through green-painted gates • Open March to Oct, daily, 10am – 6pm. Guided tours by arrangement • Entrance: IR£3, children IR£2 ◑ 🍴 WC 🐾

The life's work of Peter and Gwendoline Harold-Barry, begun in 1945, this garden has undergone a metamorphosis in the last few years as one of only 20 gardens in Ireland to be chosen for restoration funding by the Great Gardens of Ireland programme. Paths lead through woodland underplanted with rhododendron species and cultivars, and down to a walled sea estuary. A serpentine pond is now fringed with gunneras, cordylines and hydrangeas, the bold effect inspired by the paintings of 'Le Douanier' Rousseau. There are some fine tender species, including Telopea mongeansis (*T. truncata*), Datura (syn. *Brugmansia*) *sanguinea*, several varieties of abutilon and a good collection of camellias. New features are being developed, including a mixed herbaceous border, with old roses and tree peonies and areas devoted to southern-hemisphere plants and wild flowers. Note also the magnificent cryptogamic flora. In the organic walled garden there are many old varieties of fowl. Also here is a large vegetable garden with greenhouses, all being restored. A valiant garden lovingly maintained, wherein one feels the wildness is being controlled, creating a truly Irish pleasaunce, over 20 acres in all. Definitely a place for those who seek solitude and silence, far from traffic.

Derreen ★ 34

Lauragh, Killarney, Co. Kerry. Tel: (064) 83588

The Hon. David Bigham • 15m SW of Kenmare on R571 road along S of Kenmare Bay, towards Healy Pass • Open April to Sept, daily, 11am – 6pm • Entrance: IR£3, children IR£1.50 (1999 price) • Other information: Picnics on lawn near car park only ◑ 🍽 🍴 WC ♿

The broad sweep of plush lawn and the bald outcroppings of rock by the house do not prepare visitors for the lushness of the walks which weave through native woodlands and palisades of jade-stemmed bamboo. The evocatively named King's Oozy – a path that has a hankering to be a river – leads to a grove of tall, archaic tree-ferns (*Dicksonia antarctica*) with socks of filmy ferns. Wellies are the plantsman's only requirement to enjoy the large collection of rhodo-dendrons that shelter among clipped entanglements of *Gaultheria shallon*. Probably one of the wettest places in Britain and Ireland, a fact you're reminded of by the lushness (and midges in season).

The Dillon Garden ★★ 35

45 Sandford Road, Ranelagh, Dublin 6.

Helen and Val Dillon • 10 minutes drive or ½ hour walk from city centre in a cul-de-sac off Sandford Road just after Merton Road and church • Open March, daily; April to June, Sun only; July and Aug, daily; Sept, Sun only, all 2 – 6pm. Parties at any time by written arrangement • Entrance: IR£3, OAPs IR£2 • Other information: Possible for wheelchairs but limited access ◑ WC ℘

Within a walled rectangular garden, typical of Dublin's Georgian town houses, Helen Dillon has created one of the best designed and planted gardens in Ireland. As a central foil there is an immaculate lawn enhancing the colourful embroidery of the borders, which on exploration turn into a necklace of secret rooms with raised beds for rarities, such as lady's slipper orchids, or double-flowered *Trillium grandiflorum*. On the sunken terrace, terracotta pots sprout more rare plants. Clumps of *Dierama pulcherrimum* arch over the sphinxes, and a small alpine house and conservatory shelter the choicest – *Lapageria rosea*, prize-winning ferns, alpines and bulbs. The mixed borders of shrubs and herbaceous perennials are changeful, each season revealing unusual plants and exciting colour combinations. One border is planted predominantly with reds ('hot' colours), both in flowers and foliage, and the opposite one is 'cool', blues and whites. Yellows cluster under the apple tree in the corner. A listing of the plants in the Dillon's garden would not shame a large botanical garden. Each plant has its proper place, but all is ordered with no forbidding sense of contrivance. The exuberance overwhelms the formality, and the garden is both a finely designed pleasaunce and a plantsman's veritable nirvana.

Drimnagh Castle 36

Longmile Road, Dublin 12. Tel: (1) 4502530

Christian Brother Community; leased to Drimnagh Castle Committee • 3m SW of city centre. Signposted • Castle open • Garden open April to Oct, Wed, Sat, Sun and Bank Holiday Mons, 12 noon – 5pm; Nov to March, Sun and Bank Holiday Mons, 2 – 5pm, and at other times by appt • Entrance: castle and garden £1.50, OAPs and students £1, children 50p • Other information: Parking in school grounds. Guide dogs only ◐ ▆ ▆ WC ℘ ▆

Drimnagh Castle, although well known to generations of small boys, lay in semi-ruins alongside a modern brick secondary school. A local voluntary committee, aided by an Taisce and supported by the Christian Brother Community, started restoring the castle some years ago. Five years ago the Irish Garden Plant Society was approached to design a new garden to replace the derelict one, and Jim Reynolds of Butterstream (see entry) designed a seventeenth-century box garden with a hornbeam *allée* and perimeter beech hedge. This is a simple garden, intended to reflect the style of an old moated castle, which has various elements dating from the thirteenth to eighteenth centuries. Not a plantsman's place but a pleasant excursion with the castle as the main attraction.

Dunloe Castle Gardens 37

Hotel Dunloe Castle, Beaufort, Killarney, Co. Kerry. Tel: (64) 44111

Killarney Hotels Ltd • 4m W of Killarney, off Killorglin Road. Signposted • Open early May to Sept, but opening date varies – check with hotel. Parties by appt only • Entrance: individuals free, parties £50 per coach. Catalogue optional IR£1 • Other information: Toilet facilities in hotel ◑ ▭ ᕙ ⨺

On a superb site facing the Gap of Dunloe lie the imposing buildings of the Hotel Dunloe Castle, opened in 1965, surrounded by acres of parkland and gardens with magnificent and unusual trees and shrubs. Visitors and hotel guests may wander freely and appreciate the well-kept lawns, colourful planting, walled garden and the ruined fort of Dunloe Castle. The more serious garden visitor will spot such tender specimens as *Eriobotrya deflexa*, *Glyptostrobus pensilis*, *Banksia marginata* and *Telopea oreades* with the aid of a catalogue compiled by Roy Lancaster which lists trees and shrubs of note and identifies their location on a plan. Early plantings of 1920 have been continually added to and the whole is impeccably maintained. Take a two-hour stroll with the catalogue and then subject yourself to the culinary delights of a Grade-A hotel restaurant.

Earlscliffe ★★ 38

Baron's Brae, Ceanchor Road, Baily, Co. Dublin. Tel: (1) 8322556

Dr David Robinson • 5m NE of city centre on Howth. At end of Ceanchor Road, enter through last gate on left signed 'Baron's Brae' • Open for parties by appt only • Entrance: prices on application ◕ WC

Few gardens can match Earlscliffe for variety or advantage. Perched on the cliffs looking south over Dublin Bay (a view to rival the Bay of Naples) on the southern side of the Hill of Howth, a peninsula almost encircled by sea, severe frost is rare and there is an almost constant breeze – just what the most tender plants need. So the collection of plants is astonishing, and cannot be easily summarised. A forest of *Echium pininana*, the spire-shaped, blue-blossomed bugloss from the Canary Isles, is memorable; this species is naturalised at Earlscliffe (it is impolite to suggest that this astonishing six-metre tall herb could be a weed, but frequently it is). An octopus-like weeping cedar groping a thicket of the Chatham Islands daisy-bushes (*Olearia* 'Henry Travers'), a grove of bananas that flower and fruit, and waxy yellow-blossomed heathers from South Africa, greet the visitor. These are *hors-d'oeuvre*, while *Juania australis*,

Daphniphyllum macropodum, Araucaria bidwillii, Cordyline baueri – one could go on and on – are veritable sights for sore eyes. Many eucalyptus species thrive in this garden, not to mention the cupressus-like *Callitris rhomboidea* or the gigantic *Hebe* 'Lavender Queen'. Dr David Robinson's garden philosophy may disturb the ecologically-minded because, with impunity, he uses chemicals (principally simazine and glyphosate) to control weeds (*Echium pininana* is not one) in this six-acre plantsman's paradise. You may not agree with him, but you will certainly leave astonished by his plants and his audacity. Anyway, when did you last see a bunya-bunya pine growing outdoors at a latitude of 53° North?

Emo Court 39

Emo, Co. Laois. Tel: (0502) 26573

Department Arts, Heritage, Gaeltacht and the Islands Duchas • 8m NE of Portlaoise on R422 between N7 and R419 • House open mid-June to mid-Sept, daily except Mons, 10.30am – 5pm by guided tour only • Garden open all year, daily during daylight hours • Entrance: No charge for entrance to gardens only, with tours for parties if pre-booked. House entrance IR£2, OAPs IR£1.50, children IR£1, family IR£5, parties of 20 or more IR £1.50 per person (1999 prices) ○ 🍴 WC & 🐕

The garden is a splendid parkland setting for James Gandon's magnificent house, which dates, like many of the trees, from the end of the eighteenth century. There are fine specimen trees, and arrays of Irish yews stand sentry on the lawns. Varied avenues and walks have been planned through the woodland, leading to vistas of the house and a large, but neglected, lake. Statues, cunningly sited among the glades, offer pleasing surprises. There are recent plantings of trees, shrubs and perennials, particularly azaleas and magnolias.

An Féar Gorta (Tea and Garden Rooms) 40

Ballyvaghan, Co. Clare. Tel: (65) 707 7023

Catherine and Brendan O'Donoghue • In Ballyvaghan, situated on sea-front near pier • Open June to mid-Sept, Mon – Sat, 11am – 5.30pm • Entrance: free ◑ 🍴 ✕ WC &

The Burren, John Betjeman's 'Stony seaboard, far and foreign ...', is this simple garden's dramatic backdrop. Catmint spills over the native limestone, shrubby cinquefoils sparkle in the sun, butterfly bushes burst with blossom and are a-flutter with insects. There are several compartments, in front of and behind the traditional cottages, each one different but each one planted with shrubs and perennials that thrive by the edge of the sea. Catherine planted and maintains this quintessential cottage garden, while the limestone walls are Brendan's handiwork. A conservatory contains other joys, including the red banana passion flower (*Passiflora antioquiensis*) and, appropriately, the cup-and-saucer vine (*Cobaea scandens*). You can sit under their shade, sipping tea and eating scrumptious cakes, enjoying the view. From afar *The Burren* seems to be a desolate barren rockscape, but limestone weathers to rich soil and its natural fissures provide sheltered crannies for delicate, colourful Arctic and sub-tropical plants: spring gentians and mountain avens, maidenhair ferns and mountain catspaws, Irish orchids and autumn lady's tresses, rock-roses and bloody cranesbills, rowan and hazel. With comfortable, tough walking shoes and a good map, endless days can be enjoyed walking the green roads and the 'pavements grey'. Botanists abound and can be spotted easily as they peer, bottoms uppermost, into the limestone.

Fernhill ★ 41

Sandyford, Co. Dublin. Tel: (1) 295 6000

Mrs Sally Walker • 8m S of city centre on R117 Dublin – Enniskerry road • Open March to Sept, Tues – Sat, 11am – 5pm, Sun, 2 – 6pm, Bank Holiday Mons, 11am – 5pm • Entrance: IR£3, OAPs IR£2, children IR£1
◑ 🖶 WC ♿

The garden is situated on the eastern slope of the Dublin Mountains and has a laurel lawn, some fine nineteenth-century plantings and an excellent flowering specimen of *Michelia doltsopa*. The plantings of rhododendron species and cultivars provide spectacles of colour from early spring into mid-summer; many of the more tender rhododendrons flourish here. The walkways through the wooded areas wind steeply past many other shrubs, principally those that thrive on acid soil – pieris and camellias are also outstanding. There is a rock garden and a water garden near the house, and drifts of daffodils in the spring. In the summer there are the roses and a good collection of herbaceous plants, many as underplanting through the woodland.

Fota Arboretum ★ 42

Fota Trust, Carrigtohill, Co. Cork. Tel: (21) 812728

Department of Arts, Heritage, Gaeltacht and the Islands • 9m E of Cork, on Cobh road • Arboretum open Feb to Oct, daily, 10am – 6pm (Sun, 11am – 6pm) • Entrance: free for arboretum. Automatic pay barrier to car park • Other information: Refreshments and shop in Wildlife Park ◑ 🖶 WC ♿

Perhaps the wonders of Fota are best appreciated in summer when the obvious distractions like camellias, embothriums, drimys, pieris and most of the rhododendrons have finished flowering. There is no lack of colour: the walls sparkle with abutilons and cestrums, and the myrtles take on a pinkish hue. *Davidia involucrata* may be bereft of handkerchiefs, but admire instead the elaborate flowers of *Magnolia* x *wieseneri*, or the frothy white blooms of *Eucalyptus delegatensis*. Now is the time to appreciate the complicated growth of the Chilean hazel, the immense canopy of the fern-leaved beech, a perfect *Pinus montezumae* and the marvellous bark of the stone pine. Note the wickedly spiny species of colletia and the elegance of *Restio subverticillatus*. Spend a few minutes in the cool fernery. All this to the accompaniment of hoots and the chattering of exotic birds and animals in the adjacent wildlife park and the antics of the red squirrel.

Garinish Island

(see ILNACULLIN)

Glenleigh Gardens   43

Clogheen, Co. Tipperary. Tel: (52) 65251

Gypsy and Edgar Calder-Potts • 10m N of Lismore on Cahir road. Immediately outside Clogheen on 'V' road, turn right over motor grid. Signposted • Open April to Oct, daily, 10am – 6pm • Entrance: IR£3 ◑ WC ⅃

There is nothing to indicate a garden of note at the end of a somewhat unprepossessing drive, but Glenleigh's 12 acres show instinctive planting, including good specimen trees grown from seed and some unusual tender plants, creating many pleasing aspects. On the walls of the house, following on from a Banksia rose, the unusual climbers bomarea and *Mutisia decurrens* flower in early summer. Blueberries share the gently chaotic walled garden with beschornerias, and a woodland garden flourishes with orchids and ferns, including platyceriums. There is a lovely view upstream to the Knockmealdown mountains, and the overall informality of the site arouses visitors' admiration.

Glenveagh Castle ★★   44

Glenveagh National Park, Churchill, Letterkenny, Co. Donegal.
Tel: (74) 37088/37090/37262; Fax: (74) 37072

National Parks and Wildlife Service • 15m NW of Letterkenny • Castle open, IR£2 • Garden open probably 22nd April to 1st Nov, daily, 10am – 6.30pm (open to 7.30pm on Sun, June to Aug). Other times by arrangement • Entrance: IR£2, OAPs and parties per person IR£1.50, students and children IR£1 (1999 prices) • Other information: Parking at Visitor Centre. Access to garden and castle by official mini-coaches only ◑ ☕ ✕ WC

The centrepiece of the Glenveagh National Park is the garden around Glenveagh Castle. The castle is set beside a mountain lough encircled with high, peat-blanketed mountains, in the middle of windswept moorlands, a most unpromising site. But, as in so many Irish gardens, surprises are countless. The lower lawn garden has fringing shrubberies and, beyond, steep pathways wind through oak woods in which are planted scented white-flowered rhododendrons and numerous other tender shrubs from southern lands. Terraced enclosures with terracotta pots of plants and sculpture are encountered unexpectedly. The *jardin potager* at the castle has rank on rank of old Irish vegetables, ornamental vegetables and flowering herbs. This is a paradise for plantsmen and gardeners keen on seeing fine specimens of unusual aspect – *Pseudopanax ferox*, *Fascicularia bicolor*, pieris and many more. Linger, and walk the mountain sides. Then take the last bus back to the remarkable heather-roofed visitor centre with its imaginative landscaping.

Glin Castle Gardens   45

Glin, Co. Limerick. Tel: (68) 34173/34112; Fax: (68) 34364

Madam FitzGerald and the Knight of Glin • 30m W of Limerick on N69 • Castle open • Garden open May and June, daily, 10am – 12 noon, 2 – 4pm, otherwise by appt • Entrance: IR£3 (IR£2 per person for parties) • Other information: Tea shop with toilet facilities situated five-minute car ride along main road from Foynes. Bed and breakfast accommodation available ◑ WC ♨

The formal garden could not be simpler, with its lawns and two domed bays flanking a path to a sundial and an elegant *Parrotia persica*, beyond which is a meadow with daffodils and a woodland with fine old trees. Colourful in spring with magnolias and bluebells, in early summer rhododendrons are still providing a splash of colour in contrast to the cool tones of a large *Abutilon vitifolium*, while the grey walls of the castle are relieved by climbing plants. An outstanding feature is the walled garden on a steep slope, with its mathematically neat rows of vegetables and herbs, figs, fruit, roses and clematis, a castellated henhouse, rustic temple with marble incumbent, and a lovely view across the Shannon over walls and undulating slate roofs of the old battlemented, cobblestoned stableyard. If you like kitchen gardens, Glin's will please you.

Graigueconna ★   46

Old Connaught, Bray, Co. Wicklow. Tel: (1) 2822273

Mr and Mrs John Brown • 12m SE of Dublin city centre. Take N11, then slip road to Bray and turn right at traffic lights. From S take N11 towards Dublin, then slip road signed 'Bray – Shankill'. Turn left for Graigueconna • Open probably 24th June and for Wicklow Gardens Festival and from May to June, 9am – dusk by appt only for parties of four or more • Entrance: IR£3 per person (for parties of 12 or more IR£2.50 per person) • Other information: coffee provided for small groups by arrangement ◑

This three-acre garden was created early this century by Lewis Meredith, who wrote *Rock gardens – how to make and maintain them* (1906), one of the earliest 'text books' on this topic. His rock garden lies hidden at the end of a specially laid railway track along which rocks were trundled. Today, this track is a grassy path, punctuated by Irish yews and lined with excellent mixed borders of herbaceous perennials and shrubs. The rock garden, while intact, is planted for easier maintenance with ground-cover species, bulbs and ferns, along with many interesting southern-hemisphere shrubs, including towering specimens of *Crinodendron hookerianum* and *Drimys winteri*. There are numerous 'old' roses on the walls and in shrubberies; *Rosa chinensis* 'Bengal Crimson' is in bloom for months on end. Near the house are tender and unusual plants like *Beschorneria yuccoides*, and throughout the borders are uncommon herbaceous perennials, including *Astelia chathamica*, *Jovellana violacea*, and *Melanoselinum decipiens* (a giant relative of parsley from Madeira). In the conservatory is *Passiflora antioquiensis*, more tender southern-hemisphere species, and a collection of arisaema. The garden is painstakingly cared for.

Heywood Garden ★ 47

Ballinakill, Co. Laois. Tel: (502) 33563

Department of Arts, Heritage, Gaeltacht and the Islands • 3m SE of Abbeyleix. Turn E in Abbeyleix signed Ballinakill. Outside Ballinakill • Open all year, daily, during daylight hours • Entrance: free ○ ⅋ ⊲⅏

Edwin Lutyens' walled garden with pergola and lawns is acknowledged as his finest small-scale work in Ireland. It is a gem, now restored close to its original state as far as the walls and ornaments are concerned. The planting is being restored in the style of Gertrude Jekyll with the advice of Graham Stuart Thomas. On the driveway leading towards the school buildings is an eighteenth-century folly. Heywood has now been recognised as a heritage garden of historic and architectural importance.

Hilton Park 48

Scotshouse, Clones, Co. Monaghan. Tel: (47) 56007; Website: http://indigo.ie/~hiltonpk

J. and L. Madden • 10m NE of Cavan, 3m S of Clones on Ballyhaise road • Open May to Sept, daily, 1.30 – 5.30pm • Entrance: IR£2.50, party rates available • Other information: Refreshments for parties by arrangement. Picnics permitted by prior request only ◗

A curving and ascending driveway running through well-planted parkland in hilly drumlin country leads to the present house, which has seventeenth-century foundations but was re-faced in the Italian manner in the 1870s. Recently restored, the gardens offer extensive walks near the lake amongst wild flowers under fine mature trees and shrubs, the informality contrasting with the formal terraces near the house. Here the late nineteenth-century geometric flower bed designs of Ninian Niven have been revived and planted, as has the nearby rose garden. A herb garden has been added, reflecting the layout of the original eighteenth-century formal garden removed in 1868.

Ilnacullin (Garinish Island) ★★ 49

Glengarriff, Co. Cork. Tel: (27) 63040; Fax: (27) 63149

National Parks and Monuments Service, Department of Arts, Heritage, Gaeltacht and the Islands • On island in Bantry Bay • Open March and Oct, daily, 10am – 4.30pm, Sun, 1 – 5pm, April to June and Sept, daily, 10am – 6.30pm, Sun, 1 – 7pm, July and Aug, daily, 9.30am – 6.30pm, Sun, 11am – 7pm • Entrance: IR£3, OAPs IR£2, students and children IR£1.25, family IR£7.50, parties of 20 or more (1999 prices) ◗ ▆ WC

The boat trip across the sheltered inlets of Bantry Bay, past sun-bathing seals, with views of the Caha Mountains, is doubly rewarding; landing at the slipway you gain entrance to one of Ireland's gardening jewels, begun in the early 1900s. Most visitors cluster around the Casita – an Italianate garden – and reflecting pool, designed by Harold Peto, to enjoy (on clear days) spectacular scenery, and some quite indifferent annual bedding. But walk beyond, to the

Temple of the Winds, through shrubberies filled with plants usually confined indoors, tree ferns, southern-hemisphere conifers, rhododendron species and cultivars. A flight of stone steps leads to the Martello tower, and thence the path returns to the walled garden with its double-sided herbaceous border. Plant enthusiasts can spend many happy hours with such varied delights as *Lyonothamnus floribundus* var. *aspleniifolius* and myriad manukas (*Leptospermum scoparium*, the New Zealand tea tree). Take a picnic and linger; if wet, bring boots or strong shoes and an umbrella. Wonderful. If lost for a thought, ponder on the fact that 'Capability' Brown never visited Ireland.

Irish National War Memorial Park   50

Islandbridge, Dublin 8.

Department of Arts, Heritage, Gaeltacht and the Islands • In Islandbridge • Open all year, daily except 25th Dec, during daylight hours • Entrance: free ○ &

Sir Edwin Lutyens' Irish gardens (see also Heywood) are not nearly as well known as his English ones. This memorial garden (1938, dedicated 1988), restored and planted anew, is typical of his reserved, calm style, with sunken rose gardens, a simple altar stone, colonnades and formal plantings of trees. In the bookroom are volumes with the names of Irish men and women who died in World War I.

Iveagh Gardens   51

Clonmel Street, Dublin 2. Tel: (1) 6613111

Department of Arts, Heritage, Gaeltacht and the Islands • Access via Clonmel Street or National Concert Hall, Earlsfort Terrace • Open all year, Mon – Sat, 8.30am – 6pm, Suns and Bank Holiday Mons, 10am – 6pm (closes earlier Oct to March) • Entrance: free • Other information: Wheelchairs via Clonmel Street entrance only ○ & ◁

This was one of the forgotten – and almost vanished – gardens of Dublin. Originally attached to Iveagh House, home of the Earls of Iveagh, it had been allowed to decay, but is now being restored to the original Ninian Niven plans prepared for the 1865 International Exhibition palace and winter gardens which took place here. Already the Victorian fountains have been renovated and the maze replanted. The rosarium, with old varieties, is complete with chain tent, seating and a new pathway, and the American garden, rooteries and Italian parterre will be replanted soon.

Japanese Garden and St Fiachra's Garden ★   52

Irish National Stud, Tully, Kildare, Co. Kildare. Tel: (45) 521617

Irish National Stud • 25m SW of Dublin, 1m off M/N7 outside Kildare • Garden open 12th Feb to 12th Nov, daily, 9.30am – 6pm. Guided tours available • Entrance: by combined ticket for Japanese Garden, St Fiachra's Garden, Irish National Stud and Horse Museum IR£6, OAPs and students

IR£4.50, children IR£3, family (2 adults and 4 children under 12) IR£14 •
Other information: Lego area for children ☺ 🍵 ✕ <u>WC</u> ⏦ 🏬

Devised by Colonel William Hall-Walker (later Lord Wavertree), a wealthy
Scotsman of a famous brewery family, and laid out 1906-10 by the Japanese Eida
and his son Minoru, the gardens, symbolising the 'Life of Man', are acclaimed as
the finest Japanese gardens in Europe. This is not a plantsman's garden, and few
of the plants are Japanese; to be sure there are some excellent old maples, but
many of the trees and shrubs are clipped and shaped beyond reason. The
overshadowing Scots pines are exquisite. A pathway meanders through
artificial caves into a watery stream, past the tranquil ponds and on to the
weeping trees of the grave. Beautiful stone lanterns grace the site, which is in
the style of a Japanese tea garden. On a misty day with smoke from a distant
fire billowing across, this visitor recalls it as mysterious, beautiful. New in
1999 was the creation of St Fiachra's Garden, 'a garden in commemoration of
the Patron Saint of Gardeners in his home country of Ireland', as the National
Stud puts it. The entrance is via an underground stone passage, which leads
into the inner garden, another world of woodland and lakes, momentarily
leaving behind the pastures and horses of the stud farm. The woodland walk,
which meanders between lake and stream and wetland, is dominated by
waterside or aquatic plants seen within a natural setting. It creates, in effect,
a national water garden served by the natural springs of the Curragh. The
central feature is a peninsular of fissured limestone surrounded by water upon
which a stone hermitage is created, not as a relic but as a piece of sculpture,
not for archaeological reverence, but for spiritual value. Within this hermitage
is a second garden, deeper and finer but still of rock. This inner subterranean
garden is of Waterford crystal-shaped rocks and plants such as ferns and
orchids are lit by fibre optic in the darkness of the hermitage beneath the floor
in an underground passage.

John F. Kennedy Arboretum ★   53

New Ross, Co. Wexford. Tel: (051) 388171

Dúchas, The Heritage Service, Department of Arts, Heritage, Gaeltacht and the
Islands • 8m S of New Ross • Arboretum open all year, daily except 25th Dec
and 21st April: April, 10am – 6.30pm; May to Aug, 10am – 8pm; Sept, 10am
– 6.30pm; Oct to March, 10am – 5pm • Entrance: IR£2, OAPs IR£1.50,
students and children IR£1, family IR£5 (1999 prices). Heritage card available
• Other information: Refreshments available mid-March to Oct only, sometimes
Suns only. Visitor Centre with Kennedy memorial and video ○ 🍴 <u>WC</u> ♿ ⏦ 🏬

A spacious modern arboretum laid out in botanical sequence with rides; from
the summit of a nearby hill is a superb panorama not only of the arboretum but
also of parts of counties Carlow, Kilkenny, Tipperary, Waterford, Wexford
and Wicklow. Best to begin at the viewpoint – turn left just beyond the main
entrance and drive to the summit car park to see the layout. At the arboretum
be prepared for a long walk; fortunately those not keen on gardening tend to
linger near the café so that the distant reaches are quiet and empty. Planting
began in the 1960s, and now 4500 different trees and shrubs are growing,

ranging from conifers to flowering shrubs. Most species are represented by several specimens, and keen plantsmen can linger long examining the groups. Good labelling. A colourful planting of dwarf conifers is on the western side, a small lake on the east. While primarily a scientific collection, the arboretum is now achieving an established elegance.

Kilfane Glen and Waterfall 54

Thomastown, Co. Kilkenny. Tel: (56) 24558

Mrs Susan Mosse • 12m SE of Kilkenny, 4m N of Thomastown, signed off N9 • Open April to June, Sun, 2 – 6pm; July and Aug, daily, 11am – 6pm; Sept, Sun, 2 – 6pm and at other times by appt • Entrance: IR£3, OAPs IR£2.50, children IR£2, family IR£9 ◑ 🏠 **WC** ♨

This romantic woodland garden dates from 1790, when the Glen was designed to display nature in all her terrifying beauty, *à la* Wordsworth. It has the requisite romantic traits including a hermit's grotto, a *cottage orné* and a waterfall, so that present-day visitors can enjoy the beauties just as their predecessors did under the tuition of the gentry of Kilfane House. A good leaflet with a suggested walk tells the reader when to feel the *frisson*.

Killineer 55

Drogheda, Co Louth. Tel: (41) 38563

Miss Grace Carroll • 2m N of Drogheda on N1 Drogheda – Belfast road • Open to parties by appt • Entrance: donation to charity • Other information: refreshments can be provided with advance notice NEW ◐ **WC** ♿ ⬨

This is one of Ireland's last-surviving Regency gardens. The approach is through woodland, underplanted with laurel, the latter clipped each year to form a two-and-a-half-acre waist-high laurel lawn. The main garden descends in grass terraces to a sloping lawn and a lake with resident swans. In the small woodland garden nearby are moisture-loving plants such as candelabra primulas. Post-Regency features, added by the owner's father, include sculptural and architectural ornaments, a pergola, balustrading and a small pool. The kitchen garden, screened by trees and maintained in full production, includes a set of glazed wall cases for fruit.

Killruddery 56

Bray, Co. Wicklow. Tel: (1) 2863405; Tel/fax (1) 2862777

The Earl and Countess of Meath • 1m S of Bray on N11. Turn right at roundabout. Signposted • House open May, June and Sept, daily, 1 – 5pm with conducted tours and at other dates and times for pre-arranged parties • Garden open April to Sept, daily, 1 – 5pm. Guided tours for parties of 20 or more by appt • Entrance: IR£3, OAPs/ students IR£2, children IR50p (house and garden IR£4.50, OAPs/ students IR£3, children IR£1, parties of 20 or more IR£3.50 per person). All children must be accompanied • Other information: teas and meals provided for groups by arrangement ◑ **WC** ♿

The joy of Killruddery, a seventeenth-century garden with nineteenth-century embellishments, is the formal hedging, known as 'The Angles', set beside the formal canals which lead to a ride into the distant hills. There is a collection of nineteenth-century French cast statuary, a sylvan theatre created in bay, and a fountain pool enclosed in a beech hedge. The excellent nineteenth-century conservatory, alas, has a perspex dome (the cost of curved glass is horrendous). The landscape features are unique, and Killruddery deserves to be better known, but it is not a garden for keen plantsmen without designer tastes.

Kilmacurragh 57

Kilbride, Rathdrum, Co. Wicklow.

Department of Arts, Heritage, Gaeltacht and the Islands • 30m S of Dublin, 5m S of Wicklow off N11. Turn right at Old Tap pub. After 1m turn left at T-junction. Entrance through gateway with curved granite wall and sequoiadendrons • Opening dates and prices: for details write or telephone Dúchas, the Heritage Service, Department of Arts, Heritage, Gaeltacht and the Islands (1) 6613111 ●

This garden is rated highly because of its atmosphere and magnificent ancient plants. It was created by Thomas Acton in the mid- to late-nineteenth century. Behind the derelict eyesore of a house there is an incomparable avenue composed of alternating Irish yews and crimson rhododendrons — 'magical' is an overworked word, but the pattern of fallen blossoms on this pathway in May is magical. Beyond, paths wind through the arboretum, under rhododendrons taller and older than in most other gardens. The trees at Kilmacurragh include many unequalled specimens — rare conifers abound. If you can, visit it when crocus blossom is in the meadow, when the rhododendron flowers are tumbling down, at any time for elegant decrepitude. The garden has been handed over to the care of the Irish state, and will be managed, at last, as Thomas Acton always wished, as an adjunct to the National Botanic Gardens, Glasnevin (see entry).

Kilmokea 58

Great Island, Co. Wexford. Tel: (51) 388109; Fax: (51) 388209; E-mail: kilmokea@indigo.ie; Website: www.kilmokea.com

Mark and Emma Hewlett • 8m S of New Ross, 1m off R733 New Ross – Ballyhack road towards River Barrow • Open 17th March to 1st Nov, 10am – 5pm, daily • Entrance: IR£4, accompanied children under 16 free ◑ ☕ ✕ <u>WC</u> ♿ ⬥ ☙

The gardens of Kilmokea Rectory, developed over the past 45 years, have matured splendidly in the gentle microclimate of Waterford Harbour. The contrast between the formal and the informal is marvellously displayed here. It is impossible to decide which is the more inspired — a series of enclosed gardens featuring an herbaceous border, topiary and an Italian garden, etc., or the more recently developed woodland garden, which was started on the site of an old mill and where the smaller and rarer rhododendrons, candelabra primulas and tender shrubs excel beneath a canopy of conifers and exotic trees, alongside a stream and its falls. The influence of Peto can be seen here, but the imaginative hand of the previous owners, the Prices, is paramount. The present owners have spent the past two years restoring the garden. They have added many rare and tender plants including rhododendrons from Seaforde's Vietnam and China expeditions. Also pergolas, gazebos and boardwalks.

Lakemount ★ 59

Barnavara Hill, Glanmire, Co. Cork. Tel: (21) 821052

Brian Cross • 5m E of Cork, at top of Barnavara Hill above Glanmire • Open April to Sept, daily, 2 – 5pm and by appt • Entrance: IR£4 ◑ &

An immaculately maintained two-acre hillside garden, with rhododendrons, azaleas and camellias in spring and a wealth of summer interest and colour, especially hydrangeas. There are paved areas on different levels, a pool and a plant house with exotics such as *Iochroma cassia* and tibouchina, while to the rear of the house a lawn slopes gently from a rock garden to beds with a mixed planting of trees, shrubs and herbaceous plants. This is an evolving garden where new projects take shape and blend by means of skilful design and impeccable planting, which includes a wide range of unusual subjects. The perfect antidote to too many wild Irish gardens, particularly if your interest is gravel rather than grass.

Lismore Castle Gardens 60

Lismore, Co. Waterford. Tel: (58) 54424; Fax: (58) 54896

The Duke and Duchess of Devonshire • 36m SW of Waterford in Lismore • Open 22nd April to 15th Oct, daily, 1.45 – 4.45pm • Entrance: IR£3, children under 16 IR£1.50. Parties of 20 or more during working hours IR£2.50 per person, children IR£1.30 • Other information: Toilet facilities, inc. disabled, nearby ◑ ⇦

The situation of the castle overlooking the River Blackwater is stunning. There are two gardens linked by the gatehouse entrance: the upper, reached by a stairway in the gatehouse, leads to a terrace with vegetables and flowers, a reduced glasshouse by Joseph Paxton (with an interesting ridge-and-furrow roof) and a fine view from the main axis to the church spire emphasised by a new herbaceous border. In the lower garden, several steps down from the gatehouse, are a few meritricious plants, but the principal feature, an ancient yew-walk carpeted softly with the dropped needles, is wonderful. Contemporary sculpture is a recent addition. Edmund Spenser is said to have written *The Fairie Queene* here, and it is the Irish home of the Duke of Devonshire, who has Chatsworth (see entry in Derbyshire) to console him in England.

71 Merrion Square 61

Dublin 2. Tel: (1) 676 7281; Fax: (1) 676 7282

On W side of Merrion Square • House and mews previously open • Garden previously open April to Oct, Mon – Fri, and Sat and Sun by appt. Telephone to check • Entrance: mews and garden IR£4 (house, mews and garden IR£6) (1998 prices) • Other information: Refreshments by arrangement ◑ **WC**

The designer of this garden, Sybil Connolly, died in 1998, but it is hoped her creation will remain open. Thirty metres long and barely nine metres wide, it is not an easy shape to begin with, but the owner has created a beautiful town garden which belies its position in the commercial hub of Dublin. A formal terrace framed with trellis, niches and containers of box and roses leads from the eighteenth-century house down through a paved courtyard and into the garden. The old brick and blackstone walls are clothed with a fine specimen of wisteria, and roses, clematis, loniceras and actinidias add to the beauty of the old walls. Large specimens of *Cornus kousa, Pyrus salicifolia* 'Pendula', *Syringa vulgaris* 'Madame Lemoine' and *Viburnum plicatum* 'Mariesii' are stunning in season. *Paeonia* 'Joseph Rock' peeps from behind a small half-standard *Acer palmatum* 'Dissectum Atropurpureum', and three semi-circular beds house old shrub roses and perennials. An old brick pathway winds past these beds and creates an impression of width and spaciousness, edged by well-kept lawn.

Mount Congreve ★★   62

Kilmeaden, Co. Waterford. Tel: (51) 384115 (office)

Mr Ambrose Congreve • Write for directions • Open Mon – Fri, 9am – 5pm, strictly by appt. Closed Bank Holiday Mons • Entrance: IR£250 for visits organised by travel agents who specially ask for conducted tours. Individuals may go round by themselves provided they have permission from office. No small children ◐

In emulation of Exbury, Ambrose Congreve has amassed an unequalled collection of rhododendron, camellia and magnolia species and cultivars, with many other trees as icing on the cake. It is a staggering collection which cannot be described adequately in a single entry: 110 acres of shrubs, mass upon mass, since every cultivar is planted in groups. In addition to the flowering shrub collections, which include Mount Congreve hybrids, there are many other splendours, including a whole series of surprises, one of the most spectacular being a pagoda at the base of 25-metre cliffs. Highlights are memorable. In early March a forest of *Magnolia campbellii* offers pink to white goblets to the rooks. A languid walled garden, dominated by an ancient ginkgo, has a fine eighteenth-century vinery and range of glasshouses. In the borders is an extensive collection of herbaceous plants arranged in order of monthly flowering – May to July, a large arrangement for August plus a border for September and October – an unusual idea. There is far too much here to appreciate in one visit and it is satisfying to know the garden will eventually be left to the nation with a trust for maintenance for the first 25 years.

Mount Usher ★★   63

Ashford, Co. Wicklow. Tel: (404) 40116/40205/40483;
Fax: (404) 40205; E-mail: mount-usher.gardens@indigo.ie

Mrs Madelaine Jay • 30m S of Dublin, 4m NW of Wicklow, on N11 at Ashford • Open 15th March to 31st Oct, daily, 10.30am – 6pm • Entrance: IR£3.50,

OAPs, students and children IR£2.50. Special rates for parties of 20 or more. Guided tours (IR£20) must be pre-booked ◑ ☕ <u>WC</u> & ♨

The Vartry river flows through this exquisite garden over weirs and under bridges which allow visitors to meander through the collections. Mount Usher is a plant-lovers' paradise. *Pinus montezumae* is always first port of call, a shimmering tree, magnificent when the bluebells are in flower. The philosophy of Mount Usher eschews chemicals of all kinds, and the meadows are cut in a cycle which allows the bulbs and wild flowers in them to seed naturally. Throughout there are drifts of rhododendrons, fine trees and shrubs, including many that are difficult to cultivate outdoors in other parts of Britain and Ireland. The grove of eucalyptus at the lower end of the valley is memorable; a kiwi-fruit vine (*Actinidia chinensis*) cloaks the piers of a bridge, and beside the tennis court is the gigantic original *Eucryphia* x *nymansensis* 'Mount Usher'. In spring, bulbs, magnolias, a procession of rhododendrons and camellias, in summer eucryphias and leptospermums, in autumn russet and crimson leaves falling from maples – a garden for all seasons.

Muckross House and Gardens ★ 64

Killarney National Park, Killarney, Co. Kerry. Tel: (64) 31947/31440

National Parks and Wildlife Service • 4m S of Killarney, on N71 Kenmare road • House open. Admission charge • Gardens open for pedestrians all year, with car access, 8am – 5pm (July and Aug, 8am – 7pm) • Entrance: free ○ ☕ ✕ <u>WC</u> & ⬨ ♨

The garden around Muckross House is almost incidental to the spectacle of the lakes and mountains of Killarney; indeed, it is principally renowned as a viewing area for the wild grandeur of the mountains. The lawns sweep to clumps of old rhododendrons and Scots pines, and there is a huge natural rock garden. Quiet corners abound along the lough-shore walks, and anyone interested in trees and shrubs is strongly recommended to head for the recently developed arboretum area (it can be reached by car easily – follow the signpost – and is a short walk from the house). There, good specimen trees surround a wooden pergola of imaginative design, and there are plantings of tender shrubs in the wild, shaded woods beyond, which, with their unique flora and ancient yews and the almost immortal strawberry trees (*Arbutus unedo*), are enticing and magical. Useful guidebook (IR£2.50). This is a place to spend a whole day or more.

National Botanic Gardens, Glasnevin ★ 65

Glasnevin, Dublin 9. Tel: (1) 8374388

Department of Arts, Heritage, Gaeltacht and the Islands • 1m N of city centre between Finglas Road and Botanic Road close to Glasnevin Cemetery • Open all year, daily except 25th Dec, summer, 9am – 6pm, winter, 10am – 4.30pm (opens 11am Sat and Sun). Opening times for glasshouses are posted at entrance (closed 12.45 – 2pm and Sun am) • Entrance: free • Other information: Parking very limited in summer and at weekends. Access to Palm House for wheelchair users on request ○ <u>WC</u> &

A fine garden which still retains its Victorian exactitude with close-cut lawns and succulent summer carpet-bedding. The plant collections and glasshouses are undergoing restoration and renewal. Interesting new planting schemes near the entrance and around the Curvilinear Range are helping to expunge the tired image, although major building developments mean disruption in large sections of the gardens. In the winter, the glasshouses are worth visiting; by spring there are daffodil-crowded lawns and flowering cherries; the summer highlight is the double, curving herbaceous border, and in autumn the fruit-laden trees and russet foliage can be magical. The Turner conservatory (1843-69), the finest in Ireland, has been restored, and planted with cycads and related plants, with south-east Asian rhododendrons (sect. Vireya) and plants from the South African fenbos and dry temperate areas of Australia and South America. Glasnevin is undoubtedly worth visiting, especially by gardeners with a strong interest in shrubs and perennials; soil conditions preclude large-scale rhododendron planting. The Alpine House contains, in season, collections of plants of considerable interest. Highlights are hard to enumerate, but a few outstanding plants may be mentioned: *Zelkova carpinifolia* (especially in winter a marvellously architectural tree); the ancient wisteria on the Chain Tent (*c.* 1836); the weeping Atlas cedar (*Cedrus atlantica* 'Pendula'); the Chusan palms planted in 1870; orchids; *Parrotia persica* (near entrance, wonderful in February and October); and of course 'The Last Rose of Summer'. The gardens hold National Collections of *Potentilla fruticosa* and garryas.

Phoenix Park 66

Dublin 8. Tel: (1) 8213021

Department of Arts, Heritage, Gaeltacht and the Islands • N of River Liffey. From city centre follow signs to 'The West', or take No 10 bus to Phoenix Park • Open all year, daily, 7am – 11pm • Entrance: free • Other information: Guided tours of Áras an Uachtaráin, Sats from 9.45am from Visitor Centre ○ ⬤ ✕ 🗐 WC & ⬠ 🜊

This is the largest enclosed park in any European city, replete with a herd of fallow deer, some splendid monuments and great houses, most of which are accessible to the public by request, particularly Áras an Uachtaráin (the residence of the President of Ireland, and formerly the Vice-Regal Lodge), where public tours are given every Saturday (except Christmas) commencing at the Phoenix Park visitor centre. There is a new information centre, telling the history of the park, a short distance from the Phoenix monument which has been relocated to its original position on the main avenue. The planting is large-scale – the avenues of horse chestnuts, limes and beeches are spectacular in blossom and in autumn, and gas lights twinkle at night the whole way along the ceremonial avenue. The People's Garden, near the main city entrance, is the only part where there is intensive gardening, but Phoenix Park is a place to be lost in among the hawthorns and the wild flowers, far away from (but within earshot of) Dublin city centre.

Powerscourt ★ 67

Enniskerry, Co. Wicklow. Tel: (1) 2046000; Fax: (1) 2863561

Slazenger family • 12m S of Dublin, just outside Enniskerry • House open, with exhibition on history of estate and gardens • Gardens open all year, daily except 25th, 26th Dec: March – Oct, 9.30am – 5.30pm; Nov – Feb, 9.30am – dusk • Entrance: IR£5, OAPs and students IR£4.50, children (5-16) IR£3, under 5 free. Separate charge for waterfall (not part of the garden) • Other information: Guide dogs only ○ 💻 ✕ 🍴 WC ♿ 🚲 🏪 ☕

This is a 'grand garden', a massive statement of the triumph of art over the natural landscape. In its present form, with an amphitheatre of terraces and great central axis (mid-nineteenth century), the garden is largely the design of the inimitable Daniel Robertson. In some ways it is beyond compare – the axis formed by the ceremonial stairway leading down to the Triton Pond and jet, and stretching beyond to the Great Sugarloaf Mountain, is justly famous. We recommend that you walk along the terrace towards the Pepperpot, and on through the mature conifers which Lord Powerscourt collected. The Pepperpot tower has been restored and visitors can climb it to view 'the killing hollow' and the North American specimen trees in the tower valley. A tree-trail, devised by the late Alan Mitchell, has recently been opened, and will amuse dedicated dendrophiles (purchase the book when you get the entrance ticket). Wander on to the edge of the pond and look up along the stairway past the monumental terraces to the façade of the house. That's the view of Powerscourt that is breathtaking – a man-made amphitheatre guarded by winged horses. Statuary and the famous perspective gate, an avenue of monkey puzzles and a beech wood along the avenue add to the glory.

Primrose Hill ★ 68

Lucan, Co. Dublin. Tel: (1) 6280373

Mrs Cicely and Mr Robin Hall • 8m W of city centre off N4. Turn right signed Lucan, drive through village and, after Garda (police) station, take steep, narrow Primrose Lane on left. Continue to top and through black gateway • House open • Garden open Feb, daily, 1 – 5.30pm; mid-June to mid-Aug, daily, 2 – 6pm, and at other times by appt • Entrance: IR£3 ◑ 🍴 WC 🚲

The garden is approached up a beech avenue, flanked by a developing three-acre arboretum. The garden itself is not much bigger than one acre, yet it succeeds in housing a fine collection of snowdrops – the biggest and certainly the most named collection including some of their own 'Primrose Hill' seedlings which are glorious in flower. It is unusual for a garden to boast that February is its best month – but undoubtedly it is here, starting the visiting season. To return in late spring and summer when the borders are in full colour is an added joy. The herbaceous plants are lovingly cared for and planted in humus-rich compost in large clumps, giving a generous effect to the borders. Irises are high on the priority list, so are lobelias (two named ones originated here), lilies, kniphofias and, of course, *Primula auricula* 'Old Irish Blue', plus many others.

45 Sandford Road, Dublin

(see THE DILLON GARDEN)

Strokestown Park · 69

Strokestown, Co. Roscommon. Tel: (78) 33013

Westward Garage Ltd • 14m W of Longford on N5 • House open • Park open April to Oct, daily, 11am – 5.30pm. Parties by arrangement • Entrance: park free; garden IR£3.25, concessions IR£2; house, museum and garden IR£8.50, concessions IR£6.80. Separate tickets for house and museum, family tickets and rates for parties of 20 or more available (1999 prices) • Other information: Restaurant and toilet facilities at Famine Museum ◑ 🍽 ✕ 🏫 <u>WC</u> ♿ ⬤ ℗ 🎪 ♿

The neo-Palladian Strokestown Park House, entered from one of the broadest streets in Ireland, was purchased in 1979 by a local company, who set in motion a restoration plan involving the refurbishment of the house, replanting of the remaining parkland and creation of new gardens within the old walls. In the four-acre garden is one of the largest double herbaceous borders in these islands, resplendent from the top – silver, blue and white – to the bottom – purple, red and yellow – and repeated for much of its 146 metres. Handsome gates from Rockingham near Boyle have been installed, the pool and the pergola completed, a yew and beech hedge planted. The old summerhouse is close by the new maze and croquet lawn. A rose garden, a wildflower meadow and a fern walk have recently been completed, and future plans involve the Regency vinery and eighteenth-century banqueting folly in the adjoining two-acre garden. It is worth a trip from Cork just to see the herbaceous border.

Talbot Botanic Garden ★ 70

Malahide Castle, Malahide, Co. Dublin. Tel: (1) 846 2456
(or Parks Department, Dublin (1) 872 7777)

Fingal County Council • 10m N of Dublin in Malahide • Castle open • Garden open May to Sept, daily, 2 – 5pm, and to groups by appt. Conducted tour of walled garden, Wed, 2pm • Entrance: IR£2, OAPss and accompanied children under 12 free, parties IR£1.50 per person (1999 prices) ◑ 🍽 ✕ 🏫 <u>WC</u>

A 22-acre botanic garden within the 290-acre estate of Malahide with the castle centre stage. The castle was home to the Talbot family for 800 years until the death of Lord Milo Talbot in 1973; in 1976 the estate was acquired by the local authority. The garden is in two sections – the 18-acre West Lawn area of non-ericaceous plants, and a four-acre walled garden of more tender plants. with a strong emphasis on southern-hemisphere species. Genera well represented are pittosporum, euphorbia, azara, berberis, magnolia, pseudopanax and a National Collection of olearias. Plants of particular note are *Bomarea caldasii, Berberidopsis corallina, Euphorbia acanthothamnos* and *Lyonothamnus floribundus* ssp. *aspleniifolius*.

Trinity College Botanic Garden 71

Palmerston Park, Dublin 6. Tel: (1) 497 2070

School of Botany, Trinity College, Dublin • Adjacent to Palmerston Park, near Ranelagh, Dublin • Open all year, daily, Mon – Fri, 9am – 5pm. Appt preferred • Entrance: free ○ &.

This is essentially a research garden, but there is a small arboretum, order (family) beds and a collection of Irish native plants, including many national rarities, as well as some glasshouses; a fragment of *Todea barbara* from a plant donated in 1892 grows in one glasshouse. Also a collection of saxifrages, the rare Mauritius bluebell (*Nesocodon mauritianus*) and rare species recently collected from the Pitcairn group of islands. *Melianthus major* flowers well every year, and there are good specimens of *Betula utilis* 'Trinity College' and *Sorbus hibernica*.

Trinity College, Dublin 72

Dublin 2. Tel: (1) 608 1724 (Enquiries Office)

Entrances in College Green and Nassau Street. Vehicular access at Lincoln Place Gate • Open all year, daily, 8am – 12 midnight • Entrance: free ○

This 40-acre urban campus contains an eclectic collection of trees (described in a separate guidebook) in an impressive architectural setting – 600 of them, illustrating what may be grown successfully in town. The most notable subjects are the pair of *Acer macrophyllum* in Library Square, which probably originate from the earliest introduction by David Douglas; one is the largest in Europe. There are good specimens of *Trachycarpus fortunei*, *Tilia mongolica*, *Betula ermanii*, *Ostrya carpinifolia* and *Sorbus sargentiana*. Lanning Roper devised planting schemes for parts of the campus, and there are 'low-maintenance' shrubberies associated with new buildings. Some interesting modern sculptures, and a handsome campanile (1855).

Tullynally Castle 73

Castlepollard, Co. Westmeath. Tel: (44) 61159; Fax: (44) 61856

Thomas Pakenham • 1m NW of Castlepollard on R395 Granard road • Castle open • Grounds open May to Sept, daily, 2 – 6pm and at other times by appt • Entrance: IR£3, children IR£1 ○ ☕ ✕ 🖪 WC & ⬦

An elaborate early eighteenth-century formal garden of canals and basins was succeeded by romantic parkland and pleasure grounds in the best Reptonian manner. They encompass two artificial lakes and a grotto of fantastic eroded limestone from nearby Lough Derravaragh. The present owner has added new features: a Gothick summerhouse, a Chinese garden complete with pagoda and, on the upper lake, Australian black swans. Walled gardens beyond have extensive flower borders and an avenue of memorable 200-year-old yews. The energetic can undertake a mile-long walk through woodland encircling the park, offering splendid views of the castle itself.

SCOTLAND

Abbotsford 1

**Melrose, Scottish Borders TD6 9BQ. Tel: (01896) 752043;
Fax: (01896) 752916**

*Dame Jean Maxwell-Scott • 3m W of Melrose on A6091, turn SW onto B6360.
Just S of A72 • House open • Garden open 20th March to Oct, daily, 10am – 5pm
(March to May and Oct, Sun, 2 – 5pm) • Entrance: £3.50, children £1.80,
parties £2.50 per person, children £1.30 (1999 prices)* ◑ 🍺 🖫 WC ⅃ 🏛

Sir Walter Scott's magnificent house astride a river valley was built between
1817 and 1821 to satisfy his yearning to become a laird. It has a garden that is rich
in Scottish allusions. A yew hedge to the south of the house has medallions inset
from an old cross, and a fountain in the same formal garden was formed from the
same cross. The River Tweed flows past the house and there are fine views across
a stretch of garden. Herbaceous beds lead to a Gothic-type fern house filled with
other plants beside ferns.

Achamore Gardens ★ 2

Isle of Gigha, Argyll and Bute PA41 7AD. Tel: (01583) 505267

*Mr and Mrs Derek Holt • Take A83 to Tayinloan then ferry to Gigha • Open
all year, daily • Entrance: £2, children £1, collecting box • Other information:
Refreshments at hotel* ○ 🖫 WC ⊲⊳

An amazing idea to create such a superb garden on the Isle of Gigha. The
journey there is via most beautiful countryside finishing up with the ferry trip,
surrounded by squawking sea birds. In 1944 Sir James Horlick purchased the
whole island with the sole purpose of creating a garden in which to grow the
rare and unusual. This was accomplished with the advice of James Russell, and
the overall effect is tropical. A delightful woodland landscape was planted with
a vast collection of rarities from around the world. The rhododendrons are
unsurpassed in variety, quality and sheer visual magnitude, with fine specimens of tender species such as *R. lindleyii, R. fragrantissimum,* and *R. macabeanum.*
There are many varieties of camellias, cordylines, primulas and Asiatic exotica.
A great number of genera are represented by very good specimens, thriving in
Gigha's mildness. There is a fine *Pinus montezumae* in the walled garden; drifts of
Asiatic primulas feature around the especially pretty woodland pond.

Achnacloich 3

Connel, Oban, Argyll and Bute PA37 1PR. Tel: (01631) 710221

*Mrs T.E. Nelson • 3m E of Connel off A85 • Open probably April to Oct, daily,
10am – 6pm • Entrance: £1.50, OAPs £1, children free (1999 prices)* ◑ ⅃ ⊲⊳ 🐾

A small Scottish baronial house situated above the loch on a rocky cliff, with
fine views to Loch Etive and the surrounding countryside. A curved drive
sweeps past massed bulbs in spring, and later there are azaleas *(contd. on p.560)*

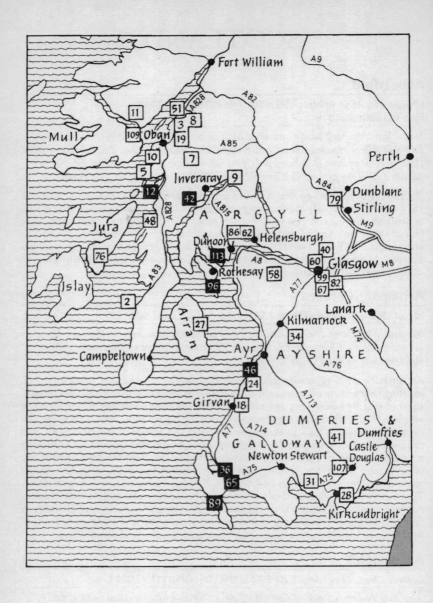

Two-starred gardens are marked on the maps with a black square.

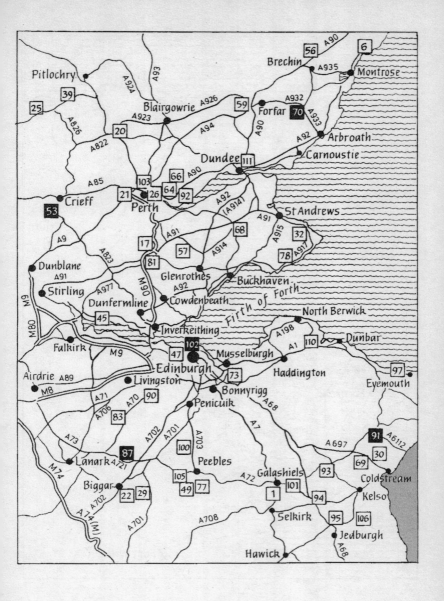

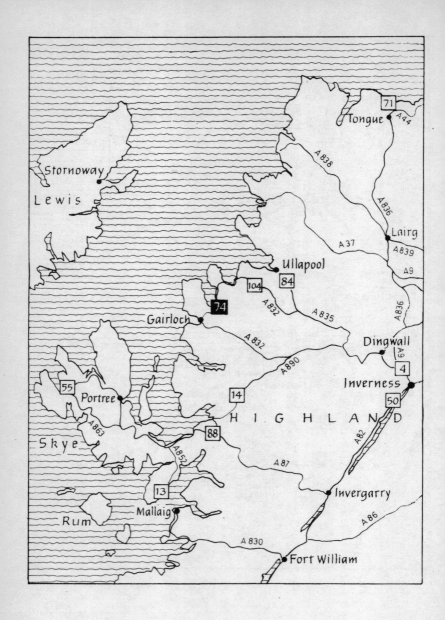

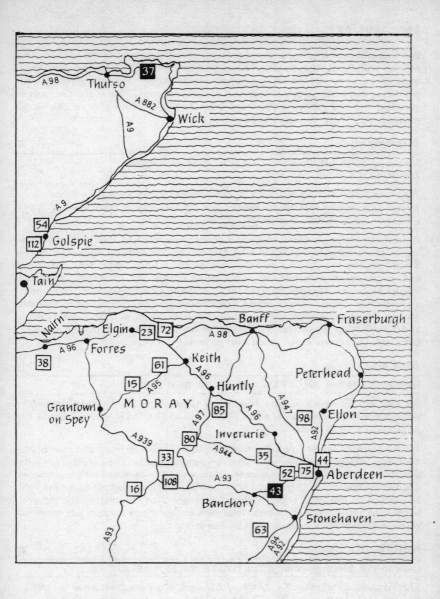

and fine Japanese maples; autumn colour is good throughout the garden. The natural woodland with its interlinked glades is beautiful in spring with bluebells, primroses and wood anemones, while other gaps are planted with primulas, magnolias, rare shrubs and rhododendrons. There are two water gardens, and the garden walks have been extended, taking in an oak wood planted with large-leaved rhododendrons.

Allangrange   4

Munlochy, Black Isle, Ross and Cromarty, Highland IV8 8NZ. Tel: (01463) 811249

Major and Mrs A. Cameron • 5m N of Inverness, signed from A9 • Open several days during summer for charity, 2 – 5.30pm and at other times by appt • Entrance: £2, children 20p ● ☕ WC ♞

A most attractive garden which spills down the hillside in a series of descending terraces merging naturally with the rolling agricultural landscape of the Black Isle. The formal part incorporates white and mauve gardens, many old and shrub roses, tree peonies and a small corner for plants of variegated foliage. In July climbing Himalayan roses, including *Rosa filipes* 'Kiftsgate', make a spectacular display. There is also a small pool garden, and to the rear of the house a woodland garden with unusual rhododendrons, primulas, meconopsis and *Cardiocrinum giganteum*. The hand of an accomplished flower painter, Elizabeth Cameron, shows itself everywhere.

An Cala   5

Easdale, Isle of Seil, Argyll PA34 4RF. Tel: (01852) 300237

Mr and Mrs Thomas Downie • 16m SW of Oban. Signed to Easdale B844 off A816 Oban – Campbelltown road • Open April to Oct, daily, 10am – 6pm • Entrance: £1.50 ◑ ㅎ ⬯

A little jewel of under five acres designed in the 1930s in front of a row of old distillery cottages, nestling into the surrounding cliffs. The stream, with its ponds and little waterfall, is an essential element in a series of different spaces filled with sophisticated colour. This is how azaleas and rhododendrons should be planted on the small scale – enhancing rather than dominating the picture. Local slate paths invite the visitor into each well-planned corner. Just over the gate, in a different world, are ocean and islands.

Arbuthnott House   6

Laurencekirk, Kincardineshire AB30 1PA. Tel: (01561) 361226

The Viscount of Arbuthnott • 22m S of Aberdeen, 3m from Inverbervie on B967 between A90 (A94) and A92 • Garden open all year, daily, 9am – 5pm • Entrance: £2, children £1 • Other information: Refreshments available at Grassic Gibbon Centre in village ○ WC

The enclosed garden dates from the late seventeenth century and with the policies is contained within the valley of the Bervie Water. The entrance drive is flanked by rhododendrons and the verges are full of primroses and celandines in spring. The drive crosses a fine bridge topped by imposing urns before reaching the house set high on a promontory, with most of the garden sloping steeply to the river. The design is unusual in that it has always been treated as an extension of the house, rather than being laid out at some distance. The sloping part has four grassed terraces and this pattern is dissected by diagonal grassed walks radiating out in a manner reminiscent of the Union Jack. This fixed structure creates long garden 'rooms' and vistas as the garden is explored. Although the garden plan is very old, much of today's mature planting was done by Lady Arbuthnott in the 1920s, and this is continued by the present Lady Arbuthnott. Herbaceous borders, old roses together with shrub roses and ramblers, shrubs underplanted with hostas, primulas, meconopsis and lilies, lilacs and viburnums provide colour throughout the summer. A metal stag for target practice stands at the bottom of the slope by the lade (millstream).

Ardanaiseig Garden and Hotel 7

Kilchrenan, Argyll and Bute PA35 1HE. Tel: (01866) 833333

4m E of Kilchrenan on B845 • Open April to Oct, 9am – 8pm • Entrance: by collection box at car park £2, OAPs and children free (1999 prices) • Other information: Refreshments at hotel. No children under 8 ◑ ⟁ ℘

A picturesque 10-mile drive from Taynuilt down the peninsular makes a fitting introduction to this traditional Argyll garden. Attractive slate paths guide the visitor round 20 acres of well-planted woodland set behind an 1834 baronial house, now a comfortable hotel, with lovely views across Loch Awe. The species and hybrid rhododendrons are particularly fine. Note the unusual curved walls of the walled garden.

Ardchattan Priory 8

Oban, Argyll and Bute PA37 1RQ. Fax: (01631) 750238

10m NE of Oban. Cross Connel Bridge on A828 N and turn first right to Ardchattan • Open April to 30th Oct, daily, 9am – 6pm • Entrance: £1.50
◑ 💭 WC ᕳ ⟁

A charming garden with spectacular views over Loch Etive. The extensive lawn to the front of the house is surrounded by herbaceous, rose and shrub borders and a rockery. Either side of the drive, the wild garden is full of roses, shrubs and ornamental trees. The garden surrounds a priory (now a private house) founded by the Valescaullian Order in 1230. The ruined chapel and early gravestones are in the care of Historic Scotland and open with the garden.

Ardkinglas Woodland Garden 9

Cairndow, Argyll and Bute PA26 8BH. Tel: (01499) 600263

Mr John Noble • On A83 Arrochar – Inveraray road. Signposted • Open all year, daily, during daylight hours • Entrance: £2, children under 16 free ◯ 💭
✕ 🖺 WC ᕳ ⟁ ℘ 🗎

The reclamation of these 25 acres continues to gather momentum. Selective felling and the eradication of undesirable regeneration have begun to restore a sense of balance and atmosphere to this dramatic landscape setting above the shores of Loch Fyne. Enjoy the renewed vigour of the historic plant collections, including the 60-metre *Abies grandis*. Amongst bluebells and ferns the next generation of plants is well and truly established. Notable tree introductions include *Cunninghamia lanceolata*, *Idesia polycarpa*, *Acer davidii* and *Rhododendron decorum*.

Ardmaddy Castle 10

By Oban, Argyll PA34 4QY. Tel: (01852) 300353

Mr and Mrs Charles Struthers • 13m SW of Oban. Signed from B844 to Easdale along narrow road • Open all year, daily, 9am – dusk • Entrance: £2
○ 🍴 WC ♿ 🐕 ⚘

The handsome but modest fifteenth-century castle, with steps up to its *piano nobile*, faces both ways — outwards with wide views to the islands and the sea, inwards on the garden side towards hanging woods and a formal walled garden. In the eighteenth century Armaddy marked the western extent of the Earl of Breadalbane's estate, enabling him to ride from one side of Scotland to the other on his own land — until all was gambled away in the early twentieth century. The walled garden set below the castle has traditional box hedge compartments and an increasing collection of herbaceous plants and flowering shrubs and trees as well as an immaculate vegetable section. A water garden with two ponds, and a woodland garden with walks add further interest. There is always a good selection of home-grown plants to buy.

Ardtornish 11

Lochaline, Morvern, Oban, Highland PA34 5UZ. Tel: (01967) 421288 (Estate Office)

Mrs John Raven • 30m SW of Corran. From Corran ferry, 9m SW of Fort William, cross to Morvern and take route left on A861 towards Lochaline, then left on A884. Gardens 2m before Lochaline on left • Open April to Oct, daily, 10am – 4.30pm • Entrance: £2, children free. Collecting box • Other information: 14 self-catering units available, 5 in house ◑ 🍴 WC 🐕 ⚘

A plantsman's garden with a particularly fine and extensive collection of unusual shrubs, deciduous trees and rhododendrons set against a background of conifers, a loch and outstanding Highland scenery. The gardens have developed over the past 100 years or more following the first house on the site, established by a distiller from London in the 1850s. They are on a steeply sloping site and rainfall is heavy. Mrs Raven's late husband wrote a book, *The Botanist's Garden*, now republished, about their other garden, Docwra's Manor (see entry in Cambridgeshire), and he assisted his wife in following her parents' footsteps in trying to establish a plantsman's paradise here. Apart from the area around the house, there is a pleasing air of informality about the gardens, which include Bob's Glen with *Rhododendron thomsonii* and *R. prattii*, and a larger glen with still more species and hybrid rhododendrons, and there is a flourishing kitchen garden.

Arduaine Garden ★★ 12

Oban, Argyll and Bute PA34 4XQ. Tel: (01852) 200366

The National Trust for Scotland • On A816, 20m S of Oban, 17m N of Lochgilphead. Joint entrance with Loch Melfort Hotel • Open all year, daily, 9.30am – sunset • Entrance: £2.50, concessions and children £1.70 (1999 prices) • Other information: Refreshments at hotel ○ ▩ WC ⑆

Arduaine – popularly pronounced Ardoony, but properly Ardooan – was conceived and planted in the early 1900s by James Arthur Campbell, possibly with advice from his friend Osgood Mackenzie, creator of Inverewe Garden (see entry). The Essex nurserymen Edmund and Harry Wright restored the garden after they acquired it in 1971 and gave it to the Trust in 1992. It consists of an outstanding 20 acres on a promontory bounded by Loch Melfort and the Sound of Jura, climatically favoured by the North Atlantic Drift or Gulf Stream – make the effort to climb to the high viewing point to enjoy the panorama. Although its fame rests largely on its outstanding rhododendrons, azaleas, magnolias and other rare trees and shrubs (the rhododendron species collection ranks high in importance in Scotland), the garden has far more than botanical interest to offer. Trees and shrubs, some over a hundred years old and thickly underplanted, tower overhead as they, and visitors, climb the glen, while at the lower level hostas, ferns, candelabra primulas and other more modest flowers and foliage cluster around lawns and along the sides of the stream.

Armadale Castle Gardens and the Museum of the Isles 13

Armadale, Sleat, Isle of Skye IV45 8RS. Tel: (01471) 844305; Website: www.cland.demon.co.uk

Clan Donald Lands Trust • 14m S of Broadford at S end of Skye, close to Mallaig ferry • Visitor Centre open April to Oct • Garden open all year, daily 9.30am – 5.30pm • Entrance: £3.85, concessions £2.40 (1999 prices) • Other information: Guided tours with head gardener available. Two electric wheelchairs available ○ ▩ ✕ ▩ WC ⑆ ⬠ ℘ ▦ ♀

This fine garden is so well groomed that it has almost the atmosphere of a city park. The cultivated areas have been sympathetically developed to include pond gardens with scree planting, a long herbaceous border with raised walk behind the ruined castle, lawns with ornamental trees and a romantic garden planted within one of the ruined sections of Armadale Castle. Surrounding the cultivated area are four miles of nature trails set within 50 acres of woodland and wildflower meadows. Although Armadale is further north than Moscow, the climate is warm and everywhere there are inspiring views up Loch Nevis to Mallaig and Knoydart. Allow plenty of time to get here: the 14-mile approach road is single-track in places and every oncoming driver must be acknowledged and thanked.

Attadale 14

Strathcarron, Wester Ross, Ross-shire IV54 8YX. Tel: (01520) 722217; Fax: (01520) 722546

Mr and Mrs Ewen Macpherson • 15m NE of Kyle of Lochalsh, on A890 between Strathcarron and Skye • Open April to Oct, daily except Sun, 10am – 5.30pm • Entrance: £3, children £1 • Other information: Disabled parking. Light refreshments and meals available 1½ m along road ◑ 🍴 **WC** ♿ ⬦ 🌱

The car park is 50 yards from the garden down the prettiest drive. Inside the gate are beautifully planted stream and ponds all along one side, including candelabra primulas, iris, giant gunneras and bamboos. A bridge over a waterfall links the water garden with a rhododendron walk with views of the sea and hills. Within the small kitchen garden is a particularly good herb plot with box hedges and stone setts. Beyond this a woodland walk has been reclaimed and replanted with drifts of meconopsis and shade-loving plants, and stone paths lead down to a dell of old rhododendrons surrounded by rocky cliffs. From there the visitor emerges into an area of shrub and ornamental tree plantings ending in a more formal sunken garden. The king of the garden is undoubtedly the 150-year-old laburnum next to the ha-ha, and the owners have now given him over 2000 new subjects planted throughout the garden. The house (not open) was built in 1755. Visitors are advised to wear waterproof shoes. There is an honesty box, maps and leaflets just inside the gate.

Ballindalloch Castle 15

Grantown-on-Spey, Banffshire, Highland AB37 9AX. Tel: (01807) 500205; Fax: (01807) 500210

Mrs Oliver MacPherson-Grant Russell • Halfway between Grantown-on-Spey and Keith on A95. Signposted • Castle open • Garden open 21st April to Sept, daily, 10am – 5pm • Entrance: grounds £2 (castle and gardens £5) • Other information: Dog walking area ◑ ☕ ✕ 🍴 **WC** ♿ 🏛 🌱

What a pleasure to find a garden of this scale and calibre set in the magnificent Spey valley. The most attractive feature is undoubtedly the 1937 rock garden, which comes tumbling down the hillside onto the most impressive lawn in the land. It takes three men two days to mow and edge it. The Russells have completely renovated all the borders over the last few years and have landscaped the old walled garden into a rose and fountain garden. The daffodil season and the river/woodland walks are particularly lovely. A small parterre at the side of the house shows how stunning humble nepeta and *Alchemilla mollis* can be when all else is eaten by the deer.

Balmoral Castle 16

Ballater, Aberdeenshire AB35 5TB. Tel: Estates Office (013397) 42334/5

H.M. The Queen • 6m W of Ballater on A93 at Crathie • Castle ballroom and carriage exhibitions open • Gardens and grounds open 17th April – July, daily,

10am – 5pm • Entrance: £4, OAPs £3, children (5-16) £1, under 5 free ◖ 🍵 🗄 WC ♿ ⬦ 🎫 🍽

Balmoral, the personal home in Scotland of Her Majesty the Queen, is Gaelic for 'majestic dwelling', and there had been earlier castles on the same site before the estate was purchased in 1852 by Prince Albert, consort to Queen Victoria. She called Balmoral 'this dear paradise', and she and the Prince immediately began making a three-acre garden about the castle and planting the grounds with rare coniferous and broad-leaved forest trees. Queen Mary added the sunken rose garden in 1932, and since 1953 the Queen and Prince Philip have made other improvements and extensions, the latest being the water garden, created in 1979 close to Queen Victoria's garden cottage. There are herbaceous borders, but generally the gardens are natural in style. Throughout the grounds there are statues and cairns in memory of Queen Victoria's family and their descendants, and also specimen trees, labelled with the names of the visiting dignitaries who planted them.

The Bank House   17

Glenfarg, Perth and Kinross PH2 9NZ. Tel: (01577) 830275

Mr and Mrs C.B. Lascelles • 10m SW of Perth off B996 between M90 junctions 8 and 9. In Glenfarg, 50 metres along Ladeside, by Glenfarg Hotel • Open by appt • Entrance: £5 ◖ 🍽 🗄 ♿ ⬦

The principal garden is approached through a paved area with additional planting above low retaining walls. An apple-and-clematis tunnel leads the visitor onwards to large curved beds set into lawns on a gently sloping site. A horseshoe-shaped yew hedge underplanted with yellow archangel and star of Bethlehem is a fine spring feature; bulbs and early-flowering herbaceous plants carry the display to summer. The owners have built up an eclectic collection of rare and unusual plants of much merit and these are grown to perfection, using organic gardening techniques. The careful planting, with great regard to colour and form, makes for an instructive visit. A smaller garden across the street, with a 'flowform cascade' water feature and a 'yin and yang' circular bed, may be visited at any time. Ornamental trees have also been planted in a newly acquired field, where a pond has been created and a wildflower meadow sown.

Bargany   18

Girvan, South Ayrshire KA26 9QL. Tel: (01465) 871249

John Dalrymple-Hamilton • 18m SW of Ayr off B734 Girvan – Dailly road • Open March to Oct, daily, 10am – 7pm (4pm in early and late season) • Entrance: by donation to collecting box ◖ 🗄 ♿ ⬦ 🌿

This is a woodland garden, densely planted with splendid ancient rhododendrons, azaleas, fine trees and conifers. Wonderfully diverse paths make for a relaxed stroll round a charming lily pond and rock garden. Good autumn colour.

Barguillean Angus Garden 19

Taynuilt, Argyll and Bute PA35 1JS. Tel: (01866) 822381; Fax: (01866) 822652

Mr Sam S. MacDonald • 5m SE of Oban, 3m SW of Taynuilt. Take minor road to Kilmore off A85 at Taynuilt Hotel • Open March to Oct, daily, 8am – 9pm. Parties welcome by prior appt in writing • Entrance: £2, children free ◑ ⟐

Nine-acre woodland garden with no formal paths or borders, but with areas of established rhododendrons, azaleas and conifers and some rare trees and shrubs on a Highland hillside overlooking a lochan with views to Ben Cruachan. Much new planting, with modern rhododendron hybrids from the NW of the United States among native birch and oak woodland, makes for interesting comparisons with established rhododendron gardens of the west coast. More plantings are planned. Described by its owner as a place of tranquillity and love, it was created by Betty Macdonald in memory of her writer/journalist son, killed in Cyprus in the 1956 troubles.

Beatrix Potter Garden 20

Birnam, Perth and Kinross PH8 0BN. Tel: (01350) 727674 (Birnam Institute)

Perthshire and Kinross Council • 13m NW of Perth via A9 in Birnam • Open all year, daily • Entrance: free ◑ 🖼 ⅋ ⟐

There is always a certain rivalry between houses where a celebrity was born and others where he or she was conceived, lived or died. So it is with authors. Beatrix Potter, it seems, may have published her famous books from the Lake District, but the characters were invented when she stayed here near the family's Dalguise House; she came here for 12 successive annual holidays and was a regular visitor to the Institute. Her diaries have revealed that Peter Rabbit and his friends were modelled on local people and animals. This new garden commemorates the connection, with bronze sculptures of some of the best-known characters amid rustic surroundings. Interest nursery rather than horticultural.

Bell's Cherrybank Gardens ★ 21

Cherrybank, Perth, Perth and Kinross PH2 0NG. Tel: (01738) 621111

UDV UK • On A9 into Perth city centre. Gardens S of main road • Open probably May to early Oct, daily, 9am – 5pm • Entrance: £1, OAPs and children 50p • Other information: Guide dogs only ◑ 🍽 WC &

This modern garden surrounding commercial offices is in fact two gardens, the first laid out in the early 1970s, plus the Scottish National Collection of heathers, begun in 1983. Their aim is to have the world's largest collection – there are now over 830 varieties, all in superb condition. Other plant collections are well maintained and beautifully designed. Interest is sustained throughout the total of 18 acres by water features, modern sculptures, pleasant vistas, a tiny putting green, tubular bells and an aviary. The children's play area includes a roundabout for wheelchair-bound children. There is a remarkable sundial designed by Ian Hamilton Finlay, the sculptor (see entry for Little Sparta). A Bell's Whisky Heritage Centre is also on the site, opening in spring 2000.

Biggar Park ★ 22

Biggar, South Lanarkshire ML12 6JS. Tel: (01899) 220185

Capt. and Mrs David Barnes • S end of Biggar on A702, 30m SW of Edinburgh • Open May to July by appt. Parties welcome by appt • Entrance: £2 • Other information: Refreshments by arrangement ● 🍴 WC & ⬥ ♀

A Japanese garden of tranquillity welcomes one to this well-planned 10-acre plantsman's garden. Sue Barnes' efficient labelling adds greatly to the enjoyment when walking through the woodland and the small arboretum and admiring the well-planted ornamental pond, all carefully designed to give year-round interest. This starts with a stunning display of daffodils, followed by glades of meconopsis, rhododendrons and azaleas in early summer before the huge herbaceous borders burst into colour. The centrepiece, however, must be the outstanding walled garden, reached through a fine rockery bank beside the eighteenth-century mansion house. The view through the wrought-iron gate stretches the length of a 45-metre double herbaceous border, attractively backed by swags of thick ornamental rope hanging from rose 'pillars', whilst either side is divided into intensively planted sections divided by pleasing grass paths.

Blackhills House 23

Lhanbryde, Elgin, Moray IV30 8QU. Tel: (01343) 842223

Mr and Mrs John Christie • 4m E of Elgin off A96. Take B9103 southwards, then minor road • Open two days in May and by appt for charity • Entrance: £2, children free (1998 prices) • Other information: Teas on open days only ● WC & ⬥

The east coast of Scotland is not, with a few exceptions, noted for its rhododendron gardens, but Blackhills in the Laich of Moray should be visited for its collection of species rhododendrons in early May and in late May for hybrids. Both sorts are spread under tree cover in a steep-sided valley with many fine specimen trees. These include a davidia, a Japanese red cedar (*Cryptomeria japonica*), Brewer's weeping spruce and a golden chestnut (*Chrysolepis chrysophylla*) – a rare chestnut relative from North America. The finest rhododendrons are those in the subsections Falconera, Grandia and Taliensia, but the genus is well represented as a whole. The wooded valley opens to reveal two lakes with plantings of maples and other Asiatic plants. Mr Thomas North Christie, who was responsible for the early planting in the 1920s, corresponded at length and exchanged the latest introductions with his neighbour the Brodie of Brodie.

Blairquhan 24

Maybole, South Ayrshire KA19 7LZ. Tel: (01655) 770239

*James Hunter Blair • 12m S of Ayr, 7m SE of Maybole on B7045. Signposted •
House open • Garden open 15th July to 13th Aug, daily except Mon, 2 –
5.30pm (last admission 4.45pm) • Entrance: £4.50, OAPs £3.50, children
£2.50 (house and garden)* ● ☕ 🖼 WC ⅄ ⬦ ℘ 🍴 ⚲

The castle is approached by a three-mile drive along the River Girvan giving
good opportunities to admire the extensive wood and parkland. The three-
acre walled garden has been redesigned with ornamental planting and there is
an 1860 Pinetum.

Bolfracks 25

Aberfeldy, Perth and Kinross PH15 2EX. Tel: (01887) 820207

*Mr J.D. Hutchison • 2m W of Aberfeldy on A827 towards Loch Tay • Open:
April to Oct, daily, 10am – 6pm • Entrance: £2.50, children free (honesty box at
gate)* NEW ◐

There has been a garden on this site for 200 years, but the present garden was
started by the owner's parents in the 1920s and reshaped by the owner over
the last 20 years. Three acres of plantsman's garden are well laid-out within a
walled enclosure and demonstrate the potential of an exposed hillside site
with a northerly aspect. Astounding views over the Tay Valley are matched by
the garden's own interesting features, including peat walls and a stream
garden. There are masses of fine bulbs in spring and good autumn colour.
Gentians do well on this soil. The walled garden contains a collection of old and
modern shrub roses.

Branklyn Garden ★ 26

116 Dundee Road, Perth, Perth and Kinross PH2 7BB. Tel: (01738) 625535

*The National Trust for Scotland • ½ m from Friarton Bridge on A90, then
A859 to Perth • Open March to Oct, daily, 9.30am – sunset • Entrance: £2.50,
OAPs and children £1.70, family £6.65. Pre-booked parties of 20 or more £2 per
person • Other information: Parking ½ m from gate. Coaches and disabled
parking at gate. Possible for wheelchairs but some paths too narrow* ◐ WC ℘ 🍴
⚲

John and Dorothy Renton created this garden nearly within sight and certainly
within sound of the centre of Perth. Work commenced in 1922, and in 1955
Dorothy was awarded the Veitch Memorial Medal by the Royal Horticultural
Society. The National Trust for Scotland took over the garden in 1968, after
the death of Dorothy in 1966 and of her husband the following year. It extends
to nearly two acres, the main interest being its Sino-Himalayan alpine and
ericaceous plants and its magnificent scree/rock gardens. There is also a
splendid collection of dwarf rhododendrons. Essential work continues to
maintain Branklyn's rightful reputation as an outstanding plantsman's garden
with its main feature which has been described as 'a plantsman's paradise'. It is

impossible to describe all the fascinating things to be found here, from the fine trees to the comprehensive collection of dwarf and smaller rhododendrons, the meconopsis to the notholirions, and the garden will repay many visits.

Brodick Castle ★ 27

Isle of Arran, North Ayrshire KA27 8HY. Tel: (01770) 302202; Fax: (01770) 302312

The National Trust for Scotland • On Isle of Arran, 2m N of Brodick. Ferry from Ardrossan or Kintyre • Castle open April to Oct, daily, 11am – 4.30pm • Gardens and country park open all year, daily, 9.30am – sunset • Entrance: £2.50, concessions £1.75, parties of 20 or more £2 per person (castle and gardens £5, concession £3.40, family £13.50, pre-booked parties of 20 or more £4 per person)(1999 prices) • Other information: Wheelchair available ○ ☕ ✕ 🏠 **WC** ◁▷ 🌿 👍 ♿

High above the shores of the Firth of Clyde and guarding the approaches to Western Scotland is this castle of locally quarried sandstone. Its garden was an overgrown jungle of rhododendrons until it was restored by the Duchess of Montrose after World War I. She was much helped after 1930 when her daughter married John Boscawen of Tresco Abbey (see entry in Cornwall). Many trees and plants arrived at that time by boat from Tresco in the Scillies; others came from subscriptions to the second generation of great plant-hunters like Kingdon-Ward and, in particular, George Forrest, one of the greatest of all collectors. Plants from the Himalayas, Burma, China and South America, normally considered tender, flourish in the mild climate. There is a good display of primulas in the bog garden. The walled formal garden to the east of the castle is over 250 years old and has recently been restored as an Edwardian garden with herbaceous plants, annuals and roses. It is impossible to list all the treasures of the woodland garden, but perhaps the most surprising is the huge size of the specimens in the lower rhododendron walk, where *R. sinogrande* are found with leaves up to 60 centimetres long.

Broughton House ★ 28

12 High Street, Kirkcudbright, Dumfries and Galloway DG6 4JX. Tel: (01557) 330437

The National Trust for Scotland • 28m SW of Dumfries. Take A75 from Dumfries past Castle Douglas, then 1m past Bridge of Dee take A711 to Kirkcudbright. Signposted • Open April to Oct, daily, 1 – 5.30pm (last admission 4.45pm). Pre-booked parties may be admitted outside opening hours • Entrance: £2.50, concessions £1.70, family £6.70, NTS/NT members free (1999 prices) ◑ **WC** 👍

Created by an artist, E.A. Hornel, who lived here from 1901 to 1933, this fascinating garden reflects an interest in oriental art following his visit to Japan and incorporates both Japanese and Scottish features. After his death the house became a museum and its surroundings were gradually restored. The garden starts with a sunken courtyard, beyond which is a pleasant hybrid, a cross between 'fantasy Japan and fantasy old-world cottage garden'. Japanese cherries blossom over skilful low-level planting in the sunken courtyard and further down are all the elements of a much larger garden: rose parterre, pergola, glasshouse, box hedges and herbaceous borders, all looking remarkably uncrowded. Charming lily pools have flat stepping stones and dramatic boulders, and are fed by an immense rainwater tank. At the end of the long central walk, beyond a hedge, is the River Dee with its mudflats and saltings.

Broughton Place   29

Broughton, Biggar, Scottish Borders ML12 6HJ. Tel: (01899) 830234

*Buchanan-Dunlop family, Mr and Mrs R.C. Carr, H. Graham and G. Reilly •
29m SW of Edinburgh, just N of Broughton on A701 Edinburgh – Moffat road.
Follow signs for Broughton Gallery • Garden open 26th March to 17th Oct, daily
except Wed, 10.30am – 6pm • Entrance: by donation to collection box • Other
information: Alternative entrance available for wheelchairs* ◑ WC & ⌇ 🏛

Winding up the towering eighteenth-century beech avenue, you come to the magnificent turreted modern mansion designed by Sir Basil Spence, cushioned into the surrounding Tweeddale hills. Although nearly 300 metres above sea level, the effects of frosts are limited by the hillside location. Jane and Graham Buchanan-Dunlop have a thriving art gallery, and it is through this that the visitor gains entry into the charming three-acre garden. Meandering paths lead up and down well-kept borders full of rare and interesting plants, mainly herbaceous. National Collections of thalictrums and tropaeolums are held here.

Bughtrig   30

**Leitholm, Coldstream, Berwickshire, Scottish Borders TD12 4JP.
Tel: (01890) 840678**

*Major General and The Hon. Mrs Charles Ramsay • 5m N of Coldstream, ¼ m
E of Leitholm on B6461 • Open June to Sept, daily, 11am – 5pm • Entrance:
£2, children under 18 £1, inc. donation to SGS • Other information: Special
arrangements for bona fide parties to garden, and occasionally house. Sometimes
possible for parties of up to 8 persons to stay in house* ◑ 🏠 ⬦

This has been owned by just three families since the fourteenth century. It is a traditional Scottish family garden, designed for amenity and support for the larder, but hedged rather than walled and close to the house. Its two-and-a-half acres contain an interesting combination of herbaceous perennials, shrubs, annuals, vegetables and fruit, surrounded by fine specimen trees which provide remarkable shelter.

Cally Gardens and Nursery   31

**Gatehouse of Fleet, Castle Douglas, Dumfries and Galloway DG7 2DJ.
Fax and information line: (01557) 815029**

*Mr Michael Wickenden · 30m SW of Dumfries via A75. Take Gatehouse
turning and turn left through Cally Palace Hotel gateway. Signposted •*

*Open 22nd April to 24th Sept, Tues – Fri, 2 – 5.30pm, Sat and Sun,
10am – 5.30pm • Entrance: £1.50, children under 13 free* ◑ WC ⓰ ⬦
ᵠ

Three hundred Glasgow children 'dug for Victory' here in World War II and
the gardens have flourished since the present owner arrived. A specialist
nursery in a two-and-three-quarter-acre, eighteenth-century walled garden
which has large beds of herbaceous plants and many unusual varieties, well
worth a visit by plant lovers. Large collection of perennial geraniums, kniphofias, crocosmias and others – 3500 varieties in all. Ninety five per cent of
the plants are propagated on the premises, some from seed collected abroad or
sent in botanic garden exchanges, and a changing selection of several hundred
is available pot-grown. A favourite with visitors is the spread of meconopsis
(Himalayan blue poppies) when in season in early June. The Cally Oak Woods
which surround the nursery have nature trails. Catalogue available (3 x 1st-
class stamps).

Cambo   32

Kingsbarns, St Andrews, Fife KY16 8QD. Tel: (01333) 450054

*Mr and Mrs P. Erskine • 6m SE of St Andrews on A917 between Kingsbarns
and Crail • Open all year, daily, 10am – dusk • Entrance: £2, children free*
○ 🖻 WC ⓰ ⬦ ᵠ

The two-and-a-half-acre walled garden is bisected by the Cambo burn, the
focal point; the sound of running water adds to the relaxing atmosphere.
This is a very productive garden with a new *potager* in one section. There
are ornamental beds of herbaceous plants, roses, and shrubs. A section of
the original glasshouses is still in good condition and fully used. In early
spring, the snowdrops are spectacular. A lilac walk of 26 varieties makes a
visit in May worthwhile, and from then until September, there is plenty of
colour and interest. Occasionally the garden next to the house is also
open.

Candacraig   33

Dinnet, Aberdeenshire AB36 8XT. Tel: (01975) 651226

*Mrs E.M. Young • 26m SW of Huntly. Take A97 Huntly – Dinnet road then
A944 (formerly B973) Strathdon – Tomintoul road • Open May to Sept, Mon –
Fri, 10am – 5pm, Sat and Sun, 2 – 6pm. At other times by appt • Entrance: by
donation* ◑ 🖻 WC ⓰ ᵠ ♀

At an altitude of 300 metres this old walled garden dates from 1820 and
covers a three-acre sheltered site in upper Donside. This is now being
systematically restored and features herbaceous borders, cottage-garden
flowers, a wide range of meconopsis and primulas, and a newly formed
spring garden with pond and meadow. There is a Victorian summerhouse in
Gothic style which, for readers so inclined, serves as the local registry office
and marriage room.

Carnell ★ 34

Hurlford, Kilmarnock, South Ayrshire KA1 5JS. Tel: (01563) 884236

Mr and Mrs J.R. Findlay and Mr James Findlay • 4m SE of Kilmarnock, NW of Mauchline on A76, 1½ m off A719 • Open 30th July, 2 – 5.30pm. Private parties by appt • Entrance: £2.50, children under 12 free (1999 prices) • Other information: Sixteenth-century pele tower ● 🍵 🖼 WC 🚻 ⟨⟩ 🌿 🏛

Eighty years ago this was a limestone quarry – now it is an exquisite example of 90 metres of linear herbaceous borders facing a rectangular pool, with informal planting as a contrast on the opposite bank. There is a new phlox and shrub border, an interesting rock garden and a walled garden. Burmese and Japanese features include a Chinese gazebo and Burmese dragons, all mementos of Commander Findlay's travels. Climbing the slope behind the pavilion in the south-east corner is the rock garden. The garden adjacent to the house has long herbaceous borders and a shrub and lily collection. The entrance to the desmesne is through an archway bedecked with a 'Kiftsgate' rose. All plants and vegetables are grown with organic compost produced *in situ*.

Castle Fraser 35

Sauchen, Inverurie, Aberdeenshire AB51 7LD. Tel: (01330) 833463

The National Trust for Scotland • 15m NW of Aberdeen, off B993 near Kemnay • Castle open Easter; May to Sept, daily; Oct, weekends • Garden open all year, daily, 9am – 6pm • Entrance: £2.10, concessions £1.40, parties £1.90 per person, school parties £1 per child (castle and garden £4.40, concessions £2.90, family £11.70, parties £3.50 per person, school parties £1 per child) (1999 prices) • Other information: Dogs on dog trail only ○ 🍵 ✕ 🖼 WC 🚻 🌿 🏛 🍴

Extensive grounds provide the setting for one of the most spectacular of the castles of Mar. It consists of a late-seventeenth-/early eighteenth-century designed landscape, with eighteenth-century agricultural improvements. The work of Thomas White (1794) was followed by 'natural-style' improvements of c. 1800, the herbaceous border restored in 1959 by James Russell and the walled garden designed by Eric Robson along traditional lines in the 1970s. There are excellent views to and from the castle, amd extensive walks in the grounds include superb views of the stunning castle in its parkland setting and outwards to nearby hills, notably Bennachie.

Castle Kennedy and Lochinch Gardens ★★ 36

Stranraer, Wigtownshire, Dumfries and Galloway DG9 8BX. Tel: (01776) 702024

The Earl of Stair and the Countess of Stair • 5m E of Stranraer on A75 • Open April to Sept, daily, 10am – 5pm • Entrance: £3, OAPs £2, children £1. Discount for parties of 20 or more ◑ 🍵 🖼 WC 🚻 ⟨⟩ 🌿 🏛

One of Scotland's most famous gardens, set on a peninsular between two lochs and well worth a visit for its sheer 75-acre magnificence and spectacular spring colour. The gardens were originally laid out in 1730 around the ruins of his castle home by Field Marshal the 2nd Earl of Stair, who used his unoccupied dragoons to effect a major remoulding of the landscape, combining large formal swathes of mown grassland with massive formal gardens, criss-crossed by avenues and *allées* of large specimen trees. The garden is internationally famous for its pinetum, currently being replanted, for its good variety of tender trees and for its species rhododendrons, including many of Sir Joseph Hooker's original introductions from his Himalayan expeditions. The monkey-puzzle avenue, now sadly a little tattered, was once the finest in the world; there is also an avenue of noble firs and another of hollies underplanted with embothriums and eucryphias. An impressive two-acre circular lily pond puts everyone else's in their proper place, and a good walk from this brings you back to the ruined castle and its walled garden, well planted with theme borders.

Castle of Mey ★★ 37

Thurso, Caithness, Highland KW14 8XH.

The Queen Elizabeth Castle of Mey Trust • 1½ m from Mey on A836 • Open probably two days in July, one day in Sept for SGS. Telephone (0131) 229 1870 for details • Entrance: £1.50, OAPs and children under 12, £1 (1999 prices) ◕

The castle dates from the late sixteenth century and was renovated by H.M. The Queen Mother in 1955. Gardening would not be possible in such an exposed position without the protection of the 'Great Wall of Mey'. Within the walled garden, she has collected her favourite flowers; many were gifts and have special meaning. The personal private feeling pervades the whole garden, which is especially well planted and well maintained. The colour schemes are very good, blending the garden with the vast natural panorama within which it is situated.

Cawdor Castle ★ 38

Cawdor, Nairn, Highland IV12 5RD. Tel: (01667) 404615

The Dowager Countess Cawdor • Between Inverness and Nairn on B9090 off A96 • Castle open • Garden open May to 8th Oct, daily, 10am – 5.30pm • Entrance: £2.80 (castle and garden £5.40, OAPs £4.40, children £2.80. Family ticket (2 adults and up to 5 children) £14.50. Parties of 20 or more £4.90 per person) (1999 prices) ◑ ☕ ✕ WC ♿

Frequently referred to as one of the Highland's most romantic castles and steeped in history, Cawdor Castle is a fourteenth-century keep with seventeenth- and nineteenth-century additions. The surrounding parkland is handsome and well kept, though not in the grand tradition of classic landscapes. To the side of the castle is the formal garden where recently added wrought-iron arches frame extensive herbaceous borders, a peony border, a very old hedge of mixed varieties of *Rosa pimpinellifolia*, the Scots or Burnet rose, a rose tunnel, old apple trees with climbing roses, interesting shrubs and lilies. An abundance of lavender and pinks complete a rather Edwardian atmosphere. The castle wall shelters exochorda, *Abutilon vitifolium*, *Carpenteria californica* and *Rosa banksiae*. Pillar-box red seats create an unusual note in this splendidly flowery garden, but the owners like them. The walled garden below the castle has been restored with a holly maze, a thistle garden, a laburnum walk and a white garden. The latter is a 'Paradise garden', preceded by Earth represented as a knot garden, and between the two lies Purgatory. There are fine views everywhere of the castle, the park and the surrounding countryside, which one can enjoy more actively by walking one of the five nature trails, varying in length from half to five miles. Further developments include the Auchindoune gardens, where Arabella Lennox-Boyd helped with the planting.

Clan Donald Visitor Centre

(see ARMADALE CASTLE GARDENS AND MUSEUM OF THE ISLES)

Cluny House ★   39

Aberfeldy, Perth and Kinross PH15 2JT. Tel: (01887) 820795

Mr J. and Mrs W. Mattingley • 32m NW of Perth. N of Aberfeldy, over Wade's Bridge, take A827 Weem – Strathtay road. House signed in 3m • Open March to Oct, daily, 10am – 6pm • Entrance: £2.50, children free ◑ 🖻 🌿

Unlike most other gardens this is as truly wild as one can find – friendly weeds grow unchecked for fear of disturbing the National Collection of Asiatic primulas. Sheltered slopes create a moist micro-climate where all the plants flourish abundantly, including a Wellingtonia with the British near-record girth of over 10 metres. In the superb woodland garden many of the plants were propagated from seed acquired by Mrs Mattingley's father on the Ludlow/Sherriff expedition to Bhutan in 1948. Special treats are the carpets of bulbs, trilliums and meconopsis, a fine selection of Japanese acers, *Prunus serrula*, hundreds of different rhododendrons, *Cardiocrinum giganteum*, massive lysichitons and many fine specimen trees.

Colzium Estate   40

Kilsyth, Glasgow G65 0PY. Tel: (01236) 825070

North Lanarkshire Council • 14m NE of Glasgow, ½ m E of Kilsyth on A803 • House and museum open by appt • Estate open all year, daily. Walled garden open April to Sept, daily, 12 noon – 7pm; Oct to March, Sat and Sun only, 12 noon – 4pm • Entrance: free ○ 🖻 **WC** ♿ 🚯

An outstanding collection of conifers, including dwarf cultivars, and rare trees in a beautifully designed large walled garden. Everything is well labelled and immaculately maintained; even gravel paths are raked. There are also 100 varieties each of snowdrops and crocuses. Other attractions include a seventeenth-century ice-house, glen walk, fifteenth-century tower house, arboretum, curling pond and clock theatre.

Corsock House   41

Corsock, Castle Douglas, Dumfries and Galloway DG7 3NJ. Tel: (01644) 440250

Mr and Mrs M.L. Ingall • 10m N of Castle Douglas on A712. Signed from A75 onto B794 • Open 28th May for charity and by appt • Entrance: £2, children 50p • Other information: Refreshments on open day only ◕

A most attractive 20-acre woodland garden with exceptionally fine plantings both of trees (*Fagus sylvatica*, Wellingtonia, oak, Douglas fir, cercidiphyllum, acer) and of rhododendrons (*R. thomsonii*, *lacteum*, *loderi*, *prattii*, *sutchuenense*). The knowledgeable owner has contributed most imaginatively to the layout of the gardens over the last 40 years, creating glades, planting vistas of azaleas and personally building a temple and *trompe-l'oeil* bridge which give the gardens a classical atmosphere. An impressive highlight is the large water garden, again cleverly laid out and with the water-edge plantings set off by a background of mature trees with good autumn colour.

Crarae Garden ★★   42

Minard, Inveraray, Argyll and Bute PA32 8YA. Tel: (01546) 886614/886388

Crarae Gardens Charitable Trust • 11m SW of Inveraray on A83 • Garden open all year, daily, 10am – 5pm or dusk if earlier • Entrance: £2.50, children £1.50, family (2 adults and 2 children) £7, wheelchair users free (1999 prices) • Other information: Possible for wheelchairs on lower slopes only ○ 🍽 🏠 WC 🐕 ♨ 🛍 🌱

The gardens were originally planned by Grace, Lady Campbell in the early part of this century, inspired by her nephew Reginald Farrer, a famous traveller and plant collector. Subsequently her son, Sir George Campbell (1894-1967), spent many years creating this superb 'Himalayan ravine' set in a Highland glen. Using surplus seed from the great plant expeditions, numerous gifts from knowledgeable friends and the shared expertise of a network of famous horticulturists, Sir George planted a variety of rare trees (his first love), exotic shrubs and species rhododendrons, which now form great canopies above the winding paths. These, together with many other plants from the temperate world, make a magnificent spectacle of colour and differing perspectives, the whole enlivened by splendid torrents and waterfalls. The autumn colouring of sorbus, acers, liriodendrons, prunus, cotoneasters and berberis is one of the great features of the garden, which now contains a National Collection of nothofagus. Another 50 acres of research arboretum developed with funding from the Millennium Commission opened in late 1999 for the millennium.

Crathes Castle Garden ★★   43

Crathes Castle, Banchory, Aberdeenshire AB31 5QJ. Tel: (01330) 844525

The National Trust for Scotland • 3m E of Banchory, 15m SW of Aberdeen on A93 • Castle open April to Oct, daily, 11am – 5.30pm (timed entry system; last admission 4.45pm). Other times by appt • Garden and grounds open all year, daily, 9.30am – dusk • Entrance: castle, garden and grounds £5, OAPs and children under 17 £3.40. Pre-booked parties of 20 or more £4 per person, children £3.40 (1999 prices) • Other information: Parking 400 metres from gardens. Dogs on nature trail in grounds only ○ 🍽 ✕ 🏠 WC ♿ ♨ 🛍 🌱

The first view of Crathes is breathtaking – a romantic castle set in flowing lawns. The building, dating from 1596, looks much as it did in the mid-eighteenth century, but there is no record of how the garden looked then, although yew topiary of 1702 survives. Sir James Burnett, who inherited the estate, was a keen collector, his wife an inspired herbaceous garden designer, and the garden today reflects their achievements. In all there are eight gardens, each with a different theme. Rare shrubs reflect Burnett's interest in the Far East, where he served in the army. Splendid wide herbaceous borders with clever plant associations were Lady Burnett's creation, the most famous of which is the white border. There are many specialist areas, such as the trough garden; the large greenhouses contain a National Collection of Malmaison carnations. Extensive wild gardens and grounds with picnic areas, with 10 miles of marked trails. Often compared to Hidcote but with evident inspiration from Jekyll, Crathes has wonders for the plantsperson, the designer and the ordinary visitor.

Cruickshank Botanic Garden 44

St Machar Drive, Aberdeen AB24 3UU. Tel: (01224) 272704

The Cruickshank Trust and University of Aberdeen • 1½ m N from city centre in Old Aberdeen. Entrance in Chanonry. Signposted • Open all year, Mon − Fri, 9am − 4.30pm; also May to Sept, Sat and Sun, 2 − 5pm • Entrance: free. Children must be accompanied by adult ○ 🖼 ⅙ ⬦

Endowed by Miss Anne H. Cruickshank in 1898 to cater for teaching and research in botany at the University of Aberdeen and for the public good, the original six acres were designed by George Nicholson of Kew. That layout disappeared with World War I. The long wall, herbaceous border and sunken garden date from 1920 but much reverted to vegetable cultivation during World War II. In 1970, the garden was extended and a new rock garden made. A terrace garden was added by the long wall in 1980, a new rose garden in 1986 and the peat walls restored in 1988. The rock garden, with a series of connecting pools, has interesting alpines, bulbs and dwarf shrubs. A small woodland area is rich in meconopsis, primulas, rhododendrons and hellebores. Proximity to the North Sea does not permit good growth of large conifers, with the exception of dawn redwood and *Pinus radiata*, but there are fine species lilacs, witch hazels, and the long wall shelters more tender exotics. The total area of the present garden is 11 acres, of which four acres are planted as an arboretum − this is reached by a path from the summit of the rock gardens.

Culross Palace 45

Culross, Dunfermline, Fife KY12 8JH. Tel: (01383) 880359

The National Trust for Scotland • 12m W of Forth Bridge off A985 • Open April to Sept, daily, 11am − 5pm • Entrance: palace and garden £4.40, children £2.90 (1999 prices) ◑ ☕ ✕ WC 🐾 🍴

A small area packed full of fascinating plants and features, including the old poultry breed, the Scots Dumpy. The atmosphere of the seventeenth-century garden is suggested by the crushed-shell paths, an abundance of herbs and period vegetables and fruit, plus attention to detail − clay watering cans, plants in baskets and hurdles.

Culzean Castle and Country Park ★★ 46

Maybole, South Ayrshire KA19 8LE. Tel: (01655) 884400

The National Trust for Scotland • 12m S of Ayr on A719 coast road • Castle open • Country park and gardens open April to Oct, daily, 10.30am – 5.30pm • Entrance: £3.50, children £2.50, parties £2.50 per person, schools £20 per bus; additional charge for castle (1999 prices) ◑ ☕ ✕ 🖾 WC ♿ ⊗ ♨ 🏛 ☕

Over 200,000 people a year visit Culzean, regarded by many as the flagship of The National Trust for Scotland. The castle was originally a medieval fortified house atop the Ayrshire cliffs, but was extensively restructured by Robert Adam from 1777 in what has become known as his 'Culzean' style. This is reflected in the many fine architectural features scattered throughout the grounds, and in particular the handsome Home Farm Courtyard, now a visitor centre. Restoration work abounds. A major undertaking has been the consolidation and partial rebuilding of Robert Adam's unique Viaduct. The Camellia House, a picturesque 1818 glasshouse, has been beautifully restored to its original use as an orangery, and the fountain in the garden below the castle has been repaired and replumbed. The Swan Pond buildings have been conserved and repaired along with the beautiful bridge to the north. More work on the gazebo and elsewhere remains to be completed, but the restored pagoda is now spectacular. The country-park landscape covers 563 acres with a network of woodland and cliff-top paths, and the gardens themselves cover a spacious 30 acres and include all the traditional elements of a grand garden at the turn of the century, the main elements being a fine fountained pleasure garden and a vast walled garden with herbaceous and vegetable plantings.

Dalmeny: The Park 47

Mons Hill, Dalmeny Estate, South Queensferry, Edinburgh. Tel: (0131) 331 1888

The Earl of Rosebery • 7m W of Edinburgh city centre off A90. Pedestrians and cars enter by Lenchold Gate and exit by Chapel Gate • Mons Hill open for charity one Sun late Feb/early March, depending on snowdrops • Entrance: admission charge ◑ ☕

Mons Hill is a partially wooded hill of semi-natural hardwoods with several acres of wild snowdrops and outstanding views towards the Pentland Hills, Edinburgh and the Firth of Forth, weather permitting. The snowdrops are over a quarter of a mile uphill from the car park and must be seen to be believed. However, Wellington boots are recommended. There is no possibility of taking wheelchairs or vehicles up the hill.

Dalmeny: The House

South Queensferry, Edinburgh EH30 9TQ. Tel: (0131) 331 1888

Grounds around Dalmeny House open when house open: July and Aug, Sun, 1 – 5.30pm, Mon and Tues, 12 noon – 5.30pm (last admission all days 4.45pm). Parties by arrangement at other times • Entrance: grounds free. House (with collection) £4, OAPs £3.50, students £3, children (10-16) £2, under 10

free. Parties of 20 or more £3 per person during opening hours (1999 prices)
● ● WC & ⬦ ⚲

Some one and a half miles from Mons Hill (see previous page) is the Garden Valley and other ornamental areas close to Dalmeny House. These feature rhododendrons, azaleas and specimen trees.

Dalnaheish 48

**Carsaig Bay, Tayvallich, Lochgilphead, Argyll and Bute PA31 8PN.
Tel: (01546) 870286**

Mrs Cynthia and Miss Jane Lambie • Telephone for directions • Open end-April to Sept by appt • Entrance: by donation ● ● ⬦

This mother-and-daughter team have devoted many years to making their one-and-three-quarter-acre seaside garden into a plantsman's pleasure. They stock it from seed, personally chosen and sent from all over the world, with the result that they have a highly original selection of hardy plants, particularly variegated and scented ones. Cynthia grows 15 varieties of fruit, and Jane specialises in aquilegias, astilbes and pittosporums. The rare cubic sundial is dated 1738. Winding up the natural stone paths and through a short woodland garden, visitors are led to what must be one of the best-positioned picnic tables in Scotland, overlooking the Atlantic Sound of Jura and magnificent surrounding mountain scenery.

Dawyck Botanic Garden ★ 49

**Stobo, Peeblesshire, Scottish Borders EH45 9JU. Tel: (01721) 760254;
Fax: (01721) 760214**

Royal Botanic Garden Edinburgh • 20m SW of Edinburgh, 8m SW of Peebles on B712 • Open March to Oct, daily, 9.30am – 6pm and at other times by arrangement • Entrance: £3, concessions £2.50, children £1, family £7. Season tickets inc. Logan and Younger Botanic Gardens (see entries) available • Other information: Guide dogs only ◐ ● WC ⬦ ⬛ ⚲

This is a specialist garden of the Royal Botanic Garden Edinburgh (see entry). With over 300 years of tree planting, Dawyck is one of the world's finest arboretums; its collections include rare Chinese conifers and the unique Dawyck beech. At the entrance is the formal azalea terrace which leads the visitor into Scrape Glen, and from here paths cross the slopes of Scrape Hill, with Scrape Burn tumbling down under the Swiss bridge in the middle of the glen. The mature specimen trees, some over 40 metres tall, stand majestically, towering above a variety of flowering trees and shrubs. From further up the hill there are magnificent views of the garden, including the beech walk with its tree-top outlook. In the Heron Wood is the first cryptogamic sanctuary and reserve for non-flowering plants; illustrated panels provide fascinating details on the essential role played by these plants. Other notable features include a fine estate chapel by William Burn and stonework and terracing on bridges, balustrades and urns produced by Italian craftsmen in the 1820s.

Dochfour Estate 50

Dochfour, Inverness, Highland IV3 6JY. Tel: (01463) 861218 (Estate Office); Fax: (01463) 861366

Hon A.J. Baillie • 6m SW of Inverness on A82 • Open April to Sept, Mon – Fri, 10am – 5pm • Entrance: £1.50, OAPs and children 50p (1999 prices) • Other information: PYO in season ◗

The estate is bounded by the River Ness to the east, and overlooked by steeply rising hills providing a dramatic backdrop to the extensive walled kitchen gardens. The formal landscaped gardens are contained within high yew hedges clipped at intervals to provide spectacular views of the loch below. Large areas of rhododendrons, terraces of daffodils, vast grass parterres and magnificent trees. Nearby is the *Abriachan Nurseries*, Loch Ness Side, Tel: (01463) 861232.

Druimavuic House Gardens 51

Appin, Argyll and Bute PA38 4BQ. Tel: (01631) 730242

Mr and Mrs Newman Burberry • 4m S of Appin on A828 Oban – Fort William road, turn L at new road bridge. Signposted • Open 9th April to 30th June, daily • Entrance: £1, children free ◗ 🍴 ⟲ ♨

A romantic site which was begun after World War I but has now been replanted and cultivated by its dedicated owners. The humorous and descriptive guide states that 'the real architect of Druimavuic Gardens is Nature', but they have certainly embellished her work most successfully. The stream garden makes an immediate impact with colourful clumps of many varieties of primulas (*florindae*, *vialii* and 'Inverewe') and meconopsis mixed in with other varied spring plantings. The well-planted woodland garden has lovely open oil-painting views of cattle watering in the loch below. There is an excellent working kitchen garden with strawberries grown at eye level. How enjoyable to see plants being propagated that you can then buy. Five miles away is *Kinlochlaich House*, primarily a walled nursery garden centre with a huge variety of good plants, shrubs and trees, approached through a quarter-acre display garden of intensively planted beds. Well worth a visit.

Drum Castle 52

Drumoak, by Banchory, Aberdeenshire AB31 5EY. Tel: (01330) 811204

The National Trust for Scotland • 10m W of Aberdeen, 3m W of Peterculter, off A93 • Castle open as garden, pm only • Garden open 21st April to Sept, daily, 10am – 6pm; Oct, weekends, 10am – 5.30pm. Grounds open all year, daily, 9.30am – sunset • Entrance: garden and grounds £2, OAPs and children £1.30 (castle, garden and grounds £4.40, OAPs and children £2.90) (1999 prices) • Garden: ◗ 🍵 ⟲ WC ♿ 🎁 ♨ *Grounds:* ○ ⟲

Within the old walled garden of the castle, the Trust has established a 'garden of historic roses' which was officially opened in June 1991 as part of its Diamond Jubilee celebrations. The four quadrants of the garden are designed and planted with roses and herbaceous or other plants appropriate to the seventeenth, eighteenth, nineteenth and twentieth centuries. The central feature is a copy of the gazebo at Tyninghame, East Lothian (see entry), and a small garden house in one corner, now restored, acts as an interpretative centre. The grounds around the castle also contain interesting conifers, spacious lawns and walks in the Old Wood of Drum, an SSSI.

Drummond Castle ★★ 53

Muthill, Crieff, Perth and Kinross PH5 2AA. Tel: (01764) 681257; Fax: (01764) 681550

Grimsthorpe and Drummond Castle Trust Ltd • 2m S of Crieff on A822 • Open 21st to 24th April; then May to Oct, daily, 2 – 6pm (last admission 5pm) • Entrance: £3, OAPs £2, children £1.50 ◑ <u>WC</u> &. ◁⅏ ⇞

The gardens to this fine castle were first laid out in 1630 by John Drummond, 2nd Earl of Perth. Next to the castle, across a courtyard, is the house and below both is the great parterre garden with, at its centre, the famous sundial made by the master mason to Charles I. When the garden was revived by Lewis Kennedy, who worked at Drummond from 1818 to 1860, he achieved what the *Oxford Companion* calls 'the re-creation of an idea of the seventeenth-century Scottish garden' with stunning effect. The long St Andrew's cross design has Italian, French and Dutch influences. Beautiful white marble Italian statuary is set in arbours along the southern borders, giving an overall sense of tranquillity and order. The fruit and vegetable gardens and glasshouses should also be visited.

Dunrobin Gardens ★ 54

Golspie, Sutherland, Highland KW10 6RR. Tel: (01408) 633177/633268; Fax: (01408) 634081

The Sutherland Trust • 1m NE of Golspie on A9 • Castle open • Garden open April to mid-Oct, Mon – Sat, 10.30am – 4.30pm, Sun, 1 – 4.30pm (last admission ½ hour before closing time) • Entrance: £5, OAPs and children £3.50, students £3.20, family £15, parties £4.50 per person, OAPs and children £3. British school parties free (1999 prices) ◑ 🍽 WC ⇞

These Victorian formal gardens were designed in the grand French style to echo the architecture of Dunrobin Castle, which rises high above them and looks out over the Moray Firth. They were created by the architect Charles Barry in 1850. Descending the stone terraces, one can see the round garden (evocative of the Scottish shield, perhaps), grove, parterre and herbaceous borders laid out beneath. The round ponds, all with fountains, are a particular feature, together with the wrought-iron Westminster gates. Roses have been replaced with hardy geraniums, antirrhinums, and *Potentilla fruticosa* 'Abbotswood'. An eighteenth-century summerhouse, converted into a museum in the nineteenth century, is now also open to the public. Other recent developments include the removal of the shrubbery and its replacement by 10 wooden pyramids covered in roses, clematis and sweet peas and interplanted with small ornamental trees to continue the French style elsewhere. In the policies (estate lands) there are many woodland walks.

Dunvegan Castle 55

Isle of Skye IV55 8WF. Tel: (01470) 521206

*MacLeod Estate • 14m NW of Portree, beyond A850/A863 junction • * Castle open • Garden open mid-March to Oct, daily, 10am – 5.30pm (last admission 5pm); Nov to mid-March, Mon – Fri, 11am – 4pm • Entrance: £3.70, children £2 (castle and gardens £5.20, concessions £4.60, children £2) (1999 prices)*
◑ 🍵 ✕ <u>WC</u> ㅤ ⓗ

A superb backcloth for the castle which stands on the shores of Loch Dunvegan, the gardens have three areas of interest. First, a round garden with a boxwood parterre of 16 triangular beds and three mixed borders for summer show, with adjacent greenhouses and fern houses. Second, an expanding woodland waterfall dell, which carries the season on past rhododendron time. The meconopsis and giant cardiocrinums are breathtaking in this setting, but note also tiny maidenhair ferns, native woodsage and other treasures. Third, an exciting two-acre walled garden, created by head gardener Tom Shephard on a long-derelict site and open to the public since 1998. Laid out on a formal plan, the four quarters each have a focus of interest: a lawn with a sorbus avenue; a raised pool with gravel surround pierced by plants; a triangle with internal yew triangle; and an unusual stepped 'temple' evocative of Mayan architecture. The surrounding paths spill over with helianthemums, cistus and other Mediterranean plants. Non-gardeners can take an exciting boat trip to the nearby seal colony – on a calm day.

Edzell Castle ★ 56

Edzell, Brechin, Angus DD9 7UE. Tel: (01356) 648631

Historic Scotland • 6m N of Brechin. Take A90 (A94) and after 2m fork left on B966 • Ruins open (closed Thurs pm and Fri in winter) • Garden open April to Sept, Mon – Sat, 9.30am – 6.30pm; Sun, 9.30am – 6.30pm; Oct to March, Mon – Sat, 9.30am – 4.30pm, Sun, 2 – 4.30pm (last admission ½ hour before closing) • Entrance: £2.30, OAPs and UB40 holders £1.75, children (5-16) £1, under 5 free) ○ 🏛 <u>WC</u> ㅤ ⬆ ♨ ⓗ ♀

In 1604 Sir David Lindsay made a remarkable small walled garden at his fortress at Edzell; as reconstructed, it gives us a clear idea of how his garden might have looked in its heyday. By the time they came into the custody of H.M. Office of Works in 1932, the garden and castle had lain in ruins for over 150 years. Although the plantings date from the 1930s, they are elaborate examples in the manner of the period of the early seventeenth century. Meticulously kept parterres of box, lawn, and bedding are contained within the original walls of unique and curious design. There are 43 panels of alternating chequered niches and sculptured symbolic figures with large recesses below for flowers. The whole is laid out to be viewed from a corner garden-house and the windows of the now-ruined castle. Edzell is quite small and a charming example of an ordered Victorian Scottish Highland village. There are shops, a tea room and two hotels. A must for lovers of the historical and the romantic.

Falkland Palace Garden 57

Falkland, Fife KY7 7BU. Tel: (01337) 857397

The National Trust for Scotland • *11m N of Kirkcaldy via A92 and A912.*
M90 junction 8 from Forth Road Bridge • *Palace open as garden (last tour of*
palace 4.30pm) • *Garden open April to Oct, Mon – Sat, 11am – 5.30pm, Sun,*
1.30 – 5.30pm • *Entrance: £2.40, OAPs and children £1.60 (palace and*
garden £4.80, OAPs and children £3.20) (1999 prices) • *Other information:*
Parking 100 metres from palace. Toilet facilities in town car park and next to
NTS shop ◑ 🅱 WC ♿

This was originally the garden at the sixteenth-century palace, which was the
hunting lodge for the Stuart monarchs. Kings and queens from James II to
Charles II enjoyed the Fife landscape and the grounds of the Renaissance
palace. During World War II the garden was a 'Dig for Victory' effort and was
thereafter remodelled by the landscape designer Percy Cane. The palace itself
lends a gracious and dignified atmosphere to this three-acre garden. The shrub
island borders are now fully mature and provide a good illustration of how to
break up large areas of lawn. The main herbaceous border, recently replanted,
runs the full depth of the garden and is maturing well, while the narrow
border, filled with delphiniums, is memorable. In addition, visitors can see the
royal tennis court (i.e. real tennis) where occasional competitions of this old
game are still staged, and an outdoor chequers game near the herb garden.
There is also an orchard. Note the interesting village houses nearby.

Finlaystone 58

Langbank, Renfrewshire PA14 6TJ. Tel/Fax: (01475) 540285;
E–mail: info@finlaystone.co.uk; Website: www.finlaystone.co.uk

Mr George Gordon MacMillan of MacMillan • *8m W of Glasgow Airport, on*
A8 W of Langbank • *House open, July, Sun, 2.30 – 4.30pm* • *Garden open all*
year, daily, 10.30am – 5pm • *Entrance: £2.50, OAPs and children £1.50* •
Other information: Doll museum and Celtic exhibition in visitor centre ○ 🍴 ✕
WC ♿ ⬥ ♿ ❢

Designed in 1900 and enhanced and tended over the last 50 years by the late Lady
MacMillan, much respected *doyenne* of Scottish gardens, and her family, this
spacious garden is imaginatively laid out over 10 acres with a further 70 acres of
mature woodland walks. There are large, elegant lawns framed by long herbaceous borders, interesting shrubberies and a mature copper beech looking down
over the River Clyde. John Knox's tree, a Celtic paving 'maze', a paved fragrant
garden with the handicapped in mind, and a bog garden are added attractions. A
walled garden is planted in the shape of a Celtic ring cross.

Glamis Castle 59

Glamis, Forfar, Angus DD8 1RJ. Tel: (01307) 840393; Fax (01307) 840733

The Earl of Strathmore and Kinghorne • *5m W of Forfar on A94* • *Castle open,*
guided tours • *Garden open April to Oct, daily, 10.30am – 5.30pm (last*

admission 4.45pm) • Entrance: £3, OAPs, students and children (5-16) £1.50, disabled persons free (castle and grounds: £6, OAPs and students £4.50, children (5-16) £3, family ticket £16.50). Reductions for parties of 20 or more
◑ ◰ ✕ 🍽 WC ⑂ ⬤ 🅿 👍 ♻

At the end of a long, tree-lined avenue and against the backdrop of mountain and moorland, the turrets and spires of Glamis Castle beckon the visitor to explore its secrets and enjoy the tranquillity of its grounds. Although much older, the park was landscaped in the 1790s by a garden designer working under the influence of 'Capability' Brown, and the avenue was replanted about 1820. On the lawn near the castle is an intriguing Baroque sundial, six and a half metres tall and with a face for every week of the year. On the east side of the castle is a two-acre Italian garden consisting of high yew hedges, herbaceous borders, fountain and seventeenth-century-style gazebos, and the creation of this quiet haven is commemorated by an engraved stone. The pinetum, planted c.1870, is now open to visitors. Glamis was the childhood home of H.M. The Queen Mother.

Glasgow Botanic Gardens   60

730 Great Western Road, Glasgow G12 0UE. Tel: (0141) 334 2422; Fax (0141) 339 6964

Glasgow City Council • Near city centre on corner of Great Western Road and Queen Margaret Drive • Open all year, daily, 7am – dusk. Kibble Palace Glasshouse open 10am – 4.45pm (4.15pm in winter). Main range open 10am – 4.45pm (from 12 noon on Sun and to 4.15pm in winter) • Entrance: free ○ 🍽
WC ⑂ ⬤ ♻

A pleasant afternoon's walk with well-maintained herbaceous, shrub and annual borders. A new and greatly extended herb garden is in the process of being developed and will include a unique feature, 'The Scottish Garden', containing plants endemic to Scotland with explanatory labels on how these plants have been utilised over centuries. The chief attraction, and well worth visiting, is the Victorian Kibble Palace. This glasshouse, built in 1872, houses temperate plants interspersed with classic marble statuary. In the nearby tropical glasshouses are displays of orchids and the National Collection of species begonias, also cacti and economic plants – all meticulously maintained. The new 'Arid Adaptations' house has on display some of the most bizarre plants in the world. The unique development of island plants is also demonstrated here. The new visitor centre has one room exhibiting the history and function of the gardens. The other room has changing horticultural exhibitions with regular displays and sales of art work.

Glen Grant Garden   61

Rothes, Aberlour, Moray AB38 7BS. Tel: (01542) 783318

Glen Grant Distillery • 10m SE of Elgin on A941, on main roundabout in Rothes • Open mid-March to Oct, daily: Mon – Sat, 10am – 4pm, Sun, 11.30 – 4pm (5pm June to Sept); Nov to mid-March by appt • Entrance: garden and distillery £2.50 (inc. £2 voucher redeemable against purchase of 70cl bottle of whisky) • Other information: Distillery tours ◗ **WC** ♿

It is hard to believe that you are further north than Moscow in this sheltered glen, originally laid out in 1886 by Major James Grant when he inherited the family business. Recently it has been well restored with exact replicas of the original rustic bridges, waterside paths and his tent-roofed dram hut. Clearly the garden will not be fully clothed until the extensive planting achieves maturity, but it is interesting to see the design in its youth. An excellent descriptive leaflet and plant list is provided.

Glenarn ★ 62

Rhu, Helensburgh, Dunbartonshire G84 8LL. Tel: (01436) 820493; Fax: (0141) 2216834

Michael and Sue Thornley • On A814 between Helensburgh and Garelochhead. Go up Pier Road to Glenarn Road • Open 21st March to 21st Sept, daily, dawn – dusk • Entrance: £2 • Other information: Refreshments certain open days only ◗ 🍴 ⏣ 🐾

Established in the 1920s by the Gibson family, this is a very special woodland garden. An earlier Victorian garden had been fed by the famous plant expeditions. Well-kept paths meander round a 10-acre sheltered bowl, sometimes tunnelling under superb giant species rhododendrons (including a *falconeri* grown from seed supplied by Hooker in 1849), sometimes allowing a glorious vista across the garden to the Clyde estuary, and sometimes stopping the visitor short to gaze with unstinted admiration at 12-metre magnolias, pieris, olearias, eucryphias and hoherias. The owners, both professional architects, acquired Glenarn some years ago and with almost no help are successfully replanting and restoring where necessary, whilst retaining the special atmosphere created by such magnificent growth. Work is about to begin on replanting large sections of the rock garden, which falls steeply down past the daffodil lawn to the house with its tall, twisting chimney pots.

Glenbervie House 63

Drumlithie, Stonehaven, Kincardineshire AB39 3YA. Tel: (01569) 740226

Mrs C.S. MacPhie • 8m NE of Laurencekirk, 6m from Stonehaven off A90 Laurencekirk – Stonehaven road. On minor road 3m W of Drumlithie • Open one day for charity, or by appt • Entrance: £2, children 80p ● 🍽 🍴 **WC** 🐾 🐾

Two very different gardens may be enjoyed here – a traditional Scottish walled garden on a slope, and a woodland garden by a stream. Occupying one wall of an enclosed garden is a fine example of a Victorian conservatory, with a great diversity of pot plants and climbers on the walls creating a spectacular display. Elsewhere in the walled area is a typical mix of herbaceous plants, fruit, vegetables and summer bedding. There are many shrub and old roses, and on walls and pillars many climbing and rambler roses. In spring there are good displays of bulbs, and the woodland garden with its drifts of primulas, ferns and interesting shrubs is beautiful in early summer. There are fine trees near the house.

Glendoick Gardens ★ 64

Glendoick, Perth, Perth and Kinross PH2 7NS. Tel: (01738) 860205 (Nursery); (01738) 860260 (Garden Centre)

Mr and Mrs Peter Cox and Kenneth Cox • 8m E of Perth, 14m SW of Dundee on A90 • Open two Suns in May for SGS and for parties by appt in May • Entrance: £2, children under 5 free • Other information: Plants for sale and toilet facilities for disabled at garden centre ● WC ఉ 🏛

One of the world's most comprehensive collections of rhododendrons is contained within the grounds of this fine Georgian mansion which has an association with Bonnie Prince Charlie, who is reputed to have visited the Laird of Glendoick one dark night in 1745. The plant collection was started by the late Euan H.M. Cox, and the present owners planted an arboretum in 1993 in memory of the 100th anniversary of his birth. They continue to visit the East in search of new varieties and grow a wide range of hybrids, and new cultivars, from elsewhere. The woodland garden, which has also been extended, is full of naturalised wild plants as well as introductions. Near the house is a conservatory, and through the walled garden the old Japanese garden has many replanted areas and fine trees. Roy Lancaster says this garden is a focal point for all who believe that plant exploration in its noblest sense is alive and well.

Glenwhan Garden ★ 65

Dunragit, Stranraer, Wigtownshire, Dumfries and Galloway DG9 8PH. Tel/Fax: (01581) 400222

Mr and Mrs Knott • 7m E of Stranraer, 1m off A75 at Dunragit. Signposted • Open 15th March to 15th Oct, daily, 10am – 5pm and by appt. Evening visits by arrangement • Entrance: £2.50, OAPs £2, children £1, toddlers free, family rate £7, conducted tours for parties of 20 or more £15 • Other information: Picnics permitted on request. Dogs strictly on leads; dog walking area. Plants for sale in nursery ◑ 🍵 ✕ 🖻 WC ఉ ⬥ 🍼

This exciting 12-acre garden has commanding views over Luce Bay and the Mull of Galloway, and is set in an area of natural beauty, with many rocky outcrops. Difficult to believe that it was only started in 1979, hewn by the owners from a hillside covered in bracken and gorse. Because of the Gulf Stream and consequent mild climate, exotic plants thrive amongst the huge collections of trees, shrubs and plants. Seats and walkways abound in the maze of hilly plantings mostly overlooking the central lakes and bog gardens. Collections, whether of genera, reminders of friends or particular themes of interest, are to be seen everywhere. The garden, now 20 years old, continues to expand and mature. It includes a woodland walk where species rhododendrons flourish amongst many different kinds of primulas, which have naturalised well.

Gowranes ★ 66

Kinnaird, Inchture, Perth and Kinross PH14 9QY. Tel: (01828) 686752

Mr and Mrs D Latham-Warde • 11m NE of Perth, 10m SW of Dundee off A90, 3m from Inchture. Signed Kinnaird • Open by appt for charity • Entrance: £3, children free ● WC

A garden full of surprises, lovingly carved out of a difficult sloping rocky site with magnificent views over the Carse of Gowrie. The house is partly surrounded by stone-flagged terraces overflowing with plants. Lower-level lawns are planted with specimen trees such as *Abies koreana* and *Prunus serrula*. From here maze-like paths lead you up and down through cool, intensive plantings of shade-loving plants, rhododendrons, camellias, azaleas, ferns, meconopsis and many others. At the bottom of the slope a rushing burn has been formed into a series of pools and waterfalls; this marks the western boundary. Great masses of primulas have seeded themselves here amongst the gunneras, hostas and *Lysichiton americanus*.

Greenbank Garden ★ 67

Flenders Road, Clarkston, Glasgow G76 8RB. Tel: (0141) 6393281

The National Trust for Scotland • From Clarkston Toll in S Glasgow take Mearns Road for 1m. Signposted • Open all year, daily except 1st, 2nd Jan and 25th, 26th Dec, 9.30am – sunset • Entrance: £3.15, concessions and children £2.10 • Other information: Refreshments summer only. Catering for parties and guided tours by arrangement. Dogs in woodland only, on lead ○ ☕ 🏠 WC ♿ 🌿 🛒 🚻

A large old walled garden of eighteenth-century house, divided into many sections, imaginatively offering practical demonstrations to illustrate the design and planting of small gardens. The colour combinations are especially good. All the plants are in good condition and admirably labelled. An old hard tennis court in the corner has been converted into a spacious and pleasant area full of ideas for disabled and infirm gardeners, with raised beds and a waist-high running-water pond. Wheelchair access to the glasshouse and potting shed allows disabled people to attend classes and work here. Woodland walks are filled with spring bulbs and shrubs and there are usually Highland cattle in the paddock. An illustrated guidebook is available.

Hill of Tarvit Mansion–House 68

Cupar, Fife KY15 5PB. Tel/Fax: (01334) 653127

The National Trust for Scotland • 2½ m S of Cupar off A916 • House open 21st to 24th April; May to Sept, daily; Oct, weekends, all 1.30 – 5.30pm (last admission 4.45pm) • Garden open all year, daily, 9.30am – 9pm (Oct to March, 4pm) • Entrance: £1, children 50p (honesty box) (house and garden £3.90, children and concessions £2.60, parties of 20 or more £3.20 per person) (1999 prices) • Other information: Shop and tea room open from 12.30pm daily ○ ☕ 🏠 WC 🛒

The garden surrounds the charming Edwardian mansion designed in 1906 for a jute magnate by Sir Robert Lorimer, who also laid out the grounds to the south of the house. There is a lovely rose garden. Good-size borders are filled with an attractive variety of perennials, annuals and heaths, and the grounds as a whole contain many unusual ornamental trees and shrubs now reaching maturity. The views over Fife are particularly fine. The plantings are regularly upgraded to include newer and more unusual specimens. A good garden for amateurs and keen plantspersons. A massive two-day plant sale is held the first weekend in October – there is no entry charge, and the public queue at the gate well before the opening.

The Hirsel 69

Coldstream, Berwickshire TD12 4LP. Tel: (01890) 882834

The Earl of Home • 9m NE of Kelso, 15m SW of Berwick-on-Tweed, W of Coldstream on A697 • Grounds open all year, daily during daylight hours • Entrance: parking charge £2 per car (1999 price) • Other information: Craft workshops ○ 🍵 🖥 WC ♿ ⌕ 🧺

Hirsel House is not open but at all seasons of the year the grounds have much of interest and enjoyment for the visitor who values the peace and ever-changing beauty of the countryside. There is something for the ornithologist, botanist, geologist, forester, zoologist, historian and archaeologist. In spring, snowdrops and aconites and then acres of daffodils herald the coming summer as the birds, resident and migrant, of which 169 have been definitely identified within the estate boundaries, start busying themselves around their nesting sites. From mid/late-May to mid-June the rhododendron wood, Dundock, is justly famous for its kaleidoscopic colouring and breathtaking scents. Rose beds, herbaceous and shrub borders follow through the summer. In October and November, the leaves turning on trees and shrubs provide attractive autumn colouring, and hundreds of duck, geese and gulls make the lake their nightly home. In winter the same trees are stark but magnificent in their skeletal forms against storm clouds and sunsets.

House of Pitmuies ★★ 70

Guthrie, By Forfar, Angus DD8 2SN. Tel: (01241) 828245

Mrs Farquhar Ogilvie • 1½ m W of Friockheim, on A932 • House open for parties by appt • Garden open April to Oct, daily, 10am – 5pm and at other times by appt • Entrance: £2.50 by collection box • Other information: Teas by arrangement for parties visiting house ◐ 🖥 WC ♿ ⌕ 🌿

In the grounds of an attractive eighteenth-century house and courtyard, these beautiful walled gardens lead down towards a small river with an informal riverside walk and two unusual buildings, a turreted dovecot and a Gothick wash-house. There are rhododendron glades with unusual trees and shrubs, but pride of place must go to the spectacular semi-formal gardens behind the house. Exquisite old-fashioned roses and a series of long borders containing a dramatic palette of massed delphiniums and other herbaceous perennials in July constitute one of the most memorable displays of its type to be found in Scotland.

House of Tongue ★   71
Tongue, Lairg, Sutherland, Highland IV27 4XH. Tel: (01847) 611209

*The Countess of Sutherland • 1m N of Tongue off A838 • Open by appt and
5th Aug for charity • Entrance: £2, children under 12 50p* ● 🖼 ⌁

Sheltered from wind and salt by tall trees, this walled garden is a haven in an
otherwise-exposed environment. Adjoining the seventeenth-century house, it
is laid out after the traditional Scottish acre, with gravel and grass walks
between herbaceous beds, hedged vegetable plots and orchard. A stepped
beech-hedged walk leads up to a high terrace which commands a fine view over
the Kyle of Tongue. The centrepiece of the garden is Lord Reay's sundial
(1714), a sculpted obelisk of unusual design.

Innes House Garden   72
Elgin, Moray IV30 3NF. Tel: (01343) 842410

*Mr and Mrs Mark Tennant • 5m E of Elgin, off A96 on B9103 Lossiemouth
road • Open to parties by appt only* ●

An extensive ornamental garden divided into compartments, the whole
framed by a wide variety of mature and interesting trees. The gardens were
partially replanned and reorientated by the present owner's great-grand-
mother in 1912, when yew hedges were planted, providing a central walk. A
charming garden has been created on the site of the original chapel. The large
trees are a major feature of the property – 47 varieties are represented, many
estimated to be over 200 years old, including rare oaks, Californian Madrona
(*Arbutus menziesii*) and Chinese beech. A complete tree list is available.

Inveresk Lodge and Village Gardens   73
Musselburgh, East Lothian EH21 6BQ. Tel: (0131) 665 1855 (office hours)

*Various owners inc. The National Trust for Scotland (Lodge) • 6m E of
Edinburgh, S of Musselburgh via A6124 • Lodge garden open all year, Mon –
Fri, 10am – 4.30pm, Sat and Sun, 2 – 5pm (closed Sat, Oct to March).
Privately owned gardens in the village open several days for SGS with teas •
Entrance: Lodge £1, honesty box; other gardens £1.50 each (1999 prices)* ○ 🖼
WC ♿ 🏺

The large seventeenth-century house in the village of Inveresk is situated on a
gently sloping site. The garden has been completely remade since it came
under the ownership of the Trust. No attempt has been made to re-create a
period style: it is 'modern' in most respects, semi-formal, well planted, well
maintained and offers a large conservatory with some good hardy ornamentals
and an aviary. The high stone retaining-walls support a wide range of climbers
and the south facing slope permits more unusual plants to be grown; a
particularly good border is devoted to shrub roses. The village itself is a
unique, unspoilt example of eighteenth-century villa development, with
houses dating from the late seventeenth and early eighteenth centuries. All
have well-laid-out gardens enclosed by high walls and containing a wide range

of shrubs and trees as well as some unusual plants. One, *Catherine Lodge*, in two acres, contains many unusual mature trees underplanted with large drifts of snowdrops, crocus and daffodils. Much of the layout, with its traditional herbaceous borders surrounding an old grass tennis court, has remained the same since the early part of this century. In the large vegetable garden, by contrast, many changes have been made: although vegetables are still grown in profusion, some of the beds have been given over to roses and in 1997 a large wildlife pond was created. The other, *Shepherd House*, was featured in Rosemary Verey's book of *Secret Gardens* in 1994, but there have been many new developments in this one-acre plantsman's garden since then. A formal rill now connects the pond to the back of the garden, where a raised pool with fountains has been created. The rill runs up the centre of the rose-arched grass path edged with nepeta. Visitors often comment that it is a garden of surprises – an alpine wall, a *potager*, an old-fashioned rose border, a shade garden, a parterre and herb gardens, all planted to capacity so as not to allow room for weeds. There is a large collection of tulips. The house (not open) is late-seventeenth-century; the Frasers have lived here and developed the garden over 40 years.

Inverewe Garden ★★ 74

Poolewe, Ross and Cromarty, Highland IV22 2LG. Tel: (01445) 781200

The National Trust for Scotland • 6m NE of Gairloch on A832 • Garden open all year, daily, 9.30am – 9pm (closes 5pm Oct to March) • Entrance: £5, concessions £3.50, parties £4 per person, senior parties £3.20 per person, family ticket £12.80 (1999 prices) • Other information: Restaurant and shop open 15th March to Oct only ○ 🍽 ✕ WC & 🌿 👜

This garden is spectacular. Created from 1865 on the shores of the sea loch, Loch Ewe, it covers the entire Am Ploc Ard peninsular. Planned as a wild garden around one dwarf willow on peat and sandstone, it has been developed as a series of walks through herbaceous and rock gardens, a wet valley, a rhododendron walk and a curved vegetable garden and orchard. It is a plantsman's garden (labelling is discreet), containing many tender species from Australia, New Zealand, China and the Americas, sheltered by mature beech and pine trees. New Zealand plants include the National Collections of olearias and ourisias. The garden is well tended and way-marked. Note: midge-repellent is advisable and on sale at the main desk.

Johnston Gardens 75

Viewfield Road, Aberdeen. Tel: (01224) 522734

Aberdeen City Council • In Aberdeen, ½ m S of Queens Road (A944 to Alford), ¼ m W of junction with ring road • Open all year, daily, 8am – one hour before dusk • Entrance: free ○ WC &

When Johnston House was demolished and the grounds sold for redevelopment, it was impossible to utilise the deepest area of the ravine. This was converted into a water and rock garden by the City of Aberdeen Parks and Recreation Department. The result is a congenial oasis of trees, shrubs and mature rhododendrons surrounding a small lake complete with an island, bridges and resident waterfowl. The rock and scree gardens have some interesting alpine plants.

Jura House 76

Ardfin, Isle of Jura, Argyll and Bute PA60 7XX. Tel: Peter Cool (01496) 820315

Riley-Smith family • On Jura, 5m SE of ferry terminal off A846. Vehicle ferries from Kennacraig by Tarbert to Port Askaig, Islay, and from Islay to Feolin, Jura • Open all year, daily, 9am – 5pm • Entrance: £2, children under 16 free. Collecting box (1999 prices) • Other information: Possible for wheelchairs but sloping gravel paths. Booklet available, 50p ○ ☕ 🍽 WC ♿ 🌱

A circular walk around the Jura House estate illustrates the rich natural history and geology of the island. Starting from the car park, the visitor walks through native woodland and follows the fuchsia-clad banks of the burn to where it plunges into a ravine, filled with ferns and lichens, over the raised beach to the sea. Spectacular views of the Islay coast accompany the steep path down to the shore. Dykes and rock formations are home to wild scree plants and scrubby trees, and here is an example of machair – dune grassland. After the climb back up the cliff, signs guide the visitor to the garden proper. This organic walled garden is a sheltered haven with many unusual plants, including a collection of Australasian origin. Linger awhile before continuing on the woodland path back to the Lodge.

Kailzie Gardens ★ 77

Peebles, Peebleshire, Scottish Borders EH45 9HT. Tel: (01721) 720007

Lady Angela Buchan-Hepburn • 2½ m SE of Peebles on B7062 • Garden and trout pond open all year, daily (in winter, during daylight hours) • Entrance: 21st April to mid-Oct: £2.50, children (5-14) 75p, groups £2.20 per person; mid-Oct to mid-March, honesty box, groups 85p per person; snowdrop days, as advertised • Other information: Gallery open probably late March to mid-Oct ○ ☕ ✕ 🍽 WC ♿ ♿ 🌱 🛍 🍴

'A Pleasure Garden' is the description in one of the advertisements for Kailzie (pronounced Kailie), and very apt it is too. The gardens of 17 acres are situated in a particularly attractive area of the beautiful Tweed Valley and are surrounded by breathtaking views. The Old Mansion Home was pulled down in 1962 and the vast walled garden, which still houses the magnificent greenhouse, has been transformed by the present owner from vegetables to a garden of meandering lawns and island beds full of interesting shrubs and plants. There are many surprises, including snowdrops in drifts in February and March, a choice flower area, secret gardens, loving seats invitingly placed under garlanded arbours and several thoughtfully sited pieces of statuary. A magnificent fountain at the end of the herbaceous borders leads on to woods and stately trees, and from here you may stroll down the Major's walk, lined with laburnum and underplanted with rhododendrons, azaleas, blue poppies and primulas. There is also a small duck pond and a fishing pond.

Kellie Castle 78

Pittenweem, Fife KY10 2RF. Tel: (01333) 720271

The National Trust for Scotland • 3m NW of Pittenweem on B9171 towards Arncroach • Castle open 21st to 24th April; May to Sept, daily; Oct, Sat and Sun, all 1.30 – 5.30pm (last admission 4.45pm) • Garden and grounds open all year, daily, 9.30am – sunset • Entrance: £1, children 50p (castle and garden extra charge) (1999 prices) • Other information: Parking 100 metres, closer for disabled. Refreshments, toilet facilities (not disabled) and shop when castle open only ○ 🍴 ♿ 🛍 ♟

The garden appears to be seventeenth-century in plan, embellished by Professor James Lorimer and his family in late Victorian times. Entered by a door in a high wall, the one-and-a-half acres inspire dreams within every gardener's reach. Simple borders, such as one of catmint, capture the imagination as hundreds of bees and butterflies work the flowers. Areas of lawn are edged with box hedges, borders, arches and trellises. In one corner, behind a trellis, is a small romantic garden within a garden. A large, green-painted commemorative seat designed by Hew Lorimer provides outstanding focal interest at the end of one of the main walks. The head gardener has established a collection of old and unusual vegetable varieties employing only organic gardening methods. Roses on trellis and on arches abound. Outside the walled garden, mown walks wind through woodland which in late spring is a haze of wild garlic.

Kilbryde Castle 79

Dunblane, Stirling, Perthshire FK15 9NF. Tel: (01786) 824897

Sir James Campbell • 9m NW of Stirling, off A820 Dunblane – Doune road • Open 9th April, 28th May, 1st Oct, 2 – 5pm for charity and also by appt • Entrance: £2, OAPs and children £1.50 • Other information: Plants for sale on open days only ◖

The 20-acre garden was created by the present owner's father and mother, whose passions were rhododendrons, azaleas, clematis and bulbs. The garden is in two parts – a partly walled upper garden with island beds full of colour on a south-facing slope, and a lovely woodland garden on either bank of a stream. The woodland garden is well planted with rhododendrons and azaleas under a canopy of mature trees. The best time to visit is spring, particularly the end of May.

Kildrummy Castle Gardens ★ 80

Alford, Aberdeenshire AB33 8RA. Tel: (019755) 71203/71277

Kildrummy Castle Garden Trust • 2m SW of Mossat, 10m W of Alford, 17m SW of Huntly. Take A944 from Alford, following signs to Kildrummy, and turn left onto A97. From Huntly turn right on to A97 • Open April to Oct, daily, 10am – 5pm • Entrance: £2, children (5-16) free (1999 prices) • Other information: Cars park inside hotel main entrance, coaches in delivery entrance. Woodland walks and children's play area ◐ 💭 ✕ 🏢 <u>WC</u> ♿ 🐾 ⛟ 🎯

The gardens are set in a deep ravine between the ruins of a thirteenth-century castle and a Tudor-style house, now a hotel. The rock garden, by Backhouse of York (1904), occupies the site of the quarry which provided the stone for the castle. The narrowest part of the ravine is crossed by a copy of the fourteenth-century Auld Brig O'Balgownie (Old Aberdeen Bridge) built by Colonel Ogston in 1900. This provides a focus for the water garden commissioned from a firm of Japanese landscape gardeners in the same period. Backhouse continued the planting. In April the reflections in the still water of pools increase the impact of the luxuriant *Lysichiton americanus*, and later come primulas and a notable *Schizophragma hydrangeoides*; there are fine maples, rhododendron species and hybrids, oaks and conifers. Although a severe frost pocket, the garden can grow embothriums, dieramas and other choice plants. The garden is especially beautiful in autumn with the colchicums and brilliant acers, all sheltered by specimen trees.

Kinross House   81

Kinross, Perth and Kinross KY13 8ET.

Mr James Montgomery • 13m N of Dunfermline, E of M90, in Kinross • Open May to Sept, daily, 10am – 7pm • Entrance: £2, children 50p (honesty box) ◐ ♿

Four acres of walled garden, all beautifully maintained, surround the mansion designed in the 1680s and restored early this century. The walls, surmounted by fine statuary, have decorative gates. This is a formal garden of spacious lawn, clipped hedging, herbaceous borders, some with colour themes, and rose borders round the fountain. There are yew hedges in interesting shapes, with well-placed seating for those in a contemplative mood or wishing to view Loch Leven Castle on the nearby island. It was here that Mary Queen of Scots was imprisoned in 1567 and though it has no garden, it would be churlish not to walk to the pier to make the short boat trip to its sombre walls.

Kittoch Mill   82

**Busby Road, Carmunnock, Glasgow G76 9BJ. Tel: (0141) 6444712;
E-mail: kittoc@globalnet.co.uk; Website: www.users.globalnet.co.uk/~kittoc**

Pat and Howard Jordan • 4m NW of East Kilbride, on B759 Busby – Carmunnock road • Open 18th, 25th June, 2 – 5pm and by appt. Prior booking for groups • Entrance: £1.50 ◕ 🐾

This charming small garden, created by the owners and set above the mill-stream waterfall adjacent to a Site of Special Scientific Interest, includes a woodland walk and Japanese-style garden. This is surely a place of pilgrimage for all hosta lovers: a National Collection of this popular plant is held here. Over 450 different varieties, all professionally labelled, grow in luxurious clumps, together with many species and cultivars of ligularia and other unusual plants.

Lawhead Croft 83

Tarbrax, West Calder, West Lothian EH55 8LW.

Sue and Hector Riddell • 12m SW of Balerno, 6m NE of Carnwath on A70 towards Tarbrax • Open for charity June to Sept, daily, at any reasonable time and for parties by written appt only • Entrance: £2, children 20p • Other information: No coaches down farm road (no turning room) ◑ 🖥 ⬡

Nearly 300 metres up in the midst of the bleak Lanarkshire moors, the present owners have planted hedges and laboriously carved out a luxuriant garden. Grass walks lead from one interesting border to another, all full of unusual plants. Colour associations and leaf contrasts are carefully thought out. There is an enchanting series of garden rooms, all with a different theme. Great ideas include an excellent bonsai collection. Recently most of the vegetable garden has been swept away and replanted in a great sweep of curved, tiered and circular beds of spectacular and original design.

Leckmelm Shrubbery and Arboretum 84

Little Leckmelm House, Lochbroom, Ullapool, Ross-shire, Highland.

Mr and Mrs Peter Troughton • 4m S of Ullapool on A835 • Open April to Sept, daily, 10am – 6pm • Entrance: £1.50 ◑ ⬨

Situated on the shore of Loch Broom, warmed by the Gulf Stream, the 10-acre arboretum planted in 1870, is full of fine species rhododendrons and mature trees, various shrubs and bamboos. It was abandoned for 50 years in the 1930s until reclamation started in 1984 and is now restored to its former Victorian glory. Note particularly the venerable old weeping beech whose spread covers at least a third of an acre, and also the largest *Chamaecyparis lawsoniana* 'Wisselii' in Europe. A map and planting plan are available in the car park.

Leith Hall ★ 85

Huntly, Aberdeenshire AB54 4NQ. Tel: (01464) 831216

The National Trust for Scotland • 34m NW of Aberdeen, 1m W of Kennethmont on B9002 • Hall open inc. exhibition: 21st to 24th April; May to Sept, daily; Oct, weekends, all 1.30 – 5.30pm (last admission 4.45pm) • Garden and grounds open all year, daily, 9.30am – dusk • Entrance: £2, OAPs and children £1.20, pre-booked parties of 20 or more £1.50 per person (hall and gardens £4, OAPs and children £2.70, pre-booked parties of 20 or more £3 per person) (1999 prices) • Other information: Dogs outside walled garden only ○ 💼 🖥 WC ⬡

The gardens of Leith Hall are being restored and it is the old garden, remote from the house, that offers the greatest pleasure to the enthusiast. This comprises long borders and a large, well-stocked rock garden. The simple, romantic design allows a tremendous display of flowers during the whole of summer and early autumn. Especially fine is the magenta *Geranium psilostemon* and a border of solid catmint running from top to bottom of the garden. There are no courtyards and no dominating architecture, just massive plantings of perennials and the odd rarity amongst the rocks. Woodland walks throughout the designed landscape, including ponds and views down the garden.

Linn Gardens 86

Cove, Helensburgh, Dunbartonshire, Argyll and Bute G84 0NR.
Tel: (01436) 842242

Mr J.H.K. Taggart • 6m S of Garelochhead, ³/₄ m N of Cove on shore of Loch Long • Open all year, daily, dawn – dusk • Entrance: £3, OAPs £2, students and teenagers £1.50, accompanied children 12 and under free • Other information: Entirely unsuitable for wheelchairs and prams. Light refreshments for organised tours. Plants for sale in adjacent nursery ○ 🏠 **WC** ♿

The garden has been developed in its present form since 1971 (the villa dates back to the 1860s), with thousands of unusual, exotic and rare plants. Water is a constant presence: in the extensive water garden, formal ponds and fountains, in the glen with its tumbling waterfall, and, beyond the garden, in the views down to the Firth of Clyde from the terrace. There are also herbaceous borders, a rockery and a cliff garden. A one-kilometre signed route takes visitors through all parts of the garden; a useful leaflet is available. If travelling towards Glasgow on A814, it may be worth stopping at *Geilston Garden*, Cardross, a walled garden and wooded glen typical of small country house estates on the banks of the Clyde [open April to Oct, daily, 9.30am – sunset].

Little Sparta ★★ 87

Dunsyre, Lanark, South Lanarkshire.

Dr Ian Hamilton Finlay • Closed at time of going to press

Sir Roy Strong has described this as the most original contemporary garden in the country, but the owner tells us it is regretfully closed to the public.

Lochalsh Woodland Garden (Balmacara Estate) 88

Lochalsh House, Balmacara, Kyle, Ross–shire, Highland IV40 8DN.
Tel: (01599) 566325; Fax: (01599) 566359

The National Trust for Scotland • 3m E of Kyle of Lochalsh off A87 • Open all year, daily, 9am – dusk • Entrance: £2, children £1 • Other information: Parking off A87 with ½ m walk to garden, closer parking by prior arrangement ○ 🏠 **WC** ♿

The garden is approached down the wooded road through the village of Glaick on the lochside. From there, across the water, rise the magnificent mountains of Skye and Knoydart. Woodland planting on this steep-sided, 11-acre site began in 1887 around Lochalsh House, and the canopy of beeches, larches, oaks and pines is now outstanding. Ornamental plantings began in the late 1950s with large-leaved rhododendrons, followed from the 1980s to the present day, by shrubs from China, Japan, the Himalayas and Australasia. Paths created through the woods give a choice of walks, of differing levels and varying lengths. Alongside these and in glades, logs have been used to build curved, raised beds for new plantings, including many hydrangeas, fuchsias, bamboos and ferns.

Logan Botanic Garden ★★ 89

**Port Logan, Stranraer, Wigtownshire, Dumfries and Galloway DG9 9ND.
Tel: (01776) 860231; Fax: (01776) 860333**

*Royal Botanic Garden Edinburgh • 14m S of Stranraer, off B7065. Signposted •
Open March to Oct, daily, 9.30am – 6pm and at other times by arrangement •
Entrance: £3, concessions £2.50, children £1, family ticket £7. Season tickets,
inc. Dawyck and Younger Botanic Gardens (see entries), available • Other
information: Discovery Centre and Sound Alive guided tours. Guide dogs only*
◑ ⬛ ✕ WC ♿ ⚲ ⛷ ⚘

This is a specialist garden of the Royal Botanic Garden Edinburgh (see entry).
In the far south-west of Scotland on a peninsula washed by the Gulf Stream,
Logan's mild climate allows a fine collection of exotic plants to be grown in the
open. Flourishing here are beautiful plants from South and Central America,
Southern Africa, Australasia and the Mediterranean which survive outside in
few other British gardens. Throughout the summer it is ablaze with colour.
One of the best Scottish collections of tender perennials includes diascias,
fuchsias and salvias. As the season progresses rhododendrons, primulas,
meconopsis and other acid-loving plants come into bloom on the peat walls,
a feature first developed here. The walled garden was established over 100
years ago and contains many smaller gardens. Major features are the water
garden with the original cabbage palms and tree ferns and the terrace garden
framed by an avenue of Chusan palms. The woodland garden is wild by
contrast, with glades of eucalyptus and magnolias surrounded by many unusual
flowering trees and shrubs. All in all, a fascinating tour of exotic plant
collections native to the southern hemisphere.

Malleny Garden 90

Balerno, Edinburgh EH14 7AF. Tel: (0131) 449 2283

*The National Trust for Scotland • In Balerno, off A70 Edinburgh – Lanark
road • Open all year, daily, 9.30am – 7pm (Nov to March closes 4pm) •
Entrance: £1, OAPs 50p (honesty box)* ◯ ⬛ WC ♿ ⚘

Aptly described as The National Trust for Scotland's secret garden, Malleny
seems an old and valued friend soon after meeting and reflects the thoughtful
planning by the head gardener and his talented wife. An impressive Deodar
cedar reigns over this three-acre walled garden, assisted by a square of early
seventeenth-century clipped yews and by yew hedges. As well as containing a
National Collection of nineteenth-century shrub roses and a permanent display from the Scottish Bonsai Association, Malleny's four-metre-wide herbaceous borders are superb, as is the large glasshouse containing a summer display
of flowering plants. Don't forget to admire the attractive herb and ornamental
vegetable garden, laid out in traditional manner.

Manderston ★★ 91

Duns, Scottish Borders TD11 3PP. Tel: (01361) 883450

Lord Palmer • 2m E of Duns on A6105 • House open • Gardens open mid-May to Sept, Sun and Thurs, and 29th May, 28th Aug, 2 – 5.30pm. Also for parties at any time of year by appt • Entrance: £5.50 (house and garden). Reduced rate for parties of 20 or more (1999 prices) ● WC ⬦ ⬛

One of the last great classic houses to be built in Britain, Manderston was modelled on Robert Adam's Kedleston Hall (see entry in Derbyshire). It was described in 1905 as a 'charming mansion inexhaustible in its attractions', and this might equally well apply to the gardens, which remain an impressive example of gardening on the grand scale. Four magnificent formal terraces planted in Edwardian style overlook a narrow serpentine lake, and a Chinoiserie bridging dam tempts one over to the woodland garden on the far side, thus elegantly effecting the transition from formal to informal. No expense was spared in creating the gardens, and this air of opulence and good quality is evident in the formal walled gardens to the north of the house. They are a lasting tribute to the very best of the Edwardian era, when 24 gardeners were employed to do what two now accomplish to the same immaculately high standard. Gilded gates open on to a panorama of colourful planting on different levels, with fountains, statuary and a charming rose pergola all complementing each other. Even the greenhouses were given lavish treatment, with the walls created from lumps of limestone to resemble an exotic planted grotto. Fifty-six acres of formal and informal beauty.

Megginch Castle 92

Errol, Perth, Perthshire PH2 7SW. Tel: (01821) 642222; Fax: (01821) 642708

Lady Strange • 8m E of Perth off A85 Perth – Dundee road • Open April to Oct, daily, 2 – 5.30pm • Entrance: £2.50, children £1, under 5 free ◗ & ⬦

Originally a fifteenth-century tower house (not open), Megginch, meaning Beautiful Island, was considerably restructured by Robert Adam in 1790 and by successive generations, and this gives the gardens and the Gothick courtyard of 1806 a timeless atmosphere. A fountain parterre to the west of the house is of particular interest for its yew and variegated holly topiary, including an unusual topiary yew crown planted to commemorate Queen Victoria's Jubilee. There are four clumps of thousand-year-old yews, at 22 metres the highest in Scotland. Try and visit Megginch during August when a stunning 110-metre double border – the length of the eighteenth-century walled garden – is a glorious blaze of annual plantings. So many dahlias can rarely have been displayed. An adjacent walled garden of the same period contains an interesting astrological garden with plants relevant to each sign. Peacocks abound.

Mellerstain ★ 93

Gordon, Scottish Borders TD3 6LG. Tel: (01573) 410225; Fax: (01573) 410636

The Earl of Haddington • 6m NW of Kelso off A6089 • House open (extra charge) • Garden open 21st April to Sept, daily except Sat, all 12.30 − 5pm (last admission 4.30pm). Parties of 20 or more at other times by arrangement • Entrance: £2, children free (house and garden £4.50, OAPs and students £3.50, children £2, parties £3.50 per person) • Other information: Craft gallery ◖ ☕ ✗ WC & ⬦ ⚐ ⚒ ⚇

The house is a unique example of the work of the Adam family; both William and his son Robert worked on the building. The garden is formal, comprised of dignified terraces, balustraded and 'lightly' planted with climbers and simple topiary, because even when labour was plentiful there were a mere six gardeners employed, though they had to supply flowers and vegetables for the London establishment as well as here. The great glory of the garden is the landscape, complete with lake and woodlands in the style of Brown and Repton, but designed early this century by Sir Reginald Blomfield. The view of the Cheviot Hills from the terraces is one of the finest to be found in this lovely area of the Scottish Borders. Mellerstain is a must for lovers of the formal, 'arranged' landscape.

Mertoun 94

St Boswells, Roxburghshire, Scottish Borders TD6 0EA. Tel: (01835) 823236

The Duke of Sutherland • 8m SE of Galashiels, 2m NE of St Boswells on B6404 • Open April to Sept, Sat, Sun and Bank Holiday Mons, 2 − 6pm • Entrance: £1.50, children 50p ☕ WC &

Overlooking the Tweed and with Mertoun House in the background, this is a lovely garden to wander round and admire the mature specimen trees, azaleas, daffodils and a most attractive ornamental pond flanked by a good herbaceous border. The focal point is the immaculate three-acre walled garden, which is everything a proper kitchen garden should be. Walking up from a 1567 dovecot, thought to be the oldest in the county, through a healthy orchard, the visitor reaches the traditional box hedges, raised beds and glasshouses of the main area. Neat rows of vegetables, herbs and bright flowers for the house vie for attention with figs and peaches in the well-stocked glasshouses.

Monteviot 95

Jedburgh, Scottish Borders TD8 6TJ. Tel: (01835) 830380 (mornings)

5m NE of Jedburgh. Turn off A68 onto B6400 to Nisbet. Entrance second turn on right • Open April to Oct, daily, 12 noon − 5pm. Parties book with Administrator • Entrance: £2, OAPs £1, children under 14 free. • Other information: Refreshments at Harestanes Countryside Visitor Centre, ½ m ◖ WC & ⬦ ⚐ ⚇

The river garden which runs down to the River Teviot has been extensively replanted with herbaceous perennials and shrubs to a more informal design.

Beside it, the semi-enclosed terraced rose gardens overlooking the river have a large collection of hybrid teas, floribundas and shrub roses. The pinetum is full of unusual trees, and nearby a water garden has recently been created, planted with hybrid rhododendrons and azaleas. A circular route has been laid out around the gardens, and there are fine views.

Mount Stuart ★★ 96

Rothesay, Isle of Bute PA20 9LR. Tel: (01700) 503877

Mount Stuart Trust • Ferry from Wemyss Bay. 5½ m S of Rothesay ferry terminal on A844 • House open as garden, 11am – 4.30pm (last admission 3.45pm) • Garden open May to mid-Oct, daily except Tues and Thurs, 10am – 5pm (last admission 4.30pm). Guided tours available • Entrance: £3.50, OAPs £3, children £2 (house and garden £6, OAPs £4.50, children £2.50) (1999 prices). Party discounts available ◖ ☕ ✕ 🛍 WC ♿ ⚲ 👜 ☕

Not counting the 300 acres of designed landscape and waymarked woodland walks, there is a wealth of horticultural interest here, and one of the most elegant drives in the country. The gardens contain a considerable mature pinetum of 1860 and a magnificent old lime tree avenue leading to the shore, but on the whole they have been restored and augmented over the last decade by the late John Bute and his wife Jennifer. In conjunction with the Royal Botanic Garden Edinburgh, they have also set aside 100 acres to grow endangered conifer species from all over the world, in order to create a seedbank for the future. Rock gardens provide decorative features near the house, but the two most important elements are the kitchen garden and the 'Wee' garden. The latter is actually eight acres of mixed and exotic plantings with emphasis on species from the southern hemisphere. It is set in the mildest part of the grounds and grows some of the most tender plants to be found outside the glasshouse, some flourishing to unusual size. The kitchen garden has been designed as an ornamental *potager* by Rosemary Verey and includes herb gardens, trellised fruit enclosure, fan-trained plum trees and mixed beech hedges. Set in the middle is the Pavilion glasshouse planted with rare flora from SE Asia. With such variety of both plants and settings this must be one of Scotland's finest gardens.

Netherbyres 97

Eyemouth, Berwickshire, Scottish Borders TD14 5SE. Tel: (018907) 50337

Colonel S.J. Furness • 8m NW of Berwick-upon-Tweed, ¼ m from Eyemouth on A1107 • Open twice yearly in April and July for charity and April to Sept for small parties by appt • Entrance: £2, children £1 ◕ ♿

Although the Victorian conservatory and vineries were demolished to make way for a modern house and conservatory, the garden is worth seeing for the unique elliptical walls, built before 1750. The present layout dates from the 1860s, and is one of the few Scottish walled gardens with a mix of fruit, flowers and vegetables still fully cultivated on traditional lines. A central gazebo feature has been added, together with a new shrub border.

Pitmedden Garden ★ 98

Pitmedden, Ellon, Aberdeenshire AB41 7PD. Tel: (01651) 842352; Fax: (01651) 843188

The National Trust for Scotland • 14m N of Aberdeen. 1m W of Pitmedden, 1m N of Udny on A920 • Gardens open May to Sept, daily, 10am – 5.30pm (last admission 5pm) • Entrance: £3.90, concessions and children £2.60 • Other information: Coaches must book. Wheelchairs supplied. Museum of farming life
◑ ☕ 🖫 WC & ᵔ 🎋 ⚑

The Great Garden exhibits the taste of seventeenth-century garden-makers and their love of patterns made to be viewed from above. The rectangular parterre garden is enclosed by high terraces on three sides and by a wall on the fourth. Simple topiary and box hedging abound. The south- and west-facing walls, lined by fine herbaceous borders, are covered by a great variety of old apple trees in both fan and espalier styles, wall growth producing nearly one ton of fruit at the end of the season. Ornamental patterns are cut in box on a grand scale, infilled with 20,000 annuals. The overall impact is striking when viewed from the original ogivally roofed stone pavilion at the north of the garden or when walking along the terraces. When the Trust acquired Pitmedden in 1952 all that survived was the masonry, and since nothing remained of the original design, contemporary seventeenth-century plans for the garden at the Palace of Holyrood in Edinburgh were used in re-creating what is seen today.

Pollok House 99

Pollokshaws Road, Glasgow G43 1AT. Tel: (0141) 616 6410

The National Trust for Scotland • 3½ m S of city centre. In Pollokshaws take A736. Signposted • House and gallery open • Garden open all year except 25th Dec and 1st Jan, Mon – Sat, 10am – 5pm, Sun, 11am – 5pm • Entrance: free (house £3.20) ◯ ☕ ✕ 🖫 WC & ◁▷ 🎋 ⚑

A visit to Pollok House offers a full day's entertainment. Next to the house is a lovely formal terrace of box parterres, beautifully planted and maintained by Glasgow Parks. There are borders near the water and a nineteenth-century woodland garden on the ridge nearby. Stone gazebos with ogee roofs. The house holds the Stirling Maxwell collection of European paintings, and in the grounds, famous for their bluebells in spring, is the Burrell Collection, one of the world's finest modern galleries, housing decorative and fine arts. The building was designed to complement the woodland and the parkland around is beautifully planted and maintained.

Portmore ★ 100

Eddleston, Peebleshire, Scottish Borders EH45 8QU. Tel: (01721) 730296

Mr and Mrs D.L. Reid • ½ m N of Eddleston, on A703 Peebles – Edinburgh road • Open for SGS in mid-July and also for parties by appt • Entrance: £2
◐ WC ◁▷

It is a joy to see an old neglected estate brought lovingly back to life here. The long drive winds up through woods, fields and little lochs to the Edwardian mansion which proudly overlooks the rolling acres. Parterres have recently been planted at the far side of the house, and shrub-filled woodland walks are being planned. The wonder of the place is the large walled garden designed and replanted by Chrissy Reid with great taste and flair — she cares particularly about colours and the effect at the entrance is magical. The soft mixture of pale greens, blues, mauves and white delights the eye in the herbaceous borders and leads the gaze to the greenhouses stuffed full of geraniums, pelargoniums, streptocarpus, fuchsias, etc. Leading off these there is an enchanting cool, dripping Victorian Italian grotto, fern-filled. The remainder of the garden is divided into squares of *potagers*, herb gardens, cherry walks, rose gardens, all surmounted with wonderful wrought-iron arches. Even the luxurious-looking fruit is protected by wire held up by three elegant arches. The whole is meticulously maintained.

Priorwood Garden 101

Melrose, Ettrick and Lauderdale, Scottish Borders TD6 9PX.
Tel: (01896) 822493

The National Trust for Scotland • On A6091 in Melrose • Open April to 24th Dec, Mon — Sat, 10am — 5.30pm, Sun, 1.30 — 5.30pm (Oct to Dec, closes 4pm) • Entrance: by donation £1 ☻ 🍴 ♿ ⬇ 🌿 👍

Purchased by The National Trust for Scotland in 1974, this was originally the walled garden belonging to Priorwood House, now Melrose Youth Hostel. The garden has been developed for the production of dried flowers, and by drying them in dessicants — as the ancient Egyptians did — the range of plants has been greatly increased to include some 700 varieties of annual and herbaceous plants. There is also an orchard, which has been designed to show the development of the apple tree in Britain, and a woodland area. The eighteenth-century garden walls are complemented by ornamental ironwork thought to be the work of Lutyens. Immediately adjacent is the *Harmony Garden*, an attractive walled garden with magnificent views of Melrose Abbey and the Eildon Hills.

Royal Botanic Garden Edinburgh ★★ 102

Inverleith Row, Edinburgh EH3 5LR. Tel: (0131) 552 7171;
Fax: (0131) 248 2901

1m N of city centre at Inverleith. Signposted • Open all year, daily except 25th Dec and 1st Jan: opens 9.30am, closes between 4pm and 7pm depending on season. Garden tours operate April to Sept, daily, 11am and 2pm from West Gate • Entrance: free, voluntary contributions invited • Other information: Exhibition hall and Inverleith House gallery open. Guide dogs only ○ ☕ ✗ WC ♿ 🌿 👍 🔦

Set on a hillside with magnificent panoramic views of the city, the Royal Botanic Garden Edinburgh is one of the finest botanic gardens in the world;

arguably the finest garden, physically, of its type in Britain. Established in the seventeenth century on an area the size of a tennis court, it now extends to 75 acres. Rhododendrons and azaleas abound, and in spring their stunning flowers provide a blaze of colour and intriguing scents. The world-renowned rock garden is probably the finest in the world. In summer marsh orchids, lilies, saxifrages and bell-shaped campanulas give brilliant colour. There are also peat and woodland gardens and a stunning herbaceous border. The arboretum sweeps along the garden's southern boundary. A relatively recent addition is the Pringle Chinese Collection on the south-facing slope of Inverleith Hill which has been four years in development. It includes a spectacular wild-water ravine, crossed by bridges, tumbling down into a tranquil pond at the bottom of the hillside. A T'ing (pavilion) provides an ideal place to relax. The Glass-house Experience, featuring Britain's tallest palm house, leads the visitor on a trail of discovery through the temperate and tropical regions of the world, featuring passion flowers, cycads (some over 200 years old) and plants that provide everyday necessities such as food, clothes and medicine. The exhibi-tions programme, centred around Inverleith House, focuses on the link between art and nature. There are also interactive hands-on exhibitions in the Exhibition Hall.

Scone Palace Pleasure Grounds   103

Perth, Perth and Kinross PH2 6BE. Tel: (01738) 552300.
Website: www.Scone-Palace.co.uk

The Earl and Countess of Mansfield • Just outside Perth on A93 Perth – Braemar road • Palace and grounds open April to Oct, daily, 9.30am – 5.15pm (last admission 4.45pm) • Entrance: £2.80, OAPs/ students £2.40, children £1.70, season ticket £5.60 (palace and gardens £5.60, OAPs/students £4.80, children £3.30, family £17) ◐ ☕ WC ⑂ ⬎ ⬛

The 100 acres of pleasure grounds, surrounding the site of Macbeth's ancient city of Scone, include the famous nineteenth-century pinetum with magni-ficent towering trees and *Sequoia giganteum* over 48 metres tall. Since 1977 a second pinetum has been planted, and there is also an acer collection, a butterfly garden, a 30-metre-long laburnum pergola and a beech maze designed by Adrian Fisher, opened in 1998, which comprises 2000 beech trees in the shape of a Murray Star. In season spectacularly massed daffodils, a primrose drive, rhododendrons and azaleas. The renowned explorer/plant collector, David Douglas, born at Scone, supplied the garden with many of his discoveries, and one of his original firs survives. There are always orchids in flower within the palace, the Earl of Mansfield having the largest collection in the country. It is also worth travelling 7m further north to marvel at the *Meikleour Beech Hedge*, now 30 metres high and a quarter of a mile long, beside the A93. Legend has it that men who planted it in 1745 were called away to fight and not one returned alive from the battle of Culloden.

Sea View
104

Durnamuck, Dundonnell, Ross-shire IV23 2QZ. Tel: (01854) 633317

Mr and Mrs Ian Nelson • 20m NW of Braemore, off A832 Dundonnell – Gairloch road. Turn at Badcaul. Signposted • Garden open May to Sept, daily, 10am – 6pm and by appt at other times • Entrance: £1 ◑ ♿ ৺

This half-acre garden, started in 1990 on the shores of Little Loch Broom, has been carved out of an inhospitable environment. The paucity of soil, only 8 inches deep, has been enriched with tons of manure and the use of raised beds, and in spite of the inherent difficulties an enchanting, varied and densely planted garden has been achieved. Among the many interesting plants is the *Rhododendron* 'Elizabeth Lockhart' with beautiful deep red new leaves, *R. camtschaticum*, grey-leaved *Olearia ilicifolia*, hebes, red-flowered *Jasminum beesianum*, flowering *Pittosporum tenuifolium* 'Tom Thumb', *Pseudowintera colorata* (the New Zealand pepper tree) and phormiums. A heather bed, rockery banks and bed, orchard, bog area and pond, the whole surrounded by hedges of escallonia, fuchsia and griselinia, complete the picture.

Stobo Castle Water Gardens
105

Peebles, Scottish Borders EH45 8NY. Tel: (01721) 760245

Hugh and Charles Seymour • 6m SW of Peebles on B712, 12m E of Biggar • Open by appt but advisable to write as phone frequently unanswered • Entrance: £1.50 ◑ 🍵 WC ♿ ৺

The enduring appeal of water is exemplified here; the planting, although most attractive, takes second place to the visual impact of clear water flowing down a series of cascades and waterfalls. Japanese bridges and stepping stones invite frequent crossings from side to side, and peaceful rills stray from the main torrent to create one huge water garden. In fine landscape-garden tradition, man has contrived to manipulate nature – in this case a large earth dam across a steep valley – into something of classical delight. The dam was faced with stone to create a magnificent waterfall and the resulting flow is impressive even in dry summers. The lovely mature trees, such as *Cercidiphyllum japonicum*, *Kalopanax pictus* var. *maximowiczii* and many Japanese maple varieties, obviously date from this period, which ended with the outbreak of World War I.

Teviot Water Garden
106

Kirkbank House, Eckford, Kelso, Scottish Borders TD5 8LE. Tel: (01835) 850734/253

Mr and Mrs Denis Wilson • Between Kelso and Jedburgh on A698 • Open April to Sept, daily, 10am – 5pm and by appt at other times • Entrance: free ◑ 🍵 ✕ WC ♿ ৺ 🛍 ♨

Created over the years from a stony riverside field, these gardens occupy a spectacular position on a steep north-west-facing bank of the River Teviot. A series of terraces linked by waterfalls displays a wide range of plants, giving a varied show throughout the summer months. Aquatic plants are a speciality, but this intimate and tranquil garden also contains a selection of choice perennials, grasses, ferns and bamboos. The shop stocks plants and other items needed by the water garden enthusiast, from fish to pumps and liners. A visit to the coffee shop and smokery completes the outing.

Threave Garden ★ 107

**Stewartry, Castle Douglas, Dumfries and Galloway DG7 1RX.
Tel: (01556) 502575**

The National Trust for Scotland • 1m W of Castle Douglas off A75 • Open all year, daily, 9.30am − dusk (walled garden and glasshouses close 5pm) • Entrance: £4.40, OAPs and children £2.90, family (2 adults, up to 6 children) £11.70, parties £3.50 per person, school parties £1 per child • Other information: Exhibition in visitor centre April to Oct, daily ○ 🍽 ✕ 🖻 WC ⴺ 🌱 ♨ ♿

The Threave estate, which extends to 1500 acres, includes the famous 65-acre garden which has been used as a school of horticulture since 1960 and caters for trainee gardeners. Numerous perennials, annuals, trees and shrubs are used in imaginative ways and are maintained by the resident horticultural students. For the visitor the principal interest is the working walled garden with its range of glasshouses, vegetables, orchard and well-trained fruit. This may be contrasted with the less formal woodland and rock gardens, heath garden and arboretum. The garden is famous for its collection of daffodils, complemented in spring by rhododendrons and flowering trees and shrubs. A £½-million programme of refurbishment has been completed at the house to allow the principal rooms to be furnished in period style; these will be open to the public in the future.

Tillypronie 108

Tarland, Aboyne, Aberdeenshire AB34 4XX. Tel: (013398) 81238

The Hon. Philip Astor • 4½ m W of Tarland via A97 Dinnet − Huntly road • Open 28th Aug for charity, 2 − 5pm • Entrance: £1, children 40p (1999 prices) ● 🍽 🖻 WC ⴺ ⬥ ♨

Set on the south-facing slope of a hill at over 300 metres above sea level, this is a cold garden, but shelter belts dating from the mid-1800s ensure that a wide range of plants can be grown; more shelter planting was added from 1925 to 1951. The overall layout was completed in the 1920s and was the work of George Dillistone of Tunbridge Wells. The terraces below the house date from the same period and support narrow herbaceous borders. The house walls provide shelter for less hardy climbers, and trained *Buddleia davidii* cultivars make a good display in August. Curved stone steps lead between extensive heather gardens to lawns sweeping down to the ponds with their colourful plantings of astilbes, filipendulas, lysichitons, primulas and ferns. There are fine specimens of *Picea breweriana* and many other conifers and an area devoted to dwarf varieties. Spectacular views over farmland and hills.

Torosay Castle and Gardens 109

Craignure, Isle of Mull, Argyll and Bute PA65 6AY. Tel: (01680) 812421; Fax: (01680) 812470

Mr Christopher James • 1½ m S from Craignure. Steamer 6 times daily April to Oct (2 to 4 times daily Nov to March) from Oban to Craignure. Motor boat during high season. Miniature steam railway from Craignure ferry. Or take Lochaline to Fishnish ferry, then travel 7m S on A849 • Castle open, April to mid-Oct, 10.30am – 5pm • Garden open all year, daily, 9am – 7pm (or dusk in winter) • Entrance: £4.50, OAPs and students £3.50, children £1.50 (castle and gardens) ○ 🍽 🏠 WC ⴕ ⟁ 🌳 ⛪

The house in baronial castle style is by Bryce (1858). The main garden is formal Italian in style, based on a series of descending terraces with an unusual statue walk. This features one of the richest collections of Italian Rococo statuary in Britain. Vaguely reminiscent of Powis Castle (see entry in Wales), this is a dramatic contrast with the rugged island scenery. The peripheral gardens around the formal terraces are also a contrast – an informal water garden and Japanese garden looking out over Duart Bay; also a small rock garden. Rhododendrons and azaleas are a feature but less important than in other west-coast gardens, and there is a collection of Australian and New Zealand trees and shrubs. A major restoration which will take 15 years is already under way, and 2000 species and cultivars have been planted over the past five years. Outside the main garden, the owners, in conjunction with The Royal Botanic Garden Edinburgh, have created a five-acre Chilean wood and are underplanting another two-acre wood with plants from the collection of the late Jim Russell.

Tyninghame House ★ 110

Tyninghame, East Linton, East Lothian EH42 1XW.

Tyninghame Gardens Ltd • 25m E of Edinburgh between Haddington and Dunbar. N of A1, 2m E of A198 • Open for charity 14th May, 9th July, 1 – 5pm • Entrance: £1.50 ○ 🍽 WC ⟁ 🌳

The gardens created by the Dowager Lady Haddington from 1947 onwards have been described as of 'ravishing beauty'. They consist of a formal rose garden, terraces, a secret garden, an Italian garden and an area of woodland. When her husband died in 1986, her son reluctantly sold the house, but the conversion and addition of two houses was handled by Kit Martin with great sensitivity. It is close to the sea, with fine views in all directions. The unique character of the garden has been maintained, perhaps enhanced, by the architectural changes around it, and by the dedicated work of Mrs Timothy Clifford and others.

University of Dundee Botanic Garden 111

Riverside Drive, Dundee DD2 1QH. Tel: (01382) 566939

University of Dundee • 2.5m from city centre on A90 Perth road. Signposted • Open: March to Oct, Mon – Sat, 10am – 4.30pm, Sun, 11am – 4pm; Nov –

Feb, Mon – Sat, 10am – 3.30pm, Sun, 11am – 3pm • Entrance: £1.50, OAPs 75p, children 75p [NEW] ◑ 🍽 WC ⚙ ♨ 👍

Founded in 1971 as a supply of plant material for teaching and research purposes, the 23-acre garden has always been open to the public for their pleasure. The planting around the glasshouse and large pond near the entrance is extremely attractive and reminiscent of a private rather than a botanical garden. The large area beyond has plants grouped according to region or habitat, including many Scottish natives; though mainly composed of trees and shrubs, the artistic layout ensures something of interest as well as beauty to see. The glasshouse is brimful of fine specimens, from tropical to temperate zones, from rainforest to desert.

West Drummuie Garden 112

West Drummuie, Golspie, Sutherland, Highland KW10 6TA. Tel: (01408) 633493

Mrs Elizabeth Woollcombe • 1m S of Golspie off A9. At white milestone, turn up hill and bear right at fork to last house • Open mid-April to early Oct, Wed only, 10.30am – 12.30pm, 2 – 4pm or at other times by appt • Entrance: free – donations welcome ◑ ♨

A smallish and beautiful private garden, on a steeply sloping hillside overlooking the Dornoch Firth. It needs to be sheltered by hedges and tall shrubs and to be rabbit-proof, but after nearly 30 years it is mature in a way that is unusual in such a location. The garden is complementary to the house and produces vegetables, fruit, firewood and free-ranging bantams which help keep the hostas slug-free. Meconopsis in variety, primulas, Chatham Island forget-me-nots (*Myosotidium hortensia*), olearias and crinodendrons thrive here.

Younger Botanic Garden Benmore ★★ 113

Dunoon, Argyll, Argyll and Bute PA23 8QU. Tel: (01369) 706261; Fax: (01369) 706369

Royal Botanic Garden Edinburgh • At Dunoon, 7m S of A885/A816 junction. Signposted • Open March to Oct, daily, 9.30am – 6pm and at other times by arrangement • Entrance: £3, concessions £2.50, children £1, family £7. Season tickets inc. Dawyck and Logan Botanic Gardens (see entries) available ◑ 🍽 ✕ WC ⚙ ♨ 👍 ♨

This specialist garden of the Royal Botanic Garden Edinburgh is a magnificent mountainside garden set in the dramatic location of the Cowal Peninsula. It is world-famous for its collections of flowering trees and shrubs. From Britain's finest avenue of giant redwoods (*Sequoiadendron giganteum*) planted in 1863, a variety of trails spreads out. More than 250 species of rhododendron and an extensive magnolia collection provide a positive array of colour on the hillside beside the River Eachaig. Other features include the formal garden with memorials and stately conifers, the Glen Massan arboretum with some of the tallest trees in Scotland, and an informal pond. A short climb leads to a stunning viewpoint looking out across the garden, Strath Eck and the Holy Loch to the Firth of Clyde and beyond.

WALES

Two-starred gardens are marked on the map with a black square.

Aberglasney 1

Llangathen, Llandeilo, Carmarthenshire SA32 8QH. Tel/Fax: (01558) 668998

Aberglasney Restoration Trust • 3m W of Llandeilo on A40. Turn S at Broak Oak junction • Open daily: April to Oct, 9.30am – 6pm; Oct to March, 10.30am – 4.30pm • Entrance: £3.95, OAPs £3.45. Guided tours £5 per person ◑ ☕ ✕ WC ♿

Here are gardens lost in time. Records for Aberglasney go back to the mid-fourteenth century, when mention was made of nine gardens, orchards and vineyards. Around 1600 the Bishop of St David's bought the estate to turn it into a private palace, and it is probably he who built the gatehouse and the marvellous cloister garden. Now, after many years of neglect, the gardens have been restored. To the side of the ruined house is a yew tunnel; bow your head and you can walk through 1000 years of history. A large walled garden is home to vegetables and soft fruit, while another walled area has a formal garden designed by Penelope Hobhouse to complement the great age of the garden. Herbaceous garden and Mediterranean plants flank the tea rooms, which in turn overlook a large pool. Pigeon House Wood is a natural, unspoilt area where you may picnic or just sit in the shade of splendid beech trees.

Ashford House 2

Talybont-on-Usk, Brecon, Powys LD3 7YR. Tel: (01874) 676271

Mr and Mrs Anderson • 6m SE of Brecon, 1m E of Talybont on B4588 • Open April to Sept, Tues, 2 – 6pm and by appt • Entrance: £2, children free ◑ ☕ WC ♿

About one acre with a further three acres of woodland and wild garden. The walled garden has a good selection of shrubs and herbaceous plants and long raised beds containing an interesting collection of alpines – one of the owners' interests. The wild garden, interplanted recently with rhododendrons and other shrubs, contains a healthy wild pool with frogs and dragonflies. Mrs Anderson propagates plants for sale.

Bodnant Garden ★★ 3

Tal-y-Cafn, Colwyn Bay, Conwy LL28 5RE. Tel: (01492) 650460

The National Trust • 8m S of Llandudno, just off A470 • Garden open mid-March to Oct, daily, 10am – 5pm (last admission 4.30pm) • Entrance: £5, children £2.50 • Other information: Parking 50 metres from garden. Plant centre (not NT) adjacent ◑ ☕ ✕ WC ♿

One of the finest gardens in the country, not only for the magnificent collections of rhododendrons, camellias and magnolias but also for its beautiful setting above the River Conwy and extensive views of the Snowdon range. The garden, which covers 80 acres, has many interesting features, the best-known being the laburnum arch, which is an overwhelming mass of bloom in late May and early June. Others include the Lily terrace, the curved and stepped pergola, the Canal terrace, Pin Mill and the Dell garden. In the Dell is the tallest redwood in the country, the 45-metre *Sequoia sempervirens*. These, together with the outstanding autumn colours, make Bodnant a garden for all seasons. The whole effect was created by four generations of the Aberconway family (who bought Bodnant in 1874), aided by three generations of the Puddle family as head gardeners.

Bodrhyddan 4

Rhuddlan, Denbighshire LL18 5SP. Tel: (01745) 590414

Lord Langford • 4m SW of Prestatyn. Take A5151 Rhuddlan – Dyserth road and turn left. Signposted • House open • Garden open June to Sept, Tues and Thurs, 2 – 5.30pm • Entrance: £4, children under 16 £2 (house and garden)
◖ ☕ WC ⌖

The main feature here is a box-edged parterre designed by William Andrews Nesfield, the father of the renowned William Eden Nesfield, who designed the 1875 alterations to the house. Other points of interest are clipped yew paths and, to the north-west, the Pleasance, known on very old maps as the Grove. This is probably because it embraces St Mary's Well, revered since pagan times and covered by a 1612 Inigo Jones pavilion, said to have been used for clandestine marriages. The Pleasance is an area of some two acres, with four ponds, fine mature trees and many new plantings; originally a Victorian shrubbery (it was abandoned due to two world wars and death duties), it has now been restored and is being extended.

Bodysgallen Hall ★ 5

Llandudno, Gwynedd LL30 1RS. Tel: (01492) 584466

Historic House Hotels • 2m S of Llandudno. At A55/A470 junction turn onto A470 towards Llandudno. Hall is 1m on right • Open all year, daily • Entrance: free to guests using hotel facilities • Other information: Refreshments in hotel ○

The Garden writes that 'there can be few better living examples of early seventeenth-century gardens anywhere in England and Wales. The limestone outcrops provide an interesting array of rockeries and terraces. One of the major features is a parterre sympathetically planted with herbs; another is a formal walled rose garden. A number of well-established and interesting trees and shrubs can be seen, including medlar and mulberry. Woodland walks add a further dimension to this magnificent award-winning garden.

Bryn Meifod 6

Graig, Glan Conwy, Colwyn Bay, Conwy LL28 5TL. Tel: (01492) 580875

Dr and Mrs K. Lever • 6m S of Llandudno, just off A470, 1½ m S of Glan Conwy. Signed 'Aberconwy Nursery' • Open by appt only • Entrance: free • Other information: Plants for sale in adjacent nursery ◑ WC

The garden, situated next to the Levers' renowned nursery, is being extended and modified. In effect a new garden is being created within the framework of an existing established one, a process of interest in itself. The planting is imaginative and includes some unusual plants in skilfully designed settings which display them to best effect. There is a lack of artificiality in what is currently a lovely garden, with the promise of even more to come. A scree area has been planted with alpines and turf beds for choice ericaceous plants. New beds are currently being worked on in a lightly wooded area at the top of the garden to accommodate the growing collection of woodland plants (epimediums, hellebores and meconopsis) and dwarf rhododendrons. *Dierama pulcherrimum* in the slate terraces around the pool is flourishing, with over 300 wands of flowers.

Brynmelyn 7

Cymerau Isaf, Ffestiniog, Gwynedd LL41 4BN. Tel: (01766) 762684

Mr and Mrs A.S. Taylor • 8m E of Porthmadog, 2m SW of Ffestiniog on A496 • Open April to Aug, 10am – 1pm, 2 – 5pm. Telephone in advance, before 10am or after 9pm • Entrance: collecting box • Other information: Parking in lay-by opposite junction to Manod (½ m to garden along path at lower gate bearing right after garage) ◑

An interesting garden, not only for its range of plant material, but also for its wild mountainside setting. It lends itself well to the overall informal style, and includes a nature reserve and woodland.

Bryn-y-Bont 8

Nantmor, Beddgelert, Caernarfon, Gwynedd LL55 4YG. Tel: (01766) 890448

Miss J. Entwisle • 6m NE of Porthmadog, 2½ m S of Beddgelert. Turn left over Aberglaslyn Bridge onto A4085. After 500 metres turn left up hill marked 'Nantmor'; house is second on right • Open by appt and for pre-booked parties • Entrance: £1.50, children free ● ● WC ◁ ℘

The well-designed two-acre garden has been created from a bracken-strewn hillside since 1978, taking full advantage of the south-facing view over Glaslyn Vale. Mixed borders, a small pond and bog garden, and rhododendron beds give way to a woodland area where trees and shrubs are being introduced to make a small arboretum and an environmentally friendly haven for wildlife.

Cae Hir ★ 9

Cribyn, Lampeter, Ceredigion SA48 7NG. Tel: (01570) 470839

Mr W. Akkermans • From Lampeter take A482 towards Aberaeron. After 5m at Temple Bar take B4337 signed Llanybydder. House is 2m on left • Open daily except Mon (but open Bank Holiday Mons), 1 – 6pm • Entrance: £2.50, OAPs £2, children 50p ◑ ● ● WC ৬ ◁ ℘ �

The aim of the gardener (a Dutch plantsman) to create a balance between the natural and the cultivated has been achieved. Six acres of sheer delight, from colour-themed subgardens and bonsai enclosure to wildflower bog areas. Fine views and plenty of seating.

Cefn Bere 10

Cae Deintur, Dolgellau, Gwynedd LL40 2YS. Tel: (01341) 422768

Mr and Mrs Maldwyn Thomas • N of A496 Barmouth road (not bypass). From Dolgellau, turn left (towards Barmouth) at top of main bridge, turn right within 100 metres, then second right behind school. Continue up hill to left-hand bend; house is fourth on right • Open spring, summer and autumn months by appt only • Entrance: by donation to collecting box ◑

This relatively small garden has a diverse plant collection amassed over the last 40 years. Planted informally but within a formal framework, it is a delight to amateur and professional gardeners alike. The alpine house, bulb and peat frames, and troughs are well worth seeing; so too are the old-fashioned roses.

Cefn Onn Park 11

Cardiff, South Glamorgan.

Cardiff City Council • From city centre take A469 under M4. Turn first right then left opposite Lisvane Station. From elsewhere, at M4 junction 32, turn S of A470. Take first left to T-junction, turn right, turn left at church, turn left at T-pass under M4, first right then left opposite Lisvane Station • Open all year, daily during daylight hours • Entrance: free ○ WC ⅏ ⬦

This park is something out of the ordinary for a city. It retains a little of the formality common in such areas, with straight gravelled paths running through the centre, but from there on the similarity ends. No large areas of bedding plants – rather, large areas of informally planted azaleas and rhododendrons. Colour and perfume, layer upon layer, reach up into the upper storey of trees, which can only be appreciated by standing on the bank opposite in order to see them at all. The camellias and magnolias here have also become trees, rather than shrubs, and the visitor may have to guard against a cricked neck trying to see everything. It may also be a little dull once the rhododendrons are over. If in the city on Sat, 10am – 12 noon or Tues, 1 – 3pm, it may also be worth calling in at *Cardiff Horticultural Society Demonstration Garden*, which has about 200 herbs, including dye and culinary plants.

Centre for Alternative Technology 12

Machynlleth, Powys SY20 9AZ. Tel: (01654) 702400; Fax: (01654) 702782

C.A.T. • 3m N of Machynlleth on A487 • Parking inc. coaches at base of site, but for elderly and disabled at top of steep drive. Also access by water-balance cliff railway from Easter to Oct • Open all year, daily except 25th Dec and mid-January, 10am – 5.30pm (4pm in winter) • Entrance: £5.70, OAPs, claimants and students £3.75, children £2.80, family ticket (2 adults and up to 4 children) £15.50 (1999 prices). Discounts for arrival by public transport or bicycle • Other information: Guide dogs only ○ ⬤ ✕ ▤ WC ⅏ ⅋ ⬛ ⬥

High in a former slate quarry, and at the heart of the environmentally friendly community here, is the most exciting garden. Compactly laid out, using natural and recycled materials to form harmoniously shaped raised beds, ponds and walks, the garden is vibrant (in June) with colour and insect life drawn to the organically grown flowers and companion planted vegetables. There are suggestions, too, for urban gardeners and displays of land reclamation, wildlife gardening, composting, weed and pest control. Wind turbines and solar fountains in different sizes and designs could be considered unusual, if highly functional, garden sculptures. Whether you want to experience the world of the worm in the underground mole hole, or wander gently by one of the lakes, be sure not to miss the view from the balcony of the water-balanced railway.

Chirk Castle ★   13

Chirk, Wrexham, Clwyd LL14 5AF. Tel: (01691) 777701

The National Trust • 10m SW of Wrexham, 2m W of Chirk off A5, 1½ m up private drive • Castle open as gardens 12 noon – 5pm (last admission 4.30pm) • Gardens only open probably Feb, weekends only (for snowdrops – but opening depends on weather so telephone to check), 12 noon – 4pm • Gardens and house open 29th March to Sept, daily except Mon and Tues (but open Bank Holiday Mondays); Oct, Wed – Sun, 11am – 5pm (last admission 4.30pm) • Entrance: Feb: £1, children 50p; other dates £2.80, children £1.40 (castle and garden £5, children £2.50, family (2 adults and 2 children) £12.50) • Other information: Parking 200 metres from garden
🕐 ☕ ✕ 🍴 WC ♿ 🎁 ☕

The castle, its walls now covered with climbing plants, dates from 1300 and is set in an eighteenth-century landscaped park. Six acres of trees and flowering shrubs, including rhododendrons and azaleas, were mostly planted by Lady Margaret Myddleton. They contrast with the yews in the formal garden, which were planted in the 1870s by Richard Biddulph. The rose garden contains mainly old cluster-flowered (floribunda) roses. From the terrace, with its fine views over Shropshire and Cheshire, the visitor passes to the classical pavilion, from which a lime tree avenue leads to a statue of Hercules. There is interesting nineteenth-century topiary, a rockery and an old hawk house, and a pleasure ground wood is now open. Chirk is described by the Trust as a 'family' garden.

Clyne Gardens ★★   14

Blackpill, Swansea, West Glamorgan SA3 5AR. Tel: (01792) 401737

Swansea City Council • From Swansea take A4067 Mumbles road and turn right at Woodman Roast Inn • Open all year, daily, 8am – dusk. Telephone for details of garden tours • Entrance: free • Other information: Refreshments in May only. Rare plants sale in May ◯ 🍴 WC ♿ ☕

Fifty acres of well-kept woodland garden to interest everyone from the beginner to the more knowledgeable. Near the entrance gates is a planting of young magnolias and a variety of rhododendrons and azaleas. This area leads on to a magnificent group of large-leaved rhododendrons, at their best in

April. The garden holds a National Collection of the rhododendron section Falconera, but even these tree-like rhododendrons are looked down upon by *Magnolia campbellii*. Clearly defined paths lead the visitor through other areas where National Collections of rhododendron section Triflora, pieris and enkianthus flourish; the perfume from *Rhododendron fragrantissimum* is heady and unforgettable. The bog garden is a prehistoric forest of *Gunnera manicata* linked by a colourful ribbon of primulas to the lake and waterfall spanned by a Japanese bridge. Many more rare and interesting trees and shrubs are there for the discerning.

Colby Woodland Garden   15

Stepaside, Amroth, Narberth, Pembrokeshire SA67 8PP. Tel: (01834) 811885

The National Trust • 10m SW of St Clear, near Amroth on Carmarthen Bay off A477 • Open April to Oct, 10am – 5pm; walled garden 11am – 5pm. Guided walks with Head Gardener • Entrance: £2.80, children £1.40, family ticket £7, parties of 15 or more £2.30 per person, children £1.15 • Other information: Parking 50 metres from garden. Disabled parking closer. Coaches by appt only. Gallery ◑ 🍽 🏠 WC ♿ 🐕 🐾 👍 🕯

This early nineteenth-century estate garden round a Nash-style house is now mainly woodland with some formal gardens. The walled garden is planted informally for ornamental effect. The woodland garden has many rhododendrons and some interesting trees. A new hydrangea bed gives further summer interest.

Cwm–Pibau   16

New Moat, Clarbeston Road, Haverfordwest, Pembrokeshire SA63 4RE. Tel: (01437) 532454

Mrs Drew • 10m NE of Haverfordwest. Take A40 through Robeston Wathen, turn left on B4313, follow signs to New Moat. 3m from Clarbeston Road on outskirts of New Moat, take concealed drive on left and continue for ½ m, keeping left • Open by appt for charity • Entrance: £1 ◐

Created by the owner since 1978, the garden has as a background mature woodland, so the long driveway is a difficult uphill walk (although on charity days it is possible to get a lift down and back to the car). Rhododendrons have been planted along the side of the drive, which leads to lawns and herbaceous plantings near the house. Paths are then signposted down through five acres of shrub plantings and along a stream fringed with moisture-lovers. This area is still young, but leads on to five more acres of woodland planted with embothriums, rhododendrons and rare shrubs.

The Dingle ★   17

Welshpool, Powys SY21 9JD. Tel: (01938) 555145

Mr and Mrs Roy Joseph • 3m NW of Welshpool. Take A490 for 1m to Llanfyllin then turn left signed 'Dingle Nursery' or 'Frochas'. After 1½ m fork

*left • Open all year, daily, except Tues and 25th Dec to 2nd Jan, 9am – 5pm •
Entrance: £1.50 for charity, children free • Other information: Possible for
wheelchairs but steep in places. Plants for sale in adjacent nursery* ○ 🍴 WC ♿
🔄 ℘

Set on the steep slopes of a verdant Welsh valley, this garden is more a
woodland creation of over 4000 carefully chosen trees and shrubs. The owners
began by damming the stream (or dingle) that flows through the site, and have
created two large pools which now set off the garden superbly. There is a
grove of acers, with many other interesting specimens such *Davidia involucrata*
and many different pittosporums. The real treat has to remain the nursery,
which is worth driving many, many miles to reach.

Dolwen ★ 18

Cefn Coch, Llanrhaeadr–ym–Mochnant, Powys SY10 0BU. Tel: (01691) 780411

*J Marriott and B Yarwood • 15m W of Oswestry, on B4580 Oswestry –
Llanrhaeadr road. Turn sharp right in Llanrhaeadr at Three Tuns Inn • Open
May to Aug by appt under new owners who may amend the times, so check
please • Entrance: £2* ◑ 🍵 WC 🔄 ℘ 🎋 🍲

A dramatic woodland and water garden situated high in the Berwyn hills with
splendid views. What started as a small cottage garden was extended by the
previous owner to two-and-a-half acres, with the extra land used to great
advantage. Striking plants in the water areas include *Salix fargesii* and *S. udensis*
'Sekka', but she was careful not to overplant the margins of the three ponds,
which she referred to as 'The Lake District'. Large boulders are sited
imaginatively and contemporary sculpture adds charm in unexpected places;
so do the bridges, some of which have unusual origins. As well as shrubs and
climbing roses, there are wonderful trees. Many of the uncommon plants here
are supplied by the *Crug Farm Nursery* near Caernarfon (see entry for Foxbrush).

Donadea Lodge 19

Babell, Flintshire CH8 8QD. Tel: (01352) 720204

*Mr and Mrs Patrick Beaumont • 8m E of St Asaph. Turn off A541 Mold –
Denbigh road at Afonwen, signed 'Babell', and at T-junction turn left; or take
A55 then B5122 to Caerwys and third turn on left • Open May to July by appt
• Entrance: £2, children 20p* ◕ WC ♿ ℘

The garden demonstrates what creative design can achieve on a very long site.
On one side an avenue of mature lime trees is a fine feature in its own right.
The other side is a mixed border of bays and small islands, each with its own
restrained and carefully thought-out colour scheme, often achieved using
unusual plants in unexpected but entirely effective combinations. A particular
feature is the use of roses and clematis.

Dyffryn Gardens ★ 20

St Nicholas, Cardiff, South Glamorgan CF5 6SU. Tel: (029) 2059 3328

*Vale of Glamorgan Council • 4m SW of Cardiff on A4232 turn S on A4050
and W to Dyffryn • Open all year, daily, 10am – dusk • Entrance: £3, OAPs
and children £2* ○

Dyffryn is one of Wales' largest landscaped gardens and has been described as
one of its best-kept secrets. An Edwardian garden, created out of a Victorian
original between 1906 and 1914, it was designed by Thomas Mawson, a leading
landscape architect rather overshadowed by his contemporary Edwin Lutyens.
Mawson's services were commissioned by the owner Reginald Cory, a distinguished horticulturist whose special interest was plants from the East, such
as those introduced to Britain by E.H. Wilson. To the south of the fine house is
a large open lawn with ornamental lily pond and, to the west, a series of
'rooms', each one enclosed by yew hedges. These are the Roman garden
(closed), the paved court, the swimming pool garden and the round garden.
Beyond these the west garden has large beds and borders and fine trees and
shrubs. There is also a Japanese garden, a lily-pool garden and a vine walk. The
arboretum, labelled as a wildlife reserve, contains some of the finest *Acer
griseum* (paperbark maple) in the country. A cacti collection is contained inside
the range of traditional display glasshouses within the walled garden. Three
million pounds of Lottery funding was given to restore the gardens to their
former glory, and a three-year refurbishment programme commenced in 1997.
New areas are planned and will include a scented garden (currently the
Mediterranean garden) and a physic garden (currently the Commonwealth
garden).

Erddig ★ 21

Wrexham, Clwyd LL13 0YT. Tel: (01978) 355314

*The National Trust • 2m S of Wrexham off A525 • House open 12 noon – 5pm
(closes 4pm from 1st Oct) • Garden open 25th March to Nov, daily except Thurs
and Fri (but open 21st April), 11am – 6pm (closes 5pm from 1st Oct).
Conducted tours for parties by prior arrangement • Entrance: £4, children £2,
pre-booked parties of 15 or more £3.20 per person, family (2 adults and 2
children) £10 (house and garden £6, children £3, family ticket £15, pre-booked
parties £5 per person) • Other information: Parking 200 metres from garden.
Wheelchairs provided. Dogs in grounds only, on lead* ◑ 💌 ✕ <u>WC</u> ♿ ✿ 🏷 🔦

The gardens, a rare example of early eighteenth-century formal design, were
almost lost along with the house, but have now been carefully restored. The
large walled garden contains varieties of fruit trees known to have been
grown there during that period and there is a canal garden and fish pool.
South of the canal walk is a Victorian flower garden, and later Victorian
additions include the parterre and yew walk. A National Collection of ivies
is here, also a narcissus collection. Apple Day is celebrated at Erddig in
October.

Farchynys Cottage 22

Bontddu, Gwynedd LL42 1TN. Tel: (01341) 430245

Mrs G. Townshend • 4m W of Dolgellau on A496 Dolgellau – Barmouth road. After Bontddu on right. Signposted • Open May to 1st Oct, daily except Sat and Wed, 2.30pm – 6pm • Entrance: £1.50 ◑

This woodland garden overlooking the Mawddach estuary is set in natural oak and conifer woodland. There is much new planting, but azaleas, rhododendrons and magnolias are well established and repay a spring visit. A small sculpture garden will mark the millennium.

Foxbrush 23

Aber Pwll, Port Dinorwic, Gwynedd LL56 4JZ. Tel: (01248) 670463

Mr and Mrs B.S. Osborne • 3m SW of Bangor on B4507 (old Caernarfon road) N of A487. Avoiding new bypass, enter village. House on left after high estate wall, opposite layby. Signed 'Felinheli' • Open12th, 26th April, 10th, 24th May, 7th, 28th June for NGS, 2 – 5pm, and by appt • Entrance: £1, children free • Other information: Cottage museum ● 🍵 🗒 WC ♿ ⬤ ⌖

A private three-acre plantswoman's garden, created single-handedly from a wilderness on the site of a sixteenth-century mill. Narrow paths meander through romantic plantings of rare treasures and sudden surprises, crossing bridges and camomile lawns, under tunnels of laburnum and a 14-metre rose and clematis pergola, past herbaceous borders, croquet lawn, river and ponds. Although essentially a spring garden (despite ferocious flooding), it is much admired throughout the summer, too. *Crug Farm Nursery*, Caernarfon, is nearby.

Glansevern Hall Gardens 24

Berriew, Welshpool, Powys SY21 8AH. Tel: (01686) 640200

Mr and Mrs R.N. Thomas • From Welshpool take A483 S. After 5m entrance on left by bridge over River Rhiew • Open May to Sept, Fri, Sat and Bank Holiday Mons, all 12 noon – 6pm • Entrance: £2, OAPs £1.50, children free ◑ 🍵 🗒 WC ♿ ⌖ 🏛

The large mature garden (it exceeds 18 acres) is set in a wider parkland on the banks of the River Severn, and is noted for its range of unusual tree species. A four-acre lake has islands where swans, ducks and other waterfowl breed. The streams, which form a water garden and feed the lake, are planted along the banks with moisture-loving plants and shrubs. A large area of lawn contains mature trees and herbaceous borders. Other notable features are the fountain with its surround and walk planted with wisteria, the restored rockery and grotto, the walled garden and the rose gardens.

Heathfield Lodge ★   25

Wiston, Haverfordwest, Pembrokeshire SA62 4PT. Tel: (01437) 731200

Wynford and Evelyn Evans • 5m NE of Haverfordwest off A40 Fishguard road. Turn right through Crundale signed 'Wiston'. In village, take Crundale road, house is on left • Open 30th May to 30th Aug, Sun and Mon, 1 – 6pm • Entrance: £1.50, children free • Other information: Coaches by appt ● WC ℗

The gardens were started about 1975 on a fold in farm land containing natural springs. The owner is a tree enthusiast, exemplified by a magnificent cedar just 20 years from planting. Mrs Evans is interested mainly in herbaceous and moisture-loving plants, as the large areas of gunneras and the borders around the house bear witness. An unusual and interesting garden still being developed but most restful and relaxing, with wide-reaching views.

Hilton Court ★   26

Roch, Haverfordwest, Pembrokeshire SA62 6AE. Tel: (01437) 710262

Mr and Mrs Peter Lynch • 6m NW of Haverfordwest off A487 St Davids road. About ¾ m beyond Simpson Cross signed on left • Open all year except Jan: Feb, daily, 10.30am – 3.30pm; March to Aug, daily, 9.30am – 6pm; Sept, daily, 10.30am – 5pm; Oct, daily, 10.30am – 3.30pm; Nov and Dec, weekends only • Entrance: £1 or donation to charity ◐ ▆ ✕ WC ℗ ⛪

The garden has been developed by the owners in the last eight years within the framework of the nine-acre grounds of an old estate, the house dating from 1735. Several lakes have been formed and the main water areas can be viewed from the decking area adjacent to the teashop. There is a two-hundred-year-old woodland walk. The garden is associated with a delightful garden centre arranged in a novel way so that plants are located near others that require similar conditions. Stone outbuildings house craft workshops. The drive to the gardens has views over the cliffs and shoreline of St Bride's Bay. The coast is subject to the gales off the Irish Sea and so a feature of the nursery is a selection of plants that can withstand both wind and salt spray. Aquatic plants are also a speciality.

Llanerchaeron   27

Aberaeron, Ceredigion SA48 8DG. Tel: Property Office (01545) 570200

The National Trust • 16m SW of Aberystwyth, 1½ m E of Aberaeron off A482 • Open April to Oct, Thurs – Sun and Bank Holiday Mons, 11am – 5pm. Guided tours Thurs, 2pm at extra charge (90p). Parkland open all year, dawn – dusk • Entrance: £2, children £1. Pre-booked parties £1.60 per person, children 80p • Other information: Dogs in parkland only, on lead ◐ ▩ WC ♿ ⚲

The Trust acquired this rare survivor of an intact Welsh gentry estate in 1994. The main house is open occasionally to see the ongoing restoration. The home farm gardens and grounds are open while restoration is in progress.

Maenan Hall 28

Llanrwst, Gwynedd LL26 0UL. Tel: (01492) 640441

The Hon. Mr and Mrs Christopher McLaren • 2m N of Llanrwst on E side of A470, ¼ m S of Maenan Abbey Hotel • Open one Sunday in May, Aug for charity, 10.30am – 5.30pm (last admission 4.30pm) • Entrance: £2, children £1 ● **WC** ◁▷ ℘

Created in 1956 by the late Christabel, Lady Aberconway, formal gardens surround the Elizabethan and Queen Anne house. Beyond are less formal gardens in mature woodland. The present owners have extended the planting of ornamental trees and shrubs in both formal and informal settings. Azaleas, rhododendrons and camellias, the latter situated in a dell at the base of a cliff, make a spring visit rewarding, while a large number of eucryphias are spectacular in late summer. A garden with many distinctive aspects, including a fine collection of roses.

Middleton Hall

(see NATIONAL BOTANIC GARDEN OF WALES)

Museum of Welsh Life and St Fagans Castle Gardens ★ 29

St Fagans, Cardiff, South Glamorgan CF5 6XB. Tel: (029) 2057 3500; Fax: (029) 2057 3490

National Museum of Wales • Near M4 junction 33. Signposted • Open all year, daily, 10am – 5/6pm • Entrance: 21st April to Oct £5.50, OAPs £3.90, children £3.20; Nov to 20th April 2001 £4.50, OAPs and children £2.65 • Other information: Dogs in grounds only, on lead ○ ● ✗ ⊟ **WC** ⅃ ⌷ ℗

An historic garden with terraces, herb and knot gardens, a hornbeam tunnel, an old grove of mulberry trees and a vinery. The Rosery of 1900 is being restored with the original varieties. Mature trees, both coniferous and broad-leaved, are an impresssive feature, as are the broad high terraces with massive stone walls hosting many climbing plants. Beneath are large fish ponds in which are carp, bream and tench farmed over the years for food for the household. In the grounds rhododendrons are underplanted with spring bulbs. The range of glasshouses is in poor condition, though the standard inside the greenhouses (as in the pleasure grounds) is high. Gardens attached to re-erected buildings from all over Wales are being developed accurately to re-create the differences in social status and period.

National Botanic Garden of Wales 30

Middleton Hall, Llanarthne, Carmarthenshire SA32 8HG. Tel: (01558) 668768; Fax: (01558) 668933

Trustees, NBGW • 8m E of Carmarthen, 7m W of Llandeilo on A48 • Due to open to the public at Easter 2000 but open now for parties (guided tours) by appt • Entrance: £3.50, concessions £3, children £1.50 ● ● **WC** ℗

This is a grand £43m project, half the money provided by the Millennium Commission's Lottery grant, and will be the first 'national' botanic garden this millennium. Though work still continues, particularly on the giant glasshouse by Foster, the garden is now 'open'. It is set in the eighteenth-century parkland of a 600-acre estate on the edge of the beautiful Towy valley with fine views. Its main path passes by a lake which will have small houses on stilts from which children will be able to study the life of the water. From here the broadwalk takes over; the right-hand side has rock outcrops of different geological ages from many areas of Wales. The left-hand side will be the largest herbaceous border in the world. So far 17,000 plants have been put in place, with a further 17,000 in holding bays, waiting for the weather. Two state-of-the-art greenhouses are already in use, and next to them the biomass boiler is under construction. Visitors should be aware that the area is a construction site and that hard hats (available on site) and suitable footwear must be worn.

Pant–yr–Holiad ★ 31

Rhydlewis, Llandysul, Ceredigion SA44 5ST. Tel: (01239) 851493

Mr and Mrs G. Taylor • 12m NE of Cardigan. Take A487 coast road to Brynhoffnant, then B4334 towards Rhydlewis for 1m, turn left and garden is second left • Open two Suns in spring for NGS, and at other times for pre-booked parties by appt • Entrance: £2, children £1 ● ● WC ●

This five-acre woodland garden, created by the owners since 1971, was started in an area of natural woodland backing onto the farmhouse. Since then hundreds of rhododendrons (species and hybrids) have been planted along the banks. Acers, eucalyptus, eucryphias and many other rare and unusual trees have now reached maturity, and the paths wander in and around to give something to please the eye wherever the visitor may care to look. A stream runs through the middle of the garden, creating a boggy area which is home for iris and primulas, numerous species of ferns and a *Rhododendron macabeanum*. A fairly recent addition is a summer walk, along which slate-edged beds are filled with herbaceous plants, including a collection of penstemons. A small pergola has a seat, surrounded by roses, from which the lovely view over the valley may be enjoyed, and the remainder of the walk is beneath arches of climbing roses. Nearer the house is a walled garden, alpine beds, a series of pools for ornamental waterfowl and a *potager*-style kitchen garden. Not far away, within a mile or two of the coast at Llangrannog, is *Pigeonsford Walled Garden*, a development about half-a-mile's walk from the nursery of the same name. It is open at Easter then May to Sept, Wed – Sun and Bank Holiday Mons, 10am – 6pm. Those interested in seeing an old garden reclaimed will want to watch progress (Tel: (01239) 654360).

Pencarreg ★ 32

Glyn Garth, Menai Bridge, Gwynedd LL59 5NS. Tel: (01248) 713545

Miss G. Jones • 1½ m NE of A545 Menai Bridge towards Beaumaris, Glan y Menai drive is turning on right, Pencarreg 100 metres on right • Open all year by appt • Entrance: charity box • Other information: Parking in layby on main road, limited parking in courtyard for small cars and disabled ● ● WC ● ●

This beautiful garden, with a wealth of species planted for all-year interest, has colour achieved by the use of common and unusual shrubs. A small stream creates another delightful and sympathetically exploited feature. The garden ends at the cliff edge and this, too, has been skilfully planted. The views are remarkable.

Penlan–Uchaf Farm Gardens 33

Gwaun Valley, Fishguard, Pembrokeshire SA65 9UA. Tel: (01348) 881388

Mr and Mrs Vaughan • 7m SE of Fishguard. Take B4313 Narberth road and after 4m turn left signed 'Cwm Gwaun/Gwaun Valley (Pontvane)'. Next to Sychpant Forest car park • Open April to early Nov (weather permitting), daily, 9am – dusk • Entrance: £2, children 50p, disabled persons and children under 3 free • Other information: Cars carrying wheelchairs may set down at main garden. Up to 25-seater coaches and minibuses permitted ◑ 🍽 🏠 WC ♿ ⟨⟩ 🐕 ♍

A medium-sized garden on a hillside near the top of the Gwaun Valley. The drive is very steep, but the view from the tea room is worth the effort. This is a young garden but the owners, realising that its position will make many trees and shrubs an impossibility, have chosen alpines and herbaceous borders and planted a 27-metre pergola with sweet peas. There are some 30,000 spring bulbs, and fuchsias, geraniums and annuals give plenty of colour later. A raised herb garden, suitable for wheelchair visitors and the blind, contains more than 100 different herbs and wild flowers. Extra-sensory area.

Penpergwm Lodge 34

Abergavenny, Monmouthshire NP7 9AS. Tel: (01873) 840208

Mrs C. Boyle • 2½ m SE of Abergavenny off B4598 Usk road. Turn left opposite King of Prussia Inn. Entrance 300 metres on left • Open April to Sept, Thurs – Sun, 2 – 6pm • Entrance: £2 (1999 price) • Other information: Teas on Sats and Suns only ◑ WC ♿ ⟨⟩ 🐕 ♍

This spacious three-acre garden forms the centrepiece for an established and successful school of gardening. Broad south-facing terraces command views over wide expanses of lawn well screened with mature trees and shrubs. A newly constructed vine pergola makes a bold statement and provides a visual link with the house, a recently planted formal garden of yew and box makes a delightful and effective enclosure. Elsewhere old-fashioned roses, herbaceous perennials and an imaginative vegetable garden contribute interest throughout the season. The nursery, Penpergwm Plants, sells unusual and interesting plants.

Penrhyn Castle ★ 35

Bangor, Gwynedd LL57 4HN. Tel: (01248) 353084; Fax: (01248) 371281

The National Trust • 1m E of Bangor on A5122 • Castle open 12 noon – 5pm (July to Aug opens 11am) (last audio tour 4pm, last admission 4.30pm) • Garden open 22nd March to 5th Nov, daily except Tues, 11am – 5.30pm (July and Aug opens 10am) • Entrance: £3.50, children £2 (castle and garden £5,

children £2.50, family ticket £12.50, parties £4 per person) • Other information:
Golf buggy available for pre-booking. Dogs in grounds only, on lead ◑ ▆ WC
& ⬥ ℘ 👍 ⌕

The large garden covers 48 acres with some fine specimen trees, shrubs and a Victorian walled garden in terraces with pools, lawns and a wild garden. Although the original house was eighteenth century, the gardens are very much early Victorian, dating from the building of the present castle by Thomas Hopper. A giant tree fern, which will dwarf any children who visit, has been sent from Tasmania to take its place in a specialist collection that also includes another giant, gunnera, and the Australian bottle brush plant. These can be found in the spectacular bog garden beyond the walled garden.

Picton Castle ★ 36

Haverfordwest, Pembrokeshire SA62 4AS. Tel: (01437) 751326

Picton Castle Trust • 4m SE of Haverfordwest off A40. Signposted • Castle open for conducted tours April to Sept. Telephone for details • Garden open April to Oct, daily except Mon (but open Bank Holiday Mons), 10.30am – 5pm • Entrance: gardens and gallery £2.75, OAPs £2.50, children £1 (castle, gardens and gallery £4, OAPs £3.50, children £1) (1999 prices) • Other information: Gallery ◑ ▆ ✕ 🗎 WC & ⬥ ℘ 👍 ⌕

The Picton grounds extend over nearly 40 acres, with woodland walks among massive oaks and giant redwoods. Rarities include the biggest *Rhododendron* 'Old Port' in existence and a metasequoia, a deciduous conifer presumed extinct but rediscovered in China in 1941. In June all these wondrously exotic shrubs reach their full splendour. In the walled garden are herb borders and summer-flowering plants, with a central pond and fountain giving a cool and calming atmosphere.

Plantasia 37

Swansea, West Glamorgan.

Swansea City Council • Signed from city centre • Open all year, daily except Mon (but open Bank Holiday Mons), 10am – 5pm • Entrance: £1.20 plus concessions (1999 prices) ◯ WC & ℘ 👍

A hothouse of over 1600 square metres divided into three zones – arid, tropical and humid – it contains over 5000 plants on permanent display from cacti to orchids.

Plas Brondanw Gardens ★ 38

Llanfrothen, Penrhyndeudraeth, Gwynedd LL48 6SW. Tel: (01766) 770484

5m NE of Porthmadog between Llanfrothen and Croesor • Open all year, daily, 9am – 5pm • Entrance: £1.50, children 25p ◯

This garden, in the grounds of the house given to Sir Clough Williams-Ellis by his father, is quite separate from the village of Portmeirion (see entry), and was created by the architect over a period of 70 years. His main objective was to provide a series of dramatic and romantic prospects inspired by the great gardens of Italy; it includes architectural features, such as the orangery. Visitors should walk up the avenue that leads past a dramatic chasm to the folly, from which there is a fine view of Snowdon — indeed mountains are visible from the end of every vista. Williams-Ellis made a prodigious investment in hedging and topiary (mostly yew) and the present-day head gardener has calculated that the former, if laid flat, would cover four acres. Hydrangeas and ferns flourish in the damp climate. The present custodian, the architect's grand-daughter, is trying to enhance the strong formal structure by flower planting.

Plas Newydd ★ 39

Llanfairpwll, Anglesey LL61 6DQ. Tel: (01248) 714795

The National Trust/The Marquess of Anglesey • 4m SW of Menai Bridge, 2m S of Llanfairpwll via A5 • House with military museum open, 12 noon – 5pm • Garden open April to 1st Nov, daily except Thurs and Fri, 11am – 5.30pm (last admission 5pm). Rhododendron garden open April to early June only. Guided tours by arrangement • Entrance: £2.50, children £1.25 (house and gardens £4.50, children £2.25, family £11, pre-booked parties of 15 or more £3.90 per person) • Other information: Parking ¼ m from garden ◑ ⬛ ✕ ▤ WC & ⚲ 👍 ♀

The eighteenth-century house by James Wyatt is also an attraction, mainly because it contains Rex Whistler's largest painting. Humphry Repton's suggestion of 'plantations... to soften a bleak country and shelter the ground from violent winds' has resulted in an informal open-plan garden, with shrub plantings in the lawns and parkland, which slopes down to the Menai Straits and frames the view of the Snowdonia peaks. There is a formal Italian-style garden to the front of the house. A new arbour has replaced a conservatory on the top terrace with a tufa mound, from which water falls to a pool on the bottom terrace. The pool has a new Italianate fountain to add to the overall Mediterranean effect of this formal area within the parkland. The influence of the Gulf Stream enables the successful cultivation of many frost-tender shrubs, and a special rhododendron garden is open in the spring when the gardens are at their best, although they are expertly tended throughout the year. Major restoration of the Italianate terrace garden continues and includes the building of a deep grotto and the replanting of the mixed borders. The marine and woodland paths along the Menai Straits have also been restored. Summer brings displays of hydrangeas, while autumn colour appears in the ever-changing arboretum of southern-hemisphere trees and shrubs, and wild flowers in season.

Plas Penhelig ★ 40

Aberdovey, Gwynedd LL35 0NA. Tel: (01654) 767577; Fax: (01654) 767783

Mr Richardson • 11m SW of Machynlleth on A43. At Aberdovey, between two railway bridges • Open mid-March to Oct, Wed – Sun, 2.30 – 5.30pm • Entrance: £2.50, children £1 ◑ ⬛ ✕ WC ⬦

A traditional Edwardian estate garden of seven acres, reclaimed over the past 10 years, includes an informal garden with lawns, terraces, pools, fountains, an orchard, a rock garden and herbaceous borders. Spring bulbs, azaleas, rhododendrons, magnolias, euphorbias, roses and some mature tree heathers of immense size command admiration. The jewel is the half-acre formal walled garden, including over 80 square metres of glass with vines and peaches. The house is now a hotel. Some 3m E of Aberdovey is *Panteidal Garden Nursery* (Tel: 01654 767322), a 150-acre landscape nursery and garden which has a favoured microclimate in the sheltered estuary and so specialises in sub-tropical or Mediterranean-type plants. Scrubland area and cottage garden. Open 2 days for NGS and otherwise by appt. Organic shop, also organic restaurant open daily, 9am – 5.30pm.

Plas–yn–Rhiw 41

Pwllheli, Gwynedd LL53 8AB. Tel: (01758) 780219

The National Trust • Near tip of Lleyn Peninsular. 12m SW of Pwllheli off B4413 on S coast road to Aberdaron. Signposted • House open (numbers limited) • Garden and snowdrop wood open some weekends Jan and Feb (telephone to check). Garden open 30th March to 15th May, Thurs – Mon; 17th May to 29th Sept, daily except Tues; all 12 noon – 5pm (last admission 4.30pm) • Entrance: Garden only £2, children £1; garden and snowdrop wood £2.50; house and garden £3.20, children £1.60, family ticket £8. Pre-booked parties in evening £1.40 extra per person • Other information: Parking 80 metres from garden. No coaches ◐ 🏠 WC ⌘ 👍 ⊕

This is essentially a cottage garden, laid out around a partly medieval manor house on the west shore of Hell's Mouth Bay. Flowering trees and shrubs, rhododendrons, camellias and magnolias are divided by formal box hedges and grass paths extending to three quarters of an acre. A snowdrop wood stands on high ground above the garden.

Portmeirion ★ 42

Penrhyndeudraeth, Gwynedd LL48 6ET. Tel: (01766) 770228 (Hotel Reception)

2m SE of Porthmadog near A487 • Open all year, daily except 25th Dec, 9.30am – 5.30pm • Entrance: £4.50, OAPs £3.60, children £2/25, under 5 free, family (2 adults and 2 children) £12, season ticket £35 • Other information: Parking at top of village. Difficult for wheelchairs as steep in places ○ 🍽 ✕ 🏠 WC ⌘ 👍

Architect Sir Clough Williams-Ellis's wild essay into the picturesque is a triumph of eclecticism, with Gothick, Renaissance and Victorian buildings arranged as an Italianate village around a harbour and set in 70 acres of sub-tropical woodlands crisscrossed by paths. This 'light opera' is played out against the backdrop of the Cambrian mountains and the vast empty sweep of estuary sands. The gentle humour of the architecture extends to the plantings in both horizontal and vertical planes – in the formal gardens and in the wild luxuriance which clings to the rocky crags. Portmeirion provides one of

Britain's most stimulating objects for an excursion, and during the period of the June festival in nearby Criccieth there are other good gardens open in the district. Write for details (with SAE) to Criccieth Festival Office, PO Box 3, 52 High Street, Criccieth LL52 0BW.

Post House Gardens ★ 43

Cwmbach, Whitland, Carmarthenshire SA34 0DR. Tel: (01994) 484213

Mrs Jo Kenaghan • 10m NW of Carmarthen off A40. Take B4298 through Meidrim. Take centre lane signed Llanboidy, turn right at crossroads signed Blaenwaun, then right at next crossroads to Cwmbach • Open May only by appt • Entrance: £2 ● 🖺 WC

Some five acres of woodland valley garden, begun in 1978, wind along the bank of the River Sien. on paths leading through shrubberies to a large pool, then across a river bridge and back by stepping stones to a bog garden. A sloping path leads to higher levels then meanders between shrubberies housing many species and hybrid rhododendrons, and on through a rose garden planted with old roses. There is also an easier path at mid-garden level which gives a good view of the shrubberies. Above the pond a summerhouse provides seating from which to admire *Rosa* 'Paul's Himalayan Musk', now rampant through and over adjacent trees; several other seats give views of different areas. Near the entrance to the garden a glasshouse (built over an old mill) and a conservatory extend the range of well-known and unusual plants, which together with the wild flowers and wooded background make up this interesting garden. Many of the rhododendrons, other shrubs and trees are grown from seed and it is often possible to buy 'extras' from the owner.

Powis Castle ★★ 44

Welshpool, Powys SY21 8RF. Tel: (01938) 554338

The National Trust • 1m S of Welshpool on A483. Signposted • Castle open as garden, 1 – 5pm • Garden open April to June, daily except Mon and Tues (but open Bank Holiday Mons); July and Aug, daily except Mon (but open Bank Holiday Mon); Sept to Oct, daily except Mon and Tues; all 11am – 6pm (last admission 5.30pm). 'Meet the gardener' tours by special arrangement • Entrance: £5, children (5-17) £2.50, under 5 free, family ticket (2 adults and 2 children) £12.50, parties £4 per person (castle, garden and museum £7.50, children (5-17) £3.75, under 5 free, family £18.75, parties £6.50 per person) • Other information: Braille guide available ◐ 🖵 🖺 WC 🌿 👜 ⓦ

The garden was originally laid out in 1720 based on earlier designs, possibly by William Winde, and the early formal design of the courtyard round the statue of Fame has been re-instated. The most notable features are the broad hanging terraces, interestingly planted and with huge clipped yews. The terraces are said to be based on those at St Germain-en-Laye near Paris, where the Catholic Marquis of Paris and his family joined James II in exile. On the second terrace, above the orangery, are fine lead urns and newly restored figures by van Nost's workshop in front of deeply recessed brick alcoves. Some fruit trees remain on the terraces, where in the nineteenth century advantage was taken of the micro-climate to grow fruit and vegetables until a kitchen garden was established; the latter is now a flower garden. Unusual and tender plants and climbers prosper in the shelter of walls and hedges. This garden is not for the faint-hearted because it is very steep, but it is well worth the effort to relish the views which are as fine as any, anywhere. There is also a good collection of old roses. The excellent guide book includes lists of plants. There has been a change of gardener here, but it is hoped that the high standard will be maintained.

Singleton Botanic Gardens ★ 45

Singleton Park, Swansea, West Glamorgan SA2 8QD. Tel: (01792) 302420

Swansea City Council • In Swansea. Entrance in Gower Road • Open all year, daily: summer, 9am – 6pm, winter, 9am – 4.30pm • Entrance: free • Other information: Refreshments during Aug only ○ **WC** ♿

A four-and-a-half-acre garden with herbaceous borders, rockeries, rose beds and an interesting collection of trees and shrubs, including tapestry hedges using a variety of different shrubs. Newly erected temperate and tropical glasshouses contain an extensive range of rare and unusual plants, including orchids, bromeliads and epiphytes.

Stammers Gardens ★ 46

Stammers Road, Saundersfoot, Pembrokeshire SA69 9HH. Tel: (01834) 813766

Mr and Mrs B. Sly • 2m N of Tenby off A478. In Saundersfoot, turn right immediately after Post Office into Stammers Road. Garden is 200 metres on right • Open 4th April to Oct, daily except Sat, 10.30am – 5pm • Entrance: £2, OAPs £1.50, accompanied children free ◑ ☕ **WC** ⚓ ✿

A pleasant surprise nestling in the heart of a typical Welsh seaside resort. Now extending to some seven acres, the gardens were first established in the late 1970s, so they have an air of maturity and are now being carefully restored, extended and replanted by the present owners. The shrubberies, ponds, stream, woodland and arboretum will be added to with a new bog garden. Refreshments can be taken while gazing out over Carmarthen Bay.

Tredegar House 47

Newport, Gwent NP10 8YW. Tel: (01633) 815880

Newport County Borough Council • 3m S of Newport. Signed from A48 and M4 junction 28 • Open 21st April to Sept, Wed – Sun, 11.30am – 5pm • Entrance: free; audio tour of gardens £2 (house and garden £3.95, concessions £3, children £2, family £10.50) • Other information: Dogs in park only, on lead ◑ ☕ ✕ 🖻 <u>WC</u> ♿ ⚓ 🏛 ♨

One of the finest Restoration houses in the country which, as restored, has a remarkable interior with pictures from Dulwich and furniture from the V&A. The reason for it being in this *Guide* is that researchers in the Orangery Garden discovered physical evidence of a unique piece of archaeology: a late-seven-teenth-century mineral parterre, using coal and brick dust, coloured sands and sea shells. It is the first to be re-created in this country and well worth seeing.

Tretower Court 48

Tretower, Crickhowell, Powys NP8 1RF. Tel: (01874) 730279

Cadw: Welsh Historic Monuments • 3m NW of Crickhowell off A479. Signed from Tretower village • Open March to Oct, daily, 10am – 6pm (4pm or 5pm depending on season). Closed Nov to March • Entrance: £2.20, OAPs and students £1.70, family £6.10 ◑ WC ♀

This late medieval house is set in the beautiful Usk valley. An earlier castle is located across an open meadow to the rear. Stretching south from the Court is a charming re-creation of a mid-fifteenth-century pleasure garden. Planted in 1991, it is maturing well and its design is faithful to the late medieval period. In previous years entertaining talks on medieval gardens have taken place from June to early August on Fridays at 2.15pm, and hopefully these continue.

Upton Castle 49

Cosheston, Pembroke Dock, Pembrokeshire SA72 4SE. Tel: (01646) 651782

Canon and Mrs H.J.N. Skelton • 2m NE of Pembroke off A477. In Cosheston turn right. Castle signed on left • Open April to Oct, daily except Sat, 10am – 5pm but check before travelling • Entrance: £1.20, children 60p, family £3 (1999 prices). Season tickets available • Other information: Approach roads very narrow. No coaches ◑ 📷 WC ⇔

The grounds of the part thirteenth-century castle were planted as a garden in the 1930s with a large collection of rhododendrons and camellia species and hybrids of the period. These have grown into large mature specimens to which the Pembrokeshire Coast National Park, which has a management agreement with the owners, has added new cultivars. Large specimens of redwood, drimys and chestnut-leaved oak, embothriums and a particularly magnificent *Magnolia campbellii*, planted in 1936, are among the 250 or more kinds of trees and shrubs growing in the grounds. A walk through the woods leads down to the Carew River. The old walled garden is now mostly grass, with fruit and vegetables and two greenhouses. There are also formal terraces with herbac-eous borders and rose beds, and a medieval chapel.

Veddw House 50

Devauden, Monmouthshire NP16 6PH. Tel: (01291) 650836

Anne Wareham and Charles Hawes • 5m NW of Chepstow off B4293. In Devauden, signed from pub on green • Open 2nd April to 1st Oct, Suns and Bank Holiday Mons, 2 – 5pm and for parties afternoon or evening by appt • Entrance: £2, children £1 ◑ 📷 WC ♨

Situated on a sheltered slope near the Wye Valley, framed by old beech woods and with views in all directions, this garden is the product of over a decade of enthusiastic labour by the owners. Some of it is still work-in-progress and no less interesting for that. There are in total two acres of flower garden and meadow and two acres of woodland. The generously planted borders include many unusual varieties. Around every corner is something of interest – a magnolia walk, a cotoneaster walk with rampant rambler roses growing through it, a philadelphus border. The formal vegetable garden and fruit cage are enclosed by borders of old scented roses and 40 varieties of clematis on trellis and arches. From here an arch leads into the orchard and the meadow, full of bulbs in spring and grasses and wild flowers in summer. Behind the house the ground slopes steeply upwards, with paths and steps leading to viewpoints. A formal garden is being created here, with yew hedges enclosing various rooms, in one of which a water feature is planned. Further up still is a hazel coppice and the wood with its superb old beech trees, sorbus and hornbeam. A detailed guide and plant list are available.

Winllan   51

Talsarn, Lampeter, Ceredigion SA48 8QE. Tel: (01570) 470612

Mr and Mrs Ian Callan • 16m S of Aberystwyth, 8m N of Lampeter on B4342 • Open for NGS May and June, daily, 2 – 6pm, and July and Aug by appt only • Entrance: £1.50, children 50p, under 12 free • Other information: Coaches by appt only ● 🖼

The six-acre garden has been created by the owners mainly as a haven for the wildlife which is disappearing so rapidly countrywide. After 20 years, the garden is home to over 200 species of wild flowers, including seven of wild orchid, and more appear all the time; these in turn attract the butterflies which thrive on the rich flora of the meadow. Similarly, dragonflies in their season enliven the pond. A small area was planted up as a woodland with some 35 species of mainly native trees in 1982; again this has its attendant wild flowers and birds. Beyond the wood is a hay meadow, and along the length of the garden the river creates another habitat. Although there is a small area of conventional garden the emphasis is on native wild plants. Visitors receive personal attention from the owners.

Wyndcliffe Court   52

St Arvans, Chepstow, Monmouthshire NP16 6EY. Tel: (01291) 622352

Mr and Mrs H.A.P. Clay • Off Wye Valley road from Chepstow • Open last Sun in May for NGS and by appt for private parties • Entrance: £2 • Other information: Garden only accessible for wheelchairs on terrace [NEW] ● 💭 🖼 WC ♿

A garden conceived in the Arts and Crafts tradition and largely unchanged since its creation in 1922. From a broad paved terrace, two flights of steps descend to the topiary terrace with its semi-circular pool; the topiary, drums of yew, are matched by ten rectangular beds of annuals. The next level is a bowling green (with clock golf, too). Beyond the charming summerhouse is a sunken garden with a long rectangular pool. Long herbaceous borders lead to the walled vegetable garden, almost an acre in size, much of it devoted to flowers and shrubs. There are several fine specimen trees and old fruit trees. David Wheeler says, 'Wyndcliffe remains secure in a romantic time warp, swathed in roses and old-world fragrance, the essence of the life of a country garden.'

Ynyshir Hall 53

Eglwysfach, Machynlleth, Powys SY20 8TA. Tel: (01654) 781209

Mr and Mrs R. Reen • 13m NE of Aberystwyth off A487 Machynlleth road. Signed in Eglwysfach • Open May, daily • Entrance: £1 (1999 price) • Other information: Refreshments and toilet facilities in hotel ○ ⬦

Although the house was once owned by Queen Victoria, the 12 acres of gardens were not really developed and extensively planted until in the hands of William Mappin, who owned the Hall from 1930-70. During this time many unusual trees were planted and the grounds landscaped. Water played an important part in the garden, and the present owners have discovered pools and a water course which are being cleared and replanted. The trees, now nearing maturity, are fine specimens which create a noble background for a variety of rhododendrons, azaleas, camellias and other shrubs. When the garden was open all year, early visitors were able to see massed plantings of daffodils and fritillaries, moving on to magnolias and other later-flowering shrubs, finishing the season with autumn colour from the maples. There is a famous 'Ironstone tree' dating from the period when Queen Victoria used to visit the Hall. The 500 acres of woodland round the house were given to the RSPB by Mappin. The Hall itself is now a hotel.

WELSH HISTORIC GARDENS TRUST
Formed in 1989, the Trust has since created a network throughout Wales. The membership has topped 600 and apart from national projects involving the Trust office, the branches undertake projects locally. Its national aims are to initiate and assist in the conservation of gardens, parks and designed landscapes that are of historic, cultural and aesthetic importance in the Welsh heritage, and to raise public awareness. The address to contact is: Plas Tyllwyd, Tanygoes, Cardigan SA43 2JD.

CHANNEL ISLANDS

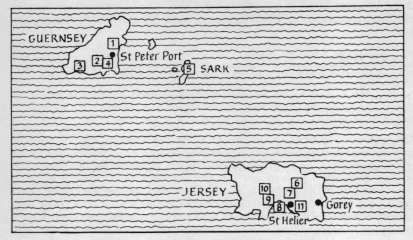

GUERNSEY AND SARK

Candie Gardens   1

Candie Road, St Peter Port, Guernsey GY1 1UG. Tel: (01481) 46263

*States of Guernsey • In St Peter Port, off Candie Road • Open all year, daily,
8am – sunset (5pm in winter) • Entrance: free • Other information: Teas, toilet
facilities, inc. disabled, shop and events in Guernsey Museum and Art Gallery*
○ 🍴 📷 WC ♿ ⬦ 👍 ⚘

Situated on a slope overlooking the harbour at St Peter Port, there are
wonderful views over the islands of Herm and Sark from these gardens.
Created over 100 years ago, they contain statues of Queen Victoria and Victor
Hugo. The lower gardens used to be the walled fruit and vegetable garden of
Candie House (now the Priaulx Library) but have since been laid out as a public
garden with palms and a maidenhair tree. Walls give shelter to *Fremontodendron
californicum*, mallows and a lemon tree. In fact a surprising variety of plants
normally grown indoors flourishes here. The first greenhouse on Guernsey is
said to have been constructed in the gardens in 1792 by Peter Mourant and two
of these greenhouses can still be seen, with thick timbers and narrow panes.
The Guernsey Museum and Art Gallery, built around an original Victorian
bandstand, and the Priaulx Reference and Genealogical Library are here.

The Hermitage   2

**Les Maindonnaux, St Martin GY4 6AH. Tel: (01481) 35256 or
Guernsey Tourist Information (01481) 723552**

*Mr and Mrs J. Webb • 1½ m S of St Peter Port • Open one or two days a year
and for private parties by appt • Entrance: £2* ◕ WC ♿

Dating from the 1750s, the house is surrounded by about three acres of landscaped gardens, dominated by a very tall Monterey cypress some 200 years old. From this vantage point visitors can view a small lake surrounded by giant gunneras, ligularias and other moisture-loving plants, fed by freshwater springs to the obvious enjoyment of the resident ducks and moorhens. Nearby azaleas, rhododendrons, camellias and fuchsias grow in abundance in a woodland setting. A walled garden offers shelter to fine specimens of *Cestrum elegans*, *Clethra arborea*, *Clianthus puniceus*, *Crinodendron hookerianum*, giant echiums and many other unusual shrubs and perennials.

Mille Fleurs 3

Rue du Bordage, St Pierre du Bois GY7 9DW. Tel: (01481) 263911 or Guernsey Tourist Information (01481) 723552

Mr and Mrs D. Russell • 6m SW of St Peter Port. 100 metres down lane from Rue de Quanteraine/Rue du Bordage junction • Open one or two days a year and for parties by appt • Entrance: £2 • Other information: Self-catering cottages available ◑

Natural country gardens of some three acres set in a peaceful, wooded conservation valley. The areas around the house and holiday cottages are a profusion of roses, clematis, penstemons and other herbaceous perennials, with sweetly scented honeysuckle and jasmine framing arches and doorways. Paths flanked by lilies, lavender and other fragrant plants meander down to the bottom of the valley, where more tender, sub-tropical plants, such as bananas, cannas and palms, flourish in the sheltered microclimate. A natural spring feeds into two ponds surrounded by mature tree ferns and giant gunneras amid huge stands of arum lilies. A large mature fig tree and a host of terracotta pots brimming with red pelargoniums and cordylines, together with banks of crocosmias, phormiums and euphorbias, lend a Mediterranean feel to the swimming-pool area.

Sausmarez Manor Exotic Woodland Garden 4

St Martins, Guernsey GY4 6SG. Tel: (01481) 35571

Mr Peter de Sausmarez • 1½ m S of St Peter Port, off Fort Road • Manor open mid-week in summer • Garden open all year, daily, 10.30am – 5.30pm or dusk if earlier. Guided tours for parties by appt • Entrance: £1.50, children 50p, disabled persons and babies free • Other information: Doll's house collection. Pitch and putt course ○ 🍽 WC ♿ 🚻 ♨

Set around two small lakes in an ancient wood is a garden which has been crammed with the unusual and rare to give an exotic feel. It is strewn with plants from many parts of the world, particularly the sub-tropics and the Mediterranean, which survive in Guernsey's mellow maritime climate. Collections of yuccas, ferns, camellias (over 300), bamboos, hebes, bananas, echiums, lilies, palm trees, fuchsias, as well as hydrangeas, hostas, azaleas, pittosporums, clematis, rhododendrons, cyclamens, impatiens, giant grasses etc., all jostle with indigenous wild flowers. No pesticides are used so wildlife flourishes and appears in season. The new sculpture trail includes works by members of the Royal Society of British Sculptors.

La Seigneurie 5

Sark GY9. Tel: (01481) 832345 (Sark Tourism)

Seigneur Mr J.M. Beaumont • ½ m NW of Creux Harbour, Sark • Open 17th April to 20th Oct, Mon – Fri, 10am – 5pm. Also Sat during July and Aug for charity • Entrance:£1, children 50p • Other information: Parking for bicycles ◑ 🚾 WC ♿

The grounds and walled garden of La Seigneurie, the residence of the Seigneurs of Sark, are beautifully maintained. Visit in spring and early summer for the camellias, azaleas and rhododendrons, later for roses, old-fashioned annuals, and in autumn for the glowing colours of dahlias and fuchsias. The walled garden contains clematis, geraniums, lapagerias, abutilons, osteospermums and many sub-tropical and tender plants. There is a *potager*, a wild pond area, a restored Victorian greenhouse with vines and bougainvilleas, a hedge maze for children, and a small outdoor museum with antique cannons. The Gothick *colombier* (the dovecot being the prerogative of the lord of the manor) may still be seen behind the house.

JERSEY

Domaine des Vaux 6

La Rue de Bas, St Lawrence JE3 1JG.

Mr and Mrs Marcus Binney • 2m N of St Helier • Open one Sun, 2 – 5pm for charity (check with Jersey Tourist Board (01534) 500700). Private parties by prior arrangement with owners in writing • Entrance: £3.50 ◐ 🍷

Marcus Binney, architectural correspondent of *The Times*, has a passion for the preservation of architecture and landscape, and these tastes are very much reflected in his and his wife Anne's delightful garden. It is in two completely contrasting parts. The top is a formal Italianate garden, set around and above a sunken rectangular lawn, and the borders here are a riot of unusual and familiar perennials and shrubs. This perfect formal garden was created by the previous generation, Sir George and Lady Binney, and designed by Walter Ison who created the strong architectural form. Lady Binney planted with an eye for colour in foliage as much as in flowers, as is evidenced by the grey and silver borders facing the yellow, gold and bronze ones. The Binneys have planted a small formal herb garden on a triangular theme and are creating a *jardinière* and a pair of long flower borders. The lower garden is a semi-wild and quite steep valley with a string of ponds connected by a stream. In spring the valley and wood are at their best, with a carpet of wild Jersey narcissi under camellias, azaleas and rhododendrons. A magnificent *Magnolia campbellii* has reached maturity and flowers abundantly in March. Of particular note are the camellias in both gardens and an interesting collection of conifers in a small arboretum. A newly created Mediterranean Garden stands at the top of the valley with a collection of planted pots which reflect the colours of the south of France and Italy.

Eric Young Orchid Foundation 7

Victoria Village, Trinity JE3 5HH. Tel: (01534) 861963

The Eric Young Charitable Trust • 1½ m N of St Helier • Open all year except 1st Jan, 25th, 26th Dec, Thurs – Sat, 10am – 4pm • Entrance: £2.50, OAPs £1.50, students and children £1 (1999 prices) • Other information: Light refreshments available from cold drinks machine. Plants for sale, when available ○ 🍵 📖 WC ♿

This exquisite collection, described as 'the finest private collection of orchids in Europe, possibly the world', was built up by the late Eric Young, who came to Jersey after World War II. In 1958 he merged his own collection with that of a Sanders nursery which was closing down, and continued to acquire new plants. The purpose-built centre, which has won many awards, consists of five growing houses and a landscaped display area where visitors may view these exotic flowers in close detail. From November to April there are cymbidiums, paphiopedilums, odontoglossums and calanthes, from May to June cattleyas, miltonias and odontoglossums and from June to October, phalaenopsis, miltonias and odontoglossums. (The beauty of these flowers is inversely proportional to the difficulties of their names.) Meanwhile, those wishing to see native orchids in season may find a walk in Les Blanches Banques, the sand dunes behind St Ouen's Bay, rewarding.

Howard Davis Park 8

St Saviour.

In St Helier, between St Clement's Road and Don Road • Open all year, daily: Oct to March, 8.30am – 4.30pm; April to May, 8am – 8pm; June to Sept, 8am – 10pm • Entrance: free (small charge for bandstand seats) ○ 🍵 📖 WC ♿ 🍴

Given by T.B. Davies, a great benefactor of the island, in memory of his son who was killed in World War I, this is the most famous of Jersey's public gardens. Colourful sub-tropical trees and plants flourish here, and the bandstand is the venue for an excellent variety of live entertainment from May to September. Other public parks in St Helier are Parade Gardens, off Parade Place, and Victoria Park, off St Aubins Road/Cheapside. Both contain interesting statues.

Jersey Lavender 9

Rue du Pont Marquet, St Brelade JE3 8DS. Tel: (01534) 742933

David and Elizabeth Christie • 3m W of St Helier near Pont Marquet Country Park • Open 22nd May to 23rd Sept, Mon – Sat, 10am – 5pm • Entrance: £2.50, children free ◑ 🍵 ✗ WC ♿ 🔁 🌿 🛍

This lavender farm was started in 1983 and now covers nine acres. Visitors are invited to walk around the main fields, planted with five varieties of lavender, to enjoy their different colours and scents. Harvesting is done by hand, starting in late June, and the distillation and perfume-bottling processes may also be seen. There is an extensive garden of herbs, including a National Collection of lavenders and a collection of 75 different species of bamboos.

Jersey Zoological Park   10

Les Augres Manor, Trinity JE3 5BP. Tel: (01534) 860000

Durell Wildlife Conservation Trust • 2½ m NW of St Helier • Open daily except 25th Dec, 9.30am – 6pm (or dusk in winter) • Entrance: £6, OAPs £5, children £3.50. Party rates available (1999 prices) ○ 🍵 ✕ 🏪 WC ♿ 🛒 ♀

Created by the author and naturalist, the late Gerald Durrell, as a sanctuary and breeding centre for endangered species, this is home to a unique collection of exotic creatures, some so rare that they may only be seen here. The 25 acres of beautiful parkland and water gardens provide a fine natural background with a rich abundance of fascinating flowers, shrubs and trees from around the world.

Samarès Manor   11

St Clement JE2 6QW. Tel: (01534) 870551; Fax: (01534) 768949

Vincent Obbard • 2m E of St Helier • Manor (guided tours daily except Sun, am. £1.80 extra) open • Garden open 22nd April to mid-Oct, daily, 10am – 5pm • Entrance: £3.70, OAPs £2.95, children £1.80, under 5 free (1999 prices) • Other information: Craft centre ◐ 🍵 ✕ 🏪 WC ♿ ☂ 🛒 ♀

The name Samarès is derived from the French for salt marsh, and indeed sea salt was once extracted from marshy land nearby. It is not known who built the existing manor house, which has passed through many owners, but the grounds have developed gradually. By 1680 they were famed for their trees. The present garden was the work of Sir James Knott, who bought the property in 1924 and had it developed, employing 40 gardeners, at a cost of £100,000. There are really two quite different gardens here: a herb garden, claimed to be one of the largest and most comprehensive in Britain, specialising in culinary and medicinal herbs in a partially walled garden leading to a lakeside area, and a Japanese garden. Of particular note are the camellias, the *Taxodium distichum* in the lake and the rocks imported from Cumberland. This is not just a garden but a whole way of life based on herbs and farm animals, with daily talks and demonstrations.

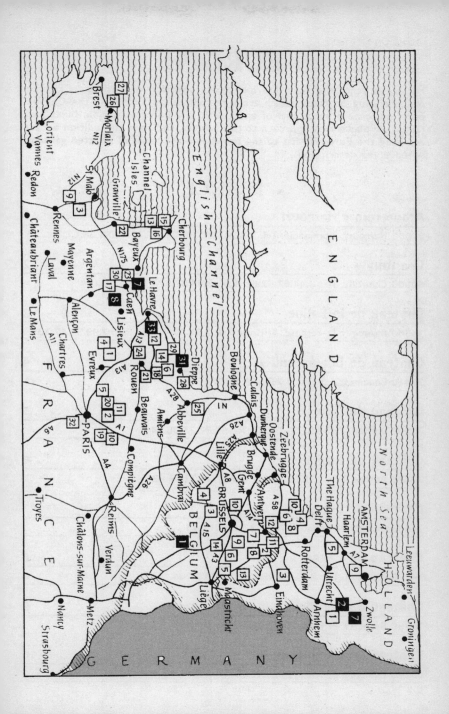

EUROPE

For some years the *Guide* has included a selection of gardens in Europe, concentrating on those which are a reasonable distance from the Channel ports or some other points of entry such as a Eurostar station. Next year (2001) we plan a new approach to this subject, and so in this edition we are reducing the European list to the names and addresses of selected gardens, without any description.

FRANCE

Arboretum d'Harcourt   1
27800 Harcourt, Normandie. Tel: 2.32.46.29.70; Fax: 2.32.46.53.38.

Chantilly ★   2
60500 Chantilly. Tel: 3.44.62.62.62; Fax: 3.44.62.62.61

Château de la Ballue   3
35560 Bazouges-la-Pérouse, Brittany. Tel: 2.99.97.47.86; Fax: 2.99.97.47.70

Château de Beaumesnil ★   4
27410 Beaumesnil. Tel/Fax: 2.32.44.40.09

Château de Bizy   5
27200 Vernon. Tel: 2.32.51.00.82; Fax: 2.32.21.66.54

Château de Bosmelet   6
76720 Auffay. Tel: 2.35.32.81.07; Fax: 2.35.32.84.62

Château de Brécy ★★   7
14480 St Gabriel-Brécy. Tel/Fax: 2.31.80.11.48

Château de Canon ★★   8
14270 Mézidon. Tel: 2.31.20.05.07/2.31.28.77.04

Château de Caradeuc   9
35190 Bécherel, Brittany. Tel: 2.99.66.77.76

Château de Compiègne ★   10
60200 Compiègne. Tel: 3.44.38.47.00; Fax: 3.44.38.47.01

Château de Corbeil-Cerf

11

60110 Corbeil-Cerf. Tel: 3.44.52.02.43

Château de Galleville ★

12

76560 Douderville, Normandie. Tel: 2.35.96.52.40

Château de Martinvast

13

50690 Martinvast. Tel: 2.33.52.02.23

Château de Miromesnil

14

Tourville sur Arques, 76550 Offranville. Tel/Fax: 2.35.85.02.80

Château de Nacqueville

15

50460 Urville-Nacqueville, Nr Cherbourg, Manche. Tel: 2.33.03.27.89/
2.33.03.56.03

Château de Vauville

16

50440 Beaumont-Hague, E. Cherbourg. Tel: 2.33.52.71.41; Fax: 2.33.52.72.31

Château de Vendeuvre

17

14170 Saint-Pierre-sur-Dives.

Clos du Coudray

18

76850 Etaimpuis, Normandie. Tel: 2.35.34.96.85

Ermenonville (Parc Jean-Jacques Rousseau) ★

19

1 rue René de Girardin, 60950 Ermenonville. Tel: 3.44.54.01.58;
Fax: 3.44.54.04.96

Jardin d'Ambleville

20

95710 Bray-et-Lû. Tel: 1.34.67.71.34

Jardin d'Angélique

21

Hameau du Pigrard, Route de Lyons, 76520 Montmain, Normandie.
Tel: 2.35.79.08.12

Jardin de Plantbessin

22

14490 Castillon, Calvados, Nr Bayeux. Tel: 2.31.92.56.03; Fax: 2.31.22.70.09

Jardin des Plantes Caen 23

Rue Desmoneux, 14000 Caen.

Jardin des Plantes Rouen 24

114 ter avenue des Martyrs de la Résistance, 76100 Rouen. Tel: 2.35.72.36.36; Fax: 2.35.72.34.55

Jardins de Valloires 25

80120 Argoules. Tel: 3.22.23.53.55

Le Jardin Exotique 26

Roscoff, Brittany. Tel: 2.98.61.29.19 (summer); Fax: 2.98.61.12.34

Le Jardin Georges Delaselle 27

29253 Ile de Batz, Finistère, Brittany. Tel: 2.98.61.75.65

Les Jardins de Cotelle et Pepinières 28

76370 Derchigny–Graincourt. Tel: 2.35.83.61.38; Fax: 2.35.04.06.00

Manoir du Fay ⋆ 29

Rue du Grand Fay, 76190 Yvetot, Normandie. Te: 2.35.56.24.73

Parc et Jardins du Château d'Harcourt 30

14220 Thury–Harcourt. Tel: 2.31.79.65.41 or 2.31.79.72.05

Parc Floral des Moutiers ⋆⋆ 31

76119 Varengeville–sur–Mer. Tel: 2.35.85.10.02; Fax: 2.35.85.46.98

Paris Gardens 32

Now that it is possible to use the Eurostar train to reach Paris in three hours from Waterloo Station the spectrum of possible garden visits expands. Even gardens in the Ile de France or the marvels at the Palace of Versailles (recently majestically restored) become more accessible for day trips if visitors catch the 6.57am train from Waterloo. We make no attempt here to provide a detailed guide but keen garden prospectors might care to consider visits to the following:

Central Paris: *The Tuileries Garden* near the Louvre (being restored, including *Le Jardin du Carrousel*. Christopher Bradley-Hole writes that the Wirtz family 'have used yew hedges, planted in an extensive *patte d'oie* converging on the Arc de Triomphe, to make sense of some of the disparate geometry of the site'); *Parc Monceau* on Boul. de Courcelles (nineteenth-century nannyland); *The Luxembourg Gardens* on the Left Bank (*grandeur ancienne*); *Jardin de Plantes* also on the Left Bank, Pont d'Austerlitz; *Place des Vosges* (Landscape architect Gordon Haynes calls this 'a masterpiece' of design and an excellent venue for picnics purchased in rue St Antoine and rue Birague to the south).

Inner suburbs: *Parc André Citroën* (the most exciting modern park in Paris); *Jardin Albert Kahn* at Boulogne Billancourt (several gardens including an authentic Japanese garden); *Fondation Cartier Sculpture Garden* in Jovy-en-Jonas (20 minutes by train or RER line B. Good café).

Outer suburbs: *Parc Caillebotte*, Yerres, near Orly (garden of the painter who launched Monet); *Roseraie de L'Hay les Roses* (famous rose garden in the corner of a large municipal park near Orly); *La Bagatelle* on the edge on the Bois de Boulogne in Neuilly (perhaps the most elegant display of roses in the world).

Ile de France: *Château de St Jean de Beauregard* at Les Ulys (a fine *potager*).

Several pundits say that one of the best gardens in France is only 60km S of Paris. This is *Château de Courances*. [Open April to Oct, Sat, Sun and public holidays, 2 – 6.30pm] Tel: 2.40.62.07.62. Potential visitors to gardens in France should try to obtain Barozzi's *Guide des 400 jardins publics de Paris*. A request for the leaflet *Visitez un Jardin Francais* to the Société Nationale d'Horticulture Française, 84 rue de Grenelle, 75007 Paris might also bring useful information. Those travelling further afield will wish to use Barbara Abbs' *French Entrée 16: Gardens of France*, available from bookshops in the UK.

Le Vasterival ★★   33

76119 St-Marguerite-sur-Mer. Tel: 2.35.85.12.05

BELGIUM

Brussels itself has a number of gardens open at all times, including *Abbaye de la Cambre*, *Bois de la Cambre*, the *Jean Massart Experimental Garden*, *Parc Leopold* on rue Belliard and the park in the City Centre. Other gardens include *Parc Tenbosch* (with outstanding trees) on chaussée de Vleurgat and *Maison d'Erasme*, 31 rue du Chapitre Auderlecht. *Parc Solvay* on chaussée de la Hulpe and *Jardins du Musée van Buuren*, 41 rue Leo Errera are in the south of the city. Ten kilometres north of Brussels is the *National Botanic Garden*, open daily 9am – sunset. Once a year, usually in April/May, the King of Belgium opens the conservatories in the *Laeken Royal Palace* on the Northern outskirts of the city. For this brief period they are open daily, except Mondays and Fridays, but there are some evening openings 9 – 11pm. Described as three acres of spectacular nineteenth-century ornamental architecture, they are well worth a visit as they house the world's oldest and most important collection of camellias.

Annevoie ★★   1

5537 Annevoie-Rouillon, Anhee.

Arboretum Kalmthout   2

Heuvel 2, B–2920 Kalmthout. Tel: 3.666.6741; Fax: 3.666.3396

Château d'Attre ★ 3
Avenue du Château, 7941 Attre, Brugelette.

Château de Belœil 4
Belil, près Mons.

Château de Hex 5
B-3870 Heers. Tel: 12.74.73.41; Fax: 12.74.49.87

Château de Leeuwergem ★ 6
B-9620 Zottegem. Tel: 93.60.08.73; Fax: 93.61.01.38

Château Fort d'Ecaussinnes (Le Potager) 7
Rue de Seneffe, 7191 Ecaussinnes-Lalaing. Tel/Fax: 67.44.24.90

Château s'Gravenwezel 8
2970 s'Gravenwezel, Schilde. Tel: 36.58.14.70; Fax: 36.58.37.81

Hof ter Weyden 11
Greefstraat 1, 2910 Essen. Tel: 36.77.22.74

Park van Beervelde 12
Beervelde-Dorp 75, B-9080 Lochristi. Tel: 93.55.55.40

Rekem Garden ★ 13
Achter St Pieter 24, 3621 Rekem-Lanaken. Tel: 89.71.46.92

Vlaamse Toontuinen (Flemish Show Gardens) 14
1 Houtmarkt, Hoegaarden 3320. Tel: 16.76.78.43/16.76.56.39;
Fax: 16.76.79.19

NETHERLANDS

Broekstraat 17 ★ 1
6999 De Hummelo. Tel: 314.38.1120; Fax: 314.38.1199

Hof van Walenburg ★★ 2

Huys de Dohm 3
De Doom 48–50, 6419 CX Heerlen. Tel: 45.571.0470

De Kempenhof 4
Zuiverseweg 4, 4357 NM Domburg. Tel: 118.58.16.47

Leiden Botanic Garden ★ 5
Hortus Botanicus, Rapenburg 73, Leiden. Tel: 71.527.7249

Middelburg Garden ★ 6
Seisdam 22, 4331 NT Middelburg. Tel: 118.62.85.74

Paleis Het Loo, National Museum ★★ 7
Koninklijk Park 1, 7315 JA Apeldoorn. Tel: 55.577.2400; Fax: 55.521.9983

Slot der Nisse 8
Dorpsplein 4443 AE, Nisse. Tel: 113.64.94.69

Dr J.P. Thijsse–Park 9
Prinses Irenelaan, Amstelveen, Amsterdam.

De Tintelhof 10
Golsteinseweg 24, 4351 SC Veere. Tel: 118.61.45.20

Specialist lists

Arboreta

Many of the gardens in the *Guide* are extensively treed, and this list concentrates on mature arboreta, in which the trees are labelled.

Bedfordshire *Swiss Garden*
Birmingham *University of Birmingham Botanic Garden*
Cheshire *Cholmondeley Castle, Ness, Tatton*
Cornwall *Pencarrow*
Cumbria *Holker, Muncaster Castle*
Derbyshire *Chatsworth, Derby Arboretum*
Devon *Bicton College, Bicton Park*
Dorset *Deans Court, Forde Abbey, Melbury House, Minterne*
Durham *Bowes Museum*
Essex *Cracknells, Saling Hall*
Gloucestershire *Batsford, Westonbirt*
Hampshire *Sir Harold Hillier Gardens and Arboretum*
Herefordshire *Hergest Croft*
Hertfordshire *Beale Arboretum*
Kent *Bedgebury, Belmont, Emmetts, Ladham House, Riverhill House*
London Area *Cannizaro Park, Isabella Plantation, Royal Botanic Gardens Kew*
Manchester Area *Haigh Hall*
Norfolk *Holkham Hall*
Oxfordshire *Harcourt Arboretum*
Shropshire *Hodnet Hall*
Suffolk *The Rookery*
Surrey *Coverwood, RHS Wisley, Winkworth*
Sussex, East *Sheffield Park*
Sussex, West *High Beeches, Leonardslee, Nymans, Wakehurst Place, West Dean*
Warwickshire *Arbury Hall*
Wiltshire *Bowood, Broadleas, Corsham Court*
Worcestershire *Eastnor Castle*
Yorkshire, North *Castle Howard, Thorp Perrow*
Yorkshire, South & West *Temple Newsam, Wentworth*
Ireland *Castlewellan, Fota, John F. Kennedy Arboretum*
Scotland *Castle Kennedy, Cruickshank Botanic, Leckmelm Shrubbery, Monteviot*

Herb Gardens

Many gardeners now grow herbs for the kitchen, and this listing is mainly devoted to those who make an ornamental feature of the necessity, though some may be purely ornamental.

Bedfordshire *Toddington Manor*
Bristol *Goldney Hall*
Cambridgeshire *Emmanuel College Cambridge*
Cheshire *Cheshire Herbs, Little Moreton Hall, Norton Priory*

Cumbria *Acorn Bank, Levens*
Derbyshire *Hardwick Hall, Herb Garden*
Dorset *Cranborne Manor, Edmondsham House, The Manor House*
Essex *Fanners Green, Tye Farm*
Gloucestershire *Alderley Grange, Barnsley House, Hullasey House, Painswick, Sudeley*
Hampshire *Gilbert White's House, Hollington Herbs, Tudor House Museum*
Hertfordshire *Hatfield, Knebworth*
Kent *Iden Croft, Leeds Castle, Long Barn, Marle Place, Scotney, Sissinghurst, Stoneacre*
Lancashire *Leighton Hall*
Lincolnshire *Doddington, Gunby*
London Area *Chelsea Physic, Hall Place, Museum of Garden History, 7 St Georges Road*
Newcastle Area *Bede's World*
Norfolk *Besthorpe Hall, Congham Hall, Norfolk Lavender*
Northamptonshire *Hill Farm, Holdenby House*
Northumberland *Herterton House, Hexham Herbs*
Nottinghamshire *Rufford Country Park*
Oxfordshire *Blenheim*
Somerset *Gaulden Manor*
Suffolk *Helmingham*
Surrey *RHS Wisley*
Sussex, East *Bateman's, Clinton Lodge, Crown House, Michelham Priory, Wellingham*
Sussex, West *Parham House*
Wiltshire *Broadleas*
Yorkshire, North *Harlow Carr*
Scotland *Falkland Palace, Kailzie, Malleny Garden, Monteviot*
Wales *Bodysgallen Hall, Pant-yr-Holiad, Penlan-Uchaf*
Channel Islands *Sausmarez Manor, Guernsey*

Herbaceous Borders

There was a time when every worthwhile garden had to have one, but now the fashionable thing is 'grasses'. None the less, these borders are the glory of the British garden, and we select some of the best, though this does not mean there are no great and good ones elsewhere.

Buckinghamshire *Cliveden*
Cambridgeshire *Anglesey Abbey*
Cheshire *Arley Hall, Tatton*
Cornwall *Lanhydrock*
Cumbria *Sizergh*
Devon *Arlington Court, Castle Drogo, Coleton Fishacre, Killerton, Knightshayes*
Dorset *Stour House*
Gloucestershire *Hidcote*
Hampshire *Bramdean House*
Kent *Sissinghurst*
Lincolnshire *Gunby*
Manchester Area *Dunham Massey*
Norfolk *Blickling, Felbrigg, Oxburgh*
Northumberland *Wallington*

Somerset *Barrington Court, Lytes Cary, Montacute, Tintinhull*
Staffordshire *Shugborough*
Suffolk *Melford Hall*
Sussex, West *Nymans*
Warwickshire *Packwood*
Wiltshire *The Courts*
Yorkshire, North *Beningbrough Hall*
Wales *National Botanic Garden of Wales, Powis Castle*

Japanese and Chinese Gardens

The influence of the oriental on British gardening tastes goes back some while, so we only list here those gardens which have a fairly full-blown connection with the Far East.

Cheshire *Tatton Park*
Cornwall *Japanese Garden and Bonsai Nursery*
Dorset *Compton Acres*
Hertfordshire *Japanese Garden*
Kent *Mount Ephraim*
London Area *Capel Manor, Holland Park, 8 Lower Merton Rise, 17 Navarino Road*
Nottinghamshire *Newstead Abbey*
Surrey *Coombe Wood*
Wiltshire *Heale, Wilton*
Yorkshire, West *Harewood*
Ireland *Japanese Garden*

Mazes

These are not, as they once were, relics of the past, but are now found in many shapes and sizes all over the country.

Birmingham *Castle Bromwich Hall Gardens*
Buckinghamshire *Chenies Manor*
Cheshire *Tatton*
Cornwall *Glendurgan*
Derbyshire *Chatsworth*
Essex *Saffron Walden Turf Maze*
Hampshire and the Isle of White *Barton Manor*
Hertfordshire *Hatfield, Knebworth*
Kent *Groombridge Place, Hever, Leeds Castle*
Lancashire *Worden Park*
London Area *Capel Manor, Crystal Palace Park, Hampton Court*
Oxfordshire *Blenheim, Greys Court*
Suffolk *Somerleyton Hall, Wyken Hall*
Sussex, West *Parham House*
Wiltshire *Longleat*
Yorkshire, North *Burton Agnes Hall*
Ireland *Carnfunnock Country Park*
Scotland *Cawdor Castle, Finlaystone, Scone Palace*
Channel Islands *La Seigneurie*

Organic Gardens

Some of those listed are 'instructional', while others are included because their owners follow the philosophy by spurning the use of chemicals, etc.

Bedfordshire *The Lodge*
Devon *Fardel Manor*
Dorset *Dean's Court, Edmondsham House*
Gloucestershire *Snowshill Manor*
Hertfordshire *Hatfield*
Kent *South Hill Farm, Yalding*
Lancashire *Pendle Heritage Centre*
Liverpool *Croxteth Hall*
Somerset *Greencombe*
Surrey *Titsey Place*
Warwickshire *Avon Cottage, Ryton Organic*
Ireland *Ballymaloe Cookery School, Creagh*
Scotland *Bank House, Carnell, Kellie Castle*
Wales *Centre for Alternative Technology*

Rock Gardens

An unusual taste for the modern gardener, so many of those listed are historic, though not necessarily anachronisms for that.

Cheshire *Arley Hall, Cholmondeley Castle, Tatton*
Cornwall *Pencarrow*
Derbyshire *Chatsworth*
Dorset *Forde Abbey*
Hampshire *Exbury Gardens*
Kent *Mount Ephraim*
Norfolk *Sandringham*
Northamptonshire *Lamport Hall*
Northumberland *Bide-a-Wee Cottage, Chillingham Castle*
Warwickshire *Warwick Castle*
Worcestershire *Spetchley Park*
Yorkshire, North *Newby Hall*
Scotland *Manderston, Torosay*

Rose Gardens

Most of the entries are for rose gardens, though some may be included because they have a number of unusual varieties although not a rose garden as such. It is hoped that owners of listed gardens have labelled their rose varieties. Many beautiful roses will of course be found in other gardens not listed here.

Berkshire *Folly Farm*
Birmingham *Botanical Gardens and Glasshouses, University Botanic*
Buckinghamshire *Chicheley, Cliveden, Manor House Bledlow*

Cambridgeshire *Elton Hall, St John's College Cambridge*

Cheshire *Bridgemere, Cholmondeley Castle, Ness, Tatton, Tirley Garth*

Cumbria *Dalemain, Graythwaite Hall, Holker*

Derbyshire *Haddon, Kedleston, 210 Nottingham Road*

Devon *Docton Mill, Rosemoor*

Dorset *Cranborne Manor, Friars Way*

Durham *Raby Castle, Westholme Hall*

Essex *Saling Hall, RHS Hyde Hall*

Gloucestershire *Abbotswood, Hunts Court, Kiftsgate Court, Misarden Park, Painswick, Stancombe, Sudeley*

Hampshire *Exbury, Fairfield House, Gilbert White's House, Mottisfont, Northcourt, Ventnor Botanic*

Herefordshire *Hergest Croft, How Caple*

Hertfordshire *Benington Lordship, Gardens of the Rose, Hatfield*

Kent *Chartwell, Emmetts, Godinton, Goodnestone Park, Hever, Leeds Castle, Mount Ephraim, Penshurst, Scotney, Sissinghurst, Squerryes Court*

Leicestershire *Belvoir*

Lincolnshire *Ayscoughfee Hall, Burghley, Doddington, Hall Farm*

Liverpool *Speke Hall*

London Area *Avery Hill Park, Cannizaro Park, Capel Manor, Fenton House, Gunnersbury Park, Hall Place, Hampton Court Palace, Priory Gardens, Queen Mary's Rose Garden, Royal Botanic Kew, Syon Park*

Manchester Area *Heaton Hall*

Norfolk *Norfolk Lavender, Mannington Hall*

Northamptonshire *Boughton, Holdenby, Kelmarsh, Rockingham Castle*

Northumberland *Belsay Hall, Chillingham, Hexham Herbs*

Nottinghamshire *Holme Pierrepoint Hall*

Oxfordshire *Blenheim, Brook Cottage, Greys Court, Oxford Botanic, Rousham, Stonor Park, Wroxton Abbey*

Rutland *Ashwell House, Old Manor House*

Shropshire *Benthall Hall, David Austin Roses, Dower House, Hodnet, Paddocks, Weston Park*

Somerset *Gaulden Manor*

Staffordshire *Eccleshall Castle, Shugborough, Trentham*

Suffolk *Euston Hall, Helmingham, Somerleyton*

Surrey *Albury Park, Loseley Park, Polesden Lacey, RHS Wisley, The Walled Garden*

Sussex, East *Crown House*

Sussex, West *Apuldram Roses, Duckyls, Hammerwood House, Nymans, Parham*

Warwickshire *Arbury Hall, Farnborough, Ilmington Manor, Ragley, Ryton, Warwick Castle*

Wiltshire *Avebury Manor, Bowood, Broadleas, Corsham Court, Heale Garden, Iford Manor, Longleat, Pound Hill House, Wilton*

Worcestershire *Eastnor Castle, Spetchley Park*

Yorkshire, North *Castle Howard, Newby Hall, Norton Conyers*

Yorkshire, South & West *Bramham Park, Nostell Priory, Temple Newsam*

Scotland *Cawdor, Drum, Dunrobin, Hill of Tarvit, Hirsel, Malleny Gardens, Manderston, Monteviot, Tyninghame*

Wales *Bodysgallen Hall*

Sculpture Gardens

Many of the gardens in the *Guide* have sculpture, but those listed have ornamental features as their primary purpose.

Cornwall *Barbara Hepworth Museum*
Surrey *Hannah Peschar Gallery*
Sussex, West *Goodwood*
Yorkshire, South & West *Yorkshire Sculpture Park*
Scotland *Little Sparta*

Water and Bog Gardens

Most of these entries are for water gardens or features; bog gardens are also included.

Berkshire *Scotlands*
Bristol *Goldney Hall*
Buckinghamshire *Manor House Bledlow (Lyde Garden), Stowe*
Cheshire *Cholmondeley Castle, Dorfold Hall, Stapeley*
Cornwall *Chyverton, Pencarrow, Trebah*
Derbyshire *Chatsworth*
Devon *Coleton Fishacre, Docton Mill, Gidleigh Park, Marwood Hill*
Dorset *Compton Acres, Forde Abbey, Mapperton, Old Mill, Stour House*
Essex *Beth Chatto Gardens, Feeringbury Manor, Glen Chantry, Magnolias, Saling Hall*
Gloucestershire *Abbotswood, Frampton Court, Hodges Barn, Lydney Park, Sezincote, Stanway House, Westbury Court*
Hampshire *Barton Manor, Exbury, Greatham Mill, Longstock Park, Spinners*
Herefordshire *Hergest Croft, How Caple, Whitfield*
Hertfordshire *Hill House, Hopleys*
Kent *Godinton Park, Ladham House, Mount Ephraim*
Lincolnshire *Burghley*
London Area *Golders Hill Park, Hampton Court, Kensington Gardens*
Manchester Area *Fletcher Moss Botanic*
Norfolk *Hoveton Hall, How Hill Farm, Lake House Water Gardens, Mannington Hall*
Northamptonshire *Lyveden New Bield*
Northumberland *Alnwick Castle, Chillingham Castle*
Nottinghamshire *Newstead Abbey*
Oxfordshire *Buscot Park*
Shropshire *Brownhill, Dudmaston, Hodnet Hall, Preen Manor*
Somerset *Gaulden Manor*
Staffordshire *Heath House*
Suffolk *Haughley Park*
Surrey *Busbridge Lakes, Coombe Wood, Coverwood, High Meadow, Pinewood House, Valley Gardens, Vann*
Sussex, East *Sheffield Park*
Sussex, West *West Dean*
Wiltshire *Bowood, Heale, Stourhead, Wilton*
Worcestershire *Croome Park, Lakeside*

Yorkshire, North *Arden Hall, Burnby Hall, Burton Constable, Newby Hall, Studley Royal and Fountains Abbey*
Yorkshire, South & West *Harewood House, Roundhay Park*
Ireland *Creagh Gardens, Fernhill, Japanese Garden*
Scotland *Corsock House, Crarae, Kilbryde Castle, Kildrummy, Manderston, Monteviot, Stobo Castle Water Gardens, Teviot, Torosay Castle*
Wales *Bodrhyddan, Cae Hir, Dolwen, Foxbrush, Glansevern, Penrhyn*

Wild Gardens and Wildernesses

The term wild garden/wilderness includes a range of types of garden, including wildlife gardens, which have been specifically designed to avoid the formal, cultivated garden. In general, the wild garden forms only a part of the total area.

Birmingham *Castle Bromwich*
Cambridgeshire *Docwra's Manor, South Farm, St John's College Cambridge*
Cheshire *Dorfold Hall, Lodge Lane*
Cornwall *Heligan, Trebah*
Cumbria *Dalemain, Hutton-in-the-Forest, Levens, Muncaster Castle*
Derbyshire *Chatsworth*
Devon *Arlington Court, Greenway House*
Dorset *Athelhampton, Dean's Court, Edmondsham House, Mapperton, Parnham House*
Essex *Olivers*
Gloucestershire *Painswick, Stancombe*
Hampshire *Manor House*
Herefordshire *How Caple*
Hertfordshire *Hatfield, Knebworth*
Kent *Godinton Park, Hole Park, Marle Place, Penshurst, Riverhill House*
Leicestershire *Belvoir*
Lincolnshire *Doddington, Fulbeck*
London Area *Camley Street Natural Park, Hampton Court, Isabella Plantation, Natural History Museum, Syon Park, Trinity Hospice, Waterhouse Plantation*
Manchester Area *Lyme Park*
Norfolk *Elsing Hall, Fairhaven Garden Trust, How Hill Farm, Mannington Hall*
Northamptonshire *Canons Ashby, Cottesbrooke, Delapre Abbey, Rockingham Castle*
Northumberland *Belsay Hall, Chillingham Castle, Hexham Herbs*
Oxfordshire *Christ Church Meadow Oxford, Mill House, Wilcote House*
Shropshire *Millichope Park*
Somerset *Hadspen*
Suffolk *Helmingham Hall, Shrubland Hall*
Surrey *Hatchlands, RHS Wisley, Savill Garden*
Sussex, East *Michelham Priory*
Sussex, West *Duckyls, Hammerwood House, High Beeches Gardens, Nymans, Stonehurst, West Dean*
Warwickshire *Charlecote Park, Ryton, Warwick Castle*
Wiltshire *Corsham Court, The Courts, Stourton House*
Yorkshire, North *Arden Hall, Constable Burton, Hackfall Wood, Norton Conyers*

Ireland *Annes Grove, Downhill*
Scotland *Ardtornish, Candacraig, Cawdor, Crarae, Crathes, Manderston, Mellerstain*
Wales *Post House, Winllan*
Channel Islands *Sausmarez Manor, Domaine des Vaux*

Index

An * indicates that the garden or nursery is mentioned in the text of another garden entry; # means that only garden names, addresses and contact details are given; col. ill. refers to a photograph in the colour insert.

654 • INDEX